Lecture Notes in Con

Shengchao Qin   Zongyan Qiu (Eds.)

Formal Methods and Software Engineering

13th International Conference
on Formal Engineering Methods, ICFEM 2011
Durham, UK, October 26-28, 2011
Proceedings

Volume Editors

Shengchao Qin
Teesside University
School of Computing
Borough Road
Middlesbrough
Tees Valley TS1 3BA, UK
E-mail: s.qin@tees.ac.uk

Zongyan Qiu
Peking University
School of Mathematical Sciences
Beijing, 100871, China
E-mail: zyqiu@pku.edu.cn

ISSN 0302-9743 e-ISSN 1611-3349
ISBN 978-3-642-24558-9 e-ISBN 978-3-642-24559-6
DOI 10.1007/978-3-642-24559-6
Springer Heidelberg Dordrecht London New York

Library of Congress Control Number: 2011937705

CR Subject Classification (1998): D.2.4, D.2, D.3, F.3, F.4.1, C.2

LNCS Sublibrary: SL 2 – Programming and Software Engineering

Typesetting: Camera-ready by author, data conversion by Scientific Publishing Services, Chennai, India

Printed on acid-free paper

Springer is part of Springer Science+Business Media (www.springer.com)

Preface

Formal engineering methods have been extensively studied over decades. Various theories, techniques, and tools have been proposed, developed, and applied in the specification, design, verification, and validation of software systems or in the construction of such systems. The challenge now is how to integrate them to effectively deal with large-scale and complex systems, e.g., cyber-physical systems, for their sound and efficient construction and maintenance. This requires us to improve the state of the art by researching effective approaches and techniques for integration of formal methods into industrial engineering practice.

The now long-established series of International Conferences on Formal Engineering Methods has provided a forum for those interested in the application of formal methods to computer systems. This volume contains the papers presented at ICFEM 2011, the 13th International Conference on Formal Engineering Methods, held during October 26–28, 2011 in Durham, UK.

There were 103 submissions from 28 countries. Each paper was reviewed by at least three Program Committee members. After extensive discussion, the Program Committee decided to accept 40 papers. The program also included three invited talks by Jifeng He, from East China Normal University, Peter O'Hearn, from Queen Mary, University of London, and Shaz Qadeer, from Microsoft Research. One invited paper and two abstracts are also included here.

ICFEM 2011 was organized mainly by the School of Computing, Teesside University. We acknowledge the financial support from our main sponsors, including Teesside University, Microsoft Research, and Formal Methods Europe. We thank our honorary chairs Cliff Hardcastle and Marc Cavazza for their support and our conference chairs Cliff Jones and Phil Brooke for their hard work during the organization of ICFEM 2011. Special thanks should be given to Angela Ackerley and Mandie Hall for their help on logistics including finance and registration.

We are grateful to all members of the Program Committee and external reviewers for their hard work. We would also like to thank all the authors of the invited and submitted papers, and all the participants of the conference. They are the main focus of the whole event. The EasyChair system was used to manage the submissions, reviewing, and proceedings production. We would like to thank the EasyChair team for a very useful tool.

August 2011

Shengchao Qin
Zongyan Qiu

Organization

Honorary Chairs

Marc Cavazza	Teesside University
Cliff Hardcastle	Teesside University

General Chairs

Phil Brooke	Teesside University
Cliff Jones	Newcastle University

Program Chairs

Shengchao Qin	Teesside University
Zongyan Qiu	Peking University

Program Committee

Bernhard K. Aichernig	TU Graz
Keijiro Araki	Kyushu University
Farhad Arbab	CWI and Leiden University
Richard Banach	University of Manchester
Nikolaj Bjorner	Microsoft Research
Jonathan P. Bowen	Museophile Limited
Michael Butler	University of Southampton
Andrew Butterfield	University of Dublin
Ana Cavalcanti	University of York
Aziem Chawdhary	University of Edinburgh
Wei-Ngan Chin	National University of Singapore
Florin Craciun	National University of Singapore
Thao Dang	VERIMAG
Jim Davies	University of Oxford
Dino Distefano	Queen Mary, University of London
Jin-Song Dong	National University of Singapore
Zhenhua Duan	Xidian University
Colin Fidge	Queensland University of Technology
J.S. Fitzgerald	Newcastle University
Leo Freitas	Newcastle University
Joaquim Gabarro	Universitat Politecnica de Catalunya
Stefania Gnesi	ISTI-CNR
Anthony Hall	Independent Consultant

Ian J. Hayes	University of Queensland
Mike Hinchey	Lero
Zhenjiang Hu	NII
Michael Jackson	Independent Consultant
Thierry Jéron	Inria Rennes - Bretagne Atlantique
Gerwin Klein	NICTA and UNSW
Laura Kovacs	TU Vienna
Kim G. Larsen	Aalborg University
Peter Gorm Larsen	Aarhus School of Engineering
Michael Leuschel	University of Düsseldorf
Xuandong Li	Nanjing University
Shaoying Liu	Hosei University
Zhiming Liu	UNU/IIST
Tiziana Margaria	University of Potsdam
Dominique Mery	Université Henri Poincaré Nancy 1 and LORIA
Stephan Merz	INRIA Lorraine
Huaikou Miao	Shanghai University
Peter Müller	ETH Zurich
Jun Pang	University of Luxembourg
Matthew Parkinson	Micrsosoft Research
Geguang Pu	East China Normal University
Shengchao Qin	Teesside University
Zongyan Qiu	Peking University
Augusto Sampaio	Federal University of Pernambuco
Thomas Santen	European Microsoft Innovation Center
Wuwei Shen	Western Michigan University
Marjan Sirjani	Reykjavik University
Bill Stoddart	Teesside University
Jing Sun	The University of Auckland
Jun Sun	Singapore University of Technology and Design
Meng Sun	Peking University
Kenji Taguchi	AIST
Tetsuo Tamai	University of Tokyo
Yih-Kuen Tsay	National Taiwan University
T.H. Tse	The University of Hong Kong
Viktor Vafeiadis	MPI-SWS
Miroslav Velev	Aries Design Automation
Laurent Voisin	Systerel
Hai H. Wang	University of Aston
Ji Wang	NUTD
Linzhang Wang	Nanjing University
Heike Wehrheim	University of Paderborn
Jim Woodcock	University of York
Hongli Yang	Beijng University of Technology
Wang Yi	Uppsala University

Naijun Zhan	Institute of Software, Chinese Academy of Sciences
Jian Zhang	Institute of Software, Chinese Academy of Sciences
Hong Zhu	Oxford Brookes University
Huibiao Zhu	East China Normal University

Publicity Chairs

Jonathan P. Bowen	Museophile Limited
Jun Sun	Singapore University of Technology and Design
Huibiao Zhu	East China Normal University

Local Organization Committee

Angela Ackerley	Teesside University
Phil Brooke	Teesside University
Steve Dunne	Teesside University
Mandie Hall	Teesside University
Shengchao Qin	Teesside University

Steering Committee

Keijiro Araki, Japan
Jin Song Dong, Singapore
Chris George, Canada
Jifeng He, China
Mike Hinchey, Ireland
Shaoying Liu (Chair), Japan
John McDermid, UK
Tetsuo Tamai, Japan
Jim Woodcock, UK

Sponsors

Formal Methods Europe (FME)
Microsoft Research Limited
Teesside University

Additional Reviewers

Aboulsamh, Mohammed
Andriamiarina, Manamiary Bruno
Andronick, June
Anh Tuan, Luu
Bauer, Sebastian
Bertolini, Cristiano
Bertrand, Nathalie
Besova, Galina
Blanchette, Jasmin Christian
Bodeveix, Jean-Paul
Bu, Lei
Carmona, Josep
Chen, Chunqing
Chen, Liqian
Chen, Xin
Chen, Zhenbang
Colley, John
Cong-Vinh, Phan
Cos, Andreea Costea
Costea, Andreea
Daum, Matthias
Dongol, Brijesh
Du, Yuyue
Edmunds, Andrew
Falcone, Ylies
Ferrari, Alessio
Ferreira, Joao F.
Gao, Ping
Gherghina, Cristian
Gotsman, Alexey
Greenaway, David
Hallerstede, Stefan
Hallestede, Stefan
Hayes, Ian
Hayman, Jonathan
He, Guanhua
Heisel, Maritta
Jaghoori, Mohammad Mahdi
Khakpour, Narges
Khamespanah, Ehsan
Kong, Weiqiang
Kreitz, Christoph
Kumazawa, Tsutomu
Kusakabe, Shigeru
Le, Quang Loc
Legay, Axel
Li, Yuan Fang
Liu, Yang
Mazzanti, Franco
Mcneile, Ashley
Meinicke, Larissa
Mochio, Hiroshi
Morisset, Charles
Moscato, Mariano
Nakajima, Shin
Nogueira, Sidney
Nyman, Ulrik
Olsen, Petur
Omori, Yoichi
Orejas, Fernando
Petersen, Rasmus Lerchedahl
Plagge, Daniel
Sabouri, Hamideh
Sewell, Thomas
Singh, Neeraj
Snook, Colin
Song, Songzheng
Stainer, Amelie
Stewart, Alan
Struth, Georg
Tiezzi, Francesco
Timm, Nils
Tounsi, Mohamed
Tsai, Ming-Hsien
Walther, Sven
Wang, Jackie
Wang, Shuling
Wang, Zheng
Welch, James
Wijs, Anton
Wu, Bin
Yamagata, Yoriyuki
Yatsu, Hirokazu
Zhang, Chenyi
Zhang, Pengcheng
Zhao, Yongxin
Zheng, Man Chun
Zheng, Manchun
Zhu, Jiaqi

Table of Contents

Invited Talks

Formal Models

Model Checking and Probability

Specification and Development

Security

Formal Verification

Cyber Physical Systems

Event-B

Verification, Analysis and Testing

Refinement

Theorem Proving and Rewriting

Towards a Signal Calculus for Event-Based Synchronous Languages

Yongxin Zhao and He Jifeng*

Shanghai Key Laboratory of Trustworthy Computing,
Software Engineer Institute,
East China Normal University, Shanghai, China
jifeng@sei.ecnu.edu.cn

Abstract. A theory of programming is intended to support the practice of programming by relating each program to the specification of what it is intended to achieve. Our intention is to develop a signal calculus for event-based synchronous languages used for specification and programming of embedded systems. In this paper, we mainly tackle conceptually instantaneous reactions, i.e., zero-time reactions. The delay-time reactions will be investigated in the follow-up work. To explore the semantic definition of instantaneous reactions (I-calculus), a set of algebraic laws is provided, which can be used to reduce all instantaneous reactions to a normal form algebraically. The normal form, surprisingly, exposes the internal implicit dependence explicitly. Consequently, that two differently written reactions happen to mean the same thing can be proved from the equations of an algebraic presentation.

1 Introduction

A theory of programming is intended to support the practice of programming by relating each program to the specification of what it is intended to achieve. A similar diversity of presentation is seen in a theory of programming, which has to explain the meaning of the notations of a programming language. The methods of presenting such a semantic definition may be classified under three headings, i.e., *denotational*, *algebraic* and *operational*.

The great merit of algebraic method is as a powerful tool for exploiting family relationships over a wide range of different theories. Algebra is well suited for direct use by engineers in symbolic calculation of parameter and structure of an optimal design. Algebraic proofs by term rewriting are the most promising way in which computers can assist in the process of reliable design. As in previous years, many researchers have applied algebraic method to investigate a large number of paradigms of computing [1,2,3,4,5,9]. But it seems that no one deals with signal-centric synchronous calculus from a algebraic perspective. Our intention is to develop a signal calculus for event-based synchronous languages used for the specification and programming of embedded systems.

* Corresponding author.

S. Qin and Z. Qiu (Eds.): ICFEM 2011, LNCS 6991, pp. 1–13, 2011.

In this paper, we mainly tackle conceptually instantaneous reactions, i.e., zero time reactions. The delay-time reactions will be investigated in the follow-up work. Technically, signals are means of communications and synchronisations between different parts of systems (agents) and between a agent and its environment. Our calculus adopts the so-called synchronous hypothesis, i.e., instantaneous reaction to signals and immediate propagation of signals in each time-instant. Note that the reaction here has to be deterministic, i.e., in every reaction, for a given set of input signals, it generates a unique set of output signals. Due to the synchronous hypothesis, each signal is consistently seen as *present* or *absent* by all agents. Thus the logical coherence of signal status leads to the semantic challenges. Further, agents can interact with each other since all generated signals are immediate sensed by all agents. As a result, the internal implicit dependence enhances the difficulty to search for an algebraic semantics.

To explore the semantic definition of the instantaneous reactions (I-calculus), a set of algebraic laws is provided, which can be used to reduce all reactions to a normal form algebraically. Consequently, that two differently written programs happen to mean the same thing can be proved from the equations of an algebraic presentation. More importantly, the internal implicitly dependence is exposed explicitly after transforming all reactions into normal forms.

The remainder of the paper is organized as follows. Section 2 gives a brief introduction to pure signals and event guards. We present our I-calculus and informally interpret the meanings of reactions in Section 3. A set of algebraic laws is provided in Section 4. The normal form for I-calculus is presented in Section 5. We prove that all reactions can be algebraically reduced to a normal form. Section 6 refers to the related work and discusses the future work.

2 Pure Signals and Event Guards

In this section, we investigate broadcast signals and introduce event guards for later discussion. In our framework, we confine ourselves to pure signals which only carry the *present* or *absent* information of signals for the purpose of precise definition and mathematical treatment[1].

Signals are means of communications and synchronisations between different agents and between a agent and its environment. In general, a signal denoted by its name has two types of statuses, i.e., either presence or absence. By default, signals are absent. A signal is present if it is an input signal that appears in the input or it is emitted as the result of an execution of the reaction. Given a signal s, we write s^+, s^- to indicate the presence and absence respectively.

Here an event is modeled as a set of signals with status. The function $sig(l)$ defines the set of signals (just names) which the event l embodies, e.g., $sig(l) = \{s, t\}$, where $l = \{s^+, t^-\}$. Note that the event in our calculus should be consistent, i.e., the status of any signal referring to the same event should be unique, which is captured by the formal definition: $\forall s \in sig(l) \bullet s^+ \notin l \vee s^- \notin l$. Hence we employ notation $l(s)$ to represent the status of signal s in event l. Finally, compatible events are defined below.

[1] Actually, the restriction is not critical; those signals which carry values of arbitrary types can be converted into our signal calculus.

Definition 1 (Compatible). *Events l_1 and l_2 are compatible if they agree with on the status of all common signals, i.e., $\forall s \in sig(l_1) \cap sig(l_2) \bullet l_1(s) = l_2(s)$. We denote it by* $\mathsf{compatible}(l_1, l_2)$.

Further, we introduce event guards to synchronise the behaviors of agents and the notation of event guards is given as follow:

$$g ::= \epsilon \mid \emptyset \mid s^+ \mid s^- \mid g \cdot g \mid g + g \mid \overline{g}$$

Now we give the meanings of event guards in Table 1. In actual, an event guard is identified as a set of events which can trigger the guard. Almost all event guards have the usual meanings and the definitions are straightforward. Intuitively, $\overline{g}$ defines all events which cannot give rise to the occurrence of any event in g.

Table 1. The Meanings of Event Guards

$$[\![\epsilon]\!] =_{df} Event \qquad [\![\emptyset]\!] =_{df} \emptyset \qquad [\![s^+]\!] =_{df} \{l \mid s^+ \in l \wedge l \in Event\}$$
$$[\![s^-]\!] =_{df} \{l \mid s^- \in l \wedge l \in Event\} \qquad [\![g_1 + g_2]\!] =_{df} [\![g_1]\!] \cup [\![g_2]\!]$$
$$[\![g_1 \cdot g_2]\!] =_{df} \{l_1 \cup l_2 \mid l_1 \in [\![g_1]\!] \wedge l_2 \in [\![g_2]\!] \wedge \mathsf{compatible}(l_1, l_2)\}$$
$$[\![\overline{g}]\!] =_{df} Event \backslash [\![g]\!]$$

In the sequel, we give a detailed discussion about event guards. Some algebraic laws about guards are listed in the following and proofs that the laws are sound with respect to semantics definition are straightforward.

Multiply $\cdot$ is idempotent, commutative, associative and distributes through addition $+$. It has $\emptyset$ as its zero and ϵ as its unit.

(multi – 1) $g \cdot g = g$ $(\cdot\ idemp)$
(multi – 2) $g_1 \cdot g_2 = g_2 \cdot g_1$ $(\cdot\ comm)$
(multi – 3) $g_1 \cdot (g_2 \cdot g_3) = (g_1 \cdot g_2) \cdot g_3$ $(\cdot\ assoc)$
(multi – 4) $g \cdot (h_1 + h_2) = g \cdot h_1 + g \cdot h_2$ $(\cdot - +\ distrib)$
(multi – 5) $\emptyset \cdot g = \emptyset$ $(\cdot - \emptyset\ zero)$
(multi – 6) $\epsilon \cdot g = g$ $(\cdot - \epsilon\ unit)$

Addition $+$ is idempotent, commutative, associative. It has $\emptyset$ as its unit and ϵ as its zero.

(add – 1) $g + g = g$ $(+\ idemp)$
(add – 2) $g_1 + g_2 = g_2 + g_1$ $(+\ comm)$
(add – 3) $g_1 + (g_2 + g_3) = (g_1 + g_2) + g_3$ $(+\ assoc)$
(add – 4) $\emptyset + g = g$ $(+ - \emptyset\ unit)$
(add – 5) $\epsilon + g = \epsilon$ $(+ - \epsilon\ zero)$
(add – 6) $g + l \cdot g = g$ $(+\ up\text{-}closed)$

Generally, we say event e_1 can give rise to event e_2 if $e_1 \supseteq e_2$. Thus event e can give rise to guard g iff the event can give rise to an event in g. Recall from the definition that if an event can give rise to a guard, a larger event can also give rise to the guard. Thus the order relation over guards is given straightforward as follows:

Definition 2. $g_1 \supseteq g_2 =_{df} [\![g_1]\!] \supseteq [\![g_2]\!]$.

Here, we also give a syntactical relation over guards.

Definition 3. *We write $g_1 \succeq g_2$ if there exists g such that $g_1 \equiv g_2 + g$, where $h_1 \equiv h_2$ indicates h_1 and h_2 are syntactically identical.*

In the following part,we use $s \in g, s \notin g$ to indicate, in syntactical, s is present and absent in g respectively. Thus the guard g can be expressed as $g_1 + g_2 \cdot s^+ + g_3 \cdot s^-$, where $s \notin g_1, g_2, g_3$. Further, we introduce the definition *up-closed*, which is crucial for our definition of normal form and is inspired by the construction of Smyth power domains [6,14].

Definition 4 (Up-Closed). *An event guard g is (syntactically) up-closed if $\forall g' \bullet g' \subseteq g \Rightarrow g' \preceq g$.*

Definition 5. *Given an event guard g, define $\uparrow g =_{df} \sum\{g' \mid g' \subseteq g\}$.*

Corollary 1. *$\uparrow g$ is up-closed and if h is up-closed and $g \subseteq h$, we have $\uparrow g \subseteq h$, i.e., $\uparrow g$ is the small up-closed guard containing g.*

Corollary 2. $g = \ \uparrow g$

Finally, we define *textual substitutions* $g[g'/s^-]$ and $g[g'/s^+]$ to derive new guards.

Definition 6 (Textual Substitution). *The textual substitutions $g[g'/s^+]$, $g[g'/s^-]$ are defined as $g_1 + g_2 \cdot g' + g_3 \cdot s^-$ and $g_1 + g_2 \cdot s^+ + g_3 \cdot g'$ respectively if $g \equiv g_1 + g_2 \cdot s^+ + g_3 \cdot s^-$, where $s \notin g_1, g_2, g_3$.*

Lemma 1. *For $g \subseteq g_1 + g_2$, there exists a decomposition $g = g_1' + g_2'$ such that $g_1' \subseteq g_1$ and $g_2' \subseteq g_2$.*

The proof may be easily validated by taking every event of guard into consideration.

3 Instantaneous Reactions: I-Calculus

In this section, we present the I-calculus for the event-based synchronous languages, which mainly tackle conceptually instantaneous reactions, i.e., zero time reactions. The syntax of I-calculus is given as follows:

$$I ::= \ !s \mid II \mid \perp \mid g\&I \mid I\backslash s \mid I \parallel I$$

Where, g is an event guard and $!s$ is an emission of signal s. The function $\mathsf{ems}(I)$ defines the set of the generated signals of reaction I.

The meanings of all reactions are accord with the common intuitions. Informally, each reaction may sense the presence of input signals and generate output signals. The reaction $!s$ emits signal s and terminates immediately; II does nothing but terminates successfully. $\perp$ represents the worst reaction which leads to a chaotic state. The reaction $g\&I$ behaves like I when the guard g is fired, otherwise it behaves like the reaction II. The reaction $I\backslash s$ declares signal s as a local signal and the emission of s becomes invisible to outside. $I_1 \parallel I_2$ immediately starts I_1 and I_2 in parallel. Note that I_1 and I_2 can interact with each other.

Example 1. Let $I_1 = s_1^+\&!s_2 \parallel (s_2^+ \cdot s_1^+)\&!s_3 \parallel s_2^-\&\perp$.

Given an input signal s_1, the guard s_1^+ can be triggered; thus signal s_2 is emitted immediately; at the time, the guard $s_2^+ \cdot s_1^+$ is also satisfied and then s_3 is generated. Hence, I would react to input signal s by emitting s_2 and s_3. For input signal s_3, I becomes chaotic since s_2 is absent in input signals and no reaction can generate it.

Example 2. Let $I_2 = s_1^+\&!s_2 \parallel (s_2^+ \cdot s_1^+)\&!s_3 \parallel s_3^+\&\perp$.

Given an input signal s_1, intuitively both signals s_2 and s_3 will be generated according to the above computation. However the reaction actually enters into chaos state since s_3^+ activates the reaction $\perp$.

As can be seen from these examples, the computation of an reaction is proceeded step by step. When input signals are given, we first inspect which guards are triggered. If the guard is fired, the involved reaction will generate the corresponding signals. Then with the generated signals, we repeat the computation until no new guard can be fired.

Indeed, the computation is tedious and subtle, which is mainly caused by the internal implicit dependence. We intend to search for a method of exposing the dependence explicitly. The algebra is obviously well suited to reveal the dependence since term rewriting (algebraic laws) preserves the equivalence of reactions.

4 Algebraic Semantics

In the section, we explore the algebraic semantics for I-calculus whose foundation is based on abstract algebras. The basic idea of the algebraic approach to semantics is to use algebraic axioms to describe the characteristic properties of the primitives and the combinators. Algebra is well-suited for direct use by engineers in symbolic calculation of parameters and the structure of an optimal design. Algebraic proof by term rewriting is the most promising way in which computers can assist in the process of reliable design [10]. From the point of view of language utility it is desirable to develop as much laws as possible, and make the laws as widely applicable as possible. Hence we state the laws in such a way.

4.1 Parallel

The parallel is commutative and associative. Consequently, the order of parallel composition is irrelevant.

par - 1 $I_1 \parallel I_2 \;=\; I_2 \parallel I_1$ $(\parallel\, comm)$

par - 2 $(I_1 \parallel I_2) \parallel I_3 \;=\; I_1 \parallel (I_2 \parallel I_3)$ $(\parallel\, assoc)$

The parallel is idempotent, due to deterministic behavior of reactions.

par - 3 $I \parallel I \;=\; I$ $(\parallel\, idemp)$

Reactions $\perp$ and II are the zero and the unit of parallel composition respectively.

par - 4 $\perp \parallel I \;=\; \perp$ $(\parallel - \perp zero)$

par - 5 $\mathit{II} \parallel I \;=\; I$ $(\parallel \;-\; \mathit{II}\; unit)$

4.2 Guard

The following law enables us to eliminate nested guards.

guard - 1 $g_1\&(g_2\&I) \;=\; (g_1 \cdot g_2)\&I$ $(\&\; multi)$

Event guards with same reaction can be combined.

guard - 2 $g_1\&I \parallel g_2\&I \;=\; (g_1 + g_2)\&I$ $(\&\; add)$

The event guard distributes through the parallel.

guard - 3 $g\&(I_1 \parallel I_2) \;=\; g\&I_1 \parallel g\&I_2$ $(\& - \parallel distrib)$

Reaction $\emptyset\&I$ behaves like II because its guard can never be fired.

guard - 4 $\emptyset\&I \;=\; \mathit{II}$ $(\& \;-\; \emptyset\; top)$

Reaction $\epsilon\&I$ always activates the reaction I.

guard - 5 $\epsilon\&I \;=\; I$ $(\& \;-\; \epsilon\; buttom)$

Reaction $g\&\mathit{II}$ never emits signals.

guard - 6 $g\&\mathit{II} \;=\; \mathit{II}$ $(\& \;-\; \mathit{II}\; void)$

4.3 Concealment

The concealment is commutative and the order is not critical.

conc - 1 $(I\backslash s)\backslash t \;=\; (I\backslash t)\backslash s$ $(\backslash\; comm)$

$\backslash s$ distributes backward over $\parallel$ when one component does not mention signal s.

conc - 2 $(I_1 \parallel I_2)\backslash s \;=\; (I_1\backslash s) \parallel I_2$ provided that $s \notin I_2$ $(\backslash - \parallel quasi\text{-}distrib)$

$\backslash s$ distributes backward over guarded reaction if s does not appear in the guard g.

conc - 3 $(g\&I)\backslash s \;=\; g\&(I\backslash s)$ provided that $s \notin g$ $(\backslash \;-\; \&\; quasi\text{-}distrib)$

4.4 Primitives

When reaction $s^-\&!s$ is triggered it behaves like $\bot$ since it violates the logical coherence between the environment assumptions (i.e., absence of signal s) and the effect of emission of signal s

prim - 1 $\quad s^-\&!s \;=\; s^-\&\bot \qquad (logical\ coherence)$

Reaction $s^+\&!s$ behaves like II because emission of s does not change the statues of s.

prim - 2 $\quad s^+\&!s \;=\; s^+\&II \qquad (axiom\ unit)$

4.5 Dependence

A guard g also triggers the reaction $s^+\&I$ if it can generate signal s. The following law is crucial for our algebraic approach since it expose the internal dependence explicitly.

depend-axiom $\quad g\&!s \parallel s^+\&I \;=\; g\&!s \parallel (s^+ + g)\&I$

4.6 Additional Laws

The following law illustrates how to eliminate the concealment.

conc - 4 $\quad (g\&!s \parallel I)\backslash s \;=\; I[g/s^+, \overline{g}/s^-]$ provided that $s \notin g$ and $s \notin \mathsf{ems}(I)$

Where, the textual substitutions $I[g/s^+]$ and $I[\overline{g}/s^-]$ can only proceed on guards.

The laws are listed above capture the properties of all primitives and the combinators. Definitely, on one hand, all the laws are consistent, i.e., no conflict can be deduced in terms of the laws. On the other hand, we advocate the laws are complete, i.e., all reactions can be reduced to a normal form defined below with the help of the laws.

Example 3. Let $I = ((s_1^+ + s_2^+ \cdot s_3^+)\&!s_2 \parallel s_2^+\&!s_4)\backslash s_2$.

We illustrate how to eliminate the concealment.

$$\begin{aligned} I &= ((s_1^+ + s_2^+ \cdot s_3^+)\&!s_2 \parallel s_2^+\&!s_4)\backslash s_2 && \{\textbf{guard-2}\} \\ &= (s_1^+\&!s_2 \parallel s_2^+ \cdot s_3^+\&!s_2 \parallel s_2^+\&!s_4)\backslash s_2 && \{\textbf{prim-2}\} \\ &= (s_1^+\&!s_2 \parallel s_2^+\&!s_4\ )\backslash s_2 && \{\textbf{conc-4}\} \\ &= s_1\&!s_4 \end{aligned}$$

5 Normal Form for I-Calculus

In the section, we investigate the normal form (unified and restricted form) for I-calculus and we prove all reactions can be algebraically reduced to normal forms. Thus additional properties of I-calculus can be simply deduced by showing them to be valid just for normal forms. The behavior equivalence of two reactions depends on the equivalence of their corresponding normal forms. More importantly, the normal form of an reaction actually exposes the internal dependency explicitly and captures the interferences in advance. Intuitively, all parallel sub-reactions in a normal form can react to environment input signals simultaneously if the input would not lead to chaos.

Definition 7 (Normal Form). *The reaction* $\|_{m\in M} g_m\&!s_m \parallel h\&\bot$ *is a norm form for I-calculus if it satisfies the two conditions below, where all* g_i *and* h *are up-closed guards, the index set* M *is finite and all signals* s_i $(i \in M)$ *are different.*

(1). $\forall m, n \in M, g \bullet (g \cdot s_n^+ \subseteq g_m \Rightarrow g \cdot g_n \subseteq g_m) \wedge (g \cdot s_n^+ \subseteq h \Rightarrow g \cdot g_n \subseteq h)$.

(2). $\forall m \in M, g_m \cdot s_m^- \subseteq h \subseteq g_m$.

Theorem 1. $g\&I \parallel h\&\bot = (g+h)\&I \parallel h\&\bot$

Proof

$$
\begin{aligned}
& (g+h)\&I \parallel h\&\bot && \textbf{(guard-2 } and \textbf{ 3)}\\
= \; & g\&I \parallel h\&(I \parallel \bot) && \textbf{(par-4)}\\
= \; & g\&I \parallel h\&\bot
\end{aligned}
$$

Theorem 2. $g\&!s = g\&!s \parallel (g \cdot s^-)\&\bot$

Proof

$$
\begin{aligned}
& g\&!s \\
= \; & (g + g \cdot s^-)\&!s && \textbf{(guard-2)}\\
= \; & g\&!s \parallel g \cdot s^-\&\bot
\end{aligned}
$$

The two theorems ensure the satisfiability of condition (2). Thus, for any m, we can always add guard $g_m \cdot s_m^-$ into h and h into g_m respectively without affecting the equivalence of reactions.

The objective of the following part is to show that all reactions in I-calculus can be reduced to normal forms. Our first step is to show that all primitives can be reduced to normal forms.

Theorem 3. *The primitive reactions* $\bot$, II *and* $!s$ *can be reduced to normal forms.*

Proof: Easily, the following computations are validated by algebraic laws.

$\bot = \epsilon\&\bot = \|_{m\in M} \uparrow\epsilon\&!s_m \parallel \uparrow\epsilon\&\bot$,

$II = \emptyset\&\bot = \|_{m\in M}\emptyset\&!s_m \parallel \emptyset\&\bot$ and

$!s = \epsilon\&!s = \epsilon\&!s \parallel s^-\&\bot = \uparrow\epsilon\&!s \parallel \uparrow s^-\&\bot$ □

Consequently, all primitives can be reduced to normal forms. Now we are going to prove that normal forms are closed under the combinators, i.e., $g\&I$, $I\backslash s$ and $I \parallel I$ since all primitive commands are already normal forms.

Lemma 2. *The reaction* $I = \|_{m\in M} g_m\&!s_m \parallel h\&\bot$ *can be reduced to normal form if condition (1) is already satisfied, i.e.,* $\forall m, n \in M, g \bullet (g \cdot s_n^+ \subseteq g_m \Rightarrow g \cdot g_n \subseteq g_m) \wedge (g \cdot s_n^+ \subseteq h \Rightarrow g \cdot g_n \subseteq h)$, *where all* s_i $(i \in M)$ *are different, all* g_i $(i \in M)$ *and* h *are up-closed guards.*

Proof: We directly construct the normal form I' which is equivalent with I.

Let $h' = h + \sum_{n\in M} g_n \cdot s_n^-$, $g'_m = g_m + h'$ and $I' = \|_{m\in M} g'_m\&!s_m \parallel h'\&\bot$.

Firstly, we show that I and I' are algebraically equivalent. Easily,

$$
\begin{aligned}
I &= \|_{m\in M} g_m \&!s_m \parallel h\&\bot && \{\textbf{thm 2}\ \textit{and}\ \textbf{guard-2}\}\\
&= \|_{m\in M} g_m \&!s_m \parallel (h + \textstyle\sum_{n\in M} g_n \cdot s_n^-)\&\bot && \{\textbf{thm 1}\ \textit{and}\ \textbf{guard-2}\}\\
&= \|_{m\in M} (g_m + h')\&!s_m \parallel h'\&\bot \\
&= \|_{m\in M} g'_m \&!s_m \parallel h'\&\bot \\
&= I'
\end{aligned}
$$

Next we prove that I' is a norm form, i.e., I' satisfies the conditions of normal form. Obviously, we have $\forall m \in M, g'_m \cdot s_m^- \subseteq h' \subseteq g'_m$ since $g_m \cdot s_m^- \subseteq h'$. i.e., reaction I' satisfies condition (2). Then we only need to prove I' also satisfies condition (1) $\forall m, n \in M, g \bullet (g \cdot s_n^+ \subseteq g'_m \Rightarrow g \cdot g'_n \subseteq g'_m) \wedge (g \cdot s_n^+ \subseteq h' \Rightarrow g \cdot g'_n \subseteq h')$. Equivalently, we show the construction from I to I' conserves the condition (1).

Suppose that $g \cdot s_n^+ \subseteq h'$ for given n, there exists a decomposition $g = h_1 + \sum_{i\in M} g'_i$ such that $h_1 \cdot s_n^+ \subseteq h$ and for any i in M, $g'_i \cdot s_n^+ \subseteq g_i \cdot s_i^-$. Thus we get $g'_i \cdot s_n^+ \subseteq g_i$ and $g'_i \subseteq s_i^-$. Hence $h_1 \cdot g_n \subseteq h \subseteq h'$ and $g'_i \cdot g_n \subseteq g_i$ are obtained by the premise. Obviously, $g'_i \cdot g_n \subseteq g_i \cdot s_i^- \subseteq h'$ is validated; that is $g \cdot g_n \subseteq h'$. Consequently, $g \cdot g'_n = g \cdot g_n + g \cdot h' \subseteq h'$.

Similarly, given m and n, suppose that $g \cdot s_n^+ \subseteq g'_m$, there exists a decomposition $g = g^1 + g^2$ such that $g^1 \cdot s_n^+ \subseteq g_m$ and $g^2 \cdot s_n^+ \subseteq h'$. Consequently, $g^1 \cdot g_n \subseteq g_m \subseteq g'_m$ and $g^2 \cdot g_n \subseteq h' \subseteq g'_m$ are obtained. Thus we have $g \cdot g'_n = g^1 \cdot g_n + g^2 \cdot g_n + g \cdot h' \subseteq g'_m + h' = g'_m$.

In a word, I' is a normal form since I' satisfies all the conditions of normal forms, i.e., I can be reduced to normal form. □

Lemma 3. *The reaction $I = \|_{n\in N} p_n \&!s_n \parallel q\&\bot$ can be equivalently reduced to the form $I = \|_{m\in M} g'_m \&!s_m \parallel h'\&\bot$ which satisfies condition (1) $\forall m, n \in M, g \bullet (g \cdot s_m^+ \subseteq g'_n \Rightarrow g \cdot g'_m \subseteq g'_n) \wedge (g \cdot s_m^+ \subseteq h' \Rightarrow g \cdot g'_m \subseteq h')$, where all s_i $(i \in M)$ are different, all g' $(i \in M)$ and h' are up-closed guards.*

Proof: see appendix. □

Theorem 4. *The statement $g\&I$ can be reduced to a normal form if I is a normal form.*

Proof: Let $I = \|_{m\in M} g_m \&!s_m \parallel h\&\bot$

Then,

$$
\begin{aligned}
g\&I &= g\&(\|_{m\in M} g_m \&!s_m \parallel h\&\bot) && \{\textbf{guard-3}\}\\
&= \|_{m\in M} g\&(g_m \&!s_m) \parallel g\&(h\&\bot) && \{\textbf{guard-1}\}\\
&= \|_{m\in M} (g \cdot s_m)\&!s_m \parallel (g \cdot h)\&\bot
\end{aligned}
$$

According to **Lemma** 4 and 3, $g\&I$ can be reduced to normal form. □

Theorem 5. *The statement $I\backslash s$ can be reduced to a normal form if I is a normal form.*

Proof: Let $I = \|_{i\in K} g_i \&!s_i \parallel h\&!\bot$

Then,

$$
\begin{aligned}
I\backslash s &= (\|_{i\in K} g_i \&!s_i \parallel g\&\bot)\backslash s && \{\textbf{guard-2}\}\\
&= (g_1\&!s \parallel g_2\&!s \parallel g_3\&!s \|_{i\in K'} g_i \&!s_i \parallel h\&\bot)\backslash s && \{\textbf{prim-1}\ \textit{and}\ \textbf{prim-2}\}\\
&= (g_1\&!s \parallel (h + g_3)\&\bot \parallel {}_{i\in K'} g_i \&!s_i)\backslash s && \{\textbf{conc-4}\}\\
&= (h + g_3)[g_1/s^+, \overline{g_1}/s^-]\&\bot \\
&\quad \parallel \|_{i\in K'} g_i[g_1/s^+, \overline{g_1}/s^-]\&s_i
\end{aligned}
$$

Where, $K' = K - \{i \mid s_i = s\}$, $s \notin g_1$, $g_2 = g_2 \cdot s^+$, and $g_3 = g_3 \cdot s^-$. According to **Lemma** 4 and 3, $I \backslash s$ can be reduced to normal form. □

Theorem 6. *The statement $I_1 \parallel I_2$ can be reduced to a normal form if both I_1 and I_2 are normal forms.*

Proof: Let $I_1 = \|_{i \in N} g_i \&!s_i \parallel h\&\bot$, $I_2 = \|_{j \in J} g'_j \&!s'_j \parallel h'\&\bot$. Without loss of generality, we assume that $N \cap J = \emptyset$.

Then,

$$\begin{aligned} I_1 \parallel I_2 &= (\|_{i \in N} g_i \&!s_i \parallel h\&\bot) \parallel (\|_{j \in J} g'_j \&!s'_j \parallel h'\&\bot) \\ &= \|_{k \in K} g_k \&!s_k \parallel (h + h')\&\bot \end{aligned}$$

Where, $K = N \uplus J$, $g_k = g_i$, $s_k = s_i$ if $k \in N$ and $g_k = g'_j$, $s_k = s'_j$ if $k \in J$. According to **Lemma** 4 and 3, $I_1 \| I_2$ can be reduced to normal form. □

Theorem 7. *All reactions can be reduced to normal forms.*

Proof: From Theorem 1-4.

In actual, the proof not only demonstrates that all reactions can be reduced to normal forms, but also shows how to translate a reaction into normal form using a unifying approach.

Example 4. Let $I = s_1^- \&!s_2 \parallel s_2^+ \&!s_3 \parallel s_3^+ \&!s_1$

We illustrate how to reduce I into normal form.

$$\begin{aligned} I &= s_1^- \&!s_2 \parallel s_2^+ \&!s_3 \parallel s_3^+ \&!s_1 && \{\textbf{depend-1}\} \\ &= s_1^- \&!s_2 \parallel (s_1^- + s_2^+)\&!s_3 \parallel s_3^+ \&!s_1 && \{\textbf{depend-1}\} \\ &= s_1^- \&!s_2 \parallel (s_1^- + s_2^+)\&!s_3 \parallel (s_1^- + s_2^+ + s_3^+)\&!s_1 && \{\textbf{thm-2}\} \\ &= s_1^- \&!s_2 \parallel (s_1^- + s_2^+)\&!s_3 \parallel (s_1^- + s_2^+ + s_3^+)\&!s_1 \\ &\quad \parallel (s_1^- + s_2^+ \cdot s_3^-)\&\bot && \{\textbf{thm-1}\} \\ &= (s_1^- + s_2^+ + s_3^+)\&!s_1 \parallel (s_1^- + s_2^+ \cdot s_3^-)\&!s_2 \\ &\quad \parallel (s_1^- + s_2^+)\&!s_3 \parallel (s_1^- + s_2^+ \cdot s_3^-)\&\bot && \{\textbf{corollary-1}\} \\ &= (\uparrow s_1^- + \uparrow s_2^+ + \uparrow s_3^+)\&!s_1 \parallel (\uparrow s_1^- + \uparrow s_2^+ \cdot \uparrow s_3^-)\&!s_2 \\ &\quad \parallel (\uparrow s_1^- + \uparrow s_2^+)\&!s_3 \parallel (\uparrow s_1^- + \uparrow s_2^+ \cdot \uparrow s_3^-)\&\bot \end{aligned}$$

Thus the behavior equivalence of two differently written reactions depends on the equivalence of their corresponding normal forms since we have prove that all reactions, however deeply structured, can be reduced to a normal form. Obviously, two reactions in normal form are behaviorally equivalent if they have the same algebraic form. The following definition captures the intuition.

Definition 8. *$NF_1 = NF_2$ iff $h \equiv h'$ and $\forall i \in M \bullet g'_i \equiv g_i$, where $NF_1 = \|_{i \in M} g_i \&!s_i \parallel h\&\bot$ and $NF_2 = \|_{i \in M} g'_i \&!s_i \parallel h'\&\bot$ are normal forms.*

As advocated in the above, normal form exposes the internal dependence explicitly. Consequently, the computation is straightforward for reactions in normal form rather than tedious computations for general algebraic forms. In particular, the computation for emission set of reaction is surprisedly simple, as shown in **theorem** 8.

Theorem 8. *For input signals S and reaction $NF = \|_{i \in M} g_i \&!s_i \parallel h\&\bot$ in normal form, we have* $\mathsf{ems}(NF) = \{s_i \mid e \notin h \wedge e \in g_i \wedge e = \{t^+ \mid t \in S\}\}$.

6 Discussion

Here we give a discussion on the related work with our study on the signal calculus. Edward *et al.* presented the tagged signal model [11] to explore the design of computational framework, where each signal represents a collection of value-tag pair. The set of tags is usually partially ordered set (poset). Thus the tagged signal model maintains the strict causality, which ensure determinacy under certain essential technical conditions.

Esterel [12,15] is an imperative synchronous language having a textual syntax somewhat along the lines of Pascal. Its distinguishing feature is the rich set of signal handing constructs for reactive programming [16]. The main semantic challenges addressed in [7,13,17] is the issue of *causality*. To solve the challenge, many research efforts are addressed to develop a diversity of constructive semantics for Esterel [12], e.g., constructive behavioral semantics, constructive operational semantics and constructive circuits.

Essentially, our signal calculus is inspired by the Esteral language. We intend to translate all Esteral statements into our calculus. For example, present s^+ then emit t_1 else emit t_2 can be expressed as $s^+\&!t_1 \parallel s^-\&!t_2$ in our calculus. Further, the sequential operator is, intentionally, not involved in this paper. In fact, all sequential instantaneous reactions can be embraced in our calculus. For instance, the sequential $g\&!t\ ;\ h\&!s$ is equivalent to $g\&!t \parallel (g\cdot(h[\epsilon/t^+, \emptyset/t^-]) + \overline{g}\cdot h)\&!s$. In other words, the extension with the sequential compositional would not enhance the expressiveness of the calculus.

In future, we will complete the signal calculus by introducing delay-time reactions. We believe that the zero-time reactions and delay-time reactions are orthogonal. Thus the extension is straightforward. The head normal form for signal calculus has the form:

$$NF = NF_1 \parallel \|_{i\in N}\ g_i\&(pause; NF)$$

Where NF_1 is the normal form of I-calculus. The reaction $pause$ means it pauses in the current instant and terminates in the next instant. The head norm form indicates that in every instant, the reaction first instantaneously reacts to the input signals and then selects the appropriate delay-time branch in the light of the guards.

Acknowledgement. This work was supported by National High Technology Research and Development Program of China (No. 2011AA010101), National Basic Research Program of China (No. 2011CB302904), National Natural Science Foundation of China (No. 61021004), Doctoral Program Foundation of Institutions of Higher Education of China (No. 200802690018). The authors also gratefully acknowledge support from the Danish National Research Foundation and the National Natural Science Foundation of China (Grant No. 61061130541) for the Danish-Chinese Center for Cyber Physical Systems. Yongxin ZHAO is also supported by ECNU Reward for Excellent Doctors in Academics (XRZZ2010027).

References

1. Goguen, J., Thatcher, J., Wagner, E., Wright, J.: Initial algebra semantics and continuous algebra. Journal of the ACM 24(1), 68–95 (1977)
2. Bergstra, J.A., Klop, J.W.: Algebra of communicating processes with abstraction. Theoretical Computer Science 37(1), 77–121 (1985)

3. Hennessy, M.C.: Algebraic Theory of Processes. MIT Press, Cambridge (1988)
4. Roscoe, A.W., Hoare, C.A.R.: The Laws of OCCAM Programming. Theoretical Computer Science 60, 229–316 (1977/1988)
5. Baeten, J.C.M., Weijland, W.P.: Process Algebra. Cambridge Tracts in Theoretical Computer Science. Cambridge University Press, Cambridge (1990)
6. Libkin, L.: An elementary proof that upper and lower powerdomain constructions commute. Bulletin EATCS 48, 175–177 (1992)
7. Berry, G., Gonthier, G.: The Esterel synchronous programming language: Design, semantics, implementation. Science of Computer Programming (SCP) 19(2), 87–152 (1992)
8. He, J., Hoare, C.A.R.: From Algebra to operational semantics. Information Processing Letter 46 (1993)
9. Maddux, R.D.: Fundamental study Relation-algebraic semantics. Theoretical Computer Science 160, 1–85 (1996)
10. Hoare, C.A.R., He, J.: Unifying Theories of Programming. Prentice Hall International Series in Computer Science. Prentice-Hall, Englewood Cliffs (1998)
11. Lee, E.A., Sangiovanni-Vincentelli, A.: A framework for comparing models of computation. IEEE Transactions on Computer-Aided Design of Integraed Circuits and Systems 17(12), 1217–1229 (1998)
12. Berry, G.: The Constructive Semantics of Pure Esterel (1999) Draft version, `ftp://ftp-sop.inria.fr/meije/esterel/papers/constructiveness3.ps.gz`
13. Tini, S: Structural Operational Semantics for Synchronous Languages. PhD thesis, Dipartimento di Informatica, Universitá degli Studi di Pisa, Pisa, Italy (2000)
14. McIver, A.K., Morgan, C.C.: Probabilistic power domains (in preparation)
15. Potop-Butucaru, D., Edwards, S.A., Berry, G.: Compiling Esterel. Springer, Heidelberg (2007)
16. Shyamasundar, R.K., Ramesh, S.: Real Time Programming: Languages, Specification and Verifcations. World Scientific Publishing, Singapore (2009)
17. Mousavi, M.: Causality in the Semantics of Esterel: Revisited. Electronic Proceedings in Theoretical Computer Science 18, 32–45 (2010)

Appendix

Proof of **Lemma** 4

Here we equivalently construct the expected form. Naturally, we can always demand that all signals s_i $(i \in N)$ are different, i.e., $\forall m, n \in N \bullet (m \neq n \Rightarrow s_m \neq s_n)$ and all g_i $(i \in M)$ and h are up-closed guards since reactions are equivalent with respect to up-closed guards. Otherwise we can equivalently transform I by removing $p_n\&!s_n$ and substituting $(p_m + p_n)\&!s_m$ and $N\backslash\{n\}$ for $p_m\&!s_m$ and N respectively. Thus we get $I = \|_{i \in M} g_i\&!s_i \parallel h\&\bot$, where all s_i $(i \in M)$ are different, all g_i $(i \in M)$ and h are up-closed guards.

Define $G =_{df} \{(g_i, s_i) \mid i \in M\}$. For any k from M, let $g_k^0 = g_k$ and $G_k = G\backslash\{(g_k, s_k)\}$, we build $H_k^1 = \{g \cdot g_i \mid \exists (g_i, s_i) \in G_k \bullet g \cdot s_i^+ \subseteq g_k^0\}$ and $g_k^1 = g_k^0 + \sum_{g \in H_k^1} g$. In general, if $g_k^r \neq g_k^{r-1}$ $(1 \leq r)$, construct $H_k^{r+1} = \{g \cdot g_i \mid \exists (g_i, s_i) \in G_k \bullet g \cdot s_i^+ \subseteq g_k^r\}$ and $g_k^{r+1} = g_k^r + \sum_{g \in H_k^{r+1}} g$. Obviously, the construction must terminate after at most $|M|$ times construction, i.e., there exists $1 \leq j_k \leq |M|$ such that $g_k^{j_k} = g_k^{j_k - 1}$. Thus we have $\forall i \in M, g \bullet g \cdot s_i^+ \subseteq g_k^{j_k} \Rightarrow g \cdot g_i \subseteq g_k^{j_k}$ and $g_k^m \subseteq g_k^n$ for $0 \leq m \leq n \leq j_k$.

We also build h^{j_h} in a similar way. Let $h^0 = h$ and $G_h = G$, we construct $H_h^1 = \{g \cdot g_i \mid \exists (g_i, s_i) \in G_h \bullet g \cdot s_i^+ \subseteq g_h^0\}$ and $g_h^1 = g_h^0 + \sum_{g \in H_h^1} g$. In general, if $g_h^r \neq g_h^{r-1}$ $(1 \leq r)$, we construct $H_h^{r+1} = \{g \cdot g_i \mid \exists (g_i, s_i) \in G_h \bullet g \cdot s_i^+ \subseteq g_h^r\}$ and $g_h^{r+1} = g_h^r + \sum_{g \in H_h^{r+1}} g$. In the same reason, there exists $1 \leq j_h \leq |M|$ such that $g_h^{j_h} = g_h^{j_h - 1}$. Thus we have $\forall i \in M, g \bullet g \cdot s_i^+ \subseteq g_h^{j_h} \Rightarrow g \cdot g_i \subseteq g_h^{j_h}$ and $g_h^m \subseteq g_h^n$ for $0 \leq m \leq n \leq j_h$.

Firstly, we show that the construction conserves the equivalence of reactions. For any $k \in M$ and $0 \leq r_k \leq j_k$, define $I_k^{r_k} = g_k^{r_k} \&!s_k \parallel I$. We state that $\forall k \in M, 0 \leq r_k < j_k \bullet I_k^{r_k} = I_k^{r_k+1}$.

$$
\begin{aligned}
I_k^{r_k} &= g_k^{r_k} \&!s_k \parallel I && \{\textbf{depend-1}\ and\ \textbf{guard-2}\} \\
&= (g_k^{r_k} + \textstyle\sum_{g \in H_k^{r_k+1}} g) \&!s_k \parallel I && \{\textbf{Def}\ of\ H_k^{r_k+1}\ and\ g_k^{r_k+1}\} \\
&= g_k^{r_k+1} \&!s_k \parallel I = I_k^{r_k+1}.
\end{aligned}
$$

Consequently, $\forall 0 \leq r_k, r_k' \leq j_k, I_k^{r_k} = I_k^{r_k'}$. Similarly, define $I^{r_h} = h^{r_h} \& \bot \parallel I$ and $\forall 0 \leq r_h, r_h' \leq j_h, I^{r_h} = I^{r_h'}$ is validated.

Let $I' = \parallel_{i \in M} g_i^{j_i} \&!s_i \parallel h^{j_h} \& \bot$. We state that $I = I'$ by the following proof,

$$
\begin{aligned}
I' &= \parallel_{i \in M} g_i^{j_i} \&!s_i \parallel h^{j_h} \& \bot && \{\textbf{guard-4}\} \\
&= \parallel_{i \in M} (g_i^{j_i} + g_i) \&!s_i \parallel (h^{j_h} + h) \& \bot && \{\textbf{guard-2}\} \\
&= \parallel_{i \in M} g_i^{j_i} \&!s_i \parallel h^{j_h} \& \bot \parallel I && \{\textbf{P-3}\} \\
&= \parallel_{i \in M} (g_i^{j_i} \&!s_i \parallel I) \parallel (h^{j_h} \& \bot \parallel I) && \{proved\} \\
&= \parallel_{i \in M} (g_i \&!s_i \parallel I) \parallel (h \& \bot \parallel I) \\
&= \parallel_{i \in M} g_i \&!s_i \parallel h \& \bot \parallel I \\
&= I \parallel I = I
\end{aligned}
$$

Finally, we prove I' satisfies the condition (1) $\forall m, n \in M, g \bullet (g \cdot s_m^+ \subseteq g_n^{j_n} \Rightarrow g \cdot g_m^{j_m} \subseteq g_n^{j_n}) \wedge (g \cdot s_m^+ \subseteq h^{j_h} \Rightarrow g \cdot g_m^{j_m} \subseteq h^{j_h})$. We first prove the statement $\forall 0 \leq r \leq j_m, g \bullet g \cdot s_m^+ \subseteq g_n^{j_n} \Rightarrow g \cdot g_m^r \subseteq g_n^{j_n}$ for given m and n by mathematical induction.

Basis When $r = 0$, obviously $\forall g \bullet g \cdot s_m^+ \subseteq g_n^{j_n} \subseteq g \cdot g_m \subseteq g_n^{j_n}$.

Induction Step Assume that $r = l$ $(0 \leq l < j_m)$, $\forall g \bullet g \cdot s_m^+ \subseteq g_n^{j_n} \Rightarrow g \cdot g_m^l \subseteq g_n^{j_n}$. When $r = l+1$, suppose $g \cdot s_m^+ \subseteq g_n^{j_n}$, we have $H_m^{l+1} = \{g \cdot g_i \mid \exists (g_i, s_i) \in G_m \bullet g \cdot s_i^+ \subseteq g_m^l\}$ and $g_m^{l+1} = g_m^l + \sum_{g \in H_m^{l+1}} g$. Recall that $\forall g' \cdot g_i \in H_m^{l+1}, g' \cdot s_i \subseteq g_m^l$. Thus $g \cdot g' \cdot g_i \subseteq g_n^{j_n}$ is validated since $g \cdot g' \cdot s_i \subseteq g \cdot g_m^l \subseteq g_n^{j_n}$. Hence, $g \cdot g_m^{l+1} = g \cdot g_m^l + g \cdot \sum_{g' \in H_m^{l+1}} g' \subseteq g_n^{j_n}$. According to the principle of mathematical induction, $\forall 0 \leq r \leq j_m, \forall g \bullet (g \cdot s_m^+ \subseteq g_n^{j_n} \Rightarrow g \cdot g_m^r \subseteq g_n^{j_n})$. In particular, $\forall g \bullet (g \cdot s_m^+ \subseteq g_n^{j_n} \Rightarrow g \cdot g_m^{j_m} \subseteq g_n^{j_n})$.

Similarly, we can prove $\forall g \bullet g \cdot s_m^+ \subseteq h^{j_h} \Rightarrow g \cdot g_m^{j_m} \subseteq h^{j_h}$.

The proof is done and $I' = \parallel_{i \in M} g_i^{j_i} \&!s_i \parallel h^{j_h} \& \bot$ satisfies the conditions. □

Reasoning about Programs Using a Scientific Method

Peter W. O'Hearn

Queen Mary University of London

Abstract. Reasoning about programs has traditionally been done using deductive reasoning, where mathematical logic is used to make proofs that connect programs with specifications. In this talk I describe an approach where an automated reasoning tool approaches program code as a scientist would in the natural world. Instead of just deductive logic, versions of abductive reasoning (generation of new hypotheses) and inductive generalization are used in an iterative fashion to discover specifications that partly describe what programs do, starting from bare code. The resulting specifications are partial or conservative, but the inference/discovery aspect makes it much easier to approach large code bases, quickly, than with the traditional deductive-only approach.

The underlying program logic in this work is separation logic, a logic for reasoning about the way that programs use computer memory, and the inference method attempts to discover a logical assertion describing the program's footprint: the collection of cells that it touches. Aiming for the footprint provides a strategy to select compact specifications, amongst the enormity of all potential specifications (which would be too many to consider). After describing the inference techniques, I report on experience using a software tool that automates the method, which has been applied to large code bases.

This talk is based on joint work with Cristiano Calcagno, Dino Distefano and Hongseok Yang.

S. Qin and Z. Qiu (Eds.): ICFEM 2011, LNCS 6991, p. 14, 2011.

Poirot—A Concurrency Sleuth

Shaz Qadeer

Microsoft Research
qadeer@microsoft.com

Abstract. Concurrent programming is difficult. The challenges are foundational: unlike sequential control flow, asynchronous control flow is difficult to understand and reason about. Not surprisingly, even expert programmers find it difficult to write concurrent software. We desperately need software engineering techniques and tools to move concurrent programming from black art to a rigorous engineering discipline. I believe that automated tools that reduce the cognitive burden of reasoning about concurrency can help tremendously in improving the productivity of concurrent programmers. In collaboration with my colleagues at Microsoft Research, I have developed Poirot (http://research.microsoft.com/en-us/projects/poirot/), a tool for answering semantic queries about a concurrent program by statically searching over its executions. Poirot exploits sequential encodings of concurrent semantics, structural under- and over-approximations for sequential control flow, and advances in automated theorem proving to search concurrent program executions efficiently. Poirot is being used in many different applications—bug detection, program understanding, and symbolic debugging. This lecture will present both a demonstration and an explanation of the techniques underlying the search engine inside Poirot.

Poirot is joint work with Akash Lal and Shuvendu Lahiri.

S. Qin and Z. Qiu (Eds.): ICFEM 2011, LNCS 6991, p. 15, 2011.

Context-Based Behavioral Equivalence of Components in Self-Adaptive Systems

Narges Khakpour[1,2], Marjan Sirjani[3], and Ursula Goltz[1]

[1] IPS, Technical University of Braunschweig, Germany
[2] Tarbiat Modares University, Iran
[3] Reykjavik University, Iceland
khakpour@ips.cs.tu-bs.de

Abstract. An important challenge to realize dynamic adaptation is finding suitable components for substitution or interaction according to the current context. A possible solution is checking behavioral equivalence of components in different contexts. Two components are equivalent with respect to a context, if they behave equivalently in that context. In this work, we deal with context-specific behavioral equivalence of PobSAM components. PobSAM is a flexible formal model for developing and modeling evolving self-adaptive systems. A PobSAM model is a collection of actors, views, and autonomous managers. Autonomous managers govern the behavior of actors by enforcing suitable context-based policies. Views provide contextual information for managers to control and adapt the actors behavior. Managers are the core components used to realize adaptation by changing their policies. They are modeled as meta-actors whose configurations are described using a multi-sorted algebra called CA. The behavior of mangers depends on the context in which they are executing. In this paper, we present an equational theory to reason about context-specific behavioral equivalence of managers independently from actors. To this end, we introduce and axiomatize a new operator to consider the interaction of managers and the context. This equational theory is based on the notion of statebased bisimilarity and allows us to reason about the behavioral equivalence of managers as well as the behavioral equivalence of the constitutes of managers (i.e., policies and configurations). We illustrate our approach through an example.

1 Introduction

Today's complex systems often need to operate in dynamic, open and heterogeneous environments, so they must be able to adapt themselves at run-time to handle varying resources, user mobility, changing user needs, and system faults. PobSAM (Policy-based Self-Adaptive Model) [8] is a flexible formal model to develop, specify and verify self-adaptive systems which uses policies as the fundamental mechanism to govern the system behavior. A PobSAM model is composed of a collection of autonomous managers, views and actors. Autonomous managers are meta-actors responsible for monitoring and handling events by enforcing suitable policies. Each manager has a set of configurations where one

S. Qin and Z. Qiu (Eds.): ICFEM 2011, LNCS 6991, pp. 16–32, 2011.

of the configurations is active at a time. The manager changes its active configuration dynamically in response to the changing circumstances according to adaptation policies. The managers monitor actors through views, i.e. views provide contextual information for the managers. One of the distinguished advantages of PobSAM is that it allows us to modify the configurations (or policies) of managers at runtime. This feature makes PobSAM a suitable model to develop evolving self-adaptive systems.

In dynamic environments such as ubiquitous computing world, many systems must cope with variable resources (bandwidth, server availability, etc.), system faults (servers and networks going down, failure of external components, etc.), and changing user priorities (high-fidelity video streams at one moment, low-fidelity at another, etc.) [3]. In such environments, the system requires to continue running with only minimal human intervention, and the component assessment and integration process must be carried out automatically. We refer to the component assessment as the problem of identifying a component with desired behavior that can replace another component or can be used for interaction in a specific context. A possible solution to this problem relies on detecting the behavioral equivalence of a particular component with desired behavior and a candidate component that could maintain that behavior. Generally, we categorize the behavioral equivalence of two components as context-independent or context-specific. The *context* of a component is defined as the environment in which the component is running. Two components that are context-independent equivalent behave equivalently in any environment, while the equivalence of two components that are context-specific equivalent, depends on the environments in which they are running.

Managers are the main components to control and adapt the system behavior in PobSAM. Thus, it is an important issue to analyze the behavioral equivalence of managers when studying the dynamic replacement and interaction of components for software adaptation. In order to ensure the correctness of the whole system behavior, we have to provide approaches to analyze the behavioral equivalence of the original manager and the adapted one.

Contribution. We previously proposed PobSAM in [8] which has a formal foundation that employs an integration of algebraic formalisms and actor-based models. The actors of PobSAM are modeled using actor-based models while the algebra CA (Configuration Algebra) is proposed to specify the configurations of managers. Due to the fact that the managers control and adapt the system behavior using dynamic policies which are context-dependent rules, the behavior of a manager depends on the context in which it is enforcing policies. We must investigate context-specific behavioral equivalence of managers. Furthermore, we can modify the policies and the configurations of a manager dynamically. Thus, this equational theory should allow us to reason about context-specific behavioral equivalence of policies and configurations as well. In this paper, we develop an equational theory to analyze context-specific behavioral equivalence of managers, based on a notion of behavioral equivalence called statebased bisimulation. The context of managers is specified by a labeled state transition system.

The context interacts with the managers by synchronous message passing. We extend CA with a new operator to consider the interaction of managers and the context. Then, we present the axioms for this operator to check behavioral equivalence of managers. In our equational theory, we can reason about context-specific behavioral equivalence of policies, configurations and managers separately. As the manager may evolve by changing its policies or configurations, this theory allows us to only reason about the modified constitutes without the need to check the whole model of the system. *An important advantage of this equational theory is that it analyzes the behavioral equivalence of the manager layer independently from the actor layer using the context.*

The remainder of this paper is organized as follows. In Section 2 we introduce an example to illustrate our approach. In Section 3, we have a brief review on PobSAM. Section 4 deals with modeling our case study in PobSAM. We introduce the notion of statebased bisimulation in Section 5. An equational theory is proposed to check context-specific behavioral equivalence of managers in Section 6. In Section 7, we give a summary of related work and Section 8 presents our conclusions.

2 Illustrating Example

We use a simple example borrowed from [16] to illustrate our approach. In this example, a team of collaborating unmanned autonomous vehicles (UAVs) are used for a search and rescue operation. Assume a person with a body sensor network (BSN) is wounded in an area and needs help. The BSN sends a help message to a mission commander. A mission is defined by the commander to save the wounded person: one or more UAVs with video cameras act as surveyors and others perform a communication relay function. The UAVs are required to adapt their behavior according to the changes of the environment. According to the role of a UAV in the mission, a set of policies is used by that UAV to control its behavior. However, the role of a UAV is not fixed, and subsequently, the policies used to control the UAV behavior must change dynamically. For instance, the video camera of a surveyor may break down and that surveyor would act as a communication relay. Thus, various sets of policies are defined for a UAV and one of those sets of policies is active at a time, i.e. adaptation is performed by changing the set of policies used to control the UAV behavior.

3 PobSAM

A PobSAM model is composed of three layers:

- The *actor layer* is dedicated to the functional behavior of the system and contains computational entities.
- The *view layer* consists of view variables that provide an abstraction of the actors' states for the managers. A view variable is an actual state variable, or a function or a predicate applied to state variables of actors.

- The main layer of PobSAM is the *manager layer* containing the autonomous managers. Managers control the behavior of actors according to the predefined policies. A manager may have different configurations and dynamic adaptation is performed by switching among those configurations. A configuration consists of two classes of policies: governing policies and adaptation policies. A manager directs the actor behavior by sending messages to the actors according to governing policies. Adaptation policies are used for dynamic adaptation by switching among configurations. However, the adaptation cannot be done immediately and when the system reaches a safe state, the manager switches to the new configuration. A new mode of operation called adaptation mode is introduced in which a manager runs before switching to the new configuration. There are two kinds of adaptations called *loose adaptation* and *strict adaptation*. Under loose adaptation, the manager handles events in the adaptation mode by enforcing the governing policies of old configuration, while in the strict adaptation mode all the events are postponed until the system passes the adaptation mode safely.

A manager is defined as a tuple $m = \langle V_m, C_m, c_{init} \rangle$, with C_m the (finite) set of configurations of m, $c_{init} \in C_m$ its initial configuration, and V_m the (finite) set of view variables observable by m. A configuration $c \in C_m$ is defined as $c = \langle g, p \rangle$, where $g = \{g_1, ..., g_n\}$ and p indicate the governing policy set and the adaptation policies of c, respectively. The constants $\top$ and $\bot$ stand for "True" and "False", respectively.

Governing Policies. A simple governing policy $g_i{=}\langle o, e, \psi \rangle \bullet a$, $1 \le i \le n$ consists of priority $o \in \mathbb{N}$, event $e \in E$ where E is an assumed set of possible events, condition ψ (a Boolean term) and an action a. The actions in the governing policies are specified using an algebra CA^a defined as follows. We let a, a', a'' denote action terms, while an (atomic) action α could be an internal action, an output action ($\alpha!$) in form of $r.msg$ (i.e. sending the message msg to actor r), or an input action ($\alpha?$).

$$a \stackrel{\text{def}}{=} a; a' \mid a \parallel a' \mid a \mathbin{|\!\lfloor} a' \mid a + a' \mid \phi :\rightarrow a \mid \alpha \mid \alpha! \mid \alpha? \mid \delta_a$$

Thus an action term can be a sequential composition (;), a parallel composition ($\parallel$), a left parallel composition ($\mathbin{|\!\lfloor}$ which is as $\parallel$ but the first action that is performed comes from the left operand), a non-deterministic choice (+), or a conditional choice ($\phi :\rightarrow a$). Moreover, we have the special constant δ_a as the deadlock action for governing policies. Operator precedences are assigned, from highest precedence to the lowest, to the conditional choice, the parallel composition operators, the sequential composition and the non-deterministic choice operators. Whenever a manager receives an event e, it identifies all simple governing policies that are triggered by that event , i.e. are of the form $\langle o, e, \psi \rangle \bullet a$ for some o, ψ, and a. For each of these activated policies, if the policy condition ψ evaluates to true and there is no other triggered governing policy with priority higher than o, then action a is executed. Table 1 shows CA^a axioms.

Adaptation Policies. Adaptation policies are specified using the algebra CA^p as follows:

Table 1. Action Algebra CA^a

$a + a' = a' + a$	A1	$a \parallel a' = a' \parallel a$	AP1
$(a + a') + a'' = a + (a' + a'')$	A2	$(a \parallel a') \parallel a'' = a \parallel (a' \parallel a'')$	AP2
$a + a = a$	A3	$(a + a') \lfloor\lfloor a'' = (a \lfloor\lfloor a'') + (a' \lfloor\lfloor a'')$	AP3
$a + \delta_g = a$	A4	$a \parallel a' = a \lfloor\lfloor a' + a' \lfloor\lfloor a$	AP4
$\delta_g; a = \delta_g$	A5	$\alpha \lfloor\lfloor a = \alpha; a$	AP5
$(a + a'); a'' = a; a'' + a'; a''$	A6	$(\alpha; a) \lfloor\lfloor a' = \alpha; (a \parallel a')$	AP6
$(a; a'); a'' = a; (a'; a'')$	A7		

$\top :\rightarrow a = a$	C1	$\bot :\rightarrow a = \delta$	C2
$\phi :\rightarrow (a + a') = \phi :\rightarrow a + \phi :\rightarrow a'$	C3	$\phi :\rightarrow (a; a') = \phi :\rightarrow a; a'$	C4
$\phi :\rightarrow (\psi :\rightarrow a) = (\phi \wedge \psi) :\rightarrow a$	C5	$(\phi \vee \psi) :\rightarrow a = \phi :\rightarrow a + \psi :\rightarrow a$	C6
$\phi :\rightarrow \delta = \delta$	C7	$\phi :\rightarrow a \lfloor\lfloor a' = \phi :\rightarrow (a \lfloor\lfloor a')$	C8

$$p \stackrel{\text{def}}{=} \langle o, e, \psi, \lambda, \phi \rangle \bullet c \mid p \oplus p \mid \delta_p$$

which consists of priority $o \in \mathbb{N}$, event $e \in E$, and a condition ψ (a Boolean term) for triggering the adaptation. Moreover, condition ϕ is a Boolean term indicating the conditions for applying the adaptation, λ is the adaptation type (loose, denoted $\bot$, or strict, denoted $\top$), and c is the new configuration. Informally, simple adaptation policy $\langle o, e, \psi, \lambda, \phi \rangle \bullet c$ indicates that when event e occurs and the triggering condition ψ holds, if there is no other triggered adaptation policy with priority higher than o, then the manager evolves to the strict or loose adaptation mode as given by λ. When the condition ϕ is true, it will perform adaptation and switch to the configuration c. The adaptation policy of a manager is defined as composition($\oplus$) of the simple adaptation policies. Furthermore, δ_p indicates the unit element for the composition operator.

4 Formal Modeling of Collaborating UAVs

Figure 1 shows the PobSAM model of a UAV partially. This model contains actors `motor, video camera, GSM` and `infrared sensors` where Rebeca[15] specification of `motor` is given in figure 1. Rebeca is an actor-based model used to specify the actor layer in [8]. The view layer has a number of views denoting the current location, speed, energy level etc of UAVs. As an example, the view `UAV1speed` indicates the speed of `UAV1` which reflects the value of the statevar `speed` of actor `UAV1motor`.

A UAV has a manager named `UAVCntrlr` for controlling different components of the UAV. A `UAVCntrlr` has three different configurations including `surveyorConf, idleConf` and `relayConf`. It enforces different sets of policies in each configuration to control the behavior of UAV. For instance, the configuration `surveyorConf` contains the adaptation policies `{p1,p2}` and the governing policy set `{g1,g2,g3}`. Assume a situation that the video camera of a surveyor breaks down and we need to use this UAV as a relay. We define the adaptation policy `p1` which informally states that "when the video camera is broken down, if the wounded person has not been found and the UAV has required capability to act as a relay, it should switch to the `relayConf` configuration". We specify this policy formally as follows in which *brokencamera* is an event. The view variable *canRelay* indicates if the UAV has required capability to act as a relay, and the view variable *success* denotes whether the wounded person has been found or not.

$$p_1 \stackrel{def}{=} \langle 1, brokenCamera, \neg success \wedge canRelay, \top, \top \rangle \bullet relayConf$$

The simple governing policy `g1` states that when the wounded person is found, the UAV must request his health information from his BSN and send a "success" message to the commander. The algebraic form of this policy is $g_1 \stackrel{\text{def}}{=} \langle 1,\ found(x,y),\ \top \rangle \bullet\ a_1$ where *found(x,y)* denotes an event that the wounded person has been found at location (x, y), and

$$\begin{aligned} a_1 = {} & BSN.reqHealthinfo()? \parallel \\ & relay1.send(success(x, y), commander)! \end{aligned}$$

5 Statebased Bisimulation

In PobSAM, the managers are running concurrently with the actors; the computation at the actor layer is reflected at the view layer, the state changing of the view layer leads to triggering and enforcing policies by the managers. Subsequently, the enforcement of policies results in new computations to be done at the actor layer. We specify the context based on specification of the view layer, the actor interfaces and possibly the interfaces of other managers. Given the formal specification of a context, we check the behavioral equivalence of managers in that context. A context is defined as follows:

Definition 1. *A context is defined as tuple* $T_c = \langle V, S_c, s_c^0, \mathcal{A}_c^I, \mathcal{A}_c^O, \mathcal{A}_c^H, \rightarrow_c \rangle$ *where*

- $V = \{v_1, ..., v_n\}$ *is the set of view variables.*
- S_c *is the set of states where a state* $s \in S_c$ *is of the form* $\langle v_1, ..., v_n \rangle$.
- s_c^0 *is the initial state.*
- $\mathcal{A}_c^I, \mathcal{A}_c^O$ *and* $\mathcal{A}_c^H$ *are disjoint sets of input, output and internal actions where* $\mathcal{A}_c = \mathcal{A}_c^I \cup \mathcal{A}_c^O \cup \mathcal{A}_c^H$.
- $\rightarrow_c \subseteq S_c \times \mathcal{A}_c \times S_c$ *is the set of transitions.*

In this paper, we extend CA^a with a new operator, called CA^a_Θ. We present a context-specific behavioral equivalence theory for CA^a_Θ. Then we use this basic theory to reason about context-specific behavioral equivalence of policies, configurations and managers. We define the operational meaning of CA^a_Θ terms by a transition system with data whose states are pairs of a CA^a term and a context state. Let A denote the set of CA^a terms. The set of all pairs over $A \times S_c$ is denoted by $S_{A \times S_c}$. We define a state transition system with data as follows:

```
manager UAVCntrlr
{
statevars {
}
configurations{
    surveyorConf=[p1,p2] [g1,g2,g3];
    //definition of relayConf and idleConf configurations
 }
policies{
  p1[strict]:on brokenCamera if (!success && canRelay)
            switchto relayConf when true priority 1 ;
   g1 : on found(x,y) if true do
(BSN.reqhealthinfo() || relay.send(success(x,y),commander))
          priority 1 ;
//definition of governing and adaptation policies
  }
}
views {
   byte UAV1speed as UAV1motor.speed;
   //definition of other views
}
Actors {
 reactiveclass motor() {
   knownobjects {}
   statevars{public byte speed; }
   msgsrv forward()  {
     ...
    }
   msgsrv stop()  {
     ...
    }
  //definition of other message servers
  }
  //definition of other reactive classes
}
```

Fig. 1. The Partial PobSAM Model of a UAV

Definition 2. *A state transition system with data defined over the context T_c, is $T(a, s_c^0) = \langle S_{A\times S_c}, \rightarrow, \mathcal{A}^I, \mathcal{A}^O, \mathcal{A}^H, (a, s_c^0)\rangle$ where $S_{A\times S_c}$ is a set of states, (a, s_c^0) is the initial state, $\rightarrow \subseteq S_{A\times S_c} \times \mathcal{A} \times S_{A\times S_c}$ and $\mathcal{A} = \mathcal{A}^I \cup \mathcal{A}^O \cup \mathcal{A}^H$.*

It worth mentioning that $\mathcal{A}_c \subseteq \mathcal{A}$, $\mathcal{A}_c^I \subseteq \mathcal{A}^I$, $\mathcal{A}_c^O \subseteq \mathcal{A}^O$ and $\mathcal{A}_c^H \subseteq \mathcal{A}^H$. We use a notion of bisimilarity called statebased bisimulation [5] for expressing context-specific behavioral equivalence of CA_Θ^a terms defined as follows:

Definition 3. ***Statebased Bisimulation*** *A binary relation $\mathcal{R} \subseteq S_{A\times S_c} \times S_{A\times S_c}$ is a statebased bisimulation iff for all $(r, s), (q, s) \in S_{A\times S_c}$ with $((r, s), (q, s)) \in \mathcal{R}$:*

- *whenever $(r, s) \xrightarrow{\alpha} (r', s')$ for some $\alpha \in \mathcal{A}$ and (r', s'), then, for some q', also $(q, s) \xrightarrow{\alpha} (q', s')$ and $((r', s'), (q', s')) \in \mathcal{R}$.*
- *Conversely, whenever $(q, s) \xrightarrow{\alpha} (q', s')$ for some $\alpha \in \mathcal{A}$ and (q', s'), then, for some r', also $(r, s) \xrightarrow{\alpha} (r', s')$ and $((r', s'), (q', s')) \in \mathcal{R}$.*

A pair $(r, s) \in S_{A\times S_c}$ is statebased bisimilar with a pair $(r', s') \in S_{A\times S_c}$ with respect to the context T_c, written by $(r, s) \underline{\Leftrightarrow}_{T_c} (r', s')$ iff $s = s'$ and there is a statebased bisimulation containing the pair $((r, s), (r', s'))$.

A state transition system with data $T(r, s) = \langle S_{A\times S_c}, \rightarrow, \mathcal{A}^I, \mathcal{A}^O, \mathcal{A}^H, (r, s)\rangle$ is statebased bisimilar with the transition system with data $T(q, s') = \langle S_{A\times S_c}, \rightarrow', \mathcal{A}'^I, \mathcal{A}'^O, \mathcal{A}'^H, (q, s')\rangle$, written by $T(r, s) \underline{\Leftrightarrow}_{T_c} T(q, s')$ iff $(r, s) \underline{\Leftrightarrow}_{T_c} (q, s')$. Furthermore, two closed terms r , q over CA^a are statebased bisimilar with respect to the context T_c, written by $r \underline{\Leftrightarrow}_{T_c} q$, iff $T(r, s) \underline{\Leftrightarrow}_{T_c} T(q, s)$ for all $s \in S_c$.

6 Context-Specific Behavioral Equivalence

In this section, we use the notion of statebased bisimulation to reason about context-specific behavioral equivalence of managers and their constituents. We introduce a new operator (Θ) to consider interactions of managers and the context. The axiom system of CA^a is extended to check statebased bisimulation of CA^a_Θ terms. Then, context-specific behavioral equivalence of policies, configurations and managers are defined based on the proposed equational theory for CA^a_Θ.

6.1 Context-Specific Behavioral Equivalence of Actions

In our model, the context and the managers run concurrently and interact by synchronous message passing. Since the conditions of an action are evaluated over the context state, therefore the concrete action carried out by the manager depends on the context. There are three types of computation steps: (i) the manager and the context synchronize on their shared input-output actions, (ii) the context performs an internal action, or (iii) the manager performs an internal action. In the cases (i) and (iii), the conditions of the action are evaluated over the state of context. We introduce the operator Θ to compute the concrete action done by a manager, regarding the interactions of the manager and a context.

Let a denote a term of CA^a which must be performed by a manager, and $T_c = \langle V, S_c, s_c^0, \mathcal{A}_c^I, \mathcal{A}_c^O, \mathcal{A}_c^H, \rightarrow_c\rangle$ denote an arbitrary context. Assume the current state of context is $s \in S_c$ and the manager starts the enforcement of action a. The operator $\Theta_s(a)$ gives the concrete action performed by the manager as the result of performing action a when the context starts its execution in state $s_c \in S_c$. The structural operational semantics of CA^a_Θ extended is described by the transition rules given in Figure 2 in addition to the transition rules proposed in [8]. The transition $a \xrightarrow{[\phi]\alpha} a'$ means that a can evolve to a' by performing action α under condition ϕ.

Figure 3 presents the axioms for Θ in which $\alpha' \in \mathcal{A}_c^H$. This axiom system together with the axioms of Table 1 are used to check context-specific behavioral equivalence of actions. We can formulate action a in form of $a = \sum_i a_i$ using the axioms presented in Table 1 where term a_i is the sequential composition of conditional actions (i.e. of the form $\phi :\rightarrow \alpha$). Thus, we give the axioms for conditional choice, non-deterministic choice and sequential composition operators. Due to the lack of space, we restrict ourselves to present axioms for output

$$\frac{a \xrightarrow{[\phi]\alpha!} \surd \quad s \xrightarrow{\alpha?} s'}{\Theta_s(a) \xrightarrow{\alpha} \surd} \sigma_s(\phi) = \top \quad \text{LTR1} \qquad \frac{a \xrightarrow{[\phi]\alpha?} \surd \quad s \xrightarrow{\alpha!} s'}{\Theta_s(a) \xrightarrow{\alpha} \surd} \sigma_s(\phi) = \top \quad \text{LTR2}$$

$$\frac{a \xrightarrow{[\phi]\alpha!} a' \quad s \xrightarrow{\alpha?} s'}{\Theta_s(a) \xrightarrow{\alpha} \Theta_{s'}(a')} \sigma_s(\phi) = \top \quad \text{LTR3} \qquad \frac{a \xrightarrow{[\phi]\alpha?} a' \quad s \xrightarrow{\alpha!} s'}{\Theta_s(a) \xrightarrow{\alpha} \Theta_{s'}(a')} \sigma_s(\phi) = \top \quad \text{LTR4}$$

$$\frac{s \xrightarrow{\alpha} s' \quad \neg((\alpha = \alpha'? \wedge a \xrightarrow{\alpha'!} a') \vee (\alpha = \alpha'! \wedge a \xrightarrow{\alpha'?} a'))}{\Theta_s(a) \xrightarrow{\alpha} \Theta_{s'}(a)} \quad \text{LTR5}$$

$$\frac{a \xrightarrow{[\phi]\alpha} a'}{\Theta_s(a) \xrightarrow{\alpha} \Theta_s(a')} \sigma_s(\phi) = \top \quad \text{LTR6}$$

Fig. 2. Transition rules for the operator Θ

and internal actions. A number of axioms similar to TA3-4 are defined for input actions. TA2 asserts that non-deterministic choice of two actions a and a' from state s is equivalent to either execution of a or execution of a' from state s. In axioms TA3-6, the fist term $\sum_{(s,\alpha',s')} \Theta_{s'}(a)$ describes the case that an internal action (α') is executed by the context, and a will be evaluated from the next state of the context (s'). If the condition of an action is evaluated to false (i.e., $\sigma_s(\psi)$), action δ_a is executed. Moreover, if ψ is evaluated to true in state s, (i) execution of $\psi :\rightarrow \alpha!$ in state s can result in performing simple action α by synchronization with $\alpha?$ of the context (TA3), (ii) execution of $\psi :\rightarrow \alpha!; a$ in state s results in execution of simple action α synchronized with $\alpha?$ in the context, followed by execution of a from next state s' (TA4), (iii) execution of $\psi :\rightarrow \alpha$ in state s can result in performing the internal action α by the manager (TA5), (iv) execution of $\psi :\rightarrow \alpha; a$ in state s leads to execution of internal action α, followed by execution of a from state s (TA6).

Proposition 1. ***(Congruence)*** *Let a_1, a_2, a'_1 and a'_2 be terms of CA^a, ψ be an arbitrary boolean formula and $T_c = \langle V, S_c, s_c^0, \mathcal{A}_c^I, \mathcal{A}_c^O, \mathcal{A}_c^H, \rightarrow_c \rangle$ indicate the context. If for all $s \in S_c$, $\Theta_s(a_1) \underline{\Leftrightarrow}_{T_c} \Theta_s(a'_1)$ and $\Theta_s(a_2) \underline{\Leftrightarrow}_{T_c} \Theta_s(a'_2)$, then for all $s \in S_c$, $\Theta_s(a_1 + a_2) \underline{\Leftrightarrow}_{T_c} \Theta_s(a'_1 + a'_2)$, $\Theta_s(a_1 \,;\, a_2) \underline{\Leftrightarrow}_{T_c} \Theta_s(a'_1 \,;\, a'_2)$, $\Theta_s(\psi :\rightarrow a_1) \underline{\Leftrightarrow}_{T_c} \Theta_s(\psi :\rightarrow a'_1)$, and $\Theta_s(a_1 \parallel a_2) \underline{\Leftrightarrow}_{T_c} \Theta_s(a'_1 \parallel a'_2)$.*

Proof. See [7].

Theorem 1. ***(Soundness)*** *Let $T_c = \langle V, S_c, s_c^0, \mathcal{A}_c^I, \mathcal{A}_c^O, \mathcal{A}_c^H, \rightarrow_c \rangle$ be a context, and a and a' indicate two arbitrary terms of CA^a. If for all $s \in S_c$, $CA^a + (\text{TA1} - \text{TA6}) \vdash \Theta_s(a) = \Theta_s(a')$ then $\Theta_s(a)$ and $\Theta_s(a')$ are statebased bisimilar with respect to T_c, i.e. $\Theta_s(a) \underline{\Leftrightarrow}_{T_c} \Theta_s(a')$.*

Proof. See [7].

6.2 Context-Specific Behavioral Equivalence of Governing Policies

We have presented an axiomatized operator to check context-specific behavioral equivalence of actions in Section 6.1. We use this proposed equational theory

$$\Theta_s(\delta_a) = \delta_a \quad \textbf{TA1} \qquad \Theta_s(a + a') = \Theta_s(a) + \Theta_s(a') \quad \textbf{TA2}$$

$$\Theta_s(\psi :\rightarrow \alpha!) = \sum_{(s,\alpha',s')} \Theta_{s'}(\psi :\rightarrow \alpha!) \;+\; \sum_{(s,\alpha?,s')} \begin{cases} \alpha & \sigma_s(\psi) = \top \\ \delta_a & \sigma_s(\psi) = \bot \end{cases} \quad \textbf{TA3}$$

$$\Theta_s(\psi :\rightarrow \alpha! \;;\; a) = \sum_{(s,\alpha',s')} \Theta_{s'}(\psi :\rightarrow \alpha! \;;\; a) \;+ \sum_{(s,\alpha?,s')} \begin{cases} \alpha;\; \Theta_{s'}(a) & \sigma_s(\psi) = \top \\ \delta_a & \sigma_s(\psi) = \bot \end{cases} \quad \textbf{TA4}$$

$$\Theta_s(\psi :\rightarrow \alpha) = \sum_{(s,\alpha',s')} \Theta_{s'}(\psi :\rightarrow \alpha) \;+\; \begin{cases} \alpha & \sigma_s(\psi) = \top \\ \delta_a & \sigma_s(\psi) = \bot \end{cases} \quad \textbf{TA5}$$

$$\Theta_s(\psi :\rightarrow \alpha \;;\; a) = \sum_{(s,\alpha',s')} \Theta_{s'}(\psi :\rightarrow \alpha \;;\; a) \;+\; \begin{cases} \alpha;\; \Theta_s(a) & \sigma_s(\psi) = \top \\ \delta_a & \sigma_s(\psi) = \bot \end{cases} \quad \textbf{TA6}$$

Fig. 3. Axioms of the operator Θ_s

to reason about context-specific behavioral equivalence of governing policies. A simple governing policy is a set of actions performed by a manager. Two simple governing policies are equivalent if and if they are activated by the same transitions of the context and their enforcement results in the same sequences of actions done by the manager.

Definition 4. *Let $T_c = \langle V, S_c, s_c^0, \mathcal{A}_c^I, \mathcal{A}_c^O, \mathcal{A}_c^H, \rightarrow_c\rangle$ denote an arbitrary context. Two simple governing policies $g_1 = \langle o_1, e, \psi_1\rangle \bullet a_1$ and $g_2 = \langle o_2, e, \psi_2\rangle \bullet a_2$ are equivalent with respect to T_c, denoted by $g_1 \overset{T_c}{\equiv} g_2$, if for all $t = (s_1, \alpha, s_2) \in \rightarrow_c$,*

(i) $t \models \tau(g_1, g) \Leftrightarrow t \models \tau(g_2, g)$ where $\tau(g_i, g), i = 1, 2,$ indicates the triggering conditions of g_i and g denotes the governing policy set of manager [9].
(ii) $\Theta_{s_2}(a_1) = \Theta_{s_2}(a_2)$

To reason about the behavioral equivalence of governing policy sets, we formulate the behavior of a governing policy set as a CA^a term. Then, we use the axiom system of CA$^a_\Theta$ to check the equivalence of corresponding action terms. Therefore, context-specific behavioral equivalence of two governing policy sets is reduced to checking context-specific behavioral equivalence of their corresponding action terms.

Definition 5. *Let g and g' indicate two arbitrary governing policy sets and $T_c = \langle V, S_c, s_c^0, \mathcal{A}_c^I, \mathcal{A}_c^O, \mathcal{A}_c^H, \rightarrow_c\rangle$ be an arbitrary context. The function $\Psi(g, t)$ returns the action term due to the enforcement of the governing policy set g, when the transition t occurs [9]. We say g and g' are equivalent with respect to T_c, denoted by $g \overset{T_c}{\equiv} g'$, iff for all $t = (s_1, \alpha, s_2) \in \rightarrow_c$, $\Theta_{s_2}(\Psi(g, t)) = \Theta_{s_2}(\Psi(g', t))$.*

Example 1. Suppose a situation that $relay_1$ becomes overloaded. The messages of a number of the surveyors which are transmitted by this relay should be transmitted through the low-loaded $relay_2$. To this end, first we have to find those

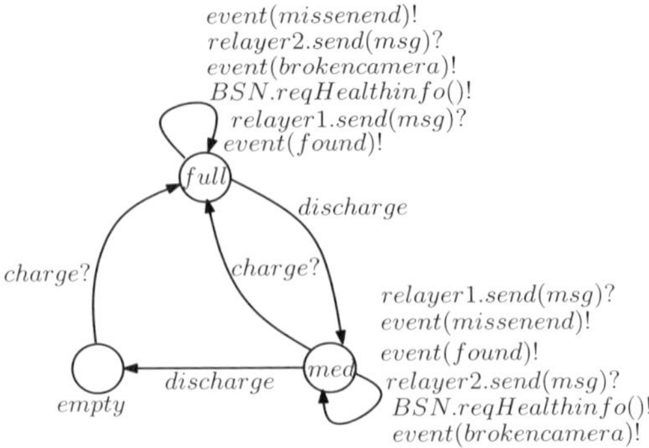

Fig. 4. The context of $surveyor_1(T_{surv})$

surveyors which transmit their messages through $relay_1$. Assume that the surveyors communicate with the relays only in the case that the wounded person is found. In order to check if a surveyor transmits its messages through $relay_1$, we check context-specific behavioral equivalence of its governing policies for transmitting data, and the simple governing policy $g_2 \stackrel{\text{def}}{=} \langle 1,\ found(x,y),\ \top\rangle \bullet a_2$ where $a_2 \stackrel{def}{=} BSN.reqHealthinfo()? \ \| \ relay1.send(msg)!$. This simple policy states that when the wounded person is found, the information should be transmitted through $relay_1$.

Suppose $surveyor_1$ has the simple governing policy $g_1 \stackrel{\text{def}}{=} \langle 1,\ found(x,y),\ \top\rangle \bullet a_1$ where

$$a_1 \stackrel{def}{=} BSN.reqHealthinfo()? \ \| \ (lowenergy :\rightarrow relay2.send(msg)! \\ +\neg lowenergy :\rightarrow relay1.send(msg)!)$$

Figure 4 shows the abstract context of $surveyor_1$ (T_{surv}) which has three states $full$ (full energy), med (medium energy) and $empty$ (no energy). Furthermore, $\{found, brokencamera, missionend\} \subseteq \mathcal{A}_c^O$ indicate the event set, $charge$ is an input action, and $discharge$ is an internal action. We should check context-specific behavioral equivalence of g_1 and g_2 with respect to T_{surv}. Both policies are triggered in the states $full$ and med in which the condition $lowenergy$ does not hold and event $found$ is activated. Hence, we must check the equations $\Theta_{full}(a_1) = \Theta_{full}(a_2)$ and $\Theta_{med}(a_1) = \Theta_{med}(a_2)$ (Definition 4). For the sake of readability, let's denote $relay1.send(msg)$ and $relay2.send(msg)$ by α_1 and α_2 respectively. According to the axiom systems in Table 1 and Figure 3,

$$\Theta_{full}(\neg lowenergy :\rightarrow \alpha_1! + lowenergy :\rightarrow \alpha_2!) \stackrel{\textbf{TA2}}{=}$$

$$\Theta_{full}(\neg lowenergy :\rightarrow \alpha_1!) + \Theta_{full}(lowenergy :\rightarrow \alpha_2!) \stackrel{\textbf{TA3,A3}}{=}$$

$$\top :\rightarrow \alpha_1 + \bot :\rightarrow \alpha_2 +$$

$$\Theta_{med}(\neg lowenergy :\rightarrow \alpha_1! + lowenergy :\rightarrow \alpha_2!) \stackrel{\mathbf{C_1,C_2}}{=}$$

$$\alpha_1 + \Theta_{med}(\neg lowenergy :\rightarrow \alpha_1! + lowenergy :\rightarrow \alpha_2!) \quad (1)$$

and

$$\Theta_{full}(\alpha_1!) = \alpha_1 + \Theta_{med}(\alpha_1!) \tag{2}$$

It is trivial to prove that

$$\Theta_{med}(\neg lowenergy :\rightarrow \alpha_1! + lowenergy :\rightarrow \alpha_2!) = \Theta_{med}(\alpha_1!) \tag{3}$$

and subsequently, the equation $\Theta_{full}(a_1) = \Theta_{full}(a_2)$ is concluded from equations (1)-(3). According to Theorem 1, the actions of g_1 and g_2 are statebased bisimilar with respect to the context T_{surv}, if they are activated in state $full$. Similarly, we can prove that the actions of g_1 and g_2 are statebased bisimilar when they are activated in state *med*. We conclude that g_1 and g_2 are equivalent according to Definition 4. Therefore, $surveyor_1$ always transmits its data through $relay_1$.

6.3 Context-Specific Behavioral Equivalence of Adaptation Policies

Informally, two simple adaptation policies are equivalent if and only if (a) they are activated by the same transitions of the context, (b) their enforcement leads to switching to the identical adaptation modes and configurations, and (c) the manager switches to the new configuration in the same set of context states:

Definition 6. *Suppose* $T_c = \langle V, S_c, s_c^0, \mathcal{A}_c^I, \mathcal{A}_c^O, \mathcal{A}_c^H, \rightarrow_c\rangle$ *be an arbitrary context. Two adaptation policies* $p_1 = \langle o_1, e_1, \psi_1, \lambda_1, \phi_1\rangle \bullet c_1$ *and* $p_2 = \langle o_2, e_2, \psi_2, \lambda_2, \phi_2\rangle \bullet c_2$ *are equivalent with respect to* T_c*, denoted by* $p_1 \overset{T_c}{\equiv} p_2$*, if for all transitions* $t = (s_1, \alpha, s_2) \in \rightarrow_c$*,*

(i) $t \models \tau(p_1, p) \Leftrightarrow t \models \tau(p_2, p)$ *where* $\tau(p_i, p), i = 1, 2$*, gives the triggering conditions of* p_i *and* p *is the adaptation policy of the manager,*
(ii) $c_1 = c_2$ *and* $\lambda_1 = \lambda_2$*,*
(iii) $s' \models \phi_1 \Leftrightarrow s' \models \phi_2$ *for all reachable states* $s' \in S_c$ *from* s_2*, where there is a path such as* σ *between* s_2 *and* s'*, and for all* $s'' \in \sigma$*,* $s'' \not\models \phi_1 \vee \phi_2$ *.*

Similar to governing policies, enforcement of adaptation policies leads to a sequence of actions carried out by the manager. We say two adaptation policies are equivalent with respect to context T_c, if their enforcement in a system with context T_c leads to the same sequence of actions carried out by the manager. We introduce the operator Ω which gives the actions done by the manager to apply an adaptation policy. Let p indicate an adaptation policy of a manager, and $p_i = \langle o, e, \psi, \lambda, \phi\rangle \bullet c$ denote an arbitrary simple adaptation policy of p, i.e. $p = p_i \oplus p'$. The function $\Omega(p_i, p)$ returns a CA^a term due to enforcing p_i, where $\tau(p_i, p)$ denotes the triggering conditions of p_i:

$$\Omega(p_i, p) = \begin{cases} \tau(p_i, p) :\rightarrow event(e)?;\ tostrict();\ \phi :\rightarrow switch(c) & \lambda = \top \\ \tau(p_i, p) :\rightarrow event(e)?;\ toloose();\ \phi :\rightarrow switch(c) & \lambda = \bot \\ \delta_a & p_i = \delta_p \end{cases}$$

The action *tostrict*() denotes an internal action performed by the manager to evolve to the strict adaptation mode, *toloose*() denotes an internal action for evolving to loose adaptation mode, and $switch(c)$ is an internal action for switching to configuration c. Furthermore, the behavior of an adaptation policy $p = p_1 \oplus ... \oplus p_n$ is defined as follows:

$$\Omega(p) = \sum_{1 \leq i \leq n} \Omega(p_i, p)$$

Given the behavior of adaptation policies as CA^a terms, we use context-specific behavioral equivalence theory of CA^a_Θ to reason about their behavioral equivalence.

Definition 7. *Let p and p' indicate two arbitrary adaptation policy and $T_c = \langle V, S_c, s_c^0, \mathcal{A}_c^I, \mathcal{A}_c^O, \mathcal{A}_c^H, \rightarrow_c \rangle$ be an arbitrary context. We say p and p' are equivalent with respect to T_c, denoted by $p \stackrel{T_c}{=} p'$, iff for all $s \in S_c$, $\Theta_s(\Omega(p)) \stackrel{T_c}{=} \Theta_s(\Omega(p'))$.*

6.4 Context-Specific Behavioral Equivalence of Configurations and Managers

A configuration consists of a set of governing policies and a set of adaptation policies. As mentioned above, we can change the configurations of a manager dynamically. Therefore, we require a theory to assure that the behavior of a configuration is equivalent to the behavior of a desired configuration, with respect to a context. In order to reason about the behavioral equivalence of two configurations, we reason about the behavioral equivalence of their governing policies as well as the behavioral equivalence of their adaptation policies:

Definition 8. *Let $c = \langle g, p \rangle$ and $c' = \langle g', p' \rangle$ be two arbitrary configurations, and $T_c = \langle V, S_c, s_c^0, \mathcal{A}_c^I, \mathcal{A}_c^O, \mathcal{A}_c^H, \rightarrow_c \rangle$ denote an arbitrary context. We say $c \stackrel{T_c}{=} c'$ iff $g \stackrel{T_c}{=} g'$ and $p \stackrel{T_c}{=} p'$.*

Example 2. Consider a situation that $surveyor_1$ breaks down, and should be replaced by another UAV with surveying capabilities, named UAV_2. Hence, we should check if the current configuration of UAV_2 (c') is equivalent to the configuration of $surveyor_1$(c) with respect to context T_{surv} shown in Figure 4. Suppose both $surveyor_1$ and UAV_2 have the same set of governing policies, i.e. $g \stackrel{T_{surv}}{=} g'$ where g indicates the governing policy set of $surveyor_1$ and g' denotes the governing policy set of UAV_2. Thus, we need to check the behavioral equivalence of their adaptation policies with respect to T_{surv}. Let p and p' indicate the adaptation policies of $surveyor_1$ and UAV_2, respectively, defined as follows:

$$\begin{aligned} p = &\langle 1, brokencamera, \neg lowenergy, \top, \top \rangle \bullet relayConf \oplus \\ &\langle 1, missionend, \top, \bot, \top \rangle \bullet idle \oplus \\ &\langle 1, found, lowenergy, \bot, \top \rangle \bullet idle \\ p' = &\langle 1, brokencamera, \top, \top, \top \rangle \bullet relayConf \oplus \\ &\langle 1, missionend, \top, \bot, \top \rangle \bullet idle \end{aligned}$$

We formulate p and p' in terms of CA^a terms as follows:

$$\begin{aligned}\Omega(p) = \neg lowenergy :\rightarrow\ & event(brokencamera)?;\ tostrict();\ switch(relayConf) + \\ \top :\rightarrow\ & event(missionend)?;\ toloose();\ switch(idleConf) + \\ \bot :\rightarrow\ & event(found)?;\ toloose();\ switch(idleConf)\end{aligned}$$

$$\begin{aligned}\Omega(p') = \top :\rightarrow\ & event(brokencamera)?;\ tostrict();\ switch(relayConf) + \\ \top :\rightarrow\ & event(missionend)?;\ toloose();\ switch(idleConf)\end{aligned}$$

For the sake of readability, we show $\Omega(p)$ and $\Omega(p')$ by a and a', respectively. When the context is in state "*full*", if the events "*discharge*" and "*found*" are raised, non of the policies p and p' are triggered, however both policies are activated when the events "*brokencamera*" and "*missionend*" are raised:

$$\begin{aligned}\Theta_{full}(a)=\Theta_{full}(a')=\ & event(brokencamera);\Theta_{med}(tostrict();\ switch(relayConf)) + \\ & event(missionend);\Theta_{med}(toloose();\ switch(idleConf))\end{aligned}$$

It is trivial to prove that $\Theta_{med}(\Omega(p)) = \Theta_{med}(\Omega(p'))$ and $\Theta_{empty}(\Omega(p)) = \Theta_{empty}(\Omega(p'))$. Consequently, according to definition 7, it is concluded that $p \overset{T_c}{=} p'$. According to definition 8, we conclude that $surveyor_1$ and UAV$_2$ are substitutable,

$$\left.\begin{array}{l} p \overset{T_c}{=} p' \\ g \overset{T_c}{=} g' \end{array}\right\} \Rightarrow c \overset{T_c}{=} c'$$

Checking context-specific behavioral equivalence of two managers is the most important part of our behavioral equivalence theory. As mentioned above, a manager runs one of its configurations at a time, and switches between the configurations to perform dynamic adaptation. Informally, two managers are behavioral equivalent with respect to T_c iff (i) the managers have equivalent initial configurations with respect to T_c, and (ii) switching from equivalent configurations leads to the equivalent configurations in both managers. We reason about the equivalence of managers in terms of behavioral equivalence of their simple configurations:

Definition 9. *Let* $m = \langle V_m, C, c_{init}\rangle$ *and* $m' = \langle V_{m'}, C', c'_{init}\rangle$ *be two managers with configuration sets* $C = \{c_1, ..., c_k\}$ *and* $C' = \{c'_1, ..., c'_{k'}\}$*, initial configurations* $c_{init} \in C$ *and* $c'_{init} \in C'$*, and set of views* V_m *and* $V_{m'}$*, respectively. Furthermore,* $T_c = \langle V, S_c, s^0_c, \mathcal{A}^I_c, \mathcal{A}^O_c, \mathcal{A}^H_c, \rightarrow_c\rangle$ *indicates an arbitrary context. We say* m *and* m' *are equivalent with respect to context* T_c*, written by* $m \overset{T_c}{=} m'$*, (i)* $c_{init} \overset{T_c}{=} c'_{init}$*, (ii) for each equivalent configurations* $c_i \in C$ *and* $c'_j \in C'$*, if the manager* m *switches from* c_i *to* c_k*, the manager* m' *must switch from* c'_j *to* $c'_l \in C'$ *where* $c_k \overset{T_c}{=} c'_l$ *and vice versa.*

Example 3. Let $surveyor_1$ has the capability to search areas with chemical hazards. The manager of this UAV is defined as $survCntrlr = \langle V, \{survconf, hazardconf, relayconf\}, survconf\rangle$ where configuration $survconf$ is used to search areas without hazardous chemicals, $hazardconf$ is used to search areas with hazards, and $relayconf$ is used for acting as a relay. Let the situation that $surveyor_1$ has to be replaced by a UAV with the manager $survCntrlr' = \langle V, \{survconf', relayconf'\}, survconf'\rangle$. Let T_s denote the context of $survCntrlr$ and $survCntrlr'$. Assume we have $survconf \stackrel{T_s}{=} survconf'$ and $relayconf \stackrel{T_s}{=} relayconf'$, if the surveying area is not contaminated with hazardous chemicals. This is due to the fact that the adaptation policies of $survconf$ and $relayconf$ for switching to $hazardconf$ are not triggered, and switching is done between $survconf$ and $relayconf$. Therefore, according to Definition 9, we conclude $survCntrlr \stackrel{T_s}{=} survCntrlr'$. It worth mentioning that if we use theses two UAVs in another context, they might not behave equivalently.

7 Related Work

Although process algebra is used for structural adaptation (e.g. see [2], [12]), however to the best of our knowledge process algebraic approaches have not been used for behavioral adaptation. Zhang et al. [19] proposed a model-driven approach using Petri Nets for developing adaptive systems. They also presented a model-checking approach for verification of adaptive system [20,18] in which an extension of LTL with "adapt" operator was used to specify the adaptation requirements. Furthermore, authors in [14,1] used labeled transition systems to model and verify embedded adaptive systems. In [10], a generic classification of the policy conflicts are presented for PobSAM models and temporal patterns expressed in LTL are provided to detect each class of conflicts. We studied the comparison of existing work in the area of formal verification of adaptive systems and PobSAM in [8].

The issue of component substitutability has already been addressed in literature with the purpose of checking compatibility of a new component with other components (e.g. [11]), substituting a component with another component with the equivalent behavior (e.g. [17]), replacing a component such that the reconfigured system preserves a specific property etc. Some approaches specify the components behavior by modeling the components interfaces while a few approaches are concerned with specifying the internal behavior of components, as we have done in this work. We use specification of components interfaces to build and specify the context of managers. Among the existing approaches, [17] uses a formalism named component-interaction automata to specify the behavior of components interfaces. They define a notion of equivalence on these automata in addition to a composition operator to prove substitutability and independent implementability properties. In a similar work, [6] specifies the components behavior using max/plus automata and defines four kinds of substitutivity considering QoS aspects. However, the main difference compared to our work is that they do not consider data states of components. Furthermore, to the best of our knowledge, none of the approaches for checking behavioral equivalence of components are based on a process algebraic formalism. The existing approaches model the components behavior using automata-based or LTS formalisms. Due to the fact that PobSAM has a different formal foundation, it requires special analysis techniques such as the equational theory presented in this paper which is not provided by other existing work.

Schaeffer-Filho et al. [13] use Alloy Analyzer [2] for formal specification and verification of policy-based systems, however they are not concerned with behavioral equivalence of components. Moreover, Georgas et al [4] uses policies as a mechanism for structural adaptation in robotic domain, but this work has no formal foundation.

8 Conclusions

In this paper, we presented an equational theory to analyze context-specific behavioral equivalence of policies, configurations and managers in PobSAM models based on the notion of statebased bisimilarity. Given the context as a labeled state transition system, we analyze context-specific behavioral equivalence of the manager layer independently from the actor layer. To this aim, we introduced and axiomatized an operator to consider interactions of the managers and the context. We demonstrated the approach using an example for search and rescue operations.

Acknowledgments. This work was funded by the NTH School for IT Ecosystems. NTH (Niedersachsische Technische Hochschule) is a joint university consisting of Technische Universitat Braunschweig, Technische Universitat Clausthal, and Leibniz Universitat Hannover.

References

1. Adler, R., Schaefer, I., SchLule, T., Vecchie, E.: From model-based design to formal verification of adaptive embedded systems. In: Butler, M., Hinchey, M.G., Larrondo-Petrie, M.M. (eds.) ICFEM 2007. LNCS, vol. 4789, pp. 76–95. Springer, Heidelberg (2007)
2. Bradbury, J.S., Cordy, J.R., Dingel, J., Wermelinger, M.: A survey of self-management in dynamic software architecture specifications. In: Proceedings of 1st ACM SIGSOFT Workshop on Self-managed Systems, pp. 28–33. ACM, New York (2004)
3. Garlan, D., Cheng, S.-W., Schmerl, B.R.: Increasing system dependability through architecture-based self-repair. In: WADS, pp. 61–89 (2002)
4. Georgas, J.C., Taylor, R.N.: Policy-based self-adaptive architectures: a feasibility study in the robotics domain. In: Proceedings of the 2008 International Workshop on Software Engineering for Adaptive and Self-managing Systems, SEAMS 2008, pp. 105–112. ACM, New York (2008)

5. Groote, J.F., Ponse, A.: Process algebra with guards: Combining hoare logic with process algebra. Formal Asp. Comput. 6(2), 115–164 (1994)
6. Heam, P.-C., Kouchnarenko, O., Voinot, J.: Component simulation-based substitutivity managing qos aspects. Electron. Notes Theor. Comput. Sci. 260, 109–123 (2010)
7. Khakpour, N.: Context-based behavioral equivalence of components in self-adaptive systems. Technical report, Technical Report of TU Bruanschweig (2011)
8. Khakpour, N., Jalili, S., Talcott, C.L., Sirjani, M., Mousavi, M.R.: Pobsam: Policy-based managing of actors in self-adaptive systems. Electr. Notes Theor. Comput. Sci. 263, 129–143 (2010)
9. Khakpour, N., Jalili, S., Talcott, C.L., Sirjani, M., Mousavi, M.R.: Formal modeling of evolving adaptive systems (submitted, 2011)
10. Khakpour, N., Khosravi, R., Sirjani, M., Jalili, S.: Formal analysis of policy-based self-adaptive systems. In: SAC, pp. 2536–2543 (2010)
11. Legond-Aubry, F., Enselme, D., Florin, G.: Assembling contracts for components. In: Najm, E., Nestmann, U., Stevens, P. (eds.) FMOODS 2003. LNCS, vol. 2884, pp. 35–43. Springer, Heidelberg (2003)
12. Mateescu, R., Poizat, P., Salaun, G.: Adaptation of service protocols using process algebra and on-the-fly reduction techniques. IEEE Transactions on Software Engineering 99(prePrints) (2011)
13. Schaeffer-Filho, A., Lupu, E., Sloman, M., Eisenbach, S.: Verification of policy-based self-managed cell interactions using alloy. In: Proceedings of the 10th IEEE International Conference on Policies for Distributed Systems and Networks, POLICY 2009, pp. 37–40. IEEE Press, Los Alamitos (2009)
14. Schneider, K., Schuele, T., Trapp, M.: Verifying the adaptation behavior of embedded systems. In: Proceedings of the 2006 International Workshop on Self-adaptation and self-managing Systems, SEAMS 2006, pp. 16–22. ACM, New York (2006)
15. Sirjani, M., Movaghar, A., Shali, A., de Boer, F.S.: Modeling and verification of reactive systems using rebeca. Fundam. Inform. 63(4), 385–410 (2004)
16. Sloman, M., Lupu, E.C.: Engineering policy-based ubiquitous systems. Comput. J. 53(7), 1113–1127 (2010)
17. Cerna, I., Varekova, P., Zimmerova, B.: Component substitutability via equivalencies of component-interaction automata. Electron. Notes Theor. Comput. Sci. 182, 39–55 (2007)
18. Zhang, J., Cheng, B.H.C.: Specifying adaptation semantics. ACM SIGSOFT Software Engineering Notes 30(4), 1–7 (2005)
19. Zhang, J., Cheng, B.H.C.: Model-based development of dynamically adaptive software. In: Proceedings of the 28th International Conference on Software Engineering, ICSE 2006, pp. 371–380. ACM, New York (2006)
20. Zhang, J., Goldsby, H., Cheng, B.H.C.: Modular verification of dynamically adaptive systems. In: Proceedings of the 8th ACM International Conference on Aspect-oriented Software Development, pp. 161–172 (2009)

Towards a Practical Approach to Check UML/fUML Models Consistency Using CSP

Islam Abdelhalim, Steve Schneider, and Helen Treharne

Department of Computing, University of Surrey
{i.abdelhalim,s.schneider,h.treharne}@surrey.ac.uk

Abstract. This work provides an underpinning for a systems modelling approach based on UML and fUML together. It uses UML state diagrams as a starting point for modelling system object behaviour abstractly, then refining each state diagram by adding the implementation decisions in a form of a fUML activity diagram. Maintaining behavioural consistency between each UML state diagram and its corresponding fUML activity diagram is an important but difficult task. In this paper we introduce a framework that automates checking such consistency in a practical way.

The framework is based on formalizing these diagrams into the process algebra CSP to do trace refinement checking using FDR2. One of the main contributions in this work is that we transform FDR2 output (counter-example in case of inconsistency) back to the UML/fUML model in a way that allows the modeller to debug the consistency problem. To be able to provide this kind of interactive feedback, the generated CSP model is augmented with traceability information. A case tool plugin based on the Epsilon model management framework has been developed to support our approach.

1 Introduction

The fUML (Foundational subset for Executable UML) standard [1] has been developed by the OMG (Object Management Group) to allow for the execution of models. This implies having more complete and precise models which in many cases lead to complicated models that include implementation decisions. However, complicated models are hard to read, browse, understand and maintain. Moreover, checking consistency between such models and their specifications (modelled as abstract models) is a very difficult task. In contrast, abstract models are not complicated, but they cannot be used for model execution.

To get the benefits of both (abstract and concrete models), the modeller starts with an abstract model and then refines it by adding more implementation detail until reaching a concrete one. This concept in the UML/fUML domain can be applied by initially modelling a system using UML in an abstract way and then refining the model to reach a concrete fUML model.

In the formal methods domain it is a common task to check consistency between abstract and concrete models using model checkers or theorem provers. However, this is not the case in the UML/fUML domain. Case tools that are

S. Qin and Z. Qiu (Eds.): ICFEM 2011, LNCS 6991, pp. 33–48, 2011.

used to draw the diagrams are concerned mainly with syntactical checking (i.e., checks if the UML/fUML diagram meets the UML/fUML standard specification). To import refinement into the UML/fUML domain, we are proposing a framework that allows checking UML/fUML model consistency. This framework is based on formalizing UML/fUML models into the CSP (Communicating Sequential Processes) [2] formal language, then performing formal model checking using FDR2 (the Failures-Divergences Refinement tool) [3]. If FDR2 detects an inconsistency it will generate a counter-example which shows a trace that led to this inconsistency. To completely isolate the modeller from dealing with the formal methods domain, our framework reflects this counter-example back to the UML/fUML model (through a model debugger).

Although checking consistency between semi-formal models (e.g., UML) has been addressed many times in the literature [4,5] using formal methods, to our knowledge, this paper is the first attempt to check consistency between non-executable and executable semi-formal models. Also the provision of a modeller friendly consistency checking feedback resulting from the model checking is one of the main contributions in this paper.

We differentiate between two types of model inconsistency based on the classification in [6]. First, intra-model inconsistency, which occurs if two (or more) diagrams with different types are not consistent (e.g., a state diagram and a related sequence diagram in the same UML model). Second, inter-model inconsistency, which occurs if two (or more) diagrams with the same type are not consistent (e.g., a version of a state diagram and a refined version represented as a state diagram as well). Our work is a combination of these two kinds of inconsistency because we start by modelling the object behaviour as an UML state diagram and refine it to a fUML activity diagram that represents the same object behaviour augmented with more implementation detail. Hence, we will refer to this as behavioral consistency.

The formalization is done automatically by transforming UML/fUML diagrams into CSP processes. We made use of Epsilon [7] as one of the available MDE (Model Drive Engineering) frameworks to support the transformation based on available UML2 [8], fUML [1] and CSP [9] meta-models. Epsilon is one of several components that build up our framework which has been implemented as a MagicDraw[1] [10] plugin to allow modellers to seamlessly use our approach during the system modelling process.

The approach has been tested using the Tokeneer ID Station [11] case study. A group of UML state and fUML activity diagrams have been developed and the consistency between them has been verified using our approach. Our previous paper [12] focused on checking deadlock between Tokeneer fUML communicated objects, however; in this work we have checked refinement between Tokeneer fUML activity and state diagrams. This work also considers the modeller-friendly checking feedback which was not addressed in [12]. Due to limitations of space

[1] MagicDraw is an (award-winning) architecture, software and system modeling case tool. It also supports additional plugins to increase its functionalities.

we will include a simple example (Microwave Oven from [13]) to illustrate the main concepts through the paper.

We assume the reader of this paper has an understanding of the UML2 standard, CSP and FDR2.

The rest of this paper is organised as follows. In Section 2, we give a background to the fUML standard and the CSP syntax used in this paper. In Section 3, we give an overview of our approach and its main components. In Section 4, we describe the Model Formalizer component and how it works. In Section 5, we describe how consistency is checked between particular UML and fUML diagrams. In Section 6, we describe how we provide the modeller with helpful feedback through a Formalization Report and the Model Debugger. In Section 7, we outline the implementation of the approach. Finally, we discuss related work and conclude in Sections 8 and 9 respectively.

2 Background

2.1 fUML

As defined by the OMG, fUML is a standard that acts as an intermediary between "surface subsets" of UML models and platform executable languages. The fUML subset has been defined to allow the building of executable models. Code-generators can then be used to automatically generate executable code (e.g., in Java) from the models. Another option is to use model-interpreters that rely on a virtual machine to directly read and run the model (e.g., fUML Reference Implementation [14]).

The fUML standard includes class and activity diagrams to describe a system's structure and behaviour respectively. Some modifications have been applied to the original class and activity diagrams in the UML2 specification [15] to meet the computational completeness of fUML. The modifications have been done by merging/excluding some packages in UML2, as well as adding new constraints, such as:

- Variables are excluded from fUML because the passing of data between actions can be achieved using object flows.
- Opaque actions are excluded from fUML since, being opaque, they cannot be executed.
- Value pins are excluded from fUML because they are redundant due to the use of value specifications to specify values.

The operational semantics of fUML is an executable model with methods written in Java, with a mapping to UML activity diagrams. The declarative semantics of fUML is specified in first order logic and based on PSL (Process Specification Language) [16].

UML/fUML Example

Throughout this paper we use a simple example of a microwave oven that consists of two classes: Controller and Heater. Figure 1 shows the state machine

(Controller_SD) that represents the Controller active object behaviour. The object can be in one of three different states (DoorOpen, ReadyToCook and Cooking) based on the incoming events (*doorClosed*, *buttonPressed*, ...). For example, if the object was in the ReadyToCook state and the *buttonPressed* event happened, it will enter the Cooking state.

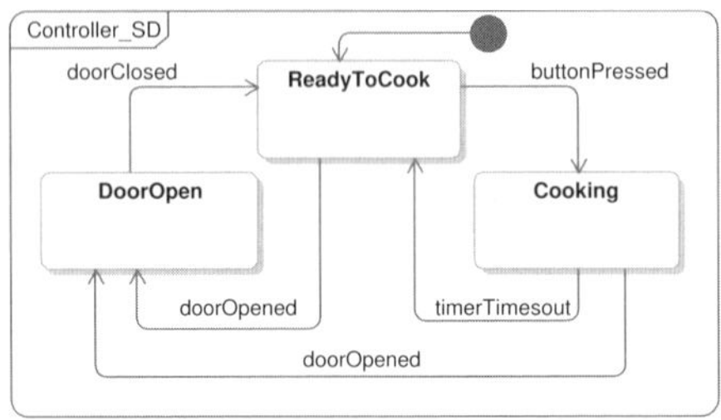

Fig. 1. UML State Diagram of the Microwave Controller

As a result of refining the Controller state digram by adding some implementation detail, we obtain the Controller fUML activity diagram depicted in Figure 2. The added implementation detail include:

- Setting the value of the class attributes (e.g., setting *isCooking* attribute to FALSE using the *valueSpecification* and *addStructuralFeatureValue* actions).
- Sending signals (equivalent to the state diagram events) to objects (e.g., sending *stopHeaterSignal* to the Heater object).
- Representing the object internal decisions (e.g., timer expiration).

Although we do not include all the implementation details for this object it is obvious that the executable model is more complicated. Our experience with modeling large systems showed that checking consistency between those two kinds of models (abstract and concrete) manually is a challenging task.

2.2 CSP

CSP is a modelling language that allows the description of systems of interacting processes using a few language primitives. Processes execute and interact by means of performing events drawn from a universal set Σ. Some events are of the form $c.v$, where c represents a channel and v represents a value being passed along that channel. Our UML/fUML formalization considers the following subset of the CSP syntax:

$$\begin{aligned} P ::= {} & a \rightarrow P \mid c?x \rightarrow P(x) \mid d!v \rightarrow P \mid P_1 \Box P_2 \\ & \mid P_1 \sqcap P_2 \mid P_1 \mathbin{{}_{A}\|_{B}} P_2 \mid P \setminus A \\ & \mid \mathit{let}\ N_1 = P_1\ , \ \ldots\ , \ N_n = P_n\ \mathit{within}\ N_i \end{aligned}$$

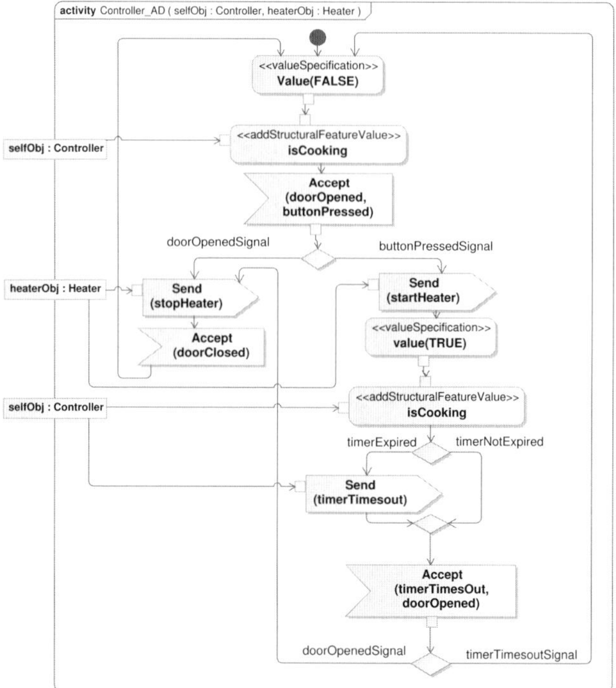

Fig. 2. fUML Activity Diagram of the Microwave Controller

The CSP process $a \rightarrow P$ initially allows event a to occur and then behaves subsequently as P. The input process $c?x \rightarrow P(x)$ will accept a value x along channel c and then behaves subsequently as $P(x)$. The output process $c!v \rightarrow P$ will output v along channel c and then behaves as P. Channels can have any number of message fields, combination of input and output values.

The choice $P_1 \, \Box \, P_2$ offers an external choice between processes P_1 and P_2 whereby the choice is made by the environment. Conversely, $P_1 \sqcap P_2$ offers an internal choice between the two processes.

The parallel combination $P_1 \underset{A\ B}{\|} P_2$ executes P_1 and P_2 in parallel. P_1 can perform only events in the set A, P_2 can perform only events in the set B, and they must simultaneously engage in events in the intersection of A and B.

The hiding operation $P \setminus A$ describes the case where all participants of all events in the set A are described in P. All these events are removed from the interface of the process, since no other processes are required to engage in them. The *let ... within* statement defines P with local definitions $N_i = P_i$.

Traces Model

Processes in CSP interact with their environment (another process, user, or combination of both) through events in their interface. A process P is refined by a process Q if the set containing all the possible traces that can be generated from process Q is a subset (or equals) of those traces of P. This definition can be expressed as: $P \sqsubseteq_T Q$.

3 Approach Overview

To automate the formalization and the feedback process, we have designed a framework that facilitates this functionality and at the same time isolates the modeller completely from the formal methods domain (CSP). Figure 3 shows the architecture of this framework and the modeller interaction points.

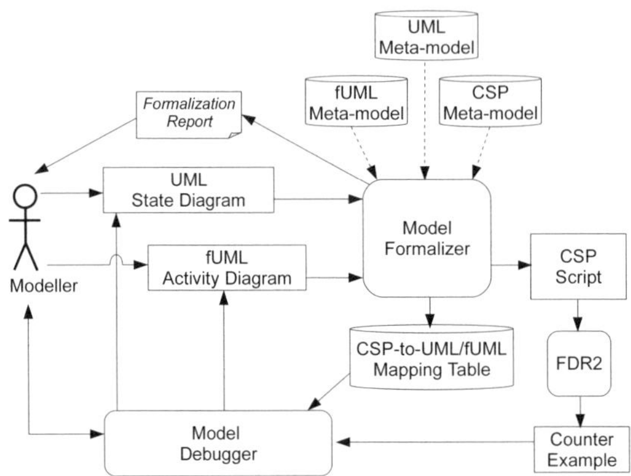

Fig. 3. Approach Architecture

Initially the modeller uses a case tool (e.g., MagicDraw) to draw the UML state diagrams and the corresponding fUML activity diagram for each active class in the system. To check consistency between the UML/fUML diagrams, the modeller should initiate the checking process. As a first step the diagrams will be converted to the XMI (XML Metadata Interchange) [17] format, thus it can be read by any MDE framework.

The Model Formalizer then processes the input diagrams and transforms them to a CSP script based on a group of transformation rules and the input UML2 [8], fUML [1] and CSP [9] existing meta-models. In case there is a problem in the formalization process, the Model Formalizer generates a Formalization Report with the error cause(s). The Model Formalizer also generates a CSP-to-UML/fUML mapping table which maps each CSP event ID to its corresponding ID for the UML/fUML element.

The generated CSP script subsequently used as an input to FDR2 that performs the consistency automatic checking. If there is a consistency problem FDR2 generates a counter-example which includes the traces (sequence of events) that led to the problem.

In case of inconsistency, the Model Debugger can be used by the modeller to trace the consistency problem source. In order to do that, the Model Debugger reads the counter-example and makes use of the CSP-to-UML/fUML mapping table to reflect the traces on the displayed diagrams in the case tool. The modeller can deal with the Model Debugger using GUI (Graphical User Interface) controls (step forward, step backward, breakpoints, etc.).

Having consistent UML/fUML diagrams will make the code generation (or model interpretation) a safer and direct process, because the modeller will be confident that the generated code from the fUML model is compatible with the system UML model.

4 The Model Formalizer

The Model Formalizer mainly transforms a source model (UML/fUML diagrams) into a formal representation (CSP script). We used Epsilon as an MDE framework to handle the transformation in two stages; firstly, a Model-to-Model transformation from the UML/fUML model to CSP model using ETL (Epsilon Transformation Language) [18] and secondly a Model-to-Text transformation from the generated CSP model to a CSP script using EGL (Epsilon Generation Language) [18]. Epsilon also requires the source/target models' meta-models, so we used the available UML2 meta-model [8] as well as the CSP meta-model used in our previous work [9].

The ETL script consists mainly of a group of transformation rules, part of them related to the UML state diagram elements (4 rules) and the others related to the fUML activity diagram elements (11 rules). Figure 4 shows a simple rule (to clarify the concept) which is used to transform a state machine (e.g., Controller_SD) to a CSP localized process (e.g., *Controller_SD_Proc*). The figure includes the ETL rule which can be understood by referring to the included UML and CSP meta-models segments.

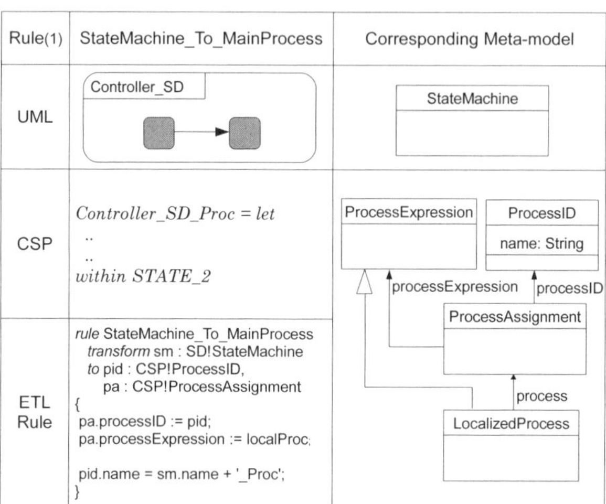

Fig. 4. Rule(1) for Transforming State Machines to CSP Localized Processes

The model elements can be accessed using the variables *SD* and *CSP* with the '!' operator. The *localProc* variable represents the main *LocalizedProcess* that all other sub-processes belongs to it. By executing this rule two CSP elements will be created (instances from: *ProcessID* and *ProcessAssignment*) and added to the CSP model. The reader can refer to [18] for more detail about the Epsilon languages and to a previous paper [12] for all the fUML activity diagram mapping rules.

After applying the ETL rules to the UML state diagram shown in Figure 1 and then applying the EGL script to the result, the CSP process in Figure 5 will be generated. According to Rule(1) in Figure 4, the state machine has been translated into a localized CSP process. Each state is translated to a CSP sub-process (e.g., ReadyToCook state translated to the process $STATE\_2$). The *inState* event is used to identify the current active state ($ST1$, $ST2$, etc.) which will be used for traceability. The *accept* event represents signals (e.g., *doorClosed*, *buttonPressed*, etc.) reception by the object to change its state.

$$
\begin{array}{l}
Controller\_SD\_Proc\ (selfObj) = let \\
\quad STATE\_1 = inState!ST1 \rightarrow \\
\quad\quad\quad accept!selfObj!doorClosed \rightarrow STATE\_2 \\
\\
\quad STATE\_2 = inState!ST2 \rightarrow (\\
\quad\quad\quad accept!selfObj!doorOpened \rightarrow STATE\_1 \\
\quad\quad\quad \Box \\
\quad\quad\quad accept!selfObj!buttonPressed \rightarrow STATE\_3) \\
\\
\quad STATE\_3 = inState!ST3 \rightarrow (\\
\quad\quad\quad accept!selfObj!timerTimesout \rightarrow STATE\_2 \\
\quad\quad\quad \Box \\
\quad\quad\quad accept!selfObj!doorOpened \rightarrow STATE\_1) \\
within\ STATE\_2
\end{array}
$$

Fig. 5. The Corresponding CSP Process for the Microwave Controller UML State Diagram

Applying the ETL rules followed by the EGL script on the fUML activity diagram, shown in Figure 2, will result in the CSP process shown in Figure 6. The main activity is translated to a localized CSP process, $Controller\_AD\_Proc$, where each node inside it is translated to a sub-process. The first three processes $AC1$, $AC2$ and $AC5$ correspond to the first three actions of the Controller_AD. $AC1$ and $AC2$ represent the *Value Specification* and *Add Structural Feature Value* actions respectively by setting *var* to FALSE and passing it $AC2$ which sets the *isCooking* attribute (structural feature) to the passed value.

According to the fUML standard, the *AcceptEvent* action registers the expected signals to a list (called *waiting event accepters*) and then waits for the signals. This logic was implemented in $AC5$ using the *registerSignals* event, then

$$
\begin{array}{l}
Controller\_AD\_Proc\ (selfObj, heaterObj) = let \\
\quad AC1 = valueSpec!selfObj?var : FALSE!NID1 \rightarrow AC2(var) \\
\quad AC2(var) = addStructFtrVal!selfObj!isCooking!var!NID3 \rightarrow \\
\qquad\qquad AC5 \\
\\
\quad AC5 = registerSignals!selfObj!rp1!NID5 \rightarrow (\\
\qquad\qquad accept!selfObj!doorOpenedSignal \rightarrow ... \\
\qquad\qquad \square \\
\qquad\qquad accept!selfObj!buttonPressedSignal \rightarrow AC12) \\
\\
\quad AC12 = send!selfObj!heaterObj!startHeaterSignal!NID9 \rightarrow ... \\
\quad\ \vdots \\
\quad ND2 = timerNotExpired!selfObj \rightarrow ... \\
\qquad\quad \sqcap \\
\qquad\quad timerExpired!selfObj \rightarrow ... \\
\quad within\ AC1
\end{array}
$$

Fig. 6. Fragment of the Corresponding CSP Process for the Microwave Controller fUML Activity Diagram (up to decision node for timer expiry)

the *accept* event. Any decision node with a control flow incoming edge is translated to a non-deterministic choice. Hence, process $ND2$ corresponds to the timer expiry decision node. Some of the events include an ID parameter (e.g., $NID1$), this ID will be used for traceability explained in Section 6.

Unlike our previous work [12,19], we do not consider inter-object communication in this paper. However, our formalization includes all the needed information to conduct inter-object behaviour analysis in the future. This is the reason for formalizing elements that will not affect the behavioural consistency checking (e.g., formalizing the *SendSignal* action in $AC12$). Nevertheless, our formalization does not cover all aspects and properties of the UML/fUML standards as we just focus on the elements included in the used case study (Tokeneer).

5 Behavioural Consistency Checking

Having the two kinds of diagrams (UML state diagram and fUML activity diagram) formalized into CSP makes the behavioural consistency checking using FDR2 a direct process. We use FDR2 to handle the model checking based on the traces refinement semantic model [2]. From one point of view of the process execution, one process is consistent with another if its behaviour are allowed by the other. Compared to other semantic models (e.g., stable failures), this one is sufficient to check if the two UML/fUML diagrams are behaviorally consistent.

Initially, the generated CSP script was augmented (by the Model Formalizer) with the following assertion to let FDR2 check the refinement between the two CSP processes. $c0$ and $h0$ represent instances of the *Controller* and *Heater* classes respectively. The set *hiddenEvents* includes all the events except the *accept* event.

$$Controller\_SD\_Proc\ (c0) \sqsubseteq_T \\ Controller\_AD\_Proc\ (c0, h0) \setminus hiddenEvents$$

However, in the case of an inconsistency, the generated counter-example (a trace leading to this inconsistency) by FDR2 includes the sequence of events from the *Controller_AD_Proc* process. As will be described in Section 6, having the traces from one side is not enough for the Model Debugger to highlight the inconsistency problem on the corresponding UML/fUML diagrams. We also need to retrieve the states that the specification has passed through. To overcome this issue, we introduce an additional process *Controller_SD_TR*.

The *Controller_SD_TR* process is a copy of the *Controller_AD_Proc* except that it stops when any *accept* event other than those allowed by the *Controller_AD_Proc* process happens. For example, the sub-process *STATE_2* in *Controller_SD_TR* is generated as follow:

$$\begin{aligned} STATE\_2 = {} & inState!ST2 \rightarrow (\\ & accept!selfObj!doorOpened \rightarrow STATE\_1 \\ & \Box \\ & accept!selfObj!buttonPressed \rightarrow STATE\_3 \\ & \Box \\ & accept!selfObj?x \rightarrow STOP) \end{aligned}$$

The refinement check (assertion) we now perform is:

$$Controller\_SD\_Proc\ (c0) \sqsubseteq_T \\ (Controller\_AD\_Proc\ (c0, h0) \underset{\{|accept|\}}{\parallel} Controller\_SD\_TR\ (c0)) \setminus hiddenEvents$$

The parallel combination above represents a process that follows the states in the *Controller_SD_Proc* process, but without affecting the refinement checking. This representation of the refinement assertion has solved the pre-described issue of debugging, as now the generated counter-example by FDR2 includes the states of the two main processes (*Controller_SD_Proc* and *Controller_AD_Proc*) which are needed to construct the appropriate feedback to the modeller. To show the effect of this technique, in the *Controller* fUML activity diagram in Figure 2, assume that the modeller (by mistake) connected the edge coming out from the *Accept*(*doorClosed*) action to the *Send*(*stopHeater*) action instead of the *Value*(*FALSE*) action. After the formalization and performing the refinement checking using FDR2, the generated counter-example is as follow:

```
<valueSpec.selfObj.FALSE.NID1,
addStructFtrVal.selfObj.isCooking.FALSE.NID3,
registerSignals.selfObj.rp1.NID5,
inState.ST2,
accept.selfObj.doorOpenedSignal,
send.selfObj.heaterObj.stopHeaterSignal.NID8,
registerSignals.selfObj.rp2.NID6,
inState.ST1,
accept.selfObj.doorClosedSignal,
send.selfObj.heaterObj.stopHeaterSignal.NID8,
registerSignals.selfObj.rp2.NID6,
inState.ST2,
accept.selfObj.doorClosedSignal>
```

The idea of using *Controller_SD_TR* derived from *Controller_SD_Proc* to track the states in the specifications, is one of this paper's contributions. We could not have been able to see the *inState* event in the above trace without this.

6 Formalization and Model Checking Feedback

The modeller will be provided with two kinds of feedback after the formalization process or behavioural consistency checking. The following sections describe them with respect to the framework components.

6.1 Formalization Report

The first kind of feedback represents the success or failure of the formalization process and it is presented to the user through a Formalization Report. In our approach, not all UML/fUML diagrams can be formalized. They have to fulfill minimum requirements in order to be formalized. These requirements include the existence of certain elements and the assignment of certain properties. For example, the Model Formalizer cannot formalize a UML state diagram that does not include a connected pseudo state, because this will prevent the Model Formalizer from setting the initial CSP sub-process in the *within* clause. Another example is not assigning the name of an edge emerging from a decision node in a fUML activity diagram. To be able to check the formalization ability of each diagram ("is formalizable?"), each transformation rule is divided into two parts. The first part checks for the required elements/assignments, and if met, the second part performs the transformation. Otherwise, a formalization error is reported to the modeller that guides him to the missing items.

6.2 Model Debugger

The second kind of feedback is provided in case of inconsistency and it represents the counter-example generated by FDR2. This feedback is provided to the modeller through the Model Debugger. As mentioned in Section 3, the Model Debug-

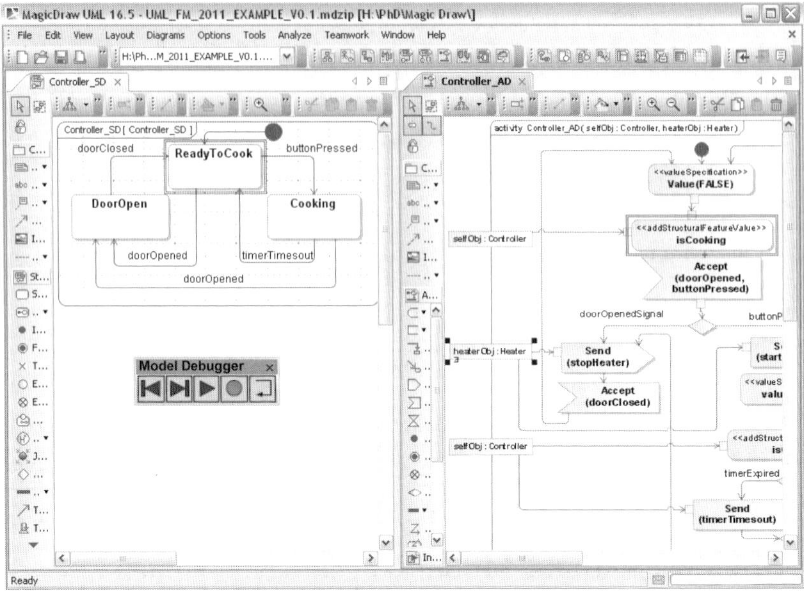

Fig. 7. Screen shot of MagicDraw Running Compass

ger component allows the modeller to interactively debug the consistency problem visually on the displayed UML/fUML activity diagram using GUI controls. The controls allow the modeller to step forward/backward (i.e., move within the sequence of traces of the counter-example with one trace forward/backward). Whilst the modeller is navigating through the events of the counter-example, the corresponding UML/fUML elements of the events are highlighted on the displayed diagrams to help him locate the source of the inconsistency. Also he can put a breakpoint on one of the UML/fUML elements and execute all events until reaching this element. Figure 7 shows the GUI controllers (inside the Model Debugger toolbar) and how the UML/fUML elements are highlighted (surrounded by a coloured square) in the diagrams.

The Model Debugger cannot work without the data that has been collected during the formalization and the model checking processes. As mentioned in Section 4, the Model Formalizer generates an ID for the CSP processes' events. It also generates the CSP-to-UML/fUML mapping table which holds the CSP events IDs and their corresponding UML/fUML element IDs (long alphanumeric references generated by MagicDraw). Table 1 shows a sample of this table which helps the Model Debugger to know which UML/fUML elements to highlight given the CSP event ID included in the counter-example. It should be clear now why we formulated the assertion statement (in Section 5) to force FDR2 to include the state diagram CSP process (*Controller_SD_TR*) traces in the counter-example.

Table 1. Sample CSP-to-UML/fUML Mapping Table

CSP Event ID	UML/fUML Element ID
ST2	_16_4_8a01c6_129197859_209692_741
NID3	_16_4_80a01c6_128715854_342172_469

We consider providing the model checking results through a Model Debugger to be another contribution of our work.

7 Approach Implementation

We have implemented our approach as a MagicDraw plugin called "Compass" (Checking Original Models means Perfectly Analyzed Systems). To use Compass, the modeller should first model the system objects' behaviour using UML state diagrams, then refine each diagram (by adding more implementation details) by modelling the same behaviour using an fUML activity diagram. At this point, the modeller can use Compass to start the consistency checking between the two kinds of diagrams and get the feedback as described in Section 6.

Figure 7 shows a screen shot of MagicDraw during debugging an inconsistency problem using the Model Debugger toolbar. The screen shows the Microwave controller UML state diagram and its corresponding fUML activity diagram with two highlighted elements (ReadyToCook state and isCooking action). There is also another window that shows the executed traces (states and actions). This is not included in the screen shot due to lack of space.

We would argue that implementing the approach in a form of a plugin to an already existing case tool is more practical for several reasons. Compared to a standalone formalization application, a plugin will allow for having a single integrated modelling environment. Also modifying the plugin to work with other case tools is a straightforward task, which means that the plugin can be made available for several case tools. This in turn will allow the modeller who is already using a certain case tool not to change his modelling environment to check his models (or even re-check legacy models).

8 Related Work

Much research work has been done on formalizing UML models to check different properties. For example, the authors in [20,19,12] used such formalizations to make sure that their UML models are deadlock free. Others, such as [21,22], used the formalization to check certain safety properties in the input models.

Intra-model consistency (i.e., are the diagrams of the same model consistent?) can be checked by formalization as well. Zhao *et al.* [23] followed that concept by checking consistency between the UML state diagram and its related sequence diagrams using Promela as a formal language.

Graw *et al.* [5] proposed inter-model consistency through checking refinement between abstract and more detailed UML state and sequence diagrams depending on cTLA (compositional Temporal Logic of Actions) as a formal representation. Ramos *et al.* [4] proposed formalizing UML-RT into Circus to prove that the model transformation preserved the original model semantics.

Most of the reviewed works in this field performs the model transformation automatically (from UML to the formal language). Some of these work depended on MDE tools to do the transformation. Varró *et al.* in [24] summarized a comparison between eleven different MDE tools used to transform from UML activity diagrams into CSP (UML-to-CSP case study [25]), as part of the AGTIVE'07 tool contest. Also Treharne *et al.* [9] used the Epsilon framework to transform UML state diagrams to CSP||B.

Providing modeller friendly feedback to report the model checking results has been addressed only a few times in the literature. The authors in [26,27] proposed presenting the model checking results (e.g., counter-example) as an object diagram that represents a snapshot of the system during the error. Alternatively, the authors in [28,29] proposed compiler style-errors with valuable feedback.

None of the reviewed works has been concerned with checking consistency between non-executable and executable semi-formal models (e.g., UML and fUML). Similarly, providing the formalization feedback interactively through a model debugger has not been developed.

9 Conclusion and Future Work

An approach to check behavioural consistency between UML state diagrams and their corresponding fUML activity diagrams has been presented in this paper. The approach depends on a framework that formalizes the UML/fUML diagrams automatically into CSP and then uses FDR2 to handle the model checking. In the case of inconsistency, the framework reflects FDR2 output (counter-example) to the original UML/fUML model through the Model Debugger.

We have developed an implementation of this framework as a MagicDraw plugin called Compass. Compass made use of the Epsilon MDE framework to translate the UML/fUML diagrams into a CSP script in two stages (Model-to-Model then Model-to-Text).

The practicality of this approach comes from several aspects. First, by its attempt to check consistency between non-executable and executable models, which we believe will be very important as fUML spreads within the normal software development process. Second, we believe that providing the model checking results through the Model Debugger is more helpful in identifying the source of the problem instead of just showing an object diagram to the modeller. Finally, by implementing the approach as a plugin to a case tool and depending on an MDE framework instead of writing our formalizer from scratch.

Validating the approach's functionality and applicability was achieved by applying it on a non-trivial case study (Tokeneer). Using MagicDraw and Compass during the system modelling helped to identify several inconsistencies between the UML abstract state diagrams and their corresponding fUML activity diagrams.

As future work, we will consider inter-object interaction to provide a similar framework that checks deadlocks and other behavioural properties. We will also aim to provide additional feedback to the user as a UML sequence diagram which visualizes the counter-examples as object interactions. Finally, we will upgrade the Model Debugger to consider the case of having more than one counter-example generated by FDR2.

Acknowledgments. Thanks to the anonymous referees for their constructive comments.

References

1. OMG: Semantics of a foundational subset for executable UML models (fUML) - Version 1.0 (February 2011), `http://www.omg.org/spec/fuml/`
2. Schneider, S.: Concurrent and Real-Time Systems: the CSP Approach. Wiley, Chichester (1999)
3. Formal Systems Oxford: FDR 2.91 manual (2010)
4. Ramos, R., Sampaio, A., Mota, A.: A semantics for UML-RT active classes via mapping into circus. In: Steffen, M., Tennenholtz, M. (eds.) FMOODS 2005. LNCS, vol. 3535, pp. 99–114. Springer, Heidelberg (2005)
5. Graw, G., Herrmann, P.: Transformation and verification of Executable UML models. Electron. Notes Theor. Comput. Sci. 101, 3–24 (2004)
6. Hnatkowska, B., Huzar, Z., Kuzniarz, L., Tuzinkiewicz, L.: A systematic approach to consistency within UML based software development process. In: Blekinge Institute of Technology, Research Report 2002:06. UML 2002. Workshop on Consistency Problems in UML-based Software Development, pp. 16–29 (2002)
7. Epsilon Project, `http://www.eclipse.org/gmt/epsilon/`
8. UML2 Project, `http://www.eclipse.org/modeling/mdt/?project=uml2`
9. Treharne, H., Turner, E., Paige, R.F., Kolovos, D.S.: Automatic generation of integrated formal models corresponding to UML system models. In: Oriol, M., Meyer, B. (eds.) TOOLS EUROPE 2009. Lecture Notes in Business Information Processing, vol. 33, pp. 357–367. Springer, Heidelberg (2009)
10. MagicDraw case tool, `http://www.magicdraw.com/`
11. Barnes, J., Chapman, R., Johnson, R., Widmaier, J., Cooper, D., Everett, B.: Engineering the tokeneer enclave protection software. In: 1st IEEE International Symposium on Secure Software Engineering (March 2006)
12. Abdelhalim, I., Sharp, J., Schneider, S.A., Treharne, H.: Formal Verification of Tokeneer Behaviours Modelled in fUML Using CSP. In: Dong, J.S., Zhu, H. (eds.) ICFEM 2010. LNCS, vol. 6447, pp. 371–387. Springer, Heidelberg (2010)
13. Mellor, S.J., Balcer, M.J.: Executable UML, A Foundation for Model-Driven Architecture. Addison-Wesley, Reading (2002)
14. OMG: fUML Reference Implementation, `http://portal.modeldriven.org`
15. OMG: Unified modeling language (UML) superstructure (version 2.3) (2010)
16. Gruninger, M., Menzel, C.: Process Specification Language: Principles and Applications. AI Magazine 24(3), 63–74 (2003)
17. Metadata Interchange (XMI), X, `http://www.omg.org/spec/XMI/`
18. Dimitrios kolovos, L.R., Paige, R.: The Epsilon Book

19. Turner, E., Treharne, H., Schneider, S., Evans, N.: Automatic generation of CSP || B skeletons from xUML models. In: Fitzgerald, J.S., Haxthausen, A.E., Yenigun, H. (eds.) ICTAC 2008. LNCS, vol. 5160, pp. 364–379. Springer, Heidelberg (2008)
20. Ng, M.Y., Butler, M.: Towards formalizing UML state diagrams in CSP. In: Cerone, A., Lindsay, P. (eds.) 1st IEEE International Conference on Software Engineering and Formal Methods, pp. 138–147. IEEE Computer Society, Los Alamitos (2003)
21. Hansen, H.H., Ketema, J., Luttik, B., Mousavi, M., van de Pol, J.: Towards model checking Executable UML specifications in mCRL2. In: ISSE, pp. 83–90 (2010)
22. Balser, M., Bäumler, S., Reif, W., Thums, A.: Interactive verification of UML state machines. In: Davies, J., Schulte, W., Barnett, M. (eds.) ICFEM 2004. LNCS, vol. 3308, pp. 434–448. Springer, Heidelberg (2004)
23. Zhao, X., Long, Q., Qiu, Z.: Model checking dynamic UML consistency. In: Liu, Z., Kleinberg, R.D. (eds.) ICFEM 2006. LNCS, vol. 4260, pp. 440–459. Springer, Heidelberg (2006)
24. Varró, D., Asztalos, M., Bisztray, D., Boronat, A., Dang, D.H., Geiss, R., Greenyer, J., Gorp, P.V., Kniemeyer, O., Narayanan, A., Rencis, E., Weinell, E.: Transformation of UML Models to CSP: A Case Study for Graph Transformation Tools. In: Schürr, A., Nagl, M., Zündorf, A. (eds.) AGTIVE 2007. LNCS, vol. 5088, pp. 540–565. Springer, Heidelberg (2008)
25. Bisztray, D., Ehrig, K., Heckel, R.: Case Study: UML to CSP Transformation. In: Applications of Graph Transformation with Industrial Relevance (2007)
26. Cabot, J., Clarisó, R., Riera, D.: Verifying UML/OCL operation contracts. In: Leuschel, M., Wehrheim, H. (eds.) IFM 2009. LNCS, vol. 5423, pp. 40–55. Springer, Heidelberg (2009)
27. Shah, S.M.A., Anastasakis, K., Bordbar, B.: From UML to Alloy and back again. In: MoDeVVa 2009: Proceedings of the 6th International Workshop on Model-Driven Engineering, Verification and Validation, pp. 1–10. ACM, New York (2009)
28. Thierry-Mieg, Y., Hillah, L.M.: UML behavioral consistency checking using instantiable Petri nets. In: ISSE, vol. 4(3), pp. 293–300 (2008)
29. Planas, E., Cabot, J., Gómez, C.: Verifying action semantics specifications in UML behavioral models. In: van Eck, P., Gordijn, J., Wieringa, R. (eds.) CAiSE 2009. LNCS, vol. 5565, pp. 125–140. Springer, Heidelberg (2009)

The Safety-Critical Java Mission Model: A Formal Account

Frank Zeyda, Ana Cavalcanti, and Andy Wellings

University of York, Deramore Lane, York, YO10 5GH, UK
{Frank.Zeyda,Ana.Cavalcanti,Andy.Wellings}@cs.york.ac.uk

Abstract. Safety-Critical Java (SCJ) is a restriction of the Real-Time Specification for Java to support the development and certification of safety-critical applications. It is the result of an international effort from industry and academia. Here we present the first formalisation of the SCJ execution model, covering missions and event handlers. Our formal language is part of the *Circus* family; at the core, we have Z, CSP, and Morgan's calculus, but we also use object-oriented and timed constructs from the *OhCircus* and *Circus Time* variants. Our work is a first step in the development of refinement-based reasoning techniques for SCJ.

Keywords: *Circus*, real-time systems, models, verification, RTSJ.

1 Introduction

Safety-Critical Java (SCJ) [11] restricts the Java API and execution model in such a way that programs can be effectively analysed for real-time requirements, memory safety, and concurrency issues. This facilitates certification under standards like DO-178B, for example. It also makes possible the development of automatic tools that support analysis and verification.

SCJ is realised within the Real-Time Specification for Java (RTSJ) [21]. The purpose of RTSJ itself is to define an architecture that permits the development of real-time programs, and SCJ reuses some of RTSJ's concepts and actual components, albeit restricting the programming interface. SCJ also has a specific execution model that imposes a rigid structure on how applications are executed.

The SCJ specification, as designed by the JSR 302 expert group, comprises informal descriptions and a reference implementation [8]. As a result, analysis tools have been developed to establish compliance with the SCJ restrictions [20].

In this paper, we complement the existing work on SCJ by presenting a formal model of its execution framework in a *Circus*-based language. The Open Group's informal account of SCJ [8] relies on text and UML diagrams, and our objective is to formalise the execution model. *Circus* [5] is a refinement notation for state-rich reactive systems. Its variants cover, for instance, aspects of time and mobility. We use its object-oriented variant, *OhCircus*, as our base notation.

Our formal model first elicits the conceptual behaviour of the SCJ framework, and secondly illustrates the translation of actual SCJ programs into their *OhCircus* specifications in a traceable manner. For now, we ignore certain aspects

S. Qin and Z. Qiu (Eds.): ICFEM 2011, LNCS 6991, pp. 49–65, 2011.

of SCJ, such as the memory model, which we discuss in a separate paper [7], and scheduling policy. Our focus is the top-level design and execution of SCJ programs, and its primary framework and application components.

The SCJ framework as designed in Java is a reflection of a general programming paradigm. It embeds a particular view of data operations, memory, and event-based versus thread-based designs [22]. Our model identifies the fundamental concepts of SCJ at a level where it can be regarded itself as a programming language. The fact that it can be realised on top of Java and the RTSJ is a bonus. It is conceivable, however, to implement specific support based on other mainstream languages, or even define an entirely new language, and formalisation is conducive to the development of such a language which is our future ambition.

What we present here is a precise semantics for core elements of SCJ. It enables formal verification of SCJ applications beyond the informal validation of statically checkable properties currently available [20]. *OhCircus* provides a notion of refinement, and our work is an essential first step to justify development and verification methods that can produce high-quality SCJ implementations.

Our work also highlights the need for a particular integration of *Circus* variants. Their Unifying Theories of Programming (UTP) [13] foundation facilitates this work. The UTP is a uniform framework in which the semantics of a variety of programming paradigms can be expressed and linked. UTP theories have already been presented for *Circus* and *Circus Time* [16,18], and also for object-orientation [17] and the SCJ memory model [7]. We thus identify the *Circus* variant necessary to formalise SCJ programs. The design of the semantic model establishes the right level of detail for reasoning about SCJ, and determines where the added expressiveness of Java should be ignored.

Finally, our work guides the construction of a platform for reasoning. Our models are free from the noise that originates from the expressiveness of Java. They allow us to reason about SCJ programs using refinement-based techniques. For verification, we can construct models of particular programs, and use the *Circus* and UTP techniques for reasoning. For development, we can start from an abstract specification, and develop implementations that follow the structure and respect the restrictions of our models.

In the next section, we introduce the SCJ framework and a case study used throughout as an example. We also provide a brief overview of our formal notation. In Section 3 we present our models and modelling approach. In Section 4, we discuss our contributions and some related work.

2 Preliminaries

In this section we present first the SCJ execution model and introduce an example: an automotive cruise controller. Afterwards, we present *Circus* and *OhCircus*.

2.1 Safety-Critical Java

SCJ recognises that safety-critical software varies considerably in complexity. Consequently, there are three compliance levels for SCJ programs and framework

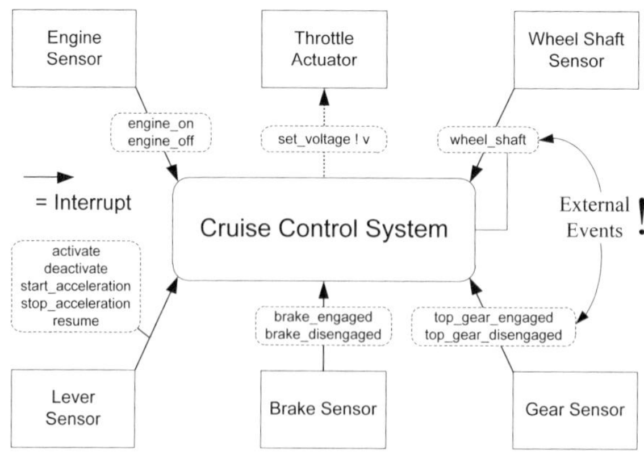

Fig. 1. ACCS interactions

implementations. In this work, we are concerned with Level 1, which, roughly, corresponds in complexity to the Ravenscar profile for Ada [4]. Level 1 applications support periodic event handlers and aperiodic event handlers.

The SCJ programming model is based on the notion of missions. They are sequentially executed by an application-specific mission sequencer provided by a safelet, the top-level entity of an SCJ application. All these concepts are realised by either interfaces or abstract classes. Namely, they are the `Safelet` interface, and the abstract classes `MissionSequencer` and `Mission` (see Fig. 2).

A Level 1 mission consists of a set of asynchronous event handlers; both periodic and aperiodic handlers are supported. Each aperiodic handler is associated with a set of events: firing of one of them causes the handler method to be scheduled for execution. Periodic event handlers, on the other hand, are controlled by a timer. Event handlers are also provided through abstract classes whose handling method must be implemented by concrete subclasses (see Fig. 2).

A Cruise Control System. As an example of an SCJ program, and to illustrate our modelling approach, we present an implementation of Wellings' automotive cruise control system (ACCS) in [21] that uses SCJ Level 1.

The goal of an ACCS is to automatically maintain the speed of a vehicle to a value set by the driver; in Fig. 1 we give an overview of its main components and commands. Explicit commands are given by a lever whose positioning corresponds to the following instructions: *activate*, to turn on the ACCS if the car is in top gear, and maintain (and remember) the current speed; *deactivate*, to turn off the ACCS; *start accelerating*, to accelerate at a comfortable rate; *stop accelerating*, to stop accelerating and maintain (and remember) the current speed; and *resume* to return to the last remembered speed and maintain it. Implicit commands are issued when the driver changes gear, operates the brake pedal, or switches on or off the engine. The ACCS is deactivated when the driver changes out of top gear, presses the brake pedal, or switches the engine off.

The speed of the vehicle is measured via the rotation of the shaft that drives the back wheels. The shaft generates an interrupt for each rotation, which causes an event being fired and an associated handler being scheduled for execution.

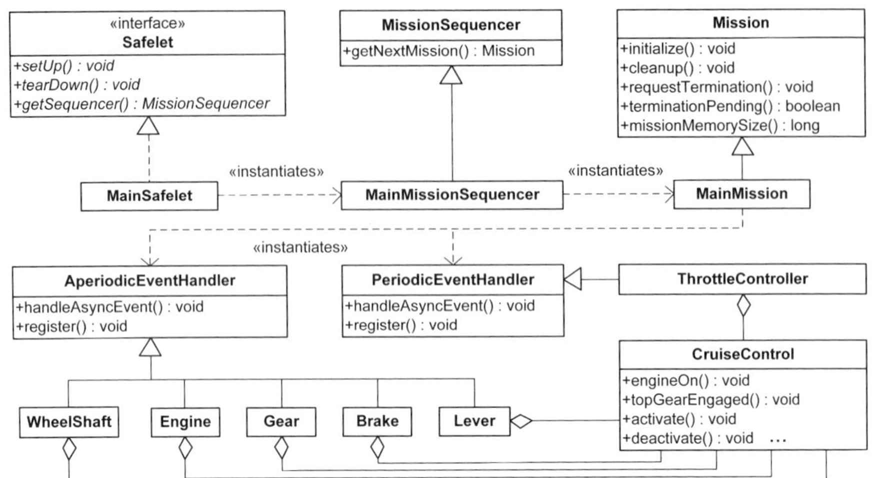

Fig. 2. UML class diagram for the cruise controller

The actual speed of the car depends on the throttle position, which is determined by the depression of the accelerator pedal and a voltage supplied by the ACCS. The combination of these values is performed outside the ACCS.

Sensors detect external happenings and generate appropriate interrupts, as illustrated in Fig. 1. These interrupts are reflected in the SCJ program by the firing of SCJ events that correspond to the possible happenings. For the setting of the throttle voltage, communication of the new voltage value to the ACCS components is realised in the program using a hardware data register.

Fig. 2 presents a UML class diagram that gives an overview of the design of the ACCS as an SCJ Level 1 safelet. As said above, `Safelet` is an interface, and the classes `MissionSequencer`, `Mission`, `AperiodicEventHandler` and `PeriodicEventHandler` are abstract. They are part of the SCJ API developed on top of the RTSJ API to capture the SCJ programming model.

`MainSafelet` is the entry point for the application. It provides the method `getSequencer()` that returns the mission sequencer. The other two methods `setUp()` and `tearDown()` are provided for initialisation and cleanup tasks. The `MainMissionSequencer` class constructs instances of the `Mission` class, by implementing `getNextMission()`. Concrete subclasses of `Mission` have to implement the `initialize()` and `missionMemorySize()` methods. The former creates the periodic and aperiodic event handlers of the mission. The handlers register themselves with the mission by way of the `register()` method.

Both periodic and aperiodic handlers implement `handleAsyncEvent()` to specify their behaviour when the handler is released. The two extra methods `requestTermination()` and `terminationPending()` cannot be overridden; they allow for the mission to be terminated by one of the handlers.

Fig. 2 does not show all components of the SCJ API. There are eight classes that realise the mission framework, twelve classes in the handler hierarchy, five classes that deal with real-time threads, seven classes concerned with scheduling, and ten classes for the memory model. The formal model that we present here abstracts from all these details of the realisation of the SCJ Level 1 programming paradigm in Java. We capture the main concepts of its novel execution model. This enables reasoning based on the core components of the SCJ paradigm.

2.2 *Circus* and *OhCircus*

The *Circus* language [5] is a hybrid formalism that includes elements from Z [19], CSP [12], and imperative commands from Morgan's calculus [15]. Several examples are provided in the next section: see Fig. 4, 5, 6, and 7, for instance.

Like in CSP, the key elements of *Circus* models are processes that interact with each other and their environment via channels. Unlike CSP, *Circus* processes may encapsulate a state. The definition of a *Circus* process hence includes a paragraph that identifies the state of the process using a Z schema.

The behaviour of a process is defined by its main action (which may reference local actions, introduced for structuring purposes). The language of actions includes all constructs from CSP, such as *Skip* and *Stop*, input and output prefixes, sequencing, parallelism, interleaving and hiding, as well as operations to modify the state. Parallelism and interleaving are parametrised in terms of the state components that each parallel action can modify to avoid potential write conflicts. State operations can be specified either by Z operation schemas or guarded commands. We explain the details of the notation as needed.

OhCircus [6] extends *Circus* with an additional notion of class. Unlike processes, objects can be used in arbitrary mathematical expressions. The permissible notation for *OhCircus* class methods includes all schema operations, guarded commands, and some additional notations used to instantiate new data objects, invoke methods, access object fields, and support inheritance.

Processes describe the active behaviour of the model (or of its components), including the whole system. Classes model passive data objects and operations performed on them. In the following section we present our model for SCJ programs. The notation we use is *OhCircus*. We, however, use a few action operators of the *Circus Time* [18] variant, and object references from our previous SCJ memory model in [7]. The latter is specified at the level of the Unifying Theories of Programming [13], the semantic framework of *Circus* and its extensions.

3 Framework and Application Models

Our model of SCJ factors into two dimensions: a generic framework model, and an application model that corresponds to a particular concrete SCJ program. We specify the semantics of safelets, the mission sequencer, missions, and aperiodic as well as periodic event handlers. To illustrate the application model, we make use of the cruise controller application as it was presented in the previous section.

Fig. 3 presents an overview of the structure of the model of a typical SCJ application — here the cruise controller. Each of the five top-level boxes refers to a process that realises a specific component of the SCJ programming model. We label these boxes with the process names. Arrows indicate the channels on

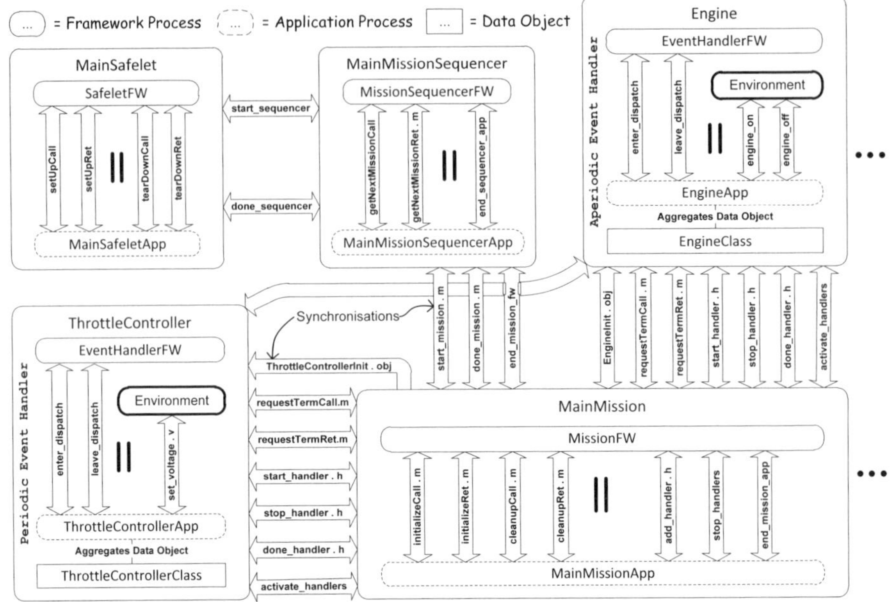

Fig. 3. Structure of the model the SCJ cruise controller

which the components communicate. For instance, the processes *MainSafelet* and *MainMissionSequencer* communicate on *start_sequencer* and *done_sequencer*.

The model of the application is obtained by parallel composition of the top-level processes, and by hiding all but the external channels. These define the interface of the system; for example, we define the event *engine_on* to represent the happening that occurs when the engine is switched on.

Each top-level process is itself defined by the parallel composition of a generic framework process (suffix *FW*), and a process that is in direct correspondence with the Java code (suffix *App*). We have an instance of the *EventHandlerFW* framework process for each handler. To obtain the model of an existing SCJ program, we can follow the strategy explained below to construct the *App* processes, and use the *FW* processes as defined later on; except only that, in the case of a handler *App* process, we need to be aware of the events the handler is bound to, and declare channels to represent them.

The following provides the definition of the *MainSafelet* process.

$$\begin{array}{l}\textbf{channelset}\ \mathit{MainSafeletChan} \mathrel{\widehat=} \\ \quad \{\!|\ \mathit{setUpCall}, \mathit{setUpRet}, \mathit{tearDownCall}, \mathit{tearDownRet}\ |\!\}\end{array}$$

$$\begin{array}{l}\textbf{process}\ \mathit{MainSafelet} \mathrel{\widehat=} \\ \quad (\mathit{SafeletFW}\ [\![\ \mathit{MainSafeletChan}\ ]\!]\ \mathit{MainSafeletApp}) \setminus \mathit{MainSafeletChan}\end{array}$$

The channels on which framework and application process communicate are hidden (operator $\setminus$). Here, these are *setUpCall*, *setUpRet*, *tearDownCall*, and *tearDownRet*. Above, a channel set *MainSafeletChan* is defined to contain all these channels. In the definition of *MainSafelet*, it is used to define the synchronisation set of the parallelism (operator $[\![\ldots]\!]$), and the set of channels to be hidden. The synchronisation set defines the channels over which communication requires synchronisation between the two parallel processes.

We differentiate between channels that represent framework events, and channels that represent method calls. Channels suffixed with *Call* and *Ret* encode method calls. Method calls are in some cases modelled by channel communications rather than mere *OhCircus* data operations to allow the framework processes to trigger or respond to those calls. A call to `requestTermination()`, for instance, has to interact with the mission framework process. We then require a *Call* and a *Ret* channel for this method.

In the following we specify each of the top-level processes.

3.1 Safelet Model

The framework process *SafeletFW* for a safelet is given below; it has no state.

$$
\begin{array}{l}
\mathbf{process}\ SafeletFW \mathrel{\widehat{=}} \mathbf{begin}\\
\quad SetUp \mathrel{\widehat{=}} setUpCall \longrightarrow setUpRet \longrightarrow Skip\\
\quad Execute \mathrel{\widehat{=}} start\_sequencer \longrightarrow done\_sequencer \longrightarrow Skip\\
\quad TearDown \mathrel{\widehat{=}} tearDownCall \longrightarrow tearDownRet \longrightarrow Skip\\
\quad \bullet\ SetUp \mathbin{;}\ Execute \mathbin{;}\ TearDown\\
\mathbf{end}
\end{array}
$$

The main action, which is given at the end after the $\bullet$, sequentially executes the *SetUp*, *Execute* and *TearDown* local actions. They correspond to the initialisation, execution, and cleanup phases of the safelet. *SetUp* and *TearDown* synchronise in sequence (prefixing operator $\longrightarrow$) on the $setUp[Call/Ret]$ and $tearDown[Call/Ret]$ channels, before terminating (basic action *Skip*). The synchronisations model calls to the methods `setUp()` and `tearDown()` of the Java class. Since the methods are parameterless and do not return any values, the communications through the channels are just synchronisations: there is no input or output. The methods themselves are specified in the application process as exemplified below: the framework process defines the flow of execution, and the application process defines specific program functionality. *Execute* raises two framework events: *start_sequencer* to start the mission sequencer, and *done_sequencer* to detect its termination. These channels are exposed by the *Safelet* component (that is, not hidden in its definition as shown above), and their purpose is to control the *MissionSequencer* component which we specify later on.

We now present the application process for the safelet in our example.

$$
\begin{array}{l}
\mathbf{process}\ MainSafeletApp \mathrel{\widehat{=}} \mathbf{begin}\\
\quad setUpMeth \mathrel{\widehat{=}} setUpCall \longrightarrow Skip \mathbin{;}\ setUpRet \longrightarrow Skip\\
\quad tearDownMeth \mathrel{\widehat{=}} tearDownCall \longrightarrow Skip \mathbin{;}\ tearDownRet \longrightarrow Skip\\
\quad Methods \mathrel{\widehat{=}} \mu X \bullet setUpMeth \mathbin{;}\ X\\
\quad \bullet\ Methods \mathbin{\triangle} tearDownMeth\\
\mathbf{end}
\end{array}
$$

$$
\begin{array}{l}
\mathbf{process}\ \mathit{MissionSequencerFW} \mathrel{\widehat=} \mathbf{begin} \\
\quad \mathit{Start} \mathrel{\widehat=} \mathit{start\_sequencer} \longrightarrow \mathit{Skip} \\
\quad \mathit{Execute} \mathrel{\widehat=} \mu X \bullet \mathit{getNextMissionCall} \longrightarrow \mathit{getNextMissionRet} \mathbin{?} \mathit{next} \longrightarrow \\
\qquad \mathbf{if}\ \mathit{next} \neq \mathit{null} \longrightarrow \mathit{start\_mission} \,.\, \mathit{next} \longrightarrow \mathit{done\_mission} \,.\, \mathit{next} \longrightarrow X \\
\qquad [\!]\ \mathit{next} = \mathit{null} \longrightarrow \mathit{Skip} \\
\qquad \mathbf{fi} \\
\quad \mathit{Finish} \mathrel{\widehat=} \mathit{end\_sequencer\_app} \longrightarrow \mathit{end\_mission\_fw} \longrightarrow \mathit{done\_sequencer} \longrightarrow \mathit{Skip} \\
\quad \bullet\ \mathit{Start} \,;\, \mathit{Execute} \,;\, \mathit{Finish} \\
\mathbf{end}
\end{array}
$$

Fig. 4. Mission sequencer framework process

The specification is trivial here since `setUp()` and `tearDown()` in `MainSafelet` do not contain any code in the ACCS implementation. More important is the modelling approach, which we adopt in all application processes. A local action *Methods* recursively (operator μ) offers a choice of actions that correspond to methods of the SCJ class; the choice is exercised by the associated framework process. For the safelet application process, the only action offered by *Methods* is *setUpMeth*. In the main action, we have a call to *Methods*. Termination occurs when there is a call to the `tearDown()` method. In the main action, this is captured by an interrupt (operator $\triangle$) that calls the *tearDownMeth* action.

A method action, here *setUpMeth* or *tearDownMeth*, synchronises on the channel that represents a call to it, *setUpCall* or *tearDownCall*, for instance, and then executes actions that correspond to the method implementation. Since, as already mentioned, `setUp()` and `tearDown()` in `MainSafelet` do not contain any code, in our example above, these actions are just *Skip*. At the end the method action synchronises on the channel that signals the return of the call, *setUpRet* or *tearDownRet*, for instance. If the method has parameters or returns a value, the call and return channels are used to communicate these values. Examples of our encoding of parametrised methods are shown below.

3.2 Mission Sequencer Model

The mission sequencer process (Fig. 4) communicates with the safelet process to determine when it has to start, and to signal its termination.

The main action executes *Start* to wait for the mission sequencer to be started, which is signalled by a synchronisation on *start_sequencer*. Afterwards, execution proceeds as specified by a recursion in the action *Execute*. In each iteration, it synchronises on the channels *getNextMissionCall* and *getNextMissionRet* to obtain the next mission via *next*. This corresponds to a call to the SCJ method `getNextMission()`. Since it returns a (mission) object, *getNextMissionRet* takes as input a value *next* of type *MissionId* (containing identifiers for the missions of an application). A special mission identifier *null* is used to cater for the case in which the method returns a Java `null` reference to signal that there are no more missions to execute. In *Execute*, a conditional checks the value of *next*. If it is not *null*, synchronisations on $\mathit{start\_mission} \,.\, \mathit{next}$ and $\mathit{done\_mission} \,.\, \mathit{next}$

are used to control the *Mission* process (defined later on) that manages execution of the particular mission *next*, and then *Execute* recurses (calls X) to handle the next mission. Otherwise, *Execute* finishes. At the end, in the *Finish* action, synchronisation on *end_sequencer_app* is used to terminate the mission sequencer application process. Next, synchronisation on *end_mission_fw* terminates the mission framework process. Finally, synchronisation on *done_sequencer* acknowledges to the safelet process that the mission sequencer has finished.

For our example, the mission sequencer application process is as follows.

$$
\begin{array}{l}
\textbf{process } \mathit{MainMissionSequencerApp} \mathrel{\widehat=} \textbf{begin} \\
\quad \textbf{state } \mathit{MainMissionSequencerState} == [\mathit{mission\_done} : \mathit{BOOL}] \\
\quad \mathit{Init} \mathrel{\widehat=} \mathit{mission\_done} := \mathit{FALSE} \\
\quad \mathit{getNextMissionMeth} \mathrel{\widehat=} \mathit{getNextMissionCall} \longrightarrow \\
\qquad \textbf{if } \mathit{mission\_done} = \mathit{FALSE} \longrightarrow \\
\qquad\quad \mathit{mission\_done} := \mathit{TRUE} \mathbin{;} \mathit{getNextMissionRet} \,!\, \mathit{MainMissionId} \longrightarrow \mathit{Skip} \\
\qquad [\!] \neg\, \mathit{mission\_done} = \mathit{FALSE} \longrightarrow \mathit{getNextMissionRet} \,!\, \mathit{null} \longrightarrow \mathit{Skip} \\
\qquad \textbf{fi} \\
\quad \mathit{Methods} = \mu X \bullet \mathit{getNextMissionMeth} \mathbin{;} X \\
\quad \bullet\ \mathit{Init} \mathbin{;} (\mathit{Methods} \mathbin{\triangle} \mathit{end\_sequencer\_app} \longrightarrow \mathit{Skip}) \\
\textbf{end}
\end{array}
$$

This is a more complete illustration of our approach to modelling SCJ classes as *Circus* processes. The member variables of the class become state components. In the above example, we have one state component *mission_done* corresponding to a variable of the same name in the SCJ class `MainMissionSequencer`. We define a free type $BOOL ::= TRUE \mid FALSE$ to support boolean values in Z.

The action *Init* specifies the constructor. Other method actions are named after the methods of the class. In the case of the mission sequencer application class modelled above, we have just the method `getNextMission()`.

The main action of an application process is always of the above shape: a call to *Init*, if present, and a call to *Methods*, with an interrupt that allows a controlling process to terminate it via a special event (here *end_sequencer_app*). In the case of the safelet application process discussed earlier, the special termination event corresponded also to a call to its `tearDown()` method.

In *MainMissionSequencerApp*, the specification of *getNextMissionMeth* is in direct correspondence with the code of `getNextMission()`. We have a conditional that, depending on the value of *mission_done* updates its value and outputs (returns) the next mission or *null*. The difference is that, instead of representing a mission by an object, we use constants of type *MissionId*. In our example, since we have only one mission, we have just one constant *MainMissionId*.

We omit the definition of the process *MainMissionSequencer*, which is a parallel composition of *MissionSequencerFW* and *MainMissionSequencerApp*, similar to that used to define *MainSafelet* at the beginning of this section.

3.3 Mission Model

The purpose of a mission process, defined by a parallelism between the mission framework process and an associated mission application process, is to create the

$$
\begin{array}{l}
\textbf{process } \mathit{MissionFW} \mathrel{\widehat=} \textbf{begin} \\
\quad \textbf{state } \mathit{MissionFWState} == [\mathit{mission} : \mathit{MissionId}, \mathit{handlers} : \mathbb{F}\, \mathit{HandlerId}] \\
\quad \mathit{Init} == [\mathit{MissionFWState}' \mid \mathit{mission}' = \mathit{null} \wedge \mathit{handlers}' = \varnothing] \\
\quad \mathit{Start} \mathrel{\widehat=} \mathit{Init} \,;\; \mathit{start\_mission} ? m \longrightarrow \mathit{mission} := m \\
\quad \mathit{AddHandler} \mathrel{\widehat=} \textbf{val } \mathit{handler} : \mathit{HandlerId} \bullet \mathit{handlers} := \mathit{handlers} \cup \{\mathit{handler}\} \\
\quad \mathit{Initialize} \mathrel{\widehat=} \mathit{initializeCall} \,.\, \mathit{mission} \longrightarrow \\
\qquad \left(\mu X \bullet \left(\begin{array}{l} \mathit{add\_handler} ? h \longrightarrow (\mathit{AddHandler}(h);\; X) \\ \Box \\ \mathit{initializeRet} \,.\, \mathit{mission} \longrightarrow \mathit{Skip} \end{array} \right) \right) \\
\quad \mathit{StartHandlers} \mathrel{\widehat=} \mathop{|||}\, h : \mathit{handlers} \bullet \mathit{start\_handler} \,.\, h \longrightarrow \mathit{Skip} \\
\quad \mathit{StopHandlers} \mathrel{\widehat=} \mathop{|||}\, h : \mathit{handlers} \bullet \mathit{stop\_handler} \,.\, h \longrightarrow \mathit{done\_handler} \,.\, h \longrightarrow \mathit{Skip} \\
\quad \mathit{Execute} \mathrel{\widehat=} \mathit{StartHandlers} ; \mathit{activate\_handlers} \longrightarrow \mathit{stop\_handlers} \longrightarrow \mathit{StopHandlers} \\
\quad \mathit{Cleanup} \mathrel{\widehat=} \mathit{cleanupCall} \,.\, \mathit{mission} \longrightarrow \mathit{cleanupRet} \,.\, \mathit{mission} \longrightarrow \mathit{Skip} \\
\quad \mathit{Finish} \mathrel{\widehat=} \mathit{end\_mission\_app} \,.\, \mathit{mission} \longrightarrow \mathit{done\_mission} \,.\, \mathit{mission} \longrightarrow \mathit{Skip} \\
\quad \bullet\, (\mu X \bullet \mathit{Start} \,;\; \mathit{Initialize} \,;\; \mathit{Execute} \,;\; \mathit{Cleanup} \,;\; \mathit{Finish} \,;\; X) \\
\qquad\quad \triangle\, \mathit{end\_mission\_fw} \longrightarrow \mathit{Skip} \\
\textbf{end}
\end{array}
$$

Fig. 5. Mission framework process

mission's event handlers, execute the mission by synchronously starting them, wait for their termination, and afterwards finish the mission. It also allows the termination of the mission by a handler at any point.

Fig. 5 presents the framework process for mission execution. Its state has two components: the identifier *mission* of the mission being executed, if any, and its finite set *handlers* of handlers. The handlers are identified by values of a type *HandlerId*. The action *Init* is a standard Z operation to initialise the state. The declaration $\mathit{MissionFWState}'$ introduces dashed versions of the state component names ($\mathit{mission}'$ and $\mathit{handlers}'$) to represent the values of the components after initialisation. *Init* defines that, initially, there is no mission executing, so that the value of *mission* is *null*, and therefore, the set of handlers is empty.

In the main action, we use again the modelling pattern where we have a sequence of actions that define the different phases of the entity life-cycle, here a mission. In the case of the mission framework process, a recursion perpetually calls this sequence of actions, because this process controls all missions in the program, and so repetitively offers its service. Termination of the service is determined by the mission sequencer process using the channel *end_mission_fw*.

The *Start* action initialises the state and waits for the mission sequencer to start a mission. Since this framework process can handle any mission, *Start* uses *start_mission* to take a mission identifier m as input, and records it in *mission*. *Finish* uses that mission identifier to terminate the application process for the mission with a synchronisation on $\mathit{end\_mission\_app} \,.\, \mathit{mission}$, and to signal to the mission sequencer that the mission has finished with $\mathit{done\_mission} \,.\, \mathit{mission}$.

The *Initialize* action models the initialisation phase which is initiated by the framework calling the `initialize()` method. It is specified using a recursion which continually accepts requests from the mission application process, through the channel *add_handler*, to add a handler h to the mission (this is achieved by the parametrised action *AddHandler*). Besides, the application process may use the event *initialiseRet* . *mission* to terminate *Initialize* at any time.

In the action *Execute*, first of all, all handlers are started with a call to the action *StartHandlers*. It uses synchronisations *start_handler*.h to start in interleaving (operator $|||$) all handlers h recorded in the state. The processes corresponding to the handlers h synchronise with the mission process on *start_handler*.

The handlers do not immediately become active after they are started. For that, the action *Start* uses a channel *activate_handlers*. All handler processes synchronise on it, but only those that previously synchronised on *start_handler* proceed to execute their active behaviour. In this way, we ensure that handlers can be initialised asynchronously, but have to start execution synchronously.

Termination of the handlers is initiated by the mission application process with a synchronisation on *stop_handlers*, raised by the action corresponding to `requestTermination()`. After that, *Execute* calls the action *StopHandlers*. For each handler h of the mission, *StopHandlers* uses *stop_handler*.h to stop it, and then waits for the notification *done_handler*.h that it actually terminated.

Finally, the *Cleanup* action calls the action of the mission application process corresponding to its `cleanup()` method. In what follows we discuss the application process, using the ACCS `MainMission` class as example.

Action methods are encoded as before; the model for `initialize()` is different, though, since it not only results in the creation of data objects, but also provides information to the framework about the handlers that have been created. Below we include an extract of its specification for the ACCS model.

$$
\begin{array}{l}
\mathit{initializeMeth} \mathrel{\widehat=} \mathit{initializeCall}\,.\,\mathit{MainMissionId} \longrightarrow \\
\quad \mathbf{var} \ldots;\ \mathit{speed} : \mathit{SpeedMonitorClass}; \\
\qquad\quad \mathit{throttle} : \mathit{ThrottleControllerClass}; \\
\qquad\quad \mathit{cruise} : \mathit{CruiseControlClass};\ \ldots \bullet \\
\qquad \mathit{throttle} := \mathbf{new}\ \mathit{ThrottleControllerClass}(\mathit{speed}, \ldots); \\
\qquad \mathit{ThrottleControllerInit}\,!\,\mathit{throttle} \longrightarrow \mathit{Skip}; \\
\qquad \mathit{add\_handler}\,.\,\mathit{ThrottleControllerHandlerId} \longrightarrow \mathit{Skip} \\
\qquad \mathit{cruise} := \mathbf{new}\ \mathit{CruiseControlClass}(\mathit{throttle}, \mathit{speedo}); \\
\qquad \mathit{engine} := \mathbf{new}\ \mathit{EngineClass}(\mathit{cruise}, \ldots); \\
\qquad \mathit{EngineInit}\,!\,\mathit{engine} \longrightarrow \mathit{Skip}; \\
\qquad \mathit{add\_handler}\,.\,\mathit{EngineHandlerId} \longrightarrow \mathit{Skip}\ ;\ \ldots \\
\quad \mathit{initializeRet}\,.\,\mathit{MainMissionId} \longrightarrow \mathit{Skip}
\end{array}
$$

This formalises the declaration of local variables *speed*, *throttle*, and so on for handler objects. These variables have a class type, and are initialised using its constructor. For instance, $\mathit{throttle} := \mathbf{new}\ \mathit{ThrottleControllerClass}(\mathit{speed}, \ldots)$ is a reference assignment to *throttle* of an object of class *ThrottleControllerClass* defined by its constructor, given *speed* and other parameters.

An important observation is that a handler is characterised not merely by (framework and application) processes, but also by a data object. In Fig. 3 this is indicated by boxes in the processes for handlers. Accordingly, we need to establish a connection between the data object and the process that aggregates it. This is achieved via a designated channel with suffix *Init*. The application process uses this channel to retrieve the data object it is connected to.

A pair of Java statements that create and register a handler with the current mission is, therefore, translated to one assignment and two communications. As already explained, the assignment constructs the handler's data object and assigns it to the appropriate local variable. Next, we have a communication like $ThrottleControllerInit\,!\,throttle$, which outputs a reference to the data object to the handler process. Finally, to record the handler as part of the mission, we have a communication like $add\_handler\,.\,ThrottleControllerHandlerId$. In the program this corresponds to a call to `register()` on the handler object.

We note, however, that not all data objects need to be wrapped in a process. For example, the *CruiseControlClass* object does not need to be associated with a process since the framework does not need to directly interact with it. It is used to aggregate other objects and has a direct translation as an *OhCircus* class.

Another method of a mission application class that needs special encoding is `requestTermination()`; it also needs to communicate with the framework process as it raises the *stop_handlers* event. All other action methods, like, for instance, the action for the `missionMemorySize()` method, and the main action are as already explained and exemplified for application processes.

3.4 Handler Models

As already noted, the application process for a handler associates application events to it. On the other hand, the specification of the framework process is similar for periodic and aperiodic handlers. In Fig. 6, we sketch the generic framework process for an event handler. It is parametrised by an identifier that must be provided when the framework process is instantiated for a particular handler. For the engine handler, for example, we use $EventHandlerFW(EngineHandlerId)$.

The state component *active* of the *EventHandlerFW* records if the handler is active in the current mission or not. The main action defines an iterative behaviour that is interrupted and terminated by the event *end_mission_fw*, which, as mentioned before, indicates the end of the mission execution.

Each iteration defines the behaviour of the handler during a mission. First, the state is initialised using *Init*. Afterwards, the handler waits to be started using the *StartHandler* action in external choice (operator $\Box$) with a synchronisation on *activate_handlers*, offered by *ActivateHandlers*. The action *StartHandler* synchronises on a particular *start_handler* event determined by the handler identifier. Afterwards, it also offers a synchronisation on *activate_handlers* (calling *ActivateHandlers*), which always occurs prior to entering the execution phase.

If the *start_handler* event occurs before *activate_handlers*, the value of *active* is *TRUE*. In this case, the handler calls the action *DispatchHandler*. It raises the *enter_dispatch* event to notify the application process that it has to enter the handler's dispatch loop in which it starts responding to the external events associated with it. The dispatch loop is interrupted after the $stop\_handler\,.\,handler$

$$
\begin{array}{l}
\textbf{process}\ EventHandlerFW \mathrel{\widehat=} handler : HandlerId \bullet \textbf{begin} \\
\quad \textbf{state}\ EventHandlerFWState == [active : BOOL] \\
\quad Init == [EventHandlerFWState' \mid active' = FALSE] \\
\quad StartHandler \mathrel{\widehat=} start\_handler\,.\,handler \longrightarrow active := TRUE \\
\quad ActivateHandlers \mathrel{\widehat=} activate\_handlers \longrightarrow Skip \\
\quad DispatchHandler \mathrel{\widehat=} enter\_dispatch \longrightarrow \\
\qquad stop\_handler\,.\,handler \longrightarrow leave\_dispatch \longrightarrow Skip \\
\quad \bullet \left(\begin{array}{l} \mu X \bullet Init; \\ \left(\begin{array}{l} ((StartHandler\ ;\ ActivateHandlers) \sqcap ActivateHandlers); \\ \textbf{if}\ active = TRUE \longrightarrow DispatchHandler \\ [\!]\ active = FALSE \longrightarrow Skip \\ \textbf{fi} \end{array} \right) ;\ X \end{array} \right) \\
\qquad\qquad \triangle\ end\_mission\_fw \longrightarrow Skip \\
\textbf{end}
\end{array}
$$

Fig. 6. Framework process for event handlers

event, by synchronising on *leave_dispatch*. If *active* is *FALSE*, the handler process skips, as in this case the handler is not part of the current mission.

As already said, the application processes for handlers are factored into a data object modelled by an *OhCircus* class, and a process that aggregates it and releases the handler. Fig. 7 presents the *OhCircus* class for the `Engine` Java class. The correspondence is direct, with member variables defined as state components, and the constructor defined in the **initial** paragraph. For methods, the only difference is that events are not treated as objects: we use event identifiers. So, *handleAsyncEvent* takes an event identifier as a value parameter, and compares it to the identifiers of the events that are handled in the class.

The application process for a handler lifts its data objects to a process that can interact with the other components of the model. We present in Fig. 8 the process for the engine handler. The object for the handler is recorded in its state component *obj*. The *Init* action initialises it with the object input through the constructor call channel: here, the channel *EngineInit* of type *EngineClass*.

The *handleAsyncEventMeth* action simply executes the corresponding data operation. We cannot adopt exactly this model when `handleAsyncEvent()` handles an output event. For instance, the throttle controller handler process has to carry out communications $set\_voltage\,!\,v$. In such cases, we cannot represent the method by just a call to a data operation like in Fig. 8, but have to encode it by an action. The *handleAsyncEventMeth* of the application process, in this case, reflects directly the Java code, but outputs a value in the correct external channel where in Java we have a device access to achieve the hardware interaction.

Since a handler the used by several missions, the application process repeatedly initialises (*Init*), executes (*Execute*), and terminates (*Terminate*) it. Execution waits for the *enter_dispatch* event, and then enters a loop that repeatedly waits for the occurrence of one of the external events associated with the

```
class EngineClass ≙ begin
  state EngineState == [private cruise : CruiseControlClass]
  initial EngineInit ≙ val cruise? : CruiseControlClass • cruise := cruise?
  public handleAsyncEvent ≙ val event : EventId •
    if event = EOnEvtId ⟶ cruise.engineOn()
    [] event = EOffEvtId ⟶ cruise.engineOff()
    fi
end
```

Fig. 7. *OhCircus* class for the `Engine` handler

```
process EngineApp ≙ begin
 state EngineState == [obj : EngineClass]
 Init ≙ EngineInit ? o ⟶ obj := o
 handleAsyncEventMeth ≙ val e : EventId • obj.handleAsyncEvent(e)
 Execute ≙ enter_dispatch ⟶ Dispatch
 Dispatch ≙
  ( μX •
     ( leave_dispatch ⟶ Skip
       □
       ( ( ( engine_on ⟶ handleAsyncEventMeth(EOnEvtId)
             □
             engine_off ⟶ handleAsyncEventMeth(EOffEvtId) ) ;
           ⊓ t : 0..EngineDeadline • wait t ) ) ) ; X )
 Terminate ≙ done_handler . EngineHandlerId ⟶ Skip
 • (μX • Init ; Execute ; Terminate ; X) △ end_mission_fw ⟶ Skip
end
```

Fig. 8. Application process for the `Engine` handler

handler. In our example, these are *engine_on* and *engine_off*. When such an event occurs, *Dispatch* calls the *handleAsyncEventMeth* action. The subsequent nondeterministic **wait** captures the permissible amount of time the program may take to execute it. The dispatch loop is abandoned when the *leave_dispatch* event occurs. Termination that follows raises a particular *done_handler . h* event to notify the mission framework process that the handler has terminated.

In the case of an application process for a periodic handler, the only difference is in *Dispatch*. It does not wait for external events and calls `handleAsyncEvent()` when an internal timer event *release* occurs. An additional parallel action *Release* generates the timer events. It is given below for `ThrottleController`.

$$
\begin{aligned}
&\mathit{Release} \mathrel{\widehat=}\\
&\quad (\mu X \bullet (\mathit{release} \longrightarrow \mathit{Skip} \blacktriangleright 0) \,;\; \mathbf{wait}\ \mathit{ThrottleControllerPeriod} \,;\; X)\\
&\qquad \vartriangle \mathit{leave\_dispatch} \longrightarrow \mathit{Skip}
\end{aligned}
$$

The *Circus Time* **wait** t action waits for the end of the period before terminating, and the ▶ operator specifies that the *release* event happens immediately afterwards. *ThrottleControllerPeriod* is a constant that specifies the period of the handler. (We have one such constant for each periodic handler.)

4 Conclusions

As far as we know, what we presented here is the first formalisation of the SCJ paradigm. Our models capture the essence of its design, and are an essential asset for analysis and development techniques for SCJ programs based on refinement.

To validate the models, we have translated them for FDR. The CSP translation encapsulates all *Circus* state into process parameters. Timing aspects are ignored, and so is the detailed application-level behaviour of handlers. We ensured that simple interaction scenarios do not result in a deadlock, and also that the mechanism for starting and terminating missions works as expected.

The direct correspondence between SCJ programs and our models enables automation in both directions. The framework processes are the same for all programs. The application processes use a fixed modelling pattern. The formalisation of the model-generation strategy discussed here, and the development of an associated tool, is work in progress. What remains to be done is to formalise the translation rules, and we believe this can be done in a compositional manner to facilitate their implementation using visitors. The tool will allow us to tackle larger industrial examples like those in Kalibera et al.'s benchmark [14].

The SCJ also incorporates a region-based memory model with restrictions on access to support safe dynamic memory management, and associated static verification techniques. We have abstracted from this here, but refined versions of our model will incorporate the language features we have formalised elsewhere [7]. For this we will further introduce constructs into the language that make explicit the memory areas in which objects are allocated. Importantly, this does not impact on any of the models presented earlier: they remain valid.

There are many approaches and tools to reason about object-oriented programs and Java [3,1], but they do not cater for the specificities of concurrency in SCJ. Brooke et al. present a CSP specification for a concurrency model for Eiffel (SCOOP) [2]. Their CSP specification shares some basic ideas with our *Circus* models, but is necessarily more complex due to its generality.

Kalibera et al.'s work in [14] is concerned with scheduling analysis and race conditions in SCJ programs, but it does not use proof-based techniques. Instead, exhaustive testing and model-checking is applied. Annotation-based techniques for SCJ can be found in [20,9]. In [20] annotations are used to check for compliance with a particular level of SCJ, and for safe use of memory. Haddad et al. define SafeJML [9], which extends JML [3] to cover functionality and timing properties; it reuses existing technology for worst-case execution-time analysis in the context of SCJ. Our model is a conceivable candidate to justify the soundness of checks supported by the annotations and carried out by the tools.

Our long term goal is the definition of refinement-based techniques for developing SCJ programs. Like in the *Circus* standard technique, we will devise a refinement strategy to transform centralised abstract *Circus Time* models into an SCJ model as described here. The development of this strategy, and the proof of the refinement rules that it will require are a challenging aspect of this endeavour. This involves the identification of refinement and modelling patterns. All this shall also provide further practical validation of our model.

Acknowledgements. This work is funded by the EPSRC grant EP/H017461/1. We have discussed our models with Chris Marriott, Kun Wei, and Jim Woodcock.

References

1. Beckert, B., Hähnle, R., Schmitt, P.H. (eds.): Verification of Object-Oriented Software. LNCS (LNAI), vol. 4334. Springer, Heidelberg (2007)
2. Brooke, P., Paige, R., Jacob, J.: A CSP model of Eiffel's SCOOP. Formal Aspects of Computing 19(4), 487–512 (2007)
3. Burdy, L., Cheon, Y., Cok, D.R., Ernst, M.D., Kiniry, J.R., Leavens, G.T., Leino, K.R.M., Poll, E.: An overview of JML tools and applications. Software Tools for Technology Transfer 7(3), 212–232 (2005)
4. Burns, A.: The Ravenscar Profile. ACM SIGAda Ada Letters XIX, 49–52 (1999)
5. Cavalcanti, A., Sampaio, A., Woodcock, J.: A Refinement Strategy for Circus. Formal Aspects of Computing 15(2-3), 146–181 (2003)
6. Cavalcanti, A., Sampaio, A., Woodcock, J.: Unifying classes and processes. Software Systems and Modeling 4(3), 277–296 (2005)
7. Cavalcanti, A., Wellings, A., Woodcock, J.: The Safety-Critical Java Memory Model: A Formal Account. In: Butler, M., Schulte, W. (eds.) FM 2011. LNCS, vol. 6664, pp. 246–261. Springer, Heidelberg (2011)
8. The Open Group. Safety Critical Java Technology Specification. Technical Report JSR-302, Java Community Process (January 2011)
9. Haddad, G., Hussain, F., Leavens, G.T.: The Design of SafeJML, A Specification Language for SCJ with Support for WCET Specification. In: JTRES. ACM, New York (2010)
10. Harwood, W., Cavalcanti, A., Woodcock, J.: A Theory of Pointers for the UTP. In: Fitzgerald, J.S., Haxthausen, A.E., Yenigun, H. (eds.) ICTAC 2008. LNCS, vol. 5160, pp. 141–155. Springer, Heidelberg (2008)
11. Henties, T., Hunt, J., Locke, D., Nilsen, K., Schoeberl, M., Vitek, J.: Java for Safety-Critical Applications. In: SafeCert (2009)
12. Hoare, C.A.R.: Communicating Sequential Processes. Prentice-Hall, Englewood Cliffs (1985)
13. Hoare, C.A.R., Jifeng, H.: Unifying Theories of Programming. Prentice-Hall, Englewood Cliffs (1998)
14. Kalibera, T., Parizek, P., Malohlava, M.: Exhaustive Testing of Safety Critical Java. In: JTRES. ACM, New York (2010)
15. Morgan, C.C.: Programming from Specifications, 2nd edn. Prentice-Hall, Englewood Cliffs (1994)
16. Oliveira, M., Cavalcanti, A., Woodcock, J.: A UTP Semantics for Circus. Formal Aspects of Computing 21(1-2), 3–32 (2009)

17. Santos, T., Cavalcanti, A., Sampaio, A.: Object-Orientation in the UTP. In: Dunne, S., Stoddart, B. (eds.) UTP 2006. LNCS, vol. 4010, pp. 18–37. Springer, Heidelberg (2006)
18. Sherif, A., Cavalcanti, A., Jifeng, H., Sampaio, A.: A process algebraic framework for specification and validation of real-time systems. Formal Aspects of Computing 22(2), 153–191 (2009)
19. Spivey, J.: The Z Notation: A Reference Manual. Prentice-Hall, Englewood Cliffs (1992)
20. Tang, D., Plsek, A., Vitek, J.: Static Checking of Safety Critical Java Annotations. In: JTRES, pp. 148–154. ACM, New York (2010)
21. Wellings, A.: Concurrent and Real-Time Programming in Java. Wiley, Chichester (2004)
22. Wellings, A., Kim, M.: Asynchronous event handling and safety critical Java. In: JTRES, ACM, New York (2010)

Is There Evolution Before Birth? Deterioration Effects of Formal Z Specifications

Andreas Bollin

Software Engineering and Soft Computing, AAU Klagenfurt, Austria
Andreas.Bollin@aau.at
http://www.aau.at/tewi/inf/isys/sesc

Abstract. Formal specifications are not an exception for aging. Furthermore, they stay valid resources only in the case when they have been kept up to date during all evolutionary changes taking place. As specifications are then not just written once, an interesting aspect is whether they do also deteriorate or not. In order to answer this question, this paper addresses the issues on various kinds of changes in the development of formal specifications and how they could be measured. For this, a set of semantic-based measures is introduced and then used in a longitudinal study, assessing the specification of the Web-Service Definition Language. By analyzing all 139 different revisions of it, it is shown that specifications can deteriorate and that it takes effort to keep them constantly at high quality. The results yield in a refined model of software evolution exemplifying these recurring changes.

1 Introduction

Would you step into a house when there is a sign saying "Enter at your own risk"? I assume not, at least if it is not unavoidable. Well, the situation is quite comparable to a lot of software systems around. Our standard software comes with license agreements stating that the author(s) of the software is (are) not responsible for any damage it might cause, and the same holds for a lot of our hardware drivers and many other applications around. Basically, we use them at our own risk.

I always ask myself: "Would it not be great to buy (and also to use) software that comes with a certificate of guarantee instead of an inept license agreement?" Of course, it would and it is possible as some companies demonstrate. It is the place where formal methods can add value to the development process. They enable refinement steps and bring in the advantages of assurance and reliable documentation.

The argument of quality is not just an academic one. Formal methods can be used in practice as companies using a formal software development process demonstrate [23]. Formal modeling is also not as inflexible as one might believe. Changing requirements and a growing demand in software involve more flexible processes and it is good to see that a combination of formal methods and the world of agile software development is possible [2]. This enables the necessary shorter development cycles, but, and this is the key issue, it also means to start thinking about evolution right from the beginning.

The questions that arise are simple: (a) Do our formal specifications really change or evolve, and (b) if this is the case, can we detect or even measure these changes? The objective of the paper is to answer these two questions. In a first step it demonstrates that

S. Qin and Z. Qiu (Eds.): ICFEM 2011, LNCS 6991, pp. 66–81, 2011.

formal specifications are not an exception for aging. Section 2 tries to make developers more receptive to this topic. And in the second step it demonstrates that there might be deterioration effects when formal specifications are undergoing constant changes. For this, Section 3 briefly introduces a set of measures that are suitable for assessing Z specifications, and Section 4 takes a closer look at 139 revisions of a large Z specification. Due to the lessons learned, a refined model of software evolution is suggested in Section 5. Finally, Section 6 summarizes the findings and again argues for a careful attention of the refined model of (specification) evolution.

2 Perfection or Decay

A formal specification describes what a system should do and as such it can be used to argue about the correctness of a candidate system. But a specification is not per se a "correct" mapping of the requirements. It needs time to create a first, useful version and, as there are affinities with traditional software development, this section starts with the model of software evolution. This model is then the basis for a – necessary – refinement, as is shown later in Section 5.

2.1 Back to the Roots

Let us start again with the analogy above: Why does one enter a house even without bothering about its safety? The answer is simple: normally, one trusts in the original design, the statics, the teams that built it and the officials that did the final checks. The trust stays the same when the house is going to be renovated, when the interior changes and when some walls are broken down (or new ones are erected). One naturally assumes that the old plans have been investigated and that structural engineers took a look at it. The same holds for our software systems. There is an overall design, there are teams that build and modify it and there are teams that test it before being sold. We trust in their professionalism. A change in requirements and needs then leads to a change in this software – it is undergoing a "renovation" process that we might call software evolution.

Bennet and Rajlich [1] introduced a staged model to describe this process in more details (see Fig. 1). Starting with the initial development and the first running version, evolutionary changes happen, leading to servicing phases and then, finally, to the phase-out and close-down versions of the software. In their article the authors also point out the important role of software change for both, the evolution and servicing phases. In fact, effort is necessary at every step of the phase to keep up with the quality standards and for keeping alive our trust in it.

Taking a closer look at our analogy of building/reconstructing a house it can be observed that there is also a chain (or network) of trust. The visitor (or owner) of the house counts on the construction company, they by themselves trust in the quality of the building materials they use, and the team that builds the house trusts in the architects (just to mention some of the links). When our evolving software is undergoing changes, then there is a similar chain of trust and dependencies.

This is now the place where formal methods come into play. To keep the trust, a change in the software has to be preceded by changes in the design documents and with

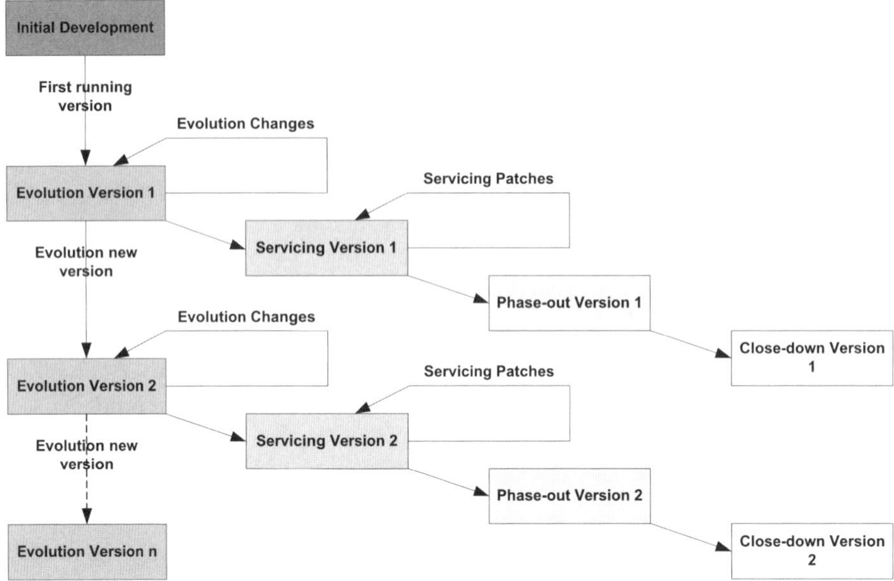

Fig. 1. The versioned staged model of Bennett and Rajlich [1]. Starting with the initial development and the first running version evolution is about to begin. The goal of the evolution phase is to adapt the software to ever changing user requirements or changes in the operating environment. When substantial changes are not possible anymore (at least not without damages to the system), then the servicing phase starts. Only small tactical changes are applied. When no more servicing is done, then the phase-out starts. Finally, with the close-down phase, the users are directed towards a new version.

it a change in the software specifications. One can also put it the other way round: when the architect does not update his or her plans, then future renovations are (hopefully) impeded.

2.2 The Role of Formal Design

Writing down requirements in a keen way is necessary, and the use of formality is not new in this respect. In their article Black et.al point out that formal methods have already been used by Ada Lovelace's and Charles Babbage's work on the analytical engine when they verified the formulas [2]. Since then several success stories of the use of formal methods have been published [8,28,23,12,11]. However, traditional formal design is commonly seen as something that is just happening at the beginning, and most of us are tempted to think about the development of just *one* formal model.

As the analogy above demonstrates, this viewpoint is probably not correct. When drawing up a plan, an architect does not only draw a single version. He or she starts with a first version, modifies it, and plays around with it. Several versions are assessed and, finally, discussed with the customer. The plans are, in addition to that, revised when the building is changed later on. The same holds for formal specifications. Their advantages not only lie in verification and validation considerations. They form the basis for incrementally pinning down the most important requirements (and eventually ongoing refinement steps). Only when kept up to date during evolutionary changes, they act as valid sources for comprehension activities. So, our formal specifications are (and should be) constantly changing during the software development phases. To think in terms of "write-once languages" (as already addressed in [16, p.243]) is for sure not appropriate.

During the last three decades there have been several advances in the field of formal software development. Specification languages were standardized and then also adapted to the world of object oriented programming. By the time new languages arise. Alloy is such an example that also allows for simulation and graphical feedback [13]. However, the main focus of the tools and languages around rests on support for writing the one and correct model (and on proving properties of it). Contrarily, in our working group we have been focusing on servicing and comprehension aspects instead [21,17], and in the last years these efforts led to a concept location model and a tool for visualization, slicing and clustering of Z specifications [4]. The resulting tools and techniques will now be used in order to find out whether (and to which extent) formal specifications do change during evolutionary activities.

3 On the Search for Measures

Formal specifications (like program code) might age during modifications and it needs effort to antagonize it. The effects of a modification should be measured in order to steer the course of change. This means to assess the specification (among other documents) at every refinement step and to consider the effect on various parameters of the specification. Looking at size-based measures only (which can be calculated easily) is for our objectives not enough. When talking about various aspects of deterioration we are more interested in measuring effects on the specifications' *quality*!

3.1 Specification Measures

The majority of specification metrics used in projects belongs to the class of size/quantity based measures. Most popular is counting lines of specification text, which, apart from looking at the time needed to write the specification, was also used as *the* basis to monitor the often-cited CICS/ESA project of IBM [9]. Counting specific specification elements is possible, too. Vinter et. al propose to count the type and number of logical constructs in Z specifications [25]. By a small case-study they demonstrate that these measures might correlate with the complexity of the specification. However, up to now a quantitative assessment of the approach is missing. Nogueira et. al suggest to use two measures expressing the complexity of each operator in the system and to calculate them by counting input and output data related to the operators [18]. Their experiences are based on a small case-study using *HOPE* as a specification language and Modula-2 for its implementation. Alternatively, Samson et. al suggest to count the number of equations in a module or per operation [24]. They observed that the number of equations required to define an operator is frequently equal to the cyclomatic complexity of code based on the specification.

Complexity considerations are relevant, but within the scope of this work quality measures are needed. Due to the declarative nature of the formal specifications under investigation, such measures (usually based on control- and data-flow) are, unfortunately, rare. The above mentioned approaches of Samson et. al or Nogueira et. al can be seen, if at all, just as possible approximations to quality considerations. But, there is one approach that could be used as a starting point. By looking at (and analyzing) the references to state variables in operations, Carrington et. al try to identify states of a module and to relate them to the top-level modular structure of an implementation [6]. With this, they are introducing the notion of cohesion within a module. They do not relate it to the quality of a specification, though, but the next section demonstrates that not so much is missing.

3.2 Slice-Based Coupling and Cohesion Measures

As mentioned in the previous section, it is hard to find suitable quality measures for formal specifications. However, for programming languages there are several approaches around. Recently, Meyers and Binkley published an empirical study demonstrating the use of slice-based measures for assessing the quality of 63 C programs [15]. Their study is based on the following situation: In a system different relations between different components can be detected. These relations make up part of the class of semantic complexity. When taking the information flow within and between these components as quality indicators, then the dual measures of coupling and cohesion are quite descriptive when assessing the quality of a program.

A practical way to calculate the needed measures is to make use of slices. Weiser [26,27] already introduced five slice based measures for cohesion, and three of them have later on been formally defined by Ott and Thuss [20]: Tightness, Coverage, and Overlap. Coupling, on the other hand, was defined as the number of local information flow entering and leaving a procedure, and Harman demonstrated in [10] that it can be calculated by the use of slices, too.

According to [15, 2:6-2:7], Tightness relates the number of statements common to all slices to the length of the module. It favors concise single thought modules where most of the statements are part of all the slices and thus affect all of the outputs. Coverage on the other hand relates the lengths of the slices to the length of the entire module. It favors large slices but does not require them to overlap and thus to indicate single thought modules. As an example, a module containing two independent slices would result in a value for Coverage of 0.5 but a value for Tightness of 0.0. Overlap measures how many statements are common to all the slices and relates the number to the size of all slices. The result is a measure that is not sensitive to changes in the size of the module, it is only related to the size of the (single) common thought in the module. Coupling between two modules is calculated by relating the inflow and outflow of a module (with respect to other modules in the program). Inflow and outflow are also calculated by making use of slices. Inter-procedural slices yield those statements of a module that are "outside", and, when examining these sets of statements mutually, their relation can be treated as "information flow". The exact semantics behind the measures (including the definitions and some impediments in calculating them) are explained in more details in the paper of Meyers and Binkley [15].

Table 1. Coupling and cohesion-related measures for Z specifications as introduced in [5]. SP is the set representing all slices SP_i of a schema ψ in a Z specification Ψ. SP_{int} is the Slice Intersection, representing the set of all predicates that are part of all slices. SU represents the Slice Union of all the slices.

Measure	*Definition*	*Description*
Tightness $\tau(\Psi, \psi)$	$\frac{\mid SP_{int}(\Psi,\psi) \mid}{\mid \psi \mid}$	Tightness τ measures the number of predicates included in every slice.
Coverage $Cov(\Psi, \psi)$	$\frac{1}{n}\sum_{i=1}^{n} \frac{\mid SP_i \mid}{\mid \psi \mid}$	Coverage compares the length of all possible specification slices SP_i ($SP_i \in SP(\Psi, \psi)$) to the length of ψ.
Overlap $O(\Psi, \psi)$	$\frac{1}{n}\sum_{i=1}^{n} \frac{\mid SP_{int}(\Psi,\psi) \mid}{\lvert SP_i \rvert}$	Overlap measures how many predicates are common to all n possible specification slices SP_i ($SP_i \in SP(\Psi, \psi)$).
Inter – Schema Flow $F(\psi_s, \psi_d)$	$\frac{\lvert (SU(\psi_d) \cap \psi_s) \rvert}{\lvert \psi_s \rvert}$	Inter-Schema flow F measures the number of predicates of the slices in ψ_d that are in ψ_s.
Inter – Schema Coupling $C(\psi_s, \psi_d)$	$\frac{F(\psi_s,\psi_d)\ \lvert \psi_s \rvert + F(\psi_d,\psi_s)\ \lvert \psi_d \rvert}{\lvert \psi_s \rvert + \lvert \psi_d \rvert}$	Inter-Schema coupling C computes the normalized ratio of the flow in both directions.
Schema Coupling $\chi(\psi_i)$	$\frac{\sum_{j=1}^{n} C(\psi_i,\psi_j)\ \lvert \psi_j \rvert}{\sum_{j=1}^{n} \lvert \psi_j \rvert}$	Schema Coupling χ is the weighted measure of inter-schema coupling of ψ_i and all n other schemas.

3.3 Specification Slicing

Slicing can be applied to formal specifications, too. The idea was first presented by Oda and Araki [19] and has later been formalized and extended by others [7,3,29]. The basic idea is to look for predicates that are part of pre-conditions and for predicates that are part of post-conditions. The general assumption is that (within the same scope) there is a "control" dependency between these predicates. "Data dependency", on the other hand, is defined as dependency between those predicates where data is potentially propagated between them. With this concept, slices can be calculated by looking at a (set of) predicates at first and then by including all other dependent predicates.

Recently, sliced-based coupling and cohesion measures have then been mapped to Z by taking the above definitions of Meyers and Binkley as initial points (see Table 1 for a summary). Based on the calculation of slice-profiles which are collections of all possible slices for a Z schema, the following measures have been assessed in [5]:

- Tightness, measuring the number of predicates included in every slice.
- Coverage, comparing the length of all possible slices to the length of the specification schema.
- Overlap, measuring how many predicates are common to all n possible specification slices.

Table 2. Pearson, Spearman, and Kendall Tau test values (including significance level p) for the correlation of size and slice-based Z specification measures. Values $\mid R \mid \in [0.8 - 1.0]$ in the mean are classified as strongly correlated, values $\mid R \mid \in [0.5 - 0.8)$ are classified as moderately correlated, and values $\mid R \mid \in [0.0 - 0.5)$ are treated as weakly correlated.

Metric Comparison (n=1123)								
Sig.			Pearson		Spearman		Kendall	
	Measure 1	*Measure 2*	*R*	*p*	*R*	*p*	*R*	*p*
Strong	*Tightness*	*Coverage*	0.830	.000	0.907	.000	0.780	.000
Moderate	*Tightness*	*Overlap*	0.809	.000	0.749	.000	0.623	.000
	Size (LOS)	*Coupling*	0.589	.000	0.686	.000	0.494	.000
	Size (LOS)	*Overlap*	-.557	.000	-.543	.000	-.415	.000
	Size (LOS)	*Tightness*	-.541	.000	-.551	.000	-.415	.000
	Coverage	*Overlap*	0.531	.000	0.566	.000	0.437	.000
Weak	*Coupling*	*Overlap*	-.343	.000	-.315	.000	-.239	.000
	Size (LOS)	*Coverage*	-.284	.000	-.447	.000	-.326	.000
	Coupling	*Tightness*	-.272	.000	-.262	.000	-.191	.000
	Coupling	*Coverage*	0.006	.829	-.102	.000	-.070	.000

– Coupling, expressing the weighted measure of inter-schema coupling (the normalized ratio of the inter-schema flow – so the number of predicates of a slice that lay outside the schema – in both directions).

In [5] it was shown that the measures are very sensitive to semantic changes in Z-schema predicates and that the changes of the values are comparable to their programming counterparts. This includes all types of operations on the specification, especially the addition, deletion or modification of predicates. The next and missing step was to look at a larger collection of sample specifications and assessing their expressiveness. The major objective was to find out which of the measures describe unique properties of a Z specification and which of them are just proxies for e.g. the lines of specification text count (LOS).

In the accompanying study more than $12,800$ lines of specification text in $1,123$ Z schemas have been analyzed and the relevant results of the analysis of the measures are summarized in Table 2. The table shows that three tests have been used: Pearson's linear correlation coefficient, Spearman's rank correlation coefficient, and Kendall's Tau correlation coefficient. The objective was to find out whether each of the measures represents some unique characteristic of the specification or not.

The Pearson's correlation coefficient measures the degree of association between the variables, but it assumes normal distribution of the values. Though this test might not necessarily fail when the data is not normally distributed, the Pearson's test only looks for a linear correlation. It might indicate no correlation even if the data is correlated in a non-linear manner. As knowledge about the distribution of the data is missing, also the Spearman's rank correlation coefficients have been calculated. It is a non-parametric test of correlation and assesses how well a monotonic function describes the association between the variables. As an alternative to the Spearman's test, the Kendall's robust correlation coefficient was used as it ranks the data relatively and is able to identify partial correlations.

The head to head comparison of the measures in Table 2 shows that the slice-based measures are not only proxies for counting lines of specification text. In fact, most of the pairs do have a weak or moderate correlation only. So, besides the size of the specification, one can select Coverage, Overlap, and Coupling as descriptors for properties of the specification, but, e.g., skip Tightness as it has the highest values of correlation to most of the other measures.

Meyers and Binkley suggested another measure based on the sizes of the generated slices and called it "deterioration" [15]. This measure has also been mapped to Z in [5] and the basic idea goes back to a simple perception: the less trains of thoughts there are in one schema, the clearer and the sharper is the set of predicates.

When a schema deals with many things in parallel, a lot of (self-contained) predicates are to be covered. This has an influence on the set of slices that are to be generated. When there is only one "crisp" thought specified in the schema, then the slice intersections cover all the predicates. On the other hand, when there are different thoughts specified in it, then the intersection usually gets smaller (as each slice only regards dependent predicates). A progress towards a single thought should therefore appear as a convergence between the size of the schema and the size of its slice-intersection, a divergence could indicate some "deterioration" of the formal specification. This measure seems to be a good candidate for checking our assumption whether specifications do age qualitatively or not, and it defined as follows:

Definition 1 Deterioration. *Let Ψ be a Z specification, ψ_i one schema out of n schemas in Ψ, and $SP_{int}(\psi_i)$ its slice intersection. Then Deterioration ($\delta(\Psi)$) expresses the average module size in respect to the average size of the slice intersections SP_{int}. It is defined as follows:*

$$\delta(\Psi) = \frac{\sum_{i=1}^{n} \mid \psi_i \mid - \mid SP_{int}(\Psi, \psi_i) \mid}{n}$$

Please note that the term "deterioration" as introduced in this paper is neither positive nor negative and one single value of deterioration is of course not very expressive. It just tells about how crisp a schema is. It does not allow for a judgement about the quality of the schema itself. Of course, we could state that all values above a pre-defined value x are to be treated as something unwanted, but it depends on the problem at hand whether we can (and should) allow for such schemas. In all, it merely makes sense to look at the differences in deterioration between two consecutive versions of the specification and thus to introduce the notion of Relative Deterioration. This measure can be defined in such a way that the relative deterioration is greater than zero when there is a convergence between schema size and slice intersection, and it is negative, when the shears between the sizes get bigger, indicating some probably unintentional deterioration. Relative Deterioration is defined as follows:

Definition 2 Relative Deterioration. *Let Ψ_{n-1} and Ψ_n be two consecutive versions of a Z specification Ψ. Then the relative deterioration ($\rho(\Psi_{n-1}, \Psi_n)$) with $n > 1$ is calculated as the relative difference between the deterioration of Ψ_{n-1} and Ψ_n. It is defined as follows:*

$$\rho(\Psi_n) = 1 - \frac{\delta(\Psi_n)}{\delta(\Psi_{n-1})}$$

4 Evaluation

With the set of measures at hand and the reasonable suspicion that specifications do age this paper is now taking a closer look at the development of a real-world specification and the effect of changes onto the measures introduced in Section 3.

4.1 Experimental Subject

One of the rare, big publicly available Z specifications is the specification of the Web Service Definition Language (*WSDL*) [22]. The document specifies the Web Services Description Language Version 2.0, which is an XML language for describing Web services. Besides natural language guidance, the specification defines the core language that is used to describe Web services based on an abstract model of what the service offers. Additionally, it specifies the conformance criteria for documents in this language. The reason for focusing on this specification is that, with 2004 onwards, a concurrent versioning system (*CVS*) has been used. *WSDL* 1.0 is not available in Z, but from November 2004 till the final release in 2007 139 versions have been checked in. The first revision is an adoption of *WSDL* 1.0, and then, successively, functionality has been added, modified, or deleted. The final revision contains 814 predicates (distributed over 1,413 lines of Z text).

This specification is now used so check whether, due to maintenance operations, there are drastic changes in the measures and whether deterioration can be detected or not. The strategy is simply to look at the changes (as documented in the code and in the *CVS* log files) and to compare them to the obtained values.

4.2 The Study

As a first step the *CVS* log was analyzed. This provided some insights to the types of changes that occurred on the way to the final release. Though there have been several changes influencing the events, the following sections and revisions are noticeable and are considered in more details:

- Up to Revision 1.005 there is a mapping of *WSDL* version 1.0 to Z. Only minor changes to the specification happen.
- Between revisions 1.005 – 1.007 there are mostly structural enhancements. Finally, model extensions take place.
- At revisions 1.020*ff* there are several refactoring steps and noticeable extension.
- At revisions 1.045*ff* there are several smaller changes to some of the concepts.
- At revisions 1.090*ff* there are massive extensions to the model and new concepts are introduced.
- Between revisions 1.096 – 1.104 the concepts in the model are simplified.

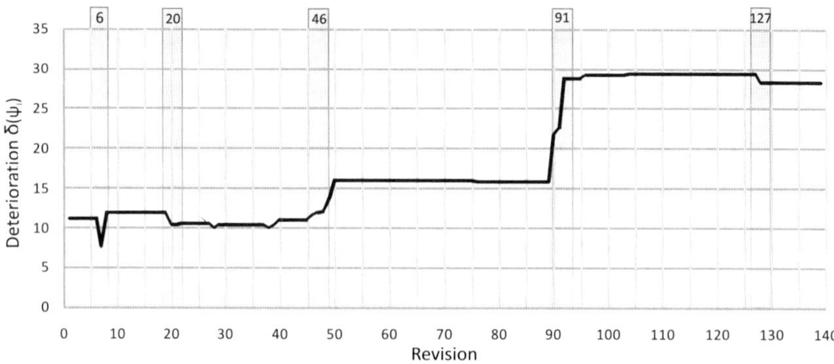

Fig. 2. Deterioration for the 139 revisions of the WSDL specification. When the value of deterioration increases, then more predicates (not closely related to each other) are introduced to schemas. This is not bad per se, but it is a hint towards a decrease in cohesion values.

– At revisions 1.127*ff* there are change requests and, thereinafter, removing features leads to a structural refactoring.

Up to revision 1.092 the interventions consisted mainly of adding new concepts (in our case Z schemas) to the specification. After revision 1.095 there are solely change requests, leading to a refactoring of the specification. Really massive changes took place at revisions 1.046 and 1.091.

When taking another closer look at the *CVS* log and the code, a specific strategy for keeping the specification constantly at a high level of quality can be detected. The recurring steps of a change request were:

1. Refactoring of the actual version.
2. Adding, removing, or modifying a concept.
3. Update of the natural language documentation.

The interesting question is now whether our measures introduced in Section 3 are able to reflect these changes and whether the measures of deterioration are able to display these changes.

4.3 Results

At first let us take a closer look at the measure called deterioration. Fig. 2 presents the value for all 139 revisions in the *CVS*. This figure indicates that the specification remarkably changes at revisions 1.046 and 1.091. In fact, the *CVS* log also documents the changes.

As absolute values (as in Fig. 2) do not perfectly describe the influence of a change, the notion of relative deterioration has been introduced in Section 3. Fig. 3 presents the value of it for all 139 revisions. Positive values indicate that the difference between the schema sizes and their slice intersections is reduced; such a deviation is assumed to be positive in respect to deterioration as the slice intersection is a measure of how strong

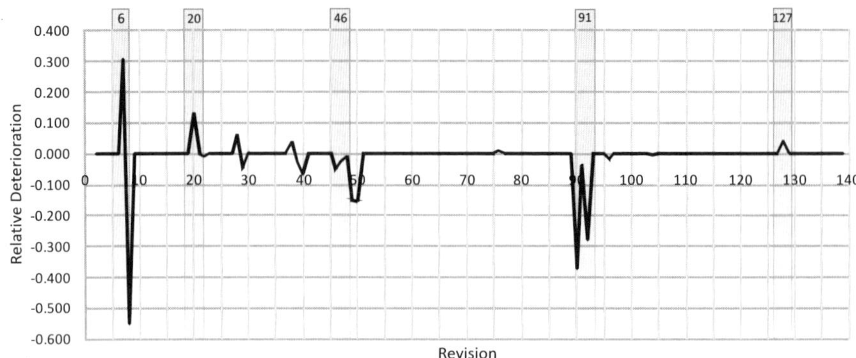

Fig. 3. The change in deterioration is better visible when looking at the relative deviation over the time. A positive value indicates an increase in cohesion, while a negative value indicates a decrease in the values of cohesion.

the predicates are interwoven in a schema. On the other hand, negative values indicate negative effects.

When taking again a look at Fig. 3 (especially between revisions 1.020 and 1.046), then the above mentioned strategy of change requests gets noticeably visible. A change is implemented by a structural improvement first (to be seen as a positive amplitude), and then it is followed by the introduction of the new concept, in most cases indicated by a negative amplitude in the diagram.

Let us now analyze the influence of a change onto the qualitative values of coupling and cohesion. By looking at Fig. 4, we see that the value for overlap decreases (on average) a bit. This indicates that, with time, the number of predicates, common to other slices, gets lower. Single Z schemas seem to deal with more independent thoughts. Refactoring these thoughts into separate schemas (which happened e.g. at revisions 1.020 and 1.127) helped a bit to improve the structure of the specification again.

The value of coverage follows more or less the fluctuation of overlap – but not at all revisions to the same extent. On the long run it definitely increases. Coverage tells us about how crisp a schema is, and in our case the developers of the specification did not manage to keep this property stable.

Finally, coupling refers to the flow between different schemas in the specification. Though the value fluctuates, the developers managed to keep coupling quite stable on the long run. Fig. 4 also shows that the value fluctuates with the values of cohesion, but not necessarily to the same extent, and not necessarily inversely (as would be assumed to be normal).

Though with the *WSDL* specification there is only one experimental subject, the results seem to substantiate that the measures are suitable for assessing this Z specification. The measures called deterioration and relative deterioration reflect the aging of the system quite well, and the measures for coupling and cohesion (a) do indicate structural changes and (b) also seem to explain some of the semantic changes in the specification.

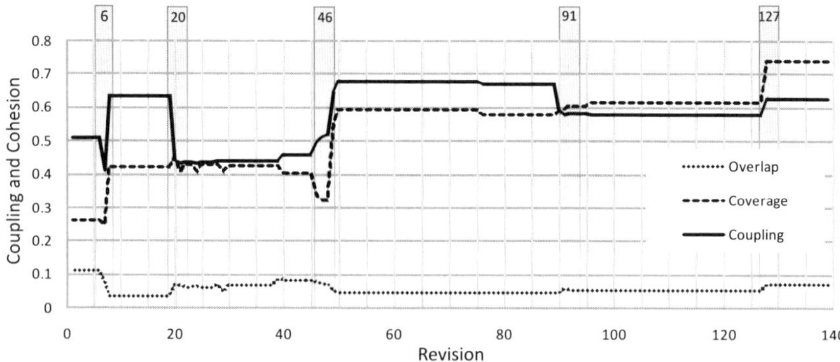

Fig. 4. The values of cohesion (expressed by the measures of overlap and coverage) and coupling for the 139 revisions of the WSDL specification. In most cases the values are subject to the same changes. However, at revisions 1.006 and 1.044 we observe changes into different directions, too.

5 An Extended Model of Evolution

As has been shown in Section 4.3, specifications keep on changing. Either one is still in the process of finding the most suitable version for our requirements, or one is modifying them due to changes in our projects' software systems. With that, a second look at the software evolution model in Fig. 1 is quite helpful – as one comes down to the following statement so far:

There is also evolution before the birth of the running version of the software system.

Fig. 5 tries to exemplify this for the initial and evolutionary versions of the software. In this figure the original model has been extended by refining the boxes of the evolutionary versions. Documents and requirements have been added so that formal specifications are made explicit (as they do belong to the set of necessary documents). They are, depending on the changing requirements, also changed. These changes either happen before one has a first running version of the software or afterwards.

The implications of this (refined) picture are manifold and should be considered when using formal specification languages in the software development lifecycle:

- Suitable size- and quality-based measures should be defined. This ensures that changes in the various documents – including formal specifications – can be detected and assessed. The slice-based measures introduced above are just an example of how it could be done for a specific specification language. For other languages the ideas might be reused. It might also be necessary to define new measures. However, the crucial point is that there is a measurement system around.
- Points of measurement should be introduced at every change/refinement loop. This ensures that the effects of changes can be assessed, and that the further direction of the development can be steered. The example of *WSDL* shows that already during the initial development changes have effects and that it takes effort to keep a specification constantly at a pre-defined level of quality. One can assume that *WSDL* is not an exception and that the observation also holds for other specification documents. By making use of a measurement system one is at least on the safe side.

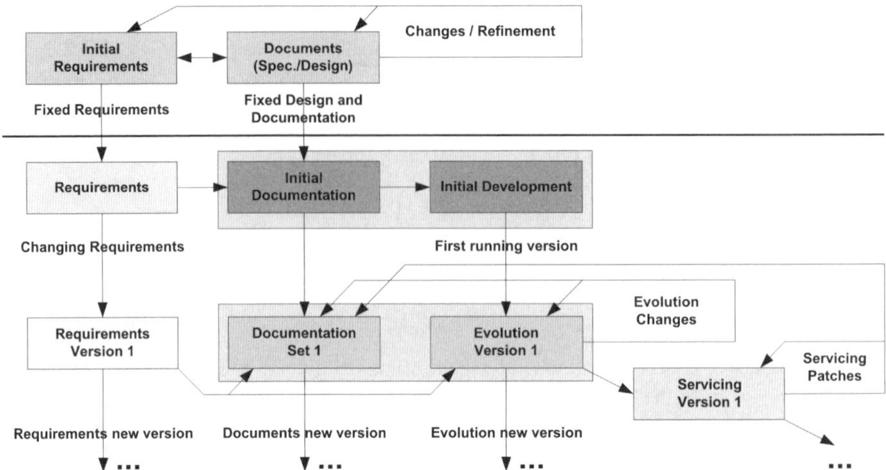

Fig. 5. A refined and extended look at the versioned stage model. Starting with a first set of initial requirements several versions of documents are created. Requirements are refined, and formal specifications are (among other design documents) also changed and modified. When the design is fixed, development is about to begin. Due to evolutionary changes after this phase, the existing documentation – including specifications and design documents – is (and has to be) changed, too. The term "evolutionary change of a formal specification" is used in a rather general sense. Apart from the classification of system types of Lehman [14], the figure illustrates that essential changes might happen to documents before and after delivery.

- The terms "Fixed Design and Documentation" just designate the conceptual border between the initial development phase and the first running version. Nevertheless, changes to the documents happen before and after this milestone in the project (as evolution is about to begin). The previously introduced measure points should also be defined for the evolutionary phases, and measures should be collected during all the evolutionary changes and servicing activities (influencing the documents and specifications).

Basically, the extended model of software evolution makes one property of specification (and other documents) explicit: they are no exception to aging. With this, it is obvious that measures, at the right point and extent, help in answering the question of what happened and, eventually, of what can be done for preventing unwanted deterioration effects.

6 Conclusion

We started with the observation that formal specifications – documents important in the very early phases of software development and later on during maintenance – might be changed more often than commonly expected and that the changes are not necessarily positive. We wanted to verify this observation, and so we mapped existing semantic-based measures to Z specification and used them to analyze a large real-world specification. The lessons learned so far are manifold.

1. Firstly, there was no suitable measurement system around. In order to understand and to assess changes, new measures had to be developed. These measures, carefully mapped to Z specifications, have been evaluated by making use of a large set of sample specifications. They are maybe not representative for all specifications around, but the statistical tests helped us in gaining at least basic confidence in the results for Z.
2. Secondly, changes onto formal specifications definitely might influence the values of the measures and there is the chance that their effects are underestimated. There is no model that enunciates this situation, which is also the reason why we borrowed from the model of evolution and refined it to cover the phases before, within, and after initial development. A closer look at the evolution of the *WSDL* specification seems to confirm the observation mentioned at the beginning of the paper: formal specifications are not just written once. They are modified, are extended, and they age.
3. Finally, the measures of coupling and cohesion (and with them deterioration and relative deterioration) seem to be a good estimate for a qualitative assessment of a specification. They are easy to calculate and seem to point out a possible loss in quality.

With that, we are able to answer our two questions that have been raised at the end of Section 1: specifications evolve and this evolution can be observed by simple semantics-based measures. The refined and extended model of evolution as presented in Section 5 is a good image of what happens when developing our systems.

The results of this contribution are interesting insofar as it turned out that, for the full benefits of a formal software development process, it makes sense to permanently take care of the quality of the underlying formal specification(s). Even when declarative specification languages are used, this can easily be done by defining suitable measures and by using them to constantly monitor the quality of the whole system. The goals for future work now include (a) taking a closer look at other formal specifications in order to verify and consolidate the findings, (b) investigating the correlation of the specification measures to code-based measures in order to come up with different prediction models, and (c) incorporating the refined model of software evolution into a formal software development process model that also considers cultural differences between the different stakeholders in a project.

Overall, the results are encouraging. Formal specifications are not necessarily restricted to the early phases of a software development process. When treated carefully (and kept up to date) they may help us in producing software systems that can be trusted, even when changed.

Acknowledgment. I am grateful to the reviewers of the FM 2011 conference and to my colleagues at AAU Klagenfurt, especially to Prof. Mittermeir, who helped me with fruitful discussions and reflections on this topic.

References

1. Bennet, K., Rajlich, V.: Software Maintenance and Evolution: a Roadmap. In: ICSE 2000: Proceedings of the Conference on The Future of Software Engineering, pp. 73–89. ACM, New York (2000)
2. Black, S., Boca, P.P., Bowen, J.P., Gorman, J., Hinchey, M.: Formal Versus Agile: Survival of the Fittest. IEEE Computer 42(9), 37–54 (2009)
3. Bollin, A.: Specification Comprehension – Reducing the Complexity of Specifications. Ph.D. thesis, AAU Klagenfurt (April 2004)
4. Bollin, A.: Concept Location in Formal Specifications. Journal of Software Maintenance and Evolution – Research and Practice 20(2), 77–105 (2008)
5. Bollin, A.: Slice-based Formal Specifiation Measures – Mapping Coupling and Cohesion Measures to Formal Z. In: Muñoz, C. (ed.) Proceedings of the Second NASA Formal Methods Symposium, NASA/CP-2010-216215, NASA, Langley Research Center, pp. 24–34 (April 2010)
6. Carrington, D., Duke, D., Hayes, I., Welsh, J.: Deriving modular designs from formal specifications. In: ACM SIGSOFT Software Engineering Notes, vol. 18, pp. 89–98. ACM, New York (1993)
7. Chang, J., Richardson, D.J.: Static and Dynamic Specification Slicing. Tech. rep., Department of Information and Computer Science, University of California (1994)
8. Clarke, E.M., Wing, J.M.: Formal Methods: State of the Art and Future Directions. Tech. rep., Carnegie Mellon University, CMU-CS-96-178 (1996)
9. Collins, B.P., Nicholls, J.E., Sorensen, I.H.: Introducing formal methods: the cisc experience with z. In: Mathematical Structures for Software Engineering, pp. 153–164. Clarendon Press, Oxford (1991)
10. Harman, M., Okulawon, M., Sivagurunathan, B., Danicic, S.: Slice-based measurement of coupling. In: Proceedings of the IEEE/ACM ICSE workshop on Process Modelling and Empirical Studies of Software Evolution, pp. 28–32. IEEE Computer Society Press, Los Alamitos (1997)
11. Hierons, R.M., Bogdanov, K., Bowen, J.P., Cleaveland, R., Derrick, J., Dick, J., Gheorghe, M., Harman, M., Kapoor, K., Krause, P., Lüttgen, G., Simons, A.J.H., Vilkomir, S., Woodward, M.R., Zedan, H.: Using formal specifications to support testing. ACM Comput. Surv. 41(2), 1–76 (2009)
12. Hinchey, M., Jackson, M., Cousot, P., Cook, B., Bowen, J.P., Margaria, T.: Software engineering and formal methods. Communications of the ACM 51(9), 54–59 (2008)
13. Jackson, D.: Software Abstractions - Logic, Language, and Analysis. The MIT Press, Cambridge (1996)
14. Lehman, M.M.: On understanding laws, evolution, and conservation in the large-program life cycle. Journal of Systems and Software 1(1), 213–221 (1979)
15. Meyers, T.M., Binkley, D.: An Empirical Study of Slice-Based Cohesion and Coupling Metrics. ACM Transactions on Software Engineering and Methodology 17(1), 2:1–2:27 (2007)
16. Mittermeir, R.T., Bollin, A.: Demand-Driven Specification Partitioning. In: Böszörményi, L., Schojer, P. (eds.) JMLC 2003. LNCS, vol. 2789, pp. 241–253. Springer, Heidelberg (2003)
17. Mittermeir, R.T., Bollin, A., Pozewaunig, H., Rauner-Reithmayer, D.: Goal-Driven Combination of Software Comprehension Approaches for Component Based Development. In: Proceedings of the ACM Symposium on Software Reusability Software Engineering Notes, SSR 2001, Software Engineering Notes, vol. 26, pp. 95–102. ACM Press, New York (2001)
18. Nogueira, J.C., Luqi, Berzins, V., Nada, N.: A formal risk assessment model for software evolution. In: Proceedings of the 2nd International Workshop on Economics-Driven Software Engineering Research, EDSER-2 (2000)

19. Oda, T., Araki, K.: Specification slicing in a formal methods software development. In: 17th Annual International Computer Software and Applications Conference, pp. 313–319. IEEE Computer Society Press, Los Alamitos (1993)
20. Ott, L.M., Thus, J.J.: The Relationship between Slices and Module Cohesion. In: 11th International Conference on Software Engineering, pp. 198–204. IEEE Computer Society, Los Alamitos (1989)
21. Pirker, H., Mittermeir, R., Rauner-Reithmayer, D.: Service Channels - Purpose and Tradeoffs. In: COMPSAC 1998: Proceedings of the 22nd International Computer Software and Applications Conference, pp. 204–211 (1998)
22. Roberto Chinnici, S.M., Moreau, J.J., Ryman, A., Weerawarana, S.: Web Services Description Language (WSDL) Version 2.0 Part 1: Core Language (2007), `http://www.w3.org/TR/wsdl20`
23. Ross, P.E.: The Exterminators. IEEE Spectrum 42(9), 36–41 (2005)
24. Samson, W., Nevill, D., Dugard, P.: Predictive software metrics based on a formal specification. Information and Software Technology 29(5), 242–248 (1987)
25. Vinter, R., Loomes, M., Kornbrot, D.: Applying software metrics to formal specifications: A cognitive approach. In: 5th International Symposium on Software Metrics, pp. 216–223. IEEE Computer Society Press, Bethesda (1998)
26. Weiser, M.: Program slices: formal, psychological, and practical investigations of an automatic program abstraction method. Ph.D. thesis, University of Michigan (1979)
27. Weiser, M.: Program slicing. In: Proceedings of the 5th International Conference on Software Engineering, pp. 439–449. IEEE Press, Piscataway (1982)
28. Woodcock, J., Davis, J.: Using Z: Specification, Refinement, and Proof. Prentice-Hall International Series in Computer Science. Prentice Hall, Hemel Hempstead (1996)
29. Wu, F., Yi, T.: Slicing Z Specifications. ACM SIGPLAN Notices 39(8), 39–48 (2004)

Asynchronous Communication in MSVL*

Dapeng Mo, Xiaobing Wang, and Zhenhua Duan**

Institute of Computing Theory and Technology,
and ISN Laboratory Xidian University,
Xi'an, 710071, P.R. China
zjmdp@foxmail.com, {xbwang,zhhduan}@mail.xidian.edu.cn

Abstract. Projection Temporal Logic (PTL) is a sound formalism for specifying and verifying properties of concurrent systems. The modeling, simulation and verification language MSVL for concurrent systems is an executable subset of PTL. However, asynchronous communication, a key component of modeling distributed system, has not been implemented in MSVL. This paper presents asynchronous communication techniques for MSVL to improve its capability for modeling and verifying distributed systems. First, a process structure is defined; then a channel structure and two pairs of communication commands are formalized; finally, an example of asynchronous communication for the contract signing protocol is demonstrated.

1 Introduction

Temporal logics [1,2,3] have been put forward as a useful tool for specifying and verifying properties of concurrent systems, and widely applied in many fields ranging from software engineering to digital circuit designs. Projection Temporal Logic(PTL)[4] is an extension of Interval Temporal Logic (ITL) and a useful formalism for system verification. The Modeling, Simulation and Verification Language (MSVL)[5] is an executable subset of PTL and it can be used to model, simulate and verify concurrent systems. To do so, a system is modeled by an MSVL program and a property of the system is specified by a Propositional Projection Temporal Logic (PPTL) formula. Thus, whether or not the system satisfies the property can be checked by means of model checking with the same logic framework.

As the complexity of distributed systems increases, a formal language for modeling and verification is desired. Although MSVL has been used to model, simulate and verify a number of concurrent systems, it could not be employed to model an asynchronous distributed system because asynchronous communication techniques have not been implemented in MSVL. For this reason, asynchronous communication construct is to be formalized.

* This research is supported by the National Program on Key Basic Research Project of China (973 Program) Grant No.2010CB328102, National Natural Science Foundation of China under Grant Nos. 60910004, 60873018, 91018010, 61003078 and 61003079, SRFDP Grant 200807010012, and ISN Lab Grant No. 201102001,Fundamental Research Funds for the Central Universities Grant No. JY10000903004.

** Corresponding author.

S. Qin and Z. Qiu (Eds.): ICFEM 2011, LNCS 6991, pp. 82–97, 2011.

Channel structure is commonly found in temporal logic languages due to its importance to describe asynchronous distributed systems. In ASDL[6], any two distinct services are impliedly connected by two unidirectional channels. It is a simple and straightforward approach to implement asynchronous communication technique. For XYZ/E[7], a channel is defined as a variable that can be a parameter of a process. This approach is flexible, but conflicts may occur when more than one process accesses a same channel at the same time. Roger Hale has implemented asynchronous communication technique for Tempura based on a shared buffer and two primitive operations[8]. The buffer is a single slot in which one message can be stored at a time. Communication in CCS[9] and CSP[10] is synchronous and there are no message buffers linking communicating agents, but asynchronous communication can be modeled by introducing buffer agents between two communicating entities. These approaches above provide us a great many ideas to implement asynchronous communication technique in MSVL.

The main contributions of this paper are as follows: 1. A process structure is defined to describe behaviors of systems. In this way, two or more processes can form a larger system with a clear structure; 2. To establish links among processes, a channel structure is presented. Channels are buffers to transport messages; 3. Communication commands, which are executed by processes to send or receive messages, are formalized. After all works above have been done, asynchronous communication is possible and a number of asynchronous concurrent systems can be modeled, simulated and verified with extended MSVL.

To inspect the practicability of our works, an example of electronic contract signing protocol is modeled and verified by the extended MSVL. Processes are used to describe all parties that participate in the protocol and channels are defined to connect all processes;then all processes run in parallel to model the protocol. With some properties specified by PPTL formulas, whether or not the protocol satisfies them are checked.

The paper is organized as follows: In section 2, the syntax and semantics of PTL are presented. In section 3, the language MSVL is briefly introduced. The formal definitions of the process structure and asynchronous communication are formalized in section 4. In section 5, an electronic contract signing protocol is modeled and verified with the extended MSVL. Conclusions are drawn in the final section.

2 Projection Temporal Logic

2.1 Syntax

Let Π be a countable set of propositions, and V be a countable set of typed static and dynamic variables. $B = \{true, false\}$ represents the boolean domain and D denotes all the data we need including integers, strings, lists etc. The terms e and formulas p are given by the following grammar:

$$
\begin{aligned}
e &::= v \mid \bigcirc e \mid \ominus e \mid f(e_1, \ldots, e_m) \\
p &::= \pi \mid e_1 = e_2 \mid P(e_1, \ldots, e_m) \mid \neg p \mid p_1 \wedge p_2 \mid \exists v : p \mid \bigcirc p \mid \ominus p \mid \\
&\quad\; (p_1, \ldots, p_m)\, prj\; p
\end{aligned}
$$

$$
\begin{aligned}
\mathcal{I}[v] &= s_k[v] = I_v^k[v] \\
\mathcal{I}[\bigcirc e] &= \begin{cases} (\sigma, i, k+1, j)[e] & \text{if } k < j \\ nil & \text{otherwise} \end{cases} \\
\mathcal{I}[\circleddash e] &= \begin{cases} (\sigma, i, k-1, j)[e] & \text{if } i < k \\ nil & \text{otherwise} \end{cases} \\
\mathcal{I}[f(e_1, \ldots, e_m)] &= \begin{cases} f(\mathcal{I}[e_1], \ldots, \mathcal{I}[e_m]) & \text{if } \mathcal{I}[e_h] \neq nil \text{ for all } h \\ nil & \text{otherwise} \end{cases}
\end{aligned}
$$

Fig. 1. Interpretation of PTL terms

where $\pi \in \Pi$ is a proposition, and v is a dynamic variable or a static variable. In $f(e_1, \ldots, e_m)$ and $P(e_1, \ldots, e_m)$, f is a function and P is a predicate. It is assumed that the types of the terms are compatible with those of the arguments of f and P. A formula (term) is called a state formula (term) if it does not contain any temporal operators ($i.e. \bigcirc, \circleddash$ and prj); otherwise it is a temporal formula (term).

2.2 Semantics

A state s is a pair of assignments (I_v, I_p) where for each variable $v \in V$ defines $s[v] = I_v[v]$, and for each proposition $\pi \in \Pi$ defines $s[\pi] = I_p[\pi]$. $I_v[v]$ is a value in D or nil (undefined), whereas $I_p[\pi] \in B$. An interval $\sigma =< s_0, s_1, \cdots >$ is a non-empty (possibly infinite) sequence of states. The length of σ, denoted by $|\sigma|$, is defined as ω if σ is infinite; otherwise it is the number of states in σ minus one. To have a uniform notation for both finite and infinite intervals, we will use extended integers as indices. That is, we consider the set N_0 of non-negative integers and ω, $N_\omega = N_0 \cup \{\omega\}$, and extend the comparison operators, $=, <, \leq$, to N_ω by considering $\omega = \omega$, and for all $i \in N_0, i < \omega$. Moreover, we define $\preceq$ as $\leq -\{(\omega, \omega)\}$. With such a notation, $\sigma_{(i..j)}(0 \leq i \preceq j \leq |\sigma|)$ denotes the sub-interval $< s_i, \ldots, s_j >$ and $\sigma(k)(0 \leq k \preceq |\sigma|)$ denotes $< s_k, ..., s_{|\sigma|} >$. The concatenation of σ with another interval (or empty string) σ' is denoted by $\sigma \cdot \sigma'$. To define the semantics of the projection operator we need an auxiliary operator for intervals. Let $\sigma =< s_0, s_1, \cdots >$ be an interval and $r_1, \ldots, r_h$ be integers $(h \geq 1)$ such that $0 \leq r_1 \leq r_2 \leq \cdots \leq r_h \preceq |\sigma|$. The projection of σ onto $r_1, \ldots, r_h$ is the interval (called projected interval), $\sigma \downarrow (r_1, \ldots, r_h) =< s_{t_1}, s_{t_2}, \ldots, s_{t_l} >$, where $t_1, \ldots, t_l$ is obtained from $r_1, \ldots, r_h$ by deleting all duplicates. For example,

$$< s_0, s_1, s_2, s_3, s_4 > \downarrow (0, 0, 2, 2, 2, 3) =< s_0, s_2, s_3 >$$

An interpretation for a PTL term or formula is a tuple $I = (\sigma, i, k, j)$, where $\sigma =< s_0, s_1, \cdots >$ is an interval, i and k are non-negative integers, and j is an integer or ω, such that $i \leq k \preceq j \leq |\sigma|$. We use (σ, i, k, j) to mean that a term or formula is interpreted over a subinterval $\sigma_{(i..j)}$ with the current state being s_k. For every term e, the evaluation of e relative to interpretation $I = (\sigma, i, k, j)$ is defined as $I[e]$, by induction on the structure of a term, as shown in Fig.1, where v is a variable and $e_1, \ldots, e_m$ are terms.

$$
\begin{array}{llllll}
empty & \stackrel{\text{def}}{=} & \neg \bigcirc true & more & \stackrel{\text{def}}{=} & \neg empty \\
halt(p) & \stackrel{\text{def}}{=} & \Box(empty \leftrightarrow p) & keep(p) & \stackrel{\text{def}}{=} & \Box(\neg empty \rightarrow p) \\
fin(p) & \stackrel{\text{def}}{=} & \Box(empty \rightarrow p) & skip & \stackrel{\text{def}}{=} & \neg empty \\
x\circ = e & \stackrel{\text{def}}{=} & \bigcirc x = e & x := e & \stackrel{\text{def}}{=} & skip \wedge x\circ = e \\
len(0) & \stackrel{\text{def}}{=} & empty & len(n) & \stackrel{\text{def}}{=} & \bigcirc len(n-1)(n>0)
\end{array}
$$

Fig. 2. Some derived formulas

The satisfaction relation for formulas $\models$ is inductively defined as follows.

1. $\mathcal{I} \models \pi$ if $s_k[\pi] = I_p^k[\pi] =$ true.
2. $\mathcal{I} \models e_1 = e_2$ if $\mathcal{I}[e_1] = \mathcal{I}[e_2]$.
3. $\mathcal{I} \models P(e_1, \ldots, e_m)$ if P is a primitive predicate other than = and, for all h, $1 \leq h \leq m$, $\mathcal{I}[e_h] \neq nil$ and $P(\mathcal{I}[e_1], \ldots, \mathcal{I}[e_m]) =$ true.
4. $\mathcal{I} \models \neg p$ if $\mathcal{I} \not\models p$.
5. $\mathcal{I} \models p_1 \wedge p_2$ if $\mathcal{I} \models p_1$ and $\mathcal{I} \models p_2$.
6. $\mathcal{I} \models \exists v : p$ if for some interval σ' which has the same length as σ, $(\sigma', i, k, j) \models p$ and the only difference between σ and σ' can be in the values assigned to variable v at k.
7. $\mathcal{I} \models \bigcirc p$ if $k < j$ and $(\sigma, i, k+1, j) \models p$.
8. $\mathcal{I} \models \ominus p$ if $i < k$ and $(\sigma, i, k-1, j) \models p$.
9. $\mathcal{I} \models (p_1, \ldots, p_m)\, prj\ q$ if there exist integers $k = r_0 \leq r_1 \leq \ldots \leq r_m \leq j$ such that $(\sigma, i, r_0, r_1) \models p_1$, $(\sigma, r_{l-1}, r_{l-1}, r_l) \models p_l$ (for $1 < l \leq m$), and $(\sigma', 0, 0, |\sigma'|) \models q$ for one of the following σ':
   (a) $r_m < j$ and $\sigma' = \sigma\downarrow(r_0, ..., r_m)\cdot\sigma_{(r_{m+1..j})}$
   (b) $r_m = j$ and $\sigma' = \sigma\downarrow(r_0, \ldots, r_h)$ for some $0 \leq h \leq m$.

A formula p is said to be:

1. *satisfied* by an interval σ, denoted $\sigma \models p$, if $(\sigma, 0, 0, |\sigma|) \models p$.
2. *satisfiable* if $\sigma \models p$ for some σ.
3. *valid*, denoted $\models p$, if $\sigma \models p$ for all σ.
4. *equivalent* to another formula q, denoted $p \equiv q$, if $\models (p \leftrightarrow q)$.

The abbreviations $true$, $false$, $\wedge$, $\rightarrow$ *and* $\leftrightarrow$ are defined as usual. In particular, $true \stackrel{\text{def}}{=} P \vee \neg P$ and $false \stackrel{\text{def}}{=} \neg P \wedge P$ for any formula P. Also some derived formulas is shown in Fig.2.

3 Modeling, Simulation and Verification Language

The Language MSVL with frame[11] technique is an executable subset of PTL and used to model, simulate and verify concurrent systems. The arithmetic expression e and boolean expression b of MSVL are inductively defined as follows:

$$
\begin{array}{l}
e ::= n \mid x \mid \bigcirc x \mid \ominus x \mid e_0\, op\, e_1 (op ::= + \mid - \mid * \mid / \mid mod) \\
b ::= true \mid false \mid e_0 = e_1 \mid e_0 < e_1 \mid \neg b \mid b_0 \wedge b_1
\end{array}
$$

where n is an integer and x is a variable. The elementary statements in MSVL are defined as follows:

Assignment: $x = e$
P-I-Assignment: $x \Leftarrow e$
Conditional: if b then p else $q \stackrel{\text{def}}{=} (b \rightarrow p) \wedge (\neg b \rightarrow q)$
While: while b do $p \stackrel{\text{def}}{=} (b \wedge p)^* \wedge \square(empty \rightarrow \neg b)$
Conjunction: $p \wedge q$
Selection: $p \vee q$
Next: $\bigcirc p$
Always: $\square p$
Termination: $empty$
Sequential: $p; q$
Local variable: $\exists x : p$
State Frame: $lbf(x)$
Interval Frame: $frame(x)$
Parallel: $p \parallel q \stackrel{\text{def}}{=} p \wedge (q; true) \vee q \wedge (p; true)$
Projection: $(p_1, \ldots, p_m)\, prj\ q$
Await: $await(b) \stackrel{\text{def}}{=} (frame(x_1) \wedge \cdots \wedge frame(x_h)) \wedge \square(empty \leftrightarrow b)$
where $x_i \in V_b = \{x | x \text{ appears in } b\}$

where x denotes a variable, e stands for an arbitrary arithmetic expression, b a boolean expression, and $p_1, \ldots, p_m$, p and q stand for programs of MSVL. The assignment $x = e$, $x \Leftarrow e$, $empty$, $lbf(x)$, and $frame(x)$ can be regarded as basic statements and the others composite ones.

The assignment $x = e$ means that the value of variable x is equal to the value of expression e. Positive immediate assignment $x \Leftarrow e$ indicates that the value of x is equal to the value of e and the assignment flag for variable x, p_x, is true. Statements of $if\ b\ then\ p\ else\ q$ and $while\ b\ do\ p$ are the same as that in the conventional imperative languages. $p \wedge q$ means that p and q are executed concurrently and share all the variables during the mutual execution. $p \vee q$ means p or q are executed. The next statement $\bigcirc p$ means that p holds at the next state while $\square p$ means that p holds at all the states over the whole interval from now. $empty$ is the termination statement meaning that the current state is the final state of the interval over which the program is executed. The sequence statement $p; q$ means that p is executed from the current state to its termination while q will hold at the final state of p and be executed from that state. The existential quantification $\exists x : p$ intends to hide the variable x within the process p. $lbx(x)$ means the value of x in the current state equals to value of x in the previous state if no assignment to x occurs, while $frame(x)$ indicates that the value of variable x always keeps its old value over an interval if no assignment to x is encountered. Different from the conjunction statement, the parallel statement allows both the processes to specify their own intervals. e.g., $len(2) \| len(3)$ holds but $len(2) \wedge len(3)$ is obviously false. Projection can be thought of as a special parallel computation which is executed on different time scales. The projection $(p_1, \ldots, p_m)\, prj\ q$ means that q is executed in parallel with $p_1, \ldots, p_m$ over an interval obtained by taking the endpoints of the intervals over which the p_i's are executed. In particular, the sequence of p_i's and q may terminate at different time points. Finally, $await(b)$ does not change any variable, but waits until the condition b becomes true, at which point it terminates.

An MSVL interpreter has been implemented in Microsoft Visual C++. An MSVL program can be transformed to a logically equivalent conjunction of the two formulaes, $Present$ and $Remains$. $Present$ consists of immediate assignments to program variables, output of program variables, $true$, $false$ or $empty$. It is executed at the current state. The formula $Remains$ is what is executed in the subsequent state (if any). The interpreter accepts well-formed MSVL programs as its input and interprets them in a serial states. If a program is reduced to $true$, it is satisfiable and a model is found, otherwise it has no model.

The interpreter can work in three modes: modeling, simulation and verification. In the modeling mode, given the MSVL program p of a system, all execution paths of the system are given as an Normal Form Graph (NFG)[5] of p. A correct path ends with a bicyclic node as shown in Fig.3(a). Under the simulation mode, an execution path of the system is output according to minimal model semantics[12] of MSVL. With the verification mode, given a system model described by an MSVL program, and a property specified by a PPTL formula, it can automatically be verified whether or not the system satisfies the property, and the counterexample will be pointed out if the system does not satisfy it. A satisfiable path ends with a circular node as shown in Fig.3(b) while an unsatisfiable path ends with a terminative node as shown in Fig.3(c).

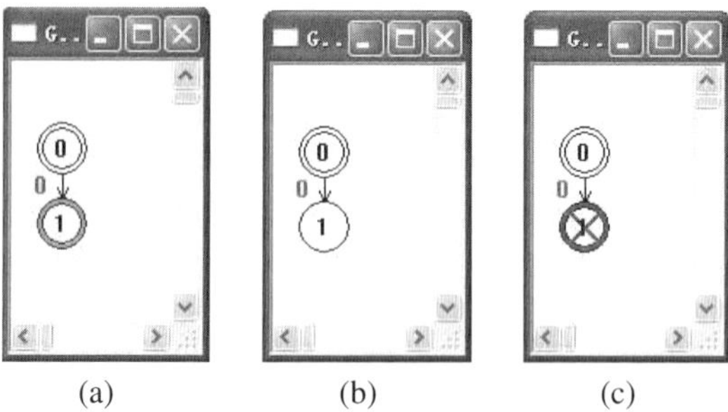

(a) (b) (c)

Fig. 3. Three types of nodes

4 Asynchronous Communication

4.1 Process

In[10], a process stands for the behavior pattern of an object. A service can be viewed as a computational entity in[6]. Similarly, we use a process to describe the manner of an object. Furthermore, process is a reasonable structure when several MSVL statements run in parallel and each independently determines the interval length. The introduction of the process structure simplifies and modularizes programming so that a complicated system can be separated into several processes. Besides, processes are viewed as communication entities and make the implementation of asynchronous communication more feasible.

The process structure consists of two parts: declaration part and calling part. The declaration part has three components: process name, formal parameters and process body. The calling part consists of process name and actual parameters.

Let $ProcName$ be the name of a process, and P, P_1, P_2 be MSVL statements. x, y are variables, and c, d denotes channel variables. The formal definitions of process are shown below:

$$\begin{aligned} proc\ ProcName(x) &\stackrel{\text{def}}{=} \{Pro\_Body\} \\ Pro\_Body &\stackrel{\text{def}}{=} x = e \mid P_1 \wedge P_2 \mid P_1 \vee P_2 \mid \bigcirc P \mid \Box P \mid \exists x : P \mid P_1 \,||\, P_2 \mid \\ &\quad\ if\, b\, then\, P_1\, else\, P_2 \mid P_1 ; P_2 \mid while\ b\, do\ P \mid frame(x) \mid \\ &\quad\ send(c,e) \mid receive(d,y) \mid empty \\ ProcName(y) &\stackrel{\text{def}}{=} (y/x)Pro\_Body_{ProcName} \end{aligned}$$

Where $proc$ is a key word, and $Proc\_Body$ is the main body of a process. The statement $ProcName(y)$ refers to call the process $ProcName$ with the actual parameter y. The semantic of $ProcName(y)$ is to replace the value of all x's in the main body of $ProcName$ by the value of y. The statement $send(c, e)$ represents to send a message(value of expression e) to channel c while the statement $receive(d, y)$ means to receive a message from channel d and assign it to the variable y.

4.2 Channel

Channel communication can be synchronous or asynchronous. For synchronous communication, a receiver blocks until a compatible party is ready to send. As to asynchronous communication, a communicating party can start a sending or receiving activity at any time without consideration of the state of the other party, because there is a buffer between them.

Before presenting formal definitions, we firstly give informal descriptions of channel communication. In MSVL, a channel is a bounded First-In-First-Out (FIFO) list where a message can be inserted at one end and received sequentially at the other. Sending a message equals appending it to the tail of the channel; receiving a message is to remove the head of the channel. Only when there is at least one empty place available in the channel will a sending activity be successful, otherwise waiting for an empty place or terminating the sending activity may be selected. A similar procedure applies to a receiving activity. As formal parameters in the declaration of a process can be channel variables, we can transfer a defined channel variable as the actual parameter to the formal parameter when calling a process. Then the process can access the channel to transport messages.

A channel is regarded as a bounded FIFO list and its declaration is given below:

$$chn\ c(n) \stackrel{\text{def}}{=} c =<> \wedge max_c = n$$

where chn is a key word and $chn\ c(n)$ declares channel c with a capacity of n. Here c is an empty list, and max_c is a static variable that represents the capacity of list c. Some list operators make it behave like a bounded FIFO.

Any process can access a channel if the channel is visible in its scope. Hence, the number of processes that a channel can connect is not restricted. Obviously, conflicts may happen when more than one process accesses a same channel at the same time and therefore some exclusion algorithms are necessary. Unfortunately, the algorithms based on hardware instructions are not workable since atomic operations are incapable of being expressed in MSVL, and the algorithms related to software are so complicated that they will make MSVL programs in confusion and barely intelligible. According to our experience, attaching exactly one process to each end of a channel will be a wise choice.

4.3 Communication Commands

For simplicity, we firstly introduce two predicates as follows:

$$\begin{aligned} isfull(c) &\stackrel{\text{def}}{=} |c| = max_c \\ isempty(c) &\stackrel{\text{def}}{=} |c| = 0 \end{aligned}$$

- $isfull(c)$ evaluates to $true$ if channel c is full, otherwise $false$.
- $isempty(c)$ evaluates to $true$ if channel c is empty, otherwise $false$.

Let x be an output expression, and y be an input variable, and c be a channel variable. Communication commands are defined as follows:

$$\begin{aligned} send(c, x) &\stackrel{\text{def}}{=} await(!isfull(c)); c := c\cdot < x > \\ receive(c, y) &\stackrel{\text{def}}{=} await(!isempty(c)); y := head(c) \wedge c := tail(c) \end{aligned}$$

- The command $send(c, x)$ will block until c has at least one empty place. If c is not full at current state, x can be inserted into the tail of c at the next state, otherwise $await(!isfull(c))$ statement will be executed repeatedly at the next state in accordance with the semantic of $await$ structure.
- If c is not empty at current state, the message at the head of c will be removed and assigned to the variable y at the next state, otherwise $await(!isempty(c))$ statement will be executed at the next state.
- The length of intervals of the two commands is 1 at least if the predicates $isfull$ and $isempty$ are $false$ at the initial state. The length, however, may be infinite if the predicates are always $true$.

An example is demonstrated to illustrate the use of $send$ and $receive$.

Example 1. A and B are two processes, and variable c is a channel between them. The pointer symbols * and & are defined in[13]. The MSVL program is given in Fig.4.

- state s_0: A gets ready to append x to the tail of c at the next state. B will execute $await(!isempty(c))$ statement again at the next state, since there is no message in c at the current state.
- state s_1: A puts x at the tail of c and then terminates. B prepares to get x at the next state since x is at the head of c at the current state.
- state s_2: B removes x from c and assigns it to the variable y. Then B terminates.

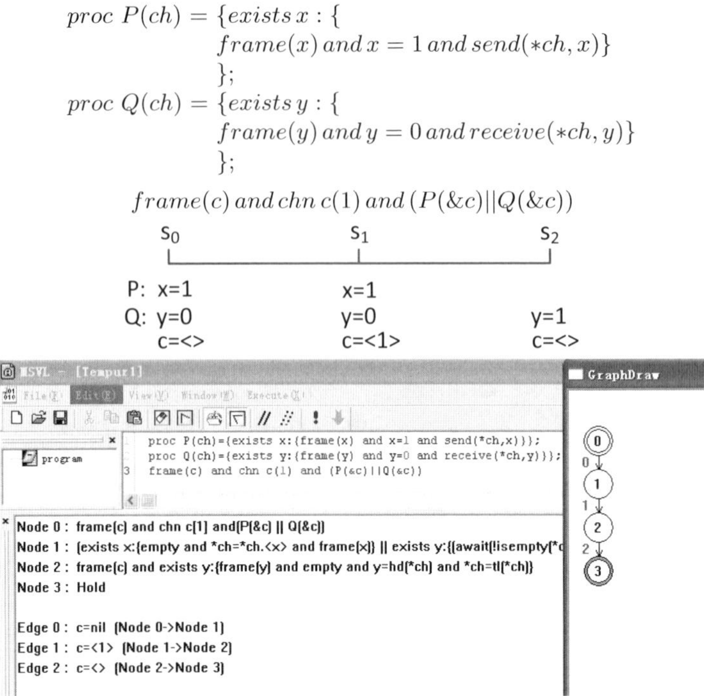

Fig. 4. Example of send and receive

While modeling a distributed system with timing constraints, some party may have to time out, which happens frequently in communication, to give up waiting if its request is not responded for a long time. The commands *send* and *receive* do not terminate until the predicates $isfull$ and $isempty$ become $false$, which implies they are not capable of handling timeout mechanism in these systems. Hence, another pair of communication commands is provided:

$$
\begin{aligned}
put(c,x) &\stackrel{\text{def}}{=} if(\,!isfull(c)\,)\; then\; \{\, c := c\cdot < x > \}\\
&\quad\;\; else\{skip\}\\
get(c,y) &\stackrel{\text{def}}{=} if(\,!isempty(c)\,)\; then\; \{\, y := head(c) \wedge c := tail(c)\,\}\\
&\quad\;\; else\{\,skip\,\}
\end{aligned}
$$

We replace the *await* structure by $if-else$ structure. If the predicate $isfull$ or $isempty$ is *true*, *skip* is executed. This pair of commands enable us to deal with timeouts in modeling the systems with timing constraints while the commands *send* and *receive* are convenient to describe the other systems. An appropriate selection should be made according to the features of the system.

5 An Application

5.1 An Example of Electronic Contract Signing Protocol

The crux of a commercial transaction is usually an exchange of one item for another. More specifically, electronic contract signing can be considered as a fair exchange of digital signatures to the same contract.

An electronic contract signing protocol allows n parties to sign a contract over networks. As the protocol relates to all parties' benefits, some critical properties need to be ensured, e.g., fairness[14]. Fairness denotes that either all parties obtain a signed contract, or nobody does. A trust third party(TTP) is necessary to guarantee the fairness, which is proved by Pagnina and Gartner in 1999[15].

The most straightforward contract signing protocol uses a TTP that first collects all signatures and then distributes the decision signed or failed. But as the third party has to be involved in all protocol executions it might easily become a reliability and performance bottleneck. To avoid such a bottleneck, optimistic protocols which do not involve a TTP in the normal, exception-less case but only involve it in the presence of faults or in the case of dishonest parties who do not follow the protocol are researched.

The optimistic multi-party contract signing protocols can run on synchronous or asynchronous networks. Basically, "synchronous"[14] means that all parties have synchronized real-time clocks, and that there is a known upper bound on the network delays. The most widely synchronous protocol is described in [16], which is to be modeled and verified with extended MSVL below. "Asynchronous"[14] means that there are no assumptions on clock synchronization and network delays. This means more precisely that a communication allows parties to respond at arbitrary times or infinite network delay. The first asynchronous optimistic multi-party contract signing protocol is described in[14]. Nevertheless, the protocols for asynchronous networks are more expensive. An improved version presented in[17] requires 2 rounds with the premise that the number of dishonest parties is less than half parties. Unfortunately, it cannot be predicted.

Before we present the protocol, some assumptions are listed as follows:

1. There is an active-time limit t, after which all parties are guaranteed that the state of the transaction is not changed. Requests for exceptions must be made before an earlier deadline. Hence, all parties have to synchronize the clocks in order to agree on the active-time limit as well as to compute local timeouts within rounds. In our model, we assume clocks of all parties are synchronized and each party may decide independently when to time out, and each step runs within a reasonable time limit.
2. The channels between the TTP and all other parties are reliable according to the conclusion that Pagnina and Gartner drew in 1999, whereas other channels may be unreliable. Namely, messages are delivered eventually between TTP and any other party, but the reliability of message passing cannot be guaranteed in other cases.
3. As already mentioned, TTP is involved in case of exceptions. Exceptions in the protocol mainly develop in two forms: receiving invalid signatures and losing

messages, which respectively are caused by dishonest parties and unreliable networks. For the simplicity of modeling, both of the two forms are regarded as some party's not sending message to others. Therefore once a message is received, it always represents a valid signature signed by the sender.

The protocol consists of main protocol and recovery protocol. If all parties are honest and no message is lost, the recovery protocol will not be involved. The details are described as follows[16]:

The Main Protocol

- *The First Round*
  - P_i sends $m_{[1,i]} = sign_i(1, c)$ to other parties
  - From all message of type $m_{[1,j]}$, P_i tries to compile vector $M_1 = (m_{[1,1]}, \ldots, m_{[1,n]})$. If this succeeds and each $m_{[1,j]}$ is a valid signature, then P_i enters the second round, otherwise P_i waits for a message from TTP.
- *The Second Round*
  - P_i sends $m_{[2,i]} = sign_i(2, c)$ to other parties
  - From all message of type $m_{[2,j]}$, P_i tries to compile vector $M_2 = (m_{[2,1]}, \ldots, m_{[2,n]})$. If this succeeds and each $m_{[2,j]}$ is a valid signature, then P_i decides signed and stops, otherwise P_i sends $m_{[3,i]}$=$sign_i(3, M_1)$ to TTP and waits for reply.

The Recovery Protocol

- TTP: If TTP receives at least one message $m_{[3,i]}$ which contains a full and consistent M_1, then TTP sends $M_{ttp} = sign_{ttp}(M_1)$ to all parties, and each P_i receiving this decides signed, otherwise TTP does not send anything, and each P_i waiting for a message from TTP decides failed if none arrives, or signed in case M_{ttp} is received, and stops.

Some explanations of the protocol are listed as follows:

1. The vector M_2 and M_{ttp} are equivalent, and they both refer to a valid contract. Assume an honest party get a valid contract. If this happens because of M_{ttp}, then TTP has distributed it to all parties, and all honest parties decide signed. Now assume an honest party V accepts because of M_2. As M_2 contains all P_i's signature $m_{[2,i]}$, P_i successfully complied M_1 in round 1. If P_i received M_2 in Round 2 it decides signed. Otherwise it initiates an recovery, which is necessarily answered by M_{ttp}, and P_i decides signed.
2. In a synchronous network, each P_i waiting for a message from TTP can correctly decide failed when times out, however, it would not be effective in a asynchronous network, as a party could not decide whether a message was not sent, or just not delivered yet.

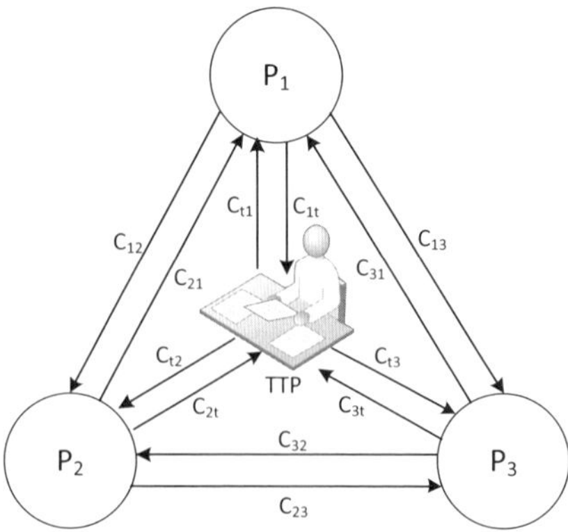

Fig. 5. Protocol structure for three parties

5.2 Modeling, Simulation and Verification with MSVL

Especially, we assume that three parties plan to sign a contract over a synchronous network by executing the protocol. TTP is included to deal with exceptions. We focus largely on the procedure of the protocol, and all messages are simplified as strings. The MSVL code of the protocol and the executable file of the interpreter can be downloaded by visiting `http://ictt.xidian.edu.cn/example.zip`.

An analysis of possible execution paths is made according to the number of parties who fail to send messages in the first round. Not sending messages is caused by two reasons mentioned above.

- Situation 1: All parties send messages to others in the first round. There are $2^3 = 8$ cases in all, according to whether the three parties send messages or not in the second round. In any case, all parties can gain a signed contract eventually.
- Situation 2: Two of them send messages but the third one fails to send in the first round. Then the third one sends a recovery request to TTP in the second round, therefore all parties will get a signed contract broadcasted by TTP. There are C_3^2x2=6 cases in all.
- Situation 3: Only one party sends messages in the first round, nobody can successfully compile M_1 to enter the second round, then all parties will time out in waiting for TTP's broadcast. Hence, there are C_3^2=3 cases in all.
- Situation 4: All parties fail to send messages in the first round. Nobody can enter the second round and there is 1 case in all.

There are 18 cases in all according to the analysis above. We run the program with extended MSVL interpreter under modeling mode and all 18 execution paths are shown in Fig.6. Due to the fact that some paths are too long to completely show in the figure, we use suspension points to represent part of them. In the modeling mode, the bicyclic nodes merely represent a successful modeling procedure since some nodes stand for a successful signing and the others represent a failed signing.

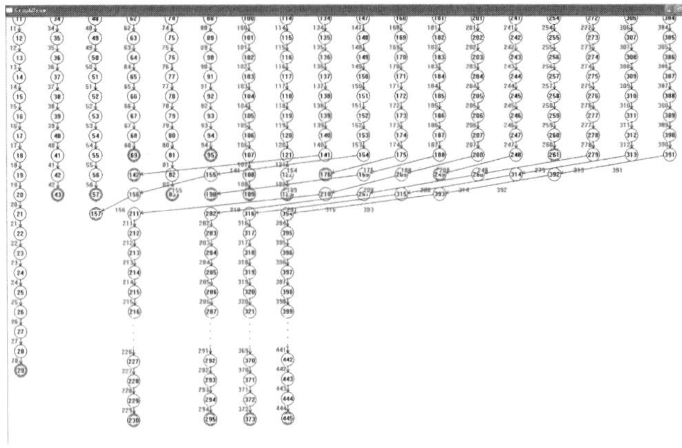

Fig. 6. Modeling result of the protocol

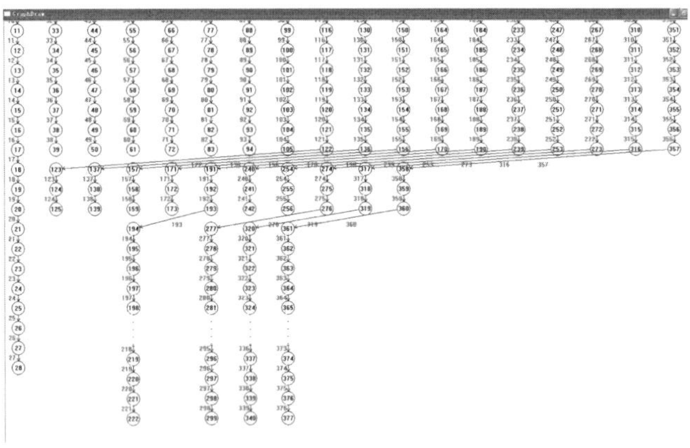

Fig. 7. Verification result of property(1)

Before verifying the properties fairness and optimism, we need to specify them by PPTL formulas. Then all works of the verification can be done automatically by means of model checking with the MSVL interpreter.

- A fairness property

$$\begin{aligned} define\ l : cont_1 &= \text{"nil"}; \\ define\ m : cont_2 &= \text{"nil"}; \\ define\ n : cont_3 &= \text{"nil"}; \\ define\ p : cont_1 &= \text{"signed"}; \\ define\ q : cont_2 &= \text{"signed"}; \\ define\ r : cont_3 &= \text{"signed"}; \end{aligned}$$

$$fin((p\ and\ q\ and\ r)\ or\ (l\ and\ m\ and\ n)) \tag{1}$$

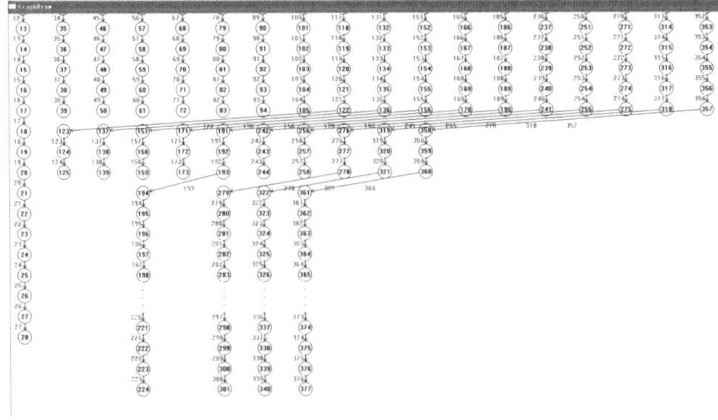

Fig. 8. Verification result of property(2)

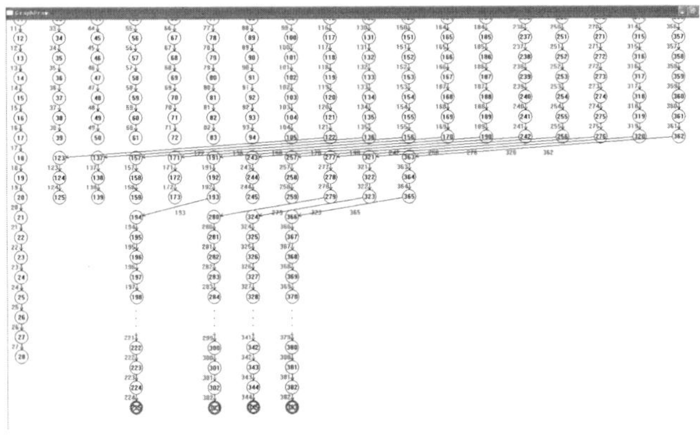

Fig. 9. Verification result of an unsatisfied PPLT formula

The proposition $cont_i$ = "$signed$" means P_i has got a valid contract while $cont_i$ = "nil" implies P_i has failed to get a valid contract. Therefore the property (1) implies either all parties obtain a signed contract, or nobody does at final states. All 18 paths ended with circular nodes in Fig.7 show that the protocol satisfies the property (1).

– An optimism property

$$define\ d : opt_1 = 1;$$
$$define\ e : opt_2 = 1;$$
$$define\ f : opt_3 = 1;$$
$$define\ g : opt \ = 1;$$

$$fin((d\ and\ e\ and\ f) \rightarrow g) \tag{2}$$

The proposition $opt_i = 1$ means P_i has compiled vector M_2 successfully. The proposition $opt = 1$ indicates TTP is not involved. Therefore the property (2) implies TTP will not participate if all parties can compile vector M_2 at final states. Fig.8 indicates the protocol satisfies the property (2).

– An unsatisfiable PPTL formula

$$fin(p\ and\ q\ and\ r) \tag{3}$$

The formula (3) means all parties will obtain a valid contract at final states. Apparently, the formula is unsatisfiable in accordance with the analysis above. Some cases will lead to a situation that nobody gets a valid contract. Fig.9 shows the protocol does not satisfy the formula (3).

6 Conclusion

In this paper, we have discussed the implementation of asynchronous communication technique in MSVL. The formal definitions of process structure, channel structure and communication commands are presented. This enables us to model and verify concurrent systems with asynchronous communications. In addition, an example of optimistic multi-party contract signing protocol has been employed to show how our method works. Its fairness and optimism have been proved satisfiable with extended MSVL. In contrast, an unsatisfiable property has also been checked and all counterexamples have been pointed out. In the future, we will further investigate the operational and axiomatic semantics of MSVL with asynchronous communication. In addition, we will also try to model and verify some larger example to our approach.

Acknowledgment. We would like to thank Miss Qian Ma and Miss Xia Guo for their useful help. In particular, Guo's help on MSVL interpreter and Ma's suggestion on the verification example are very appreciated.

References

1. Pnueli, A.: The temporal semantics of concurrent programs. In: Proceedings of the 18th IEEE Symposium Foundations of Computer Science, pp. 46–67 (1997)
2. Karp, Alan, R.: Proving failure-free properties of concurrent systems using temporal logic. ACM Trans. Program. Lang. Syst. 6, 239–253 (1984)
3. Cau, A., Moszkowski, B., Zedan, H.: Itl and tempura home page on the web, `http://www.cse.dmu.ac.uk/STRL/ITL/`
4. Tian, C., Duan, Z.: Propositional projection temporal logic, buchi automata and ω-regular expressions. In: Agrawal, M., Du, D.-Z., Duan, Z., Li, A. (eds.) TAMC 2008. LNCS, vol. 4978, pp. 47–58. Springer, Heidelberg (2008)
5. Duan, Z., Tian, C.: A unified model checking approach with projection temporal logic. In: Liu, S., Araki, K. (eds.) ICFEM 2008. LNCS, vol. 5256, pp. 167–186. Springer, Heidelberg (2008)
6. Solanki, M., Cau, A., Zedan, H.: Asdl: A wide spectrum language for designing web services. In: WWW, pp. 687–696 (2006)
7. Tang, Z.: Temporal Logic Program Designing and Engineering, vol. 1. Sicence Press, Beijing (1999)
8. Hale, R.: Programming in Temporal Logic. Cambridge University, Cambridge (1988)
9. Milner, R.: A Calculus of Communicating Systems. Springer, Heidelberg (1980)

10. Hoare, C.A.R.: Communicating sequential processes (August 1978)
11. Duan, Z., Koutny, M.: A framed temporal logic programming language. Journal Computer Science and Technology 19(3), 341–351 (2004)
12. Duan, Z., Yang, X., Koutny, M.: Framed temporal logic programming. Science of Computer Programming 70, 31–61 (2008)
13. Duan, Z., Wang, X.: Implementing pointer in temporal logic programming languages. In: Proceedings of Brazilian Symposium on Formal Methods, Natal, Brazil, pp. 171–184 (2006)
14. Baum-waidner, B., Waidner, M.: Optimistic asynchronous multi-party contract signing (1998)
15. Pagnia, H., Gartner, F.C.: On the impossibility of fair exchange without a trusted third party. Darmstadt University of Technology, Tech. Rep. Technical Report: TUD-BS-1999-02 (1999)
16. Asokan, N., Baum-waidner, B., Schunter, M., Waidner, M.: Optimistic synchronous multi-party contract signing (1998)
17. Baum-Waidner.: Optimistic asynchronous multi-party contract signing with reduced number of rounds (2001)

Verification of Orchestration Systems Using Compositional Partial Order Reduction*

Tian Huat Tan[1], Yang Liu[2], Jun Sun[3], and Jin Song Dong[2]

[1] NUS Graduate School for Integrative Sciences and Engineering
tianhuat@comp.nus.edu.sg
[2] School of Computing, National University of Singapore
{liuyang,dongjs}@comp.nus.edu.sg
[3] Singapore University of Technology and Design
sunjun@sutd.edu.sg

Abstract. *Orc* is a computation orchestration language which is designed to specify computational services, such as distributed communication and data manipulation, in a concise and elegant way. Four concurrency primitives allow programmers to orchestrate site calls to achieve a goal, while managing timeouts, priorities, and failures. To guarantee the correctness of *Orc* model, effective verification support is desirable. *Orc* has a highly concurrent semantics which introduces the problem of state-explosion to search-based verification methods like model checking. In this paper, we present a new method, called Compositional Partial Order Reduction (CPOR), which aims to provide greater state-space reduction than classic partial order reduction methods in the context of hierarchical concurrent processes. Evaluation shows that CPOR is more effective in reducing the state space than classic partial order reduction methods.

1 Introduction

The advent of multi-core and multi-CPU systems has resulted in the widespread use of concurrent systems. It is not a simple task for programmers to utilize concurrency, as programmers are often burdened with handling threads and locks explicitly. Processes can be composed at different levels of granularity, from simple processes to complete workflows. The *Orc* calculus [17] is designed to specify orchestrations and wide-area computations in a concise and structured manner. It has four concurrency combinators, which can be used to manage timeouts, priorities, and failures effectively [17]. The standard operational semantics [29] of *Orc* supports highly concurrent executions of *Orc* sub-expressions. Concurrency errors are difficult to discover by testing. Hence, it is desirable to verify *Orc* formally. The highly concurrent semantics of *Orc* can lead to state space explosion and thus pose a challenge to model checking methods.

In the literature, various state reduction techniques have been proposed to tackle the state space explosion problem, including on-the-fly verification [15], symmetry reduction [7,11], partial order reduction (POR) [8,22,12,28,5,23], etc. POR works by exploiting the independency of concurrently executing transitions in order to reduce the

* This research is supported in part by Research Grant IDD11100102 of Singapore University of Technology and Design, IDC and MOE2009-T2-1-072 (Advanced Model Checking Systems).

S. Qin and Z. Qiu (Eds.): ICFEM 2011, LNCS 6991, pp. 98–114, 2011.

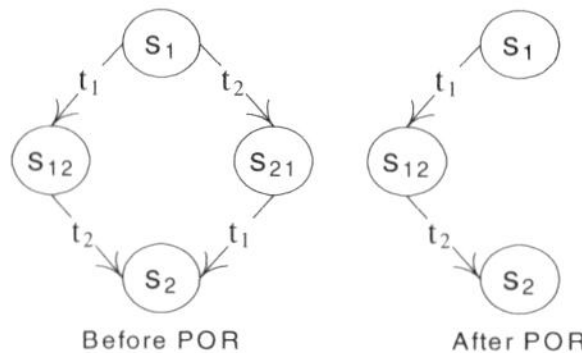

Fig. 1. Partial Order Reduction

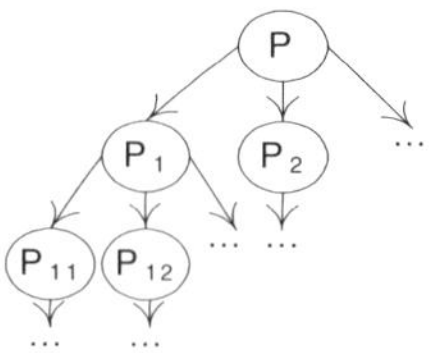

Fig. 2. Hierarchical Concurrent Processes

number of possible interleavings. For example, consider the transition system in Figure 1 where t_1 and t_2 are independent transitions. This means that executing either t_1t_2 or t_2t_1 from state s_1 will always lead to state s_2. POR will detect such independency, and choose only t_1t_2 for execution, thus reducing the explored state space. Classic POR algorithms, such as [28,12,8,22,5], work by identifying a subset of outgoing transitions of a state which are sufficient for verification. In this paper, we denote such subsets as *ample sets* – see [8,5].

Many concurrent systems are designed using a top-down architecture, and concurrent processes are structured in a hierarchical way. In Figure 2, process P contains subprocesses P_i (i = 1, 2, etc.) that are running concurrently. Moreover, each process P_i also contains subprocesses P_{ij} (j = 1, 2, etc.) that are running concurrently. We refer to concurrent processes of this kind as hierarchical concurrent processes (HCP). There are many real-life examples of HCP. Consider a browser that supports tabbed browsing. Multiple browser windows could be opened at the same time, each browser window could contain multiple opened tabs, and each opened tab could download several HTML elements in parallel. *Orc* processes provide another example of HCP.

Classic POR algorithms, such as [28,12,8,22,5], assume that *local transitions* within the participated processes are dependent. In the context of HCP (Figure 2), if POR is applied on process P, transitions within processes P_1, P_2, etc. will be considered as *local transitions*, and be assumed to be dependent. Nevertheless, many local transitions may be independent. In this work, we propose a method called Compositional Partial Order Reduction (CPOR), which extends POR to the context of HCP. CPOR exploits the independency within local transitions. It applies POR recursively for the hierarchical concurrent processes, and several possible ample sets are composed in a bottom-up manner. In order to apply CPOR to *Orc*, we first define the HCP structure of an *Orc* process. Subsequently, based on the HCP structure, we established some local criteria that could be easily checked by CPOR algorithm. Experimental results show that CPOR can greatly reduce the explored state space when verifying Orc models.

Paper Outline. Section 2 introduces *Orc* language. Section 3 elaborates on CPOR and shows how it can be applied to *Orc* models. Section 4 gives several experimental results. Section 5 surveys the related work. Finally, Section 6 discusses the extensibility of CPOR with possible future work and concludes the paper.

2 Orchestration Language Orc

2.1 Syntax

Orc is a computation orchestration language in which multiple services are invoked to achieve a goal while managing time-outs, priorities, and failures of services or communication. Following is the syntax of *Orc*:

$$
\begin{array}{llll}
\textit{Variable} & x ::= & \textit{variable name} & \\
\textit{Value} & m ::= & \textit{value} & \\
\textit{Parameter} & p ::= & x \mid m & \\
\textit{Expression} & E ::= & M(\overline{p}) & \text{– site call} \\
& \mid & E \mid E & \text{– parallel} \\
& \mid & E > x > E & \text{– sequential} \\
& \mid & E < x < E & \text{– pruning} \\
& \mid & E \; ; \; E & \text{– otherwise}
\end{array}
$$

Site. The simplest *Orc* expression is a site call $M(\overline{p})$, where M is the service's name and $\overline{p}$ is a list of parameters. Sites are the basic units of *Orc* language. A site can be an external service (e.g. *Google* site) which resides on a different machine. For example, *Google*(*"Orc"*) is an external site call that calls the external service provided by *Google* and its response is the search results for keyword *"Orc"* by the *Google* search engine. A site can also be a local service (e.g. *plus* site) which resides on the same machine. For example, a site call *plus*$(1,1)$ calls the local *plus* service and its response is the summation of the two arguments. Since a site in *Orc* is essentially a service, henceforth, we would use the term *site* and *service* interchangeably. Some services maintain a state, those services are denoted as *stateful services*. An example is *Buffer* site, which provides the service of First-In-First-Out (FIFO) queue. We denote the data structure that constitutes the state of a stateful service as *state object* of the stateful service. A site call (e.g. a dequeue operation on *Buffer* site) for a certain stateful service may change the corresponding state object (e.g. a FIFO queue). Thus, multiple site calls with the same arguments to the same stateful service might result in different responses. Services that do not have any state are called *stateless services*. An example is *plus* site, which takes two numbers as input and returns their summation. Multiple calls with the same arguments to a stateless service will always result in the same response.

Combinators. There are four combinators: parallel, sequential, pruning, and otherwise combinators. The parallel combinator $F \mid G$ defines a parallel expression, where expressions F and G execute independently, and its published value can be the value published either by F or by G or both of them. The sequential combinator $F > x > G$ defines a sequential expression, where each value published by F initiates a separate execution of G wherein x is bound to the published value. The execution of F is then continued in parallel with all these executions of G. The values published by the sequential expression are the values published by the executions of G. For example, $(\textit{Google}(\text{“}\textit{Orc}\text{”}) \mid \textit{Yahoo}(\text{“}\textit{Orc}\text{”})) > x > \textit{Email}(\textit{addr}, x)$ will call Google and Yahoo sites simultaneously. For each returned value, an instance of x will be bound to it, and an email will be sent to *addr* for each instance of x. Thus, up to two emails will be sent. If x is not used in G, $F \gg G$ can be used as a shorthand for $F > x > G$.

The pruning combinator $F < x < G$ defines a pruning expression, where initially F and G execute in parallel. However, when F needs the value of x, it will be blocked until G publishes a value to bind x and G terminates immediately after that. For example, $Email(addr, x) < x < (Google(\text{“}Orc\text{”}) \mid Yahoo(\text{“}Orc\text{”}))$ will get the fastest searching result for the email sending to *addr*. If x is not used in F, $F \ll G$ can be used as a shorthand for $F < x < G$. The otherwise combinator $F \;\; ; \;\; G$ defines an otherwise expression, where F executes first. The execution of F is replaced by G if F halts without any published value, otherwise G is ignored. For example, in the expression $(Google(\text{“}Orc\text{”}) \;\; ; \;\; Yahoo(\text{“}Orc\text{”})) > x > Email(addr, x)$, Yahoo site is used as a backup service for searching *“Orc”* and it will be called only if the site call $Google(\text{“}Orc\text{”})$ halts without any result for *“Orc”*.

Functional Core Language (Cor). *Orc* is enhanced with functional core language (Cor) to support various data types, mathematical operators, conditional expressions, function calls, etc. Cor structures such as conditional expressions and functions are translated into site calls and four combinators [17]. For example, conditional expression *if E then F else G*, where E, F, and G are *Orc* expressions would be translated into expression $(if(b) \gg F \mid if(\sim b) \gg G) < b < E$ before evaluation.

Example - Metronome. Timer is explicitly supported in *Orc* by introducing time-related sites that delay a given amount of time. One of such sites is *Rtimer*. For example, *Rtimer* $(5000) \gg$ *“Orc”* will publish “Orc” at exactly 5 seconds. Functional core (Cor) defines functions using the keyword *def*. Following is a function that defines a metronome [17], which will publish a *signal* value every t seconds. *signal* is a value in *Orc* that carries no information. Note that the function is defined recursively.

$$def\ metronome(t) \;=\; (signal \;\mid\; Rtimer(t) \gg metronome(t))$$

The following example publishes “tick” once per second, and publishes “tock” once per second after an initial half-second delay.

$$(metronome(1000) \gg \text{“}tick\text{”}) \mid (Rtimer(500) \gg metronome(1000) \gg \text{“}tock\text{”})$$

Thus the publications are “tick tock tick $\cdots$” where “tick” and “tock” alternate each other. One of the properties that we are interested is whether the system could publish two consecutive “tick”s or two consecutive “tock”s which is an undesirable situation. In order to easily assert a global property that holds throughout the execution of an *Orc* program, we extend *Orc* with auxiliary variables. The value of an auxiliary variable could be accessed and updated throughout the *Orc* program. Henceforth, we will simply refer to the extended auxiliary variables as *global variables*. A global variable is declared with the keyword *globalvar* and a special site, *\$GUpdate*, is used to update a global variable. We augment the metronome example with a global variable *tickNum*, which is initialized to zero. *tickNum* is increased by one when a “tick” is published, and is decreased by one when a “tock” is published.

$$\begin{array}{l} globalvar\ tickNum = 0 \\ def\ metronome(t) = (signal \mid Rtimer(t) \gg metronome(t)) \\ (metronome(1000) \gg \$GUpdate(\{tickNum = tickNum + 1\}) \gg \text{“}tick\text{”}) \\ \mid (Rtimer(500) \gg metronome(1000) \gg \$GUpdate(\{tickNum = tickNum - 1\}) \\ \gg \text{“}tock\text{”}) \end{array}$$

With this, we are allowed to verify whether the system could publish two consecutive "tick"s or two consecutive "tock"s by checking the temporal property such that whether the system is able to reach an undesirable state that satisfying the condition $(tickNum < 0 \vee tickNum > 1)$.

2.2 Semantics

This section presents the semantic model of *Orc* based on Label Transition System (LTS). In the following, we introduce some definitions required in the semantic model.

Definition 1 (System Configuration). *A system configuration contains two components (Proc,Val), where Proc is a Orc expression, and Val is a (partial) variable valuation function, which maps the variables to their values.*

A variable in the system could be an *Orc*'s variable, or the global variable which is introduced for capturing global properties. The value of a variable could be a primitive value, a reference to a site, or a state object. The three primitive types supported by *Orc* are boolean, integer, and string. All variables are assumed to have finite domain. Two configurations are equivalent iff they have the same process expression *Proc* and same valuation function *Val*. *Proc* component of system configuration is assumed to have finitely many values.

Definition 2 (System Model). *A system model is a 3-tuple $\mathcal{S} = (Var, init_G, P)$, where Var is a finite set of global variables, $init_G$ is the initial (partial) variable valuation function and P is the Orc expression.*

Definition 3 (System Action). *A system action contains four components (Event, Time, EnableSiteType, EnableSiteId). Event is either publication event, written !m or internal event, written τ. EnableSiteType, EnableSiteId are the type and unique identity of the site that initiates the system action. Time is the total delay time in system configuration before the system action is triggered.*

Every system action is initiated by a site call, and we extend the system action defined in [29] with two additional components, *EnableSiteType* and *EnableSiteId*, to provide information for CPOR. A publication event !*m* communicates with the environment with value *m*, while an internal event τ is invisible to the environment. There are three groups of site calls. The first two groups are site calls for stateless and stateful services respectively. And the third are the site calls for $GUpdate which update global variables. These three groups are denoted as *stateless*, *stateful*, and *GUpdate* respectively, and those are the possible values for *EnableSiteType*. Every site in the system model is assigned a unique identity which ranges over non-negative integer value. Discrete time semantics [29] is assumed in the system. *Time* ranges over non-negative integer value and is assumed to have finite domains.

Definition 4 (Labeled Transition System (LTS)). *Given a model $\mathcal{S} = (Var, init_G, P)$, let Σ denote the set of system actions in P. The LTS corresponding to $\mathcal{S}$ is a 3-tuple $(C, init, \rightarrow)$, where C is the set of all configurations, init $\in C$ is the initial system configuration $(P, init_G)$, and $\rightarrow \subseteq C \times \Sigma \times C$ is a labeled transition relation, and its definition is according to the operational semantics of Orc [29].*

To improve readability, we write $c \xrightarrow{a} c'$ for $(c, a, c') \in \rightarrow$. An action $a \in \Sigma$ is *enabled* in a configuration $c \in C$, denoted as $c \xrightarrow{a}$, iff there exists a configuration $c' \in C$, such that $c \xrightarrow{a} c'$. An action $a \in \Sigma$ is *disabled* in a configuration $c = (P, V)$, where $c \in C$, iff the action a is not enabled in the configuration c, but it is enabled in some configurations (P, V'), where $V' \neq V$. $Act(c)$ is used to denote the set of enabled actions of a configuration $c \in C$, formally, for any $c \in C$, $Act(c) = \{a \in \Sigma \mid c \xrightarrow{a}\}$. $Enable(c, a)$ is used to denote the set of reachable configurations through an action $a \in \Sigma$ from a configuration $c \in C$, that is, for any $c \in C$ and $a \in \Sigma$, $Enable(c, a) = \{c' \in C \mid c \xrightarrow{a} c'\}$. $Enable(c)$ is used to denote the set of reachable configurations from a configuration $c \in C$, that is, for any $c \in C$, $Enable(c) = \{c' \in Enable(c, a) \mid a \in \Sigma\}$. $Ample(c)$ is used to denote the ample set (refer to Section 3) of a configuration $c \in C$. $AmpleAct(c)$ is defined as the set of actions that caused a configuration $c \in C$ transit into the configurations in $Ample(c)$, that is, for any $c \in C$, $AmpleAct(c) = \{a \in \Sigma \mid c \xrightarrow{a} c', c' \in Ample(c)\}$. $PAct(c)$ is used to denote the set of enabled and disabled actions of a configuration c, and $Act(c) \subseteq PAct(c)$. We use TS to represent the original LTS before POR is applied and $\widehat{TS}$ to represent the reduced LTS after POR is applied. TS_c is used to represent the LTS (before any reduction) that starts from c, where c is a configuration in TS. An *execution fragment* $l = c_0 \xrightarrow{a_1} c_1 \xrightarrow{a_2} \ldots$ of LTS is an alternating sequence of configurations and actions. A *finite execution fragment* is an execution fragment ending with a configuration.

We are interested in checking the system against two kinds of properties. The first kind is deadlock-freeness, which is to check whether there does not exist a configuration $c \in C$ in TS such that $Enable(c) = \varnothing$. The second kind is temporal properties that are expressible with LTL without Next Operator (LTL-X) [5]. For any LTL-X formula ϕ, prop(ϕ) denotes the set of atomic propositions used in ϕ. In the metronome example which augmented with a global variable *tickNum*, prop(ϕ)=$\{(tickNum < 0), (tickNum > 1)\}$. An action $a \in \Sigma$ is *ϕ-invisible* iff the action does not change the values of propositions in prop(ϕ) for all $c \in C$ in TS.

2.3 Hierarchical Concurrent Processes (HCP)

The general structure of a hierarchical concurrent process P is shown graphically using a tree structure in Figure 3. Henceforth, we denote such a graph as a HCP graph, or simply HCP if it does not lead to ambiguity.

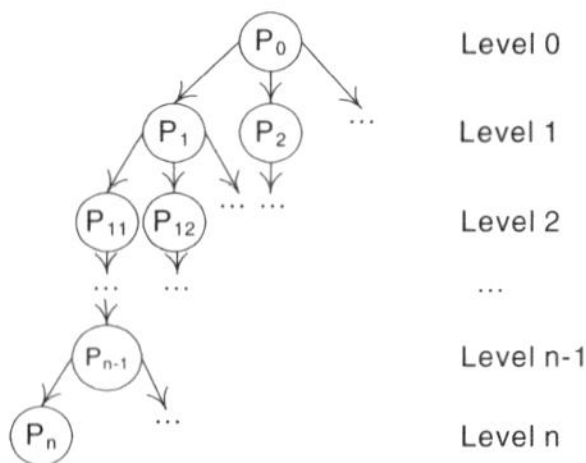

Fig. 3. The general structure of HCP

Figure 3 shows that process P_0 contains subprocesses P_1, P_2, etc that are running concurrently. Process P_1 in turn contains subprocesses P_{11}, P_{12}, etc that are running concurrently. This goes repeatedly until reaching a process P_n which has no subprocesses. Each process P in the hierarchy will have its associated level, starting from level 0. A process without any subprocess (e.g. process P_n) is denoted as *terminal process*, otherwise the process is denoted as *non-terminal process*. Furthermore, process P_0 at level 0 is denoted as *global process*, while processes at level i, where $i > 0$, are denoted as *local processes*. The *parent process* of a local process P' is a unique process P such that there is a directed edge from P to P' in the HCP graph. When P is the parent process of P', P' is called the *child process* of P. *Ancestor processes* of a local process P' are the processes in the path from global process to P'. *Descendant processes* of process P are those local processes that have P as an *ancestor process*.

An *Orc* expression P could be viewed as a process that is composed by HCP. This could be formalized by constructing the HCP according to syntax of P, assigning process identity to each sub-expression of P, and defining how the defined processes evolve during the execution of expression P. In the following, we illustrate this in detail. An *Orc* expression can be either a site call or one of the four combinators and their corresponding HCPs are shown in Figure 4. A site call is a terminal process node, while each of the combinators has either one or two child processes according to their semantics (refer to Section 2), and the HCPs of respective child process nodes are defined recursively. We denote expressions A and B as LHS process and RHS process for each combinators in Figure 4. For example, a pruning combinator ($A < x < B$) contains two child nodes because its LHS process and RHS process could be executed concurrently. Each of the process nodes in HCP is identified by a unique process identity (*pid*), and node values in HCP are prefixed with their *pid* (e.g. p_0, p_1, etc.). In Figure 5, an expression $(S_1 \ll S_2) \mid (S_3 \ll S_4)$, where S_1, S_2, S_3, and S_4 are site calls, could be viewed as a process composed by HCP of three levels.

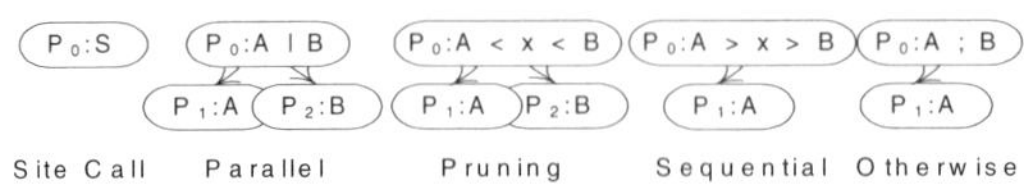

Fig. 4. HCP of general Orc Expressions

P0:(S1 << S2) | (S3 << S4)
P1:S1 << S2
P2:S3 << S4
P3:S1
P4:S2
P5:S3
P6:S4
(S1 << S2) | (S3 << S4)

Fig. 5. An example

Consider a transition $(P, V) \xrightarrow{a} (P', V')$, where a is some action. We abuse the notation by using P and P' to denote the HCPs before and after the transition. In fact, P' could have different tree structures from P, and processes could be added or deleted in P'. In order to have a clear relation of processes between P and P', we define the relation of processes between P and P' over each rule of the operational semantics of *Orc* [27], some of which are presented in Figure 6 for illustration purpose. There are two HCPs under each rule. HCPs on the left and right are the HCPs before and after triggering the action initiated by respective rules. Two process nodes on different HCPs belong to the same process if they have the same *pid* value, and an arrow is used to relate them. Processes that could only be found in HCP on the right or left are the processes that are newly added or deleted respectively. In SEQ1V, the transition of f to f' produces an

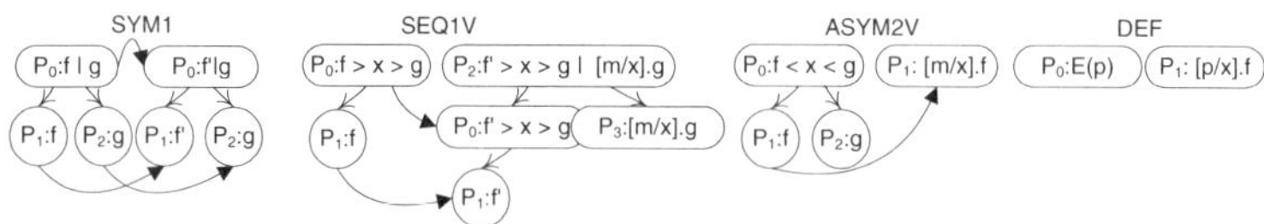

Fig. 6. Relation of Processes between P and P'

$$A = (userdb.put(\text{“}user1\text{”}) \mid userdb.put(\text{“}user2\text{”})) < userdb < Buffer()$$
$$B = (flightdb.put(\text{“}CX510\text{”}) \mid flightdb.put(\text{“}CX511\text{”})) < flightdb < Buffer()$$

Fig. 7. Execution of *Orc* process $P = A \mid B$

output value m, and notation $[m/x].g$ is used to denote that all the instances of variable x in g are replaced with value m.

A site S is *private in* $P_1[P]$, if the reference of site S could not be accessed by all processes other than process P_1 and its descendant processes under HCP graph of global process P. Otherwise, site S is *shared in process* $P_1[P]$. A site S is *permanently private in* $P_1[c]$, if for any configuration $c' = (P', V')$ that is reachable by c, if P' has P_1 as its descendant process, site S must be private in process $P_1[P']$.

The example in Figure 7 shows an *Orc* process $P = A \mid B$. Variables *userdb* and *flightdb* will be initialized to different instances of site *Buffer*, which provides the service of FIFO queue. In process A, two string values *user*1 and *user*2 are enqueued in the buffer referenced by *userdb* concurrently. *Buffer* site that is referenced by *userdb* is *private* in $A[P]$, since *userdb* could only be accessed by process A. Now consider at some level j of HCP graph of global process P, where $j > 1$, we have processes $P_{j_1} = userdb.put(\text{“}user1\text{”})$ and $P_{j_2} = userdb.put(\text{“}user2\text{”})$. *Buffer* site that is referenced by *userdb* is *shared* in $P_{j_1}[P]$, since *userdb* could be accessed by P_{j_2} which is not a descendant process of P_{j_1}.

3 Compositional Partial Order Reduction (CPOR)

The aim of Partial Order Reduction (POR) is to reduce the number of possible orderings of transitions by fixing the order of independent transitions as shown in Figure 1. The notion of *indepedency* plays a central role in POR, which is defined below by following [13].

Definition 5 (Independency). *Two actions a_1 and a_2 in an LTS are independent if for any configuration c such that $a_1, a_2 \in Act(c)$:*
1. $a_2 \in Act(c_1)$ where $c_1 \in Enable(c, a_1)$ and $a_1 \in Act(c_2)$ where $c_2 \in Enable(c, a_2)$,
2. Starting from c, any configuration reachable by executing a_1 followed by a_2, can also be reached by executing a_2 followed by a_1.
Two actions are dependent iff they are not independent.

Given a configuration, an ample set is a subset of outgoing transitions of the configuration which are sufficient for verification, and it is formally defined as follow:

Definition 6 (Ample Set). *Given an LTL-X property ϕ, and a configuration $c \in C$ in TS, an* ample set *is a subset of the enable set which must satisfy the following conditions [5]:*
(A1) Nonemptiness condition: *$Ample(c) = \varnothing$ iff $Enable(c) = \varnothing$.*
(A2) Dependency condition: *Let $c_0 \xrightarrow{a_1} c_1 \xrightarrow{a_2} \ldots \xrightarrow{a_n} c_n \xrightarrow{a} t$ be a finite execution fragment in TS. If a depends on some actions in $AmpleAct(c_0)$, then $a_i \in AmpleAct(c_0)$ for some $0 < i \leq n$.*
(A3) Stutter condition: *If $Ample(c) \neq Enable(c)$, then any $\alpha \in AmpleAct(c)$ is ϕ-invisible.*
(A4) Strong Cycle condition: *Any cycle in $\widehat{TS}$ contains at least one configuration c with $Ample(c)$=$Enable(c)$.*

To be specific, reduced LTS generated by the ample set approach needs to satisfy conditions A1 to A4 in order to preserve the checking of LTL-X properties. However, for the checking of deadlock-freeness, only conditions A1 and A2 are needed [12]. Henceforth, our discussion will be focused on the checking of LTL-X property, but the reader could adjust accordingly for the checking of deadlock-freeness.

Conditions A1, A3, and A4 are relatively easy to check, while condition A2 is the most challenging condition. It is known that checking condition A2 is equivalent to checking the reachablity of a condition in the full transition system TS [8]. It is desirable that we could have an alternative condition A2' that only imposes requirements on the current configuration instead of all traces in TS, and satisfaction of condition A2' would guarantee the satisfaction of condition A2. Given a configuration $c_g = (P_g, V_g)$, and P_d as a descendant process of P_g, with associated configuration $c_d = (P_d, V_d)$, we define a condition A2' that based solely on c_d, and its soundness will be proved in Section 3.3.

(A2')Local Criteria of A2. For all configurations $c_a \in Ample(c_d)$ and $c_a = (p_a, v_a)$ the following two conditions must be satisfied:
(1) The enable site for the action a that enable c_a must be either stateless site, or stateful site *private in* $p_a[P_g]$;
(2) p_a is not a descendant process of the RHS process of some pruning combinators or the LHS process of some sequential combinators.

Notice that we define an ample set as a set of enabled configurations rather than a set of enabled actions like [5]. The reason is due to in references like [5], action-deterministic system is assumed. This entails that for any configuration $c \in C$ and any action $a \in \Sigma$, c has at most one outgoing transition with action a, formally, $c \xrightarrow{a} c'$ and $c \xrightarrow{a} c''$ implies $c' = c''$. Therefore, the enabled configurations could be deduced by the enabled actions. Nonetheless, an *Orc* system is not action-deterministic, the main reason is because some events in *Orc* are internal events that are invisible to the environment. By defining ample set as a set of configurations, with their associated enabled actions, the requirement of action-deterministic system is no longer needed.

3.1 Classic POR and CPOR

Classic POR methods assume that local transitions of a process are dependent, and in the context of HCP, it means that actions within individual processes from level 1

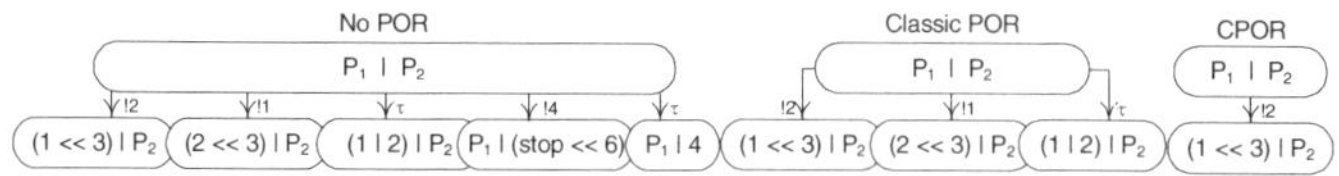

Fig. 8. LTS of *Orc* Process $P = (P_1 \mid P_2), P_1 = ((1 \mid 2) \ll 3), P_2 = (4 \ll 6)$

onwards are *simply assumed to be dependent*. In Figure 8, three LTSs of the process P are given. No POR shows the set of all initial transitions of process P; classic POR shows how the state-space of a parallel composition can be reduced when its component processes are independent; and CPOR reduces the initial actions further by examining internal process structure. For simplicity, system configuration is represented only by process expression. When no POR is applied, all interleavings of transitions are considered, and there are five branches after the initial state. When the classic POR is applied, since P_1 and P_2 are active processes, assume that it checks process P_1 first. All transitions of P_1 are assumed to be dependent by the classic POR. For this reason the resulting ample set of P is $\{((1 \ll 3) \mid P_2), ((2 \ll 3) \mid P_2), ((1 \mid 2) \mid P_2)\}$, which is a valid ample set after checking for conditions A1-A4. Therefore, there are three branches from initial state when classic POR is applied. Different from classic POR, when CPOR is applied, POR is again applied to process $(1 \mid 2)$. We define $Amples(P)$ as a set of ample sets of process P that satisfy conditions A1 and A2, but yet to be checked for conditions A3 and A4. $Amples((1 \mid 2)) = \{\{1\}, \{2\}\}$ and $Amples(P_1)$ is $Amples((1 \mid 2))$ after restructuring by the semantics of P_1, which is $\{\{1 \ll 3\}, \{2 \ll 3\}\}$. $Amples(P)$ is $Amples(P_1)$ after restructuring by the semantics of P, which is $\{\{1 \ll 3 \mid P_2\}, \{2 \ll 3 \mid P_2\}\}$. Each ample set in $Amples(P)$ will then be checked for conditions A3 and A4, and both ample sets turn up to be valid, therefore the ample set $\{1 \ll 3 \mid P_2\}$ is chosen nondeterministically to be the returned value. Thus there is only a single branch after the initial state when CPOR is applied. There are a total of 31, 14 and 5 states for LTS of process P in the situations where no POR, classic POR and CPOR are applied respectively.

3.2 CPOR Algorithm

In this section, we discuss the procedures for CPOR as given in Algorithm 1. *CAmple* returns an ample set which is a subset of enabled configurations from the configuration $c = (P, V)$, and *Visited* is the stack of previously visited configurations. Each configuration c_a in the ample set, where $c_a = (Proc, Val)$, is associated with an action $a_a = (Event, Time, EnableSiteType, EnableSiteId)$, which caused the transition from c to c_a, that is $c \xrightarrow{a_a} c_a$. Henceforth, we use the dot-notation such as $c_a.Proc$, $c_a.Event$, etc to denote the component values of c_a as well as the component values of its associated action a_a. $P.Amples$ (line 2) is a set that stores ample set candidates that satisfy conditions A1 and A2, but yet to check for conditions A3 and A4. Procedure $enableSubProcs(P)$ (line 3) returns the set of enabled child processes according to HCP graph of *Orc* expressions P as shown in Figure 4, with an exception that for sequential process $P_s = A > x > B$, it returns an empty set $\{\}$ instead of $\{A\}$, and for pruning process $P_p = A < x < B$, it returns $\{A\}$ instead of $\{A, B\}$. This exception is applied in order to satisfy the condition A2'(2). Procedure $fillAmpleRec(P,V)$ (line 17) retrieves the ample set candidates under valuation V and assigns it to $P.Amples$. In line 18, $Enable(c)$ where $c = (P,V)$ gives the set of all enabled configurations from the configuration c. Procedure $checkA2Local(config)$ checks whether configuration *config* satisfies A2'(1). Procedure *isPrivate* (line 32) checks whether the site with *config.EnableSiteId* as unique identity is *private* in $Proc[P_G]$ where *Proc* is the process component of *config* and P_G is the argument P of procedure *CAmple* provided by user, which is the global process that has *Proc* as descendant process. The checking is done by syntax analysis. In *Orc*, P is a terminal process (line 20) iff it is a site call. Procedure $composeAmples(P, sP, V)$ (line 26) combines $sP.Amples$ back into $P.Amples$ under valuation V. Procedure *reformAmples* $(sP.Amples, P)$ (line 27) restructures configurations within *sp.Amples* by operational semantics of *Orc*. For example, consider $P = (1 + x < x < 2)$, and $sP = 2$. After making a transition, $sP.Amples = \{\{c\}\}$, where c is the configuration $(stop, \varnothing)$ with $c.Event = !2$. After restructuring by $reformAmples(sP.Amples, P)$, c becomes $(1 + 2, \varnothing)$, and $c.Event = \tau$, according to rule $ASYM2V$ as stated below.

$$\frac{(2,\varnothing) \xrightarrow{!2} (stop,\varnothing)}{(1+x<x<2,\varnothing) \xrightarrow{\tau} (1+2,\varnothing)} \quad [\,ASYM2V\,]$$

When $P = sP$, $reformAmples(sP.Amples, P)$ will simply return $sP.Amples$. Subsequently, ample sets that are empty sets are filtered away (line 28). We continue on the discussion of procedure *CAmple*. To analyze whether an ample set *ample* is valid, the algorithm checks whether all configurations within satisfy conditions A3 and A4 (line 9, 10). If it turns out to be true, a valid ample set is found, and it will be returned immediately (line 14, 15). If no valid ample set has been found in line 3-15, all the enabled configurations from current configuration $c = (P,V)$ will be returned (line 16). Regarding checking of condition A3 (line 9), there are two kind of actions that might not be ϕ-*invisible*, which are actions that contain publication events or actions that involved the update of global variables. Consider the metronome example, if we are checking property like whether *!tick* event can be executed infinitely often, an action a with $a.Event = !tick$ is not ϕ-*invisible*. Another example is when we are checking whether $tickNum < 0$ is true in all situations, where *tickNum* is a global variable, an action a with $a.EnableSiteType = GUpdate$ is not ϕ-*invisible*.

3.3 Soundness

Lemma 1. *Given any two actions a_1 and a_2 in the system, and let s_1 and s_2 be the enable sites of actions a_1 and a_2 respectively. If sites s_1 and s_2 are not descendant processes of the RHS process of some pruning combinators and state objects of sites s_1 and s_2 are disjoint, then action a_1 is independent of action a_2.*

Proof. Actions a_1 and a_2 are dependent only when (a) action a_1 could disable action a_2 or vice versa or (b) starting from the same configuration, transitions a_1a_2 and a_2a_1 could result in different configurations. Situation (a) could happen if site s_1 could possibly modify the state object of site s_2 or vice versa, or when sites s_1 and s_2 are the descendant processes of the RHS process of some pruning combinators. For the latter

```
procedure CAmple(P, V, Visited)
    P.Amples := ∅;
    foreach sP ∈ enableSubProcs(P) do                          // A2'(2)
        fillAmpleRec(sP, V);
        composeAmples(P, sP, V);
        foreach ample ∈ P.Amples do
            validAmple := true;
            foreach config ∈ ample do
                if ¬ config satisfies A3                          // A3
                  ∨ config ∈ Visited                              // A4
                then
                    validAmple := false;
                    break;
            if validAmple then
                return ample;
    return Enable((P, V));
procedure fillAmpleRec(P, V)
    P.Amples := {{config : Enable((P, V))
                | checkA2Local(config)}};                         // A2'(1)
    if P is terminal process then
        composeAmples(P, P, V);
    else
        foreach sP ∈ enableSubProcs(P) do
            fillAmpleRec(sP, V);
            composeAmples(P, sP, V);
procedure composeAmples(P, sP, V)
    P.Amples := P.Amples ∪ reformAmples(sP.Amples, P);
    P.Amples := P.Amples \ {∅};                                   // A1
procedure checkA2Local(config)
    return(config.EnableSiteType is stateless ∨
            config.EnableSiteType is stateful ∧
            isPrivate(config.EnableSiteId)) ;
```

Algorithm 1: CAmple

case, consider $x < x < (s_1 \mid s_2)$, if site s_1 published a value, site s_2 will be disabled immediately. Nevertheless, this case is ruled out by the assumption. Condition (b) could happen when sites s_1 and s_2 contain a common state object which they may modify and depend on. Therefore, conditions (a) and (b) are the results of having a common state object between sites s_1 and s_2. This implies that if sites s_1 and s_2 have disjoint state objects, actions a_1 and a_2 are independent to each other. □**end.**

Lemma 2. *Given a configuration $c = (P,V)$, and process P_1 as a descendant process of P. If P_1 is not a descendant process of the LHS process of some sequential combinators, then a site S that is private in $P_1[P]$, is permanently private in $P_1[c]$ as well.*

Proof. We prove by inspecting each rule in the operational semantics of *Orc* [29]. Only rule SEQ1V of operational semantics of *Orc* is possible to transfer the site reference from a process p to other processes, while retaining process p. Consider HCPs under rule SEQ1V in Figure 6, a site S that is private in $P_1[P_0]$ may not be private in $P_1[P_2]$, since P_3 might have the access to the reference of site S. Therefore, if we exclude this situation by assuming P_1 is not a descendant process of the LHS process of some sequential combinators, we prove the lemma. □ **end.**

We define several notions here. Given a configuration $c_g = (P_g, V_g)$, and P_d as a descendant process of P_g, with associated configuration $c_d = (P_d, V_d)$. $\mathbb{C}_{c_g}$ is defined as the set of configurations reachable by c_g in LTS; $\mathbb{P}_{c_g}$ is defined as $\{P \mid c = (P,V) \wedge c \in \mathbb{C}_{c_g}\}$; $HCP(\mathbb{P}_{c_g})$ is defined as the HCPs for each global process in $\mathbb{P}_{c_g}$; $\mathbb{H}_{c_g}$ is defined as the union of processes within each HCP in $HCP(\mathbb{P}_{c_g})$; $\mathbb{H}_{c_g}[P_d]$ is the set of processes that contain process P_d and its corresponding descendant processes in respective HCPs in $HCP(\mathbb{P}_{c_g})$, and $\mathbb{H}_{c_g}[P_d] \subseteq \mathbb{H}_{c_g}$.

Lemma 3. *If an action $a \in Act(c_d)$ satisfies A2' then the action is independent of any action $b \in Act(c')$, where $c' = (P', V')$, such that $P' = \mathbb{H}_{c_g}/\mathbb{H}_{c_g}[P_d]$, and V' is any valuation.*

Proof. Assume an action $a \in Act(c_d)$ satisfies A2', and assume the action is dependent to an action $b \in Act(c')$. Let sites s_a and s_b be the enable sites of actions a and b respectively. By A2'(1), site s_a is a stateless site or stateful site that is private in $p_a[P_g]$. Site s_a could not be a stateless site since a stateless site does not have a state object, and thus action a is trivially independent to any actions in the system by Lemma 1 and A2'(2). Therefore, site s_a is a stateful site that is private in $p_a[P_g]$. By Lemma 2 and A2'(2), site s_a is also permanently private in $p_a[c_g]$. By definition, state objects of site s_a and s_b are disjoint. By Lemma 1 and A2'(2), actions a and b are independent, a contradiction. □ **end.**

Theorem 1. *If any action $a \in Act(c_d)$ satisfies A2', then $AmpleAct(c_g) = Act(c_d)$ satisfies A2 for all traces in TS_{c_g}.*

Proof. Assume any action $a \in Act(c_d)$ satisfies A2', and $AmpleAct(c_g) = Act(c_d)$ does not satisfies A2 for some traces in TS_{c_g}. This means that there exists a finite execution fragment $l = c \xrightarrow{a_1} c_1 \xrightarrow{a_2} \ldots \xrightarrow{a_n} c_n \xrightarrow{a_{n+1}} \ldots$,where actions $a_1, \ldots, a_n \notin Act(c_d)$ and action a_{n+1} depends on some actions in $AmpleAct(c_g) = Act(c_d)$. Since Lemma 3 holds, action a_{n+1} must be from $PAct(c_d)/Act(c_d)$, we denote the enable site of action a_{n+1} as S_{n+1}. Since site S_{n+1} is disabled initially in c_d, it means that it is enabled later by a site call from a process $p' \in \mathbb{H}_{c_g}/\mathbb{H}_{c_g}[P_d]$. For sites in process P_d, site calls from a process $p' \in \mathbb{H}_{c_g}/\mathbb{H}_{c_g}[P_d]$ could only enable the sites that are shared in $p_d[P'_g]$, where P'_g is the global process of p'. We denote the set of state objects of the sites that are shared in $p_d[P'_g]$ as $\mathbb{D}_{share}$, and state object of S_{n+1} is in $\mathbb{D}_{share}$. On the other hand, by Lemma 2 and A2'(2), any action $a \in Act(c_d)$ is enabled by a site that is permanently private in

$p_a[c_g]$. By definition, state object of the enable site of any action $a \in Act(c_d)$ must not be found in $\mathbb{D}_{share}$. Therefore, action a_{n+1} is independent to all actions in $Act(c_d)$ by Lemma 1 and A2'(2), a contradiction. □ **end.**

Theorem 2. *Algorithm CAmple is sound.*

Proof. To show the soundness of the algorithm, we need to show that the returned ample set satisfies conditions A1-A4. Checking of condition A1 is done at line 28. Conditions A3 and A4 are checked at the global process level (line 9, 10) at *CAmple* since they are only concerned with the property of global process configurations, i.e. whether their actions are ϕ-*invisible* and whether they have been visited before. By Theorem 1, satisfaction of condition A2' leads to satisfaction of condition A2. Condition A2'(1) is checked at line 19. Condition A2'(2) is guaranteed by constraining the procedure *enableSubProcs*(P) (line 3) not to return LHS process of a sequential process and RHS process of a pruning process. □ **end.**

4 Evaluation

Our approach has been realized in the ORC Module of Process Analysis Toolkit (PAT) [1]. PAT is designed for systematic validation of distributed/concurrent systems using state-of-the-art model checking techniques [25,26]. It can be considered as a framework for manufacturing model-checkers. The data are obtained with Intel Core 2 Quad 9550 CPU at 2.83GHz and 4GB RAM. ORC module supports verification of deadlock-freeness and Linear Temporal Logic (LTL) [24] property base on [21]. In Table 1 (A), three situations are compared: *CPOR* is the scenario where Compositional POR approach as described in Section 3 is applied; *POR* is the scenario where the classic approach of POR that only considered the concurrency of processes at level 1 is applied; *No POR/CPOR* is the scenario where neither POR nor CPOR is applied. In the table, ✓ and ✗ means the property is satisfied and violated respectively. The results are omitted (shown as "-") for states and times, if it takes more than eight hours for verification.

Model *Concurrent Quicksort* is a variant of the classic quicksort algorithm and emphasizes its concurrent perspective, as described in [18]. For model *Concurrent Quicksort*, *size* denotes the number of elements in the array to be sorted. Property (1.1) is used to verify whether elements in the array will eventually be sorted, and once sorted, it will remain sorted. Model *Readers-Writers Problem* is a famous computer science problem as described in [9], for which *size* denotes the number of readers. Property (2.1) verifies whether the model is possible to reach a state that violates the mutual exclusion condition. Model *Auction Management* is the case study in [2] which includes the use of external services. Please refer to [27] for the details of modeling external services in our work. Property (3.1) is used to verify that if an item has a bid on it, it will eventually be sold; Property (3.2) is used to verify that every item is always sold to a unique winner. Part (B) is the comparison of the effectiveness of our model checker for Orc and that of the model checker Maude [3,4]. Figures for number of rewrites and time usage for Maude model checker are from [4], which was run under 2.0GHz dual-core node with 4GB of memory. The experiments show that CPOR provides greater-scale reduction than classic POR for HCPs. In addition, our implementation with CPOR is more efficient than Maude [3,4].

Table 1. Performance evaluation on model checking *Orc*'s model

(A) Comparing difference POR methods

Model	Property	Size		States			Time(s)		
				CPOR	POR	No POR/CPOR	CPOR	POR	No POR/CPOR
Concurrent Quicksort	(1.1)	2	✓	58	1532	10594	0.08	1.13	5
		3	✓	69	3611	36794	0.11	8.48	74
		5	✓	237	-	-	0.68	-	-
Readers-Writers Problem	(2.1)	2	✗	106	1645	7620	0.07	1.12	4
		3	✗	152	18247	142540	0.11	14.86	101
		10	✗	472	-	-	0.49	-	-
Auction Management	(3.1)	N.A.	✓	869	-	-	0.6	-	-
	(3.2)	N.A.	✓	883	-	-	0.75	-	-

(B) Comparing Our Model Checker and Maude

Model	Property		States/Rewrites		Time(s)	
			Our	Maude	Our	Maude
Auction Management	(3.1)	✓	869	7052663	0.6	14.4
	(3.2)	✓	883	8613539	0.75	19.8

5 Related Work

This work is related to research on applying POR to hierarchical concurrent systems. Lang et al. [20], proposed a variant of POR using compositional confluence detection. The proposed method works by analyzing the transitions of the individual process graphs as well as the synchronization structure to identify the confluent transitions in the system graph. Transitions within the individual process graphs (at level 1) are assumed to be dependent, thus all possible transitions will be generated for individual process graphs. While in our work, we further exploit the independency within each process recursively. Basten et al. [6], proposed an approach to enhance POR via process clustering. The proposed method combines processes (at level 1) in clusters, and applies partial order reduction at proper cluster-level to achieve more reduction. Krimm et al. [19], proposed an approach to compose the processes (at level 1) of an asynchronous communicating system incrementally, and at the same time apply POR for the generated LTS. Both approaches of [6] and [19] have the assumption that the local transitions of each process (at level 1) are dependent. To the best of the author's knowledge, there is no existing work that applies POR in the context for HCP. The reason for not including orthogonal approaches such as [20,6,19] for comparisons in Section 4 is because they optimized POR by restructuring or leveraging the information of processes at level 1, while CPOR is aimed to extend POR for HCP. This means that they could be similarly used to optimize CPOR, in the same way they are used to optimize classic POR.

This work is also related to research on verifying *Orc*. Liu et al. [10], proposed an approach to translate the *Orc* language to Timed Automata, and use model checker like UPPAAL for verification. However, no reduction is considered. Alturki et al. [2,3], proposed an approach to translate the *Orc* language to rewriting logic for verification. An operational semantics of *Orc* in rewriting logic is defined, which is proved to be semantically equivalent to the operational semantics of *Orc*. To make the formal analysis more efficient, a reduction semantics of *Orc* in rewriting logic is further defined, which is proved to be semantically equivalent to the operational semantics of *Orc* in rewriting logic. We have compared the efficiency of our model checker with theirs in Section 4.

6 Conclusion

In this paper, we proposed a new method, called Compositional Partial Order Reduction (CPOR), which aims to provide the reduction with a greater scale than current partial order reduction methods in the context of hierarchical concurrent processes. It has been used in model checking *Orc* programs. Experiment results show that CPOR provide significant state-reduction for *Orc* programs. There are many languages other than *Orc* that could have the structure of HCP such as process algebra languages (e.g. CSP [14]) or service orchestration languages (e.g. BPEL [16]). Similar to classic POR method, the main challenge of applying CPOR for a language is to find an appropriate local criteria of A2 for that language. In addition, Algorithm 1 in the paper needs to be adjusted according to the semantics of the specific language. As for future works, we would further evaluate CPOR by applying it for verifying programs in other languages.

References

1. PAT: Process Analysis Toolkit, `http://www.comp.nus.edu.sg/~pat/research/`
2. AlTurki, M., Meseguer, J.: Real-time rewriting semantics of orc. In: PPDP, pp. 131–142 (2007)
3. AlTurki, M., Meseguer, J.: Reduction semantics and formal analysis of orc programs. Electr. Notes Theor. Comput. Sci. 200(3), 25–41 (2008)
4. AlTurki, M., Meseguer, J.: Dist-Orc: A Rewriting-based Distributed Implementation of Orc with Formal Analysis. Technical report, The University of Illinois at Urbana-Champaign (April 2010), `https://www.ideals.illinois.edu/handle/2142/15414`
5. Baier, C., Katoen, J.P.: Principles of Model Checking. The MIT Press, Cambridge (2007)
6. Basten, T., Bosnacki, D.: Enhancing partial-order reduction via process clustering. In: ASE, pp. 245–253 (2001)
7. Clarke, E.M., Filkorn, T., Jha, S.: Exploiting Symmetry In Temporal Logic Model Checking. In: Courcoubetis, C. (ed.) CAV 1993. LNCS, vol. 697, pp. 450–462. Springer, Heidelberg (1993)
8. Clarke, E.M., Grumberg, O., Peled, D.A.: Model Checking. The MIT Press, Cambridge (2000)
9. Courtois, P.J., Heymans, F., Parnas, D.L.: Concurrent control with "readers" and "writers". Commun. ACM 14(10), 667–668 (1971)
10. Dong, J.S., Liu, Y., Sun, J., Zhang, X.: Verification of computation orchestration via timed automata. In: Liu, Z., Kleinberg, R.D. (eds.) ICFEM 2006. LNCS, vol. 4260, pp. 226–245. Springer, Heidelberg (2006)
11. Emerson, E.A., Sistla, A.P.: Utilizing Symmetry when Model-Checking under Fairness Assumptions: An Automata-Theoretic Approach. ACM Transactions on Programming Languages and Systems (TOPLAS) 19(4), 617–638 (1997)

12. Godefroid, P.: Partial-Order Methods for the Verification of Concurrent Systems. LNCS, vol. 1032. Springer, Heidelberg (1996)
13. Håkansson, J., Pettersson, P.: Partial order reduction for verification of real-time components. In: Raskin, J.-F., Thiagarajan, P.S. (eds.) FORMATS 2007. LNCS, vol. 4763, pp. 211–226. Springer, Heidelberg (2007)
14. Hoare, C.A.R.: Communicating Sequential Processes. International Series on Computer Science. Prentice-Hall, Englewood Cliffs (1985)
15. Holzmann, G.J.: On-the-fly model checking. ACM Comput. Surv. 28(4es), 120 (1996)
16. Jordan, D., Evdemon, J.: Web Services Business Process Execution Language Version 2.0. (April 2007), `http://www.oasis-open.org/specs/#wsbpelv2.0`
17. Kitchin, D., Quark, A., Cook, W., Misra, J.: The orc programming language. In: Lee, D., Lopes, A., Poetzsch-Heffter, A. (eds.) FMOODS 2009. LNCS, vol. 5522, pp. 1–25. Springer, Heidelberg (2009)
18. Kitchin, D., Quark, A., Misra, J.: Quicksort: Combining concurrency, recursion, and mutable data structures. Technical report, The University of Texas at Austin, Department of Computer Sciences
19. Krimm, J.-P., Mounier, L.: Compositional state space generation with partial order reductions for asynchronous communicating systems. In: Graf, S. (ed.) TACAS 2000. LNCS, vol. 1785, pp. 266–282. Springer, Heidelberg (2000)
20. Lang, F., Mateescu, R.: Partial order reductions using compositional confluence detection. In: Cavalcanti, A., Dams, D.R. (eds.) FM 2009. LNCS, vol. 5850, pp. 157–172. Springer, Heidelberg (2009)
21. Liu, Y.: Model Checking Concurrent and Real-time Systems: the PAT Approach. PhD thesis, National University of Singapore (2010)
22. Peled, D.: Combining partial order reductions with on-the-fly model-checking. In: Dill, D.L. (ed.) CAV 1994. LNCS, vol. 818, pp. 377–390. Springer, Heidelberg (1994)
23. Peled, D.: Ten years of partial order reduction. In: Vardi, M.Y. (ed.) CAV 1998. LNCS, vol. 1427, pp. 17–28. Springer, Heidelberg (1998)
24. Sistla, A.P., Clarke, E.M.: The complexity of propositional linear temporal logics. J. ACM 32(3), 733–749 (1985)
25. Sun, J., Liu, Y., Dong, J.S., Pang, J.: PAT: Towards flexible verification under fairness. In: Bouajjani, A., Maler, O. (eds.) CAV 2009. LNCS, vol. 5643, pp. 709–714. Springer, Heidelberg (2009)
26. Sun, J., Liu, Y., Roychoudhury, A., Liu, S., Dong, J.S.: Fair model checking with process counter abstraction. In: Cavalcanti, A., Dams, D.R. (eds.) FM 2009. LNCS, vol. 5850, pp. 123–139. Springer, Heidelberg (2009)
27. Tan, T.H., Liu, Y., Sun, J., Dong, J.S.: Compositional Partial Order Reduction for Model Checking Concurrent Systems. Technical report, National Univ. of Singapore (April 2011), `http://www.comp.nus.edu.sg/pat/fm/cpor/CPORTR.pdf`
28. Valmari, A.: The state explosion problem. In: Petri Nets, pp. 429–528 (1996)
29. Wehrman, I., Kitchin, D., Cook, W., Misra, J.: A timed semantics of orc. Theoretical Computer Science 402(2-3), 234–248 (2008)

Domain-Driven Probabilistic Analysis of Programmable Logic Controllers

Hehua Zhang[1], Yu Jiang[2], William N.N. Hung[3], Xiaoyu Song[4], and Ming Gu[1]

[1] School of Software, TNLIST, Tsinghua University, China
[2] School of Computer Science, TNLIST, Tsinghua University, China
[3] Synopsys Inc., Mountain View, California, USA
[4] Dept. ECE, Portland State University, Oregon, USA

Abstract. Programmable Logic Controllers are widely used in industry. Reliable PLCs are vital to many critical applications. This paper presents a novel symbolic approach for analysis of PLC systems. The main components of the approach consists of: (1) calculating the uncertainty characterization of the PLC systems, (2) abstracting the PLC system as a Hidden Markov Model, (3) solving the Hidden Markov Model using domain knowledge, (4) integrating the solved Hidden Markov Model and the uncertainty characterization to form an integrated (regular) Markov Model, and (5) harnessing probabilistic model checking to analyze properties on the resultant Markov Model. The framework provides expected performance measures of the PLC systems by automated analytical means without expensive simulations. Case studies on an industrial automated system are performed to demonstrate the effectiveness of our approach.

Keywords: PLC, Hidden Markov Model, Probabilistic Analysis.

1 Introduction

Programmable Logic Controllers are widely used in industry. Many PLC applications are safety critical. There are a lot of studies on the modeling and verification of PLC programs. Most of them transfer PLC programs to automata [3,9,1] or Petri nets [7]. Formal methods [16,6,14]are also proposed for analysis. Most of these methods consider the static individual PLC program that is isolated from its operating environment and verify some functional properties based on traversing the transferred model. The existent deterministic analysis of PLC programs are valuable, but the uncertain errors caused by noise, environment, or hardware should not be neglected [11].

In this paper, we present a symbolic framework for the formal analysis of PLC system.[1] We develop a probabilistic method to model the inherent uncertainty property of the PLC system. Then, we abstract the PLC system as a Hidden Markov Model, and generalize the Baum-Welch algorithm to solve the Hidden

[1] This research is sponsored in part by NSFC Program (No.91018015, No.60811130468) and 973 Program (No.2010CB328003) of China.

S. Qin and Z. Qiu (Eds.): ICFEM 2011, LNCS 6991, pp. 115–130, 2011.

Markov Model using domain knowledge of its dedicated operating environment. After that, we combine the solved Hidden Markov Model with uncertainty characterization of the PLC system to form an integrated Markov model. We harness probabilistic model checking to analyze properties on the regular Markov Model through PRISM [8]. Our framework also allows us to obtain some performance measures of the PLC system, such as the reliability and some other time related properties. Case studies demonstrate the effectiveness of our approaches.

2 Preliminaries

Ladder diagram (LD) is a widely used graphical programming language for PLCs. The language itself can be seen as a set of connections between logical checkers (contacts) and actuators (coils). If a path can be traced between the left side of the rung and the output, through asserted contacts, the rung is true and the output coil storage bit is asserted true. If no path can be traced, then the output coil storage bit is asserted false. Fig. 1 shows a simple ladder program with some common instructions. It is made up of four ladder rungs.

The symbol $-|\ |-$ is a normal open contact, representing a primary input. When the value of SW_1 is 1, the contact stays in the closed state, and the current flows through the contact. The symbol $-|/|-$ is a normal close contact. When the value of SW_3 is 0, the contact stays in the closed state, and the current flows through the contact. $-|\ |-|\ |-$ represents a serial connection of two kinds of contacts. Similarly, in the third rung, b_1 and V_3 are connected in parallel. When at least one value of them is 1, the current can flow through the trace. There is also a timer instruction in Fig. 1. More details can be found in [10].

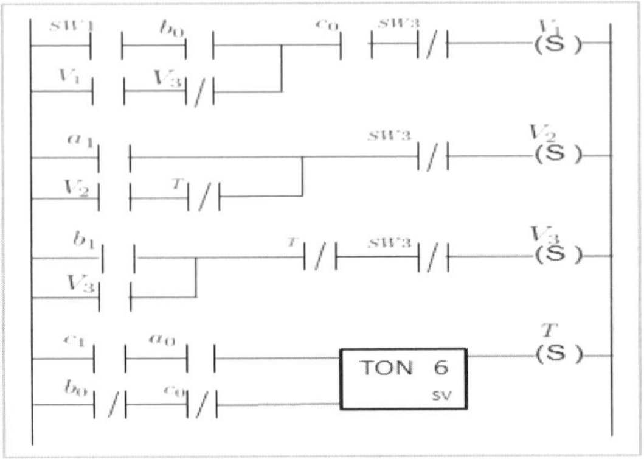

Fig. 1. A simple ladder

The simplest Markov model is the Markov chain which is a random process with the property that the next state depends only on the current state. It models the state of a system with a random variable that changes over time. A discrete time Markov model can be defined as a tuple $\langle S, \pi, A, L \rangle$, where

- $S = \{S_1 \cdots S_N\}$ is a set of states. We use q_t to denote the state of the system at time $t (t \in N^+)$.
- $\pi = \{\pi_1 \cdots \pi_N\}$ is the initial state distribution, where $\pi_i = Pr[q_1 = S_i]$ is the probability that the system state at time unit 1 is S_i.
- $A = \{a_{ij}\} (\forall i, j \in N)$ is the state transition probability matrix for the system and $a_{ij} = Pr[q_{t+1} = S_j | q_t = S_i]$.
- L is a set of atomic propositions labeling states and transitions.

In a regular Markov model, the state is directly visible to the observer, and therefore the state transition probabilities are the only parameters. This model is too restrictive to be applicable to many problems of interest. Here, we extend the concept of Markov model to include the case where the observation is a probabilistic function of the state. In a Hidden Markov Model, the state is not directly visible, but the output, dependent on the state, is visible. Each state has a probability distribution over the possible output observations. Hence the sequence of observations generated by a hidden Markov model gives certain information about the sequence of states.

Formally, a Hidden Markov Model is defined as a tuple $M = \langle S, O, \pi, A, B, L \rangle$. The items S, π, A and L are defined as above. The remaining two items of the tuple are defined as:

- $O = \{O_1 \cdots O_M\}$ is a set of observations that the system can generate. We use v_t to denote the observation generated by the system at time $t (t \in N^+)$.
- $B = \{b_{ik}\}$ is the observation state probability matrix of the system: $b_{ik} = Pr[v_t = O_k | q_t = S_i] (\forall S_i \in S, \forall O_k \in O)$, which means the probability that the system generates observation O_k in state S_i.

Given an observation sequence $Q_o = O_1 O_2 \cdots O_t$, in our framework, we need to consider the following problem:

- How to adjust the model parameters A, B to maximize $Pr(Q_o | M)$.

The problem has been solved by an iterative procedure such as the Baum-Welch method [2,5] and equivalently the EM method [4] or gradient techniques [12]. In this paper, we generalize Baum-Welch method with additional weights.

3 Symbolic Framework

We present a symbolic framework for the formal analysis of PLC systems. The framework is applicable from the implementation process to the deployment process of the system. It contains three main procedures: (1) Uncertainty characterization of a PLC ladder program, which can reflect the inner quality of the system. (2) Hidden Markov Model construction and its solution, which can reflect the actual operating environment of the PLC system. (3) Reward based probabilistic model checking to analyze the performance properties of the system on the integrated Markov model. The components of the framework are shown in Fig. 2.

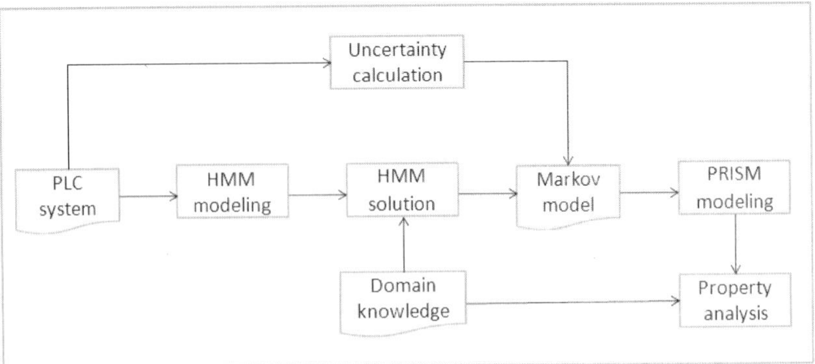

Fig. 2. Validation Process

3.1 Modeling Uncertainty of PLC Systems

In a PLC, the program is executed through periodic scanning. In each cycle, the inputs are first sampled and read. Then, the program instructions are executed. Finally, the outputs are updated and sent to the actuators. The uncertainty characterization calculation refers to evaluating the effects of errors caused by input sampling and program execution. The sampling error happens when the actual input is 1 (or 0), but the sensor samples a 0 (or 1). Program execution error happens when the output of each ladder logic is 1 (or 0), mainly for the *AND* logic ($a \wedge b$) and *OR* logic ($a \vee b$), but the actual output of the logic execution turns out to be 0 (or 1). The probability of these two kinds of errors depends on noise, environment, hardware, etc.

The uncertainty calculation can be divided into three steps. We first define the output of each rung on the logic checkers and the output of instructions such as timer and counter. They are connected by ladder logic ($a \wedge b$, $a \vee b$). Then, we build an abstract syntax tree (AST) for the output expression, with which we can give a topological sort for each ladder logic ($\wedge(a,b)$, $\vee(a,b)$). Finally, we can use the third algorithm presented in the technical report [17] to process each node in the abstract tree, until we arrive at the root node. The uncertainty characterization of this ladder rung can be described as follows:

$$f(o) = P_o^0 P_\varepsilon(0 \to 1) + P_o^1 P_\varepsilon(1 \to 0)$$

The first factor denotes the probability that the output of this ladder rung should be 0 (denoted by P_o^0), but the root node of the abstract syntax tree propagates a $P_\varepsilon(0 \to 1)$ error. The second factor is similar. An example is shown in Fig. 3. Because each ladder logic diagram may have many ladder rungs, we can get the following theorem:

Theorem 1. *The uncertainty characterization of the whole PLC system f is*

$$f = 1 - \prod_{i=1}^{i=n} (1 - f(o)_n)$$

Where $f(o)_n$ means the uncertainty characterization of the n-th ladder rung.

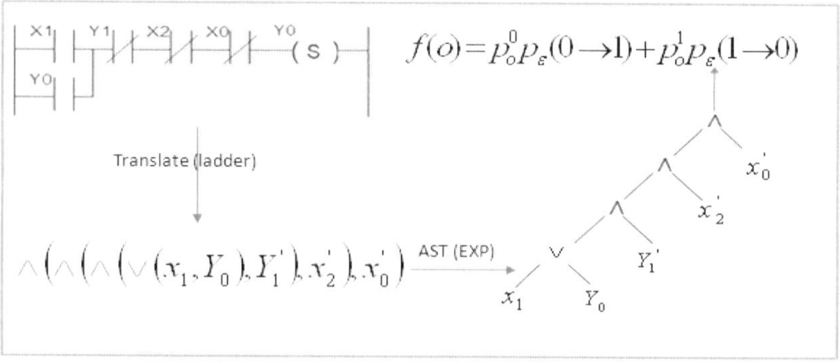

Fig. 3. Uncertainty Calculation

3.2 Construction of Hidden Markov Model

Unlike the previous methods which consider an individual PLC program that is isolated from its operating environment, we construct a Hidden Markov Model (HMM) to reflect the control principle of the whole PLC system. Our model manifests the dynamic characteristics of all the possible execution paths of the PLC system. The HMM depicts how the PLC system transfers from one state to another with a hidden probability.

As mentioned in Section 2, a HMM can be defined as a tuple $\langle S, O, \pi, A, B, L \rangle$. We abstract the PLC system as a tuple. S is the set of normal states of the PLC system. Each state of the PLC system is composed of the states of the physical devices which are actuated by the PLC ladder program. Then, each state of the PLC system can be identified by the primary outputs of the PLC ladder rungs. O contains the observations corresponding to the state set S. It is a probabilistic function of the state and can be abstracted from basic functional requirements and from events corresponding to the physical outputs of the system. L is a set of atomic propositions $\{L\}$ labeling states and transitions. Since the PLC works in a periodic scanning manner and there may be timer instructions in the ladder logic diagram, we extend the label with time attribute to reflect the time property of the PLC system. The recursive syntax of the label is defined as:

$$L \rightarrow I|T|O; \; I \rightarrow I0|I1|0|1; \; T \rightarrow n \in N^{+}$$

It is composed of three components. The first component I is the sequence of the primary inputs of the PLC ladder program. The sequence will determine the outgoing transitions of each state. The second component T is the time attribute related to the timer instructions in the ladder program, which means the corresponding state S_i transfers to state S_j with a time delay T. The value of T is a positive integer N^{+}. O is the set of observations that the primary input will trigger in the dedicated state S_j of the transition.

3.3 Solving the Hidden Markov Model

After we obtain the knowledge about the PLC systems' observations, states, and transitions among those states, we need to solve the unknown parameters of the HMM, especially for the parameters of the state transition probability A. We give two methods to solve the HMM by using three kinds of domain knowledge. If the domain knowledge is from a domain expert or the runtime monitoring method, the problem can be addressed by the extended Baum-Welch algorithm.

Extended Baum-Welch Method. The extended Baum-Welch algorithm is based on two kinds of domain knowledge. The first kind of knowledge relies on domain expert. In a particular application, this can be done by asking the domain expert to directly provide a set of sequences of the PLC system's observations. The observation sequences are representative of the expert's knowledge of the PLC system's actual operating environment. The second kind of domain knowledge is from runtime monitoring. If the PLC has been deployed on the system, the system is already in use, we can observe the execution of the system many times to attain the observations.

After we get the observation sequence $O(O_1O_2 \cdots O_tO_{t+1}O_{t+2} \cdots O_T)$ of the HMM from time unit 1 to T, we need to adjust the model parameters $M\ (A, B, \pi)$ to maximize the probability of the observation sequence. The Baum-Welch algorithm applies a dynamic programming technique to estimate the parameters. It makes use of a forward-backward procedure based on two variables:

$$\alpha_t(i) = P(O_1O_2 \cdots O_t, q_t = S_i|M) \qquad \beta_t(i) = P(O_{t+1}O_{t+2} \cdots O_T|q_t = S_i, M)$$

$\alpha_t(i)$ is the probability of the partial observation sequence $O_1O_2 \cdots O_t$, and system model is in state S_i at time unit t, and $\beta_t(i)$ is the probability of the partial observation sequence from $t+1$ to the end, given state S_i at time unit t and the model M. We compute the parameter a_{ij} as follows:

$$\gamma_t(i) = P(q_t = S_i|O, M) = \frac{\alpha_t(i)\beta_t(i)}{\sum\limits_{i=1}^{N} \alpha_t(i)\beta_t(i)}$$

$\gamma_t(i)$ is the probability of the system in state S_i at time t, given the observation sequence O and the model M.

$$\xi_t(i,j) = P(q_t = S_i, q_{t+1} = S_j|O, M) = \frac{\alpha_t(i)a_{ij}b_j(O_{t+1})\beta_{t+1}(j)}{\sum\limits_{i=1}^{N}\sum\limits_{j=1}^{N} \alpha_t(i)a_{ij}b_j(O_{t+1})\beta_{t+1}(j)}$$

$\xi_t(i,j)$ is the probability of the system in state S_i at time t and in state S_j at time t+1, respectively, with M and O. $b_j(O_{t+1})$ denotes the probability that the system is in state j, and the observations is O_{t+1}.

Then, the expected number of all the transitions from S_i and the transitions from S_i to S_j can be defined as $\sum_{t=1}^{T-1} \gamma_t(i)$ and $\sum_{t=1}^{T-1} \xi_t(i,j)$, respectively. The expected number of observing observation O_k in state S_i can be defined as $\sum_{t=1,v_t=O_k}^{T} \gamma_t(i)$. For a single observation sequence, the iterative calculation formulas for state transition and observation probabilities can be defined as:

$$\overline{a_{ij}} = \frac{\sum\limits_{t=1}^{T-1} \xi_t(i,j)}{\sum\limits_{t=1}^{T-1} \gamma_t^(i)} \qquad \overline{b_{ij}} = \frac{\sum\limits_{t=1,v_t=O_j}^{T} \gamma_t(i)}{\sum\limits_{t=1}^{T} \gamma_t(i)}$$

The numerator of $\overline{a_{ij}}$ denotes the expected number of transitions from state S_i to S_j, the denominator of $\overline{a_{ij}}$ denotes the expected number of transitions going out of state S_i. The numerator of $\overline{b_{ij}}$ denotes expected number of times in state S_i and observing symbol O_j, the denominator of $\overline{b_{ij}}$ denotes the expected number of times in state S_i.

For different observation sequences $Os = [O^1, O^2 \cdots, O^s]$, where $O^k = [O_1^k, O_2^k \cdots O_T^k]$ is the k_{th} observation sequence, the other symbols are similar. We need to adjust the model parameter of model M to maximize $P(Os|M)$. We extend the method presented in [13] with a weight W_k for each O^k. W_k is the frequency of the sequence O^k. We define $P_k = P(O^k|M)$ and $P(Os|M) = \prod_{k=1}^{k} P_k W_k$. Then, the iterative calculation formulas for state transition and observation probabilities can be changed to:

$$\overline{a_{ij}} = \frac{\sum\limits_{k=1}^{k} \frac{1}{P_k W_k} \sum\limits_{t=1}^{T-1} \xi_t^k(i,j)}{\sum\limits_{k=1}^{k} \frac{1}{P_k W_k} \sum\limits_{t=1}^{T-1} \gamma_t^k(i)} \qquad \overline{b_{ij}} = \frac{\sum\limits_{k=1}^{k} \frac{1}{P_k W_k} \sum\limits_{t=1,v_t=O_j}^{T} \gamma_t^k(i)}{\sum\limits_{k=1}^{k} \frac{1}{P_k W_k} \sum\limits_{t=1}^{T} \gamma_t^k(i)}$$

The meaning of the numerator and denominator of the extended formulas are the same with the original formula described above. Then, we can choose an initial model $M = (A, B, \pi)$ and use the initial model to compute the right side of the iterative calculation formulas. Once we get the new model $\overline{M} = (\overline{A}, \overline{B}, \pi)$, we can use $\overline{M}$ to replace M and repeat this procedure until the probability of observation sequence $P(Os|\overline{M})$ and $P(Os|M)$ are equal or $|P(Os|\overline{M}) - P(Os|M)| < \theta$, θ is the precision limit you want.

With these two methods, we can build the solved HMM to show the real operating environment in an particular application. We can get value of the state transition matrix, each element a_{ij} is also identified with a label L, $L \rightarrow I/T/O$.

3.4 Construction of Combined Regular Markov Model

The uncertainty characterization of the PLC system itself shows the inherent behaviors of the system, which evaluates the effects of the errors from input sampling and the errors from program execution. The solved HMM shows the operating environment of the system in a particular application with the use of normal states and the transitions. Then, we construct a new Markov model to combine these two properties.

The first step is to add the abnormal state caused by the uncertainty characterization. Since the system would go into an abnormal state from any normal states, we build an abnormal state (U) for all normal states (S_n). When a normal state transits to an abnormal state, it can be recovered by the system itself or by human intervention, and reset to the initial state. We also need to add these two kinds of transitions into the solved HMM. Then, we can get all the nodes and transitions of the new Markov model M'.

The second step is to initiate the transition matrix of the new model M'. We need to assign values to different transitions. The probability of a normal state transmitting to the abnormal state depends on the value of the uncertainty calculation. The recovering transitions depends on the design of the system or the workers. After we add these states and transitions to the matrix A, the value of a_{ij} based on operating environment needs to be adjusted, by multiplying with a coefficient. The matrix A and A' are given by:

$$\mathbf{A} = \begin{pmatrix} a_{00} & a_{01} & \dots & a_{0n} \\ a_{10} & a_{11} & \dots & a_{1n} \\ \vdots & \vdots & \ddots & \vdots \\ a_{n0} & a_{n1} & \dots & a_{nn} \end{pmatrix} \quad \mathbf{A}^{'} = \begin{pmatrix} a_{00}(1-f) & a_{01}(1-f) & \dots & a_{0n}(1-f) & f \\ a_{10}(1-f) & a_{11}(1-f) & \dots & a_{1n}(1-f) & f \\ \vdots & \vdots & \ddots & \vdots & \\ a_{n0}(1-f) & a_{n2}(1-f) & \dots & a_{nn}(1-f) & f \\ r_{U0} & 0 & \dots & 0 & 1-r_{U0} \end{pmatrix}$$

In the new matrix, the last row and the last column are for the abnormal state U, the remaining rows and columns are for the normal states S_n. The probability from the normal states to the abnormal state is f, which is the value of the uncertainty characterization. We know that the error probability is the same for all the normal states, because uncertainty characterization f is the inner quality of the PLC ladder program. The recovering transition probability from abnormal state U to the initial state is r_{U0}, The system will remain in the abnormal state with a probability $1 - r_{U0}$ in case of some uncertainty that can-not be recovered by the system or the operators. The transition probability between the normal states is $a_{ij}(1 - f)$. a_{ij} is the transition probability between the normal states when the system is without uncertainty. The result of a_{ij} multiplied by the coefficient $1 - f$ is the transition probability combined with the uncertainty characterization.

Theorem 2. The new transition matrix $A^{'}$ satisfies the property of regular Markov model

Proof. According to the solved HMM's matrix A:$a_{00} + a_{01} + \cdots + a_{0n} = 1$

$$\begin{aligned} a^{'}_{00} + a^{'}_{01} + \cdots + a^{'}_{0n} &= a_{00}(1-f) + a_{01}(1-f) + \cdots + a_{0n}(1-f) + f \\ &= a_{00} + a_{01} \cdots + a_{0n} - (a_{00} + a_{01} \cdots + a_{0n})f + f \\ &= 1 + f - f = 1 \end{aligned}$$ □

The new Markov model combines the inherent property and the operating environment of the PLC system. It closely mimics the actual execution of the PLC in real life applications. Based on this model, we can analyze the runtime properties of the PLC system using model-checking technology.

3.5 Property Analysis with PRISM

After building the integrated Markov model, we can perform probabilistic model checking using PRISM [8]. First, we need to specify the Markov model in PRISM modeling language. Second, the rewards used to specify additional quantitative measures of interest should be added into the model. Finally, we specify the properties about the PLC system.

A PRISM model comprises a set of modules which represent different aspects of the system. The behavior of the PRISM model is specified by guarded commands. Synchronization between different modules can be implemented by augmenting guarded commands with action labels. We now describe the combined Markov model $\langle S^{'}, \pi^{'}, A^{'}, L^{'} \rangle$ in PRISM manner. The module is derived from the transition matrix $A^{'}$ of the model. We declare a variable S, whose value range from [0, n+1]. Then, we build a label command for each arrow of the matrix $A^{'}$ on this variable.

$$[L_i]S = i \rightarrow (a^{'}_{i0} : S^{'} = 0) + (a^{'}_{i1} : S^{'} = 1) + \ldots (a^{'}_{in} : S^{'} = n) + (f : S^{'} = n + 1)$$

Then, we focus on extending the model with rewards. There are two kinds of rewards and the structure is:

rewards *"reward_name"* *component* **endrewards**

The component for state rewards is *guard* : *reward* and the component for transitions is [*Label*] *guard* : *reward*. The *guard* is a predicate over the state variables, *Label* is the command label in each module, and the *reward* is a real-valued expression that will assign quantitative measures we care about the states and the transitions that are satisfied with the guard.

In the domain of PLC system, the main properties we care about are the timing and the reliability of the system. So, we define two representative **rewards** for the model. The first is about the time property. It can be derived from the element T of the transition label L. We add a *reward* component $[L_i]$ *true* : T for each transition into the **reward**. The reward reflects the elapsed time of each transition in the model. The other is a state **reward**. We associate a number 1 to all the normal states with the *reward* component S : 1. These can be used to get the long-run availability of the system. We can also define other kinds of **reward**, such as power consumption of each transition and state.

After we describe the probabilistic model and rewards in PRISM manner, we can analyze some properties of the model. We can specify the properties in PRISM's specification language. We can use the P and S operator to specify quantitative time instant or long-run properties respectively. For example, we can use the following specification to describe the execution state of the PLC system in the long-run (U denote the abnormal state of the system, S denote the normal state of the system):

Property 1: $S_{=?}[!U]$, the probability that the PLC system is not in failure in the long-run.

We can extend the above property with bounded variant of time. The following two properties specifications describe the reliability of the PLC system in a time period:

Property 2: $P_{=?}[G^{[0,t]}\ !U]$, the probability that the PLC system has no error during t time units.

We can also use the R operator to get the expected value defined in terms of a reward structure. We can get many performance measures of the system. Based on the two rewards defined above, we specify two properties about time:

Property 3: $R_{"S"=?}[C^{\leq t}]$, the cumulative time of the system being in normal states during the t time units.
Property 4: $R_{"T"=?}[F\ U]$: the cumulative time of the system passed before the first uncertainty state happens.

4 Case Studies

We apply our framework to an actual industrial PLC system which was originally published in [15]. The system is shown in Fig. 4. It consists of three pistons (A, B, C) which are operated by solenoid valves (V_1, V_2, V_3). Each piston has two corresponding normally open limit sensor contacts. Three push buttons are provided to start the system (switch $SW1$), to stop the system normally (switch $SW2$) and to stop the system immediately in emergency (switch $SW3$). In a manufacturing facility [15], such piston systems can be used to load/unload parts from a machine table, or to extend/retract a cutting tool spindle, etc.

Piston A is controlled by valve V_1. When the value of V_1 is 1 and the piston is at the left side, the piston will move from left to the right, and the movement is denoted by A^+. When the value of V_1 is 0 and the piston is at the right side, the piston will move back to the left side, and the movement is denoted by A^-. We can see that the movement of A will affect the value of sensors (a_0, a_1). Initially, piston A is at the left side and the normally open sensor contact a_0 is closed. Hence, the value of a_0 is 1, a_1 is 0. When V_1 turns out to be 1 at this time, the piston will move to the right side (A^+). Then, the open sensor contact a_0 will break and the sensor contact a_1 will close. Hence, the value of a_0 changes to 0 and a_1 changes to 1, automatically. We can use this property to design ladder programs to control the system.

There are many PLC ladder programs that can be used to control this system. Let us see the example in Fig. 1. The ladder program is the same as the third ladder diagram in [15]. It contains four ladder rungs, which includes 8 primary input contacts $(SW1, SW3, a_0, a_1, b_0, b_1, c_0, c_1)$. $SW1$ and $SW3$ are changed by human operation, the others are automatically changed by movements of the pistons. We can construct an automata model for the operating principle of the PLC system. The state is denoted by the outputs of the ladder. The system has

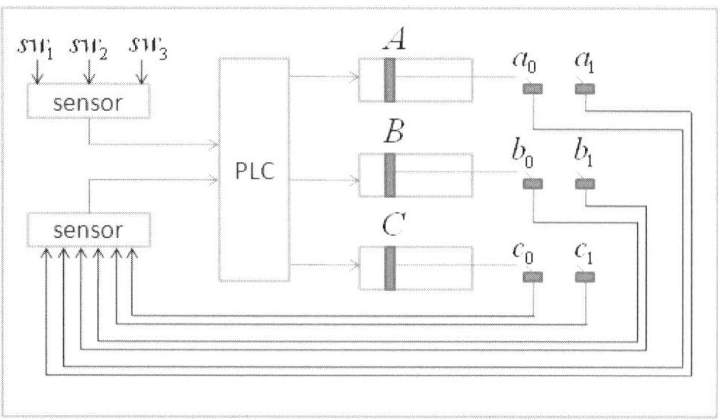

Fig. 4. Industrial automated system originally published in [15]

six normal states ($S_0, S_1, S_2, S_3, S_4, S_5$), and an uncertainty state corresponding to the all kinds of failure caused by the uncertainty characterization. The six normal states are the states of the Hidden Markov Model. In the Fig. 5, each normal state has some corresponding observations linked by dotted line. In this system, the four states have only one corresponding observation and state S_5 has 3 corresponding observations. The transitions are labeled with the primary input sequences. The time unit for each transition is 1 time unit except that the transition between state S_3 and S_4 is 6 time units. We introduce the control theory of the model with more detail below.

At first, the system is in a blank state named S_0. In this state, the pistons stay at the left side. So, the values of $(a_0, a_1, b_0, b_1, c_0, c_1)$ are $(1, 0, 1, 0, 1, 0)$. In the first execution cycle of the PLC system, when the worker press the start switch($SW1$), the system is activated. The values of (V_1, V_2, V_3, T) are $(1, 0, 0, 0)$. The piston A will move to the right side(A^+). The values of $(a_0, a_1, b_0, b_1, c_0, c_1)$ change to $(0, 1, 1, 0, 1, 0)$. The second execution cycle, the values of (V_1, V_2, V_3, T) are $(1, 1, 0, 0)$. The piston B will move to the right side(B^+). The values of $(a_0, a_1, b_0, b_1, c_0, c_1)$ changes to $(0, 1, 0, 1, 1, 0)$. The third execution cycle, the values of (V_1, V_2, V_3, T) are $(0, 1, 1, 0)$. The piston A will move back to the left and the piston C will move to the right side simultaneously (A^-C^+). The values of $(a_0, a_1, b_0, b_1, c_0, c_1)$ changes to $(1, 0, 1, 0, 0, 1)$. If we press $SW3$, the pistons B and A will move to the left side (A^-B^-). The fourth execution cycle, since the value of c_1 and a_0 are 1, the timer instruction is activated. In the next five time units, the value for output (V_1, V_2, V_3, T) will not change. Then, the system will keep static for five time units. At the sixth time units, the values of (V_1, V_2, V_3, T) are $(0, 0, 0, 1)$. Then, Pistons B and C will move to the left side (B^-C^-). The values of $(a_0, a_1, b_0, b_1, c_0, c_1)$ changes to $(1, 0, 1, 0, 1, 0)$.

We can build the Hidden Markov Model for the PLC system using the operating principle presented in Fig. 5. The states of the Hidden Markov Model are the normal states in the automata. The transition Label L between two hidden states is also derived from the figure. Element I is the eight primary inputs on the automata label. Element T is the time for each state transition of the original

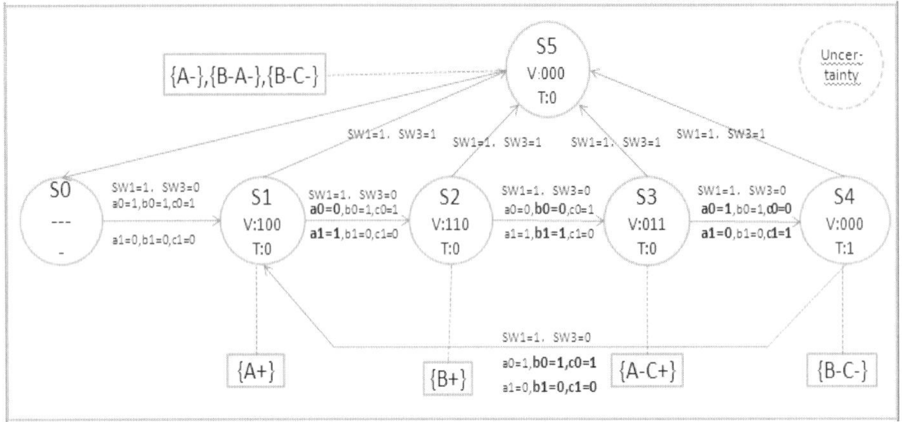

Fig. 5. Work theory

automata. The set of Observations is composed of the content in the rectangle of the Fig. 5. Hence, we can get the matrix A, B for the hidden markov model:

$$\mathbf{A} = \begin{pmatrix} & S_0 & S_1 & S_2 & S_3 & S_4 & S_5 \\ S_0 & a_{00} & a_{01} & a_{02} & a_{03} & a_{04} & a_{05} \\ S_1 & a_{10} & a_{11} & a_{12} & a_{13} & a_{14} & a_{15} \\ S_2 & a_{20} & a_{21} & a_{22} & a_{23} & a_{24} & a_{25} \\ S_3 & a_{30} & a_{31} & a_{32} & a_{33} & a_{34} & a_{35} \\ S_4 & a_{40} & a_{41} & a_{42} & a_{43} & a_{44} & a_{45} \\ S_5 & a_{50} & a_{51} & a_{52} & a_{53} & a_{54} & a_{55} \end{pmatrix} \quad \mathbf{B} = \begin{pmatrix} & A^+ & B^+ & C^+A^- & B^-C^- & A^- & B^-A^- \\ S_0 & b_{00} & b_{01} & b_{02} & b_{03} & b_{04} & b_{05} \\ S_1 & b_{10} & b_{11} & b_{12} & b_{13} & b_{14} & b_{15} \\ S_2 & b_{20} & b_{21} & b_{22} & b_{23} & b_{24} & b_{25} \\ S_3 & b_{30} & b_{31} & b_{32} & b_{33} & b_{34} & b_{35} \\ S_4 & b_{40} & b_{41} & b_{32} & b_{43} & b_{44} & b_{45} \\ S_5 & b_{50} & b_{51} & b_{52} & b_{53} & b_{54} & b_{55} \end{pmatrix}$$

The element a_{23} means the probability that the state S_2 transmit to state S_3. The element b_{10} means the probability that we can observe that piston A moves to the right when the system is in state S_1. The semantic of the other elements are the same.

There is a real-life application that the operating environment of the system is representative of one movement sequence O: $[A^+, B^+, C^+A^-, B^-C^-]$. Hence, we need to solve the matrix A and B using the Baum-Welch algorithm or by simulation to get a maximum $P(O|M)$. Then, we need to combine the solved Hidden Markov Model M with the uncertainty state caused by the uncertainty characterization. We assume that the sampling error for each primary input contacts is 0.05, and the execution error for each ladder logic unit is 0.3. Using the method in Section 3.1, the uncertainty characterization of the PLC system is 9.80%. That means the system will go into an uncertainty state with probability 0.098 from any normal states. The system will recover to the initial state with probability 0.9 from the uncertainty state. The combined matrix is as follows:

$$\mathbf{A}^{'} = \begin{pmatrix} & S_0 & S_1 & S_2 & S_3 & S_4 & U \\ S_0 & 0 & 0.902 & 0 & 0 & 0 & 0.098 \\ S_1 & 0 & 0 & 0.902 & 0 & 0 & 0.098 \\ S_2 & 0 & 0 & 0 & 0.902 & 0 & 0.098 \\ S_3 & 0 & 0 & 0 & 0 & 0.902 & 0.098 \\ S_4 & 0 & 0.902 & 0 & 0 & 0 & 0.098 \\ U & 0.9 & 0 & 0 & 0 & 0 & 0.1 \end{pmatrix}$$

For a more complex example, whose operating environment is representative of three kinds of observation sequences. The observation sequences O_1, O_2, and O_3 are $[A^+, A^-], [A^+, B^+, B^- A^-]$ and $[A^+, B^+, A^- C^+, B^- C^-]$, respectively. In one thousand observations, O_1 appear 200 times, O_2 appear 200 times, and O_3 about 600 times. Then, we use the Baum-Welch algorithm for multiple observation sequences described in Section 3.3 and combined it with uncertainty characterization as follows:

$$\mathbf{A}^{'} = \begin{pmatrix} & S_0 & S_1 & S_2 & S_3 & S_4 & S_5 & U \\ S_0 & 0 & 0.902 & 0 & 0 & 0 & 0 & 0.098 \\ S_1 & 0 & 0 & 0.722 & 0 & 0 & 0.180 & 0.098 \\ S_2 & 0 & 0 & 0 & 0.677 & 0 & 0.225 & 0.098 \\ S_3 & 0 & 0 & 0 & 0 & 0.902 & 0 & 0.098 \\ S_4 & 0 & 0.902 & 0 & 0 & 0 & 0 & 0.098 \\ S_5 & 0.902 & 0 & 0 & 0 & 0 & 0 & 0.098 \\ U & 0.9 & 0 & 0 & 0 & 0 & 0 & 0.1 \end{pmatrix}$$

We can describe the model of this example in PRISM as described in Section 3.5. We extend the model with rewards to help us analyze the system. The time property is derived from the time element T of the Markov model transition label L. In addition, we present a reward *power* for each state. The reward denote the power consumption for valid piston movements in each state.

At last, we can initiate some properties that we care about the system model. The first property is based on the reward *oper*, and denote the long term availability of the system. The second property is based on the reward *time*, and denote the first time that it is in failure. The third property is based on the reward *power*, and denote the valid power consumption during 1000 time units.

– $S_{=?}[S < 6]$ $\quad R_{\{"time"\}=?}[F\ S = 6]$ $\quad R_{\{"power"\}=?}[C^{\leq 1000}]$

We can do more experiments on the system presented in [15]. There are four ladder programs presented in that paper. Although the four PLC programs have the same sampling error and execution error probability, their inner property are different due to different arrangements of primary inputs and logic executions. We set the input sampling error probability to 0.05 and change the value of execution error probability, denoted by ε. Using the method presented in Section 3.1, we can obtain the uncertainty characterization for the four ladder programs in Table 1.

Table 1. Uncertainty Characterization

ladder	$\varepsilon = 0.01$	$\varepsilon = 0.05$	$\varepsilon = 0.1$	$\varepsilon = 0.15$	$\varepsilon = 0.2$	$\varepsilon = 0.25$	$\varepsilon = 0.3$
ladder1	0.67%	16.87%	13.67%	12.54%	10.23%	8.69%	5.51%
ladder2	0.70%	17.63%	13.89%	13.21%	11.82%	10.57%	6.62%
ladder3	1.08%	28.04%	25.36%	24.57%	22.03%	21.18%	9.80%
ladder4	1.15%	30.13%	26.51%	25.82%	24.65%	22.83%	10.94%

Table 2. Uncertainty Characterization By Random Simulation

ladder	$\varepsilon = 0.01$	$\varepsilon = 0.05$	$\varepsilon = 0.1$	$\varepsilon = 0.15$	$\varepsilon = 0.2$	$\varepsilon = 0.25$	$\varepsilon = 0.3$
ladder1	0.69%	17.02%	13.82%	12.66%	10.29%	8.75%	5.54%
ladder2	0.74%	17.82%	14.05%	13.35%	11.91%	10.63%	6.67%
ladder3	1.12%	28.22%	25.51%	24.71%	22.14%	21.27%	9.89%
ladder4	1.21%	30.37%	26.68%	25.98%	24.78%	22.95%	11.16%

Table 3. Property Results

property	env	U=0.01	U=0.03	U=0.05	U=0.07	U=0.09	U=0.1	U=0.15	U=0.2	U=0.25
oper	1	0.989	0.968	0.947	0.928	0.909	0.900	0.857	0.818	0.783
oper	2	0.990	0.971	0.952	0.934	0.917	0.908	0.868	0.830	0.795
time	1	233	98	43	32	27	21	18	8	6
time	2	198	73	38	30	23	21	13	9	7
power	1	1462	1391	1325	1261	1200	1171	1032	908	797
power	2	1234	1181	1130	1081	1034	1011	903	804	714

We have also devised random simulations to confirm the correctness of the uncertainty characterization. The values get by random simulations is presented in Table 2. A more visual representation for ladder3 is shown in Fig.6.

In the following, we will show how operating environment affect the performance of one PLC system. We use the example described in Fig. 1, which is also the same as the third ladder diagram in [15]. We have described two operating environment examples above, which are denoted by two sets of observation sequences. We compare the three properties in these two operating environment with the help of PRISM. The results are shown in Table 3.

From Table 3, we can see the long term availability for the second example (env=2) is always better than the first example. The first failure time for the second example come faster than the first one. The total number of valid piston movements for the first operating environment is bigger than the second. A more visual representation is shown in Fig.7,8,9 (the green line is for the second application environment). We can come to the conclusion that: for the same PLC system, properties of the system are different in different application operating environment.

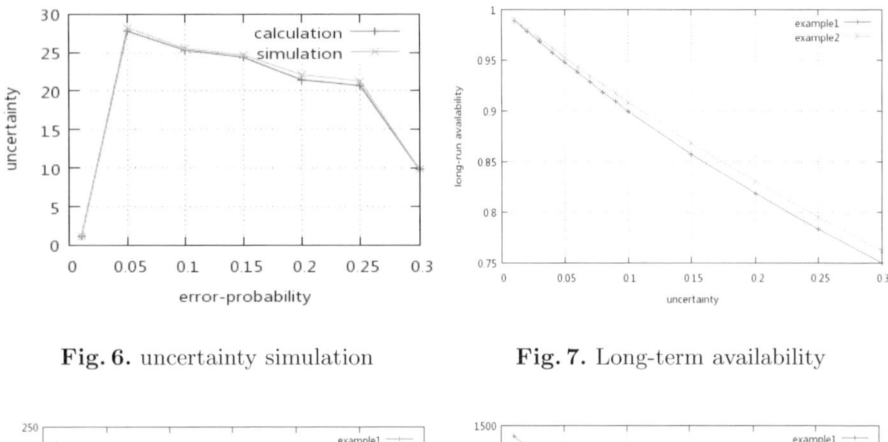

Fig. 6. uncertainty simulation

Fig. 7. Long-term availability

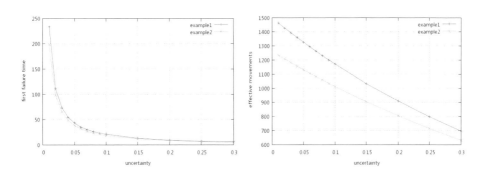

Fig. 8. Failure-Time

Fig. 9. Total-movements

5 Conclusion

This paper presents a symbolic framework for the formal analysis of PLC systems. The framework is based on the uncertainty calculation of the PLC system itself and the Hidden Markov Model of the whole PLC system. We solve the Hidden Markov Model by extending the Baum-Welch algorithm or simulation to reflect the particular operating environment of the system's application. With the help of PRISM we can perform probabilistic model checking on the combined Markov Model. The techniques used in our framework allows us to obtain expected performance measures of the PLC system, which are more accurate and closer to the real-world run-time state, by automated analytical means. We can compare the performance of different PLC system designs for an particular application. Our future effort focus on the automatic techniques that transfer PLC into Hidden Markov Model and a more accurate calculation of the uncertainty characterization of PLC.

References

1. Bauer, N., Engell, S., Huuck, R., Lohmann, S., Lukoschus, B., Remelhe, M., Stursberg, O.: Verification of PLC Programs Given as Sequential Function Charts. In: Ehrig, H., Damm, W., Desel, J., Große-Rhode, M., Reif, W., Schnieder, E., Westkämper, E. (eds.) INT 2004. LNCS, vol. 3147, pp. 517–540. Springer, Heidelberg (2004)
2. Baum, L.E., Sell, G.R.: Growth transformations for functions on manifolds. Pacific Journal of Mathematics 27(2), 211–227 (1968)
3. Canet, G., Couffin, S., Lesage, J.J., Petit, A., Schnoebelen, P.: Towards the automatic verification of PLC programs written in instruction list. In: Proc. IEEE Conf. Systems, Man and Cybernetics, Nashvill, TN, USA, pp. 2449–2454 (October 2000)
4. Dempster, A., Laird, N., Rubin, D., et al.: Maximum likelihood from incomplete data via the EM algorithm. Journal of the Royal Statistical Society. Series B (Methodological) 39(1), 1–38 (1977)
5. Ephraim, Y., Dembo, A., Rabiner, L.R.: A minimum discrimination information approach for hidden Markov modeling. IEEE Transactions on Information Theory 35(5), 1001–1013 (2002)
6. Frey, G., Litz, L.: Formal methods in PLC programming. In: Proc. IEEE Conf. Systems, Man, and Cybernetics, vol. 4, pp. 2431–2436 (2000)
7. Hanisch, H.-M., Thieme, J., Luder, A., Wienhold, O.: Modeling of PLC behaviour by means of timed net condition/event systems. In: IEEE Int. Symp. Emerging Technologies and Factory Automation (EFTA), pp. 361–369 (1997)
8. Hinton, A., Kwiatkowska, M., Norman, G., Parker, D.: PRISM: A tool for automatic verification of probabilistic systems. In: Hermanns, H. (ed.) TACAS 2006. LNCS, vol. 3920, pp. 441–444. Springer, Heidelberg (2006)
9. Willems, H.X.: Compact timed automata for PLC programs. Technical report csi-r9925, University of Nijmegen, Computing Science Institute (1999)
10. International Electrotechnical Commission (IEC): IEC 61131-3 Standard (PLC Programming Languages), 2.0 edn. (2003)
11. Johnson, T.L.: Improving automation software dependability: A role for formal methods? Control Engineering Practice 15(11), 1403–1415 (2007)
12. Levinson, S., Rabiner, L., Sondhi, M.: An introduction to the application of the theory of probabilistic functions of a Markov process to automatic speech recognition. The Bell System Technical Journal 62(4), 1035–1074 (1983)
13. Rabiner, L.: A tutorial on hidden Markov models and selected applications in speech recognition. Proceedings of the IEEE 77(2), 257–286 (1989)
14. Rausch, M., Krogh, B.H.: Formal verification of PLC programs. In: Proc. American Control Conference (1998)
15. Venkatesh, K., Zhou, M., Caudill, R.J.: Comparing ladder logic diagrams and petri nets for sequence controller design through a discrete manufacturing system. IEEE Transactions on Industrial Electronics 41(6), 611–619 (1994)
16. Younis, M.B., Frey, G.: Formalization of existing PLC programs: A survey. In: Proc. Computational Engineering in Systems Applications, CESA (2003)
17. Zhang, H., Jiang, Y., Hung, W.N.N., Yang, G., Gu, M.: On the uncertainty characterization of programmable logic controllers (2011), `http://web.cecs.pdx.edu/~song/research/paper_hehua_final_2.pdf`

Statistical Model Checking for Distributed Probabilistic-Control Hybrid Automata with Smart Grid Applications

João Martins[1,2], André Platzer[1], and João Leite[2]

[1] Computer Science Department, Carnegie Mellon University, Pittsburgh PA
{jmartins,aplatzer}@cs.cmu.edu
[2] CENTRIA and Departamento de Informática, FCT, Universidade Nova de Lisboa
jleite@di.fct.unl.pt

Abstract. The power industry is currently moving towards a more dynamical, intelligent power grid. This *Smart Grid* is still in its infancy and a formal evaluation of the expensive technologies and ideas on the table is necessary before committing to a full investment. In this paper, we argue that a good model for the Smart Grid must match its basic properties: it must be hybrid (both evolve over time, and perform control/computation), distributed (multiple concurrently executing entities), and allow for asynchronous communication and stochastic behaviour (to accurately model real-world power consumption). We propose Distributed Probabilistic-Control Hybrid Automata (DPCHA) as a model for this purpose, and extend Bounded LTL to Quantified Bounded LTL in order to adapt and apply existing statistical model-checking techniques. We provide an implementation of a framework for developing and verifying DPCHAs. Finally, we conduct a case study for Smart Grid communications analysis.

1 Introduction

The ultimate promise of the Smart Grid is that of a more stable, energy-efficient, adaptable, secure, resilient power grid, while delivering cheaper electricity. Currently, energy consumption follows fairly predictable patterns that need to be very closely matched by power generation (otherwise blackouts or damage to the infrastructure may occur). There are peak hours (e.g., people arrive home on a hot summer day and turn on the AC), and low hours (e.g., during the night). Certain power generators run permanently at 100% capacity, providing support to what is known as the base load. More adaptable but more expensive generators change their output to match demand, varying the price of energy throughout the day. During peak hours, it might be necessary to turn on highly adaptable and expensive peak load generators, making energy extremely expensive for those few hours.

One of the core ideas of the Smart Grid is that generators will no longer passively adapt to consumption. Instead, power consumers both at the lower level (e.g., appliances such as washing machines) and higher level (utilities serving

S. Qin and Z. Qiu (Eds.): ICFEM 2011, LNCS 6991, pp. 131–146, 2011.

some geographical area) will feed their desired consumption back into the Grid. Indeed, utilities and home-owners have already begun deploying smart meters and appliances that make available more detailed, up-to-date energy consumption information. This gives the smarter Grid better foresight, increasing its robustness and its ability to reschedule non-critical appliances (e.g., the dishwasher) to off-peak hours, reducing energy costs.

Given the size and criticality of the power infrastructure, it is clear that Smart Grid technologies have to be analysed very carefully. Furthermore, the cost of providing real test-beds for all technologies is prohibitive, especially if the infrastructure can sustain damaged when things go wrong. Formal verification, on the other hand, allows us to study a *model* of the system in question, sidestepping the above issues. Given an appropriate model, we may then check the system for properties: how much can be saved with appliance rescheduling? Do Smart Meters help in predicting and optimizing load? Does that prediction help balance load across generators? Not only are the answers to these questions useful in furthering our understanding of the technologies, they also give us hints about how they may be improved upon before real-world deployment.

For the above reasons, we believe that formal verification of new technologies is fundamental for the Smart Grid. The first step in this endeavour is to find adequate models for the Grid. The models need to be flexible and generic so they can be reused for multiple projects and ideas, yet match the nature and properties of the Grid. Forcing models that do not fit the properties of the Grid lead to modelling idiosyncrasies, effectively making modelling and verification much harder than they need to or should be (humanly and computationally).

What, then, are the properties of the Smart Grid? Most importantly, it is a *cyber-physical* system. Its infrastructure exists in the real-world and follows the laws of physics (e.g., a generator increasing its output), but it also contains control components that make decisions and change the state instantaneously. Thus, it is a hybrid system, i.e., has both continuous and discrete dynamics. Some mathematical models and verification techniques for hybrid systems extend automata theory by allowing continuous evolution to occur in each state (e.g., [6,3,1]), but verification is known to be undecidable for most cases [3]. Differential Dynamic Logic ($d\mathcal{L}$) allows the specification of both the properties and the behaviour of a hybrid system [9] and provides a proof calculus for verification.

Another property of the Smart Grid is that it is *distributed*. The Grid is not one monolithic system, but composed of a large number of distributed and *communicating* entities, from the power generators down to electrical substations to the utilities, households, appliances and meters. All of these elements coexist, communicate and cooperate with one another in real-time. Most automata models support the notion of composition, allowing a fixed number of automata to execute concurrently. The Grid, however, is *dynamically* distributed: appliances are turned on and off, power lines can be cut, and meters may fail. The model must allow entities/elements to enter, leave and communicate as part of the system dynamics. Dynamic I/O Automata [5] allow a dynamic number of elements, but are not hybrid. Quantified Differential Dynamic Logic ($Qd\mathcal{L}$) [10] also allows a dynamic number of elements and is hybrid, but like Dynamic I/O automata, has a shared-memory communication model. Proposals for Smart Grid communication are currently based on IP and message-passing protocols, so that forcing a fundamentally different shared-memory paradigm appears unwise.

Finally, the Grid exhibits *stochastic behaviour*. As we have seen, power consumption follows known but not completely fixed patterns so that using non-determinism to model these patterns encodes little information about the actual behaviour of the Grid. Hybrid system models are generally non-deterministic, attempting to verify safety properties that hold even in the worst-case. In the Grid, worst-case scenarios (e.g., all lines cut at the same time, all appliances always on) are sure to bring about a complete collapse, and most safety properties *will not* hold! Alternatively, a probabilistic model enables 1) a more detailed and accurate representation of the Grid's consumption patterns and 2) a more comprehensive quantitative study. Since we know most interesting properties are not always true, we may *estimate the probability* that they hold. This precludes $Qd\mathcal{L}$ [10], which is not stochastic, whereas Stochastic $d\mathcal{L}$ [11] is not distributed. I/O Automata have a stochastic extension, but it is not distributed [5].

Petri Nets are inherently dynamically distributed and there have been stochastic and differential extensions [12,2]. However, the notion of markings flowing place to place is not one that we find when designing the participants of the Smart Grid. They would be composed of multiple markings scattered over different places of the Petri graph. Several entities of the same class (e.g., microwaves), sharing the same "control" graph, would create a multitude of markings superimposed in the same places. Markings would have to be associated with one another to keep track of the entities as a whole, instead of considering an entity as an indivisible structure. There is also no immediately available communication mechanism for transmitting messages (with a payload). In conclusion, while many Petri Net variants feature mechanisms very similar to those of the Smart Grid, it is our belief their actual implementation is generally differs enough to warrant the Grid a model of its own.

In [8] the state of the system is given by a composition of objects and messages. All objects evolve continuously as long as no invariant is violated, and fire probabilistic discrete transitions when they are. Asynchronous communication is achieved by assigning a delivery time to all messages upon creation. The decision to do a discrete or continuous transition depends exclusively on whether an invariant is violated, making the dynamics of this model very restricted.

In summation, we need a model that is composed of many different entities. These entities should be able to enter and leave the system at will, representing failures and appliances being turned on or off. Furthermore, the entities must be able to communicate asynchronously: given the scale of the Grid and the impact of message delivery delays, it is unrealistic to assume synchronous (instant) communication. Finally, the system must be able to behave probabilistically, in order to encode uncertain environments, e.g., power consumption. To the best of our knowledge, no existing model naturally incorporates all of these properties.

In this paper, we propose Distributed Probabilistic-Control Hybrid Automata (DPCHA) as such a model. We take care that the system can be easily sampled from (to obtain execution traces), with the objective of applying existing efficient statistical verification techniques.

Previous work has shown that statistical model checking (SMC) is a promising approach for the verification of probabilistic systems [4,15,14]. Given a property and a model, SMC techniques will repeatedly sample traces from the model and check if they satisfy the property. Every new result provides more information on whether the property holds for arbitrary traces. While known to be unsound, SMC can arbitrarily approximate the *probability* that the property holds very efficiently, making many otherwise intractable problems accessible.

Logics traditionally used in the specification of properties for these hybrid systems generally consider a fixed state-space. This makes them insufficient for the representation of properties of distributed systems. We propose Quantified Bounded Linear Temporal Logic, an extension to Bounded Linear Temporal Logic that handles the dynamic state space of DPCHA using quantification over the elements of the system. A similar phenomenon has been studied in the context of Java threads [13], for example, but not for cyber-physical systems.

The main contribution of this paper is the proposal of a model that naturally adapts to Smart Grid scenarios and for which these techniques are applicable, enabling meaningful studies of the system.

We present some technical background in Section 2, and our DPCHA model in Section 3. To specify properties we define QBLTL in Section 4. We briefly explain Bayesian statistical model checking in Section 5, and develop an initial case study in the Smart Grid domain in Section 6. We conclude in Section 7.

2 Preliminaries

Before developing the distributed model, we will begin by introducing how a single entity behaves (e.g., microwave, generator). Thus, we briefly recall discrete-time hybrid automata (DTHA) [15]. Each entity must have a *state*, e.g., current and desired power output of a generator. The entity is in a *location* that specifies how the state should *flow* as time passes, e.g., spooling up generator to match desired output. Finally, the entity may decide to *jump* from one location to another, e.g., the microwave switches to "defrost". We refer to an entity's *situation* as the pair of its location and state. Thus, DTHA are hybrid because they allow continuous evolution (time passing) and discrete transitions between locations.

Definition 1 (DTHA). *A discrete-time hybrid automaton consists of*

- $\langle Q, E\rangle$, *a "control graph" with* Q *as* locations *and* $E \subseteq Q \times Q$ *as the* edges
- $\mathbb{R}^n$ *is the state space of the automaton's state*
- $\mathit{jump}_e : \mathbb{R}^n \rightharpoonup \mathbb{R}^n$, *a partial function defining how the state changes when jumping along edge* e
- $\varphi_q : \mathbb{R}_{\geq 0} \times \mathbb{R}^n \to \mathbb{R}^n$, flows. $\varphi_q(t;x)$ *is the result of a continuous evolution at location* $q \in Q$ *after time* t *when starting in state* $x \in \mathbb{R}^n$
- $(q_0; x_0) \in Q \times \mathbb{R}^n$, *an initial situation*

Suppose an entity is in a situation $(q; x)$. It may jump along an edge e originating from q, updating its state according to $\texttt{jump}_e$. Or it may remain in q for some time t, updating its state according to the flow φ_q (which can be, for instance, the solution of a differential equation system). Since there might be multiple options for the next step, the automaton is non-deterministic.

Definition 2 (Transition relation for DTHA). *The transition relation for a DTHA is defined as:*

$$(q; x) \xrightarrow{\alpha} (\overline{q}; \overline{x}), \text{ where}$$

- *When* $\alpha = t \in \mathbb{R}_{\geq 0}$ *is a time, then* $(q; x) \xrightarrow{t} (q; \overline{x})$ *iff* $\overline{x} = \varphi_q(t; x)$
- *When* $\alpha = e \in E$ *is an edge from* q *to* $\overline{q}$, *then* $(q; x) \xrightarrow{e} (\overline{q}; \overline{x})$ *iff* $\overline{x} = \mathit{jump}_e(x)$

It is only possible to jump along an edge e if the entity's state is in the domain of $\texttt{jump}_e$. In this case, we say that e is *enabled* and that $\texttt{jump}_e$ works as a *guard* for e. A *scheduler* $\delta : Q \times \mathbb{R}^n \rightarrow \mathbb{R}_{\geq 0} \cup E$ that, given a situation $(q; x)$, decides the next action α (a flow or an edge to jump), can be applied repeatedly to an entity's situation to obtain a *trace* for that entity.

We now have defined the dynamics of a single entity. To make it behave probabilistically, all we need to do is to make $\delta : Q \times \mathbb{R}^n \rightarrow \mathcal{D}(E \cup \mathbb{R}_{\geq 0} \cup \mathbb{R}_{\geq 0})$ return a *probability distribution* over all possible actions instead of a single action α. Sampling from this distribution gives the entity its next step.

3 Distributed Probabilistic Control Hybrid Automata

A single entity's behaviour is given by its control graph, flows and jumps. We have mentioned that traditional notions of automata composition are not dynamic enough for the Grid. *Configuration automata* [5] keep track of multiple executing entities (also automata) that can enter and leave the system, resulting in two layers of automata that have no particular intuition in the Grid. Furthermore, the automata force communication to be immediate and synchronous.

Instead, like in Petri Nets, we assume all the control graphs are given, so we understand how microwaves (for example) behave, but are not required to know how many. With these control graphs, jumps and flows for each type of entity (e.g., microwave, meter), it is trivial to encode the behaviour of all types of entities in one global control graph.

The global control graph accommodates several entities, not unlike Petri Net markings. These entities are characterised by their situation and execute like a single entity from the previous section. This is the basic intuition for the notions of Distributed Discrete-Time Hybrid Automata (DDTHA) and Distributed Probabilistic Control Hybrid Automata (DPCHA) that we define below.

To maintain a sensible global notion of time, the DDTHA will do a continuous transition only if all executing entities decide to do so. If any entity decides to do a jump, then the other entities must either jump as well or *flounder* (i.e. doing a discrete transition with no effect), keeping time unchanged. In this sense, discrete transitions take precedence over continuous transitions, but consume no time.

We must still address the ability to communicate and to allow entities to enter or exit the system. We reduce these two concerns (communication and dynamic number of entities) to five elementary *actions*: $\texttt{new}[N]$, $\texttt{die}$, $\texttt{snd}[l][T]$, $\texttt{recv}[l][R]$, $\texttt{jmp}$. Each edge in the control graph features an action. When an entity jumps along that edge, its action is executed. $\texttt{jmp}$ is a null action so that the entity simply follows $\texttt{jump}_e$. $\texttt{new}[N]$ additionally creates a new entity with a situation specified by a function N, and $\texttt{die}$ makes the jumping entity exit the system. $\texttt{snd}[l][T]$ and $\texttt{recv}[l][R]$ send and receive messages through a *channel* determined by function l. The content of the sent message is given by function T, whereas the receiving entity's state is updated according to R, taking into account both its current state and message content. To achieve asynchronous communication, sent messages are stored at the global automaton level in a "buffer", and are removed later when received. The content of messages is a real vector computed by function T, and affects the receiver's state according to R. Thus, each action is characterised by functions determining exactly how it is executed. We let $\mathcal{A}_e$ denote the action of edge e, which happens in addition to the effects of $\texttt{jump}_e$.

In summary, the control graph retains its general structure, but annotates each edge with actions for communication and dynamism. Instead of a single initial situation, we have an initial set of active entities and an initial situation for each entity. Active entities all evolve time-synchronously, each following the rules of DTHA. As entities jump along edges, they execute the associated actions, enabling communication and complex interactions.

Definition 3 (DDTHA). *A Distributed Discrete-Time Hybrid Automaton is composed of*

- $\mathbb{R}^n$, *the state space for each entity, with* $n \in \mathbb{N}$
- $\mathbb{R}^{n_m}$, *the state space of each message's content, with* $n_m \in \mathbb{N}$
- $\mathcal{A} = \{\texttt{new}[N], \texttt{die}, \texttt{snd}[l][T], \texttt{recv}[l][R], \texttt{jmp}\}$, *the set of all actions, with channel specification functions* $l : \mathbb{R}^n \to C$, *new entity creation functions* $N : \mathbb{R}^n \to Q \times \mathbb{R}^n$, *message transmission functions* $T : \mathbb{R}^n \to \mathbb{R}^{n_m}$ *and message reception functions* $R : \mathbb{R}^{n_m} \times \mathbb{R}^n \to \mathbb{R}^n$
- $\langle Q, E\rangle$, *control graph with locations* Q *and edges* $E \subseteq Q \times \mathcal{A} \times Q$
- $\texttt{jump}_e : \mathbb{R}^n \times \mathbb{R}^n$, *a relation when* $\mathcal{A}_e = \texttt{recv}$ *or function* $\texttt{jump}_e : \mathbb{R}^n \to \mathbb{R}^n$ *otherwise, defining acceptable state updates when jumping along edge* e
- φ_q, *as in Def. 1*
- L*: a (countable) set of entity identifiers*
- $A_0 \subset L$*: a finite set of initial* active entities
- $S_0 : A_0 \to Q \times \mathbb{R}^n$, *a function with a* situation *for each initial active entity*
- C, *a (countable) set of communication channels*

The state of a DDTHA consists of the situations of all its entities, active and past. Information about past entities is kept so that checking properties of them is well-defined. The state also maintains a set of "in transit" messages (sent but not received), enabling asynchrony of communication.

Definition 4 (State of a DDTHA). *The state of a DDTHA is given by* $AS = (A, S, M)$ *with*

– $A \subset L$ *a finite set of the labels of active entities*
– $S : L \rightharpoonup Q \times \mathbb{R}^n$, *a partial function with the situation of active/past entities*
– $M \subseteq C \times \mathbb{R}^{n_m}$, *a set of unreceived messages and respective channels*

One interesting issue arises when an entity a decides (through a scheduler) to flow for t time units but sometime at $t' < t$ some other entity b finishes its own flow and schedules a jump. In this situation, the DDTHA also schedules a discrete transition, but a cannot be allowed to reevaluate its previous decision to flow for t time (e.g., the washing machine should not stop because someone turned on the TV). Therefore, we assume without loss of generality that each entity stores in its state (e.g., in its first coordinate) how long it must still flow, denoted by δ-time. In state (A, S, M), an entity a's δ-time is denoted $\delta\text{-time}^S(a)$. When the DDTHA schedules a discrete transition, any entity with non-zero δ-time will flounder, thus only truly rescheduling once its flow decision finishes executing.

Another important element of discrete transitions is message reception. There must be an injective mapping from "in transit" messages to receiving entities so that they get exactly one message. Injection ensures each receiving entity gets at most one message. Of course, the entities must react accordingly, and received/sent messages are removed/added to M.

The following example justifies our choice of probabilities and asynchronous communication and illustrates a simplified modelling of the Smart Grid.

Example 1. Newest generation smart meters feed up-to-date information into the Grid, including power consumption from the appliance level up to substation and utility levels and so on; the Grid also needs to match generator output with power consumption. There is a Grid control infrastructure that maintains this fragile balance.

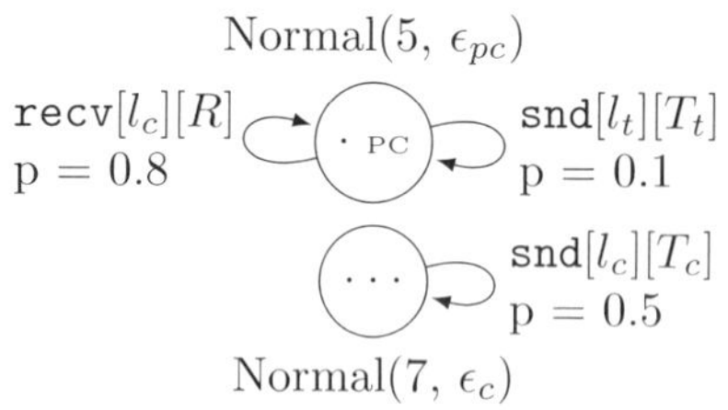

Normal(5, ϵ_{pc})
recv[l_c][R] p = 0.8
PC
snd[l_t][T_t] p = 0.1
...
snd[l_c][T_c] p = 0.5
Normal(7, ϵ_c)

Fig. 1. Simplified Smart Grid

An ideal model for this scenario would have entities representing appliances, consuming energy, shutting off and powering on, and sending messages into the Grid through channel l_c. Another (unique) entity, called the Power Controller (PC), would react to messages from l_c and control generator output by sending it messages through l_t. Unfortunately, it is computationally infeasible to model every appliance in a country-wide Grid (except maybe Monaco or Nauru!). A sensible simplification instead represents *classes* of appliances that get turned on at around the same time for a very similar duration, like ACs/computers in offices, the TVs at home, etc. Ideally, the exact times and durations are given by probability distributions, simulating real-world behaviour. We obtain a much more manageable number of entities by using *classes* of appliances instead of *individual* appliances.

Real networks become congested so that messages are not delivered instantly. Probabilities can be used to simulate this delay: the PC's choice for flow time, for instance, could be given as a normal random variable Normal(5, ϵ_{pc}). The PC then waits around 5s before getting the message. We may assign its individual scheduler a 0.8 probability of jumping along a `recv` edge, so that there is a 0.2 chance it will be further delayed (simulating message loss and retransmission or congestion). These remaining 0.2 can be split between sending control messages to generators or deciding to do another flow.

To justify our choice of asynchronous communication, suppose that whenever an appliance class entity sends a message, the PC is forced to ignore its δ-time and synchronise to receive that message. The PC is deviating from its original specification of continuous evolution according to a Normal RV, which would make the semantics, meaning and usefulness of the model unclear.

Definition 5 (Transition for DDTHA). *The transition relation of a DDTHA is defined inductively as*

$$(A, S, M) \xrightarrow{\alpha} (\overline{A}, \overline{S}, \overline{M})$$

where A is non-empty, $\alpha \in \mathbb{R}_{\geq 0} \cup (A \to (E \cup \mathbb{R}_{\geq 0} \cup \{F\}))$, iff

- *If $\alpha = t \in \mathbb{R}_{\geq 0}$, then $\forall_{a \in A}\ a \in \overline{A}$, $S(a) \xrightarrow{t} \overline{S}(a)$, $\delta\text{-}time^{\overline{S}}(a) = \delta\text{-}time^{S}(a) - t$ and $\delta\text{-}time^{\overline{S}}(a) \geq 0$*
- *If $\alpha = \tau : A \to E \cup \mathbb{R}_{\geq 0} \cup \{F\}$, then there are partial injective mappings $\mu_c : \{(c, \mathbb{R}^{n_m}) \in M\} \to \{a \in A : \tau(a) = (q, \texttt{recv}[l][R], \overline{q})\}$ from messages of each channel to entities scheduled to receive on that channel, $\overline{M} = (M \setminus \bigcup\{range(\mu_c) : c \in C\}) \cup \{(l(S(a)), T(S(a))) : a \in A, \tau(a) = (q, \texttt{snd}[l][T], \overline{q})\}$ and $\forall_{a \in A}$ if $\delta\text{-}time^{S}(a) > 0$, then $\tau(a) = F$, $a \in \overline{A}$ and $S(a) = \overline{S}(a)$; otherwise if $\delta\text{-}time^{S}(a) = 0$*
  - *If $\tau(a) = t \in \mathbb{R}_{\geq 0}$, then $S(a) = \overline{S}(a)$ except $\delta\text{-}time^{\overline{S}}(a) = t$*
  - *If $\tau(a) = (q, \texttt{jmp}, \overline{q}) \in E$, then $a \in \overline{A}$ and $S(a) \xrightarrow{(q,\overline{q})} \overline{S}(a)$*
  - *If $\tau(a) = (q, \texttt{new}[N], \overline{q}) \in E$, then $a \in \overline{A}$, $S(a) \xrightarrow{(q,\overline{q})} \overline{S}(a)$, and there exists a completely new $\overline{a} \notin A$, $\overline{a} \in \overline{A}$ such that $\overline{S}(\overline{a}) = N(S(a))$*
  - *If $\tau(a) = (q, \texttt{die}, \overline{q}) \in E$, then $a \notin \overline{A}$ and $S(a) \xrightarrow{(q,\overline{q})} \overline{S}(a)$*
  - *If $\tau(a) = (q, \texttt{snd}[l][T], \overline{q}) \in E$, then both $a \in \overline{A}$, $S(a) \xrightarrow{(q,\overline{q})} \overline{S}(a)$ and $(l(S(a)), T(S(a))) \in \overline{M}$*
  - *If $\tau(a) = (q, \texttt{recv}[l][R], \overline{q}) \in E$, then $\mu_c(a) = (c, y) \notin \overline{M}$ with $c = l(S(a))$, $a \in \overline{A}$ and $(S(a), R(y, S(a))) \in \texttt{jump}_{\tau(a)}$ and $\overline{S}(a) = R(y, S(a))$*

There may be multiple messages to deliver to an entity, and vice-versa. To remove this source of non-determinism, we simply use a combination of lexicographical and temporal ordering to choose a single assignment.

Given a single-entity scheduler $\delta : Q \times \mathbb{R}^n \to \mathbb{R}_{\geq 0} \cup E$ like those of DTHA, we define a DDTHA scheduler Δ for an automaton state (A, S, M) as follows

1. If $\forall_{a \in A}\ \delta(S(a)) \in \mathbb{R}$, then $\Delta(AS) = \min\{\delta(S(a)) : a \in A\}$
2. If $\exists_{a \in A}\ \delta(S(a)) \in E$, then $\Delta(AS) = \tau$, where for each $a \in A$:

$$\tau(a) = \begin{cases} \delta(S(a)) & , \delta\text{-time}^S(a) = 0 \\ F & , \delta\text{-time}^S(a) > 0 \end{cases}$$

Each scheduler Δ yields a single execution of the system. These valid executions are called traces, and are formalised as follows.

Definition 6 (Trace of a DPCHA). *A* trace *of a DPCHA is a sequence* $\sigma = (AS_0, t_0), (AS_1, t_1), ...,$ *with* AS_i *as in Def. 4,* $t_i \in \mathbb{R}_{\geq 0}$ *such that 1)* $AS_0 = (A_0, S_0, \emptyset)$ *and 2) for each* $i \in \mathbb{N}_{>0}$ *(up to the size of the trace if it is finite):*

1. $AS_{i-1} \xrightarrow{\Delta(AS_{i-1})} AS_i$
2. $t_{i-1} = \begin{cases} \Delta(AS_{i-1}) & , \text{if } \Delta(AS_{i-1}) \in \mathbb{R}_{\geq 0} \\ 0 & , \text{if } \Delta(AS_{i-1}) \in (L \to E \cup \{F\}) \end{cases}$

Given the priority of discrete transitions, we make the assumption of *divergence of time*, i.e., we do not consider schedulers whose traces have infinitely many transitions in finite time. This ensures there is no infinite sequence of jumps, i.e. that time actually passes and the system evolves.

To obtain DPCHA, we probabilise the single entity scheduler δ, from which the global scheduler Δ is obtained. In effect, we sample from each entity's distribution sequentially until all entities have decided on their course of action. From this set of actions we construct the global action, and the distribution of the global DPCHA action is derived from the distribution of the entities' actions. This results in *Distributed Probabilistic-Control Hybrid Automata*, allowing us to formally specify the model in Example 1.

4 Quantified Bounded Linear Temporal Logic

The next step towards applying SMC techniques is to define a way to specify properties and to check whether they are satisfied by the execution traces of the system. These properties must deal with the distributed nature of the Grid. For example, we want to be able to aggregate power demand, or how much power is being generated in total.

We start from Bounded Linear Temporal Logic (BLTL), featuring a strong *bounded until* $\mathbf{U}^t$ operator to deal with time. $\phi_1 \, \mathbf{U}^t \phi_2$ states that ϕ_1 must hold until ϕ_2 holds and ϕ_2 holds before the time bound t. It does not require ϕ_1 to hold when ϕ_2 first holds, but it does require ϕ_2 to hold at some point before t.

It has been proven that that BLTL formulae can be checked with only finite traces as long as the system guarantees divergence of time [15]. Unfortunately, BLTL lacks the capability to express properties about a system with a dynamic number of entities, and existing alternatives are domain-specific or bounded [13]. Each entity contains its variables (e.g., refrigerator temperature), but to refer to those variables we must first get a handle on the entity itself. We do this by allowing for quantification over active entities in the system (i.e. actualist quantification). Similarly, we allow any computable aggregation function to range over the entities and return some aggregate value (e.g., max, $\sum$). This results in Quantified Bounded linear Temporal Logic, whose syntax is defined as follows:

Definition 7 (Syntax of QBLTL). *Formulae of QBLTL are given by the following grammar, with* $* \in \{+, -, \div, \times, \hat{}\}$ *and* $\sim \in \{\leq, \geq, =\}$*:*
$\theta ::= c \mid \theta_1 * \theta_2 \mid \pi_i(e) \mid \mathsf{E}(e) \mid \boldsymbol{ag}[e](\theta)$, *with* $i \in \mathbb{N}, c \in \mathbb{Q}$
$\phi ::= \mathsf{E}(e) \mid \theta_1 \sim \theta_2 \mid \phi_1 \vee \phi_2 \mid \neg\phi_1 \mid \phi_1\ \boldsymbol{U}^t \phi_2 \mid \exists e.\phi_1$

In the above, e is a variable denoting an entity. $\pi_i(e)$ is the ith variable of entity e. $\mathbf{ag}[e](\theta)$ stands as a template for *any* computable, associative and commutative aggregation function (e.g., $\sum[e](\pi_{\text{temp}}(e))$). We abuse notation to define $\mathsf{E}(e)$ as 1) an indicator function for whether e is active, 2) formula evaluating to true iff e is active. This is useful for filtering out entities in aggregations and specifying properties quantifying over entities that exit the system. For example, $\sum[e](\mathsf{E}(e))$ evaluates to the number of active entities in the automaton.

As usual, we define the other logical operators from Def. 7, e.g., $\phi_1 \wedge \phi_2 \equiv \neg(\neg\phi_1 \vee \neg\phi_2)$, and temporal operators such as $\mathbf{F}^t\phi \equiv \text{true}\,\mathbf{U}^t\phi$ (eventually ϕ holds before t) and $\mathbf{G}^t\phi \equiv \neg\mathbf{F}^t\neg\phi$ (ϕ always holds until t).

The semantics of QBLTL are given with respect to traces and a variable assignment $\eta : Vars(\phi) \to L$ to entity labels (cf. Def. 3), where $Vars(\phi)$ is the set of variables occurring in ϕ. η is used to keep track of which entity variables refer to, as in first order logic.

Let $\sigma = (AS_0, t_0), (AS_1, t_1), ...$ be a trace of a DPCHA. We define that trace σ and assignment η satisfy a formula ϕ by a relation $\sigma, \eta \models \phi$. Let σ^i be the trace suffix of σ starting at position i, e.g., $\sigma^0 = \sigma$ and $\sigma^k = (AS_k, t_k), (AS_{k+1}, t_{k+1}), ...$ Let $[\![\theta]\!]^\eta_{\sigma^k}$ represent the value of interpreting θ under AS_k and assignment η, and $AS_i = (A_i, S_i, M_i)$ for all $i \geq 0$.

Definition 8 (Semantics of QBLTL). *The semantics of QBLTL for a trace* $\sigma^k = (AS_k, t_k), (AS_{k+1}, t_{k+1}), ...$ *are defined by the interpretation of terms:*

- $[\![c]\!]^\eta_{\sigma^k} = c$,
- $[\![\theta_1 * \theta_2]\!]^\eta_{\sigma^k} = [\![\theta_1]\!]^\eta_{\sigma^k} * [\![\theta_2]\!]^\eta_{\sigma^k}$, *interpreting the syntactic operator * by the corresponding semantic operator *,*
- $[\![\pi_i(e)]\!]^\eta_{\sigma^k} = x_i$, *where* $S_k(\eta(e)) = (q; x) \in Q \times \mathbb{R}^n$, *and* x_i *is the projection to the* i*th coordinate of* x,
- $[\![\mathsf{E}(e)]\!]^\eta_{\sigma^k} = 1$ *if* $\eta(e) \in A_k$ *and* 0 *otherwise.*
- $[\![\boldsymbol{ag}[e](\theta)]\!]^\eta_{\sigma^k} = \boldsymbol{ag}\left([\![\theta]\!]^{\eta\{e\mapsto l_1\}}_{\sigma^k}, \boldsymbol{ag}\left(..., [\![\theta]\!]^{\eta\{e\mapsto l_n\}}_{\sigma^k}\right)\right)$, *where* $(l_1, l_2, ..., l_n)$ *is some ordering of* A_k *(well-defined since* $\boldsymbol{ag}$ *is associative and commutative),*

and the following relation:

- $\sigma^k, \eta \models \mathsf{E}(e)$ *iff* $\eta(e) \in A_k$
- $\sigma^k, \eta \models \theta_1 \sim \theta_2$ *iff* $[\![\theta_1]\!]^\eta_{\sigma^k} \sim [\![\theta_2]\!]^\eta_{\sigma^k}$, *extending the syntactic comparison operator* $\sim$ *to the corresponding semantic* $\sim$,
- $\sigma^k, \eta \models \phi_1 \vee \phi_2$ *iff* $\sigma^k, \eta \models \phi_1$ *or* $\sigma^k, \eta \models \phi_2$,
- $\sigma^k, \eta \models \neg\phi_1$ *iff* $\sigma^k, \eta \not\models \phi_1$ *or it is false that* $\sigma^k, \eta \models \phi_1$,
- $\sigma^k, \eta \models \phi_1\ \boldsymbol{U}^t \phi_2$ *iff there exists* $i \in \mathbb{N}$ *such that 1)* $\sum_{l=0}^{i} t_{k+l} \leq t$, *2) for all* j *such that* $0 \leq j < i$, $\sigma^{k+j}, \eta \models \phi_1$ *and 3)* $\sigma^{k+i}, \eta \models \phi_2$,
- $\sigma^k, \eta \models \exists e.\phi_1$ *iff there exists* $l \in A_k$ *such that* $\sigma^k, \eta\{e \mapsto l\} \models \phi_1$

As usual in logic, $\sigma^k, \eta \models \phi$ is only well-defined if η contains an assignment for every free variable of ϕ. In $\exists e$, e is a variable ranging over *currently existing* entities. However, these entities may leave the system in the future, leaving us with a "dangling" variable. We illustrate this next.

Example 2. Consider a model where a consumer entity is created whenever an appliance is turned on, and that disappears when it is turned off. While verifying this model we may want to check that some appliances are always running at high power, e.g., a refrigerator with a consumption minimum of 300 watts. This property can be expressed in the following QBLTL formula $\exists e.\mathbf{G}^{24\cdot 3600}\pi_{\text{consumption}}(e) \geq 300$.

Given a trace for a sample day, we attempt to evaluate the formula. For instance, suppose e represents a washing machine that is running at first, but finishes its program and leaves the active Grid sometime later. What is the meaning of $\pi_{\text{consumption}}(e) \geq 300$ after the washing machine leaves the system?

The actualist semantics that we chose achieve what we believe is a good compromise that avoids semantic pitfalls, in the same vein as [10]. The key is to keep track of past entities' state in S so that the semantics are well-defined even with exiting entities. The main point, however, is that the special predicate/term $\mathsf{E}(\cdot)$ can be used to handle entities that have left the system. The property above should have been $\exists e.\mathbf{G}^{24\cdot 3600}\mathsf{E}(e) \wedge \pi_{\text{consumption}}(e) \geq 300$, i.e. is there an entity that is permanent and that is always consuming above 300.

We have made sure that our extensions are compatible with earlier SMC approaches so that we can lift the theory of SMC directly to our scenario. First, we guarantee that finite simulations are sufficient for checking whether a QBLTL formula is satisfied, because we cannot run infinite simulations. Due to our setting, this is a straightforward extension of results from [15]. We define a bound $\#(\phi)$ of a QBLTL formula by having $\#(\theta) = 0$ for any term θ. For any other logical connective excluding the until operator (e.g., $\neg\phi_1, \phi_1 \vee \phi_2$), we define the bound as the maximum of the bound of its direct subformulae, e.g., $\#(\phi_1 \vee \phi_2) = \max(\#(\phi_1), \#(\phi_2))$, and $\#(\exists e.\phi) = \#(\phi)$. Finally, $\#(\phi_1 \, \mathbf{U}^t \phi_2) = t + \max(\#(\phi_1), \#(\phi_2))$. We can now show that ϕ is satisfied by two infinite traces as long as the prefixes bounded by $\#(\phi)$ of those traces are the same.

Lemma 1 (QBLTL has bounded simulation traces). *Let ϕ be a QBLTL formula and $k \in \mathbb{N}$. Then for any two infinite traces $\sigma = (AS_0, t_0), (AS_1, t_1), \ldots$ and $\overline{\sigma} = (\overline{AS}_0, \overline{t}_0), (\overline{AS}_1, \overline{t}_1), \ldots$ with $AS_{k+I} = \overline{AS}_{k+I}$ and $t_{k+I} = \overline{t}_{k+I}$, for all $I \in \mathbb{N}$ with $\sum_{0 \leq l < I} t_{k+l} \leq \#(\phi)$ we have that $\sigma^k \models \phi$ iff $\overline{\sigma}^k \models \phi$.*

The proof is done by induction on QBLTL formulae. The original proof for BLTL [15] extends directly to our additions. It then follows that sampling can be bounded with $\#(\phi)$.

Lemma 2 (Bounded sampling). *The problem $\sigma \models \phi$ is well defined and can be checked for QBLTL formulae ϕ and traces σ based only on a finite prefix of σ of bounded duration.*

Again, thanks to our compatible setting, the proof for this lemma lifts directly from [15]. Without this result, SMC would not be applicable in our scenario.

5 Bayesian Statistical Model Checking

Statistical Model Checking [4,15,14] is a simple technique that has received attention due to its application to many practical situations. We follow the presentation of a Bayesian approach to the method closely, as presented in [15].

SMC tries to determine the probability p that an arbitrary trace of an automaton satisfies a QBLTL formula ϕ. Two core Bayesian approaches have been proposed: interval estimation and hypothesis testing. These methods diverge from the traditional model checking problem in that a trace that does not satisfy a formula ϕ is not a counter-example, but instead *evidence* that $p < 1$. For simplicity, we present the hypothesis testing algorithm and refer to [15] for an interval estimation algorithm, which is directly applicable in our scenario.

The hypothesis testing algorithm attempts to solve the problem "is the probability that property ϕ holds greater or equal to θ", also represented as $P_{\geq\theta}\phi$. That is, we compare the null hypothesis $H_0 : p \geq \theta$ with the alternate hypothesis $H_1 : p < \theta$. We can represent the result of each sampled trace satisfying ϕ by Bernoulli random variables with the real probability p. After n samples, we have $d = \{x_1, ..., x_n\}$ draws from those Bernoulli RV's, and each result gives us further evidence either for H_0 or for H_1. Since these hypothesis are mutually exclusive, we can assume that the prior probabilities add to 1, $P(H_0)+P(H_1) = 1$. Bayes' theorem gives us the posterior probabilities as $P(H_i|d) = \frac{P(d|H_i)P(H_i)}{P(d)}$ with $i \in \{0, 1\}$, for every d with $P(d) = P(d|H_0)P(H_0) + P(d|H_1)P(H_1) > 0$, which is always the case in this instance.

Definition 9 (Bayes factor). *The Bayes factor $\mathcal{B}$ of sample d and hypotheses H_0, H_1 is $\frac{P(d|H_0)}{P(d|H_1)}$.*

The value of the Bayes factor as defined above, obtained from data d by sampling and testing the property, can be seen as evidence in favour of the acceptance of hypothesis H_0. The inverse $\frac{1}{\mathcal{B}}$, on the other hand, is evidence in favour of H_1. We can then choose a threshold T for how much evidence is required before we accept one of the hypotheses.

From [15], we know an efficient way to calculate the Bayes factor for H_0, H_1:

$$\mathcal{B}_n = \frac{1 - \int_\theta^1 g(u)du}{\int_\theta^1 g(u)du}\left(\frac{1}{F_{(x+\alpha,n-x+\beta)}(\theta)} - 1\right),$$

in the case of beta priors, where x is the number of successes in the draws $d = (x_1, ..., x_n)$ and $F_{(s,t)}(\cdot)$ is the Beta distribution function with parameters s, t. The actual algorithm can be found in Figure 2.

The algorithm samples traces from the DPCHA, then checks them against the given formula ϕ. Since the result of these checks can be seen as drawing from a Bernoulli RV with the desired probability, the algorithm then uses the Bayes factor to calculate how much evidence is in favour of either H_0 or H_1. The amount of evidence changes with each new draw, resulting in an algorithm that adapts termination to the amount of information it can extract at each

Input: DPCHA automaton A, QBLTL property ϕ, probability θ, threshold $T \geq 1$ and Beta prior density g for unknown parameter p

```
n := 0                                   {// Total number of traces drawn}
x := 0                                   {// Total number of traces satisfying φ}
loop
  σ := sample trace from DPCHA A {// according to probabilistic Δ, cf. Sect. 3}
  n := n + 1
  if σ ⊨ φ then {// according to Def. 8}
    x := x + 1
  end if
  B := BayesFactor(n, x)
  if B > T then
    return H_0 accepted
  else if B < 1/T then
    return H_1 accepted
  end if
end loop
```

Fig. 2. Bayesian Statistical Model Checking for estimation

iteration. Eventually, enough evidence is amassed for one of the hypotheses, and it is accepted. More details about this and a more sophisticated *estimation* algorithm (that we use in the following) can be found in [15].

6 Case Study: Smart Grid

We now develop a case study using a simplified Smart Grid model. We show the versatility of our model, how smoothly it fits to the verification methods defined previously, and how easily SMC can be used to check important properties. Recall that the Smart Grid is a fusion of the Power Grid and the Cyber Grid. The hope is that communication capabilities and direct feedback from the consumer level will allow the Smart Grid to provide energy more efficiently and cost-effectively. We use the techniques implemented in our framework to study what properties of the communications layer of the Grid are important for achieving this goal. We focus on the trade-offs between cost-relevant parameters of the network and overall system performance and safety.

As in the examples above, consumer entities represent *classes* of appliances. Their demand follows a bell-shaped curve over time, representing a number of individual appliances being gradually turned on, then off and exiting the system. Consumers are managed by a Consumer Controller, which is the environment's probabilistic core. It spawns and maintains consumer entities, ensuring Grid consumption follows the patterns we observe in real life. The probability of creating a consumer (and its characteristics) depends on the hour of the day. Consumers appearing during the night or late evening request less energy but last for longer (2-3h vs 7-8h). The Power Controller (PC) receives feedback about consumption and matches generator output to demand. The generator only changes its output acceleration, so timing is essential. Refer to [7] for details.

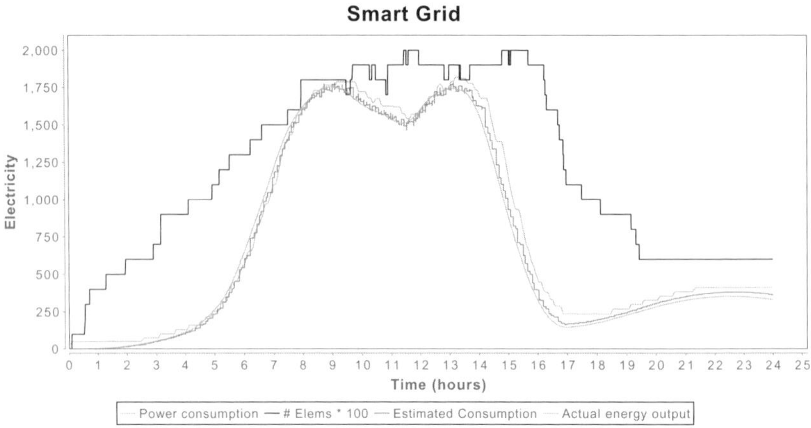

Fig. 3. Smart Grid scenario with one generator

Figure 3 shows aggregate power consumption, generator output, the PC's estimated consumption and the number of active consumer entities during one day. The shape of sample curves matches the patterns observed in reality, with peak times and a break for lunch. This indicates that our model, even simplified, simulates reasonable Grid behaviour. The intervals between control decisions for the consumers, generator and PC are given by Normal random variables with mean of 5 and variance between 1 and 3. During these control decisions, the entity decides whether not to jump along a `recv` edge, emulating message loss.

We wish to investigate what the impact of network reliability on the system level properties is by checking how resilient the Grid is to message loss. We use a benchmark of two core properties. Property (1) $\mathbf{G}^{1440}|\sum[e](Gen(e)\cdot\pi_{\text{output}}(e))-\sum[e](Cons(e)\cdot\pi_{\text{consumption}}(e))| < 400$ states that the output of the generator is always within 400 units of energy of the actual demand within the horizon of observation (1440 time units). Property (2) $\mathbf{G}^{1440}|\sum[e](Gen(e)\cdot\pi_{\text{output}}(e)) - \sum[e](PC(e)\cdot(\pi_0(e)+...+\pi_{19}(e)))| < 250$ states that the PC's estimate of power consumption is not too far from the truth. The PC's variables 0 through 19 store how much the consumers tell the PC they are consuming. Here, PC, Gen and $Cons$ are simply indicator functions for whether the element is the power controller, a generator or a consumer. We would expect that property (2) is a prerequisite to property (1), because regulating generator output depends on having good estimates of the demand.

In our experiments to test message loss resilience, we vary the delivery probability of messages for the PC. In other words, whenever there is a control decision the probability that the PC will receive a message (indicating there was no message loss) can be 0.9, 9.95, 0.97, 0.98, 0.99 and 1.00. To test these properties we use Bayesian interval estimation [15], which is a variation of the algorithm in Section 5. This algorithm returns a confidence interval where the probability that the properties are satisfied lie. We can specify the size of the interval, as well as the confidence coefficient, allowing it to be used for cursory and in-depth

Table 1. Experimental results for Bayesian hypothesis testing for Smart Grid

	(1) 1.00	(2) 1.00	(1) 0.99	(2) 0.99	(1) 0.98	(2) 0.98
Prob.	[0.89, 0.93]	[0.95, 0.99]	[0.87, 0.91]	[0.91, 0.95]	[0.86, 0.90]	[0.86, 0.90]
# correct/total	508/557	180/183	582/651	399/426	634/720	608/685
	(1) 0.97	(2) 0.97	(1) 0.95	(2) 0.95	(1) 0.9	(2) 0.9
Prob.	[0.83, 0.86]	[0.82, 0.86]	[0.75, 0.79]	[0.66, 0.70]	[0.28, 0.32]	[0.16, 0.20]
# correct/total	745/879	754/893	914/1180	998/1461	431/1423	169/971

analyses. Table 1 summarises the results for intervals of 0.04 and a confidence coefficient of 0.95.

As one would expect, a higher probability of message delivery errors will exponentially decrease the probability that the Grid is "safe" by making the generator output deviate too far from what the actual consumption is. In this scenario, we could now focus on the message delivery probability interval between 0.97 and 1.00. This helps companies and utilities decide whether to invest in more reliable communication infrastructures or not, depending on what they perceive the risk to be. It is unclear whether higher levels justify investment in 0.99 or 0.995 reliable infrastructures, because they are more expensive at Grid scale.

We also see that the stronger property (1) holds less often than the weaker (2), as we foresaw. Furthermore, the discrepancy is proportional to the error rate. This tells us that communication is central in the Smart Grid. Property (1), by requiring communication from consumers to the PC to the generator, is clearly affected by compounded delays of two hops, while (2) only requires one.

Network bandwidth is another very configurable network parameter that greatly affects deployment costs. The Grid industry still deploys networks that send a few thousand bits *per day*. Using the above model with 0.98 message delivery probability but *doubling* the consumer feedback interval from 5 to 10 minutes, we obtain the following intervals: for property (1), [0.80, 0.84] and for (2), [0.78, 0.82], a much lower performance decrease than we expected. We omit a similar analysis to the one above due to space constraints, and refer to [7].

7 Conclusions

In order to check for desirable properties of Smart Grid technologies, we defined Distributed Probabilistic-Control Hybrid Automata as a model for hybrid systems with a dynamic number of probabilistic elements, and Quantified Bounded Linear Temporal Logic to specify properties in the distributed scenario. We also showed that Bayesian statistical model checking techniques are applicable in this context for verifying QBLTL properties. Finally, we developed a Smart Grid case study where even a preliminary study revealed important cost-benefit relations relevant to full-scale deployment.

References

1. Alur, R., Courcoubetis, C., Henzinger, T.A., Ho, P.H.: Hybrid automata: An algorithmic approach to the specification and verification of hybrid systems. In: Grossman, R.L., Ravn, A.P., Rischel, H., Nerode, A. (eds.) HS 1991 and HS 1992. LNCS, vol. 736, Springer, Heidelberg (1993)
2. Demongodin, I., Koussoulas, N.: Differential Petri nets: representing continuous systems in a discrete-event world. IEEE Transactions on Automatic Control 43(4), 573–579 (1998)
3. Henzinger, T.A.: The theory of hybrid automata. In: LICS (1996)
4. Legay, A., Delahaye, B., Bensalem, S.: Statistical model checking: An overview. In: Barringer, H., Falcone, Y., Finkbeiner, B., Havelund, K., Lee, I., Pace, G., Roşu, G., Sokolsky, O., Tillmann, N. (eds.) RV 2010. LNCS, vol. 6418, pp. 122–135. Springer, Heidelberg (2010)
5. Lynch, N.A.: Input/Output automata: Basic, timed, hybrid, probabilistic, dynamic,.. In: Amadio, R.M., Lugiez, D. (eds.) CONCUR 2003. LNCS, vol. 2761, pp. 187–188. Springer, Heidelberg (2003)
6. Lynch, N.A., Segala, R., Vaandrager, F.W., Weinberg, H.B.: Hybrid I/O automata. In: Alur, R., Sontag, E.D., Henzinger, T.A. (eds.) HS 1995. LNCS, vol. 1066, Springer, Heidelberg (1996)
7. Martins, J., Platzer, A., Leite, J.: Statistical model checking for distributed probabilistic-control hybrid automata in the smart grid. Tech. Rep. CMU-CS-11-119, Computer Science Department, Carnegie Mellon University (2011)
8. Meseguer, J., Sharykin, R.: Specification and analysis of distributed object-based stochastic hybrid systems. In: Hespanha, J.P., Tiwari, A. (eds.) HSCC 2006. LNCS, vol. 3927, pp. 460–475. Springer, Heidelberg (2006)
9. Platzer, A.: Differential dynamic logic for hybrid systems. J. Autom. Reas. 41(2), 143–189 (2008)
10. Platzer, A.: Quantified differential dynamic logic for distributed hybrid systems. In: Dawar, A., Veith, H. (eds.) CSL 2010. LNCS, vol. 6247, pp. 469–483. Springer, Heidelberg (2010)
11. Platzer, A.: Stochastic differential dynamic logic for stochastic hybrid programs. In: Bjørner, N., Sofronie-Stokkermans, V. (eds.) CADE 2011. LNCS, vol. 6803, pp. 431–445. Springer, Heidelberg (2011)
12. Trivedi, K.S., Kulkarni, V.G.: FSPNs: Fluid stochastic Petri nets. In: Ajmone Marsan, M. (ed.) ICATPN 1993. LNCS, vol. 691, pp. 24–31. Springer, Heidelberg (1993)
13. Yahav, E., Reps, T., Sagiv, M.: LTL model checking for systems with unbounded number of dynamically created threads and objects. Tech. Rep. TR-1424, Computer Sciences Department, University of Wisconsin (2001)
14. Younes, H.L.S., Simmons, R.G.: Statistical probabilistic model checking with a focus on time-bounded properties. Inf. Comput. 204(9), 1368–1409 (2006)
15. Zuliani, P., Platzer, A., Clarke, E.M.: Bayesian statistical model checking with application to Simulink/Stateflow verification. In: Johansson, K.H., Yi, W. (eds.) HSCC, pp. 243–252. ACM, New York (2010)

PRTS: An Approach for Model Checking Probabilistic Real-Time Hierarchical Systems*

Jun Sun[1], Yang Liu[2], Songzheng Song[3], Jin Song Dong[2], and Xiaohong Li[4]

[1] Singapore University of Technology and Design
sunjun@sutd.edu.sg
[2] National University of Singapore
{liuyang,dongjs}@comp.nus.edu.sg
[3] NUS Graduate School for Integrative Sciences and Engineering
songsongzheng@nus.edu.sg
[4] School of Computer Science and Technology, Tianjin University
xiaohongli@tju.edu.cn

Abstract. Model Checking real-life systems is always difficult since such systems usually have quantitative timing factors and work in unreliable environment. The combination of real-time and probability in hierarchical systems presents a unique challenge to system modeling and analysis. In this work, we develop an automated approach for verifying probabilistic, real-time, hierarchical systems. Firstly, a modeling language called PRTS is defined, which combines data structures, real-time and probability. Next, a zone-based method is used to build a finite-state abstraction of PRTS models so that probabilistic model checking could be used to calculate the probability of a system satisfying certain property. We implemented our approach in the PAT model checker and conducted experiments with real-life case studies.

1 Introduction

With the development of computing and sensing technology, information process and control software are integrated into everyday objects and activities. Design and development of control software for real-life systems are notoriously difficult problems, because such systems often have complex data components or complicated hierarchical control flows. Furthermore, control software often interacts with physical environment and therefore depends on quantitative timing. In addition, probability exhibits itself commonly in the form of statistical estimates regarding the environment in which control software is embedded. Requiring a system always to function perfectly within any environment is often overwhelming. Standard model checking may produce 'unlikely' counterexamples which may not be helpful.

Example 1 (A motivating example). Multi-lift systems heavily rely on control software. A multi-lift system consists of a hierarchy of components, e.g., the system contains multiple lifts, floors, users, etc.; a lift contains a panel of buttons, a door and a lift

* This research was partially supported by research grant "SRG ISTD 2010 001" from Singapore University of Technology and Design.

S. Qin and Z. Qiu (Eds.): ICFEM 2011, LNCS 6991, pp. 147–162, 2011.

controller; a lift controller may contain multiple control units. It is complex in control logic as behavior of different components must be coordinated through a software controller. Ideally, the system shall be formally verified to satisfy desirable properties. For instance, one of the properties is: *if a user has requested to travel in certain direction, a lift should* not *pass by, i.e., traveling in the same direction without letting the user in.* However, this property is not satisfied. Typically, once a user presses a button on the external panel at certain floor, the controller assigns the request to the '*nearest*' lift. If the '*nearest*' lift is not the first reaching the floor in the same traveling direction, the property is violated. One counterexample that could be returned by a standard model checker is that the lift is held by some user for a long time so that other lifts pass by the floor in the same direction first. Designing a multi-lift system which always satisfies the property is extremely challenging. One way is to re-assign all external requests every time a lift travels to a different floor. Due to high complexity, many existing lift systems do not support re-assigning requests. The question is then: *what is the probability of violating the property, with typical randomized arrival of user requests from different floors or from the button panels inside the lifts*? If the probability is sufficiently low, then the design may be considered as acceptable. Further, can we prove that choosing the 'nearest' lift is actually better than assigning an external request to a random lift?

The above example illustrates two challenges for applying model checking in real-life systems. Firstly, an expressive modeling language supporting features like real-time, hierarchy, concurrency, data structures as well as probability, may be required to model complex systems. Secondly, the models should be efficiently model checkable for widely used properties, such as reachability checking and Linear Temporal Logic(LTL) checking. One line of work on modeling complicated systems is based on integrated formal specification languages [10,23]. These proposals suffer from one limitation, i.e., there are few supporting tools for system simulation or verification. Existing model checkers are limited because they do not support one or many of the required system features. For instance, SPIN [17] supports complex data operations and concurrency, but not real-time or probability. UPPAAL [7] supports real-time, concurrency and recently data operations as well as probability (in the extension named UPPAAL-PRO), but lacks support for hierarchical control flow and is limited to maximal probabilistic reachability checking. PRISM [15] is popular in verifying systems having concurrency, probability and the combination of real-time and probability in its latest version [19]. However, it does not support hierarchical systems, but rather networks of flat finite state systems. In addition, most of the tools support only simple data operations, which could be insufficient in modeling systems which have complicated structures and complex data operations, such as the multi-lift system.

Contribution. Compared to our previous work [28,27], the contributions of this work are threefold. First, we develop an expressive modeling language called PRTS, combining language features from [28,27]. PRTS is a combination of data structures, hierarchy, real-time, probability, concurrency, etc, and it is carefully designed in order to be expressive and also model checkable for different properties. Second, a fully automated method is used to generate abstractions from PRTS models. We show that the infinite states caused by real-time transitions could be reduced to finitely zones, which are then subject to probabilistic model checking. The abstraction technique proposed in [27] is extended to PRTS and shown to be probability preserving. Third, we implement a dedicated model checker as a part of the PAT model checker [26], which supports editing, simulating and verifying PRTS models. The tool has been applied to the multi-lift system and benchmark systems.

Organization. The paper is structured as follows. Section 2 recalls background. Section 3 introduces the proposed modeling language PRTS. Section 4 defines its operational semantics. Section 5 describes zone-based abstraction technique, which leads to the model checking approach in Section 6. The evaluation is reported in Section 7. Section 8 surveys related work. Section 9 concludes the paper and discusses future work.

2 Basic Concepts

In this section, we recall some basic concepts and definitions of model checking techniques [5] that will be used throughout the rest of the paper. When modeling probabilistic systems (particularly, discrete-time stochastic control processes), MDP is one of the most widely used models. An MDP is a directed graph whose transitions are labeled with events or probabilities. The following notations are used to denote different transition labels. $\mathbb{R}_+$ denotes the set of non-negative real numbers; $\epsilon \in \mathbb{R}_+$ denotes the event of idling for exactly ϵ time units; τ denotes an unobservable event; Act denotes the set of observable events such that $\tau \notin Act$; Act_τ denotes $Act \cup \{\tau\}$. Given a countable set of states S, a distribution is a function $\mu : S \to [0, 1]$ such that $\Sigma_{s \in S}\, \mu(s) = 1$. μ is a *trivial* distribution or is trivial if and only if there exists a state $s \in S$ such that $\mu(s) = 1$. Let $Distr(S)$ be the set of all distributions over S. Formally,

Definition 1. *An MDP is a tuple $\mathcal{D} = (S, init, Act, Pr)$ where S is a set of states; $init \in S$ is the initial state; $Pr : S \times (Act_\tau \cup \mathbb{R}_+) \times Distr(S)$ is a transition relation.*

An MDP $\mathcal{D}$ is *finite* if and only if S and $Distr(S)$ are finite. For simplicity, a transition is written as: $s \xrightarrow{x} \mu$ such that $s \in S$; $x \in Act_\tau \cup \mathbb{R}_+$ and $\mu \in Distr(S)$. If μ is trivial, i.e., $\mu(s') = 1$, then we write $s \xrightarrow{x} s'$. There are three kinds of transitions. A time-transition is labeled with a real-valued constant $\epsilon \in \mathbb{R}_+$. An observable transition is labeled with an event in Act. An un-observable transition is labeled with τ. Throughout the paper, *MDPs are assumed to be deadlock-free following the standard practice.* A deadlocking MDP can be made deadlock-free by adding self loops labeled with τ and probability 1 to the deadlocking states, without affecting the result of probabilistic verification.

A state of $\mathcal{D}$ may have multiple outgoing distributions, possibly associated with different events. A scheduler is a function deciding which event and distribution to choose. A Markov Chain [5] can be defined given an MDP $\mathcal{D}$ and a scheduler δ, which is denoted as $\mathcal{D}^\delta$. A Markov Chain is an MDP where only one event and distribution is available at every state. Intuitively speaking, given a state s, firstly an enabled event and a distribution are selected by the scheduler, and then one of the successor states is reached according to the probability distribution. A rooted run of $\mathcal{D}^\delta$ is an alternating sequence of states and events $\pi = \langle s_0, x_0, s_1, x_1, \cdots \rangle$ such that $s_0 = init$. The sequence $\langle x_0, x_1, \cdots \rangle$, denoted as $trace(\pi)$, is a trace of $\mathcal{D}^\delta$. Let $runs(\mathcal{D}^\delta)$ denote the set of rooted runs of $\mathcal{D}$. Let $traces(\mathcal{D}^\delta)$ denote the set of traces of $\mathcal{D}^\delta$. Given $\mathcal{D}^\delta$ and $s_i \in D$, let μ_i be the (only) distribution at s_i. The probability of exhibiting π in $\mathcal{D}^\delta$, denoted as $\mathcal{P}_{\mathcal{D}^\delta}(\pi)$, is $\mu_0(s_1) * \mu_1(s_2) * \cdots$.

It is often useful to find out the probability of $\mathcal{D}$ satisfying a property ϕ. Note that with different schedulers, the result may be different. For instance, if ϕ is reachability of a state s, then s may be reached by different scheduling with different probability. The measurement of interest is thus the maximum and minimum probability of satisfying ϕ. The maximum probability is defined as follows.

$$\mathcal{P}_{\mathcal{D}}^{max}(\phi) = \sup_\delta \mathcal{P}_{\mathcal{D}}(\{\pi \in runs(\mathcal{D}^\delta) \mid \pi \text{ satisfies } \phi\})$$

Note that the supremum ranges over all, potentially infinitely many, schedulers. Intuitively, it is the maximum of probability of satisfying ϕ with any scheduler. The minimum is defined as: $\mathcal{P}_{\mathcal{D}}^{min}(\phi) = \inf_\delta \mathcal{P}_{\mathcal{D}}(\{\pi \in runs(\mathcal{D}^\delta) \mid \pi \text{ satisfies } \phi\})$ which yields the best lower bound that can be guaranteed for the probability of satisfying ϕ. For different classes of properties, there are different methods to calculate the maximum and minimum probability, e.g., reachability by solving a linear program or graph-based iterative methods; LTL checking by identifying end components and then calculating reachability probability [5].

3 Syntax of PRTS

The choice of modeling language is an important factor in the success of the entire system analysis or development. The language should cover several facets of the requirements and the model should reflect exactly (up to abstraction of irrelevant details) a system. In this work, we draw upon existing approaches [16,21,2,27] and create the single notation PRTS. In the following, we briefly introduce the syntax of a core subset of PRTS. Interested readers can refer to PAT user manual for a complete list of constructs and detailed explanation.

A PRTS model (hereafter model) is a 3-tuple (Var, σ_i, P) where Var is a finite set of finite-domain global variables; σ_i is the initial valuation of Var and P is a process which captures the control logic of the system. A process is defined in form of $Proc(\overline{para}) = PExpr$ where $Proc$ is a process name; $\overline{para}$ is a vector of parameters and $PExpr$ is a process expression. A rich set of process constructs are defined to capture different features of various systems, as shown in the following.

$$\begin{aligned} P = & \ Stop \mid Skip \mid e \rightarrow P \mid P \Box Q \mid P \sqcap Q \mid P;\ Q \mid P \parallel Q \mid P \mid\mid\mid Q \\ & \mid P \setminus \{X\} \mid if\ b\ then\ P\ else\ Q \mid a\{program\} \rightarrow P \mid Wait[d] \\ & \mid P\ timeout[d]\ Q \mid P\ interrupt[d]\ Q \mid P\ deadline[d] \mid P\ within[d] \\ & \mid pcase\{pr_0 : P_0;\ pr_1 : P_1;\ \cdots;\ pr_k : P_k\} \mid ref(Q) \end{aligned}$$

Hierarchical Control Flow. A number of the constructs are adapted from the classic CSP [16] to support modeling of hierarchical systems. Process $Stop$ and $Skip$ are process primitives, which denote inaction and termination respectively. Process $e \rightarrow P$ engages in an abstract event e first and then behaves as process P. Event e may serve as a multi-party synchronization barrier if combined with parallel composition $\parallel$. A variety of choices are supported, e.g., $P \Box Q$ for unconditional choice; and *if* b *then* P *else* Q for conditional branching in which b is a boolean expression composed by process parameters and variables in Var. Process $P;\ Q$ behaves as P until P terminates and then behaves as Q. Parallel composition of two processes is written as $P \parallel Q$, where P and Q may communicate via multi-party event synchronization. If P and Q only communicate through variables[1], then it is written as $P \mid\mid\mid Q$. Process $P \setminus \{X\}$ hides occurrence of any event in $\{X\}$. Recursion is supported by referencing a process name with concrete parameters. The semantics of the constructs is defined in [29].

Data Structures and Operations. Different from CSP, a PRTS model is equipped with a set of variables Var. Variables can be of simple types like Boolean or integer or arrays of simple types. In order to support arbitrary complex data structures and operations, user-defined data types are allowed. A user-defined data type must be defined externally (e.g., as a C# library), and imported in a model. The detailed explanation of the interface methods and examples of creating/using C# library can be found in PAT user manual. Note that in order to guarantee that model checking is terminating, each data object must have only finitely many different values and *all data operations must be terminating*, both of which are users' responsibility. Furthermore, users are recommended to apply standard programming techniques like using assertions to ensure correctness of the data operations. Data operations are invoked through process expression $a\{program\} \rightarrow P$, which generates an event a and atomically executes program $program$ at the same time, and then behaves as P. In other words, $program$ is a *transaction*. Variable updates are allowed in $program$. In order to prevent data race, event a with an attached program will not to be synchronized by multiple processes.

Real-Time. A number of timed process constructs are supported in PRTS to cover common timed behavioral patterns. Process $Wait[d]$ idles for exactly d time units, where d an integer constant. In process $P\ timeout[d]\ Q$, the first observable event of P shall occur before d time units elapse (since the process is *activated*). Otherwise, Q takes over control after exactly d time units. Process $P\ interrupt[d]\ Q$ behaves exactly as P (which may engage in multiple observable events) until d time units elapse, and then Q takes over control. PRTS extends Timed CSP [25] with additional timed process constructs. Process $P\ deadline[d]$ constrains P to terminate before d time units. Process $P\ within[d]$ requires that P must perform an observable event within d time units. Constant d associated with the timed process constructs are referred as the *parameter of the timed process construct*. Note that real-time systems modeled in PRTS can be fully hierarchical, whereas Timed Automata based languages (e.g., the one supported by Uppaal) often have the form of a network of flat Timed Automata.

Probability. In order to randomized behaviors (i.e., unreliable environment or cognitive aspects of user behaviors), probabilistic choices are introduced as follows.

$$pcase\ \{pr_0 : P_0;\ pr_1 : P_1;\ \cdots;\ pr_k : P_k\}$$

where pr_i is a positive integer constant to express the probability weight. Intuitively, it means that with $\frac{pr_i}{pr_0+pr_1+\cdots+pr_k}$ probability, the system behaves as P_i. Note that the

[1] Or synchronous/asynchronous channels. The details are skipped for simplicity.

```
1. #define NoOfFloors 2;
2. #define NoOfLifts 2;
3. #import "PAT.Lib.Lift";
4. var<LiftControl> ctrl = new LiftControl(NoOfFloors,NoOfLifts);
5. Users() = pcase {
6.            1 : extreq.0.1{ctrl.Assign_External_Up_Request(0)} -> Skip
7.            1 : intreq.0.0.1{ctrl.Add_Internal_Request(0,0)} -> Skip
8.            1 : intreq.1.0.1{ctrl.Add_Internal_Request(1,0)} -> Skip
9.            1 : extreq.1.0{ctrl.Assign_External_Down_Request(1)} -> Skip
10.           1 : intreq.0.1.1{ctrl.Add_Internal_Request(0,1)} -> Skip
11.           1 : intreq.1.1.1{ctrl.Add_Internal_Request(1,1)} -> Skip
12.        } within[1]; Users();
13. Lift(i, level, direction) = ...;
14. System = (||| x:{0..NoOfLifts-1} @ Lift(x, 0, 1)) ||| Users();
```

Fig. 1. A lift system model

```
public void Assign_External_Up_Request(int level) {
    ...
    int minimumDistance = int.MaxValue;
    int chosenLift = -1;
    for (int i = 0; i < LiftStatus.Length; i++) {
       int distance;
       if (LiftStatus[i] >= 0) {
           if (LiftStatus[i] <= level) {
                distance = level - LiftStatus[i];
           } else {
                distance = NoOfFloors - LiftStatus[i] + NoOfFloors - level;
           }
       } else {
           distance = LiftStatus[i] * -1 + level;
       }
       if (distance < minimumDistance) {
           chosenLift = i;
           minimumDistance = distance;
       }
    }
    ExternalRequestsUp[level] = chosenLift;
}
```

Fig. 2. A data operation example

sum of all the probabilities in one *pcase* is guaranteed to be 1. Process P_i can be any process and thus PRTS supports fully hierarchical probabilistic systems.

Example 2. We use the lift system example to illustrate modeling with PRTS. The model (in ASCII format as supported in PAT) is shown in Figure 1. Line 1 and 2 define two constants which denote the number of floors and lifts respectively. Line 3 imports a C# library, which defines a data type *LiftControl* encapsulating all data components and operations of the lift system. Note that it is a design decision whether to maintain the data externally in the C# library or in the model itself. A *LiftControl* object contains multiple data structures, e.g., an integer array for user requests from external button panels, a two dimensional array for requests for internal button panels, etc. Interested readers can refer to PAT (version 3.0 or later, open with PAT's C# editor and compiler) for its details. The *LiftControl* class also defines multiple data operations. For instance, one of them is shown in Figure 2 which assigns an external request for traveling upwards to a lift. The idea is to assign a request to a lift which can reach the requesting floor by traveling the minimum number of floors (without changing direction except at the top or bottom floor). Note that $level$ denotes the requesting floor and $LiftStatus$ is an array maintaining status of the lifts, i.e., $ListStatus[i] = -2$ means that i-th lift is at level 2 traveling downwards. In Figure 1, line 4 of the lift model creates a $LiftControl$ object named $ctrl$. Line 5 to 12 defines a process $Users()$, which models behavior of the users. In this (overly) simplified model, user requests are assumed to arrive periodically with uniform probabilistic distribution[2]. There are 6 different requests with 2 floors and 2 lifts (two of which are external requests). Each is given $\frac{1}{6}$ probability, as modeled using $pcase$ at line 5-12 in Figure 1. For instance, event $extreq.0.1$ models an external request at 0-floor for traveling upwards. The event is associated with a program which invokes the method for assigning requests to lifts through object $ctrl$. Note that user behaviors are subject to real-time constraint, i.e., a request is requested within 1 second, modeled using $within[1]$. At line 13, process $Lift$ which is composed of sub-processes models an individual lift. We skip its details for the sake of space. At the top level, the system is the interleaving of users and lifts at line 14.

4 Operational Semantics

The semantics of a PRTS model is an MDP, due to its mixture of nondeterminism and probabilistic choices. In order to define the operational semantics, we define the notion of a configuration to capture the global system state during the execution, referred as *concrete configurations*. This terminology distinguishes the notion from the abstract configurations which will be introduced in Section 5.

Definition 2. *A concrete system configuration is a tuple $c = (\sigma, P)$ where σ is a variable valuation and P is a process.*

Given a model, the probabilistic transition relation of its MDP semantics can be defined by associating a set of firing rules with every process construct, which are also known as *concrete firing rules*. In the following, the rules for process $Wait[d]$, $P\ timeout[d]\ Q$ and $pcase$ are exemplified in Figure 3. The rest are similarly defined (available in [29]). The top two rules capture behaviors of process $Wait[d]$. The first rule states that through a time-transition, a process may idle for any amount of time as long as it is less than or equal to d time units. Note that no variable update is not possible in time-transitions. The second rule states that the process terminates immediately after d becomes 0. The next four rules capture semantics of process $P\ timeout[d]\ Q$. If an observable event e can be performed by P, then $P\ timeout[d]\ Q$ becomes P' (the first rule). That is, once an observable event is engaged before d time units, time-out never occurs. If d is 0, Q may take over control and the whole process becomes Q via a τ-transition (the second rule). Note that it is possible that an observable event occurs when d is 0. Only that when d is 0, time-transition is not allowed before the τ-transition. If an unobservable transition is generated by P, the $timeout$ operator remains (the third rule). If P may idle for less than or equal to d time units, so is $P\ timeout[d]\ Q$. All above transitions result in trivial distributions. The resultant distribution of the $pcase$ process is defined such that the probability of becoming P_i is pr_i. Note that neither variable valuation

[2] A realistic user model can be obtained by mining data of actual lift systems.

$$\frac{\epsilon \leq d}{(\sigma, Wait[d]) \xrightarrow{\epsilon} (\sigma, Wait[d - \epsilon])} \qquad \frac{}{(\sigma, Wait[0]) \xrightarrow{\tau} (\sigma, Skip)}$$

$$\frac{(\sigma, P) \xrightarrow{e} (\sigma', P'), e \in Act}{(\sigma, P\ timeout[d]\ Q) \xrightarrow{e} (\sigma', P')} \qquad \frac{}{(\sigma, P\ timeout[0]\ Q) \xrightarrow{\tau} (\sigma, Q)}$$

$$\frac{(\sigma, P) \xrightarrow{\tau} (\sigma', P')}{(\sigma, P\ timeout[d]\ Q) \xrightarrow{\tau} (\sigma', P'\ timeout[d]\ Q)}$$

$$\frac{(\sigma, P) \xrightarrow{\epsilon} (\sigma, P'), \epsilon \leq d}{(\sigma, P\ timeout[d]\ Q) \xrightarrow{\epsilon} (\sigma, P'\ timeout[d - \epsilon]\ Q)}$$

$$\frac{}{\begin{array}{l}(\sigma, pcase\ \{pr_0 : P_0;\ pr_1 : P_1;\ \cdots;\ pr_k : P_k\}) \xrightarrow{\tau} \mu \\ \quad \text{s.t. } \mu((\sigma, P_i)) = \frac{pr_i}{pr_0 + pr_1 + \cdots + pr_k} \text{ for all } i \in [0,\ k]\end{array}} \ [\ pcase\ ]$$

Fig. 3. Concrete firing rules

nor time change. Rule *pcase* is the only rule which produces a nontrivial distribution. *We remark that different from Probabilistic Timed Automata(PTA) [14,21], probability and time are separated in PRTS, i.e., a transition can be either time-consuming or has trivial probability but never both.*

Definition 3. *Let $M = (Var, \sigma_{init}, P)$ be a model. $\mathcal{D}_M$ is an MDP $(S, init, Act, Pr)$ such that S is a set of concrete system configurations; $init = (\sigma_{init}, P)$; and Pr : $S \times (Act_\tau \cup \mathbb{R}_+) \times Distr(S)$ is defined by the firing rules.*

$\mathcal{D}_M$ is referred to as the *concrete semantics of M*. Because PRTS has a dense-time semantics, $\mathcal{D}_M$ has infinitely many states. In order to apply model checking techniques, a finite-state abstract MDP is required.

5 Abstraction

In this section, we present a fully automated approach to generate a finite-state abstract MDP from a model. Without loss of generality, *we assume that every process reachable from the initial configuration is finite-state (as defined in [24])*. As a result, in a process which has finitely many process constructs, the only source of infinity is timing, or equivalently, the infinitely many possible values for parameters of timed process constructs. For instance, given process $Wait[1]$, there are infinitely many processes that can be reached by a time-transition, e.g., $Wait[0.9]$, $Wait[0.99]$, $Wait[0.999]$, etc. One observation is that for certain properties, the exact value of the parameters is not important, i.e., they can be grouped into equivalent classes. This leads to the idea of using a constraint to capture the value of the parameters. In the following, we summarize *dynamic zone abstraction* [27] and prove that it can be applied to PRTS models without changing the results of probabilistic properties.

In order to distinguish parameters associated with different process constructs, the first step of the abstraction is to associate timed process constructs with clocks. Constraints on the clocks are then used to capture values of the respective parameters. For simplicity of presentation, we assume that each process construct is associated with a unique clock[3]. For instance, let $P\ timeout[d]_c\ Q$ denote that process $P\ timeout[d]\ Q$ is associated with clock c. $P\ timeout[d]_c\ Q$ with a constraint $c \leq 5$ represents any process $P\ timeout[d']\ Q$ with $d' \leq 5$. This gives the notion of abstract system configurations, which compose the abstract MDP.

Definition 4. *Given a concrete system configuration (σ, P), the corresponding abstract system configuration is a triple (σ, P_T, D) such that P_T is a process obtained by associating P with a set of clocks; and D is a zone over the clocks.*

There are usually multiple timed process constructs in a process P. Nonetheless, at one moment not all of the timed constructs are activated, i.e., only some of them are ready to take over control and perform a transition. We write $cl(P)$ to denote the set of clocks activated in P and $X = 0$ where X is a set of clocks to denote the conjunction of $c = 0$ for all $c \in X$.

A zone D is the conjunction of multiple primitive constraints over a set of clocks. A primitive constraint is of the form $t \sim d$ or $t_i - t_j \sim d$ where t, t_i, t_j are clocks, d is a constant and $\sim$ is either, $\geq$, $=$ or $\leq$[4]. Intuitively, a zone is the maximal set of clock valuations satisfying the constraint. A zone is empty if and only if the constraint is unsatisfiable. An abstraction configuration (σ, P_T, D) is valid if and only if D is not empty. The following zone operations are relevant. Let D denote a zone. $D^{\uparrow}$ denotes the zone obtained by delaying arbitrary amount of time. Note that all clocks proceed at the same rate. For instance, let c be a clock, $(c \leq 5)^{\uparrow}$ is $c \leq \infty$. Given a set of clocks X, $D[X]$ denotes the set of valuations of clocks in X which satisfy D. Zones can be equivalently represented as Difference Bound Matrices(DBMs) and zone operations can be translated into DBMs manipulation [12,8].

In order to define the abstract MDP, we define abstract firing rules. To distinguish from concrete transitions, an abstract transition is written in the form: $(\sigma, P_T, D) \overset{e}{\rightsquigarrow} (\sigma', P'_T, D')$. Figure 4 shows the abstract rules for process $Wait[d]$, $P\ timeout[d]\ Q$ and $pcase$ as examples. Given process P which is associated with clocks, $idle(P)$ is defined to be the maximum zone such that P can idle before performing an event-transition. For instance, $idle(P\ deadline[5]_c) = idle(P) \wedge c \leq 5$, i.e., $P\ deadline[5]_c$ can idle as long as P can idle and the reading of c is no bigger than 5. Refer to [29] for the detailed definition of $idle(P)$ and the rest of the abstract firing rules. Rule ade in Figure 4 states that process $Wait[d]$ idles for exactly d time units and then engages in event τ and the process transforms to $Skip$. Note that the zone of the target configuration is $D^{\uparrow} \wedge c = d$. Intuitively, it means that the transition occurs sometime in

[3] For practice, clocks are renamed dynamically so that they are shared by processes which are activated at the same time. Refer to details in [27].

[4] In our setting, the clock constraints are always closed.

the future (captured by $D^{\uparrow}$) when c reads d (captured by $c = d$). It should be clear that this is 'equivalent' to the concrete firing rules. Rule $ato1$, $ato2$ and $ato3$ capture the abstract semantics of P $timeout[d]$ Q. Depending on when the first event of P takes place and whether it is observable, process P $timeout[d]$ Q behaves differently in three ways. Rule $ato1$ states that if P generates a τ-transition, the *timeout* construct remains. Furthermore, the target zone $D' \wedge c \leq d$ constrains that the transition must take place no later than d time units. In contrast, rule $ato2$ states that if P generates an observable transition, then the *timeout* construct is removed. Similarly, it is constrained that the transition must occur no later than d time units. Rule $ato3$ captures the case when timeout occurs. Namely, timeout occurs if and only if the reading of c is exactly d and, further, P must be able to idle until c reads d. Rule *apcase* captures the abstract semantics of *pcase*. *Note that this τ-transition is instantaneous.*

Definition 5. *Let $M = (Var, \sigma_{init}, Proc)$ be a model. $\mathcal{D}^a_M = (S_a, init_a, Act, Pr_a)$ is the abstract MDP such that S_a is a set of valid abstract system configurations; $init_a = (\sigma_{init}, Proc, D_{init})$ is the initial abstract configuration where D_{init} is $cl(Proc) = 0$; and Pr_a is the smallest transition relation such that: for all $s \in S_a$, if $s \overset{a}{\rightsquigarrow} \mu$, then $(s, a, \mu') \in Pr_a$ such that: if $\mu((\sigma, P, D)) > 0$, then $\mu'((\sigma, P, D')) = \mu((\sigma, P, D))$ where $D' = D[cl(Q)] \wedge cl(Q) - cl(P) = 0$.*

Informally, for any (σ, P_T, D) obtained by applying an abstract firing rule, D' is obtained by firstly pruning all clocks which are not in $cl(Q)$ and then setting clocks associated with newly activated processes (i.e., $cl(Q) - cl(P)$) to be 0. The construct of $\mathcal{D}^a_M$ is illustrated in the following example.

Example 3. Assume a model $M = (\varnothing, \varnothing, P)$ such that process P is defined as follows.

$$P = (pcase\ \{1 : Wait[2]_{c_0};\ 3 : Wait[5]_{c_1}\})\ timeout[3]_{c_2}\ exit \rightarrow P$$

The abstract MDP is shown as follows.

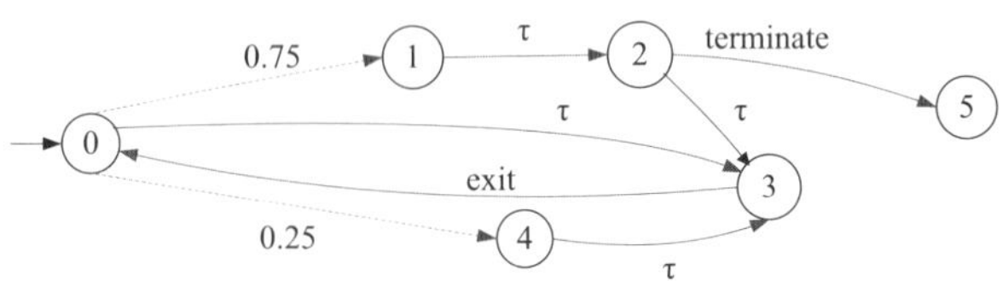

A transition is labeled with an event (with a skipped probability 1) or a probability less than 1 (with a skipped event τ). Note that all transitions with resulting in a non-trivial distribution is labeled with τ, whereas all transitions labeled with an event other than τ has probability 1. The initial configuration state 0 is $(\varnothing, P, c_2 = 0)$ where clock c_2 is associated with $timeout[3]$ in P. Applying rule $ato3$, we get the transition from state 0 to state 3. Note that clock c_2 is pruned after the transition because it is no longer associated with any process constructs. Applying rule *apcase*, we get the transitions from state 0 to state 1 and 4, which belong to the same distribution. Note that clock c_2 is not pruned during both transitions. State 4 is as follows: $(\varnothing, Wait[5]_{c_1}\ timeout[3]_{c_2}\ exit \rightarrow P, c_2 = 0 \wedge c_1 = 0)$. By rule *apcase*, the τ-transition is instantaneous and thus $c_2 = 0$. Note that $c_2 = c_1$ since c_1 starts when

$$\frac{}{(\sigma, Wait[d]_c, D) \overset{\tau}{\rightsquigarrow} (\sigma, Skip, D^{\uparrow} \wedge c = d)} \; [\, ade \,]$$

$$\frac{(\sigma, P, D) \overset{\tau}{\rightsquigarrow} (\sigma', P', D')}{(\sigma, P \; timeout[d]_c \; Q, D) \overset{\tau}{\rightsquigarrow} (\sigma', P' \; timeout[d]_c \; Q, D' \wedge c \leq d)} \; [\, ato1 \,]$$

$$\frac{(\sigma, P, D) \overset{e}{\rightsquigarrow} (\sigma', P', D'), e \neq \tau}{(\sigma, P \; timeout[d]_c \; Q, D) \overset{e}{\rightsquigarrow} (\sigma', P', D' \wedge c \leq d)} \; [\, ato2 \,]$$

$$\frac{}{(\sigma, P \; timeout[d]_c \; Q, D) \overset{\tau}{\rightsquigarrow} (\sigma, Q, c = d \wedge idle(P))} \; [\, ato3 \,]$$

$$\frac{}{\begin{array}{l}(\sigma, pcase \; \{pr_0 : P_0; \; pr_1 : P_1; \; \cdots; \; pr_k : P_k\}, D) \overset{\tau}{\rightsquigarrow} \mu \\ \quad \text{s.t. } \mu((\sigma, P_i, D)) = \frac{pr_i}{pr_0 + pr_1 + \cdots + pr_k} \text{ for } i \in [0, k]\end{array}} \; [\, apcase \,]$$

Fig. 4. Abstract firing rules

$c_2 = 0$. Two rules can be applied to state 4, i.e., $ato3$ so that timeout occurs or otherwise $ato2$. Applying rule $ato3$, we obtain the transition from state 4 to state 3. Applying rule $ato2$, we obtain the following zone: $c_1 = 5 \wedge c_2 \leq 3 \wedge c_1 = c_2$. It can be shown that the zone is empty and hence the transition is infeasible. Other transitions are similarly obtained. Note that the event *terminate* is generated by the process *Skip* which is in term generated from $Wait[2]$ (rule ade). □

6 Verification

We show that the abstraction model can be verified with standard probabilistic model checking techniques. Given a model M, $\mathcal{D}^a_M$ must be finite so as to be model checkable.

Theorem 1. *$\mathcal{D}^a_M$ is finite for any model M.* □

A proof sketch is as follows. The number of states in $\mathcal{D}^a_M$ is bounded by the number of 1) variable valuations, 2) process expressions and 3) zones. By assumption, 1) is finite. Because clocks are associated with timed process constructs and we assume that every reachable process P is finite, $cl(P)$ is finite. It can be shown that by reusing clocks, finitely many clocks are sufficient. Combined with our assumption, 2) is finite. By previous work on zone abstraction [9], 3) is finite[5].

Furthermore, the abstract semantics $\mathcal{D}^a_M$ must be 'sufficiently' equivalent to the concrete semantics $\mathcal{D}_M$ so that verification results based on $\mathcal{D}^a_M$ apply to $\mathcal{D}_M$. In the following, we show that our abstraction is probability preserving with respect to one popular class of properties: (untimed) LTL-X (i.e., LTL without the 'next' operator)[6].

[5] Zone normalization is not necessary as all clocks are bounded from above. Refer to [29].

[6] The next operator is omitted because its semantics for real-times systems can be confusing.

Assume that ϕ is an LTL-X formula, constituted by temporal operators, logic operators and atomic propositions on variables. Given a run π of an MDP and ϕ, satisfaction of ϕ by π is defined in the standard way. Let $\mathcal{P}_{\mathcal{D}}^{max}(\phi)$ be the maximum probability of MDP $\mathcal{D}$ satisfying ϕ; $\mathcal{P}_{\mathcal{D}}^{min}(\phi)$ be the minimum probability satisfying ϕ. The following establishes that it is sound and complete to model-check LTL-X against $\mathcal{D}_M^a$.

Theorem 2. *Let M be a model.* $\mathcal{P}_{\mathcal{D}_M^a}^{max}(\phi) = \mathcal{P}_{\mathcal{D}_M}^{max}(\phi)$ *and* $\mathcal{P}_{\mathcal{D}_M^a}^{min}(\phi) = \mathcal{P}_{\mathcal{D}_M}^{min}(\phi)$. □

A proof sketch is as follows. Refer to [29] for a complete proof. This theorem is proved by showing that: for every run ex of $\mathcal{D}_M$, there is a run ex' of $\mathcal{D}_M^a$(and vice versa) such that (1) ex and ex' are stutter equivalent in terms of variable valuations; (2) ex and ex' have the same probability. Intuitively, (1) is true because variable valuations do not change through time transitions and all that our abstract does is to encapsulate time transitions (while preserving event transitions). (2) is true because time-transitions always have probability 1. We remark that it is known that forward analysis of PTA [21] is not accurate (e.g., the maximum probability returned is an over-approximation) because zone graphes generated from Timed Automata do not satisfy (pre)-stability. We show in [29] that dynamic zone abstraction (for Stateful Timed CSP [27] and ergo PRTS) generates zone graphes which are time-abstract bi-similar to the concrete transition systems and satisfy (pre-)stability. As a result, forward analysis of $\mathcal{D}_M^a$ is accurate.

We adopt the automata-based approach [5] to check LTL-X properties. Firstly, a deterministic Rabin automaton equivalent to a given LTL-X formula is built. The product of the automaton and the abstract MDP is then computed. Thirdly, *end components* in the product which satisfy the Rabin acceptance condition are identified. Lastly, the probability of reaching any state of the end components is calculated, which equals the probability of satisfying the property.

7 Implementation and Evaluation

System modeling, simulation and verification in PRTS have been supported (as a module) in PAT[7]. PAT has user-friendly editor, simulator and verifier and works under different operating systems. After inputting PRTS model in the editor, users could simulate the system behaviors step by step or generate the whole state space if the number of states is under some constraint. For verification, besides the LTL-X checking, PRTS also supports reachability checking, and refinement checking (i.e., calculating the probability of a probabilistic system exhibiting any behaviors of a non-probabilistic specification).

To answer the question on our motivating example, we verify the lift model and compare two ways of assigning external requests. One is to assign the request to a *random* lift. The other is that an external request is always assigned to the 'nearest' lift. For simplicity, we assume external requests are never re-assigned. A lift works as follows. It firstly checks whether it should serve the current floor. If positive, it opens its door and then repeats from the beginning later. If negative, it checks whether it should continue traveling in the same direction (if there are internal requests or assigned external requests on the way) or change direction (if there are internal or assigned external

[7] http://www.patroot.com

Table 1. Experiments: Lift System

System	Random		Nearest	
	Result(pmax)	Time(s)	Result(pmax)	Time(s)
lift=2; floor=2; user=2	0.21875	3.262	0.13889	2.385
lift=2; floor=2; user=3	0.47656	38.785	0.34722	18.061
lift=2; floor=2; user=4	0.6792	224.708	0.53781	78.484
lift=2; floor=2; user=5	0.81372	945.853	0.68403	223.036
lift=2; floor=3; user=2	0.2551	12.172	0.18	6.757
lift=2; floor=3; user=3	0.54009	364.588	0.427	119.810
lift=2; floor=3; user=4	0.74396	11479.966	0.6335	1956.041
lift=2; floor=4; user=2	0.27	27.888	0.19898	13.693
lift=3; floor=2; user=2	0.22917	208.481	0.10938	88.549
lift=3; floor=2; user=3	OOM	OOM	0.27344	3093.969

requests on the other direction) or simply idle (otherwise). Note that it is constrained (using $within$) to react regularly. The property that a lift should not pass by without serving a user's external request is verified through probabilistic reachability analysis, i.e., what is the maximal probability of reaching a state such that a lift is passing by a requested floor in the requested direction. Table 1 summarizes the experiment results, where OOM means out of memory. The experiment testbed is a PC running Windows Server 2008 64 Bit with Intel Xeon 4-Core CPU×2 and 32 GB memory. Details about our experiments are available at $http://www.comp.nus.edu.sg/\tilde{}pat/icfem/prts$.

The parameters of the model denote the number of *lifts*, the number of *floors* and number of *user requests* respectively. We limit the number of user requests so as to check how the probability varies as well as to avoid state space explosion. It is inf when there is no limit. Column $Random$ and $Nearest$ shows the *maximum* probability of violating the property with $random$ assignment and '$nearest$' assignment respectively. Note that it can be shown that the minimum probability is always 0 (i.e., there exists a scheduler which guarantees satisfaction of the property). The following conclusion can be made. Firstly, it takes at least two external requests, two lifts and two floors to constitute a bad behavior, e.g., one lift is at top floor (and later going down to serve a request), while a request for going down at the top floor is assigned to the other lift. Secondly, the more user requests, the higher the probability is. Intuitively, this means that with more requests, it is more likely that the bad behavior occurs. Similarly, the probability is higher with more floors. Lastly, 'nearest' assignment performs better than random assignment as expected, i.e., the maximum probability of exhibiting a bad behavior with the former is always lower than with the latter in all cases.

The statistics on memory consumption is skipped as PAT only generates an estimated memory usage for each verification run because memory usage is managed by .NET framework. In average, our current implementation processes 11K states per second (or millions in one hour) in these experiments, which is less than other explicit-state model checkers like SPIN. This is expected given the complexity in handling PRTS. State space explosion occurs when there are more than 3 lifts and more than 4 floors. This, however, should not be taken as the limit of PAT, as many optimization techniques are yet to incorporated.

Table 2. Experiments: PAT vs PRISM

System	Property	Result	PAT(s)	PRISM(s)
ME (N=5)	LTL	1	9.031	7.413
ME (N=8)	LTL	1	185.051	149.448
RC (N=4,K=4)	LTL	0.99935	4.287	33.091
RC (N=6,K=6)	LTL	1	146.089	2311.388
CS (N=2, K=4)	LTL	0.99902	9.362	1.014
CS (N=3, K=2)	LTL	0.85962	212.712	7.628

Next, the PRTS checker is compared with state-of-the-art probabilistic model checker PRISM on verifying benchmark systems based on MDP. The results are summarized in Table 2. We use existing PRISM models; re-model them using PRTS and verify them. The models are a mutual exclusion protocol (ME), a randomized consensus algorithm(RC), and the CSMA/CD protocol (CS). We use the iterative method in calculating the probability and set termination threshold as relative difference 1.0E-6 (same as PRISM). Our implementation is better for CS, slightly slower than ME and significantly slower for RC. The main reason that PAT could outperform PRISM in some cases is that models in the PRTS have much fewer states than their respective in PRISM - due to difference in modeling language design. In general, PRISM handles more states per time unit than PAT. The main reason is the complexity in handling hierarchical models. Note that though these models have simple structures, there is overhead for maintaining underlying data structures designed for hierarchical systems. PRISM is based on MTBDD or sparse matrix or a hybrid approach, whereas PAT is based on explicit state representation currently. Symbolic methods like BDD are known to handle more states. Applying BDD techniques to hierarchical complex languages like PRTS is highly non-trivial. It remains as one of our ongoing work.

8 Related Work

There are several modeling methods and model checking algorithms for real-time probabilistic systems. Alur, Courcoubetis and Dill presented a model-checking algorithm for probabilistic real-time systems to verify TCTL formulae of probabilistic real-time systems [1]. Their specification is limited to deterministic Timed Automata, and its use of continuous probability distributions (a highly expressive modeling mechanism) does not permit the model to be automatically verified against logics which include bounds on probability. Remotely related is the line of work on Continuous-Time Markov Chains (CTMC) [4]. Different from CTMC, our work is based on discrete probability distributions. A method based on MTBDD for analyzing the stochastic and timing properties of systems was proposed in [3]. Properties are expressed in a subset of PCTL. The method was not based on real-time but in the realm of discrete time. Similar work using discrete time includes [13,20].

Research on combining quantitative timing and probability has been mostly based on Probabilistic Timed Automata (PTA) [14,21]. PTA extends Timed Automata [2] with nondeterministic choices, and discrete probability distributions which are defined over a finite set of edges. It is a modeling formalism for describing formally both nondeterministic and probabilistic aspects of real-time systems. Based on PTA, symbolic verification techniques [22] are developed using MTBDDs. In [6], Beauquier proposed another model of probabilistic Timed Automata. The model in [6] differs from PTA in that it allows different enabling conditions for edges related to a certain action and it uses Büchi conditions as accepting conditions. In [18], probabilistic timed program (PTP) is proposed to model real-time probabilistic software (e.g., SystemC). PTP is an extension of PTA with discrete variables. PTA and PTP are closely related to PRTS with some noticeable differences. Firstly, time transitions and probabilistic transitions are separated in PRTS. Secondly, (Stateful) Timed CSP is equivalent to closed Timed Automata (with τ-transitions) [24] and therefore strictly less expressive, which implies that PRTS is less expressive than PTA. Lastly, different from PRTS, models based on PTA or PTP often have a simple structure, e.g., a network of automata with no hierarchy.

Verification of real-time probabilistic systems often uses a combined approach, i.e., combination of real-time verifiers with probabilistic verifiers [11]. Our approach is a combination of real-time zone abstraction with MDP, which has no extra cost of linking different model checkers. This work is related to our previous works [27,28] with the following new contribution: the two languages proposed in [27,28] are combined to form PRTS and dynamic zone abstraction is seamlessly combined with probabilistic model checking to verify PRTS models.

9 Conclusion

We proposed a modeling language PRTS which is capable of specifying hierarchical complex systems with quantitative real-time features as well as probabilistic components. We show that dynamic zone abstraction results in probabilistic preserving finite-state abstractions, which are then subject to probabilistic model checking. In addition, we have extended our PAT model checker to support this kind of systems so that the techniques are easily accessible. As for future work, we are investigating state space reduction techniques such as symmetry reduction, bi-simulation reduction in the setting of PRTS. We are also exploring other classes of properties such as timed property.

References

1. Alur, R., Courcoubetis, C., Dill, D.L.: Model-checking for Probabilistic Real-time Systems. In: Leach Albert, J., Monien, B., Rodríguez-Artalejo, M. (eds.) ICALP 1991. LNCS, vol. 510, pp. 115–126. Springer, Heidelberg (1991)
2. Alur, R., Dill, D.L.: A Theory of Timed Automata. Theoretical Computer Science 126, 183–235 (1994)
3. Baier, C., Clarke, E.M., Garmhausen, V.H., Kwiatkowska, M.Z., Rya, M.: Symbolic Model Checking for Probabilistic Processes. In: Degano, P., Gorrieri, R., Marchetti-Spaccamela, A. (eds.) ICALP 1997. LNCS, vol. 1256, pp. 430–440. Springer, Heidelberg (1997)
4. Baier, C., Haverkort, B.R., Hermanns, H., Katoen, J.: Model-Checking Algorithms for Continuous-Time Markov Chains. IEEE Trans. Software Eng. 29(6), 524–541 (2003)
5. Baier, C., Katoen, J.: Principles of Model Checking. The MIT Press, Cambridge (2008)
6. Beauquier, D.: On Probabilistic Timed Automata. Theor. Comput. Sci. 292(1), 65–84 (2003)
7. Behrmann, G., David, A., Larsen, K.G., Håkansson, J., Pettersson, P., Yi, W., Hendriks, M.: UPPAAL 4.0. In: QEST, pp. 125–126. IEEE, Los Alamitos (2006)

8. Behrmann, G., Larsen, K.G., Pearson, J., Weise, C., Yi, W.: Efficient timed reachability analysis using clock difference diagrams. In: Halbwachs, N., Peled, D.A. (eds.) CAV 1999. LNCS, vol. 1633, pp. 341–353. Springer, Heidelberg (1999)
9. Bengtsson, J., Yi., W.: Timed Automata: Semantics, Algorithms and Tools. In: Lectures on Concurrency and Petri Nets, pp. 87–124 (2003)
10. Butterfield, A., Sherif, A., Woodcock, J.: Slotted-circus. In: Davies, J., Gibbons, J. (eds.) IFM 2007. LNCS, vol. 4591, pp. 75–97. Springer, Heidelberg (2007)
11. Daws, C., Kwiatkowska, M., Norman, G.: Automatic Verification of the IEEE 1394 Root Contention Protocol with KRONOS and PRISM. International Journal on Software Tools for Technology Transfer 5(2-3), 221–236 (2004)
12. Dill, D.L.: Timing Assumptions and Verification of Finite-State Concurrent Systems. In: Automatic Verification Methods for Finite State Systems, pp. 197–212 (1989)
13. Garmhausen, V.H., Aguiar Campos, S.V., Clarke, E.M.: ProbVerus: Probabilistic Symbolic Model Checking. In: ARTS, pp. 96–110 (1999)
14. Gregersen, H., Jensen, H.E.: Formal Design of Reliable Real Time Systems. PhD thesis (1995)
15. Hinton, A., Kwiatkowska, M.Z., Norman, G., Parker, D.: PRISM: A Tool for Automatic Verification of Probabilistic Systems. In: Hermanns, H. (ed.) TACAS 2006. LNCS, vol. 3920, pp. 441–444. Springer, Heidelberg (2006)
16. Hoare, C.A.R.: Communicating Sequential Processes. Prentice-Hall, Englewood Cliffs (1985)
17. Holzmann, G.J.: The Model Checker SPIN. IEEE Trans. on Software Engineering 23(5), 279–295 (1997)
18. Kwiatkowska, M., Norman, G., Parker, D.: A Framework for Verification of Software with Time and Probabilities. In: Chatterjee, K., Henzinger, T.A. (eds.) FORMATS 2010. LNCS, vol. 6246, pp. 25–45. Springer, Heidelberg (2010)
19. Kwiatkowska, M., Norman, G., Parker, D.: PRISM 4.0: Verification of probabilistic real-time systems. In: Gopalakrishnan, G., Qadeer, S. (eds.) CAV 2011. LNCS, vol. 6806, pp. 585–591. Springer, Heidelberg (2011)
20. Kwiatkowska, M., Norman, G., Parker, D., Sproston, J.: Performance Analysis of Probabilistic Timed Automata using Digital Clocks. In: FMSD, vol. 29, pp. 33–78 (2006)
21. Kwiatkowska, M., Norman, G., Segala, R., Sproston, J.: Automatic Verification of Real-time Systems with Discrete Probability Distributions. Theoretical Computer Science 282(1), 101–150 (2002)
22. Kwiatkowska, M., Norman, G., Sproston, J., Wang, F.: Symbolic Model Checking for Probabilistic Timed Automata. Information and Computation 205(7), 1027–1077 (2007)
23. Mahony, B.P., Dong, J.S.: Blending Object-Z and Timed CSP: An Introduction to TCOZ. In: ICSE, pp. 95–104 (1998)
24. Ouaknine, J., Worrell, J.: Timed CSP = Closed Timed Safety Automata. Electrical Notes Theoretical Computer Science 68(2) (2002)
25. Schneider, S.: Concurrent and Real-time Systems. John Wiley and Sons, Chichester (2000)
26. Sun, J., Liu, Y., Dong, J.S., Pang, J.: PAT: Towards Flexible Verification under Fairness. In: Bouajjani, A., Maler, O. (eds.) CAV 2009. LNCS, vol. 5643, pp. 709–714. Springer, Heidelberg (2009)
27. Sun, J., Liu, Y., Dong, J.S., Zhang, X.: Verifying Stateful Timed CSP Using Implicit Clocks and Zone Abstraction. In: Breitman, K., Cavalcanti, A. (eds.) ICFEM 2009. LNCS, vol. 5885, pp. 581–600. Springer, Heidelberg (2009)
28. Sun, J., Song, S.Z., Liu, Y.: Model Checking Hierarchical Probabilistic Systems. In: Dong, J.S., Zhu, H. (eds.) ICFEM 2010. LNCS, vol. 6447, pp. 388–403. Springer, Heidelberg (2010)
29. Sun, J., Song, S.Z., Liu, Y., Dong, J.S.: PRTS: Specification and Model Checking. Technical report (2010), `http://www.comp.nus.edu.sg/pat/preport.pdf`

Integrating Prototyping into the SOFL Three-Step Modeling Approach

Fauziah binti Zainuddin and Shaoying Liu

Department of Computer Science
Hosei University, Tokyo, Japan
fauziahz@ump.edu.my, sliu@hosei.ac.jp

Abstract. Writing formal specifications in a practical software project is likely to increase the time for requirements analysis and/or abstract design and to postpone the implementation, which is often hard to be accepted by the user and/or the manager of the project. Prototyping provides an agile approach for communication between the user and the developer but is unable to deal with all aspects of the system precisely and completely. In this paper, we put forward a new development approach resulting from integrating prototyping techniques into the SOFL three-step modeling approach. The new approach is aimed at achieving a quality development process through promoting the facilities for user-friendly communication between the user and the developer and for exploring all possible aspects of the system precisely. We have applied the approach to develop an IC card software for the Japan railway service system and present the recorded data as the result of the study. Compared to our previous experiences using both formal and informal methods, our study suggests that the new approach can be more practical than existing formal specification methods and more effective in achieving the completeness and accuracy of the user's requirements than informal specification methods.

Keywords: Low-fidelity prototype, high-fidelity prototype, SOFL.

1 Introduction

Formal methods have been considered as an effective approach to developing high quality software for safety critical systems [1], but whether they can be easily adopted by today's software industry as a routine technique is controversial. In his recent article [2], Parnas discusses why the well-known current formal software development methods have not been widely employed by industry. One of the challenges is that existing formal methods do not seem to provide suitable user orientation platform for the user to interact directly with the developer and to give full contribution in the formal specification construction process. Constant user contributions are very important to ensure that the developer develops the application software as required by the end user and stakeholder. An analysis on a few literatures shows that user participation has general positive impact on system success and user satisfactions [3], but existing formal methods focus only on the preciseness in expressions; they do not pay attention to the importance of how user-developer communication is facilitated in the formalization process.

S. Qin and Z. Qiu (Eds.): ICFEM 2011, LNCS 6991, pp. 163–178, 2011.

This issue has motivated us to develop a more practical approach to requirements analysis and design. The new approach is derived from combination of the existing SOFL three-step modeling approach [4] with prototyping techniques that are commonly used for requirements analysis in industry [5]. The SOFL three-step approach advocates that a complete and precise specification of a software system is achieved through three steps: *informal*, *semi-formal*, and *formal specifications*. Although this structure provides more opportunities for the user to access the process of specification construction than directly writing the specification using a formal notation, yet our experience shows that users in general still feel difficult to understand the documentation, since it is hard for them to imagine how the potential system looks like by merely reading the textual, even precise, documentation. In the end, the developer has to go forward alone and the construction process tends to be longer than conventional software development process. The result of the process is a formal specification that requires a validation against the user's requirements, which has proved to be challenging in practice as well [4].

In this paper, we put forward an integrated approach to using prototyping techniques in the SOFL three-step modeling approach for requirements and design specifications. In this approach, prototyping techniques are used to: (1) demonstrate the potential dynamic features of the system under development based on the currently developed documentation (either informal, semi-formal or formal specification) to end user, aiming to capture more user's feedbacks; (2) facilitate the developer in constructing comprehensive and well defined specifications at different levels; by examine all possible aspects of the requirements and/or design.

The rest of the paper is organized as follows. In Section 2, we highlight the related work to motivate our research in this paper. Section 3 gives a brief introduction to the SOFL three-step approach and discusses its problems, and in Section 4, we give general idea about prototype. In Section 5, we present our integrated approach, and in Section 6, we present a case study. In Section 7 we discuss our experience gained from the case study and the unsolved issues for future research, and finally in Section 8, we draw the conclusions.

2 Related Work

The idea of combining formal methods with prototyping techniques was highlighted by Liu in his book on the SOFL Formal Engineering Method [4]. He brought up the idea of using prototyping as medium or technique in visualizing dynamic features of the system in order to effectively capture the user's requirements in the early phases of system development. He believes that the result from using this kind of technique can serve as the fundamental for developing an entire system using formal methods, especially on the functional behavior. Peter *et al.* reported a work on integrating formal methods and prototyping using component-based approach to construct and verify user interface [6]. In their approach, a single specification is used to construct both implementations (prototypes) for experimentation and models for formal reasoning. Prototypes are expressed directly as specification in the formal notation and their behavior is observed by animating the specification. This approach provides the user interface designer with a set of primitive components and a dataflow-based formalism for connecting them. Hall [7] reported his previous company success story using formal methods in developing cost critical systems. In the report, he mentioned about the need of making formal methods to be more accessible to the user and suggested using prototyping, particularly in the early stage of the development life cycle. In his another publication, Hall listed seven myths of formal methods that he believed not to be true [8]. One of the listed myths is that formal methods are unacceptable to users. Although he disagreed with this myth, he expressed his concern about the style of formal specifications, suggesting the idea of animating and prototyping formal specifications for user access. However, there was no specific suggestion on how prototyping techniques can be used in combination with formal methods in his publications.

Our work described in this paper aims to establish an engineering approach using both formal specification and prototyping in a manner that utilizes their advantages and reduces the impact of their weaknesses. Instead of using formal specifications for prototyping purpose (e.g., by automatically transforming a formal specification into an executable prototype program), our approach is to integrate prototyping techniques into the SOFL three-step modeling approach so that both prototyping and writing specifications at different levels can play complementary roles in the process of obtaining complete and accurate requirements and/or design. Before going to the details of our approach in Section 4, we first briefly introduce the SOFL three-step modeling approach next.

3 SOFL Three-Step Approach and Its Problems

3.1 SOFL Three-Step Approach

The *S*tructured *O*bject-oriented *F*ormal *L*anguage (SOFL) is a kind of formal engineering method (FEM) introduced by the second author about 15 years ago. FEM approach differs from traditional formal methods (FM) such as VDM, Z, and B-method, in such a way that SOFL emphasizes more engineering disciplines and techniques to be implemented in software development process [4, 9]. In other words, SOFL promotes practical ways to use formal techniques while preserving the advantages of formal methods such as preciseness and effectiveness in facilitating the development of tool construction [10]. For the sake of space, we focus only on the three-step modeling approach of the SOFL method in this section. A comprehensive introduction of SOFL is described in the second author's book [4].

As shown in Figure 1, the three-step modeling approach starts with writing an *informal specification* in a natural language that is supposed to document clearly and concisely major desired functions, data resources and necessary constraints on both functions and resources. The goal of this specification is to collect "complete" requirements (from the coverage's point of view) from the user and to present them in a hierarchical structure on an abstract level for comprehensibility. Since all of the terms used in the specification and the relations among functions, data resources and constraints are all described informally, their meaning are however not precisely defined. To clarify these issues, the second step is to refine the informal specification into a *semi-formal specification*. To this end, three things must be done: (1) to organize the related functions, data resources and constraints into each SOFL module; (2) to formally define the data resources in each module using the well-defined data types to set up a foundation for specifying the functions; (3) to define each informal function as a SOFL *process* and define its function using informally presented pre- and post-conditions. Since the semi-formal specification is still expected to serve as a medium to facilitate the communication between the developer and the user, it is appropriate to keep the functional description informal.

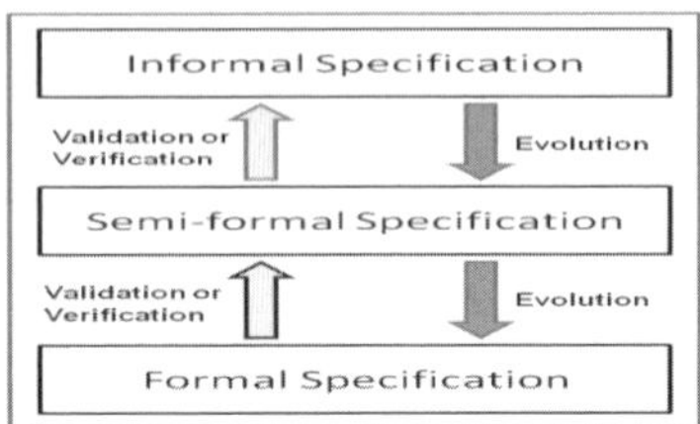

Fig. 1. SOFL Three-step Approach

The final step is to construct a complete *formal specification* based on previous semi-formal specification, by connecting all defined processes using a formalized data flow diagram, called condition data flow diagram (CDFD), to form the architecture of the whole system and by formalizing all the informal parts in the semi-formal specification using predicate logic formulas. During this formalization, all of the ambiguities of informal descriptions would have been removed and the final specification offers a firm foundation for implementation and verification of the program. These three steps relate to each other in restrict refinement and evolutions depends on the phase of development and will go through certain validation and verification process.

3.2 Problem Descriptions

Even though there is sufficient evidence resulting from various research previously [8, 11] to suggest that the SOFL three-step modeling technique be effective in ensuring software quality and reducing cost for information system development, there is no indication that it can facilitate the developer-user interaction or cooperation. With regard of this issue, we have raised three questions about the SOFL three-step approach.

Firstly, how can we ensure that the user involves in the entire or at least in the first two steps of the SOFL three-step approach? Based on Kujala *et al.* [12], the user's involvement becomes the key concept of achieving positive effects on system success and user satisfaction. Kujala [3] and Damoron [13] list benefits that can be derived from user's effective involvement. The benefits include: (1) improved quality of the system arising from more accurate user requirements, (2) avoidance of costly system features that the user does not want or cannot use, (3) improvement of the level of acceptance of the system, (4) greater understanding of the system by the user that is likely to result in more effective use, and (5) increased participation in decision-making within the organization. Even though all of the benefits are specifically focused on system design, yet it aptly illustrates the advantages for system development as a whole and we also believe that we are sharing the same aim in our new approach.

Secondly, how can we guarantee that all the system requirements are covered during the system specification process? This issue has been highlighted by Alaga and Kourkopolous more than a decade ago [14] and recently by Liu [15] and Nancy [16]. They perceive the completeness of a specification as an important and desired property of a specification for the guarantee of a valid and correct implementation. A specification is considered complete if and only if its consequence closure is equivalent to that of the set of the user's intended requirements [15], which is extremely difficult to be formally verified because the concept is related to human judgments. User's feedback is perhaps the most important source of human judgment in any software development process. If this source is eliminated from early development phase, it will lead to information misinterpretation by the developer. Sometimes it may end up with the developer building something that is not needed by the user.

Finally, how can we effectively obtain ideas on system design or dynamic features of the system? Writing any kind of specification in the SOFL three-step modeling approach would not effectively demonstrate dynamic features of the system under development. Without seeing those features, the user may not know exactly about the system functions and/or performance.

4 Prototyping

Prototyping has been chosen rather than other techniques because of the nature of prototype: an activity with the purpose of creating a manifestation that, in its simplest form, filters the qualities in which designers are interested, without distorting the understanding of the whole [17].

Prototypes can be classified into two types: *low-fidelity prototype* and *high-fidelity prototype*. Low-fidelity prototypes were defined by Sefelin *et al.* [18] to be the visualization of design ideas at very early stages of the design process. Therefore they usually have limitations in terms of functions and interaction prototyping efforts [19]. Low-fidelity prototypes are constructed to deliberately depict concepts, design alternatives and screen layouts. There are several suggested tools to develop the low-fidelity prototype such as paper, informal tools and development tools. However in choosing the right tool, a few elements need to be considered [20]: (1) requirements of the project, (2) expertise of design team, (3) access to relevant libraries, and (4) balance investment with effectiveness.

Unlike low-fidelity prototypes, high-fidelity prototypes have complete functionality and are interactive [19]. This kind of prototype is always used for exploration and testing, besides the end user can operate the prototype as if it were the final product. From the end users perspective high-fidelity prototype can help them to understand how the system will operate, therefore it is easy to get user interface improvement and recommendations from them. For the programmer, a prototype acts as a living specification of the functional and operating requirements. Whenever the design guidance is needed, the prototype will be referred to determine the design detail.

In our approach, evolutionary prototyping is strongly recommended to be implemented along with high-fidelity prototype. According to Davis [21], evolutionary prototyping has a few characteristics (that suit our proposed approach most): (1) it implements only confirmed requirements, (2) it is built in a quality manner (including software requirement specification, design documentation and thorough test set), (3) it is used to determine what unconsidered but necessary requirements exist (one of the goal of adopting prototype in our proposed approach).

5 Proposed Framework for Integration

To overcome the weaknesses of the SOFL three-step approach highlighted in the previous section and achieve a both speedy and quality software development, we believe that integrating prototyping techniques into the SOFL three-step approach will provide a solution.

The framework for integration is illustrated in Figure 2. The goal of the framework is to establish a "user-centered'' approach to software development using prototyping and the SOFL three-step specification method. The essential idea of the framework includes three points: (1) using early specifications (i.e., informal and semi-formal specifications) to capture user's requirements and to help build effective prototypes, (2) using the constructed prototype to obtain further feedbacks from the user by demonstrating the required functions in the specification and to help evolve the current specification to a more complete and/or precise specification, and (3) evolving the latest prototype into the final product based on the formal specification in an incremental manner. These three points are realized in three phases.

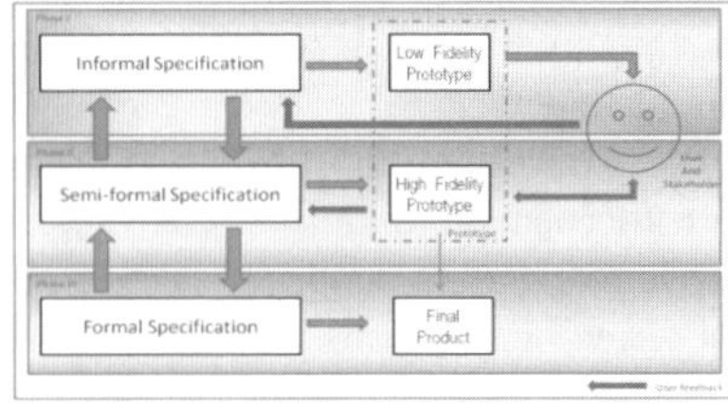

Fig. 2. Proposed SOFL-Prototyping framework

5.1 Phase I

In the first phase of the framework, informal specification is integrated with low-fidelity prototyping. The informal specification is used to document the user's requirements at an abstract level by the developer, which may be incomplete and imprecise, and are usually difficult to explain to the user. A low-fidelity prototype is then built, based on the contents of the informal specification and the developer's experience, to show the user an image of the potential functions required in an "animated" manner. This prototype usually allows the user and the developer communicates more effectively and efficiently, and the feedbacks from the user can be adopted in evolving the informal specification into a more complete one (but may still be expressed informally and abstractly).

To build the low-fidelity prototype, we find that the following process is effective. Firstly, divide the functions in the informal specification into two groups: (1) *major functions* that mostly interest the user and needs to interact with the end-user, (2) all of the other functions, known as *internal functions*, which may help realize those major functions. For example, in the IC card system for Japan railway service adopted in our case study (Section 6), *Recharging card* (by updating its balance) is a major function, but *Checking card validity* and *Checking recharging limit* can be internal functions because these two help realize the two major functions, respectively. Secondly, build the prototype with a structure of two layers: (1) the first layer is a visualized user-machine interface that demonstrates each of the selected major functions, and (2) the second layer is a set of internal functions attached to the relevant major functions, describing which major function is supported by which internal functions, as illustrated in Figure 3.a. The interface can be structured in a flat or hierarchical manner, as shown in Figure 3.b and 3.c respectively, depending on the developer's engineering judgment, but generally it may be the mixture of the two at some level. Further, user interface components such as *filter*, *update*, *display button* components (components listed in User Interface Simple Pattern [22,23]) can facilitate developer on basic operation for the associated user interface, while the profile of the potential user will assist developer on user interface design. The design for user interface should be simple, using pleasant color, with minimum yet clear information on it for its usability.

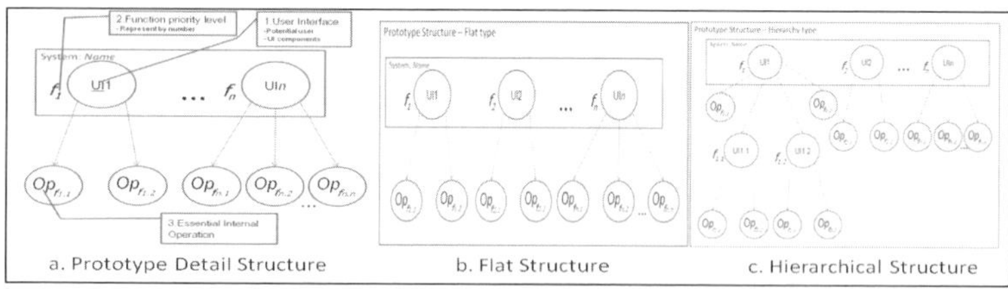

Fig. 3. Prototype Structure

Let us take the functions related to recharging the IC card in the case study for example. Since *recharging card by cash* and *recharging card from bank account* are two major functions, we create two buttons for choosing the functions on the user-machine interface of the low-fidelity prototype, as illustrated in Fig. 4, and connect each of the choice to a graphical representation of the related internal functions, such as *checking the recharging limit* and *updating card balance*. For the sake of space, we omit these details in Figure 4.

After the low-fidelity prototype is demonstrated to the user, feedbacks from him or her may be obtained based on which the developer will evolve the informal specification accordingly. If the feedbacks effect on major structure of the informal specification, the prototype structure may also need to be evolved properly. This cycle may continue several times until both the user and the developer reaches an agreement.

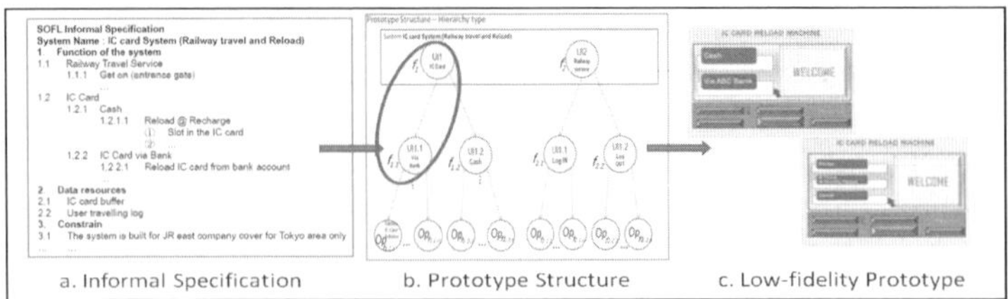

Fig. 4. Phase I Transformation Example

5.2 Phase II

To further understand the user's requirements and clarify the ambiguities in the informal specification, and to prepare for the implementation of the system, the informal specification is evolved into a semi-formal specification in which all of the related functions, data resources and constraints are organized into modules and defined more precisely.

The decision for creating modules can be made based on two sources: the informal specification and the low-fidelity prototype. The informal specification provides all of the necessary functions, data resources, and constraints for consideration, while the prototype supplies the information about the relation between the major functions and the internal functions, as mentioned previously. One of the ways to create modules is to put a major function and its associated internal functions in the same module because they may share the same data resources and constraints. In each module, necessary types, variables, and constants are declared using the formal notation to define the meaning of the corresponding data resources listed in the informal specification; invariants are defined to reflect the corresponding constraints; and processes are created to define the corresponding functions given in the informal specification. The characteristic of the semi-formal specification is that all of the logical expressions, such as pre- and post-conditions of processes, are written informally while data declarations and process interfaces are defined formally.

On the basis of the semi-formal specification and the low-fidelity prototype, a high-fidelity prototype will be implemented using a programming language like Java. The following guidelines are usually considered in building the high-fidelity prototype:

1. Evolving the user-machine interface of the low-fidelity prototype into a more effective or appropriate style for the high-fidelity prototype. The idea for the new interface usually comes from two sources: (1) low-fidelity prototype, because it was designed according to the required elements and demonstrated to the user for feedbacks, and (2) semi-formal specification, since more complete and precisely defined functions are documented based on the user's feedbacks. For example, the originally defined flat structure of the user-machine interface may need to be improved to a more hierarchical structure for usability.
2. For each module in the semi-formal specification, creating a class to implement it in the prototype. Each process defined in the module can be implemented as a static or instance method in the class. This principle also applies to (mathematical) functions defined in the module. Further, transform all of the data types and/or

state variables into an appropriate concrete data structures in the prototype. For example, a composite data type in the module can be implemented as a class; a set, sequence, or map can be implemented as an array or array list data structure, depending on the developer's engineering judgment.

3. Implementing the *major functions-internal functions* structure adopted in the low-fidelity prototype in a more effective or appropriate style in the high-fidelity prototype. Since this is still a prototype, there is no need to implement all of the existing internal functions for each major function; the most important ones that may draw the user's attention can be selected for implementation and all the rest can be arranged for future implementation. For each internal function, its full functionality may not need to be implemented; only the most interesting part may be sufficient for the prototype. Thus, the related functions of interest are connected together properly in the prototype.

Continuing the same example described in Phase 1, we produce a high-fidelity prototype by following the above guidelines, as shown in Fig. 6, which is part of our case study content in Section 6 (the figure is not repeated here for the sake of space).

5.3 Phase III

The major tasks of Phase III are twofold: producing a formal specification and evolving the high-fidelity prototype into a final product. The formal specification in SOFL basically consists of two parts: (1) a hierarchy of Condition Data Flow Diagrams (CDFDs) and (2) a corresponding hierarchy of modules. Each CDFD is associated with a module. The CDFD describes the architecture of the module, showing how the processes in the same module are integrated based on data flows to perform the overall behavior of the module, while the module offers a facility to define precisely all the components of the CDFD, such as processes, data flows, and data stores. All data flows and stores are declared with well-defined types; their constraints are defined using invariants; and each process is specified using pre- and post-conditions in the formal notation.

The formal specification is completed on the basis of the semi-formal specification, the feedbacks from the user after the demonstration of the high-fidelity prototype, and the major function-internal function structure of the high-fidelity prototype. Specifically, it includes the following points:

- The idea of constructing a hierarchy of CDFDs may partly come from the structure of the high-fidelity that shows how the related functions are connected and partly come from the semi-formal specification. All of the modules in the semi-formal specification must be properly integrated into the CDFD hierarchy.
- The precise formal specification for each process occurring in the CDFD may be written by "evolving" its semi-formal specification ("refinement", extension, or modification) [24] based on the user's feedbacks and the developer's understanding.

After the formal specification is completed, it will be used to evolve the high-fidelity prototype in an incremental manner by doing the following:

1. Evolve the user-machine interface of the high-fidelity prototype based on the CDFDs in the formal specification. Since a high level CDFD is usually used to describe the relation between major processes (corresponding to user's major functions) and the decomposed CDFD of a high level process shows how the related internal processes (corresponding to the user's internal functions) are integrated, the information contained in the CDFD hierarchy can be effectively used to improve the user interface and the structure of the prototype.
2. Extend and improve the algorithm and data structures of the program code of each method (operation) in the prototype based on the corresponding process specification. Since the formal process specification usually presents a more precise and complete definition of the functionality, it can assist the developer to improve the code.
3. Inspect and test the code to detect bugs using formal specification-based inspection and testing techniques [25]. Model checking is a so called light weight formal method for verification [26], but it is still impractical in dealing with real software systems. Inspection and testing are much more practical; they cannot guarantee the correctness, but would help the developer increase the confidence in the functional consistency between the code and the specification.
4. Demonstrate the improved behavior of the current prototype to the user for validation. If there is any need for further improvement, the developer can directly incorporate that feedback into the code of the prototype.

These activities can be repeated incrementally until a final product is ready for delivery. Since the formal specification is a well-defined and organized document, the evolution process would be unlikely to encounter any chaotic situation. This is a significant advantage over many agile methods based on the evolutionary process model as mentioned by Kent [27]. Further, because new implementations or improvements can be demonstrated to the user frequently after they are completed, the user's role in providing feedbacks can be efficiently incorporated into the development process to ensure the quality of the final product.

Note that since our purpose of writing the formal specification is to help evolve the current prototype, we do not advocate the approach of automatically transforming a formal specification into an executable prototype taken by some other researchers [28]. There are two reasons. One is that such an automatic transformation approach is only limited to an executable subset of the formal notation. The other is that even if the prototype can be produced in that way, the efficiency of the prototype (i.e., runtime speed and memory) is usually lower than the one produced by the developer. This result does not fit for our purpose in our approach.

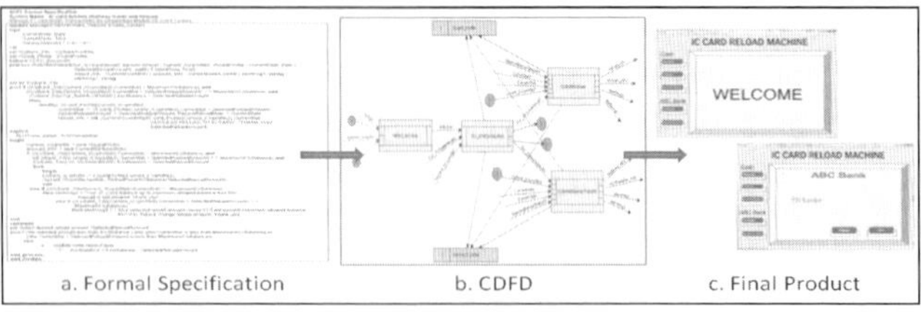

a. Formal Specification b. CDFD c. Final Product

Fig. 5. Phase III Transformation Example

Figure 5 illustrates the relation between the formal specification and the evolution of the high-fidelity prototype produced in the previous phase. For the sake of space, we omit the explanation of the details.

6 Case Study

We have conducted a case study on the proposed framework by developing an IC card system for Japan railway service in Tokyo using the framework to gain experience and to identify issues for further improvement. The system offers similar functions to those of the currently deployed SUICA system. SUICA stands for "*S*uper *U*rban *I*ntelligent *C*ard" [29], and has been widely used by Japan Railway (JR). The initial user requirements document of the IC card system was available, as shown in Figure 3, before the case study began. The IC card system can be used for multipurpose, including (1) going in and out of a railway station, (2) buying a train ticket, (3) recharging the card by cash or through the customer's bank account, and (4) using as a fixed period railway pass for a defined station interval.

6.1 Phase I

The first job we did in the case study was to translate the initial user's requirements document into a SOFL informal specification. (Refer to Figure 4, shows tasks flow in this phase). The informal specification was written in a well-organized form, clearly and concisely describing functions to be implemented, a list of data resources to be used and necessary constraints on both functions and resources. Secondly, we transformed the informal specification into prototype structure. Finally, based on this structure, we built a low-fidelity prototype. Computer-based low-fidelity prototype was preferable by the subject as being concluded by Sefelin *et al.* [19] in their research, comparing computer-based and paper-based low-fidelity prototypes; both of them lead to almost same quantity and quality of critical user statements. For this reason, we choose a computer-based low-fidelity prototype using Microsoft PowerPoint. The ease of use of this presentation software and the ability for constructing animation have provide advantages for us in simulating the functional architecture of the IC card system to the user. In a very short period of time we were able to convert the informal specification into a kind of system like presentation.

We then demonstrated the prototype to the end users for their feedback. Each major functional scenario of the requirements was demonstrated and explained, and the user sometimes pointed out mistakes or told his opinions on the "implemented" functions. The most important feedback gained from the user in the first cycle of the presentation is that the user discovered a misinterpreted IC card and ATM card functionality. The user was expecting to see the IC card to have the same function as an ATM card (this aspect was not mentioned in the user's initial requirements document), but this function was built differently in the prototype. Through three such presentation cycles the user is completely satisfied with the functions provided in the prototype.

Table 1 shows all of the relevant data concerned with efforts and cost in this phase, which include performed tasks, the number of iterations (only up to three cycles), planned time for each task and actual used time.

Table 1. Recorded System Development Related Data – Phase I

No.	Task	No Of Iteration	Planned		Actual	
			Days	Hours	Days	Hours
1	**PHASE I**					
1.1	**Informal Specification / Low fidelity Prototype**					
1.1.1	Contruct informal specification	1	3	24	2.5	20
1.1.2	*Design low-fidelity prototype*	1	5	40	5	40
1.1.3	Gain user feedback (presentation)	1	0.04	1	0.04	1.5
1.1.4	Reconstruct informal specification	2	2	16	1	8
1.1.5	*Redesign low fidelity prototype*	2	3	24	2	16
1.1.6	Gain user feedback (presentation)	2	0.04	1	0.04	1
1.1.7	Reconstruct informal specification	3	1	8	0.5	4
1.1.8	*Redesign low fidelity prototype*	3	1	8	1	8
1.1.9	Gain user feedback (presentation)	3	0.04	1	0.04	1

As a result of phase I, the developer gained a deep understanding of what the end users really wants for the system and they obtained a clear picture of what the system can provide and how it looks likes on abstract level.

6.2 Phase II

The system requirements analysis continues in phase II, as being illustrated in Figure 6, we first evolved the informal specification into a semi-formal specification, then revised on the prototype structure and finally build a high-fidelity prototype. We adopt C# .Net platform for our high-fidelity prototype as requested by the stakeholder.

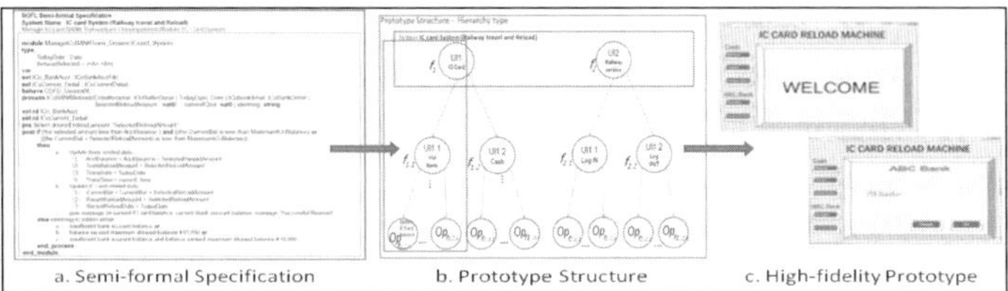

Fig. 6. Phase II Transformation Example

Generally, adopting evolutionary prototyping technique is likely to force us to experience a few iterations. However, in our case study we only experienced one iteration before proceed to the next phase, even though we discovered new requirement from end user (extra charges required for every single transaction related with bank account). Since it relate with computational issue in internal operation, so we decided to add the new requirement in next phase. As shown in Table 2. This is mainly attributed to the early user involvement and approval in phase I, which leads to entire system acceptance and reducing the development time by almost 56% from the estimated time. The time reduction is due to development team no need to think on user interface design issue since it was approved in previous phase, so more focus on other issue such as programming. As shown in Figure 6.c, user interface screen capture taken from the high-fidelity prototype, the design is consistent with the user interface design in low-fidelity prototype.

Table 2. Recorded System Development Related Data – Phase II

No.	Task	No Of Iteration	Planned		Actual	
			Days	Hours	Days	Hours
2	**PHASE II**					
2.1	**Semi-formal Specification / High-Fidelity Prototype**					
2.1.1	Construct semi-formal specification	*1*	8	64	8	64
2.1.2	*Design high-fidelity prototype*	*1*	10	80	12	96
2.1.3	Gain user feedback (presentation)	*1*	0.04	1	0.04	1.5
2.1.4	Reconstruct semi-formal	*2*	5	40	0	0
2.1.5	*Redesign high-fidelity prototype*	*2*	7	56	0	0
2.1.6	Gain user feedback (presentation)	*2*	0.04	1	0	1
2.1.7	Reconstruct semi-formal	*3*	3	24	0	0
2.1.8	*Redesign high-fidelity prototype*	*3*	4	32	0	0
2.1.9	Gain user feedback (presentation)	*3*	0.04	1	0	1

6.3 Phase III

In contrast to informal and semi-formal specifications, the formal specification in SOFL represents the architecture of the entire system and functional definitions of its components. As being briefly explain in sub-section 5.3.

Comparing to our previous experiences using SOFL in several system development projects, the developer usually needs to construct CDFD several times in order to conform to the required system structure. However, by using this prototype integration approach, the developer can visualize basic system structure according to the prototype structure in previous phase. This helps the developer to construct the CDFD much easier, faster and match with the entire desired system structure.

The development of high-fidelity prototype in phase II helps the developer considerably in constructing the detailed design specification (called explicit specification in SOFL). During building the high-fidelity prototype, the developer is forced to experience object-oriented programming to certain extent, thus the same developer can significantly benefit from this experience in constructing the formal detailed design specification. For example, the classes and methods defined in the high-fidelity prototype can be reused in writing the specification. This leads to shortening the total time for constructing the formal specification.

Table 3. Recorded System Development Related Data – Phase III

No.	Task	No Of Iteration	Planned		Actual	
			Days	Hours	Days	Hours
2	**PHASE III**					
2.1	**Formal Specification**					
2.1.1	Construct formal specification	*1*	10	80	7	56

As shown in Table 3, total allocation time for formal specification construction was reduced by almost 30% from the estimated time. For actual product construction, development was done incrementally and final revised high-fidelity became construction fundamental.

7 Discussion

The case study allows us to identify the benefits and unresolved issues of the integrated approach presented in this paper by intuitively comparing with our previous experiences using either prototyping techniques or formal methods for software development, for example, the experience gathered from developing a Parcel Delivery System for industry. This system was fully developed using SOFL, but we encountered difficulties in explaining the system details to the stakeholder. The hardest thing was that the stakeholder could not follow the detail of our explanation based on the static textual documentation; he could not easily build an image of the potential system only based on the documentation and our explanation. Sometimes some textual formal process specifications are hard to explain. This scenario leads to prolonging the development period. Ideally, we should run a control experiment to rigorously compare the development results with and without prototyping. Unfortunately, this kind of experiment requires a lot of resources which are currently not available. We plan to continue our investigation of this kind in the future.

The benefits can be classified into three categories. First, the integrated approach can bring the user into the process of specification construction, thus avoiding "directional" mistakes in defining functions and operation interfaces in early stages. Second, the prototype can significantly help the developer write both semi-formal and formal specifications that tend to be more useful for future program verification due to the operation interface consistency than the specifications written without referring to any prototype. Finally, using prototypes allows the developer to demonstrate his or her progress to the user in a vivid and agile manner, thus creating a high possibility to enhance the user's confidence in the ongoing project.

The case study also allowed us to find two important issues for future research. First, we understand that the integrated approach could improve the quality, efficiency and productivity of the system under development, but have not collected enough hard evidence to support this claim. To find out the truth, a systematic controlled experiment must be conducted. This will form an independent study, and will be one of our future researches. Second, to efficiently apply our approach in practice, an effective tool support would be important. This will also become another goal of our future research.

8 Conclusion

We describe a new practical approach to software development that integrates prototyping techniques into the SOFL three-step modeling approach. The informal specification is used to capture "complete" but abstract user requirements while the low-fidelity prototype built based on the informal specification is used to demonstrate the preliminary behavior of the potential system for accurate understanding of the requirements by both the user and the developer. A semi-formal specification is built based on both the informal specification and the prototype, and serves as a foundation for building a high-fidelity prototype. To achieve a systematic and precise documentation that reflects both the requirements and the system architecture, a formal design specification is eventually constructed for implementation and its verification. This formal specification is effectively used as a foundation for incremental evolution of the high-fidelity prototype. We have applied the integrated approach in a case study and presented its benefits in facilitating communication between the user and the developer and avoiding directional mistakes in early stages. We have also identified two important issues for future research, as described at the end of Section 7.

Acknowledgement. This work is supported by NII Collaborative Research Program. It is also partly supported by the NSFC Grant (No. 60910004), 973 Program of China Grant (No. 2010CB328102) and, Science and Technology Commission of Shanghai Municipality under Grant No. 10510704900.

References

1. Woodcock, J., Larsen, P.G., Bicarregui, J., Fitzgerald, J.: Formal Methods: Practice and Experience. ACM Computing Surveys 41(4), 19:1–19:36 (2009)
2. Parnas, D.: Really Rethinking of "Formal Methods". Computer, 28–34 (2010)
3. Kujala, S.: User Involvement: A Review of Benefits and Challenges. In: Behaviour & Information Technology, pp. 1–16 (2003)
4. Liu, S.: Formal Engineering for Industrial Software Development Using the SOFL Method. Springer, Heidelberg (2004)
5. Litcher, H., Schneider-Hufschmidt, M., Zullighoven, H.: Prototyping in Industrial Software Projects – Bridging the Gap between Theory and Practice. IEEE Transaction on Software Engineering, 825–832 (1994)
6. Bumbulis, P., Alencer, P.S.C., Cowan, D.D., Lucena, C.J.P.: Combining Formal Technique and Prototyping in User Interface Construction and Verification. In: 2nd Eurographics Workshop on Design, Specification, Verification of Interactive Systems (DSV-IS 1995), pp. 7–19. Springer, Heidelberg (1995)
7. Hall, A.: What Does Industry Need from Formal Specification Techniques? In: Second IEEE Workshop on Industrial Strength Formal Specification Techniques, pp. 2–7 (1999)
8. Hall, A.: Seven Myths of Formal Methods. IEEE Software, 11–19 (1990)
9. Liu, S., Asuka, M., Koyama, K., Nakamura, Y.: Applying SOFL to Specify A Railway Crossing Controller for Industry. In: Industrial Strength Formal Specification Techniques, 2nd IEEE Workshop on Digital Object Identifier, pp. 16–27 (1998)
10. Cheng, B.H.C., France, R.: A Discussion about Integrated Techniques. In: Second IEEE Workshop on Industrial Strength Formal Specification Techniques, pp. 65–72 (1998)
11. Mat, A.R., Liu, S.: Applying SOFL to Construct Formal Specification an Automatic Automobile Driving Simulation System. In: International Conference on Software Technology and Engineering, pp. 42–48. World Scientific Publishing, Singapore (2009)
12. Kujala, S., Kauppinen, M., Lehtola, L., Kojo, T.: The Role of User Involvement in Requirement Quality and Project Success. In: 13th IEEE International Conference on Requirement Engineering, pp. 75–84 (2005)
13. Damodaran, L.: User Involvement in the System Design Process – A Practical Guide for Users. Behaviour & Information Technology, 363–377 (1996)
14. Alagar, V.S., Kourpoulos, D.: Completeness in Specification. Information and Software Technology, 331–342 (1994)
15. Liu, S.: Utilizing Test Case Generation to Inspect Formal Specifications for Completeness and Feasibility. In: 10th High Assurance Systems Engineering Symposium, pp. 349–356 (2007)
16. Leveson, N.: Completeness in Formal Specification Language Design for Process-Control Systems. In: Formal Methods in Software Practice, pp. 75–87. ACM Press, New York (2000)
17. Youn-Kyung Lim, Erik, S., Josh, T.: The anatomy of prototypes: Prototypes as filters, prototypes as manifestations of design ideas. ACM Trans. Comput.-Hum. Interact. 15(2), 7–33 (2008)

18. Sefelin, R., Tscheligi, M., Giller, V.: Paper prototyping - what is it good for? A comparison of paper- and computer-based low-fidelity prototyping. In: Conference on Human Factors in Computing Systems CHI 2003, pp. 778–779. ACM Press, New York (2003)
19. Rudd, J., Stern, K., Isensee, S.: Low vs. High-fidelity Prototyping Debate. ACM Interactions 3(1), 76–85 (1996)
20. Low fidelity Prototype, `http://social.cs.uiuc.edu/class/cs465/lectures/lofidelity.pdf`
21. Davis, A.M.: Operational prototyping: a new development approach. IEEE Software, 70–78 (1992)
22. Gao, T., Shi, Q.: A Complex Interface Modeling Approach Based on Presentation Style. In: IEEE International Conference Intelligent Computing and Intelligent Systems, ICIS 2009, pp. 233–237 (2009)
23. Nguyen, T., Tram, Q., Tai, C.G.T., Thuy, D.T.B.: User Interface Design Pattern Management System Support for Building Information System. In: 1st International IEEE Conference on Digital Information Management, pp. 99–101 (2007)
24. Liu, S.: Evolution: A More Practical Approach than Refinement for Software Development. In: Proceedings of Third IEEE International Conference on Engineering of Complex Computer Systems, pp. 142–151. IEEE Computer Society Press, Los Alamitos (1997)
25. Liu, S.: Integrating Specification-Based Review and Testing for Detecting Errors in Programs. In: Butler, M., Hinchey, M.G., Larrondo-Petrie, M.M. (eds.) ICFEM 2007. LNCS, vol. 4789, pp. 136–150. Springer, Heidelberg (2007)
26. Duan, Z., Tian, C.: A Unified Model Checking Approach with Projection Temporal Logic. In: Liu, S., Araki, K. (eds.) ICFEM 2008. LNCS, vol. 5256, pp. 167–186. Springer, Heidelberg (2008)
27. Beck, K.: Embracing Change with Extreme Programming. Computer 32(10), 70–77 (1999)
28. Chachkov, S., Buchs, D.: From Formal Specifications to Ready-to-Use Software Components: The Concurrent Object Oriented Petri Net Approach. In: IEEE International Conference on Application of Concurrency to System Design, pp. 99–110 (2001)
29. Shirakawa, Y.: JR East contactless IC card automatic fare collection system "Suica". In: 7th IEEE International Symposium on Digital Object Identifier High Assurance Systems Engineering, pp. 3–10 (2002)

A Deterministic Interpreter Simulating a Distributed Real Time System Using VDM

Kenneth Lausdahl[1], Peter Gorm Larsen[1], and Nick Battle[2]

[1] Aarhus School of Engineering, Dalgas Avenue 2, DK-8000 Aarhus C, Denmark
[2] Fujitsu Services, Lovelace Road, Bracknell, Berkshire. RG12 8SN,UK

Abstract. The real time dialect of VDM, called VDM-RT, contains constructs for describing concurrent threads, synchronisation of such threads and the distribution of object instances and their threads over multiple CPUs with busses connecting them. Tools that simulate an executable subset of VDM-RT models benefit from being deterministic so that problems are reproducible and can be more easily investigated. We describe the deterministic scheduling features of our VDM-RT interpreter, and show how multi-threaded models can also be debugged deterministically.

Keywords: VDM, interpreter, deterministic, scheduler, real time, multiple processors, semantics.

1 Introduction

The power of formal methods traditionally lies in being able to write a specification, and to analyse and refine that specification formally to produce a target implementation that is verified. However, formal models can also be used for direct simulation of a system under construction. Benefit can be gained from exploring design options through simulation, even before any formal analysis of the model has been carried out [34]. One way for efficiently finding problems with a formal model is to evaluate expressions making use of the definitions from the model [35]. In the event that such expressions do not yield the expected values, it is essential to be able to deterministically reproduce the problem, for example by debugging the model using a deterministic interpreter.

In VDM-RT a model represents a potentially infinite set of semantic models due to the looseness [37] present in the language. This allows the modeller to gain abstraction and to avoid implementation bias. To perform a model simulation, tool support must provide an interpreter for the model language, and a debugging environment that allows the designer to investigate problems. Given a specification with looseness, the tool support must also provide a *deterministic* interpreter and debugger, otherwise problems with the model would not be reproducible and so could not be investigated easily.

Programming language interpreters and compilers are typically not deterministic when the language includes concurrency, and this is even less likely for debuggers, where the interference of the user can easily change the behaviour of the program being debugged. Existing work has examined the problems of the deterministic execution of programming languages with threads [3]. Others have added assertions to check the determinism of multi-threaded applications at the programming language level [7].

S. Qin and Z. Qiu (Eds.): ICFEM 2011, LNCS 6991, pp. 179–194, 2011.

In this paper we demonstrate how it is possible to interpret and debug formal models written in VDM-RT in a deterministic manner. We hope that others can benefit from our experience and produce similar tools for executable subsets of other formal languages.

The paper starts off with an overview of the VDM technology in Section 2. Afterwards, Section 3 briefly explains how the sequential part of VDM can be interpreted. Section 4 continues with an explanation about how the concurrent aspects of the VDM interpreter are made deterministic. This is followed by Section 5 which explains how the interaction with a debugger interface can be made deterministic. Section 6 provides related work and finally Section 7 provides concluding remarks.

2 The VDM Technology

The Vienna Development Method (VDM) [4,19,11] was originally developed at the IBM laboratories in Vienna in the 1970's and as such it is one of the longest established formal methods. The VDM Specification Language is a language with a formally defined syntax, static and dynamic semantics [31,26]. Models in VDM are based on data type definitions built from simple abstract types such as **bool**, **nat** and **char** and type constructors that allow user-defined product and union types and collection types such as (finite) sets, sequences and mappings. Type membership may be restricted by predicate invariants which means that run-time type checking is also required from an interpreter perspective. Persistent state is defined by means of typed variables, again restricted by invariants. Operations that may modify the state can be defined implicitly, using standard pre- and post-condition predicates, or explicitly, using imperative statements. Such operations denote relations between inputs and pre-states and outputs and post-states, allowing for nondeterminism. Functions are defined in a similar way to operations, but may not refer to state variables. Recursive functions can have a **measure** defined for them to ensure termination [33]. Arguments passed to functions and operations are always passed by value, apart from object references.

Three different dialects exists for VDM: The ISO standard VDM Specification Language (VDM-SL) [12], the object oriented extension VDM++ [13] and a further extension of that called VDM Real Time (VDM-RT) [41,17]. All three dialects are supported by the open source tool called Overture [23] as well as by VDMTools [14]. These tools, among other features, include standard parsers and type checkers that produce Abstract Syntax Trees (ASTs). Such ASTs form the basic input of the interpreter presented in this article.

None of these dialects are generally executable since the languages permits the modeller to use type bindings with infinite domains, or implicitly defined functions and operations, but the dialects all have subsets that can be interpreted [24]. In addition some commonly used implicit definitions can be executed in principle [16]. A full description of the executable subset of the language can be found in [25].

In this paper we focus on the ability to execute a simulation when looseness is present in the specification in such a way that the results are deterministic and reproducible. This means that our interpreter's result will correspond to a valid value from one model of the specification, and it will always produce that value. All valid models can be collected [22], however our industrial experience indicates that the ability to investigate multiple models is mainly of academic value. Loose specifications arise because specifications generally need to be stated at a higher level of abstraction than that of the final implementation. Looseness enables the modeller to express that it does not matter which particular value a certain expression yields, as long as it fulfils certain requirements [22].

VDM++ and VDM-RT allow concurrent *threads* to be defined. Such threads are synchronised using *permission predicates* that are associated with any operations that cannot allow concurrent execution. Where pre-conditions for an operation describe the condition the caller must ensure before calling it, the permission predicate describes the condition that must be satisfied before the operation can be activated, and until that condition is satisfied the operation call is blocked. The permission predicates can refer to instance variables as well as *history counters* which indicate the number of times an operation has been requested, activated or completed for the current object. In VDM-RT, the concurrency modelling can be enhanced by deploying objects on different CPUs with busses connecting them. Operations called between CPUs can be asynchronous, so that the caller does not wait for the call to complete. In addition, threads can be declared as *periodic*, so that they run autonomously at regular intervals. For periodic threads it is also possible to express jitter, start time offset as well as the minimum arrival time between occurences of the operation used in a periodic thread[1].

VDM-RT has a special **system** class where the modeller can specify the hardware architecture, including the CPUs and their bus communication topology; the dialect provides two predefined classes for the purpose, `CPU` and `BUS`. CPUs are instantiated with a clock speed (Hz) and a *scheduling policy*, either *First-come, first-served (FCFS)* or *Fixed priority (FP)*. The initial objects defined in the model can then be deployed to the declared CPUs using the CPU's `deploy` and `setPriority` operations. Buses are defined with a transmission speed (bytes/s) and a set of CPUs which they connect. Object instances that are not deployed to a specific CPU (and not created by an object that is deployed), are automatically deployed onto a `virtual CPU`. The virtual CPU is connected to all real CPUs through a `virtual bus`. Virtual components are used to simulate the external environment for the model of the system being developed.

The semantics of VDM-RT has been extended with the concept of discrete time, such that all computations a thread performs take time, including the transmission of messages over a bus. Time delays can be explicitly specified by special **duration** and **cycles** statements, allowing the modeller to explicitly state that a statement or block consumes a known amount of time. This can be specified as a number of nanoseconds or a number of CPU cycles of the CPU on which the statement is evaluated. All virtual resources are infinitely fast: calculation can be performed instantaneously consuming no time, though if an explicit duration statement is evaluated on a virtual CPU, the system time will be incremented by the duration.

The formal semantics of the kernel of VDM-RT is provided in [40] in an operational semantics style. This uses an interleaving semantics without restricting non-deterministic choices; in particular there is no requirement for specific scheduling policies. Thus, the

[1] In the current version of the VDMJ interpreter the allowable jitter is a simple random distribution but it is expected that the user in the future will be able to specify a desired jitter distribution.

semantics enables multiple different interleavings and as such the deterministic execution provided by the VDMJ [2] interpreter described here can be seen as one possible scheduling of a model containing non-determinism. Effectively, all the other models are ignored from the interpreter's perspective.

The VDM interpreter in Overture is a Java implementation called VDMJ. It implements the scheduling and debug principles presented in this paper. It supports all VDM dialects, allowing deterministic interpretation of sequential, multi-threaded and distributed VDM models.

3 Interpreting Sequential VDM Models

In order to simulate the evaluation of functions or operations from a VDM model an interpreter first needs to be initialised with the definitions declared in the model. This is achieved with a tree traversal of the AST produced by the parser. Essentially, the syntactic definitions must be transformed into their semantic equivalent representations. However, since VDM is not designed to be interpreted, this transformation can be quite complicated, because of the potential dependencies between different definitions. Note however that the interpreter presented here operate with specific values and not symbolic values [20].

The initialization of a specification amounts to the evaluation of the state of the system, either in VDM-SL state definitions or VDM++ and VDM-RT static class definitions. This involves the evaluation of initialization clauses for the various state definitions, guided by their definition dependency ordering. VDM does not define a syntactic order for the evaluation of definitions, but rather the order is inferred from the definitions' dependencies on each other: definitions that do not depend on others are initialized first, in any order; then definitions that depend on those are initialized, and so on[2]. Every time a specification is re-initialized, it returns to the same initial state.

When the initialisation is complete, the interpreter is ready to start the evaluation of a test expression, making use of the definitions and state from the VDM model. In order to perform such a test evaluation, the interpreter creates a runtime *context* that initially contains the values defined in the state (if any). The evaluation then proceeds by evaluating any arguments, by direct recursive traversal evaluation of the argument expressions in the AST, and then executing the function or operation body in a new stack frame that is linked to the state context. The evaluation evolves in a natural recursive fashion, reflecting the function or operation call structure of the specification on one particular thread.

The interpreter is also able to check all pre- and post-conditions, type and state invariants, recursive measures and performs general runtime type checking. The additional checks can be switched on or off whenever the user requires additional checking. Extra checking naturally has an impact on the performance of the interpreter but this may be a faster way to discover problems in VDM models. Semantically, bottom values (denoting undefined) will result from different kinds of run-time errors from the interpreter depending upon whether such checks are performed or not, but the behaviour

[2] There are some dependency orders which are perfectly legal VDM, but which cannot be calculated by the interpreter.

will always be deterministic. The special check for termination of recursive functions may be worth a special mention, since this is (as far as we know) not performed by any other interpreters. In VDM it is possible to define so-called **measure** functions that must be monotonically decreasing for recursive calls. This can be checked at run-time by the interpreter such that infinite recursion will always be detected.

These additional checks, based on predicates, correspond to the kind of checking carried out in JML [6]. This can be illustrated using the conventional `Factorial` function (in the post-condition here a basic library function from the `MATH` library is used). The ordering of the additional checking can be seen in Figure 1.

Some VDM expressions contain looseness, for example a choice construct called a let-be expression looks like: **let** a **in set** {1,2} **in** a. This expression denotes either 1 or 2 but it is deliberately left as an implementation choice for the implementer

```
public Factorial: nat -> nat1
Factorial(n) ==
  if n = 0
  then 1
  else n * Factorial(n - 1)
pre n >= 0
post RESULT = MATH`fac(n)
measure Id;

Id : nat -> nat
Id(n) == n;
```

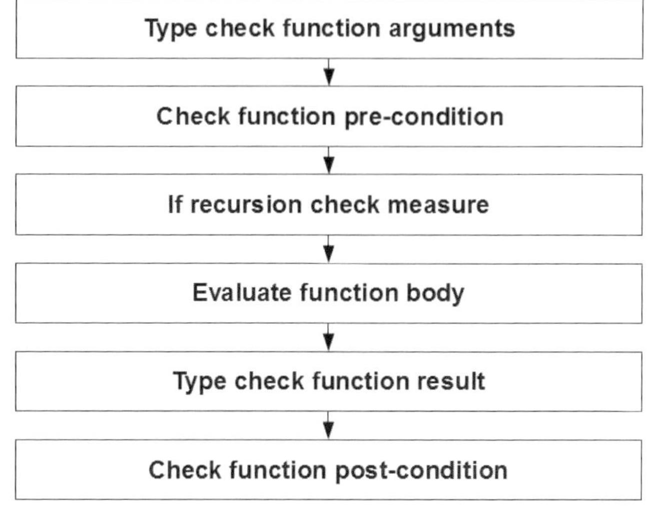

Fig. 1. Additional predicate checking in function evaluation

from a refinement perspective. In order to be able to reproduce executions, the interpreter must thus choose one of the possible semantic models in order to produce a deterministic interpretation. In the same way iterations over a set of elements must be performed in the same order every time to ensure a deterministic result. As a result, the evaluation of any sequential VDM model by the interpreter will always produce the same result value, even if looseness means that the result cannot be predicted (easily) ahead of time.

With respect to the interpretation of logical expressions it is also worth mentioning that the standard left to right evaluation used in most programming languages are used. This means that from a semantic perspective it is equivalent to McCarthy logic [28] instead of the standard Logic of Partial Functions (LPF) handling of undefinedness in VDM [18,10]. Alternatively one could start parallel threads interpreting each subexpression in a logical expression and then only yield a run-time error (denoting undefined) in the event that none of them yield a result that is sufficient to determine the truth value of the logical operator according to the traditional LPF rules. However, it has been decided that the extra complexity of this would not be worthwhile.

4 Interpreting Concurrent Real-Time Models

All VDM-SL specifications and non-threaded VDM++ specifications result in a simple single threaded evaluation, as described above. Their execution will always produce the same result because VDMJ treats all loose operations as under-determined rather than non-deterministic [26].

VDM-RT simulates distributed systems and thus the initialisation process explained for sequential VDM models above also needs to deal with the deployment of object instances to `CPU`s, for example. The user indicates the intended deployment in the special **`system`** class and so the interpreter needs to extract the necessary information from the AST of that class. In addition, the interpreter needs to make use of the deployment information to determine whether interprocess communication over a `BUS` is necessary. It is also worthwhile noting that if an object instance creates new object instances (using the **`new`** constructor) during the interpretation, those new instances must be deployed on the same `CPU` by the interpreter.

Note that the interpreter here abstracts away from the challenges of being able to determine the global state in a distributed system [1]. Since the interpreter always will have consistent information about all the `CPU`'s at any point of time, the traditional issues with unsynchronised clocks and dependability in distributed systems [21] are abstracted away.

VDM++ and VDM-RT specifications can have multiple threads of execution, and their evaluation can easily become non-deterministic since the thread scheduling policy is deliberately left undefined in the VDM semantics. In order to eliminate this looseness, VDMJ uses a scheduler which coordinates the activity of all threads in the system and allows them to proceed, according to a policy, in a deterministic order. This guarantees repeatable evaluations even for highly threaded VDM specifications.

VDMJ implements VDM threads using Java threads as opposed to a stack machine. Previous experience [14] with an implementation of a single threaded stack machine turned out to be slower because of e.g. swap overhead. The Java language does not define the operation of the underlying JVM thread scheduler. Instead, Java places various constraints on the ordering of events that must occur between threads, in the light of synchronization primitives that control access to shared resources. This means that although a given Java program will have a well defined partial ordering of some of its operations, the JVM thread scheduler has a great deal of freedom regarding how to execute threads that are not using synchronized access to variables or methods. In particular, there is no way to control which thread gets control of which (real) CPU in the system.

In order to ensure that the VDMJ interpreter is fully independent of the JVM scheduler we need to use Java synchronization primitives to enforce the semantics of the various VDM language features to control concurrency (permission predicates and mutexes), and to control the scheduling order and duration of timeslices allocated to different threads.

VDMJ scheduling is controlled on the basis of multiple *Resources* by a *Resource Scheduler*. A Resource is a separate limited resource in the system, such as a CPU or a bus (see Figure 2). These are separate in the sense that multiple CPUs or busses may exist, and limited in the sense that one CPU can only run one thread at a time, and one bus can only be transmitting one message at a time. Therefore there is a queue of activity that should be scheduled for each Resource – threads to run on a CPU, or messages to be sent via a bus. The Resource Scheduler is responsible for scheduling execution on the Resources in the system.

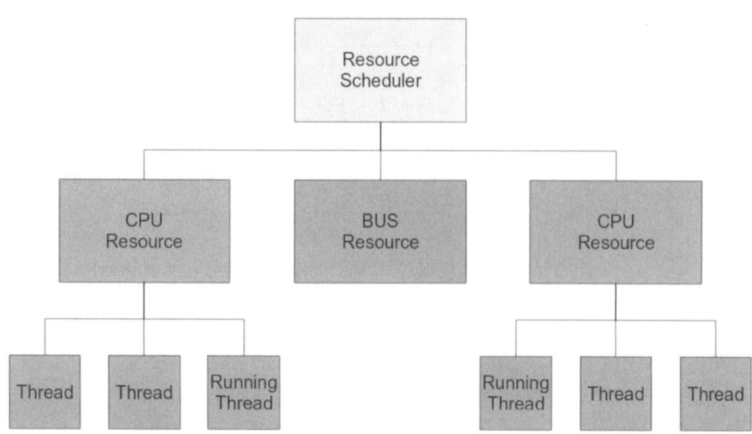

Fig. 2. Overview of the VDM-RT resource scheduler

An interpreter (of any VDM dialect) has a single Resource Scheduler. A VDM-SL or VDM++ simulation will have only one CPU Resource (called a virtual CPU) and no bus Resources; a VDM-RT system will have as many CPUs and busses as are defined in the `system` class.

Every Resource has a scheduling policy[3] potentially different for each instance of the Resource. A policy implements methods to identify the thread that is best to run next and for how long it is to be allowed to run (its timeslice).

With VDM-RT, in the event that the active thread is trying to move system time, the Resource will identify this fact. The Resource Scheduler is responsible for waiting until *all* Resources are in this state, and then finding the minimum time step that would satisfy at least one of the waiting threads. System time is moved forward at this point, and those threads that have their time step satisfied are permitted to continue, while those that need to wait longer remain suspended. This reflects the semantics of VDM-RT as defined in [40,17].

For example, if there are two threads running (on two CPUs), the Resource Scheduler will offer each of them timeslices in turn. When one thread wishes to move system time by (say) 10 units, its CPU Resource will indicate this to the Resource Scheduler, which will stop including it in the scheduling process, allowing the other CPU's thread to run. Eventually, the second thread will also want to move system time (typically at the end of a statement), say by 15 units, and its CPU Resource will also indicate this to the Resource Scheduler. At this point, all active threads want to move time, one by 10 and the other by 15. The minimum time step that will satisfy at least one thread is a step of 10 units. So the Resource Scheduler moves system time by 10, which releases the first thread; the second thread remains trying to move time, but for the remaining 5 units that it needs. By default, all statements take a duration of 2 cycles, calculated with reference to the speed of the CPU on which the statement is executed. Statements (or blocks of statements) can have their default times overridden by **duration** and **cycles** statements. The core of the scheduler is illustrated by:

```
progressing := false;
for all resource in set resources do
  -- record if at least one resource is able to progress
  progressing := CanProgress(resource) or progressing;
let timesteps = {resource.getTimestep()
                | resource in set resources}\{nil}
in
  -- nobody can progress and nobody is waiting for time
  if not progressing and timesteps = {}
  then error -- deadlock is detected
  -- nobody can progress and somebody is waiting for time
  elseif not progressing and timesteps <> {}
  then let mintime = Min(timesteps)
       in
         (SystemClock.advance(mintime);
          for all resource in set resources do
            AdvanceTime(resource,mintime))
  else -- continue scheduling
```

[3] As described in Section 2, this can currently be either a "*First Come First Served*" or a "*Fixed Priority*" scheduling policy, but more could be added in the future and parameterisation of these can be imagined.

The initial loop establishes whether any resources can progress. The `CanProgress` operation does a compute step for the Resource, if possible. The `progressing` flag will be **`true`** if any Resource was able to progress. The `getTimestep` operation either returns the timestep requested by the Resource, or **`nil`**, indicating that it is not currently waiting for time to advance. If no Resource can progress and no Resource is waiting for a timestep, the system is *deadlocked*. Otherwise, if no Resource can progress and at least one is waiting for a timestep, then system time can advance by the *smallest* requested amount. In this event, every Resource is adjusted by the minimum step, which will result in at least one Resource being able to progress. This scheduling process continues until the original expression supplied by the user completes its evaluation.

The critical point, for deterministic behaviour, is that only one Java thread is ever running at a given point of time: either a thread associated with a CPU or a bus Resource, or the Resource Scheduler itself (which runs in the main thread). Furthermore, threads run in a deterministic order and for deterministic timeslices, since the scheduling policies are deterministic. Timeslices are deterministic because they are implemented as the execution of a specific number of VDM statements or expressions, rather than a period of time.

In VDM++ and VDM-RT threads are synchronised using permission predicates and this adds to the complexity of the VDMJ interpreter. As explained in Section 2 permission predicates can depend on the value of instance variables and history counters. An object's history counters contain information about the history of requests, invocations and completions of all operations for the object. Here it is important to ensure that threads that have been blocked are awoken in a deterministic fashion. Given that the threads are otherwise running in a deterministic fashion, this is easily arranged since all the threads waiting for a history counter change (or a state variable value change) already have a fixed position in their CPU Resource's scheduling list. When the waiting threads are signalled, all applicable threads are signalled at the same time, and no new threads can be scheduled until this is complete. So the way that the scheduling evolves after a history event (or state change) is deterministic, since the threads waiting at any point is also deterministic and the scheduling is deterministic.

Finally, threads that are defined as periodic also need to be taken into account in the scheduling. A simple periodic thread will calculate that it needs to wait until system time has moved (say) 100 time units before it should execute its body again. The thread does this calculation when it is scheduled to run, which is deterministic since the scheduler is deterministic; the thread is re-scheduled when the required time is reached, which again is deterministic because the movement of time only occurs when there is no scheduling activity. Periodic threads can also have more complex repeat semantics, limiting the inter-run period for example, or adding random jitter to the period. However these calculations are still deterministic since a seedable pseudo-random number generator is used for the jitter. The generator is re-seeded whenever the specification is re-initialized. This guarantees the overall execution will be the same, given the same sequence of evaluations after an initialization.

5 Creating a Deterministic Debugger

In order to get a deterministic debugger for an interpreted language the interpreter naturally needs to be deterministic in itself as explained above. However, when a language includes concurrent threads, debuggers which have a deterministic interpreter are not necessarily deterministic since the debugging may effect the execution. Conventional debuggers for multi-threaded applications are usually non-deterministic because threads suspended for debug do not share their actual thread state and are just excluded from the scheduling, letting other threads carry on as normal. An example of such a debugger is the Java debugger in Eclipse and the C# debugger in Visual Studio. In the Java Virtual Machine (VM) a thread can be suspended through the Java Debug Wire Protocol (JDWP) [29] for inspection. However, the state of the suspended thread is not changed while the thread is stopped, making any other thread unable to detect that the thread was suspended. This causes non-deterministic scheduling since the suspended thread can no longer be scheduled, thus decreasing the number of threads in the scheduling algorithm by one. Even though the VM supports a total suspend of the entire VM, the problem still applies, since it makes use of the same internal mechanism, suspending one thread at a time, risking non-deterministic scheduling during the suspend process.

5.1 Deterministic Debugging

In VDMJ, deterministic scheduling is guaranteed during debugging. This ensures that threads will always be scheduled in the same order, independent of any debug actions made by the user. In relation to conventional debuggers, this is like a suspend of the VM causing the scheduling order to be preserved during debug. The main difference is that no single thread can be suspended, while others continue. If a thread hits a breakpoint which forces it into debug mode, its execution will be suspended and a signal will be sent simultaneously to all other threads to do the same. Similarly, no thread can continue before all threads have returned from debug mode. The debugger allows all threads to be inspected while in debug mode, because in effect, they all stopped at the same breakpoint. In order for interpretation to continue, all threads must be signalled and receive the same continue command from the user interface. The order in which the commands are sent to the threads is irrelevant because interpretation can only be continued after all threads have received the signal. Great care is taken not to lose signals during this process. The thread which initiated the debug session is signalled last during a resume, so that the other threads are in the state that they were before we hit the breakpoint. The thread order of this signal communication cannot affect the scheduling order, since it is strictly controlled and independent of the debugging session.

5.2 Debugging User Interface

A debugging interface must be both compelling and simple. However it must provide enough information and control of the model being debugged to determine if the inspected behaviour is correct. In Overture, the debug interface is based on the *Debug* feature of the Eclipse platform, allowing a simple, standardized interaction during debugging. A protocol is required to connect the debug interface with the interpreter

(VDMJ). The chosen protocol in Overture is Xdebug DBGP[4] [32]. This protocol supports the debugging of multi-threaded models and provides commands for both control and retrieval of state information from the executing model. The protocol is designed to keep the debugger as simple as possible, using simple text commands for control with more complex XML responses to the user interface with information about the model or the general state of the interpreter. To integrate the DBGP protocol with the Eclipse Debug feature, a *Debug Target* is required which defines the connection between the debug interface included in Eclipse and the protocol. The debug target is responsible for sending commands to the interpreter and decoding responses either as state change of the interpreter, or as information representing threads, stack frames, variables and values.

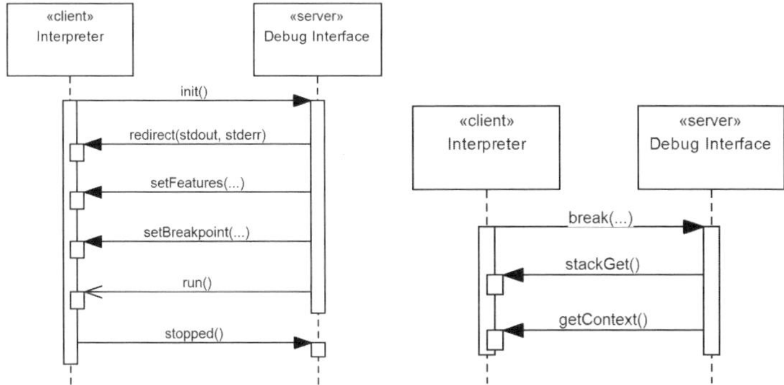

(a) Normal flow of the debug protocol. **(b)** Break in the debug protocol.

Fig. 3. Sequence diagrams of interaction with the debugger

In Figure 3a the normal flow of debugging is shown for a single thread. When the thread connects to the debug target it sends an `init` command with a session id. This causes the debug target to initialize a debugging session and subsequently start the configuration of the debugger, redirecting output and setting debugger features and breakpoints followed by a `run` command starting the executing. This will allow the debugger to start the interpretation of the model, then the interpreter either hits a breakpoint shown in Figure 3b or runs to completion sending a `stopped` command to the debug target signalling the end of the debugging session. If a multi-threaded model is executed only the main thread will send the `init` command while other threads created later just connect with the session id which allows the debug target to group them into the same debug session. The server will always configure all threads after a connection has been established.

Figure 3b shows the case where a breakpoint is hit in a thread. This causes the thread to send a `break` message notifying that a breakpoint was hit. When this happens the debugger will start populating the user interface with call stack through `stackGet` and variables which are in scope per selected stack frame by the `getContext` command. Threads with a short lifetime and with no breakpoints only report their existence if they

[4] A common debugger protocol for languages and debugger UI communication.

exist when a breakpoint is hit, this avoids overloading of the debugging protocol in case many **async** operations and **periodic** threads are part of the model. This may seem trivial but in order to achieve a resonable performance of the interpretation of a VDM-RT model in the debugger this is a paramount design decision.

5.3 Debugging Multi-threaded Applications

Concurrent VDM models makes use of permission predicates to control concurrent behaviour, by allowing synchronization of operations to be explicitly specified. However if thread execution is restricted by predicates, which includes history counters, then it is generally difficult to determine why a certain thread is blocked. To improve the debugging of multi-threaded models, VDMJ keeps track of all threads and all associated history counters and provides this information through the debug interface. This allows a user to inspect threads blocked by permission predicates as shown in Figure 4. All history counters associated with a thread will be available with the current value and operation name e.g. **#fin**(ClientListen).

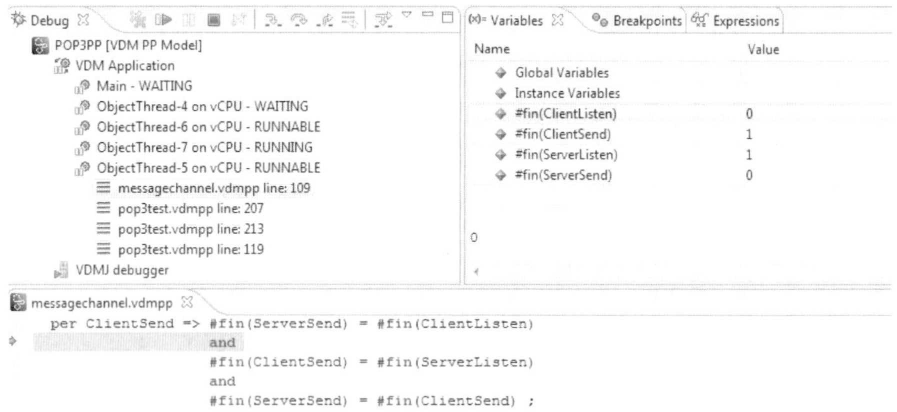

Fig. 4. Debug UI Showing history counter values

The permission predicate shown in Figure 4 from the POP3 client/ server application [13], guards the operation ClientSend to ensure a balance between send and received messages. The permission predicate includes several history counters, thus the variables view provides information about these. In Figure 4 it is easy to deduce the reason why a permission predicate may be blocked. From a usability perspective this is a very important feature making it much easier for users to deduce the reasons why a concurrent model is not behaving as imagined.

6 Related Work

The development that is closely related to the sequential part of this work is clearly the interpreter from VDMTools [24]. That interpreter has internally defined its own virtual machine and ensures its deterministic execution by simply having one master scheduler that controls all threads. However from a performance point of view the VDMJ interpreter is usually significantly faster than the interpreter from VDMTools, the exceptions being test cases that use higher order functions.

The B-Method is also a model-oriented formal method and here the ProB tool [27] is related to the work presented here. Among other features ProB contains an animator feature. Since B focus on implicit definitions the executable subset is smaller than what we are able to cope with in this paper, and concurrency and distributed systems cannot be incorporated since it is not included in the B notation. The ProB interpreter is also deterministic but focus is more put on enabling the user to apply operations that have acceptable pre-conditions interactively rather than on traditional testing which is enabled with the VDMJ interpreter presented here.

The ProB tool has also been used to animate Z specifications [30]. For Z many others have also produced interpreters/translators to programming languages for subsets of the notation [9,39,5,36]. Common to all these papers is that they do not include concurrency in the Z notation and thus do not have the challenges created for keeping determinism as presented in this paper.

The POOSL approach has significant similarities with VDM-RT in its ability to describe a distributed system in a model-oriented fashion [38,15]. Here they have decided to resolve non-determinism by always selecting the first option when a finite collection of possibilities exists, though it is stated that it is possible that this way of interpreting the non-determism can be changed in the future. However, they do not have the interactive debugging functionality described in this paper, but are limited to logging primitives.

A significantly different approach for interpreting formal models can be found in Maude [8]. However this technology is based on algebraic approaches using term rewriting and thus it is not really comparable to the approach presented in this paper.

7 Concluding Remarks

Deterministic interpreters for distributed concurrent models are essential for repeatability of test executions. In this paper we have presented one approach for implementing an interpreter in Java for an executable subset of VDM, and a scheduling algorithm which takes distribution over resources and scheduling of threads within resources into account to provide deterministic execution. We have also presented how VDMJ is different to conventional debuggers by enabling debug without affecting the scheduling of threads. We believe that this property is essential in order for users to be able to discover why a VDM model with concurrency behaves in a specific way. In addition we have explained some of design decisions taken both to increase performance as well as for increasing the usability. We believe that the same principles can be adapted to interpreters for other formal modelling languages such as Circus [42].

Ongoing work on the semantics of a core kernel of VDM is currently being carried out. It is expected that the results of this effort will provide a more rigorous presentation of the material presented here. This will include mappings from the different VDM dialects to VDM Core as well as considerations for the models that are being ignored by the interpreter as well.

Regarding the GUI debugger, we expect to improve the functionality by creating better ways of providing overviews of the status of all threads at all CPUs simulated in a VDM-RT model. Such improvements will make it easier for the user to quickly deduce the underlying reasons behind potential issues.

Acknowledgements. The work reported in this paper have partly been carried out in the DESTECS project which have partially been funded by the European Commission. In addition we would like to thank Marcel Verhoef, Sune Wolff and the anonymous reviewers for valuable input on the work presented here.

References

1. Babaoglu, Ö., Marzullo, K.: Consistent Global States of Distributed Systems: Fundamental Concepts and Mechanisms. Tech. Rep. UBLCS-93-1, University of Bologna, Piazza di Porta S. Donato, 5, 40127 Bologna (Italy) (January 1993)
2. Battle, N.: VDMJ User Guide. Tech. rep., Fujitsu Services Ltd., UK (2009)
3. Bergan, T., Anderson, O., Devietti, J., Ceze, L., Grossman, D.: CoreDet: A Compiler and Runtime System for Deterministic Multithreaded Execution. In: ASPLOS 2010. ACM, New York (2010)
4. Bjorner, D., Jones, C.B. (eds.): The Vienna Development Method: The Meta-Language. LNCS, vol. 61. Springer, Heidelberg (1978)
5. Breuer, P., Bowen, J.: Towards correct executable semantics for z. In: Bowen, J., Hall, J. (eds.) Z User Workshop, pp. 185–209. Springer, Heidelberg (1994)
6. Burdy, L., Cheon, Y., Cok, D., Ernst, M.D., Kiniry, J.R., Leavens, G.T., Leino, K.R.M., Poll, E.: An overview of JML Tools and Applications. Intl. Journal of Software Tools for Technology Transfer 7, 212–232 (2005)
7. Burnin, J., Sen, K.: Asserting and checking determinism for multithreaded programs. In: 17th ACM SIGSOFT Symposium on the Foundations of Software Engineering (FSE). ACM, New York (2009)
8. Clavel, M., Durán, F., Eker, S., Lincoln, P., Martí-Oliet, N., Meseguer, J., Talcott, C.L. (eds.): All About Maude - A High-Performance Logical Framework, How to Specify, Program and Verify Systems in Rewriting Logic. LNCS, vol. 4350. Springer, Heidelberg (2007)
9. Dick, A., Krause, P., Cozens, J.: Computer aided transformation of Z into Prolog. In: Nicholls, J. (ed.) Z User Workshop, Workshops in Computing, pp. 71–85. Springer, Heidelberg (1990)
10. Fitzgerald, J.S.: The Typed Logic of Partial Functions and the Vienna Development Method. In: Bjørner, D., Henson, M.C. (eds.) Logics of Specification Languages. EATCS Monographs in Theoretical Computer Science, pp. 427–461. Springer, Heidelberg (2007)
11. Fitzgerald, J.S., Larsen, P.G., Verhoef, M.: Vienna Development Method. Wiley Encyclopedia of Computer Science and Engineering. John Wiley & Sons, Inc., Chichester (2008)
12. Fitzgerald, J., Larsen, P.G.: Modelling Systems – Practical Tools and Techniques in Software Development, 2nd edn. Cambridge University Press, Cambridge (2009); ISBN 0-521-62348-0
13. Fitzgerald, J., Larsen, P.G., Mukherjee, P., Plat, N., Verhoef, M.: Validated Designs for Object–oriented Systems. Springer, New York (2005), `http://www.vdmbook.com`
14. Fitzgerald, J., Larsen, P.G., Sahara, S.: VDMTools: Advances in Support for Formal Modeling in VDM. ACM Sigplan Notices 43(2), 3–11 (2008)

15. Florescu, O., Voeten, J., Verhoef, M., Corporaal, H.: Reusing Real-Time Systems Design Experience Through Modelling Patterns. In: Forum on specification and Description Languages (FDL). ECSI (2006); received the best paper award at FDL 2006. This paper is available on-line at, `http://www.es.ele.tue.nl/premadona/publications/FVVC06.pdf`
16. Fröhlich, B.: Towards Executability of Implicit Definitions. Ph.D. thesis, TU Graz, Institute of Software Technology (September 1998)
17. Hooman, J., Verhoef, M.: Formal semantics of a VDM extension for distributed embedded systems. In: Dams, D., Hannemann, U., Steffen, M. (eds.) Concurrency, Compositionality, and Correctness. LNCS, vol. 5930, pp. 142–161. Springer, Heidelberg (2010)
18. Jones, C.B.: Program Specification and Verification in VDM. Logic of Programming and Calculi of Discrete Design F36, 149–184 (1987)
19. Jones, C.B.: Systematic Software Development Using VDM, 2nd edn. Prentice-Hall International, Englewood Cliffs (1990); ISBN 0-13-880733-7
20. Kneuper, R.: Symbolic Execution as a Tool for Validation of Specifications. Ph.D. thesis, Department of Computer Science, Univeristy of Manchester (March 1989), technical Report Series UMCS-89-7-1
21. Lamport, L.: Time, Clocks, and the Ordering of Events in a Distributed System. Communications of the ACM 21(7), 558–565 (1978)
22. Larsen, P.G.: Evaluation of underdetermined explicit expressions. In: Naftalin, M., Bertrán, M., Denvir, T. (eds.) FME 1994. LNCS, vol. 873, pp. 233–250. Springer, Heidelberg (1994)
23. Larsen, P.G., Battle, N., Ferreira, M., Fitzgerald, J., Lausdahl, K., Verhoef, M.: The Overture Initiative – Integrating Tools for VDM. ACM Software Engineering Notes 35(1) (January 2010)
24. Larsen, P.G., Lassen, P.B.: An Executable Subset of Meta-IV with Loose Specification. In: Prehn, S., Toetenel, H. (eds.) VDM 1991. LNCS, vol. 551, Springer, Heidelberg (1991)
25. Larsen, P.G., Lausdahl, K., Battle, N.: The VDM-10 Language Manual. Tech. Rep. TR-2010-06, The Overture Open Source Initiative (April 2010)
26. Larsen, P.G., Pawłowski, W.: The Formal Semantics of ISO VDM-SL. Computer Standards and Interfaces 17(5-6), 585–602 (1995)
27. Leuschel, M., Butler, M.J.: ProB: an automated analysis toolset for the B method. STTT 10(2), 185–203 (2008)
28. McCarthy, J.: A Basis for a Mathematical Theory of Computation. In: Braffort, P., Hirstberg, D. (eds.) Western Joint Computer Conference, then published in: Computer Programming and Formal Systems, pp. 33–70. North Holland, Amsterdam (1967)
29. Microsystems, S.: Java Debug Wire Protocol. 1.5.0 edn. Sun Microsystems, Inc, (2004), `http://download.oracle.com/javase/1.5.0/docs/guide/jpda/jdwp-spec.html`
30. Plagge, D., Leuschel, M.: Validating Z Specifications Using the ProB Animator and Model Checker. In: Davies, J., Gibbons, J. (eds.) IFM 2007. LNCS, vol. 4591, pp. 480–500. Springer, Heidelberg (2007)
31. Plat, N., Larsen, P.G.: An Overview of the ISO/VDM-SL Standard. Sigplan Notices 27(8), 76–82 (1992)
32. Rethans, S.C.A.D.: A Common Debugger Protocol for Languages and Debugger UI Communication. XDEBUG, 2 edn. (2011), `http://www.xdebug.org/docs-dbgp.php`
33. Ribeiro, A., Larsen, P.G.: Proof obligation generation and discharging for recursive definitions in VDM. In: Dong, J.S., Zhu, H. (eds.) ICFEM 2010. LNCS, vol. 6447, pp. 40–55. Springer, Heidelberg (2010)
34. Rushby, J.: Formal Methods: Instruments of Justification or Tools for Discovery? In: Nordic Seminar on Dependable Computing System 1994. The Technical University of Denmark, Department of Computer Science (August 1994)

35. Rushby, J.: Disappearing formal methods. In: Fifth IEEE International Symposium on High Assurance Systems Engineering, HASE 2000. IEEE, Los Alamitos (2000)
36. Sherrell, L.B., Carver, D.L.: Experiences in Translating Z Designs to Haskell Implementations. Software Practice and Experience 24(12), 1159–1178 (1994)
37. Søndergaard, H., Sestoft, P.: Non-determinism in Functional Languages. The Computer Journal 35(5), 514–523 (1992)
38. Theelen, B., Florescu, O., Geilen, M., Huang, J., van der Putten, P., Voeten, J.: Software/hardware engineering with the parallel object-oriented specification language. In: Proceedings of the ACM-IEEE International Conference on Formal Methods and Models for Codeesign (MEMOCODE), pp. 139–148. IEEE Computer Society, Los Alamitos (2007)
39. Valentine, S.: Z^{--}, an executable subset of Z. In: Nicholls, J. (ed.) Z User Workshop, Workshops in Computing, pp. 157–187. Springer, Heidelberg (1992)
40. Verhoef, M.: Modeling and Validating Distributed Embedded Real-Time Control Systems. Ph.D. thesis, Radboud University Nijmegen (2008); ISBN 978-90-9023705-3
41. Verhoef, M., Larsen, P.G., Hooman, J.: Modeling and Validating Distributed Embedded Real-Time Systems with VDM++. In: Misra, J., Nipkow, T., Karakostas, G. (eds.) FM 2006. LNCS, vol. 4085, pp. 147–162. Springer, Heidelberg (2006)
42. Woodcock, J.C.P., Cavalcanti, A.L.C.: A concurrent language for refinement. In: Butterfield, A., Pahl, C. (eds.) IWFM 2001: 5th Irish Workshop in Formal Methods. BCS Electronic Workshops in Computing, Dublin, Ireland (July 2001)

On Fitting a Formal Method into Practice*

Rainer Gmehlich[1], Katrin Grau[1], Stefan Hallerstede[2], Michael Leuschel[2], Felix Lösch[1], and Daniel Plagge[2]

[1] Robert Bosch GmbH, Stuttgart, Germany
[2] Heinrich-Heine-University of Düsseldorf, Germany

Abstract. The development of the Event-B formal method and the supporting tools Rodin and ProB was guided by practical experiences with the B-Method, the Z specification notation, VDM and similar practical formal methods. The case study discussed in this article — a cruise control system — is a serious test of industrial use. We report on where Event-B and its tools have succeeded, where they have not. We also report on advances that were inspired by the case study. Interestingly, the case study was not a pure formal methods problem. In addition to Event-B, it used Problem Frames for capturing requirements. The interaction between the two proved to be crucial for the success of the case study. The heart of the problem was tracing informal requirements from Problem Frames descriptions to formal Event-B models. To a large degree, this issue dictated the approach that had to be used for formal modelling. A dedicated record theory and dedicated tool support were required. The size of the formal models rather than complex individual formulas was the main challenge for tool support.

1 Introduction

This article recounts an attempt to apply Event-B [1] to an industrial specification problem in a methodologically heterogenous environment without prior use of formal methods. This required integration within an existing, evolving development methodology. This means the methodology cannot be dictated to follow customs and conventions that have arisen within formal methods such as Event-B.

We believe some of the problems we encountered will be typical for industrial deployment of formal methods in general. In particular, this concerns problems related to the different cultures, customs and conventions in industry and academia. At times, these problems (appear to) become more severe than all technical problems taken together. It seems advisable to be prepared for this, assuming the different cultures are unavoidable.

The article presents a non-chronological digest of an experiment carried out at Bosch: to develop a model of a cruise control system. The focus of this experiment

* This research was carried out as part of the EU FP7-ICT research project DEPLOY (Industrial deployment of advanced system engineering methods for high dependability and productivity) http://www.deploy-project.eu

S. Qin and Z. Qiu (Eds.): ICFEM 2011, LNCS 6991, pp. 195–210, 2011.

was to apply Event-B to an industrial problem in an industrial environment. In that environment, Problem Frames [8] are used to deal with informal requirements. Initially, the academics did not yet grasp the central importance of this: formal methods seem to have a tendency to take over whole development processes and dictate what should be done instead. However, here formal methods were only a piece in a bigger puzzle. Other parts of the puzzle dealt with continuous control (which is provided by specialised design methods) or real time (which is considered more a matter of code generation). Note that such issues enter the case study in the form of assumptions at various places. We have learned that excluding parts of a problem can be a challenge for formal methods. The claim of correctness will only be with respect to a large set of assumptions, the justifications of which are unavailable.

The core of the formal modelling problem of the experiment concerns only the switching behaviour of the cruise control. The main difficulties are to fit Event-B into the overall development scheme, while finding the appropriate abstractions to express the formal model of the cruise control. In [16], a formal development of a cruise control in Event-B is presented. The development is more ambitious than our development, but it does neither support traceability of Problem Frames descriptions nor hazard analysis. It also does not respect the boundaries described above about what not to model. One would also think that hybrid modelling of the cruise control (for instance, [15]) should be of advantage. But again, our problem is the switching behaviour of the cruise control. We want to avoid duplicating work already carried out by other engineers. In principle, one could also use an approach based on StateMate [6]. We believe, however, that tracing of requirements and matching formal models with Problem Frames would be difficult. In particular, although Event-B refinement is not satisfactory for matching Problem Frames elaboration, it gave us a means to express what we wanted.

We believe our observations and findings would apply in similar form to other formal methods used in place of Event-B. In this context, note again the exclusion of certain aspects such as continuity or real time. Not everything is under control of the formal method. Our contribution is an approach for tracing requirements by matching Problem Frames with formal Event-B models using a dedicated way of modelling and instantiating records. We also have made progress in checking large models for deadlocks using constraint-solving techniques.

Industrial use is impossible without having supporting tools. For Event-B the Rodin tool [2] has been developed. In short, it deals with editing and proof obligation generation. It has a plugin architecture that permits its extension with new functionality. One plugin provided is ProB [11], a tool for model animation, model checking and constraint checking.

Overview. Section 2 describes how Event-B was fitted into an industrial development process. The following sections focus on specific problems of the integration. Section 3 discusses integration with Problem Frames. Section 4 discusses a specific aspect of that integration: the relationship of Problem Frames elaboration and Event-B refinement. Section 5 discusses a scaling problem by way of deadlock analysis. A conclusion follows in Section 6.

2 Event-B in an Industrial Development Process

The case study we discuss in this article is carried out within the Deploy research project. The project's main objective is to make major advances in engineering methods for dependable systems through the deployment of formal engineering methods. One work package of the project deals with the deployment of formal methods, in particular, Event-B and ProB in the automotive sector. The case study applies Event-B to the modelling of a *cruise control system*. A cruise control system is an automotive system implemented in software which automatically controls the speed of a car. It is part of the engine control system which controls actuators of the engine (such as injectors, fuel pumps or throttle valve) based on the values of specific sensors (such as the accelerator pedal position sensor, the airflow sensor or the lambda sensor).

The cruise control system consists of a discrete part describing the control logic and continuous parts describing the actual closed loop controllers required to adjust the speed of the car. In the case study we focus exclusively on the discrete part, that is, the switching behaviour of the cruise control system. The continuous control part is provided by other design methods.

2.1 Event-B

Event-B models are composed of *contexts* and *machines*. Contexts capture static aspects of a model expressed in terms of *carrier sets*, *constants* and *axioms*. Consequences of the axioms can be stated as *theorems* (that need to be proved). Fig. 5 and 7 below show two contexts. The *concrete* context of Fig. 7 is said to *extend* the *abstract* context of Fig. 5: all carrier sets, constants, axioms and theorems of the context being extended are visible in the extending context.

Machines capture dynamic aspects of a model (see Fig. 6). The state of a machine is described in terms of *variables*. The possible values of the variables are constrained by *invariants* (see *inv1* and *inv2* of Fig. 6). Possible state changes are modelled by *events*. Each event consists of a collection of *parameters* p, of *guards* g and of *actions* a (a collection of simultaneous update statements). We use the following schema to describe events: any p when g then a end. An event may cause a state change if its guard is true for a choice of parameters. Event-B does not make any fairness assumptions about event occurrences. *Refinement* is used to specify more details about a machine. For instance, the *concrete* machine of Fig. 8 is a refinement of the *abstract* machine of Fig. 6. The state of the abstract machine is related to the state of the concrete machine by a *gluing invariant* associated with the concrete machine that relates abstract variables to concrete variables (see invariant *inv3* in Fig. 8). Each event of the abstract machine is *refined* by one or more concrete events. Roughly speaking, the events of the abstract machine must be capable of simulating the behaviour of the events of the concrete machine. The Rodin tool can generate proof obligations to verify properties such as invariant preservation or refinement.

2.2 Fitting Event-B into Development Practice

Introducing the formal development method Event-B into industrial practice (in the automotive sector) requires integration with existing development processes and tools. Fig. 1 shows a sketch of a development process which includes Event-B. This article deals with the use of Event-B at the position indicated in the figure. The main challenge encountered in this respect is concerned with the relationship of Event-B and Problem Frames.

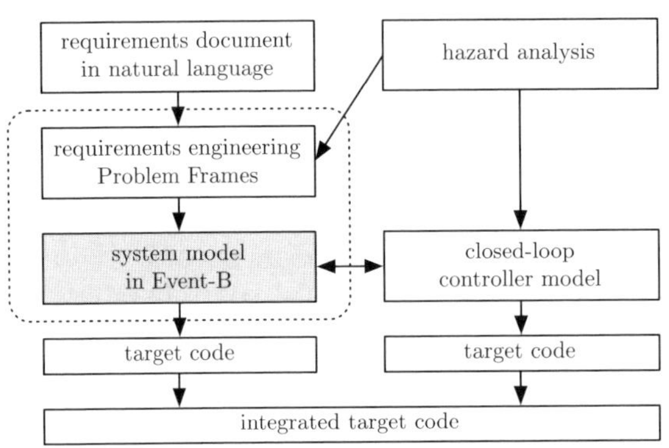

Fig. 1. Overview of the development process

We comment briefly on the phases of the development process, to give an impression of the general picture and the constraints imposed. Development begins with natural language requirements that tend to be unstructured and difficult to relate to a formal model. A hazard analysis yields safety requirements to be incorporated. Requirements engineering and hazard analysis go hand in hand. The development of the closed loop controller is done by control engineers. Verifying closed loop controllers requires reasoning about continuous time behaviour. Since specialised methods are already in place we did not study modelling of continuous time behavior in the case study. We modelled the discrete part of the system in Event-B making a contribution to the existing design process. Another work package of the Deploy project focused on the task of generating code from Event-B models [3].

The need for Problem Frames for requirements engineering had been recognised early on with formal system modelling in view. The decision to use Problem Frames was made after a first attempt to directly model natural language requirements in Event-B resulted in a large gap between the requirements document and the Event-B model. The gap between the two documents was too large to permit maintaining them consistently: it is indispensable to validate by means of a review, say, that an Event-B model adequately captures what is stated in the requirements. And tracing this information seemed out of reach. Furthermore, the Bosch engineers had made good experiences with using the Problem Frames approach for structuring requirements as well. It is important to note here, that the conditions determining a decision to use a certain method in industry are considerably different from those in academia: the method chosen in industry must not only fit a single problem it must also be understandable for a large variety of engineers who are not directly involved in solving the problem at hand. The Problem Frames approach looked very promising to the Bosch engineers because it could easily be understood by the development engineers.

The Problem Frames approach enabled the Bosch engineers to validate the Event-B model with respect to the requirements and provided an easier way of tracing requirements in the Event-B model. With the introduction of the Problem Frames approach they obtained two simpler validation problems:

(1) to validate whether the problem frames capture the natural language requirements
(2) to validate whether the Event-B model corresponds to the problem frames.

Each of the two validation problems appeared to be feasible as opposed to the direct approach from natural language requirements to Event-B models.

The insight we gained from the early phase of the case study is that introducing Event-B in industry on its own is difficult. Introducing Event-B in conjunction with supporting Problem Frames greatly reduces the entry barrier for engineers to use Event-B. Similar observations have been made with UML-B before [14].

2.3 Problem Frames

Problem Frames is an informal graphical requirements engineering method developed by Michael Jackson [8]. The immediate focus of Problem Frames, as its name suggests, is on software development as a problem to be solved. The problem to be solved is hereby visualized using *problem diagrams* that contain a *machine*, i.e., the system to be built, the *problem world*, i.e., the environment the system is interacting with and the *requirements* which are expressed in terms of the problem world. The requirements engineering process usually starts with a *context diagram*, an abstract problem diagram, which describes the main elements of the problem world as well as the overall requirement the system shall fulfill. Fig. 2 shows a simple *context diagram* of the cruise control system.

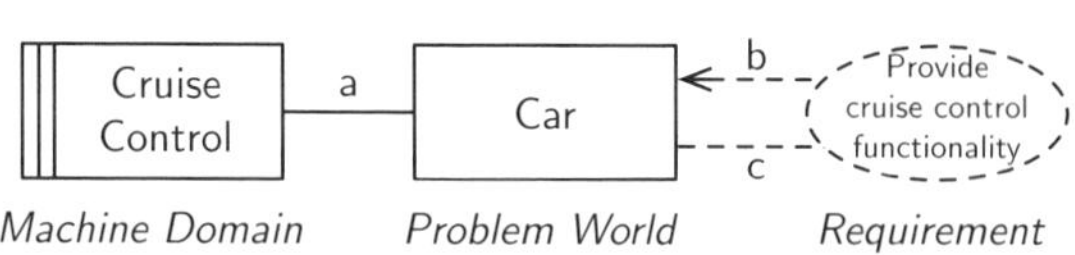

Fig. 2. Context diagram for cruise control system

The machine interacts with the problem world by *shared phenomena* at the interface *a*. Typically, these *phenomena* are events and states, controlled either by the problem world or by the machine and shared at input-output ports of the machine. Requirements are described only in terms of the phenomena of the problem world which are shared between the problem world and the requirements at interfaces *b* and *c*.

Projections of this context diagram, called *subproblems*, are then used to describe different aspects of the problem. A more detailed description of the concepts of Problem Frames can be found in [8].

We extended the original Problem Frames approach [9,13] by an additional operation called *elaboration* as well as an adapted version of the already existing projection operation. In an *elaboration* of an abstract problem diagram the environment, the phenomena and the requirements are described in more detail. For example, the problem diagram in Fig. 4 is an elaboration of the problem diagram in Fig. 3. Elaboration in Problem Frames thus serves a similar purpose as refinement in Event-B, i.e., to relate abstract descriptions of the system to more concrete descriptions.

2.4 The Cruise Control System

In the following we describe the control logic of the cruise control system in more detail. The behaviour of the cruise control system is determined by three different operating modes: NOCTRL, CTRL, ACTRL. In the NOCTRL mode the system is inactive, that is, it is not actively regulating the speed of the car. In the CTRL mode the system is either maintaining or approaching a previously defined target speed. In the ACTRL mode the system is either accelerating or decelerating by a predefined value. The three modes of the system can be switched by the driver using the *control interface* or by the software in case the control software detects an error. In the latter case the mode is always switched to NOCTRL.

There are two ways of a driver to control the behaviour of the cruise control system: (i) using the brake pedal or clutch pedal to (temporarily) deactivate the cruise control system, and (ii) using the control elements provided by the operating lever. The operating lever usually has the following buttons: (a) SET to define a target speed, (b) RESUME to resume a previously defined target speed, (c) TIPUP to increase the target speed, (d) TIPDN to decrease the target speed, (e) ACC to accelerate, (f) DEC to decelerate. Furthermore, there is a dedicated switch for switching the cruise control system ON or OFF.

Depending on commands given by the driver or signals received by sensors the cruise control system switches between the modes. In order to distinguish the different operational states of the system the three major modes are further partitioned into a number of ten submodes as shown in Table 1.

3 Relating Problem Frames to Event-B Models

A major obstacle during the case study was to understand how the gap between Problem Frames and Event-B could be closed. If the informal requirements could not be traced into the formal models, the development method would be of no use for the engineers. A close correspondence between concepts of Problem Frames and Event-B was needed to arrive at a systematic approach to requirements tracing. Feedback from the analysis of the formal models should suggest

Table 1. Modes and submodes of the cruise control system

Mode	Submode	Description
NOCTRL	UBAT_OFF	Ignition is off and engine not running
	INIT	Ignition is on and cruise control is being intialized
	OFF	Ignition is on, cruise control initialized and switched off
	ERROR	An irreversible error has occurred
	STANDBY	Cruise control has been switched on
	R_ERROR	A reversible error has occurred
CTRL	CRUISE	Cruise control is maintaining the target speed
	RESUME	Target speed is approached from above or from below
ACTRL	ACC	Cruise control is accelerating the car
	DEC	Cruise control is decelerating the car

improvements to the informal requirements. For example, missing requirements were identified by using deadlock checking in ProB.

The central concern was to relate the elaboration and projection operations provided by the extended Problem Frames approach to the notion of refinement in Event-B. In order to illustrate this problem we use a small example which describes a fragment of the cruise control system both at an abstract level (see Fig. 3) and a more concrete (elaborated) level (see Fig. 4). Note that some aspects (e.g. Ignition) are ignored.

3.1 Problem Frames Description of the Cruise Control

Fig. 3 shows an abstract problem diagram of the pedal subproblem for the cruise control system. The diagram of Fig. 3 shows the machine domain CrCtl Pedals, the given domain Pedals, the designed domain State Model, and the requirement R1. The phenomena shared between the machine, the domains, and the requirement are shown in Fig. 3 under *interfaces* with the following syntax: *[Name of the interface]: [Domain controlling the phenomenon]!{list of shared phenomena}*. For example, the line "L1 : Pedals!{P_Env_PedalSignals}" means that the phenomenon *P_Env_PedalSignals* controlled by the domain Pedals is shared with the machine CrCtl Pedals. The requirement R1 states that "depending on the status of the pedals (P_Env_PedalSignals), the internal mode of the cruise control system (P_CrCtl_Mode) should change to the mode R_ERROR or ERROR."

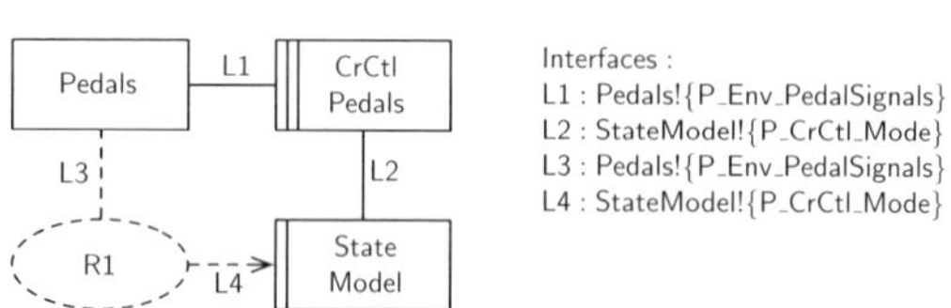

Fig. 3. Abstract problem diagram for pedals

Fig. 4 shows the elaborated version of the abstract problem diagram of Fig. 3. The abstract given domain Pedals has now been elaborated into the given domains Brake Pedal, Clutch Pedal, and Accelerator Pedal as well as the abstract phenomena shown in Fig. 3. For example, the abstract phenomenon

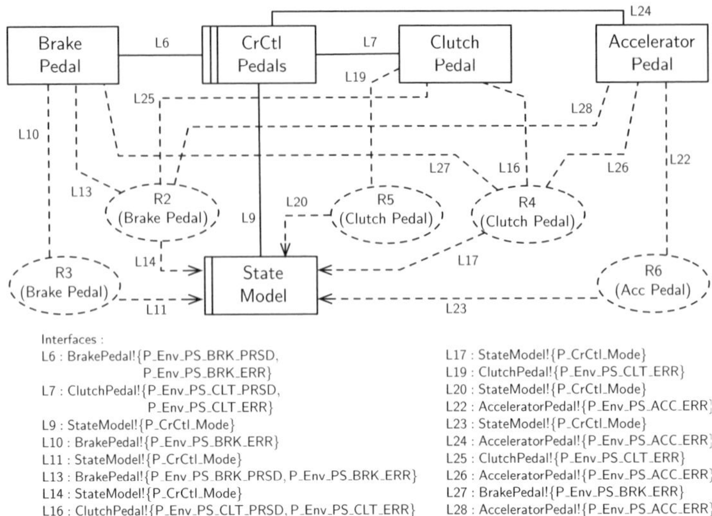

Fig. 4. Elaborated problem diagram for pedals

P_Env_PedalSignals has been elaborated into the concrete phenomena P_Env_BRK_PRSD, P_Env_BRK_ERR, P_Env_CLT_PRSD, P_Env_CLT_ERR, and P_Env_PS_ACC_ERR. The requirement R1 of Fig. 3 has also been elaborated into the requirements R2, R3, R4, R5, R6.

For illustration we state the requirements R2 and R3. Requirement R2 is: "If the brake pedal is pressed (P_Env_PS_BRK_PRSD) and no pedal error is present (P_Env_PS_BRK_ERR = FALSE, P_Env_PS_CLT_ERR = FALSE, P_Env_PS_ACC_ERR = FALSE), the mode (P_CrCtl_Mode) must change to R_ERROR." Requirement R3 is: "If a brake pedal error is present (P_Env_PS_BRK_ERR), the mode (P_CrCtl_Mode) must change to ERROR." R4 states the same as R2 for the clutch pedal (P_Env_CLT_PRSD) and R5 the same as R3 for the clutch pedal error (P_Env_PS_CLT_ERR). R6 states the same as R3 for the accelerator pedal error (P_Env_PS_ACC_ERR). Pressing the accelerator pedal (P_Env_PS_ACC_PRSD) is part of a different subproblem and therefore not dealt with in Fig. 4.

3.2 Relating Problem Frames Concepts to Event-B Concepts

To support traceability of requirements in problem diagrams to formal elements of Event-B models we relate Problem Frames concepts one-to-one to Event-B concepts. This simple approach to relating Problem Frames descriptions to Event-B models is a key to the feasibility problem of requirements tracing mentioned in Section 2.2. Table 2 indicates how the concepts are matched. The transition from Problem Frames descriptions to Event-B models is still a manual step in the design process. However, starting from the natural language requirements this intermediate step provides enough guidance to obtain a suitable Event-B model that captures the requirements and permits tracing them into that model.

Table 2. Mapping of Problem Frame Elements to Event-B Elements

Problem Frames	Event-B
Problem diagram	Machine and context
Phenomena	Variables, constants or carrier sets
Types of phenomena	Carrier sets or constants
Requirements	Events and/or invariants
Elaboration of a problem diagram	Refinement of a machine or context
Projection of a problem diagram	Decomposition of a machine or context
Elaboration of phenomena	Data refinement

The first three correspondences for problem diagrams, phenomena and their types do not pose problems. Requirements state properties that must hold for the system: if they are dynamic, they are best matched by events; if they are static, they are best matched by invariants. Determining the relationship of elaboration and refinement is more involved. In particular, an approach to record instantiation was needed on top of Event-B refinement for the correspondence to work. Dealing with projection and decomposition is still more complicated because in Problem Frames projection is used as early as possible in system description whereas in Event-B decomposition is usually delayed so that system-wide properties can be verified before decomposition.

3.3 A Matching Event-B Model of the Cruise Control

Using the mapping from Problem Frames to Event-B described in Section 3.2 we developed an Event-B model of the cruise control. Problem Frames are used to structure requirements and support their (informal) analysis. Requirements and domain properties can be stated in any way that appears convenient like Table 1. Fig. 5 shows a context that captures the table with OK representing all submodes except R_ERROR and ERROR.[1] The two constants PS_SET

constants OK R_ERROR ERROR PS_SET PS_ERROR
sets T_Mode T_Env_PedalSignals
axioms @*axm1* $\mathrm{PS\_SET} \subseteq \mathrm{T\_Env\_PedalSignals}$
@*axm2* $\mathrm{PS\_ERROR} \subseteq \mathrm{T\_Env\_PedalSignals}$
@*axm3* $\mathrm{PS\_SET} \cap \mathrm{PS\_ERROR} = \varnothing$
@*axm4* $\mathit{partition}(\mathrm{T\_Mode}, \mathrm{OK}, \{\mathrm{R\_ERROR}\}, \{\mathrm{ERROR}\})$ [2]

Fig. 5. Context of abstract model

and PS_ERROR are abstractions for specific pedal signal combinations not expressible in the abstract model. The abstract machine (that corresponds to the abstract diagram of Fig. 3) is shown in Fig. 6. Depending on the pedal signals

[1] We have abstracted from the remaining submodes for the sake of brevity.
[2] The predicate *partition* states that the sets OK, {R_ERROR} and {ERROR} are a set-theoretical partition of the set T_Mode.

variables $\mathrm{P\_Env\_PedalSignals}$ $\mathrm{P\_CrCtl\_Mode}$
invariants @*inv1* $\mathrm{P\_Env\_PedalSignals} \in \mathrm{T\_Env\_PedalSignals}$
@*inv2* $\mathrm{P\_CrCtl\_Mode} \in \mathrm{T\_Mode}$
events
event $\mathrm{CrCtl\_Chg\_Mode\_PedalSignals\_R1}$
when $\mathrm{P\_Env\_PedalSignals} \in \mathrm{PS\_SET} \vee \mathrm{P\_Env\_PedalSignals} \in \mathrm{PS\_ERROR}$
then $\mathrm{P\_CrCtl\_Mode} :\in \{\mathrm{R\_ERROR}, \mathrm{ERROR}\}$ end

Fig. 6. Abstract machine

the mode is changed. This is stated informally in the Problem Frame diagram of Fig. 3. Close correspondence between the diagram and the Event-B model is important for traceability of the requirements and validation of the formal model.

Correspondence of the abstract diagrams and models is straightforward. Relating elaborated problem diagrams to Event-B models is less obvious because close correspondence remains crucial. Refinement permits to introduce more details into a model as needed for elaboration. However, it does not allow to relate abstract and concrete phenomena systematically. What is needed is closer to "instantiation" of abstract phenomena by concrete phenomena. Refinement is powerful enough to emulate the intended effect of such an "instantiation": we can state the mathematics of it (see Fig. 7). Although refinement does not suit

constants $\mathrm{iEnv\_PS}$ $\mathrm{iEnv\_PS\_SET}$ $\mathrm{iEnv\_PS\_ERROR}$
axioms
@*axm5* $\mathrm{iEnv\_PS} \in \mathbb{B} \times \mathbb{B} \times \mathbb{B} \times \mathbb{B} \times \mathbb{B} \twoheadrightarrow \mathrm{T\_Env\_PedalSignals}$
@*axm6* $\mathrm{iEnv\_PS\_ERROR} = \mathrm{iEnv\_PS}^{-1}[\mathrm{PS\_ERROR}]$
@*axm7* $\mathrm{iEnv\_PS\_ERROR} =$
$(\mathbb{B} \times \{\mathbf{T}\} \times \mathbb{B} \times \mathbb{B} \times \mathbb{B}) \cup (\mathbb{B} \times \mathbb{B} \times \mathbb{B} \times \{\mathbf{T}\} \times \mathbb{B}) \cup (\mathbb{B} \times \mathbb{B} \times \mathbb{B} \times \mathbb{B} \times \{\mathbf{T}\})$
theorem @*thm1* $\forall a, b, c, d \cdot$
$\mathrm{iEnv\_PS}(a \mapsto b \mapsto c \mapsto d \mapsto e) \in \mathrm{PS\_ERROR} \Leftrightarrow b = \mathbf{T} \vee d = \mathbf{T} \vee e = \mathbf{T}$
@*axm8* $\mathrm{iEnv\_PS\_SET} = \mathrm{iEnv\_PS}^{-1}[\mathrm{PS\_SET}]$
@*axm9* $\mathrm{iEnv\_PS\_SET} = (\{\mathbf{T}\} \times \{\mathbf{F}\} \times \mathbb{B} \times \{\mathbf{F}\} \times \{\mathbf{F}\}) \cup (\mathbb{B} \times \{\mathbf{F}\} \times \{\mathbf{T}\} \times \{\mathbf{F}\} \times \{\mathbf{F}\})$
theorem @*thm2* $\forall a, b, c, d, e \cdot \mathrm{iEnv\_PS}(a \mapsto b \mapsto c \mapsto d \mapsto e) \in \mathrm{PS\_SET} \Leftrightarrow$
$(a = \mathbf{T} \wedge b = \mathbf{F} \wedge d = \mathbf{F} \wedge e = \mathbf{F}) \vee (b = \mathbf{F} \wedge c = \mathbf{T} \wedge d = \mathbf{F} \wedge e = \mathbf{F})$

Fig. 7. Context of concrete model

our needs perfectly we can use it to develop the notion of "elaboration in Event-B" that will suit it. Here refinement is used for the development of a development method. Refinement in its generality may not be part of the final development method that could be used at Bosch for the modelling of discrete systems. The general technique refinement allowed us experiment with different notions using an available software tool, the Rodin tool. We are aware that the approach using refinement for instantiation that we describe in the following would be too complicated to scale. Of course, we intend that records and record instantiation be incorporated directly into the formal notation of Event-B so that refinement

```
variables P_Env_PS_BRK_PRSD P_Env_PS_BRK_ERR P_Env_PS_CLT_PRSD
          P_Env_PS_CLT_ERR P_Env_PS_ACC_ERR P_CrCtl_Mode
invariants @inv3 P_Env_PedalSignals = iEnv_PS(
    P_Env_PS_BRK_PRSD ↦ P_Env_PS_BRK_ERR ↦ P_Env_PS_CLT_PRSD ↦
    P_Env_PS_CLT_ERR ↦ P_Env_PS_ACC_ERR)
events
  event CrCtl_Chg_Mode_PedalSignals_R2 refines CrCtl_Chg_Mode_PedalSignals_R1
    when P_Env_PS_BRK_PRSD = T ∧ P_Env_PS_BRK_ERR = F∧
         P_Env_PS_CLT_ERR = F ∧ P_Env_PS_ACC_ERR = F
    then P_CrCtl_Mode := R_ERROR end
  event CrCtl_Chg_Mode_PedalSignals_R3 refines CrCtl_Chg_Mode_PedalSignals_R1
    when P_Env_PS_BRK_ERR = T then P_CrCtl_Mode := ERROR end
  event CrCtl_Chg_Mode_PedalSignals_R4 refines CrCtl_Chg_Mode_PedalSignals_R1
    when P_Env_PS_CLT_PRSD = T ∧ P_Env_PS_BRK_ERR = F
         P_Env_PS_CLT_ERR = F ∧ P_Env_PS_ACC_ERR = F
    then P_CrCtl_Mode := R_ERROR end
  event CrCtl_Chg_Mode_PedalSignals_R5 refines CrCtl_Chg_Mode_PedalSignals_R1
    when P_Env_PS_CLT_ERR = T then P_CrCtl_Mode := ERROR end
  event CrCtl_Chg_Mode_PedalSignals_R6 refines CrCtl_Chg_Mode_PedalSignals_R1
    when P_Env_PS_ACC_ERR = T then P_CrCtl_Mode := ERROR end
```

Fig. 8. Concrete machine

would not have to be used to imitate it. However, we found it instructive to determine first what kind of record concept would be needed for our purposes.

Our main insight here is that refinement seems to function as an enabler for the invention of the required technology. It may not itself be the required technology. The development of the concept of elaboration in Event-B is discussed in the next section.

4 Elaboration in Event-B

Dealing with elaboration in Event-B was the central problem to be solved to deal adequately with traceability of requirements from problem diagrams. Its solution required a dedicated record theory, an instantiation method and a tool improvement that could master the refinement-based modelling of the former.

A Convention for Modelling Records. When elaborating Problem Frame diagrams each abstract phenomenon is replaced by a set of more concrete phenomena. For example, in the cruise control model the abstract phenomenon P_Env_PedalSignals is replaced by the concrete phenomena

P_Env_PS_BRK_PRSD	Brake pedal pressed,
P_Env_PS_BRK_ERR	Brake pedal error,
P_Env_PS_CLT_PRSD	Clutch pedal pressed,
P_Env_PS_CLT_ERR	Clutch pedal error,
P_Env_PS_ACC_ERR	Accelerator pedal error.

This problem appeared to be solved in the form of existing record theories for Event-B [4] or VDM [10]. However, after some experimentation with [4] we also shied away from trying [10]. The theories appeared too powerful. Simple facts —and we only needed simple facts— were comparatively difficult to prove. We wanted them to be proved automatically without further interaction. It took a while until we realised that we should formulate a simple effective theory of limited expressiveness that would satisfy our needs (but not more). The approach that we use now (see Fig. 7 and 8) does permit nearly fully automatic proofs. We use a restricted form of data refinement for records based on a convention to model records loosely by lists of variables. Refinement of such records is done by instantiating abstract variables by lists of concrete variables and similarly for parameters. The instantiation is expressed by means of invariants, for instance, *inv3* in Fig. 8. Function iEnv_PS is a bijection from the concrete variables to the abstract variables.[3] This function facilitates all refinement proofs. By means of it abstract constants are mapped to concrete constants that specify relationships between data values in more detail. For instance, by *axm6* of Fig. 7 the concrete set iEnv_PS_ERROR corresponds to the abstract set PS_ERROR. The concrete set iEnv_PS_ERROR is then specified in more detail in *axm7*. Theorem *thm1* formulates the set-theoretical equation in terms of an equivalence. In fact, theorem *thm1* is more useful in proofs. The approach of specifying iEnv_PS_ERROR by two axioms has been chosen in order to avoid introducing contradicting statements in contexts. Important facts such as theorem *thm1* are proved. Note that the shape of the theorems matches the needs of the refinement proof. For instance, theorem *thm2* is geared towards the refinement proof of event CrCtl_Chg_Mode_PedalSignals_R2. Letting a = P_Env_PS_BRK_PRSD, b = P_Env_PS_BRK_ERR and so on, using *inv3* we can infer

$$\begin{aligned} & \text{P\_Env\_PS\_BRK\_PRSD} = \mathbf{T} \land \text{P\_Env\_PS\_BRK\_ERR} = \mathbf{F} \land \\ & \text{P\_Env\_PS\_CLT\_PRSD} = \mathbf{T} \land \text{P\_Env\_PS\_CLT\_ERR} = \mathbf{F} \land \\ & \text{P\_Env\_PS\_ACC\_ERR} = \mathbf{F} \\ \Rightarrow\ & \text{P\_Env\_PedalSignals} \in PS\_SET \ , \end{aligned}$$

which establishes that the concrete guard implies the abstract guard. We have solved the problem concerning refinement *proofs* of record instantiation.

Tool Issues. The full model of the cruise control turned out to be difficult to model check. The extra theory provided in the contexts for the instantiation reduced the efficiency of the associated tools used for model checking and constraint solving (see Section 5). To solve the problem of instantiation a preprocessing step is applied to the model to automatically detect records usage. We begin by searching for axioms of the form $iAP \in CP \rightarrowtail\!\!\!\!\twoheadrightarrow AP$ where iAP is a constant, the "instantiation mapping", AP a carrier set, the abstract phenomenon to be instantiated, and CP a Cartesian product, modelling the list of concrete phenomena. Axiom @*axm5* in the concrete model above (Fig. 7) is such an axiom. Using $iAP \in CP \rightarrowtail\!\!\!\!\twoheadrightarrow AP$ we can safely assume the set AP to be equal

[3] This is even stronger than functional data-refinement.

to CP because of the existence of the bijection iAP. Technically, the concerned axiom is removed, the set AP turned into a constant and the axioms $AP = CP$ and $iAP = \mathrm{id}(CP)$ are added.

A Method for Records and Record Instantiation. The mathematical model and its treatment by the tool can be used to formulate a method for dealing with records and instantiation: All records are non-recursive. They may contain some constraints, for instance, "maximal speed" > "minimal speed". For the instantiation of fields, we simply state which concrete fields instantiate which abstract fields. Constants like PS_ERROR can be instantiated by specifying a corresponding subset of the concrete record. Abstract properties like @*axm3* have to proved for the instantiated subsets.

Discussion. We do not believe that a general theory and method can be found that would satisfy all the needs of different industrial domains. We need specific theories and tools that work well in specific domains, for instance, the automotive domain. Similar experiences have been made in the railway domain at Siemens Transportation Systems [12], where ProB was improved to deal with large relations and sets. These arose in the modelling and validation of track topologies. Our quiet hope is that still some theory and technology can be shared. It just does not seem reasonable anymore to seek expressly a general theory with supporting technology.

5 Verifying Deadlock Freedom

Besides invariant preservation, the absence of deadlocks is crucial in this case study, as it means that the engineers have thought of every possible scenario. In other words, a deadlock means that the system can be in a state for which no action was foreseen by the engineers.

Deadlock Freedom. An event is *enabled* in a state if there are values for its parameters p that make its guard g true in that state. We denote the *enabling predicate* $(\exists p \cdot g)$ of an event e by G_e. Event-B provides a way to verify the deadlock freedom of model: the (DLF) proof obligation of [1]: $A \wedge I \Rightarrow G_{e_1} \vee \ldots \vee G_{e_n}$, where A are the axioms, I are invariants and G_{e_ℓ} $(\ell \in 1 \,..\, n)$ the enabling predicates of the events e_ℓ of the considered machine. For the machine of Fig. 8 this proof obligations is:[4]

$$
\begin{array}{l}
\text{"all axioms and theorems of Fig. 5 and Fig. 7"} \wedge \\
\text{"all invariants of Fig. 6 and Fig. 8"} \\
\Rightarrow (\mathrm{P\_Env\_PS\_BRK\_PRSD} = \mathbf{T} \wedge \mathrm{P\_Env\_PS\_BRK\_ERR} = \mathbf{F} \wedge \\
\quad\ \mathrm{P\_Env\_PS\_CLT\_ERR} = \mathbf{F} \wedge \mathrm{P\_Env\_PS\_ACC\_ERR} = \mathbf{F}) \vee \\
\quad \mathrm{P\_Env\_PS\_BRK\_ERR} = \mathbf{T} \vee \\
\quad (\mathrm{P\_Env\_PS\_CLT\_PRSD} = \mathbf{T} \wedge \mathrm{P\_Env\_PS\_BRK\_ERR} = \mathbf{F} \wedge \\
\quad\ \mathrm{P\_Env\_PS\_CLT\_ERR} = \mathbf{F} \wedge \mathrm{P\_Env\_PS\_ACC\_ERR} = \mathbf{F}) \vee \\
\quad \mathrm{P\_Env\_PS\_CLT\_ERR} = \mathbf{T} \vee \mathrm{P\_Env\_PS\_ACC\_ERR} = \mathbf{T}
\end{array}
$$

[4] Currently, this proof obligation is not generated by the Rodin tool. We have generated it by means of the Flow-Plugin [7].

The (DLF) proof obligation in general quickly becomes very complex, in particular, if the involved events have parameters. As long as it holds and is discharged by an automatic theorem prover this is not a problem. The more common situation is, however, that it cannot be proved. As a matter of fact, this is also the more interesting situation because it may point to errors in the model. For example, the (DLF) proof obligation above could not be proven: an event for covering the case in which all pedal signals are set to FALSE was missing.

We need the tool in order to find errors in our model and expect support for correcting the model. To put this into perspective: the real model of the case study from which the example has been extracted has 78 constants with 121 axioms, 62 variables with 59 invariants and has 80 events with 855 guards. When the proof of this proof obligation fails, it is not clear at all why this is. Analysis of a large failed (DLF) proof obligation by interactive proof is very time consuming. Maybe we simply do not find the proper proof; maybe there is a deadlock; maybe the invariant is too weak. Counter examples can provide vital clues where to look for problems.

A different approach is needed to check for deadlocks. The most immediate is to animate the model and see whether we encounter a state in which no event is enabled. Another one is to model-check it. Model checking can provide fast feedback, but is also associated with known problems: in many applications the state space is either infinite or much too large to explore exhaustively. In the case study model checking did not produce satisfactory results. Neither proof nor model-checking worked.

Constraint Checking. Finally, we did achieve good results using constraint checking. We have implemented a dedicated constraint checker to deal with deadlock-freedom [5]. It is not based on model execution but yields a solution to the (DLF) proof obligation, providing a counter example if (DLF) does not hold. On sub-models with about 20 events constraint checking was very effective in helping to develop a correct deadlock-free model. But on the large proof obligation mentioned above it did not help to resolve all problems. Constraint solving computed counterexamples to (DLF) but eventually it became too time consuming to see how the model could be corrected. No obvious improvement to ProB could have solved this problem. Independently of the modelling method, the large number of constants and variables makes it difficult to interpret deadlocked states and understand how the model has to be corrected. We believe that refinement can be used to address the inherent complexity of the model. This way deadlock-freedom could be analysed for models whose size is increased in small increments: we have already seen that dealing with about 20 events at once is effectively possible.

Lessons Learned. The lesson we learned is that the problem could only be solved by using multiple verification techniques, such as proof, model checking and animation, in order to analyse, understand and debug the formal model. Matching Problem Frames with Event-B may have to be relaxed allowing for refinement in Event-B to cater for a stepwise introduction of records. The most interesting insight we gained from the case study was the need for strong tools to allow for large models and at the same time the need for appropriate techniques to reduce the size of those models. We plan to redo some parts of the modelling to find a good measure for that mix. The case study was important as a driver for tool improvements, in particular, of ProB. The scale of the case study was the key to this.

6 Conclusion

When we started the case study we asked whether Event-B is fit for industrial use. We had to be more specific about our question. There are too many factors besides Event-B so that we should have asked whether Event-B fits into a suitable methodology for development (at Bosch). We have seen that Event-B allowed us to think about properties of the cruise system model that would be difficult to achieve non-formally. We have matched Problem Frames elaboration formally using Event-B refinement. The resulting method of Event-B elaboration supported by theory and tools is novel and was crucial for the use of Event-B in the targeted development process. We have successfully analysed the model with respect to deadlock-freedom, but saw the difficulty of using the counter examples to develop a non-trivial deadlock-free system. We believe that refinement will be the key to overcome this difficulty: the model must be analysed and constructed piecemeal to provide better feedback to the engineers. In future work, we would like to check more properties. For instance, check wether the choice between the events of a machine is deterministic. Only one event should be enabled at any time: we expect an implementation of a cruise control controller to be predictable. We also would like to analyse certain sequences of actions using temporal (LTL) formulas. Some requirements do not fit into the simple scheme of events and invariants.

What about the answer to our question? In the case study we could see that we can clearly profit from the use of formal methods in the development process. Checking the model for consistency and deadlock-freedom uncovered many errors in the model and led to various improvements of the requirements. For example, deadlock checking identified many cases in which requirements had been missing. Event-B with its tools Rodin and ProB can be useful for improving the quality of requirements and of models that can serve as blue prints for implementations. We have also seen that we have profited in "unintended" ways. We did not follow the method described in [1] but had to develop our own, in particular, to work with Problem Frames for the management of complex requirements.

Acknowledgements. We are especially grateful to Cliff Jones who coordinated the work of the academic partners in this case study. We are also grateful for the fruitful interactions with Rezazadeh Abdolbaghi, Jean-Raymond Abrial, Michael Butler, Alexei Iliasov, Michael Jackson, Sascha Romanovsky, Matthias Schmalz, and Colin Snook.

References

1. Abrial, J.-R.: Modeling in Event-B: System and Software Engineering. Cambridge University Press, Cambridge (2010)
2. Abrial, J.-R., Butler, M.J., Hallerstede, S., Hoang, T.S., Mehta, F., Voisin, L.: RODIN: an open toolset for modelling and reasoning in Event-B. STTT 12(6), 447–466 (2010)
3. Edmunds, A., Butler, M.J.: Tool support for Event-B code generation (2009)
4. Evans, N., Butler, M.J.: A proposal for records in event-B. In: Misra, J., Nipkow, T., Karakostas, G. (eds.) FM 2006. LNCS, vol. 4085, pp. 221–235. Springer, Heidelberg (2006)
5. Hallerstede, S., Leuschel, M.: Constraint-Based Deadlock Checking of High-Level Specifications. In: Proceedings ICLP 2011 (to appear, 2011)
6. Harel, D., Lachover, H., Naamad, A., Pnueli, A., Politi, M., Sherman, R., Shtull-Trauring, A., Trakhtenbrot, M.: STATEMATE: A working environment for the development of complex reactive systems. IEEE Transactions on Software Engineering SE-16(4), 403–414 (1990)
7. Iliasov, A.: On Event-B and Control Flow. Technical Report CS-TR-1159, University of Newcastle (2009)
8. Jackson, M.: Problem Frames: Analyzing and structuring software development problems. Addison-Wesley Longman Publishing Co., Inc., Amsterdam (2001)
9. Jones, C.B.: DEPLOY Deliverable D15: Advances in Methodological WPs
10. Jones, C.B.: Systematic Software Development Using VDM. Prentice-Hall, Englewood Cliffs (1990)
11. Leuschel, M., Butler, M.J.: ProB: an automated analysis toolset for the B method. STTT 10(2), 185–203 (2008)
12. Leuschel, M., Falampin, J., Fritz, F., Plagge, D.: Automated property verification for large scale B models. In: Cavalcanti, A., Dams, D.R. (eds.) FM 2009. LNCS, vol. 5850, pp. 708–723. Springer, Heidelberg (2009)
13. Loesch, F., Gmehlich, R., Grau, K., Jones, C.B., Mazzara, M.: DEPLOY Deliverable D19: Pilot Deployment in the Automotive Sector
14. Snook, C.F., Butler, M.J.: UML-B: Formal modeling and design aided by UML. ACM Trans. Softw. Eng. Methodol. 15(1), 92–122 (2006)
15. Stursberg, O., Fehnker, A., Han, Z., Krogh, B.H.: Verification of a cruise control system using counterexample-guided search. Control Engineering Practice 12(10), 1269–1278 (2004)
16. Yeganefard, S., Butler, M.J., Rezazadeh, A.: Evaluation of a Guideline by Formal Modelling of Cruise Control System in Event-B. In: Muñoz, C. (ed.) NFM 2010, NASA/CP-2010-216215 (April 2010)

A Formal Engineering Approach to High-Level Design of Situation Analysis Decision Support Systems*

Roozbeh Farahbod[1], Vladimir Avram[2], Uwe Glässer[2], and Adel Guitouni[1]

[1] Defence R&D Canada – Valcartier, Québec, Canada
{roozbeh.farahbod,adel.guitouni}@drdc-rddc.gc.ca
[2] Computing Science, Simon Fraser University, British Columbia, Canada
{vavram,glaesser}@cs.sfu.ca

Abstract. We apply the Abstract State Machine (ASM) method and the CoreASM tool to design and analysis of Situation Analysis Decision Support (SADS) systems. Realistic situation analysis scenarios routinely deal with situations involving multiple mobile agents reacting to discrete events distributed in space and time. SADS system engineering practices call for systematic formal modeling approaches to manage complexity through modularization, refinement and validation of abstract models. We explore here SADS system design based on ASM modeling techniques paired with CoreASM tool support to facilitate analysis of the problem space and reasoning about design decisions and conformance criteria so as to ensure they are properly established and well understood prior to building the system. We provide an extension to CoreASM for the Marine Safety & Security domain, specifically for capturing rendezvous scenarios. The extension yields the necessary background concepts, such as mobile sensors and shipping lanes, and offers runtime visualization of simulation runs together with an analyzer to measure success of various rendezvous detection strategies used in the model. We illustrate the application of the proposed approach using a sample rendezvous scenario.

1 Introduction

In this paper we explore a formal approach to model-driven engineering (MDE) of situation analysis decision support (SADS) systems. Situation Analysis (SA) is viewed as a process to provide and maintain a state of *situation awareness* for the decision maker. Situation awareness is essential for decision-making activities; it is about our perception of the elements in the environment, the comprehension of their meaning, and the projection of their status in the near future [12]. Computational models of situation analysis processes are in many cases distributed in nature, comprising multiple autonomously operating *agents* that react in an asynchronous manner to discrete events distributed in space and time. Agents cooperate in developing a global understanding of a situation as it unfolds by exchanging information related to their local perception of events.

* This research has been funded by Defence R&D Canada, MDA Corp. and NSERC.

S. Qin and Z. Qiu (Eds.): ICFEM 2011, LNCS 6991, pp. 211–226, 2011.

Best engineering practice calls for systematic modeling approaches that build on established design methods to manage complexity through modularization, refinement, validation and verification of abstract models. The focus here is on requirements analysis and design validation of asynchronous SADS system models by analytical and experimental means. For this purpose we combine the Abstract State Machine (ASM) method [6] with the extensible CoreASM tool environment [15] for rapid prototyping of abstract executable models. The ASM method provides a flexible framework for formalizing abstract operational concepts and requirements in modeling dynamic system properties.

The goal of our combined ASM/CoreASM approach is to link fundamental aspects of SADS systems design with rapid prototyping of abstract executable models in order to facilitate *1)* analysis of the problem space and *2)* reasoning about design decisions, and also to *3)* derive conformance criteria for checking the validity of SADS domain models. The proposed approach is intended to ensure that the key system attributes are properly established and well understood prior to building the system. Taking advantage of the innovative CoreASM plugin mechanism, we provide a customized extension to CoreASM for the domain of Marine Safety & Security, specifically for capturing *rendezvous scenarios*. This extension yields the necessary background concepts, such as mobile sensors and shipping lanes, and also offers runtime visualization of simulation runs together with an analyzer for measuring the effectiveness of various rendezvous detection strategies defined as part of the model. We illustrate our solution using a sample rendezvous scenario, and critically evaluate our approach in light of joint projects [23,16] with Defence R&D Canada and MDA Corp., Richmond, BC, a leader in Canada's defence and space technology.

Section 2 frames the problem scope and discusses related work. Sections 3 and 4 recall key aspects of the ASM method and CoreASM tool architecture. Section 5 illustrates the SADS application scenario and Section 6 the CoreASM SA plugin developed for this type of scenarios. Section 7 concludes the paper.

2 Problem Description

Experienced decision makers rely on situation awareness in order to make informed decisions. As Endsley puts it, *decisions are formed by situation awareness and situation awareness is formed by decisions* [20]. Situation awareness is a state of mind maintained by the process of *situation analysis*. Therefore, in this work, we focus on situation analysis decision support.

Despite situation awareness and decision making being intimately related, they form distinct parts of a dynamic decision making process. Situation awareness as a product of situation analysis provides input to the decision making process. A situation analysis decision support system is usually composed of the following components: *1)* situation information collection (e.g., sensors and sensors networks), *2)* knowledge base on the situation, *3)* reasoning scheme (engine) about the situation, *4)* human-computer interface, and *5)* controls. Figure 1 illustrates a basic representation of such a system. Decision making influences the situation analysis process by adjusting its control parameters as illustrated in Figure 1. Finally, this feedback loop results in the state of situation awareness being constantly adjusted in response to the goals and requirements of decision making.

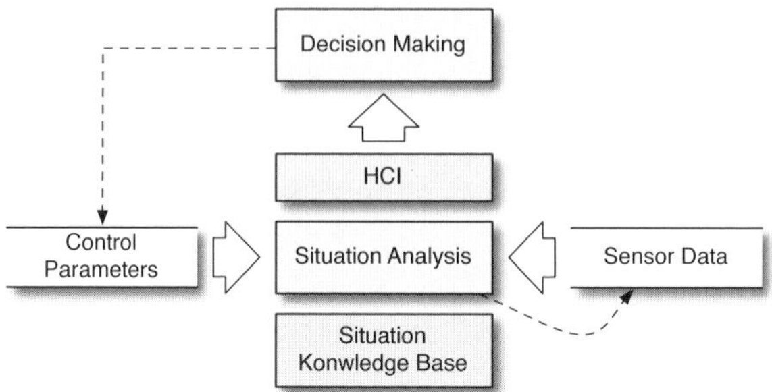

Fig. 1. Situation Analysis and Decision Support

2.1 Design and Validation of SADS Systems

Realistic situation analysis scenarios routinely deal with convoluted and intricate event patterns and interdependencies to interpret and reason about complex situations, assess risks and predict how a situation may evolve over time. Decision support systems for situation analysis can be very complex with numerous resources, distributed computing agents, and events distributed in space and time. Design and development of SADS systems face two fundamental questions:

1. How can we formulate the problem in a precise and yet understandable form?
2. How can we express and evaluate a solution before actually building it into a system?

Rapidly increasing complexity of decision-making problems and elaborate contextual situations have altered the nature of decision support. Interactive decision-making, to be facilitated by decision support systems, has become a complex multifaceted process—decision-makers must engage in solving various semi-structured, or even ill-structured, problems involving multiple attributes, objectives and goals. As a result, SADS system design is not an intuitive deterministic task [31,28].

A comprehensive formal systems design approach is needed to address the nondeterministic complexities arising from today's real-world decision-making requirements [28]. Such an approach should facilitate design and development of model-based decision support systems through three stages: formulation, solution and analysis. Formulation refers to generating a model of the problem space, the solution stage refers to the development of a solution, and the analysis stage refers to 'what-if' analyses and validation of solutions [33].

Formal frameworks proposed for modeling of SADS systems, such as [8] and [29], mainly focus on specific and mostly theoretical aspects of developing SADS systems and leave a gap for practical systems design. We believe that a comprehensive formal framework in this context would have two purposes [16]:

1. facilitate exploration of the problem space and the key aspects to be addressed;
2. provide an experimental platform that allows one to evaluate and compare feasible solutions.

Thus, any such framework ought to support adaptive and evolutionary design approaches that encompass dynamic modeling, simulation and validation in an interactive and iterative fashion.

2.2 Related Work

There are three known major approaches to design and development of SADS systems, which can be characterized as using: *1)* general purpose formal logics [2,32]; *2)* methods like machine learning and ontologies [9,11]; and *3)* approaches specifically designed for SA, such as dynamic Case Based Reasoning and State Transition Data Fusion (STDF) [25,29]. None of these specifically supports the early phases of problem formulation and system design, while making implementation commitments prior to rigorous requirements analysis and validation of design specifications.

For example, the approach in [2] attempts to make their decision support system operational by employing the reasoners which are associated with the specific logics. An SADS system necessarily must be able to reason about data over time, an aspect which is not supported by the applied reasoners. As a result, the authors were forced to design their framework to work around this issue. However, even though these approaches may not lend themselves well to decision support system design as addressed here, it is important to realize they can play an important part in the process, and each have their own strengths and benefits. This is one of the reasons why we are proposing an integrated framework [16] which makes use of existing approaches such as STDF [29] and Interpreted Systems (IS) [26].

There is a neccessity for broader and more integrated approaches to designing of decision support systems for complex domains [28]. We believe, as McDermid put it, that "Large, complex systems are hard to evolve without undermining their dependability. Often change is disproportionately costly..." [30] and thus system architectures are pivotal in meeting this challenge [28].

3 Abstract State Machines

This section briefly outlines basic concepts of the ASM method for high-level design and analysis of distributed systems. For further details, we refer to [6,24]. Abstract State Machines are a versatile mathematical framework for modeling of discrete dynamic systems that aims at bridging the gap between formal and empirical approaches by linking specification methods and computation models. Building on common notions from discrete mathematics and computational logic, static and dynamic aspects of systems are modeled at any desired level of abstraction by combining the concept of *abstract states* with *transition systems*. ASMs have been used in modeling of architectures, languages, protocols and virtually all kinds of sequential, parallel and distributed systems with a notable orientation toward applied system engineering [21,5,22,34].[1]

A fundamental challenge in designing SADS systems for real-life applications is understanding the problem (the *formulation* phase). The inherent complexity of the design task calls for continual analysis and validation of both the problem formulation and potential solutions (the *analysis* phase) as part of a progressing design process. To adequately capture the problem and devise feasible solutions, we propose an explorative modeling approach that supports the development of abstract models, the appropriateness and validity of which can be established analytically and experimentally early in the design process. To achieve this, a model should be concise and easily readable both for domain experts and system designers, and should come with a precise semantics allowing to resolve potential ambiguities and identify loose ends. In this context, freedom of abstraction plays an important role as it enables designers to stress on the essential aspects of problem solutions rather than encoding insignificant details. Executability of abstract and even incomplete models is often a desirable feature for experimental validation of complex system models in early design stages to obtain feedback from domain experts. Besides, freedom of abstraction ought to be paired with well-defined refinement techniques that make it easy to cross levels of abstraction and link models at different levels through incremental steps all the way down to a concrete model serving as a reliable blueprint for construction.

ASM models are in essence rigorously defined "pseudo-programs" operating on abstract data structures [6]; this way, they support writing of concise and intelligible specifications with a precise semantic foundation. The ASM framework comes with a sound and powerful notion of stepwise refinement [7] that helps in structuring the design of a system into suitable levels of abstraction and linking them down to a concrete model. In addition, the ASM framework is open to integrate domain-specific concepts and flexible to be combined with other modeling approaches as needed by the application domain [16,3].

3.1 ASM Systems Engineering Method

The ASM method aims at industrial system design and development by integrating precise high-level, problem-domain oriented modeling into the design and development cycle, and by systematically linking abstract models down to executable code. The method consists of three essential elements: *a)* capturing the requirements into a precise yet abstract operational model, called a *ground model* ASM, *b)* systematic and incremental refinement of the ground model down

[1] See also the ASM website at `www.asmcenter.org` and the overview in [6].

to the implementation, and *c)* experimental model validation through simulation or testing at each level of abstraction. This process emphasizes freedom of abstraction as a guiding principle, meaning that original ideas behind the design of a system can be expressed in a direct and intuitive way so as to enable system designers to stress on the essential aspects of design rather than encoding insignificant details. To this end, it is crucial that the method allows for and actually encourages language conventions to be established, as in the typical "in the following, we use the notation ...to mean ...". It is also understood that authors can use the full extent of mathematics and computer science notations if that is instrumental to express themselves clearly. Any executable implementation must thus allow for similar extensibility, which constitute a significant design challenge in itself.

Starting from a ground model and applying the process of step-wise refinement [7], a hierarchy of intermediate models can be created that are systematically linked down to the implementation. At each step, the refined model can be validated and verified to be a correct implementation of the abstract model. The resulting hierarchy serves as design documentation and allows one to trace requirements down to the implementation.

3.2 Distributed ASMs

The original notion of *basic ASM* was defined to formalize simultaneous parallel actions of a single computational agent. A basic ASM M is defined as a tuple of the form $(\Sigma, \mathcal{I}, \mathcal{R}, P_M)$, where Σ is a finite set of function names and symbols, $\mathcal{I}$ is a set of initial states for Σ, $\mathcal{R}$ is a set of transition rule declarations, and $P_M \in \mathcal{R}$ is a distinguished rule, called the *main rule* or the Program of M.

A state $\mathfrak{A}$ for Σ is a non-empty set X together with an interpretation $f^{\mathfrak{A}} : X^n \mapsto X$ for each function name f in Σ. Functions can be *static* or *dynamic*. Interpretations of dynamic functions can change from state to state. The evaluation of a transition rule in a given state produces a finite set of *updates* of the form $\langle (f, \langle a_1, \ldots, a_n \rangle), v \rangle$ where f is an n-ary function name in Σ and $a_1, \ldots, a_n, v \in X$. An update $(f, args, v)$ prescribes a change to the content of location $f(args)$ taking effect in the next state.

A distributed ASM (DASM) M_D is defined by a dynamic set AGENT of autonomously operating computational *agents*, each executing a basic ASM. This set may change dynamically over runs of M_D, as required to model a varying number of computational resources. Agents of M_D interact with each other, and also with the operational environment of M_D, by reading and writing shared locations of a global machine state. The underlying semantic model resolves potential conflicts according to the definition of *partially ordered runs* [22,24].

M_D interacts with its operational environment—the part of the external world visible to M_D—through actions/events observable at external interfaces, formally represented by controlled and monitored functions. Of particular interest are *monitored functions*, read-only functions controlled by the environment. A typical example is the abstract representation of global system time in terms of a monitored function *now* taking values in a linearly ordered domain TIME. Values of *now* increase monotonically over runs of M_D.

4 The CoreASM Extensible Architecture

CoreASM [13,18] is a environment for writing, running, and validation of executable specifications according to the ASM method.[2] It has been designed with an extensible plugin-based architecture that offers a great deal of flexibility for customizing its language definition and execution engine depending on the application context. The CoreASM environment consists of a platform-independent engine for executing CoreASM specifications and a GUI for interactive visualization and control of simulation runs. The engine comes with a sophisticated interface enabling future development and integration of complementary tools, e.g., for symbolic model checking and automated test generation [13].

Over several years, CoreASM has been put to the test in a range of applications in the private and public sectors, spanning computational criminology, coastal surveillance, situation analysis, decision support systems, and Web services. The diversity of application fields has been invaluable to examine the practicability of using CoreASM for requirements analysis, design specification and rapid prototyping of abstract executable models [17,16,10].

Abstract state machines are used in diverse application domains, some of which require the introduction of special rule forms and data structures. Consequently, CoreASM is designed to be flexibly extensible by third parties in order to meet diverse application requirements. Besides, to ensure freedom of experimentation, CoreASM allows various modeling tools and environments to closely interact with the engine and also enables researchers to experiment with variations to CoreASM. The design of a *plugin-based architecture* with a minimal kernel for the CoreASM language and modeling environment offers the extensibility of both the language and its simulation engine. A micro-kernel (the *core* of the language and engine) contains the bare essentials. Most of the constructs of the language and the functionalities of the engine come in the form of plugins extending the kernel. This concept is explored in detail in [14,18].

4.1 Extensible Language

Language extensibility is not a new concept. There are a number of programming languages that support some form of extensibility ranging from introducing new macros to the definition of new syntactical structures. However, what CoreASM offers is the possibility of extending and modifying the syntax and semantics of the language, keeping only the bare essential parts invariable. In order to achieve this goal, plugins can extend the grammar of the core language by providing new grammar rules together with their semantics. As a result, to load each specification, the CoreASM engine builds a language and a parser for that language to parse the specification based on the set of plugins that the specification uses.

[2] CoreASM is an Open Source project and is readily available at www.coreasm.org.

4.2 Extensible Engine

There are two different mechanisms for extending the CoreASM engine. Plugins can either extend the functionality of specific engine components (such as the parser or the scheduler), or they extend the control state ASM of the engine by interposing their own code in between state transitions of the engine. The latter mechanism enables a wide range of extensions of the engine's execution cycle for the purpose of implementing various practically relevant features, such as adding debugging support, adding a C-like preprocessor, or performing statistical analysis of the behavior of the simulated machine (for instance, through coverage analysis, profiling and the like).

In the extensible Control State ASM [15] of the engine, each state transition is associated with an *extension point*. Plugins can extend the engine's control state ASM by registering for these extension points. At any extension point, if there is any plugin registered for that point, the code contributed by the plugin for that transition is executed before the engine proceeds to the next control state. As an example, the eCASM of Figure 2(a) can be executed with a set of extension point plugins $\{p_1, p_2\}$ contributing rules $PRule_1$ and $PRule_2$ that (potentially) extend the execution of the machine to the control state ASM of Figure 2(b).

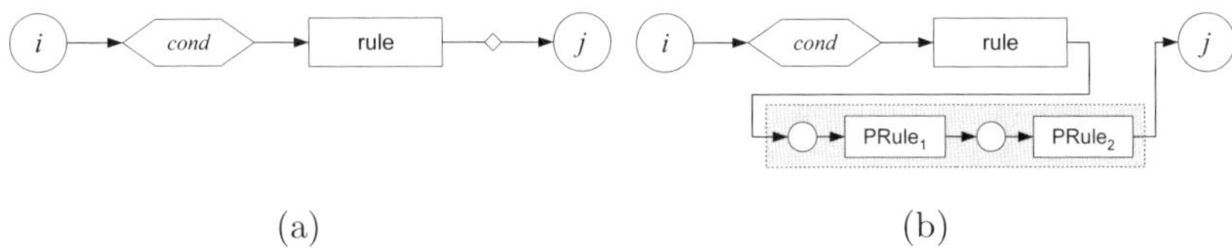

Fig. 2. (a) An Extensible Control State ASM and (b) its extended form

5 Application Scenario

This section illustrates a rendezvous scenario to showcase the application of high-level modeling of an SADS system using ASMs and CoreASM. We model the scenario, including both the environment and the proposed SADS system, using multi-agent ASMs and utilize the CoreASM environment to validate both models with respect to Marine Safety & Security operational concepts.

There are vessels traveling along shipping lanes (see Figure 3). Each vessel V_i moves along a particular shipping lane L_i. A vessel V_i may send a *request-for-rendezvous* to a non-deterministically chosen vessel V_j suggesting a point of rendezvous in the future. If V_j accepts the rendezvous request, the two vessels will meet at the agreed point, staying close for at least a minimum time T^r_{min} and then moving back to their shipping lanes continuing their journey.

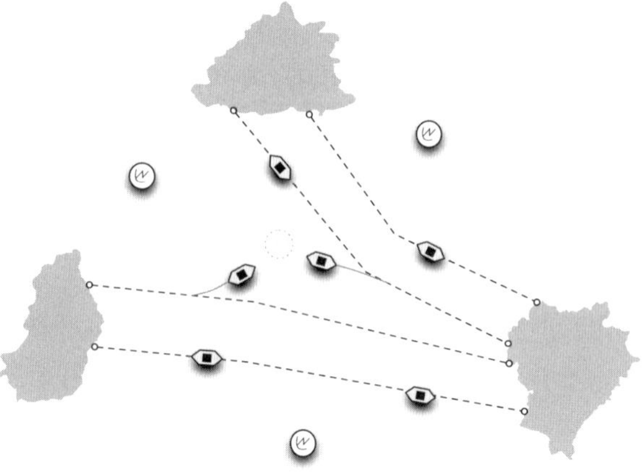

Fig. 3. Rendezvous Scenario

A number of observers O_i in the environment (depicted by ⓦ) monitor the location of vessels within sight using sensors S_{ij} that each have observation errors. The idea is to build a simple decision support system that can warn the user of potential rendezvous.

5.1 Vessels

Vessels and observers are modeled as Nodes that can move in the environment according to their controlled velocity. The following ASM specification abstractly models vessel behavior:

```
VesselProgram ≡
  NodeProgram
  if rendezvousActive(self) then
    MaintainRendezvous
  else
    StayOnLane
  RendezvousCommunications
```

The rule NodeProgram, which is the common behavioral aspect of all nodes, updates the location of the vessel according to simulation time and its velocity. If a rendezvous is in progress, MaintainRendezvous ensures that the vessel's velocity directs it towards the rendezvous point and if there, keeps it at the point for at least a minimum time T^r_{min}; otherwise, StayOnLane keeps the velocity of the vessel aligned to its shipping lane. In parallel, RendezvousCommunications maintains the communication between vessels in arranging rendezvous. As an example, the StayOnLane rule is defined as follows:

```
StayOnLane ≡
  if ¬isPointOnPath(loc, shipLane, d_e) then
    velocity := speedVector(loc, closestPointOnPath(loc, shipLane, dirOnLane), v_unit)
    isOnLane := false
  else
    MoveOnLane
```

The above rule indicates that if the vessel is not within distance d_e of its lane, it should adjust its velocity such that it steers towards the lane; otherwise, it should keep moving on the lane.[3]

5.2 Observers

Every observer is modeled as an instance of an Observer agent which extends the functionalities of a Node with Situation Analysis behavior following the core idea of the STDF process model for situation awareness and applying the IS view of knowledge representation. The abstract behavior of an Observer node is specified by the following ASM rule:

```
ObserverProgram ≡
  NodeProgram
  MaintainOptimumLocation
  STDFProgram

STDFProgram ≡
  stepwise {Detection Observation Comprehension Projection UpdateSTDFState}
```

where the STDFProgram models the main STDF activities in order to achieve a situation awareness by detecting and observing the nodes, comprehension of the situation, projection of the events into the future and updating the current understanding of the events based on the newly observed information.

In this scenario, the Detection rule creates a typical 2-dimensional Kalman [27] filter for every vessel in the environment. The Observation rule maintains a history of observations for every observed vessel. The Comprehension rule updates the value of predicates of interest (such as $pShipOnLane_i$ probability of a vessel V_i being on a shipping lane, or $pFutureRendezvous_{ij}$ probability of a future rendezvous between two vessels V_i and V_j). The Projection rule uses Kalman filters to project future locations of the vessels and the UpdateSTDFState corrects Kalman filters based on the last observations.

```
Projection ≡
  forall n in observedNodes(self) do
    projectedLoc(self, n) := predict_tkf(kalmanFilter(self, n), undef)
```

[3] To improve readability, we assume the parameter *self* to be implicitly passed to the functions *loc*, *shipLane*, *dirOnLane*, and *isOnLane*.

UpdateSTDFState $\equiv$
forall n **in** $observedNodes(self)$ **do**
$kalmanFilter(self, n) := correctFilter_{tkf}(kalmanFilter(self, n), observedLoc(self, n))$

5.3 Rendezvous Awareness

In order to demonstrate how the ASM engineering method facilitates design exploration of SADS systems, in our example we evaluate four different rendezvous detection strategies. Because it is not the aim of this work to come up with new rendezvous prediction algorithms, so far, we have only implemented basic rendezvous prediction and detection algorithms.

The first model depicted in Figure 4(a) attempts to predict if and where a rendezvous will take place between two vessels. It starts by computing trajectories, based on current and projected locations, for both vessels currently being analyzed. If there is an intersection of the computed trajectories and it is detected that the vessels are not on their sea lanes, then a new line is calculated in between the two currently observed locations of the vessels. If the shortest distance d in between this line and the previously computed trajectory intersection point of the vessels is below a certain threshold the model assumes that a rendezvous will occur. Finally the predicted rendezvous location is set to the midpoint between the vessels and the rendezvous probability is set to a function of the distance between the line joining the two vessels and the intersection point of their trajectories.

The second model uses the exact same method for predicting rendezvous occurrences and locations as the first model. However, instead of using the last observed location for vessels when computing their trajectories it utilizes an average last location based on n previously observed vessel locations.

The third model uses a hybrid approach between the first model and a model utilizing vessel headings (Figure 4(b)). Using these headings the angle θ in between the directions is calculated and if it is considered to be close to 180 degrees the model assumes that the vessels are currently heading in opposite directions. Once the model identifies that the vessels are moving towards each other, it uses the exact same approach as in the first model to determine the location and the probability of the rendezvous. The main advantage of this model is that it excludes ships with intersecting paths that are moving away from each other.

The fourth model only makes use of heading data. It first uses the same approach as in the third model to detect whether or not two vessels are heading towards each other. Once this is established, the model tries to ensure that the vessels are heading towards each other on the same path within a threshold which is specified in degrees (Figure 4(c)). This is achieved by drawing a straight line between the currently observed positions of the two vessels in question and observing the angles θ_A and θ_B which this path creates with the current headings of the vessels. If the average of the angles for the two vessels is below a certain threshold then the model assumes they are heading towards a rendezvous point and calculates this as the midpoint between their current locations.

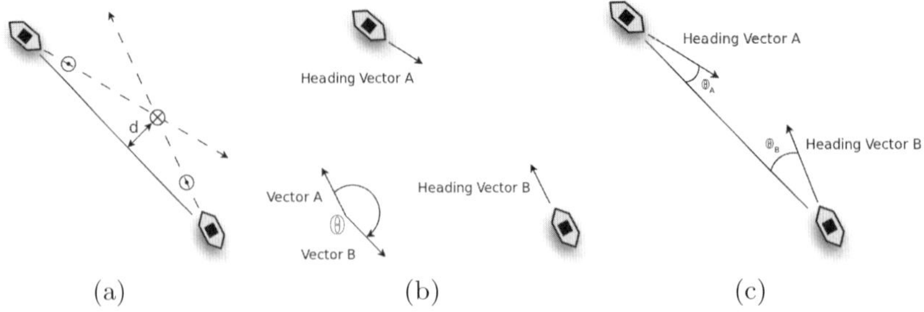

Fig. 4. Detection of Rendezvous Location: Models 3 and 4

6 The SA Plugin

In order to facilitate modeling and analysis of SADS systems in the context of marine safety and security, in particular the application scenario described in Section 5, we have extended the CoreASM modeling environment with a special-purpose plugin, called the SA Plugin, that provides the following components:

1. necessary background concepts such as the domain of sensor, Kalman filter, geographical location, and shipping lane together with related operations;
2. a visualizer that provides a runtime visualization of simulation runs by monitoring the states of the simulated machine;
3. an analyzer that reports on measure of success of various rendezvous detection strategies used in the model.

The rest of this section briefly explores the design and development of this plugin.

6.1 Extending the CoreASM Engine

The SA Plugin extends the CoreASM engine in two ways: First, it extends the initial vocabulary of CoreASM with domains of Sensor, Kalman filter, 2D Point and Path and related operations on these domains such as binding sensors to other *observable* functions, defining error parameters on sensors, correction and prediction operations on Kalman filters, and distance and projection on Paths and Points.

Second, it extends the control flow of the CoreASM engine and injects visualization and analysis code after successful completion of every computation step. The code updates the 3D visual representation of the state of the simulated system (location of vessels, markers for detected rendezvous, etc.) and, in addition, gathers statistical information on the effectiveness of each observer in detecting rendezvous with respect to the actual events in the environment. In addition to updating the visualization, the plugin produces a live log of the actual events happening in the environment, and observers' reactions to those events, in an external file that can later be used for analysis of the strategies.

6.2 Visualization

As soon as the engine completes the first step of the simulation, the SA Plugin opens its visual interface window (see Figure 5). The main component of this window is a real-time 3D visualization of the scenario ① based on the states of the CoreASM simulation. In the snapshot presented in Figure 5 one can see four vessels (labeled A to D) and five observer nodes (labeled O-1 to O-5) where O-1 to O-4 each employ rendezvous detection models 1 to 4 (see Section 5.3) and O-5 employs an integration of all 4 observations. On the right ②, there is a list of observer nodes in the model. If an observer is selected, the 3D visualizer shows the world-view of the selected observer, including its observed position of vessels ③ (which has a non-deterministic error), and its detected or projected rendezvous areas ④, marked by red cones. The size of each cone is inversely proportional to the probability of a rendezvous in that area.

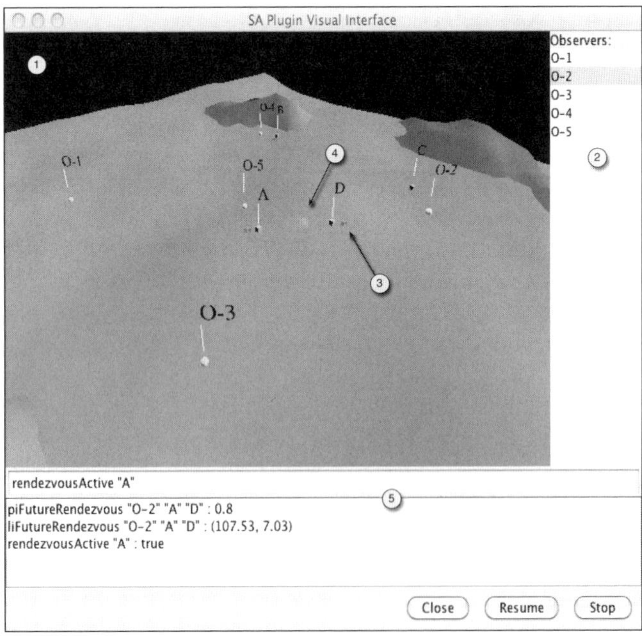

Fig. 5. A Snapshot of the CoreASM SA Plugin

6.3 Situation Analysis

The lower section of the visual interface window ⑤ provides a textual interface to query the runtime values of various predicates captured in the abstract model. A parser is used to parse the queries provided in the input line into CoreASM expressions, the values of which are retrieved using the Control API of the CoreASM engine and printed out in the output panel below.

Table 1. Performance of Rendezvous Detection Methods over 100 incidents

	Detections	Delay	First Dist.	First Prob.	Final Dist.	Final Prob.
O1	100%	33.69	19.11	0.53	7.85	0.68
O2	96%	39.90	27.87	0.56	6.03	0.81
O3	54%	45.84	8.22	0.52	5.40	0.65
O4	96%	35.30	9.99	1.00	2.24	1.00
O5	99%	28.42	28.52	0.85	4.00	0.92

Upon termination of the simulation run, for every observer, the following values are reported: number of observations, average detection delay, average distance from predicted rendezvous location to real rendezvous location (at the first and final detection), and average detection probability (at the first and final detection). Table 1 presents a summary of the observation reports over a run of our scenario with 100 rendezvous incidents.[4] Farahbod et al. [19] provide additional experimental results and a Receiver Operating Characteristic (ROC) curve for the rendezvous detection models.

7 Conclusions and Future Work

In this paper we propose a hybrid formal framework for interactive modeling and experimental validation of SADS scenarios in the Marine Safety & Security domain. The proposed framework captures common concepts and notions of situation analysis and situation awareness, allows for reasoning about knowledge, uncertainty and belief change, and enables rapid prototyping of abstract executable decision support system models.

Albeit the sample rendezvous scenarios studied here are relatively simple when compared to other typical rendezvous pattern, the intrinsic complexity of such scenarios already demands systematic approaches that facilitate development of executable formal models in order to explore the problem space, reason about design decisions and investigate feasible solutions. Yet the application presented in this paper demonstrates how the framework facilitates a seamless mapping of functional system requirements into an abstract executable ground model [4] which can be analyzed through simulation and animation to check its validity and appropriateness. To this end, the proposed framework complements purely analytical means that focus on verification of internal properties such as consistency and completeness of a model (not further detailed here), and provides a sensible way of linking formal and empirical aspects in model-driven engineering of SADS systems. Experimental study of SA scenarios as presented here can considerably enhance our insight into intricate system dynamics and simplify the challenging task of deriving meaningful conformance criteria for checking the validity of SADS domain models against established operational concepts of Marine Safety & Security.

This work is a first step towards building a framework for design and development of SADS systems. Specifically, we are planning to extend the background

[4] This report excludes false positives.

concepts supported by the framework, improve the user interface and visualization capabilities, and enhance the analysis method using the scripting features of the CoreASM Bârun plugin [1]. In addition, we consider importing real data to ground the validation phase in actual real-world scenarios.

References

1. Altenhofen, M., Farahbod, R.: Bârun: A scripting language for coreASM. In: Frappier, M., et al. (eds.) ABZ 2010. LNCS, vol. 5977, pp. 47–60. Springer, Heidelberg (2010)
2. Baader, F., et al.: A novel architecture for situation awareness systems. In: Giese, M., Waaler, A. (eds.) TABLEAUX 2009. LNCS, vol. 5607, pp. 77–92. Springer, Heidelberg (2009)
3. Börger, E.: Why Use Evolving Algebras for Hardware and Software Engineering? In: Bartosek, M., Staudek, J., Wiedermann, J. (eds.) SOFSEM 1995. LNCS, vol. 1012, pp. 236–271. Springer, Heidelberg (1995)
4. Börger, E.: The ASM ground model method as a foundation of requirements engineering. In: Dershowitz, N. (ed.) Verification: Theory and Practice. LNCS, vol. 2772, pp. 145–160. Springer, Heidelberg (2004)
5. Börger, E., Glässer, U., Müller, W.: Formal Definition of an Abstract VHDL 1993 Simulator by EA-Machines. In: Delgado Kloos, C., Breuer, P.T. (eds.) Formal Semantics for VHDL, pp. 107–139. Kluwer Academic Publishers, Dordrecht (1995)
6. Börger, E., Stärk, R.: Abstract State Machines: A Method for High-Level System Design and Analysis. Springer, Heidelberg (2003)
7. Börger, E.: Construction and analysis of ground models and their refinements as a foundation for validating computer based systems. Formal Aspects of Computing 19(2), 225–241 (2007)
8. Bossé, É., Jousselme, A.L., Maupin, P.: Situation analysis for decision support: A formal approach. In: Proc. of the 10th Intl. Conf. on Information Fusion (2007)
9. Brannon, N.G., Seiffertt, J.E., Draelos II, T.J., Wunsch, D.C.: Coordinated machine learning and decision support for situation awareness. Neural Networks 22(3), 316–325 (2009)
10. Brantingham, P.L., Glässer, U., Jackson, P., Vajihollahi, M.: Modeling criminal activity in urban landscapes. In: Memon, N., Farley, J.D., Hicks, D.L., Rosenoørn, T. (eds.) Mathematical Methods in Counterterrorism, pp. 9–31. Springer, Heidelberg (2009)
11. Chmielewski, M.: Ontology applications for achieving situation awareness in military decision support systems. In: Nguyen, N.T., Kowalczyk, R., Chen, S.-M. (eds.) ICCCI 2009. LNCS, vol. 5796, pp. 528–539. Springer, Heidelberg (2009)
12. Endsley, M.R.: Theoretical underpinnings of situation awareness: A critical review. In: Endsley, M.R., Garland, D.J. (eds.) Situation Awareness Analysis and Measurement, LEA (2000)
13. Farahbod, R., Gervasi, V., Glässer, U.: CoreASM: An extensible ASM execution engine. Fundamenta Informaticae, 71–103 (2007)
14. Farahbod, R., Gervasi, V., Glässer, U., Ma, G.: coreASM plug-in architecture. In: Abrial, J.-R., Glässer, U. (eds.) Rigorous Methods for Software Construction and Analysis. LNCS, vol. 5115, pp. 147–169. Springer, Heidelberg (2009)
15. Farahbod, R., Glässer, U.: The CoreASM modeling framework. Software: Practice and Experience 41(2), 167–178 (2011)

16. Farahbod, R., Glässer, U., Bossé, E., Guitouni, A.: Integrating abstract state machines and interpreted systems for situation analysis decision support design. In: Proc. of the 11th Intl. Conf. on Information Fusion, Köln, Germany (July 2008)
17. Farahbod, R., Glässer, U., Khalili, A.: A multi-layer network architecture for dynamic resource configuration & management of multiple mobile resources in maritime surveillance. In: Proc. of SPIE Defense & Security Symposium, Orlando, Florida, USA (March 2009)
18. Farahbod, R.: CoreASM: An Extensible Modeling Framework & Tool Environment for High-level Design and Analysis of Distributed Systems. Ph.D. thesis, Simon Fraser Univ., BC, Canada (May 2009)
19. Farahbod, R., Avram, V., Glässer, U., Guitouni, A.: Engineering situation analysis decision support systems. In: European Intelligence and Security Informatics Conference, Athens, Greece (2011)
20. Garland, D.J., Endsley, M.R.: Situation Awareness: Analysis and Measurement. CRC Press, Boca Raton (2000)
21. Glässer, U., Gotzhein, R., Prinz, A.: The formal semantics of SDL-2000: Status and perspectives. Computer Networks 42(3), 343–358 (2003)
22. Glässer, U., Gurevich, Y., Veanes, M.: Abstract communication model for distributed systems. IEEE Trans. on Soft. Eng. 30(7), 458–472 (2004)
23. Glässer, U., et al.: A collaborative decision support model for marine safety and security operations. In: Hinchey, M., et al. (eds.) DIPES 2010. IFIP AICT, vol. 329, pp. 266–277. Springer, Heidelberg (2010)
24. Gurevich, Y.: Evolving Algebras 1993: Lipari Guide. In: Börger, E. (ed.) Specification and Validation Methods, pp. 9–36. Oxford University Press, Oxford (1995)
25. Jakobson, G., Lewis, L., Buford, C., Sherman, C.: Battlespace situation analysis: The dynamic cbr approach. In: Military Communications Conf., vol. 2, pp. 941–947 (October 2004)
26. Jousselme, A.L., Maupin, P.: Interpreted systems for situation analysis. In: Proc. of the 10th Intl. Conf. on Information Fusion, Québec, Canada (July 2007)
27. Kalman, R.E.: A new approach to linear filtering and prediction problems. Transactions of the ASME–Journal of Basic Engineering 82(Series D), 35–45 (1960)
28. Klashner, R., Sabet, S.: A DSS design model for complex problems: Lessons from mission critical infrastructure. Decision Support Systems 43, 990–1013 (2007)
29. Lambert, D.A.: STDF model based maritime situation assessments. In: Proc. of the 10th Intl. Conf. on Information Fusion (July 2007)
30. McDermid, J.: Science of software design: Architectures for evolvable, dependable systems. In: NSF Workshop on the Science of Design: Software and Software-Intensive Systems, Airlie Center, VA (2003)
31. Nemati, H., Steiger, D., Iyer, L., Herschel, R.: Knowledge warehouse: an architectural integration of knowledge management, decision support, artificial intelligence and data warehousing. Decision Support Systems 33(2), 143–161 (2002)
32. Ryu, Y.U.: Constraint logic programming framework for integrated decision supports. Decision Support Systems 22(2), 155–170 (1998)
33. Shim, J.P., Warkentin, M., Courtney, J.F., Power, D.J., Sharda, R., Carlsson, C.: Past, present, and future of decision support technology. Decision Support Systems 33(2), 111–126 (2002)
34. Stärk, R., Schmid, J., Börger, E.: Java and the Java Virtual Machine: Definition, Verification, Validation. Springer, Heidelberg (2001)

Conformance Checking of Dynamic Access Control Policies

David Power, Mark Slaymaker, and Andrew Simpson

Oxford University Computing Laboratory
Wolfson Building, Parks Road, Oxford OX1 3QD, UK

Abstract. The capture, deployment and enforcement of appropriate access control policies are crucial aspects of many modern software-based systems. Previously, there has been a significant amount of research undertaken with respect to the formal modelling and analysis of access control policies; however, only a limited proportion of this work has been concerned with *dynamic* policies. In this paper we explore techniques for the modelling, analysis and subsequent deployment of such policies—which may rely on external data. We use the Alloy modelling language to describe constraints on policies and external data; utilising these constraints, we test static instances constructed from the current state of the external data. We present Gauge, a constraint checker for static instances that has been developed to be complementary to Alloy, and show how it is possible to test systems of much greater complexity via Gauge than can typically be handled by a model finder.

1 Introduction

Large-scale data-oriented systems dominate much of our lives: as employees, as consumers, as patients, as travellers, as web surfers, and as citizens. The nature of much of this data, coupled with an increased awareness of relevant security and privacy issues, means that it is essential that effective tools, technologies and processes are in place to ensure that any and all access is appropriate. Our concern in this paper is the construction of access control policies that rely on context to inform decisions. (Arguments as to the potential benefits of *context-sensitive access control* have been made by, for example, [1], [2], and [3].) Specifically, our concern is what might be termed *evolving access control*—whereby access control decisions are made on the basis of state.

We utilise formal models for the construction and analysis of such dynamic policies. In this respect, our work has much in common with that of [4], which defines a framework to capture the behaviour of access control policies in dynamic environments. (In common with our approach, the authors also separate the policy from the environment.) Importantly, our work is driven by practical concerns. The policies that are constructed and analysed are subsequently deployed to instances of the *sif* (service-oriented interoperability framework) middleware framework [5,6] to support the secure sharing and aggregation of data.

S. Qin and Z. Qiu (Eds.): ICFEM 2011, LNCS 6991, pp. 227–242, 2011.

The framework supports relatively straightforward policies that conform to the role-based access control (RBAC) model [7]; it also supports more complex policies in the expressive XACML (eXtensible Access Control Markup Language) policy language.[1]

Of course, the use of access control policies can bring many benefits when managing complex systems: by centralising all authorisation decisions, consistency of access can be maintained, and updating a single access control policy is much simpler than modifying multiple components. Nevertheless, creating and updating access control policies is still a potentially time-consuming task. Going further, policy languages such as XACML support access to external data—which may be updated independently of the policy. While this simplifies the task of maintaining policies, it greatly complicates their analysis and also necessitates controls on the modification of external data.

As demonstrated by many authors, formal methods have a role to play in this area, with examples including the work of [8] and [9]—both of which are concerned with the modelling and analysis of XACML. Even when the requirements for an access control policy are well understood, it is still possible for mistakes to be made: the flexibility of policy languages increases the potential for mistakes due, in part, to their expressiveness.

We utilise the Alloy Modelling Language [10] in this paper to build models of policies and external data. Using the Alloy Analyzer we are able to test properties of those models. By constructing instances of policies and external data, we are able to evaluate the constraints described in the Alloy model.[2] However, the Alloy Analyzer is only capable of analysing models of bounded size; this and a lack of support for the large integers needed to model times, dates and monetary values has led some researcher to avoid using the Alloy Modelling Language [16]. To address these problems, we have developed a tool for checking constraints on large policies which also has the potential to support large integers and other data types.

While, in general, it is not possible to say if a policy is 'correct' (due to the 'safety problem' of [17]), it is possible to test for certain healthiness conditions, such as separation of duty constraints in role-based policies. Of course, there are many other possible constraints which may be appropriate in role-based policies, such as the absence (or presence) of a user with all permissions, or all users having at least one role.

To this end, we concern ourselves with RBAC models and policies as a means of illustrating the contribution. Specifically, we build on the RBAC model of [18], which has been utilised in the policy editing tool described in [19]. It should be noted that the modelling and analysis of RBAC constraints has a rich history, with the work of [20] and [21] being of particular note.

---

[1] See `http://www.oasis-open.org/committees/xacml/`

[2] Other work that has built policy analysis tools on Alloy include the contributions of [11], [12] and [13]. Also relevant in terms of related work is the DynAlloy tool [14,15], which extends Alloy to handle dynamic specifications.

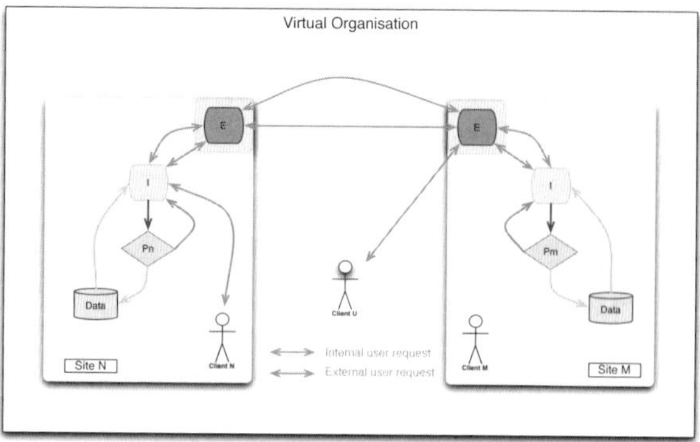

Fig. 1. The sif view of a distributed system

The structure of the remainder of this paper is as follows. In Section 2 we describe the motivation for, and context of, our work: the capture, analysis and enforcement of dynamic access control policies that make reference to external state. Then, in Section 3, we describe the modelling and analysis of constraints via Alloy. In Section 4 we introduce Gauge—our tool for the evaluation of Alloy predicates and expressions. Finally, in Section 5, we summarise the contribution of this paper and outline potential areas of future work.

2 Context

In this section we present the background to our work. We start by introducing the sif framework, before giving consideration to what we term *evolving access control*. We then briefly introduce our RBAC policy editing tool.

2.1 sif

sif (service-oriented interoperability framework) is concerned with supporting secure data sharing and aggregation in a fashion that doesn't require organisations to throw away existing data models or systems, change practices, or invest in new technology. The philosophy behind sif was originally described in [22]. There, a virtual organisation—spread across two or more geographically or physically distinct units—was characterised as per Figure 1. Deployments communicate via their external interfaces (represented by E), with data being accessed via an internal interface, I. The permitted access to the data is regulated by policies (P): each organisation has control over its data, which means that the responsibility for defining policies resides a local level.

sif offers support for three types of 'plug-in'—data plug-ins, file plug-ins and algorithm plug-ins—and it is these plug-ins that facilitate interoperability. By using a standard plug-in interface, it becomes possible to add heterogeneous

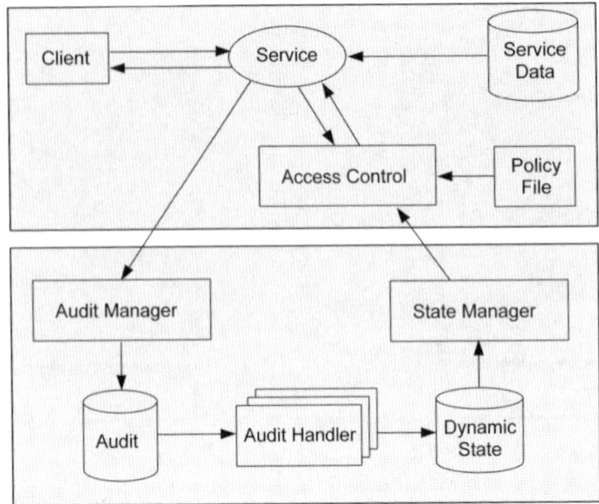

Fig. 2. Evolving access control architecture

resources into a virtual organisation. If, in a distributed, heterogeneous context, a user runs a query across several data nodes, then the middleware will distribute that query to the nodes and aggregate the results. The middleware exposes as much to the user as the developer considers useful for the application in question: it may be appropriate to expose the whole underlying data structure, allowing users to construct SQL queries; alternatively, a simple interface supporting pre-formulated queries might be appropriate.

2.2 Evolving Access Control

The middleware framework of the previous section has the potential to support what might be termed *evolving access control*: what may be accessed by users and applications may change dynamically, depending on context. Examples of such policies might include "if there has been no contact from Officer X for over 30 minutes then access should be denied from her device," "Professor Y can access up to 10 of these images," and "Dr Z can access data provided that the network capacity is sufficient." *Meta-policies* prescribe the relationship between policies: after Officer X has been out of contact for over 30 minutes, any access that was previously possible is now denied; once Professor Y has accessed 10 images, she can access no more of them; when the network capacity increases, Dr Z can access data to his heart's content.[3] Thus, these meta-policies are necessarily written at a higher level of abstraction than policies—and, as such, are intended to be closer to the level at which requirements might be captured or guidelines might be stated.

Of course, providing a system with the functionality to adapt access control policies automatically means that the need for assurance that the *correct* policy

[3] Note that our notion of meta-policy—describing the relationship between policies—differs from that of [23]—where the concern is 'policies about policies'.

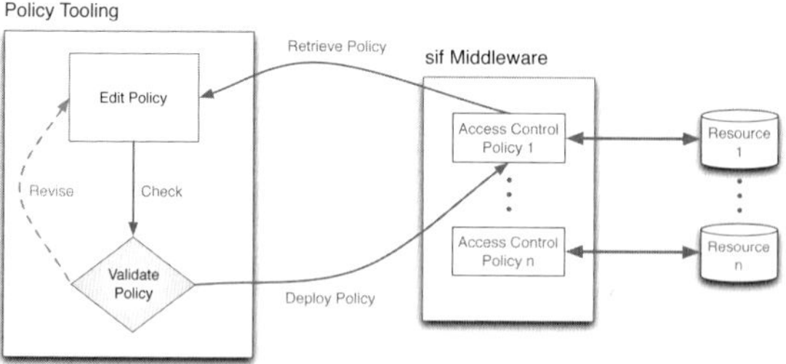

Fig. 3. Policy editing and validation workflow

is in place necessarily increases: ensuring that certain fundamental properties hold in every potential state, for example, is essential—we would not want our protection mechanism to evolve into a state that provided little protection, for example. Hence the driver for a *model-driven* approach to evolving access control: raising the level of abstraction for data owners and policy writers, with a view to giving a degree of assurance that data sharing is appropriate.

In this paper, our concern is the modelling and analysis of external data referenced by access control policies. Ideally, it would be possible not only to analyse the current state of external data but to model the modifications of that data. This is possible with our evolving access control deployments, where the combination of policy and external state evolve in accordance with a meta-policy.

The architecture of the existing evolving access control system is presented in Figure 2. Here, an audit of client activity and other events of significance is handled by an audit manager. Handlers monitor the audit and update the dynamic state in accordance with the rules of the meta-policy. When the server makes an access control request, external data can be accessed via a state manager which reads the dynamic state.

2.3 RBAC Policy Editing Tool

The sif middleware can support a number of different types of access control policies, with the associated RBAC editing tool of [19] allowing the creation and modification of RBAC policies. An illustration of how formal modelling and analysis is incorporated into the overall RBAC policy workflow is given in Figure 3.

Once modified, the policy is converted into an Alloy instance and then validated against an Alloy model using the Alloy Evaluator. The tool tests each policy against 12 different constraints; if a constraint does not hold, the user is informed of the reason why so that the policy can be revised. The process of creating instances is discussed in more detail in Section 4, in which we also describe an alternative method of evaluating constraints.

3 Constraints and Requirements

The work described in the following is motivated by the desire to be able to ensure that policy level constraints hold in the presence of dynamically changing data—assuming that we are aware of potential changes to the external data and, as such, can perform constraint checking before the changes are made. The simplest solution to this problem is to treat the entire policy as external data and to check all of the constraints whenever there is a potential change. However, a more efficient approach is to check just the constraints that are dependent on the external data; this approach assumes that any constraints that are independent of the external data have been checked at the time of policy construction.

We start by describing the model for RBAC policies that we leverage to illustrate our contribution.

3.1 RBAC

The underlying principle upon which role-based access control is based is the association of permissions with the roles that users may hold within an organisation. There are four standard components in the ANSI standard for role-based access control systems [7].

- *Core RBAC* is mandatory in any RBAC system, and associates permissions with roles and roles with users.
- Any combination of the following can be utilised in a particular system.
  1. *Role hierarchies* define what amounts to an inheritance relation between roles. As an example, role r_1 inherits from role r_2 if all privileges associated with r_2 are also associated with r_1.
  2. A *static separation of duty* (SSD) constraint is characterised by a role set, rs, such that $\# rs \geq 2$, and a natural number, n, such that $2 \leq n \leq \# rs$, and ensures that no user can be authorised for n or more roles in rs.
  3. A *dynamic separation of duty* (DSD) constraint is concerned with sessions: a DSD constraint ensures that no user can be associated with n or more roles in rs in a particular session.

3.2 An Alloy Representation of RBAC

We present a model for core RBAC with hierarchy and static separation of duty constraints. The model is based on that of [18], which presents a formal description of RBAC using the formal description language, Z [24,25].

First, we introduce `User`, `Role`, `Action` and `Resource`, with `Action` and `Resource` being used to define the contents of a `Permission`.

```
sig User, Role, Action, Resource {}

sig Permission {
  action : Action,
  resource : Resource
}
```

The MER signature represents a mutually exclusive roles constraint which restricts the combinations of roles a user can be associated with. The signature consists of an integer, limit, and a set of roles, roles. The MER signature also has a constraint, which states that the value of limit ranges between 2 and the cardinality of the roles set.

```
sig MER {
  limit : Int,
  roles : set Role
} {
  2 <= limit
  limit <= (# roles)
}
```

The fact uniquePermission ensures that each Permission is unique, i.e. no two different (signified by disj) elements of Permission have the same action–resource pair. This simplifies the subsequent definitions in the RBAC model.

```
fact uniquePermission {
  all disj pb1, pb2 : Permission |
    pb1.action != pb2.action || pb1.resource != pb2.resource
}
```

The Hierarchy signature represents an RBAC system with a role hierarchy and static separation of duty constraints. It contains the sets USERS, ROLES and PRMS, which represent the particular users, roles and permissions to which the policy relates. It also contains the relations UA, PA and RH, which represent the user-role, role-permission and role hierarchy mappings. The set SC is a set of static separation of duty constraints, the roles of which must be a subset of ROLES. The relation RH must be acyclic, which is ensured by no (^RH & iden). The composition UA.*RH.PA creates a user–permission relation which relates users and their reachable permissions taking into account the role hierarchy.

```
sig Hierarchy {
  USERS :  set User,
  ROLES : set Role,
  PRMS : set Permission,
  UA : USERS -> ROLES,
  RH : ROLES -> ROLES,
  PA : ROLES -> PRMS,
  SC : set MER
} {
  no (^RH & iden)
  all s : SC | s.roles in ROLES
}
```

We now describe a number of constraints that can be used to validate policies. The applicability of each constraint will depend, of course, upon the context of the deployed policy. In total, there are 12 constraints that are checked by our RBAC policy construction tool, three of which are presented below.

The first example is a constraint on any individual user having all permissions, represented as a fact called `NobodyCanDoEverything` affecting all elements of `Hierarchy`. This fact could have been included in the signature of `Hierarchy`, but is written as a separate fact to promote modularity and (consequently) to allow it to be tested independently.

```
fact NobodyCanDoEverything {
  all h : Hierarchy, u : h.USERS |
    u.(h.UA).*(h.RH).(h.PA) != h.PRMS
}
```

Similarly, the enforcement of static separation of duty constraints is written as a separate fact called `NobodyBreachesSC`. If the constraint does not hold, the tool evaluates the function `fun_NobodyBreachesSC` which returns a set containing (`Hierarchy`, `MER`, `User`) triples indicating, for each hierarchy, the particular static separation of duty of constraint which has been breached and the user that breaches it. Similar functions exist for the other constraints.

```
fact NobodyBreachesSC {
  all h : Hierarchy, s : h.SC, u : h.USERS |
      #(s.roles & u.(h.UA).*(h.RH)) < s.limit
}

fun fun_NobodyBreachesSC() : Hierarchy -> MER -> User {
  { h : Hierarchy, s : h.SC, u : h.USERS |
      #(s.roles & u.(h.UA).*(h.RH)) >= s.limit }
}
```

There are also constraints relating to redundancy in the model. One such example is `NoRedundantPermissions`, which prevents a role from being assigned a permission that it already holds due to inheritance.

```
fact NoRedundantPermissions {
  all h : Hierarchy, r : h.ROLES |
    no (r.(h.PA) & r.^(h.RH).(h.PA))
}
```

3.3 Adding Sessions

We now consider how sessions can be added to the RBAC model so as to allow us to divide a policy into static and dynamic parts. We assume that the dynamic parts of the policy are stored as external data.

The signature `Session` extends `Hierarchy`. The relation `AR` contains the currently active roles for each user; this represents the dynamic part of the policy. The set `DC` is a set of dynamic separation of duty constraints, which restrict the active roles of a user (it is assumed that the set DC does not change dynamically). As was the case for static separation of duty constraints, it is assumed that all dynamic separation of duty constraints refer only to roles from the set ROLES. The composition AR.PA is now used to relate users to their current permissions.

```
sig Session extends Hierarchy {
   AR : USERS -> ROLES,
   DC : set MER
} {
   all d : DC | d.roles in ROLES
}
```

The value of the relation AR needs to meet two criteria: each user–role pair has to represent a role that the user has access to, and the dynamic separation of duty constraints must be met. These criteria are captured in the fact DynamicFact.

```
fact DynamicFact {
   all s : Session |
     s.AR in (s.UA).*(s.RH) &&
     all d : s.DC , u : s.USERS |
       #(d.roles & u.(s.AR)) < d.limit
}
```

As none of the constraints on Hierarchy make reference to AR they will not need to be checked when AR changes, which reduces the amount of dynamic constraint checking required. It is possible to add extra constraints that do depend on the AR relation. For example, it is possible to modify the fact NobodyCanDoEverything to only depend on the currently activated roles.

```
fact NobodyCanCurrentlyDoEverything {
  all s : Session, u : s.USERS |
    u.(s.AR).(s.PA) != s.PRMS
}
```

4 Gauge

In this section we discuss Gauge, a means of evaluating Alloy predicates and expressions that has been developed as a companion tool to the Alloy Analyzer. Unlike the Alloy Analyzer, Gauge is not a model finder and can only work with known instances. Specifically, Gauge is designed for instances built from real world data which are too large for a model finder to handle; it is also capable of handling large integers and other data types which are commonly found in practice.

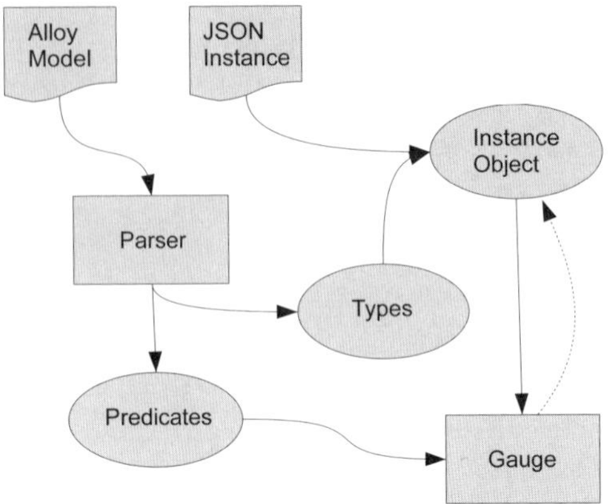

Fig. 4. Parsing and evaluation process

4.1 Overview

The first stage of using Gauge involves creating an Alloy model and using the Alloy Analyzer to check the suitability of the model. Once this has been done, it is then possible to construct a JavaScript Object Notation (JSON) instance of the data using the signatures defined in the model.

Figure 4 shows how the Alloy model and JSON instance are processed. The Alloy model is parsed using a modified version of the parser used by the Alloy Analyzer; this creates both type information for the signatures and predicate information for the facts and other constraints. The type information is used to turn the JSON instance into an object representation (considered further in the next section). Once the instance object has been created, the predicates can then be evaluated. In certain circumstances, Gauge can extend the instance by adding new atoms; this is represented by the dotted arrow.

4.2 Instances

An instance consists of three types of data: atoms, signature relations and field relations. Atoms are the basic building blocks of an instance and each atom has a signature type. The signature relations are sets of atoms of a certain signature type. Where one signature extends another, atoms of the subtype will appear in both signature relations. Field relations are sets of tuples, the first element of which is the atom to which the field relates.

In a JSON instance, each atom is introduced as a separate object. The `id` field is used as a unique identifier for the atom and the `type` field represents the signature type of the atom. If the atom has any field values, these are listed in `fields` where each field name is associated with an array of arrays of atom identifiers. The inner arrays are necessary as field values could be of any arity.

Shown below is an example of JSON instance containing a MER atom and its associated roles.

```
{ id : role1, type : Role },
{ id : role2, type : Role },
{ id : mer1, type : MER,
  fields : {
    limit : [[2]],
    roles : [[role1],[role2]]}
}
```

When loaded, the following atoms, signature relations and field relations are created, including the univ signature relation which all signatures extend. Integers are identified using a decimal string representation.

$$\begin{aligned}
&Atoms = \{role1, role2, mer1, 2\}\\
&Signatures = \{Role \rightarrow \{role1, role2\}, MER \rightarrow \{mer1\},\\
&\qquad Int \rightarrow \{2\}, univ \rightarrow \{role1, role2, mer1, 2\}\}\\
&Fields = \{limit \rightarrow \{(mer1, 2)\}, roles \rightarrow \{(mer1, role1), (mer1, role2)\}\}
\end{aligned}$$

4.3 Evaluation

Each predicate that is to be evaluated is constructed from a number of expressions. When evaluated, an expression can have either a Boolean value, a relational value, or a primitive integer value. For relational operators, such as composition (`.`) or union (`+`), Gauge first evaluates the two sub-expressions and then combines the resulting relations using the operator specified. When reference is made to a signature or field, the associated relation is retrieved from the instance.

For Boolean operators such as (`&&`) or (`||`), a 'short-circuit' approach is used whereby sub-expressions are evaluated from left to right as required. Similarly, when evaluating quantifiers such as `some` or `all` evaluation stops as soon as a definitive result is found.

Some expressions introduce variables, the simplest of which is `let`. To store the current values of variables, a mapping is maintained between variables and the relations they represent. For a `let` expression, the value of the variable is fixed within each evaluation. After evaluating the body of the `let` expression, the variable is removed from the mapping before the result is returned. For quantifiers, the value of each variable is drawn from a set, the body of the quantifier is evaluated separately for each combination of variable values. Set comprehensions work similarly to quantifiers with successful combinations of variable values being turned into tuples and added to the resulting relation.

Calls to predicates and functions are handled dynamically during evaluation. The arguments are first calculated and added to the variable mapping. The body of the called predicate or function is then evaluated. As a natural consequence of this evaluation method, Gauge is capable of evaluating certain types of recursively defined functions and predicates.

4.4 Types

While it is possible to model specific aspects of data types when constructing an Alloy model, a certain amount of abstraction is needed if one wishes to use the model-finding capabilities of the Alloy Analyzer. An example of this is the representation of integers, where the bit width is restricted. When testing for counterexamples, the restriction of the bit width is not normally a problem; however, real world data is, of course, likely to exceed the bit width used for modelling.

There are many other data types that would be of relevance in an access control system, including times, dates, strings and X.509 certificates. Each of these would be impossible to model completely in Alloy but are simple to handle in a general purpose programming language.

Such types are handled in a straightforward manner in Gauge by casting between Alloy atoms and native representations as necessary. As a simple example, part of the Gauge time module is presented below. Here, `currentTime` refers to the current time, and the predicate `Time_lte` is used for comparisons.

```
sig Time {}
one sig currentTime extends Time {}

pred Time_lte(t1, t2 : Time) {
  lte[t1,t2]
}
```

As a simple example, the predicate `NineToFive` can be used to check if the time of evaluation is in 'normal office hours': between 9am and 5pm.

```
pred NineToFive() {
  Time_lte[T_9_0_0,currentTime]
  Time_lte[currentTime,T_17_0_0]
}
```

When evaluating `NineToFive`, Gauge will recognise the predicate `Time_lte` as a predicate on time and, instead of expanding its definition, will perform the comparison using native Java objects. For atoms such as `T_9_0_0`, Gauge will create a time object with the three numbers representing hours, minutes and seconds. The atom `currentTime` is also recognised as a special case and a new atom is created which represents the current time.

It is possible to use the same methods to allow time arithmetic, such as adding an hour or calculating the difference between two times. These will potentially add new atoms to the instance. Without the ability to add new atoms, all intermediate results would need to form part of the initial instance.

4.5 Scalability

While the model finder used by Alloy is capable of dealing with the case when the relations are all fixed, it still is restricted by internal data structures which

Users	Atoms	Static time	Dynamic time
256	530	41ms	8ms
512	995	88ms	14ms
1024	1925	189ms	24ms
2048	3785	544ms	110ms
4096	7505	1.78s	169ms
8192	14945	6.71s	591ms
16384	29825	27.5s	2.29s
32768	59585	122s	8.38s
65536	119105	553s	35.6s

Fig. 5. Scalability results

put a limit on the total number of atoms of $2^{31/n}$ (where n is the largest arity of any relation in the model). In our RBAC model, the `UA`, `PA` and `RH` field relations are all of arity 3, which imposes a limit of approximately 1,000 total atoms. Gauge, on the other hand, does not have any restrictions on the size of the instance other than the memory needed to store it.

To test scalability, instances of policies were created, and the time taken to test the 12 static and 2 dynamic constraints were recorded. A simple role hierarchy was created, with all apart from one role being connected in a binary tree. One user was allocated the 'separate role', with all others being randomly allocated between one and three roles from the tree. For each role, there were exactly four permissions, each having a unique action and resource. There was a single separation of duty constraint for every 16 roles—with each such constraint involving two roles, one of which was the 'separate role'. By allocating the roles, permissions and constraints in this fashion, it was possible to ensure that all but one of the constraints held, maximising the amount of work required. The constraint that did not hold pertained to a role being senior to multiple roles.

There were 16 times as many users as roles, and 8 times as many active roles. The number of users is listed in Figure 5, together with the total number of atoms. The total number of atoms includes 64 integers and the atom representing the policy, but otherwise is proportional to the number of users.

4.6 Optimisation

To achieve the times listed in Figure 5, the constraints were modified so that they could be evaluated more efficiently. As discussed previously, Gauge uses a simple evaluation strategy for quantifiers where the body is evaluated separately for each combination of variable values. This can lead to an expression being evaluated multiple times for the same values. By using `let` statements, it is possible to store the results of expressions so they can be reused. Shown below is `DynamicFact` rewritten using `let` statements.

```
fact DynamicFact {
  all s : Session |
    let sess = s.AR |
      sess in (s.UA).*(s.RH) &&
      all d : s.DC |
        let lim = d.limit |
          let rol = d.roles |
            all u : s.USERS | #(rol & u.sess) < lim
}
```

In this case the difference in performance is significant: with 8192 users, the evaluation took 454 seconds without the `let` statements and 0.795 seconds with the `let` statements. Other optimisations are less obvious; for example, `uniquePermission` can be rewritten to remove the quantifiers completely.

```
fact uniquePermission {
  (action.~action & resource.~resource) in iden
}
```

Again, the difference in performance is significant: with 2048 permissions, the original `uniquePermission` took 14 seconds to evaluate compared with 0.022 seconds for the alternative version.

Another potential area of performance gain when evaluating the dynamic constraints comes from using an incremental approach to evaluation. In the current example, the deactivation of a role can never result in the breaching of a constraint and the activation of a role can only result in breaches related to the user doing the activating and the role(s) being activated. A combination of storing the value of expressions related to the static part of the policy (such as `(s.UA).*(s.RH)`) and only evaluating quantifiers for the parts of the dynamic policy that have changed (removing `all u : s.USERS`) would have a dramatic effect on performance.

5 Conclusions and Further Work

In this paper we have discussed methods for the modelling and analysis of access control policies which reference external data. The referencing of external data is of particular relevance when dealing with dynamic access control policies which are constantly modified in response to user activity or system events. By building models of access control policies in the Alloy modelling language, we are able to describe policy constraints and test existing policies. By directly creating Alloy instances, it becomes possible to test more complex policies than might be handled by the Alloy model finder. We have described a prototype evaluator called Gauge which is capable of handling large instances and also has limited support for real world data types.

By decomposing a model of an access control policy into static and dynamic parts, we have shown how it is possible to test just a small set of constraints when the dynamic parts of a policy change. It is possible to test the suitability of a set of constraints by using the model-finding capabilities of the Alloy Analyzer; once a set of constraints has been found to be suitable, a simple evaluation of a new instance is sufficient.

The long-term goal is to be able to analyse changes in dynamic state in real time. While this is currently feasible for policies which have hundreds or even thousands of users, the evaluation time for larger policies starts to become prohibitive. By providing a facility for the persistent storage of instances it will be possible to cache results and to only evaluate constraints related to changes in the dynamic state. With such a system in place, it should be possible to handle significantly larger policies.

For changes to the static parts of policies, there is the potential to increase the speed of evaluation by decomposing the problem and utilising parallel evaluation; with the advent of cloud computing infrastructures, such approaches are now more feasible than ever before, and we intend exploring the potential for benefitting from such developments in the near future. Finally, while the development of Gauge has been driven by the needs of a particular domain, we consider it to be a general purpose evaluator; as such, we will be giving consideration to further application areas in the coming months.

References

1. Kumar, A., Karnik, N., Chafle, G.: Context sensitivity in role-based access control. ACM SIGOPS Operating Systems Review 36(3), 53–66 (2002)
2. Bhatti, R., Bertino, E., Ghafoor, A.: A trust-based context-aware access control model for web-services. Distributed and Parallel Databases 18(1), 83–105 (2005)
3. Hulsebosch, R.J., Salden, A.H., Bargh, M.S., Ebben, P.W.G., Reitsma, J.: Context sensitive access control. In: Proceedings of the 10th ACM Symposium on Access Control Models and Technologies (SACMAT 2005), pp. 111–119 (2005)
4. Dougherty, D.J., Fisler, K., Krishnamurthi, S.: Specifying and reasoning about dynamic access-control policies. In: Furbach, U., Shankar, N. (eds.) IJCAR 2006. LNCS (LNAI), vol. 4130, pp. 632–646. Springer, Heidelberg (2006)
5. Simpson, A.C., Power, D.J., Russell, D., Slaymaker, M.A., Kouadri-Mostefaoui, G., Ma, X., Wilson, G.: A healthcare-driven framework for facilitating the secure sharing of data across organisational boundaries. Studies in Health Technology and Informatics 138, 3–12 (2008)
6. Slaymaker, M.A., Power, D.J., Russell, D., Simpson, A.C.: On the facilitation of fine-grained access to distributed healthcare data. In: Jonker, W., Petković, M. (eds.) SDM 2008. LNCS, vol. 5159, pp. 169–184. Springer, Heidelberg (2008)
7. Ferraiolo, D.F., Sandhu, R.S., Gavrilla, S., Kuhn, D.R., Chandramouli, R.: Proposed NIST standard for role-based access control. ACM Transactions on Information and Systems Security 4(3), 224–274 (2001)
8. Zhang, N., Ryan, M., Guelev, D.P.: Synthesising verified access control systems in XACML. In: Proceedings of the 2nd ACM Workshop on Formal Methods in Security Engineering (FMSE 2004), pp. 56–65 (2004)
9. Bryans, J.W., Fitzgerald, J.S.: Formal engineering of XACML access control policies in VDM++. In: Butler, M., Hinchey, M.G., Larrondo-Petrie, M.M. (eds.) ICFEM 2007. LNCS, vol. 4789, pp. 37–56. Springer, Heidelberg (2007)

10. Jackson, D.: Software Abstractions: Logic, Language, and Analysis. MIT Press, Cambridge (2006)
11. Schaad, A., Moffett, J.D.: A lightweight approach to specification and analysis of role-based access control extensions. In: Proceedings of the 7th ACM Symposium on Access Control Models and Technologies (SACMAT 2002), pp. 13–22 (2002)
12. Hughes, G., Bultan, T.: Automated verification of access control policies. Technical Report 2004-22, University of California, Santa Barbara (2004)
13. Fisler, K., Krishnamurthi, S., Meyerovich, L., Tshantz, M.C.: Verification and change-impact analysis of access-control policies. In: Inverardi, P., Jazayeri, M. (eds.) ICSE 2005. LNCS, vol. 4309, pp. 196–205. Springer, Heidelberg (2006)
14. Frias, M.F., Galeotti, J.P., Pombo, C.G.L., Aguirre, N.M.: DynAlloy: upgrading Alloy with actions. In: Inverardi, P., Jazayeri, M. (eds.) ICSE 2005. LNCS, vol. 4309, pp. 442–451. Springer, Heidelberg (2006)
15. Frias, M.F., Pombo, C.G.L., Galeotti, J.P., Aguirre, N.M.: Efficient analysis of DynAlloy specifications. ACM Transactions on Software Engineering and Methodology (TOSEM) 17(1), Article number 4 (2007)
16. Shaikh, R.A., Adi, K., Logrippo, L., Mankovski, S.: Inconsistency detection method for access control policies. In: Proceedings of 6th International Conference on Information Assurance and Security (IAS 2010), pp. 204–209 (2010)
17. Harrison, M.A., Ruzzo, W.L., Ullman, J.D.: Protection in operating systems. Communications of the ACM 19(8), 461–471 (1976)
18. Power, D.J., Slaymaker, M.A., Simpson, A.C.: On formalizing and normalizing role-based access control systems. The Computer Journal 52(3), 305–325 (2009)
19. Power, D.J., Slaymaker, M.A., Simpson, A.C.: Automatic conformance checking of role-based access control policies via alloy. In: Erlingsson, Ú., Wieringa, R., Zannone, N. (eds.) ESSoS 2011. LNCS, vol. 6542, pp. 15–28. Springer, Heidelberg (2011)
20. Ahn, G.J., Sandhu, R.S.: Role-based authorization constraint specification. ACM Transactions on Information and Systems Security 3(4), 207–226 (2000)
21. Crampton, J.: Specifying and enforcing constraints in role-based access control. In: Proceedings of the 8th ACM Symposium on Access Control Models and Technologies (SACMAT 2003), pp. 43–50 (2003)
22. Power, D.J., Politou, E.A., Slaymaker, M.A., Simpson, A.C.: Towards secure grid-enabled healthcare. Software: Practice and Experience 35(9), 857–871 (2005)
23. Hosmer, H.H.: Metapolicies I. ACM SIGSAC Review 10(2-3), 18–43 (1992)
24. Spivey, J.M.: The Z Notation: A Reference Manual. Prentice-Hall, Englewood Cliffs (1992)
25. Woodcock, J.C.P., Davies, J.W.M.: Using Z: Specification, Refinement, and Proof. Prentice-Hall, Englewood Cliffs (1996)

A Knowledge-Based Verification Method for Dynamic Access Control Policies

Masoud Koleini and Mark Ryan

University of Birmingham,
Birmingham, B15 2TT, UK
{m.koleini,m.d.ryan}@cs.bham.ac.uk

Abstract. We present a new approach for automated knowledge-based verification of access control policies. The verification method not only discovers if a vulnerability exists, but also produces the strategies that can be used by the attacker to exploit the vulnerability. It investigates the information needed by the attacker to achieve the goal and whether he acquires that information when he proceeds through the strategy or not. We provide a policy language for specifying access control rules and the corresponding query language that is suited for expressing the properties we aim to verify. The policy language is expressive enough to handle integrity constraints and policy invariants. Finally, we compare the results and enhancements of the current method - implemented as a policy verification tool called *PoliVer* - over similar works in the context of dynamic access control policy verification.

1 Introduction

Social networks like Facebook and LinkedIn, cloud computing networks like Salesforce and Google docs, conference paper review systems like Easychair and HotCRP are examples of the applications that huge numbers of users deal with every day. In such systems, a group of agents interact with each other to access resources and services. Access control policies in such multi-agent systems are dynamic (state-based) [1,2,3,4], meaning that the permissions for an agent depend on the state of the system. As a consequence, permissions for an agent can be changed by the actions of other agents.

For complex systems, reasoning by hand about access control policies is not feasible. Automated verification is a solution and enables policy designers to verify their policies against properties needed. For instance, in Google docs, we need to verify "if Alice shares a document with Bob, it is not possible for Bob to share it with Charlie unless Alice agrees", or in HotCRP, "if Bob is not chair, it is not possible for him to promote himself to be a reviewer of a paper submitted to the conference". If such properties do not hold, it can imply a security hole in the system and needs to be investigated and fixed by policy designers.

Knowledge - the information that an agent or group of agents has gained about the system - plays an important role in exploiting vulnerabilities by the attacker. For instance in Facebook, consider a situation in which Alice is a friend of Bob,

S. Qin and Z. Qiu (Eds.): ICFEM 2011, LNCS 6991, pp. 243–258, 2011.

and she has excluded non-friends from seeing her photos and her list of friends. Bob has tagged Alice on some photos of him, which are publicly available. Eve is interested in finding some photos of Alice. If Eve knows that Alice and Bob are friends, then the pseudocode below demonstrates how she can proceed:

```
foreach (photo ∈ Bob.photos)
  if (photo.isAccessibleBy(Eve) and Alice ∈ photo.tags)
    Output photo;
```

Although this vulnerability exists, Eve still needs to find some of Alice's friends to exploit it. The required information may be a prior knowledge, or gained by exploring the system. In both cases, a verification method that investigates how the agents can gain information about the system, share it with other agents and use the information to achieve the goal is valuable in debugging access control policies.

This paper proposes a dynamic access control model supporting knowledge-based verification through reasoning about readability. In this context, an agent knows the value of a proposition[1] (for instance, areFriends(Alice, Bob)) if he has previously read the proposition, or performed an action that has altered its value. This abstraction of knowledge results in a simpler model, which makes the verification efficient, and is powerful enough to model knowledge in access control systems. Using this definition of knowledge, we are able to efficiently verify a property - as a vulnerability - over access control systems, and if the property is satisfied, produce an output which demonstrates how an agent can execute a sequence of actions to achieve the goal, what information he requires to safely proceed through the strategy and what are the risky situations where he needs to guess what action to perform.

As an important feature in this paper, we are interested in finding the system propositions in which the strategy for the attacker to achieve the goal is different according to whether the proposition is true or false. We call those propositions *effective*. The values of effective propositions are needed by the attacker to determine the appropriate strategy. If the attacker does not know the value of the effective proposition, he could still guess the value. In the case of wrong guess, he may be able to backtrack to the guessing state and select the right strategy. However, backtracking has two main disadvantages: firstly, it may not be possible to backtrack or undo the actions already performed and secondly, unauthorized actions may be logged by the system. So, the attacker needs to minimize guessing to get the goal.

The proposed algorithm is able to:

- Verify a property (or equivalently, goal) over an access control system which is characterised by a dynamic policy.
- Provide the strategy together with the information required for an attacker to achieve the goal, if the goal is found to be achievable.

[1] In the context of this paper, a proposition refers to a boolean variable in the system, and a state is a valuation of all system propositions.

- Find out if the attacker can gain the required knowledge while he traverses through the strategy.

Our Contribution: We propose a policy language with corresponding verification algorithm that handles integrity constraints - rules that must remain true to preserve integrity of data. The policy language enables users to define action rules and also read permission rules to represent agent knowledge in the system. We provide a verification algorithm (with respect to effective propositions) which is able to find the strategy in a more efficient way than the guessing approach in a similar knowledge based verification framework [1]. The algorithm verifies knowledge by reasoning about readability. This approach approximates knowledge, finds errors efficiently and is easier to automate. Finally, we present case studies for strategy finding and knowledge verification algorithm and compare the performance with similar methods.

The rest of this paper is organized as follows. Related work is discussed in Section 2. Formal definitions of access control policy, access control system and query language are introduced in Section 3. Model-checking strategy is explained in Section 4. Knowledge-based verification of the strategies is presented in Section 5. Experimental results are provided in section 6 and conclusions and future work are explained in Section 7.

Notation 1. *To enhance readability, for the rest of this paper,* letters with no index *such as* u *and* a *used as the arguments will represent* variables. indexed letters *such as* u_1 *and* a_1 *will be used for* objects *(instantiated variables).*

2 Related Work

Although there is lots of research in the area of stateless access control system verification [5,6,7], we only mention several important related papers in the context of dynamic policy verification.

One of the first works is the security model of Bell and LaPadula designed in 1976 [8]. This model is a state transition framework for access control policies in a multi-level security structure and is based on security classification of objects and subjects. In general, the model is not fine-grained, not all access control policies can be modelled and also contains several weaknesses [9].

Dougherty et al. [3] define a datalog-based verification of access control policies. They have separated static access control policy from the dynamic behaviour and defined a framework to represent the dynamic behaviour of access control policies. They consider an *environment* consisting of the facts in the system. Performing each action adds some facts or removes some other from the environment. They perform formal analysis for *safety* and *availability* properties on their access control model.

In terms of verifying knowledge, RW [1] is the most similar framework to ours[2]. "Read" and "write" rules in RW define the permissions for read/write

[2] RW is implemented as a tool named AcPeg (Access Control Policy Evaluator and Generator).

access to the system propositions. RW considers agent knowledge propositions in state space. So, an agent can perform an action if he knows he is able to perform it. RW suffers from the restriction that only one proposition can be updated at a time in every write action. Our policy language allows defining actions with bulk variable update. As a practical limitation, the state space in RW grows in a greater context than conventional model-checkers, which makes the verification of complex policies difficult. Our method is more efficient as it abstracts knowledge states and and uses a fast post-processing algorithm for knowledge verification.

SMP [10] is a logic for state-modifying policies based on transaction logic. Although SMP provides an algorithm that finds the optimal sequence of transitions to the goal, it suffers from restricted use of negation in preconditions, which is not the case in our proposed algorithm.

Becker [2] has designed a policy language (DynPAL) that is able to verify safety properties over dynamic access control policies with an unbounded number of objects. The paper proposes two methods for reasoning about *reachability* and *policy invariants*. For reachability, the policy can be translated into PDDL syntax [11] and verified using a planner. Safety properties can be verified using a first order logic theorem prover and by translating the policy and invariance hypothesis into the first order logic validity problem. According to the experimental results [2], the planner may not be successful in finding if a property is an invariant in a reasonable time. Also initial states are not considered in safety property verification.

3 Definitions

3.1 Access Control Policy

In a multi-agent system, the agents authenticate themselves by using the provided authentication mechanisms, such as login by username and password, and it is assumed that the mechanism is secure and reliable. Each agent is authorized to perform actions, which can change the system state by changing the values of several system variables (in our case, atomic propositions). Performing actions in the system encapsulates three aspects: the agent request for the action, allowance by the system and system transition to another state. In this research, we consider agents performing different actions asynchronously; a realistic approach in computer systems. We present a simple policy language that is expressive enough to model an asynchronous multi-agent access control system.

Syntax Definition: Let T be the set of *types* which includes a special type "Agent" for agents and $Pred$ be a set of *predicates* such that each n-ary predicate has a type $t_1 \times \cdots \times t_n \rightarrow \{\top, \bot\}$, for some $t_i \in T$. Let V be a set of variables. Every variable in set V has a type. Consider $\boldsymbol{v}$ as a sequence of distinct variables. If $w \in Pred$, then $w(\boldsymbol{v})$ is called an *atomic formula*. L is a *logical formula* and consists of atomic formulas combined by logical connectives and existential and universal quantifiers. In the following syntax, *id* represents the identifier for the rules, and u is a variable of type Agent.

The syntax of access control policy language is as follows:

$$L ::= \top \mid \bot \mid w(\boldsymbol{v}) \mid L \vee L \mid L \wedge L \mid L \rightarrow L \mid \neg L \mid \forall v : t\, [L] \mid \exists v : t\, [L]$$
$$W ::= +w(\boldsymbol{v}) \mid -w(\boldsymbol{v}) \mid \forall v : t.\, W$$
$$W_s ::= W \mid W_s, W$$
$$\text{ActionRule} ::= id(\boldsymbol{v}) : \{W_s\} \leftarrow L$$
$$\text{ReadRule} ::= id(u, \boldsymbol{v}) : w(\boldsymbol{v}) \leftarrow L$$

Given a logical formula L, we define $fv(L) \subseteq V$ to be the set of all variables in atomic formulas in L, which occur as free variables in L. We extend fv to the set $\{W_s\}$ in the natural way.

An *action rule* has the form "$\alpha(\boldsymbol{v}) : E \leftarrow L$" such that logical formula L represents the condition under which the action is permitted to be performed. The set of signed atomic formulas E represents the effect of the action. $+w(\boldsymbol{v})$ in the effect means executing the action will set the value of $w(\boldsymbol{v})$ to true and $-w(\boldsymbol{v})$ means setting the value to false. In the case of $\forall v : t.W$ in the effect, the action updates the signed atom in W for all possible values of v. $\alpha(\boldsymbol{v})$ represents the name of the action rule. We can refer to the whole action rule as $\alpha(\boldsymbol{v})$.

We also stipulate for each action rule $\alpha(\boldsymbol{v}) : E \leftarrow L$ where $\boldsymbol{v} = (v_1, \ldots, v_n)$:

- v_1 is of type Agent and presents the agent performing the action.
- $fv(E) \cup fv(L) \subseteq \boldsymbol{v}$.
- $\{+w(\boldsymbol{x}), -w(\boldsymbol{x})\} \not\subseteq E$ where $\boldsymbol{x}$ is a sequence of variables.

A *read permission rule* has the form "$\rho(u, \boldsymbol{v}) : w(\boldsymbol{v}) \leftarrow L$" such that the logical formula L represents the condition under which the atomic proposition $w(\boldsymbol{v})$ is permitted to be read and $\rho(u, \boldsymbol{v})$ represents the name of the read permission rule. We can refer to the whole read permission rule as $\rho(u, \boldsymbol{v})$.

We also stipulate for each read permission rule $\rho(u, \boldsymbol{v}) : w(\boldsymbol{v}) \leftarrow L$ where $\boldsymbol{v} = (v_1, \ldots, v_n)$:

- u is of type Agent and presents the agent reading $w(\boldsymbol{v})$.
- $fv(L) \subseteq \{u, v_1, \ldots, v_n\}$.

Definition 1. *(Access control policy). An* access control policy *is a tuple* $(T, Pred, A, R)$ *where* T *is the set of* types, $Pred$ *is the set of* predicates, A *is the set of* action rules *and* R *is the set of* read permission rules.

Example 1. A conference paper review system policy contains the following properties for unassigning a reviewer from a paper:

- A chair is permitted to unassign the reviewers.
- If a reviewer is removed, all the corresponding subreviewers (subRev) should be removed from the system at the same time.

The unassignment action can be formalized as follows:

$$\text{delRev}(u, p, a) : \{\text{-rev}(p, a), \forall b : \text{Agent. -subRev}(p, a, b)\} \leftarrow \text{chair}(u) \wedge \text{rev}(p, a)$$

Example 1 shows how updating several variables synchronously can preserve integrity constraints. The RW framework is unable to handle such integrity constraint as it can only update one proposition at a time.

3.2 Access Control System

Access control policy is a framework representing authorizations, actions and their effect in a system. Access control systems can be presented by a policy, a set of objects and corresponding substitutions.

We define Σ as a *finite set of objects* such that each object in Σ has a type. $\Sigma_t \subseteq \Sigma$ is the set of objects of type t. If V is the *set of variables*, then a *substitution* σ is a function $V \rightarrow \Sigma$ that respects types.

Definition 2. *(Atomic propositions). The set of* atomic propositions *P is defined as the set of predicates instantiated with the objects in Σ:*

$$P = \{w(\boldsymbol{v})\sigma \mid w \in Pred, \boldsymbol{v} \in V^* \text{ and } \sigma \text{ is a substitution}\}$$

A *system state* is a valuation of atomic propositions in P. A state s can be defined as a function $P \rightarrow \{\top, \bot\}$. We use $s[p \mapsto m]$ to denote the state that is like s except that it maps the proposition p to value m.

Instantiation of the Rules: When a substitution applies to an action rule in the policy, it will extend to the variables in arguments, effects and logical formula in the natural way. If $a : e \leftarrow f$ is the instantiation of $\alpha(\boldsymbol{v}) : E \leftarrow L$ under the substitution σ, then $a = \alpha(\boldsymbol{v})\sigma$, $e = E\sigma$ and $f = L\sigma$.

This is the same for applying a substitution to the read permission rules in the policy. If $r : p \leftarrow f$ is the instantiation of $\rho(u, \boldsymbol{v}) : w(\boldsymbol{v}) \leftarrow L$ under the substitution σ, then $r = \rho(u, \boldsymbol{v})\sigma$, $p = w(\boldsymbol{v})\sigma$ and $f = L\sigma$.

Definition 3. *(Action, read permission). An* action *is an instantiation of a policy action rule. A* read permission *is an instantiated read permission rule.*

Since the number of objects is finite, each quantified logical formula will be expanded to a finite number of conjunctions (for $\forall$ quantifier) or disjunctions (for $\exists$ quantifier) of logical formulas during the instantiation phase. The universal quantifiers in the effect of actions will be expanded into a finite number of signed atomic propositions.

Definition 4. *(Access control system). An* access control system *is an access control policy instantiated with the objects in Σ.*

Definition 5. *(Action effect). Let $a : e \leftarrow f$ be an action in the access control system. Action a is* permitted to be performed *in state s if f evaluates to true in s. We also define:*

$$effect_+(a) = \{p \mid +p \in e\} \qquad effect_-(a) = \{p \mid -p \in e\}$$
$$effect(a) = effect_+(a) \cup effect_-(a)$$

3.3 Query Language

Verification of the policy deals with the *reachability problem*, one of the most common properties arising in temporal logic verification. A state s is *reachable* if it can be reached in a finite number of transitions from the initial states.

In multi-agent access control systems, the transitions are made by the agents performing actions.

The query language determines the *initial states* and the *specification*. The syntax of the *policy query* is:

$$L ::= \top \mid \bot \mid w(\boldsymbol{v}) \mid \langle w(\boldsymbol{v})\rangle \mid L \vee L \mid L \wedge L \mid L \rightarrow L \mid \neg L \mid \forall v : t\ [L] \mid \exists v : t\ [L]$$
$$W ::= w(\boldsymbol{v}) \mid w(\boldsymbol{v})* \mid w(\boldsymbol{v})! \mid w(\boldsymbol{v})*! \mid \neg W$$
$$W_s ::= \text{null} \mid W_s, W$$
$$G ::= C : (L) \mid C : (L \text{ THEN } G)$$
$$\text{Query} ::= \{W_s\} \rightarrow G$$

where $w(\boldsymbol{v})$ is an atomic formula and C is a set of variables of type Agent.

In the above definition, G is called a nested goal if it contains the keyword THEN, otherwise it is called a simple goal. C is a *coalition of agents* interacting together to achieve the goal in the system. Also the agents in a coalition share the knowledge gained by reading system propositions or performing actions. The specification $\langle w(\boldsymbol{v})\rangle$ means $w(\boldsymbol{v})$ is readable by at least one of the agents in the coalition. *Initial states* are the states that satisfy the literals in $\{W_s\}$. Every literal W is optionally tagged with * when the value of atomic formula is fixed during verification, and/or tagged with ! when the value is initially known by at least one of the agents in the outermost coalition.

Example 2. One of the properties for a proper conference paper review system policy is that the reviewers (rev) of a paper should not be able to read other submitted reviews (submittedR) before they submit their own reviews. Consider the following query:

$$\{\text{chair}(c)*!, \neg\text{author}(p, a)*, \text{submittedR}(p, b), \text{rev}(p, a), \neg\text{submittedR}(p, a)\} \rightarrow$$
$$\{a\} : (\langle\text{review}(p, b)\rangle \wedge \neg\text{submittedR}(p, a) \text{ THEN } \{a, c\} : (\text{submittedR}(p, a)))$$

The query says "starting from the initial states provided, is there any reachable state that agent a can promote himself in such a way that he will be able to read the review of the agent b for paper p while he has not submitted his own review and after that, agent a and c collaborate together so that agent a can submit his review of paper p?". If the specification is satisfiable, then there exists a security hole in the policy and should be fixed by policy designers. In the above query, the value of chair(c) and author(p, a) is fixed and chair(c) is known to be true by the agent a at the beginning.

Instantiation of the Policy Query: An *instantiated query* or simply *query* is the policy query instantiated with a substitution. The query $i \rightarrow g$ is the instantiation of policy query $I \rightarrow G$ with substitution σ if $i = I\sigma$ and $g = G\sigma$.

For the query $i \rightarrow g$, we say g is *satisfiable* in an access control system if there exists a conditional sequence of actions called *strategy* (defined below) that makes the agents in the coalitions achieve the goal beginning from the initial states. The strategy is presented formally by the following syntax:

$$\textit{strategy} ::= \text{null} \mid a; \textit{strategy} \mid \text{if}(p)\ \{\textit{strategy}\}\ \text{else}\ \{\textit{strategy}\}$$

In the above syntax, p is an atomic proposition and a is an action. If a strategy contains a condition over the proposition p, it means the value of p determines the next required action to achieve the goal. p is known as an *effective proposition* in our methodology.

Definition 6. *(Transition relation). Let $s_1, s_2 \in S$ where S is the set of states, and ξ be a strategy. We use $s_1 \rightarrow_\xi s_2$ to denote "strategy ξ can be run in state s_1 and result in s_2", which is defined inductively as follows:*

- $s \rightarrow_{null} s$.
- $s \rightarrow_{a;\xi_1} s'$ *if*
  - *a is permitted to be performed in state s and*
  - *$s'' \rightarrow_{\xi_1} s'$ where s'' is the result of performing a in s.*
- $s \rightarrow_{if(p)\{\xi_1\}\ else\ \{\xi_2\}} s'$ *if:*
  - *If $s(p) = \top$ then $s \rightarrow_{\xi_1} s'$ else $s \rightarrow_{\xi_2} s'$.*

A set of states st_2 is reachable *from set of states st_1 through strategy ξ ($st_1 \rightarrow_\xi st_2$) if for all $s_1 \in st_1$ there exists $s_2 \in st_2$ such that $s_1 \rightarrow_\xi s_2$.*

Definition 7. *(State formula). If S is the set of states and $st \subseteq S$ then:*

- *f_{st} is a formula satisfying exactly the states in st: $s \in st \leftrightarrow s \models f_{st}$.*
- *st_f is the set of states satisfying f: $s \in st_f \leftrightarrow s \models f$.*

4 Model-Checking and Strategy Synthesis

Our method uses backward search to find a strategy. The algorithm begins from the goal states st_g and finds all the states with transition to the current state, called pre-states. The algorithm continues finding pre-states over all found states until it gets all the initial states (success) or no new state could be found (fail).

The model-checking problem in this research is not a simple reachability question. As illustrated in Figure 1, the strategy is successful only if it works for all the outcomes of reading or guessing a proposition in the model. Thus, reading/guessing behaviour produces the need for a universal quantifier, while actions are existentially quantified. The resulting requirement has an alternation of universal and existential quantifiers of arbitrary length, and this cannot be expressed using standard temporal logics such as CTL, LTL or ATL.

Notation 2. *Assume f is a propositional formula. Then $p \in prop(f)$ if proposition p occurs in all formulas equivalent to f.*

Definition 8. *(Transition system). If action a is defined as $a : e \leftarrow f$ and st is a set of states, $PRE_a^\exists(st)$ is the set of states in which action a is permitted to perform and performing the action will make a transition to one of the states in st by changing the values of the propositions in the effect of the action. Let Lit^* be the set of literals that are tagged by $*$ in the query. Then:*

$$PRE_a^\exists(st) = \left\{ s \in S \mid s \models f, \forall l \in Lit^* : s \models l, s[p \mapsto \top \mid +p \in e][p \mapsto \bot \mid -p \in e] \in st \right\}$$

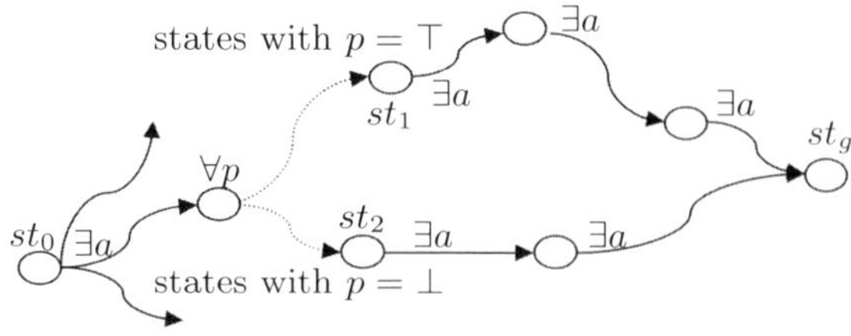

Fig. 1. Strategy finding method. Ovals represent sets of states. Solid lines show the existence of an action that makes a transition between two sets of states. Dashed lines are universally quantified over the outcome of reading or guessing the value of proposition p.

4.1 Finding Effective Propositions

Definition 9. *(Effective proposition). Atomic proposition p is* effective *with respect to st_0 as the set of initial states and st_g as the set of goal states if there exist a set of states st and strategies ξ_0, ξ_1 and ξ_2 such that $\xi_1 \neq \xi_2$ and:*

- $st_0 \rightarrow_{\xi_0} st$,
- $st \cap \{s \mid s(p) = \top\} \rightarrow_{\xi_1} st_g$,
- $st \cap \{s \mid s(p) = \bot\} \rightarrow_{\xi_2} st_g$ *and*
- $st \cap \{s \mid s(p) = \top\} \neq \emptyset,\ st \cap \{s \mid s(p) = \bot\} \neq \emptyset$.

Effective propositions are important for the following reason:

The value of proposition p is not specified in the query and is not known by the agents at the beginning. The agents need to know the value of p to select the appropriate strategy to achieve the goal. In the states of st, if the agent (or coalition of agents) knows the value of p, he will perform the next action without taking any risk. Otherwise, he needs to guess the value of p. This situation is risky and in the case of a wrong decision and may not be repeatable.

The algorithm provided in this paper is capable of finding effective propositions while searching for strategies, and then, is able to verify the knowledge of the agents about effective propositions in the decision states.

Proposition 1. *Let st_1, st_2 and st_g be sets of states and ξ_1 and ξ_2 be strategies such that $st_1 \rightarrow_{\xi_1} st_g$ and $st_2 \rightarrow_{\xi_2} st_g$. Suppose $p \in prop(f_{st_1}) \cap prop(f_{st_2})$, $st_d = st_{f_{st_1[\top/p]}} \cap st_{f_{st_2[\bot/p]}}$ and $s \in st_d$. Then if $s(p) = \top$, we conclude that $s \rightarrow_{\xi_1} st_g$, otherwise $s \rightarrow_{\xi_2} st_g$ will be concluded.*

Proof. A complete proof using structural induction is provided in [12].

Let st_g in proposition 1 be the set of goal states, st_d the set of states found according to the proposition 1 and st_0 the set of initial states. If there exist a strategy ξ_0 such that $st_0 \rightarrow_{\xi_0} st_d$, then by definition 9, the atomic proposition p is an effective proposition and therefore $st_d \rightarrow_{\text{if}(p)\ \{\xi_1\}\ \text{else}\ \{\xi_2\}} st_g$. The states in st_d are called *decision states*.

Example 3. Let $(T, Pred, A, R)$ be a simple policy for changing password in a system, where:

$$T = \{\text{Agent}\}$$
$$Pred = \{\text{permission}(a : \text{Agent}), \text{trick}(a : \text{Agent}), \text{passChanged}(a : \text{Agent})\}$$
$$A = \{\text{setTrick}(a) : \{+\text{trick}(a)\} \leftarrow \neg\text{permission}(a),$$
$$\text{changePass}(a) : \{+\text{passChanged}(a)\} \leftarrow \text{permission}(a) \vee \text{trick}(a)\}$$

We have excluded read permission rules, as they are not required in this particular example. In the above policy, the administrator of the system has defined a permission for changing password. The permission declares that one of the propositions permission(a) or trick(a) is needed for changing password. permission(a) is write protected for the agents and no action is defined for changing it. If an agent does not have permission to change his password, he can set trick(a) to true first and then, he will be able to change the password. This can be seen as a mistake in the policy.

Consider that we have just one object of type Agent in the system ($\Sigma_{Agent} = \{a_1\}$) and we want to verify the query $\{\} \rightarrow \{a\} : (\text{passChanged}(a))$. The only possible instantiation of the query is when a is assigned to a_1. As the initial condition is empty, the set of initial states contain all the system states ($st_0 = S$). The following procedures show how the strategy can be found:

$$f_{st_g} = \text{passChanged}(a_1)$$

We can find one set of states as the pre-state of st_g:

$$f_{PRE^{\exists}_{\text{changePass}(a_1)}(st_g)} = f_{st_1} = \text{permission}(a_1) \vee \text{trick}(a_1)$$

$$st_1 \rightarrow_{\text{changePass}(a_1)} st_g$$

f_{st_g} and f_{st_1} don't share any proposition and hence, there is no effective proposition occurring in both of them together. For the set st_1, we can find one pre-set:

$$f_{PRE^{\exists}_{\text{setTrick}(a_1)}(st_1)} = f_{st_2} = \neg\text{permission}(a_1)$$

$$st_2 \rightarrow_{\text{setTrick}(a_1);\text{changePass}(a_1)} st_g$$

The next step is to look for effective propositions occurring in f_{st_1} and f_{st_2}. For $p = \text{permission}(a_1)$ we have:

$$f_{st_1}[\top/p] = \top, f_{st_2}[\bot/p] = \top, f_{st_1}[\top/p] \wedge f_{st_2}[\bot/p] = \top$$

$$st_3 = st_\top = S \qquad st_3 \rightarrow_\xi st_g$$

$$\xi = \text{if}(\text{permission}(a_1))\{\text{changePass}(a_1)\} \text{ else } \{\text{setTrick}(a_1); \text{changePass}(a_1)\}$$

Since $st_0 \subseteq st_3$, the goal is reachable and we output the strategy.

Backward Search Transition Filtering: If an action changes a proposition, the value of the proposition will be known for the rest of the strategy. So in backward search algorithm, we filter out the transitions that alter effective propositions before their corresponding decision states are reached.

4.2 Pseudocode for Finding Strategy

Consider P as the set of atomic propositions, A_C the set of all the actions that the agents in coalition C can perform, st_0 the set of initial states and st_g the set of goal states for simple goal g. K_C contains the propositions known by the agents in coalition C at the beginning (tagged with ! in the query). The triple (st, ξ, efv) is called *state strategy* which keeps the set of states st found during backward search, the strategy ξ to reach the goal from st and the set of effective propositions efv occurring in ξ. The pseudocode for the strategy finding algorithm is as follows:

input: P, A_C, st_0, st_g, K_C
output: strategy
state_strategies:=$\{(st_g, \text{null}, \emptyset)\}$
states_seen:=$\emptyset$
old_strategies:=$\emptyset$

while old_strategies$\neq$state_strategies **do**
  old_strategies:=state_strategies
  for all $(st_1, \xi_1, efv_1) \in state\_strategies$ **do**
    for all $a \in A_C$ **do**
      if $effect(a) \cap efv_1 = \emptyset$ **then**
        $PRE := PRE_a^{\exists}(st_1)$
        if $PRE \neq \emptyset$ and $PRE \not\subseteq states\_seen$ **then**
          $states\_seen := states\_seen \cup PRE$
          $\xi :=$ "a;" $+ \xi_1$
          $state\_strategies := state\_strategies \cup \{(PRE, \xi, efv_1)\}$
          if $st_0 \subseteq PRE$ **then**
            output ξ
          end if
        end if
      end if
    end for

    for all $(st_2, \xi_2, efv_2) \in state\_strategies$ **do**
      for all $p \in P \backslash K_C$ **do**
        if $p \in prop(f_{st_1}) \cap prop(f_{st_2})$ **then**
          $PRE := st_{f_{st_1[\top/p]}} \cap st_{f_{st_2[\bot/p]}}$
          if $PRE \neq \emptyset$ and $PRE \not\subseteq states\_seen$ **then**
            $states\_seen := states\_seen \cup PRE$
            $\xi :=$ "if(p)" $+ \xi_1 +$ "else" $+ \xi_2$
            $state\_strategies := state\_strategies \cup \{(PRE, \xi, efv_1 \cup efv_2 \cup \{p\})\}$
            if $st_0 \subseteq PRE$ **then**
              output ξ
            end if
          end if

```
            end if
          end for
        end for
      end for
    end while
```

The outermost while loop checks the fixed point of the algorithm, where no more state (or equivalently, state strategy) could be found in backward search. Inside the while loop, the algorithm traverses the state strategy set that contains $(st_g, \text{null}, \emptyset)$ at the beginning. For each state strategy (st, ξ, efv), it finds all the possible pre-states for st and appends the corresponding state strategies to the set. It also finds effective propositions and decision states by performing pairwise analysis between all the members of the state strategy set based on the proposition 1. The strategy will be returned if the initial states are found in backward search. The proof for the termination, soundness (If the algorithm outputs a strategy, it can be run over st_0 and results in st_g) and completeness (If some strategy exists from st_0 to st_g, then the algorithm will find one) is provided in [12].

Verification of the Nested Goals: To verify a nested goal, we begin from the inner-most goal. By backward search, all backward reachable states will be found and their intersection with the states for the outer goal will construct the new set of goal states. For the outer-most goal, we look for the initial states between backward reachable states. If we find them, we output the strategy. Otherwise, the nested goal is unreachable.

5 Knowledge vs. Guessing in Strategy

Agents in a coalition know the value of a proposition if: they have read the value before, or they have performed an action that has affected that proposition[3]. If a strategy is found, we are able to verify the knowledge of the agents over the strategy and specifically for effective propositions, using read permissions defined in the policy. Read permissions don't lead to any transition or action, and are used just to detect if an agent or coalition of agents can find out the way to the goal with complete or partial knowledge of the system. The knowledge is shared between the agents in a coalition.

To find agent knowledge over effective propositions, we begin from the initial states, run the strategy and verify the ability of the coalition to read the effective propositions. If at least one of the agents in the coalition can read an effective proposition before or at the corresponding decision states, then the coalition can find the path without taking any risk. In the lack of knowledge, agents should guess the value in order to find the next required action along the strategy.

Pseudocode for Knowledge Verification over the Strategy: Let g be a simple goal and $(st_0, \xi, \mathit{efv})$ be the state strategy where st_0 is the set of initial

[3] In this research, we do not consider reasoning about knowledge like the one in interpreted systems. This approach makes the concept of knowledge weaker, but more efficient to verify.

states, $st_0 \rightarrow_\xi st_g$ and *efv* is the set of effective propositions occurring in ξ. If C is the coalition of agents and K_C the knowledge of the coalition at the beginning, then the recursive function "KnowledgeAlgo" returns an annotated strategy with a string "Guess:" added to the beginning of every "if" statement in ξ, where the coalition does not know the value of the proposition inside if statement.

```
input: st_0, ξ, efv, C, K_C
output: Annotated strategy ξ'

function KnowledgeAlgo(st, ξ, efv, C, K_C)
  if ξ=null then
    return null
  end if
  for all p ∈ efv, u_1 ∈ C do
    for all read permissions ρ(u_1, o) : p ← f do
      if st ⊨ f then
        K_C := K_C ∪ {p}
      end if
    end for
  end for
  if ξ = a; ξ_1 then
    st' :=result of performing action a in st
    return "a;"+
        KnowledgeAlgo(st', ξ_1, efv, C, K_C ∪ effect(a))
  else if ξ = if(p){ξ_1} else {ξ_2} then
    if p ∈ K_C then
      str :=""
    else
      str :="Guess: "
    end if
    return str+ "if(p){"+
       KnowledgeAlgo(st_{f_st ∧ p}, ξ_1, efv\{p}, C, K_C) + "} else {"+
       KnowledgeAlgo(st_{f_st ∧ ¬p}, ξ_2, efv\{p}, C, K_C) +"}"
  end if
end function
```

Knowledge Verification for Nested Goals: To handle knowledge verification over the strategies found by nested goal verification, we begin from the outermost goal. We traverse over the strategy until the goal states are reached. For the next goal, all the accumulated knowledge will be transferred to the new coalition if there exists at least one common agent between the two coalitions. The algorithm proceeds until the strategy is fully traversed.

	RW(Algo-1)		PoliVer algorithm	
Query	Time	Memory	Time	Memory
Query 4.2	2.05	18.18	0.27	3.4
Query 4.3	0.46	9.01	0.162	6.68
Query 4.4	6.45	59.95	0.52	6.61
Query 6.4	9.10	102.35	0.8	12.92
Query 6.8	20.44	222.02	0.488	7.30

Fig. 2. A comparison of query verification time (in second) and runtime memory usage (in MB) between RW and PoliVer

6 Experimental Results

We implemented the algorithms as a policy verification tool called *PoliVer* by modifying the AcPeg model-checker, which is an open source tool written in Java. First, we changed the parser in order to define actions and read permissions in the policy as in section 3.1. The query language also changed to support queries of the form defined in section 3.3. Second, we implemented the strategy finding algorithm in the core of AcPeg and then, applied knowledge verification algorithm over strategies found.

One of the outcomes of the implementation was the considerable reduction of binary decision diagram (BDD) variable size compared to RW. In RW, there are 7 knowledge states per proposition and therefore, an access control system with n propositions contains 7^n different states. Our simplification of knowledge-state variables results in 2^n states. The post-processing time for knowledge verification over found strategies is negligible compared to the whole process of strategy finding, while produces more expressive results.

We encoded authorization policies for a conference review system (CRS), employee information system (EIS) and student information system (SIS) in [1] into our policy language. We compared the performance in terms of verification time and memory usage for the queries: Query 4.2 for CRS with 7 objects (3 papers and 4 agents) that looks for strategies which an agent can promote himself to become a reviewer of a paper, Query 4.3 for CRS which is a nested query that asks if a reviewer can submit his review for a paper while he has read the review of someone else before, Query 4.4 with 4 objects for CRS with five-level nested queries that checks if an agents can be assigned as a pcmember by the chair and then resign his membership, Query 6.4 with 18 objects for EIS which evaluates if two managers can collaborate to set a bonus for one of them and Query 6.8 for SIS with 10 objects that asks if a lecturer can assign two students as the demonstrator of each other.

Figure 2 shows a considerable reduction in time and memory usage by the proposed algorithm compared to Algo-1 in RW (Algo-1 has slightly better performance and similar memory usage compared to Algo-0). As a disadvantage for both systems, the verification time and state space grow exponentially when more objects are added. But this situation in our algorithm is much better than RW. Our experimental results demonstrates the correctness of our claim in

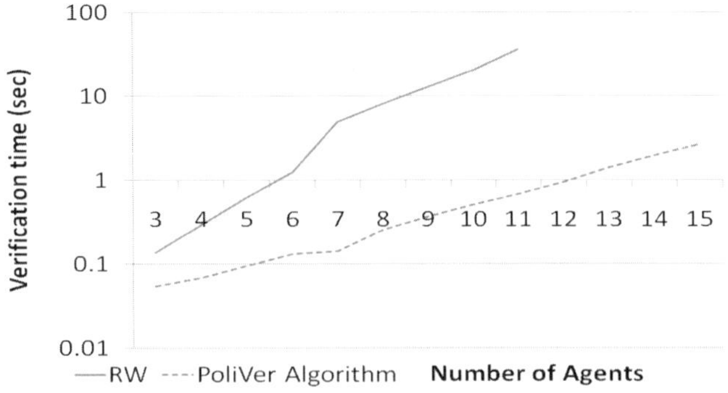

Fig. 3. Verification time vs. number of agents for RW and PoliVer (Query 6.8)

practice by comparing the verification time of Query 6.8 for different number of agents. Figure 3 sketches the verification time for both algorithms for different number of agents in logarithmic scale. The verification time in RW increases as 2.5^n where n is the number of agents added, while the time increases as 1.4^n in our algorithm. Note that this case study does not show the worst case behaviour when the number of agents increases[4].

7 Conclusion and Future Work

Our language and tool is optimised for analysing the access control policies of web-based collaborative systems such Facebook, LinkedIn and Easychair. These systems are likely to become more and more critical in the future, so analysing them is important. More specifically, in this work:

- We have developed a policy language and verification algorithm, which is also implemented as a tool. The algorithm produces evidence (in the form of a strategy) when the system satisfies a property.
- We remove the requirement to reason explicitly about knowledge, approximating it with the simpler requirement to reason about readability as it is sufficient in many cases. Compared to RW that has 7^n states, we have only 2^n states in our approach (where n is the number of propositions). Also, complicated properties can be evaluated over the policy by the query language provided.
- We detect the vulnerabilities in the policy that enable an attacker to discover the strategy to achieve the goal, when some required information is not accessible. We introduce the concept of effective propositions to detect such vulnerabilities.
- A set of propositions can be updated in one action. In the RW framework, each write action can update only one proposition at a time.

[4] The tool, case studies and technical reports are accessible at: `http://www.cs.bham.ac.uk/ mdr/research/projects/11-AccessControl/poliver/`

Future Work: For the next step, we intend to cover large applications like Facebook and Easychair in our case studies.

Acknowledgements. We would like to thank Microsoft Research as Masoud Koleini is supported by a Microsoft PhD scholarship. We also thank Moritz Becker and Tien Tuan Anh Dinh for their useful comments and Joshua Phillips for the performance and quality testing of the release version of PoliVer.

References

1. Zhang, N., Ryan, M., Guelev, D.P.: Synthesising verified access control systems through model checking. J. Comput. Secur. 16(1), 1–61 (2008)
2. Becker, M.Y.: Specification and analysis of dynamic authorisation policies. In: CSF 2009: Proceedings of the 2009 22nd IEEE Computer Security Foundations Symposium, pp. 203–217. IEEE Computer Society, Washington, DC, USA (2009)
3. Dougherty, D.J., Fisler, K., Krishnamurthi, S.: Specifying and reasoning about dynamic access-control policies. In: Furbach, U., Shankar, N. (eds.) IJCAR 2006. LNCS (LNAI), vol. 4130, pp. 632–646. Springer, Heidelberg (2006)
4. Naldurg, P., Campbell, R.H.: Dynamic access control: preserving safety and trust for network defense operations. In: SACMAT 2003: Proceedings of the Eighth ACM Symposium on Access Control Models and Technologies, pp. 231–237. ACM, New York (2003)
5. Fisler, K., Krishnamurthi, S., Meyerovich, L.A., Tschantz, M.C.: Verification and change-impact analysis of access-control policies. In: ICSE 2005: Proceedings of the 27th International Conference on Software Engineering, pp. 196–205. ACM, New York (2005)
6. Becker, M.Y., Gordon, A.D., Fournet, C.: SecPAL: Design and semantics of a decentralised authorisation language. Technical report, Microsoft Research, Cambridge (September 2006)
7. Li, N., Mitchell, J.C., Winsborough, W.H.: Design of a role-based trust management framework. In: Proceedings of the 2002 IEEE Symposium on Security and Privacy, pp. 114–130. IEEE Computer Society Press, Los Alamitos (2002)
8. Bell, D., LaPadula., L.J.: Secure computer systems: Mathematical foundations and model. Technical report, The Mitre Corporation (1976)
9. Bell, D.E.: Looking back at the bell-la padula model. In: ACSAC 2005: Proceedings of the 21st Annual Computer Security Applications Conference, pp. 337–351. IEEE Computer Society, Washington, DC, USA (2005)
10. Becker, M.Y., Nanz, S.: A logic for state-modifying authorization policies. ACM Trans. Inf. Syst. Secur. 13(3), 1–28 (2010)
11. Fox, M., Long, D.: Pddl2.1: An extension to pddl for expressing temporal planning domains. Journal of Artificial Intelligence Research 20, 61–124 (2003)
12. Koleini, M., Ryan, M.: A knowledge-based verification method for dynamic access control policies. Technical report, University of Birmingham, School of Computer Science (2010), http://www.cs.bham.ac.uk/~mdr/research/projects/11-AccessControl/poliver/

Validation of Security-Design Models Using Z

Nafees Qamar[1,2], Yves Ledru[1], and Akram Idani[1]

[1] UJF-Grenoble 1/Grenoble-INP/UPMF-Grenoble2/CNRS, LIG UMR 5217, F-38041, Grenoble, France
{Muhammad-Nafees.Qamar,Yves.Ledru,Akram.Idani}@imag.fr
[2] INRIA Rhône Alpes, Grenoble, France

Abstract. This paper is aimed at formally specifying and validating security-design models of an information system. It combines graphical languages and formal methods, integrating specification languages such as UML and an extension, SecureUML, with the Z language. The modeled system addresses both functional and security requirements of a given application. The formal functional specification is built automatically from the UML diagram, using our RoZ tool. The secure part of the model instanciates a generic security-kernel written in Z, free from applications specificity, which models the concepts of RBAC (Role-Based Access Control). The final modeling step creates a link between the functional model and the instanciated security kernel. Validation is performed by animating the model, using the Jaza tool. Our approach is demonstrated on a case-study from the health care sector where confidentiality and integrity appear as core challenges to protect medical records.

1 Introduction

In secure information systems, specifications include functional aspects, describing how information is processed, and security aspects, modelling a security policy. Security policies are often described using access control rules. In this paper, we focus on the use of SecureUML [3], a UML profile for RBAC (Role-Based Access Control) [7] to describe access control rules. Separation of concerns tends to separate functional and security models. But, in SecureUML, authorization rules of the security model may refer to contextual elements of the functional one. One of the key considerations in secure systems development is thus to produce an integrated model of functional and non-functional aspects. This gives rise to the concept of security-design models (e.g.,[9], [3]). Such models can be used to validate the security policy, in the context of the functional model, and to study how the integrated system would react to attacks.

This paper tries to incorporate the precision of formal languages into intuitive graphical models. SecureUML [3] expresses functional and security models as UML diagrams. In this paper, we show how these diagrams can be translated into a single formal specification, expressed in the Z language [16]. We then use Jaza [18] to animate the model and contribute to its validation. Validation is performed by asking queries about the access control rules, as done in the SecureMova tool [4], and by playing scenarios, which lead the system through several

S. Qin and Z. Qiu (Eds.): ICFEM 2011, LNCS 6991, pp. 259–274, 2011.

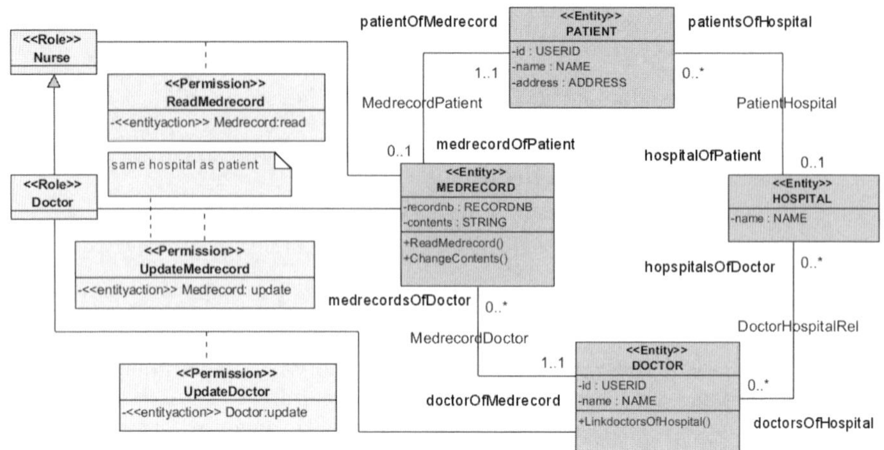

Fig. 1. Security policy model using SecureUML

state changes and involve both security and functional models. Such dynamic scenarios can exhibit security flaws, which cannot be detected by static queries. A companion paper [11] describes these validation activities using animation, while the current paper focuses on the underlying Z specification.

In the past, we developed RoZ, a tool which transforms a UML class diagram, annotated with Z assertions, into a Z specification [6]. The resulting Z specifications can be animated using Jaza [10]. Our mid-term goal is to upgrade RoZ in order to address security concerns in our UML models. Our security model is based on SecureUML [3], a UML profile for RBAC [7]. Several works [7],[1],[13] attempt to specify RBAC in Z. Most of them specify the RBAC meta-model. As far as we know, none of these has been used in conjunction with an animator in order to validate a given security policy. So our goal is not to model or validate RBAC itself, but to validate security policies expressed as RBAC rules in the context of a functional specification. Several tools exploit OCL in order to validate RBAC rules. Sohr et al [15] have adapted the USE OCL tool for the analysis of security policies. SecureMova [4],a tool dedicated to SecureUML, allows one to query the security policy, and to evaluate which actions are permitted for a given role in a given context, depicted as an object diagram. Still, both tools don't animate the operations of the functional model, making it difficult to evaluate how evolutions of the functional state can impact authorization rules.

This paper presents our translation of functional and security models into Z and how these can be validated, using the Jaza animator. Our approach has the following goals: (1) to start from an intuitive graphical specification which features both functional and security models, 2) to systematically construct a formal specification of the integrated system from the graphical model, and 3) to use queries and animation to validate the integrated model. It must be noted that we currently focus on validation, i.e. confront our model to the user, and

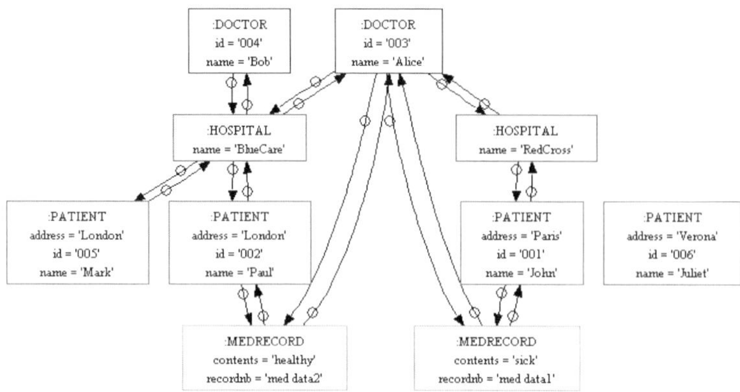

Fig. 2. Object diagram for the functional model produced from the output of Jaza

ensure that it exhibits the expected behaviour. Although we use formal methods, we don't address verification (i.e. prove that the system is right) at this stage.

The paper is structured as follows. Sect. 2 introduces an illustrative example. Sect. 3 recalls the principles of the translation of the functional model, while Sect. 4 features the specification of the security kernel. The integration of both models is described in Sect. 5. Sect. 6 features the validation activities, based on animation. Finally, Sect. 7 and 8 present related work and conclusion.

2 Illustrative Example: Medical Information System

Fig. 1 models a simple medical information system using SecureUML [3]. The figure has two sides where functional features on the right, are decoupled from security features on the left. The functional part describes four classes : patients, doctors, hospitals and medical records. Each medical record corresponds to exactly one patient. Its field *contents* stores confidential information whose integrity must be preserved. The functional part also records the current hospital hosting the patient, the doctors working in this hospital, and the one responsible for the patient's medical record. Fig. 2 gives an object diagram corresponding to this functional model. It features 4 patients, 2 doctors (Alice and Bob), 2 medical records, and 2 hospitals. Alice is linked to both hospitals, while Bob only works for one of them.

The left part of Fig. 1 describes the access control rules of the information system. In SecureUML and RBAC, users of the system are abstracted into roles, and permissions are granted to roles. Fig. 1 features two roles : *Nurse* and *Doctor*. An inheritance relation links *Doctor* to *Nurse*, expressing that doctors inherit all permissions of nurses. Confidentiality and integrity must be ensured for medical records. Two permissions rule the access to class *MEDRECORD*. Permission *ReadMedRecord* is granted to nurses (and inherited by doctors). It expresses that nurses and doctors have read access to medical records. It refers to *entity action read* which designates operations accessing the class without modifying it. Although the security part of Fig. 1 uses the graphical syntax of UML (classes and association classes), elements stereotyped as roles or permissions only make sense for security concerns. For example, there will not be objects of type *Nurse* in our animations, but there will be users playing this role. Similarly, the associative class *ReadMedrecord* is simply a graphical notation to express the permissions associated to nurses and related to medical records.

Permission *UpdateMedrecord* grants additional rights to doctors, who may update medical records. Constraint "*Same hospital as patient*" restricts this permission to the doctors linked to the same hospital as the patient. In Fig. 2, it means that only Alice may modify the medical record of John, numbered "med data1", because she is the only doctor linked to RedCross hospital. In SecureUML, such constraints are expressed in OCL; here, they will be expressed in the Z language. In Fig. 1, a third permission named *UpdateDoctor* grants to all doctors full access, i.e. read and update access, to objects of class *DOCTOR*.

Validation studies normal and malicious behaviours. In this paper, besides some nominal scenarios, we study the following attack: Bob, a malicious doctor, wants to corrupt the integrity of John's medical record. Since Bob is not working for RedCross hospital, the access control rules should forbid this modification.

3 Translating the Functional Model into Z

The following sections describe how the integrated graphical model of Fig. 1 is translated into a Z specification. First, the RoZ tool automatically translates the functional model, corresponding to the right part of Fig. 1. RoZ [6] transforms a UML class diagram, annotated with Z assertions, into a single Z specification. An optional feature of the tool also generates basic operations such as setters and getters for the attributes and the associations. These basic operations are often implicitly included in a class diagram; so the tool avoids the analyst to manually specify each of these operations. One may fear that, in a security context, these additional operations augment the "attack surface" of the application. In such a case, the analyst can choose to disable their optional generation, or to exclude them from the set of operations linked to the access control model (Sect. 5).

Here are some elements of the formal specification generated from the functional diagram of the medical record information system. First, the types of the class attributes are introduced as given types.

$[NAME, USERID, STRING, RECORDNB]$

```
┌─ MEDRECORD ─────────────────
│ recordnb : RECORDNB
│ contents : STRING
└─────────────────────────────

┌─ DOCTOR ────────────────────
│ id : USERID
│ name : NAME
└─────────────────────────────

┌─ MedrecordExt ──────────────
│ Medrecord : 𝔽 MEDRECORD
└─────────────────────────────

┌─ DoctorExt ─────────────────
│ Doctor : 𝔽 DOCTOR
└─────────────────────────────
```

Every class is translated into two Z schemas. The first one, a schema type, describes the type of the elements of the class. This schema corresponds to the class intent and lists the class attributes. Schemas *MEDRECORD* and *DOCTOR* describe the intent of the corresponding classes. A second schema describes the extension of the class, i.e. the set of objects belonging to the class. Schemas *MedrecordExt* and *DoctorExt* correspond to these extensions; each of these includes a finite set of objects corresponding to the type of the class.

During a Jaza animation, each object is represented as a list of pairs *attribute* == *value*. The list is enclosed between $\lblot \ldots \rblot$. Here is the Jaza representation of sets *Doctor* and *Medrecord* corresponding to the state of Fig. 2.

$$\begin{array}{l} Doctor' == \{\lblot\ id == \text{"003"}, name == \text{"}Alice\text{"}\ \rblot, \lblot\ id == \text{"004"}, name == \text{"}Bob\text{"}\ \rblot\} \\ Medrecord' == \{\lblot\ contents == \text{"}healthy\text{"}, recordnb == \text{"}meddata2\text{"}\ \rblot, \\ \qquad\qquad\qquad \lblot\ contents == \text{"}sick\text{"}, recordnb == \text{"}meddata1\text{"}\ \rblot\} \end{array}$$

UML associations are translated by RoZ as a pair of functions corresponding to both roles of the association. For example, functions *hospitalsOfDoctor* and *doctorsOfHospital* describe the association between doctors and hospitals. Their domain and range are constrained by predicates of the schema. Additional predicates express that the inverse role can be constructed from the direct one.[1]

DoctorHospitalRel

$$\begin{array}{l} HospitalExt;\ DoctorExt \\ hospitalsOfDoctor : DOCTOR \pfun \mathbb{F}\, HOSPITAL \\ doctorsOfHospital : HOSPITAL \pfun \mathbb{F}\, DOCTOR \\ \hline \mathrm{dom}\, hospitalsOfDoctor \subseteq Doctor \land \bigcup(\mathrm{ran}\, hospitalsOfDoctor) \subseteq Hospital \\ \ldots \end{array}$$

Here is how Jaza represents role *doctorsOfHospital* corresponding to Fig. 2.

$$\begin{array}{l} doctorsOfHospital' == \\ \qquad \{(\lblot\ name == \text{"}BlueCare\text{"}\ \rblot, \{\lblot\ id == \text{"003"}, name == \text{"}Alice\text{"}\ \rblot, \\ \qquad\qquad\qquad \lblot\ id == \text{"004"}, name == \text{"}Bob\text{"}\ \rblot\}), \\ \qquad (\lblot\ name == \text{"}RedCross\text{"}\ \rblot,\ \{\lblot\ id == \text{"003"}, name == \text{"}Alice\text{"}\ \rblot\})\} \end{array}$$

Finally, we give several specifications of operations. *MRChangeContents* is a setter for field *contents*. This operation, which works on the type of medical records, must be "promoted" to impact the actual contents of the class extension, and to modify the related associations. *MRChangeContentsP*, the promoted operation takes an additional input $x?$ designating the object to modify[2].

MRChangeContents

$$\begin{array}{l} \Delta MEDRECORD \\ newcontents? : STRING \\ \hline contents' = newcontents? \land recordnb' = recordnb \end{array}$$

$$MRChangeContentsP == MRChangeContents \land \ldots$$

[1] These predicates are omitted for space reasons.

[2] For more information on operation promotion please refer to Wordsworth's text [19] page 137.

Operation *DRLinkDoctors* creates a link between a doctor and an hospital. Its predicates distinguish between the case where a first doctor is linked to the hospital, and the case where doctors were already linked to this hospital.

$$
\begin{array}{l}
\textbf{DRLinkDoctors} \\
\hline
\Xi HospitalExt;\ \Xi DoctorExt;\ \Delta DoctorHospitalRel \\
hospital? : HOSPITAL;\ doctor? : DOCTOR \\
\hline
(hospital? \notin \operatorname{dom} doctorsOfHospital) \Rightarrow \\
\quad (doctorsOfHospital' = doctorsOfHospital \oplus \{hospital? \mapsto \{doctor?\}\}) \\
(hospital? \in \operatorname{dom} doctorsOfHospital) \Rightarrow \\
\quad (doctorsOfHospital' = doctorsOfHospital \oplus \{hospital? \mapsto \\
\qquad (doctorsOfHospital(hospital?) \cup \{doctor?\})\})
\end{array}
$$

These operations are sufficiently detailed to animate the model with Jaza. After several steps, one may end up with a state corresponding to Fig. 2. Nevertheless, these operations don't take into account the access control rules. In particular, they are not aware of which user is executing them. This will be the responsibility of the security kernel described in the next section.

4 The Security Kernel

The translation process proceeds with the security part of Fig. 1. Our approach is based on a reusable security kernel which specifies the main concepts of RBAC in Z. This security kernel is instantiated with the roles, permissions, resources and operations of the SecureUML diagram.

4.1 Permissions

A *permission assignment* links a *role* to an *operation* on a given *class*, also called the protected *resource*. These four types are introduced in Z as given types or as enumerated types. When considering enumerated types, the values of the type must be extracted from the UML diagram in order to instantiate the security kernel. Here are the type declarations corresponding to Fig. 1. Schema *Sets* includes sets of values corresponding to each of these types.

$$
\begin{array}{l}
[PERMISSION] \\
ROLE ::= Doctor \mid Nurse \\
RESOURCE ::= Medrecords \mid Patients \mid \\
\quad Doctors \mid Hospitals \\
ABS\_ACTION ::= EntityRead \mid \\
\quad EntityUpdate \mid EntityFullAccess
\end{array}
$$

$$
\begin{array}{l}
\textbf{Sets} \\
\hline
role : \mathbb{F}\, ROLE \\
resource : \mathbb{F}\, RESOURCE \\
permission : \mathbb{F}\, PERMISSION \\
abs\_action : \mathbb{F}\, ABS\_ACTION \\
\hline
\end{array}
$$

Here are the values of these variables during the Jaza animation, as they appear after the initialisation step.

$abs\_action' == \{EntityFullAccess, EntityRead, EntityUpdate\},$
$permission' == \{"ReadMedrecord", "UpdateDoctor", "UpdateMedrecord"\},$
$resource' == \{Doctors, Hospitals, Medrecords, Patients\},$
$role' == \{Doctor, Nurse\},$

Schema *ActionAssignment* links roles to a tuple made of the name of the permission, the abstract action allowed by the permission and the kind of resource associated to this permission.

$$\begin{array}{l} \text{\_ActionAssignment \_\_\_} \\ action\_Asmt : ROLE \leftrightarrow (PERMISSION \times ABS\_ACTION \times RESOURCE) \end{array}$$

The permissions of Fig. 1 are stored during a Jaza session as:

$$\begin{array}{l} action\_Asmt' == \{(Doctor, ("UpdateDoctor", EntityFullAccess, Doctors)), \\ \quad (Doctor, ("UpdateMedrecord", EntityUpdate, Medrecords)), \\ \quad (Nurse, ("ReadMedrecord", EntityRead, Medrecords))\} \end{array}$$

4.2 Role Hierarchy

RBAC allows us to define hierarchical relations between roles. This is captured by schema *RoleInherits*. The predicates forbid circularity in the role hierarchy, and forbid the use of roles not declared in set *role*.

$$\begin{array}{l} \text{\_RoleInherits \_\_\_} \\ Sets \\ role\_Inherits : ROLE \leftrightarrow ROLE \\ \hline role\_Inherits^{+} \cap \mathrm{id}\, role = \varnothing \\ \mathrm{dom}\, role\_Inherits \subseteq role \wedge \mathrm{ran}\, role\_Inherits \subseteq role \end{array}$$

Fig. 1 features a simple role hierarchy, where role *Doctor* inherits all permissions of *Nurse*. This is expressed in Jaza as:

$role\_Inherits' == \{(Doctor, Nurse)\},$

Schema *InheritAssignment* computes *comp_Asmt* which is *action_Asmt* combined with the inherited permissions.

$$\begin{array}{l} \text{\_InheritAssignment \_\_\_} \\ RoleInherits \\ ActionAssignment \\ comp\_Asmt : ROLE \leftrightarrow (PERMISSION \times ABS\_ACTION \times RESOURCE) \\ \hline comp\_Asmt = \{r : \mathrm{dom}\, action\_Asmt;\ x : role;\ a : \mathrm{ran}\, action\_Asmt \\ \quad \mid ((x \mapsto r) \in ((role\_Inherits^{+}) \cup (\mathrm{id}\, role))) \wedge ((r \mapsto a) \in action\_Asmt) \bullet (x \mapsto a)\} \end{array}$$

In our example, permission *ReadMedrecord* is inherited by doctors from nurses. Relation *comp_Asmt* is initialized by Jaza as:

$$\begin{array}{l} comp\_Asmt' == \{(Doctor, ("ReadMedrecord", EntityRead, Medrecords)), \\ \quad (Doctor, ("UpdateDoctor", EntityFullAccess, Doctors)), \\ \quad (Doctor, ("UpdateMedrecord", EntityUpdate, Medrecords)), \\ \quad (Nurse, ("ReadMedrecord", EntityRead, Medrecords))\}, \end{array}$$

4.3 Action Hierarchy

Permissions of Fig. 1 refer to abstract actions, such as *read* or *update*. These must be linked to their concrete counterparts. Our security kernel expresses this link in *action_Relation*, as well as an action hierarchy (*action_Hierarchy*), defining abstract actions in terms of other abstract actions (e.g. *EntityFullAccess* includes *EntityUpdate* and *EntityRead*). These relations are expressed in schema *ActionsRelation*. We first introduce the enumerated type of atomic actions, corresponding to the methods of *PATIENT* and *MEDRECORD* in Fig. 1.

$ATM\_ACTION ::= MRReadMedrecord1 \mid DRLinkDoctors1 \mid MRChangeContentsP1$

ActionsRelation

$Sets$
$action\_Hierarchy : ABS\_ACTION \leftrightarrow ABS\_ACTION$
$atm\_action : \mathbb{F}\ ATM\_ACTION$
$action\_Relation : ABS\_ACTION \leftrightarrow (ATM\_ACTION \times RESOURCE)$

$action\_Hierarchy^{+} \cap \mathrm{id}\ abs\_action = \varnothing$
$\mathrm{dom}\ action\_Hierarchy \subseteq abs\_action \wedge \mathrm{ran}\ action\_Hierarchy \subseteq abs\_action$
$\mathrm{dom}\ action\_Relation \subseteq abs\_action \wedge \mathrm{ran}\ action\_Relation \subseteq (atm\_action \times resource)$

It must be noted that the correspondance between abstract and concrete actions takes into account the class on which the abstract action is performed. For example, concrete operation *MRReadMedrecord*1 only makes sense for medical records. These relations are instantiated as follows in our example.

$$
\begin{aligned}
action\_Hierarchy' == & \{(EntityRead, EntityFullAccess),\\
& (EntityUpdate, EntityFullAccess)\},\\
action\_Relation' == & \{(EntityRead, (MRReadMedrecord1, Medrecords)),\\
& (EntityUpdate, (MRChangeContentsP1, Medrecords)),\\
& (EntityUpdate, (DRLinkDoctors1, Doctors))\},
\end{aligned}
$$

abstract_Asmt unfolds the hierarchy of abstract actions in *comp_Asmt*. Then *concrete_Asmt* replaces abstract actions by their concrete counterparts for the given kind of resource.

ComputeAssignment

$InheritAssignment;\ ActionsRelation$
$abstract\_Asmt : ROLE \leftrightarrow (PERMISSION \times ABS\_ACTION \times RESOURCE)$
$concrete\_Asmt : ROLE \leftrightarrow (PERMISSION \times ATM\_ACTION \times RESOURCE)$

...

$$
\begin{aligned}
concrete\_Asmt' == &\\
& \{(Doctor, (\text{"}ReadMedrecord\text{"}, MRReadMedrecord1, Medrecords)),\\
& (Doctor, (\text{"}UpdateDoctor\text{"}, DRLinkDoctors1, Doctors)),\\
& (Doctor, (\text{"}UpdateMedrecord\text{"}, MRChangeContentsP1, Medrecords)),\\
& (Nurse, (\text{"}ReadMedrecord\text{"}, MRReadMedrecord1, Medrecords))\},
\end{aligned}
$$

For example, this table tells us that nurses may call *MRReadMedrecord* on class *MEDRECORD*.

Table 1. Three sessions

Session	User	Role	User Id
sess1	Alice	Doctor	003
sess2	Bob	Doctor	004
sess3	Jeck	Nurse	007

4.4 Roles, Users and Sessions

Users of the security kernel must be linked to roles, through sessions. Schema *RoleAssignment* introduces a set of users and relation *role_Asmt* lists the roles a user can take. *SessionRoles* defines sessions and user ids. Type *USERID* already appeared in the functional model and is used to make a link between users taking a role featured in the security part of the model (e.g. *Doctor*), and the classes representing these users in the functional model (e.g. *DOCTOR*). Injective function *accessRights* links user ids to users. Function *session_User* links a session to some user, who has activated a set of roles, recorded in *session_Role*. These roles must correspond to roles allowed to this particular user in *role_Asmt*. Several predicates (omitted for space reasons), associated to these schemas, check the consistency between these variables. Table 1 features several sessions with associated users, roles and ids.

$[USER, SESSION]$

RoleAssignment

$Sets$
$user : \mathbb{F}\ USER$
$role\_Asmt : USER \leftrightarrow ROLE$

...

SessionRoles

$RoleAssignment$
$uid : \mathbb{F}\ USERID;$
$session : \mathbb{F}\ SESSION$
$accessRights : USERID \rightarrowtail\!\!\!\!\!\rightarrow USER$
$session\_User : SESSION \nrightarrow USER$
$session\_Role : ROLE \leftrightarrow SESSION$

...

4.5 Putting It All Together

Schema *PermissionAssignment* computes an entire table of the graphical model given in Fig. 1. It constructs a relation between user identity, user, role and the respective permissions, atomic actions, and the resources. This is achieved using the *concrete_Asmt* relation and linking roles to their users and user ids.

PermissionAssignment

$SessionRoles;\ RoleAssignment;\ ComputeAssignment$
$perm\_Asmt : (USERID \times USER \times ROLE) \leftrightarrow (PERMISSION \times ATM\_ACTION \times RESOURCE)$

$$perm\_Asmt = \{uid : \mathrm{dom}\ accessRights;\ u : \mathrm{dom}\ role\_Asmt;\ r : \mathrm{ran}\ role\_Asmt;\ b : \mathrm{ran}\ concrete\_Asmt \mid (uid, u) \in accessRights \land (u, r) \in role\_Asmt \land (r, b) \in concrete\_Asmt \bullet ((uid, u, r) \mapsto b)\}$$

In our example, *perm_Asmt* is initialized as follows:

$perm\_Asmt' ==$
$\{(("003", "Alice", Doctor), ("ReadMedrecord", MRReadMedrecord1, Medrecords)),$
$(("003", "Alice", Doctor), ("UpdateDoctor", DRLinkDoctors1, Doctors)),$
$(("003", "Alice", Doctor), ("UpdateMedrecord", MRChangeContentsP1, Medrecords)),$
$(("004", "Bob", Doctor), ("ReadMedrecord", MRReadMedrecord1, Medrecords)),$
$(("004", "Bob", Doctor), ("UpdateDoctor", DRLinkDoctors1, Doctors)),$
$(("004", "Bob", Doctor), ("UpdateMedrecord", MRChangeContentsP1, Medrecords)),$
$(("007", "Jeck", Nurse), ("ReadMedrecord", MRReadMedrecord1, Medrecords))\},$

We can now use this table, and the information about sessions, to specify the basis for secure operations. *SecureOperation* actually does nothing: it does neither update the state nor computes a result. It simply states preconditions to allow *user?*, with id *uid?*, acting in a given *role?*, during a given *session?* to perform a given *action?* on a *resource?*, as stated by *permission?*.

SecureOperation

$\Xi SessionRoles;\ \Xi PermissionAssignment$
$session? : SESSION;\ resource? : RESOURCE;\ atm\_action? : ATM\_ACTION$
$role? : ROLE;\ user? : USER;\ uid? : USERID;\ permission? : PERMISSION$

$(session?, user?) \in session\_User$
$(role?, session?) \in session\_Role$
$((uid?, user?, role?), (permission?, atm\_action?, resource?)) \in perm\_Asmt$

SecureOperation will be used in the next section in combination with operations of the functional model.

Another use of tables *perm_Asmt* and *concrete_Asmt* is to perform queries on the access control policy. In a companion paper [11], we feature six such queries, inspired by SecureMova [4]. For example, query *EvaluateActionsAgainstRoles* returns a table listing all roles allowed to perform a given action, and the corresponding permission.

EvaluateActionsAgainstRoles

$\Xi Sets;\ \Xi ComputeAssignment$
$atm\_action? : ATM\_ACTION$
$z\_roles! : ROLE \leftrightarrow (PERMISSION \times ATM\_ACTION \times RESOURCE)$

$z\_roles! = \{r : \mathrm{dom}\, comp\_Asmt;\ p : permission;\ rsrc : resource \mid$
$(r \mapsto (p, atm\_action?, rsrc)) \in concrete\_Asmt \bullet (r \mapsto (p, atm\_action?, rsrc))\}$

This can be evaluated using Jaza. For example, the following query questions about the permissions to call *MRChangeContentsP1*. The answer tells us that only role doctor is allowed to perform this action on medical records.

$;\ EvaluateActionsAgainstRoles[atm\_action? := MRChangeContentsP1]$
$\ldots$
$z\_roles! == \{(Doctor, ("UpdateMedrecord", MRChangeContentsP1, Medrecords))\}$

5 Linking Functional and Security Models

SecureOperation is meant to be included, as a precondition, in the secured version of the operations of the functional model. For example, let us consider the setter method for *contents*, named *MRChangeContentsP*. A secured version of this operation includes the schema of the operation and *SecureOperation*. Schemas *PatientHospitalRel* and *DoctorHospitalRel* are also included to get read access to the associations between hospitals, patients and doctors.

$$
\begin{array}{l}
\textit{SecureMRChangeContentsP} \\
\hline
\textit{SecureOperation} \\
\textit{MRChangeContentsP} \\
\Xi \textit{PatientHospitalRel};\ \Xi \textit{DoctorHospitalRel} \\
\hline
\textit{atm\_action?} = \textit{MRChangeContentsP1} \wedge \textit{resource?} = \textit{Medrecords} \\
\exists\, \textit{hospital} : \textit{Hospital} \mid \textit{hospitalOfPatient}(\textit{patientOfMedrecord}(x?)) = \textit{hospital} \bullet \\
\quad \exists\, \textit{doctor} : \textit{Doctor} \mid \textit{accessRights}^{-1}(\textit{session\_User}(\textit{session?})) = \textit{doctor.id} \bullet \\
\qquad \textit{doctor} \in \textit{doctorsOfHospital}(\textit{hospital})
\end{array}
$$

The first predicate links this operation to the corresponding atomic action and resource in the security model. It can be generated automatically. The other predicate expresses constraint *Same hospital as patient*: "the medical record may only be updated by a doctor working in the current hospital of the patient". It retrieves *hospital*, the hospital corresponding to the patient of medical record $x?$. Then it retrieves the *DOCTOR* object corresponding to the id of the user of the current session. Finally, it checks that this doctor works for *hospital*. This constraint, expressed informally in Fig. 1 must be added manually by the analyst.

This operation inherits all input parameters of schema *SecureOperation*. Most of these parameters can be deduced by Jaza once *session?* has been fixed. Therefore, we define a new version of the schema hiding these parameters.

$$
\begin{array}{l}
\textit{SecureMRChangeContentsP2} == \\
\quad \textit{SecureMRChangeContentsP} \setminus (\textit{uid?}, \textit{user?}, \textit{abs\_action?}, \textit{atm\_action?}, \textit{resource?}, \\
\qquad\qquad \textit{permission?}, \textit{role?})
\end{array}
$$

Secure versions of *ReadMedicalRecord* and *LinkDoctors* are defined similarly.

Constraint "*Same hospital as patient*" links information from the security model (the id of the current user) to the state of the functional model (the hospital of the patient). Its evaluation depends on the states of both models and can thus evolve if any of these states evolves. As we will see in Sect. 6, this makes the analyses and validation of the security policy more complex.

6 Validating and Animating Secure Operations

Graphical models such as Fig. 1 remain rather abstract. Moreover, complex interactions between functional and security models may either forbid one to play a nominal behaviour, or allow an attack to succeed. This would reveal that the detailed specifications don't model the user's intent. Animation can help convince the user that the model corresponds to his intent. Our validation of security properties uses the Jaza tool[18]. Jaza can animate a large subset of constructs of the Z language. It uses a combination of rewriting and constraint solving to find a final state and outputs from a given initial state and inputs. If the initial state and inputs don't satisfy the precondition of the operation, the tool returns *"No Solutions"*. The tool can be further queried to find out which constraint could not be satisfied. ZLive[3] is a more recent tool which should eventually replace Jaza. But its current version (1.5.0) has an insufficient coverage of the Z language to animate the specifications generated by our tools.

In the sequel, we start from the state of Fig. 2 and Table 1. We first show that normal behaviours are permitted by the security model. We then investigate the attempts of a malicious doctor to corrupt the integrity of a medical record.

6.1 Normal Behaviour

Our first tests play nominal scenarios. Their success will show that the combination of security and functional models allows normal behaviours to take place.

Scenario I: *A doctor reads a medical record.*

$; \ SecureMRReadMedrecord2$
$Input\ session? = "sess1"$
$Input\ r? = "meddata2"$

This first scenario tests whether a doctor, here Alice using $sess1$, may read medical record $meddata2$. This tests the inheritance of permission $ReadMedrecord$ from nurses to doctors. Jaza animation succeeds and gives the following result:

$x! == \{\langle\!|\ contents == "healthy", recordnb == "meddata2"\ |\!\rangle\}$

Scenario II: *A doctor updates the medical record of a patient in the same hospital.* In this scenario, doctor Alice wants to update some medical record. Since Alice belongs to the same hospital as the patient, this modification is allowed.

$; \ SecureMRChangeContentsP2$
$Input\ x? = \langle\!|\ contents == "healthy", recordnb == "meddata2"\ |\!\rangle$
$Input\ newcontents? = "severe"$
$Input\ session? = "sess1"$

The output shows that the medical record's contents have changed to *"severe"*.

$$Medrecord' == \{\langle\!|\ contents == "severe", recordnb == "meddata2"\ |\!\rangle, \\ \langle\!|\ contents == "sick", recordnb == "meddata1"\ |\!\rangle\}$$

These two examples show that the security kernel does not block licit operations. They can be shown to stakeholders of the information system to validate that the right behaviour was captured.

6.2 Analysing a Malicious Behaviour

Security analysis must also evaluate the system's ability to block unauthorized behaviour. Here, let us consider a malicious doctor, Bob, who tries to corrupt the integrity of medical record $meddata1$, calling operation $MRChangeContentsP1$.

[3] http://czt.sourceforge.net/zlive/index.html

As we have seen in Sect. 4.5, a query tells us that only doctors are allowed to perform this operation. Still, animations go beyond the results of queries presented in Sect. 4.5, because queries don't take into account constraints such as *Same hospital as patient* which may restrict the access to some operations. We will thus try a scenario where Bob attempts to modify medical record *meddata*1.

Scenario III.A: *A doctor attempts to update the medical record of a patient of another hospital.*

; *SecureMRChangeContentsP*2
Input x? = ⦇ *contents* == "*sick*", *recordnb* == "*meddata*1" ⦈
Input newcontents? = "*cured*"
Input session? = "*sess*2"

Hopefully, Jaza answers that this execution is not allowed by the model.

No Solutions

A closer look at the constraints tells us that Bob's hospital is not the same as the one of the patient. The query tool told us that only doctors are allowed to change the contents of a medical record. But Jaza animation also confirmed that a constraint requires the doctor to work in the same hospital as the patient. Since Bob does not work in the same hospital, there are two ways for him to change the outcome of this constraint. Either he moves the patient to his hospital, or he joins the hospital of the patient. Let us study the latter solution, and query the model about which roles are allowed to change the affiliation of a doctor.

; *EvaluateActionsAgainstRoles*[*atm_action*? := *DRLinkDoctors*1]
...
z_roles! == {(*Doctor*, ("*UpdateDoctor*", *DRLinkDoctors*1, *Doctors*))}

The query tells us that doctors are allowed to call this operation. Let us try it!

Scenario III.B: *The doctor first attempts to change his hospital association using one of the class methods and he succeeds in his attempt.*

; *SecureDRLinkDoctors*2
Input session? = "*sess*2"
Input hospital? = ⦇ *name* == "*RedCross*" ⦈
Input doctor? = ⦇ *id* == "004", *name* == "*Bob*" ⦈

The output tells us that Bob is now working for both hospitals.

doctorsOfHospital′ ==
{(⦇ *name* == "*BlueCare*" ⦈, {⦇ *id* == "003", *name* == "*Alice*" ⦈,
⦇ *id* == "004", *name* == "*Bob*" ⦈}),
(⦇ *name* == "*RedCross*" ⦈, {⦇ *id* == "003", *name* == "*Alice*" ⦈,
⦇ *id* == "004", *name* == "*Bob*" ⦈})}

Scenario III.C: *The doctor makes the malicious changes to the medical record*

; *SecureMRChangeContentsP*2
Input x? = ⦇ *contents* == "*sick*", *recordnb* == "*meddata*1" ⦈
Input newcontents? = "*cured*"
Input session? = "*sess*2"

Bob did succeed and compromised the integrity of the medical record.

$$Medrecord' == \{\langle\!| \ contents == "cured", recordnb == "meddata1" \ |\!\rangle, \\ \langle\!| \ contents == "severe", recordnb == "meddata2" \ |\!\rangle\},$$

It means that the current access control rules allow any doctor to join the hospital of any patient. Constraint "*Same hospital as patient*" is thus useless!

Our approach supports three kinds of validation activities: (a) answering standard queries about the access rules (leaving out the constraints), (b) checking that a given operation may be performed by a given user in a given state, (c) sequencing several operations for given users from a given state. Our scenarios show that the three kinds of activities are useful. State of the art tools such as SecureMova or OCL/USE only allow (a) and (b), which are mainly of static nature. Our tool covers (c), adding a dynamic character to validation activities and allowing to explore attack scenarios.

Constructing a sufficiently complete set of scenarios is essential to perform a suitable validation. This construction is outside the scope of the current paper that focuses on making such scenarios animatable.

7 Related Work

Our previous works [6],[10] on RoZ are the roots to our present work. Amalio [2] gives an overview of the alternate approaches to translate UML into Z.

SecureUML[3] is a security profile for UML. It has already been presented and it is the basis of our approach. The works of Sohr [15], and the SecureMova tool [4] are the closest to our approach, and have deeply influenced it. In Sect. 6, we showed several queries similar to the ones handled by these tools. In addition, our tool can handle sequences of operations involving both security and functional models. UMLSec [9] is another UML profile that focuses on secrecy and cryptographic protocols. Our work does not target secrecy aspects, but addresses a more abstract level focusing on access control.

Hall [8] used Z to specify a formal security policy model for an industrial project. Likewise, ISO standardized RBAC has widely been described by researchers using Z. A few notable propositions elsewhere [1],[12],[20] offer generic formal representation of RBAC. Yet, these works focus on meta-model foundations of RBAC, while we target the animation of application level models.

Various validation and verification of security properties based on RBAC are given in previous work [12],[5]. Abdallah [1] defines a security administration using access monitor for core RBAC and distinguishes among various concepts of RBAC. Boswell [5], describes a security policy model in Z, for NATO Air Command and Control System (ACCS). The author shares learned lessons from manual validation of this large, distributed, and multi-level-secure system. Morimoto et al., [12] chose a common-criteria security functional requirements taken from ISO/IEC-15408 and proposed a process to verify Z specifications by the Z/EVES theorem prover. Sohr [14] has proposed protecting clinical information systems to overcome risks by using first-order LTL supported by Isabelle/HOL for formal verification of security policy for RBAC.

Toahchoodee et al [17] merge functional and security models into a single UML model which is translated into Alloy. Alloy can then be used to find a state which breaks a given property. The properties they describe [17] are mainly of static nature, i.e. they focus on the search for a state which breaks a property, and don't search for sequences of actions leading to such a state.

8 Conclusion and Future Work

We have presented an approach to validate security design models using Z assertions. The graphical notation of security rules is inspired by SecureUML. Our proposal goes through three steps: (a) automated generation of functional specifications using RoZ [6], (b) the use of a generic security kernel, instantiated by the security model, and specified in Z, and (c) the link between the kernel and the operations of the functional model. Animation of the specifications makes it possible to check that normal behaviours are authorized by the security model and to analyze potential attacks. This is based on the evaluation of standard queries about the security policy and the animation of user-defined scenarios. Using Jaza brings a dynamic dimension to these analyses which is not covered by state of the art tools such as SecureMova and USE. It must be noted that the goal of our animation is to validate the rules of a given security policy, not the RBAC model itself. Further work should address the validation of the generic security kernel described in Sect. 4, i.e. to establish that this generic kernel conforms to the RBAC standard[7]. We intend to evaluate it by the animation of several case studies documented in the RBAC litterature.

Our current tool automatically translates the functional model, but requires manual instantiation of the security kernel, and manual definition of the link between both models. Our next step is to generate this information automatically, from the security part of the SecureUML diagram and a description of the action hierarchy. Also, the security kernel can be improved to take into account additional concepts such as delegation or organisation.

An adequate choice of nominal and attack scenarios is essential to guarantee the quality of the validation activities. Perspectives include the definition of metrics for the coverage of the model by these scenarios, and the automated generation of scenarios that systematically explore the model. This could benefit from the use of verification techniques like model-checking.

Acknowledgment. We first want to thank the reviewers of ICFEM for their constructive comments. This research is partly supported by the ANR Selkis and TASCCC Projects under grants ANR-08-SEGI-018 and ANR-09-SEGI-014.

References

1. Abdallah, A.E., Khayat, E.J.: Formal Z Specifications of Several Flat Role-Based Access Control Models. In: Proceedings of the 30th Annual IEEE/NASA Software Engineering Workshop (SEW 2006), pp. 282–292. IEEE Computer Society, Los Alamitos (2006)

2. Amálio, N., Polack, F.: Comparison of Formalisation Approaches of UML Class Constructs in Z and Object-Z. In: Bert, D., Bowen, J., King, S. (eds.) ZB 2003. LNCS, vol. 2651, pp. 339–358. Springer, Heidelberg (2003)
3. Basin, D., Doser, J., Lodderstedt, T.: Model Driven Security: From UML Models to Access Control Infrastructures. ACM TOSEM 15(1), 39–91 (2006)
4. Basin, D.A., Clavel, M., Doser, J., Egea, M.: Automated Analysis of Security Design Models. Information and Software Technology, Special issue on Model Based Development for Secure Information Systems 51(5) (2009)
5. Boswell, A.: Specification and Validation of a Security Policy Model. IEEE Transactions on Software Engineering 21(2), 63–68 (1995)
6. Dupuy, S., Ledru, Y., Chabre-Peccoud, M.: An Overview of RoZ: A Tool for Integrating UML and Z Specifications. In: Wangler, B., Bergman, L.D. (eds.) CAiSE 2000. LNCS, vol. 1789, pp. 417–430. Springer, Heidelberg (2000)
7. Ferraiolo, D.F., Sandhu, R.S., Gavrila, S.I., Kuhn, D.R., Chandramouli, R.: Proposed NIST standard for Role-based Access Control. ACM Transactions on Information and System Security, 224–274 (2001)
8. Hall, A.: Specifying and Interpreting Class Hierarchies in Z. In: Proceedings of the Z User Workshop, pp. 120–138. Springer/BCS (1994)
9. Jürjens, J.: Secure Systems Development with UML. Springer, Heidelberg (2004)
10. Ledru, Y.: Using Jaza to Animate RoZ Specifications of UML Class Diagrams. In: Proceedings of the 30th Annual IEEE/NASA Software Engineering Workshop (SEW-30 2006), pp. 253–262. IEEE Computer Society, Los Alamitos (2006)
11. Ledru, Y., Qamar, N., Idani, A., Richier, J.L., Labiadh, M.A.: Validation of security policies by the animation of Z specifications. In: 16th ACM Symposium on Access Control Models and Technologies, SACMAT 2011, pp. 155–164. ACM, New York (2011)
12. Morimoto, S., Shigematsu, S., Goto, Y., Cheng, J.: Formal verification of security specifications with common criteria. In: Proceedings of the 22nd Annual ACM Symposium on Applied Computing (SAC 2007), pp. 1506–1512. ACM, New York (2007)
13. Power, D., Slaymaker, M., Simpson, A.: On Formalizing and Normalizing Role-Based Access Control Systems. The Computer Journal 52(3), 305–325 (2009)
14. Sohr, K., Drouineaud, M., Ahn, G.: Formal Specification of Role-based Security Policies for Clinical Information Systems. In: Proc. of the 20th Annual ACM Symposium on Applied Computing, pp. 332–339. ACM, New York (2005)
15. Sohr, K., Drouineaud, M., Ahn, G.J., Gogolla, M.: Analyzing and managing role-based access control policies. IEEE Trans. Knowl. Data Eng. 20(7), 924–939 (2008)
16. Spivey, J.M.: The Z Notation: A reference manual, 2nd edn. Prentice Hall, Englewood Cliffs (1992)
17. Toahchoodee, M., Ray, I., Anastasakis, K., Georg, G., Bordbar, B.: Ensuring spatio-temporal access control for real-world applications. In: SACMAT 2009, 14th ACM Symp. on Access Control Models and Technologies. ACM, New York (2009)
18. Utting, M.: JAZA: Just Another Z Animator (2005), `http://www.cs.waikato.ac.nz/~marku/jaza/`
19. Wordsworth, J.: Software Development with Z: a practical approach to formal methods. Addison-Wesley, Reading (1992)
20. Yuan, C., He, Y., He, J., Zhou, Z.: A Verifiable Formal Specification for RBAC Model with Constraints of Separation of Duty. In: Lipmaa, H., Yung, M., Lin, D. (eds.) Inscrypt 2006. LNCS, vol. 4318, pp. 196–210. Springer, Heidelberg (2006)

Mutation in Linked Data Structures*

Ewen Maclean and Andrew Ireland

School of Mathematical and Computer Sciences,
Heriot-Watt University
Edinburgh, UK
{E.A.H.Maclean,A.Ireland}@hw.ac.uk

Abstract. Separation logic was developed as an extension to Hoare logic with the aim of simplifying pointer program proofs. A key feature of the logic is that it focuses the reasoning effort on only those parts of the heap that are relevant to a program - so called local reasoning. Underpinning this local reasoning are the *separating conjunction* and *separating implication* operators. Here we present an automated reasoning technique called *mutation* that provides guidance for separation logic proofs. Specifically, given two heap structures specified within separation logic, mutation attempts to construct an equivalence proof using a difference reduction strategy. Pivotal to this strategy is a generalised decomposition operator which is essential when matching heap structures. We show how mutation provides an effective strategy for proving the functional correctness of iterative and recursive programs within the context of weakest precondition analysis. Currently, mutation is implemented as a proof plan within our CORE program verification system. CORE combines results from shape analysis with our work on invariant generation and proof planning. We present our results for mutation within the context of the CORE system.

1 Introduction

Separation logic [13,14] was developed as an extension to Hoare logic with the aim of simplifying pointer program proofs, but in general is applicable when reasoning about dynamically allocated objects. A key feature of the logic is that it focuses the reasoning effort on only those parts of the heap that are relevant to a program – so called local reasoning. Underpinning this local reasoning are the *separating conjunction* and *separating implication* operators. In general, to support proof automation within separation logic requires automated reasoning techniques that can deal with both operators. Here we present *mutation* which is such a technique. Specifically, given two heap structures specified within separation logic, mutation attempts to construct a functional equivalence proof. To give an intuition for the technique, mutation is analogous to the task of assembling jigsaw pieces as illustrated in Fig 1. That is, when proving functional equivalence one needs to consider both the *shape* and *data* associated with the jigsaw pieces. Mutation constrains proof search by the use of a difference reduction strategy

* The research reported in this paper is supported by EPSRC grant EP/F037597. Our thanks go to Gudmund Grov for his feedback and encouragement with this work.

S. Qin and Z. Qiu (Eds.): ICFEM 2011, LNCS 6991, pp. 275–290, 2011.

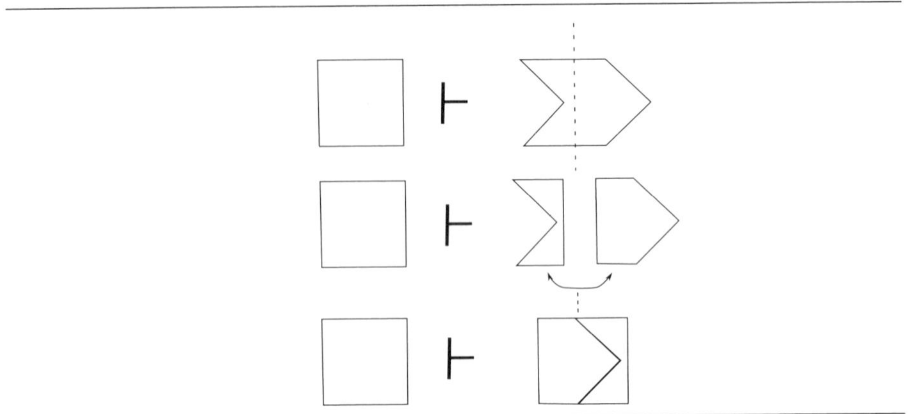

Fig. 1. Jigsaw analogy for reasoning about heap equivalence

that attempts to match heap structures. Pivotal to mutation is a generalised decomposition operator which is essential when matching heap structures, and corresponds to the need for non-structural inductive lemmas which arise when reasoning about the heap [3]. While the jigsaw analogy works well for shape, it is less effective in communicating the functional part. Essentially, by establishing the shape properties, mutation as a side-effect calculates pure functional proof obligations. Currently, mutation is implemented as a proof plan within our CORE program verification system. Mutation provides an effective strategy for proving the functional correctness of iterative and recursive programs within the context of a weakest precondition analysis. CORE combines results from shape analysis with our work on invariant generation and proof planning. In particular, the functional proof obligations mentioned above are discharged using IsaPlanner [8], a proof planner for the Isabelle proof development environment [12], which embodies a state-of-the-art inductive theorem proving strategy, i.e. rippling [5]. We present our results for mutation within the context of the CORE system.

The rest of the paper is structured as follows. In §2 we give a brief introduction to separation logic. Mutation and its application to loop based code is described in detail in §3. §4 describes how the approach can be generalised, while our implementation and results are presented in §5. Related and future work is covered in §6 and our conclusions are presented in §7.

2 Separation Logic

The development of separation logic was influenced by early work on program reasoning by Burstall [6] and the Logic of Bunched Implications by O'Hearn and Pym. Here we give a brief introduction to separation logic, for a full account see [14].

Separation logic extends predicate calculus with new forms of assertions for describing the heap:

- empty heap: the assertion *emp* holds for a heap that contains no cells.
- singleton heap: the assertion $X \mapsto E$ holds for a heap that contains a single cell, *i.e.* X denotes the address of a cell with contents E.
- separating conjunction: the assertion $P * Q$ holds for a heap if the heap can be divided into two disjoint heaps H_1 and H_2, where P holds for H_1 and Q holds for H_2 simultaneously.
- separating implication: the assertion $P \mathrel{-\!\!*} Q$ holds for a heap H_1, if whenever H_1 is extended with a disjoint heap H_2, for which P holds, then Q holds for the extended heap.

Typically one wants to assert that a pointer variable, say X, points to E within a larger group of heap cells. This can be represented by $(X \hookrightarrow E)$, which is an abbreviation for $(true * (X \mapsto E))$ – which asserts that the heap can be divided into two parts: A singleton heap, for which $(X \mapsto E)$ holds; and the rest of the current heap, for which *true* holds. Note that *true* holds for any heap. In what follows we will focus on pointers that reference a pair of adjacent heap cells. So we will use $(X \mapsto E_1, E_2)$ as an abbreviation for $(X \mapsto E_1) * (X + 1 \mapsto E_2)$. This pair notation can be generalised to any product type, and to records which can be seen as labelled product types. Central to the logic is the *frame rule*:

$$\frac{\{P\}C\{Q\}}{\{R * P\}C\{R * Q\}}$$

Note that the frame rule imposes a side condition, *i.e.* no variable occurring free in R is modified by C – where R denotes the frame invariant mentioned earlier. It is the frame rule that supports local reasoning. Within the context of goal directed proof, it allows us to focus on the correctness of C within a tight specification, expressed by assertions P and Q. An important role for the frame rule is in reasoning about recursively defined procedures.

We will also make significant use of the following rule which expresses the relationship between separating conjunction and separating implication:

$$\frac{P * Q \vdash R}{Q \vdash P \mathrel{-\!\!*} R} \qquad (1)$$

3 Mutation: Reasoning about Shape and Data

The mutation proof pattern we describe below is applicable to the verification of both iterative and recursive programs. For reasons of space, however, we focus here on its application to iterative code, i.e. the verification of a loop body with respect to a given loop invariant[1]. While the technique has been tested on

[1] In the recursive case the loop invariant is replaced by a frame invariant. A full account of mutation and invariant generation is available as a Technical Report, see [9].

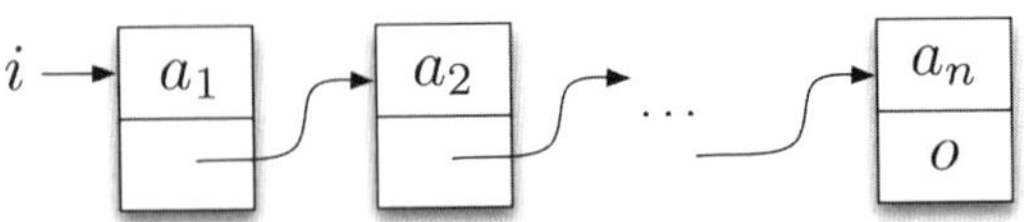

The picture above corresponds to $data\_lseg(a, i, o)$, where i and o delimit the singly linked-list segment representing a, *i.e.* the sequence $[a_1, a_2, \ldots, a_n]$.

Fig. 2. An acyclic singly linked-list segment

programs that manipulate acyclic singly-linked lists, we describe in §4 some experiments on binary trees, and how it can be extended to arbitrary recursively defined linked list data structures. Consider the following iterative version of in-place list reversal:

$\{(\exists a.\ data\_lseg(a, i, null) \wedge a_0 = a)\}$
```
o = null;
while (i != null) {
   t = i->tl;
   i->tl = o;
   o = i;
   i = t; }
```
$\{(\exists b.\ data\_lseg(b, o, null) \wedge a_0 = rev(b))\}$

Note that the program variables `i` and `o` point to the initial and reversed linked lists respectively. Note also that we use `i->tl` to de-reference the next pointer field of `i`, while `i->hd` de-references the data field. Turning to the pre- and postconditions, we use the inductively defined predicate `data_lseg` to specify an acyclic singly-linked list segment:

$$data\_lseg([], Y, Z) \leftrightarrow emp \wedge Y = Z \quad (2)$$
$$data\_lseg([W|X], Y, Z) \leftrightarrow (\exists p.\ (Y \mapsto W, p) * data\_lseg(X, p, Z)) \quad (3)$$

Note that the first argument denotes a sequence, where sequences are represented using the Prolog list notation. The second and third arguments delimit the corresponding linked-list segment structure. Note also that the definition excludes cycles. The *data_lseg* predicate is illustrated in Fig 2. Finally, we use *rev* to denote sequence reversal which is defined in terms of *app*, list concatenation, i.e.

$$rev([]) = [] \qquad\qquad app([], Z) = Z$$
$$rev([X|Y]) = app(rev(Y), [X]) \qquad\qquad app([X|Y], Z) = [X|app(Y, Z)]$$

In order to verify the code a *loop invariant* is required which needs to specify two disjoint lists, i.e. the list pointed to by i, representing the segment that remains to be reversed, and the list pointed to by o, representing the segment that has been reversed so far. In separation logic, such an invariant can be represented as follows:

$$(\exists a, b.\ data\_lseg(a, i, null) * data\_lseg(b, o, null) \wedge a_0 = app(rev(b), a)) \quad (4)$$

Using *weakest precondition* (WP) analysis, intermediate assertions can be calculated for the code given above as follows:

$\{(\exists a, b.\ data\_lseg(a, i, null) * data\_lseg(b, o, null)$
$\qquad \wedge\ a_0 = app(rev(b), a)) \wedge \neg(i = null)\}$
$\{(\exists a, b.\ (i \mapsto \mathcal{F}_1, \mathcal{F}_2) * ((i \mapsto \mathcal{F}_1, o) \multimap (data\_lseg(a, \mathcal{F}_4, null) * data\_lseg(b, i, null)$
$\qquad \wedge\ (t \hookrightarrow \mathcal{F}_3, \mathcal{F}_4)\ \wedge\ a_0 = app(rev(b), a))\}$

```
t = i->tl;
```

$\{(\exists a, b.\ (i \mapsto \mathcal{F}_1, \mathcal{F}_2) * ((i \mapsto \mathcal{F}_1, o) \multimap (data\_lseg(a, t, null) * data\_lseg(b, i, null)$
$\qquad \wedge\ a_0 = app(rev(b), a))\}$

```
i->tl = o;
```

$\{(\exists a, b.\ data\_lseg(a, t, null) * data\_lseg(b, i, null)\ \wedge a_0 = app(rev(b), a))\}$

```
o = i;
```

$\{(\exists a, b.\ data\_lseg(a, t, null) * data\_lseg(b, o, null)\ \wedge a_0 = app(rev(b), a))\}$

```
i = t
```

$\{(\exists a, b.\ data\_lseg(a, i, null) * data\_lseg(b, o, null)\ \wedge a_0 = app(rev(b), a))\}$

Note that $\mathcal{F}_1$, $\mathcal{F}_2$, $\mathcal{F}_3$ and $\mathcal{F}_4$ denote meta-variables. Verification corresponds to proving that the precondition implies the calculated WP, i.e.

$$\begin{aligned}&data\_lseg(\mathcal{X}_a, i, null) * data\_lseg(\mathcal{X}_b, o, null) \wedge \\ &\qquad a_0 = app(rev(\mathcal{X}_b), \mathcal{X}_a))\ \wedge \neg(i = null) \vdash \\ &(i \mapsto \mathcal{F}_1, \mathcal{F}_2) * ((i \mapsto \mathcal{F}_1, o) \multimap \\ &\qquad data\_lseg(\mathcal{F}_a, \mathcal{F}_4, null) * data\_lseg(\mathcal{F}_b, i, null) \wedge \\ &\qquad\qquad (i \hookrightarrow \mathcal{F}_3, \mathcal{F}_4)\ \wedge a_0 = app(rev(\mathcal{F}_b), \mathcal{F}_a)\end{aligned} \quad (5)$$

Note that the existential variables a and b within the hypotheses are replaced by the skolem constants $\mathcal{X}_a$ and $\mathcal{X}_b$ respectively, while in the goal they are replaced by meta variables $\mathcal{F}_a$ and $\mathcal{F}_b$ respectively.

Proving such a *verification condition* (VC) gives rise to the following patterns of reasoning:

$$\begin{array}{ccc} \vdash (\ldots R \mathrel{-\!\!*} Q \ldots) & & \ldots P \ldots \vdash S * Q \\ \vdots & & \vdots \\ \vdash (\ldots R \mathrel{-\!\!*} (S * Q') \ldots) & & \ldots R * P' \ldots \vdash S * Q \\ \vdash \ldots Q' \ldots & & \ldots P' \ldots \vdash (R \mathrel{-\!\!*} (S * Q)) \\ & & \ldots P' \ldots \vdash Q \end{array}$$

Note that both patterns contain a common core – the selection, attraction and cancellation of heaplets R and S. Crucially R and S are unifiable, and occur on either side of the $\mathrel{-\!\!*}$ operator. The pivotal cancellation step corresponds to an application of the following rewrite rule[2]

$$(X \mathrel{-\!\!*} (X * Y)) :\Rightarrow Y \tag{6}$$

Such a cancellation step is required in order to achieve a match between a goal and a given hypothesis – typically this is referred to as *fertilisation*. Note that this pattern arises when reasoning about programs that mutate the heap, i.e. programs that allocate or update heaplets. We have represented this pattern of reasoning as a proof strategy which we call *mutation*. As a difference reduction strategy, mutation is strongly influenced by *rippling* [5]. While mutation focuses on the cancellation of heaplets, rippling focuses on the elimination of induction terms. As indicated above, the pattern may involve just the goal, but also a given hypothesis. In order to explain the mutation proof strategy, we introduce meta-level annotations. Specifically, we will refer to a heaplet X that occurs on the left-hand side of a $\mathrel{-\!\!*}$ as an *anti-heaplet*, and annotate it as $\boxed{X}^{-}$, alternatively if X occurs on the right-hand side of a $\mathrel{-\!\!*}$ it will be annotated as $\boxed{X}^{+}$. Using these meta-level annotations, the general pattern of mutation is illustrated in Fig 3.

As will be illustrated later, for a given verification, multiple applications of the mutation strategy will be required in order to complete a proof. But first we will describe in more detail mutation in terms of its lower level parts, i.e. heaplet analysis, attraction and cancellation.

3.1 Heaplet Analysis and Heap Decomposition

The process of identifying a heaplet R that cancels an anti-heaplet S may involve choice. In the presentation that follows we give example healpets and anti-heaplets as pointer cells, but in general a heaplet and anti-heaplet can be any structure existing within the heap. Below we list the heuristics that we use in identifying such heaplets[3]:

---

2 We use $:\Rightarrow$ to denote the rewrite relation and $\rightarrow$ to denote logical implication.

3 In order to simplify our description we exploit the fact that $P \vdash Q$ and $\vdash P \mathrel{-\!\!*} Q$ are equivalent (see rule (1)).

$$\vdash (\ldots \boxed{R}^{-} \mathrel{-\!\!*} Q \ldots)$$
$$\vdots$$
$$\vdash (\ldots \boxed{R}^{-} \mathrel{-\!\!*} (\boxed{S}^{+} * Q') \ldots)$$
$$\vdash \ldots Q' \ldots$$

goal mutation

$$\ldots P \ldots \vdash \boxed{S}^{+} * Q$$
$$\vdots$$
$$\ldots \boxed{R}^{-} * P' \ldots \vdash \boxed{S}^{+} * Q$$
$$\ldots P' \ldots \vdash (\boxed{R}^{-} \mathrel{-\!\!*} (\boxed{S}^{+} * Q))$$
$$\ldots P' \ldots \vdash Q$$

hypothesis mutation

Fig. 3. General pattern of mutation

1. **Explicit case:** there exists a heaplet and anti-heaplet which unify, i.e.

$$(\ldots * \boxed{(x \mapsto y, z)}^{-} * \ldots) \mathrel{-\!\!*} (\ldots * \boxed{(x' \mapsto y', z')}^{+} * \ldots)$$

where x, y, z and x', y', z' unify respectively.
2. **Implicit case:** there exists a heaplet but no explicit anti-heaplet which unifies, or vice versus:
   (a) **Simple decomposition:** Where an explicit anti-heaplet $\boxed{(x \mapsto \_, y)}^{-}$ exists a complementary heaplet may be identified by unfolding the "head" of a *data_lseg* predicate, i.e.

$$\ldots \mathrel{-\!\!*} (\ldots * \mathit{data\_lseg}(\_, \boxed{x}^{+}, \_) * \ldots)$$

   decomposes to give:

$$\ldots \mathrel{-\!\!*} (\ldots * (\boxed{(x \mapsto \_, T)}^{+} * \mathit{data\_lseg}(\_, T, \_)) * \ldots)$$

   Alternatively the "tail" of a *data_lseg* predicate, i.e.

$$\ldots \mathrel{-\!\!*} (\ldots * \mathit{data\_lseg}(\_, \_, \boxed{y}^{-}) * \ldots)$$

   decomposes to give:

$$\ldots \mathrel{-\!\!*} (\ldots * (\mathit{data\_lseg}(\_, \_, T) * \boxed{(T \mapsto \_, y)}^{-}) * \ldots)$$

   The same pattern holds for an explicit heaplet, where no explicit anti-heaplet occurs.
   (b) **General decomposition:** In general, the (anti-)heaplet may be embedded within a *data_lseg*, and progress towards a proof will then require a *general decomposition* step. When applied to the goal, this involves the

introduction of meta-variables ($\mathcal{F}_i$), place-holders that will be instantiated by fertilisation:

$$\ldots * \mathit{data\_lseg}(\mathcal{F}_1, \boxed{x}^{+}, \_) * \ldots$$

decomposes to give:

$$\ldots * \mathit{data\_lseg}(\mathcal{F}_2, \boxed{x}^{+}, \boxed{\mathcal{F}_3}^{+}) * \boxed{(\mathcal{F}_3 \mapsto \mathcal{F}_4, \mathcal{F}_5)}^{+} *$$
$$\mathit{data\_lseg}(\mathcal{F}_6, \boxed{\mathcal{F}_5}^{+}, \_) * \ldots \qquad \wedge\ \mathcal{F}_1 = \mathit{app}(\mathcal{F}_2, [\mathcal{F}_4|\mathcal{F}_6])$$

At the level of annotations, we use a dotted box to emphasise the potential for unfolding heaplets, e.g. $\boxed{\mathcal{F}_j}^{+}$. Note that when rewriting a hypothesis, the general decomposition step introduces skolem constants, i.e. $\mathcal{X}_j$. The notion of simple and general decomposition for *data_lseg* described above are illustrated diagrammatically in Fig 4.

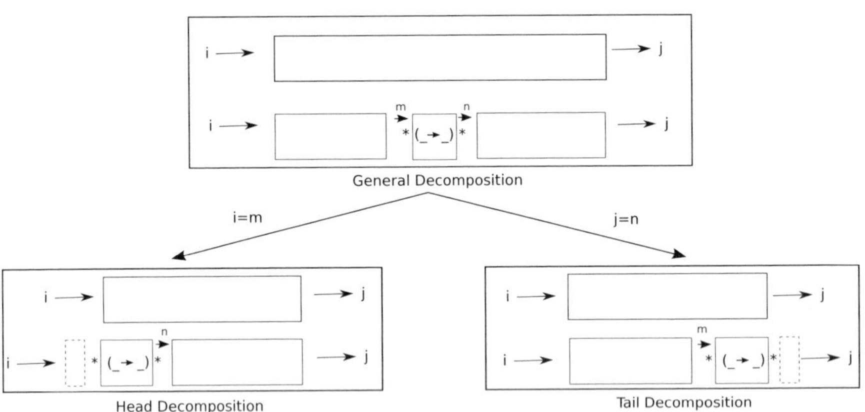

Note that "head" and "tail" decomposition are special cases of the general decomposition step.

Fig. 4. Simple and general decomposition for *data_lseg*

3.2 Heaplet Attraction, Cancellation and Fertilisation

Once heaplet analysis is complete, rewriting is used to attract the selected heaplet and anti-heaplet so as to enable a cancellation step:

$$((\ldots) * \boxed{(x \mapsto y, z)}^{-} * (\ldots)) \twoheadrightarrow ((\ldots) * \boxed{(x' \mapsto y', z')}^{+} * (\ldots))$$
$$\vdots \qquad \vdots$$
$$((\ldots) * (\ldots) * (\boxed{(x \mapsto y, z)}^{-} \twoheadrightarrow (\boxed{(x' \mapsto y', z')}^{+} * ((\ldots) * (\ldots))))$$
$$\text{by (6)}$$
$$((\ldots) * (\ldots)) \ \twoheadrightarrow\ ((\ldots) * (\ldots))$$

The rewriting that proceeds the cancellation step involves the application of rewrite rules which are derived from basic properties of separation logic, *e.g.*

$$X * Y :\Rightarrow Y * X \tag{7}$$

$$pure(Z) \rightarrow (X \wedge Z) * Y :\Rightarrow X * (Z \wedge Y) \tag{8}$$

$$(X * Y) * Z :\Rightarrow X * (Y * Z) \tag{9}$$

where *pure* is a predicate which denotes that its argument has no shape content.

Attraction selects rewrite rules which reduce the term tree distance between a heaplet and its anti-heaplet. There is no search in this process. To illustrate this consider the term tree manipulation shown in Fig 5. The term $\boxed{S}^{+}$ is moved within the term $a*(b*(\boxed{S}^{+}\wedge c))$ and transformed into the term $\boxed{S}^{+}*((c\wedge b)*a)$, in order that rule (6) can apply. To illustrate an informal argument for the termination of attraction, assume the position of a term within a term tree is given by a list of branch indices, starting at 1. Application of commutativity rules such as (7) reduces the number of occurrences of the index 2 within the position tree. Application of associativity rules such as (9) reduces the length of the position tree. The process terminates when the position tree [1] is reached, indicating that the desired term is at the top of the tree.

Note that in general, mutation is an iterative strategy, where a successful pattern of attraction and cancellation may require additional decomposition steps in order to achieve fertilisation. This is potentially a non-terminating process so a depth bound is used to control the search.

Now we return to the list reversal example presented earlier, and VC (5). Using the mutation annotations described above, the VC becomes:

$$\begin{array}{l} data\_lseg(\mathcal{X}_a, \boxed{i}^{-}, null) * data\_lseg(\mathcal{X}_b, \boxed{o}^{-}, null) \wedge \\ \quad a_0 = app(rev(\mathcal{X}_b), \mathcal{X}_a)) \wedge \neg(i = null) \vdash \\ \boxed{(i \mapsto \mathcal{F}_1, \mathcal{F}_2)}^{+} * (\boxed{(i \mapsto \mathcal{F}_1, o)}^{-} \mathrel{-\!\!*} \\ \quad data\_lseg(\mathcal{F}_a, \boxed{\mathcal{F}_4}^{+}, null) * data\_lseg(\mathcal{F}_b, \boxed{i}^{+}, null) \wedge \\ \qquad \boxed{(i \hookrightarrow \mathcal{F}_3, \mathcal{F}_4)}^{+} \wedge a_0 = app(rev(\mathcal{F}_b), \mathcal{F}_a) \end{array} \tag{10}$$

Proving (10) requires three applications of the mutation strategy. Here we only sketch the high-level pattern. The first application focuses on the goal:

$$\ldots \vdash \ldots * (\boxed{(i \mapsto \mathcal{F}_1, o)}^{-} \mathrel{-\!\!*} \ldots * data\_lseg(\mathcal{F}_b, \boxed{i}^{+}, null)) \wedge \ldots$$

$$\begin{array}{l} \ldots \vdash \ldots * (\boxed{(i \mapsto \mathcal{F}_1, o)}^{-} \mathrel{-\!\!*} \ldots * (\boxed{(i \mapsto \mathcal{F}_{b_{hd}}, \mathcal{F}_6)}^{+} * \\ \qquad data\_lseg(\mathcal{F}_{b_{tl}}, \mathcal{F}_6, null)) \wedge \ldots \end{array}$$

$$\begin{array}{l} \ldots \vdash \ldots * (\boxed{(i \mapsto \mathcal{F}_1, o)}^{-} \mathrel{-\!\!*} (\boxed{(i \mapsto \mathcal{F}_{b_{hd}}, \mathcal{F}_6)}^{+} * (\ldots * \\ \qquad data\_lseg(\mathcal{F}_{b_{tl}}, \mathcal{F}_6, null)))) \wedge \ldots \end{array}$$

$$\ldots \vdash \ldots * (\ldots * data\_lseg(\mathcal{F}_{b_{tl}}, \mathcal{F}_6, null)) \wedge \ldots$$

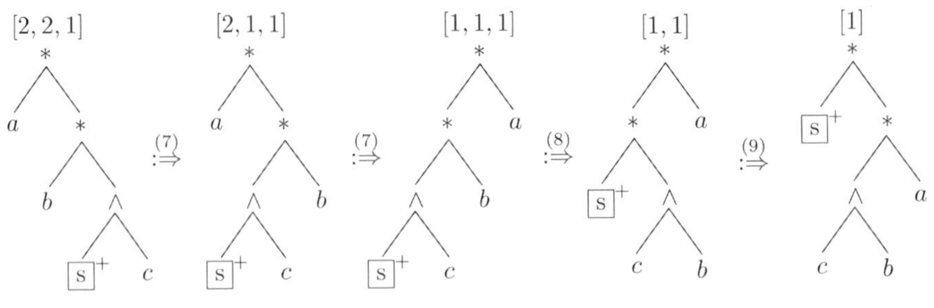

$a*(b*(\boxed{S}^{+}\wedge c))$ $a*((\boxed{S}^{+}\wedge c)*b)$ $((\boxed{S}^{+}\wedge c)*b)*a$ $(\boxed{S}^{+}*(c\wedge b))*a$ $\boxed{S}^{+}*((c\wedge b)*a)$

Selective rewriting (anti-)heaplets, with the overall aim of reducing the term tree distance between healpets and anti-heaplets.

Fig. 5. Mutation guided rewriting

The above rewriting is justified by (3), (9) and (6). The second application applies to both the hypotheses and goal. Focusing on the left conjunct within the goal, we obtain the following high-level pattern:

$$\begin{array}{rl}
\ldots data_lseg(\mathcal{X}_a, \boxed{i}^{-}, null) * \ldots \vdash & (\boxed{(i \mapsto \mathcal{F}_1, \mathcal{F}_2)}^{+} * \ldots) \\
\ldots(\boxed{(i \mapsto \mathcal{X}_{a_{hd}}, \mathcal{X}_1)}^{-} * data_lseg(\mathcal{X}_{a_{tl}}, \mathcal{X}_1, null)) * \ldots \vdash & (\boxed{(i \mapsto \mathcal{F}_1, \mathcal{F}_2)}^{+} * \ldots) \\
\ldots * data_lseg(\mathcal{X}_{a_{tl}}, \mathcal{X}_1, null) * \ldots \vdash & (\boxed{(i \mapsto \mathcal{X}_{a_{hd}}, \mathcal{X}_1)}^{-} -\!\!* \\
& (\boxed{(i \mapsto \mathcal{F}_1, \mathcal{F}_2)}^{+} * \ldots)) \\
\ldots * data_lseg(\mathcal{X}_{a_{tl}}, \mathcal{X}_1, null) * \ldots \vdash & (\ldots)
\end{array}$$

where $\mathcal{F}_1$ and $\mathcal{F}_2$ are instantiated to be $\mathcal{X}_{a_{hd}}$ and $\mathcal{X}_1$ respectively. Here the rewriting is justified by (3), (1) and (6). Turning to the right conjunct we require a third application of mutation:

$$\begin{array}{l}
\boxed{(i \mapsto \mathcal{X}_{a_{hd}}, \mathcal{X}_1)}^{-} * \ldots \vdash \boxed{(i \hookrightarrow \mathcal{F}_3, \mathcal{F}_4)}^{+} \wedge \ldots \\
\boxed{(i \mapsto \mathcal{X}_{a_{hd}}, \mathcal{X}_1)}^{-} * \ldots \vdash (\boxed{(i \mapsto \mathcal{F}_3, \mathcal{F}_4)}^{+} * true) \wedge \ldots \\
\qquad \ldots \vdash \boxed{(i \mapsto \mathcal{X}_{a_{hd}}, \mathcal{X}_1)}^{-} -\!\!* ((\boxed{(i \mapsto \mathcal{F}_3, \mathcal{F}_4)}^{+} * true) \wedge \ldots) \\
\qquad \ldots \vdash \boxed{(i \mapsto \mathcal{X}_{a_{hd}}, \mathcal{X}_1)}^{-} -\!\!* (\boxed{(i \mapsto \mathcal{F}_3, \mathcal{F}_4)}^{+} * (true \wedge \ldots)) \\
\qquad \ldots \vdash true \wedge \ldots
\end{array}$$

where $\mathcal{F}_3$ and $\mathcal{F}_4$ are instantiated to be $\mathcal{X}_{a_{hd}}$ and $\mathcal{X}_1$ respectively. This rewriting is justified by (1), (9) and (6). As noted in the §1, a side-effect of manipulating the shape is a functional residue. In the case of list reversal, the residue takes the form:

$$\vdash app(rev(\mathcal{X}_b), [\mathcal{X}_1|\mathcal{X}_3]) = app(rev([\mathcal{X}_1|\mathcal{X}_b]), \mathcal{X}_3)$$

As noted in §1, we use IsaPlanner [8] to discharge these proof obligations.

3.3 An Example General Decomposition

Note that in the list reversal example, the decomposition step involved splitting off the head of the heap structure. As highlighted in §3.1, a more general form of decomposition may be required. To motivate this point, consider the following specification of list concatenation:

$\{data\_list(a, x) * data\_list(b, y) \ \wedge a_0 = a \ \wedge \ b_0 = b\}$

```
local n,t;
if (x == null) {
   x = y; }
else {
   t = x;
   n = t->tl;
   while (n != null) {
      t = n;
      n = t-> tl; }
t->tl = y; }
```

$\{(\exists c.\ data\_list(c, x) \ \wedge \ c = app(a_0, b_0))\}$

where we use the abbreviation *data_list* to denote a null-terminated linked-list segment via:

$$data\_list(A, I) \leftrightarrow data\_lseg(A, I, null) \tag{11}$$

In this example, the loop invariant takes the form:

$$(\exists \alpha, \beta, h.\ data\_lseg(\alpha, x, t) * (t \mapsto h, n) * data\_list(\beta, n) * data\_list(b_0, y) \wedge \\ x \neq n \ \wedge \ a_0 = app(\alpha, [h|\beta]))$$

The annotated version of the VC resulting from proving the loop invariant implies the postcondition takes the form:

$$data\_lseg(\mathcal{X}_\alpha, \boxed{x}^-, t) * \boxed{(t \mapsto \mathcal{X}_h, null)}^- * data\_lseg(\mathcal{X}_b, \boxed{y}^-, null) \wedge \\ x \neq null \wedge \mathcal{X}_a = app(\mathcal{X}_\alpha, [\mathcal{X}_h|null]) \vdash \\ \boxed{(t \mapsto \mathcal{F}_1, \mathcal{F}_2)}^+ * (\boxed{(t \mapsto \mathcal{F}_1, y)}^- \mathrel{-\!\!*} data\_lseg(\mathcal{F}_3, \boxed{x}^+, null) \\ \wedge \mathcal{F}_3 = app(\mathcal{X}_a, \mathcal{X}_b)) \tag{12}$$

Focusing on the goal associated with (12), and in particular the anti-heaplet $\boxed{(t \mapsto \mathcal{F}_1, y)}^{-}$, then mutation guides us to apply a general decomposition step to $data\_lseg(\mathcal{F}_3, \boxed{x}^{+}, null)$ in order to generate a heaplet that will cancel the anti-heaplet, i.e.

$$\begin{aligned}\ldots \vdash & \boxed{(t \mapsto \mathcal{F}_1, \mathcal{F}_2)}^{+} * (\boxed{(t \mapsto \mathcal{F}_1, y)}^{-} \mathrel{-\!\!*} \\ & data\_lseg(\mathcal{F}_4, \boxed{x}^{+}, \mathcal{F}_5) * \boxed{(\mathcal{F}_5 \mapsto \mathcal{F}_6, \mathcal{F}_7)}^{+} * data\_lseg(\mathcal{F}_8, \boxed{\mathcal{F}_7}^{+}, null) \\ & \wedge \mathcal{F}_3 = app(\mathcal{F}_4, [\mathcal{F}_6|\mathcal{F}_8]) \wedge \mathcal{F}_3 = app(\mathcal{X}_a, \mathcal{X}_b))\end{aligned} \quad (13)$$

Note that to achieve the cancellation two attraction steps, corresponding to commutativity and associativity are required.

4 Towards a Generalisation of Mutation

So far we have described *mutation* within the context of an acyclic singly linked list segment as represented by the inductively defined predicate *data_lseg*. We now describe how the basic approach could be generalised for other inductively defined predicates. In particular, we illustrate the generalisation via some experiments in applying the strategy to binary trees.

As an example of generalising mutation beyond linked lists, consider the following inductive definition of a binary tree:

$$\begin{aligned} data\_tree(t_0, X) &\leftrightarrow emp \wedge X = null \\ data\_tree(t(H, TL, TR), Y) &\leftrightarrow (\exists l, r.\ (Y \mapsto H, l, r) * \\ & \qquad data\_tree(TL, l) * data\_tree(TR, r)) \end{aligned}$$

The tree representation for the functional content is defined as

$$tree ::= t_0 \mid t(int, tree, tree)$$

where t_0 denotes the empty tree. To illustrate this representation, consider the following program fragment which isolates the left branch of a binary tree:

$\{data\_tree(t(1, t(2, t_0, t_0), t(3, t_0, t_0)), i)\}$

```
j = i->l;
i->l = null;
```

$\{data\_tree(t(2, t_0, t_0), j) * data\_tree(t(1, t_0, t(3, t_0, t_0)), i)\}$

In terms of mutation, this leads to the following VC:

$$\begin{aligned} & data\_tree(t(1, t(2, t_0, t_0), t(3, t_0, t_0)), \boxed{i}^{-}) \vdash \\ & \quad \boxed{(i \mapsto \mathcal{F}_1, \mathcal{F}_2, \mathcal{F}_3)}^{+} * (\boxed{(i \mapsto \mathcal{F}_1, null, \mathcal{F}_3)}^{-} \mathrel{-\!\!*} \\ & data\_tree(t(2, t_0, t_0), \boxed{\mathcal{F}_5}^{+}) * data\_tree(t(1, t(3, t_0, t_0), t_0), \boxed{i}^{+}) \wedge \\ & \quad \boxed{(i \hookrightarrow \mathcal{F}_4, \mathcal{F}_5, \mathcal{F}_6)}^{+}) \end{aligned}$$

Comparing this VC with (10) we see that the shape and distribution of heaplets and anti-heaplets is similar, and that heaplet analysis, decomposition, attraction and cancellation are applicable.

To generalise mutation completely, we must introduce rules for general decomposition. In the case of linked lists we extend the definitions (2) and (3) via the rule:

$$\begin{aligned}&\mathit{data\_lseg}(D,W,Z)\ \wedge\ D\neq[]\ \leftrightarrow W\neq Z\ \wedge\\ &\quad(\exists d_1,d_2,d_3,x_1,x_2.\ (\mathit{data\_lseg}(d_1,W,x_1)\ *\ (x_1\mapsto d_2,x_2)\ *\\ &\qquad\mathit{data\_lseg}(d_3,x_2,Z))\wedge D=\mathit{app}(d_1,[d_2|d_3]))\end{aligned}\qquad(14)$$

which is illustrated by the general case in Fig. 4. Note that we record the place at which the linked list segment was decomposed by using existential variables. The components of the decomposition are two linked list segments, a heaplet and a functional constraint. The functional constraint $D = \mathit{app}(d_1, [d_2|d_3])$ is sufficient to describe how the data given by the existential variables is composed.

In the case of trees, we introduce a predicate *data_tseg*, which is analogous to *data_lseg*, and record the decomposition via existential variables and a position within the tree. *data_tseg* generalises *data_tree* by introducing a "trailing pointer" indicating where the tree is decomposed. Similarly to the list segment example (14), the components of binary tree decomposition are three tree segments, a heaplet and a functional constraint. The functional constraint uses a function *tree_join* which uses the position data and existential variables to describe how the tree is composed, this is analogous to append, i.e. *app*. As the decomposition is not linear, it is necessary to introduce a position argument for the functional composition of the data. We give the general decomposition rule for tree segments as:

$$\begin{aligned}\mathit{data\_tseg}(t_0,Y,(Z,\_))\ &\leftrightarrow\ \mathit{emp}\ \wedge\ Y=Z\\ \mathit{data\_tseg}(T,X,(Y,P))\wedge\ T\neq t_0\ &\leftrightarrow\ X\neq Y\ \wedge(\exists i,j,k,p_1,p_2,p_3,t_2,t_3,d_1,t_l,t_r.\\ &\quad\mathit{data\_tseg}(t_1,X,(i,p_1))\ *\ (i\mapsto d_1,tl,tr)\ *\\ &\qquad\mathit{data\_tseg}(t_2,t_l,(j,p_2))\ *\ \mathit{data\_tseg}(t_3,t_r,(k,p_3))\ \wedge\\ &\qquad T=\mathit{tree\_join}(t_1,d_1,t_2,t_3,p_1)\ \wedge\ Y=c(P,p_1,p_2,p_3,j,k))\end{aligned}$$

where c denotes a function that calculates where the initial trailing pointer Y lies after the decomposition. The rule for defining *data_tseg* in terms of *data_tree* takes the form:

$$\mathit{data\_tree}(T,I)\leftrightarrow(\exists p.\ \mathit{data\_tseg}(T,I,(\mathit{null},p)))$$

which is analogous to the linked-list abbreviation given by (11).

5 Implementations and Results

We now describe briefly the parts of the CORE system [10] that are relevant to the mechanisation of mutation. Moreover, we give the results of our experiments with mutation on programs which manipulate linked lists.

The CORE system incorporates different components, but the principal component relevant to the work presented here is the proof planner. We use a verified VC generator [1], and our proof planner which manipulates the VCs. Proof planning is a technique which supports abstract reasoning, by decoupling proof search and proof checking – for more details see [4]. In the work we present here, mutation is an example of an abstract reasoning technique. Heaplet analysis, as described via meta-level annotations in §3 is implemented via a heuristic scoring technique – where each possible match is assigned a score according to the likelihood of mutation cancelling heaplet/anti-heaplet pairs.

Table 1 shows the results of applying mutation to annotated programs which manipulate pointers. Mutation was successful at dealing with all the example programs and was fully automatic. Indicated in the table are the type of program – iterative (I), recursive (R) and involving a function call (F). Also indicated are the types of decomposition step required - H indicates taking an element from the head of a linked list, while T indicates taking an element from the tail, and G is the general case – all three cases are illustrated in Fig 4.

Table 1. Results of applying mutation to linked list programs

Name	Type	Mutation			Name	Type	Mutation		
		H	G	T			H	G	T
split_list	S	✔			double_list	R	✔		✔
copylist	R	✔		✔	list_copy	I	✔		✔
list_reverse	I	✔			list_traverse	R	✔		✔
list_traverse	I	✔		✔	list_deallocate_rec	R	✔		✔
list_insert_rec	R	✔	✔	✔	list_deallocate	I	✔		✔
list_length	I	✔		✔	list_min	R	✔		✔
list_append	I	✔	✔	✔	list_append_rec	R	✔	✔	✔
list_remove	R	✔	✔	✔	list_reverse_rec	R	✔		✔
push	S	✔			list_replace_last	R	✔		✔
enqueue	F	✔			list_rotate	IF	✔		✔
pop_dequeue	S	✔			sortlist	RF	✔	✔	✔

6 Related and Future Work

Our work adds a functional dimension to the shape analysis results of Smallfoot [2]. Specifically, mutation provides proof guidance when combining shape and functional properties. Holfoot [15] embeds Smallfoot style analysis within the HOL proof development environment, and also supports functional reasoning. Like Smallfoot, Holfoot supports forward proof which is in contrast to our backward (WP) style of reasoning. In terms of automation, Holfoot is able to automatically generate frame invariants, but loop invariants must be supplied, as is the case with Smallfoot. A related system, JStar [7] which targets the verification of Java programs, makes use of abstract interpretation for the generation of loop invariants. For the purposes of explaining mutation, we have included the loop invariants. However, it should be noted that mutation is used within the context of the CORE system which supports the automatic generation of the functional loop invariants via term synthesis. Another approach to extending shape analysis is described in [11] where user defined shape predicates are also used to describe size. It should also be noted that mutation has similarities with the rewrite strategy used within SmallfootRG, although with a different goal in mind, i.e. rely/guarantee style reasoning. Finally, with regards to our general decomposition steps. While these are handcrafted, we know of no system which automates the construction of such lemmas.

In terms of future work, we aim to further investigate mechanised support for the construction of general decomposition rules. The CORE system currently supports the visualisation of heap structures. One way forward would be to build upon the visualiser, and provide a tool in which a user can input decomposition rules via diagrams.

7 Conclusion

We have introduced mutation, an automated reasoning technique that is designed to prove the equivalence of linked data structures specified in separation logic. This is a challenging problem, made even more challenging if there is a necessity to prove equivalence of the data held within these structures. We have shown that the technique works well for linked list structures. In addition, we have also illustrated how it can be generalised for more complicated data types. By implementing mutation via a proof planner, it can potentially be integrated within other separation logic theorem provers.

References

1. Atkey, R.: Amortised resource analysis with separation logic. In: 19th European Symposium on Programming, pp. 85–103 (2010)
2. Berdine, J., Calcagno, C., O'Hearn, P.: Smallfoot: Modular automatic assertion checking with separation logic. In: de Boer, F.S., Bonsangue, M.M., Graf, S., de Roever, W.-P. (eds.) FMCO 2005. LNCS, vol. 4111, pp. 115–137. Springer, Heidelberg (2006)
3. Berdine, J., Calcagno, C., O'Hearn, P.: Symbolic execution with separation logic. In: Yi, K. (ed.) APLAS 2005. LNCS, vol. 3780, pp. 52–68. Springer, Heidelberg (2005)
4. Bundy, A.: The use of explicit plans to guide inductive proofs. In: Lusk, R., Overbeek, R. (eds.) CADE 1988. LNCS, vol. 310, pp. 111–120. Springer, Heidelberg (1988)
5. Bundy, A., Basin, D., Hutter, D., Ireland, A.: Rippling: Meta-level Guidance for Mathematical Reasoning. Cambridge University Press, Cambridge (2005)
6. Burstall, R.M.: Some techniques for proving correctness of programs. In: Machine Intelligence, vol. 7, pp. 23–50. Edinburgh University Press, Edinburgh (1972)
7. Distefano, D., Parkinson, M.J.: jstar: towards practical verification for java. In: Proceedings of the 23rd ACM SIGPLAN Conference on Object-Oriented Programming Systems Languages and Applications, OOPSLA 2008, pp. 213–226. ACM, New York (2008)

8. Dixon, L., Fleuriot, J.D.: IsaPlanner: A prototype proof planner in isabelle. In: Baader, F. (ed.) CADE 2003. LNCS (LNAI), vol. 2741, pp. 279–283. Springer, Heidelberg (2003)
9. Ireland, A., Maclean, E., Grov, G.: Verification and synthesis of functional correctness of pointer programs. Research Memo HW-MACS-TR-0087, School of Mathematical and Computer Sciences, Heriot-Watt University (2011)
10. Maclean, E., Ireland, A., Grov, G.: The core system: Animation and functional correctness of pointer programs, Under review as a ASE-11 Tool Demonstration paper (2011)
11. Nguyen, H.H., David, C., Qin, S., Chin, W.N.: Automated verification of shape and size properties via separation logic. In: Cook, B., Podelski, A. (eds.) VMCAI 2007. LNCS, vol. 4349, pp. 251–266. Springer, Heidelberg (2007)
12. Nipkow, T., Paulson, L.C., Wenzel, M.T.: Isabelle/HOL — A Proof Assistant for Higher-Order Logic. LNCS, vol. 2283. Springer, Heidelberg (2002)
13. O'Hearn, P., Reynolds, J., Hongseok, Y.: Local reasoning about programs that alter data structures. In: Fribourg, L. (ed.) CSL 2001 and EACSL 2001. LNCS, vol. 2142, pp. 1–19. Springer, Heidelberg (2001)
14. Reynolds, J.C.: Separation logic: A logic for shared mutable data structures. In: Logic in Computer Science, pp. 55–74. IEEE Computer Society, Los Alamitos (2002)
15. Tuerk, T.: A formalisation of smallfoot in HOL. In: Berghofer, S., Nipkow, T., Urban, C., Wenzel, M. (eds.) TPHOLs 2009. LNCS, vol. 5674, pp. 469–484. Springer, Heidelberg (2009)

Contract-Based Verification of Simulink Models*

Pontus Boström

Department of Information Technologies, Åbo Akademi University,
Joukahaisenkatu 3-5, 20520 Turku, Finland
pontus.bostrom@abo.fi

Abstract. This paper presents an approach to compositional contract-based verification of Simulink models. The verification approach uses Synchronous Data Flow (SDF) graphs as a formalism to obtain sequential program statements that can then be analysed using traditional refinement-based verification techniques. Automatic generation of the proof obligations needed for verification of correctness with respect to contracts, as well as automatic proofs are also discussed.

1 Introduction

Model-based design has become a widely used design method to create embedded control software. In this approach, the controller is developed together with a simulation model of the plant to be controlled. This enables simulation of the complete system and thereby some degree of evaluation and testing of the controller without using a prototype. One of the most popular tools for model-based design of control systems is Simulink [17].

Simulink has a user-friendly graphical modelling notation based on data flow diagrams, as well as good simulation tools for testing and validating controllers together with models of the controlled plant. The complexity of control systems is increasing rapidly as more functionality in many applications, such as anti-locking brakes and fuel-injection systems, is implemented in software. As the systems become more complex, the size of the Simulink models used in their design also quickly grows. Hence, there is a continuing need to better manage the complexity of models. Since control systems also often have high reliability requirements, there is also a need to analyse the models for correctness. One approach that we have explored to address the problems above is to use contracts to aid the decomposition of models into smaller parts with well defined interfaces and to aid the analysis of those parts and their interaction for correctness.

The aim of this paper is to propose a new compositional technique for verifying functional correctness of Simulink models with respect to contracts. Contracts here refer to pre- and postconditions for programs or program fragments. Contract-based design has become a popular method for object-oriented software development [18,11,6]. This suggests contracts could be useful for Simulink data flow diagrams also. Furthermore, the interaction between components in

* Work done in the EFFIMA program coordinated by Fimecc.

S. Qin and Z. Qiu (Eds.): ICFEM 2011, LNCS 6991, pp. 291–306, 2011.

Simulink data flow diagrams is simpler than between objects in object-oriented systems, which means that automated formal verification can potentially be easier to do.

We have earlier developed contracts and contract-based verification methods for Simulink models [9,10,7]. Here we give more expressive contracts, similar in expressiveness to the contracts for reactive components in [16]. In addition features in [9,10,7], the contracts here can model internal state of components and relate it to the concrete state used in the Simulink diagrams. A new compositional method to verify correctness of Simulink models with respect to these contracts is also given. The formal analysis methods for Simulink models with contracts are based on translating the models to functionally equivalent sequential statements that can be analysed by traditional, refinement-based, techniques [1,3,4]. To obtain the sequential program statements, Simulink diagrams are viewed as synchronous data flow (SDF) graphs [15,14]. The benefit of using SDF graphs compared to the more ad-hoc approach in [9,10,7] is that the mapping of these data flow graphs to the sequential programs used in the analysis has been thoroughly studied. The approach is supported by a tool [8] that can automatically verify that Simulink models satisfy their contracts. Contract-based design in Simulink has been applied to larger examples [9,7]. The contracts were found to be useful both when structuring the system and for verification.

The paper starts with an overview of Simulink, as well as the proposed contract format. Then SDF graphs are presented with the translation procedure to the sequential programming notation used for analysis. This is followed by discussion of translation correctness. Representation of Simulink diagrams as SDF graphs is then discussed, followed by a presentation of methods for analysis of correctness with respect to contracts, as well as tool support. To illustrate the approach, contract-based verification is used on a small example.

2 Simulink

The language used to create models in Simulink is based on hierarchical data flow diagrams [17]. A Simulink diagram consists of functional blocks connected by signals (wires). The blocks represent transformations of data, while the signals give the flow of data between blocks. The blocks have in- and out-ports that act as connection points for signals. The in-ports provide data to the blocks, while the out-ports provide the results computed by the blocks. Blocks can be parameterised with parameters that are set before model execution and remain constant during the execution. Blocks can also contain memory. Hence, their behaviour does not only depend on the current values on the in-ports and the parameter values, but also on previous in-port values.

Here only discrete Simulink models with one rate are considered. This means that a model is evaluated periodically with a given sampling rate. At each sampling instant, all blocks in the diagram are evaluated in the order given by the signals between them. The models are also assumed to be non-terminating, which is a common assumption for control systems.

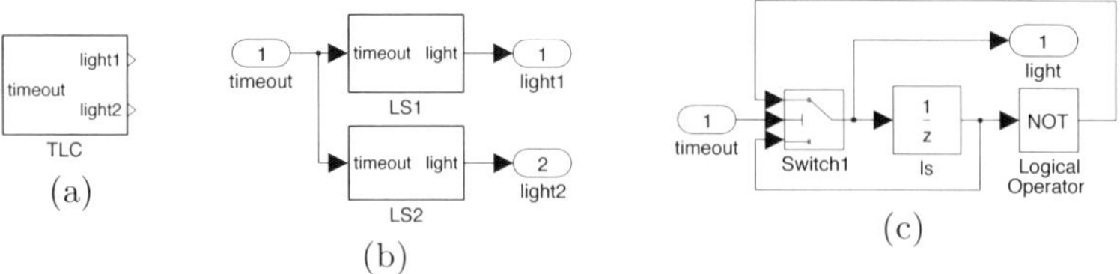

Fig. 1. (a) A subsystem that contains a simple traffic light controller, (b) its contents consisting of two individual light controllers and (c) the individual light controllers

In its most general form, a discrete Simulink block b contains a list of in-ports u, a list of out-ports y, parameters c and a state vector (internal memory) x [17]. The behaviour of the block is given by the difference equation in (1).

$$\begin{aligned} y.k &= f.c.(x.k).(u.k) \\ x.(k+1) &= g.c.(x.k).(u.k) \end{aligned} \tag{1}$$

Here f denotes the function that updates the out-ports y at sample k and g the function that updates the state x. Consider, e.g., the *Logical Operator*-block and the *Unit Delay*-block (marked by $1/z$) in Fig. 1 (c). In this case the *Logical Operator*-block negates the input, while a *Unit Delay*-block delays the input with one sampling time. The behaviour of the *Logical Operator*-block is then given by the equation $y.k = \neg u.k$. Note that this block has no internal state. A *Unit Delay*-block then has the behaviour given as $y.k = x.k \wedge x.(k+1) = u.k$. Information about other blocks can be found in the Simulink documentation [17]. The diagrams can also be hierarchically structured using the notion of subsystem blocks, which are blocks that themselves contain diagrams.

To illustrate the use of Simulink, a small example that consists of a controller for a simplified traffic light system is given. The system consists of two lights that can be either *green* (true) or *red* (false). However, both lights should not be green at the same time. When a timeout signal has the value true, the lights change. The subsystem block *TLC* in Fig. 1 (a) contains the traffic light controller. A new light configuration is computed separately for each light by the subsystems *LS1* and *LS2* (Fig. 1 (b)) at each sampling instant. Both lights are switched in case *timeout* is true otherwise they retain their values (Fig. 1 (c)).

3 Contracts in Simulink

Simulink diagrams for advanced control systems can contain thousands of blocks. For example, in the system discussed in [9], the controller contains more than 4000 blocks. To effectively manage the complexity of such large models, there is a need to better make explicit the division of responsibility between subsystems. To make verification scalable, it is also useful to reason about the interaction between subsystems at a higher level of abstraction than their detailed content, which often consist of deep hierarchies of diagrams containing hundreds of blocks.

contract :
parameters : $(c : t)+$
inports : $(u : t)+$
outports : $(y : t)+$
memory : $(x : t)+$
paramcondition : Q^{param}
precondition : Q^{pre}
postcondition : Q^{post}
initicondition : Q^{init}
postconditionm : Q^{postm}
refrel : Q^{refrel}
end

(a)

contract :	**postcondition** :
inports :	$\sim light1 \,\|\| \sim light2$
timeout : *boolean*	**postconditionm** :
outports :	$s' ==$ **if** *timeout* **then** $\sim s$
light1 : *boolean*;	**else** s **end**
light2 : *boolean*	**initcondition** :
memory :	$s == false$
s : *boolean*	**refrel** :
	$s ==$ v.$(LS1/ls)$ &&
	v.$(LS2/ls) \sim=$ v.$(LS1/ls)$
	end

(b)

Fig. 2. (a) The abstract syntax of contracts and (b) an example contract that describes the traffic light controller subsystem

Our proposed solution to the problems above is to use contracts to describe subsystems. This enables verifying subsystem hierarchies one layer at the time, where each layer relies on the contract descriptions of the subsystems in the layer below. The contracts are mainly intended for expressing properties of control logic. System level properties such as, e.g. stability and performance, are best handled by other means.

An (atomic) subsystem can essentially be considered to be a block of the form in (1), where the internal diagram implements f and g and the state x is provided by the memories of the blocks inside the subsystem. A contract contains conditions to describe this type of behaviour. Our proposed contracts have the abstract syntax given in Fig. 2 (a). There c, u, y and x are identifiers, t is a type in the set $\{\mathsf{double}, \mathsf{int}, \mathsf{boolean}\}$, $z+$ denotes one or more occurrences of z and Q denotes a predicate. The contract first declares the parameters, in- and out-ports of the subsystem, as well as internal state (specification) variables. These are all given as lists of identifier-type pairs. The behaviour of the subsystem is described by a set of conditions. Here Q^{param} describes the block parameters used in the subsystem, Q^{init} describes the initial values of the variables x, Q^{pre} is the precondition, Q^{post} is the postcondition constricting the out-ports and Q^{postm} the postcondition constricting the new values x' of x. The specification variables in the contracts give an abstract view of the block memories inside the subsystem. The block memories in turn represent the concrete state of the Simulink model. The condition Q^{refrel} is then used to describe how the specification variables relate to block memories. In order to refer to block memories in the internal diagram, we use a naming scheme based on block naming policy in Simulink [8]. The contracts here have a similar structure and describe the same type of behaviour as the ones for reactive components in [16].

To give an idea of how contracts can be used, a contract describing the functionality of the traffic light system from Section 2 is given in Fig. 2 (b). A specification variable s is used to model the state of the first light. The initialisation of this light is here assumed to be red (false). The postconditions then encode the desired behaviour of the controller. Both lights should not be green (true) at the same time. Note that for brevity the postcondition does not consider that the output depends on s. The refinement relation then describes how the memory in the *Unit delay*-blocks in the subsystems *LS1* and *LS2* relate to s. Here a function v is used to map block memories to variable identifiers. This mapping is discussed more in Section 6. The concrete syntax used in the contract conditions is inspired by the syntax of Matlab expressions [8].

4 Synchronous Data Flow Graphs

The goal is to verify functional correctness of Simulink models with respect to contracts. Program analysis for sequential programs have been studied extensively, e.g., [3,4]. To reuse this work, we translate the Simulink diagrams to functionally equivalent sequential programs. Furthermore, this allows us to also handle imperative constructs from Matlab, which are often used in conjunction with Simulink. To obtain such sequential programs from Simulink diagrams, we represent the diagrams as synchronous data flow (SDF) graphs [15,14] since compilation of such graphs to sequential or parallel code has been studied extensively.

A data flow program is described by a directed graph where data flows between nodes along the edges. Synchronous data flow programs are a special case where the communication between nodes is synchronous, i.e., the size of the communication buffers is known in advance. The paradigm in [15,14] is intended for heterogenous systems where the nodes can be implemented either by other data flow graphs or in some other programming notation. A node can produce a new value on its outgoing edges when data is available on all incoming edges. A node with no incoming edges can fire at any time. Nodes have to be side-effect free. The data flow graphs presented here are used for sampled signal processing systems, i.e., the nodes in the diagrams are executed periodically with a fixed sampling rate. Furthermore, the SDF programs are never supposed to terminate.

We use a similar notation as in [15,14] to describe our synchronous data flow graphs. An example is given in Fig. 3. The program computes the (exponential) moving average v of the input u over time, $v.k = aw.k + (1 - a)D.v.k$. Here $D.v.k$ denotes the delay of v with one sampling time, $D.v.k = v.(k - 1)$.

Each node is labelled with the in- and out-port names, as well as the update statement inside the node that describes how the out-ports are modified each time the node is executed. The triangle shaped nodes are input or output nodes. They are used to model input and output of data from outside of the graph. The input blocks are assumed to always have data available [15]. The number n on an edge adjacent to the source node denotes that the node will output n pieces of data, while the number m near the destination node denotes that the block will read m pieces of data when it fires. This gives a convenient way to also handle multi-rate data flow networks. Since we only consider single-rate graphs here, n and m are always 1. The D on an edge denotes that the edge delays the data by one sampling time. Each delay also has an identifier, here d.

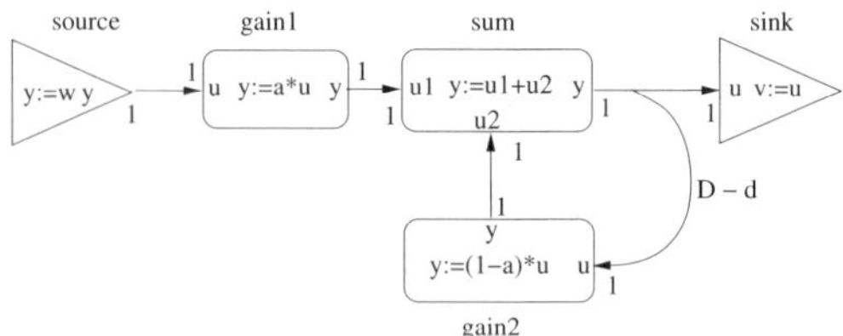

Fig. 3. Example of a simple SDF program

The nodes in the SDF graph can be statically scheduled to obtain sequential or parallel programs [15]. Here we will only present the algorithm [15] for obtaining a minimal *periodic admissible sequential schedule* (PASS), which represents the shortest repeating sequential program. To describe the scheduling, we first construct a *topology matrix* for the SDF graph. This matrix describes how the data availability on the edges change during the execution of the graph. As an example, consider the graph G in Fig. 3. We first number the nodes using a function n_n and edges using n_e according to:

$$\begin{aligned} n_n.source &= 1 \\ n_n.gain1 &= 2 \\ n_n.sum &= 3 \\ n_n.gain2 &= 4 \\ n_n.sink &= 5 \end{aligned} \quad \text{and} \quad \begin{aligned} n_e.(source, gain1) &= 1 \\ n_e.(gain1, sum) &= 2 \\ n_e.(gain2, sum) &= 3 \\ n_e.(sum, gain2) &= 4 \\ n_e.(sum, sink) &= 5 \end{aligned}$$

The element $(n_e.e, n_n.n)$ of the topology matrix Γ for G in Fig. 3 then describes how many data items node n produces on edge e when it fires.

$$\Gamma = \begin{bmatrix} 1 & -1 & 0 & 0 & 0 \\ 0 & 1 & -1 & 0 & 0 \\ 0 & 0 & -1 & 1 & 0 \\ 0 & 0 & 1 & -1 & 0 \\ 0 & 0 & 1 & 0 & -1 \end{bmatrix} \tag{2}$$

The node n run at step k is specified with a vector $v.k$ that contains 1 in the position given by the number $n_n.n$ and 0 elsewhere. For example, if the node *source* is run then $v.k$ is $v.k = \begin{bmatrix} 1\,0\,0\,0\,0 \end{bmatrix}^T$. Using the vector $v.k$ for the node executed at step k, the amount of data on the edges at step $k+1$, $b.(k+1)$, is now given as:

$$b.(k+1) = b.k + \Gamma v.k \tag{3}$$

The change to the buffers is given as the product of the topology matrix and the current $v.k$. The initial amount of data on an edge is given by the number of delays on the edge. For the graph G, the initial state is given by $b.0 = \begin{bmatrix} 0\,0\,0\,1\,0 \end{bmatrix}^T$. The vectors q in the null-space[1] of Γ then give the number of times the nodes can be executed in order to return the buffers to the initial state.

$$b.0 = b.0 + \Gamma q \tag{4}$$

[1] The null-space of a matrix A is the set of all vectors q, such that $Aq = \mathbf{0}$.

In case the graph is schedulable, the least [15], non-zero, integer vector in the null-space of Γ gives the number of times each node is executed in the minimal PASS. This gives an algorithm for scheduling the nodes.

1. Find the smallest integer vector q in the null-space of Γ
2. Construct a set S of all nodes in the graph
3. For each $\alpha \in S$, schedule α if it is runnable and then update the state $b.(k+1)$ in (3) according to v for α. A node is runnable if it has not yet been run q_α times and if execution of α does not make any $b_i.(k+1)$ in (3) negative.
4. If each node α is scheduled q_α times, then stop
5. If no node in S can be scheduled, return error else go to step 3.

5 The Sequential Language

The computation inside nodes is described with a simple imperative programming language. This language is also the target language when translating the SDF graph to a sequential program. The focus is here on verification and a language designed for this purpose is therefore used [3].

Since the analysis methods are based on the refinement calculus [3], a short introduction is needed. Each program statement is a predicate transformer from predicates on the output state space to predicates on the input state space. A predicate transformer S applied to a predicate q gives the weakest predicate describing the states from where S is guaranteed to establish q. The syntax of the statement language is given as:

$$\begin{array}{llll} S ::= & x := E \ (\text{Assignment}) \ | & x : |P \ \ (\text{Non}-\text{deterministic assignment}) & | \\ & [g] \quad\ \ (\text{Assumption}) \ | & S_1 ; S_2 \ \ (\text{Sequential composition}) & | \\ & \{g\} \quad\ (\text{Assertion}) \quad | & S_1 \sqcap S_2 \ (\text{Non}-\text{deterministic choice}) & \end{array} \tag{5}$$

Here x is a list of variables, E a list of expressions, while g and P are predicates. For an arbitrary postcondition q we have that:

$$\begin{array}{llll} (x := E).q = q[x/E] & & x : |P(x, x').q = \forall x' \cdot P(x, x') \Rightarrow q[x/x'] & \\ [g].q & = g \Rightarrow q & (S_1; S_2).q & = S_1.(S_2.q) \\ \{g\}.q & = g \wedge q & (S_1 \sqcap S_2).q & = S_1.q \wedge S_2.q \end{array} \tag{6}$$

Each statement is thus a predicate transformer that transforms a post-condition q into the weakest precondition for the statement to establish condition q. A statement S terminates properly, if it is executed in a state where it can reach the weakest post-condition *true*. These states are described by the condition $S.true$, which is referred to as the termination guard of S, $\mathsf{t}.S \mathrel{\hat{=}} S.true$. In states where $S.true$ does not hold the statement is said to abort. A statement S is said to behave miraculously, if executed in a state where $S.false$ holds. The statement S can then establish any post-condition. The condition that describes the states where S will not behave miraculously is called the guard of S, $\mathsf{g}.S \mathrel{\hat{=}} \neg S.false$. All statements in (5) are monotonic [3]. A statement S is monotonic, if it preserves the ordering given by implication: $S.q \Rightarrow S.p$, if $q \Rightarrow p$.

A refinement relation $\sqsubseteq$ can be defined for the predicate transformers: $S \sqsubseteq R \mathrel{\hat{=}} \forall q \cdot S.q \Rightarrow R.q$. This relation states that if S can establish a postcondition q, then q can also be established by R. Since all statements are *monotonic*, refinement of an individual statement in a program leads to the refinement of the whole program [3]. We can also introduce the concept of *data refinement*. Data refinement is used when two programs do not necessarily work on the same state-space and we like to prove that one refines the other. To prove the refinement, we use a decoding statement Δ that maps the concrete state space to the abstract state space [1,4]. Data refinement of S by R under decoding Δ, $S \sqsubseteq_\Delta R$, is defined as: $S \sqsubseteq_\Delta R \mathrel{\hat{=}} \Delta; S \sqsubseteq R; \Delta$. The decoding Δ is normally assumed to have the form $\Delta \mathrel{\hat{=}} \{+a - c|Q\}$ [1], where $\{+a - c|Q\}$ denotes non-deterministic *angelic* assignment that removes the concrete variables c from the state space and adds the abstract variables a to the state space in manner such that Q relates a and c [1]. An angelic relational assignment statement has the semantics: $\{+a - c|Q\}.q = \exists a' \cdot Q[a/a'] \wedge q[a/a']$ (see [1,4]).

Due to the quantification over predicates, the formulation of refinement above is not very convenient to use. We here use a condition that allows generation of proof obligations for refinement in first order logic when the abstract statement has a specific format, $S = \{g\}; a, z : |P$. Using $\Delta = \{+a - c|Q\}$, rule (7) can be used to prove $S \sqsubseteq_\Delta R$, see [1].

$$Q \wedge g \wedge z, a = z_0, a_0 \Rightarrow R.(\exists a' \cdot Q[a/a'] \wedge P[a, a', z, z'/a_0, a', z_0, z]) \qquad (7)$$

Here a again denotes the abstract variables, c denotes the concrete variables and z common variables. The intuition is that if the precondition g holds in the abstract initial state then the concrete statement R will reach a state corresponding to an abstract state reachable by $a, z : |P$.

Simulink is used to develop control systems, where the interaction of programs with their environment rather than their input-output behaviour is important. Hence, we are here interested in *reactive systems*. Consider two systems constructed from iteration of statements S and S', $init;$ **do** S **od** and $init';$ **do** S' **do** . The behaviour of the systems can then be defined by the traces of the observable states generated during execution [2]. Data refinement can be used to show *trace refinement* [2], $init;$ **do** S **od** $\sqsubseteq_{tr}$ $init';$ **do** S' **do** , between the two systems if they have the same observable state. Hence, that all traces generated by the concrete system can also be generated by the abstract system. Assume we have a decoding statement Δ that states how the unobservable state of the two systems relate. It is then sufficient to prove [2]: $\Delta; init \sqsubseteq init'; \Delta$ and $\Delta; S \sqsubseteq S'; \Delta$ if S' is strict, g.$S = true$. This provides a mechanism to prove correctness of the system over all executions by only analysing the iterated statements. Note also that the decoding statement can be used to provide essentially a loop invariant on the observable and concrete state, see (7).

6 Translation of SDF Graphs

An SDF graph can be translated to a functionally equivalent sequential program by utilising the scheduling in Section 4. Here we will only consider single-rate

Simulink models. Hence, in the systems we consider all data-rates are one and there is also at most one delay on each edge. First we need to introduce the buffers needed for the communication between the nodes. In principle the communication is handled through FIFO-buffers [14]. However, to make the proof obligations simpler, we would like to have static buffers (shared variables). Due to the restrictions on delays and data rates, static buffering is straightforward to implement. All ports and delays are first translated as variables.

Definition 1. *Let the function* v *be an injective function from node and port or delay to variable identifier. Then* $\mathsf{v}.n.p$ *maps a node* n *and port* p *to a unique identifier, while* $\mathsf{v}.d$ *then maps a delay* d *to a unique variable identifier.*

Using the unique variable identifiers, an SDF graph can be translated to a statement in the imperative programming language in (5).

Definition 2. *Let* trans *be a function from an SDF graph to a sequential statement. The translation* $\mathsf{trans}.G$ *of SDF graph* G *is obtained as follows:*

1. *For each node* n *in* G*: Each out-port* p *in* n *is translated to a unique variable* $\mathsf{v}.n.p$*. Each unconnected in-port* p *in* n *is also translated to a unique variable* $\mathsf{v}.n.p$*.*
2. *Each delay* d *is also translated to a unique variable* $\mathsf{v}.d$*.*
3. *The sequential statements from the nodes in* G *are scheduled according to the algorithm in Section 4.*
4. *For each delay* d *on an edge* e *an update statement* $\mathsf{v}.d := \mathsf{v}.n.p$*, where* $\mathsf{v}.d$ *is the variable obtained from* d *and port* p *in* n *is the source port of* e*, is added after the statements from the source and destination nodes of* e*.*

Since we only consider a special case in this paper, the data is handled as if FIFO-buffers were used. If there is no delay on an edge, then the required buffer size is one, since for each data element produced on the edge one will be consumed. The variable obtained from the out-port then corresponds directly to a buffer with one element. In case there is one delay on an edge the required buffer size is two, since both the delayed value and the value produced by the source node have to fit into the buffer. In this case the delay variable corresponds to the head of the buffer and the variable obtained from the out-port in the source node corresponds to the tail element. Fig. 4 illustrates this situation.

Consider the SDF graph G in Fig. 3. This graph is translated to the sequential statement $\mathsf{trans}.G$ given below:

$$\begin{aligned}\mathsf{trans}.G \mathrel{\hat{=}}\ & \mathsf{v}.source.y := \mathsf{v}.G.w;\\ & \mathsf{v}.gain1.y := a * \mathsf{v}.source.y;\\ & \mathsf{v}.gain2.y := (1-a) * \mathsf{v}.d;\\ & \mathsf{v}.sum.y := \mathsf{v}.gain1.y + \mathsf{v}.gain2.y;\\ & \mathsf{v}.d := \mathsf{v}.sum.y;\\ & \mathsf{v}.G.v := \mathsf{v}.sum.y\end{aligned} \tag{8}$$

The statements are obtained from the nodes and scheduled according to Definition 2. Here we assume that w and v in the in and out nodes are ports of a node

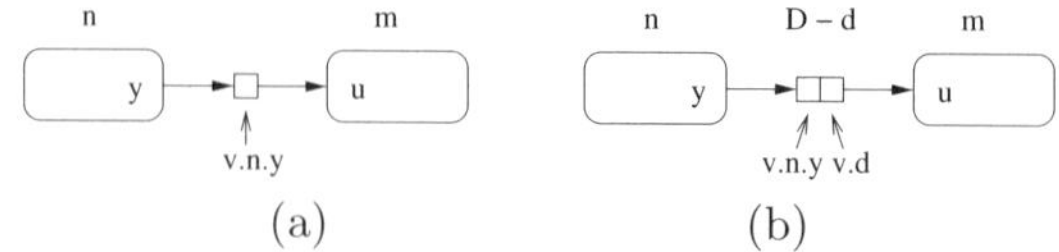

Fig. 4. (a) The buffer of an edge from n to m without a delay and (b) the buffer of an edge with one delay d

G that contains the graph. Note that we have directly replaced every in-port with the out-port variable or delay variable it is connected to.

We can now give a semantics to complete SDF graphs [8], i.e., graphs with no unconnected inputs. The semantics of a complete SDF graph G is here given by the traces of observable behaviour of the system obtained from the minimal PASS, $init$; **do** trans.G **od** . Hence, we can observe the state between repetitions of shortest repeating program statement. This semantics has been chosen to match the semantics of discrete single-rate Simulink, where at each sampling instant the entire model is evaluated.

6.1 Correctness of the Translation

A minimal PASS obtained with the algorithm in Section 4 is not necessarily unique. In order for the translation from SDF graph to sequential statement to be correct, all minimal PASS for the same graph should yield functionally equivalent statements. Different schedules can only be created during scheduling if several nodes are runnable at the same time, i.e., the nodes are independent. Changing the order in which the nodes are chosen then corresponds to swapping the nodes in the resulting schedule. We can thus generate all possible minimal schedules by repeated pairwise swapping of independent nodes. In order to transform a minimal PASS into any other, we then have to show that for any two statements S_1 and S_2 obtained from two independent nodes, $S_1; S_2 = S_2; S_1$. This does not hold in general even though statements from independent nodes use disjoint sets of variables. Consider for example $S_1 = \{false\}$ and $S_2 = [false]$. However, we have that $\{\mathsf{g}.(S_1; S_2)\}; S_1; S_2 = \{\mathsf{g}.(S_2; S_1)\}; S_2; S_1$. Thus for two statements T_1 and T_2 obtained from two different PASS for the same SDF graph we have: $\{\mathsf{g}.T_1\}; T_1 = \{\mathsf{g}.T_2\}; T_2$. Note that when we have a deterministic program T then it is non-miraculous [3], i.e., $\mathsf{g}.T = true$

7 SDF Graph Representation of Simulink Models

To give a semantics to Simulink models, they are mapped to SDF graphs. Discrete Simulink models consist of graphical data flow diagrams, which are similar to SDF graphs. However, a Simulink block is not exactly the same as a node in the SDF notation. In this section we present how to map the most fundamental blocks to their corresponding SDF representation.

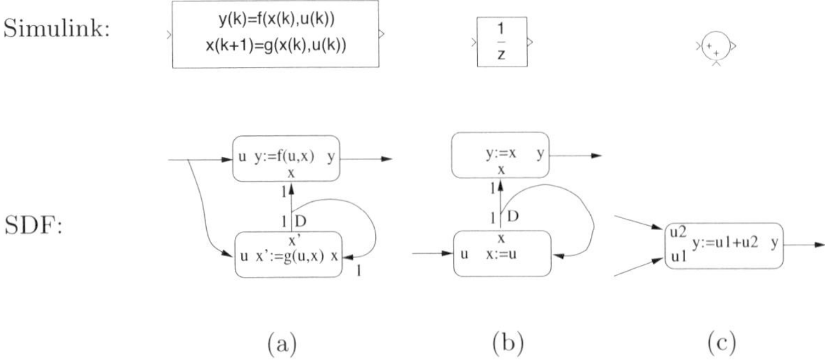

Fig. 5. The SDF representation of (a) a general Simulink block, (b) a *Unit delay*-block and (c) a *Sum*-block

7.1 Mapping Simulink Blocks to Nodes

We can differentiate between the following important Simulink blocks: *Functional blocks*, *In and out blocks* and *Subsystem blocks.*

Functional blocks. These blocks in the Simulink library directly encapsulates a difference equation. Consider again a Simulink block with the general form in (1). The implementation of the block as an SDF graph is shown in Fig. 5 (a). The behaviour of the block is described by two equations, which are not necessarily executed together. All Simulink functional blocks are then special cases of this general pattern: consider, e.g., the *Unit delay*-block and the *Sum*-block shown with their SDF representations in Fig. 5 (b) and (c), respectively. Note that we here only consider Simulink blocks that do not have side effects.

In and out blocks. These blocks are used to obtain inputs from in-ports of the containing subsystem, as well as export values to the out-ports. In and out blocks correspond to in and out nodes in the SDF graphs.

Subsystem blocks. Subsystem blocks that are used for structuring Simulink diagrams. The diagrams are structured using *virtual* and *atomic* subsystem blocks. Virtual subsystems are only used to syntactically group different blocks together and they do not have any affect on the behaviour of the Simulink models. Since execution of blocks from two virtual subsystems might have to be interleaved, we cannot translate virtual subsystem blocks individually and then compose the result. To handle this problem, the virtual subsystem hierarchy is flattened during the translation of the diagrams. This flattening might lead to scalability problems in the verification, and atomic subsystems should be preferred instead. The atomic subsystems are mapped to SDF nodes themselves. The content of an atomic subsystem is translated recursively to an SDF graph, which then become the content of the SDF node corresponding to the subsystem. Consider an atomic subsystem S with in-ports u and out-ports y in Fig. 6. Its SDF representation (denoted $\mathsf{sdf}.S$) is obtained by recursively translating its content.

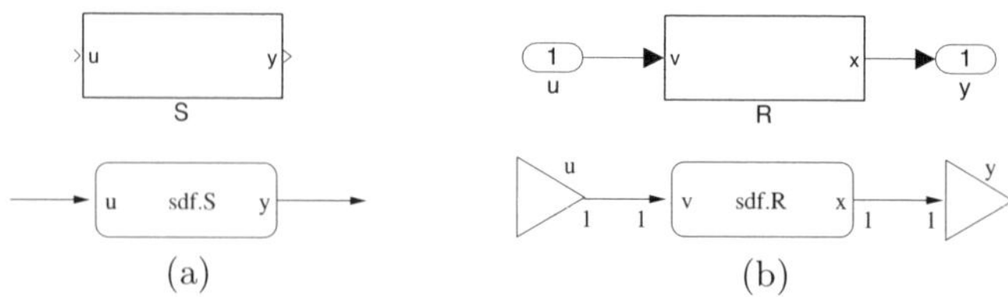

Fig. 6. (a) A Simulink atomic subsystem S and the corresponding SDF node and (b) the contents of S and its corresponding SDF representation

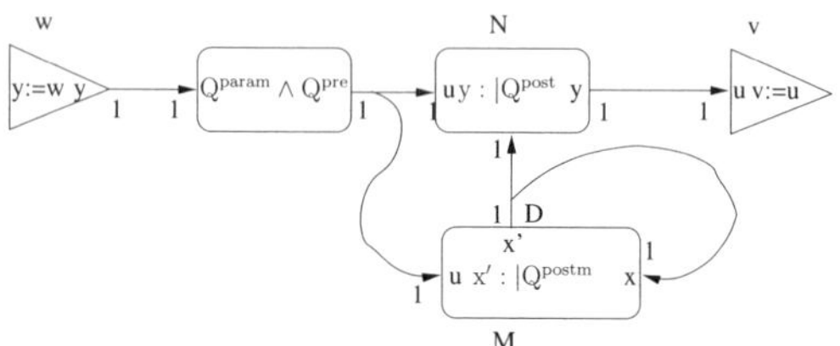

Fig. 7. SDF graph obtained from the contract specification of an atomic subsystem

7.2 Mapping a Subsystem Contract Description to an SDF Graph

One goal of the method given in this paper is to use the contract descriptions of (atomic) subsystems as abstractions of the subsystem behaviours when analysing models. From the contract description we can directly obtain the most abstract statement that satisfies the contract. The most abstract statement that satisfies a specification concerning variables x with precondition Q^{pre} and a postcondition Q^{post}, is $\{Q^{pre}\}; x : |Q^{post}$, see [3].

Assume we have subsystem S in Fig. 6 (a), which is described by the contract C in Fig. 2 (a). We then get the SDF graph representation, $\mathsf{sdf}.C$, shown in Fig. 7 for the contract. This is the most abstract description of S that can be used when analysing models where the subsystem is used. Note that this is very similar to the translation of the general Simulink block in Fig. 5 (a). The reason is that the contract gives an abstract description of the same type of behaviour.

A functionally equivalent sequential program statement $\mathsf{trans}.(\mathsf{sdf}.C)$ can now be obtained. This is again done using the translation procedure in Definition 2.

$$\begin{aligned}\mathsf{trans}.(\mathsf{sdf}.C)] \mathrel{\hat{=}}\ & \mathsf{v}.w.y := \mathsf{v}.S.w; \{Q^{param}[u/\mathsf{v}.w.y] \wedge Q^{pre}[u/\mathsf{v}.w.y]\}; \\ & \mathsf{v}.N.y : |Q^{post}[x, u, y/\mathsf{v}.d, \mathsf{v}.w.y, \mathsf{v}.N.y]; \mathsf{v}.S.v := \mathsf{v}.N.y; \\ & \mathsf{v}.M.x' : |Q^{postm}[x, u, x'/\mathsf{v}.d, \mathsf{v}.w.y, \mathsf{v}.M.x'']; \mathsf{v}.d := \mathsf{v}.M.x'\end{aligned} \tag{9}$$

As in (8), references to the inports are directly substituted by the variable obtained from the connected outport or delay. Note that again the variables w and v in the in and out nodes are considered ports in the containing subsystem S.

8 Verification with Respect to Contracts

In order to do compositional verification of Simulink models, we need to show that the use of a subsystem implementation instead of its contract description (Fig. 7) preserves the behaviour, i.e. refines, the complete system. Assume we have a Simulink model $\mathcal{M}$ containing an atomic subsystem M with contract C. The semantics of the Simulink model is given by the translation to sequential statements. The abstract statement obtained from the model $\mathcal{M}$ where M is used can be written as $\mathsf{trans.(sdf.}\mathcal{M}) \mathrel{\hat{=}} S_1; \mathsf{trans.(sdf.}C)[\mathsf{v.}M.p_i/\mathsf{v.(conn.}p_i)]; S_2$. The concrete statement is then given as $\mathsf{trans.(sdf.}\mathcal{M}') \mathrel{\hat{=}} S_1; \mathsf{trans.(sdf.}M)[\mathsf{v.}M.p_i/\mathsf{v.(conn.}p_i)]; S_2$. In the complete translation all connected in-ports of M are replaced by the port or block memory they are connected to (see Section 6). This is here denoted with the substitution $[\mathsf{v.}M.p_i/\mathsf{v.(conn.}p_i)]$, where p_i are in-ports of subsystem M and $\mathsf{conn.}p_i$ denotes the out-ports or delays those ports are connected to. According to Section 5, in order to prove trace refinement $init; \mathbf{do}\ \mathsf{trans.(sdf.}\mathcal{M})\ \mathbf{od} \sqsubseteq_{tr} init'; \mathbf{do}\ \mathsf{trans.(sdf.}\mathcal{M}')\ \mathbf{od}$ it is sufficient to prove data refinement of the initialisation and the statement inside the loop. The observable state is considered to be all variables except the ones internal to subsystem M and contract C. For the statement we thus need to prove:

$$\begin{aligned} &\Delta; S_1; \mathsf{trans.(sdf.}C)[\mathsf{v.}M.p_i/\mathsf{v.(conn.}p_i)]; S_2 \\ &\sqsubseteq S_1; \mathsf{trans.(sdf.}M)[\mathsf{v.}M.p_i/\mathsf{v.(conn.}p_i)]; S_2; \Delta \end{aligned} \tag{10}$$

Since the refinement only concerns the internals of M, the decoding Δ refers only to the internal variables of $\mathsf{trans.(sdf.}C)$ and $\mathsf{trans.(sdf.}M)$. Here it has the form $\Delta \mathrel{\hat{=}} \{-\mathsf{v.}b_n.p_n, \mathsf{v.}d_n + \mathsf{v.}x, \mathsf{v.}b_o.p_o | Q^{refrel}\}$, where p_n denotes the new out-ports, p_o denotes old out-ports, d_n denotes new delays obtained from Simulink block memories and x denotes specification variables in contract C. Recall that Q^{refrel} (see Fig. 2 (b)) is a predicate that relates the specification variables in contract C with the block memories and specification variables in the diagram inside M.

Since the variables of Δ and S_1, as well as Δ and S_2 are disjoint, we have that $\Delta; S_1 \sqsubseteq S_1; \Delta$ and $\Delta; S_2 \sqsubseteq S_2; \Delta$. To prove (10) we then need to show that:

$$\Delta; \mathsf{trans.(sdf.}C) \sqsubseteq \mathsf{trans.(sdf.}M); \Delta \tag{11}$$

Proof.

$$\begin{aligned} &\Delta; S_1; \mathsf{trans.(sdf.}C)[\mathsf{v.}M.p_i/\mathsf{v.(conn.}p_i)]; S_2 \\ \sqsubseteq\ &\{\text{Assumption above}\} \\ &S_1; \Delta; \mathsf{trans.(sdf.}C)[\mathsf{v.}M.p_i/\mathsf{v.(conn.}p_i)]; S_2 \\ =\ &\{\mathsf{v.}M.p_i, \mathsf{v.(conn.}p_i) \text{ not free in } \Delta\} \\ &S_1; (\Delta; \mathsf{trans.(sdf.}C))[\mathsf{v.}M.p_i/\mathsf{v.(conn.}p_i)]; S_2 \\ \sqsubseteq\ &\{\text{Assumption (11) and } \mathsf{v.(conn.}p_i) \text{ not free in } \mathsf{trans.(sdf.}M)\} \\ &S_1; (\mathsf{trans.(sdf.}M); \Delta)[\mathsf{v.}M.p_i/\mathsf{v.(conn.}p_i)]; S_2 \\ =\ &\{\mathrm{v.M.p_i}, \mathsf{v.(conn.}\mathrm{p_i}) \text{ not free in } \Delta\} \\ &S_1; \mathsf{trans.(sdf.}M); [\mathsf{v.}M.p_i/\mathsf{v.(conn.}p_i)]; \Delta; S_2 \\ \sqsubseteq\ &\{\text{Assumption above}\} \\ &S_1; \mathsf{trans.(sdf.}M)[\mathsf{v.}M.p_i/\mathsf{v.(conn.}p_i)]; S_2; \Delta \end{aligned}$$

□

Note also that if all subsystems are implemented as deterministic diagrams, then the corresponding statements do not behave miraculously [3]. The SDF graph obtained from the Simulink model is thus non-terminating, which is the requirement for correct translation stated in Subsection 6.1.

8.1 Tool Support

Prototype tool support for this approach has been developed [8]. The tool takes a Simulink model annotated by contracts written down as text in the *Description*-field of the subsystems as argument. The tool then automatically checks that each atomic subsystem (with a contract) satisfies its contract using the approach described in this paper. Currently the tool supports virtual, atomic and enabled subsystems, a wide variety of mathematical and logical blocks, delay and memory blocks, as well as switch blocks. However, this list of handled Simulink constructs is expanding. To prove (11), the final proof obligation is after simplifcations generated using formula (7). To increase scalability when verifying that a subsystem conforms to its contract, the verification tool uses the abstractions given by the contract descriptions of the subsystems at lower levels in the subsystem hierarchy as discussed earlier. We have used the SMT solver Z3 [13] to automate the proofs. The constructs that are supported (e.g. the types of arithmetic) and the scalability of the verification is thus largely dependent on this tool.

8.2 Example of Subsystem Refinement

To give an example of the translation of Simulink models and the analysis methods, the simple traffic light controller from Section 2 is used. The subsystem, *TLC*, implementing the controller is shown in Fig. 1 (a). The contract C associated with the subsystem is given in Fig. 2 (b). The contract specification of the subsystem is translated to a sequential program statement as described in (9):

$$\begin{array}{l}\mathsf{trans.}(\mathsf{sdf.}C) \mathrel{\hat{=}} \\ \quad \mathsf{v.}\mathit{Timeout.y} := \mathsf{v.}\mathit{TLC.timeout}; \\ \quad \mathsf{v.}N.\mathit{light}1, \mathsf{v.}N.\mathit{light}2 : |\neg \mathsf{v.}N.\mathit{light}1' \vee \neg \mathsf{v.}N.\mathit{light}2'; \\ \quad \mathsf{v.}\mathit{TLC.light}1 := \mathsf{v.}N.\mathit{light}1; \mathsf{v.}\mathit{TLC.light}2 := \mathsf{v.}N.\mathit{light}2; \\ \quad \mathsf{v.}M.s' : |\mathsf{v.}M.s'' = \mathbf{if}\ \mathsf{v.}\mathit{Timeout.y}\ \mathbf{then}\ \neg \mathsf{v.}s\ \mathbf{else}\ \mathsf{v.}s\ \mathbf{end}; \mathsf{v.}s := \mathsf{v.}M.s'\end{array}$$

The statement above should then be refined by the translation of the diagram inside the subsystem *TLC*, which is shown in Fig. 1 (b). One possible translation of the diagram is then given as:

$$\begin{array}{rl}\mathsf{trans.}(\mathsf{sdf.}\mathit{TLC}) \mathrel{\hat{=}} & \mathsf{trans.}(\mathsf{sdf.}\mathit{LS1})[\mathsf{v.}\mathit{LS1.timeout}/\mathsf{v.}\mathit{TLC.timeout}]; \\ & \mathsf{trans.}(\mathsf{sdf.}\mathit{LS2})[\mathsf{v.}\mathit{LS2.timeout}/\mathsf{v.}\mathit{TLC.timeout}]; \\ & \mathsf{v.}\mathit{TLC.light}1 := \mathsf{v.}\mathit{LS}1.\mathit{light}; \\ & \mathsf{v.}\mathit{TLC.light}2 := \mathsf{v.}\mathit{LS}2.\mathit{light};\end{array}$$

The translation proceeds recursively through subsystems *LS1* and *LS2*. In case they would have contracts, their contract description would be used in the translation. The block memories from the unit delay blocks in *LS1* and *LS2* relate to the specification variable s as described by Q^{refrel} in Fig. 2 (b). The refinement rule (11) for subsystem refinement leads to the condition:

$$\{-\mathsf{v}.(LS1/ls), \mathsf{v}.(LS2/ls), \ldots + \mathsf{v}.s, \ldots | Q^{refrel}\}; \mathsf{trans}.(\mathsf{sdf}.C)$$
$$\sqsubseteq \mathsf{trans}.(\mathsf{sdf}.TLC); \{-\mathsf{v}.(LS1/ls), \mathsf{v}.(LS2/ls), \ldots + \mathsf{v}.s, \ldots | Q^{refrel}\}$$

The tool we have developed [8] has been used to verify this refinement. Whenever subsystem TLC is used in a model we can now use the simpler contract description when analysing the rest of the model. Since we have property (10) and we proved property (11) above, the behaviour of the complete model when the internal diagram of the subsystem is used will refine the behaviour of the model when contract description is used.

9 Conclusions

This paper presents one approach to automatically verify that Simulink models satisfy contracts stating functional properties. The method is based on representing Simulink diagrams as SDF graphs to obtain a functionally equivalent sequential program statements that can be analysed using traditional refinement-based methods. This gives an approach to compositionally verify large models. As a by-product, we also obtain a method for contract-based verification for any SDF-based notation. The approach has also been implemented in a tool [8].

Other formalisations of Simulink supported by verification tools exist in Lustre [19] and Circus [12]. However, these approaches do not consider compositional, contract-based, verification. Contracts could be analysed in those frameworks also, but our approach gives a convenient way to separately reason about both pre- and post-conditions, as well as refinement. Our method can also easily handle the imperative constructs from Matlab that are often used in conjunction with Simulink, which would problematic in Lustre. The tool with the goals closest to ours is *Simulink Design Verifier* (SLDV) [17]. This tool can verify that discrete Simulink models satisfy properties given as special blocks in the diagrams. However, it does not provide a method to systematically build correctness arguments for large models as we do with contracts. SLDV verifies that from a given initial state a state violating the given properties cannot be reached, while our approach is an inductive argument stating that if we start from a state satisfying the refinement relation the model will again end up in such a state and behave according to the contract description. Furthermore, SDLV cannot handle non-linear arithmetic, which Z3 can handle to some degree. This makes it limited for verification of complex properties involving arithmetic. Its main focus is perhaps also more on verifying control logic that involves Stateflow [17].

The work can extended in several directions. Multi-rate systems and more of the Simulink modelling language should be considered. SDF graphs already support multi-rate systems. However, the SDF multi-rate notion does not directly correspond to the one in Simulink. Boogie [5] should also be investigated as a tool for automatic verification of the sequential statements obtained by our translation process, since it is already a very mature tool for this purpose. As a conclusion, SDF graphs in conjunction with the theory of refinement seem to give a good basis for contract-based verification of Simulink models, since mature automatic verification tools and techniques can be used.

References

1. Back, R.-J.R., von Wright, J.: Refinement calculus, part I: Sequential nondeterministic programs. In: de Bakker, J.W., de Roever, W.-P., Rozenberg, G. (eds.) REX 1989. LNCS, vol. 430, pp. 42–66. Springer, Heidelberg (1990)
2. Back, R.-J.R., von Wright, J.: Trace refinement of action systems. In: Jonsson, B., Parrow, J. (eds.) CONCUR 1994. LNCS, vol. 836, pp. 367–384. Springer, Heidelberg (1994)
3. Back, R.-J.R., von Wright, J.: Refinement Calculus: A Systematic Introduction. Springer, Heidelberg (1998)
4. Back, R.-J.R., von Wright, J.: Encoding, decoding and data refinement. Formal Aspects of Computing 12, 313–349 (2000)
5. Barnett, M., Chang, B.Y.E., Deline, R., Jacobs, B., Leino, K.R.M.: Boogie: A modular reusable verifier for object-oriented programs. In: de Boer, F.S., Bonsangue, M.M., Graf, S., de Roever, W.-P. (eds.) FMCO 2005. LNCS, vol. 4111, pp. 364–387. Springer, Heidelberg (2006)
6. Barnett, M., Fähndrich, M., Leino, K.R.M., Müller, P., Schulte, W., Venter, H.: Specification and verification: The Spec# experience. Communications of the ACM 54(6) (2011)
7. Boström, P.: Formal design and verification of systems using domain-specific languages. Ph.D. thesis, Åbo Akademi University (TUCS) (2008)
8. Boström, P., Grönblom, R., Huotari, T., Wiik, J.: An approach to contract-based verification of Simulink models. Tech. Rep. 985, TUCS (2010)
9. Boström, P., Linjama, M., Morel, L., Siivonen, L., Waldén, M.: Design and validation of digital controllers for hydraulics systems. In: The 10th Scandinavian International Conference on Fluid Power, pp. 227–241 (2007)
10. Boström, P., Morel, L., Waldén, M.: Stepwise Development of Simulink Models Using the Refinement Calculus Framework. In: Jones, C.B., Liu, Z., Woodcock, J. (eds.) ICTAC 2007. LNCS, vol. 4711, pp. 79–93. Springer, Heidelberg (2007)
11. Burdy, L., Cheon, Y., Cok, D., Ernst, M., Kiniry, J., Leavens, G.T., Leino, K.R.M., Poll, E.: An overview of JML tools and applications. International Journal on Software Tools for Technology Transfer 7(3), 212–232 (2005)
12. Cavalcanti, A., Clayton, P., O'Halloran, C.: Control law diagrams in circus. In: Fitzgerald, J.S., Hayes, I.J., Tarlecki, A. (eds.) FM 2005. LNCS, vol. 3582, pp. 253–268. Springer, Heidelberg (2005)
13. de Moura, L., Bjørner, N.: Z3: An efficient SMT solver. In: Ramakrishnan, C.R., Rehof, J. (eds.) TACAS 2008. LNCS, vol. 4963, pp. 337–340. Springer, Heidelberg (2008)
14. Lee, E.A., Messerschmitt, D.G.: Static scheduling of synchronous data flow programs for digital signal processing. IEEE Trans. on Computers C-36(1) (1987)
15. Lee, E.A., Messerschmitt, D.G.: Synchronous data flow. Proceedings of the IEEE 75(9) (1987)
16. Maraninchi, F., Morel, L.: Logical-time contracts for reactive embedded components. In: EUROMICRO 2004. IEEE Computer Society, Los Alamitos (2004)
17. Mathworks Inc.: Simulink (2010), http://www.mathworks.com
18. Meyer, B.: Object-Oriented Software Construction, 2nd edn. Prentice-Hall, Englewood Cliffs (1997)
19. Tripakis, S., Sofronis, C., Caspi, P., Curic, A.: Translating discrete-time Simulink to Lustre. ACM Trans. on Embedded Computing Systems 4(4), 779–818 (2005)

Exploiting Abstraction for Efficient Formal Verification of DSPs with Arrays of Reconfigurable Functional Units*

Miroslav N. Velev** and Ping Gao

Aries Design Automation
miroslav.velev@aries-da.com
http://www.miroslav-velev.com

Abstract. We compare two approaches for efficient formal verification of the integration of pipelined processor cores with arrays of reconfigurable functional units. The processors are modeled at a high level of abstraction, using a subset of Verilog, in a way that allows us to exploit the property of Positive Equality that results in significant simplifications of the solution space, and orders of magnitude speedup relative to previous methods. The presented techniques allow us to formally verify the integration of pipelined processors, including complex Digital Signal Processors (DSPs), with arrays of reconfigurable functional units of any size, where the reconfigurable functional units have any design, and for any topology of the connections between them. Such architectures are becoming increasingly used because of their much higher performance and reduced power consumption relative to conventional processors. One of the compared two approaches, which abstracts the entire array of reconfigurable functional units, results in at least 3 orders of magnitude speedup relative to the other approach that models the exact number of reconfigurable functional units and abstracts the design of each and the network that connects them, such that the speedup is increasing with the size of the array. To the best of our knowledge, this is the first work on automatic formal verification of pipelined processors with arrays of reconfigurable functional units.

1 Introduction

Many reconfigurable processor architectures have been proposed—see [19] for a detailed discussion of several. Semiconductor companies are increasingly using reconfigurable processors [4, 5, 12, 13, 15], because of their much higher performance and reduced power consumption relative to conventional processors. Efficient formal verification of such processors is a challenge.

The contribution of this paper is a method for efficient formal verification of pipelined processors with arrays of reconfigurable functional units. The presented abstraction techniques allow us to formally verify the integration of pipelined processor cores with arrays of reconfigurable functional units, where the arrays can have any size, and the reconfigurable functional units any design and any topology of the connections between them. The resulting techniques can be viewed as *design for formal*

* This research was partially funded by the U.S. NSF and NASA.
** Corresponding author.

S. Qin and Z. Qiu (Eds.): ICFEM 2011, LNCS 6991, pp. 307–322, 2011.

verification, and produce at least 3 orders of magnitude speedup, which is increasing with the number of reconfigurable functional units in the array.

In this paper we formally verify variants of the ADRES reconfigurable architecture [22] with increasing numbers of reconfigurable functional units in their arrays. The processors are modeled at a high level of abstraction, using a subset of Verilog, in a way that allows us to exploit the property of Positive Equality to achieve significant simplifications of the solution space, and orders of magnitude speedup relative to previous methods. Correctness is proved with Correspondence Checking [9, 30, 44]—a highly automatic method for formal verification of pipelined/superscalar/VLIW implementation processors by comparison with a non-pipelined specification, based on an inductive correctness criterion and symbolic simulation. This approach is exhaustive, in contrast to assertion-based formal verification, where many properties are proved without guaranteeing that they cover all possible execution scenarios.

Every time the design of computer systems has shifted to a higher level of abstraction, productivity has increased. The logic of Equality with Uninterpreted Functions and Memories (EUFM) [9] allows us to abstract functional units and memories, while completely modeling the control of a processor. In our earlier work on applying EUFM to formal verification of pipelined and superscalar processors, we imposed some simple restrictions [29, 30] on the modeling style for defining such processors, resulting in correctness formulas where most of the terms (abstracted word-level values) appear only in positive equations (equality comparisons) that are called p-equations. Such terms, called p-terms (for positive terms), can be treated as distinct constants [7], thus significantly pruning the solution space, and resulting in orders of magnitude speedup of the formal verification; this property is called Positive Equality. The speedup from Positive Equality is at least 5 orders of magnitude for elaborate dual-issue superscalar designs, and increases with the complexity of the microprocessor under formal verification [44]. On the other hand, equations that appear in negative polarity, or in both positive and negative polarity, are called g-equations (for general equations), and their arguments g-terms. G-equations can be either true or false, and can be encoded with Boolean variables [16, 25, 36, 48] by accounting for the property of transitivity of equality [8], when translating an EUFM correctness formula to an equivalent Boolean formula.

The modeling restrictions and the resulting scalability, together with techniques to model multicycle functional units, exceptions, and branch prediction [31], allowed an earlier version of our tool flow to be used to formally verify a model of the M•CORE processor at Motorola [20], and detect three bugs, as well as corner cases that were not fully implemented. We also applied this method to formally verify an out-of-order superscalar processor, where the reorder buffer could hold up to 1,500 instructions in various stages of execution, and the issue and retire logic could dispatch and complete, respectively, up to 128 instructions per clock cycle [34]. A VLIW processor imitating the Intel Itanium [18, 27] in many features, and that could have more than 200 RISC-like instructions in execution, was formally verified in [32, 44]. Techniques to formally verify pipelined processors with data-value prediction were presented in [46], and with delayed branches in [47]. An efficient method for debugging in Correspondence Checking was proposed in [49]. An approach for automatic formal verification of pipelined processors with hardware mechanisms for soft-error tolerance [6, 11] was presented in [50].

Our tool flow consists of: 1) a symbolic simulator for a subset of Verilog, used to symbolically simulate a pipelined, or superscalar, or VLIW implementation processor and its non-pipelined specification, and produce an EUFM correctness formula; 2) a decision procedure for the logic of EUFM that exploits Positive Equality and other optimizations to translate the EUFM correctness formula to a satisfiability-equivalent Boolean formula; and 3) an efficient Boolean Satisfiability (SAT) solver.

Recent dramatic improvements in SAT-solvers [17, 23, 24, 26] significantly sped up the solving of Boolean formulas generated in formal verification of microprocessors. However, as found in [35], the new efficient SAT-solvers would not have scaled for solving these Boolean formulas if not for the property of Positive Equality. Efficient translations to CNF [37, 38, 40 – 43], exploiting the special structure of EUFM formulas produced with the modeling restrictions, resulted in additional speedup of 2 orders of magnitude.

2 Background

2.1 Using Positive Equality to Formally Verify Pipelined Processors

We use a two-step methodology for formal verification of pipelined, superscalar, or VLIW processors. In step one, all functional units and memories are formally verified individually, in isolation from the rest of the processor. We assume that this step is already performed when the individual modules are implemented; the technology for formal verification of individual functional units and memories is very mature, and is already used in industry. In step two, which is the focus of this paper, we prove that the correct functional units and memories are integrated correctly with control mechanisms in a processor pipeline in a way that preserves the sequential instruction semantics during the concurrent execution of any combination of instructions from any possible state.

For step two above, we perform formal verification by *Correspondence Checking* —comparing a pipelined implementation against a non-pipelined specification, using controlled flushing [10] to automatically compute an *abstraction function*, *Abs*, that maps an implementation state to an equivalent specification state. The *safety property* (see Fig. 1) is expressed as a formula in the logic of EUFM, and checks that one step of the implementation corresponds to between 0 and k steps of the specification, where k is the issue width of the implementation, i.e., the maximum number of instructions that an implementation processor can start executing in a clock cycle; $k > 1$ in superscalar processors. F_{Impl} is the transition function of the implementation, and F_{Spec} is the transition function of the specification. We will refer to the sequence of first applying *Abs* and then F_{Spec} as the *specification side* of the diagram in Fig. 1, and to that of first applying F_{Impl} and then *Abs* as the *implementation side*.

The safety property is the inductive step of a proof by induction, since the initial implementation state, Q_{Impl}, is completely arbitrary. If the implementation is correct for all transitions that can be made for one step from an arbitrary initial state, then the implementation will be correct for one step from the next implementation state, Q_{Impl}, since that state will be a special case of an arbitrary state as used for the initial state, and so on for any number of steps. For some processors, e.g., where the control logic is optimized by using unreachable states as don't-care conditions, we might have to impose a set of *invariant constraints* for the initial state, Q_{Impl}, in order to exclude unreachable states. Then, we need to prove that those constraints will be satisfied in the implementation state after one step, Q_{Impl}, so that the correctness will hold by induction for that state, and so on for all subsequent states. The reader is referred to [39, 45] for efficient ways to prove liveness of pipelined processors, and to [1, 2] for a discussion of correctness criteria. We can prove liveness by a modified version of the safety correctness criterion [39, 45].

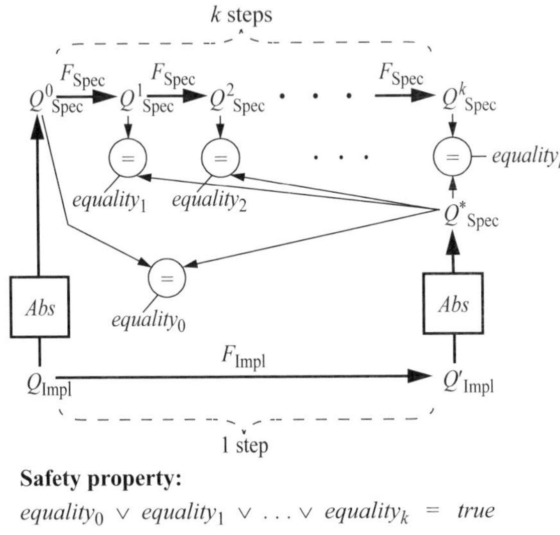

Fig. 1. The safety correctness property for an implementation processor with issue width k: one step of the implementation should correspond to between 0 and k steps of the specification, when the implementation starts from an arbitrary initial state Q_{Impl} that is possibly restricted by a set of invariant constraints

The syntax of EUFM [9] includes *terms* and *formulas*. Terms are used to abstract word-level values of data, register identifiers, memory addresses, as well as the entire states of memories. A term can be an Uninterpreted Function (UF) applied to a list of argument terms, a term variable, or an *ITE* operator selecting between two argument terms based on a controlling formula, such that *ITE*(*formula*, $term_1$, $term_2$) will evaluate to $term_1$ when *formula* = *true*, and to $term_2$ when *formula* = *false*. The syntax for terms can be extended to model memories by means of functions *read* and *write* [9, 33]. Formulas are used to model the control path of a processor, as well as to express a correctness condition. A formula can be an Uninterpreted Predicate (UP) applied to a list of argument terms, a Boolean variable, an *ITE* operator selecting between two argument formulas based on a controlling formula, or an equation (equality comparison) of two terms. Formulas can be negated and combined with Boolean connectives. We will refer to both terms and formulas as *expressions*. If we exclude functions *read* and *write* from the syntax of EUFM, we obtain the logic of Equality with Uninterpreted Functions.

UFs and UPs are used to abstract the implementation details of functional units by replacing them with "black boxes" that satisfy no particular properties other than that of *functional consistency*. Namely, that equal combinations of values to the inputs of the UF (or UP) produce equal output values. Thus, we will solve a more general problem—proving that the processor is correct for any functionally consistent implementation of its functional units. However, this more general problem is easier to solve.

Function *read* takes two argument terms serving as memory state and address, respectively, and returns a term for the data at that address in the given memory. Function *write* takes three argument terms serving as memory state, address, and data, and returns a term for the new memory state. Functions *read* and *write* satisfy the *forwarding property of the memory semantics*: *read*(*write*(*mem*, *waddr*, *wdata*), *raddr*) is equivalent to *ITE*((*raddr* = *waddr*), *wdata*, *read*(*mem*, *raddr*)).

We classify the equations that appear negated as *g-equations* (for general equations), and as *p-equations* (for positive equations) otherwise. We classify all terms that appear as arguments of g-equations as *g-terms* (for general terms), and as *p-terms* (for positive terms) otherwise. We classify all applications of a given UF as g-terms if at least one application of that UF appears as a g-term, and as p-terms otherwise.

In [29, 30], the style for modeling high-level processors was restricted in order to increase the terms that appear only in positive equations or as arguments to UFs and UPs, and reduce the terms that appear in both positive and negated equations. First, equations between data operands, where the result appears in both positive and negated polarity—e.g., determining whether to take a branch-on-equal instruction—are abstracted with a new UP in both the implementation and the specification. Second, the Data Memory is abstracted with a conservative model, where the interpreted functions *read* and *write* are replaced with new UFs, *DMem_read* and *DMem_write*, respectively, that do not satisfy the forwarding property. This property is not needed, if both the implementation and the specification execute the same sequence of operations that are not stalled based on conditions that depend on equations between addresses for that memory [33]. The property of functional consistency of UFs and UPs can be enforced by Ackermann constraints [3], or nested *ITE*s [28]. In our decision procedure, we use nested *ITE*s, because this translation method allows us to treat more terms as p-terms, and thus to exploit Positive Equality more fully [7].

The modeling restrictions result in a monotonically positive structure of the correctness formula that contain p-equations and applications of UFs and UPs. Such formulas have to be valid for any interpretation of the p-terms, including the maximally diverse interpretation, where each p-term is replaced with a distinct constant. However, because of the monotonically positive structure of a correctness formula, its validity under a maximally diverse interpretation of the p-terms implies the validity of the formula under any interpretation of the p-terms. The resulting property of Positive Equality produces a significant pruning of the solution space, and orders of magnitude speedup. The focus of the current paper is how to exploit Positive Equality to efficiently formally verify complex pipelined processors with large arrays of reconfigurable functional units.

2.2 Abstracting a Single Reconfigurable Functional Unit

In our recent work [51], we proposed a method to abstract a single reconfigurable functional unit with the placeholder shown in Fig. 2.

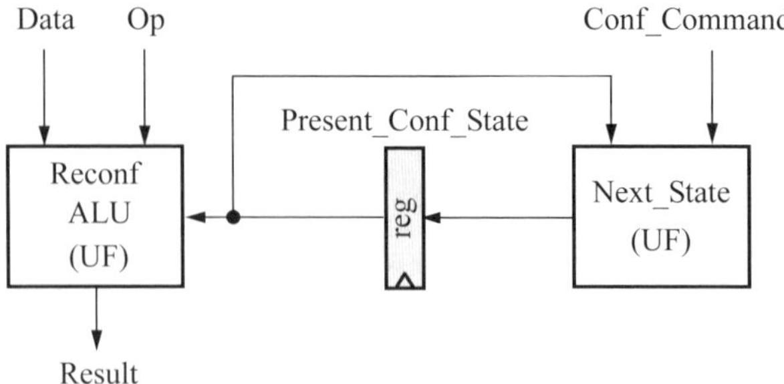

Fig. 2. Placeholder for abstracting one reconfigurable functional unit

The entire state of the configuration memory that stores the configuration contexts of this functional unit was abstracted with one term stored in the latch Present_Conf_State. The next state of that latch was produced by UF Next_State that takes as inputs the present state of the latch and term Conf_Command that abstracts the current configuration command. Depending on the ISA, the latch that abstracts the present state of the configuration memory could be updated conditionally, based on an enable signal (not shown in the figure) produced by the decoding logic of the processor. UF Reconf ALU abstracts the computation of a word-level result as a function of the current state of the configuration memory, the input data term (there can be as many input data terms as required for the given reconfigurable functional unit), and the opcode term Op that is assumed to specify both the computation to be performed and the configuration context to be used from the configuration memory.

If a reconfigurable functional unit produces several word-level or bit-level output values, the computation of each will be abstracted with a different UF or UP, respectively, that all have the same inputs. For a given reconfigurable functional unit, the same placeholder (consisting of UFs and UPs with the same names for the computation of the results and the next state of the configuration memory) is used to abstract that reconfigurable functional unit in both the pipelined/superscalar/VLIW implementation processor and the non-pipelined specification.

2.3 The ADRES Reconfigurable Architecture

In the ADRES reconfigurable architecture [22] (see Fig. 3.a), a VLIW processor core interacts with an array of reconfigurable functional units. Each reconfigurable functional unit (FU) has its dedicated register file (RF), configuration memory (Conf. RAM), and configuration counter (conf. counter) that selects a configuration context from the configuration memory to control the FU in each clock cycle (see Fig. 3.b). A reconfigurable functional unit takes as inputs two data operands, src1 and src2, a 1-bit predicate value, pred, and the currently selected configuration context, and produces as results one word-level value, dst1, and two 1-bit predicate values, pred_dst1 and pred_dst2 that will be used for predication of later computations. The word-level result is written to that functional unit's dedicated register file, as controlled by the currently selected configuration context. A network on a chip with a specific topology of connections is used to send results from each of these functional units to any of the other reconfigurable functional units, and to the integer functional units in the VLIW core. The configuration of the connections in the network is controlled by the currently selected configuration contexts of all reconfigurable functional units. The configuration contexts, their selection with the configuration counter, and the communication between the reconfigurable functional units in the array is orchestrated by the compiler.

The ADRES architecture is a template in that its specific design can be optimized for a given set of applications by varying: the architecture of the VLIW processor core, the number of reconfigurable functional units in the array, the computational power of each reconfigurable functional unit (they do not have to be identical), the size of the configuration memory and register file of each of these functional units, and the topology of the communication network between them, among other factors.

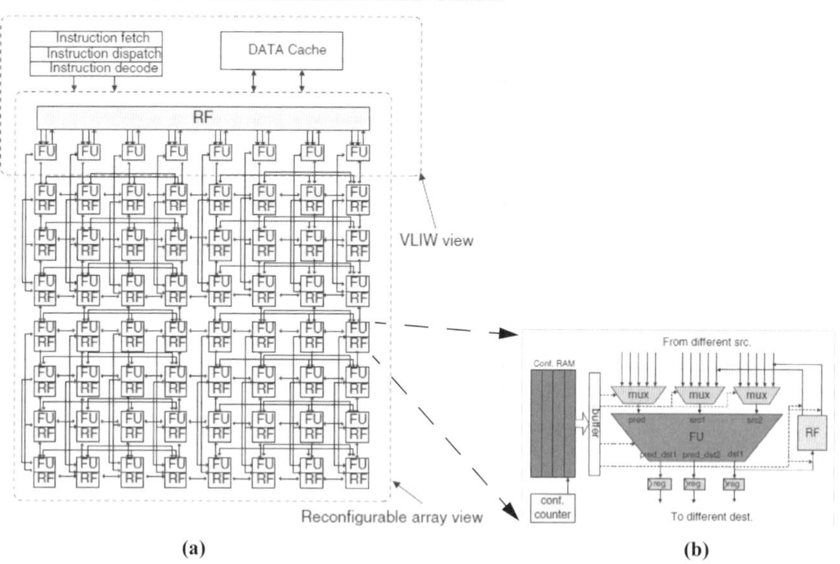

Fig. 3. (a) The ADRES architecture template; and (b) an example of a reconfigurable functional unit (FU) in ADRES with its dedicated Register File (RF), and configuration memory (Conf. RAM)

3 Techniques for Abstracting Arrays of Reconfigurable Functional Units

3.1 Detailed Abstract Modeling of the Array of Reconfigurable Functional Units

We start by presenting a method for detailed abstract modeling of the array of reconfigurable functional units in the ADRES architecture, using abstraction techniques that allow us to exploit the property of Positive Equality. We use an uninterpreted function (UF) to abstract the network that selects each predicate operand or data operand for one of the reconfigurable functional units, regardless of the topology of that network and its selection mechanism. This is done with a different UF for each predicate or data operand of each reconfigurable functional unit, thus modeling a possibly different topology and mechanism for selecting each operand. Such an UF has as inputs all possible sources of predicate or data operands, respectively, including the outputs of functional units in the main pipeline of the processor, results computed by the other reconfigurable functional units in the array in the previous clock cycle and stored in the registers after those reconfigurable functional units, and the register file of the given reconfigurable functional unit. Furthermore, each such UF that models the selection of an operand has as input a term that abstracts the control bits selecting an operand from the possible sources in the current clock cycle; this term abstracts the control bits that are extracted from the current configuration context in order to select the data operand in the given UF.

The detailed abstract model of one reconfigurable functional unit in the array of the ADRES architecture is shown in Fig. 4. The UFs that abstract the selection of the one predicate and two data operands for a given reconfigurable functional unit are in the top center and are labeled, respectively, Select Pred Operand, Select Data Operand 1, and Select Data Operand 2. The computation of the two predicate and one data results is abstracted with uninterpreted functions Compute pred_dst1, Compute pred_dst2, and Compute dst1, respectively, shown at bottom center.

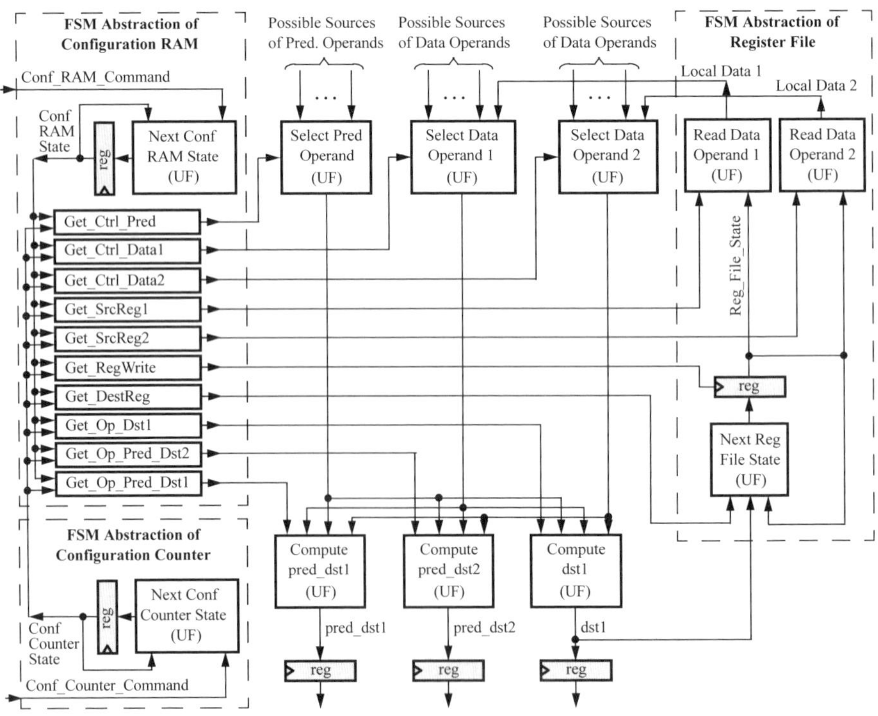

Fig. 4. Detailed abstract model of one reconfigurable functional unit in the array of the ADRES architecture

The Configuration Counter is abstracted with a Finite State Machine (FSM), shown in the lower left corner of Fig. 4, where the current state is abstracted with term Conf Counter State, stored in a register, and the next state is computed with UF Next Conf Counter State, which takes as operands the term for the current state and term Conf_Counter_Command that abstracts a command for updating/modifying the current state that comes from the main processor pipeline, and produces a term for the next state of the Configuration Counter. The Configuration RAM is abstracted with another FSM, shown in the middle and top on the left side, where the current state is abstracted with term Conf RAM State, stored in a register, and the next state is computed with UF Next Conf RAM State, which takes as operands the term for the current state and term Conf_RAM_Command that abstracts a command for updating/modifying the current state that comes from the main processor pipeline.

Extracting the various command fields and control bits from the current Configuration RAM state, as pointed to by the current state of the Configuration Counter, is done with nine UFs and one UP, that all take as arguments the terms for the current state of the Configuration RAM and for the current state of the Configuration Counter, and produce abstractions of the corresponding control fields. For example, UF Get_Ctrl_Pred extracts a term that abstracts the control signals selecting the predicate operand, as abstracted by UF Select Pred Operand. Similarly, UFs Get_Ctrl_Data1 and Get_Ctrl_Data2 extract terms that abstract the control signals selecting the first and the second data operands, respectively, as abstracted by UFs Select Data Operand 1 and Select Data Operand 2. UFs Get_SrcReg1, Get_SrcReg2, and Get_DestReg extract terms that represent the two source register identifiers and one destination register identifier that are used to, respectively, read two data operands from the local register file, and write the word-level result when computed at the end of the current clock cycle. Uninterpreted Predicate (UP) Get_RegWrite extracts a control bit that indicates whether the word-level result dst1 that will be computed in the current cycle will be written to the local register file. Finally, UFs Get_Op_Pred_Dst1, Get_Op_Pred_Dst2, and Get_Op_Dst1 extract terms that abstract the control bits selecting operations to be performed when computing the two predicate and one data results.

The local register file is abstracted with another FSM (see the right side of Fig. 4), where the entire state is abstracted with term Reg_File_State. The reading of the two data operands is abstracted with UFs Read Data Operand 1 and Read Data Operand 2, respectively, that both take as an argument the term for the current state of the register file, as well as the term that abstracts the corresponding source register identifier, as produced by UFs Get_SrcReg1 and Get_SrcReg2, respectively. The next state of the register file is abstracted with a term produced by UF Next Reg File State that takes as arguments the term for the current register file state, the term for the destination register identifier, and the term for the current data result, dst1, whose computation is abstracted with UF Compute dst1. From [33], we can use such an FSM abstraction of the local register file, since both the implementation and the specification processors execute the same sequence of memory operations for each such register file, and these operations are not stalled based on conditions that depend on equations between addresses (register identifiers) for that register file. This is the case, because in the ADRES architecture all computations are orchestrated by the compiler and there is no stalling in the array of reconfigurable functional units.

The entire array of reconfigurable functional units is modeled by using the detailed abstraction from Fig. 4 for each reconfigurable functional unit. The models for the different functional units are linked together by using the two predicate and one data results, computed by each of these functional units at the end of the previous clock cycle, as possible sources of the one predicate and two data operands for all functional units in the array. The same abstraction of the array is used in both the pipelined/superscalar/VLIW implementation processor, and in its non-pipelined specification. Note that each reconfigurable functional unit in the array contributes 6 architectural state elements—the 6 registers that are shaded in Fig. 4—to the set of architectural state elements, for which the automatic tool has to compare for equality the symbolic expressions produced by both sides of the commutative correctness diagram in Fig. 1.

As an optimization, which we applied, we can use different names for the 20 UFs and one UP that are used to abstract each reconfigurable functional unit in the array. This allows us to model potentially different topologies of the networks for selecting operands, potentially different logic for extracting control signals from the currently selected configuration context from the Configuration RAM, and potentially different implementations of the functional units, as well as of the Configuration RAM and register file of each functional unit. Also, this results in much simpler symbolic expressions when UFs and UPs are eliminated in translation of the EUFM correctness formula to CNF, since functional consistency will be enforced only for different applications of an UF or an UP for the same reconfigurable functional unit, as opposed to for all reconfigurable functional units.

We can prove the following lemma, where a *conservative approximation* means an abstraction that omits some properties of the original model in a conservative way that may only lead to a falsification of the correctness condition; however, if the correctness condition is satisfied with the conservative approximation, then the correctness condition will also be satisfied with the original model that also satisfies the omitted properties (that were not necessary for the correctness proof).

Lemma 1. The presented detailed abstract model of one reconfigurable functional unit, as shown in Fig. 4, when used with different names for the 20 UFs and one UP that abstract each reconfigurable functional unit in the array, is a conservative approximation.

Proof: Follows from the construction of the model in Fig. 4 and using different names for the UFs and UPs used for different reconfigurable functional units in the array. □

3.2 Abstracting the Entire Array of Reconfigurable Functional Units with One FSM

We can also abstract the entire array of reconfigurable functional units with just one FSM, where the present state is represented with term Present_State stored in a register, and the next state is a term produced by uninterpreted function Next_State that takes as arguments the term for the present state, the terms Conf_Counter_Command and Conf_RAM_Command that abstract the commands from the main processor pipeline for updating, respectively, the Configuration Counters and the Configuration RAMs in the array, and any additional terms that abstract operands supplied by the main processor pipeline, as shown in Fig. 5.

The present state of the FSM from Fig. 5 is used not only for computing the next state of the FSM, but also in the main processor pipeline as an argument to all UFs and UPs that in the detailed model from Sect. 3.1 had as arguments terms from any of the state elements in the array of reconfigurable functional units. In this way, we can view each of these UFs and UPs as both abstracting the same computation as in the detailed processor model from Sect. 3.1 and extracting the field from the present state of the array that was used as an argument to the corresponding UF or UP in the processor pipeline from Sect. 3.1.

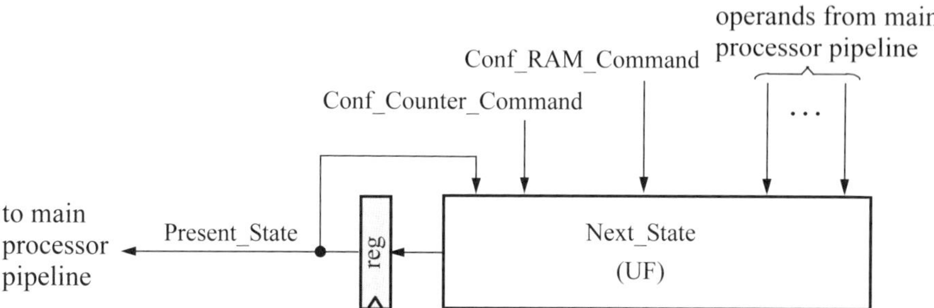

Fig. 5. An FSM that can be used to abstract the entire array of reconfigurable functional units

The same abstraction of the array is used in both the pipelined/superscalar/VLIW implementation processor, and in its non-pipelined specification. Now only one new architectural state element is introduced, regardless of the size of the array.

LEMMA 2. The presented abstraction of the entire array of reconfigurable functional units, as shown in Fig. 5, is a conservative approximation.

Proof: Follows from the construction of the model in Fig. 5, where term Present_State can be viewed as abstracting the concatenation of all state elements from the detailed model in Sect. 3.1, and UF Next_State can be viewed as abstracting the combined operation of all UFs and UPs from the detailed model of the array of reconfigurable functional units.

The above abstraction is based on the assumption that the correctness of the array of reconfigurable functional units is proved separately. This has to be done for the approaches from both Sect. 3.1 and 3.2 when proving that a specific algorithm is correctly mapped onto the array of reconfigurable functional units, based on given specific contents of the Configuration RAMs and Configuration Counters, as well as specific implementations of all logic blocks in the array of reconfigurable functional units. Such a proof will be carried out for each implementation of an algorithm that is mapped onto an array of reconfigurable functional units, and is beyond the scope of this paper. The focus of this paper is a method for proving the correctness of the integration of an array of reconfigurable functional units with a given pipelined, superscalar, or VLIW processor pipeline.

4 Results

The experiments were conducted on a computer with two 3.47-GHz six-core Intel Xeon x5690 processors and 64 GB of memory, running Red Hat Enterprise Linux v6.1. (Each experiment used only a single core, and had access to 32 GB of memory.) We applied our industrial tool, combined with a proprietary SAT solver that is faster than the best publicly available SAT solvers by at least a factor of 2. The computation of the abstraction function in the inductive correctness criterion of safety from Fig. 1 was done with controlled flushing [10]. Translation to CNF was done with block-level methods, where blocks of logic gates are translated to CNF without intermediate CNF variables for internal values [37, 38, 40, 42, 43].

The experiments were to formally verify safety of processors, starting with DSP_base, the original DSP design before its extension with an array of reconfigurable functional units in the style of the ADRES architecture. That processor has 5 pipeline stages with up to 9 RISC-like instructions in each stage, for a total of up to 45 RISC-like instructions in execution. DSP_base implements predicated execution for each instruction, based on the value of a qualifying predicate register from a predicate register file. There are separate integer and floating-point register files. The processor implements branch prediction, exceptions, and has multicycle functional units—the instruction memory interface, the floating-point functional units in the Execution stage, and the data memory interface can each take multiple clock cycles to complete an operation.

As shown in the first line of Table 1, the formal verification of the original design, DSP_base, results in a Boolean correctness formula with 4,238 Boolean variables, and its CNF translation has 14,540 CNF variables, 743,481 literals, and 214,842 clauses. The symbolic simulation according to the correctness diagram in Fig. 1 took 0.03 s, the translation of the EUFM correctness formula to CNF 0.6 s, and the SAT solving 3.8 s, for a total of 4.4 s.

We wrote a script that automatically extends the original DSP with detailed abstract models of arrays of reconfigurable functional units, as described in Sect. 3.1. Another script was used to add the same detailed model of the array to the non-pipelined specification processor. The size of the array varied from 1 to 2,048. As discussed in Sect. 3.1, each reconfigurable functional unit had 6 flip-flops in its abstract model that were considered to be part of the architectural state elements of the extended processor. The experiments for these models are presented in the middle section of Table 1. As can be seen, the processors with arrays of up to 16 reconfigurable functional units result in CNF correctness formulas that are comparable in size to that from the original processor, and so are their respective total times for formal verification. However, after the processor with an array of 256 reconfigurable functional units, the numbers of literals and clauses in the CNF correctness formulas increase by a factor of 3 or more, and the total formal verification time by approximately a factor of 5 with each doubling of the number of reconfigurable functional units. Our decision procedure ran out of memory (given the 32 GB available to it) in the translation of the EUFM correctness formula to CNF for the model with an array of 2,048 reconfigurable functional units, and so the formal verification of that design did not complete in 10,236 s.

The last row of Table 1 presents the results for the DSP where the entire array of reconfigurable functional units is abstracted with a single FSM in a way that is a conservative approximation, for any number of reconfigurable functional units in the

Table 1. Experimental results. The formal verification of the DSP with an array of 2,048 reconfigurable functional units ran out of memory in the translation of the EUFM correctness formula to CNF, given the 32 GB of memory that were accessible by the tool. Boolean variables are those that are arguments of the Boolean correctness formula before its translation to CNF.

Benchmark	CNF Formula					Time [s]			
	Bool Vars	CNF Vars	Literals	Clauses	Size [MB]	Symbolic Simu-lation	Transl. to CNF	SAT Solving	Total
DSP_base	4,238	14,540	743,481	214,842	4.9	0.03	0.6	3.8	4.4
DSP_array_1	4,247	14,782	749,278	216,785	4.9	0.03	0.6	4.1	4.7
DSP_array_2	4,252	14,843	751,842	217,580	4.9	0.03	0.6	4.0	4.6
DSP_array_4	4,262	14,965	757,096	219,206	4.9	0.04	0.6	4.0	4.6
DSP_array_8	4,286	15,255	770,726	223,248	5.0	0.04	0.7	4.4	5.1
DSP_array_16	4,322	15,697	792,148	229,970	5.2	0.06	0.9	3.9	4.9
DSP_array_32	4,242	16,656	844,635	244,688	5.5	0.12	1.2	5.5	6.8
DSP_array_64	4,562	18,625	992,836	290,306	6.5	0.19	2.3	6.8	9.3
DSP_array_128	4,882	22,662	1,416,702	416,415	9.5	0.45	6.9	13.2	20.6
DSP_array_256	5,522	30,337	2,763,268	808,130	19	1.37	29	25	55
DSP_array_512	6,802	46,071	7,542,856	2,192,512	53	4.9	163	138	306
DSP_array_1024	9,362	77,280	25,362,823	7,316,482	180	28	1,212	550	1,790
DSP_array_2048	—	—	—	—	—	108	>10,128	—	>10,236
DSP_array_fsm	4,242	14,706	747,155	216,120	4.9	0.03	0.61	4.6	5.2

array, for any design of these functional units, and any topology of the connections between them, as presented in Sect. 3.2. The entire state of the array was abstracted with one term stored in a flip-flop that was considered part of the architectural state. As can be seen, the CNF correctness formula had approximately the same size as that from formal verification of the original processor without an array of reconfigurable functional units. The total formal verification time was 5.2 s. This represents at least *3 orders of magnitude speedup* relative to the formal verification of the processor with an array of 2,048 reconfigurable functional units, and the speedup is increasing with the size of the array. Thus, the formal verification time becomes invariant, regardless of the size of the array of reconfigurable functional units, their design, the sizes of their register files and configuration memories, or the topology of the connections between them.

5 Conclusion

We presented abstraction techniques to formally verify the integration of pipelined processors with arrays of reconfigurable functional units in the style of the ADRES architecture. Our techniques allow us to formally verify the integration of pipelined processor cores with arrays of reconfigurable functional units of any size, where the reconfigurable functional units have any design, and are connected with a network of any topology. These abstraction techniques result in at least 3 orders of magnitude speedup relative to formal verification without them, and the speedup is increasing with the number of reconfigurable functional units in the array. To the best of our knowledge, this is the first work on automatic formal verification of pipelined processors with arrays of reconfigurable functional units.

References

[1] Aagaard, M.D., Day, N.A., Lou, M.: Relating Multi-Step and Single-Step Microprocessor Correctness Statements. In: Aagaard, M.D., O'Leary, J.W. (eds.) FMCAD 2002. LNCS, vol. 2517, pp. 123–141. Springer, Heidelberg (2002)

[2] Aagaard, M.D., Cook, B., Day, N.A., Jones, R.B.: A Framework for Superscalar Microprocessor Correctness Statements. Software Tools for Technology Transfer (STTT) 4(3), 298–312 (2003)

[3] Ackermann, W.: Solvable Cases of the Decision Problem. North-Holland, Amsterdam (1954)

[4] Anglia, STMicroelectronics Adds DSP to Reconfigurable-Processor SoC for Wireless Infrastructure Applications (March 2006), http://www.anglia.com/newsarchive/904.asp?article_id=1750

[5] Asia and South Pacific Design Automation Conference (ASP-DAC 2009), Panel Discussion: Near-Future SoC Architectures—Can Dynamically Reconfigurable Processors be a Key Technology? (January 2009)

[6] Blaauw, D., Das, S.: CPU, Heal Thyself: A Fault-Monitoring Microprocessor Design Can Save Power or Allow Overclocking. IEEE Spectrum 46(8), 40–43 (2009), http://spectrum.ieee.org/semiconductors/processors/cpu-heal-thyself/0

[7] Bryant, R.E., German, S., Velev, M.N.: Processor Verification Using Efficient Reductions of the Logic of Uninterpreted Functions to Propositional Logic. ACM Transactions on Computational Logic 2(1), 93–134 (2001)

[8] Bryant, R.E., Velev, M.N.: Boolean Satisfiability with Transitivity Constraints. ACM Transactions on Computational Logic (TOCL) 3(4), 604–627 (2002)

[9] Burch, J.R., Dill, D.L.: Automated Verification of Pipelined Microprocessor Control. In: Dill, D.L. (ed.) CAV 1994. LNCS, vol. 818, pp. 68–80. Springer, Heidelberg (1994)

[10] Burch, J.R.: Techniques for Verifying Superscalar Microprocessors. In: Design Automation Conference (DAC 1996), pp. 552–557 (June 1996)

[11] Das, S., Tokunaga, C., Pant, S., Ma, W.-H., Kalaiselvan, S., Lai, K., Bull, D.M., Blaauw, D.T.: RazorII: In Situ Error Detection and Correction for PVT and SER Tolerance. IEEE Journal of Solid-State Circuits 44(1), 32–48 (2009)

[12] DPReview, Casio Introduces Exilim EX-ZR10 with Back-Illuminated Sensor (September 2010), http://www.dpreview.com/news/1009/10092015casioexzr10.asp

[13] EDACafe, Panasonic Deploys Reconfigurable Logic in Professional AV Products (November 2007), http://www10.edacafe.com/nbc/articles/view_article.php?section=CorpNews&articleid=462449

[14] Eén, N., Sörensson, N.: MiniSat: A SAT Solver with Conflict-Clause Minimization. In: Bacchus, F., Walsh, T. (eds.) SAT 2005. LNCS, vol. 3569, pp. 61–75. Springer, Heidelberg (2005)

[15] Free Press Release, Sony Details PSP Chip Specs (PlayStation Portable Game Player) (June 2007), http://www.free-press-release.com/news/200706/1182092979.html

[16] Goel, A., Sajid, K., Zhou, H., Aziz, A., Singhal, V.: BDD Based Procedures for a Theory of Equality with Uninterpreted Functions. Formal Methods in System Design 22(3), 205–224 (2003)

[17] Goldberg, E., Novikov, Y.: BerkMin: A Fast and Robust Sat-Solver. In: Design, Automation and Test in Europe (DATE 2002), pp. 142–149 (March 2002)

[18] Intel Corporation, IA-64 Application Developer's Architecture Guide (May 1999), http://developer.intel.com/design/ia-64/architecture.htm
[19] Kim, Y., Mahapatra, R.N.: Design of Low-Power Coarse-Grained Reconfigurable Architectures. CRC Press, Boca Raton (2011)
[20] Lahiri, S., Pixley, C., Albin, K.: Experience with Term Level Modeling and Verification of the M·CORE ^{TM} Microprocessor Core. In: International Workshop on High Level Design, Validation and Test (HLDVT 2001), pp. 109–114 (November 2001)
[21] Le Berre, D., Simon, L.: Results from the SAT 2004 SAT Solver Competition. In: SAT 2004 (May 2004)
[22] Mei, B., De Sutter, B., Vander Aa, T., Wouters, M., Dupont, S.: Implementation of a Coarse-Grained Reconfigurable Media Processor for AVC Decoder. Journal of Signal Processing Systems 51, 225–243 (2008)
[23] Moskewicz, M.W., Madigan, C.F., Zhao, Y., Zhang, L., Malik, S.: Chaff: Engineering an Efficient SAT Solver. In: 38th Design Automation Conference (DAC 2001) (June 2001)
[24] Pipatsrisawat, K., Darwiche, A.: A Lightweight Component Caching Scheme for Satisfiability Solvers. In: Marques-Silva, J., Sakallah, K.A. (eds.) SAT 2007. LNCS, vol. 4501, pp. 294–299. Springer, Heidelberg (2007)
[25] Pnueli, A., Rodeh, Y., Strichman, O., Siegel, M.: The Small Model Property: How Small Can It Be? Journal of Information and Computation 178(1) (2002)
[26] Ryan, L.: Siege SAT Solver, http://www.cs.sfu.ca/~loryan/personal
[27] Sharangpani, H., Arora, K.: Itanium Processor Microarchitecture. IEEE Micro. 20(5), 24–43 (2000)
[28] Velev, M.N., Bryant, R.E.: Bit-Level Abstraction in the Verification of Pipelined Microprocessors by Correspondence Checking. In: Gopalakrishnan, G.C., Windley, P. (eds.) FMCAD 1998. LNCS, vol. 1522, pp. 18–35. Springer, Heidelberg (1998)
[29] Velev, M.N., Bryant, R.E.: Exploiting Positive Equality and Partial Non-Consistency in the Formal Verification of Pipelined Microprocessors. In: 36th Design Automation Conference (DAC 1999), pp. 397–401 (June 1999)
[30] Velev, M.N., Bryant, R.E.: Superscalar Processor Verification Using Efficient Reductions of the Logic of Equality with Uninterpreted Functions to Propositional Logic. In: Pierre, L., Kropf, T. (eds.) CHARME 1999. LNCS, vol. 1703, pp. 37–53. Springer, Heidelberg (1999)
[31] Velev, M.N., Bryant, R.E.: Formal Verification of Superscalar Microprocessors with Multicycle Functional Units, Exceptions, and Branch Prediction. In: DAC 2000, pp. 112–117 (June 2000)
[32] Velev, M.N.: Formal Verification of VLIW Microprocessors with Speculative Execution. In: Emerson, E.A., Sistla, A.P. (eds.) CAV 2000. LNCS, vol. 1855, pp. 86–98. Springer, Heidelberg (2000)
[33] Velev, M.N.: Automatic Abstraction of Memories in the Formal Verification of Superscalar Microprocessors. In: Margaria, T., Yi, W. (eds.) TACAS 2001. LNCS, vol. 2031, pp. 252–267. Springer, Heidelberg (2001)
[34] Velev, M.N.: Using Rewriting Rules and Positive Equality to Formally Verify Wide-Issue Out-Of-Order Microprocessors with a Reorder Buffer. In: Design, Automation and Test in Europe (DATE 2002), pp. 28–35 (March 2002)
[35] Velev, M.N., Bryant, R.E.: Effective Use of Boolean Satisfiability Procedures in the Formal Verification of Superscalar and VLIW Microprocessors. Journal of Symbolic Computation (JSC) 35(2), 73–106 (2003)
[36] Velev, M.N.: Automatic Abstraction of Equations in a Logic of Equality. In: Cialdea Mayer, M., Pirri, F. (eds.) TABLEAUX 2003. LNCS, vol. 2796, pp. 196–213. Springer, Heidelberg (2003)

[37] Velev, M.N.: Using Automatic Case Splits and Efficient CNF Translation to Guide a SAT-Solver When Formally Verifying Out-of-Order Processors. In: Artificial Intelligence and Mathematics (AI&MATH 2004), pp. 242–254 (January 2004)
[38] Velev, M.N.: Efficient Translation of Boolean Formulas to CNF in Formal Verification of Microprocessors. In: Asia & South Pacific Design Autom. Conf., pp. 310–315 (January 2004)
[39] Velev, M.N.: Using Positive Equality to Prove Liveness for Pipelined Microprocessors. In: Asia and South Pacific Design Automation Conference, pp. 316–321 (January 2004)
[40] Velev, M.N.: Exploiting Signal Unobservability for Efficient Translation to CNF in Formal Verification of Microprocessors. In: Design, Automation and Test in Europe (DATE 2004), pp. 266–271 (February 2004)
[41] Velev, M.N.: Encoding Global Unobservability for Efficient Translation to SAT. In: International Conference on Theory and Applications of Satisfiability Testing (May 2004)
[42] Velev, M.N.: Comparative Study of Strategies for Formal Verification of High-Level Processors. In: Int'l. Conf. on Computer Design (ICCD 2004), pp. 119–124 (October 2004)
[43] Velev, M.N.: Comparison of Schemes for Encoding Unobservability in Translation to SAT. In: Asia & South Pacific Design Automation Conference (ASP-DAC 2005), pp. 1056–1059 (January 2005)
[44] Velev, M.N., Bryant, R.E.: TLSim and EVC: A Term-Level Symbolic Simulator and an Efficient Decision Procedure for the Logic of Equality with Uninterpreted Functions and Memories. Int'l. Journal of Embedded Systems 1(1/2), 134–149 (2005)
[45] Velev, M.N.: Automatic Formal Verification of Liveness for Pipelined Processors with Multicycle Functional Units. In: Borrione, D., Paul, W. (eds.) CHARME 2005. LNCS, vol. 3725, pp. 97–113. Springer, Heidelberg (2005)
[46] Velev, M.N.: Using Abstraction for Efficient Formal Verification of Pipelined Processors with Value Prediction. In: International Symposium on Quality Electronic Design (2006)
[47] Velev, M.N.: Formal Verification of Pipelined Microprocessors with Delayed Branches. In: ISQED 2006, pp. 296–299 (March 2006)
[48] Velev, M.N., Gao, P.: Exploiting Hierarchical Encodings of Equality to Design Independent Strategies in Parallel SMT Decision Procedures for a Logic of Equality. In: High Level Design Validation and Test Workshop (HLDVT 2009), pp. 8–13 (November 2009)
[49] Velev, M.N., Gao, P.: A Method for Debugging of Pipelined Processors in Formal Verification by Correspondence Checking. In: ASP-DAC 2010, pp. 619–624 (January 2010)
[50] Velev, M.N., Gao, P.: Method for Formal Verification of Soft-Error Tolerance Mechanisms in Pipelined Microprocessors. In: Dong, J.S., Zhu, H. (eds.) ICFEM 2010. LNCS, vol. 6447, pp. 355–370. Springer, Heidelberg (2010)
[51] Velev, M.N., Gao, P.: Automatic Formal Verification of Reconfigurable DSPs. In: Asia and South Pacific Design Automation Conference (ASP-DAC), pp. 293–296 (January 2011)

Architectural Verification of Control Systems Using CSP

Joabe Jesus[1], Alexandre Mota[1], Augusto Sampaio[1], and Luiz Grijo[2]

[1] Centro de Informática - Universidade Federal de Pernambuco (UFPE)
Recife - PE - Brazil
{jbjj,acm,acas}@cin.ufpe.br

[2] Empresa Brasileira Aeronáutica (Embraer)
São José dos Campos - SP - Brazil
luiz.grijo@embraer.com.br

Abstract. Although validation of complex dynamic systems can be realised using checklists and simulations provided by tools such as Simulink, these techniques usually do not cover all system behaviours. Moreover, the control laws are rarely modelled together with the system architecture. This integration can reveal defects which are only detected in final stages of the development. This work presents two major contributions: a strategy to validate the integration of a proposed architecture with control laws, based on the *CSP* process algebra; and the validation of a Fly-by-wire Elevator Control System designed by Embraer. The results show that the strategy helps finding defects in early stages of the development, saving time and costs.

1 Introduction

Correct design and implementation of complex dynamic systems is a technical challenge. The validation activities necessary to guarantee the correctness of a system design are very complex, whereas exhaustive verification of a system implementation using a test suite is commonly impractical [1]. Even the usage of system engineering process models focused on validation and verification (V&V), such as the V-Model provided by the *SAE International* in its Aerospace Recommended Practice (ARP) number 4754 [2], need improvements and additional processes to help industry to reach the "time to market". Moreover, V&V techniques of simulation and testing as well as complementary processes mentioned in [2], such as the certification activities (DO-178B checklists) and the safety assessment process (ARP4761) do not guarantee the absence of system faults (caused by errors and observed as failures).

To guarantee the correctness of such systems the use of formal methods is highly indicated [1]. For example, aviation companies, such as Embraer and Airbus, space agencies such as NASA, and their partners and suppliers have been applying formal methods and model driven development to improve their systems [3,4]. One of their main challenges is transforming the V-Model into an improved model (Y-Model [5]) in which model-based design is used to produce

S. Qin and Z. Qiu (Eds.): ICFEM 2011, LNCS 6991, pp. 323–339, 2011.

better products and help finding defects as early as possible, reducing the number of change cycles in the development.

This work uses formal models as a basis to analyse dynamic systems. Our key idea is to analyse the system design both at a more abstract level as well as when embedded into different architectures, similar to what is performed in hardware-software *codesign* methodologies [6]. We propose the use of the process algebra *CSP* (Communicating Sequential Processes) [7] to specify and analyse the architectural and the operational requirements together with the control law diagrams, by considering the *Simulink* model as the software part and the arquitecture models as the hardware part. We also define a strategy for integrating these system models into *CSP* and use data abstraction techniques to allow verification using model-checking. Particularly, by considering the environment (external devices and equipments such as sensors and actuators) and the processors where the system will be scheduled, our strategy allows the engineer to analyse whether the design satisfies some properties before starting the coding and manufacturing phases inside the components layer of the V-Model, thus saving costs. Moreover, we define translation rules that automatically transform control laws (discrete time Simulink block diagrams [8]) into machine readable *CSP* (CSP_M) [7], the *CSP* version used in tools, and an integration pattern for analysis. In this way we take advantage of existing tools, and particularly the Failures-Divergences Refinement (FDR) model-checker [7], for checking desired properties of the system design.

This paper is organised as follows. Section 2 briefly discusses the problem of verification of control models described in Simulink. In Section 3 we present our strategy to verify control systems as well as the automatic translation of control law diagrams into *CSP* and our approach to the integration of these diagrams and the system architectural requirements into *CSP*. Afterwards, Section 4 presents the application of our strategy to the Fly-By-Wire (FBW) industrial case study. Finally, Section 5 discusses related work and Section 6 presents our conclusions and future work. We assume basic knowledge about Simulink and *CSP*, although we explain some constructs as the need arises.

2 Simulink and the Verification of Control Systems

A wide variety of activities of the aviation industry, such as the airplane design, are regulated by federal organisations. Moreover, some certification standards must be fulfilled by an aircraft for it to be allowed to fly [9]. Essentially, these regulations require an aircraft to be safely controllable and manoeuvrable during all flight phases. The process consists basically in checking the safety/operational requirements for the aircraft systems and its equipments as well as the *nominal behaviour*[1]. In this Section we brifly discuss verification of control system designs described in *Simulink*.

The concept of control is important for a variety of dynamic systems and the use of block diagrams is an established technique to model a control system.

[1] The behaviour the system/equipament must exhibit if none of its components fail.

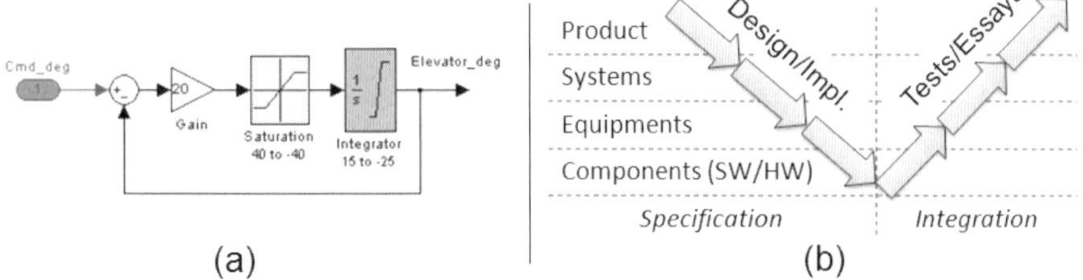

Fig. 1. (a) An actuator control system in Simulink; (b) The V-Model

A control law diagram is a visual model that consists, essentially, of a set of blocks and lines (signals) connecting them. It models the equations of the entire system using simple logical and arithmetic blocks (see Fig. 1(a)).

In this context, well established *simulation environments* such as Simulink [8] (a graphical front-end for Matlab) support the design of complex systems, involving a continuous or discrete model (control law) for each operational condition.

Simulink allows defining subsystems (parameterised through mask variables) which can be grouped into block libraries. Moreover, it provides several predefined libraries and blocksets (domain specific libraries). These features and rich sets of blocks help desiging complex systems at a high level of abstraction. Blocks are usually polymorphic (operate on several datatypes). When copied to a diagram, they are instantiated to the particular context (refer to [8] for further details).

2.1 Verification of Control Systems

The V-Model, in Fig. 1(b), defines two legs which separate the specification and the integration activities, respectively. The V&V activities relate the specification and integration activities through the analysis and identification of errors in each level (product, systems, equipaments and components). However, during the development, the costs for modifications increase tremendously, not only due to the repetition of work in the design departments, but also in related disciplines. So, when a defect is found, the project must return to its specification activities, increasing costs and delaying the schedule.

According to [9], control computers include several basic functions that are of direct interest to test engineers during the verification activities, for instance: control laws, sensor processing functions, actuator interfaces, redundancy management, failure monitoring and reporting systems. In this context, the verification of the system architecture is often realised during the integration leg of the V-Model, instead of being realised in the specification leg.

In some companies, like *Embraer*, V&V activities are performed in a host computer and in target computers. A host computer, running Simulink, is used during design and to check whether a discrete model, corresponding to the continuous model, can produce adequate outputs (such as system response analysis).

Whereas target computers are used in a test laboratory (such as an "iron bird rig" — a skeleton of the final aircraft), in a (flight) simulator and in operational tests. Nevertheless, these target environments require a considerable investment in equipment and facilities [9]. This has motivated our approach to carry out verification in an early stage, abstracting both the host and the target computers into an integrated CSP model.

3 A Strategy to Verify Control System Designs

The key idea of our strategy is to generate an integrated formal model from the requirements (architectural and operational) and control laws design; and use model checkers to investigate the desired properties of the system. Thus, defects are found as early as possible. Moreover, it is possible to reduce the number of change cycles realised to correct these defects because they are usually found during integration tests.

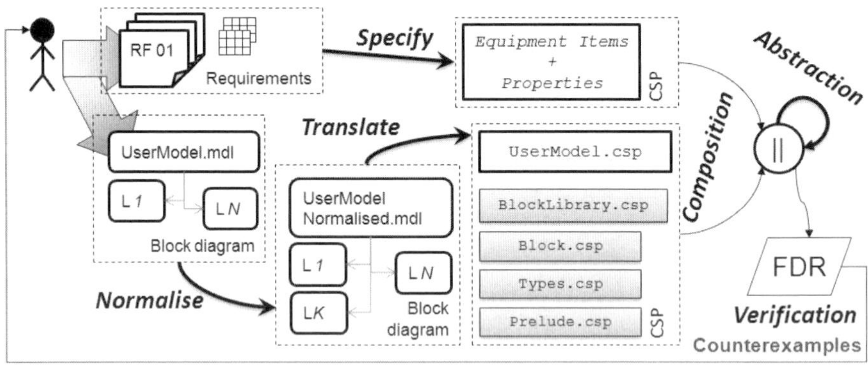

Fig. 2. Verification strategy steps

Fig. 2 depicts our strategy. It starts with the automatic translation from a normalised Simulink block diagram to a *CSP* specification. Complementary, the system architectural requirements (equipments descriptions and operational conditions) are also specified in *CSP* (a non-automatic step yet). These specifications are manually combined to build a complete specification that has all controller components and the *nominal behaviour* of the architectural components of the system. Then, desired properties of the system are described in *CSP* as well. The complete specification is abstracted to avoid the state-explosion problem and analysed using the FDR model-checker. If a given property is not satisfied, the analysis will produce a counter-example used as input to change the specifications (block diagram and architecture) of the system. A more detailed description of each step is presented below.

3.1 Mapping Control Law Diagrams to *CSP*

In this section we present our translation rules from Simulink to *CSP*. An important contribution of this work is our set of algebraic rules to systematically map a Simulink model into a *CSP* specification. We propose rules that are compositional. This allows one to create a *CSP* specification by translating the hierarchy of blocks, in an incremental fashion. It is important to note that Simulink has no formal semantics in which we can formally guarantee the correctness of the rules we are proposing. Therefore, we are indeed giving a semantics to Simulink via a mapping into *CSP*. The proposed semantics is based on the informal descriptions provided in the Simulink manuals [8], like other works do [10,11].

The process algebra *CSP* [7] is suitable for describing the behaviour of systems formally through the definition of sequential processes. These processes are defined using operators over *events* (atomic computations) and can be combined to form more elaborate processes, using a rich repertoire of operators, such as choice, sequential and parallel composition. Besides all these elements, CSP_M (the machine-readable version[2] of *CSP*) also provides functional programming features, such as parameters, local definitions and abstract datatypes; and support for manipulating booleans, integers, tuples, sets and sequences. Moreover, events are defined through channels (families of events), which can carry data from a specified type.

As already mentioned, Simulink blocks are usually polymorphic. However, CSP_M only provides a few types and it has no such a notion of polymorphic channels. To fill this gap, we define an infrastructure in CSP_M composed of four incremental layers (`Prelude.csp`, `Types.csp`, `Blocks.csp` and `BlockLibrary.csp`) to help defining Simulink blocks as CSP processes. With these layers we can define our normalisation rules and our translation rules, whose generated processes are heavily defined in terms of the infrastructure of our layers. Details about our design decisions and other abstractions can be found in [12].

The first set of rules is used to simplify block diagrams. These **normalisation rules** are inspired in some refactoring rules for programming languages. The key idea is to eliminate subsystem duplications. That is, convert the original replicas into references to a single copy of the subsystem. These simplifications are helpful to minimise the size of the original system; this is crucial for using model checking.

The second set of rules (**mapping rules**) is applied to a normalised model. The translation is performed in a bottom-up order by applying the translation function Ψ. The mapping rules are presented as equations, whose left-hand side represents the application of Ψ to an element of Simulink and the right-hand side is the CSP_M script produced by this particular application of the function. Therefore, our set of mapping rules is an inductive definition of Ψ on the hierarchical structure of a Simulink model. The translation strategy can be thought of as a term rewriting system that exhaustively applies the rules that progressively replace Simulink elements with *CSP* constructs. Figure 3 summarises the overall

[2] `http://www.fsel.com/documentation/fdr2/html/index.html`

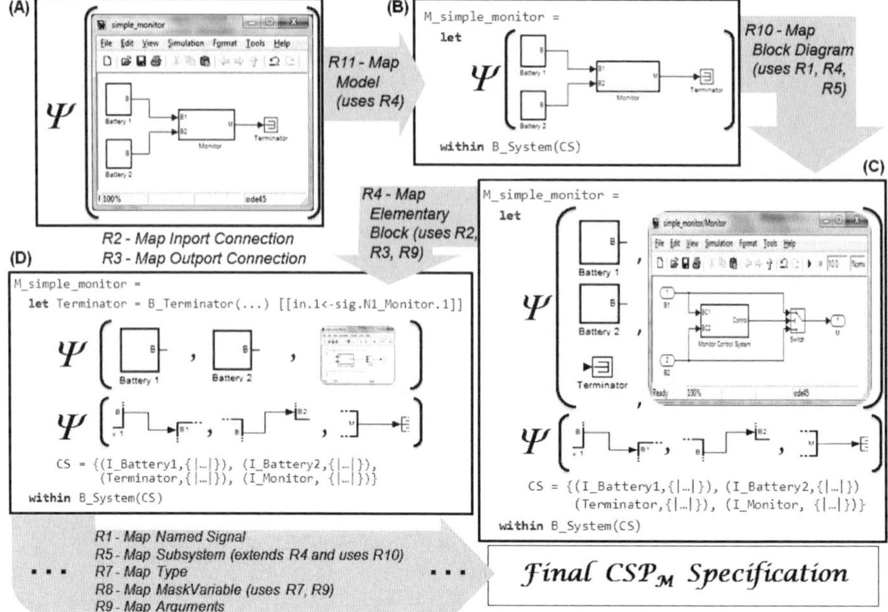

Fig. 3. Strategy to translate Simulink elements into CSP constructs

strategy and illustrates that, given a Simulink model as input, we can produce a corresponding CSP_M specification.

In Figure 3, window (A) shows how our strategy starts by applying Rule 5 of Ψ to a Simulink model. Thus, window (B) presents the generated *CSP* specification composed of a single process `M_simple_monitor` corresponding to the result of this application of Ψ. Rule 5 uses the Rule 4 to define the local definitions corresponding to the model diagram elements (blocks, signals and connections). Besides, several rules are listed in the figure to indicate their relationships.

Before presenting our translation rules we need to discuss the representation of signals. Signals of the user block diagrams (model or subsystems) are mapped into indexed references of a channel that we call `sig`. This indexed reference is realised through a unique identifier (`PortId`) composed of the block identifier (`BlockId`) and the number (`Int`) of the port that produces the signal.

```
datatype BlockId = N1_BlockName1 | ... | N1_BlockNamei
                 | N2_BlockName1 | ... | N2_BlockNamej
                 | Nm_BlockName1 | ... | Nm_BlockNamek

nametype PortId = BlockId.Int
channel sig: PortId.T
```

To explicitly capture the origin of the signals we use a datatype `BlockId` that defines a tag for each block in the user model. Also, in order to distinguish blocks with the same name in different subsystems, a block identifier (tag from `BlockId`) is prefixed with a *namespace identifier* (`N1_`, `N2_` and `Nm_` in the

`BlockId` definition) defined incrementally by traversing the model using a depth-first algorithm. For instance, a signal produced by the first port of a **Demux** block named **Demultiplex** inside a (sub)system identified by m $(1 \leq m \leq M)$ becomes `sig.N`m`_Demultiplex.1`.

The channel `sig` just describes how data exchanged between two or more block processes are captured as events, but it still does not connect the blocks. The synchronous semantics of *CSP* guarantees that the value read by the destination processes is the same written by the source process at any time step. The following rule summarises how we translate a signal:

Rule 1 (Map Named Signal)

Ψ (

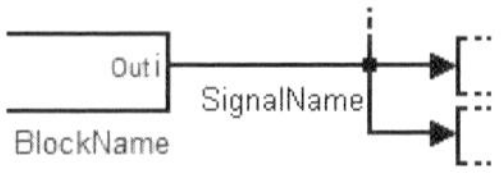

) $(N_m) =$

```
sig_SignalName =
      sig.Nm_BlockName.i
```

(1)

Signals are translated as declarations (aliases) by prefixing the name given by the user with "`sig_`". In addition, we also map inport and outport connections to *CSP* renamings referencing our channels `in` and `out`, respectivelly.

Rule 2 (Map Inport Connection)

Ψ (

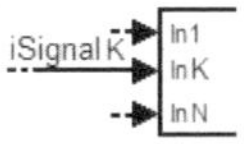

) $(N_m) =$ `in.K <- sig_iSignalK` (2)

The following is the main rule to map elementary blocks:

Rule 3 (Map Elementary Block)

Ψ (

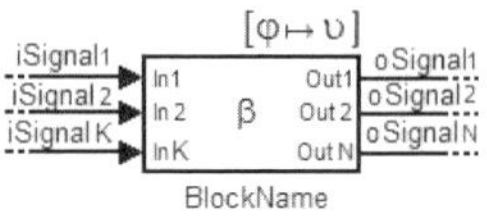

) $(N_m) =$

`BlockName =`
`BlockType(`$\Psi([\varphi \mapsto \upsilon])(N_m)$`) [[`
$\Psi(cs)(N_m)$ `]]`

(3)

Where `BlockType` $\in$ `BlockLibrary`; `BlockType` *is associated to the Simulink block* β*; the arguments are obtained from* $\Psi([\varphi \mapsto \upsilon])(N_m)$*; and* cs *is a list of inport and outport connections.*

This rule generates a reference to a process of our `BlockLibrary` layer with arguments translated from arguments (υ) of the block. The translation function Ψ takes two factors into account to choose a process from our `BlockLibrary` that is appropriate to model the Simulink block: the block type and the block sample time configuration (see details in [12]).

To exemplify the translation, assume that β is a Unit Delay block from the Simulink Discrete Library and that $[\varphi \mapsto \upsilon]$ associates the value 1 to the parameter **initial condition** (**x0**) and the value 1/64 to the parameter **SampleTime**, then $\Psi(\beta[\varphi \mapsto v])$ results in `B_UnitDelay(I.1)(Sampler__64Hz)` as presented in Fig. 4. Furthermore, we use a renaming to identify the connection of the block process to the translated signals, obtained by applying Ψ to the named or unnamed signals that surround the block.

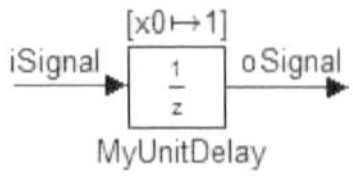

Ψ ([x0↦1] iSignal → $\frac{1}{z}$ → oSignal MyUnitDelay) $(N_m) =$

```
MyUnitDelay =
   B_UnitDelay( Ψ([x0 ↦ 1])(N_m) ) [[
      in.1 <- Ψ(iSignal)(N_m),
      out.1 <- Ψ(oSignal)(N_m) ]]
```

Fig. 4. Applying Rule 3 to an elementary UnitDelay block

Now, we can translate a normalised block diagram δ containing a list *bks* of blocks, a list *sgs* of signals and a list *cs* of connections using the next rule:

Rule 4 (Map Block Diagram)

$$\Psi\begin{pmatrix}\delta \\ [\quad bks, sgs, cs \quad]\end{pmatrix}(N_m) = \begin{array}{l}\Psi(\ bks\ )(N_m)\\ \Psi(\zeta(sgs))(N_m)\\ \texttt{CS = \{ (}p_1\texttt{, }\Gamma(cs(\!|\ b_1\ |\!))\texttt{),}\\ \quad\quad\texttt{(}p_2\texttt{, }\Gamma(cs(\!|\ b_2\ |\!))\texttt{), ...,}\\ \quad\quad\texttt{(}p_N\texttt{, }\Gamma(cs(\!|\ b_N\ |\!))\texttt{) \}}\end{array} \tag{4}$$

Where *$cs(\!|\ b_k\ |\!)$ is the list of connections involving the block b_k; and $\Gamma(cs(\!|\ b_k\ |\!))$ is a set of events of channel* `sig` *that will be consumed by the process p_k.*

In this rule, Ψ is first applied to the list of blocks (*bks*), that is, to every block (b_1, b_2 and b_N) of the list *bks*, producing a list of respective process declarations (referenced in `CS` as p_1, p_2 and p_N). Then, Ψ is applied to the named signals obtained by applying a filter (ζ) over *sgs*. Finally, we apply an auxiliary function Γ to each block to produce a relation `CS` that associates the generated processes to the set of events of channel `sig` consumed by the process, similar to what is done with CLawSP [10].

The following rule concludes the translation by mapping the user model, which has an internal diagram δ, to a process definition:

Rule 5 (Map Model)

$$\Psi\begin{pmatrix}ModelName \\ \delta \\ [\quad bks, sgs, cs \quad]\end{pmatrix}(\_) = \begin{array}{l}\texttt{M\_ModelName =}\\ \quad\texttt{let } \Psi(\ \delta\ )(N_1)\\ \quad\texttt{within B\_System(CS)}\end{array} \tag{5}$$

Where `B_System(CS) = || (p,chs): CS @ [ chs ] p`*, that is, an indexed (replicated) alphabetised parallel expression in which the processes (*`p`*) are restricted to the set of events (*`chs`*).*

This translation maps the entire Simulink model as a unique process whose name is given by the name of the Simulink system prefixed by "M_". We firstly apply Ψ to the internal block diagram δ, producing the declarations of the system

— note that the first namespace (N_1) is defined here. Then, the relation CS, from Rule 4, is passed as argument to the process B_System from our BlockLibrary, performing the connections of the processes through an indexed alphabetised parallel.

Furthermore, we also have rules to handle Simulink subsystems, enable ports and reference blocks (see [12]) — omitted here due to space restrictions.

3.2 Mapping Architectural Requirements to *CSP*

The requirements of a product are separated into several groups such as safety, certification, product, system and functional. In this work we focus on *nominal behaviour*. Thus, functional and system requirements are our main interest. Functional requirements describe the functions designed in Simulink and performed on the *(flight) control computers*. System requirements describe the architecture and operation modes of the system (usually associated to architectural components like command switches), as well as restrictions on the physical implementation of the system, such as limits on data communicated between items of equipment [9].

Thus, the really important requirements to translate are those describing the system architecture. Typical architectures of control systems include items of equipment such as sensors and transducers, displays, actuators, electrical, mechanical and hydraulic components. To translate these items to *CSP* we can use almost all expressions provided by CSP_M, including the usage of our provided infraestructure.

As long as the requirements are *domain specific*, we connect them with the translated Simulink model. To achieve this, we first define a process that represents a (computer) clock that listens to tock events and consequently execute a simulation loop when it generates tick events.

```
channel tock
Clock = tock -> tick -> Clock
```

Then, we declare the set of channels aTick, containing the event tick; and aClock, including the events tick and tock;

```
aTick = {| tick |}
aClock = {| tick, tock |}
```

and define a process ControlComputer, in which the model process is embedded.

```
ControlComputer(Model) = ( Model [| aTick |] Clock ) \ aClock
```

Through the parallel composition of the model (Model) and the Clock, synchronising on the event tick (inside aTick), the computer process controls when each Simulink loop iteration occurs. Moreover, by hiding the clock events (aClock), we define the control computer as a "black box" component, as long as the environment will only have access to the input and output defined by the process Model.

Although the control computers are the main equipments responsible to execute the control logic, other interesting items used in a control system architecture are the data buses that transmit data between other items using specific communication protocols. To represent such a kind of item one can use similar ideas from those used in [13]. For a detailed explanation about data buses and flight control systems architecture refer to [14].

Using our approach for other equipments of the system it is possible to model the logic of an equipament in *Simulink* and specify its architecture using the power of CSP_M operators. In particular, indexed (replicated) process operators can be used to specify complex architectures involving characteristics such as redundancy and monitoring.

3.3 Defining Properties

According to [7], parallel composition can be used in two ways: to synchronise processes to carry out a task concurrently or to be equivalent to the conjunction (for instance, logical "and") of trace specifications. In this second usage *CSP* acts more than a simple specification language and the parallel process is supposed to be used on the left-hand side of a refinement check. If we take the entire *CSP* model of a control system, as previously showed, and compose it in parallel with *CSP* processes that reveal non expected behaviours in our system, we can find defects of the system architecture or of the system design.

We define a channel `defectFound` of a user defined datatype `Defect` to allow the definition of properties using the following template

```
channel defectFound: Defect
DefectK = [events of interest] -> if [verification mechanism]
                                  then defectFound.DEFECT_ID_K -> STOP
                                  else DefectK
```

By providing just the desired events of interest, which are produced by system, and a verification mechanism to verify a given property, it is possible to define many kinds of properties. Moreover, the template process deadlocks if the defect is found. Thus, our validation strategy results are obtained by assertions like

```
assert (System [|{|[events of interest]|}|] DefectK) :[deadlock free [F]]
```

This idea of putting a process to watch another process for defects is also discussed in details in [15]. Moreover, `System` can also have deadlocks, but, in this case, the Simulink design or architecture is supposed to deadlock as well.

3.4 Abstraction and Validation

After composing the *CSP* specifications generated from the Simulink model, from the system architecture and from specified properties, some simplifications must be performed, since most real systems have infinite domains that are not directly supported by a model checker like FDR. Although user may need to carry out some abstractions, the state-space explosion problem can be avoided in our strategy by using the ideas of [16,17] and changing/tunning the type parameter (`Tin`) of our library processes, see [12]. However, this latter abstraction must be accomplished not only by reducing the data domains used by the process, but also between block processes.

A detailed discussion about the optimisations we perform during our translation can be found in [12]. Basically, we reduce the size of our library block processes and also reduce the size of the final specification using ideas such as factorisation and compression algorithms of FDR [7].

3.5 Tool Support and Completeness

To be able to translate complex Simulink models, we implemented our rules in a prototype tool (**Sim2Csp**). This tool automatically generates a CSP_M from a Simulink model (MDL file). It was implemented in Java reusing the Simulink file parser of Circus Producer [10] and using concepts of model transformation.

Concerning completeness, our translation rules deal with all concepts identified in discrete Simulink models, as depicted in Fig. 3, although we still do not have a complete block library. Furthermore, even if we can translate a complete *Simulink* diagram to CSP_M, this does not guarantee that the CSP_M specification is analysable by model-checking due to limitations of FDR. This can be the case even after the abstraction process. Nevertheless, this is a fundamental problem related to model-checking [17]. Regarding soundness, as already mentioned, our mapping into CSP actually defines a semantics for Simulink. Even so, we checked the expected equivalence of certain *Simulink* blocks using the *data independence* technique [16] (see details in [12]), such as Memory and UnitDelay; as well as errors also identified in Simulink. For instance, in *algebraic loops* (deadlocks cause by *direct feedthrough*) [8].

4 Verifying a Fly-by-Wire Elevator Control System

In most aircrafts, the pitching movement (the up-and-down motion of the aircraft's nose) is controlled by two *elevator* surfaces at the rear of the fuselage. The Elevator Control System (ECS) is a command augmentation system and it is responsible to one of the essential primary functions of an aircraft: the pitch function. The main goal of the ECS is to control these two surfaces, augmenting the commands of the pilots when the aircraft is in air, to decrease pilot workload [9]. Moreover, it can be operated in *direct* mode, if the pilot has direct control of a surface; or in *alternate* mode, otherwise.

Fig. 5 shows an architectural overview of the ECS. The system is composed of Inceptors, Display, Sensors, Controllers and Actuators. Inceptors (side-sticks) capture commands from the pilots: priorities, from push-buttons (PB); and longitudinal side-stick deflections (in degrees), from Linear Variable Differential Transformers (LVDT). These signals are processed by four controllers, which also consider the state of the airplane to generate commands to the associated actuator (PCU). The flight conditions are derived from three airplane state variables: pitch rate (in degrees per second), aircraft location ("on ground" or "in air") and flap position (retracted or deployed). These signals are provided by three Inertial Reference Units (IRUs), four Weight-On-Wheels (WOW) sensors (two for each landing gear below the wings) and the Flap-Slat Actuator Control Electronics (FSACE), respectively.

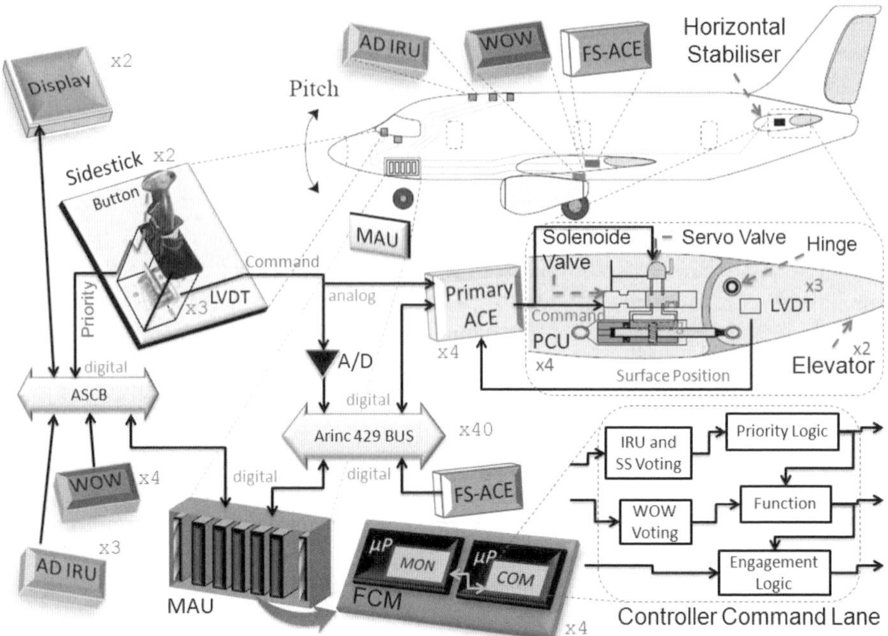

Fig. 5. The Elevator Control System - Architecture Overview

The system captures commands or intents from pilots through *inceptors* and then processes these signals in the *controller* component, which also receives feedback inputs from three rate gyros (IRUs) *sensors*, from *actuator* raw LVDT and from *surface* deflection LVDTs. As most flight control actuation systems on current aircrafts, the ECS actuators are electrically signalled (engaged or disengaged by solenoid valves) and hydraulically powered (forces are regulated by servo valves). These actuators drive the surface movements according to the commands sent, via electrical wiring, from the controllers. Each controller is embedded into a *primary computer* — Flight Control Module (FCM). Controllers are defined in *Simulink* and have several subsystems, including the control law function (control algorithm) to send the command signals to the associated actuator. It is important to highlight that every surface has two attached actuators, which are associated to a specific replica of the controller.

We point out that many equipments illustrated in Fig. 5 such as side-sticks, sensors and actuators are physical devices designed by suppliers of the manufacturer and integrated to the aircraft. Thus, their descriptions are restricted to their operation requirements. Just the controller components embedded into Flight Control Modules (FCM) are designed by Embraer. So, we use our tool to apply normalisation rules and translate the normalised model to *CSP*, generating a specification containing: 286 instances of library processes, 30 definitions of subsystem processes, 539 usages of the channel `sig` and 1 process definition for a Stateflow chart. Afterwards, we properly represented the architectural components and operation requirements in *CSP*.

4.1 Validation and Results

The flight control laws inside the **Control Logic** subsystem describe what changes in the system plant must be done to satisfy the pilot commands. When designing the laws, control engineers define the required frequencies of the signals consumed by the controller to guarantee stability of the feedback control. Moreover, they also verify whether the commands sent to the actuator drive the elevator correctly.

In parallel to the control law design, the architecture is defined with redundancy and voting mechanisms, creating replicas of the controller that must share the same input signals. However, if replicas of the controller are not synchronised they can drive the *elevators* "correctly" (as designed) in opposite directions. This is an important property, as long as this would cause a *rolling* moment at the aircraft tail and an undesired *spin* movement of the aircraft. In particular, elevators are usually projected for the longitudinal control of the airplane whereas such a movement (lateral control) is controlled by the two *aileron* surfaces, located at the trailing edges of the wings.

Observing the **Priority Logic** subsystem we think that if the controllers embedded into FCMs are not synchronised they can receive different values of the priorities from the pilots. This can produce different commands to the surfaces, as long as the side-sticks of the captain and the first-officer can be in opposite directions. Thus, our verification goal is to check whether this property can be violated. We design an `Observer` process based on the process `Defect` from Section 3.3.

```
Observer = surfacePos?x?s1Pos:Ts_Surface ->
             surfacePos?y:diff({1,2},{x})?s2Pos:Ts_Surface ->
               if (neq(s1Pos, s2Pos)) then defect -> STOP
               else Observer
```

It receives the positions `s1Pos` and `s2Pos` (of type `Ts_Surface`) of the two elevator surfaces `x` and `y` ($\in \{1, 2\}$) and checks the property by comparing these positions. When the surfaces have different positions (described by the *inequality* `neq(s1Pos,s2Pos)`), the observer produces a `defect` event and then deadlocks (**STOP**).

Finally, the `Observer` is combined in parallel with the `System` and the verification reduced to an assertion that should not reveal a deadlock.

```
ObservedSystem = ECS [| {| surfacePos.i.x | i<-{1,2}, x<-Ts_Surface |} |] Observer
assert ObservedSystem :[deadlock free [F]]
```

Intuitively, a deadlock can occur because the **Priority Logic** subsystems can give control to different pilots if the controllers are not synchronised to read the priorities and debounce them.

After specifying all those components in *CSP* as well as the desired property, the `ObservedSystem` presents a huge state space (the *state explosion* problem) due to the manipulated data types. To overcome this problem we need to perform some simplifications. We use the data abstraction approach proposed in [17] to find the minimum values of the data types (the abstract domains) that are relevant to capture the system's behaviour of interest. This reveals, for example, that abstracting the pitch rate signals produced by the IRUs or the side-stick LVDT signal as `Tinteger` values ranging between -64 and 64, instead of the floating precision numbers with 18 bits of accuracy, results in five (discrete) values: -25, -1, 0, 1 and 25, corresponding to the positions LOWER, NEGATIVE, NEUTRAL, POSITIVE and HIGHER. So, we just modify the set `T_LVDT` as follows:

```
T_LVDT = { I.x | x<-{ -25, -1, 0, 1, 25 }}
```

Moreover, as the Controllers depend on the `LVDT` signals, they are also abstracted to finite domains. We applied this technique to each component of the system and also to the interactions between them.

The verification of the model (**A1**) performed with FDR founds a deadlock — confirming our intuition that the architecture can interfere in the design (Simulink model) — because the four FCMs are not executing the **Priority Logic** subsystems synchronously. Following our strategy, we performed a change in the design using a simplified architecture (**A2**), with only two controllers embedded into a two FCMs and reading the priorities synchronously; then the property was satisfied. Table 1 shows the results of the analysis. We observed that simplifying the architecture reduced the verification time. All experiments were performed on an Intel Core 2 Duo T5750 processor, 2Gb RAM and OS Kubuntu Linux 8.10 inside VirtualBox 3.2.

Table 1. Formal verification results

	Processes	**Approx. Time**	**Deadlock free**
A1	2680	12 hours	Fail
A2	1368	9 hours	Pass ✓

Table 2. Test-based verification

	Simulation	**Tests**	**"Iron bird rig" Test Laboratory**
Computer Type	Host	Host	Target
Equipment Type	Simulated	Simulated	Real (Final)
Approx. Time	1 hour	2 hours	1 hour + $\sim$ 4 months (construction)

As previously said, in a standard V-Model, the design is verified in several phases of the development with different techniques such as simulation in a host computer and tests in a prototype laboratory with a target (micro)processor and real equipments (RIG test). According to *Embraer*, as we see in Table 2, the estimated time to execute tests that cover this same property is about four hours. However the time elapsed from the end of the design phase — after the tests in a target computer with simulated equipments — to the analysis of the "Iron bird" test results is approximately four working months, due to the construction of the necessary laboratory facilities. Moreover, as we said, if a problem is found during a RIG test, for example, the correction cycle is very costly. In this way, our work significantly reduces the costs of manufacturing and testing incorrect designs, since our validation is done during the initial phases of the development.

5 Related Work

We identified several related works [11,18,10,3,19,20] that aim to guarantee correctness of control systems. However, none of these works have considered a systematic translation from Simulink to *CSP*, based on compositional rules, nor the influence of architectural requirements on the system in a formal way. They only define the steps to create a complete model in their formal notations informally, hiding the translation details into tools that implement their informal descriptions. Our tool support is based on our normalisation and translation rules.

The work reported in [11] is close to the works of CLawZ [18] and Circus [10] with respect to proposing a systematic translation from Simulink into some formal language. But [11] defines a new language based on time intervals. These works differ from ours because they use theorem proving. Thus, in most cases, it is not possible to automatically check a property, whereas in our strategy one can automatically prove a system property, provided the model is correctly abstracted. Moreover, [18] and [10] address checking code against model, rather than model against requirements.

Concerning the translation from Simulink into a formal notation but aiming at checking safety properties, normally stated in terms of boolean formulas, we can find the works [3,19]. They use NuSMV as the target formal language and do not provide any comments on how to handle state-explosion.

The work reported in [20] is similar to our *Simulink* translation approach. However, Lustre is used as the formal notation to represent *Simulink* blocks. This can also be regarded as a formalisation of *Simulink* as long as Lustre, like *CSP*, is equipped with a formal semantics. They also report the development of a strategy (without rules) and a translator utility. Nevertheless, the purpose of their approach is to produce correct implementations.

Furthermore, tools like the Simulink Validation and Verification [21] contribute to the work of certifying the model compliance with DO-178B [22]. It allows monitoring the model signals during extensive testing, so that correct designs are created.

Moreover, the formal models produced by our strategy can also be analysed using other tools for *CSP*, such as the Process Analysis Toolkit (PAT) model-checker[3]. Furthermore, the CSP-Prover[4] can be used to apply our strategy to continuous systems, as long as the CSP-Prover provides built-in real numbers and can deal with infinite models. By using the CSP-Prover, our work immediately extends the work of [11] in terms of supported formal analysis techniques.

6 Conclusion

In this work we have shown that a Simulink control diagram can be represented formally as a process in the process algebra *CSP*. We accomplished this by

[3] `http://www.comp.nus.edu.sg/~pat/`

[4] `http://staff.aist.go.jp/y-isobe/CSP-Prover/CSP-Prover.html`

defining an infrastructure that provides useful constructions to represent control diagrams, and an automatic translation of the system designs in Simulink to the top-level components of this infrastructure. Furthermore, our layered infrastructure helps defining a formal semantics to Simulink elements (blocks, signals, subsystems and timing features).

One of the key points of our infrastructure are the template processes that represent the Simulink main elements. For instance, we have a process `Block` that describes a generic Simulink discrete block, a `Sampler` process that behaves as a limited counter (quickly compiled by FDR) and integrated to the `Block` by the function `Sampled`. Moreover, Simulink loops are captured by the `tick` events synchronised by all processes.

Another important point to observe is about minimising the state-space of the *CSP* specification. Our template processes allow the factorisation of the block timing features, reducing state explosion. This was possible due to the definition of the timing controlling events (`tick`, `step` and `sampleStep`) triggered by `Samplers` and listened by `Sampled`. Furthermore, we proposed normalisation rules to simplify Simulink models, avoiding duplicated definitions — this minimises the generated *CSP* specification.

As discussed in [12], some processes of our library are data independent and can be easily abstracted using the technique of Lazić's work [16]; we did this in the ECS. Other blocks are data dependent and need the ideas of data abstraction [17]. For instance, the type parameter `Tin` is used to restrict the inputs of the block [12].

By defining properties as observer processes and using deadlock analysis, we can also check the system design. This idea was inspired, for example, in [7] about parallel composition as conjunction. This allowed us to find a defect when integrating the Simulink model of the Elevator Control System with its proposed architecture.

Finally, our rules are implemented in our prototype tool **Sim2Csp**. This tool automatically generates a CSP_M model from a Simulink model file, and was implemented in Java reusing the core of Circus Producer [10].

As future work we intend to improve our block library, our tool (**Sim2Csp**) and apply data independece and data abstraction automatically. We also intend to realise a deeper investigation on how the formal techniques of data abstraction, abstract interpretation and data independence can be supported in our strategy.

Acknowledgements. This work was supported by INES[5], funded by CNPq and FACEPE, grants 573964/2008-4 and APQ-1037-1.03/08, by CNPq grant 482462/2009-4 and by the Brazilian Space Agency (UNIESPAÇO 2009).

References

1. Holloway, C.M.: Why engineers should consider formal methods. In: Proceedings of the 16th AIAA/IEEE Digital Avionics Systems Conference, Irvine CA, vol. 1, pp. 1.3-16 – 1.3-22 (October 1997)

[5] `http://www.ines.org.br`

2. Certification Considerations for Highly-Integrated or Complex Aircraft Systems. Technical Report ARP4754, SAE International, Warrendale, PA (December 1999)
3. Bernard, R., Aubert, J., Bieber, P., Merlini, C., Metge, S.: Experiments in model-based safety analysis: flight controls. In: 1st IFAC workshop on Dependable Control of Discrete Systems (2007)
4. Bozzano, B., Villafiorita, A.: Improving system reliability via model checking: The fSAP/NuSMV-SA safety analysis platform. In: Anderson, S., Felici, M., Littlewood, B. (eds.) SAFECOMP 2003. LNCS, vol. 2788, pp. 49–62. Springer, Heidelberg (2003)
5. Camus, J.-L., Dion, B.: Efficient development of airborne software with Scade suite. Esterel Technologies (2003), http://www.esterel-technologies.com
6. Silva, L., Sampaio, A., Barros, E.: A constructive approach to hardware/software partitioning. Form. Methods Syst. Des. 24(1), 45–90 (2004)
7. Roscoe, A.: The Theory and Practice of Concurrency. Prentice Hall PTR, Englewood Cliffs (1997)
8. The MathWorks Inc. Simulink User's Guide (2008)
9. Pratt, R.: Flight Control Systems: Pratical Issues in Design and Implementation. The Institution of Electrical Engineers, UK (2000)
10. Zeyda, F., Cavalcanti, A.: Mechanised Translation of Control Law Diagrams into *Circus*. In: Leuschel, M., Wehrheim, H. (eds.) IFM 2009. LNCS, vol. 5423, pp. 151–166. Springer, Heidelberg (2009)
11. Chen, C., Dong, J.S.: Applying Timed Interval Calculus to Simulink Diagrams. In: Liu, Z., Kleinberg, R.D. (eds.) ICFEM 2006. LNCS, vol. 4260, pp. 74–93. Springer, Heidelberg (2006)
12. Jesus, J.: Designing and formal verification of fly-by-wire flight control systems. Master's thesis, UFPE (2009), joabe.ecomp.poli.br/msc/jbjj-msc.pdf.
13. Roscoe, A., Broadfoot, P.: Proving Security Protocols With Model Checkers by Data Independence Techniques (1999)
14. Grijo, L.: Architectures of Flight Control and Autopilot for Civil Aircraft. Master's thesis, Aeronautical Institute of Technology, São José dos Campos (2004)
15. Halbwachs, N., Lagnier, F., Raymond, P.: Synchronous Observers and the Verification of Reactive Systems. In: Third Int. Conf. on Algebraic Methodology and Software Technology, AMAST 1993. Springer, Heidelberg (1993)
16. Lazic, R., Roscoe, A.: Data independence with generalised predicate symbols. In: PDPTA 1999, vol. I, pp. 319–325. CSREA Press (1999)
17. Farias, A., Mota, A., Sampaio, A.: Compositional Abstraction of CSPZ Processes. Journal of the Brazilian Computer Society 14(2) (June 2008)
18. Arthan, R.D., Caseley, P.: Colin O'Halloran, and A. Smith. ClawZ: Control Laws in Z. In: Proc. 3rd IEEE ICFEM 2000, York, pp. 169–176 (September 2000)
19. Meenakshi, B., Bhatnagar, A., Roy, S.: Tool for Translating Simulink Models into Input Language of a Model Checker. In: Liu, Z., Kleinberg, R.D. (eds.) ICFEM 2006. LNCS, vol. 4260, pp. 606–620. Springer, Heidelberg (2006)
20. Tripakis, S., Sofronis, C., Caspi, P., Curic, A.: Translating discrete-time Simulink to Lustre. ACM Trans. Embed. Comput. Syst. 4(4), 779–818 (2005)
21. The MathWorks Inc. Simulink Validation and Verification 2 User's Guide (2008)
22. Software considerations in airborne systems and equipment certification. DO 178B, RTCA Inc., Washington D.C. (December 1992)

Symbolic Execution of Alloy Models

Junaid Haroon Siddiqui and Sarfraz Khurshid

The University of Texas at Austin

Abstract. Symbolic execution is a technique for systematic exploration of program behaviors using symbolic inputs, which characterize classes of concrete inputs. Symbolic execution is traditionally performed on imperative programs, such as those in C/C++ or Java. This paper presents a novel approach to symbolic execution for declarative programs, specifically those written in Alloy – a first-order, declarative language based on relations. Unlike imperative programs that describe *how* to perform computation to conform to desired behavioral properties, declarative programs describe *what* the desired properties are, without enforcing a specific method for computation. Thus, symbolic execution does not directly apply to declarative programs the way it applies to imperative programs. Our insight is that we can leverage the fully automatic, SAT-based analysis of the Alloy Analyzer to enable symbolic execution of Alloy models – the analyzer generates instances, i.e., valuations for the relations in the model, that satisfy the given properties and thus provides an execution engine for declarative programs. We define symbolic types and operations, which allow the existing Alloy tool-set to perform symbolic execution for the supported types and operations. We demonstrate the efficacy of our approach using a suite of models that represent structurally complex properties. Our approach opens promising avenues for new forms of more efficient and effective analyses of Alloy models.

1 Introduction

Symbolic execution [5, 14] is a technique first presented over three decades ago for systematic exploration of behaviors of imperative programs using symbolic inputs, which characterize classes of concrete inputs. The key idea behind symbolic execution is to explore (feasible) execution paths by building *path conditions* that define properties required of inputs to execute the corresponding paths. The rich structure of path conditions enables a variety of powerful static and dynamic analyses. However, traditional applications of symbolic execution have largely been limited to small illustrative examples, since utilizing path conditions in automated analysis requires much computation power, particularly for non-trivial programs that have long execution paths with complex control flow. During recent years, many advances has been made in constraint solving technology [7] and additionally, raw computation power has increased substantially. These advancements have led to a resurgence of symbolic execution, and new variants that perform *partial* symbolic execution have become particularly popular for systematic bug finding [4] in programs written in commonly used languages such as C/C++, C#, and Java.

S. Qin and Z. Qiu (Eds.): ICFEM 2011, LNCS 6991, pp. 340–355, 2011.

While symbolic execution today lies at the heart of some highly effective and efficient approaches for checking imperative programs, the use of symbolic execution in declarative programs is uncommon. Unlike imperative programs that describe *how* to perform computation to conform to desired behavioral properties, declarative programs describe *what* the desired properties are, without enforcing a specific method for computation. Thus, symbolic execution, or execution per se, does not directly apply to declarative programs the way it applies to imperative programs.

This paper presents a novel approach to symbolic execution for declarative programs written in the Alloy modeling language [11]. Alloy is a first-order declarative logic based on sets and relations, and is supported by its fully automatic, SAT-based analyzer. The Alloy tool-set is rapidly gaining popularity for academic research and teaching as well as for designing dependable software in industry. The powerful analysis performed by the analyzer make Alloy particularly attractive for modeling and checking a variety of systems, including those with complex structural constraints – SAT provides a particularly efficient analysis engine for such constraints.

Our insight into symbolic execution for Alloy is that path conditions in symbolic execution, which by definition are constraints (on inputs), can play a fundamental role in effective and efficient analysis of declarative programs, which themselves are constraints (that describe "what"). The automatic analysis performed by the Alloy tool-set enables our insight to form the basis of our approach. Given an Alloy model, the analyzer generates *instances*, i.e., concrete valuations for the sets and relations in the model, which satisfy the given properties. Thus, the analyzer, in principle, already provides an *execution engine* for declarative programs, which bears resemblance to concrete execution of imperative programs. Indeed, a common use of the analyzer is to *simulate* Alloy predicates and iterate over concrete instances that satisfy the predicate constraints [11]. The novelty of our work is to introduce *symbolic execution* of Alloy models, which is inspired by traditional symbolic execution for imperative programs. Specifically, we introduce symbolic types and symbolic operators for Alloy, so that the existing Alloy Analyzer is able to perform symbolic execution for the supported types and operations. To illustrate, symbolically simulating an Alloy predicate using our approach allows generating a *symbolic instance* that consists of a concrete valuation, similar to a traditional Alloy instance, as well as a symbolic valuation that includes a constraint on symbolic values, similar to a path condition.

We demonstrate the efficacy of our approach using a suite of models that represent a diverse set of constraints, including structurally complex properties. Our approach opens promising avenues for new forms of more efficient and effective analyses of Alloy models. For example, our approach allows SAT to be used to its optimal capability for structural constraint solving, while allowing solving of other kinds of constraints to be delegated to other solvers. As another example, our approach allows Alloy users to view multiple instances simultaneously without the need for enumeration through repeated calls to the underlying solver: a symbolic instance represents a class of concrete instances.

This paper makes the following contributions:

- **Symbolic execution for declarative programs.** We introduce the idea of symbolic execution for declarative programs written in analyzable notations, similar to symbolic execution of imperative programs.
- **Symbolic execution for Alloy models.** We present our approach for symbolic execution of Alloy, and provide an extensible technique to support various symbolic types and operators.
- **Demonstration.** We use a suite of small but complex declarative models to demonstrate the efficacy of our approach and the promise it holds in laying the foundation of novel methodologies for automated analysis of declarative programs.

2 Background and Illustrative Example

This sections presents background on symbolic execution and Alloy and an example of symbolic execution for Alloy technique using a sorted linked list.

2.1 Symbolic Execution Basics

Forward symbolic execution is a technique for executing a program on symbolic values [14]. There are two fundamental aspects of symbolic execution: (1) defining semantics of operations that are originally defined for concrete values and (2) maintaining a *path condition* for the current program path being executed – a path condition specifies necessary constraints on input variables that must be satisfied to execute the corresponding path.

As an example, consider the following program that returns the absolute value of its input:

```
       static int abs(int x) {
L1.      int result;
L2.      if (x < 0)
L3.        result = 0 - x;
L4.      else result = x;
L5.      return result;      }
```

To symbolically execute this program, we consider its behavior on a primitive integer input, say `X`. We make no assumptions about the value of `X` (except what can be deduced from the type declaration). So, when we encounter a conditional statement, we consider both possible outcomes of the condition. To perform operations on symbols, we treat them simply as variables, e.g., the statement on `L3` updates the value of `result` to be `0-X`. Of course, a tool for symbolic execution needs to modify the type of `result` to note updates involving symbols and to provide support for manipulating expressions, such as `0-X`.

Symbolic execution of the above program explores the following two paths:

```
path 1:    [X < 0] L1 -> L2 -> L3 -> L5
path 2:    [X >= 0] L1 -> L2 -> L4 -> L5
```

Note that for each path that is explored, there is a corresponding path condition (shown in square brackets). While execution on a concrete input would have followed exactly one of these two paths, symbolic execution explores both.

2.2 Alloy Basics

Alloy is a first-order relational language [11]. An Alloy specification is a sequence of paragraphs that either introduce new types or record constraints on *fields* of existing types. Alloy assumes a universe of atoms partitioned into subsets, each of which is associated with a basic type. Details of the Alloy notation and of the Alloy Analyzer can be found in [11].

Acyclic lists can be modeled in Alloy with the following specification (called `SortedList` for consistency with the example in the following section):

```
one sig SortedList {
  header: lone Node,
  size: Int }
sig Node {
  data: Int,
  nextNode: lone Node }
pred Acyclic(l: SortedList) {
  all n: l.header.*nextNode | n !in n.^nextNode }
```

The *signature* declarations `SortedList` and `Node` introduce two uninterpreted types, along with functions `header : SortedList` → `Node`, `size : SortedList` → `Int`, `data : Node` → `Int`, and `nextNode : Node` → `Node`. `header` and `nextNode` are partial functions, indicated by the declaration `lone`.

The Alloy *predicate* Acyclic, when invoked, constrains its input `l` to be acyclic. The dot operator '`.`' represents relational image, '`~`' represents transpose, '`^`' represents transitive closure, and '`*`' denotes reflexive transitive closure.

The quantifier `all` stands for universal quantification. For instance, the constraint `all n: l.header.*nextNode | F` holds if and only if evaluation of the *formula* `F` holds for each atom in the transitive closure of `nextNode` starting from `l.header`. Formulas within curly braces are implicitly conjoined. The quantifier `lone` stands for "at most one". There are also quantifiers `some` and `no` with the obvious meaning.

Given an Alloy specification, the Alloy Analyzer automatically finds *instances* that satisfy the specification, i.e., the valuations of relations and signatures that make all the facts in the specification true. Alloy Analyzer finds instances within a pre-specified *scope* – the maximum number of atoms in each basic signature. Alloy Analyzer can also enumerate all non-isomorphic instances.

2.3 Illustrative Example: Symbolic Execution for Alloy

This section presents an example of symbolic execution of Alloy formulas using a sorted linked list. In Section 2.2 we presented the Alloy specification for a linked list. To make it into a sorted linked list, we use the following predicate.

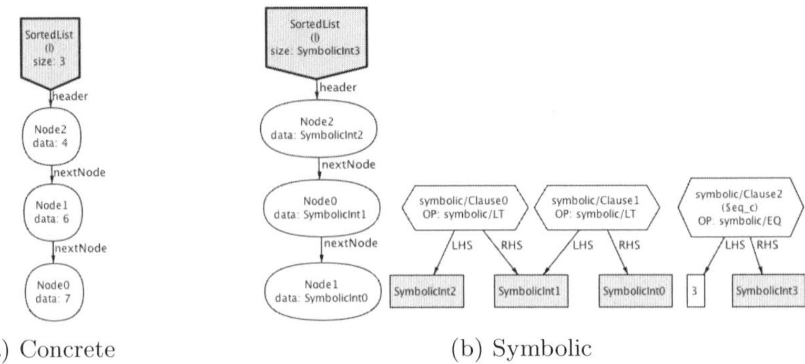

(a) Concrete (b) Symbolic

Fig. 1. Visualizing a sorted linked list with three nodes

```
pred RepOk(l: SortedList) {
  all n: l.header.*nextNode| n !in n.^nextNode -- acyclicity
  #l.header.*nextNode = l.size -- size ok
  all n: l.header.*nextNode |
    some n.nextNode => n.data < n.nextNode.data } -- sorted
```

The Alloy Analyzer can be used on this model to find instances of a sorted linked list. We add the following commands to our model to test the `RepOk` predicate for three nodes.

```
fact { SortedList.header.*nextNode = Node } -- no unreachable Node
run RepOk for 3 -- maximum 3 atoms of each kind
```

As a result of executing this model, Alloy Analyzer produces an instance. The user can get more and more instances by clicking next. One example instance is shown in Fig. 1(a). This sorted linked list represents the sequence $\langle 4, 6, 7 \rangle$. The Alloy Analyzer produces many more instances with three nodes with different sorted arrangements of integers in the domain of Alloy integers.

Symbolic execution of Alloy (Section 3) is a technique to produce instances with symbolic variables and a set of constraints over those symbolic variables. These individual constraints are called *clauses* in our models. The technique is implemented as (1) Alloy library module, (2) a set of guidelines for the user on how to write their Alloy formulas, (3) a set of mechanically generated rules, and finally (4) a mechanism to invoke the Alloy Analyzer. To use symbolic execution of Alloy, the user writing the model has to include the `symbolic` module:

```
open symbolic
```

The user changes any uses of `Int` they wants to make symbolic to `SymbolicInt`. The updated signature declarations for our example look like this:

```
one sig SortedList {
  header: lone Node,
  size: SymbolicInt }
```

```
sig Node {
  data: SymbolicInt,
  nextNode: lone Node }
```

Lastly, the user changes any operations performed on the symbolic variables to use the predicates provided by the `symbolic` module (e.g. `eq`, `lt`, `gt`, etc.). We follow the predicate names introduced by the Alloy 4.2 release candidate in its `integer` module for concrete operations on integers. If the user uses these predicates, no changes are required for predicate invocation. The Alloy Analyzer's type checking finds out whether a symbolic operation is needed or a concrete operation. The updated `RepOk` predicate looks like this:

```
pred RepOk(l: SortedList) {
  all n: l.header.*nextNode| n !in n.^nextNode -- acyclicity
  (#l.header.*nextNode).eq[l.size] -- size ok
  all n: l.header.*nextNode |
    some n.nextNode => (n.data).lt[n.nextNode.data] } -- sorted
```

As the next step, the Alloy module is transformed and a new `fact` is mechanically generated. This fact ensures that the symbolic integers used are all unique. For sorted linked list, this fact is:

```
fact {
  #SymbolicInt = (#SortedList).plus[#Node]
  SymbolicInt = SortedList.size + Node.data }
```

Finally, when this updated model is run through Alloy Analyzer, models with a set of constraints on these symbolic integers are generated. An example instance with three nodes is given in Fig. 1(b). This time, however, it is the only instance with three nodes. Other instances either have fewer or more nodes. This helps the user visualize the model in a more efficient manner. Also a symbolic instance more explicitly states the relationship between data nodes.

3 Symbolic Execution of Alloy Formulas

This section presents the four key parts of our approach: (1) Alloy library module that introduces symbolic variables and operations on them as well as a representation for clauses that define constraints on symbolic fields, (2) changes required in the user model to introduce symbolic fields, (3) mechanically generated facts that enable consistent usage of symbolic values, and (4) Alloy Analyzer usage to restrict any redundant clauses from being generated.

3.1 Symbolic Alloy Module

This section presents the Alloy module that enables symbolic execution. The module starts by the module declaration and a few signatures:

```
module symbolic

abstract sig Expr {}
sig SymbolicInt, SymbolicBool extends Expr {}

abstract sig RelOp {}
one sig lt, gt, lte, gte, eq, neq, plus, minus extends RelOp {}
```

Expr atoms represent expressions that can be symbolic variables or expressions on symbolic variables and plain integers. RelOp are single atoms (because of the one modifier) that represents a few binary operations we demonstrate. Next we define the Clause atom, which is an expression combining two symbolic variables, standard Alloy integers, or expressions.

```
abstract sig Clause extends Expr {
  LHS: Expr+Int,
  OP: RelOp,
  RHS: Expr+Int }
```

Next, we have a set of predicates that require certain clauses to exist. For example the following lt and eq predicates would require that appropriate Clause atoms must exist. These Clause atoms in the final output show us the relationship enforced on symbolic variables in the model.

```
pred lt(e1: Expr+Int, e2: Expr+Int) {
  some c: Clause | c.LHS = e1 && c.OP = LT && c.RHS = e2 }
pred eq(e1: Expr+Int, e2: Expr+Int) {
  some c: Clause | c.LHS = e1 && c.OP = EQ && c.RHS = e2 }
```

Similar predicates exist for all supported operations and Alloy functions exist to combine plus and minus operators to form more complex expressions.

3.2 User Modifications to Alloy Model

This section describes the changes required of the user in their model. Some such changes were discussed in Section 2.3 in the context of a sorted linked list.

The first change is a call to use the symbolic module. This imports the library signatures, predicates, and functions discussed in the previous section.

```
open symbolic
```

Next the user changes Int to SymbolicInt and Bool to SymbolicBool. These are the only primitive types supported by the Alloy Analyzer and we enable symbolic analysis for both of them.

Lastly, the user has to change all operations on symbolic variables to use one of the predicates or functions in the symbolic module. However, the names we used are the same as those used in the built-in Alloy integer module. The new recommended syntax of Alloy 4.2 release candidate is already to use such predicates. Specifically, for plus and minus predicates, the old syntax is no longer allowed. The + and - operators exclusively mean set union and set difference now.

We follow the lead of this predicate-based approach advocated in the Alloy 4.2 release candidate and support `eq`, `neq`, `lt`, `gt`, `lte`, `gte`, `plus`, and `minus` in our `symbolic` module. If the user is using old Alloy syntax, he has to change to the new syntax as follows:

```
a = b  ⇒  a.eq[b]
a < b  ⇒  a.lt[b]
a > b  ⇒  a.gt[b]
a + b  ⇒  a.plus[b]
a - b  ⇒  a.minus[b]
```

The `plus` and `minus` operations in our `symbolic` library come in two forms: as a predicate and as a function. The predicate requires the clause to exist and the function returns the existing clause. For example, to convert an expression `a+b>c` the user first converts it to new syntax i.e. `(a.plus[b]).gt[c]`. Then he adds the plus operation as a separate predicate as well i.e. `a.plus[b] && (a.plus[b]).gt[c]`. The compiler recognizes the first invocation as a predicate that requires a new clause to exist and the second invocation as returning that clause. If the predicate is omitted, the function returns no clause and no satisfying model is found. We include two case studies that show how it is used (Section 4.3 and Section 4.4).

3.3 Mechanically Generated Facts

This section presents the Alloy facts that our technique mechanically generates to ensure soundness of symbolic execution. These facts ensure that symbolic variables are not shared among different objects. For example, two `Node` atoms cannot point to the same `SymbolicInt` atom as `data`. Otherwise, we cannot distinguish which nodes's symbolic variable a `Clause` is referring to. Note that this does not prevent two nodes to contain the same integer value.

We use two mechanically generated facts to ensure uniqueness of symbolic variables. To form these facts, we find all uses of symbolic variables (`SymbolicInt` and `SymbolicBool`). We describe the generation of facts for `SymbolicInt`. Similar facts are generated for `SymbolicBool`.

Consider a `sig A` where `B` is a field of type `SymbolicInt` – i.e. `B` is a relation of the type `A`→`SymbolicInt`. We form a list of all such relations {(`A1`, `B1`), (`A2`, `B2`), (`A3`, `B3`), ...} and then generate two facts.

The first fact ensures that all `SymbolicInt` atoms are used in one of these relations and the second fact ensures that we exactly have as many `SymbolicInt` atoms as needed in these relations. If any `SymbolicInt` atom is used in two relations, then some `SymbolicInt` atom is not used in any relation (because of second fact), but unused `SymbolicInt` atoms are not allowed (because of first fact). Thus the two facts are enough to ensure unique symbolic variables.

```
SymbolicInt = A1.B1 + A2.B2 + A3.B3 + ...
#SymbolicInt = #A1 + #A2 + #A3 + ...
```

Note that if some `sig` has more than one `SymbolicInt`, then for some i, j, `Ai = Aj`. The particular `sig` will be counted twice in the second fact. Also note that the new Alloy syntax requires the second fact to be written using the `plus` function as the + operator is dedicated to set union operation.

```
#SymbolicInt = (#A1).plus[(#A2).plus[(#A3).plus[ ... ]]]
```

3.4 Alloy Analyzer Usage

This section discusses a practical issue in analyzing a model that contains symbolic clauses instead of concrete integers. The key problem is to deal with redundant clauses that may exist in a symbolic instance because they are allowed by the chosen scope, although not explicitly enforced by the constraints, i.e., to separate redundant clauses from enforced clauses. Recall that the Alloy Analyzer finds valid instances of the given model for the given scope. Any instance with redundant clauses within given bounds is still valid. These redundant clauses are not bound to any particular condition on the symbolic variables and can take many possible values resulting in the Alloy Analyzer showing many instances that are only different in the values of redundant clauses. We present two approaches to address this problem.

Iterative Deepening. The first approach is to iteratively run the Alloy Analyzer on increasing scopes for `Clause` atoms until we find a solution. The predicates in `symbolic` module require certain `Clause` atom to exist. If the scope for `sig Clause` is smaller than the number of required clauses, then the Alloy Analyzer will declare that no solutions can be found. This separate bound on `sig Clause` can be given as:

```
run RepOk for 3 but 1 Clause
```

There are three considerations in this approach. The first is performance. Performance is an issue for large models where the bound on `Clause` has to be tested from zero to some larger bound. However, for most models, Alloy analysis is often performed for small sizes. Thus the repetitions required for testing different values is also expected to be small. Still, this incurs a performance overhead.

The second consideration is how to decide an upper bound on number of clauses. The user may use multiple clauses on each symbolic variable. We can enumerate to twice the number of symbolic variables as a safe bound and then inform the user that there may be instances with more clauses but none with fewer clauses. If the user knows that their model needs more clauses, then they can give a higher bound for the clauses to find such instances.

The third consideration is if we find a solution with n clauses, there may be solutions with more than n clauses. For example, the user can write a predicate like:

```
a.eq[b] || (a.eq[c] && c.eq[b])
```

Such an expression can result in one to three clauses. If Alloy Analyzer finds a solution with n clauses, there might be solutions with $n + 1$ and $n + 2$ clauses. Because of this, when we find a valid solution, we inform the user that there might be solutions with more clauses. Again, the user – with knowledge of the model – can force a higher bound on clauses or rewrite such predicates.

Skolemization. The second approach for handling the bound on `Clause` atoms uses *skolemization* in Alloy. According to Alloy's quick guide, "Often times, quantified formulas can be reduced to equivalent formulas without the use of quantifiers. This reduction is called *skolemization* and is based on the introduction of one or more skolem constants or functions that capture the constraint of the quantified formula in their values."

The important aspect of skolemization for our purpose is that skolemized atoms are identified explicitly in Alloy Analyzer's output. If we ensure that all generated clauses are skolemized we can start with a large bound for `Clause` atoms and easily identify redundant `Clause` atoms in the output.

Additionally, Alloy Analyzer's code can be modified to generate only skolemized atoms of one kind. This eliminates all issues related with bounds on the number of clauses. Only enforced clauses will be generated.

The only drawback to this scheme is that the user needs to ensure all predicates can be converted by skolemization. For example, the ordering check for sorted list in Section 2.3 does not produce skolemized results the way it is written. However the following equivalent predicate does:

```
some tail: l.header.*nextNode | no tail.nextNode
  && all n: l.header.*nextNode-tail | (n.data).lt[n.nextNode.data]
```

Instead of an implication, we have to use universal and existential quantifiers. The new sorting check for linked list works with skolemization.

Skolemization translates existential quantifier based expressions. In the future, it should be investigated if the technique associated with skolemization – that renames an atom generated to satisfy a predicate – can be separately used for symbolic execution of Alloy. This would require changing the Alloy Analyzer implementation and only allowing `Clause` atoms that are generated to satisfy predicates in the `symbolic` module. Such `Clause` atoms would be generated regardless of how the predicate in `symbolic` module was invoked.

4 Case Studies

This section presents four small case studies that demonstrate that our technique enables novel forms of analysis of Alloy models using the Alloy Analyzer.

4.1 Red-Black Trees

Red-black trees [6] are binary search trees with one extra bit of information per node: its color, which can be either red or black. By restricting the way nodes are colored on a path from the root to a leaf, red-black trees ensure that the tree is balanced, i.e., guarantee that basic dynamic set operations on a red-black tree take O(lg n) time in the worst case.

A binary search tree is a red-black tree if:

1. Every node is either red or black.
2. Every leaf (NIL) is black.

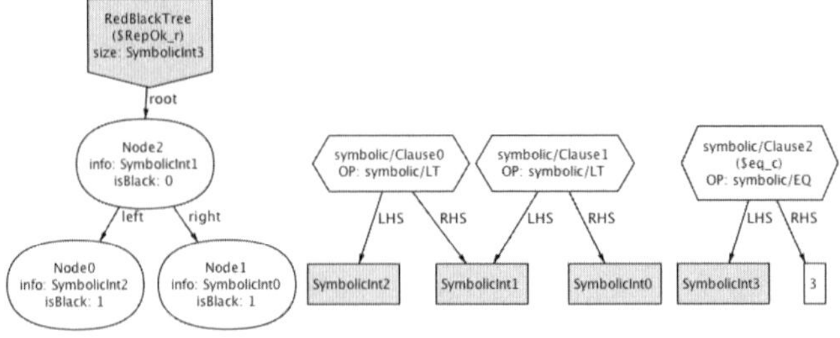

Fig. 2. Visualizing the constraints on data in a red-black tree with three nodes

3. If a node is red, then both its children are black.
4. Every path from the root node to a descendant leaf contains the same number of black nodes.

All four of these red-black properties are expressible in Alloy [13]. Each node is modeled as:

```
sig Node {
  left: Node,
  right: Node,
  data: SymbolicInt,
  isBlack: Bool }
```

The core binary tree properties are:

```
pred isBinaryTree(r: RedBlackTree) {
  all n: r.root.*(left + right) {
    n !in n.^(left + right)     -- no directed cycle
    lone n.~(left + right)      -- at most one parent
    no n.left & n.right }}      -- distinct children
```

We show how symbolic execution of Alloy formulas helps in generating and visualizing red-black tree instances. Using symbolic execution for `size` is similar to sorted linked list. We now show how to make `data` symbolic and write the binary search tree ordering constraints using predicates in the `symbolic` module.

```
pred isOrdered(r: RedBlackTree) {
  all n: r.root.*(left+right) { -- ordering constraint
    some n.left => (n.left.info).lt[n.info]
    some n.right => (n.info).lt[n.right.info] }}
```

Next, we consider the `isBlack` relation. The constraints to validate color are:

```
pred isColorOk(r: RedBlackTree) {
  all e: root.*(left + right) | -- red nodes have black children
    e.isBlack = false && some e.left + e.right =>
      (e.left + e.right).isBlack = true
```

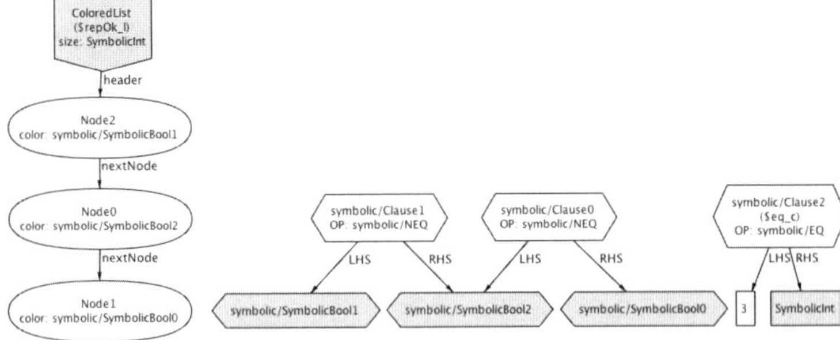

Fig. 3. Visualizing the constraints on a list with alternating colors. Presents an example with symbolic booleans.

```
  all e1, e2: root.*(left + right) | --all paths have same #blacks
    (no e1.left || no e1.right) && (no e2.left || no e2.right) =>
      #{ p: root.*(left+right) |
        e1 in p.*(left+right) && p.isBlack = true } =
      #{ p: root.*(left+right) |
        e2 in p.*(left+right) && p.isBlack = true }
}
```

We don't want `isBlack` to be symbolic because `isBlack` ensures that the generated trees are balanced. If we allow `isBlack` to be symbolic, the Alloy Analyzer will give instances with unbalanced trees combined with a set of unsolvable constraints for `isBlack`. To avoid such instances we keep `isBlack` concrete.

In Fig. 2, an example of a red-black tree instance produced by symbolic execution of the above model is shown. The `root` node is red while both children are black. The constraints show that `data` in `left` node has to be less than data in `root` node which has to be less than data in the `right` node. Another constraint shows that `size` has to be three for this red-black tree.

4.2 Colored List

In this example, we consider a list where no two successive elements have the same color. This example presents a case where symbolic booleans are used.

The `Node sig` is defined as:

```
sig Node {
 nextNode: lone Node,
 color: SymbolicBool }
```

The check for alternate colors in the list can be written as

```
pred ColorsOk(l: ColoredList) {
  all n: l.header.*nextNode |
    some n.nextNode => (n.color).neq[n.nextNode.color] }
```

When this Alloy model is symbolically executed, one instance we get is shown in Fig. 3. There are expressions that restrict the value of each boolean to be *not equal* to either its predecessor's data or its successor's data.

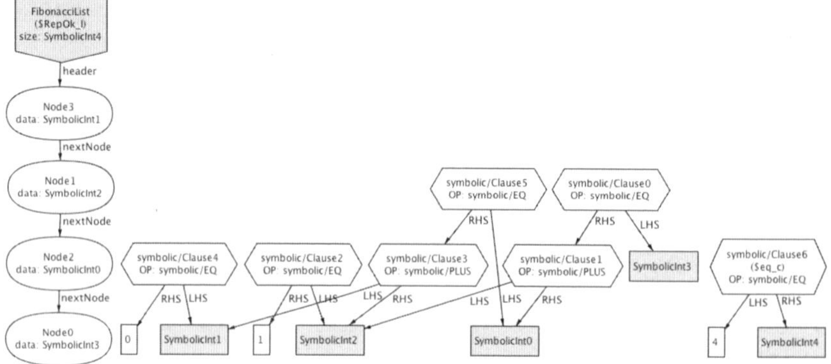

Fig. 4. Visualizing the constraints on data in a fibonacci sequence. Presents an example of non-trivial numeric constraints.

Such a models help in visualizing the structure of a model and understanding the relationships between various elements. Since each symbolic instance corresponds to a class of concrete instances, we are able to visualize more structures and build a better understanding of the model in much less time.

4.3 Fibonacci Series

This example presents how symbolic execution of Alloy models is able to allow non-trivial numeric operations and help avoid integer overflow. Because of Alloy's SAT-based analysis, the domain of integers used has to be kept small and integer overflow is a well-recognized issue. The Alloy 4.2 release candidate supports an option that disables generation of instances that have numeric overflow. Our approach provides an alternative solution since we build constraints on symbolic fields and do not require SAT to perform arithmetic.

This example considers a fibonacci series stored in a linked list. The first two elements are required to contain zero and one. Anything after that contains the sum of last two elements. This can be modeled in Alloy as:

```
pred isFibonacci(l: SortedList) {
  some l.header => (l.header.data).eq[0]
  some l.header.nextNode => (l.header.nextNode.data).eq[1]
  all n: l.header.*nextNode |
    let p = n.nextNode, q = p.nextNode |
      some q => (n.data).plus[p.data] &&
      (q.data).eq[(n.data).plus[p.data]] }
```

The first two constraints ensure that if the `header` and its `next` exist, they should be equal to 0 and 1 respectively. The third constraint works on all nodes (`n`) thats that have two more nodes (`p` and `q`) in front of them. It generates a `plus` clause between `n` and `p` and then generates an equality clause between the `plus` clause and `q`. This covers all restrictions on data in a fibonacci series.

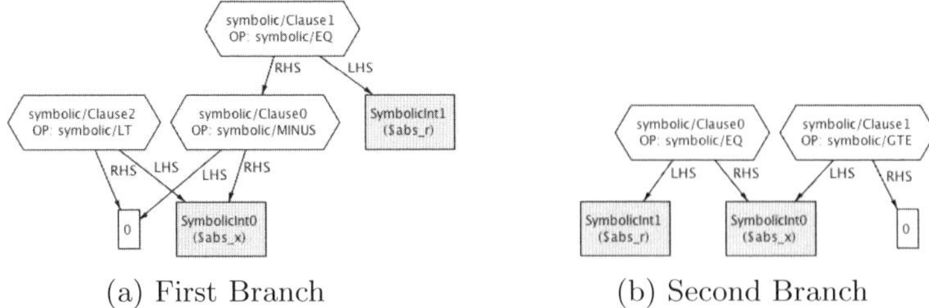

(a) First Branch (b) Second Branch

Fig. 5. Visualizing constraints on two paths within a small imperative function. Presents an example of visualizing traditional path conditions using Alloy.

Fig. 4 shows an instance of the fibonacci list with four nodes. The conditions show that the third and fourth node have to contain the sum of the previous two, while the first two nodes can only contain 0 and 1. This shows the expressive power of symbolic execution for Alloy models and the way it shows a whole class of concrete inputs in a single visualization.

4.4 Traditional Symbolic Execution of Imperative Code

This section demonstrates an example of a small imperative function that is translated to Alloy and is symbolically executed using the Alloy Analyzer. This shows a non-conventional application of the Alloy Analyzer. Consider the `abs` function from Section 2.1 that returns the absolute value of its input.

```
static int abs(int x) {
  int result;
  if (x < 0)
    result = 0 - x;
  else result = x;
  return result;      }
```

This function can modeled in Alloy as:

```
pred abs(x: Int, result: Int) {
  x.lt[0] => 0.minus[x] && result.eq[0.minus[x]]
    else x.gte[0] && result.eq[x] }
```

The predicate takes `x` and `result` where `x` is the original input and `result` models the return value of this function. Symbolic execution of this function explores two paths with conditions `x<0` on one path and `x>=0` on the other path.

When we run this model using symbolic execution for Alloy models, we find both these paths in the output of Alloy Analyzer. The visualization of these paths is shown in Fig. 5. Within the correct bounds and when redundant clauses are prevented, these are the only two results generated by the Alloy Analyzer.

This case study is one of the novel applications of symbolic execution in Alloy. It shows that Alloy can even provide a symbolic execution engine for traditional symbolic execution. It is yet to be seen how feasible Alloy would be in comparison with other symbolic execution engines for analysis of imperative programs.

5 Related Work

Clarke [5] and King [14] pioneered traditional symbolic execution for imperative programs with primitive types. Much progress has been made on symbolic execution during the last decade. PREfix [1] is among the first systems to show the bug finding ability of symbolic execution on real code. Generalized symbolic execution [12] shows how to apply traditional symbolic execution to object-oriented code and uses *lazy initialization* to handle pointer aliasing.

Symbolic execution guided by concrete inputs is one of the most studied approaches for systematic bug finding during the last five years. DART [10] combines concrete and symbolic execution to collect the branch conditions along the execution path. DART negates the last branch condition to construct a new path condition that can drive the function to execute on another path. DART focuses only on path conditions involving integers. To overcome the path explosion in large programs, SMART [9] introduced inter-procedural static analysis techniques to reduce the paths to be explored by DART. CUTE [15] extends DART to handle constraints on references. CUTE can in principle be used with preconditions on structural inputs.

EGT [2] and EXE [3] also use the negation of branch predicates and symbolic execution to generate test cases. They increase the precision of the symbolic pointer analysis to handle pointer arithmetic and bit-level memory locations. All the above approaches consider symbolic execution for imperative constraints.

Symbolic Execution has been applied outside the domain of imperative programs. Thums and Balser [16] uses symbolic execution to verify temporal logic and statecharts. They consider every possible transition and maintain the symbolic state. Wang et al. [18] use symbolic execution to analyze behavioral requirements represented as Live Sequence Charts (LSC). LSC are executable specifications that allow the designer to work out aberrant scenarios. Symbolic execution allows them to group a number of concrete scenarios that only differ in the value of some variable. These are novel applications of symbolic execution, however, they translate the problem from some domain to a sequence of events with choices. This is essentially a sequential operation. To our knowledge symbolic execution has not yet been applied to declarative logic programs.

The Alloy Analyzer uses the Kodkod tool [17], which provides the interface to SAT. The Alloy tool-set also includes JForge [8], which is a framework for analyzing a Java procedure against strong specifications within given bounds. It uses Kodkod for its analysis. JForge translates an imperative Java program to its declarative equivalent. We believe JForge can provide an enabling technology to transform our technique for symbolic execution of Alloy models to handle imperative programs.

6 Conclusion

This paper introduced a novel technique for symbolic execution of declarative models written in the Alloy language. Our insight is that the fully automatic SAT-based analysis that the Alloy tool-set supports, provides a form of execution that can be leveraged to define symbolic execution for Alloy. We demonstrated the efficacy of our technique using a variety of small but complex Alloy models, including red-black trees, colored lists, Fibonacci series, as well as a model of an imperative program. We believe our work opens exciting opportunities to develop more efficient and effective analyses of Alloy. For example, the constraints on symbolic fields can be solved using specialized solvers that directly support the corresponding theories. Moreover, a symbolic instance summarizes a number of concrete instances and thus our technique provides an efficient mechanism for the user to enumerate and inspect desired instances.

Acknowledgments. This work was funded in part by the Fulbright Program, the NSF under Grant Nos. IIS-0438967 and CCF-0845628, and AFOSR grant FA9550-09-1-0351.

References

1. Bush, W.R., et al.: A Static Analyzer for Finding Dynamic Programming Errors. Softw. Pract. Exper. 30 (2000)
2. Cadar, C., Engler, D.: Execution generated test cases: How to make systems code crash itself. In: Godefroid, P. (ed.) SPIN 2005. LNCS, vol. 3639, pp. 2–23. Springer, Heidelberg (2005)
3. Cadar, C., et al.: EXE: Automatically Generating Inputs of Death. In: CCS 2006 (2006)
4. Cadar, C., et al.: Symbolic Execution for Software Testing in Practice Preliminary Assessment. In: ICSE Impact (2011)
5. Clarke, L.A.: Test Data Generation and Symbolic Execution of Programs as an aid to Program Validation. PhD thesis, University of Colorado at Boulder (1976)
6. Cormen, T.T., et al.: Introduction to Algorithms. MIT Press, Cambridge (1990)
7. de Moura, L., Bjørner, N.: Z3: An efficient SMT solver. In: Ramakrishnan, C.R., Rehof, J. (eds.) TACAS 2008. LNCS, vol. 4963, pp. 337–340. Springer, Heidelberg (2008)
8. Dennis, G., Yessenov, K.: Forge website, `http://sdg.csail.mit.edu/forge/`
9. Godefroid, P.: Compositional Dynamic Test Generation. In: POPL (2007)
10. Godefroid, P., et al.: DART: Directed Automated Random Testing. In: PLDI (2005)
11. Jackson, D.: Software Abstractions: Logic, Language, and Analysis. The MIT Press, Cambridge (2006)
12. Khurshid, S., et al.: Generalized symbolic execution for model checking and testing. In: Garavel, H., Hatcliff, J. (eds.) TACAS 2003. LNCS, vol. 2619, pp. 553–568. Springer, Heidelberg (2003)
13. Khurshid, S., Marinov, D.: TestEra: Specification-Based Testing of Java Programs using SAT. Automated Softw. Eng. J. 11 (2004)
14. King, J.C.: Symbolic Execution and Program Testing. Commun. ACM 19 (1976)
15. Sen, K., et al.: CUTE: A Concolic Unit Testing Engine for C. In: ESEC/FSE (2005)
16. Thums, A., Balser, M.: Interactive verification of statecharts. In: Ehrig, H., Damm, W., Desel, J., Große-Rhode, M., Reif, W., Schnieder, E., Westkämper, E. (eds.) INT 2004. LNCS, vol. 3147, pp. 355–373. Springer, Heidelberg (2004)
17. Torlak, E., Jackson, D.: Kodkod: A relational model finder. In: Grumberg, O., Huth, M. (eds.) TACAS 2007. LNCS, vol. 4424, pp. 632–647. Springer, Heidelberg (2007)
18. Wang, T., et al.: Symbolic Execution of Behavioral Requirements. In: Pract. Aspects Decl. Lang. (2004)

Distributed Theorem Proving for Distributed Hybrid Systems*

David W. Renshaw, Sarah M. Loos, and André Platzer

Carnegie Mellon University, Computer Science Department, Pittsburgh, PA, USA

Abstract. Distributed hybrid systems present extraordinarily challenging problems for verification. On top of the notorious difficulties associated with distributed systems, they also exhibit continuous dynamics described by quantified differential equations. All serious proofs rely on decision procedures for real arithmetic, which can be extremely expensive. Quantified Differential Dynamic Logic (Qd$\mathcal{L}$) has been identified as a promising approach for getting a handle in this domain. Qd$\mathcal{L}$ has been proved to be complete relative to quantified differential equations. But important questions remain as to how best to translate this theoretical result into practice: how do we succinctly specify a proof search strategy, and how do we control the computational cost? We address the problem of automated theorem proving for distributed hybrid systems. We identify a simple mode of use of Qd$\mathcal{L}$ that cuts down on the enormous number of choices that it otherwise allows during proof search. We have designed a powerful strategy and tactics language for directing proof search. With these techniques, we have implemented a new automated theorem prover called KeYmaeraD. To overcome the high computational complexity of distributed hybrid systems verification, KeYmaeraD uses a distributed proving backend. We have experimentally observed that calls to the real arithmetic decision procedure can effectively be made in parallel. In this paper, we demonstrate these findings through an extended case study where we prove absence of collisions in a distributed car control system with a varying number of arbitrarily many cars.

1 Introduction

Hybrid systems with joint discrete and continuous dynamics have received considerable attention by the research community, including numerous model checking [11,2,9] and some theorem proving approaches [18,22,23]. Unfortunately, even though hybrid systems verification is already very challenging, not all relevant cyber-physical systems can be modeled as hybrid systems. Hybrid systems cannot represent physical control systems that are distributed or form a multi-agent system, e.g., distributed car control systems. Such systems form *distributed hybrid systems* [8,15,25] with discrete, continuous, and distributed dynamics. Distributed hybrid systems combine the challenges of

* This material is based upon work supported by the National Science Foundation under NSF CAREER Award CNS-1054246, Grant Nos. CNS-0926181, CNS-0931985, CNS-1035800, by the ONR award N00014-10-1-0188, by DARPA FA8650-10C-7077. The second author was supported by an NSF Graduate Research Fellowship.

S. Qin and Z. Qiu (Eds.): ICFEM 2011, LNCS 6991, pp. 356–371, 2011.

hybrid systems and distributed systems, which are both undecidable. Validation technology for distributed hybrid systems had been mostly limited to simulation [8,20] and semantic considerations [28,15]. Very recently, a verification logic, called *quantified differential dynamic logic* (Qd$\mathcal{L}$) has been introduced, along with a proof calculus for distributed hybrid systems [25]. This calculus is compositional and has been proved to be complete relative to quantified differential equations [25]. Yet, several questions need to be addressed to translate this theoretical result into practice. We consider questions of automation in a theorem prover in this paper.

The most important question is how to structure and traverse the proof search space for distributed hybrid systems. We develop a range of techniques to control the proof search space in practice. Our first improvement over the Qd$\mathcal{L}$ base calculus [25] is that we cut down the branching factor during proof search significantly. The Qd$\mathcal{L}$ base calculus allowed rules to be applied anywhere within a formula, which leads to a substantial amount of unnecessary nondeterminism in proof search. We develop a proper sequent calculus and reduce rule application to top-level formulas in the sequent whenever possible. We dispense with the big step arithmetic rule from [25] and introduce modular arithmetic rules that are more amenable to automation. Instead of recursive first-order substitutions [25], we introduce new proof rules for quantified assignments, which are the distributed and first-order equivalent of Hoare's assignment rule.

These improvements reduce the unnecessary nondeterminism in proof search substantially. Yet, the distributed hybrid systems verification problem also leads to inherent nondeterminisms during proof search. In theory, this concerns only the (in)variant search [25], but, in practice, there are also influential choices in how to handle the arithmetic [24]. The heavy computational cost (doubly exponential) of real arithmetic places quite a burden on the proof search procedure. Especially, common heuristics like "if this branch does not close after 5 min, it (practically) never will" are remarkably unsuccessful in distributed hybrid systems. We need more advanced strategies that consider all proof options in a fair way and timeshare limited computation resources efficiently.

For hybrid systems theorem proving [22], we know several proof strategies that can be successful depending on the property to be shown [24]. We expect different and even more varied proof search strategies to be of relevance in distributed hybrid systems theorem proving. We, thus, develop a strategy language in which new strategies can be expressed easily. In an extended case study, we also show that this strategy language has its merits for scripting local proof tactics for arithmetically difficult parts of a proof.

We take the nondeterminisms in proof search at face value. We develop a proof procedure with built-in and/or-branching. Alternatives in proof rule application produce or-branches. The premises of a particular proof rule produce and-branches. Our approach follows all proof search alternatives in parallel. An alternative will only be discarded if it became irrelevant (an or-sibling has been proved or an and-sibling disproved). Proof search may also temporarily disfavor a proof branch that it considers less promising at the moment but may dynamically revisit this choice later.

We have implemented this approach in a new automated theorem prover called *KeYmaeraD* that has a distributed (multiple cores and computers) proof engine for distributed (multi-agent) hybrid systems. Note that our distributed prover does not just prove one of the distributed agents on each of the distributed cores. This coarse-grained parallelism is terribly inefficient and not even sufficient, because the systems we consider have an unbounded number of agents, which then could not be proved on a finite computer.

To show that our approach is successful in practice, we consider an extended case study and prove collision freedom in a distributed car control system. Thanks to the distributed proof search procedures in KeYmaeraD, we found a simpler proof than we previously found manually [16]. This observation shows that the approach presented in this paper can be quite useful. Our previous prover, KeYmaera [27], for hybrid systems cannot handle distributed hybrid systems. In previous work on car control verification [16], we, thus, came up with a proof about two cars in KeYmaera and then used a sophisticated modular proof argument showing how safety of the distributed system could be concluded in a modular way. This lifting effort was a formal but fully manual paper-proof and required modularization proof rules that can only be used in some scenarios. In this paper we consider a more systematic approach that makes it possible to verify systems like distributed car control in a fully mechanized theorem prover for distributed hybrid systems, not just hybrid systems. Our contributions are as follows:

- We identify a mode of using Qd$\mathcal{L}$ proof rules that is suitable for automation and limits the proof search space significantly by reducing unnecessary nondeterminisms.
- We present a systematic proof search framework with and/or-branching that reflects the problem structure in distributed hybrid systems verification naturally.
- We implement our framework in KeYmaeraD, the first verification tool for distributed hybrid systems.
- We present a flexible combinator approach to proof strategies.
- We formally verify collision freedom in a challenging distributed car control system and present the first mechanized proof of distributed car control.

2 Related Work

Hybrid Systems. Process-algebraic approaches, like χ [3], have been developed for modeling and simulation. Verification is still limited to small fragments that can be translated directly to other verification tools like PHAVer or UPPAAL, which do not support distributed hybrid systems.

Automated Theorem Proving. Theorem provers designed in the so-called *LCF style* focus on the construction of objects of a distinguished type called *thm*, the constructors of which correspond exactly to the proof rules of the logic of interest. This provides an intrinsic mechanism for ensuring that any theorem object represents a valid proof, and it reduces the trusted code base to the implementation of the proof rules. Proof search then centers on the use of *tactics*, which are high-level scripts succinctly describing the expected structure of a proof.

Prominent examples of provers in the LCF style include Isabelle [21] and NuPRL [13]. These systems can be used to encode and reason about object logics such as Qd$\mathcal{L}$, they permit users to call external decision procedures, and there has been serious work in using parallelism to improve Isabelle's performance [19]. For these reasons, Isabelle is an attractive candidate for our intended applications. However, the work on parallelism has primarily focused on speeding up the checking of proofs, rather than assisting in the construction of proofs. We would like to use a parallelism model tuned to our particular workflow, and to retain flexibility to modify it in the future. Moreover, we want to move away from the command-line interfaces common to LCF-style provers, instead opting for a more point-and-click interface, akin to that of KeYmaera [27].

Car Control Case Study. Major initiatives have been devoted to developing safe next-generation automated car control systems, including the California PATH project, the SAFESPOT and PReVENT initiatives, the CICAS-V system, and many others. With the exception of [16], safety verification for car control systems has been for specific maneuvers or systems with a small number of cars [29,1,6,17]. Our formal verification of collision-freedom applies to a generic, distributed control for arbitrarily many cars.

Other projects have attempted to ensure the safety of more general systems with simulation and other non-formal methods [7,10,5,14]. Our techniques follow a formal, mechanized, proof calculus, which tests safety completely, rather than using a finite number of simulations which can only test safety partially. We build on the work of [16], which presented a cumbersome, manual proof of collision-freedom for a highway system. We generate a semi-automated, mechanized proof safety for a lane of an arbitrary number of cars, where cars may merge into and exit the system. In this case study, mechanization not only provides a more convincing proof, but also allows us to find simpler proofs of safety.

3 Preliminaries: Quantified Differential Dynamic Logic

As a system model for distributed hybrid systems, $\mathsf{Qd}\mathcal{L}$ uses *quantified hybrid programs* (QHP) [25]. Note that we use a slightly simplified fragment of $\mathsf{Qd}\mathcal{L}$ here that is more amenable to automation. QHPs are defined by the following grammar (α,β are QHPs, θ terms, i a variable of sort C, f is a function symbol, s is a term with sort compatible to f, and H is a formula of first-order logic):

$$\alpha,\beta \ ::= \ \forall i\!:\!C\ \mathcal{A} \mid \forall i\!:\!C\ \{\mathcal{D}\ \&\ H\} \mid ?H \mid \alpha \cup \beta \mid \alpha;\beta \mid \alpha^*$$

where $\mathcal{A}$ is a list of assignments of the form $f(s) := \theta$ and nondeterministic assignments of the form $f(s) := *$, and $\mathcal{D}$ is a list of differential equations of the form $f(s)' = \theta$. When an assignment list does not depend on the quantified variable i, we may elide the quantification for clarity.

The effect of *assignment* $f(s) := \theta$ is a discrete jump assigning θ to $f(s)$. The effect of *nondeterministic assignment* $f(s) := *$ is a discrete jump assigning *any value* to $f(s)$. The effect of *quantified assignment* $\forall i\!:\!C\ \mathcal{A}$ is the simultaneous effect of all assignments in $\mathcal{A}$ for all objects i of sort C. The QHP $\forall i\!:\!C\ a(i) := a(i) + 1$, for example, expresses that all cars i of sort C simultaneously increase their acceleration. The effect of *quantified differential equation* $\forall i\!:\!C\ \mathcal{D}\,\&\,H$ is a continuous evolution where, for all objects i of sort C, all differential equations in $\mathcal{D}$ hold and formula H holds throughout the evolution (i.e. the state remains in the region described by *evolution domain constraint* H). The dynamics of QHPs changes the interpretation of terms over time: for an $\mathbb{R}$-valued function symbol f, $f(s)'$ denotes the derivative of the interpretation of the term $f(s)$ over time during continuous evolution, not the derivative of $f(s)$ by its argument s. We assume that f does not occur in s. In most quantified assignments/differential equations s is just i. For instance, the following QHP expresses that all cars i of sort C drive by $\forall i{:}C\ x(i)'' = a(i)$ such that their position $x(i)$ changes continuously according to their respective acceleration $a(i)$.

The effect of *test* $?H$ is a *skip* (i.e., no change) if formula H is true in the current state and *abort* (blocking the system run by a failed assertion), otherwise. *Nondeterministic choice* $\alpha \cup \beta$ is for alternatives in the behavior of the distributed hybrid system. In the *sequential composition* $\alpha;\beta$, QHP β starts after α finishes (β never starts if α continues indefinitely). *Nondeterministic repetition* α^* repeats α an arbitrary number of times, possibly zero times.

The formulas of Qd$\mathcal{L}$ [25] are defined as in first-order dynamic logic plus many-sorted first-order logic by the following grammar (ϕ, ψ are formulas, θ_1, θ_2 are terms of the same sort, i is a variable of sort C, and α is a QHP):

$$\phi, \psi \ ::= \ \theta_1 = \theta_2 \mid \theta_1 \geq \theta_2 \mid \neg\phi \mid \phi \wedge \psi \mid \phi \vee \psi \mid \forall i{:}C\ \phi \mid \exists i{:}C\ \phi \mid [\alpha]\phi \mid \langle\alpha\rangle\phi$$

We use standard abbreviations to define $\leq, >, <, \rightarrow$. The real numbers $\mathbb{R}$ form a distinguished sort, upon which are defined the rigid functions + and $\times$. Sorts $C \neq \mathbb{R}$ have no ordering and hence $\theta_1 = \theta_2$ is the only relation allowed on them. For sort $\mathbb{R}$, we abbreviate $\forall x{:}\mathbb{R}\ \phi$ by $\forall x\, \phi$. In the following, all formulas and terms have to be well-typed. Qd$\mathcal{L}$ formula $[\alpha]\phi$ expresses that *all states* reachable by QHP α satisfy formula ϕ. Likewise, $\langle\alpha\rangle\phi$ expresses that *there is at least one state* reachable by α for which ϕ holds.

For the formal semantics of Qd$\mathcal{L}$ and QHPs, we refer to [25].

Example 1. Let C be the sort of all cars. By $x(i)$, we denote the position of car i, by $v(i)$ its velocity and by $a(i)$ its acceleration. Then the Qd$\mathcal{L}$ formula

$$(\forall i : C\ \ x(i) \geq 0) \rightarrow [\forall i : C\ \ \{x(i)' = v(i), v(i)' = a(i)\ \&\ v(i) \geq 0\}](\forall i : C\ \ x(i) \geq 0)$$

says that, if all cars start at a point to the right of the origin and we only allow them to evolve as long as all of them have nonnegative velocity, then they end up to the right of the origin. In this case, the QHP just consists of a quantified differential equation expressing that the position $x(i)$ of car i evolves over time according to the velocity $v(i)$, which evolves according to its acceleration $a(i)$. The constraint $v(i) \geq 0$ expresses that the cars never move backwards, which otherwise would happen eventually in the case of braking $a(i) < 0$. This formula is indeed valid, and KeYmaeraD would be able to prove it.

4 Revised Qd$\mathcal{L}$ Proof Calculus

Our desire during verification is to prove that a given formula is valid, that is, true under all interpretations of function symbols. We do this by finding a tree of rule applications (i.e. a proof) within a formal proof calculus (i.e. a set of proof rules), reducing our formula to known facts. In broad strokes, our typical approach is to divide proof search

$$\frac{}{\Gamma,\phi \Rightarrow \phi,\Delta}(close) \quad \frac{\Gamma \Rightarrow \Delta}{\Gamma,\phi \Rightarrow \Delta}(hide\text{-}L) \quad \frac{\Gamma \Rightarrow \Delta}{\Gamma \Rightarrow \phi,\Delta}(hide\text{-}R)$$

$$\frac{\Gamma,\phi \Rightarrow \Delta}{\Gamma \Rightarrow \neg\phi,\Delta}(\neg R) \quad \frac{\Gamma \Rightarrow \phi,\psi,\Delta}{\Gamma \Rightarrow \phi \vee \psi,\Delta}(\vee R) \quad \frac{\Gamma \Rightarrow \phi,\Delta \quad \Gamma \Rightarrow \psi,\Delta}{\Gamma \Rightarrow \phi \wedge \psi,\Delta}(\wedge R) \quad \frac{\Gamma,\phi \Rightarrow \psi,\Delta}{\Gamma \Rightarrow \phi \rightarrow \psi,\Delta}(\rightarrow R)$$

$$\frac{\Gamma \Rightarrow \phi,\Delta}{\Gamma,\neg\phi \Rightarrow \Delta}(\neg L) \quad \frac{\Gamma,\phi \Rightarrow \Delta \quad \Gamma,\psi \Rightarrow \Delta}{\Gamma,\phi \vee \psi \Rightarrow \Delta}(\vee L) \quad \frac{\Gamma,\phi,\psi \Rightarrow \Delta}{\Gamma,\phi \wedge \psi \Rightarrow \Delta}(\wedge L)$$

$$\frac{\Gamma \Rightarrow \phi,\Delta \quad \Gamma,\psi \Rightarrow \Delta}{\Gamma,\phi \rightarrow \psi \Rightarrow \Delta}(\rightarrow L) \quad \frac{x_1 \textbf{ fresh} \qquad \Gamma \Rightarrow \phi(x_1),\Delta}{\Gamma \Rightarrow \forall x\!:\!C\ \phi(x),\Delta}(\forall R) \quad \frac{\Gamma,\forall x\!:\!C\ \phi(x),\phi(\theta) \Rightarrow \Delta}{\Gamma,\forall x\!:\!C\ \phi(x) \Rightarrow \Delta}(\forall L)$$

$$\frac{[\alpha][\beta]\phi}{[\alpha;\beta]\phi}(\,;) \quad \frac{[\alpha]\phi \wedge [\beta]\phi}{[\alpha \cup \beta]\phi}(\cup) \quad \frac{\chi \rightarrow \phi}{[?\chi]\phi}(?) \quad \frac{\Gamma \Rightarrow \psi,\Delta \quad \Gamma,\psi \Rightarrow [\alpha]\psi,\Delta \quad \Gamma,\psi \Rightarrow \phi,\Delta}{\Gamma \Rightarrow [\alpha^*]\phi,\Delta}(^*)$$

Fig. 1. Common rules for Qd$\mathcal{L}$

into three phases. First we transform and decompose our formula according to any QHPs that it contains. Then we use the nullarize rule (cf. Section 4.6) to get rid of index variables. Finally, we deal with the remaining first-order real arithmetic using quantifier elimination in real-closed fields (which does not support general function symbols [22]).

Taking the proof rules in [25] as a starting point, we have designed new proof rules with several aims in mind. Primarily, we have aimed for a set of proof rules that makes proof search amenable to automation. We have also favored rules that are simple enough that their proof of soundness is readily understood. Pictured in Figure 1 are the proof rules that we leave unmodified (but cf. the caveat in the next subsection), and the standard rules for a classical sequent calculus. Instead of dealing with raw formulas, we deal with *sequents* of the form $\Gamma \Rightarrow \Delta$, denoting that the conjunction of the formulas in the list Γ implies the disjunction of the formulas in Δ, where Γ and Δ are finite sets of formulas. Note that in this paper we concentrate on the $[\alpha]$ modality and universal quantification. Similar ideas apply to the $\langle\alpha\rangle$ modality and existential quantification.

4.1 Working Outside-In

In the proof calculus given in [25], most of the rules for dealing with QHPs can be applied deep within formulas. For example, if we were trying to prove the formula

$$[?x > 30][y := 0 \cup y := x][x := x + 1; ?(y < 10)]\ x = y$$

we could apply the (?) rule, the ($\cup$) rule, or the (;) rule. (In this formula, x and y are nullary functions. For brevity, we do not notationally distinguish between nullary functions and free variables.) In our approach, we only consider the outermost part of a formula unless we are forced otherwise. So we would use the (?) rule on this formula. This greatly cuts down on the number of choices at each step of proof search. One downside is that sometimes our approach (and-)branches more than is strictly necessary. We find in practice that the benefit from reducing the (or-)branching factor outweighs this cost.

4.2 A Note about Capture

Recall that instead of having a separate syntactic category for state variables, we allow functions to change their interpretation during the execution of a QHP; this is where a program's state is stored. One consequence of this setup is that performing a substitution is not as straightforward as in ordinary first-order logic. We have to worry about functions being captured by assignments inside of modalities. For example, we can incur capture by "substituting" the term $x(i)$ for the variable Y in the formula

$$[\forall j : C\ x(j) := x(j) + 1]\ 0 = Y,$$

even though $x(i)$ does not appear in this formula. If we are not careful, this could lead to unsoundness of our proof rules. Therefore, we use a notion of substitution *admissibility* that excludes substitutions like the above one. We will not formally define admissibility here, but refer to [25].

4.3 Assignment

Proof rules for assignment are central to our approach. We want a proof rule to allow us to work on formulas such as $[x := 1]\phi$. This formula means that ϕ holds after execution of the QHP $x := 1$. One approach to working on this formula would substitute 1 for x in ϕ. Indeed, when doing so is an admissible substitution, this gives us a sound rule. This rule should be familiar to readers familiar with Hoare Logic. If the substitution is not admissible, as in the case when we are trying to prove $[x := 1][x := 0]x = 1$, then this approach fails. In this case, however, we can introduce a new nullary function x_1, rename x to x_1 in ϕ, and instead prove $[x := 1][x_1 := 0]x_1 = 1$, by applying a now-trivial substitution. But then what should we do with formulas such as

$$[x := 1][x := 1 \cup ?(true)]x = 1$$

where it is not clear how to rename in a way that will make the substitution admissible? The approach that we take is to delay substitution, encoding its information into a new assumption. Thus, to prove the above formula, we can prove the equivalent

$$(x_1 = 1) \rightarrow [x_1 := 1 \cup ?(true)]x_1 = 1.$$

We can write our rule as follows:

$$\frac{\textsf{A fresh} \qquad \Gamma, updates(\mathcal{A}, \mathsf{A}) \Rightarrow rename(\mathcal{A}, \mathsf{A}, \phi), \Delta}{\Gamma \Rightarrow [\mathcal{A}]\phi, \Delta}\ (:=)$$

where A is a set of fresh names for $\mathcal{A}$'s assigned functions. The formula $rename(\mathcal{A}, \mathsf{A}, \phi)$ is ϕ with all occurences of $\mathcal{A}$'s assigned functions renamed by their fresh counterparts (from A). Also, $updates(\mathcal{A}, \mathsf{A})$ is a set of formulas that relates $\mathcal{A}$'s assigned functions to their fresh counterparts in the appropriate way. The exact form $updates(\mathcal{A})$ depends on the form of the assignments contained in it. We show some examples in Figure 2.

$\mathcal{A}$	A	$updates(\mathcal{A}, \mathsf{A})$	$rename(\mathcal{A}, \mathsf{A}, x = f(k))$
$x := x + 1$	x_1	$x_1 = x + 1$	$x_1 = f(k)$
$x := y + 1, y := x$	x_1, y_1	$x_1 = y + 1$ and $y_1 = x$	$x_1 = f(k)$
$\forall i : C\ f(i) := f(i) + 1$	f_1	$\forall i : C\ f_1(i) = f(i) + 1$	$x = f_1(k)$
$f(j) := 3$	f_1	$f_1(j) = 3$ and $\forall i : C\ i \neq j \rightarrow f_1(i) = f(i)$	$x = f_1(k)$

Fig. 2. Examples for the (:=) rule

4.4 Equality Substitution

The assignment rule ends up adding many new function symbols along with assumptions about them. It is desirable that we have a way to simplify this information. Suppose that θ_1 and θ_2 are closed terms and we know $\theta_1 = \theta_2$. Suppose furthermore that we are trying to prove $\Gamma \Rightarrow \Delta$, where Γ and Δ are modality-free. Then we may replace any occurrence of θ_1 in Γ or Δ with θ_2. Often we want to perform all possible replacements so as to eliminate a particular function. For this common case, we have the following proof rule:

$$\frac{\Gamma_{\theta_1}^{\theta_2} \Rightarrow \Delta_{\theta_1}^{\theta_2}}{\theta_1 = \theta_2, \Gamma \Rightarrow \Delta}(=)$$

Here, $\Gamma_{\theta_1}^{\theta_2}$ means Γ with every occurrence of θ_1 replaced by θ_2. This is not a substitution in the ordinary sense of the word, because θ_1 is a term, not a variable. We emphasize that it is important that Γ and Δ be modality-free. Otherwise the rule could incur capture and be unsound.

4.5 Differential Equations

Suppose that the QHP we need to deal with is a set of quantified differential equations $\mathcal{D}$, and suppose furthermore that $\mathcal{D}$ has a set of symbolic solutions $S(t)$. The usual proof rule to apply in this situation, as put forth in [25], is

$$\frac{\forall t \geq 0\ ((\forall 0 \leq \tilde{t} \leq t\ [S(\tilde{t})]H) \rightarrow [S(t)]\phi)}{[\forall i : C\ \{\mathcal{D}\ \&\ H\}]\phi}(=')$$

which is essentially a direct translation of the semantics of $\mathcal{D}$. The premise can be understood informally as follows: for all future times t, if the solution remains in the domain constraint H up to time t, then the postcondition is true at time t. This premise has the undesirable characteristic of containing a nested quantification on the left of an implication. Often, the following rule (with a simpler, but stronger premise) suffices:

$$\frac{\forall t \geq 0\ [S(t)](H \rightarrow \phi)}{[\forall i : C\ \{\mathcal{D}\ \&\ H\}]\phi}(='_{endpoint})$$

This premise states that, for all future times t, if the solution is in the domain constraint H at t, then the postcondition is true at t. We call this the *endpoint* version of the rule.

4.6 Eliminating Index Variables

The first order theory of real numbers is decidable only for formulas that have no uninterpreted non-nullary function symbols. Therefore, in order to use a backend decision procedure, we need to get rid of such functions. In [25], this task was accomplished in a proof rule that eliminated all non-nullary functions in a single proof rule application. This had the potential to cause an exponential blowup in the size of the sequent.

In contrast, we take a more local approach. We use what we call the *nullarize* proof rule, which looks for occurrences of a given closed term θ, and replaces them with a new nullary function. We write the rule as follows.

$$\frac{g_1 \textbf{ fresh} \qquad \Gamma_\theta^{g_1} \Rightarrow \Delta_\theta^{g_1}}{\Gamma \Rightarrow \Delta}(null)$$

Recall that this is not substitution—it is a replacement operation. It is important that θ be a closed term. We may not, for example, use the rule to get rid of $f(i)$ in the formula

$$\forall i : C \ \ f(i) > 0,$$

If this formula occurred on the left of the sequent, then we can nullarize f only after we have used the $(\forall L)$ rule to instantiate i.

4.7 Real Arithmetic

Nullary functions can be understood as being implicitly universally quantified. In contrast, we consider any *variables* that are free to be implicitly existentially quantified (inside of the universal quantification of functions). For example, if Y is a free variable and x is a nullary function, then the formula $x = Y$ means for all interpretations of x there exists a value for Y such that $x = Y$. This particular formula is valid.

Thus, once we have eliminated modalities and non-nullary functions, we are left with a sequent that is equivalent to a formula in the first-order theory of real closed fields. This is a decidable theory. Note that there is a subtle distinction here—first-order logic over the reals, with uninterpreted functions, is undecidable. However, first-order arithmetic, with only the rigid arithmetic functions, is decidable. Therefore, when we have reached this point, we invoke a decision procedure for this theory.

5 Proving in KeYmaeraD

In order to make use of the above proof calculus, we have implemented KeYmaeraD, a new theorem prover. KeYmaeraD's design is inspired by the LCF approach to theorem proving. At any given time there is a tree called the *proof state*, which the user is trying to build into a proper proof. Each node in the tree represents a proof goal (i.e. a sequent). The only way the user has of changing the proof state is to apply one of the proof rules, as pictured in Figure 3. Applying a proof rule to a goal does one of three things:

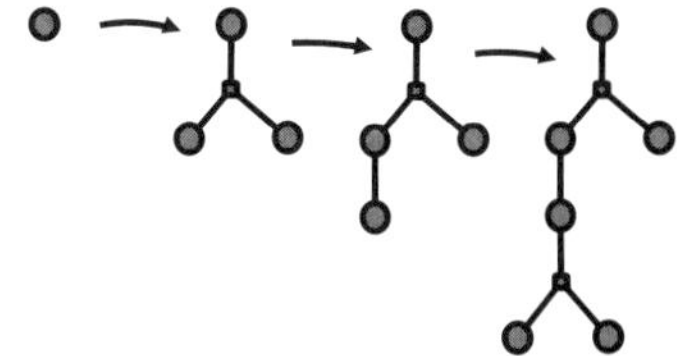

Fig. 3. Application of proof rules to nodes (the circles) leads to and-branching (the squares)

1. fails, in which case the proof state is left unchanged,
2. succeeds in closing the goal,
3. breaks the goal into one or more conjunctive subgoals.

One way in which KeYmaeraD differs from many LCF-style provers is that it allows or-branching on the proof state itself, rather than only at the level of tactics. (We will discuss tactics later.) This allows the user to explore multiple possible proofs simultaneously, as pictured in Figure 4. If any or-branch successfully closes, KeYmaeraD automatically marks the others as irrelevant, as pictured in Figure 5.

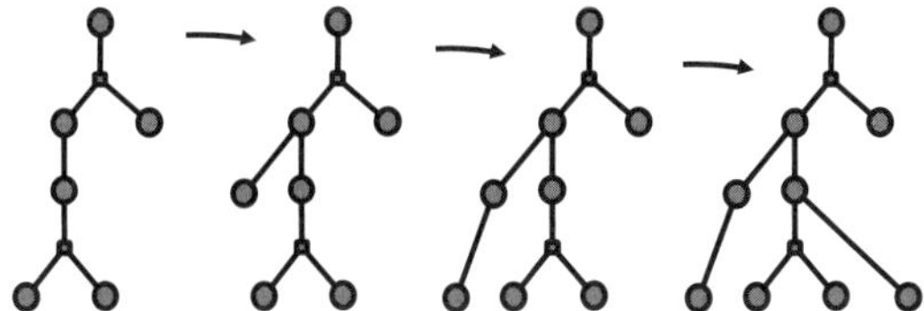

Fig. 4. Application of different rules at the same node leads to or-branching, shown here as circle nodes with two children

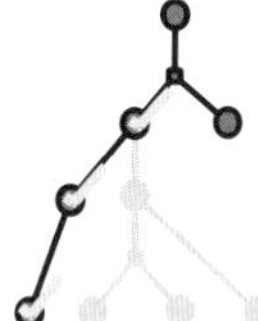

Fig. 5. Closing an or-branch

The typical strategy we use to try to prove a Qd$\mathcal{L}$ formula in KeYmaeraD is as follows: We want to use the proof rules to get rid of modalities and the indices. Then we will be left with arithmetic, which is decidable. For dealing with the QHPs in the modalities, we have found that it often suffices to work from the outside in, as discussed in the previous section. In this way, we do not have to think about which rule to apply. The hard part in this phase is choosing invariants for loops and differential equations (if they do not have symbolic solutions; see [26]). The or-branching is useful for trying different invariants and remembering why particular branches fail to close.

Next, we get rid of indices. The hard part here is choosing instantiations. If our goal has no modalities and no indices, we can pass it to the arithmetic backend. This procedure will return asynchronously and KeYmaeraD will appropriately update the proof state to reflect its success or failure.

One key observation is that giving the arithmetic solver *too much* information can cause it to take too long (even by > 3 orders of magnitude). We often need to decide what parts of the sequent to include. A common pattern in our workflow is the following. We let the arithmetic decision procedure work on a sequent as soon as we have gotten rid of modalities and indices. In the meantime, we start an or-branch that hides believed-to-be-irrelevant formulas in the sequent before again invoking the procedure. Sometimes the original call returns before we even get to making a second call. Sometimes the second call returns immediately and makes the first call irrelevant.

6 Strategy Language

Using KeYmaeraD to apply proof rules one by one—a task that is already much easier than manipulating Qd$\mathcal{L}$ formulas on paper—quickly becomes tedious. To increase the user's power, we introduce tactics, which are a way to script proof search. Our ultimate aim is to allow Qd$\mathcal{L}$ theorem proving to be as automated as possible. We envision that future versions of KeYmaeraD will be able to perform successful proof searches that take on the order of days or weeks using a cluster of tens or hundreds of computers running the arithmetic backend. Carefully designed tactics should provide a modular way to work toward this aim.

KeYmaeraD has an embedded language of base tactics and tactic-combinators ("tacticals" in the jargon). Tactics can be built from provided tactics. We also allow tactics to use arbitrary code in the Scala language, which is the implementation language of KeYmaeraD. In this latter case, tactics can read and do whatever analysis they like on the entire proof state. In keeping with our LCF-style design, the only way that a tactic can change the proof state, however, is to apply proof rules. Hence, tactics are not soundness-critical, only important for completeness.

The type of a tactic is as follows:

$$Node \rightarrow Option[List[Node]]$$

A tactic takes a node of the proof state. It does some computation that might have effects on the proof state. Then, it either returns `None`, signaling failure, or it succeeds and returns a list of nodes. Note that this success does not necessarily signify that the tactic has proved any particular goal—it just means that the tactic did what it was meant to do on this node. The list of returned nodes is intended to be used for the composition of tactics. A typical mode of use is for this list to be a conjunctive list of subgoals— if they are all valid then the original sequent is valid. However, the soundness of the system does not depend on tactics being used only in this way. Indeed, the tactic `arithT`, as explained below, does not follow this pattern. Some common tactics and tactic combinators are shown in Figure 6.

6.1 Example: Instantiation

Here we explain one kind of tactic that we have found useful. Suppose we have several formulas with universal quantifiers on the left in our sequent. To make use of these formulas, we will need to use the ($\forall L$) rule, which instantiates the formulas. We may want to think carefully about what terms we will use for the instantiations. If so, we might, e.g. use a tactic that looks for formulas of the form $i = j$ uses these matched terms

Tactics	
`nilT`	Always fails.
`unitT`	Always succeeds, returning the given node (no-op).
`tryruleatT(rl,pos)`	Tries to apply the rule `rl` at the position `pos`.
`tryruleT(rl)`	Tries to apply the rule `rl` at all positions until it succeeds.
`tryrulepT(rl,prd)`	Tries the rule on a top-level formula where the predicate is true.
Tactic Combinators	
`eitherT(t1,t2)`	First tries `t1`. Upon failure, tries `t2`.
`composeT(t1,t2)`	Tries `t1` and then, upon success, applies `t2` to all the returned nodes.
`repeatT(t)`	Tries `t` until it fails, returning the result of the final success.
`branchT(t,ts)`	Tries `t`. Upon success, maps the returned nodes to `ts`.

Fig. 6. Tactics and Tactic Combinators

to instantiation. At the other extreme, we may just want to instantiate the quantified formulas with any and all terms that could possibly make sense. (This is often feasible for sorts other than the real numbers, where no functions are predefined and the only relation is equality.) This is often useful in sequents that are light on arithmetic. But exhaustive instantiation quickly chokes the arithmetic solvers. Tactics that take either of these tacks are used heavily in our case study.

6.2 Arithmetic

The decision procedure for arithmetic returns asynchronously. We have a tactic called `arithT` that fails if the goal cannot be passed to the procedure. (This happens if there are any modalities or indices left.) Otherwise it succeeds, returning the empty list. When the procedure returns with a result, KeYmaeraD will automatically update the proof state to reflect the new information. To better understand this protocol, consider the composed tactic `eitherT(arithT, myOtherTactic)`. If `arithT` fails, then we need to continue to work on the sequent to get rid of modalities or indices. Therefore, in that case we continue with `myOtherTactic`. Otherwise, we do not need to do anything other than wait for the decision procedure to return. So the tactic succeeds, even if the procedure eventually returns "false."

6.3 Input Formulas

Some important proof rules such as (*) are parametrized by a formula. Because of our renaming method for dealing with assignments, sometimes it is impossible for the writer of a proof script to know in advance what name some functions will have when such a rule needs to be applied. Therefore, we provide a unification function `unify` that can be invoked in tactics. The result of `unify(fm1,fm2)` is either failure or a substitution function which, when applied to `fm2` will return `fm1`. Note that we do not use `unify` to synthesize invariant formulas, we merely use it to get a handle on formulas as they shift names.

7 Case Study

In this section we present a mechanized, formal verification of a distributed adaptive cruise control and automatic braking system as a complex case study of the KeYmaeraD theorem prover. Major initiatives have been devoted to developing safe next-generation automated car control systems, including the California PATH project, the SAFESPOT and PReVENT initiatives, the CICAS-V system, and many others. Chang et al. [4], for instance, propose CICAS-V in response to a report that crashes at intersections in the US cost \$97 Billion in the year 2000.

Providing a formal verification of safety-critical cyber-physical systems is vital to ensure safety as the public adopts these systems into daily use. However, before KeYmaeraD, formal verification of large-scale, distributed, hybrid systems was only possible manually. Manual proofs not only require ample skilled man-power, but are also prone to errors. Applying the powerful verification methods of $\mathsf{Qd}\mathcal{L}$ to a broad range of distributed hybrid systems is not possible without automation and mechanization, which KeYmaeraD provides.

In this section, we present the first semi-automated and fully mechanized proof of an arbitrary number of cars driving under distributed controllers along a straight lane.

Modeling. Model 1 is a QHP for an arbitrary number of cars following distributed, discrete and continuous dynamics along a straight lane. In addition, the model allows cars to appear and disappear at any time and in any safe location, simulating lane changes. The discrete control consists of three possible choices, modeled as a nondeterministic assignment in $ctrl(i)$; see line (3). Braking is allowed at all times, and is the only option if certain safety constraints are not met. Car i may accelerate only if the constraint $\mathbf{Safe}_\varepsilon(i)$ holds, meaning that the cars in front of car i are far enough away for car i to accelerate for at least ε time units. Here, ε represents the upper bound on sensor/communication update delay. Additionally, if the car is stopped, it can always continue to stand still.

Every car on the lane is associated with three real values: position, velocity, and acceleration. Since cars may also appear and disappear, we add a fourth element: existence. The existence field is a bit that flips on ($\mathsf{E}(n) := 1$) when a car appears on the lane and off ($\mathsf{E}(n) := 0$) when a car disappears. Any number of cars may disappear from the road (simulating merging into an adjacent lane or exiting the highway) at any time. To accomplish this, the model non-deterministically chooses an existing car and flips its existence bit to off; see line (8). Modeling cars merging into the lane is almost as simple; however, before a car can merge, it must check that it will be safely in front of or behind all previously existing cars on the lane; see line (9).

This model is similar to the `lhc` model proved manually in [16], but with a few simplifications. First, we assume in line (4) that the cars have omniscient sensing, i.e., each car receives data about the position and velocity of all the cars on the lane, as opposed to just the car directly ahead. Second, we assume that when the car accelerates, it applies maximum acceleration, and when it brakes it applies maximum braking, rather than choosing from a bounded range of acceleration and braking forces.

Model 1. Local highway control (lhc)

$$
\begin{aligned}
\texttt{lhc} &\equiv ((ctrl^n; dyn^n)^* \cup delete^* \cup create^*)^* && (1)\\
ctrl^n &\equiv \forall i : C\ \ a(i) := *;\ ?(\forall i : C\ \ \mathrm{E}(i) = 1 \rightarrow ctrl(i)) && (2)\\
ctrl(i) &\equiv a(i) = -B\ \vee\ (\mathbf{Safe}_\varepsilon(i) \wedge a(i) = A)\ \vee\ (v(i) = 0 \wedge a(i) = 0) && (3)\\
\mathbf{Safe}_\varepsilon(i) &\equiv \forall j : C\ \ x(i) \leq x(j) \wedge i \neq j \rightarrow && (4)\\
& \qquad x(i) + \frac{v(i)^2}{2B} + \left(\frac{A}{B} + 1\right)\left(\frac{A}{2}\varepsilon^2 + \varepsilon v(i)\right) < x(j) + \frac{v(j)^2}{2B} && (5)\\
dyn^n &\equiv (t := 0;\ \forall i : C\ \{dyn(i)\}) && (6)\\
dyn(i) &\equiv x(i)' = v(i),\ v(i)' = a(i), t' = 1\ \&\ (t \leq \varepsilon\ \wedge\ (\mathrm{E}(i) = 1 \rightarrow v(i) \geq 0)) && (7)\\
delete &\equiv n := *;\ ?(\mathrm{E}(n) = 1);\ \mathrm{E}(n) := 0 && (8)\\
create &\equiv n := new;\ ?(\forall i : C\ \ E(i) = 1 \rightarrow (i \ll n) \wedge (n \ll i)) && (9)\\
(n := new) &\equiv n := *;\ ?(\mathrm{E}(n) = 0 \wedge v(n) \geq 0);\ \mathrm{E}(n) := 1 && (10)\\
(i \ll n) &\equiv (x(i) \leq x(n) \wedge i \neq n) \rightarrow \left(x(i) < x(n) \wedge x(i) + \frac{v(i)^2}{2B} < x(n) + \frac{v(n)^2}{2B}\right) && (11)
\end{aligned}
$$

Verification. Now that we have described a suitable model for a lane of cars in a highway (Model 1), we identify a set of safety requirements and prove that the model never violates them. Safety verification must ensure that, at all times, every car on the road is safely behind all the cars ahead of it in its lane. We say that car i is safely following car j if $(i \ll j)$, as defined in line (11). To capture the notion that the cars should be safe at all times, we use the $[\alpha]$ modality, as shown in Proposition 1.

Proposition 1 (Safety of local highway control lhc). *Assuming the cars start in a controllable state (i.e. each car is a safe distance from the cars ahead of it on the lane), the cars may move, appear, and disappear as described in the* (lhc) *model, then no cars will ever collide. This is expressed by the following provable* Qd$\mathcal{L}$ *formula:*

$$
\begin{aligned}
&(\forall\, i : C\ \forall j : C\ (\mathrm{E}(i) = 1 \wedge \mathrm{E}(j) = 1) \rightarrow ((i \ll j) \wedge v(i) \geq 0 \wedge v(j) \geq 0)) \rightarrow\\
&\quad [\texttt{lhc}](\forall i : C\ \forall j : C\ (\mathrm{E}(i) = 1 \wedge \mathrm{E}(j) = 1) \rightarrow ((i \ll j) \wedge v(i) \geq 0 \wedge v(j) \geq 0)))
\end{aligned}
$$

Our final tactic script is about 400 lines. At the end of its execution, the proof state has 1134 nodes. On a MacBook Pro with a 2.86GHz Core 2 Duo processor, using Mathematica 7.0.0 for the real arithmetic backend, the proof takes 40 seconds to complete with one worker, and 33 seconds with two workers. This includes the time it takes to compile and load the tactic script— approximately 13 seconds.

In the course of developing this proof, we discovered that the endpoint rule for differential equations suffices for this formula—a simplification which greatly increases the computational efficiency of our proof.

Because KeYmaeraD uses a tactics-based approach rather than real-time interactions, verification requires fewer human inputs and lends itself to reusability. The two car case for this model, for instance, required far fewer tactics when implemented in KeYmaeraD than the hundreds of human-interactions needed by KeYmaera. The tactics were also robust enough to be applied to multiple proof branches. Moreover, we initially proved a version that omitted $x(i) < x(j)$ in the invariant. Then, after realizing that the invariant did not obviously imply the safety condition we wanted, we added this condition. With only minimal changes to the tactics script, the updated model was easily verified.

The manual proof presented in [16] relies heavily on modular proof structure principles to get the proof complexity to a manageable size. With KeYmaeraD, we can improve on that modular structure by employing modular proof tactics. This approach still simplifies the resulting proof structure as before, but, unlike dedicated modularity arguments, it also maintains better robustness to changes in the model.

8 Conclusions and Future Work

We introduce automation techniques for theorem proving for distributed hybrid systems using quantified differential dynamic logic. We have implemented KeYmaeraD, the first formal verification tool for distributed hybrid systems. As a major case study in KeYmaeraD, we have formally verified collision freedom in a sophisticated distributed car control system with an unbounded (and varying) number of cars driving on a straight lane.

References

1. Althoff, M., Althoff, D., Wollherr, D., Buss, M.: Safety verification of autonomous vehicles for coordinated evasive maneuvers. In: IEEE IV 2010, pp. 1078–1083 (2010)
2. Alur, R., Courcoubetis, C., Halbwachs, N., Henzinger, T.A., Ho, P.H., Nicollin, X., Olivero, A., Sifakis, J., Yovine, S.: The algorithmic analysis of hybrid systems. Theor. Comput. Sci. 138(1), 3–34 (1995)
3. van Beek, D.A., Man, K.L., Reniers, M.A., Rooda, J.E., Schiffelers, R.R.H.: Syntax and consistent equation semantics of hybrid Chi. J. Log. Algebr. Program. 68(1-2), 129–210 (2006)
4. Chang, J., Cohen, D., Blincoe, L., Subramanian, R., Lombardo, L.: CICAS-V research on comprehensive costs of intersection crashes. Tech. Rep. 07-0016, NHTSA (2007)
5. Chee, W., Tomizuka, M.: Vehicle lane change maneuver in automated highway systems. PATH Research Report UCB-ITS-PRR-94-22, UC Berkeley (1994)
6. Damm, W., Hungar, H., Olderog, E.R.: Verification of cooperating traffic agents. International Journal of Control 79(5), 395–421 (2006)
7. Dao, T.S., Clark, C.M., Huissoon, J.P.: Optimized lane assignment using inter-vehicle communication. In: IEEE IV 2007, pp. 1217–1222 (2007)
8. Deshpande, A., Göllü, A., Varaiya, P.: SHIFT: A formalism and a programming language for dynamic networks of hybrid automata. In: Hybrid Systems, pp. 113–133 (1996)
9. Frehse, G.: PHAVer: algorithmic verification of hybrid systems past HyTech. STTT 10(3), 263–279 (2008)
10. Hall, R., Chin, C.: Vehicle sorting for platoon formation: Impacts on highway entry and troughput. PATH Research Report UCB-ITS-PRR-2002-07, UC Berkeley (2002)
11. Henzinger, T.A., Nicollin, X., Sifakis, J., Yovine, S.: Symbolic model checking for real-time systems. In: LICS, pp. 394–406 (1992)
12. Hespanha, J.P., Tiwari, A. (eds.): Hybrid Systems: Computation and Control, 9th International Workshop, HSCC 2006. LNCS, vol. 3927. Springer, Heidelberg (2006)

13. Howe, D.J.: Automating Reasoning in an Implementation of Constructive Type Theory. Ph.D. thesis, Cornell University (1988)
14. Jula, H., Kosmatopoulos, E.B., Ioannou, P.A.: Collision avoidance analysis for lane changing and merging. PATH Research Report UCB-ITS-PRR-99-13, UC Berkeley (1999)
15. Kratz, F., Sokolsky, O., Pappas, G.J., Lee, I.: R-charon, a modeling language for reconfigurable hybrid systems. In: Hespanha, J.P., Tiwari, A. (eds.) HSCC 2006. LNCS, vol. 3927, pp. 392–406. Springer, Heidelberg (2006)
16. Loos, S.M., Platzer, A., Nistor, L.: Adaptive cruise control: Hybrid, distributed, and now formally verified. In: Butler, M., Schulte, W. (eds.) FM 2011. LNCS, vol. 6664, pp. 42–56. Springer, Heidelberg (2011)
17. Lygeros, J., Lynch, N.: Strings of vehicles: Modeling safety conditions. In: Henzinger, T.A., Sastry, S.S. (eds.) HSCC 1998. LNCS, vol. 1386, Springer, Heidelberg (1998)
18. Manna, Z., Sipma, H.: Deductive verification of hybrid systems using STeP. In: Henzinger, T.A., Sastry, S.S. (eds.) HSCC 1998. LNCS, vol. 1386, pp. 305–318. Springer, Heidelberg (1998)
19. Matthews, D.C.J., Wenzel, M.: Efficient parallel programming in Poly/ML and Isabelle/ML. In: DAMP (2010)
20. Meseguer, J., Sharykin, R.: Specification and analysis of distributed object-based stochastic hybrid systems. In: Hespanha, J.P., Tiwari, A. (eds.) HSCC 2006. LNCS, vol. 3927, pp. 460–475. Springer, Heidelberg (2006)
21. Paulson, L.C.: The foundation of a generic theorem prover. Journal of Automated Reasoning 5 (1989)
22. Platzer, A.: Differential dynamic logic for hybrid systems. J. Autom. Reas. 41(2), 143–189 (2008)
23. Platzer, A.: Differential-algebraic dynamic logic for differential-algebraic programs. J. Log. Comput. 20(1), 309–352 (2010)
24. Platzer, A.: Logical Analysis of Hybrid Systems: Proving Theorems for Complex Dynamics. Springer, Heidelberg (2010)
25. Platzer, A.: Quantified differential dynamic logic for distributed hybrid systems. In: Dawar, A., Veith, H. (eds.) CSL 2010. LNCS, vol. 6247, pp. 469–483. Springer, Heidelberg (2010)
26. Platzer, A.: Quantified differential invariants. In: Frazzoli, E., Grosu, R. (eds.) HSCC. ACM, New York (2011)
27. Platzer, A., Quesel, J.D.: KeYmaera: A hybrid theorem prover for hybrid systems (System description). In: Armando, A., Baumgartner, P., Dowek, G. (eds.) IJCAR 2008. LNCS (LNAI), vol. 5195, pp. 171–178. Springer, Heidelberg (2008)
28. Rounds, W.C.: A spatial logic for the hybrid p-calculus. In: Alur, R., Pappas, G.J. (eds.) HSCC 2004. LNCS, vol. 2993, pp. 508–522. Springer, Heidelberg (2004)
29. Stursberg, O., Fehnker, A., Han, Z., Krogh, B.H.: Verification of a cruise control system using counterexample-guided search. Control Engineering Practice (2004)

Towards a Model Checker for NesC and Wireless Sensor Networks*

Manchun Zheng[1], Jun Sun[2], Yang Liu[1], Jin Song Dong[1], and Yu Gu[2]

[1] School of Computing, National University of Singapore
{zmanchun,liuyang,dongjs}@comp.nus.edu.sg
[2] Singapore University of Technology and Design
{sunjun,jasongu}@sutd.edu.sg

Abstract. Wireless sensor networks (WSNs) are expected to run unattendedly for critical tasks. To guarantee the correctness of WSNs is important, but highly nontrivial due to the distributed nature. In this work, we present an automatic approach to directly verify WSNs built with TinyOS applications implemented in the NesC language. To achieve this target, we firstly define a set of formal operational semantics for most of the NesC language structures for the first time. This allows us to capture the behaviors of sensors by labelled transition systems (LTSs), which are the underlying semantic models of NesC programs. Secondly, WSNs are modeled as the composition of sensors with a network topology. Verifications of individual sensors and the whole WSN become possible by exploring the corresponding LTSs using model checking. With substantial engineering efforts, we implemented this approach in the tool NesC@PAT to support verifications of deadlock-freeness, state reachability and temporal properties for WSNs. NesC@PAT has been applied to analyze and verify WSNs, with *unknown* bugs being detected. To the best of our knowledge, NesC@PAT is the first model checker which takes NesC language as the modeling language and completely preserves the interrupt-driven feature of the TinyOS execution model.

1 Introduction

Wireless sensor networks (WSNs) are widely used in critical areas like military surveillance, environmental monitoring, seismic detection [2] and so forth. Such systems are expected to run unattendedly for a long time in environments that are usually unstable. Thus it is important for them to be highly reliable and correct. TinyOS [16] and NesC [7] have been widely used as the programming platform for developing WSNs, which adopt a low-level programming style [13]. Such a design provides fine-grained controls over the underlying devices and resources, but meanwhile makes it difficult to understand, analyze or verify implementations. The challenges of modeling and formally verifying WSNs with NesC programs are listed as follows.

- The syntax and semantics of NesC are complex [7] compared to those of formal modeling languages. To the best of our knowledge, there has not been any formal semantics for the NesC language. Thus establishing formal models from NesC programs is non-trivial.

* This research is supported in part by Research Grant IDD11100102 of Singapore University of Technology and Design, IDC and MOE2009-T2-1-072 (Advanced Model Checking Systems).

S. Qin and Z. Qiu (Eds.): ICFEM 2011, LNCS 6991, pp. 372–387, 2011.

- TinyOS provides hardware operations on motes (i.e. sensors) which can be invoked by NesC programs including messaging, sensing and so on [16,6]. Therefore, modeling NesC programs (executing on TinyOS) requires modeling the behaviors of hardware at the same time.
- TinyOS adopts an interrupt-driven execution model, which introduces local concurrency (i.e. intra-sensor concurrency) between tasks and interrupts, which increases the complexity of model checking NesC programs.

Related Work. A number of approaches and tools have been published on analyzing, simulating, debugging and verifying WSN applications or WSNs. W. Archer et al. presented their work on interface contracts for TinyOS components in [3], which exposed bugs and hidden assumptions caused by improper interface usages, and added plentiful safety conditions to TinyOS applications. Nguyet and Soffa proposed to explore the internal structure of WSN applications using control flow graphs, but without any error detection [23]. V. Menrad et al. proposed to use Statecharts to achieve readable yet more precise formulations of interface contracts [22]. These approaches contribute to the correctness of usages of interfaces, but are incapable of verifying any specific property like safety or liveness.

The tool *FSMGen* [13] presented by N. Kothari et al. infers compact, user-readable Finite State Machines from TinyOS applications and uses symbolic execution and predicate abstraction for static analysis. This tool captures highly abstract behaviors of NesC programs and has revealed some errors. However, low-level interrupt driven code is not applicable since the tool is based on a coarse approximation of the TinyOS execution model. Some essential features like loops are not supported and the tool provides no supports for analyzing the concurrent behaviors of a WSN (rather than a single sensor).

Bucur and Kwiatkowska proposed *Tos2CProver* [4] for debugging and verifying TinyOS applications at compile-time, checking memory-related errors and other low-level errors upon registers and peripherals. Checking run-time properties like the unreachability of error states is not supported in *Tos2CProver*. Again, this approach only checks errors for single-node programs and lacks the ability to find network-level errors.

Hanna et al. proposed *SLEDE* [8,9] to verify security protocol implementations in the NesC language by extracting PROMELA [11] models from NesC implementations. This approach is translation-based, and abstracts away certain NesC features like the concurrency between tasks and interrupts, thus failing to find concurrency-related bugs that are significant. Moreover, *SLEDE* is dedicated to security protocols, and not applicable for verifying non-security properties like liveness.

T-Check [18] is built upon the TinyOS simulator TOSSIM [15] and uses explicit model checking techniques to verify safety and liveness properties. *T-Check* revealed several bugs of components/applications in the TinyOS distribution, however, it has limited capability in detecting concurrent errors due to the limitation of TOSSIM, e.g., in TOSSIM, events execute atomically and are never preempted by interrupts. Moreover, the assertions of *T-Check* are specified in propositional logic, which is incapable of specifying important temporal properties like the infinitely often release of a buffer or the alternate occurrences of two events.

While the existing approaches have contributed a lot to analyzing and finding bugs of TinyOS applications or WSNs, few of them simulate or model the interrupt-driven execution model of TinyOS. Further, only a few are dealing with WSNs, which are obviously more complex than individual sensors. In this paper, we propose a systematic and self-contained approach to verify WSNs built with TinyOS applications (i.e. NesC programs). Our work includes a component model library for hardware, and the formalized definitions of NesC programs and the TinyOS execution model. Based on these, the labelled transition systems (LTSs) of individual sensors are constructed directly from NesC programs. With a network topology that specifies how the sensors are connected, the LTS of a WSN is then composed (on-the-fly) from the LTSs of individual sensors. Model checking algorithms are developed to support verifications of deadlock-freeness, state reachability and temporal properties specified as linear temporal logic (LTL) [21] formulas. Both the state space of a WSN and that of an individual sensor can be explored for verifications. With substantial engineering efforts, our approach has been implemented as the NesC module in PAT [19,25,20], named NesC@PAT (available at http://www.comp.nus.edu.sg/~pat/research). In this paper, we use NesC@PAT to verify the Trickle [17] algorithm of WSNs. A bug of the algorithm is found and has been confirmed by implementing a WSN using real sensors (e.g., Iris motes). This shows that our approach can assist developers for behavioral analysis, error detection, and property verification of WSNs.

Contribution. We highlight our contributions in the following aspects.

- Our approach works directly on NesC programs, without building (abstract) models before applying verification techniques. Manual construction of models is avoided, which makes our approach useful in practice.
- We formally define the operational semantics of NesC and TinyOS as well as WSNs. New semantic structures are introduced for modeling the TinyOS execution model and hardware-related behaviors like timing, messaging, etc.
- The interrupt-driven feature of the TinyOS execution model is preserved in the sensor models generated in our approach. This allows concurrency errors between tasks and interrupts to be detected.
- Our approach supports verifications of deadlock-freeness, state reachability and temporal properties. This provides flexibility for verifying different properties to guarantee the correctness of sensor networks. Moreover, the expressive power of LTL has allowed to define significant temporal properties (e.g., the infinite often occurrences of a event).

The rest of the paper is organized as follows. Section 2 introduces NesC and TinyOS, and discusses the complexity and difficulty caused by specific features of NesC and TinyOS. The formal definitions of sensors and the operational semantics of TinyOS applications are presented in Section 3. Section 4 defines WSNs formally and introduces how the LTS of a WSN is obtained. Section 5 presents the architecture of our tool NesC@PAT and experimental results of verifying the Trickle algorithm. Finally, Section 6 concludes the paper with future works.

2 Preliminaries

This section briefly introduces the NesC programming language and the TinyOS operating system. Section 2.1 illustrates the specific features of NesC which make it complex

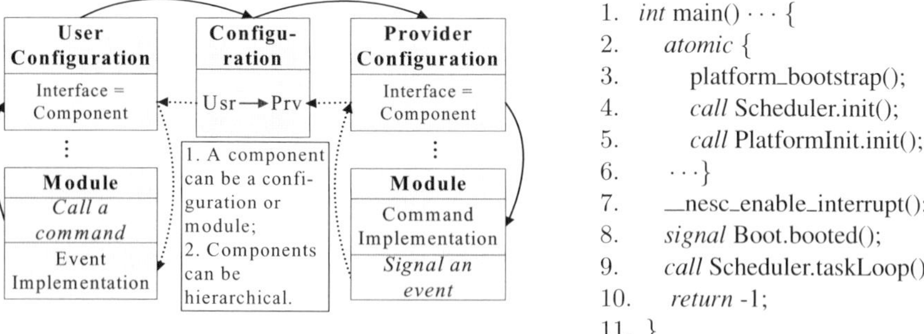

Fig. 1. Call graph of NesC programs

```
int main() ··· {
    atomic {
        platform_bootstrap();
        call Scheduler.init();
        call PlatformInit.init();
    ···}
    __nesc_enable_interrupt();
    signal Boot.booted();
    call Scheduler.taskLoop();
    return -1;
}
```

Fig. 2. TinyOS Boot Sequence

to directly verify NesC programs. Section 2.2 introduces TinyOS with an explanation of its execution model and its hardware abstraction architecture.

2.1 The NesC Language

The programming language NesC (Nested C) [7] is proposed for developing WSNs. NesC is a dialect of C, which embodies the structural concepts and the execution model of TinyOS applications. NesC has two basic modular concepts: interface and component. An *interface* declares a number of commands and events. A *command* denotes the request for an operation, and an *event* indicates the completion of that operation. Thus, NesC achieves a non-blocking programming convention, implementing operations as split-phase. In other words, the request of a operation and its completion are separated.

An interface can be either *provided* or *used* by a component. In NesC, there are two types of *component*, i.e. configuration and module. A *configuration* indicates how components are wired to one another via interfaces. A *module* implements the *commands* declared by its provided interfaces and the *events* declared by its used interfaces. Commands and events are two types of functions, and *task* is the third. A component may call a command or signal an event of an interface. Table 1 exemplifies the common-used constructs of the NesC language, and the corresponding operational semantics will be discussed in Section 3.

A call graph describes the wiring relation between components. Fig. 1 illustrates a general call graph of NesC programs. Inside a configuration, a second-level configuration can be wired to a third component, where the second-level configuration itself contains a wiring relation between a set of components. Thus, the call graph of a NesC program might be a hierarchical 'tree' of components, where intermediate nodes are configurations and leaves are modules.

NesC is an extension of the C language. It does not support advanced C features like dynamic memory allocation, function pointer, multi-thread and so on, which makes it an 'easier' target for formal verification. Nonetheless, it supports almost the same set of operators, data types, statements and structures as C does and, in addition, NesC-specific features such as calling a command, signaling an event, posting a task and so forth. Verifying NesC programs is thus highly non-trivial, as illustrated in the following.

Table 1. Common-used NesC Constructs

NesC Construct	Example	Remark
Command	*command* error_t AMControl.start() {⋯}	There are commands, events and tasks besides ordinary functions. The only difference among them is the way of invocation. A task is a parameterless function without any return value.
Event	*event* message_t* Receive.receive (message_t* msg, ⋯, uint8_t len) {⋯ return msg; }	
Task	*task* void setLeds() {⋯}	
Call	*call* Timer.startPeriodic(250);	Call, signal and post are function calls, invoking commands, events and tasks, respectively.
Signal	*signal* Timer.fired();	
Post a task	*post* setLeds();	
Atomic	*atomic*{x = x + 1; call AMSend.send(dst, pkt);}	Interrupts are disabled within an atomic block.

- Function calls like calling a command or signaling an event could be complex if the module invoking the command/event and that implementing it are wired via a hierarchical call graph.
- NesC allows local variables declared in functions or even in blocks of functions, just like C does. A traditional way to analyze local variables is to use stacks. Dealing with local variables significantly increases the complexity of verification.
- NesC is a typed programming language, and all data types of C including array and struct are supported. There are also type operations (e.g. type casting) supported by NesC. Therefore, modeling NesC should take into account typed aspects.
- There are other expressive features of NesC, which are inherited from C, however make it complex. Examples of such features include pointers, parameters being types, definition of types, pre-compilation, etc.

We remark that our approach targets at NesC programs and does not necessarily support the verification of C programs. In the following, we briefly explain how we support the above 'troubling' features.

Fortunately, NesC is static [7], i.e. there is no dynamic memory allocation or function pointer. Thus the variable access and the call graph can be completely captured at compile time. In our work, we treat pointers as normal variables, the value of which is a reference to a certain variable. We develop a parser to produce the call graph of a NesC program with the function (command, event, task or normal function) bodies defined by each component. A nested search algorithm is designed to traverse the call graph for fetching the corresponding function body once a function is invoked.

Local variables are modeled statically in our approach, with a renaming method to avoid naming conflicts. Nested function calls are supported with the assumption that there are no circles within the calling stacks. This is because that we rename local variables according to the positions of their declarations. Thus distinguishing the local variables between two invocations of the same function can be tricky and costly. However, the restriction is modest. The reason is that the most common invocation circle of NesC programs lies in the split-phase operations, i.e. when a command finishes it signals an event and in that event when it is completed it calls back the command again. However, [14] recommends NesC programmers to avoid such a way of programming. Even in this situation we can still get rid of naming conflicts of local variables because a new invocation of a function is always assured to be at the end of the previous one.

Typed information is captured and we distinguish variables declared as different types and analyze functions with parameters being types. Our work also supports defining new types by *struct* and *typedef*. Moreover, pre-compilation is supported, as well as capturing information from *.h* files. More details of tackling NesC language features can be found in our technical report in [1].

2.2 TinyOS and Its Execution Model

TinyOS [6,16] is the run-time environment of NesC programs. The behavior of a NesC program is thus highly related to the interrupt-driven execution model of TinyOS [14]. Tasks are deferred computations, which are scheduled in FIFO order. Tasks always run till completion, i.e. only after a task is completed, can a new task start its execution. In contrast, interrupts are preemptive and always preempt tasks. In our work, this interrupt-driven feature is captured using an interrupt operator ($\triangle$), as discussed in Section 3.

The operating system TinyOS is implemented in NesC, with a component library for hardware operations like sensing, messaging, timing, etc. The TinyOS component library adopts a three-layer Hardware Abstraction Architecture (HAA), including Hardware Presentation Layer (HPL), Hardware Adaptation Layer (HAL) and Hardware Interface Layer (HIL) [16,6]. The design of HAA gradually adapts the capabilities of the underlying hardware platforms to platform-independent interfaces between the operating system and the application code. Specific semantic structures are introduced for modeling hardware devices, which will be discussed in Section 3.

Since TinyOS 2.0, each NesC application should contain a component *MainC* (predefined by TinyOS), which implements the boot sequence of a sensor [14]. Fig. 2 sketches the function that implements the boot sequence. At first, the scheduler, hardware platform and related software components are initialized (line 3-5). Then interrupts are enabled (line 7) and the event *booted* of interface *Boot* (*Boot.booted*) is signaled (line 8), after which the scheduler recurrently runs tasks that have been posted (line 9). The execution of line 2 to 7 is usually short and always decided by TinyOS thus our approach assumes that this part is always correct and begins modeling the behaviors of a sensor at the execution of event *Boot.booted*.

3 Formalizing Sensors with NesC Programs

This section presents the formalization of sensors running TinyOS applications. In particular, we present the operational semantics of the NesC programming constructs, and introduce dedicated semantic structures for capturing the TinyOS execution model and hardware behaviors and then the LTS semantics of sensors.

The behaviors of a sensor are determined by the scheduler of tasks and the concurrent execution between tasks and device interrupts.

Definition 1 (Sensor Model). *A sensor model $\mathcal{S}$ is a tuple $\mathcal{S} = (A, T, R, init, P)$ where A is a finite set of variables; T is a queue which stores posted tasks in FIFO order; R is a buffer that keeps incoming messages sent by other sensors; init is the initial valuation of the variable set A; and P is a program, composed by the running NesC program M that can be interrupted by various devices H, i.e., $P = M \bigtriangleup H$.*

H models (and often abstracts) the behaviors of hardware devices such as Timer, Receiver and Reader (i.e. the sensing device). Because tasks are deferred computations, when posted they are pushed into the task queue T for scheduling in FIFO order. We remark that T and R are empty initially for any sensor model $\mathcal{S}$. The interrupt operator ($\bigtriangleup$) is introduced to capture the interrupt-driven feature of the TinyOS execution model, which will be explained later in this section.

The variables in A are categorized into two groups. One is composed of variables declared in the NesC program, which are further divided into two categories according to their scopes, i.e. component variables and local variables. Component variables are defined in a component's scope, whereas local variables are defined within a function's or a block's scope. In this work, all variables including local variables are loaded to the variable set A at initialization. To avoid naming conflicts, the name of each variable is first prefixed with the component name. A local variable is further renamed with the line number of its declaration position. The other is a set of *device status variables* that capture the states of hardware devices. For example, *MessageC.Status* is introduced to model the status of the messaging device. A status variable is added into A after the compilation if the corresponding device is accessed in the NesC program.

Example 1. **Trickle** [17] is a code propagation algorithm which is intended to reduce network traffic. Trickle controls message sending rate so that each sensor hears a small but enough number of packets to stay up-to-date. In the following, the notion *code* denotes large-size data (e.g. a route table) each sensor maintains, while *code summary* denotes small-size data that summarizes the *code* (e.g. the latest updating time of the route table). Each sensor periodically broadcasts its code summary, and

- stays quiet if it receives an identical code summary;
- broadcasts its code if it receives an older summary;
- broadcasts its code summary if it receives an newer summary.

We have implemented this algorithm in a NesC program *TrickleAppC* (available in [1]), with the modification that a sensor only broadcasts the summary initially (instead of periodically) and if it receives any newer summary. The struct *MetaMsg* is defined to encode a packet with a summary, and *ProMsg* is defined to encode a packet with a summary and the corresponding code. Initially, each node broadcasts its summary (a *MetaMsg* packet) to the network . If an incoming *MetaMsg* packet has a newer summary, the sensor will broadcast its summary; if the received summary is outdated, the sensor will broadcast its summary and code (a *ProMsg* packet). An incoming *ProMsg* packet with a newer summary will update the sensor's summary and code accordingly.

Assume that a sensor executes *TrickleAppC*. By Definition 1, the corresponding sensor model is $\mathcal{S} = (A, T, R, init, P)$. In *TrickleAppC*, component *TrickleC* is referred as *App*, so *App* is used for renaming its variables. The variable set after renaming is $A = \{$ *MessageC.Status*, *App.summary*, *App.code*, *App.34.pkt*, $\cdots\}$, where

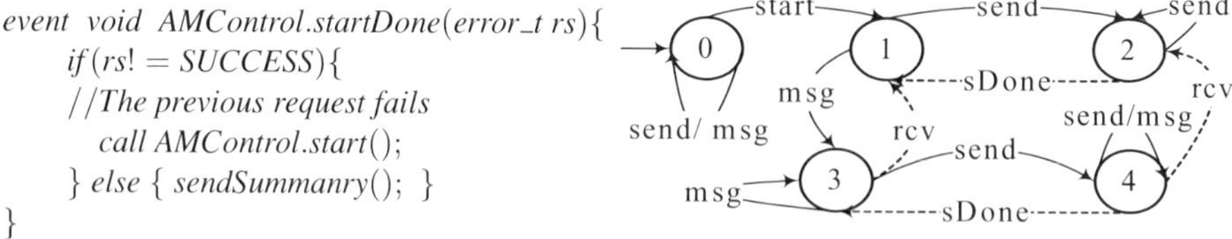

```
event void AMControl.startDone(error_t rs){
    if(rs! = SUCCESS){
    //The previous request fails
      call AMControl.start();
    } else { sendSummanry(); }
}
```


Fig. 3. Event *AMControl.startDone*

Fig. 4. The *MessageC* Model

variables with two-field names (e.g. *App.summary*) are component variables, except for *MessageC.Status* (a device status variable) and those with three-field names (e.g. *App.34.pkt*) are local variables. *init* is the initial valuation where $MessageC.Status = OFF$, $App.summary = 0$, $App.code = 0$, $App.34.pkt = null, \cdots$. In *TrickleAppC*, only the messaging device *MessageC* is accessed, therefore, initially the program *P* is event *Boot.booted* interrupted by the messaging device, i.e., $P = M_b \bigtriangleup MessageC$. Event *Boot.booted* is implemented by *TrickleC*, and the following is its function body.

```
event void Boot.booted(){
    call AMControl.start(); //Start the messaging device
}
```

Calling *AMControl.start* will execute the corresponding command implemented by *ActiveMessageC*. Component *ActiveMessageC* is defined in the TinyOS component library for activating the messaging device. When *AMControl.start* is completed, the event *AMControl.startDone* (implemented by *TrickleC*) will be signaled. If *AMControl. start* returns *SUCCESS*, the function *sendSummary* is called for sending the summary. Otherwise, the command *AMControl.start* is re-called, as shown in Fig. 3. We use a model *MessageC* to describe the behaviors of the messaging device of a sensor. If *AMControl.start* is performed successfully, the program *P* of $\mathcal{S}$ will become $P = M_b' \bigtriangleup MessageC'$, and the value of *MessageC.Status* will be modified. □

The models of the hardware devices are developed systematically. According to the TinyOS component library, we develop a component model library for most common-used components like *AMSenderC*, *AMReceiverC*, *TimerC*, etc[1]. We currently model hardware at HAA's top layer, i.e. Hardware Interface Layer, ignoring differences between the underlying platforms. For example, components *ActiveMessageC*, *AMSenderC* and *AMReceiverC* from the TinyOS component library are designed for different operations on the messaging device, such as activation, message transmission and message reception. Although there may be multiple *AMSenderC*'s or *AMReceiverC*'s in a NesC program, they all share the same messaging device. In Fig. 4, action *start* is a command from *ActiveMessageC*, action *send* is a request for sending a message from an *AMSendderC*, and action *msg* is the arrival of an incoming message. Action *sDone* and action *rcv* are interrupts triggered by *MessageC*, which signal the *sendDone* event of *AMSenderC* and the *receive* event of *AMReceiverC*, respectively.

Definition 2 (Sensor Configuration). *Let* $\mathcal{S} = (A, T, R, init, P)$ *be a sensor model. A sensor configuration* C *of* $\mathcal{S}$ *is a tuple* (V, Q, B, P) *where* V *is the valuation of variables*

[1] The current component library is not yet complete but sufficient for many NesC programs.

A; Q is a sequence of tasks, being the content of T; B is a sequence of messages, being the content of R; P is the executing program.

For a sensor model $\mathcal{S} = (A, T, R, init, P)$, its initial configuration $C^{init} = (init, \varnothing, \varnothing, P)$, in respect that initially task queue T and message buffer R are empty. A transition is written as $(V, Q, B, P) \xrightarrow{e} (V', Q', B', P')$ (or $C \xrightarrow{e} C'$ for short). Next, we define the behavior of a sensor as an LTS.

Definition 3 (Sensor Transition System). *Let $\mathcal{S} = (A, T, R, init, P)$ be a sensor model. The transition system of $\mathcal{S}$ is defined as a tuple $\mathbb{T} = (\mathbb{C}, init, \rightarrow)$, where $\mathbb{C}$ is the set of all reachable sensor configurations and $\rightarrow$ is the transition relation.*

The transition relation is formally defined through a set of firing rules associated with each and every NesC programming construct. The firing rules for *post* and *call* are presented in Fig. 5 for illustration purpose. The complete set of firing rules can be found in [1]. The following symbols are adopted to define the firing rules.

- $^\frown$ is sequence concatenation.
- $\checkmark$ simply denotes the termination of the execution of a statement.
- τ is an event label denoting a silent transition.
- $Impl(f, L_{arg})$ returns the the body of function $(\{F\})f$ with arguments L_{arg}.
- $FstFnc(L_{arg})$ returns the first element in L_arg which contains function calls.
- $L_{arg}[a'/a]$ replaces argument a with a' in the argument list L_{arg}.
- I is a status variable in A, denoting whether interrupts are allowed. Interrupts are only disabled within an *atomic* block thus I is set *off* only during an *atomic* block.

Rules *post*1 and *post*2 describe the semantics of the statement *post tsk*(). The task *tsk* will be pushed to the task queue Q if there are no identical tasks pending in Q (rule *post*1), otherwise the task is simply dropped (rule *post*2). Rules *call*1 and *call*2 capture the semantics of a command call $call\ intf.cmd(L_{arg})$, where L_{arg} is the list of arguments. If the arguments contain no function calls, the execution of a command call will transit directly to the execution of the corresponding function body (rule *call*1). Otherwise, the function calls in the arguments will be executed first (rule *call*2), also step by step.

Apart from the firing rules for NesC structures, we adopt several operators and semantic structures from process algebra community [10] to capture the execution model of TinyOS and hardware behaviors. Some of these firing rules are presented in Fig. 6, and the complete set can be found in [1]. The interrupt operator ($\triangle$) is used to formalize the concurrent execution between tasks and interrupts, and interrupts always preempt tasks, denoted by rules *itr*1. Further, when a task (M) completes its completion, a new task will be fetched from Q for execution (rule *itr*3). Interrupts are always enabled in rules *itr*3 and *itr*4 because no atomic blocks are executing. A sensor will remain *idle* when no interrupts are triggered by devices (i.e. *H is idle*) and no tasks are deferred (rule *itr*4), and it can be activated by an interrupt like the arrival of a new message.

A hardware interrupt is modeled as an atomic action which pushes a task to the top of the task queue, and thus the task has a higher priority than others. This task will signal the corresponding event for handling the interrupt. This is exactly the way that TinyOS deals with hardware interrupts. For example, when an interrupt is triggered by an incoming message, a task (t_{rcv}) will be added at the head of Q for signaling a *receive*

$$\frac{e = s.post.t,\ t \notin Q,\ Q' = Q^\frown \langle t \rangle}{(V,\ Q,\ B,\ post\ tsk()) \xrightarrow{e} (V,\ Q',\ B,\ \checkmark)}\ [\ post1\ ]$$

$$\frac{e = s.post.t,\ t \in Q}{(V,\ Q,\ B,\ post\ tsk()) \xrightarrow{e} (V,\ Q,\ B,\ \checkmark)}\ [\ post2\ ]$$

$$\frac{FstFnc(L_{arg}) = \epsilon,\ F = Impl(intf.cmd, L_{arg})}{(V,\ Q,\ B,\ call\ intf.cmd(L_{arg})) \xrightarrow{e} (V,\ Q,\ B,\ \{F\})}\ [\ call1\ ]$$

$$\frac{FstFnc(L_{arg}) = a,\ a \neq \epsilon,\ (V,\ Q,\ B,\ a) \xrightarrow{e} (V',\ Q',\ B',\ a')}{(V,\ Q,\ B,\ call\ intf.cmd(L_{arg})) \xrightarrow{e} (V',\ Q',\ B',\ call\ intf.cmd(L_{arg}[a'/a]))}\ [\ call2\ ]$$

Fig. 5. Firing Rules for NesC Structures

event (rule *rcv*). Semantic structures *Send* and *Rcv* are defined to model the behaviors of sending and receiving a message respectively. *Send* is defined as (s, dst, msg), where s is the identifier of the sensor which sends a message, *dst* is the list of receivers and *msg* is the message itself.

Notice that devices such as Timer, Receiver, Reader (Sensor) and so on 'execute' concurrently, because they can trigger interrupts independently. This is captured using an interleave operator $|||$, which resembles the interleave operator in CSP [10].

4 Formalizing Wireless Sensor Networks

In this section, we formalize WSNs as LTSs. A sensor network $\mathcal{N}$ is composed of a set of sensors and a network topology[2]. From a logical point of view, a network topology is simply a directed graph where nodes are sensors and links are directed communications between sensors. In reality, a sensor always broadcasts messages and only the ones within its radio range would be able to receive the messages. We introduce radio range model to describe network topology, i.e. whether a sensor is able to send messages to some other sensor. Let $\mathbb{N} = \{0, 1, \cdots, i, \cdots, n\}$ be the set of the unique identifier of each sensor in a WSN $\mathcal{N}$. The radio range model is defined as the relation $\mathcal{R} : \mathbb{N} \leftrightarrow \mathbb{N}$, such that $(i, j) \in \mathcal{R}$ if and only if sensor j is within sensor i's radio range. We define a WSN model as the parallel of the sensors with its topology, as shown in Definition 4.

Definition 4 (WSN Model). *The model of a wireless sensor network $\mathcal{N}$ is defined as a tuple$(\mathcal{R}, \{\mathcal{S}_0, \cdots, \mathcal{S}_n\})$ where $\mathcal{R}$ is the radio model (i.e. network topology), $\{\mathcal{S}_0, \cdots, \mathcal{S}_n\}$ is a finite ordered set of sensor models, and $\mathcal{S}_i$ $(0 \leqslant i \leqslant n)$ is the model of sensor i.*

Sensors in a network can communicate through messaging, and semantic structures *Send* and *Rcv* are defined to model message transmission among sensors. WSNs are

[2] We assume that the network topology for a given WSN is fixed in this work.

$$\frac{V(I) = on,\ (V,\ Q,\ B,\ H) \xrightarrow{e} (V',\ Q',\ B',\ H')}{(V,\ Q,\ B,\ M \triangle H) \xrightarrow{e} (V',\ Q',\ B',\ M \triangle H')} \quad [\,itr1\,]$$

$$\frac{H \text{ is idle or } V(I) = \mathit{off},\ (V,\ Q,\ B,\ M) \xrightarrow{e} (V',\ Q',\ B',\ M')}{(V,\ Q,\ B,\ M \triangle H) \xrightarrow{e} (V',\ Q',\ B',\ M' \triangle H)} \quad [\,itr2\,]$$

$$\frac{H \text{ is idle},\ M = Impl(t, \varnothing)}{(V,\ \langle t \rangle ^\frown Q',\ B,\ \checkmark \triangle H) \xrightarrow{e} (V,\ Q',\ B,\ M \triangle H)} \quad [\,itr3\,]$$

$$\frac{H \text{ is idle}}{(V,\ \varnothing,\ B,\ \checkmark \triangle H) \xrightarrow{s.idle} (V,\ \varnothing,\ B,\ \checkmark \triangle H)} \quad [\,itr4\,]$$

$$\frac{B = \langle msg \rangle ^\frown B',\ t_{rcv} \notin Q,\ Q' = \langle t_{rcv} \rangle ^\frown Q}{(V,\ Q,\ B,\ Rcv) \xrightarrow{s.rcv\_msg} (V,\ Q',\ B',\ Rcv)} \quad [\,rcv\,]$$

$$\frac{t_{sendDone} \notin Q,\ Q' = \langle t_{sendDone} \rangle ^\frown Q}{(V,\ Q,\ B,\ Send(s, msg)) \xrightarrow{s.send.msg} (V,\ Q',\ B,\ \checkmark)} \quad [\,send\,]$$

Fig. 6. Firing Rules for Concurrent Execution and Hardware Behaviors

highly concurrent as all sensors run in parallel, i.e. the network behaviors are obtained by non-deterministically choosing one sensor to execute at each step.

Definition 5 (WSN Configuration). *Let $\mathcal{N} = (\mathcal{R}, \{\mathcal{S}_0, \cdots, \mathcal{S}_n\})$ be a WSN model. A configuration of $\mathcal{N}$ is defined as the finite ordered set of sensor configurations: $\mathcal{C} = \{C_0, \cdots, C_n\}$ where C_i ($0 \leqslant i \leqslant n$) is the configuration of $\mathcal{S}_i$.*

Definition 5 formally defines a global system state of a WSN. Next, the semantics of sensor networks can be defined in LTSs, as follows.

Definition 6 (WSN Transition System). *Let $\mathcal{N} = (\mathcal{R}, \{\mathcal{S}_0, \cdots, \mathcal{S}_n\})$ be a sensor network model. The WSN transition system corresponding to $\mathcal{N}$ is a 3-tuple $\mathcal{T} = (\Gamma, init, \hookrightarrow)$ where Γ is the set of all reachable WSN configurations, $init = \{C_0^{init}, \cdots, C_n^{init}\}$ (C_i^{init} is the initial configuration of $\mathcal{S}_i$) being the initial configuration of $\mathcal{N}$, and $\hookrightarrow$ is the transition relation.*

Example 2. Fig. 7 presents a WSN with three nodes (i.e., $\mathcal{S}_0$, $\mathcal{S}_1$ and $\mathcal{S}_2$), each of which is implemented with application *TrickleAppC* (*Tk* for short) of Example 1. The radio range of each senor is described by a circle around it, and the network topology model can be abstracted as $\mathcal{R} = \{(0,1), (1,2), (2,0)\}$.

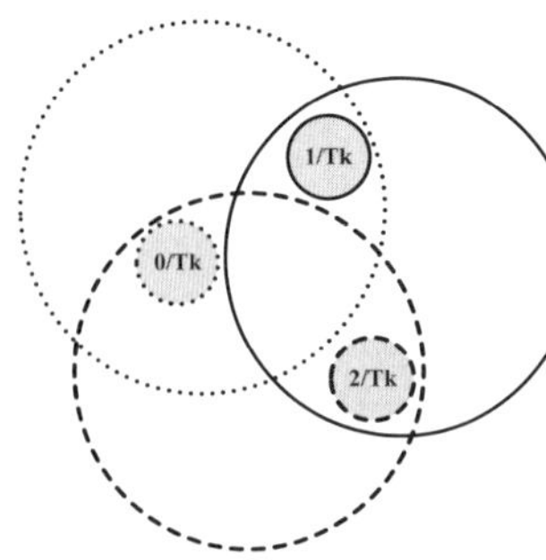

Fig. 7. A WSN Example

A transition of a WSN is of the form $\mathcal{C} \overset{e}{\hookrightarrow} \mathcal{C}'$, where $\mathcal{C} = \{C_0, \cdots, C_i, \cdots, C_n\}$ and $\mathcal{C}' = \{C'_0, \cdots, C'_i, \cdots, C'_n\}$. The transition relation is obtained through a set of firing rules, which are shown in Fig. 8. Rule *network*1 describes the concurrent execution betweens sensors, i.e. the network non-deterministically chooses a sensor to perform a transition. Rule *network*2 is dedicated for communication. Function $Radio(i)$ returns the set of sensors that are within sensor i's radio range. Function $InMsg(msg, C_j)$ enqueues the message msg to sensor j, i.e. $C'_j = InMsg(dst, msg, C_j) \Leftrightarrow (j \in dst \Rightarrow C'_j = C_j[B_j \frown \langle msg \rangle / B_j]) \wedge (j \notin dst \Rightarrow C'_j = C_j)$. Thus a sensor sending a message will not only change its local state but also change those of the sensors in the destination list, by enqueuing the message to their message buffers.

$$\frac{C_i \overset{e}{\rightarrow} C'_i,\ e \neq s_i.send.dst.msg,\ e \neq s_i.idle}{\{C_0, \cdots, C_i, \cdots, C_n\} \overset{e}{\hookrightarrow} \{C_0, \cdots, C'_i, \cdots, C_n\}} \quad [\,network1\,]$$

$$\frac{C_i \overset{e}{\rightarrow} C'_i,\ e = s_i.send.msg,\ \forall j \in [0, i) \cup (i, n] \bullet C'_j = InMsg(Radio(i), msg, C_j)}{\{C_0, \cdots, C_i, \cdots, C_n\} \overset{e}{\hookrightarrow} \{C'_0, \cdots, C'_i, \cdots, C'_n\}} \quad [\,network2\,]$$

Fig. 8. Firing Rules for Sensor Networks

5 Implementation and Evaluation

Our approach has been implemented in the model checking framework PAT as the NesC module, which is named NesC@PAT. Fig. 9 illustrates the architecture of NesC@PAT. There are five main components, *i.e.* an editor, a parser, a model generator, a simulator and a model checker. The editor allows users to input different NesC programs for sensors and to draw the network topology, as well as to define assertions (i.e. verification goals). The parser compiles all inputs from the editor. The model generator generates sensor models based on the NesC programs and the built-in hardware model collection (i.e. the component model library). Furthermore, it generates WSN models. Both the sensor models and the network models are then passed to the simulator and the model checker for visualized simulation and automated verification respectively.

NesC@PAT supports both sensor-level and network-level verifications, against properties including deadlock-freeness, state reachability, and liveness properties expressed in linear temporal logic (LTL) [21]. Deadlock-freeness and state reachability are checked by exhaustively exploring the state space using Depth-first search or Breadth-first search algorithms. We adopt the approach presented in [25] to verify LTL properties. First, the negation of an LTL formula is converting into an equivalent Büchi automaton; and then accepting strong connected components (SCC) in the synchronous product of the automaton and the model are examined in order to find a counterexample. Notice that the

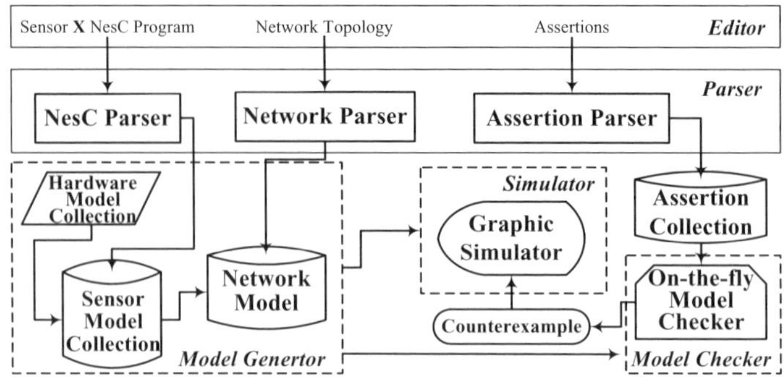

Fig. 9. Architecture of NesC@PAT

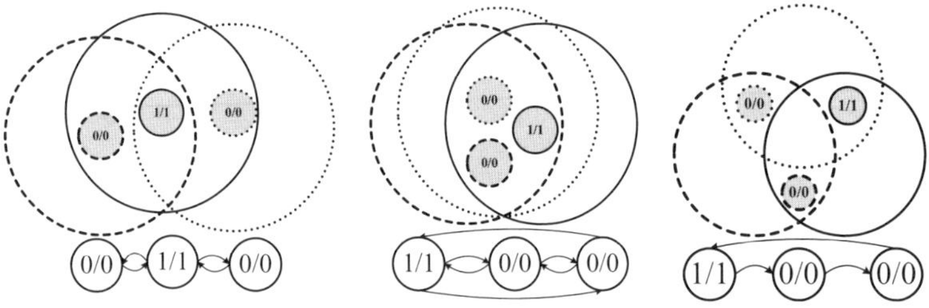

Fig. 10. Network Topology: Star, Ring, Single-track Ring

SCC-based algorithm allows us to model check with fairness [27], which often plays an important role in proving liveness properties of WSNs.

NesC@PAT was used to analyze WSNs deployed with the Trickle algorithm presented in Example 1. We studied WSNs with different topologies including star, ring and single-tracked ring (short for SRing). The settings of WSNs are presented in Fig. 10, where $1/1$ stands for *new* code/*new* summary and $0/0$ stands for *old* code/*old* summary and a directed graph is used to illustrate the logical view for each network. Two safety properties (i.e. *Deadlock free* and *Reach FalseUpdat* $-$ *ed*) and two liveness properties (i.e. $\Diamond$*AllUpdated* and $\Box\Diamond$*AllUpdated*) are verified. Property *Reach FalseUpdated* is a state reachability checking, which is valid if and only if the state *FalseUpdated* where a node updates its code with an older one can be reached. Property $\Diamond$*AllUpdated* is an LTL formula which is valid if and only if the state *AllUpdated* where all nodes are updated with the new code can be reached *eventually*, while $\Box\Diamond$*AllUpdated* requires state *AllUpdated* to be reached *infinitely often*.

A server with Intel Xeon 4-Core CPU*2 and 32 GB memory was used to run the verifications, and the results are summarized in Table 2. The results show that the algorithm satisfies the safety properties, i.e. neither a deadlock state nor a *FalseUpdated* state is reachable. As for the liveness property, both ring and star networks work well, which means that every node is eventually updated with the new code. However, the single-tracked-ring (SRing) network fails to satisfy either liveness property. The counterexample produced by NesC@PAT shows that only one sensor can be updated with the new code. By simulating the counterexample in NesC@PAT, we can find the reason

(a) Initial Setting

(b) Star/Ring network

(c) SRing network

Fig. 11. Real Executions on Iris Motes

of this bug. On one hand, the initially updated node A receives old summary from node C thus broadcasting its code but only node B can hear it. On the other hand, after node B is updated it fails to send its code to node C because node B never hears an older summary from node C. We also increased the number of sensors for SRing networks, and the results remained the same.

We ran the Trickle program on Iris motes to study whether this bug could be evidenced in real executions. The *TrickleAppC* was modified by adding operations on leds to display the changes of code (available in [1]):

1. Initially sensor A has the new code $(1/1)$ and has its red led on, while sensor B and C have the old code $(0/0)$ and have their yellow leds on, as shown in Fig. 11a.
2. A sensor will turns on its red led when it is updated with the new code.
3. Different topologies are achieved by specifying different *AM id* for each sensor's *AMSenderC* and *AMReceiverC*, details of which are in [1].

The revised *TrickleAppC* was executed on real sensors with star, ring and single-tracked ring topologies. Fig. 11b shows that the star/ring network is able to update all nodes, and Fig. 11c shows that the single-tracked ring network fails to update one node, which confirms that the bug found by NesC@PAT could be evidenced in reality.

Discussion. The results in Table 2 show that a WSN of Trickle algorithm with three nodes has a state space of $10^6 \sim 10^7$, and the state space grows exponentially with the network topology and the number of nodes. One direction of our future work is to introduce reduction techniques such like partial order reduction [24] and symmetry reduction [5] to improve the scalability of our approach. Hardware-related behaviors are abstracted and manually modeled based on real sensors, i.e. Iris motes. This manual abstraction of hardware is simple to implement, but lacks the ability to find errors due to hardware failures, as the hardware is assumed to be always working.

6 Conclusion

In this work, we present an initial step towards automatic verifications of WSNs at implementation level. Semantic models, i.e. event-based LTS, of WSNs are generated directly and automatically from NesC programs, avoiding manual construction of models. To the best of our knowledge, our approach is the first complete and systematical approach to verify networked NesC programs. Moreover, our approach is the first to

Table 2. Experimental Results

Network	Property	Size	Result	#State	#Transition	Time(s)	Memory(KB)
Star	Deadlock free	3	✓	300,332	859,115	49	42,936
	Reach FalseUpdated		×	300,332	859,115	47	23,165
	$\Diamond$AllUpdated		✓	791,419	2,270,243	148	25,133
	$\Box\Diamond$AllUpdated		✓	1,620,273	6,885,511	654	13,281,100
Ring	Deadlock free	3	✓	1,093,077	3,152,574	171	80,108
	Reach FalseUpdated		×	1,093,077	3,152,574	161	27,871
	$\Diamond$AllUpdated		✓	2,127,930	6,157,922	389	78,435
SRing	Deadlock free	3	✓	30,872	85,143	5	19,968
		4	✓	672,136	2,476,655	170	72,209
	Reach FalseUpdated	3	×	30,872	85,143	5	23,641
		4	×	672,136	2,476,655	156	62,778
	$\Diamond$AllUpdated	3	×	42	73	<1	19,290
		4	×	52	113	<1	19,771
	$\Box\Diamond$AllUpdated	3	×	146	147	<1	51,938
		4	×	226	227	<1	51,421
		8	×	746	747	<1	59,900
		20	×	4,126	4,127	2	148,155

model the interrupt-driven execution model of TinyOS. This is important since it allows concurrency errors at sensor level to be detected. Model checking algorithms have been implemented for verifying various properties.

Our work currently adopts a non-threaded execution model of TinyOS. Recently, new models have been proposed, e.g., TOSThread [12] has been proposed to allow user threads in TinyOS. Our future work thus includes designing approach for modeling TOSThread. Moreover, the current component model library of NesC@PAT only models a subset of the TinyOS component library. Another future direction is to generate comprehensive timing models using techniques [26,20] and to take failures into account by probabilistic modeling techniques [28]. We also plan to apply reduction techniques [29] for optimizing the usage of time and memory at verification phase.

References

1. NesC@PAT, `http://www.comp.nus.edu.sg/~pat/NesC/`
2. Akyildiz, I.F., Su, W., Sankarasubramaniam, Y., Cayirci, E.: Wireless sensor networks: a survey. Computer Networks 38, 132–138 (2001)
3. Archer, W., Levis, P., Regehr, J.: Interface contracts for TinyOS. In: IPSN, pp. 158–165 (2007)
4. Bucur, D., Kwiatkowska, M.Z.: Software verification for TinyOS. In: IPSN, pp. 400–401 (2010)
5. Emerson, E.A., Jha, S., Peled, D.: Combining Partial Order and Symmetry Reductions. In: Brinksma, E. (ed.) TACAS 1997. LNCS, vol. 1217, pp. 19–34. Springer, Heidelberg (1997)
6. Gay, D., Levis, P., Culler, D.E.: Software design patterns for TinyOS. ACM Trans. Embedded Comput. Syst. 6(2) (2007)

7. Gay, D., Levis, P., Behren, R.v., Welsh, M., Brewer, E., Culler, D.: The nesC Language: A Holistic Approach to Networked Embedded Systems. In: PLDI, pp. 1–11 (2003)
8. Hanna, Y., Rajan, H.: Slede: Framework for automatic verification of sensor network security protocol implementations. In: ICSE Companion, pp. 427–428 (2009)
9. Hanna, Y., Rajan, H., Zhang, W.: Slede: a domain-specific verification framework for sensor network security protocol implementations. In: WISEC, pp. 109–118 (2008)
10. Hoare, C.A.R.: Communicating Sequential Processes. Prentice-Hall, Englewood Cliffs (1985)
11. Holzmann, G.J.: Design and Validation of Protocols: A Tutorial. Computer Networks and ISDN Systems 25(9), 981–1017 (1993)
12. Klues, K., Liang, C.-J.M., Paek, J., Musaloiu-Elefteri, R., Levis, P., Terzis, A., Govindan, R.: TOSThreads: thread-safe and non-invasive preemption in TinyOS. In: SenSys, pp. 127–140 (2009)
13. Kothari, N., Millstein, T.D., Govindan, R.: Deriving State Machines from TinyOS Programs Using Symbolic Execution. In: IPSN, pp. 271–282 (2008)
14. Levis, P., Gay, D.: TinyOS Programming, 1st edn. Cambridge University Press, Cambridge (2009)
15. Levis, P., Lee, N., Welsh, M., Culler, D.E.: TOSSIM: Accurate and Scalable Simulation of Entire TinyOS Applications. In: SenSys, pp. 126–137 (2003)
16. Levis, P., Madden, S., Polastre, J., Szewczyk, R., Woo, A., Gay, D., Hill, J., Welsh, M., Brewer, E., Culler, D.: TinyOS: An operating system for sensor networks. In: Ambient Intelligence. Springer, Heidelberg (2004)
17. Levis, P., Patel, N., Culler, D.E., Shenker, S.: Trickle: A Self-Regulating Algorithm for Code Propagation and Maintenance in Wireless Sensor Networks. In: NSDI, pp. 15–28 (2004)
18. Li, P., Regehr, J.: T-check: bug finding for sensor networks. In: IPSN, pp. 174–185 (2010)
19. Liu, Y., Sun, J., Dong, J.S.: An Analyzer for Extended Compositional Process Algebras. In: ICSE Companion, pp. 919–920. ACM, New York (2008)
20. Liu, Y., Sun, J., Dong, J.S.: Developing Model Checkers Using PAT. In: Bouajjani, A., Chin, W.-N. (eds.) ATVA 2010. LNCS, vol. 6252, pp. 371–377. Springer, Heidelberg (2010)
21. Manna, Z., Pnueli, A.: The Temporal Logic of Reactive and Concurrent Systems:Specification. Springer, Heidelberg (1992)
22. Menrad, V., Garcia, M., Schupp, S.: Improving TinyOS Developer Productivity with State Charts. In: SOMSED (2009)
23. Nguyen, N.T.M., Soffa, M.L.: Program representations for testing wireless sensor network applications. In: DOSTA, pp. 20–26 (2007)
24. Peled, D.: Combining Partial Order Reductions with On-the-fly Model-Checking. Formal Methods in System Design 8(1), 39–64 (1996)
25. Sun, J., Liu, Y., Dong, J.S., Pang, J.: PAT: Towards Flexible Verification under Fairness. In: Bouajjani, A., Maler, O. (eds.) CAV 2009. LNCS, vol. 5643, pp. 709–714. Springer, Heidelberg (2009)
26. Sun, J., Liu, Y., Dong, J.S., Zhang, X.: Verifying Stateful Timed CSP Using Implicit Clocks and Zone Abstraction. In: Breitman, K., Cavalcanti, A. (eds.) ICFEM 2009. LNCS, vol. 5885, pp. 581–600. Springer, Heidelberg (2009)
27. Sun, J., Liu, Y., Roychoudhury, A., Liu, S., Dong, J.S.: Fair model checking with process counter abstraction. In: Cavalcanti, A., Dams, D.R. (eds.) FM 2009. LNCS, vol. 5850, pp. 123–139. Springer, Heidelberg (2009)
28. Sun, J., Song, S., Liu, Y.: Model Checking Hierarchical Probabilistic Systems. In: Dong, J.S., Zhu, H. (eds.) ICFEM 2010. LNCS, vol. 6447, pp. 388–403. Springer, Heidelberg (2010)
29. Zhang, S.J., Sun, J., Pang, J., Liu, Y., Dong, J.S.: On Combining State Space Reductions with Global Fairness Assumptions. In: Butler, M., Schulte, W. (eds.) FM 2011. LNCS, vol. 6664, pp. 432–447. Springer, Heidelberg (2011)

Formal Analysis of a Scheduling Algorithm for Wireless Sensor Networks

Maissa Elleuch[1,2], Osman Hasan[2], Sofiène Tahar[2], and Mohamed Abid[1]

[1] CES Laboratory, National School of Engineers of Sfax, Sfax University
Soukra Street, 3052 Sfax, Tunisia
maissa.elleuch@ceslab.org,
mohamed.abid@enis.rnu.tn

[2] Dept. of Electrical & Computer Engineering, Concordia University
1455 de Maisonneuve W., Montreal, Quebec, H3G 1M8, Canada
{melleuch,o_hasan,tahar}@ece.concordia.ca

Abstract. In wireless sensor networks (WSNs), scheduling of the sensors is considered to be the most effective energy conservation mechanism. The random and unpredictable deployment of sensors in many WSNs in the open fields makes the sensor scheduling problem very challenging and thus randomized scheduling algorithms are used. The performance of these algorithms is usually analyzed using simulation techniques, which do not offer 100% accurate results. Moreover, probabilistic model checking, when used, does not include a strong support to reason accurately about statistical quantities like expectation and variance. In this paper, we overcome these limitations by using higher-order-logic theorem proving to formally analyze the coverage-based random scheduling algorithm for WSNs. Using the probabilistic framework developed in the HOL theorem prover, we formally reason about the expected values of coverage intensity, the upper bound on the total number of disjoint subsets, for a given expected coverage intensity, the lower bound on the total number of nodes and the average detection delay inside the network.

Keywords: Probabilistic reasoning, Theorem proving, Higher-order-logic, Wireless sensor networks, Scheduling, Coverage.

1 Introduction

Wireless sensor networks (WSNs) [24] have been proposed as an efficient solution to monitor a field without any continuous human surveillance. Such networks are composed of small tiny devices wirelessly connected over the field. The main task of sensors consists in taking measurements of the monitored event. According to these measurements, a decision procedure is made at the base station. The WSNs are extensively being deployed these days in a variety of applications like detection of natural disasters or biological attacks and military tracking.

Minimizing energy requirements for the sensor nodes is very critical given the fact that these nodes are always stand-alone and battery powered. Scheduling [14] of the nodes is one of the most widespread solutions to preserve energy. It

S. Qin and Z. Qiu (Eds.): ICFEM 2011, LNCS 6991, pp. 388–403, 2011.

consists in splitting the network on several sub-networks, which work alternatively. The biggest challenge involved in this approach is the ability to provide continuous coverage, i.e., reliable monitoring or tracking by sensors.

For inhospitable fields where the sensors are arbitrarily deployed, the trend is to use a random scheduling scheme. As the study of random scheduling algorithms for WSNs is recent, the focus is to investigate more in developing new models that can satisfy the coverage constraint. In general, a theoretical paper-and-pencil based model of the proposed scheduling algorithm is developed and analyzed. After that, performance evaluation by simulation is done in order to illustrate the theoretical results. Nevertheless, the results obtained by simulation can never be totally accurate. Thus, simulation cannot be considered as a reliable solution for the probabilistic analysis of WSNs especially when applied to validate WSNs for mission-critical applications like military, health, disaster relief and environmental monitoring.

In order to overcome the common drawbacks of simulation, formal methods [6] have been proposed as an efficient solution to validate a wide range of hardware and software systems. Formal methods increase the system reliability by rigorously using mathematical techniques to analyze the mathematical model for the given system. They have the advantage to find out subtle errors that cannot be revealed by traditional simulation. The need of formal methods in the context of WSNs is illustrated in [19]. However, formal methods seem very restricted when used to validate probabilistic systems. The random components of the system cannot be directly modeled within traditional formal tools. For example, it will be impossible to reason precisely about statistical properties, such as expectation and variance, in the case of state-based approaches. Furthermore, huge proof efforts are usually expected to be involved in reasoning about random components of a wireless system in the case of theorem proving.

Due to the recent developments in the formalization of probability theory concepts in higher-order-logic [12,7], the analysis of a variety of wireless systems with random components in a higher-order-logic theorem prover [5] can be handled with reasonable amount of proof efforts. In this paper, we propose to use the probabilistic framework developed in the HOL theorem prover [7] to formally analyze the coverage-based random scheduling algorithm of [18]. Due to the high expressiveness of the underlying logic and the inherent soundness of theorem proving, this framework overcomes the common limitations of probabilistic model checking, which are the state space explosion and the inaccuracy in the reasoning about statistical quantities. Particularly, we aim at verifying the expected values of coverage intensity, and deducing the upper bound on the total number of disjoint subsets, given expected coverage intensity for the given scheduling algorithm. We also verify the lower bound on the total number of nodes and the average detection delay inside the network.

The remainder of this paper is organized as follows. First, we discuss related work. Then, we present an overview of HOL probabilistic analysis foundations. Sections 4 and 5 provide the formal specification and verification of the coverage-based random scheduling algorithm, respectively. Finally, we conclude the paper.

2 Related Work

Due to its wide applicability, the random scheduling algorithm has been analyzed using various approaches in the open literature. The most commonly used approach is simulation, where a computer based mathematical model of the given algorithm is built and then evaluated through rigorous sampling. The simulation tools must essentially provide some probabilistic features in order to perform realistic simulations. In [18], a coverage-based random scheduling algorithm has been analyzed by a mathematical model, which coverage has been subsequently enhanced in [17] by eliminating some blind points. The evaluation of the two previous works within a Java simulator has restricted the monitored region to 200mx200m, the detection range to 10m, and the number of sub-networks to 6. Due to the inherent nature of simulation coupled with the usage of computer arithmetic, the probabilistic analysis results attained by the simulation approach can not be termed as completely accurate.

Probabilistic model checking is one of the first formal methods to be used for probabilistic analysis of wireless systems [22]. It has the same principle as traditional model checking: the mathematical model of the probabilistic system is exhaustively tested to check if it meets a set of probabilistic properties. This technique has been successfully used to validate many aspects of WSNs. The authors of [20] performed the formal analysis of the OGDC algorithm in the RT-Maude rewriting tool [21]. They have successfully analyzed the common performance metrics, such as, the network coverage intensity and lifetime. The probabilistic model checker PRISM [15] has also been used quite frequently for the verification of medium access control (MAC) protocols designed for WSNs, such as the S-MAC [1] and ECO-MAC [25] protocols. For the first protocol, the authors have verified, within PRISM, the reachability of packets to the sink node for a simple network model of 3-hops. They have also evaluated the expected communication latency and energy consumption of the model. Regarding the probabilistic model checking of ECO-MAC, it has especially verified properties related to the number of packet retransmissions.

In addition to its accuracy, the main advantage of probabilistic model checking method is its mechanization. However, it also suffers from some major shortcomings like the common problem of state space explosion [2] and the inability to reason accurately about statistical properties. For instance, during the verification of the OGDC [20] algorithm, the network model has been limited to 6 nodes on a surface of 15mx15m. Similarly, in [1], the network hops have been restricted to 3 and the number of scheduled subsets to 2 so that the built model can be accepted in PRISM. Finally, while verifying the ECO-MAC [25] protocol, the authors have been also obliged to readjust some parameters by a reduction factor in order to avoid a state explosion problem which was completely unpredictable. On the other hand, the reasoning support for statistical quantities in probabilistic model checker like PRISM is not so accurate. In [1], the authors have given expected values of communication latency and energy consumption by running several experiments on the proposed model of S-MAC. These values were specific to the chosen configuration and can not be considered as general in any way. Another limitation of some classical model checkers trying to model probabilities can be also identified in [20], where the probability modeling was very approximative within the RT-Maude tool. The authors have just used a random function which is assumed to be 'good' to generate such behavior. For Uniform distributions, they have selected a sampling value generated by the same random function on a given interval. Such kind of analysis is not exhaustive and thus cannot be termed as formally verified.

In this paper, we overcome the limitations of both simulation and model checking techniques by using the probabilistic framework developed in the HOL theorem prover to validate a variant of the randomized scheduling of nodes in the context of WSNs. This framework, which is a theorem proving based probabilistic analysis framework, has already shown its practical effectiveness on a lot of case studies. Indeed, Hurd successfully verified the Miller-Rabin primality test; a well-known and commercially used probabilistic algorithm [13]. Hasan et al. verified the stop-and-wait protocol [9], a stuck-at fault model for reconfigurable memory arrays [8] and the automated repeat request (ARQ) mechanism at the logic link control (LLC) layer of the General Packet Radio Service (GPRS) standard for Global System for Mobile Communications (GSM) [10]. The HOL probabilistic framework is principally founded on Hurd's PhD thesis [12] where the formalization of some discrete random variables along with their verification, based on the corresponding PMF properties is presented [12]. In [7], Hurd's formalization framework has been extended with a formal definition of expectation. This definition is then utilized to formalize and verify the expectation and variance characteristics associated with discrete random variables that attain values in positive integers only. Statistical properties of continuous random variables have been also verified in [11]. To the best of our knowledge, none of the past works dealing with the random scheduling algorithm for WSNs or one of its variant has incorporated a formal probabilistic technique based on model checking or theorem proving.

3 Preliminaries

In this section, we describe the main theoretical elements upon which the probabilistic framework developed in the HOL theorem prover is built [7]. Particularly, we present the formalization of discrete random variables in HOL and the verified probabilistic properties that will be needed later. The general methodology that we have to follow for analyzing a wireless system within the probabilistic framework developed in the HOL theorem prover can be found in [10].

3.1 Formalization of Discrete Random Variables and Verification of their PMF

A random variable is called discrete if its range, i.e., the set of values that it can attain, is finite or at most countably infinite [23]. Discrete random variables are mathematically specified by their Probability Mass Functions (PMF) which is the probability that a random variable X is exactly equal to some value x, i.e., $Pr(X = x)$. In higher-order-logic, discrete random variables are formalized as deterministic functions with access to an infinite Boolean sequence $\mathbf{B}^\infty$; a source of infinite random bits with data type $(num \rightarrow bool)$[12]. According to the result of popping the top most bit in the infinite Boolean sequence, these deterministic functions make random choices. They may pop as many random bits as they need for their computation. At the end of the computation, they return the result along with the remaining portion of the infinite Boolean sequence to be used by other functions. Thus, a random variable that takes a parameter of type α and ranges over values of type β can be represented in HOL by the function:

$$\mathcal{F} : \alpha \rightarrow B^\infty \rightarrow \beta \times B^\infty.$$

As an example, the $Bernoulli(\frac{1}{2})$ random variable that returns 1 or 0 with equal probability can be modeled as follows

```
⊢ bit = λs. (if shd s then 1 else 0, stl s).
```

where the variable s represents the infinite Boolean sequence and the functions `shd` and `stl` are the sequence equivalents of the list operation *'head'* and *'tail'*. The function `bit` accepts the infinite Boolean sequence and returns a pair with the first element equal to either 0 or 1 and the second element equal to the unused portion of the infinite Boolean sequence, which in this case is the tail of the sequence.

Random variables can also be expressed in a more compact form using the general state-transforming monad where the states are the infinite Boolean sequences.

```
⊢ ∀ a,s. unit a s = (a,s)
⊢ ∀ f,g,s. bind f g s = g (fst (f s)) (snd (f s)).
```

The HOL functions `fst` and `snd` above return the first and second components of a pair, respectively. The `unit` operator is used to lift values to the monad, and the `bind` is the monadic analogue of function application. All monad laws hold for this definition, and the notation allows us to write functions without explicitly mentioning the sequence that is passed around, e.g., function `bit` can be defined as

```
⊢ bit_monad = bind sdest (λb. if b then unit 1 else unit 0).
```

where, `sdest` gives the head and tail of a sequence `s` as a pair (*shd* `s`, *stl* `s`).

The measure theory formalization of [12] can be used to define a probability function `prob`, which transforms sets of infinite Boolean sequence to the set of real number between 0 and 1. The domain of `prob` is the set $\mathcal{E}$ of probability events. Consequently, the formalization of `prob` and $\mathcal{E}$ can be used together to prove probabilistic properties of random variables such as:

$$\vdash \texttt{prob}\ \{\texttt{s}\ |\ \texttt{fst (bit s) = 1}\} = \frac{1}{2}.$$

where the HOL function `fst` selects the first component of a pair and $\{x|C(x)\}$ represents a set of all elements x that satisfy the condition C.

By following the methodology described above, most of the commonly used discrete random variables which are frequently used have been specified in the HOL theorem prover. The corresponding PMF of each of these discrete random variables has been also verified. For example, HOL definitions and PMF theorems for the Bernoulli, Uniform, Binomial and Geometric random variables can be found in [12,7].

3.2 Formalization and Verification of Expectation Properties for Discrete Random Variables in HOL

The expectation of a discrete random variable, which attains values in the positive integers only, is specified as follows [16]:

$$Ex\_fn[f(R)] = \sum_{n=0}^{\infty} f(n)Pr(R = n). \tag{1}$$

where R is the discrete random variable and f represents a function of the random variable R. The function f maps the random variable R to a real value. The above definition of expectation holds only if the summation is well defined, i.e., finite. The above equation can be formalized in HOL as follows:

Definition 1
⊢ ∀ f R. expec_fn f R = suminf (λn.(f n)prob {s | (fst (R s)=n)}).

The HOL function `suminf` represents the infinite summation of a real sequence. The function `expec_fn` accepts two parameters, the function `f` of type ($num \rightarrow real$) and the positive integer valued random variable `R` and returns a real number.

The expectation of a discrete random variable that attains values in positive integers would be a particular case of the above definition where the function `f` is instantiated by the identity function (`λn.n`).

Definition 2
⊢ ∀ R. expec R = expec_fn (λn.n) R.

For illustration purposes, the formalization of expectation of a positive valued discrete random variable was used to verify the expectation of the Bernoulli, Uniform, Binomial and Geometric random variables [7]. It was also very interesting to check the correctness of some related properties, which greatly facilitates the theorem proving based probabilistic analysis. For example, the proof of the linearity of expectation, specified in (2), has been provided in [7].

$$Ex\_fn[af(R) + b] = aEx\_fn[f(R)] + b \tag{2}$$

4 Coverage-Based Randomized Scheduling Algorithm

According to the probabilistic framework, proposed in [10], the formal analysis of wireless systems is composed of two main steps, i.e., the formalization of the given wireless system, while modeling its random components by the formalized random variables, and using this model to formally verify properties of interest as higher-order-logic theorems. In this section, we develop a HOL formalization of the coverage-based random scheduling algorithm for WSNs, which corresponds to the first step outlined above. This formalization is basically inspired by the paper-and-pencil based analytical analysis presented in [18].

4.1 Overview of the Coverage-Based Randomized Scheduling Algorithm

We consider a WSN that deploys n sensors over a field of size a. All sensors have the same task; gathering data and routing it back to the base station. The deployment of nodes over the two-dimensional field is random and thus no location information is available. The size of the sensing area of each sensor is denoted by r. A sensor can only sense the environment and detect events within its sensing range. We say that a point of the monitored field is covered when any event occurring at this point can be detected by at least one active sensor. The probability q that each sensor covers a given point is r/a. The random scheduling of the nodes assigns each sensor to one of the k sub-networks with equal probability $1/k$. During a time slot Ti, only the nodes belonging to the sub-network i will be active and can cover an occurring event. Hence, the disjoint sub-networks created will work alternatively. We denote also by: Si, the set of sensors that belongs to the sub-network i and covers a specific point inside the field, S, the set of nodes covering a specific point inside the field, and, c, the cardinality of S.

For illustration purposes, Fig. 1 shows how the scheduling algorithm splits arbitrarily a network containing eight sensor nodes to two sub-networks. The eight nodes, randomly deployed in the monitored region, are identified by IDs ranging from 0 to 7. The two sub-networks are called *S0* and *S1*. Each node chooses at random between 0 and 1 in order to be assigned to one of these two

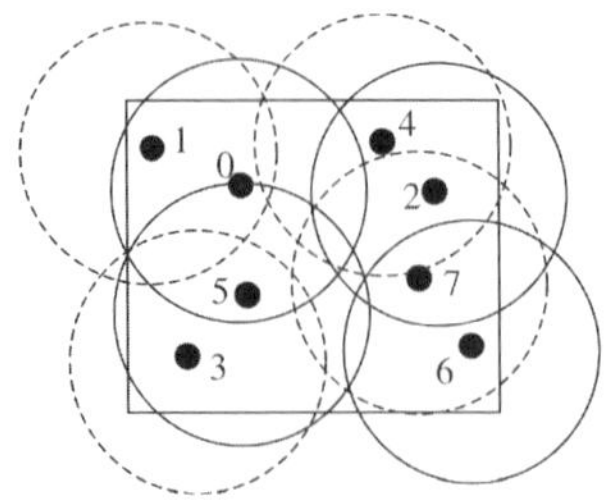

Fig. 1. An example of the randomized coverage-based algorithm [18]

sub-networks. Suppose that nodes 0; 2; 5; 6 select the number 0 and join the subset S0 and nodes 1; 3; 4; 7 choose the number 1 and join the subset *S1*. Thus, the two sub-networks will work alternatively. In other words, when the nodes 0; 2; 5; 6, which sensing ranges are denoted by the solid circles, are active, the nodes 1; 3; 4; 7 illustrated by the dashed circles will be idle and vice versa.

4.2 Formalization of the Network Coverage Intensity

The challenge in the random scheduling algorithm described below, is to select a value of k so that the energy can be saved with a good coverage. Therefore, the performance of this algorithm depends essentially on the chosen value of k. A large k will imply a lot of sub-networks which would in turn result in few nodes in each of these sub-networks, and hence a poor coverage. However, a small k will imply few sub-networks with a lot of points covered simultaneously by a lot of nodes, so a waste of energy.

The random scheduling algorithm involves several random variables. The first one distributes uniformly the nodes over the sub-networks. It is formalized by the HOL function `rd_subsets`:

Definition 3

```
⊢ (∀ k. rd_subsets 0 k = []) ∧
  (∀ c,k. rd_subsets (c+1) k = (prob_uniform k)::(rd_subsets c k)).
```

which generates recursively a list of Uniform random variables, and accepts two parameters: c, the number of sensors that covers a specific point inside the field, and k, the number of sub-networks. In this definition, we use the predefined HOL function `prob_uniform` which takes as input a natural k and generates a Uniform (k) random variable.

Let X be the random variable denoting the total number of non-empty subsets *Sj*. X is defined as follows:

$$X = \sum_{j=0}^{k-1} Xj. \tag{3}$$

where *Xj* is the Bernoulli random variable describing a non-empty subset. The variable *Xj*, expressed by the following HOL function, is based on the recursive HOL predicate `subset_empty` which describes an empty subset by looking for an index j in the list generated by the function `rd_subsets`.

Definition 4

```
⊢ ∀ j,c,k. subset_non_empty j c k = bernoulli_num
   (prob bern {s | fst (subset_empty j (rd_subsets c k) s) = F}).
```

The function `subset_non_empty` takes three parameters: j, a natural number, c, the number of sensors that covers a specific point inside the field, and k, the number of sub-networks. The set `{s | fst (subset_empty j (rd_subsets c k) s) = F}`, used in this function, formally models the set of events when the subset Sj is non-empty.

In order to define the random variable X, given in (3), we first define a function which recursively generates a list of Xj's by accepting the parameters: k, the length of the list, c, the number of sensors that covers a specific point inside the field, and m, the number of sub-networks. After that, a pre-defined function of the HOL probability theory, called `sum_rv_lst`, accepts this list of random variables and returns their sum as a single random variable.

Definition 5

```
⊢ (∀ c,m. subset_non_empty_lst 0 c m = [subset_non_empty 0 c m]) ∧
  (∀ k,c,m. subset_non_empty_lst k c m =
  (subset_non_empty (k+1) c m)::(subset_non_empty_lst k c m)).
```

The coverage intensity for a specific point Cp can now be defined as the average time during which the point is covered by the total length of the scheduling cycle.

$$Cp = \frac{E[X] \times T}{k \times T}. \tag{4}$$

where $E[X]$ denotes the expectation of the random variable X defined in (3). The variable Cp is formalized in HOL as follows:

Definition 6

```
⊢ ∀ c,k. cvrge_intsty_pt c k =
  (expec (sum_rv_lst (subset_non_empty_lst k c (k+1))))/(k+1).
```

The above definition specifies the coverage intensity for a specific point using the HOL function `cvrge_intsty_pt`. This function takes as parameters: c, the number of sensors that covers a specific point inside the field, and k, the number of sub-networks. Added to the function `subset_non_empty_lst`, this definition uses two other predefined HOL functions which are `expec`, for the expectation of a discrete random variable (Definition 2), and `sum_rv_lst`, for the summation over random variables. More details about these two functions can be found in the preliminaries section and in [7].

It has been shown in [18] that Cp is equal to:

$$\left[1 - \left(1 - \frac{1}{k}\right)^{c}\right]. \tag{5}$$

We recall that the variable c is initially the number of nodes covering a specific point inside the field. Covering a point or not can be assimilated to a Bernoulli trial with the probability q. If we consider the variable c among the n nodes of the network, it becomes a Binomial random variable with the following probability:

$$Pr(c = j) = \frac{n!}{j!\,(n-j)!} q^{j} (1-q)^{n-j}. \tag{6}$$

where q is the probability that each sensor covers a given point.

Thereafter, Cp is also a random variable. Particularly, Cp is a function of the random variable c. Since the random deployment strategy distributes independently the nodes over the area and the random scheduling makes a uniform distribution of the same sensors, the expectation of Cp for any point inside the area is the same and its value is Cn. The variable Cn is defined as follows:

$$Cn = Ex\_fn[Cp] \tag{7}$$

where Ex_fn designates the expectation of a function of a random variable. The corresponding HOL function formalizing (7) is:

Definition 7

```
⊢ ∀ q,n,k. cvrge_intsty_network q n k =
  expec_fn (λx. 1 + (-1)×(1 - 1/(k+1))^x) (prob_binomial_p n q).
```

The above function `cvrge_intsty_network` accepts as inputs q, the probability that a sensor covers a point, n, the number of sensors deployed inside the field, and k, the number of sub-networks. This function specifies the expectation of a function of random variable and thus needs two parameters: the input function which basically describes the variable Cp and the random variable which is the Binomial of (6).

4.3 Formalization of the Average Detection Delay

The average detection delay is another performance metric which can be relevant in evaluating the random scheduling algorithm. It is defined as the expectation of the time elapsed from the occurrence of an event to the time when the event is detected by some sensor nodes. The average detection delay for an event arriving at any time slot with equal probability and lasting for duration longer than $(k-1) \times T$, is defined as:

$$delays = \sum_{i=1}^{k-1} \int_{0}^{T} \frac{1}{T} \times \Pr(H0 \cap H1 \cap ... \cap \overline{Hi}) \times (i \times T - t)dt. \tag{8}$$

where Hi is the event that none of the c covering sensor nodes belongs to the working subset i, $\overline{Hi}$ is the event that at least one of the c covering sensors belongs to the working subset i, T is the duration of a time slot, and k is the number of disjoint subsets.

Defining the HOL theorem corresponding to the verification of the average detection delay requires the formalization of the set $(H0 \cap H1 \cap ... \cap H(i-1) \cap \overline{Hi})$ as a higher-order-logic function. The proposed idea consists in dividing this set into two parts: the first one defines the intersection of the $(i-1)$ first events while the second models the event that *'the ith working sub-network is non-empty within Ti'*.

The function `compl_intersection`, given in Definition 8, illustrates the first part of the required final set.

Definition 8

```
⊢ ∀ i,c,k. compl_intersection i c k =
          bind (indep_rv_list (subset_non_empty_rv_list i c k))
                                        (λx. unit (disj_list x)).
```

This builds the intersection of events describing the $(i-1)$ first empty subsets. The idea is to first make a list of the required random variables (function `subset_non_empty_rv_list`) by satisfying the independence criteria (function `indep_rv_list`), and then create the conjunction of all the elements of the list as required. The function `compl_intersection` takes as parameters: i, a natural index, c, the number of sensors that covers a specific point inside the field, and k, the number of sub-networks. The HOL definitions of the the two functions used within the function `compl_intersection` can be found in [4].

The second part of the final set is described by the Bernoulli random variable used in (3) which also expresses the event of an empty subset. Thus, the final set is described by the following HOL function `final_set` which takes the same parameters as the function `compl_intersection`.

Definition 9

```
⊢ ∀ i,c,k. final_set i c k =
                bind (compl_intersection i c k) (λx.
                bind (subset_non_empty (k-i-1) c (k-i)) (λy.
                unit (¬x ∧ (y = 1)))).
```

5 Formal Verification of the Random Scheduling Algorithm

We use the defined HOL functions in order to formally verify the main statistical properties regarding the network coverage intensity and the average detection delay. We have described the verified theorems in a backward chaining approach, i.e., we present the main goal first and then the corresponding proofs.

5.1 Formal Verification of the Network Coverage Intensity

We have already noticed from the specification section that the network coverage intensity is defined as a statistical measure of the coverage intensity for a specific point (see (7)). Hence, we need to verify first that the coverage intensity for a specific point, defined in (4), is really equal to the expression given in (5). The HOL theorem corresponding to this property can be expressed as follows:

Theorem 1

```
⊢ ∀ c,k. cvrge_intsty_pt c k = 1 - (1 - (1/(k+1)))^c.
```

The verification of the above theorem is based on Theorem 2, which gives the expectation of the random variable specified in (3).

Theorem 2

```
⊢ ∀ c,k. expec (sum_rv_lst (subset_non_empty_lst k c (k+1))) =
        (k+1)×(1 - (1 - (1/(k+1)))^c).
```

The proof of Theorem 2 is mainly based on the application of the expectation property stating that the expectation of the sum of discrete random variables is equal to the sum of their respective expectation, and the verification of the expectation of each element of the list `subset_non_empty_lst` [4].

Next, we have to verify the second main theorem related to the network coverage intensity Cn. It has been shown in [18] that Cn is equal to:

$$1 - \left(1 - \frac{q}{k}\right)^n. \tag{9}$$

which is formalized in HOL by the following theorem:

Theorem 3

$\vdash \forall$ `n,q,k.` `(0` $\leq$ `q)` $\wedge$ `(q` $\leq$ `1)` $\wedge$ `(1` $\leq$ `n)` $\Rightarrow$
`(cvrge_intsty_network q n k = (1 - (1-(q/(k+1)))`^{n}`)).`

The proof of Theorem 3 is primarily based on the application of the linearity of expectation property (see (2)) which further requires the independence of the Binomial random variable, already verified in [7], and the proof of the finite summation of the corresponding function multiplied by the probability. Besides that, the proof of Theorem 3 needed a lot of mathematical reasoning related to the real summation especially for the Binomial theorem for reals which was not available in the existing HOL libraries and thus, we had to prove it.

Theorem 3 gives a clear relationship between the network coverage intensity, the number of nodes n and the number of disjoint sub-networks k. As a result, two important corollaries can be deduced. Given a number k, we require that the minimum of the network coverage intensity Cn is t, and we can deduce the lower bound on the necessary number of sensor nodes in the whole network which is:

$$n \geq \left\lceil \frac{\ln(1-t)}{\ln\left(1-\frac{q}{k}\right)} \right\rceil. \tag{10}$$

The above corollary has been successfully verified in HOL by using intermediate results associated to the two mathematical functions of power and logarithm.

Similarly, we can deduce that for a given n and providing a network coverage intensity of at least t, the upper bound on the number of disjoint subsets k is:

$$k \leq \frac{q}{1 - e^{\frac{\ln(1-t)}{n}}}. \tag{11}$$

The proof of the above corollary was straightforward and is based on pre-verified theorems from the two HOL theories of real and exponential.

The second corollary, given in (11), is very useful in dynamically adjusting the coverage of a sensor network after it is deployed. When the total number of sensor nodes is fixed, the network coverage intensity can be adjusted by changing the number of disjoint subsets k. A simple message flooding can be done to inform all sensor nodes about the new value of k.

5.2 Formal Verification of the Average Detection Delay

It has been shown in [18] that the average detection delay for an event, occurring at a point covered by c sensor nodes and lasting for duration longer than $(k-1) \times T$, is equal to:

$$delays = \frac{T}{2} \times \left[\left(\frac{k-1}{k} \right)^c + 2 \times \sum_{i=2}^{k-1} \left(\frac{k-i}{k} \right)^c \right]. \tag{12}$$

We have successfully verified the theorem formalizing the above equation. The proof has been based on an important result, verified in Theorem 4, along with some reasoning based on derivatives, and the corresponding details can be found in [4].

Theorem 4

```
⊢ ∀ i c k. (2 ≤ k) ∧ (1 ≤ (k - i)) ⇒
         (prob bern {s | fst (final_set i c k s) = T} =
         product 0 i (λj. (1-(1/(k-j)))^c)×(1-(1-1/(k-i))^c)).
```

This theorem reduces the probability of a set of independent events to the product of their respective probabilities. The function `product`, used in the above theorem, is a recursive function that gives the product of a sequence of elements of the same function. The proof of Theorem 4 required reasoning related to the transformation of probabilistic sets and to the independence theorem of probability. Under some assumptions, this last theorem transforms the probability of the intersection of two independent events into the product of their respective probabilities.

Our results demonstrate the effectiveness of the probabilistic theorem proving based approach for the verification of randomized scheduling algorithms for WSNs. We have been able to formally verify the most important probabilistic properties of interest associated with the network coverage intensity and the average detection delay. While other techniques, like simulation and model checking, are restricted by the number of simulated nodes n, the number of disjoint subsets k, the sensing range r, and the surface a, our results are completely generic, i.e., the verified theorems are universally quantified for all values of n, k, r and a.

Moreover, the inherent soundness of theorem proving certifies that the obtained results are 100% accurate. Based on the discussion in Sections 1 and 2 of this paper, it is clear that other techniques can never have this flexibility. Indeed, previous simulation work have given non-exhaustive results which are valid for specific network configurations. Similarly, probabilistic model checking have been frequently forced to restrict the values of the two first parameters in order to avoid a state space explosion problem. Finally, compared to probabilistic model checkers, a major novelty provided in this paper is the ability to perform formal and accurate reasoning about statistical properties of the problem. Hence, it was possible to verify the network coverage intensity which is a statistical measure of the coverage intensity for a specific point. This possibility is mainly due to the strong theoretical support for probability modeling available within the HOL probabilistic framework and the high expressibility of higher-order logic.

The above mentioned additional benefits, associated with the theorem proving approach, are attained at the cost of the time and effort spent, while formalizing the randomized scheduling algorithm and formally reasoning about its properties, by the user. This analysis consumed approximately 200 man-hours and 1500 lines of HOL code by an expert user.

The major challenges faced in this work include the learning of the HOL probabilistic framework that primarily requires prior familiarization with the theorem proving technique and a good background on the probability theory. Higher-order-logic formalization also required a lot of intuition in selecting the right random variables. Similarly, an exhaustive set of assumptions is required for the verification as missing any assumption leads to verification failure due to the inherent soundness of the underlying theorem proving approach. Nevertheless, the fact that we were building on top of already verified probability theory related results helped significantly in this regard. In this paper, a lot of intermediate results have been omitted in order to meet page limits. The interested reader can refer to [4] for more details about all the theorems.

6 Conclusions

Due to the deployment constraints of WSNs, we are more motivated to provide algorithms characterized by a probabilistic behavior. Such a characteristic is impossible to cover using classic validation procedures like simulation, which do not ascertain 100% accuracy. The purpose of this paper was to provide a reliable analysis by using an accurate formal probabilistic reasoning based on the general purpose HOL theorem prover. We formally analyzed the coverage and the average detection delay of a scheduling algorithm designed for randomly deployed wireless sensor networks. We particularly verified the expected values of the coverage intensity, the upper bound on the total number of disjoint subsets, the lower bound on the total number of nodes and the average detection delay inside the network.

To the best of our knowledge, this paper presents the *first* formal analysis of a randomized scheduling problem using a probabilistic formal method. Obtained results have the advantages to be exhaustive and completely generic, i.e., valid for all parameter values, which cannot be attained in simulation or probabilistic model checking based approach. In addition, the successful formal reasoning about statistical properties clearly demonstrates the practical effectiveness of the proposed approach compared to probabilistic model checking, where such a feature is not available.

It is important to note that the usability of the HOL probabilistic framework for the WSN context is not limited to the current case study. Indeed, the whole framework can be efficiently used to formally analyze several probabilistic routing algorithms for WSNs. One such example is the Reverse Path Forwarding (RPF) algorithm [3]. Once the HOL probabilistic framework is enriched with possibilities to reason about statistical properties of multiple continuous random variables, it will be promising to extend the formal analysis of the coverage-based scheduling algorithm. We can, for example, think to formally verify the network lifetime which is a crucial aspect in the WSNs context or the impact of clock asynchrony on the coverage quality.

References

1. Ballarini, P., Miller, A.: Model Checking Medium Access Control for Sensor Networks. In: International Symposium on Leveraging Applications of Formal Methods, Verification and Validation, pp. 255–262. IEEE Press, New York (2006)
2. Clarke, E.M., Grumberg, O., Peled, D.A.: Model Checking. The MIT Press, Cambridge (2000)
3. Dalal, Y., Metcalfe, R.: Reverse Path Forwarding of Broadcast Packets. Commun. of ACM 21(12), 1040–1048 (1978)
4. Elleuch, M., Hasan, O., Tahar, S., Abid, M.: Formal Probabilistic Analysis of the Coverage-based Random Scheduling Algorithm for WSNs. Technical Report. ENIS, Sfax University, Tunisia (2011), http://www.ceslab.org/publications/TR_FPARSAWSN_v1.3.pdf
5. Gordon, M.J.C.: Mechanizing Programming Logics in Higher-Order Logic. In: Current Trends in Hardware Verification and Automated Theorem Proving, pp. 387–439. Springer, Heidelberg (1989)
6. Gupta, A.: Formal Hardware Verification Methods: A Survey. Formal Methods in System Design 1(2-3), 151–238 (1992)
7. Hasan, O.: Formal Probabilistic Analysis using Theorem Proving. PhD Thesis, Concordia University, Montreal, QC, Canada (2008)
8. Hasan, O., Tahar, S., Abbasi, N.: Formal Reliability Analysis using Theorem Proving. IEEE Transactions on Computers 59(5), 579–592 (2010)
9. Hasan, O., Tahar, S.: Performance Analysis and Functional Verification of the Stop-and-Wait Protocol in HOL. Journal of Automated Reasoning 42(1), 1–33 (2009)
10. Hasan, O., Tahar, S.: Probabilistic Analysis of Wireless Systems using Theorem Proving. Electronic Notes in Theoretical Computer Science 242(2), 43–58 (2009)
11. Hasan, O., Abbasi, N., Akbarpour, B., Tahar, S., Akbarpour, R.: Formal Reasoning about Expectation Properties for Continuous Random Variables. In: Cavalcanti, A., Dams, D.R. (eds.) FM 2009. LNCS, vol. 5850, pp. 435–450. Springer, Heidelberg (2009)
12. Hurd, J.: Formal Verification of Probabilistic Algorithms. PhD Thesis, University of Cambridge, Cambridge, UK (2002)
13. Hurd, J.: Verification of the Miller-Rabin Probabilistic Primality Test. J. of Logic and Algebraic Programming 50(1-2), 3–21 (2003)
14. Jain, S., Srivastava, S.: A Survey and Classification of Distributed Scheduling Algorithms for Sensor Networks. In: International Conference on Sensor Technologies and Applications, pp. 88–93. IEEE Press, New York (2007)
15. Kwiatkowska, M., Norman, G., Parker, D.: PRISM: Probabilistic Model Checking for Performance and Reliability Analysis. ACM SIGMETRICS Performance Evaluation Review 36(4), 40–45 (2009)
16. Levine, A.: Theory of Probability. Addison-Wesley series in Behavioral Science, Quantitative Methods. Addison-Wesley, Reading (1971)
17. Lin, J.W., Chen, Y.T.: Improving the Coverage of Randomized Scheduling in Wireless Sensor Networks. IEEE Transactions on Wireless Communications 7(12), 4807–4812 (2008)
18. Liu, C., Wu, K., Xiao, Y., Sun, B.: Random Coverage with Guaranteed Connectivity: Joint Scheduling for Wireless Sensor Networks. IEEE Transactions on Parallel and Distributed Systems 17(6), 562–575 (2010)

19. McIver, A.K., Fehnker, A.: Formal Techniques for the Analysis of Wireless Networks. In: International Symposium on Leveraging Applications of Formal Methods, Verification and Validation, pp. 263–270. IEEE Computer Society, Washington, DC, USA (2006)
20. Ölveczky, P.C., Thorvaldsen, S.: Formal Modeling and Analysis of the OGDC Wireless Sensor Network Algorithm in Real-Time Maude. In: Bonsangue, M.M., Johnsen, E.B. (eds.) FMOODS 2007. LNCS, vol. 4468, pp. 122–140. Springer, Heidelberg (2007)
21. The Real-Time website, `http://heim.ifi.uio.no/peterol/RealTimeMaude/`
22. Rutten, J., Kwaiatkowska, M., Normal, G., Parker, D.: Mathematical Techniques for Analyzing Concurrent and Probabilisitc Systems. CRM Monograph Series, vol. 23. American Mathematical Society, Providence (2004)
23. Yates, R.D., Goodman, D.J.: Probability and Stochastic Processes: A Friendly Introduction for Electrical and Computer Engineers. Wiley, Chichester (2005)
24. Yick, J., Mukherjee, B., Ghosal, D.: Wireless Sensor Network Survey. J. Computer Networks 52, 2292–2330 (2008)
25. Zayani, H., Barkaoui, K., Ben Ayed, R.: Probabilistic Verification and Evaluation of Backoff Procedure of the WSN ECo-MAC Protocol. J. of Wireless & Mobile Networks 2(2), 156–170 (2010)

An Abstract Model for Proving Safety of Multi-lane Traffic Manoeuvres*

Martin Hilscher[1], Sven Linker[1], Ernst-Rüdiger Olderog[1], and Anders P. Ravn[2]

[1] Department of Computing Science, University of Oldenburg, Germany
{martin.hilscher,sven.linker,olderog}@informatik.uni-oldenburg.de
[2] Department of Computer Science, Aalborg University, Denmark
apr@cs.aau.dk

Abstract. We present an approach to prove safety (collision freedom) of multi-lane motorway traffic with lane-change manoeuvres. This is ultimately a hybrid verification problem due to the continuous dynamics of the cars. We abstract from the dynamics by introducing a new spatial interval logic based on the view of each car. To guarantee safety, we present two variants of a lane-change controller, one with perfect knowledge of the safety envelopes of neighbouring cars and one which takes only the size of the neighbouring cars into account. Based on these controllers we provide a local safety proof for unboundedly many cars by showing that at any moment the reserved space of each car is disjoint from the reserved space of any other car.

Keywords: Multi-lane motorway traffic, lane-change manoeuvre, collision freedom, abstract modelling, spatial interval logic, timed automata.

1 Introduction

To increase the safety of road traffic many individual driving assistant systems based on suitable sensors have been developed for cars. The next step is to utilize car to car communication to combine such individual system to build up more advanced assistance functionalities. In this paper we study one such functionality, lane-change assistance for cars driving on a multi-lane motorway. The challenge is to develop lane-change controllers based on suitable sensor and communication facilities such that the *safety* (*collision freedom*) of multi-lane motorway traffic can be demonstrated if all cars are equipped with such a controller. This is ultimately a problem of hybrid system verification, where the car dynamics, the car controllers, and suitable assumptions together should imply safety.

In the California PATH (Partners for Advanced Transit and Highways) project automated highway systems for car platoons including lane change have been designed. Lygeros et al. [1] sketch a safety proof taking car dynamics into account, but admitting *safe collisions*, i.e., collisions at a low speed. Not all scenarios of multi-lane traffic are covered in the analysis. Jula et al. [2] provide calculations

* This research was partially supported by the German Research Council (DFG) in the Transregional Collaborative Research Center SFB/TR 14 AVACS.

S. Qin and Z. Qiu (Eds.): ICFEM 2011, LNCS 6991, pp. 404–419, 2011.

of safe longitudinal distances between cars based on car dynamics. Werling et al. [3] study car traffic in urban scenarios and an abstract representation of several car manoeuvres. In their analysis cars are assumed to drive with constant speed. To simplify safety proofs controller patterns are exploited in Damm et al. [4], where a proof rule for collision freedom of two traffic agents based on criticality functions is proposed. This proof rule has for instance been applied to verify a distance controller. However, it is not clear how to extend this approach to deal with arbitrarily many cars on a motorway. Our paper is inspired by approaches to controller design for hybrid systems that *separate* the dynamics from the control layer. Raisch et al. [5,6] introduce abstraction and refinement to support a hierarchical design of hybrid control systems. Van Schuppen et al. [7] introduce synthesis of control laws for piecewise-affine hybrid systems based on simplices.

Our key idea for coping with the safety of many cars on a motorway is to show that different cars occupy and reserve disjoint spaces. To this end, we introduce an abstract model of multi-lane motorway traffic based on spatial properties of local views of cars. The properties are expressed in a new dedicated *Multi-Lane Spatial Logic* (MLSL) inspired by Moskowski's interval temporal logic [8], Zhou, Hoare and Ravn's Duration Calculus [9], and Schäfer's Shape Calculus [10]. MLSL is a two-dimensional extension of interval temporal logic, where one dimension has a continuous space (the position in each lane) and the other has a discrete space (the number of the lane). In MLSL we can for instance express that a car E has reserved a certain space on its lane. However, that the size of this reservation covers the braking distance of E is not part of the spatial logic. This would come into the picture only when refining the spatial properties to the car dynamics, which is not part of this paper. By using MLSL, we separate the purely spatial reasoning from the car dynamics.

As we shall see, spatial properties needed for the safety proof can be expressed very concisely in MLSL. We shall use formulas of MLSL as guards and state invariants of abstract lane-change controllers. In a technical realisation of such controllers, the properties that may appear in the formulas stipulate suitable sensors of the cars, for instance distance sensors.

The contributions of our paper are follows:

- we introduce an abstract model of motorway traffic with lane-change manoeuvres and a suitable spatial interval logic MLSL (Sect. 2);
- we provide two variants of lane-change controllers, a simple one with perfect knowledge of the safety envelopes of neighbouring cars and an elaborated one which takes only the extension of the neighbouring cars into account, but requires communication with a helper car (Sect. 3);
- we conduct proofs of safety (collision freedom) for both controllers (Sect. 4).

Finally, in Sect. 5 we conclude and discuss more related and future work.

2 Abstract Model

Usually, road traffic is modelled as a dynamical system, where each vehicle has a trajectory in the plane defined by its position, its speed and its acceleration [1].

However, to conduct a proof of safety of many cars on a multi-lane motorway, this is a far too detailed description of traffic. Thus we introduce a more abstract model which is based on local views of cars as shown in Fig. 1.

We start from a global picture of multi-lane motorway traffic, where the road has an infinite extension with positions represented by the real numbers and where lanes are represented by natural numbers $0, 1, \ldots, n$. At each moment of time each car, with a unique identity denoted by letters A, B, ..., has its position *pos*, speed *spd*, and acceleration *acc*. We assume that all traffic proceeds in one direction, with increasing position values, in the pictures shown from left to right. The abstract model is introduced by allowing for each car only local views of this traffic. A view of a car E comprises a contiguous subset of lanes, and has a bounded extension. A view containing all lanes with an extension up to a given constant, the *horizon*, will be called *standard view*.

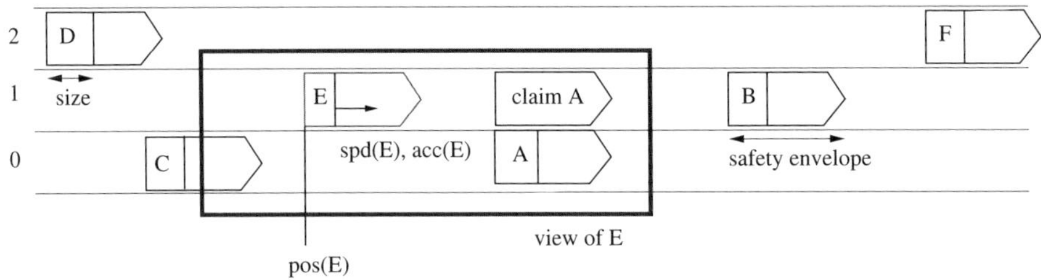

Fig. 1. View of car E comprising a bounded extension of lanes 1 and 0. Car E sees its own reservation, both the reservation and the claim of car A ahead, which is preparing for a change from lane 0 to lane 1, and part of the reservation of car C driving on a neighbouring lane behind E. It does not see the cars B, D and F because they are driving outside of its view.

What a car "knows" of its view is expressed by formulas in a dedicated multi-lane spatial logic, which extends interval temporal logic [8] to two dimensions, one with a continuous space (the position in each lane) and the other with a discrete space (the number of the lane). Such a formula consists of a finite list of lanes, where each lane is characterized by a finite sequence of segments. A segment is either occupied by a car, say E, or it is empty (*free*). For instance, in the view of car E shown in Fig. 1, the following formula ϕ holds:

$$\phi \equiv \left\langle \begin{array}{c} \mathit{free} \frown E \frown \mathit{free} \frown cl(A) \frown \mathit{free} \\ C \frown \mathit{free} \frown re(A) \frown \mathit{free} \end{array} \right\rangle$$

Here $\frown$ is the *chop operator* of interval temporal logic; it serves to separate adjacent segments in a lane. In the logic we can distinguish whether a car A has *reserved* a space in a lane ($re(A)$) or only *claimed* a space ($cl(A)$) for a planned lane change manoeuvre. We stipulate that reserved and claimed spaces have the extension of the *safety envelopes* of the cars, which include at each moment the speed dependent braking distances. The key idea of our approach is that we abstract from the exact values of these distances in our safety proof.

2.1 Traffic Snapshot

We introduce a formal model $\mathcal{TS}$ of a traffic snapshot, which describes the traffic on the motorway at a given point in time. Henceforth we assume a globally unique identifier for each car and take $\mathbb{I}$ as the set of all such *car identifiers*, with typical elements $A, B, \ldots$. Furthermore, $\mathbb{L} = \{0, \ldots, N\}$, for some fixed $N \geq 1$, denotes the set of motorway lanes, with typical elements l, m, n.

Definition 1 (Traffic Snapshot). *A* traffic snapshot $\mathcal{TS}$ *is a structure*

$$\mathcal{TS} = (res, clm, pos, spd, acc),$$

where res, clm, pos, spd, acc are functions

- $res : \mathbb{I} \to \mathcal{P}(\mathbb{L})$ *such that $res(C)$ is the set of lanes C reserves,*
- $clm : \mathbb{I} \to \mathcal{P}(\mathbb{L})$ *such that $clm(C)$ is the set of lanes C claims,*
- $pos : \mathbb{I} \to \mathbb{R}$ *such that $pos(C)$ is the position of car C along the lanes,*
- $spd : \mathbb{I} \to \mathbb{R}$ *such that $spd(C)$ is the current speed of the car C,*
- $acc : \mathbb{I} \to \mathbb{R}$ *such that $acc(C)$ is the current acceleration of the car C.*

We denote the set of all traffic snapshots by $\mathbb{TS}$.

Definition 2 (Transitions). *The following* transitions *describe the changes that may occur at a traffic snapshot $\mathcal{TS} = (res, clm, pos, spd, acc)$. Note that we use the overriding notation $\oplus$ of Z for function updates [11].*

$$\mathcal{TS} \xrightarrow{t} \mathcal{TS}' \Leftrightarrow \mathcal{TS}' = (res, clm, pos', spd', acc) \wedge \forall C \in \mathbb{I}\colon pos'(C) = pos(C) + spd(C) \cdot t + \tfrac{1}{2} acc(C) \cdot t^2 \wedge \forall C \in \mathbb{I}\colon spd'(C) = spd(C) + acc(C) \cdot t \quad (1)$$

$$\mathcal{TS} \xrightarrow{\mathsf{c}(C,n)} \mathcal{TS}' \Leftrightarrow \mathcal{TS}' = (res, clm', pos, spd, acc) \wedge |clm(C)| = 0 \wedge |res(C)| = 1 \wedge \{n+1, n-1\} \cap res(C) \neq \emptyset \wedge clm' = clm \oplus \{C \mapsto \{n\}\} \quad (2)$$

$$\mathcal{TS} \xrightarrow{\mathsf{wd\ c}(C)} \mathcal{TS}' \Leftrightarrow \mathcal{TS}' = (res, clm', pos, spd, acc) \wedge clm' = clm \oplus \{C \mapsto \emptyset\} \quad (3)$$

$$\mathcal{TS} \xrightarrow{\mathsf{r}(C)} \mathcal{TS}' \Leftrightarrow \mathcal{TS}' = (res', clm', pos, spd, acc) \wedge clm' = clm \oplus \{C \mapsto \emptyset\} \wedge res' = res \oplus \{C \mapsto res(C) \cup clm(C)\} \quad (4)$$

$$\mathcal{TS} \xrightarrow{\mathsf{wd\ r}(C,n)} \mathcal{TS}' \Leftrightarrow \mathcal{TS}' = (res', clm, pos, spd, acc) \wedge res' = res \oplus \{C \mapsto \{n\}\} \wedge n \in res(C) \wedge |res(C)| = 2 \quad (5)$$

$$\mathcal{TS} \xrightarrow{\mathsf{acc}(C,a)} \mathcal{TS}' \Leftrightarrow \mathcal{TS}' = (res, clm, pos, spd, acc') \wedge acc' = acc \oplus \{C \mapsto a\} \quad (6)$$

In (1) time can pass, which results in the cars moving along the motorway according to their respective speeds and accelerations. A car may *claim* a neighbouring lane n *iff* it currently does not already claim another lane or is in the progress of changing the lane and therefore reserves two lanes (2). Furthermore a car may *withdraw* a claim (3) or *reserve* a previously claimed lane (4) or withdraw the reservation of all but one of the lanes it is moving on (5). Finally a car may change its acceleration (6).

Example. The following trace shows a car C driving for t_1 seconds on lane 1 or 3, then claiming lane 2, driving for t_2 seconds while claiming lane 2, reserving lane 2, driving for t_{lc} seconds on both lanes (moving over) and then withdrawing all reservations but the one for lane 2.

$$\mathcal{TS}_1 \xrightarrow{t_1} \mathcal{TS}_2 \xrightarrow{\mathsf{c}(C,2)} \mathcal{TS}_3 \xrightarrow{t_2} \mathcal{TS}_4 \xrightarrow{\mathsf{r}(C)} \mathcal{TS}_5 \xrightarrow{t_{lc}} \mathcal{TS}_6 \xrightarrow{\mathsf{wd\ r}(C,2)} \mathcal{TS}_7$$

2.2 View

For our safety proof we will restrict ourselves to finite parts of a traffic snapshot $\mathcal{TS}$ called views, the intuition being that the safety of manoeuvres can be shown using local information only.

Definition 3 (View). *A* view V *is defined as a structure* $V = (L, X, E)$, *where*

- $L = [l, n] \subseteq \mathbb{L}$ *is an interval of lanes that are visible in the view,*
- $X = [r, t] \subseteq \mathbb{R}$ *is the extension that is visible in the view,*
- $E \in \mathbb{I}$ *is the identifier of the car under consideration.*

A subview *of* V *is obtained by restricting the lanes and extension we observe. For this we use sub- and superscript notation:* $V^{L'} = (L', X, E)$ *and* $V_{X'} = (L, X', E)$, *where* L' *and* X' *are subintervals of* L *and* X, *respectively.*

For a car E *and a traffic snapshot* $\mathcal{TS} = (res, clm, pos, spd, acc)$ *we define the standard view of* E *as*

$$V_s(E, \mathcal{TS}) = (\mathbb{L}, [pos(E) - h, pos(E) + h], E) \enspace ,$$

where the horizon h *is chosen such that a car driving at maximum speed can, with lowest deceleration, come to a standstill within the horizon* h.

Sensor Function. Subsequently we will use a car dependent sensor function $\Omega_E : \mathbb{I} \times \mathbb{TS} \to \mathbb{R}_+$ which, given a car identifier and a traffic snapshot, provides the length of the corresponding car, as perceived by E. In Section 3 we will give safety proofs for two sensor function instantiations, one delivering the *safety envelope* of all cars (perfect knowledge) and one delivering only the actual *size* of cars. See Fig. 1 for illustration.

Abbreviations. For a given view $V = (L, X, E)$ and a traffic snapshot $\mathcal{TS} = (res, clm, pos, spd, acc)$ we use the following abbreviations:

$$\begin{aligned} I_V &= \{C \mid C \in \mathbb{I} \wedge (\exists l \in L : l \in res(C) \vee l \in clm(C)) \\ &\quad \wedge [pos(C), pos(C) + \Omega_E(C, \mathcal{TS})] \cap X \neq \emptyset\} && (7) \\ res_V &= res \cap (I_V \times \mathcal{P}(L)) && (8) \\ clm_V &= clm \cap (I_V \times \mathcal{P}(L)) && (9) \\ len_V &: \begin{cases} I_V \rightarrow \mathcal{P}(X) \\ C \;\mapsto [pos(C), pos(C) + \Omega_E(C, \mathcal{TS})] \cap X \end{cases} && (10) \end{aligned}$$

The set (7) is constructed in the following way: a car C is in I_V *iff* it occupies (intends to change to) a lane considered in this view and C's occupation of the road as perceived by E intersects with the extension considered in the view. The functions (8) and (9) are restrictions of their counterparts in $\mathcal{TS}$ to the sets of lanes and identifiers considered in this view. The function (10) gives us the part of the motorway car E perceives occupied by a car cut on the edges of the view's extension.

2.3 A Multi-lane Spatial Logic

In this section we will define the syntax and semantics of the spatial logic used in the definition of the lane change controller. Since we are interested in the safety of manoeuvres on a motorway with multiple lanes, we call this logic *multi-lane spatial logic* (MLSL). We employ five different atoms, boolean connectors and first-order quantification. Furthermore we use two *chop* operations. The first chop is denoted by $\frown$ like for interval logics, while the second chop operation is given only by the vertical arrangement of formulae.

Their intuitions are as follows. A formula $\phi_1 \frown \phi_2$ is satisfied by a view V with the extension $[r, t]$, if V can be divided at a point s into two subviews V_1 and V_2, where V_1 has the extension $[r, s]$ and satisfies ϕ_1 and V_2 has the extension $[s, t]$ and satisfies ϕ_2, respectively. A formula $\genfrac{}{}{0pt}{}{\phi_2}{\phi_1}$ is satisfied by V with the lanes l to n, if V can be split along a lane m into two subviews, V_1 with the lanes l to m and V_2 with the lanes $m+1$ to n, where V_i satisfies ϕ_i for $i = 1, 2$.

The set of variables ranging over car identifiers is denoted by Var, with typical elements c, d, u and v. To refer to the car owning the current view, we use a special variable ego $\in$ Var.

Definition 4 (Syntax). *The syntax of the* multi-lane spatial logic MLSL *is given by the following formulae:*

$$\phi ::= true \mid u = v \mid free \mid re(\gamma) \mid cl(\gamma) \mid \phi_1 \wedge \phi_2 \mid \neg\phi_1 \mid \exists v \colon \phi_1 \mid \phi_1 \frown \phi_2 \mid \genfrac{}{}{0pt}{}{\phi_2}{\phi_1}$$

where γ is a variable or a car identifier, and u and v are variables. We denote the set of all MLSL formulae by Φ.

Definition 5 (Valuation and Modification). *A* valuation *is a function* $\nu\colon \mathrm{Var} \to \mathbb{I}$. *For a valuation* ν *we use the overriding notation* $\nu \oplus \{v \mapsto \alpha\}$ *to denote the* modified valuation, *where the value of* v *is modified to* α.

Since the semantics is defined with respect to both views and valuations, we will only consider valuations ν which are *consistent* with the current view $V = (L, X, E)$, which means that we require $\nu(\mathrm{ego}) = E$. In the following definition, observe that we require that the spatial atoms may only hold on a view with exactly one lane and an extension greater than zero. In the semantics of *free*, we abstract from cars visible only at the endpoints of the view.

Definition 6 (Semantics). *In the following, let* u *and* v *be variables and* γ *a variable or a car identifier. The* satisfaction *of formulae with respect to a traffic snapshot* $\mathcal{TS}$, *a view* $V = (L, X, E)$ *with* $L = [l, n]$ *and* $X = [r, t]$, *and a valuation* ν *consistent with* V *is defined inductively as follows:*

$$
\begin{array}{lcl}
\mathcal{TS}, V, \nu \models \mathit{true} & & \text{for all } \mathcal{TS}, V, \nu \\
\mathcal{TS}, V, \nu \models u = v & \Leftrightarrow & \nu(u) = \nu(v) \\
\mathcal{TS}, V, \nu \models \mathit{free} & \Leftrightarrow & |L| = 1 \text{ and } |X| > 0 \text{ and} \\
 & & \forall i \in I_V : \mathit{len}_V(i) \cap (r, t) = \emptyset \\
\mathcal{TS}, V, \nu \models \mathit{re}(\gamma) & \Leftrightarrow & |L| = 1 \text{ and } |X| > 0 \text{ and } \nu(\gamma) \in I_V \text{ and} \\
 & & \mathit{res}_V(\nu(\gamma)) = L \text{ and } X = \mathit{len}_V(\nu(\gamma)) \\
\mathcal{TS}, V, \nu \models \mathit{cl}(\gamma) & \Leftrightarrow & |L| = 1 \text{ and } |X| > 0 \text{ and } \nu(\gamma) \in I_V \text{ and} \\
 & & \mathit{clm}_V(\nu(\gamma)) = L \text{ and } X = \mathit{len}_V(\nu(\gamma)) \\
\mathcal{TS}, V, \nu \models \phi_1 \wedge \phi_2 & \Leftrightarrow & \mathcal{TS}, V, \nu \models \phi_1 \text{ and } \mathcal{TS}, V, \nu \models \phi_2 \\
\mathcal{TS}, V, \nu \models \neg\phi & \Leftrightarrow & \text{not } \mathcal{TS}, V, \nu \models \phi \\
\mathcal{TS}, V, \nu \models \exists v \colon \phi & \Leftrightarrow & \exists \alpha \in I_V : \mathcal{TS}, V, \nu \oplus \{v \mapsto \alpha\} \models \phi \\
\mathcal{TS}, V, \nu \models \phi_1 \frown \phi_2 & \Leftrightarrow & \exists s \colon r \leq s \leq t \text{ and} \\
 & & \mathcal{TS}, V_{[r,s]}, \nu \models \phi_1 \text{ and } \mathcal{TS}, V_{[s,t]}, \nu \models \phi_2 \\
\mathcal{TS}, V, \nu \models \begin{array}{c}\phi_2 \\ \phi_1\end{array} & \Leftrightarrow & \exists m \colon l - 1 \leq m \leq n + 1 \text{ and} \\
 & & \mathcal{TS}, V^{[l,m]}, \nu \models \phi_1 \text{ and } \mathcal{TS}, V^{[m+1,n]}, \nu \models \phi_2
\end{array}
$$

We write $\mathcal{TS} \models \phi$ *if* $\mathcal{TS}, V, \nu \models \phi$ *for all views* V *and consistent valuations* ν.

For the semantics of the vertical chop, we set the interval $[l, m] = \emptyset$ if $l > m$. A view V with an empty set of lanes may only satisfy *true* or an equality formula. We remark that both chop modalities are associative. For the definition of the controller we employ some abbreviations. In addition to the usual definitions of $\vee, \rightarrow, \leftrightarrow$ and $\forall$, we use a single variable or car identifier γ as an abbreviation for $\mathit{re}(\gamma) \vee \mathit{cl}(\gamma)$. Furthermore, we use the notation $\langle \phi \rangle$ for the two-dimensional modality *somewhere* ϕ, defined in terms of both chop operations:

$$\langle \phi \rangle \equiv true \frown \begin{pmatrix} true \\ \phi \\ true \end{pmatrix} \frown true.$$

In the following, the main application of the somewhere modality is to abstract the exact positions on the road from formulae, e.g., to identify overlaps of claims and safety envelopes. If a view V satisfies the formula $\exists c\colon \langle cl(\text{ego}) \wedge re(c)\rangle$, then there is a part on some lane in V occupied by both the claim of the car under consideration and the safety envelope of some car c.

In the safety proof we exploit that somewhere distributes over disjunction:

$$\langle \phi_1 \vee \phi_2 \rangle \equiv \langle \phi_1 \rangle \vee \langle \phi_2 \rangle \,. \tag{11}$$

This equivalence is an immediate consequence of the semantics.

3 Controllers

We now present two lane-change controllers, one with perfect knowledge of the safety envelopes (covering the necessary braking distances) of neighbouring cars and one which takes only the physical size of the neighbouring cars into account.

The controllers are specified as *timed automata* [12] with clocks ranging over $\mathbb{R}$ and data variables ranging over $\mathbb{L}$ and $\mathbb{I}$. The semantics is a transition system, where a configuration $\mathcal{C}$ consists of a traffic snapshot $\mathcal{TS}$, the standard view V of a car, a valuation ν (also of clocks and data variables), and the current state q of the controller, i.e. $\mathcal{C} = (\mathcal{TS}, V, \nu, q)$. To restrict the transitions which are allowed in a lane-change manoeuvre, like the creation of new claims and the extension and shrinking of reservations, suitable MLSL formulae will appear in transition guards and state invariants. We take care that none of our controllers introduces a timelock, which would prevent time from progressing unboundedly.

Timed automata working in parallel can communicate with each other via *broadcast channels* as in UPPAAL [13]. Using a CSP-style notation [14], sending a value val over a channel p is denoted by $p!val$; receiving a value over p and binding it to a variable c appearing free in a guard ϕ is denoted by $p?c\colon \phi$. Formally, $\mathcal{TS}, V, \nu \models p?c\colon \phi$ *iff* $\mathcal{TS}, V, \nu \oplus \{c \mapsto val\} \models \phi$, where val is the value simultaneously sent via $p!val$ by another automaton. A message sent by a car C is broadcast to all cars within the extension of the standard view of C.

3.1 Changing Lanes with Perfect Knowledge

Let us first assume that every car can perceive the full extension of claims and reservations of all cars within its view. In other words, every car has *perfect knowledge* of the status of the road within its view. This assumption is formalised through the sensor function Ω_E, which defines the extension of the cars seen by the owner E of a view. Putting $\Omega_E(I, \mathcal{TS}) = se(I, \mathcal{TS})$ models that the sensors return the whole safety envelope for all cars. This implies that a car E perceives a car C as soon as C's safety envelope enters the view of E.

Intuitively, a car C on lane n, in the following called the *actor*, can claim a space on a target lane m next to n to start the manoeuvre. This does not yet imply that C actually changes the lane. It corresponds to setting the direction indicator to prepare for a lane change. The goal of the actor is to safely convert its claim into a reservation of m. If the space claimed by the actor is already occupied or claimed by another car (*potential collision check*), C removes its claim and continues driving on its current lane. Even though we assume instantaneous transitions, we allow time to pass up to a certain time bound to between claiming and reserving a lane. If no potential collision occurs, the actor communicates its new reservation and starts its manoeuvre. Since we abstract from the exact form of changing the lane, we just assume that the manoeuvre takes at most t_{lc} time to finish. Finally, the actor shrinks its reservation to solely m.

This intuition is formalised by the lane-change controller LCP in Fig. 2. At the initial state q_0, we assume that the car has reserved exactly one lane, which is saved in the variable n. Furthermore, we employ an auxiliary variable l to store the lane the actor wants to change to. The *collision check* cc expresses the disjointness of the actor's reservation and the reservations of all other cars:

$$cc \equiv \neg\exists c\colon c \neq \text{ego} \wedge \langle re(\text{ego}) \wedge re(c)\rangle\,,$$

the *potential collision check* $pc(c)$ for a car c expresses the overlapping of the actor's claim with (the reservation or claim of) c:

$$pc(c) \equiv c \neq \text{ego} \wedge \langle cl(\text{ego}) \wedge c\rangle\,.$$

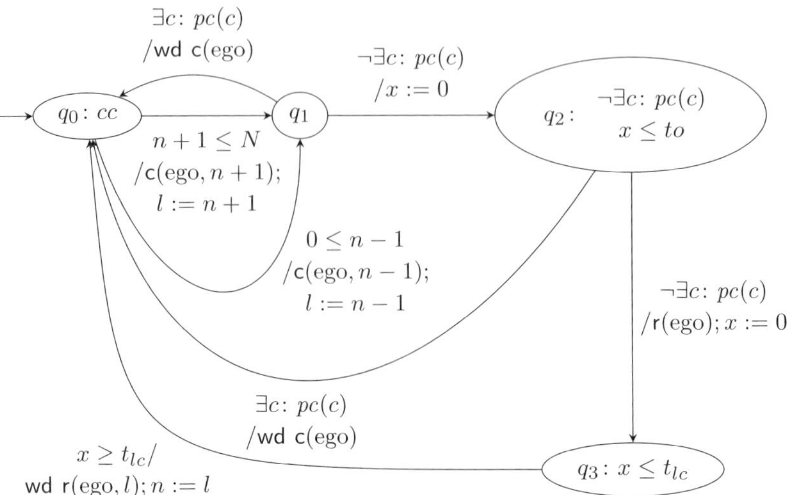

Fig. 2. Controller LCP for the Lane-Change Manoeuvre with Perfect Knowledge

3.2 A More Realistic Approach for Changing Lanes

The assumption that every car can perceive every safety envelope within its view is very strong. In this section, we define a controller which accomplishes a lane-change manoeuvre with much less information: each car knows only the size of the other cars, while it still knows its own safety envelope. Hence the sensor function for a view $V = (L, X, E)$ is defined conditionally by

$$\Omega_E(I, \mathcal{TS}) \equiv \mathsf{if}\ I = E\ \mathsf{then}\ se(I, \mathcal{TS})\ \mathsf{else}\ size(I)\ \mathsf{fi}.$$

In this setting, the potential collision check is not sufficient for the safety of the manoeuvre, since the actor cannot know whether the safety envelope of a car on the lane the actor wants to occupy overlaps with its own safety envelope. Our approach to overcome this problem is the definition of a *helper controller* HC (Fig. 4) implemented in addition to the lane-change controller LC (Fig. 3).

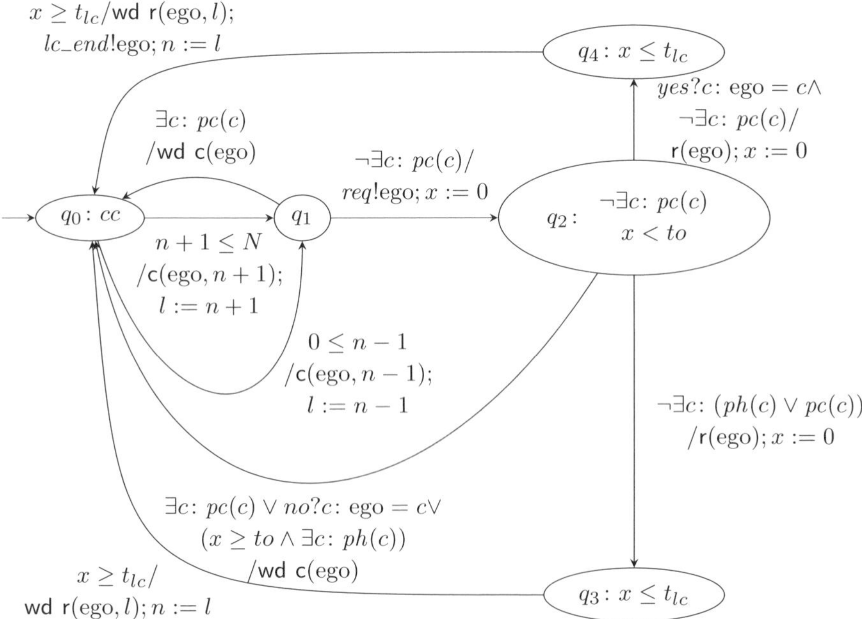

Fig. 3. Controller LC for the Lane-Change Manoeuvre with a Helper Car

The idea of the lane-change manoeuvre with the help of these controllers is similar to the previously described manoeuvre. The actor sets a claim and checks whether this claim overlaps with already existing claims and reservations. However, since the actor can perceive via $re(c)$ only the physical size of other cars c and not the whole of their safety envelopes, it cannot know whether its claim overlaps with a car driving behind the actor on the target lane. Hence the

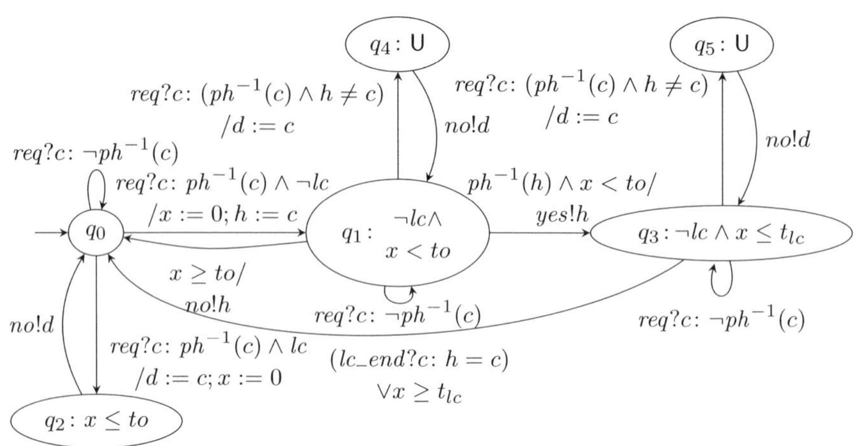

Fig. 4. Controller HC for Helper Car

actor broadcasts a request *req* to find a potential helper. Such a *helper car* has to fulfill three conditions. It has to be on the target lane m, it has to be behind the actor, and it must not already be involved in a lane-change manoeuvre.

The formula to identify such a car from the viewpoint of the actor is called *potential helper check*:

$$ph(c) \equiv \langle re(c) \frown free \frown cl(\text{ego})\rangle \,.$$

If a such helper car is approached by a broadcast request *req* from the actor, its controller HC checks for disjointness of its own reservation and the actor's claim, using the *inverse potential helper check* defined by

$$ph^{-1}(c) \equiv \langle re(\text{ego}) \frown free \frown cl(c)\rangle \,,$$

and that it is not performing a lane-change manoeuvre, expressed by the formula

$$lc \equiv \left\langle \begin{matrix} \text{ego} \\ \text{ego} \end{matrix} \right\rangle .$$

If these two conditions are satisfied, it responds with the acknowledgment *yes*. Afterwards, it ensures that no other car may enter the lane in between the helper and the actor. This is done in the urgent states [13] q_4 and q_5 of the controller HC. Then, the actor may safely change the lane by extending its reserved space to lane m and remove its claim. Otherwise, if no helper is available, the actor waits for a certain time *to* without getting any response. Afterwards, it has to check, whether a car entered its view on lane m, before possibly extending its reservation to lane m. If m is free within the actor's horizon, the reservation gets extended, otherwise the actor removes its claim and returns to the initial state, since it cannot guarantee the disjointness of its claim and the reservation of the new car. After successfully changing the lane, the actor removes its reservation of lane n and drives solely on lane m.

4 Safety Proof

The desired safety property is that at any moment the spaces reserved by different cars are disjoint. To express this property we consider the formula

$$Safe \equiv \forall c, d : c \neq d \Rightarrow \neg \langle re(c) \wedge re(d) \rangle \,,$$

which states that in each lane any two different cars have disjoint reserved spaces. The quantification over lanes arises implicitly by the negation of the somewhere modality in *Safe*. We call a traffic snapshot $\mathcal{TS}$ *safe* if $\mathcal{TS} \models Safe$ holds. The safety property depends on the following three assumptions.

Assumption A1. There is an *initial safe* traffic snapshot $\mathcal{TS}_0$.

Assumption A2. Every car C is equipped with a *distance controller* that keeps the safety property invariant under time and acceleration transitions, i.e., for every transition $\mathcal{TS} \xrightarrow{t} \mathcal{TS}'$ and $\mathcal{TS} \xrightarrow{\mathsf{acc}(C,a)} \mathcal{TS}'$ if $\mathcal{TS}$ is safe also $\mathcal{TS}'$ is safe.

Informally, this means that the distance controller admits a positive acceleration of C only if the space ahead permits this. Also, if the car ahead is slowing down, the distance controller has to initiate braking (with negative acceleration) of C to reduce the extension of its reservation (the safety envelope).

Assumption A3. Every car is equipped with a controller LCP as in Fig. 2.

Then the safety property is formalised by the following theorem.

Theorem 1 (Safety of LCP). *Suppose that the assumptions* A1–3 *hold. Then every traffic snapshot* $\mathcal{TS}$ *that is reachable from* $\mathcal{TS}_0$ *by time and acceleration transitions and transitions allowed by the controller LCP in Fig. 2 is safe.*

Proof. It suffices to prove safety from the perspective of each car, i.e., that there is no other car with intersecting reserved space. Formally, we fix an arbitrary car E and show that for all traffic snapshots $\mathcal{TS}$ reachable from $\mathcal{TS}_0$, all views V of E, and all valuations with $\nu(\text{ego}) = E$:

$$\mathcal{TS}, V, \nu \models Safe', \text{ where } Safe' \equiv \neg\exists\, c \neq \text{ego} \wedge \langle re(\text{ego}) \wedge re(c) \rangle \,. \tag{12}$$

We proceed by induction on the number k of transitions needed to reach $\mathcal{TS}$ from $\mathcal{TS}_0$.

Induction basis: $k = 0$. Then $\mathcal{TS} = \mathcal{TS}_0$ and (12) holds by A1.

Induction step: $k \to k + 1$. Consider some $\mathcal{TS}_1$ that is reachable from $\mathcal{TS}_0$ by k transitions and thus satisfy (12) by induction hypothesis. Let $\mathcal{TS}$ result from $\mathcal{TS}_1$ by one further transition, which we now examine.

For a transition $\mathcal{TS}_1 \xrightarrow{t} \mathcal{TS}$ or $\mathcal{TS}_1 \xrightarrow{\mathsf{acc}(C,a)} \mathcal{TS}$ of any car C property (12) holds for $\mathcal{TS}$ by A2. Of all other transitions allowed by the LCP controller of E, only a reservation transition $\mathcal{TS}_1 \xrightarrow{\mathsf{r}(E)} \mathcal{TS}$ could possibly violate property (12). In the LCP controller of E shown in Fig. 2 the only reservation transition starts in state q_2. This state satisfies the invariant

$$\neg\exists\, c : c \neq \text{ego} \wedge \langle cl(\text{ego}) \wedge c \rangle \,,$$

which implies $\neg\exists c : c \neq \text{ego} \wedge \langle cl(\text{ego}) \wedge re(c)\rangle$. By taking the induction hypothesis (12) for $\mathcal{TS}_1$ into account, we thus have

$$\begin{aligned}\mathcal{TS}_1, V, \nu \models \quad & \neg\exists c : c \neq \text{ego} \wedge \langle cl(\text{ego}) \wedge re(c)\rangle \\ & \wedge \neg\exists c : c \neq \text{ego} \wedge \langle re(\text{ego}) \wedge re(c)\rangle\,.\end{aligned}$$

We transform this formula:

$$\begin{aligned} & (\neg\exists c : c \neq \text{ego} \wedge \langle cl(\text{ego}) \wedge re(c)\rangle) \wedge (\neg\exists c : c \neq \text{ego} \wedge \langle re(\text{ego}) \wedge re(c)\rangle) \\ \leftrightarrow\ & \neg\exists c : (c \neq \text{ego} \wedge \langle cl(\text{ego}) \wedge re(c)\rangle) \vee (c \neq \text{ego} \wedge \langle re(\text{ego}) \wedge re(c)\rangle) \\ \leftrightarrow\ & \neg\exists c : c \neq \text{ego} \wedge (\langle cl(\text{ego}) \wedge re(c)\rangle \vee \langle re(\text{ego}) \wedge re(c)\rangle) \\ \leftrightarrow\ & \{\text{somewhere distributes over disjunction: see (11)}\} \\ & \neg\exists c : c \neq \text{ego} \wedge \langle (cl(\text{ego}) \wedge re(c)) \vee (re(\text{ego}) \wedge re(c))\rangle \\ \leftrightarrow\ & \neg\exists c : c \neq \text{ego} \wedge \langle (cl(\text{ego}) \vee re(\text{ego})) \wedge re(c)\rangle\,. \end{aligned}$$

Applying the Reservation Lemma 1 to the latter formula yields

$$\mathcal{TS}, V, \nu \models \neg\exists c : c \neq \text{ego} \wedge \langle re(\text{ego}) \wedge re(c)\rangle\,,$$

which shows that (12) holds for $\mathcal{TS}$. □

We now connect formulae about reservations with the fact, that a newly created reservation occupies the same space as a previous claim (A proof is contained in the long version of this paper [15]).

Lemma 1 (Reservation). *Consider a reservation transition* $\mathcal{TS} \xrightarrow{\mathsf{r}(C)} \mathcal{TS}'$ *and an MLSL formula* ϕ' *not containing* $cl(\gamma)$ *as a subformula. Let* ϕ *result from* ϕ' *by replacing every occurrence of* $re(\gamma)$ *by* $re(\gamma) \vee cl(\gamma)$. *Then for all views* $V = (L, X, E)$ *with* $C \in I_V$ *and valuations* ν *with* $\nu(\gamma) = C$ *the following holds:*

$$\mathcal{TS}, V, \nu \models \phi \;\text{ if and only if }\; \mathcal{TS}', V, \nu \models \phi'.$$

4.1 Safety Proof for Changing Lanes with Help

As for the controller LCP, we want to prove that the property *Safe* is an invariant of the allowed transitions, but now the with assumption A3 modified as follows:

Assumption A3. Every car is equipped with the controllers LC as in Fig. 3 and HC of Fig. 4 running in parallel.

Since this scenario incorporates communication between two cars, the helper and the actor, we have to assume that a car changing a lane can perceive all cars whose safety envelopes reach up to its position.

Assumption A4. The horizon h of the standard view (Def. 3) is at least the length of the safety envelope of the fastest car with the smallest braking force.

Theorem 2 (Safety of LC and HC). *Suppose that the assumptions* A1–4 *hold. Then every traffic snapshot* $\mathcal{TS}$ *that is reachable from* $\mathcal{TS}_0$ *by time and acceleration transitions and transitions allowed by the controller LC in Fig. 3 and the helper controller HC in Fig. 4 is safe.*

Proof. We refine the proof of Theorem 1. Fix an arbitrary car E and show that for all traffic snapshots $\mathcal{TS}$ reachable from $\mathcal{TS}_0$, all helper cars H, standard views V of E and V_H of H, and valuations ν and ν' consistent with the respective views: $\mathcal{TS}, V, \nu \models \mathit{Safe}'$ and $\mathcal{TS}, V_H, \nu' \models \mathit{Safe}'$. Again, we proceed by induction on the number k of transitions needed to reach $\mathcal{TS}$ from $\mathcal{TS}_0$.

Induction basis: $k = 0$. Then $\mathcal{TS} = \mathcal{TS}_0$ and (12) holds by A1.

Induction step: $k \to k+1$. Consider some $\mathcal{TS}_1$ that is reachable from $\mathcal{TS}_0$ by k transitions and thus satisfy (12) by induction hypothesis. Let $\mathcal{TS}$ result from $\mathcal{TS}_1$ by one further transition, which we now examine. As in the proof of Theorem 1, the only possibly dangerous transition is a reservation transition $\mathcal{TS}_1 \xrightarrow{\mathsf{r}(E)} \mathcal{TS}$. In the controller LC of car E shown in Fig. 3 there are two such transitions, both starting in state q_2. Observe that in q_2, whenever there is a potential collision the manoeuvre is aborted. Hence, if a car D creates a new claim overlapping with E's claim, D or E withdraws its claim. Now, consider the transition from q_2 to q_3. By A4 and since the safety envelope starts at the position of its car, we may proceed as in the proof of Theorem 1.

Next, consider the transition from q_2 to q_4. We have to show that E's claim does not overlap with the reservation of the helper H. Let V_H be the standard view of H and ν' be a valuation consistent with V_H. Since the controller HC sends to E the message *yes*!E, it has taken the transition with the guard $ph^{-1}(E)$, exiting state q_1 of HC, so $\mathcal{TS}_1, V_H, \nu' \models \langle re(\text{ego}) \frown \mathit{free} \frown cl(E)\rangle$.

Since the state q_1 of HC has the invariant lc, the subformula *free* is satisfied by a subview with an extension greater than zero, and claims of E cannot overlap with existing reservations of E, this implies

$$\mathcal{TS}_1, V_H, \nu' \models \neg \langle re(\text{ego}) \wedge (cl(E) \vee re(E))\rangle .$$

Since $\nu'(E) = E$, we can apply the Reservation Lemma 1, which yields

$$\mathcal{TS}, V_H, \nu' \models \neg \langle re(\text{ego}) \wedge re(E)\rangle .$$

□

5 Conclusion

The novelty in our paper is the identification of a level of abstraction that enables a purely spatial reasoning on safety. We proved safety for arbitrarily many cars on the motorway locally, by considering at most two cars at a time.

More on related work. Manoeuvres of cars have been extensively studied in the California PATH (Partners for Advanced Transit and Highways) project [16], which aimed at an Automated Highway System (AHS) to increase safety and throughput on highways. The project introduced the concept of a *platoon*, a tightly spaced convoy of cars driving on a motorway at a relatively high speed.

In Hsu et al. [17] the architecture of the AHS system is outlined, and at the platoon layer three manoeuvres are investigated: merge and split of platoons as well as lane change of free traffic agents, i.e., single cars. For these manoeuvres protocols are modelled as communicating finite state machines and tested within the automata-based tool COSPAN by R. Kurshan. The protocol for lane change does not take all possible traffic scenarios on neighbouring lanes into account. For example, the scenario where cars are driving on both the target lane and the lane next to it is not considered.

In Lygeros et al. [1] the analysis of [17] is refined by taking the hybrid controllers as the model. Sufficient conditions on the car dynamics are established for showing safety of the AHS system at the coordination layer (for communication and cooperation between cars) and the regulation layer (for hybrid controllers performing the traffic manoeuvres). The lane change manoeuvre is explicitly investigated in a multi-lane safety theorem. However, its proof, based on an induction argument on the number of cars, is only outlined. Moreover, the possible scenarios of lane change in dense traffic are only partially covered. The scenario where two cars wish to change to a common target lane is not taken into account.

The safety problem has also been studied for railway networks, which are simpler to handle because the movements of trains are more constrained than those of cars. Haxthausen and Peleska [18] give manual safety proof for trains driving in an arbitrary railway network. Faber et al. [19] provide an automatic verification of safety properties in railway networks.

Future work. On the application side we want to pursue an extension of the scope of our work. For example, we intend to study the scenarios of urban traffic as in [3]. Also, we would like to study variations of the assumptions made in our safety proofs. On the foundational side we would like to investigate the connection of MLSL with more traditional spatial logics based on topological models [20] and its meta properties like decidability. Here proof ideas from [21] might be helpful. This leads to question of automatic verification of the safety properties. Here the approach of [19] could be considered.

The semantics of MLSL may be extended to include a length measurement. Let ϕ^θ denote that ϕ holds for a length θ, where θ is a first-order term denoting a real value. The semantics on p. 410 is extended by

$$\mathcal{TS}, V, \nu \models \phi^\theta \qquad\qquad \Leftrightarrow \quad \mathcal{TS}, V, \nu \models \phi \text{ and } |X| = \nu(\theta).$$

The initial definition of MLSL semantics contained this case, but to our own surprise, we did not make use of this measurement in the controllers and the safety proofs, respectively. This is due to the fact that we reason at a very abstract level, and that differences in lengths are only taken care of in the assumptions.

To link our work to hybrid systems, a refinement of the spatial reasoning in this paper to the car dynamics is of interest. There we could benefit from the approaches in [5,6,7,4] and expect that length measurements are needed.

References

1. Lygeros, J., Godbole, D.N., Sastry, S.S.: Verified hybrid controllers for automated vehicles. IEEE Transactions on Automatic Control 43, 522–539 (1998)
2. Jula, H., Kosmatopoulos, E.B., Ioannou, P.A.: Collision avoidance analysis for lane changing and merging. Technical Report UCB-ITS-PRR-99-13, California Partners for Advanced Transit and Highways (PATH), Univ. of California at Berkeley (1999)

3. Werling, M., Gindele, T., Jagszent, D., Gröll, L.: A robust algorithm for handling traffic in urban scenarios. In: Proc. IEEE Intelligent Vehicles Symposium, Eindhoven, The Netherlands, pp. 168–173 (2008)
4. Damm, W., Hungar, H., Olderog, E.R.: Verification of cooperating traffic agents. International Journal of Control 79, 395–421 (2006)
5. Moor, T., Raisch, J., O'Young, S.: Discrete supervisory control of hybrid systems based on l-complete approximations. Discrete Event Dynamic Systems 12, 83–107 (2002)
6. Moor, T., Raisch, J., Davoren, J.: Admissiblity criteria for a hierarchical design of hybrid systems. In: Proc. IFAD Conf. on Analysis and Design of Hybrid Systems, St. Malo, France, pp. 389–394 (2003)
7. Habets, L.C.G.J.M., Collins, P., van Schuppen, J.: Reachability and control synthesis for piecewise-affine hybrid systems on simplices. IEEE Transactions on Automatic Control 51, 938–948 (2006)
8. Moszkowski, B.: A temporal logic for multilevel reasoning about hardware. Computer 18, 10–19 (1985)
9. Zhou, C., Hoare, C., Ravn, A.: A calculus of durations. Information Processing Letters 40, 269–276 (1991)
10. Schäfer, A.: A Calculus for Shapes in Time and Space. In: Liu, Z., Araki, K. (eds.) ICTAC 2004. LNCS, vol. 3407, pp. 463–477. Springer, Heidelberg (2005)
11. Woodcock, J., Davies, J.: Using Z – Specification, Refinement, and Proof. Prentice-Hall, Englewood Cliffs (1996)
12. Alur, R., Dill, D.L.: A theory of timed automata. TCS 126, 183–235 (1994)
13. Behrmann, G., David, A., Larsen, K.G.: A tutorial on UPPAAL. In: Bernardo, M., Corradini, F. (eds.) SFM-RT 2004. LNCS, vol. 3185, pp. 200–236. Springer, Heidelberg (2004)
14. Hoare, C.A.R.: Communicating sequential processes. CACM 21, 666–677 (1978)
15. Hilscher, M., Linker, S., Olderog, E.R., Ravn, A.P.: An abstract model for proving safety of multi-lane traffic maenoeuvres. Report 79, SFB/TR 14 AVACS (2011); ISSN: 1860-9821, avacs.org
16. Varaija, P.: Smart cars on smart roads: problems of control. IEEE Transactions on Automatic Control AC-38, 195–207 (1993)
17. Hsu, A., Eskafi, F., Sachs, S., Varaija, P.: Protocol design for an automated highway system. Discrete Event Dynamic Systems 2, 183–206 (1994)
18. Haxthausen, A.E., Peleska, J.: Formal development and verification of a distributed railway control system. IEEE Trans. on Software Engineering 26, 687–701 (2000)
19. Faber, J., Ihlemann, C., Jacobs, S., Sofronie-Stokkermans, V.: Automatic Verification of Parametric Specifications with Complex Topologies. In: Méry, D., Merz, S. (eds.) IFM 2010. LNCS, vol. 6396, pp. 152–167. Springer, Heidelberg (2010)
20. van Benthem, J., Bezhanishvili, G.: Modal logics of space. In: Aiello, M., Pratt-Hartmann, I., Benthem, J. (eds.) Handbook of Spatial Logics, pp. 217–298. Springer, Heidelberg (2007)
21. Schäfer, A.: Axiomatisation and decidability of multi-dimensional duration calculus. Information and Computation 205, 25–64 (2007)

Formal Derivation of a Distributed Program in Event B

Alexei Iliasov[1], Linas Laibinis[2], Elena Troubitsyna[2], and Alexander Romanovsky[1]

[1] Newcastle University, UK
[2] Åbo Akademi University, Finland
{alexei.iliasov,alexander.romanovsky}@ncl.ac.uk,
{linas.laibinis,elena.troubitsyna}@abo.fi

Abstract. Achieving high dependability of distributed systems remains a major challenge due to complexity arising from concurrency and communication. There are a number of formal approaches to verification of properties of distributed algorithms. However, there is still a lack of methods that enable a transition from a verified formal model of communication to a program that faithfully implements it. In this paper we aim at bridging this gap by proposing a state-based formal approach to correct-by-construction development of distributed programs. In our approach we take a systems view, i.e., formally model not only application but also its environment – the middleware that supports it. We decompose such an integrated specification to obtain the distributed program that should be deployed on the targeted network infrastructure. To illustrate our approach, we present a development of a distributed leader election protocol.

1 Introduction

Development of distributed systems remains one of the more challenging engineering tasks. The complexity caused by concurrency and communication requires sophisticated techniques for designing distributed systems and verifying their correctness. Active research in this area has resulted in a large variety of distributed protocols and approaches for their verification. However, these techniques emphasise the creation of a mathematical model establishing algorithm properties and per se do not provide an unambiguous recipe on how to develop a distributed program that would correctly implement a desired algorithm. Moreover, these techniques often ignore the impact of deploying the developed software on a particular network infrastructure. In this paper we present a complete formal development of a distributed protocol (a fairly common variation of leader election [9]) and demonstrate how state-based modelling and refinement help to alleviate these problems.

The main technique for mastering system complexity is abstraction and decomposition. Our development starts from creating an abstract centralised system specification. In a chain of correctness preserving refinement steps we build

S. Qin and Z. Qiu (Eds.): ICFEM 2011, LNCS 6991, pp. 420–436, 2011.

```
MACHINE M
  SEES Context
  VARIABLES v
  INVARIANT Inv(c, s, v)
  INITIALISATION ...
  EVENTS
    E1 = any vl where g(c, s, vl, v) then S(c, s, vl, v, v') end
    ...
END
```

Fig. 1. Structure of Event B model

the details of the distributed algorithm and communication scheme. Our modelling adopts a systems approach: the specification defines not only the behaviour and properties of the algorithm but also the essential assumptions about the network infrastructure. The final step of our refinement chain is decomposition. We rely on the modularisation extension of Event B [2] to decompose the specification into separate modules representing the communicating processes and the middleware. The obtained specification of processes may be further refined into runnable specifications and treated as programs. Alternatively, a translation may be done into a programming language. Our formal development ensures that the resulting distributed program will behave correctly when deployed on the middleware that satisfies the assumptions explicitly stated in the formal model.

2 Background

We start by briefly describing our development framework. The Event B formalism [2,16] is a specialisation of the B Method [1], a state-based formal approach that promotes the correct-by-construction development paradigm and formal verification by theorem proving. Event B enables modelling of event-based (reactive) systems by incorporating the ideas of the Action Systems formalism [4] into the B Method. Event B is actively used within the FP7 ICT project DEPLOY [12] to develop dependable systems from various domains.

2.1 Modelling and Refinement in Event B

The Event B development starts from creating an abstract system specification. The general form of an Event B model is shown in Figure 1. Such a model encapsulates a local state (program variables) and provides operations on the state. The actions (called *events*) are defined by a list of new local variables (parameters) vl, a state predicate g called *event guard*, and a next-state relation S called *substitution* (see the **EVENTS** section in Figure 1). Event parameters and guards may be sometimes absent leading to the respective syntactic shortcuts starting with keywords **when** and **begin**.

The event guard g defines the condition or a set of states when the event is *enabled*. The relation S is expressed as either a deterministic or non-deterministic assignment to the model variables. One form of a non-deterministic assignment used in the paper is the selection of a value from a set expression, written as $v :\in Set$, where Set is an non-empty set of possible values.

The **INVARIANT** clause contains the properties of the system (expressed as state predicates) that should be preserved during system execution. These define the *safe states* of a system. In order for a model to be consistent, invariant preservation should be formally demonstrated (i.e., proved). Data types s, constants c and relevant axioms are defined in a separate component called *context* (clause **SEES** in Figure 1).

The cornerstone of the Event B method is *refinement* – the process of transforming an abstract specification by gradually introducing implementation details while preserving correctness. It allows us to transition from an abstract, non-deterministic model to a detailed, deterministic program implementing a system. Since Event B models are state-based, data refinement – a technique of reinterpreting a model using different state models – is at the core of most refinement proofs. For a refinement step to be valid, every possible execution of a refined machine must correspond to some execution step of its abstract machine.

The consistency of Event B models, i.e., verification of well-formedness and invariant preservation as well as correctness of refinement steps, should be formally demonstrated by discharging relevant *proof obligations*, which collectively define the *proof semantics* of a model [2]. The Rodin platform [18], a tool supporting Event B, is an integrated environment that automatically generates necessary proof obligations and manages a collection of automated provers that would try to autonomously discharge the generated theorems. At times a user intervention would be necessary to guide the provers or construct a complete proof in an interactive proving environment. The level of automation in proving is high enough to make realistic development practical. On average, the rate of assisted proofs is about 20%, of which only a small percentage goes beyond giving one or two hints to the provers.

2.2 Modelling Modular Systems in Event B

Recently the Event B language and tool support have been extended with a possibility to define modules [11,17] – components containing groups of callable atomic operations. Modules can have their own (external and internal) state and the invariant properties. The important characteristic of modules is that they can be developed separately and, when needed, composed with the main system.

A module description consists of two parts – *module interface* and *module body*. Let M be a module. A module interface MI is a separate Event B component. It allows the user of module M to invoke its operations and observe the external variables of M without having to inspect the module implementation details. MI consists of external module variables w, constants c, sets s, the external module invariant $M\_Inv(c, s, w)$, and a collection of module operations, characterised by their pre- and postconditions, as shown below.

INTERFACE MI
SEES $MI\_Context$
VARIABLES w
INVARIANT $M\_Inv(c, s, w)$
INITIALISATION ...
PROCESS
PE_1 = **any** vl **where** $g(c, s, vl, w)$ **then** $S(c, s, vl, w, w')$ **end**
...
OPERATIONS
O_1 = **any** p **pre** $Pre(c, s, vl, w)$ **post** $Post(c, s, vl, w, w')$ **end**
...
END

Fig. 2. Interface Component

The primed variables in the operation postcondition stand for the final variable values after operation execution. If some primed variables are absent, this means that the corresponding variables are unchanged by an operation.

In addition, a module interface description may contain a group of standard Event B events under the **PROCESS** clause. These events model autonomous module thread of control, expressed in terms of their effect on the external module variables. In other words, the module process describes how the module external variables may change between operation calls.

A module development starts with the design of an interface. Once an interface is defined, it cannot be altered in any manner. This ensures that a module body may be constructed independently from the model relying on the interface of the module. A module body is an Event B machine. It implements the interface by providing the concrete behaviour for each of the interface operations. The interface process specification may be further refined like a normal subset of Event B events. A set of additional proof obligations are generated to guarantee that an operation has a suitable implementation in the implementing machine.

When module M is imported into another Event B machine, the importing machine may invoke the operations of M and access (read) the external (interface) variables of M. To make a specification of a module generic, in $MI\_Context$ we can define some constants and sets (types) as parameters. Their properties then define the constraints to be verified when a module is instantiated.

Next we present a formal development of a distributed system that illustrates the various aspects of modelling and refinement in Event B.

3 Modelling of a Leader Election Protocol

The main goal of this paper is to present an entire formal development of a distributed system in Event B. The system implements a leader election protocol, i.e., its purpose is to elect a single leader among all the participating processes. The solution is inspired by the bully algorithm [9]. In its simple interpretation the algorithm ensures that the process with a largest id wins from all the processes willing to become a leader.

Our development strategy is as follows. The development starts from a trivial high-level specification that "magically" elects the leader. In a number of steps we obtain a model of a centralised leader election algorithm. Then we gradually decentralise this model by refining its data structure and behaviour. Several refinement steps aim at decoupling the data structures of the individual processes and introducing the required communication mechanism.

In this last, more challenging refinement step, we decompose the specification to separate the model of communication environment (middleware) from the models of constituent processes. To achieve this, we rely on the modularisation extension of Event B. Finally, we show how the process specifications may be converted into runnable code. Due to a space limit we do not present the complete specifications produced at each refinement step. Instead we describe the more interesting aspects of each particular model. The complete Event B development is available at [14].

3.1 Abstract Model of Leader Election

Abstract Specification. Our development starts with creating an abstract model that defines a single variable *leader* and one-shot leader election abstraction. Assume that the system has n processes and the process ids are from $1..n$. The leader election protocol is made of a single event that atomically selects a new leader value:

$$elect = \textbf{any}\ nl\ \textbf{where}\ nl \in 1..n\ \textbf{then}\ leader := nl\ \textbf{end}$$

First Refinement. In the first refinement step we start to introduce some localisation properties of the algorithm. Each process is able to decide (vote) on whether it wants to become a new leader or not. Such a decision is made by a process independently of other processes and is recorded in a global vector of decisions: $decision : 1..n \mathrel{+\!\!\!\rightarrow} 0..n$.

When a process votes, it puts into the decision vector either its id (process identifier), indicating that it is willing to be a new leader, or 0, indicating the opposite: $\forall i \cdot i \in dom(decision) \Rightarrow decision(i) \in \{0, i\}$.

To determine the leader among the set of willing processes, we compare their "bully" id's. A new leader is a process with the maximal id among the processes that are willing to be leaders. Assuming the decision vector is complete, the new leader is the process with the largest id, i.e., $max(ran(decision))$, where ran is the function range operator.

Unfortunately, all the processes may refuse being a leader and then the election has to be restarted. This means that a protocol round is potentially divergent. To avoid this, we exclude the situation when every process decides not to be a leader. This is achieved by requiring that any process willing to initiate the protocol is also committing to be a leader. The corresponding invariant property states that, whenever the decision vector is not empty, there is a process willing to be a new leader: $card(decision) \geq 1 \Rightarrow max(ran(decision)) \in 1..n$.

This invariant guarantees that after a voting round, when the decision vector has records for all the processes, there is a new leader. The protocol may be initiated by any process that has not yet voted (event *initiate*). As soon as a new election is initiated, i.e., $dom(decision) \neq \varnothing$, the remaining processes are free to choose or decline to be a new leader (event *decide*).

$initiate =$ **any** idx **where**
$\quad idx \in 1 \,..\, n$
$\quad idx \notin dom(decision)$
then
$\quad decision(idx) := idx$
end

$decide =$ **any** idx, d **where**
$\quad idx \in 1 \,..\, n$
$\quad idx \notin dom(decision)$
$\quad d \in \{idx, 0\}$
$\quad decision \neq \varnothing$
then
$\quad decision(idx) := d$
end

Even after the protocol has been initiated, the processes can still continue to "initiate" the election. This effectively corresponds to expressing willingness to become a new leader. The abstract event elect is now refined by the following a deterministic event, computing the new leader id from the vector of process decisions.

$elect =$ **when** $dom(decision) = 1 \,..\, n$ **then** $leader := max(ran(decision))$ **end**

3.2 Decentralising Leader Election

Second Refinement. After the first refinement the leader election is modelled in a centralised way – processes are able to access the global decision vector *decision*. It yields a simple model but prevents a distributed implementation. Our next refinement step aims at decentralising the model (and thus the localisation of model state). For each process i, we introduce $other(i)$ – a local, process-specific version of the global decision vector: $other \in 1 \,..\, n \rightarrow \mathbb{P}(0 \,..\, n)$.

Based on the information contained in $other(i)$, the process i should be able compute an overall leader without consulting the global vector *decision*. In the invariant we postulate that a local knowledge of a process is a part of the global decision vector: $\forall i \cdot i \in 1 \,..\, n \Rightarrow other(i) \subseteq ran(\{i\} \lhd decision)$, where $\lhd$ is the domain subtraction operator. At the same time, $other(i)$ does not include the process decision stored separately.

To populate their local versions of the decision vector, the processes have to communicate between each other. Once the process has voted, it starts communicating its vote to other processes. Symmetrically, a process populates its local knowledge by receiving messages from the other processes. As a simple model of communication, for each process i, we introduce the set $recv(i)$ – a set of the processes from which it has received their vote messages, and the set $pending(i)$ – a set of the processes that it has committed to communicate its decision to. A process must communicate its decision to all other processes.

We do not consider here process and communication failures. Process crashes and message loss do not affect the correctness properties but make it impossible to demonstrate the progress (convergence) of the protocol (unless, of course, there is an upper bound on the number of process and message failures). We prefer to produce a stronger, convergent model first and then consider a case where individual communications steps cannot be proven convergent due to potentially infinite retransmission attempts recovering from lost messages. Our intention is to deal with process and communication failures in the model of the middleware introduced after the decomposition step.

In the following invariant we define the properties of our communication scheme. The messages committed by one process to be sent are not yet received by another process:

$$\forall i, j \cdot i \in 1 \mathinner{..} n \land j \in 1 \mathinner{..} n \Rightarrow (i \in pending(j) \Rightarrow j \notin recv(i))$$

Moreover, for each process, the local version of the decision vector $other(i)$ is an exact slice of the global decision vector, formed from the received messages:

$$\forall i \cdot i \in 1 \mathinner{..} n \Rightarrow decision[recv(i)] = other(i)$$

where [...] is the relational image operator.

The behavioural part of the communication model comprises two new events: send and receive. The event send models sending a decision message to some destination process to. The event is potentially divergent. It will be made convergent in the next refinement step. The event receive models the reception of a decision message. It uses the message to update the local knowledge ($other(to)$) of a process as well as the sets of the received and pending messages.

$send =$	$receive =$
any idx, to **where**	**any** idx, to **where**
$\quad idx \in dom(decision)$	$\quad idx \in dom(pending)$
$\quad to \in 1 \mathinner{..} n \setminus \{idx\}$	$\quad to \in pending(idx)$
$\quad idx \notin recv(to)$	**then**
then	$\quad recv(to) := recv(to) \cup \{idx\}$
$\quad pending(idx) :=$	$\quad other(to) := other(to) \cup \{decision(idx)\}$
$\qquad pending(idx) \cup \{to\}$	$\quad pending(idx) := pending(idx) \setminus \{to\}$
end	**end**

The purpose of the decentralisation performed at this refinement step is to ensure that, once the local decision vector is completely populated, a process can independently elect the leader. To represent the locally selected leaders, we split (data refine) the abstract variable *leader* into a vector of leaders, one for each process. We define the gluing invariant that connects the new vector $leaders$ with the abstract variable $leaders \in 1 \mathinner{..} n \nrightarrow 1 \mathinner{..} n$ such that $\forall i \cdot i \in dom(leaders) \Rightarrow leaders(i) = leader$.

The central property of this refinement step is that the leader id is determined from the local knowledge is the actual leader defined by the global decision vector:

$$\forall i \cdot i \in 1 \mathinner{..} n \ \land \ recv(i) = dom(\{i\} \lhd decision) \ \Rightarrow \\ max(ran(decision)) = max(other(i) \cup \{decision(i)\})$$

This is an essential property with respect to the protocol correctness. It also justifies refining the event *elect* into its decentralised version, where each process is able to compute the common leader once *other(i)* contains the decisions of all other processes: $leaders(idx) := max(other(idx) \cup \{decision(idx)\})$.

3.3 Refining Inter-process Communication

Third Refinement. Our next refinement steps aims at achieving further decoupling of process data structures. Currently, to send a decision message, a process should access the *recv* variable of the targeted recipient to check that it has not received this message. Such an access to the process local data can be avoided if for each process i we introduce a history of the recipients of messages sent by i – $sent(i)$, where $sent \in 1\,..\,n \rightarrow \mathbb{P}(1\,..\,n)$. Correspondingly, event **send** is refined as follows

$$
\begin{array}{l}
send = \textbf{any } idx, to \textbf{ where} \\
\quad \ldots \\
\quad \underline{to \notin sent(idx)} \;//\; \textbf{instead of } idx \notin recv(to) \\
\textbf{then} \\
\quad sent(idx) := sent(idx) \cup \{to\} \\
\quad \ldots \\
\textbf{end}
\end{array}
$$

Since *sent(i)* includes all the messages currently being transmitted, the pending messages constitute the subset of the outgoing messages history: $\forall i \cdot i \in 1\,..\,n \Rightarrow pending(i) \subseteq sent(i)$. Now we can formulate the following property central to the model of communication mechanism.

$$\boxed{\forall i, j \cdot i \in 1\,..\,n \Rightarrow (j \in sent(i) \setminus pending(i) \Leftrightarrow i \in recv(j))}$$

It postulates that if a process j has received a message from a process i then the process i has sent the message to j and this message is not currently in transition (not in the set *pending*). The same property holds in the other direction: what has been sent and is not being transmitted has been received. This allows us to conclude that the combination of *sent*, *pending* and *recv* describes a *one-to-one asynchronous communication channel.*

Fourth Refinement. As a result of introducing the message history *sent*, the vector *recv* becomes redundant. Therefore, it may be data refined by a simpler data structure, *irec*, storing only the number of received messages. This simplifies the model, e.g., by allowing to replace adding elements to a set by incrementing the message count *irec*, where $irec \in 1\,..\,n \rightarrow 0\,..\,(n-1)$ and $\forall i \cdot i \in 1\,..\,n \Rightarrow irec(i) = card(recv(i))$.

Fifth Refinement. The final step towards achieving the localisation of process data is to avoid direct access to the memory of another agent[1]. One remaining case is an action of the *receive* event updating variable $other(i)$ (see the complete event *receive* definition above): $other(to) := other(to) \cup \underline{\{decision(idx)\}}$.

[1] The sole exception we are going to allow in our model concerns the values of $pending(i)$, which may be read by another process j. Around this exception we are going to build a model of inter-process communication.

Our solution is to communicate the decision of the sending process along with the id of the destination process. The value $decision(idx)$ becomes embedded into a message sent by the process idx to the process to. We refine the history of sent messages $sent$ by an extended version $xsent$: $xsent \in 1\,..\,n \rightarrow (1\,..\,n \leftrightarrow 0\,..\,n)$ such that $\forall i \cdot i \in 1\,..\,n \Rightarrow sent(i) = prj1[xsent(i)]$. A similar relation is defined for $pending(i)$. The decision of the sender is contained in the second projection: $\forall i \cdot i \in 1\,..\,n \wedge xsent(i) \neq \varnothing \Rightarrow \{decision(i)\} = prj2[xsent(i)]$.

Let us now analyse the information presented in $xsent$. The domain of $xsent$ is the name of a sending process, while its range is a set of pairs of the form of ($target\ process$, $process\ decision$). $xsent$ is a set of triplet that have the structure of a simple network protocol message:

$\langle source\_address \rangle \mid \langle target\_address \rangle \mid \langle payload \rangle$

The address fields are process names and the decision of a sending process. The result of this refinement step is a model that reflects the essential features of a distributed system. Namely, it separates the private and externally visible memory of the processes and explicitly defines inter-process communication. The communication is based on message passing in a point-to-point network protocol.

4 Deriving Distributed Implementation

Before presenting the decomposition of the model of leader election, we first describe the general structure of a distributed system that we aim at.

Our goal is to implement a distributed software that will operate on top of the existing hardware and some network infrastructure (*middleware*). We assume that middleware is a generic platform component and its sole functionality is to deliver messages between processes. In our model we make the following assumptions about the middleware behaviour:

- the middleware implements a simple point-to-point communication protocol; as a message it expects a data structure containing source and target addresses of the network points as well as the data to be delivered to the target point;
- for any message sent, it is guaranteed that the message is eventually delivered[2];
- when a message is delivered, the sender gets a delivery receipt;
- the middleware is not able to access the internal memory of a process; it only observes the buffer of output messages.

The description fits any packet-oriented protocol that has the capability of acknowledging the reception of a message, i.e., TCP/IP. While modelling a distributed system, we consider the communications among the processes as observations of the messages sent and received by the processes. The communication

[2] In reality, this means that the failure to deliver a message aborts the whole protocol. The consequences of this are outside of the scope of this paper.

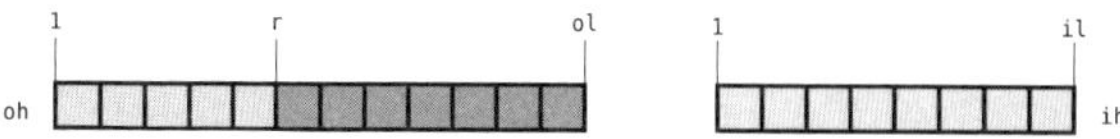

Fig. 3. Output history (oh), output queue (the darker part of oh) and input history (ih)

history of an individual process is represented by two message sequences – for sent and received messages respectively.

We define the following data structures:

$il \in \mathbb{N}$	index of the last message in input history
$ol \in \mathbb{N}$	index of the last message in otput history
$ih \in 1 \ldots il \rightarrow MSG$	input history sequence
$oh \in 1 \ldots ol \rightarrow MSG$	output history sequence
$r \in \mathbb{N}$	index of the last sent message in input history

where MSG is an type of process messages. The current queue of outgoing messages is then a particular slice of the output history:

$(r + 1 \,..\, ol \lhd oh)$	output queue
$ol - r \leq L$	output queue length constraint

where L is the maximum length of the output queue (that is, the sender buffer size). At any given point of time the output message history consists of the messages already sent and the messages produced but not yet delivered. The variable r points at the last message that has been reported as delivered by the environment. When an environment successfully delivers a message, the variable r is incremented. The out-of-order message delivery is possible but for simplicity we focus on a simpler, ordered delivery (the protocol itself is insensitive to out-of-order delivery). The oldest message awaiting delivery is located at index $r+1$ in the output history. Consequently, the restriction of the output history $r + 1 \,..\, ol \lhd oh$ gives us a sequence of all the messages awaiting delivery. The middleware constantly observes the changes made to the output histories of processes and reacts on the appearance of a new message awaiting delivery[3].

To model process communication, we define callable operations for each process. These operations will be invoked by the middleware every time a message is delivered or received. We specify these operations in the style described in subsection 2.2. Each process has two such operations, receive_msg and deliver_msg:

$receive\_msg$ = **any** m **pre**
$\quad m \in MSG$
post
$\quad ih' = ih \cup \{il + 1 \mapsto m\} \wedge$
$\quad il' = il + 1$
end

$deliver\_msg$ = **pre** $ol > r$ **post** $r' = r + 1$ **end**

[3] Event B does not have a notion of fairness so it is possible that the middleware delays the delivery of a message for as long as there are other messages to deliver. We have proven that this does not affect the protocol progress.

The operation receive_msg is invoked when a new message is delivered to a process. The operation saves the message into the input history. An invocation of deliver_msg by the middleware informs a process about the delivery of the oldest message in the output queue.

Let P, Q be processes and P_pid, Q_pid be their ids (names). The process communication is modelled via the operations P_receive_msg and Q_deliver_msg that correspond respectively to the P and Q instances of receive_msg and deliver_msg. The asynchronous communication between P and Q is specified by two symmetric middleware events Q_to_P and P_to_Q, where

$$
\begin{array}{ll}
Q\_to\_P = \textbf{any } msg \textbf{ where} & \\
\quad msg \in 0..n & \\
\quad Q\_ol > Q\_r & \text{//process has an undelivered message} \\
\quad P\_pid \mapsto msg = Q\_oh(Q\_r + 1) & \\
\textbf{then} & \\
\quad nil := \mathsf{P\_receive\_msg}(msg) & \text{// the message is delivered to P} \\
\quad nil := \mathsf{Q\_deliver\_msg} & \text{// and removed from the queue of Q} \\
\textbf{end} &
\end{array}
$$

Here nil is a helper variable to save a void result of a operation call. The event P_to_Q is defined similarly. Both Q_to_P and P_to_Q are refinements of the abstract event receive.

Above we considered the case with two processes, P and Q. However, the presented approach can be generalised to any number of processes[4].

4.1 System Architecture

The goal of the planned decomposition refinement step is to derive the distributed architecture that supports the communication scheme described above. The general representation of the system architecture after decomposition (in a simple case with only two processes) is shown in Figure 4. The abstract, monolithic model is refined by a model representing the communication middleware, which references the involved processes realised as separate modules. The middleware accesses the modules via the provided generic interface (hence, all the processes are based on the single interface). The interface of a module includes not only the operations receive_msg and deliver_msg but also the specification of an autonomous process thread of control (or, simply, a process thread).

In this part of an interface we define the effect of a process thread on the interface variables. In a distributed system, the specification of a process thread should at least define how and when the process adds messages to the output queue. We also require that a process does not change the input history and the part of output history preceding the output queue. Also, the output message queue may only be extended by a process thread (that is, the middleware would

[4] At the moment one has to fix the number of processes at a decomposition step. We are working on improvements to Rodin that would allow us to model generic decomposition steps and later instantiate them with any number of processes.

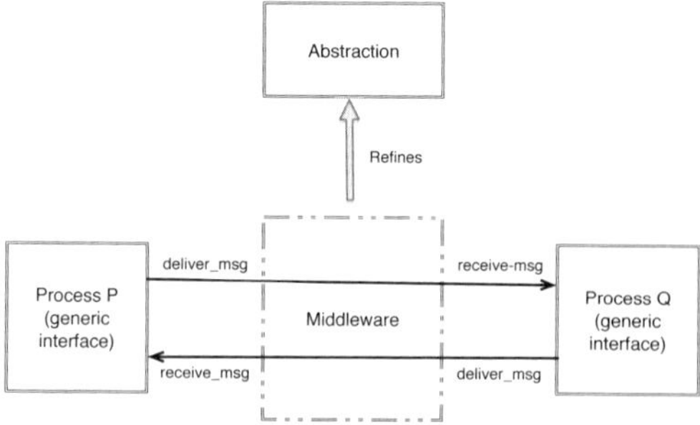

Fig. 4. Decomposition architecture

not create messages on its own). These conditions are mechanically generated as additional proof obligations for a model.

A process thread is defined via a number of events. At the decomposition level, these events define how the process thread may update the interface variables. Since the interface variables are used to replace the abstract model variables, it is necessary to link the interface events with the abstracts events of the model before decomposition. Such a link is defined at the point of module import (in the middleware model). It is necessary to specify which interface events are used to refine abstract model events. There are two typical scenarios to achieve this: (i) distributing the abstract events among the interface events, or (ii) splitting the same abstract event into several interface events. In our model it is the latter case as we move the behaviour of a process into its own module.

Next we present how this general decomposition strategy can be applied to derive a distributed implementation of the leader election protocol.

4.2 Decomposition of the Leader Election Model

The essence of the decomposition refinement step is the data refinement of the various data structures of the leader election protocol into input and output message histories of the individual processes. For the sake of simplicity, the election is done among two process called P and Q, which differ, at the interface level, only by their process id.

The overall scheme of the accomplished decomposition refinement is shown in Figure 5. The result of the fifth refinement, elect5, is refined by the middleware model elect6. This model imports two instances of the generic module interface *Node*. All the variables and most of operations of the interface corresponding to processes P and Q appear with the prefixes $P\_$ and $Q\_$ respectively. This is a feature of the modularisation extension that helps to avoid name clashes when importing several interfaces. The variables of the abstract model elect5 are split into two groups. The variables *decision* and *leaders* become internal, "phantom" variables of the process instances, i.e., they cannot be accessed by middleware. These variables are only used in the process thread. The other variable group including *other*, *irec*, *xsent*, and *xpending* is replaced (data refined) by the corresponding input and output histories of the process instances.

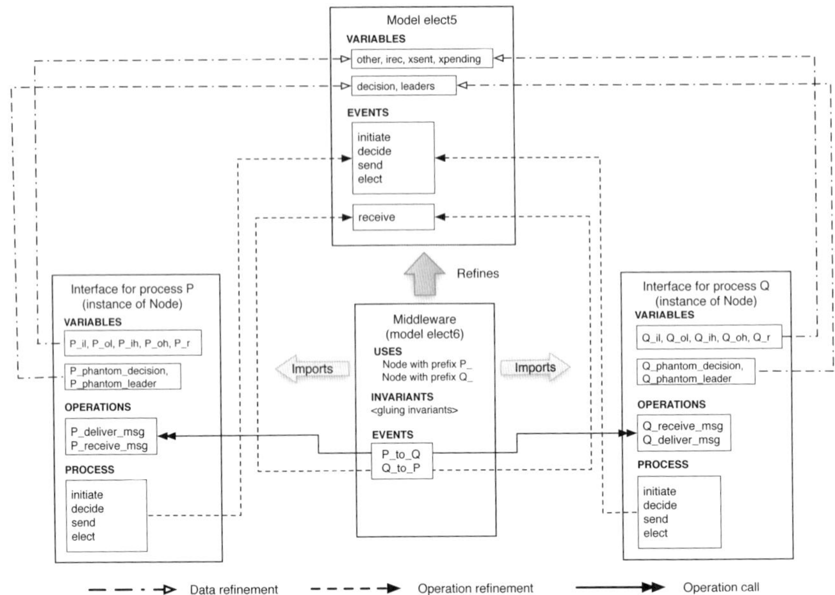

Fig. 5. The structure of the decomposition refinement

The number of message received from other process is related to the length of the input history of a process, while the local knowledge of a process is same as the information contained in its input history. The following are the data refinement conditions for these two variables (for the case of process P).

$$irec(P\_pid) = P\_il$$
$$other(P\_pid) = ran(P\_ih)$$

The process output history, oh, is a suitable replacement for $xsent$. The abstract notion of not yet delivered messages ($xpending$) maps into the output message queue. The refinement relation for $xsent$ and $xpending$ is the following:

$$xsent(P\_pid) = ran(P\_oh)$$
$$xpending(P\_pid) = ran(P\_r + 1 \mathinner{..} P\_ol \lhd P\_oh)$$

From earlier refinement steps we know that $xpending(P\_pid) \subseteq xsent(P\_pid)$. This coincides with the definition of the output queue as a subset of the output history. Such simple mapping between message histories and the variables of the previous (centralised) model is possible because they describe the same idea – asynchronous communication – albeit in differing terms.

The events of the abstract model are also split into two groups. The event receive is now refined by the middleware events implementing the point-to-point process communication, P_to_Q and Q_to_P. The remaining events, initiate, decide, send, and elect, become a part of the process thread of each process. Therefore, these events are also distributed, each dedicated to the functionality of a single process.

4.3 Towards Runnable Code

The decomposition step leaves us with a specification of a process separated from the specification of the middleware. To implement the model as a software system, we have to achieve the following goals: (i) ascertain that the middleware model is compatible with the deployment infrastructure; (ii) convert the process specification into process software. The former task may be approached by using the middleware model as a blueprint to be matched against the existing middleware implementation, e.g, via model-based testing. A logically simpler, though normally impractical, alternative is to pursue the top-down approach and refine the middleware model all the way to machine code or even hardware description. For the latter task, one normally employs a code generator, which essentially accomplishes a large-scale unproven refinement step relating two formal languages: a target programming language and our modelling language, Event B. Unfortunately, no such tool is yet available for Event B. Nevertheless, we have conducted a manual, line-by-line translation into Java [15]. Let us note that, whichever approach we take, we have to make a transition from a completely proven artefact to a system with an unproven, informal part. One way to reduce the gap between a model and its runnable version is to treat a deterministic model as a program. For this, it suffices to build an Event B model interpreter, which, in principle, can be achieved by first defining an Event B operational semantics.

Let v be the variables, E the set of events and Σ_0 the set of initial states of an Event B model. Also, let the set of model states be defined as $\Sigma = \{v \mid I(v)\}$, where $I(v)$ is the model invariant and $\Sigma_0 \subseteq \Sigma$. A distinguished value nil $\notin \Sigma$ denotes the state of an uninitialised model. An event $e \in E$ is interpreted as a next-state relation $e : \Sigma \leftrightarrow \Sigma$. The behaviour of the model is then given by a transition system $(\Sigma \cup \{\text{nil}\}, \rightarrow)$ where $\rightarrow$ is defined by the following rules:

$$\frac{v \in \Sigma_0}{(\text{nil}) \rightarrow (v)} \qquad\qquad \frac{v \mapsto v' \in \bigcup E}{(v) \rightarrow (v')}$$

The first rule initialises the model. The second one describes state transitions defined by a combination of all the model events. It may be proven that the proof semantics of Event B implies that, unless a deadlock is reached, there is always a next state v' and it is a safe state. A tool for this style of code generation is available for Event B [6]. Rather than simply interpreting models, it produces equivalent C code.

To obtain a complete operational code, it is necessary to do an 'assembly' step linking the program of a process with the program of the existing networking infrastructure. At the moment this step is completely manual.

4.4 Proof Statistics

The proof statistics (in terms of generated proof obligations) for the presented Event B development is shown below. The numbers here represent the total number of proof obligations, the number of automatically and manually proved ones, and the percentage of manual effort. Here the models elect0-elect6 are the protocol refinement steps. IProcess is the process module interface component. QuickPrg is one specific realisation of the process module body that may learn the overall leader before the completion of the protocol. Other process implementations (found in [14]) do not incur any proof obligations. Two models stand out in terms of proof effort: elect2 is an important step giving the proof of the protocol correctness, while elect6 accomplishes model decomposition. About 35% of total manual proofs are related to the decomposition step.

Step	Total	Auto	Manual	Manual %
elect0	3	3	0	0%
elect1	16	13	3	19%
elect2	76	61	15	20%
elect3	23	23	0	0%
elect4	19	12	7	37%

Step	Total	Auto	Manual	Manual %
elect5	37	29	8	22%
elect6	131	106	25	19%
IProcess	53	44	9	17%
QuickPrg	19	16	3	16%
Overall	377	307	70	19%

5 Conclusions

In this paper we have presented an application of Event B and its modularisation extension to the derivation of a correct-by-construction distributed program. The formal model construction is a top-down refinement chain, based on the ideas pioneered in Dijkstra's work on program derivation [7]. We start with a centralised and trivially correct model and end up with a localised, deterministic model of a process. Small abstraction gaps between models constructed at each refinement step have simplified protocol verification and allowed us to better manage the complexity traditionally associated with distributed programs.

In the domain of refinement-driven development, the closest work is the development of distributed reference counting algorithm [5] and also topology discovery model [10]. Both present verification of fairly intricate protocols and propose developments starting with a simple, centralised abstraction that is gradually replaced by a complex of communicating entities. The focus of these works is on the investigation of the consistency properties of the relevant protocols. In contrast, we place an emphasis on the role of refinement as an engineering technique to obtain correct-by-construction software.

Another closely related work is derivation of a distributed protocol by refinement in [3]. The development finishes with a formal model of a program to be run by each process. Our approach has a number of significant distinctions. Firstly, we perform the actual decomposition and separate processes from middleware. Secondly, we explicitly define our assumptions about the middleware providing the correct infrastructure for deploying the derived distributed program.

Walden [19] has investigated formal derivation of distributed algorithms within the Action Systems formalism [4], heavily relying on the superposition refinement technique. These ideas, while not supported by an integrated toolkit, are very relevant in the domain of Event B.

Butler et al. [13,8] have presented a number of formal developments addressing refinement of distributed systems. The presented work focuses on Event B modelling of a range of two-process communication primitives.

There are a number of model checking approaches to verifying distributed protocols. Model checking is a technique that verifies whether the protocol preserves certain properties (e.g., deadlock freeness) by fully exploring its (abridged) state space. Refinement approaches take a complementary view – instead of verifying a model extracted from an existing program, they promote a derivation of a program with in-built properties. The correct-by-construction development allows us to increase the complexity of a formal model gradually. This facilitates comprehension of the algorithm and simplifies reasoning about its properties.

The main contribution of this paper is a complete formal development of a distributed program implementing a leader election protocol. The formal development has resulted in creating not only a mathematical model of distributed software but also its implementation. The systems approach that we have adopted has allowed us not only create the programs to be run by network processes but also explicitly state the assumptions about the middleware behaviour. These assumptions allow the designers to choose the appropriate type of middleware on which the derived program should be deployed. We have conducted a code generation experiment and ascertained that the constructed program behaves as expected [15]. With a tool support, obtaining runnable code would be straightforward. As a continuation of this work we plan to model and derive the code of a fully operational distributed control system.

Acknowledgments. This work is supported by the FP7 ICT DEPLOY Project and the EPSRC/UK TrAmS platform grant.

References

1. Abrial, J.R.: The B-Book. Cambridge University Press, Cambridge (1996)
2. Abrial, J.R.: Modelling in Event-B. Cambridge University Press, Cambridge (2010)
3. Abrial, J.R., Cansell, D., Mery, D.: A mechanically proved and incremental development of IEEE 1394. Formal Aspects of Computing 14, 215–227 (2003)
4. Back, R., Sere, K.: Superposition refinement of reactive systems. Formal Aspects of Computing 8(3), 1–23 (1996)
5. Cansell, D., Méry, D.: Formal and incremental construction of distributed algorithms: on the distributed reference counting algorithm. Theoretical Computer Science 364, 318–337 (2006)
6. Degerlund, F., Walden, M., Sere, K.: Implementation issues concerning the action systems formalism. In: Proceedings of the Eighth International Conference on Parallel and Distributed Computing Applications and Technologies (PDCAT 2007). IEEE Computer Society, Los Alamitos (2007)
7. Dijkstra, E.: A Discipline of Programming. Prentice-Hall International, Englewood Cliffs (1976)
8. Fathabadi, S., Butler, M.: Applying Event-B Atomicity Decomposition to a Multi Media Protocol. In: de Boer, F.S., Bonsangue, M.M., Hallerstede, S., Leuschel, M. (eds.) FMCO 2009. LNCS, vol. 6286, pp. 89–104. Springer, Heidelberg (2010)
9. Garcia-Molina, H.: Elections in distributed computing systems. IEEE Transactions on Computers 31(1) (1982)
10. Hoang, T., Kuruma, H., Basin, D., Abrial, J.R.: Developing topology discovery in Event B. Science of Computer Programming 74 (2009)

11. Iliasov, A., Troubitsyna, E., Laibinis, L., Romanovsky, A., Varpaaniemi, K., Ilic, D., Latvala, T.: Supporting Reuse in Event B Development: Modularisation Approach. In: Frappier, M., Glässer, U., Khurshid, S., Laleau, R., Reeves, S. (eds.) ABZ 2010. LNCS, vol. 5977, pp. 174–188. Springer, Heidelberg (2010)
12. IST FP7 project DEPLOY, http://www.deploy-project.eu/
13. Butler, M., Yadav, D.: An incremental development of the Mondex system in Event B. Formal Aspects of Computing 20, 61–77 (2008)
14. Protocol, L.E.: Event B specification (2011), http://iliasov.org/modplugin/leaderel2commented.zip
15. Protocol, L.E.: Java implementation (2011), http://iliasov.org/modplugin/leaderel_program.zip
16. Rigorous Open Development Environment for Complex Systems (RODIN): Deliverable D7, Event B Language, http://rodin.cs.ncl.ac.uk/
17. RODIN modularisation plug-in: Documentation, http://wiki.event-b.org/index.php/Modularisation_Plug-in
18. The RODIN platform, http://rodin-b-sharp.sourceforge.net/
19. Walden, M.: Formal Reasoning About Distributed Algorithms. Åbo Akademi University, Finland, ph.D. Thesis (1998)

From Requirements to Development: Methodology and Example

Wen Su[1], Jean-Raymond Abrial[2], Runlei Huang[3], and Huibiao Zhu[1]

[1] Software Engineering Institute, East China Normal University
{wensu,hbzhu}@sei.ecnu.edu.cn
[2] Marseille, France
jrabrial@neuf.fr
[3] Alcatel-Lucent Shanghai Bell
runleihuang@alcatel-sbell.com.cn

Abstract. The main destination of this paper is the industrial milieu. We are concerned with the difficulties encountered by industrial developers who are willing to apply "new" approaches to software engineering (since they always face the same problem for years: how to develop safe software) but are in fact disappointed by what is proposed to them. We try to characterize what the relevant constraints of industrial software projects are and then propose a *simple methodology* able to face the real problem. It is based on the usage of Event-B [1] and is illustrated by means of an *industrial project*.

1 Introduction

We believe that, for a long time, software engineering has been considered either a theoretical discipline in certain circles of Academia, while a rather purely technical discipline in others. In the former case, the focus is put mainly on the mathematical semantics of the programming language that is used, while in the second case the focus is put on the informal modeling of the problem at hand using semantically meaningless boxes and arrows. In our opinion, none of these approaches is very useful for the working software developer facing industrial problems. This is because a vast majority of industrial software development project is characterized as follows:

1. The problem is usually not mathematically involved.
2. The industrial "Requirement Document" of the project is usually very poor and difficult to exploit.
3. The main functions of the intended system are often quite simple.
4. However, many special cases make things complicated and difficult to master.
5. The communication between the software and its environment involves complicated procedures.

As a result, the developer is very embarrassed because he/she does not know how to "attack" the project development. This is particularly frustrating because, from a certain point of view, the function of the final system seems to be very simple (case 3 above).

S. Qin and Z. Qiu (Eds.): ICFEM 2011, LNCS 6991, pp. 437–455, 2011.

For solving these difficulties, industrial managements have developed some "processes" defining the various phases that engineers have to follow in order to achieve the intended result, namely to have a final software satisfying its specification. Roughly speaking, the various phases of such industrial development processes are usually as follows:

1. Choose a programming language to code the software.
2. Write the software specifications, using various semi-formal approaches.
3. Design the system by cutting it into pieces with "well defined" communication mechanisms.
4. Code the various pieces using the chosen programming language.
5. Verify the code by means of various testing approaches.
6. Deliver the documentation of the system.

Note that phase 1 (programming language choice) is usually not an explicitly written part of the development process although it is implicitly very often decided quite early as indicated here. The discipline imposed by such a development process is certainly not a bad habit. However, in our opinion, it does not solve the real difficulty faced by the developer: how to structure the development approach so that one can have a strong feeling that the final product is indeed the one that was intended.

The purpose of this paper is to propose a systematic approach able to help the industrial developer to solve the mentioned difficulties. We think that such an approach or a similar one is not used by industrial practitioners, this is the reason why we think it is worth proposing it here. We shall first present our simple methodology in section 2 and then illustrate it by means of a real industrial project in section 3.

2 Methodology

The key ingredient of this methodology is derived from the observation that the system we intend to build is *too complicated*: it has therefore to be initially simplified (even very much simplified) and then *gradually* made more complicated in order to take account in a smooth fashion of all its peculiarities.

However, one of the main difficulties here for people to adopt such a practice is that they are not usually used to consider first a system that is simpler than the one they have to develop: they try to immediately take into account all the complexities of the system at once. Also the usage of a top-down approach is in fact very rare in industry. The practice of heavy testing has made people writing code and only then trying to validate it.

2.1 The Requirement Document

But, of course, in order to figure out what the real complications of the system we intend to build are, we cannot in general rely on the industrial requirement document that is at our disposal. As said in the Introduction, this document is quite often very difficult to exploit. So, our first action is to *rewrite this document*: this is to be done of course together with the people who wrote the initial one.

It is important to state that we do not consider that the initial requirement document is useless: most of the time, it contains all the details of the future system. We just say that it is difficult to read and exploit for doing our initial engineering work. In section 3.2, we shall explain more on the requirement document while presenting our example.

2.2 The Refinement Strategy

As said in the previous section, the key idea of this approach is to proceed by successive approximations. For doing this, it is important to prioritize the way we are going to take account of the requirements that have been carefully identified in the new requirement document. When we say "to take account of the requirements", we are not very clear here. To take account of them in order to do what?

1. To write the code. But how can we write software code by successive approximation? **NO**, writing the code is far too early a phase at this stage.
2. To reshape once again the requirement document. **NO**, one rewriting is sufficient.
3. To write a specification document by translating the requirements into boxes and arrows. **NO**, we are not sure that it will add something to the requirements that we have been very careful to write by simple natural language statements: experience shows that such translations, far from making things clearer, quite often make things very obscure and therefore difficult to exploit later to write the final code.
4. To write a specification document by using a mathematical language for translating the requirements. **NO**, the term "translation" is not adequate here. The requirements are usually not amenable to a direct translation.
5. To write successive mathematical models defining gradually some *mathematical simulations* of the dynamic system we intend to build. **YES**, that will be our approach. This notion of model will be developed in the next section.

2.3 Some Rules

Now that we have defined (at least vaguely for the moment) what is to be done after taking account of the requirements, we have now to give some rules by which this choice among all the requirements can be performed in various steps. This is not easy to do so, for the very good reason that there is not in general a single "obvious" choice. However, we can give some **rules of thumb**:

R0. Take a short number of requirements at a time.
R1. Take account of a requirement partially only if it seems too complicated to be swallowed in one step.
R2. Introduce the other parts of a complicated requirement in further steps.
R3. As a special case of the previous rules, when a condition depends on many different cases, first abstract it with a non determinate boolean condition and then make it concrete and deterministic in further steps.
R4. Introduce gradually the functions of the system.
R5. Start with the most abstract requirements of *the whole system*: its main functions.
R6. Introduce the most concrete requirements at the very end of the choice process.
R7. Try to balance the requirements of the software and those of its environment.
R8. Be careful not to forget any requirements.
R9. If a requirement cannot (for some reason) be taken into account, remove it from the document.

It is clear that this initial ordering of the requirements is not the last word concerning this question. We might discover later that our initial choice is not technically adequate. We might also discover that some requirements are simply impossible to achieve, or badly expressed, or be better modified, etc. We must feel free to modify our choices and to modify our requirement document as well. In section 3.4, we shall explain more about the refinement strategy of our example.

2.4 Modeling with Event-B [1] and Proving with the Rodin Platform [2]

Equipped with the "road map" (Requirement Document and Refinement Strategy) defined in previous sections[1], we can now enter our next phase: modeling.

Modeling versus Programming
The first thing to understand about modeling is that it is *quite different* from programming. In the latter, we describe the way a computer must behave in order to fulfill a certain task, while in the former we describe the way a system can be *observed*: the emphasis is put on the global simulation of an *entire system* taking account of the properties that must be obeyed. This is clearly something that is not part of the programming of a piece of software. In other words, the modeling we envisage is not that of the future software alone but rather the modeling of this software together with its surrounding environment. This aspect will be made clearer in the illustrating example presented in section 3.

Successive Approximations
Another important difference between modeling and programming is that modeling can be developed by successive approximations while this is clearly impossible, and even dangerous, with programming: every programmer knows very well how perilous it is to modify or extend a piece of software as one has no guarantee not to introduce subtle bugs in doing so.

Mathematical Modeling
The simulations done in our approach are not realized by using a simulation language: we rather build mathematical models of discrete transition systems. All this is described in details in [1] where this approach is called "Event-B". Next is a brief informal description of Event-B, which was largely inspired by Action Systems [4] [5].

Event-B
Roughly speaking, a mathematical model (a simulation) done with Event-B is simply defined by means of a *state* and some *transitions* on this state (the events). The state is defined by means of variables together with some permanent properties that these variables must be fulfilled: such properties are called the *invariants* of the state. Each transition is defined by means of two items: the *guard* defining the necessary conditions for the transition to occur and the *actions* defining the way the state is modified by the

[1] These two first phases of our approach can take a significant time, i.e. several months, for important projects.

transition. As can be seen, any "state machine" (which is nothing else but a transition system) can be defined in this way. Some *proofs* must be performed in order to ensure that each transition indeed maintains the properties of the state variables (the invariants).

Superposition Refinement

A model described in the way we have just mentioned is able to be *extended*: this is done by adding more variables (and thus more invariants) and more events to it. This technique is called *superposition refinement* [3]. Besides extending the state and adding events, some extensions can also be performed in two more ways on already existing events: (1) by strengthening their guards, and (2) by extending their actions. It means that an existing transition can be made more precise in a superposition refinement by giving additional constraints to it.

Proofs

Invariant preservation proofs may have to be performed while doing a refinement. Moreover, in a refinement, proofs of guards strengthening have also to be added to those of invariant preservations. The important thing to understand here is that proofs already done in a previous model (the one that is extended) *remain valid after the extension*, and so on while doing further refinements. In other words, we can *accumulate* progressive proof work in a safe way.

Deadlock Freeness

An important property of a state transition system is *deadlock freeness*. A system (or some part of it) is said to be deadlocked if no transition can occur any more. Most of the time, we are interested in modeling systems that never deadlock. It is simply done by proving that a transition can always occur. As the conditions for an event to occur are defined by its guard, deadlock freeness is thus ensured by proving that the disjunction of the guards of the concerned events is always true.

The Rodin Platform

In the previous sections, we mention the necessity of proving things about models: invariant preservation, guard strengthening, and deadlock freeness. In a typical industrial project there might be several thousands proofs[2]. It is obviously out of the question to manually generate what is to be proved and to manually prove all of them. A tool has been built for doing this: the Rodin Platform [2]. It has been developed over the last seven years by means of European Projects fundings. The Rodin Platform is constructed on top of Eclipse. It contains many plug-ins among which some important ones are the Proof Obligation Generator and the Prover. The former is able to generate the statements to be proved by analyzing the models. The latter is able to prove the various statements generated by the previous plug-in either automatically or interactively (i.e. helped by the human user giving some hints to the automatic prover)[3].

[2] In the example developed in this paper, we have 439 proofs.

[3] In the example developed in this paper, all 439 proofs are done automatically (except two of them done interactively) by the prover of the Rodin Platform.

Finding Errors while Proving
An important aspect of this proving effort is that we might encounter problems in attempting to perform some of the proofs: we might discover that they simply cannot be proven automatically nor interactively. This is the indication that something is wrong in our model. This might be corrected by modifying, removing or adding some invariants, or by doing the same on events guards or actions.

Proving versus Testing
What can be seen here is that proving plays for models the same role as that played by testing for programs. However, the big difference between the two is that proving is not performed at the end of the modeling phase but in the middle of it, more precisely at each refinement step. This means that proving is indeed part of modeling. In doing this, we might also figure out that certain requirements are in some cases impossible to achieve: this is where it might be advisable to return to the requirement document and modify it. We might also figure out that our refinement strategy has to be re-thought: some requirements might be taken in a different order so as to improve the proving process.

Checking Models against the Requirement Document
While developing the various successive models of a system, we have to follow what we prescribe in the refinement strategy. This is done by checking that, at each refinement step, we take account of the various requirements that were chosen. At the end of the modeling phase we must have taken all requirements into account.

Data Refinement
The next step is to envisage how the part of the model dealing with the future software can be translated into executable code. Before doing that however, it might be necessary to envisage other kinds of refinements needed to transform the data structures used in the model into implementable data structures. This kind of refinement is called *data refinement* [6]. It is not considered in this paper and not used in the example of section 3.

2.5 After Modeling

Once the modeling phase is finished, that is when in the last refinement we can figure out that we have taken successfully all requirements and done all proofs, then we can envisage to go into the next phase: coding and executing. This will be done by using automatic plug-ins of the Rodin Platform.

Concerning execution, some interesting plug-ins are also available on the Rodin Platform: these are AnimB and ProB [7]. They are able to directly animate (without prior translation) and also model-check some Event-B models. Such animations are quite useful: they allow users to see how the global model of the system can behave.

3 The Example

In this section, we propose to illustrate the methodology we have just briefly presented in the previous section. This will be done thanks to a real industrial example. In developing this example, we shall give more information than the general one we already gave on the way each phase is performed. We shall follow the various phases that were mentioned in the previous section:

1. Re-writing the requirement document in section 2.1.
2. Make precise the refinement strategy in section 2.2.
3. Develop the various models in section 2.4.

Our example is extracted from the software controlling the behavior of a train. This software is called the "Vehicle OnBoard Controller (for short VOBC): the part we shall develop is called the "Mode Selection Subsystem", it is a module of the VOBC.

3.1 Main Purpose of System

The purpose of the system under study is to detect the *driving mode* wished by the train driver (he has some buttons at his disposal to do that) and decide accordingly whether this mode is feasible so that the current mode of the train could be (or not be) that wished by the driver. The different modes are the following:

1. OFF: train stops,
2. Restricted Manual Forward (RMF): forward manual drive, no train protection,
3. Restricted Manual Reverse (RMR): backward manual drive, no train protection,
4. Train Protection Manual (ATPM): forward manual drive, train protection,
5. Automatic Mode (ATO): forward automatic drive, train protection.

The “train protection" is a special automatic procedure taking care of dangerous situations (like trespassing a red light). In certain circumstances, the VOBC shall trigger the emergency brake (EB) of the train in case the request made by the driver might put the train in a dangerous situation. When such a special case vanishes then the VOBC can resume with a normal behavior.

As can be seen, this system seems to be quite straightforward. It is indeed. However we shall discover in the sequel that there is a vast number of special cases and also some peculiar equipments so that the system becomes complicated to develop. In fact, we face exactly the difficulty that was mentioned at the beginning of this article: a complicated and intricate situation without any sophisticated mathematics.

3.2 The Requirement Document

The requirement document takes the form of two embedded texts: the *explanatory* text and the *reference* text. They are both written in English. The former contains general explanations about the project we want to develop: it is supposed to help a new reader to understand the problem. The latter is made of short (dry) labelled and numbered statements listing the precise requirements that must be fulfilled by the concerned system: these statements should be self-contained[4].

Some of the "requirements" are mainly assumptions concerning the equipment rather than, strictly speaking, genuine requirements. They are nevertheless very important as they define the *environment* of our future software.

---

[4] The example treated here is a simplified version of a real example. We simplify it in order to cope with the size of this paper.

1) Requirement Labelling

We shall adopt the following labels for our assumptions and requirements: TR_ENV (train environment), DR_ENV (driver environment), VOBC_ENV (VOBC environment), and VOBC_FUN (VOBC functions).

2) The Main Actors

Here are the various "actors" of our system: a train, a train driver, and the VOBC (a software controller). In the sequel, we shall first define some assumptions about these actors and then focus on the main function of the VOBC.

3) Train Assumptions

The following assumptions are concerned with the devices, equipment, and information that are relevant to our project in the train: the cabin, the mode button, the emergency brake, and speed information.

A train has two cabins (cabin A and B), each one is either active or inactive.	TR_ENV-1

Each cabin contains a Mode Selection Switch (MSS), with available modes: - Off (OFF) - Restricted Manual Forward (RMF) - Automatic Mode (ATO) - Restricted Manual Reverse (RMR)	TR_ENV-2

Each cabin contains an Automatic Train Protection Manual button (ATPM).	TR_ENV-3

It seems strange, a priori, to have the mode ATPM not defined as another alternative in the MSS button: this makes things complicated. We shall see how in the development, we might first simplify this situation by considering that the switch has an ATPM position in order to focus more easily on the main problem. Here are more train assumptions:

The train has an Emergency Brake	TR_ENV-4	The train may be stationary	TR_ENV-5

4) Driver Assumptions

The following assumptions are concerned with the actions the driver can do and that are relevant to our problem: requiring a mode modification.

The MSS is used by the driver of an active cabin to request a certain mode	DR_ENV-1

The ATPM button is for the driver to request the Automatic Train Protection Manual Mode (ATPM)	DR_ENV-2

5) VOBC Assumptions

Next are a series of assumptions concerning the information the VOBC can receive from its environment.The next requirement shows that the VOBC can receive a large number of information: clearly we shall have to formalize this gradually. It is also mentioned that the VOBC works on a cycle basis. In other words, the VOBC periodically checks this information and then takes some relevant decisions.

The VOBC has a periodic interrogation (cycle) to the train for the conditions: - The MSS position (OFF, RMR, RMF, ATO) - The state of the driver screen (TOD) - The active cab (cab A or cab B, no cab) - The state of Brake Release - The speed (stationary,non-stationary) - The ATPM button depressed - The position - A valid LMA (Limit of Movement Authorization) - The orientation - The startup tests completed - The possible calibrated wheel - Trainline Healthy - The Brake/Motor output (normal, failure)	VOBC_ ENV-1

The next requirement shows a complicated encoding of the information received by the VOBC. As will be seen below, we shall take into account this complex coding at the very end of our development only.

The VOBC has a periodic interrogation to the validation of Mode Selector, it is communicated the MSS position by means of the boolean below: (VOBC_ ENV-2)

MSS	Mode 1	Mode 2	ACA	ACB	FWDCS	REVCS
OFF	0	0	X	X	X	X
FWD	1	0	1	0	1	0
FWD	1	0	0	1	0	1
REV	1	0	1	0	0	1
REV	1	0	0	1	1	0
ATO	0	1	X	X	X	X

* *X means input does not play a part in determination of the mode.*

One active cab is required to be detected except OFF mode (zero or one)
All other boolean combinations are considered Mode Selector invalid.

The mention "FWD" and "REV" in this table for the "MSS" position come from the industrial document. More precisely, "FWD" stands for "RMF" and "REV" stands for "RMR".

Here is one the main output of the VOBC: triggering of the emergency brake.

The Emergency Brake is activated by the VOBC.	VOBC_ENV-3

6) VOBC Functionalities

In this section, we carefully define the various functional requirements of the VOBC.

· **Active and passive state of the VOBC**

In this section, we encounter a large number of cases where the VOBC can enter into the "passive" state. Obviously, we have to take such cases gradually only.

The VOBC can be in a passive or active state. On start-up, it is passive.	VOBC_FUN-1

After start-up, if the VOBC receives the startup tests completion then the VOBC shall move to active state.	VOBC_FUN-2

The VOBC moves to passive state if one of the following conditions is met: - Trainline is not healthy. - The mode selector input is invalid (VOBC_ENV-2) - The cabin combination is invalid (VOBC_ENV-2) - The Brake/Motor output is failure when the VOBC is in ATO mode. - The selected direction is towards the train rear when in ATO or ATPM mode - The position is lost when the mode is ATPM or ATO. - The mode transition required is detected but the transition fails - The current mode is ATPM or ATO but this current mode is not available (see below **Mode Availability** VOBC_FUN-7,8)	VOBC_ FUN-5

If the VOBC is in the passive state, then when the conditions for this are over, the VOBC tests the transition of the selected MSS mode: - If the test succeeds, it changes to the required mode in active state. - Otherwise, it stays in passive state	VOBC_ FUN-4

The previous requirement covers the case where the passive state was entered while in the ATPM mode. It goes back "naturally" in the RMF mode.

When the VOBC moves from active state to passive state, the emergency brake must be triggered.	VOBC_FUN-3

· **Mode Availabilities**

Here are some further requirements of the VOBC. We shall see that sometimes the ATO or ATPM modes are said to be "not available". Such complicated cases, again, will be taken into account gradually.

The ATPM and ATO modes can be *available* or *not available* by the VOBC.	VOBC_FUN-6

These conditions are required by an active VOBC to make the ATPM mode available: - Train position and orientation established - Wheels calibrated - Selected direction not reverse - Valid LMA received. - TOD is not failure	These conditions are required by an active VOBC to make the ATO mode available: - Train position and orientation established - Wheels calibrated - Selected direction not reverse - Valid LMA received - No Brake/Motor Effort failure detected - No Brake Release failure detected
VOBC_FUN-7	VOBC_FUN-8

· Mode Transitions (Basic Functionalities)

Here, at last, we reach the basic functionalities of the VOBC: the mode transition decisions. When in an active state, the role of the VOBC is to validate the mode required by the driver.

The VOBC provides the following operating modes for the train: - Off (OFF) - Automatic Mode (ATO) - Automatic Train protection Manual (ATPM) - Restricted Manual Forward (RMF) - Restricted Manual Reverse (RMR)	VOBC_FUN-9

The VOBC can accept a mode change requested by the driver only if it has detected that the train is stationary	VOBC_FUN-10

If the VOBC detects a mode change requested by the driver while the train is not stationary then: - it activates the Emergency Brake - it maintains the current train mode of operation	VOBC_FUN-11

If the VOBC detects a stationary train, it releases the Emergency Brake due to mode changes only when the VOBC is not in passive state	VOBC_FUN-12

If the active VOBC receives a driver's mode request, it will not test the mode transition (see VOBC_FUN-14-19) until the train is stationary. - If the test succeeds, transit to the required mode - If it fails, transit to the passive state	VOBC_FUN-13

Some of the following requirements about RMF or ATPM mode transition are complicated due to the presence of the ATPM button. This will not be taken into account at the beginning of the development.

The VOBC can transition to RMF mode while not in ATPM mode if the conditions below are met: - One cab is active. - The MSS is in the RMF position - The train is stationary.	VOBC_FUN-14

The VOBC can transition to RMF mode while in ATPM mode if the following conditions are met: - One cab is active. - The MSS is in the RMF position. - The train is stationary. - The ATPM button is activated.	VOBC_FUN-15

The VOBC can transition to RMR if the conditions below are met: - One cab is active. - The MSS is in the RMR position. - The train is stationary.	VOBC_FUN-16

The VOBC can change to ATPM from RMF if all below are met: - One cab is active. - The MSS is in the RMF position. - The train is stationary. - The ATPM button is activated. - ATPM mode is available.	VOBC_FUN-17

The VOBC can transition to ATO if the conditions below are met: - One cab is active. - The MSS is in the ATO position. - The train is stationary. - ATO mode is available.	VOBC_ FUN-18	The VOBC can transition to OFF if the conditions below are met: - One cab is active. - The MSS is in the OFF position. - The train is stationary.	VOBC_ FUN-19

3.3 Comments about the Previous Requirements

A Large Number of Requirements

We have 29 requirements to take account of. Notice however that the real example has far more requirements: more than one hundred. But even with this restricted number of requirements, we can figure out that things have become quite complicated to handle. It is not clear how we can treat this situation in a decent fashion. The difficulty comes from the large number of variables we have to take into account. Again, this situation is *very typical* of industrial projects. We face here the exact situation that we want to solve in this article.

The Difficulty

At first glance, it seems very difficult to simplify things as we recommended in section 2 describing our methodology in general terms. It seems that the only approach we can use here is one where everything is defined at the same level. This is the case because all requirements are heavily related to each others: a typical case is VOBC_FUN_5 mentioning mode availability and VOBC_FUN_7,8 describing these availabilities.

The Solution: Abstraction, Refinement, and Proofs

We shall see in the next section how the introduction of abstraction and refinement will solve this difficult question: when some conditions are quite heavy (e.g. those making the VOBC state "passive" in VOBC_FUN-5), we shall abstract them by a simple boolean variable which will be later expanded. We shall see also that such an approach will have a strong influence on the *design* of our system.

Moreover, as explained in section 2.4, we perform some proofs at each refinement step allowing us to check that our system is consistent. Such proofs help us correcting errors that we might have introduced while modeling. Again, proving is part of modeling.

3.4 Refinement Strategy

In this section, we shall obey all the **rules** mentioned in section 2.3 as guidelines. We present here how to choose among all the requirements and perform them in various steps.

Initial Model: Normal Behavior

The idea is to start by *eliminating all complicated cases*, as mentioned in **R5**: only consider the main functions of the whole system, namely checking the consistency between the mode wished by the driver and the mode that is acceptable by the VOBC system. Here, we almost ignore all the noises, just use a most abstract one: a non-deterministic event standing for all the noises.

For instance, we shall suppose that the MSS button has an ATPM alternative: we can thus (temporarily) remove the ATPM button from the cabin (it was defined in requirement TR_ENV-3). This button will be re-introduced in the fifth refinement below. We can forget about the particularly complicated encoding between the train and the VOBC (defined in requirement VOBC_ENV-2).

We also eliminate all special cases where the emergency brake is possibly triggered (requirements VOBC_FUN-3 and VOBC_FUN-5).

Finally, we forget about the initialization of the VOBC (see VOBC_FUN-2).

The net result of all these simplifications is that we only consider the *normal case* where the wish of the train driver is positively received by the VOBC: this is the initial model.

In subsequent refinements we shall gradually re-introduce all the complicated cases we eliminated in this initial model. In doing this, we follow our rule **R4** concerned with the progressive introduction of the system functions.

First Refinement: Non-stationary Case

In this level, we take account of the most important special case that influences the system decision. By reading carefully the requirement document, it seems that this most important special case is the one where the wish of the driver is done while the train is not stationary (VOBC_FUN-10). We introduce this special case in this refinement. Here again, we follow our rule **R4**.

Second Refinement: Elementary Non-availabilities

Similarly to the previous refinement taking account of rule **R4**, we present here special cases inside the system decision. We also obey rule **R0**: taking a small number of requirements at a time. These special cases are the non-availabilities of the ATPM or ATO modes that are introduced in requirements VOBC_FUN-7,8 by some complex conditions.

For the moment, we shall follow our rule **R3** telling us that we can abstract a complex condition with a boolean variable: so, we only introduce the very fact that these modes might be unavailable by using abstract boolean variables obtained non-deterministically, without relying on the corresponding details. By doing so, we also follow our rule **R1** stipulating that we could take account of a requirement in a partial way only. These boolean variables will be given more deterministic concrete understanding in the sixth refinement below.

Note that the order of this refinement and the previous one could be interchanged as they do not depend on each other.

Third Refinement: Active and Passive States, Initialization

In this level, we extend our development of the VOBC by adding a system state (passive and active). This corresponds to requirements VOBC_FUN-1,2,3,4. Following **R1**, **R2**, **R3**, and **R4**, we take account in a partial way of the state of the VOBC by means of a boolean variable. Partially only because, again, all the fine details of the "passivity" are too complicated (they will be introduced in the sixth refinement). However, the availabilities of the ATPM and ATO mode are taken into account (see requirements VOBC_FUN-3) by means of the boolean variabIes introduced in the previous refinement.

We also take account of the initialization of the VOBC. Moreover, we consider the fact that only one cabin is active for accepting a transition.

Fourth Refinement: Emergency Brake

Here we focus on an important output of the VOBC which is influenced by all the special cases: we introduce the emergency brake (introduced in VOBC_FUN-3 and VOBC_FUN-11). It is triggered by all the special cases we have now considered (at least partially): non-stationarity (first refinement), non-availabilities (second refinement), and possible passivity (third refinement).

Until now, we took account of all the functions of the system in an abstract way. The following refinements consider now the very concrete requirements related to a large number of variables.

Fifth Refinement: Handling of the ATPM Button

In the initial model, we were cheating by having the ATPM button inside the MSS switch. This was done for simplification. We are now ready to introduce the special properties of ATPM button for handling this particular mode. For this reason, we introduce special TRAIN variables and events. As mentioned in **R7**, we do introduce the environment variable in a way that is balanced with the VOBC development. This is what we do here: introducing the train variables only when we need it.

Sixth Refinement: Completion of Non-availabilities and Passive State Cases

We are now able to complete all cases of non-availabilities of the ATPM or ATO modes (VOBC_FUN-7,8). We also consider all cases of passivity (VOBC_FUN-5).

Seventh Refinement: Encoding of the Cabin and MSS button

We consider the encoding of the communication between the train and the VOBC, now taking partial account of requirement VOBC_ENV-2.

Eighth Refinement: Last Encoding

This refinement takes account of the last requirement of VOBC_ENV-2.

3.5 Refinement Strategy Synthesis

The following table maps the initial model and the eight refined models to the related requirements which are taken into account.

Refinement	VOBC Function	Train	Driver	VOBC
Initial	VOBC_FUN-9,14-19(p)	TR_ENV-2(p)	DR_ENV-1,2(p)	VOBC_ENV-1(p)
First	VOBC_FUN-10,11-19(p)	TR_ENV-5	–	VOBC_ENV-1(p)
Second	VOBC_FUN- 5(p), 6, 17(p), 18(p)	–	–	–
Third	VOBC_FUN-1,2,4,5(p),14-19(p)	TR_ENV-1	–	VOBC_ENV-1(p)
Fourth	VOBC_FUN-3,11,12	TR_ENV-4	–	VOBC_ENV-3
Fifth	VOBC_FUN-15,17	TR_ENV-2,3	DR_ENV-2	VOBC_ENV-1(p)
Sixth	VOBC_FUN-5,7,8	–	–	VOBC_ENV-1,2(p)
Seventh	–	–	–	VOBC_ENV-2(p)
Eighth	–	–	–	VOBC_ENV-2

* *(p) means the related requirement is PARTIALLY taken into account.*

As it is shown in this table, at each level we only take a short number of requirements, this follows **R0**. We also find many partial accounts. This follows **R1** and **R2**: we take account of complicated requirements partially only and leave the other parts for further steps. The whole refinement strategy follows **R5** and **R6**: start from the very abstract requirements and end with the concrete ones. After this refinement strategy is obtained, we take **R8** into account: to make sure no requirement has been forgotten, and then, following **R9**, remove all requirements that cannot be considered.

3.6 Formal Development

The formal development presented in this paper is only very short due to some lack of space. The interested reader can download the complete formal development of this example from the Event-B website [2]. In the following, we present some diagrams describing in a simple manner the events of each step. Such events are implicitly represented in some boxes standing for the various phases that will be executed. We follow exactly what was presented in section 3.4 describing our refinement strategy.

In the initial model, we have essentially two sets of events corresponding to the TRAIN Input phase where an abstract MSS might be changed and the VOBC Decision phase where the modification of the abstract MSS made by the driver is accepted:

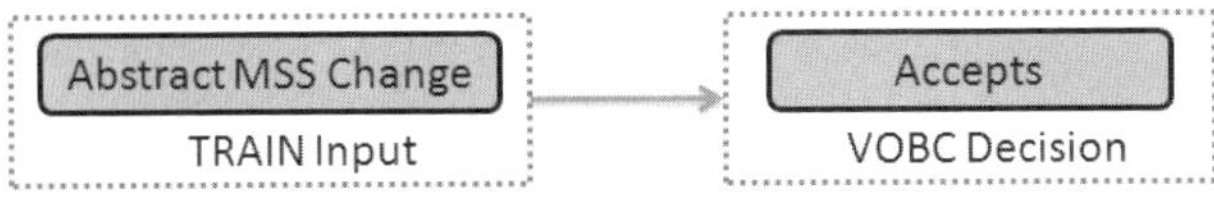

In the first refinement, we take account of the speed of the TRAIN and the corresponding possible rejection made by the VOBC:

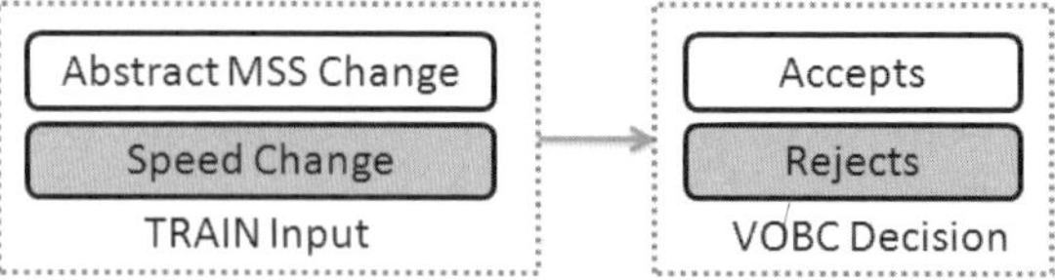

In the second refinement, we introduce some boolean variables dealing with the ATPM and ATO availabilities. These boolean variables are *non-deterministically* assigned in the VOBC Checks phase. The boolean variables are then used (read) in the VOBC Decision phase:

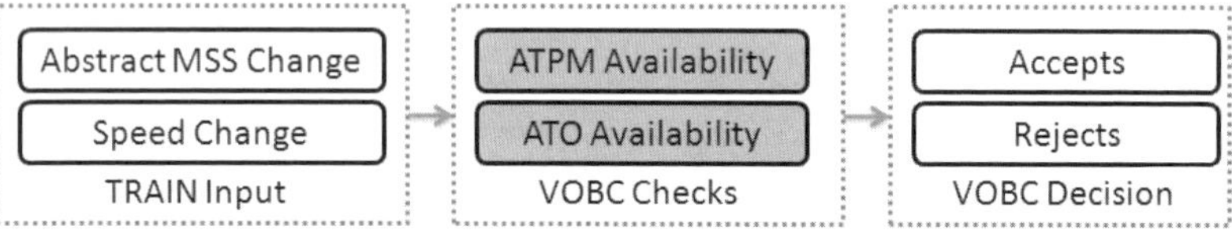

In the third and fourth refinements, we introduce a similar boolean variable for the "passivity" state and we deal with the Emergency Brake handling in the VOBC Decision phase:

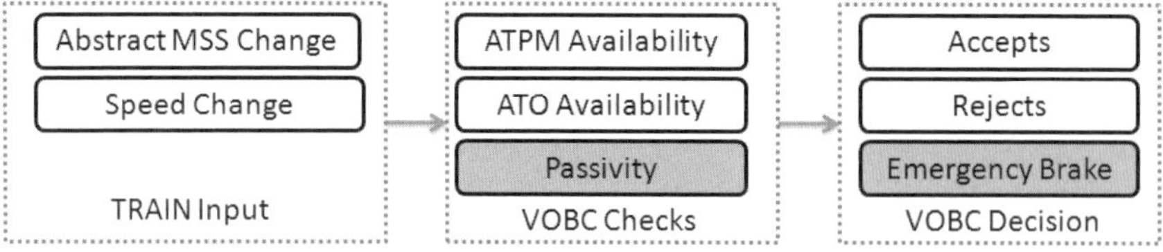

In the fifth refinement, we make the driver switch and button more concrete. More precisely, we now separate the ATPM button from the abstract MSS:

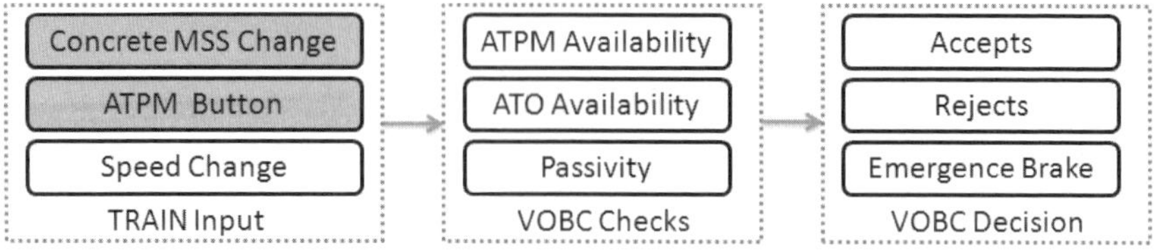

In the sixth refinement, we introduce a large number of various inputs in the TRAIN Inputs phase allowing us to make *deterministic* the assignments to the availabilities and passivity boolean variables in the VOBC Checks phase. An important aspect of what is done here is that the boolean variables introduced in the second and third refinements in the VOBC Checks phase are still used (read) in the VOBC Decision phase, which is thus *not modified*.

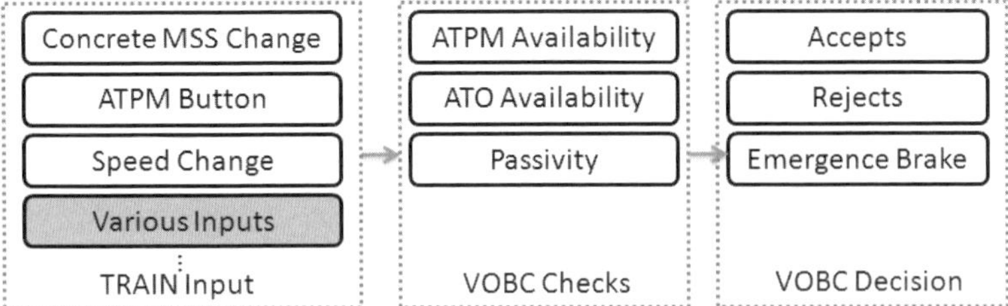

In the seventh and eighth refinements, we introduce more TRAIN Inputs and thus implement the MSS switch as well as the ATPM button. This introduces an intermediate TRAIN Checks phase. We have now a clear separation between the part of the model dealing with the future software and that dealing with the environment:

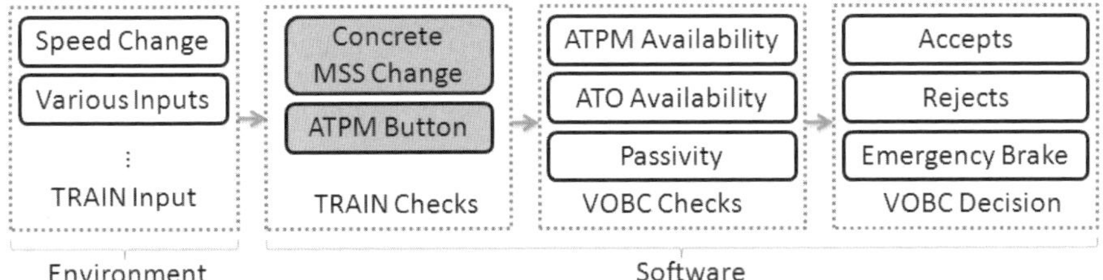

3.7 Proof Statistics

The entire formal development with the Rodin Platform generated 439 proof obligations all automatically discharged except two of them requiring a very light manual intervention (one click).

3.8 Timing and Determinism Issues

In the real industrial system, there are some important timing issues that have not been taken into account in this paper because of the lack of space. However, it its possible to give some information on how this can be formalized in our model. The problem is as follows: the driver MSS button change or ATPM button depression should last for a certain time in order to be taken into account by the VOBC. This is to avoid some outside troubles. The problem can be simply formalized by ensuring that any change in these buttons has to last continuously for at least some cycles ("8" is a typical number) before being taken into account by the VOBC. This could have been incorporated at the end of the development.

Determinism (for the VOBC) is another important issue in industry. It means that exactly one event (of the VOBC) has its guard true. So, it is a theorem we can prove. Deadlock freeness means there is at least one guard true, determinism is one step more precise: there is exactly exactly one guard that is true. It can be checked in any refinement, but it is more interesting to check it at the end.

4 Related Work

There have been recently several papers [8] [9] [10] on topics similar to the ones presented in this paper. They are all concerned with defining some guidelines for modeling complex systems. They treat problems that are more complex that the one envisaged here: how to structure the refinements of systems where a future software controller has to master an environment by means of some sensors and actuators. Their main message is to start by defining the environment together with the properties to be ensured on it, and then (and only then) to study how a controller can handle the situation although it will base its decision on a fuzzy picture (due to the transmission time) of the real environment.

The case studied here is simpler than the one studied in these papers in that our controller is just there to decide whether the driver has the right to require a new mode. We do not control a complex situation. However, we treat a problem that is not so much studied in their examples, namely that of the presence of a large number of special cases and special equipments, transforming an apparently simple problem into one that becomes quite complicated (but not complex).

5 Conclusion

In this paper, we briefly recall a simple methodology to be used for industrial software developments. The main points we wanted to insist on are the following: (1) the importance of having a well-defined requirement document, (2) the need to enter in a formal model construction before the coding phase, and (3) the usage of superposition refinement in this modeling phase so that the system can be first drastically simplified and then gradually extended to fulfill its requirements.

This methodology was illustrated by a simple example representing a typical problem encountered in industry (although slightly simplified). In this example, we show a more important point, namely how the usage of superposition refinement leads naturally to the design of our system into successive phases enriching gradually the "contents" of its main variables until one can reach a final decision phase that is independent from the many more basic variables.

Acknowledgement. The authors gratefully acknowledge support from the Danish National Research Foundation and the National Natural Science Foundation of China (Grant No. 61061130541) for the Danish-Chinese Center for Cyber Physical Systems. This work was also supported by National Basic Research Program of China (No. 2011CB302904), National High Technology Research and Development Program of China (No. 2011AA010101) and National Natural Science Foundation of China (No. 61021004).

References

1. Abrial, J.R.: Modeling in Event-B: System and Software Engineering. Cambridge University Press, Cambridge (2010)
2. Rodin Platform, http://www.event-b.org

3. Back, R.J.R., Sere, K.: Superposition Refinement of Reactive Systems. Formal Aspect of Computing (1995)
4. Back, R.J.R., Kurki-Suonio, R.: Distributed Cooperation with Action Systems. ACM Transaction on Programming languages and Systems (1988)
5. Butler, M.J.: Stepwise Refinement of Communication Systems. Science of Computer Programming (1996)
6. Hoare, C.A.R.: Proof of Correctness of Data Representation. Acta Informatica (1972)
7. Leuschel, M., Butler, M.: ProB: An Automated Analysis Toolset for the B Method. International Journal on Software Tools for Technology Transfer (2008)
8. Hoang, T.S., Hudon, S.: Defining Control Systems with Some Fragile Environment. Working Report 723 ETH (2011)
9. Butler, M.J.: Towards a Cookbook for Modelling and Refinement of Control Problems. Working paper (2009), `http://deploy-eprints.ecs.soton.ac.uk/108/`
10. Yeganefard, S., Butler, M.J., Rezazadeh, A.: Evaluation of a guideline by formal modelling of cruise control system in Event-B. In: Proceedings of NFM (2010)

Reasoning about Liveness Properties in Event-B*

Thai Son Hoang[1] and Jean-Raymond Abrial[2]

[1] Department of Computer Science,
Swiss Federal Institute of Technology Zurich (ETH-Zurich), Switzerland
htson@inf.ethz.ch
[2] Marseille, France
jrabrial@neuf.fr

Abstract. Event-B is a formal method which is widely used in modelling safety critical systems. So far, the main properties of interest in Event-B are safety related. Even though some liveness properties, e,g, termination, are already within the scope of Event-B, more general liveness properties, e.g. progress or persistence, are currently unsupported. We present in this paper proof rules to reason about important classes of liveness properties. We illustrate our proof rules by applying them to prove liveness properties of realistic examples. Our proof rules are based on several proof obligations that can be implemented in a tool support such as the Rodin platform.

Keywords: Event-B, liveness properties, formal verification, tool support.

1 Introduction

Event-B [1] is a formal modelling method for discrete state transition systems and is based on first-order logic and some typed set theory. The backbone of the method is the notion of step-wise refinement, allowing details to be gradually added to the formal models. An advantage of using refinement is that any (safety) properties that are already proved to hold in the early models are guaranteed to hold in the later models. This is crucial in a method for developing systems correct-by-construction. System development using Event-B is supported by the RODIN platform [2]. It is an open and extensible platform containing facilities for modelling and proving Event-B models.

So far, most of the properties that are proved in Event-B are safety properties, i.e., something (bad) never happens, which are usually captured as invariants of the models. Although it is essential to prove that systems are safe, it might not be sufficient. Considering an elevator system, an important safety property is that *the door must be closed while the elevator is moving*. However, an unusable non-moving elevator also satisfies this safety property. Hence, it is desirable to be able to specify and prove that the system also satisfies some *liveness* properties, e.g., it is always that case that a request will eventually be served.

Currently, besides safety properties that are captured as *invariants*, Event-B can only be used to model certain liveness properties, e.g., *termination*. More general classes of liveness properties, such as *progress* or *persistence* are unsupported. On the one hand,

* Part of this research was supported by DEPLOY project (EC Grant number 214158).

S. Qin and Z. Qiu (Eds.): ICFEM 2011, LNCS 6991, pp. 456–471, 2011.

we want to increase the set of properties that can be specified and verified in Event-B. On the other hand, we aim to keep the reasoning practical, so that we can easily have tool support to generate and discharge obligations.

We propose a set of *proof rules* for reasoning about three different classes of liveness properties. The rules are based on some basic *proof obligations*, that can be conveniently implemented in the supporting Rodin platform of Event-B. The first proof rule is for proving *existence* properties stating that something will *always eventually* occur ($\Box \Diamond P$). The second proof rule is for reasoning about *progress* properties: something must eventually happen if some condition becomes true ($\Box(P_1 \Rightarrow \Diamond P_2)$). The third proof rule is for proving *persistence* properties: *eventually*, something *always* holds ($\Diamond \Box P$).

The rest of the paper is organised as follows. Section 2 gives an overview of the Event-B modelling method and temporal logic. Our main contribution is in Section 3 including proof rules for the previously mentioned properties. Section 4 illustrates the applicability of our rules to some realistic examples. We briefly elaborate our ideas for tool supports in Section 3.3. Finally, we draw some conclusion (Section 6), discuss related work (Section 5), and investigate future research directions (Section 6.1).

2 Background

2.1 The Event-B Modelling Method

A model in Event-B, called *machine*, contains a vector of state variables v and a set of events $\mathsf{evt_i}$. Each event has the form $\mathsf{evt_i} \mathrel{\widehat{=}}$ **any** x **where** $G_i(x, v)$ **then** $A_i(x, v, v')$ **end**, where x are parameters of the event, $G_i(x, v)$ is the guard and $A_i(x, v, v')$ is the action. The guard of an event is the necessary condition for the event to be enabled. The action of an event comprises several assignments, each has one of the following forms: $v := E(x, v)$, $v :\in E(x, v)$, and $v :\mid Q(x, v, v')$.

Assignments of the first form deterministically update variables v with values of $E(x, v)$. Assignments of the latter two forms are nondeterministic. They update variable v to be either some member of a set $E(x, v)$ or satisfying a before-after predicate $Q(x, v, v')$. The first two forms of assignment can be represented using the last form with the corresponding before-after predicates $v' = E(x, v)$ and $v' \in E(x, v)$. Assignments of an action are supposed to be executed in parallel. Each event therefore corresponds to a before-after predicate $\mathsf{A}(x, v, v')$ by conjoining the before-after predicate of all assignments and the predicate $u = u'$ where u is the set of variables unchanged by the action. A dedicated event, called init, without parameters and guard is used as the initialisation of the machine. An after predicate Init is associated with init.

Variables v are constrained by invariant $I(v)$ which needs to be proved to hold in every reachable state of the system. This is guaranteed by proving that the invariant is *established* by the initialisation init and subsequently *preserved* by all events.

To overcome the complexity in system development, Event-B advocates the use of *refinement*: a process of gradually adding details to a model. A development in Event-B is a sequence of machines, linked by some refinement relationship: an *abstract* machine is refined by the subsequent *concrete* machine. Abstract variables v are linked to concrete variables w by some *gluing invariant* $J(v, w)$. Any behaviour of the concrete model must be *simulated* by some behaviour of the abstract model, with respect to the gluing invariant $J(v, w)$.

An Event-B machine corresponds to a state transition system: the states s are captured as tuples $\langle \overline{v} \rangle$, representing the values of variables v; and the events correspond to transitions between states. An event evt is said to be *enabled* in a state s if there exists some parameter x such that the guard G of the event hold in that state s. Otherwise, the event is said to be *disabled*. A machine M is said to be *deadlocked* in s if all its events are disabled in that particular state.

Given an event evt, we say a state t is an evt-*successor state* of s if t is a possible after-state of the execution of evt from the before-state s. Lifting the definition to a machine M, we say that t is an M-*successor state* of s if there exists an event evt of M such that t is an evt-successor of s.

A *trace* σ of a machine M is a sequence of states (either finite or infinite) $s_0, s_1, \ldots$ satisfying the following conditions.

- s_0 is an initial state, i.e., satisfying the initial after predicate Init.
- For every two successive states s_i and s_{i+1}, s_{i+1} is an M-successor state of s_i.
- If the sequence is finite and ends in some state s_{final} then machine M is deadlocked in s_{final}.

Finally, a machine M is associated with a set of traces $\mathcal{T}(\mathsf{M})$ denoting all of its possible traces.

2.2 Temporal Logic

We give a summary of the (propositional) LTL temporal logic similar to the one defined by Manna and Pnueli [10]. We will consider temporal formulas to be interpreted over the sequences of states arising from machine traces.

The basic element of the language is a *state formula* P: any first-order logic formula. It describes some property that holds in some state s. It is built from terms and predicates over the program variables v. The extended temporal formulas are constructed from these basic state formulas by applying the Boolean operators $\neg, \wedge, \vee, \Rightarrow$ and temporal operators: always ($\Box$), eventually ($\Diamond$) and until ($\mathcal{U}$).

Let σ be a non-empty, finite or infinite, sequence of states of the form $s_0, s_1, \ldots$. We use the standard notation $\sigma \models \phi$ to denote that σ satisfies formula ϕ. We first define some notations that will be used in the interpretation of temporal formulas.

- States satisfying a state formula P are called P-states.
- The length of the trace σ denoted as $l(\sigma)$ is defined as follows. If σ is finite, i.e., of the form $s_0, \ldots, s_k$, $l(\sigma) = k + 1$. If σ is infinite, $l(\sigma) = \omega$, the least infinite ordinal number.
- Given a number $0 \leq k < l(\sigma)$, a k-suffix sequence of states of σ denoted as σ^k is the sequence of states obtained by dropping the first k elements from σ, i.e., $\sigma^k = s_k, s_{k+1}, \ldots$.

The interpretation of the LTL formulas over σ is as follows.

- For a state formula P, $\sigma \models P$ iff s_0 is a P-state.

– The Boolean operators are interpreted intuitively.

$$\begin{array}{lll} \sigma \models \phi_1 \land \phi_2 & \text{iff} & \sigma \models \phi_1 \text{ “and” } \sigma \models \phi_2 \,, \\ \sigma \models \phi_1 \lor \phi_2 & \text{iff} & \sigma \models \phi_1 \text{ “or” } \sigma \models \phi_2 . \\ \sigma \models \neg\phi & \text{iff} & \text{“not” } \sigma \models \phi \,, \\ \sigma \models \phi_1 \Rightarrow \phi_2 & \text{iff} & \sigma \models \phi_1 \text{ “then” } \sigma \models \phi_2 \,. \end{array}$$

– The temporal operators are interpreted as follows.

$$\begin{array}{lll} \sigma \models \Box\,\phi & \text{iff} & \text{for all } k \text{ where } 0 \leq k < l(\sigma), \text{ we have } \sigma^k \models \phi. \\ \sigma \models \Diamond\,\phi & \text{iff} & \text{there exists } k \text{ where } 0 \leq k < l(\sigma), \text{ such that } \sigma^k \models \phi. \\ \sigma \models \phi_1\,\mathcal{U}\,\phi_2 & \text{iff} & \text{there exists } k, \text{ where } 0 \leq k < l(\sigma), \text{ such that} \\ & & \quad \sigma^k \models \phi_2, \text{ and} \\ & & \quad \text{for all } i \text{ such that } 0 \leq i < k, \text{ we have } \sigma^i \models \phi_1. \end{array}$$

In the case where we have some state predicates P, P_1, P_2, the combination with the temporal operators can be understood as follows.

$$\begin{array}{lll} \sigma \models \Box\,P & \text{iff} & \text{every state in } \sigma \text{ are } P\text{-state.} \\ \sigma \models \Diamond\,P & \text{iff} & \text{there exits some } P\text{-state in } \sigma. \\ \sigma \models P_1\,\mathcal{U}\,P_2 & \text{iff} & \text{there exists some } P_2\text{-state } s_k \text{ in } \sigma, \\ & & \text{and every state until } s_k \text{ (excluding } s_k\text{) is } P_1\text{-state.} \end{array}$$

Definition 1. *A machine* M *is said to satisfy property* ϕ *(denoted as* $\mathsf{M} \models \phi$*) if all its traces satisfy* ϕ*, i.e.,* $\forall \sigma \in \mathcal{T}(\mathsf{M}) \cdot \sigma \models \phi$.

In subsequent proof rules, we use the notation $\mathsf{M} \vdash \phi$ to denote that $\mathsf{M} \models \phi$ *is provable*.

3 Proof Rules

In this section we present some proof rules to reason about important classes of liveness properties. We progress by first presenting some basic proof obligations as building blocks for the later proof rules. We assume here that there is a machine M with events of the general form mentioned in Section 2.1.

3.1 Proof Obligations

Machine M Leads from P_1 to P_2. Given two state formulas P_1, P_2, we say M *leads from* P_1 *to* P_2 if for any pair of successor states (s_i, s_{i+1}) of any trace of M, if s_i is a P_1-state then s_{i+1} is a P_2-state. We first define the *leads from* notion for events.

An event evt leads from P_1 to P_2 if starting from any P_1-state, execution of every event leads to a P_2-state. This is guaranteed by proving the following (stronger) condition.

$$P_1(v) \land G(x, v) \land \mathsf{A}(x, v, v') \Rightarrow P_2(v')$$

(We adopt the convention that free variables in proof obligations are universally quantified.)

Given the above definition, M *leads from* P_1 *to* P_2 if every event evt of M leads from P_1 to P_2.

Proof. From the definition of machine trace in 2.1 and of *leads from* notion for events.

In subsequent proof rules, we use the notation $\mathsf{M} \vdash P_1 \curvearrowright P_2$ to denote that this fact is provable. Note that the property can be stated in terms of k-suffix as follows. For any pair of successor state s_i, s_{i+1} of any k-suffix of any trace of M, if s_i is a P_1-state then s_{i+1} is a P_2-state.

Machine M is Convergent in *P*. The obligation allows us to prove that any trace of M *does not end with an infinite sequence of P-states*. Equivalently, the property can be stated as: any k-suffix of any trace of M also *does not end with an infinite sequence of P-state*. This can be guaranteed by reasoning about the *convergence* property of the events in M as follows.

- An integer expression $V(v)$ (called the *variant*) is defined.
- For every event evt of M, we prove that
  1. When in a P-state, if evt is enabled, $V(v)$ is a natural number[1].

$$P(v) \wedge G(x,v) \Rightarrow V(v) \in \mathbb{N}$$

  2. An execution of evt from a P-state decreases $V(v)$.

$$P(v) \wedge G(x,v) \wedge \mathsf{A}(x,v,v') \Rightarrow V(v') < V(v)$$

Proof. If a trace ends with an infinite sequence of P-states, then $V(v)$ will be decreased infinitely (condition 2). However, since in P-states, $V(v)$ is a member of a well-founded set (condition 1), this results in a contradiction.

In the subsequent proof rules, we use $\mathsf{M} \vdash \downarrow P$ to denote that this fact (i.e., M is convergent in P) is provable.

Machine M is Divergent in *P*. This obligation allows us to prove that any infinite trace of M *ends with an infinite sequence of P-states*. An equivalent property is that any infinite k-suffix of any trace of M also ends with an infinite sequence of P-states.

- An integer expression $V(v)$ (called the *variant*) is defined.
- For every event evt of M, we prove the following conditions.
  1. When in a $\neg P$-state, if evt is enabled, $V(v)$ is a natural number.
  2. An execution of evt from a $\neg P$-state decreases the value of the variant.

$$\neg P(v) \wedge G(x,v) \wedge \mathsf{A}(x,v,v') \Rightarrow V(v') < V(v)$$

  3. An execution of evt from a P-state *does not increase* $V(v)$ if the new value of the variant $V(v')$ is a natural number.

$$P(v) \wedge G(x,v) \wedge \mathsf{A}(x,v,v') \wedge V(v') \in \mathbb{N} \Rightarrow V(v') \leq V(v)$$

Proof. Condition 1 and 2 guarantees that the variant V is a member of an well-founded set (e.g., $\mathbb{N}$) and decreases when $\neg P$ holds, and condition 3 ensures that this decreasing *cannot be undone* when P holds. Hence if M has an infinite trace, then $\neg P$-states will eventually disappear from it.

In the subsequent proof rules, we use $\mathsf{M} \vdash \nearrow P$ to denote that this fact (i.e., M is divergent in P) is provable.

[1] More generally, the variant can be a member of any well-founded set.

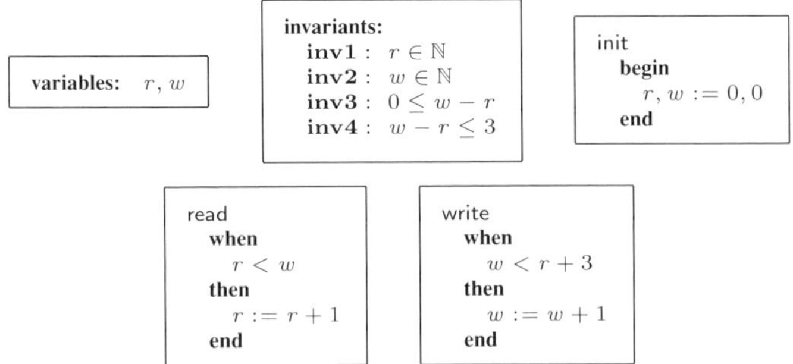

Fig. 1. Machine RdWr: Reader/Writer

Machine M is Deadlock-Free in P. This obligation allows to prove that any (finite) trace of M does not end in a P-state. This is guaranteed by proving that in a P-state, at least one event of M is enabled, i.e., M is deadlock-free in any P-state.

$$P(v) \quad \Rightarrow \quad \bigvee_i (\exists x \cdot G_i(x, v))$$

Proof. From the definition of machine trace in Section 2.1.

Note that an equivalent property is as follows: any k-suffix of any trace of M is also deadlock-free in P, i.e., does not end in a P-state.

In the subsequent proof rules, we use $\mathsf{M} \vdash \circlearrowleft P$ to denote that this fact is provable.

3.2 Proof Rules

We are going to use the example of Reader/Writer in **Fig.** 1 to illustrate our proof rules in this section. The machine models a system with two processes *Reader* and *Writer* sharing a common bounded buffer. The machine has two variables, namely r and w (both initialised to 0), representing the current pointer of the reader and the writer. The "buffer" is the range $[r + 1, w]$ representing the data that have been written but not yet read. The size of the buff is $w - r$. Assuming that the buffer can hold a maximum of 3 pieces of data, we must have $0 \leq w - r$ and $w - r \leq 3$ as invariants of the model.

There are two events: read and write for reading and writing, respectively. Event read increases the read pointer r by 1, when there are some unread data. Similarly, event write advances the writer pointer w, when there is still some space in the buffer.

Invariance. Safety properties are usually captured in Event-B machine as invariants. The proof rules for invariance properties are well-known and already *built-into* for Event-B. They are also used in [10]. We restate the rules mentioned in Section 2.1 in terms of the above proof obligations as follows.

$$\frac{\vdash \mathsf{Init} \Rightarrow I \qquad \mathsf{M} \vdash I \curvearrowright I}{\mathsf{M} \vdash \Box I} \quad \mathbf{INV_{induct}}$$

The above rule $\mathbf{INV_{induct}}$ allows us to prove invariance properties which are inductive. Otherwise, i.e. when invariance properties are not inductive, the following proof rule can be used.

$$\frac{\begin{array}{l} \vdash J \Rightarrow I \\ \mathsf{M} \vdash \Box J \end{array}}{\mathsf{M} \vdash \Box I} \quad \mathbf{INV_{theorem}}$$

Informally, rule $\mathbf{INV_{theorem}}$ allows us to prove that I is an invariance property relying on a stronger additional invariant J. Subsequently, we can make use of the inductive rule $\mathbf{INV_{induct}}$ to prove that J is an invariance property,

Invariance properties are important in reasoning about the correctness of our models since it limits the set of reachable states. In the subsequent proof rules, we adopt the convention that already proved invariance properties can be assumed and hence, do not mention them explicitly.

Existence. An existence property states that some (good) property, say P, will *always eventually* hold. The following proof rule allows us to prove that a machine M satisfies an existence property $\Box\Diamond P$ by reasoning about convergence and deadlock-freedom.

$$\frac{\begin{array}{l} \mathsf{M} \vdash \downarrow \neg P \\ \mathsf{M} \vdash \circlearrowleft \neg P \end{array}}{\mathsf{M} \vdash \Box\Diamond P} \quad \mathbf{LIVE_{\Box\Diamond}}$$

Proof. Consider a trace σ of machine M. Consider a k-suffix σ^k of σ. If σ^k is an infinite sequence of states, according to the first antecedent, it cannot end with an infinite sequence of $(\neg P)$-states, hence a P-state eventually appears. The second antecedent ensures that in the case where σ^k is finite, it does not end in a $(\neg P)$-state, i.e., it must end in a P-state.

Example 1. *We want to prove that for* RdWr, *eventually* $r \geq L$ *for some natural number* L. *Our reasoning is as follows.*

$$\boxed{\mathsf{RdWr} \vdash \Box\Diamond r \geq L} \xrightarrow{\mathbf{LIVE_{\Box\Diamond}}} \begin{cases} \boxed{\mathsf{RdWr} \vdash \downarrow (\neg r \geq L)} & (1) \\ \boxed{\mathsf{RdWr} \vdash \circlearrowleft (\neg r \geq L)} & (2) \end{cases}$$

(1) RdWr $\vdash \downarrow (\neg r \geq L)$ *: we propose a variant* $V_1 = (L - r) + (L + 3 - w)$, *a sum of two terms, which are decreased accordingly by* read *and* write. *The fact that the variant is a natural number when the events are enabled in a* $(\neg r \leq L)$*-state is a consequence of invariant* **inv4**.

(2) RdWr $\vdash \circlearrowleft (\neg r \geq L)$ *: According to the proof obligation for proving deadlock-freedom, we have to prove that* $\neg r \geq L \Rightarrow r \neq w \vee w \neq r + 3$ *which holds trivially.*

Progress. A progress property states that a P_1-state must always be followed eventually by a P_2-state. For a machine M, the property can be formalised as follows $\mathsf{M} \vdash \Box(P_1 \Rightarrow \Diamond P_2)$. In order to reason about progress properties, we introduce two proof rules. The first one **Until** deals with a special form of progress properties where P_1 is stable (i.e., holds until P_2 holds). The second one $\mathbf{LIVE_{progress}}$ deals with a more general form of progress properties by "inventing" an auxiliary property.

$$\frac{\mathsf{M} \vdash (P_1 \land \neg P_2) \curvearrowright (P_1 \lor P_2) \qquad \mathsf{M} \vdash \Box\Diamond(\neg P_1 \lor P_2)}{\mathsf{M} \vdash \Box(P_1 \Rightarrow (P_1 \,\mathcal{U}\, P_2))}\ \mathbf{Until}$$

$$\frac{\mathsf{M} \vdash \Box(P_1 \land \neg P_2 \Rightarrow P_3) \qquad \mathsf{M} \vdash \Box(P_3 \Rightarrow (P_3 \,\mathcal{U}\, P_2))}{\mathsf{M} \vdash \Box(P_1 \Rightarrow \Diamond P_2)}\ \mathbf{LIVE_{progress}}$$

Proof. The rules are justified as follows.

- **Until**: Consider a trace σ of machine M. Consider a k-suffix σ^k of σ where s_k is a P_1-state. We have to prove that there exists a state P_2-state s_m in trace σ (with $k \leq m$) such that any state between s_k and s_m (excluding s_m) is a P_1-state.
  - If s_k is also a P_2-state, then we can take m to be k.
  - If s_k is a $\neg P_2$-state, then it is also a $(P_1 \land \neg P_2)$-state. From the second antecedent, we know that eventually, there is a $(\neg P_1 \lor P_2)$-state. Let s_m be the first such state (hence $k \leq m$). We will prove that s_m is indeed the state that we are looking for.
    * Since s_m is the first state after s_k satisfying $\neg P_1 \lor P_2$, any state in between s_k and s_m excluding s_m is a $(P_1 \land \neg P_2)$-state, i.e., is a P_1-state.
    * Since s_k is a $(P_1 \land \neg P_2)$-state, and s_m is a $(\neg P_1 \lor P_2)$-state, they must be different, i.e., $k \neq m$, hence s_{m-1} is a state in between s_k and s_m. Subsequently, s_{m-1} must be a $(P_1 \land \neg P_2)$-state. Together with the first antecedent of the rule, s_m is a $(P_1 \lor P_2)$-state. Since s_m is both a $(\neg P_1 \lor P_2)$-state and a $(P_1 \lor P_2)$-state, it must be a P_2 state.
- $\mathbf{LIVE_{progress}}$: Rule $\mathbf{LIVE_{progress}}$ relies on auxiliary state predicate P_3 and its justification is as follows. The first antecedent states that $P_1 \land \neg P_2 \Rightarrow P_3$ is an invariant of machine M and the second antecedent states an until-property where P_3 holds until eventually P_2 holds. Consider any k-suffix σ^k of a trace σ of machine M, where s_k is a P_1-state. If s_k is also a P_2-state then the progress property holds trivially. Otherwise, i.e., if s_k is a $\neg P_2$-state, according to the first antecedent, s_k must be a P_3-state. The second antecedent then allows us to conclude that there exits a P_2-state s_m where $k \leq m$.

Example 2. *Consider machine* RdWr. *We want to prove that the reader can always make some progress, which is formalised by* $\mathsf{RdWr} \vdash \Box(w = L \Rightarrow \Diamond\, r = L)$ *, for some natural number* L*. Our reasoning starts by applying rule* $\mathbf{LIVE_{progress}}$ *with the auxiliary state predicate* P_3 *to be* $r < L$.

$$\mathsf{RdWr} \vdash \Box(w = L \Rightarrow \Diamond\, r = L) \xrightarrow{\mathbf{LIVE_{progress}}} \begin{cases} \mathsf{RdWr} \vdash \Box(w = L \land \neg r = L \Rightarrow r < L) & (3) \\ \mathsf{RdWr} \vdash \Box(r < L \Rightarrow (r < L \,\mathcal{U}\, r = L)) & (4) \end{cases}$$

(3) *The fact that* $w = L \land \neg r = L \Rightarrow r < L$ *is a consequence of invariant* **inv3**, *i.e. proved by rule* $\mathbf{INV_{theorem}}$.

(4) *We apply rule* **Until** *as follows.*

$$\boxed{\mathsf{RdWr} \vdash \Box(r < L \Rightarrow (r < L \, \mathcal{U} \, r = L))}$$

$$\xrightarrow{\textbf{Until}} \begin{cases} \boxed{\mathsf{RdWr} \vdash (r < L \land \neg r = L) \curvearrowright (r < L \lor r = L)} & (4.1) \\ \boxed{\mathsf{RdWr} \vdash \Box\Diamond(\neg r < L \lor r = L)} & (4.2) \end{cases}$$

(4.1) *This sub-goal can be simplified as* $\mathsf{RdWr} \vdash (r < L) \curvearrowright (r \leq L)$, *i.e., we must prove that* read *and* write *lead from* $r < L$ *to* $r \leq L$, *which is trivial. For* read, *we need to prove* $r < L \land r \neq w \Rightarrow r + 1 \leq L$.

(4.2) *This sub-goal is equivalent to* $\mathsf{RdWr} \vdash \Box\Diamond(r \geq L)$ *which we proved in* ***Example** 1.*

Persistence. A persistence property states that P must eventually hold forever. Formally, this is expressed for a machine M as $\mathsf{M} \vdash \Diamond\Box P$.

$$\boxed{\dfrac{\mathsf{M} \vdash \nearrow P \qquad \mathsf{M} \vdash \circlearrowleft \neg P}{\mathsf{M} \vdash \Diamond\Box P} \quad \textbf{LIVE}_{\Diamond\Box}}$$

Proof. Consider any trace σ of machine M. The first antecedent guarantees that if the σ is infinite, it will end with an infinite sequence of P-states. The second antecedent ensures that if σ is finite, it cannot end with a $(\neg P)$-state. Together, we know that the σ ends with (finite or infinite) sequence of P-states.

Example 3. *Consider machine* RdWr. *We want to prove that* $\Diamond\Box(L \leq w)$ *for some natural number* L. *We start by applying rule* $\textbf{LIVE}_{\Diamond\Box}$.

$$\boxed{\mathsf{RdWr} \vdash \Diamond\Box(L \leq w)} \xrightarrow{\textbf{LIVE}_{\Diamond\Box}} \begin{cases} \boxed{\mathsf{RdWr} \vdash \nearrow (L \leq w)} & (5) \\ \boxed{\mathsf{RdWr} \vdash \circlearrowleft (\neg L \leq w)} & (6) \end{cases}$$

(5) *We use* $V_2 = (L - w) + (L - r)$ *as our variant.*

1. *In* $(\neg L \leq w)$*-states,* V_2 *is a natural number (thanks to invariant* $r \leq w$*).*
2. *Both* read *and* write *decrease* V_2, *hence, they satisfy conditions for decreasing the variant in* $(\neg L \leq w)$*-states and not increasing the variant in* $L \leq w)$*-states.*

(6) *We have to prove that* $\neg L \leq w \Rightarrow r \neq w \lor w \neq r + 3$, *which is trivial.*

3.3 Tool Support

Our proof rules are based on several basic proof obligations that can be easily realised in a tool support such as the Rodin platform. In particular, the proof obligations related to our illustrated examples in Section 4 are indeed simulated within the current Rodin platform, relying on the standard proof obligation generators. For example, the proof obligations for proving that *a machine* M *is convergent in* P is encoded by adding P to guards of all events and prove the new events are convergent with some variant V. Other proof obligations, e.g., deadlock-freedom, are mostly encoded as *theorems* in the models. The generated obligations are discharged using the current proving support within the platform.

We propose to extend the Event-B models with clauses corresponding to the different liveness properties. For example, the existence property in Example 1 can be specified as follows.

```
existence:
  exst1 :  r ≥ L
           variant (L − r) + (L + 3 − w)
```

Note that we also need to include the declaration for the variant used in proving convergence properties. With this declaration, related proof obligations for ensuring the existence property can be generated accordingly.

Similarly, we can define the following clauses for progress and persistence properties. Note that we also indicate the auxiliary invariant for the progress property, in addition to the declaration of the variant.

```
progress:
  prog1 :  from w = L to r = L
           invariant r < L
           variant (L − r) + (L + 3 − w)
```

```
persistence:
  stbl1 :  L ≤ w
           variant (L − w) + (L − r)
```

We are working on extending the Rodin platform to include these newly proposed clauses.

4 Examples

We illustrate our application of proof rules for *existence* and *progress* properties with Peterson's mutual exclusion algorithm (Section 4.1). The proof rule for *persistence* is illustrated in our example of a device calibration in Section 4.2.

4.1 Peterson's Algorithm

Description. Peterson's algorithm [13] involves two processes P_a and P_b. It is a mutual exclusion algorithm: at most one process shall be in the, so-called, "critical section". It uses three variables: w_a, w_b, and $turn$, elements of the set $\{0, 1\}$.

When $w\_a = 1$ (resp. $w\_b = 1$), it means that P_a (resp. P_b) wishes to enter the critical section or is in the critical section. When $turn = 0$, it means that it is P_a's turn to enter the critical section (if it wishes to do so), and similarly with $turn = 1$ for P_b.

Initially, we have $w\_a = 0$, $w\_b = 0$ (i.e., no process wishes to enter the critical section), and $turn$ takes any value in $\{0, 1\}$. Here are the skeletal sequential programs supposed to be executed concurrently:

```
P_a
  while true do
    // Wishing to Enter the Critical Section
    w_a := 1;
    turn := 1;
    // Busy Waiting
    while ¬ (w_b = 0 ∨ turn = 0) do
      SKIP
    end
    // Enter Critical Section
    ...
    w_a := 0
    // Leave Critical Section
    ...
  end
```

```
P_b
  while true do
    // Wishing to Enter the Critical Section
    w_b := 1;
    turn := 0;
    // Busy Waiting
    while ¬ (w_a = 0 ∨ turn = 1) do
      SKIP
    end
    // Enter Critical Section
    ...
    w_b := 0
    // Leave Critical Section
    ...
  end
```

As can be seen, each process enters a "busy waiting" loop before entering the critical section. Each of them waits until the proper conditions to enter the critical section hold. For P_a, it corresponds to waiting either that P_b does not wish to enter the critical section ($w\_b = 0$) or that it is P_a's turn to enter the critical section ($turn = 0$). We have similar busy waiting conditions for P_b.

We would like to prove two things:

Mutual exclusion. At most one process can be in the critical section at a time.
Progress. A process wishes to enter the critical section will eventually do so.

Refinement Strategy. We shall proceed with three models. The initial model will handle the **mutual exclusion** problem: it is independent from the Peterson's algorithm. The first refinement deals with Peterson's algorithm: we shall have to prove that this refinement indeed refines the initial model and thus obeys the mutual exclusion property. Finally, the second refinement deals with the **progress** property.

The Initial Model

Variables and Invariants. In this initial model, besides variables w_a and w_b as defined in the description, we introduce two more variables, a and b, members of the set $\{0, 1\}$. When $a = 1$, it means that P_a is in the critical section, and similarly with b for P_b.

variables: a, b, w_a, w_b

invariants:
- **inv0_1** : $w\_a = 0 \Rightarrow a = 0$
- **inv0_2** : $w\_b = 0 \Rightarrow b = 0$
- **inv0_3** : $a = 0 \lor b = 0$

Invariant **inv0_1** says that when P_a does not wish to enter the critical section ($w\_a = 0$) then it is certainly not in the critical section ($a = 0$). Invariant **inv0_2** defines a similar property for P_b. Invariant **inv0_3** formalises the mutual exclusion property: at most one process can be in the critical section at a time.

Events. All variables are initialised with 0. Next are events associated with P_a. There are three events describing the way P_a can enter and leave each phase: wishing to enter the critical section, entering the critical section, or leaving it. The sequentiality of the events is ensured by the fact that P_a can be in exactly one situation at a time, either $w\_a = 0$ or $w\_a = 1 \land a = 0$ or $w\_a = 1 \land a = 1$.

wish_a
when
$w\_a = 0$
then
$w\_a := 1$
end

enter_a
when
$w\_a = 1$
$a = 0$
$b = 0$
then
$a := 1$
end

leave_a
when
$a = 1$
then
$a := 0$
$w\_a := 0$
end

The events for P_b are similar. The two processes are obviously concurrent as there is clearly some non-determinacy between the events of one and those of the other.

As can be seen, process P_a enters the critical section if it is not in it ($a = 0$) and if process P_b is also not in it ($b = 0$): the mutual exclusion property is ensured. However, we have two problems here: (1) the checking by P_a of the situation of P_b by looking at b, (2) we have no guarantee that one process does not always enter the critical section while the other one wants to do it as well. These problems will be addressed in the subsequent refinements.

Proofs. There are 25 proof obligations all discharged automatically by the Rodin prover.

First Refinement

Variables and Invariants. Besides variables introduced in the initial model, we add now the variable $turn$ as defined in the description.

variables: ...
$turn$

invariants:
inv1_1 : $turn = 0 \wedge w\_a = 1 \Rightarrow b = 0$
inv1_2 : $turn = 1 \wedge w\_b = 1 \Rightarrow a = 0$

Invariant **inv1_1** is needed in order to prove guard strengthening in event enter_a. This is because in this event we remove the reference to variable b. Invariant **inv1_2** plays a similar role for P_b.

Events. These events deal with P_a. In the event enter_a, the guard $b = 0$ has been replaced by the guard $w\_b = 0 \vee turn = 0$ that does not make any reference to b.

wish_a
when
$w\_a = 0$
then
$w\_a := 1$
$\underline{turn := 1}$
end

enter_a
when
$w\_a = 1$
$a = 0$
$\underline{w\_b = 0 \vee turn = 0}$
then
$a := 1$
end

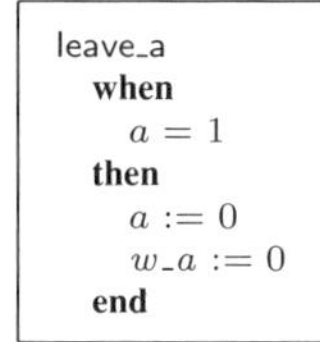

leave_a
when
$a = 1$
then
$a := 0$
$w\_a := 0$
end

We have similar events for P_b which are omitted.

Proofs. The Proof Obligation Generator of the Rodin platform produces 18 proof obligations all discharged automatically.

Second Refinement. In this refinement, we shall prove the progress property for process P_a by encoding the proof obligations in the Rodin platform (see Section 3.3). The property can be stated as follows:

$$\mathsf{Peterson} \vdash \Box(w\_a = 1 \Rightarrow \Diamond\, a = 1)$$

i.e. if process P_a wishes to enter the critical section ($w\_a = 1$) then it will eventually be able to do so. In fact P_a remains wishing to enter the critical section until it enters it. Hence we can apply proof rule $\mathbf{LIVE_{progress}}$ with $w\_a = 1$ as the auxiliary invariant. The first subgoal is trivial, proving that $w\_a = 1 \wedge \neg a = 1 \Rightarrow w\_a = 1$, the second subgoal is $\mathsf{Peterson} \vdash \Box(w\_a = 1 \Rightarrow w\_a = 1\ \mathcal{U}\ a = 1)$.

According to rule **Until**, we have to prove the following two statements:

$$\mathsf{Peterson} \vdash (w\_a = 1 \ \wedge\ a = 0) \curvearrowright (w\_a = 1 \ \vee\ a = 1)$$
$$\mathsf{Peterson} \vdash \Box\Diamond(w\_a = 0 \ \vee\ a = 1)$$

The first statement generates 6 proof obligations that are all discharged trivially. According to the proof rule $\mathbf{LIVE}_{\Box\Diamond}$, the second statement leads to the following:

$$\mathsf{Peterson} \vdash \downarrow (w\_a = 1 \ \wedge\ a = 0)$$
$$\mathsf{Peterson} \vdash \circlearrowleft (w\_a = 1 \ \wedge\ a = 0)$$

The first of these statement requires finding a decreasing variant, which we propose

$$V_3 = 2 * w\_b + 3 * turn - b - a$$ [2]

The fact that this variant is a natural number whenever an event is enabled and under the assumption $w\_a = 1 \ \wedge\ a = 0$ generates 6 proof obligations that are easily discharged. The fact that this variant is decreased by every event under the assumption $w\_a = 1 \ \wedge\ a = 0$ generates 6 proof obligations that are easily discharged provided we add the following additional invariant: $w\_a = 1 \wedge w\_b = 0 \Rightarrow turn = 1$. The second statement requires to prove that the model is deadlock free under the assumption $w\_a = 1 \ \wedge\ a = 0$. It is easily discharged.

Proofs. We have to prove 24 proof obligations. The prover of the Rodin platform proves them all automatically except two easy ones that were proved interactively. All in all, we have 67 proof obligations all proved automatically except two of them.

At this level of details, our Event-B model allows common variables to be accessed and modified concurrently. If we are interested in the precise atomicity assumption on common variables, e.g. $turn$, it is possible to decompose the events wish_a, wish_b, enter_a, and enter_b so that some new events treat with $turn$ only (together with some address counters for sequencing). Introducing these details would only add some complication to the illustration of our proof rules.

4.2 Device Calibration

We now consider a second example. A certain device can be either *on* or *off*. Calibration allows the device to be adjusted. During calibration, the status of the device can alternate. We assume that the duration of the calibration process is limited and model the system as follows. A Boolean variable s denotes the status of the device, and an integer variable t denote the current time, initialised to be 0. The machine Calibration contains three events, each of them advances t by 1. When t is less than some constant M then calibration happens, alternating the status s between *on* and *off* (events

[2] V_3 is a lexicographic variant: $(turn, w\_b, -(a + b))$, with decreasing order of precedences.

calibrate_on and calibrate_off). When t is greater than M and the device is on then the device works normally, no more calibration occurs, only the time t advances (event working)

calibrate_on	calibrate_off	working
when $s = off$, $t \leq M$ **then** $s := on$, $t := t + 1$ **end**	**when** $s = on$, $t < M$ **then** $s := off$, $t := t + 1$ **end**	**when** $s = on$, $M \leq t$ **then** $t := t + 1$ **end**

We want to prove that eventually, the device will be persistent in the on state, i.e. Calibration $\vdash \Diamond \Box s = on$. Applying our $\mathbf{LIVE}_{\Diamond \Box}$ results in two sub-goals.

- Calibration $\vdash \nearrow (s = on)$. We propose the following variant $V_4 = M - t$.
  - To prove that V_4 is a natural number when $\neg s = on$, we add the following invariant **inv0_1** stating that $s = off \Rightarrow t \leq M$.
  - All events increase t hence decrease the variant V_4, hence they certainly decrease V_4 when $\neg s = on$ and do not increase V_4 when $s = on$.
- Calibration $\vdash \circlearrowleft (s = off)$. For this, we must prove that when $s = off$ then one of the events is enabled, and in our case, it is calibrate_on, according to **inv0_1**.

We encode the verification conditions in the Rodin platform, resulting in 19 proof obligations, all of them are discharged automatically by the built-in provers.

5 Related Work

The idea of combining different reasoning features, e.g., *invariant*, *event convergence* and *deadlock-freedom* to prove liveness properties has been presented in our earlier work [8]. There we prove liveness properties characterising when a system reaches stable states. Here, we extend this idea to prove some other important classes of liveness properties. In designing our proof rules, we have been inspired by the pioneering work of Chandy and Misra [4], of Lamport [9], and in particular of Manna and Pnueli [10].

Our proof rules for *progress* properties are similar to that of Manna and Pnueli [10], in the sense that we both use the variant technique to reason about convergence of events. However, our **Until** rule for proving $P_1 \Rightarrow (P_1 \, \mathcal{U} \, P_2)$ has the additional assumption $\neg P_2$ in its sub-goals, i.e., we need to prove the sub-goal only when the desirable condition P_2 has not yet been established. The use of the variant technique is clearly an advantage over the proof lattices approach from Owicki and Lamport [12] when the systems have infinitely many states. In UNITY [4], reasoning about progress properties is embedded within its logic by several proof rules. Our proof rules are comparable to a combination of their transitivity, implication and induction rules. An important motivation for us is to be able to realise the reasoning about liveness properties in a tool support. In our opinion the rules from [10,4] are not at the level which can be realised practically.

In [3], Abrial and Mussat have addressed the problem of verifying *progress* properties, by formulating the problem in terms of proving loops termination. Our proof rules are stronger than those in [3]. In particular when proving $P_1 \Rightarrow (P_1 \,\mathcal{U}\, P_2)$, we allow the triggering condition P_1 to be invalidated as soon as the desirable condition P_2 holds, i.e., proving that $\mathsf{M} \vdash (P_1 \wedge \neg P_2) \curvearrowright (P_1 \vee P_2)$, whereas in [3], a stronger condition was proposed, i.e., $\mathsf{M} \vdash (P_1 \wedge \neg P_2) \curvearrowright P_1$.

Within our knowledge, there are no practical proof rules existing for *persistence* properties. A stronger persistence property can be defined in the work of Chandy and Misra [4] by combining an *existence* property, e.g., $\diamond P$ and a *stable* properties, e.g., $P \Rightarrow \Box P$. Whereas in their work a persistence predicate remains hold once it holds, we allow a persistence predicate to be invalidated, before becoming stable. In particular, our notion *divergence* by proving a *non-increasing variant* is novel.

Proving general LTL properties in Event-B has been consider in [6]. The approach taken is to encode in B the Büchi automata equivalent to the LTL properties, and then synchronise the resulting machine with the original event system. Several analyses are done on the combined machine, including proving that eventually some accepting state of the Büchi automata will be reached. The downside of this approach is that the reasoning is done on the combined machine containing the original machine with the representation of the LTL property, which increases the complexity of the verification process, for example, finding the appropriate variant.

6 Conclusions

We have presented our proposed proof rules for reasoning about three types of liveness properties in Event-B: *existence*, *progress* and *persistence*. These classes cover a significant numbers of properties that are used in practice. According to the survey done by Dwyer, Avrunin and Corbett [5], amongst over 500 examples of property specifications that they have collected, 27% are invariance properties (in terms of global *absence* and *universality* properties). The class of existence and progress properties cover 45%. Altogether with our extension, we can model in Event-B 72% instead of 27% of the collected properties.

Another practical aspect of our proof rules is that they rely on some basic reasoning obligations which can be implemented straight away in a tool support such as the Rodin platform. This requires only to add to the platform a new declaration and to extend the proof obligation generator for generating appropriate proof obligations. These conditions can be proved within the scope of the existing provers, i.e., there is no need for extending the proving support of the platform.

6.1 Future Work

The main difference between our proof rules and those in [10,12,4] is that we have not yet considered (strongly/weakly) fairness assumptions. This will be necessary later, especially in modelling concurrent and distributed systems. At the moment, we regard this as future work and expect to have some proof rules using similar proof obligations.

In this paper, we do not attempt to have a complete set of proof rules (even for the set of properties under consideration). We rather to come up with some practical rules for some reasonable important subset of properties. Future work along the direction of having a relative complete set of rules can be inspired from [11].

A direct extension of our proof rules is to include the notion of *probabilistic* convergence [7]. This allows us to model systems with *probabilistic* behaviours and reason about properties such as "eventually certain condition holds with *probability one*". An example is the proof of Rabin's choice coordination algorithm to guarantee that eventually, with probability one, all processes agree on a particular alternative [14].

An important future research direction is to investigate how liveness properties can be maintained during refinement. While safety properties are maintained by refinement in Event-B, more investigation need to be done to ensure that liveness properties are preserved during refinement with the possibility of strengthening the refinement notion. In [6], the author proposes a notion of refinement *oriented by the property*. Since the definition depends on the LTL property of interest, references to this property will need to be carried along the refinement chain. We are looking for a notion of refinement preserving our interested set of liveness properties without confining to similar restriction.

Acknowledgement. We would like to thank anonymous reviewers for their constructive comments. We also thank David Basin, Andreas Fürst, Dominique Méry and Matthias Schmalz for their help with various drafts of the paper.

References

1. Abrial, J.-R.: Modeling in Event-B: System and Software Engineering. Cambridge University Press, Cambridge (2010)
2. Abrial, J.-R., Butler, M., Hallerstede, S., Hoang, T.S., Mehta, F., Voisin, L.: Rodin: an open toolset for modelling and reasoning in Event-B. International Journal on Software Tools for Technology Transfer (STTT) 12(6), 447–466 (2010)
3. Abrial, J.-R., Mussat, L.: Introducing dynamic constraints in B. In: Bert, D. (ed.) B 1998. LNCS, vol. 1393, pp. 83–128. Springer, Heidelberg (1998)
4. Chandy, K.M., Misra, J.: Parallel Program Design: A Foundation. Addison-Wesley, Reading (1988)
5. Dwyer, M., Avrunin, G., Corbett, J.: Patterns in property specifications for finite-state verification. In: ICSE, pp. 411–420 (1999)
6. Groslambert, J.: Verification of LTL on B event systems. In: Julliand, J., Kouchnarenko, O. (eds.) B 2007. LNCS, vol. 4355, pp. 109–124. Springer, Heidelberg (2006)
7. Hallerstede, S., Hoang, T.S.: Qualitative probabilistic modelling in event-B. In: Davies, J., Gibbons, J. (eds.) IFM 2007. LNCS, vol. 4591, pp. 293–312. Springer, Heidelberg (2007)
8. Hoang, T.S., Kuruma, H., Basin, D., Abrial, J.-R.: Developing topology discovery in Event-B. Sci. Comput. Program. 74(11-12), 879–899 (2009)
9. Lamport, L.: The temporal logic of actions. ACM Trans. Program. Lang. Syst. 16(3), 872–923 (1994)
10. Manna, Z., Pnueli, A.: Adequate proof principles for invariance and liveness properties of concurrent programs. Sci. Comput. Program. 4(3), 257–289 (1984)
11. Manna, Z., Pnueli, A.: Completing the temporal picture. Theor. Comput. Sci. 83(1), 91–130 (1991)
12. Owicki, S., Lamport, L.: Proving liveness properties of concurrent programs. ACM Trans. Program. Lang. Syst. 4(3), 455–495 (1982)
13. Peterson, G.: Myths about the mutual exclusion problem. Inf. Process. Lett. 12(3), 115–116 (1981)
14. Yilmaz, E., Hoang, T.S.: Development of Rabin's choice coordination in Event-B. Technical report, University of Dusseldorf, Proceedings of AVoCS 2010 (2010)

Extracting Significant Specifications from Mining through Mutation Testing

Anh Cuong Nguyen and Siau-Cheng Khoo

Department of Computer Science, National University of Singapore
{anhcuong,khoosc}@comp.nus.edu.sg

Abstract. Specification mining techniques are used to automatically infer interaction specifications among objects in the format of call sequences, but many of these specifications can be meaningless or insignificant. As a consequence, when used in program testing or formal verification, the presence of these leads to false positive defects, which in turn demand much effort for manual investigation. We propose a novel process for determining and extracting significant specifications from a set of mined specifications using *mutation testing*. The resulting specifications can then be used with program verification to detect defects with high accuracy. To our knowledge, this is the first fully automatic approach for extracting significant specifications from mining using program testing. We evaluate our approach through mining significant specifications for the Java API and use them to find real defects in many systems.

Keywords: Specification mining, mutation testing, formal specifications.

1 Introduction

Specification mining is a process that enables the inference of candidate interaction protocols between objects in a program from its execution traces or source code. One important type of these specifications is the class of temporal logic properties over function or method call sequences. These specifications can be efficiently used to describe interesting reliability and safety properties of software system such as lock acquisition and release, or resource ownership properties like "all calls to `read(f)` must exist between calls to `open(f)` and `close(f)`."

Specifications reflecting legitimate usage protocols can be used in program testing or formal verification to detect defects in systems. A system is said to have defects if it does not respect one or more legitimate protocols. A common issue pertaining to specification mining approach, however, is that there are typically many meaningless and insignificant specifications discovered by the mining process. As a consequence, when insignificant specifications are used for detecting defects, they usually lead to false reports and demand expensive effort for manual investigation. To illustrate this problem, consider the experiment done by Wasylkowski et al. for detecting anomalies in AspectJ, a compiler for the AspectJ language, using *object usage model* mined from a specification miner called Jadet [19]. Among 276 anomalies and 790 violations detected, only 7

S. Qin and Z. Qiu (Eds.): ICFEM 2011, LNCS 6991, pp. 472–488, 2011.

violations from 6 anomalies lead to real system defects. Aside from Wasylkowski experiment, many other experiments also show that verify systems against specifications obtained from mining may lead to many violations, but only a few of them actually associated with real defects. [17,12,10].

How can one mine specifications against violations of which can lead to real defects rather than false ones? In this paper, we propose a novel technique that employs *mutation tests* to determine significant specifications from a set of mined specifications. The resulting specifications can then be used in program verification to detect defects with high precision.

Specifically, given a mined specification that attempts to describe a behavior of a method, we perform a mutation operation on the method body so that it intentionally violates the given specification. We then execute the method with specific input to determine if such a violation of specification will lead to exception being thrown at appropriate program points. When that happens, we deem the mined specification to be significant. Otherwise, we deem it insignificant.

We have implemented a prototype to test our proposal on the Java API, and discovered significant specifications with 100% of precision and at least 80% of recall. We then supplied the resulting significant specifications to a model checker to help find real defects. Our experiment shows that specifications deemed as significant can drastically expedite the discovery of real defects in programs that use the corresponding API.

Our main contributions are as follows:

1. We put the definition of *specification significance* on a firmer theoretical ground. We assess the significance of a specification by its ability to exhibit bad system behaviours when it is violated (Sec. 2). To our knowledge, this is the first work looking into this issue.
2. We introduce a novel approach for determining significant specifications using *mutation testing*.
3. We demonstrate the effectiveness of this approach by implementing a prototype to test on Java API.

The outline of this paper is as follows: In Section 2, we provide an overview of specification mining and formal representation of specification. We then provide a theoretical formulation of the notion of "significant specification" in Section 3. This is followed by a detailed description of our "mutation test" approach (Section 4) and an experiment on its effectiveness (Section 5). Finally, we discuss related work in Section 6 before concluding in Section 7.

2 Background

We begin with a brief overview on how specification mining can produce an insignificant specification and then detect false defects from it. Suppose that we want to mine *call sequence usages* of the **Stack** object in each method body, using either their execution traces or source codes. Consider the following code snippet, which is taken from APACHE FOP, a print formatter for XSL formatting objects.

```
1  private Stack nestedBlockStack = new Stack();
2  public void handleWhiteSpace(...) {
3          ...
4          if (nestedBlockStack.empty() || fo != nestedBlockStack.peek()) {
5                  ...
6                  nestedBlockStack.push(currentBlock);
7          } else {
8                  nestedBlockStack.pop();
9          }
10         ...
11         if (!nestedBlockStack.empty())
12                 nestedBlockStack.pop();
13         ...
14 }
```

The execution flow from line 4 to line 8 in the above snippet introduces a specification stating that a stack must be peeked before it is popped: `pop` $\hookrightarrow$ `peek`[1]. In addition, lines 11 and 12 introduce another specification stating that a stack must be checked for its emptiness before it can be popped: `pop` $\hookrightarrow$ `empty`. We shall refer to these two rules as $\mathbf{R_1}$ and $\mathbf{R_2}$, in that respective order.

Intuitively, $\mathbf{R_2}$ is a more preferable candidate for the process of checking and finding defects. Still, a closer analysis on the code reveals that $\mathbf{R_1}$ is also a meaningful specification in the current context. It can be interpreted that a stack should check (by peeking) for the existence of an object before it actually executes a pop operation. However, this usage protocol is not universally required for well-behaved stack objects. Different from $\mathbf{R_1}$, $\mathbf{R_2}$ states a rule that a stack should strictly follow. A precondition for a stack to perform a pop is that the object stack must be at a non-empty state. Therefore a call to `empty` checks for the legal state of stack object before it can perform a pop. Without checking the object stack for emptiness, the program may crash when trying to perform a pop operation. For this reason, defects found by a violation to $\mathbf{R_2}$ are likely to be true defects, whereas defects found by a violation to $\mathbf{R_1}$ are likely to be false ones.

The specification miner is unfortunately clueless about this intuition. Currently, a common solution to this problem is to determine the specification significance based on the notion of confidence and support, which are linked to the number of occurrences of the pattern in the given sequences. However, this solution can be ineffective in many cases because an insignificant rule may have a high occurrence. For example, $\mathbf{R_1}$ can have a very high occurrence if the code accidentally uses the rule frequently throughout an execution (which is indeed the case for FOP where our experiment discovered 122 occurrences of $\mathbf{R_1}$.)

In this paper, we propose a novel technique to ascertain the significance of system specifications: A specification is deemed significant when violating the specification during program execution can make the participating objects misbehave, which lead to bad system behavior, exhibited by a system crash. It

[1] Section 2.1 explains the notation in detail.

should be noted that our definition of significance centers on the behavior of the participating objects found in the specification, and referenced in the code.

For the remaining of this section, we describe the type of system specification we use throughout the paper (Sec. 2.1). In Sec. 3, we formalize various definitions of specification significance and give an overview of our solution for identifying significant specifications (Sec. 3.1).

2.1 Past-Time Temporal Specification

Past-time temporal specifications are rules stating that "whenever a series of events occurs, previously another series of events must have happened" [14]. Specifications of this format are commonly found in practice and useful for program testing and verification. Indeed in our empirical study with the Java API, we found a large number of significant rules obeying past-time temporal logic, for example, `next` $\hookrightarrow$ `hasNext`, `pop` $\hookrightarrow$ `empty` or `get` $\hookrightarrow$ `size`.

In our work, past-time temporal specifications discovered are always constructed from two components, a *consequence* and a *premise*, each consists of a series of events. A specification is denoted as `consequence` $\hookrightarrow$ `premise` and states that whenever a series of consequence events occurs it must be preceded by another series of premise events. Each past-time temporal specification can be mapped to its corresponding Linear-time Temporal Logic (LTL) expression. Examples of such correspondences are shown in Table 1, which we borrow from [14]. In addition, all past-time temporal specification in our work must obey

Table 1. Specifications and their Past-time LTL Equivalences

Specification	LTL Notation
$a \hookrightarrow b$	$G(a \rightarrow X^{-1}F^{-1}b)$
$\langle a, b\rangle \hookrightarrow c$	$G((a \wedge XFb) \rightarrow X^{-1}F^{-1}c)$
$a \hookrightarrow \langle b, c\rangle$	$G(a \rightarrow X^{-1}F^{-1}(c \wedge X^{-1}F^{-1}b))$

another condition, which is all events in the specification must be method calls coming from the same object. This condition is not strictly required for our technique for detecting significant specifications, but it is appropriate for a preliminary study. A technique that handles specifications across multiple objects can be extended straightforwardly from ours.

Finally, a violation of a past-time temporal specification can happen when one or more events in the premise are missing while all events in the consequence occur in the correct order. We use the notation $\overset{v}{\hookrightarrow}$ to symbolize violation. Examples of violations of specifications used in Table 1 are shown in Table 2.

3 Specification Significance

To have a sense of how specification significance can be defined, let's consider the following scenario. Suppose that a programmer makes use of a new API library

Table 2. Specification Violations and their Past-time LTL Equivalences

Specification Format	Violation	LTL of Violation Notation
$a \hookrightarrow b$	$a \overset{v}{\hookrightarrow} \neg b$	$F(a \wedge X^{-1}G^{-1}\neg b)$
$\langle a, b\rangle \hookrightarrow c$	$\langle a, b\rangle \overset{v}{\hookrightarrow} \neg c$	$F((a \wedge XFb) \wedge X^{-1}G^{-1}\neg c)$
$a \hookrightarrow \langle b, c\rangle$	$a \overset{v}{\hookrightarrow} \langle \neg b, c\rangle$ $a \overset{v}{\hookrightarrow} \langle b, \neg c\rangle$ $a \overset{v}{\hookrightarrow} \langle \neg b, \neg c\rangle$	$F(a \wedge X^{-1}G^{-1}(c \rightarrow X^{-1}G^{-1}\neg b))$

and she must follow some call sequence usage specifications specified by the library, which are sometimes documented, sometimes not. She would be prone to make mistake by not obeying some of the usage specifications. When this happens, one or more objects defined in the specification will behave wrongly, and this leads to bad program behaviours.

The definition of specification significance simulates this real life scenario. Firstly, when determining the significance, we look at three components that make of a specification: the *method calls* that make of the event series, the *participating objects* and the relevant *code* that the specification resides in. Then the significance of a specification can be viewed as its ability to cause a participating object to misbehave when the call series does not occur correctly, and that leads to bad code behaviours. Particularly in this work, we consider an object misbehaviour as a thrown exception, and a bad behaviour as a code crash due to the exception. We will discuss further in Sec. 7 how we can determine other kinds of bad code behaviour by incorporating more code checking systems. Concretely we define 3 levels of specification significance as follows, of which the latter two are goals attainable by our method.

Usage Significance. Rules belonging to this set are meaningful and important for use in some specific contexts. An example is `File.delete()` $\hookrightarrow$ `File.isDirectory()`, which is used to delete system directories. Violations of these rules are though harmful in some specific usages, they are safe in other usages. Therefore when these rules are used for testing software, their violations may lead to many false positive defects. We do not deal with these rules here.

Object Significance. Rules belonging to this set are not only important for the usage code but also important for the object participating in the usage. An example is `Stack.pop()` $\hookrightarrow$ `Stack.empty()`. When these rules are violated, some calls in the rule will likely throw exceptions. The rule premise can be seen as a check for the object state validity, before the object can use a call in the rule consequence. Therefore if the check fails (the object state is invalid) but the object still uses a call in consequence, the call will trigger an exception.

Definition 1 (Object Significance). *A specification* Spec *is object significant if and only if there exist a code* C *and its input* I *such that code* C *when executed* *with* I *will crash, due to the violation of* Spec, *by throwing an exception at a call* c *occurred in consequent component of* Spec.

$$\texttt{Spec}.sig() \Leftrightarrow \exists\ \texttt{C,I}\ \exists\ \texttt{c} \in \texttt{Spec}.cons: \quad \big(\texttt{C}.exec(I) \wedge \texttt{Spec}.violate()\big) \wedge \lightning@c$$

The notation $\lightning@c$ denotes throwing of an exception at call c.

Is one code crash sufficient to determine the object significance of a specification? Generally, not all programs that violate an object significant specification will lead to crashes. For example, one may not need to call `Stack.empty()` before `Stack.pop()` if she knows that the stack is not empty. Nevertheless, we found that the definition using the existence of at least one code crash is useful enough to detect object significant specifications in practice.

Universe Significance. Rules belonging to this set are dictators for every code. An example is `InputStream.reset()` $\hookrightarrow$ `InputStream.mark(int)`, which states that the `InputStream` need to be marked before "repositioning" can be performed on the input stream to the most previous mark (by calling `reset`). The rule premise in this case is meant to bring the object to a valid state for using a call in the rule consequence. Violation of these rules will most likely cause exceptions (unless, for example, the call in premise is replaced by its definition).

Definition 2 (Universe Significance). *A specification* Spec *is universe significant if and only if for all code* C *and its input* I, *when* C *is executed with* I *and the specification* Spec *is violated, the code will crash by an exception thrown by a call* c *occurred in consequent component of* Spec.

$$\texttt{Spec}.sig() \Leftrightarrow \forall\ \texttt{C,I}\ \forall\ \texttt{c} \in \texttt{Spec}.cons: \quad \big(\texttt{C}.exec(\texttt{I}) \wedge \texttt{Spec}.violate()\big) \rightarrow \lightning@c$$

3.1 Identifying Significant Specifications

In this work we introduce a method for identifying object and universe significant specifications in an API library. An overview of our method is shown in Fig. 1. Concretely the method works as follows.

- In the first step, the API-client (back-end software) is fetched into a past-time temporal specification miner. The miner returns a set of raw specifications of the API, which contains both significant and insignificant specifications.
- For each specification, we simulate the specification violation by *suppressing* one or more calls occurring in its premise; the suppression is achieved by creating mutated programs. We use codes of the API-clients as candidate programs for mutation.
- Mutated programs are executed. If one of the programs crashes by an exception caused by a call in the specification consequence component, we deemed the corresponding specification to be significant, otherwise it is insignificant. Finally we collect all significant specifications and output to the user.

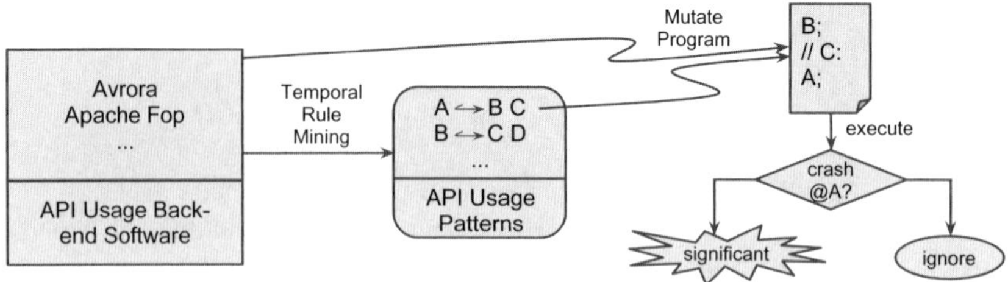

Fig. 1. Extract Significant Specifications from an API Library

4 Mutation Testing

We are now ready to discuss the realization of our mutation testing technique as a practical and effective tool for extracting significant specifications. Our goal is to express opinions about which design choices we prefer and discuss both advantages and shortcomings of these decisions.

We begin by employing a temporal specification miner called LM [6]. LM takes in a set of execution traces. Based on the user-specified minimum thresholds of *support* and *confidence*, LM generates a set of past-time temporal specifications, such as the example below:

```
<org/apache/fop/fo/XMLWhiteSpaceHandler.handleWhiteSpace(Lorg/apache/
    fop/fo/FObjMixed;Lorg/apache/fop/fo/FONode;Lorg/apache/fop/fo/FONode
    ;)V:97,106 ...>
(122, 1.0)
PREMISE:
        java/util/Stack.empty()Z
CONSEQUENCE:
        java/util/Stack.pop()Ljava/lang/Object;
```

The specification states that any `Stack` object must follow the rule `pop` $\hookrightarrow$ `empty`. The rule has a support of 122 (instances from the collection of traces) and a full confidence of 1.0, and one instance of the rule occurs inside the method body of `XMLWhiteSpaceHandler.handleWhiteSpace()` at source line 97 and 106. We call the method body *a container of the specification*.

4.1 Simulating Specification Violation through Program Mutation

We simulate a specification violation by mutating the original program. We use containers of the specification as candidate codes for injecting mutations. The idea behind mutation is to suppress specific calls in the containers that also appear in the specification premise, so that when the container is executed, it causes the program to crash due to violation of the specification.

There are several challenging design issues in program mutation:

Issue 1. Each past-time temporal specification can be violated in many ways. A challenge here is to efficiently represent and manipulate all these violations.

Issue 2. Method call under suppression may occur multiple times in a container. Which occurrence should we suppress to effectively violate the specification?

Issue 3. We mutate the suppressed call by replacing it with an object of identical return type to ensure smooth running of the code. There can be many candidate objects for replacement, which one should we use?

Generally a specification premise can contain several calls. However, an error may occur only when a particular combination of calls are suppressed. For example, the specification `pop` $\hookrightarrow$ $\langle$`empty peek`$\rangle$ about a `Stack` object only yields error at `pop` when `empty` is missing (suppressing `peek` yields no errors). Simulating violation by suppressing all combinations of calls in the premise can be expensive: we need to generate $2^n - 1$ mutated programs when a premise contains n calls. This complexity can be mitigated in two ways. First, we check only *closed temporal rules*[14], which are intuitively rules with "maximal" length. Second, we mutate the container of a closed rule by simultaneously suppressing all calls in the premise. For example, for all three rules `pop` $\hookrightarrow$ $\langle$`empty peek`$\rangle$, `pop` $\hookrightarrow$ `peek` and `pop` $\hookrightarrow$ `empty` (the first rule is closed while the other two can be *subsumed* by the first), we need only one check by suppressing both `empty` and `peek` at the same time. Intuitively, if the closed rule is detected as insignificant (call to `pop` does not yield error), we can safely claim that the rule itself and all subsumed rules are insignificant. On the other hand, if the closed rule is detected as significant, the rule itself or some of its subsumed rules may also be significant (here `pop` $\hookrightarrow$ `empty` is also significant). Later when we have detected a succinct set of significant rules, we can analyze them further to see which subsumed rules are also significant. This will be studied in Sec. 4.4.

For design issues 2 and 3, we illustrate our design decisions through an example. Consider the specification given in the beginning of Sec. 4 and its container shown in Sec. 2. Suppose that we want to simulate a violation `pop` $\hookrightarrow$ $\neg$`empty`. Following is a suitable mutation for the container.

```
private Stack nestedBlockStack = new Stack();
public void handleWhiteSpace(...) {
    ...
    if (nestedBlockStack.empty() || fo != nestedBlockStack.peek()) {
        ...
        nestedBlockStack.push(currentBlock);
    } else {
        nestedBlockStack.pop();
    }
    ...
    if (!false) % Replaces (!nestedBlockStack.empty())
        nestedBlockStack.pop();
    ...
}
```

We mutate the container by replacing the call `nestedBlockStack.empty()` at line 11 to a concrete value `false`. This example exposes two problems: the call under suppression (e.g. `empty`) can appear many times (issue 2) and it can be replaced by many concrete values (e.g. `true` or `false`) (issue 3).

We address the second issue by relaxing the definition of violation in the following way: a specification is violated when one (rather than all) of its instances is violated. Thus, when there are many candidate calls for suppression, we only need to suppress those calls that appear in the specification instances. In case of LM, the specification instances are *iterative patterns* [15], which can be uniquely identified from the traces. It becomes natural to use instances to determine a specification violation. In our example above, assuming that line 8 is not executed, the only iterative pattern instance that supports the specification is `empty@11 pop@12`. This instance is thus subject to mutation.

Furthermore, when the mutated code crashes due to an exception, we check whether the exception is raised by a call that is (i) defined in specification consequence, and (ii) part of the instance used for mutation. Only when both conditions are satisfied can we conclude that the specification is significant. In our example above, we need to check that the exception is raised by `pop@12` but not by other occurrences of `pop`.

Finally, a suppressed call can be replaced by many different concrete values, and some might be more suitable than others. For example, in the mutation above, it is more suitable to use `false` as a replacement value because using `true` will make the call `pop` at line `12` non-executable. Ideally one would want to try all possible replacement values, but this is infeasible in practice. In our implementation, we try to simulate as many values as possible using randomly created objects. We discuss the mechanism for creating objects further in Sec. 4.2. Quantitatively, we create one mutation for one replacement object. Thus, if a specification has i instances, its premise contains n calls and each call has maximum r replacement objects, we generate at most ir mutated programs. In Sec. 4.3 we described how the number of mutated programs can be further reduced, thus improving the performance of our technique.

We implement our mutation technique for Java language to work on Java bytecode programs. Bytecode manipulations are done using the ASM bytecode manipulation framework [3]. We omit the details due to space constraint.

4.2 Generating Replacement Objects

Our mutation technique requires replacing the suppressed call by an object of its return type (except for `void`, which we simply skip the call). We generate these objects by first creating an *object pool* for each object type. An object pool is a set of bytecode instruction sequences that generate objects on the fly. For each type, the content of object pool is randomly created. Generation mechanism can be characterized by three types of input object: primitive types, classes with public constructors and arrays.

We partition the object pool for any primitive type with wide value range into distinct pre-defined sets. For `int`, these are: large negative, small negative,

0, small positive and large positive numbers. For each value range, we only create a small number of objects. Bytecode instructions are used to construct objects within each value range of the corresponding primitive type, as shown in Table 3.

Table 3. Object Pool and Value Ranges for Primitive Type

Primitive Type	Bytecode Instructions	Value Ranges
byte, short, int	{bipush $val}	[MIN,-100];[-50,-1];0; [1,50];[100,MAX]
long, float, double	{ldc $val}	[MIN,-100.0];[-50.0,-1.0];0.0 [1.0,50.0];[100.0,MAX]
boolean	{iconst_0}, {iconst_1}	false; true
char	{bipush $val}	[a-z]; [A-Z]; [0-9]; [^a-zA-Z0-9]

Object pool of a class that has public constructors is generated inductively and component-wise using object pool of the primitive types. In order to prevent the inductive generation from going into a loop, when initializing an object, we choose constructors that do not involve any *parent objects* of the current object or the object itself as parameters.

For object pool of array type, we firstly assign a random size to each array dimension. Elements of the array are either a primitive type or a normal class and can be randomly generated as usual.

One shortcoming of this approach is that we cannot generate any objects of classes that do not have public constructors, or constructors that require parameters that cannot be generated, as well as array of these classes. These cases rarely occur in our experiment. When they happen, we mark the specification for manual review.

4.3 Exploring Early Pruning

The complexity of our algorithm depends on the run time of containers and the number of mutations under inspection. To reduce the number of mutations and the containers' run time, we utilize two effective pruning strategies.

Duplicated Instances Avoidance. For two specifications $\mathbf{R_1}$ and $\mathbf{R_2}$ that have the same premise but $\mathbf{R_1}$'s consequence is a super-sequence of $\mathbf{R_2}$, we always check $\mathbf{R_1}$ first. To illustrate this, consider an example with two specifications pertaining to `Rectangle2D` object which are mined from Apache Fop, $\mathbf{R_1} = \langle$ `getWidth, getY, getHeight` $\rangle \hookrightarrow$ `getX` and $\mathbf{R_2} =$ `getY` $\hookrightarrow$ `getX`. Set of instances for $\mathbf{R_1}$ is `{transfrom:22,22,22,22}` while for $\mathbf{R_2}$ is `{transfrom:22,22; generate:56,56}`. Since the instance for $\mathbf{R_1}$ also re-occurs as one for $\mathbf{R_2}$, we remember the instance and only check it once, at rule $\mathbf{R_1}$.

Early Termination. Figure 2 shows how a container is being mutated. Aside from suppressing calls in rule premise, we also insert try-catch block around every call in the rule consequence. Each try-catch block does not only record the specification as significant, but also forces early termination of the execution once its significance is determined. In addition, we also force termination of execution (by inserting `System.exit(0)`) when the container exits, if all calls in the instance under check have been executed.

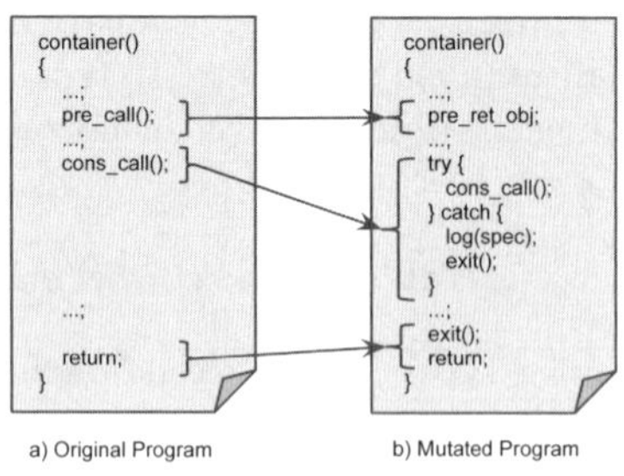

Fig. 2. Mutation of a Container

4.4 Specification Refinement

We show here how the significance of the temporal rules identified by our method can be further improved, leading to a reduction in the number of false positives when used in software testing and/or verification.

Disjunctive Premise. It is common for a call sequence to be preceded by multiple choices of premises. Therefore, given two specifications that have same consequence but different premises, we combine them using disjunction. For example we combine two rules `pop` $\hookrightarrow$ `empty` and `pop` $\hookrightarrow$ `push` into a single, but more precise rule `pop` $\hookrightarrow$ `empty|push`.

Conjunctive Premise. For specifications with multiple calls in the premise, some of these calls may not be required for the consequence, and thus may be dropped. Given such a specification, we re-apply the check on the specification, by suppressing each call in the premise one by one. If a call suppression does not lead to throwing of exceptions, we can safely remove it. For example with the rule `pop` $\hookrightarrow \langle$ `peek, empty` $\rangle$, we can remove `peek` to obtain the rule `pop` $\hookrightarrow$ `empty`.

5 Evaluation

We have built a system described in this paper as a plug-in, called SpecCheck, for the Lm miner. Fig. 3 depicts its system architecture. SpecCheck plugin is implemented as a Java agent that would be invoked by the Java Virtual Machine during load time of the target application. We evaluated SpecCheck on the DaCapo 2009 benchmarks [2] to address the following concerns:

– What proportion of the specifications labelled by SpecCheck as significant are indeed significant (precision)?
– What proportion of significant specifications has been labelled by SpecCheck as such (recall)?

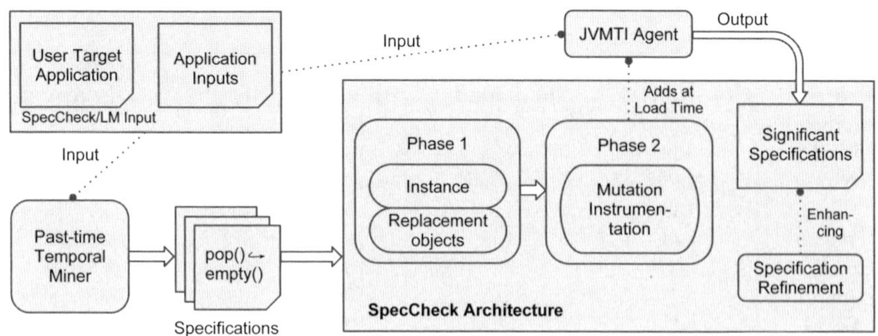

Fig. 3. SpecCheck High-level Architecture

– How efficient are the significant specifications, compared to the original specifications, in detecting system defects?

DaCapo 2009 benchmark suite consists of 14 complex Java systems that range over a diverse set of application domains. We select from DaCapo 7 single-thread driven benchmarks to evaluate the effectiveness of SpecCheck (see Table 4). We use the test harness provided by the benchmark suite and perform evaluation for traces of all calls to the Java API library (Sec. 5.1). Finally we evaluate the effectiveness of extracted rules in finding defects in Sec. 5.1.

5.1 Java API Rules

Mining Setup. The set of traces for each Java class varies pretty much in size and some can be very large due to code looping. We keep the traces as they are but use different support and confidence threshold settings for each trace depending on its size. Concretely we set support and confidence thresholds to 5 and 40% respectively for trace files less than 100KB, 50 and 40% respectively for trace files less than 1MB, 100 and 60% respectively for trace files less than 5MB, and ignore all trace files larger than that. Using these settings, the mining process can finish within minutes.

Evaluation Results. Throughout the suite, Lm infers a large number of specifications, among them an average of 6% (38/633) are determined by SpecCheck as significant (Table 4). The ratio of specifications marked as significant to all mined specifications is small, but this is consistent with many past studies that the number of mined specifications which lead to real defects are normally small [17,12,10].

We end up with 22 significant specifications after specification refinement step: 21 of them are object significant and 1 of them is universe significant.

To assess the precision and recall of SpecCheck, we employed three programmers to independently and manually extract significant rules from mined rules. Based on this result, precision and recall achieved by SpecCheck are very encouraging, as depicted in Table 4.

Table 4. Significant Java API Rules Extracted from DaCapo 2009 Benchmarking Suite

Benchmark Project	Mined Spec Considered	Significant Spec Identified	Precision	Recall	Spec Discarded
avrora	28	3	100%	100%	89.2%
batik	369	16	100%	80.0%	95.3%
eclipse	145	10	100%	100%	93.1%
fop	132	11	100%	100%	91.6%
jython	193	14	100%	87.5%	93.2%
luindex	34	4	100%	100%	88.2%
pmd	61	9	100%	100%	85.2%
Total	633	38	100%	86.0%	93.9%
After Spec Refinement:		**No. of Object Spec : 21**		**No. of Universe Spec : 1**	

In the assessment of "recall", we have missed a few significant rules (6/44), which correctly reflect some limitations of our mutation techniques. Firstly we may not have generated the correct replacement objects which can cause exceptions. Secondly we may never reach a designated consequence call which we would like to check during execution, as the program threw exception earlier than expected. Finally we may miss some significant rules that produce errors, but without throwing the anticipated exceptions (e.g. null pointer creation, memory leak, *etc.*)

A sampling of significant specifications is displayed in Table 5. The sample shows that we can detect rules whose significance *cannot* be trivially judged by looking at name similarities (e.g. `pop` $\hookrightarrow$ `empty`). We can also detect rules of length greater than 2 (e.g. `getPixels` $\hookrightarrow \langle$ `getMinX, getMinY, getHeight` $\rangle$). Finally we find one universe significant rule. It is `reset` $\hookrightarrow$ `mark`, which has been explained in Sec. 3.

Performance. Without applying any optimizations described in Sec. 4.3, the checking step does not complete even after several hours for most benchmarks.[2] This is expected, for example in ECLIPSE case, where a single run of the application can take up to 2 minutes. The dataset consists of 145 specifications for checking, each specification has at least two instances and each instance generates at least two mutated programs. The number of mutated programs can be up to 580 and running all of them takes approximately 1160 minutes (which is 19 hours!). Fortunately, with the pruning techniques described in Sec. 4.3, checking of specifications mined from ECLIPSE took only around 15 minutes (6 seconds per rule in average). This confirms that our pruning strategy is necessary and efficient.

5.2 Verification Using Java API Rules

In order to ascertain that the specifications we have identified are indeed significant, we compare their ability to detect defects or code smells against those we

[2] We conduct the experiment in an Intel Core i5 M460 computer with 2GB memory running Linux Mint 10 Julia.

Table 5. A Sampling of Java API Significant Specifications from the DaCapo suite

Java Class	Specification
	Object Signifiance
`FlatteningPathIterator`	`currentSegment([F)I` ↪ `isDone()Z`
`Raster`	`getPixels(IIII[I)[I` ↪ `getMinX()I getWidth()I| getMinX()I getMinY()I getHeight()I`
`ByteBuffer`	`get()B` ↪ `hasRemaining()Z`
`Stack`	`pop()Object` ↪ `empty()Z|push(Object)Object`
`LinkedList`	`get(I)Object` ↪ `size()I|add(Object)Z`
`String`	`substring(II)String` ↪ `length()I|indexOf(C)I`
	Universe Significance
`InputStream`	`reset()V` ↪ `mark(I)V`

Table 6. Significant Specifications Show More True Positives and Fewer False Positives

		Significant Specs			Insignificant Specs		
Benchmark	**Classes**	**Anomalies**	**True**	**False**	**Anomalies**	**True**	**False**
avrora	1838	3	2	2	19	0	61
batik	2430	3	2	1	34	0	154
eclipse	527	3	1	2	22	0	108
fop	1314	2	2	0	11	0	57
jython	2816	1	0	1	24	0	103
luindex	536	1	1	2	10	0	62
pmd	727	2	5	3	13	0	68
Total	9652	7	13	11	60	0	613

have classified as insignificant. We only choose those insignificant specifications with high confidences (> 80%). There are 368 of them in total. We employ JFTA [4] to perform static verification.

For those identified significant specifications, running JFTA over the seven DACAPO benchmarks reported only a few violations; many of them were true positives. This is in line with our hypothesis that the specifications are significant. On the other hand, verifying using insignificant specifications reported a large number of anomalies and violations (nearly 1000 violations for most projects). However, we observed that majority of violations came from certain Java API classes (e.g. `StringBuilder` and rules `toString` ↪ `append`). Thus we only selected and reported the maximum 10 violations of different anomalies from each API class in case of insignificant specifications. Nevertheless, these specifications still produced much more error reports compared to those produced by significant specifications. Table 6 shows the result of our comparison. It reports the number of anomalies (ie., violation of specifications), true and false code smells (codes that indicate something may go wrong [19]) or defects. (Recall that one anomaly may consist of several defects, each in a different method.)

We inspected all violations manually and reported either defects or code smells as true positives and the rest as false positives. When we are not sure if a violation is a defect/code smell, we conservatively count it as false positive. We also do not consider violations that are already handled directly by a try-catch block in the code. Aside from keeping the amount of false positives small, we are also interested in finding real defects. Among seven projects, 54% of error reports uncover real defects or code smells, which is a considerably high rate for a specification-based bug detection tool (e.g. compared to [10,19]). A more detailed analysis of these errors is available in our technical report [16].

6 Related Work

The integration of *data mining* into *software engineering* has attracted much interest in the past decade. The field is dynamically evolving. Many projects on specification mining produce either an automation [1,13] or frequent patterns of software behaviours [15,12]. PERRACOTTA [20] mines two-event temporal logic rules that match a given template, which is later extended by JAVERT to mine more complex specifications [7]. On mining object-oriented behaviours, JADET and ADABU respectively use static and dynamic analysis to mine intra-procedural object usage models [19,5]. Finally, the specification miner LM we used mines *live sequence charts*, inter-object behaviours of arbitrary sizes [6].

Specification mining can infer many specifications but many of them can be meaningless or irrelevant. This limitation creates a big hurdle for introducing specification mining into real practices. Many interesting research has been proposed to mitigate this hurdle. Thummalapenta and Xie opine that rules exhibiting exceptional conditions can lead to discovery of real defects, and propose to mine exception-handling rules [17]. OCD automatically learns, enforces and determines anomalies using online statistical learning [8]. JADET, and later CHECK-MYCODE, determine anomalies based on various heuristic ranking [19,10]. Goues and Weimer also introduce a method to mine specifications with few false positives. Their method uses software artifacts like repository and source code to select only input traces with acceptable trustworthiness metrics [9]. Our method inherits advantages from all cited methods: we also mine specifications and detect anomalies with few false positives, allow arbitrary temporal specifications and only require the software itself as input. Finally Dallmeier et al. introduce TAUTOKO tool, which also performs mutation operations, but for the purpose of test case generation [4].

7 Conclusion

We have presented the first mutation testing-based algorithm that identifies significant specifications from a set of mined specifications. We implemented our algorithm in an efficient and practical tool called SPECCHECK. Initial evaluation on DACAPO benchmarks shows encouraging result: we are able to identify significant Java API specifications with high precision and recall; significant specifications can be used to detect defects with high accuracy. In comparison, use of those specifications not identified as significant leads to a large number of false positives.

In future we would like to apply our technique to a wider range of projects to gain better statistical results, and to collect significant specifications as a database for bug detection purpose, probably similar to [10]. We also want to detect significance based on program errors aside from exceptions; one way to do this is to incorporate with verification tools such as Cork [11] or Jpf [18], which can detect memory leaks and concurrency errors.

Acknowledgements. We thank Zhao Lin, Shafeeq Ahmed and Quang Huynh for their help on the evaluation of SpecCheck. We thank the anonymous reviewers for their valuable feedbacks. Additional thanks go to Hugh Anderson, David Lo, Sandeep Kumar, Chengnian Sun, Narcisa Milea and Zhiqiang Zuo for their inputs and discussions on the preliminary versions for this work. This research is partially supported by the research grants R-252-000-403-112 and R-252-000-318-422.

References

1. Ammons, G., Bodík, R., Larus, J.R.: Mining specifications. In: POPL 2002, pp. 4–16 (2002)
2. Blackburn, S.M., Garner, R., Hoffmann, C., Khang, A.M., McKinley, K.S., Bentzur, R., Diwan, A., Feinberg, D., Frampton, D., Guyer, S.Z., Hirzel, M., Hosking, A., Jump, M., Lee, H., Moss, J.E.B., Moss, B., Phansalkar, A., Stefanović, D., VanDrunen, T., von Dincklage, D., Wiedermann, B.: The dacapo benchmarks: java benchmarking development and analysis. In: OOPSLA 2006, pp. 169–190 (2006)
3. Bruneton, E., Lenglet, R., Coupaye, T.: Asm: A code manipulation tool to implement adaptable systems. In: Adaptable and Extensible Component Systems, Grenoble, France (2002), `asm.objectweb.org/current/asm-eng.pdf`
4. Dallmeier, V., Knopp, N., Mallon, C., Hack, S., Zeller, A.: Generating test cases for specification mining. In: ISSTA 2010, pp. 85–96 (2010)
5. Dallmeier, V., Lindig, C., Wasylkowski, A., Zeller, A.: Mining object behavior with adabu. In: WODA 2006, pp. 17–24 (2006)
6. Doan, T.A., Lo, D., Maoz, S., Khoo, S.C.: Lm: a miner for scenario-based specifications. In: ICSE 2010, pp. 319–320 (2010)
7. Gabel, M., Su, Z.: Javert: fully automatic mining of general temporal properties from dynamic traces. In: SIGSOFT 2008/FSE, vol. 16, pp. 339–349 (2008)
8. Gabel, M., Su, Z.: Online inference and enforcement of temporal properties. In: ICSE 2010, pp. 15–24 (2010)
9. Goues, C., Weimer, W.: Specification mining with few false positives. In: Kowalewski, S., Philippou, A. (eds.) TACAS 2009. LNCS, vol. 5505, pp. 292–306. Springer, Heidelberg (2009)
10. Gruska, N., Wasylkowski, A., Zeller, A.: Learning from 6,000 projects: lightweight cross-project anomaly detection. In: ISSTA 2010, pp. 119–130 (2010)
11. Jump, M., McKinley, K.S.: Cork: dynamic memory leak detection for garbage-collected languages. In: POPL 2007, pp. 31–38 (2007)

12. Livshits, B., Zimmermann, T.: Dynamine: finding common error patterns by mining software revision histories. In: ESEC/FSE, vol. 13, pp. 296–305 (2005)
13. Lo, D., Khoo, S.C.: Smartic: towards building an accurate, robust and scalable specification miner. In: SIGSOFT 2006/FSE, vol. 14, pp. 265–275 (2006)
14. Lo, D., Khoo, S.C., Liu, C.: Mining past-time temporal rules from execution traces. In: WODA 2008, pp. 50–56 (2008)
15. Lo, D., Khoo, S.C., Wong, L.: Non-redundant sequential rules-theory and algorithm. Inf. Syst. 34, 438–453 (2009)
16. Nguyen, A.C., Khoo, S.C.: Extracting significant specifications from mining through mutation testing. Tech. Rep. TRA7/11, Department of Computer Science, National University of Singapore (July 2011)
17. Thummalapenta, S., Xie, T.: Mining exception-handling rules as sequence association rules. In: ICSE 2009, pp. 496–506 (2009)
18. Visser, W., Havelund, K., Brat, G., Park, S., Lerda, F.: Model checking programs. Automated Software Engineering 10, 203–232 (2003)
19. Wasylkowski, A., Zeller, A., Lindig, C.: Detecting object usage anomalies. In: ESEC-FSE 2007, pp. 35–44 (2007)
20. Yang, J., Evans, D., Bhardwaj, D., Bhat, T., Das, M.: Perracotta: mining temporal api rules from imperfect traces. In: ICSE 2006, pp. 282–291 (2006)

Developer-Oriented Correctness Proofs

A Case Study of Cheney's Algorithm

Holger Gast

Wilhelm-Schickard-Institut für Informatik
University of Tübingen
gast@informatik.uni-tuebingen.de

Abstract. This paper examines the problem of structuring proofs in functional software verification from a novel perspective. By aligning the proofs with the operational behaviour of the program, we allow the formalization of the underlying concepts and their properties to reflect informal correctness arguments. By splitting the proof along the different aspects of the code, we achieve re-use of both theories and proof strategies across algorithms, thus enabling reasoning by analogy as employed in software construction. We demonstrate the viability and usefulness of the approach using a low-level C implementation of Cheney's algorithm.

1 Introduction

Proofs in functional software verification are usually complex and technically involved. In the case of automatic verification, they require the maintenance of abstract state in ghost-variables (e.g. [1,2]), auxiliary intermediate assertions (e.g. [3]), and suitable axioms and triggers to guide the specific prover ([4]; e.g. [2, §4.3], [1, §7]). While interactive software verification can in principle lead to more readable and understandable proofs (e.g. [5, §1.2], [6]) even in the most carefully structured larger case studies (e.g. [7,8,9,10]), the presentation is limited to the specifications and invariants, while proofs are expressly excluded ([7,8]), or are only surveyed at a very high level (e.g. [10]). The implicit underlying strategy is to reduce most occurring goals to forms that the available automatic provers can handle (e.g. [7,10]). Even allowing for necessary abbreviations for space reasons, the gap between the concrete code and the formal proof is still tremendous and often needs to be bridged at a technical level.

This paper proposes to approach the problem of finding and structuring correctness proofs from the developer's (or software engineer's) perspective. The immediate motivation for this choice is the fact that developers seem to be able to produce code that is basically correct (except for failures in unforeseen circumstances), so their mode of reasoning can be considered overall successful. By emulating it at a more formal level, one would arrive at proofs that are more precise versions of the developers' correctness arguments, thus bridging the gap between the formal and the informal.

We show that it is possible carry out this agenda by verifying a moderately complex algorithm, a C implementation of Cheney's collector [11]. Herein, we apply the following strategies derived from a developer's point of view.

S. Qin and Z. Qiu (Eds.): ICFEM 2011, LNCS 6991, pp. 489–504, 2011.

- Developers rely on experience with similar algorithms. For a novel problem, they identify familiar parts or aspects and apply the corresponding coding idioms and reasoning patterns. We therefore structure the proof around previously known aspects: graphs of memory objects, including reachability, are shared with the Schorr-Waite algorithm [12] and the collector's work queue is treated as a linked lists from [13,14]. The algorithm's distinguishing forwarding pointers reduce to the *map* datatype from the Isabelle/HOL library.
- A major strength of interactive theorem proving is the possibility to develop self-contained theories independently of concrete verification conditions (e.g. [5], [10], [6]). As an experiment, we have therefore formalized the mentioned aspects by considering the algorithm's code and expected behaviour alone, without looking at the concrete verification conditions. The derived lemmas thus follow a developer's mental execution of the code, and the actual verification was found to consist of applying these lemmas.
- We unify the overall proof by applying the *split/join* reasoning pattern throughout. The pattern complements the separation lemmas of classical approaches [6] and extends the automatic unfoldings of [15]: before the code manipulates a memory object, the pre-condition must be split such that separation lemmas prove the parts unchanged; for the post-condition, the split parts are joined together. Beyond automatic unfoldings, the formulation of split/join theorems reflects the information available at their point of application (e.g. §3.2) and boundary parameters (§2.5–2.7, §3.2) are introduced to enable the split. The reasoning pattern resembles a developer's drawing of pointer diagrams to make explicit the manipulated entities.

The proof is carried out in lightweight separation, which is described in detail in [12,16,13] and is developed as a conservative extension of Isabelle/HOL. For the purposes of this paper, it can be treated as a usual verification environment based on Hoare logic. We introduce the notation and concepts as needed. The proof document is available from the author's homepage [17].

The contributions of the paper are the following:

- The aspect-oriented proof style enables the re-use of extensive and non-trivial generic theories across algorithms that implement different specifications and only share the specific aspects of their correctness arguments. The re-use also comprises reasoning patterns building on the re-used theories.
- Since the aspects are mostly independent of one another, the different parts of the proof can equally be developed, understood, and maintained independently. We have found this useful in adjusting the details of the formalization during development, as is usually necessary for any larger case study.
- All parts of the proof exhibit a direct link to an informal understanding of the code and the high-level steps are connected by a few straightforward arguments about equalities, sets, and maps.

Overview. Section 2 formalizes the different independent aspects of Cheney's algorithm and exhibits the theory re-use from earlier developments. Section 3 assembles the aspects into a common invariant and correctness proof of the overall algorithm. Section 4 surveys related work. Section 5 concludes.

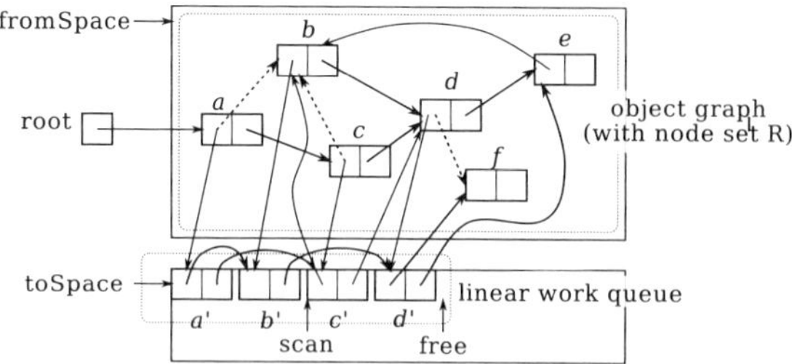

Fig. 1. Overview over the Collector State

2 Dissecting Cheney's Algorithm

This section summarizes Cheney's collector [11,9,18] and formalizes its three main aspects: the object graph, the work queue, and the forwarding map. The final aspect captures that the to-space is large enough for receiving all necessary copies of objects.

Following the earlier studies [9,18], we restrict the algorithm to objects with two fields, which may contain pointers or atomic data, and to a single root reference. The machine representation of pointers, values, and objects follows [9].

2.1 The Three Main Aspects of the Algorithm

Figure 1 depicts the general idea of Cheney's collector. The algorithm works on two equal-size half-spaces, the *from-space* and the *to-space*. (They are depicted here in different sizes to save vertical space.) At the beginning of a collection, the from-space contains all objects allocated by the program, while the to-space is empty. The collector's task is to copy all objects still required by the program into the to-space and to declare the from-space unused.

The algorithm's first aspect is the graph formed by the objects in the from-space, with the pointers in their fields as the successors. The graph is accessed from a single cell `root`, which represents the root set in the program's run-time stack. The central point here is the notion of reachability: an object is required by the program iff it is reachable in the graph starting from the root cell.

Further, the algorithm uses the copied objects between the addresses `toSpace` and `free` as a work queue. These objects are divided by the `scan` pointer: the objects before `scan`, i.e. a', b' , are processed completely, i.e. their fields already point to copies of their original successor objects. The objects after `scan`, i.e. c', d', have been copied but their fields have not been updated.

The final aspect of the algorithm is the forwarding map: objects in the from-space that have already been copied, i.e. objects a to d, contain a forwarding pointer to their copies in their first word. These pointers are crucial for handling aliasing and cycles. For instance, when processing c', the algorithm finds that its successor a has already been copied because its first field is a pointer to the to-space, and it therefore sets the first field of c' to a'. By the same mechanism, the cycle from e to b will lead to a cycle from the later copy e' to b'.

```
1 void collect(void **r) {
2   void *tmp = fromSpace;
3   fromSpace = toSpace;
4   toSpace = tmp;
5   free = toSpace;
6   scan = free;
7
8   copy_ref(r);
9   while (scan != free) {
10    copy_ref((void**)scan);
11    copy_ref((void**)(scan + 4));
12    scan = scan + 8;
13  }
14 }
```

```
1 void copy_ref(void **p) {
2  if (*((int*)p) & 1 == 0 &&
3      *(void**)p != null) {
4   void *obj = *p;
5   int fwd = *(int*) obj;
6   if (fwd & 1 == 0 &&
7       toSpace <= (void*)fwd &&
8       (void*)fwd < toSpace+spaceSz){
9     *(void**)p = (void*)fwd;
10  } else {
11    void *newObj = free;
12    free = free + 8;
13    *(int*)newObj = *(int*)obj;
14    *(int*)(newObj + 4) =
15          *(int*)(obj + 4);
16    *(void**)obj = newObj;
17    *(void**)p = newObj;
18  } } }
```

Fig. 2. The Collector's Code

2.2 Implementation

Figure 2 shows the collector's code (in the C dialect of [12,16]). It is organized around the idea of copying *references*, i.e. memory words that contain either an atomic value or a pointer to an object. Values and pointers are distinguished by the least-significant bit in their byte-representation [9]. Both the root cell and the two fields of an object constitute references in this sense, which is expressed in the factoring the basic step into the `copy_ref` function.

The function `copy_ref` mainly performs a case distinction. Lines 2–3 identify pointers by checking the bit-representation of the reference. Nothing is done for atomic values and the `null` pointer. Lines 4–8 read the first word of the referenced object and check for a forwarding pointer. If the object `obj` has already been copied, reference `p` is set to the existing copy (Line 9). The final case in Lines 11–17 allocates an object at `free`, copies `obj`, and sets `p` to the new object.

At an informal level, `copy_ref` is correct since it maintains the situation of Figure 1 and guarantees that after execution the reference `p` is handled completely, i.e. it contains the "correct" atomic value or the "correct" pointer to the copy of the original object. We will subsequently make this general idea precise enough for formal verification while maintaining the link to the informal view.

The `collect` function drives the overall process. It is called when the to-space is exhausted and the objects still used by the program must be copied to the empty from-space. Lines 2–6 reverse the roles of the half-spaces and initialize the collection. Line 8 copies the root reference, Lines 9–13 process newly copied objects until no more such objects remain. Intuitively, the loop invariant should be a formalization of Figure 1, which we achieve in the remainder of the paper.

2.3 Values, Pointers, and Objects

We will now make the informal view presented so far precise enough for formal verification, while maintaining close links to the informal arguments. We start by introducing some basic definitions that abstract over the low-level representation of values and pointers (to-int and to-ptr convert the byte-representation into a `word` [19] or the wrapper type `addr` [12], respectively).

is-atomic v $\equiv$ to-int v AND $1 \neq 0 \vee$ to-ptr v = null
is-ptr v $\equiv$ to-int v AND $1 = 0 \wedge$ to-ptr v $\neq$ null

The memory objects handled by the collector consist of two adjacent machine words. The constant obj-fields yields the byte-representations of these words in a list (`[ ]` denotes a HOL list; `rd` $ctx\ p\ t\ M$ reads the byte-representation of type t at address p in memory M; $\oplus$ is address offset; ctx is the context containing the type definitions; `gctx` is a global context fixed for the development).

obj-fields p M $\equiv$ [rd gctx p TInt M, rd gctx (p $\oplus$ 4) TInt M]

Lightweight separation [12] requires a symbolic formalization of the memory layout in the form of *covers*. An object is covered by a block of 8 consecutive bytes.

obj-cover p $\equiv$ block p 8

To access the fields, we prove that an object may be split [12] into its two fields («$p{:}t$» is a block at p with the size of type t; $\|$ is the disjoint union of covers).

obj-cover p = «p:TInt» $\|$ «p $\oplus$ 4:TInt»

The core idea of lightweight separation is to prove the result of memory accesses unchanged after a modification by the program by reasoning about the disjointness of covers [16]. We therefore show (automatically) that the memory accessor obj-field p depends only on the object at p.

declare_accessor "obj-fields p" "obj-cover p"

Since the constants introduced subsequently have straightforward accessed regions and the proofs are automatic, we omit the corresponding declarations.

2.4 The Structure of the Half-Spaces

The collector's overall memory layout is given by global variables `toSpace`, `fromSpace`, `spaceSz`, and `free`. We therefore define constants to access them, according to this template (rdv is a `rd` with the address and type of a variable):

toSpace M $\equiv$ to-ptr (rdv (in-globals gctx) "toSpace" M)

The layout obeys the following invariant: from- and to-space are given by non-`null` pointers such that the spaces are contiguous and non-overlapping ({a..<b} is the half-open interval $[a, b)$; to-Ptr converts an addr to its byte-representation).

space-vars-inv M $\equiv$
  fromSpace M $\neq$ null $\wedge$ toSpace M $\neq$ null $\wedge$
  is-ptr (to-Ptr (fromSpace M)) $\wedge$ is-ptr (to-Ptr (toSpace M)) $\wedge$
  fromSpace M $\leq$ fromSpace M $\oplus$ spaceSz M $\wedge$
  toSpace M $\leq$ toSpace M $\oplus$ spaceSz M $\wedge$
  {fromSpace M ..< fromSpace M $\oplus$ spaceSz M}
    $\cap$ {toSpace M ..< toSpace M $\oplus$ spaceSz M} = {}

Pointers into the to-space play a special role of forwarding pointers, and we introduce the following constants:

toSpace-range M ≡ { toSpace M ..< toSpace M ⊕ spaceSz M }
to-space-ref p M ≡ is-ptr (rd gctx p TInt M) ∧ to-ptr (rd gctx p TInt M) ∈ toSpace-range M

2.5 Queue Structure

We now turn to the structure of the work queue. The algorithm splits the objects between `toSpace` and `free` into two groups at `scan` and advances `scan` linearly through the objects. It thus treats the copied objects as two linear lists, one of "jobs already done" and one of "jobs that need to be done".

Linear lists are, of course, a common structure that developers are familiar with. We have therefore developed a generic library of lists [14], building on [13]. The library is expressed as a *locale* [20], Isabelle's form of parameterized theories. The list locale takes two parameters: the cover node for the list nodes and a function succ reading the *next*-pointer from a node. The node cover is, of course, the `obj-cover` from §2.3; the *next*-link is computed from the objects' size:[1]

queue-succ p M ≡ p ⊕ 8

The library furthermore assumes that the next-link only depends on the object under consideration, which is proven automatically. Re-using the library as a locale instance q takes 20 lines of straightforward Isabelle code; the queue-structure can then be expressed by the constant nodes in q: there are nodes B (for "black" [9]) and Q (for "queue") such that

q.nodes (toSpace M) (scan M) B M ∧ q.nodes (scan M) (free M) Q M ∧ set B ∩ set Q = {}

The library also provides theorems for reasoning about the defined lists. For instance, the loop in `collect` starts with configuration (a) below, then takes one object off the front of list Q in (b), works on it, and adds it to list B in (c).

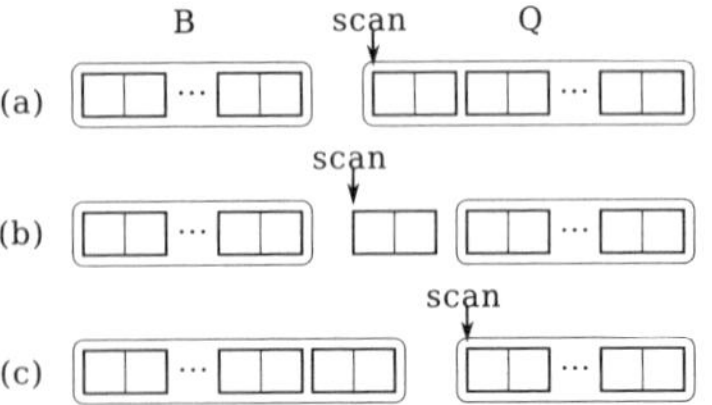

These are very common operations lists. The library therefore provides theorem (1) for unfolding the first node of a lists and theorem (2) for folding a node into the end of a list. (The complementary theorems are available, too. The parameter succ will be replaced by queue-succ in the specific local instance.)

$$\frac{p \neq q}{\text{nodes } p\ q\ xs\ M \ = (\exists ys.\ \text{nodes } (\text{succ } p\ M)\ q\ ys\ M \wedge xs = p \# ys \wedge p \notin \text{set } ys)} \quad (1)$$

$$\frac{\text{nodes } p\ r\ ys\ M \quad \text{succ } r\ M = q \quad q \notin \text{set } (ys\ @\ [r])}{\text{nodes } p\ q\ (ys\ @\ [r])\ M} \quad (2)$$

[1] For objects of arbitrary length, the successor could be computed by reading the object's header field. The used list structure is thus not overly general.

Note also that premise of (1) and the first premise of (2) directly relate to the while-test and operations of `collect`. The second premise of (2) is given by the disjointness condition in the above formalization of the work queue. By applying the theorems as suggested, both the structure of the queue and the correctness proofs are thus related to a developer's familiar concept of lists.

2.6 The Object Graph

Developers naturally think of memory objects a set of entities that are linked by pointers. In programming languages with garbage collection, the runtime system guarantees that all objects reachable from the program variables will always be retained in memory and that there are no dangling pointers.

We make this general idea more precise by using a generic library from an earlier case study of the Schorr-Waite algorithm [12]. The locale parameters here are the object's memory layout, which is given by the constant obj-cover (§2.5), and a function that reads the successor-pointers from a given object. That function is defined directly using obj-fields (§2.3): the object successors are precisely the pointers stored in the object fields. (Note that is-ptr `null` is false.)

obj-succs p M ≡ map to-ptr (filter is-ptr (obj-fields p M))

Creating the instance g of the object graph locale takes 16 lines. The library then provides extensive automatic proof support [12, §5.1] for establishing disjointness of sets of objects in the graph by set-theoretic arguments about their base-pointers and Burstall-style [21] disjointness proofs on individual fields.

We can now introduce and motivate the split/join proof strategy announced in §1. For the queue structure in §2.5, it was natural to split off the "current" node from the list Q to modify its content while standard separation lemmas [6] prove the remainder of Q unchanged. Analogously in the case of an object graph, assertions about reachability may be invalidated by modifications to individual objects. It therefore becomes necessary to split the graph at particular objects.

The splitting of lists into fragments is enabled by an explicit end node. The graph library thus introduces a *boundary set* Q into the definition of reachability: reachable P Q R M denotes that in memory state M, there are paths starting in set P to all nodes in set R that never touch Q. In particular, Q and R are disjoint.

The collector uses the reachability predicate in two places: first, the specification (§3.1) defines the set of objects R reachable in the initial state (with an empty boundary set). Second, and more interestingly, we can capture that all objects that have not been copied so far (predicate forw-obj, see §2.7) are reachable from the work queue, without ever crossing an already copied object:

g.reachable (g.Succs (set Q) M ∪ S) {p ∈ R. forw-obj p M} {p ∈ R. ¬ forw-obj p M} M

This formalization is particularly interesting as it mirrors the following conjunct of the Schorr-Waite loop invariant ([12, Figure 4], [6, i4,i6]): all unmarked nodes are reachable from the stack without crossing marked nodes (or `null` pointers).

reachable ({t}∪ set (map (λn. to-ptr (cell-r-rd n M)) S))
    {n. n = null ∨ n∈N ∧ marked n M} {n∈N. ¬marked n M} M

At this point, we thus see the re-use of a proof strategy between algorithms that are only linked by the aspects of a work queue and reachability in object graphs.

Using the boundary set, the library provides the splitting theorem (3) ([12, (44)]): the reachable set R can be split at some subset D into parts R1 and R2 and D. Note that both R1 and R2 are disjoint from D, such that nodes in D can be manipulated without influencing reachability within R1 and R2.

$$\frac{\text{reachable } \Gamma \text{ P Q R M} \qquad \text{D} \subseteq \text{R} \qquad \text{D} \cap \text{Q} = \{\}}{\begin{array}{l}(\exists \text{R1 R2. reachable } \Gamma \text{ P } (\text{Q} \cup \text{D}) \text{ R1 M} \wedge \\ \quad \text{reachable } \Gamma \text{ (Succs } \Gamma \text{ D M) } (\text{Q} \cup \text{D}) \text{ R2 M} \wedge \\ \quad \text{R} = \text{R1} \cup \text{R2} \cup \text{D})\end{array}} \tag{3}$$

Conversely, two parts of a object graph thus created can be joined together:

$$\frac{\text{reachable P Q R M} \qquad \text{reachable P' Q R' M}}{\text{reachable } (\text{P} \cup \text{P'}) \text{ Q } (\text{R} \cup \text{R'}) \text{ M}} \tag{4}$$

Both theorems apply in the verification of the `copy_ref` function: before setting the forwarding pointer of `obj` in Line 16, the reachability of un-copied nodes is split using (3) to expose the object obj. At the end, the split parts are joined by (4), using the fact that `obj` has now been copied.

This reasoning succeeded immediately, because it mirrors the Schorr-Waite proof [12, §5.2.4]. The proximity to an informal argument is also interesting: one would draw a pointer diagram, highlight the object to be manipulated, and think about the reachability by paths that might cross the object.

The specification of copying collectors rests on the notion of a *graph isomorphism* [18,22,9], i.e. a one-to-one mapping from the original object graph to its copy that respects the pointer structure. The definition can be given at the level of the existing graph library as follows, and it will be equally re-usable.

First, the isomorphism will map addresses, while object fields can contain either pointers or atomic values. Following [18], we hide the case distinction by an auxiliary function *pointer map*, which is the identity on atoms.

pmap $\varphi \equiv \lambda$v. if is-ptr v
    then (if to-ptr v $\in$ dom φ then Some (to-Ptr (the (φ (to-ptr v)))) else None)
    else Some v

Then, a *morphism* is a mapping between object sets that respects the successor relations; an *isomorphism* is an injective morphism ($\circ$ is function composition).

morph φ A fieldsA B fieldsB $\equiv$
    dom φ = A $\wedge$ ran φ = B $\wedge$
    ($\forall$a $\in$ A. fieldsB (the (φ a)) = map (the $\circ$ pmap φ) (fieldsA a))
iso φ A fieldsA B fieldsB $\equiv$ morph φ A fieldsA B fieldsB $\wedge$ inj-on φ A

2.7 The Forwarding Pointers

The forwarding pointers established by the algorithm are used to handle aliasing and cycles. Beyond this technical role, they bear a relation to the specification (cf. §3.1) as they constitute the graph isomorphism that a copying collector constructs [18,22]. As this aspect touches all parts of Figure 1, it is the most complex one. Nevertheless, it can be tackled using the proposed split/join strategy and arguments following the algorithm's operational behaviour.

The basis for the development is a predicate for forwarded objects. An object is forwarded iff its first field is a to-space reference (§2.4, Figure 1).

$$\mathsf{forw\text{-}obj\ p\ M} \equiv \mathsf{to\text{-}space\text{-}ref\ p\ M}$$

The forwarding pointers can be read as a (partial) mapping from the original objects from the set R of reachable objects (§2.6) to the copies, if these exist (Isabelle *maps* are functions to the option type to encode partiality):

$$\begin{aligned}\mathsf{forw\text{-}map\ R\ M} \equiv \lambda \mathsf{p}.\ & \mathsf{if\ p} \in \mathsf{R} \wedge \mathsf{forw\text{-}obj\ p\ M}\\ & \mathsf{then\ Some\ (to\text{-}ptr\ (rd\ gctx\ p\ TInt\ M))}\\ & \mathsf{else\ None}\end{aligned}$$

We are now going to capture the consistency conditions expressed visually in Figure 1 in a predicate Forw φ R B C Q M0 M. It relates the parts B, Q and R from Figure 1 in the initial state M0 and current state M. The set C of "current" objects plays the role of a boundary set of §2.5 and §2.6: it may contain the objects that have been removed temporarily from the queue for processing (§2.5).

$$\begin{aligned}&\mathsf{Forw}\ \varphi\ \mathsf{R\ B\ C\ Q\ M0\ M} \equiv\\ &\quad \varphi = \mathsf{forw\text{-}map\ R\ M} \ \wedge\ \mathsf{ran}\ \varphi = \mathsf{B} \cup \mathsf{C} \cup \mathsf{Q} \wedge \mathsf{inj\text{-}map}\ \varphi\ \wedge\\ &\quad (\forall\, \mathsf{r} \in \mathsf{dom}\ \varphi.\ \mathsf{the}\ (\varphi\ \mathsf{r}) \in \mathsf{B} \longrightarrow\\ &\quad\ \mathsf{set\ (obj\text{-}succs\ r\ M0)} \subseteq \mathsf{dom}\ \varphi\ \wedge\\ &\quad\ \mathsf{obj\text{-}fields\ (the}\ (\varphi\ \mathsf{r}))\ \mathsf{M} = \mathsf{map\ (the} \circ \mathsf{pmap}\ \varphi)\ \mathsf{(obj\text{-}fields\ r\ M0))} \wedge\\ &\quad (\forall\, \mathsf{r} \in \mathsf{dom}\ \varphi.\ \mathsf{the}\ (\varphi\ \mathsf{r}) \in \mathsf{Q} \longrightarrow\\ &\quad\ \mathsf{obj\text{-}fields\ (the}\ (\varphi\ \mathsf{r}))\ \mathsf{M} = \mathsf{obj\text{-}fields\ r\ M0)}\end{aligned}$$

The forwarding map φ is thus injective and targets the entire queue. For the objects in the black part B, their successors are also copied and the object fields are mapped by φ. For the queue part Q, the object fields are copies of the source object under φ. Note how all of these relationships are derived directly from Figure 1 and capture the aspects of the "forwarding" and "copying" completely.

As with the previous aspects, we now consider the split/join theorems for Forw. They will be applied in Line 17 of `copy_ref`, the only point where the forwarding map is modified. According to the preceding if-conditions, the object `obj` has not been forwarded at this point, so we can extract it by the splitting rule (5), thus making it accessible for modification.

$$\frac{\neg\ \mathsf{forw\text{-}obj\ p\ M}}{\mathsf{Forw}\ \varphi\ \mathsf{R\ B\ C\ Q\ M0\ M} = \mathsf{Forw}\ \varphi\ (\mathsf{R}\ \text{-}\ \{\mathsf{p}\})\ \mathsf{B\ C\ Q\ M0\ M}} \tag{5}$$

After the update of Line 17, the object `obj` *is* forwarded, the forwarding map has therefore been extended, and the queue contains a newly copied object. The extension of the forwarding map is expressed by the following constant (where operator ++ from the Isabelle library denotes the merge of two maps).

$$\mathsf{extend\text{-}forw\ ctx}\ \varphi\ \mathsf{p\ M} = \varphi\ {+}{+}\ [\ \mathsf{p} \mapsto \mathsf{to\text{-}ptr\ (rd\ ctx\ p\ TInt\ M)}\ ]$$

The join theorem (6) then expresses the reasoning necessary for deriving that the forwarding map is consistent after `copy_ref`. Note how the first premise reflects the conclusion of (5) while the others capture the operational behaviour of the algorithm, as gleaned from the code.

$$\frac{\begin{array}{c}\mathsf{Forw}\ \varphi\ (\mathsf{R}\ \text{-}\ \{\mathsf{p}\})\ \mathsf{B}\ \mathsf{C}\ \mathsf{Q}\ \mathsf{M0}\ \mathsf{M} \\ \mathsf{p} \in \mathsf{R} \quad \mathsf{forw\text{-}obj\ p\ M} \\ \mathsf{obj\text{-}fields\ (to\text{-}ptr\ (rd\ ctx\ p\ TInt\ M))\ M} = \mathsf{obj\text{-}fields\ p\ M0} \\ \mathsf{to\text{-}ptr\ (rd\ ctx\ p\ TInt\ M)} \notin \mathsf{B} \cup \mathsf{C} \cup \mathsf{Q} \\ \mathsf{same\text{-}static\ ctx\ gctx}\end{array}}{\mathsf{Forw\ (extend\text{-}forw\ ctx}\ \varphi\ \mathsf{p\ M)\ R\ B\ C}\ (\mathsf{Q} \cup \{\ \mathsf{to\text{-}ptr\ (rd\ ctx\ p\ TInt\ M)}\ \})\ \mathsf{M0\ M}} \quad (6)$$

The final code location concerned with the forwarding map is Line 12 of `collect`, which advances `scan` and thus moves the "current" object to the "black" part of the work queue (§2.5). At this point, both fields of the object at `scan` must be "completely processed". Using the function pmap from §2.6, we can express this assertion concisely: a reference is "done", under a given mapping φ, if in current state M its previous content in M' has been overwritten with the correct word:

$$\mathsf{done\text{-}ref\ p}\ \varphi\ \mathsf{M'\ M} \equiv (\mathsf{pmap}\ \varphi\ (\mathsf{rd\ gctx\ p\ TInt\ M'}) = \mathsf{Some\ (rd\ gctx\ p\ TInt\ M)})$$

The constant is, however, more than an auxiliary. Consider the two calls in the `collect` loop. Each guarantees in its post-condition `done_ref` for its passed object field, but each possibly extends the map φ. It therefore became clear immediately that (7) was needed at the end of the loop body; by proving it directly, we could check the background theory about the algorithm before attempting the verification. ($\leq_\mathsf{m}$ from the Isabelle library defines extensions of maps.)

$$\frac{\mathsf{done\text{-}ref\ p}\ \varphi\ \mathsf{M'\ M} \quad \varphi \leq_\mathsf{m} \varphi'}{\mathsf{done\text{-}ref\ p}\ \varphi'\ \mathsf{M'\ M}} \quad (7)$$

Theorem (8) then verifies the correctness of Line 17 of `collect`: the forwarding map is left intact if both object fields are "done":

$$\frac{\begin{array}{c}\mathsf{Forw}\ \varphi\ \mathsf{R\ B}\ \{\mathsf{p}\}\ \mathsf{Q\ M0\ M} \\ \mathsf{obj\text{-}fields\ p\ M'} = \mathsf{obj\text{-}fields\ (the\ (inv\text{-}map}\ \varphi\ \mathsf{p))\ M0} \\ \mathsf{done\text{-}ref\ p}\ \varphi\ \mathsf{M'\ M} \quad \mathsf{done\text{-}ref}\ (\mathsf{p} \oplus 4)\ \varphi\ \mathsf{M'\ M}\end{array}}{\mathsf{Forw}\ \varphi\ \mathsf{R\ (insert\ p\ B)}\ \{\}\ \mathsf{Q\ M0\ M}} \quad (8)$$

We wished to be sure early in proof development that the overall goal of constructing the graph isomorphism (§2.6) would be attained. Immediately after deriving the definition of Forw from Figure 1, we therefore proved (9) to ensure that the consistency conditions are strong enough: when the algorithm's work queue becomes empty after the loop, and all objects have been forwarded, then the forwarding map is an isomorphism.

$$\frac{\mathsf{Forw}\ \varphi\ \mathsf{R\ B}\ \{\}\ \{\}\ \mathsf{M0\ M} \quad \forall \mathsf{p} \in \mathsf{R}.\ \mathsf{forw\text{-}obj\ p\ M}}{\mathsf{iso}\ \varphi\ \mathsf{R}\ (\lambda \mathsf{p}.\ \mathsf{obj\text{-}fields\ p\ M0})\ \mathsf{B}\ \ (\lambda \mathsf{p}.\ \mathsf{obj\text{-}fields\ p\ M})} \quad (9)$$

In summary, even the complex aspect of the forwarding map has been derivable from the code and informal arguments, without referring to the generated verification conditions. The search for split/join theorems has led to understandable reasoning steps, whose application during the verification is clear.

2.8 Remaining Free Space

The collector copies objects out of the from-space into the to-space. Since both spaces have the same size, the to-space will be large enough to receive all copies. In order to be satisfied that this reasoning will be sufficient, we proved (10) before proceeding further (region-size A is the size of the region covered by A; $\triangleright$ denotes allocatedness [16]). Its premises reflect the situation in Line 11 of `copy_ref`: as an invariant, the space occupied by all non-copied objects is no greater than the remaining free-block (i.e. the remainder of the to-space after free); both the free-block and the non-copied objects are allocated; and some object p among these has not been copied. The conclusion asserts that one object can be extracted to maintain the invariant and to split the free-block; furthermore moving the free-pointer forward will leave it inside the to-space, ready for further allocations.

$$\frac{\begin{array}{l}\text{region-size}\,(\text{g.nodes}\ \{p \in R.\ \neg\ \text{forw-obj p M}\}) \leq \text{region-size}\,(\text{free-block M})\\ \text{M} \triangleright \text{free-block M} \parallel \text{g.nodes}\ \{p \in R.\ \neg\ \text{forw-obj p M}\}\\ p \in R \quad \neg\ \text{forw-obj p M}\end{array}}{\begin{array}{l}\text{region-size}\,(\text{g.nodes}\ \{p' \in R.\ p' \neq p \wedge \neg\,\text{forw-obj p' M}\}) + 8 \leq \text{region-size}\,(\text{free-block M}) \wedge\\ \text{free-block M} = \text{obj-cover}\,(\text{free M})\\ \qquad\qquad \parallel \text{block}\,(\text{free M} \oplus 8)\ (\text{spaceSz M - (free M} \ominus \text{toSpace M) - 8}) \wedge\\ \text{free M} < \text{free M} \oplus 8 \wedge \text{free M} \oplus 8 \leq \text{toSpace M} \oplus \text{spaceSz M}\end{array}} \quad (10)$$

3 Assembling the Correctness Proof

Section 2 has formalized the aspects of Cheney's algorithm along with theorems for reasoning about them, and has indicated precisely how to apply the theorems in verification. It remains to assemble the available parts into the correctness proof. This mode of presentation reflects our way of proceeding: we finished most of the base work before being concerned with the verification conditions.

3.1 The Specification of `collect`

The pre-condition of the collector is the expected one: the memory consists of the two half-spaces (§2.4) and the objects R reachable from the root `r` (§2.6) are contained in the (exhausted) to-space. Finally, the two spaces are laid out according to §2.4, the global definitions in the current context match those in gctx, and the auxiliary (or logical) variable M0 is bound to the initial state (► denotes that the cover describes the entire memory layout):

$$\begin{array}{l}\text{M} \blacktriangleright \langle\!\langle \text{r:TInt} \rangle\!\rangle \parallel \text{gc-vars} \parallel \text{to-block M} \parallel \text{from-block M} \wedge\\ \text{g.reachable (ref-set r M)}\ \{\}\ \text{R M} \wedge \text{g.nodes R} \preceq \text{to-block M} \wedge\\ \text{space-vars-inv M} \wedge \text{same-static ctx gctx} \wedge \text{M0} ::= \text{M}\end{array}$$

The post-condition specifies the same memory layout, but the object graph is copied to the new to-space into a set R' of objects, whose graph structure is isomorphic to that of the initial graph R [18,22]:

$$\begin{array}{l}\text{M} \blacktriangleright \langle\!\langle \text{R0:TInt} \rangle\!\rangle \parallel \text{gc-vars} \parallel \text{to-block M} \parallel \text{from-block M} \wedge \text{space-vars-inv M} \wedge\\ (\exists \varphi\ \text{R'}.\ \text{iso}\ \varphi\ \text{R}\ (\lambda \text{p. obj-fields p M0})\ \text{R'}\ (\lambda \text{p. obj-fields p M}) \wedge\\ \qquad\qquad \text{g.nodes R'} \preceq \text{to-block M})\end{array}$$

$$
\begin{array}{l}
\text{gc-inv root sc sc' R S B C Q } \varphi \text{ M0 M} \equiv \\
\quad \text{space-vars-inv M} \wedge \\
\quad \text{is-ptr (to-Ptr (free M))} \wedge \text{free M} \in \{ \text{toSpace M .. toSpace M} \oplus \text{spaceSz M} \} \wedge \\
\quad \text{q.nodes (toSpace M) sc B M} \wedge \text{q.nodes sc' (free M) Q M} \wedge \\
\quad \text{set B} \cap (\text{set C} \cup \text{set Q}) = \{\} \wedge \text{set C} \cap \text{set Q} = \{\} \wedge \\
\quad (\text{set B} \cup \text{set C} \cup \text{set Q}) \subseteq \{..< \text{free M} \} \wedge \\
\quad \text{Forw } \varphi \text{ R (set B) (set C) (set Q) M0 M} \wedge \\
\quad \text{g.reachable (ref-set root M0) } \{\} \text{ R M0} \wedge \\
\quad \text{g.nodes R} \preceq \text{from-block M} \wedge \\
\quad \text{to-block M} = \text{g.nodes (set B} \cup \text{set C} \cup \text{set Q)} \parallel \text{free-block M} \wedge \\
\quad \text{g.reachable (g.Succs (set Q) M} \cup \text{S)} \{\text{p} \in \text{R. forw-obj p M}\} \{\text{p} \in \text{R. } \neg \text{forw-obj p M}\} \text{ M} \wedge \\
\quad \text{region-size (g.nodes } \{\text{p} \in \text{R. } \neg \text{ forw-obj p M}\}) \le \text{region-size (free-block M)} \wedge \\
\quad (\forall \text{p} \in \text{R. } \neg \text{ forw-obj p M} \longrightarrow \text{obj-fields p M} = \text{obj-fields p M0})
\end{array}
$$

Fig. 3. The Collector's Invariant

3.2 The Loop Invariant and Proof of `collect`

The main invariant of `collect` (Figure 3), which together with the memory layout from the pre-condition forms the loop invariant, relates the parts of Figure 1 and has four further parameters S, C, sc and sc', which act as boundaries in the formulation of split/join theorems. The invariant gathers the aspects from §2: it captures the half-spaces (§2.4) with the additional `free` pointer and the queue structure (§2.5), whose fragments are delimited by the boundary parameters. In the forwarding map, it leaves C open in the same way as §2.7. It keeps the definition of R as the set of objects reachable in the initial state M0, and the split of the (swapped) from- and to-spaces. Finally, the invariant on sizes (§2.8) and the reachability of un-copied nodes (§2.6) guarantee that the algorithm can make progress. The un-copied objects remain unmodified from the initial state, which again imitates the invariant of the Schorr-Waite algorithm [12,6].

Like the separate aspects, the invariant enjoys split and join theorems that guide the verification. The split theorem (11) is applied at the beginning of the `collect` loop body, where the invariant holds and the queue is not empty. It moves the object `scan` to the current nodes C and makes explicit the information that was known before: its successors may lead to un-copied nodes, and its fields are just copied from some original object (given by φ^{-1}), such that the successors are contained in R (by reachable sets being closed).

$$
\frac{\text{gc-inv root (scan M) (scan M) R S B [] Q } \varphi \text{ M0 M} \qquad \text{scan M} \neq \text{free M}}{\begin{array}{l}
\exists \text{Q'. gc-inv root (scan M) (queue-succ (scan M) M) R} \\
\qquad\qquad\qquad (\text{S} \cup \text{set (obj-succs (scan M) M)) B [scan M] Q' } \varphi \text{ M0 M} \wedge \\
\quad \text{Q} = \text{scan M \# Q'} \wedge \text{scan M} \notin \text{set Q'} \wedge \\
\quad \text{obj-fields (scan M) M} = \text{obj-fields (the (inv-map } \varphi \text{ (scan M))) M0} \wedge \\
\quad \text{set (obj-succs (scan M) M)} \subseteq \text{R}
\end{array}} \tag{11}
$$

After the loop body, the `scan` object is re-integrated into the overall structure by the join theorem (12). Therein, M' designates the memory state before the loop body, such that the first three premises mirror the conclusion of the split theorem (11) and the advancing of `scan` (Line 12). The real proof obligation is in the last line: both fields of the object must be "done" (§2.7). In the conclusion, the scan object is now "black".

$$\frac{\begin{array}{l}\text{gc-inv root (scan M') (scan M) R (set (obj-succs (scan M') M')) B [scan M'] Q } \varphi \text{ M0 M}\\ \text{obj-fields (scan M') M'} = \text{obj-fields (the (inv-map } \varphi \text{ (scan M'))) M0}\\ \text{scan M} = \text{scan M'} \oplus 8\\ \text{done-ref (scan M') } \varphi \text{ M' M} \qquad \text{done-ref (scan M'} \oplus 4) \ \varphi \text{ M' M}\end{array}}{\text{gc-inv root (scan M) (scan M) R \{\} (B @ [scan M']) [] Q } \varphi \text{ M0 M}} \tag{12}$$

The proof of both theorems (11) and (12) are direct using the split/join theorems for the constituent aspects from §2. For instance, the last two premises of (12) are obviously needed to apply (8).

The verification of `collect` is now clear: in the beginning, gc-inv holds trivially for the empty queue and empty forwarding map. The helper `copy_ref` will be proven in §3.3 to maintain gc-inv and to guarantee that its argument is a done-ref (§2.7) after execution. For `collect`, we therefore split gc-inv at the beginning of the loop body by (11) and join it after the two calls by (12) (using (7)).

In summary, the overall correctness proof is only an application of reasoning steps derived from informal arguments of the code's behaviour and consistency conditions in §2, and the developer's intention of factoring out the copying of a single reference is reflected in the proof structure.

3.3 The `copy_ref` Function

Informally, the auxiliary function `copy_ref` must process a single reference completely, i.e. convert it to a done-ref (§2.7), without violating gc-inv. Its specification merely makes this notion precise. The pre-condition assumes the invariant memory layout and gc-inv, and binds a few auxiliary variables to initial values.

$\exists$ 'B Q. gc-inv root sc sc' R S B C Q φ M0 M $\wedge$ proper-ref p R M $\wedge$
M ► gc-vars ‖ g.nodes R ‖ g.nodes (set B $\cup$ set Q) ‖ free-block M ‖ « p :TInt » ‖ F $\wedge$
same-static ctx gctx $\wedge$ P0 := p $\wedge$ M1 ::= M $\wedge$ wf-cover F

The post-condition asserts gc-inv (albeit with a possibly changed queue) and an unmodified layout (although the free-block may be different). Furthermore, it has processed the given reference as required (§2.7), has at most extended the forwarding map, and has not modified the space variables, the pointer `scan` and F, which contains the remainder of the memory (the frame conjunct [12]).

$\exists$ 'B Q φ'. gc-inv root sc sc' R S B C Q φ' M0 M $\wedge$
M ► gc-vars ‖ g.nodes R ‖ g.nodes (set B $\cup$ set Q) ‖ free-block M ‖ « P0 :TInt » ‖ F $\wedge$
done-ref P0 φ' M1 M $\wedge$ map-le φ φ' $\wedge$
frame (space-vars ‖ gvar-block "scan" ‖ F) M1 M

As in the case of `collect`, the correctness proof of `copy_ref` follows the indications from §2: in the first case (Lines 7–9), only the reference p is modified, and the post-condition can be derived by extracting knowledge about the copied pointer from gc-inv. The second case (Lines 11–17) is the interesting one: we split the graph R by (3), the forwarding map by (5), and the free-block by (10). To derive the post-condition, the complementary join theorems (4) and (6) are invoked to re-assemble gc-inv and the post-condition.

4 Related Work

We have proposed strategies for structuring a correctness proof from a developer's perspective. To the best of our knowledge, neither the alignment of the proof with different aspects of the algorithm, nor the unifying strategy of high-level split/join theorems with dedicated boundary parameters have been discussed before. Further, no other study has attempted theory re-use across algorithms through generic formalizations of shared aspects. We now discuss related case studies on garbage collectors, focussing on recent low-level implementations.

Myreen [7] verifies Cheney's collector by refinement, proving successively more detailed specifications correct relative to the previous one. The intention is to re-use higher levels, which express the core of copying collection, to verify other collectors. This re-use is, however, not demonstrated, and it applies only to algorithms with the same specification. Our approach of factoring the proof into aspects has enabled the re-use of extensive theories across algorithms with different specifications. Myreen explicitly excludes the discussion of the proofs beyond mentioning that his approach is a reduction to set-theoretic arguments.

Varming/Birkedal [23, §4.1] formalize the earlier pen-and-paper development [18] in Isabelle/HOLCF based on higher-order separation logic. Their structure of the invariants and specifications is complementary to ours, in that they use the separating conjunction to specify disjoint parts of the heap independently, while we formalize the unifying aspects across the entire heap. Their definitions of the invariants refer to the memory content directly, and no intermediate levels are introduced. The overall structure of the substantial development is not discussed.

McCreight [9, Ch. 6] gives a detailed proof of Cheney's collector in separation logic. He structures the specifications and invariants carefully by a number of auxiliary predicates and motivates their definitions in relation to the code (e.g. [9, §6.2, Fig. 6.7]). His loop invariant is developed in several steps (Figs. 6.16, 6.17, 6.18, 6.21). Following the idea of local reasoning, each definition leaves open a parameter for the remainder of the memory, which is instantiated in the subsequent definitions. The development is thus, again, complementary to ours by splitting the assertions along the memory layout, as prescribed by separation logic. Independent lemmas about the auxiliary predicates are not discussed, and McCreight mentions (§6.3.3; p. 122; §6.4.3) that the actual proofs involve a substantial amount of manual, low-level manipulation.

Hawblitzel and Petrank [2] verify several practical collectors using the Boogie/Z3 tool-suite. The collectors are written in BoogiePL, are translated to assembly language, and can be applied to existing benchmarks. Their specifications follow the framework [22], but exclude the central aspect of reachability [2, §4.1.1]. The proofs are discussed briefly along the verification conditions, which are also related back to the code. For the SMT prover to succeed, however, a substantial amount of further annotations as well as detailed technical considerations on triggers [2, §4.3] are necessary.

Mehta and Nipkow [6] verify the related Schorr-Waite graph marking algorithm. Their elegant Isar proof [6, §7.2] is discussed down to individual verification conditions. However, no attempt at structuring the proof further is made and the level of detail is limited by the used high-level language. Hubert and Marché [10] verify a C implementation of the same algorithm. Their description of the proof in [10, §4] is limited to the explanation of the invariant.

5 Conclusion

We have approached the verification of a low-level C implementation of Cheney's collector from a developer's perspective: by formalizing and reasoning about the different aspects of the algorithm independently, by choosing the aspects to be familiar from other contexts, and by unifying the development using the introduced split/join reasoning pattern, a strong relationship between the proof and an informal understanding of the code's operational behaviour was maintained throughout. The verification then consisted in applying the derived lemmas, and the overall proof appears as a precise version of informal correctness arguments.

The development [17] consists of 2590 lines, which is comparable to [7] and substantially smaller than [9]. Of these lines, 1230 are re-used from previous studies (lists: 330; object graphs: 650 (+750 ML); byte-level memory: 250). The new part consists of 280 lines for basic definitions and library instantiation (§2.4–§2.6); 580 for proofs about the aspects (§2.5–2.8); 60 for code and specification; 440 for the verification conditions (§3). This relative distribution underlines the degree of re-use, as well as the largely self-contained treatment of the identified aspects of the algorithm.

The proposed approach has shown several benefits. First, we have achieved high-level proof re-use across different algorithms: two aspects, the work queue and reachability in object graphs, were solved completely by generic theories from previous developments. Isabelle locales were found to be a suitable mechanism for accomplishing such re-use. Second, the strong relation between the proof structure and the code greatly aided the development, since proofs could be derived from the informal correctness arguments as used by developers. Finally, the fact that the reasoning about the different aspects is independent has enhanced the maintainability of the proof during development.

We have chosen an interactive prover for our development because of its support for structured theory development. The application of the derived lemmas was, however, mostly automatic and consisted in discharging side-conditions in set-theory by simple tactic invocations. As future work, we therefore propose to investigate the application of our approach in the context of the Boogie and SMT solver integration [5] available with the current Isabelle distribution.

References

1. Banerjee, A., Barnett, M., Naumann, D.A.: Boogie meets regions: A verification experience report. In: Shankar, N., Woodcock, J. (eds.) VSTTE 2008. LNCS, vol. 5295, pp. 177–191. Springer, Heidelberg (2008)
2. Hawblitzel, C., Petrank, E.: Automated verification of practical garbage collectors. SIGPLAN Not. 44(1), 441–453 (2009)

3. Zee, K., Kuncak, V., Rinard, M.: Full functional verification of linked data structures. SIGPLAN Not. 43(6), 349–361 (2008)
4. Moskal, M.: Programming with triggers. In: Dutertre, B., Strichman, O. (eds.) SMT 2009: Proceedings of the 7th International Workshop on Satisfiability Modulo Theories. ACM, New York (2009)
5. Böhme, S., Moskal, M., Schulte, W., Wolff, B.: HOL-Boogie–An interactive prover-backend for the Verifying C Compiler. J. Autom. Reason. 44, 111–144 (2010)
6. Mehta, F., Nipkow, T.: Proving pointer programs in higher-order logic. Inf. Comput. 199(1-2), 200–227 (2005)
7. Myreen, M.O.: Reusable verification of a copying collector. In: Leavens, G.T., O'Hearn, P., Rajamani, S.K. (eds.) VSTTE 2010. LNCS, vol. 6217, pp. 142–156. Springer, Heidelberg (2010)
8. Marti, N., Affeldt, R.: Formal verification of the heap manager of an operating system using separation logic. In: Liu, Z., Kleinberg, R.D. (eds.) ICFEM 2006. LNCS, vol. 4260, pp. 400–419. Springer, Heidelberg (2006)
9. McCreight, A.: The Mechanized Verification of Garbage Collector Implementations. PhD thesis, Department of Computer Science, Yale University (2008)
10. Hubert, T., Marché, C.: A case study of C source code verification: the Schorr-Waite algorithm. In: Aichernig, B.K., Beckert, B. (eds.) SEFM. IEEE, Los Alamitos (2005)
11. Cheney, C.J.: A nonrecursive list compacting algorithm. Commun. ACM 13, 677–678 (1970)
12. Gast, H.: Reasoning about memory layouts. Formal Methods in System Design 37(2-3), 141–170 (2010)
13. Gast, H., Trieflinger, J.: High-level Reasoning about Low-level Programs. In: Roggenbach, M. (ed.) Automated Verification of Critical Systems 2009. Electronic Communications of the EASST, vol. 23 (2009)
14. Gast, H.: Verifying the L4 kernel allocator in lightweight separation (2010), `http://www-pu.informatik.uni-tuebingen.de/users/gast/proofs/kalloc.pdf`
15. Berdine, J., Calcagno, C., O'Hearn, P.W.: Smallfoot: Modular automatic assertion checking with separation logic. In: de Boer, F.S., Bonsangue, M.M., Graf, S., de Roever, W.-P. (eds.) FMCO 2005. LNCS, vol. 4111, pp. 115–137. Springer, Heidelberg (2006)
16. Gast, H.: Lightweight separation. In: Mohamed, O.A., Muñoz, C., Tahar, S. (eds.) TPHOLs 2008. LNCS, vol. 5170, pp. 199–214. Springer, Heidelberg (2008)
17. Gast, H.: A developer-oriented proof of Cheney's algorithm (2011), `http://www-pu.informatik.uni-tuebingen.de/users/gast/proofs/cheney.pdf`
18. Torp-Smith, N., Birkedal, L., Reynolds, J.C.: Local reasoning about a copying garbage collector. ACM Trans. Program. Lang. Syst. 30(4), 1–58 (2008)
19. Dawson, J.E.: Isabelle theories for machine words. In: 7th International Workshop on Automated Verification of Critical Systems (AVOCS 2007). ENTCS, vol. 250 (2009)
20. Kammüller, F., Wenzel, M., Paulson, L.C.: Locales - A sectioning concept for isabelle. In: Bertot, Y., Dowek, G., Hirschowitz, A., Paulin, C., Théry, L. (eds.) TPHOLs 1999. LNCS, vol. 1690, pp. 149–166. Springer, Heidelberg (1999)
21. Burstall, R.: Some techniques for proving correctness of programs which alter data stuctures. In: Meltzer, B., Michie, D. (eds.) Machine Intelligence, vol. 7. Edinburgh University Press, Edinburgh (1972)
22. McCreight, A., Shao, Z., Lin, C., Li, L.: A general framework for certifying garbage collectors and their mutators. SIGPLAN Not. 42(6), 468–479 (2007)
23. Varming, C., Birkedal, L.: Higher-order separation logic in Isabelle/HOLCF. Electron. Notes Theor. Comput. Sci. 218, 371–389 (2008)

Static Analysis of String Values

Giulia Costantini[1], Pietro Ferrara[2], and Agostino Cortesi[1]

[1] University Ca' Foscari of Venice, Italy
{costantini,cortesi}@dsi.unive.it
[2] ETH Zurich, Switzerland
pietro.ferrara@inf.ethz.ch

Abstract. In this paper we propose a unifying approach for the static analysis of string values based on abstract interpretation, and we present several abstract domains that track different types of information. In this way, the analysis can be tuned at different levels of precision and efficiency, and it can address specific properties.

1 Introduction

Strings are widely used in modern programming languages. Their applications vary from providing an output to a user to the construction of programs executed through reflection. For instance, in PHP strings can be a way of communicating programs, while in Java they are widely used as SQL queries, or to access information about the classes through reflection. The execution of `str.substring(str.indexOf('a'))` raises an exception if `str` does not contain an `'a'` character: in this case, it would be useful being able to track the characters surely contained on the variable `str`. As another example, when dealing with SQL queries, what happens if we execute the query "`DELETE FROM Table WHERE ID =` " + `id` when `id` is equal to "`10 OR TRUE`"? The content of `Table` would be permanently erased! It's clear that a wrong manipulation of strings could lead not only to subtle exceptions, but to dramatic and permanent effects as well [20].

For all these reasons, the interest on approaches that automatically analyse and discover bugs on strings is constantly raising. On the other hand, the state-of-the-art in this field is still limited: approaches that rely on automata and use regular expressions are precise but slow, and they do not scale up [14,24,21,13], while many other approaches are focused on particular properties or class of programs [10,18,12]. Genericity and scalability are the main advantages of the abstract interpretation approach [4,5], though its instantiation to textual values has been quite limited up to now.

The main contribution of this paper is the formalisation of a *unifying* abstract interpretation based framework for string analysis, and its instantiations with *four different domains* that track distinct types of information. In this way, we can tune the analysis at diversified levels of *accuracy*, yielding to faster and rougher, or slower but more precise string analyses.

S. Qin and Z. Qiu (Eds.): ICFEM 2011, LNCS 6991, pp. 505–521, 2011.

```
var query = "SELECT '$\$$' ||
  (RETAIL/100) FROM INVENTORY WHERE ";
if (l != null)
 query = query+"WHOLESALE > "+l+" AND ";

var per = "SELECT TYPECODE, TYPEDESC FROM
  TYPES WHERE NAME = 'fish' OR NAME = 'meat'";
query = query+"TYPE IN (" + per + ");";
return query;
```

(a) The first running example

```
string x = "a";
while(cond)
  x = "0" + x + "1";
return x;
```

(b) The second running example

Fig. 1. The running examples

We inspired our work looking at the approach adopted for numerical domains for static analysis of software [7,11,19]. The interface of a numerical domain is nowadays standard: each domain has to define the semantics of arithmetic expressions (like $\mathtt{i} + 5$) and boolean conditions (like $\mathtt{i} < 5$). Similarly, we consider a limited list of basic string operators that can be easily extended to the various programming languages. The concrete semantics of these operators is approximated in the four different abstract domains. In addition, after 30 years of practice with numerical domains, it is clear that a monolithic domain precise on any program and property (e.g., Polyhedra [7]) gives up in terms of efficiency, while to achieve scalability we need specific approximations on a given property (e.g., Pentagons [17]) or class of programs (e.g., ASTRÉE [6]). With this scenario in mind, we develop several domains inside the same framework to tune the analysis at different levels of precision and efficiency w.r.t. the analysed program and property. Other abstractions are possible and welcomed, and we expect our framework to be generic enough to support them.

The paper is structured as follows. In the rest of this Section we introduce two running examples, and we recall some basics of abstract interpretation. Section 2 defines the syntax of the string operators we will consider. Section 3 introduces the concrete semantics, while in Section 4 the abstract domains are formalised. Finally, Section 5 discusses the related work, and Section 6 concludes.

1.1 Running Examples

Along the paper, we will always refer to the two examples reported in Tables 1(a) and 1(b). The first `Java` program is taken from [10], and it dynamically builds an SQL query by concatenating some strings. One of these concatenations applies only if a certain value (unknown at compile time) is not null. We are interested in checking if the SQL query resulting by the execution of such code is well formed. For the sake of readability, we will use some shortcuts to identify string constants of this program, as reported in Table 1. The second program modifies a string inside a `while` loop whose condition cannot be statically evaluated. Therefore, we will need to apply a widening operator [2] to force the convergence of the analysis. Intuitively, this program produces strings in the form "$0^n a 1^n$".

Table 1. Shortcuts of string constants in the first running example

Name	String constant
s_1	"SELECT '\$' || (RETAIL/100) FROM INVENTORY WHERE "
s_2	"WHOLESALE > "
s_3	" AND "
s_4	"SELECT TYPECODE, TYPEDESC FROM TYPES WHERE NAME = 'fish' OR NAME = 'meat'"
s_5	"TYPE IN ("
s_6	"); "

1.2 Abstract Interpretation

Abstract interpretation is a theory to define and soundly approximate the semantics of a program [4,5], focusing on some runtime properties of interest. Usually, each concrete state is composed by a set of elements (e.g., all the possible computational states), that is approximated by an unique element in the abstract domain. Formally, the concrete domain $\wp(\mathsf{D})$ forms a complete lattice $\langle \wp(\mathsf{D}), \subseteq, \emptyset, \mathsf{D}, \cup, \cap \rangle$. On this domain, a semantics $\mathbb{S}$ is defined. In the same way, an abstract semantics is defined, and it is aimed to approximate the concrete one in a computable way. Formally, the abstract domain $\overline{\mathsf{A}}$ has to form a complete lattice $\langle \overline{\mathsf{A}}, \leq_{\overline{\mathsf{A}}}, \bot_{\overline{\mathsf{A}}}, \top_{\overline{\mathsf{A}}}, \sqcup_{\overline{\mathsf{A}}}, \sqcap_{\overline{\mathsf{A}}} \rangle$. The concrete elements are related to the abstract domain by a concretization $\gamma_{\overline{\mathsf{A}}}$ and an abstraction $\alpha_{\overline{\mathsf{A}}}$ functions. In order to obtain a sound analysis, we require that the abstraction and concretization functions above form a Galois connection. An abstract semantics $\overline{\mathbb{S}}$ is defined as a sound approximation of the concrete one, i.e., $\forall \overline{\mathsf{a}} \in \overline{\mathsf{A}} : \alpha_{\overline{\mathsf{A}}} \circ \mathbb{S}[\![\gamma_{\overline{\mathsf{A}}}(\overline{\mathsf{a}})]\!] \leq_{\mathsf{A}} \overline{\mathbb{S}}[\![\overline{\mathsf{a}}]\!]$.

When abstract domains do not satisfy the ascending chain condition, a widening operator $\nabla_{\overline{\mathsf{A}}}$ is required in order to guarantee the convergence of the fixed point computation. This is an upper bound operator such that for all increasing chains $\overline{\mathsf{a}}_0 \leq_{\overline{\mathsf{A}}} \ldots \overline{\mathsf{a}}_n \leq_{\overline{\mathsf{A}}} \ldots$ the increasing chain defined as $\overline{\mathsf{w}}_0 = \overline{\mathsf{a}}_0, \ldots, \overline{\mathsf{w}}_{i+1} = \overline{\mathsf{w}}_i \nabla_{\mathsf{A}} \overline{\mathsf{a}}_{i+1}$ is not strictly increasing.

2 Syntax

Different languages define different operators on strings, and usually each language supports a huge set of such operators: in Java 1.6 the `String` class contains 65 methods plus 15 constructors, `System.Text` in .Net contains about 12 classes that work with Unicode strings, and PHP provides 111 string functions. Considering all these operators would be quite verbose, and in addition the most part of them perform similar actions using slightly different data. We restrict our description on a small but representative set of common operators. We chose these operators looking at some case studies. Other operators can be easily added to our approach. For each operator, this would mean to define its concrete semantics, and its approximations on the different domains we will introduce.

Table 2. The concrete semantics, where $\top_B$ represents that the condition could be evaluated to true or false depending on the string in S_1 we are considering

$$\mathbb{S}[\![\texttt{new String(str)}]\!]() = \{\texttt{str}\}$$
$$\mathbb{S}[\![\texttt{concat}]\!](S_1, S_2) = \{s_1 s_2 : s_1 \in S_1 \wedge s_2 \in S_2\}$$
$$\mathbb{S}[\![\texttt{readLine}]\!]() = S$$
$$\mathbb{S}[\![\texttt{substring}_b^e]\!](S_1) = \{c_b..c_e : c_1..c_n \in S_1 \wedge n \geq e \wedge b \leq e\}$$
$$\mathbb{B}[\![\texttt{contains}_c]\!](S_1) = \begin{cases} \text{true} & \text{if } \forall s \in S_1 : c \in \mathit{char}(s) \\ \text{false} & \text{if } \forall s \in S_1 : c \notin \mathit{char}(s) \\ \top_B & \text{otherwise} \end{cases}$$

A common operation is the creation of a new constant string (`new String(str)` where `str` is a sequence of characters). Usually programs concatenate strings (`concat(s1, s2)` where `s1` and `s2` are strings), read inputs from the user (`readLine()`), and take a substring of a given string ($\texttt{substring}_b^e(\texttt{s})$, where s is a string, and b and e are integer values) as well. A common test is to check if a string contains a character ($\texttt{contains}_c(\texttt{s})$, where `s` is a string and `c` is a character).

3 Concrete Domain and Semantics

3.1 Concrete Domain

Our concrete domain is simply made of strings. Given an alphabet K, that is a finite set of characters, we define strings as (possibly infinite) sequences of characters. Formally, $S = K^*$, where A^* is an ordered sequence of elements in A, that is, $A^* = \{a_1 \cdots a_n : \forall i \in [1..n] : a_i \in A\}$. A string variable in our program could have different values in different executions, and our goal is to approximate all these values (potentially infinite, e.g., when dealing with user input) in a finite, computable, and hopefully efficient manner. Our lattice will be made of sets of strings. As usual in abstract interpretation, the partial order is the set inclusion. Formally, our concrete domain is defined by $\langle \wp(S), \subseteq, \emptyset, S, \cup, \cap \rangle$.

3.2 Semantics

Table 2 formalises the concrete semantics. For each statement of the language we introduced in Section 2, we define its semantics. For the first four statements, we define a semantics $\mathbb{S}$ that, given the statement and eventually some sets of concrete string values in S, returns a set of strings resulting from that operation. The semantics of `new String(str)` returns a singleton containing `str`, while the semantics of `readLine` returns a set containing all the possible strings, since we may read any string from the standard input. The semantics of `concat` returns all the possible concatenations of a string taken from the first set and a string taken from the second set (we denote by $s_1 s_2$ the concatenation of strings s_1 and s_2), while the semantics of $\texttt{substring}_b^e$ returns all the substrings from the b-th to e-th character of the given strings (note that if one of the strings is too short, there is not any substring for it in the resulting set, since this would cause a runtime error without producing any value). For $\texttt{contains}_{\mathsf{c}}$ we define a particular semantics $\mathbb{B} : [\wp(\mathsf{S}) \rightarrow \{\mathsf{true}, \mathsf{false}, \top_{\mathsf{B}}\}]$ that, given a set of strings, returns true if all the strings contains the character c, false if none contains this character, and $\top_{\mathsf{B}}$ otherwise. This special boolean value represents a situation in which the boolean condition may be evaluated to true some times, and to false other times. We denoted by *char* a function that returns the set of characters contained in the string in input.

4 Abstract Domains and Semantics

What is the *relevant* information contained in a string? How can we approximate it in an *efficient* way? Tracking both sound and precise information at compile time on strings in an efficient way is infeasible. Then we need to introduce *approximation*. We want to track information precise enough to efficiently analyse the behaviours of interest, considering the string operators we defined in the previous section. Our purpose is to approximate strings as much as we can, preserving the information we deem relevant.

4.1 Character Inclusion

For the first abstract domain we aim at approximating a string through the characters we know it surely contains or it could contain. This information could be particularly useful to track if the indexes extrapolated from a string with operators like indexOf(c) could be used to cut the string (because c is surely contained in the string), or they could be invalid (e.g., -1). A string will be represented by a pair of sets: the set of *certainly* contained characters $\overline{\mathsf{C}}$ and the set of *maybe* contained characters $\overline{\mathsf{MC}}$ ($\overline{\mathcal{CI}} = \{(\overline{\mathsf{C}}, \overline{\mathsf{MC}}) : \overline{\mathsf{C}}, \overline{\mathsf{MC}} \in \wp(\mathsf{K}) \wedge \overline{\mathsf{C}} \subseteq \overline{\mathsf{MC}}\} \cup \bot_{\overline{\mathcal{CI}}}$). The partial order $\leq_{\overline{\mathcal{CI}}}$ on $\overline{\mathcal{CI}}$ is the following one:

$$(\overline{\mathsf{C}}_1, \overline{\mathsf{MC}}_1) \leq_{\overline{\mathcal{CI}}} (\overline{\mathsf{C}}_2, \overline{\mathsf{MC}}_2) \Leftrightarrow (\overline{\mathsf{C}}_1, \overline{\mathsf{MC}}_1) = \bot_{\overline{\mathcal{CI}}} \vee (\overline{\mathsf{C}}_1 \supseteq \overline{\mathsf{C}}_2 \wedge \overline{\mathsf{MC}}_1 \subseteq \overline{\mathsf{MC}}_2)$$

This is because the more information we have on the string (that is, the more characters are certainly contained and the less characters are maybe contained), the less number of strings we are representing. For example the abstract element represented by the pair $(\{a\}, \{a\})$ is more precise than the one represented by $(\emptyset, \{a, b\})$. In fact, the first pair represents the concrete set of strings $\{a, aa, aaa, \dots\}$ while the second pair corresponds to $\{\epsilon, a, b, aa, bb, ba, ab, \dots\}$.

For these reasons, the least upper bound is defined by $\sqcup_{\overline{\mathcal{CI}}}((\overline{\mathsf{C}}_1, \overline{\mathsf{MC}}_1), (\overline{\mathsf{C}}_2, \overline{\mathsf{MC}}_2)) = (\overline{\mathsf{C}}_1 \cap \overline{\mathsf{C}}_2, \overline{\mathsf{MC}}_1 \cup \overline{\mathsf{MC}}_2)$, and the greatest lower bound is defined by $\sqcap_{\overline{\mathcal{CI}}}((\overline{\mathsf{C}}_1, \overline{\mathsf{MC}}_1), (\overline{\mathsf{C}}_2, \overline{\mathsf{MC}}_2)) = (\overline{\mathsf{C}}_1 \cup \overline{\mathsf{C}}_2, \overline{\mathsf{MC}}_1 \cap \overline{\mathsf{MC}}_2)$. The widening operator corresponds to the $\sqcup_{\overline{\mathcal{CI}}}$ operator, and it ensures the convergence of the analysis since we supposed that the alphabet is finite. The top element of the lattice is $\top_{\overline{\mathcal{CI}}} = (\emptyset, \mathsf{K})$, while the bottom element $\bot_{\overline{\mathcal{CI}}}$ corresponds to a "failure" state.

The function which abstracts a single string s is: $\alpha'_{\overline{\mathcal{CI}}}(\mathsf{s}) = (char(\mathsf{s}), char(\mathsf{s}))$. The abstraction function takes us from a set of strings to an element in $\overline{\mathcal{CI}}$, and

Table 3. The abstract semantics of $\overline{\mathcal{CI}}$

$$\overline{\mathbb{S}_{\mathcal{CI}}}[\![\texttt{new String(str)}]\!]() = (char(\mathsf{str}), char(\mathsf{str}))$$
$$\overline{\mathbb{S}_{\mathcal{CI}}}[\![\texttt{concat}]\!]((\overline{\mathsf{C}}_1, \overline{\mathsf{MC}}_1), (\overline{\mathsf{C}}_2, \overline{\mathsf{MC}}_2)) = (\overline{\mathsf{C}}_1 \cup \overline{\mathsf{C}}_2, \overline{\mathsf{MC}}_1 \cup \overline{\mathsf{MC}}_2)$$
$$\overline{\mathbb{S}_{\mathcal{CI}}}[\![\texttt{readLine}]\!]() = (\emptyset, \mathsf{K})$$
$$\overline{\mathbb{S}_{\mathcal{CI}}}[\![\texttt{substring}_{\mathsf{b}}^{\mathsf{e}}]\!]((\overline{\mathsf{C}}_1, \overline{\mathsf{MC}}_1)) = (\emptyset, \overline{\mathsf{MC}}_1)$$
$$\overline{\mathbb{B}_{\mathcal{CI}}}[\![\texttt{contains}_{\mathsf{c}}]\!]((\overline{\mathsf{C}}_1, \overline{\mathsf{MC}}_1)) = \begin{cases} \mathsf{true} \ \text{ if } \mathsf{c} \in \overline{\mathsf{C}}_1 \\ \mathsf{false} \text{ if } \mathsf{c} \notin \overline{\mathsf{MC}}_1 \\ \top_{\mathsf{B}} \quad \text{otherwise} \end{cases}$$

#I	Var	$\overline{\mathcal{CI}}$
1	query	$\alpha'_{\overline{\mathcal{CI}}}(\mathsf{s}_1)$
3	l	$(\emptyset, \mathsf{K})$
3	query	$(\pi_1(\alpha'_{\overline{\mathcal{CI}}}(\mathsf{s}_1)) \cup \pi_1(\alpha'_{\overline{\mathcal{CI}}}(\mathsf{s}_2)) \cup \pi_1(\alpha'_{\overline{\mathcal{CI}}}(\mathsf{s}_3)), \mathsf{K})$
4	query	$(\pi_1(\alpha'_{\overline{\mathcal{CI}}}(\mathsf{s}_1)), \mathsf{K})$
5	per	$\alpha'_{\overline{\mathcal{CI}}}(\mathsf{s}_1)$
7	query	$(\pi_1(\alpha'_{\overline{\mathcal{CI}}}(\mathsf{s}_1)) \cup \pi_1(\alpha'_{\overline{\mathcal{CI}}}(\mathsf{s}_4)) \cup \pi_1(\alpha'_{\overline{\mathcal{CI}}}(\mathsf{s}_5)) \cup \pi_1(\alpha'_{\overline{\mathcal{CI}}}(\mathsf{s}_6)), \mathsf{K})$

(a) First running example

#I	Var	$\overline{\mathcal{CI}}$
1	x	$(\{a\}, \{a\})$
3	x	$(\{0, a, 1\}, \{0, a, 1\})$
4	x	$(\{a\}, \{0, a, 1\})$

(b) Second running example

Fig. 2. The results of $\overline{\mathcal{CI}}$

it returns the upper bound of the abstraction of all the concrete strings. Let π_i be the projection on the i-th component of a tuple.

$$\alpha_{\overline{\mathcal{CI}}}(\mathsf{S}_1) = \bigsqcup_{\overline{\mathcal{CI}}, \mathsf{s} \in \mathsf{S}_1} \alpha'_{\overline{\mathcal{CI}}}(\mathsf{s}) = (\bigcap_{\mathsf{s} \in \mathsf{S}_1} \pi_1(\alpha'_{\overline{\mathcal{CI}}}(\mathsf{s})), \bigcup_{\mathsf{s} \in \mathsf{S}_1} \pi_2(\alpha'_{\overline{\mathcal{CI}}}(\mathsf{s})))$$

Semantics. Table 3 defines the abstract semantics of the operators introduced in Section 2 on the abstract domain $\overline{\mathcal{CI}}$. We denote by $\overline{\mathbb{S}_{\mathcal{CI}}}$ and $\overline{\mathbb{B}_{\mathcal{CI}}}$ the abstract counterparts of $\mathbb{S}$ and $\mathbb{B}$ respectively.

When we evaluate a string, we know that the characters that are surely or maybe included are exactly the ones that appear in the string. The concatenation of two strings will contain all the characters that are surely or maybe contained in the two strings. `readLine` returns a top value, while if we take a substring of a given string, the result will possibly contain all the characters that are possibly contained in the initial string, while we know nothing about the surely contained characters. Finally, the semantics of $\texttt{contains}_{\mathsf{c}}$ is quite precise, as it checks if a character is surely contained or not contained respectively through $\overline{\mathsf{C}}$ and $\overline{\mathsf{MC}}$.

Running Example. Consider the examples introduced in Section 1.1. The results of the analysis of the first program using $\overline{\mathcal{CI}}$ are depicted in Figure 2(a). At the beginning, variable `query` is related to a state that contains the abstraction of c_1, that is, both $\overline{\mathsf{C}}$ and $\overline{\mathsf{MC}}$ contain all the characters of s_1. Since we do not know the value of `l`, we compute the least upper bound between the abstract values of `query` after instructions 1 and 3. In this way, we obtain that after the `if` statement the abstract value of `query` contains the abstraction of s_1 in the $\overline{\mathsf{C}}$ component (since it surely contains all the characters of that constant string), and the top value in the

$\overline{\mathsf{MC}}$ component (since we may have concatenated a string that may contain any character). At the end of the given code, `query` surely contains the characters of $\mathsf{s}_1, \mathsf{s}_4, \mathsf{s}_5$, and s_6, and it may contain any character, since we possibly concatenated in `query` an input string (the `l` variable).

As for the second program, in Figure 2(b) we see that after instruction `1` `x` surely contains 'a'. Inside the loop (line `3`), `x` surely contains 'a', '0' and '1'. In line `4` we report the least upper bound between the value of `x` *before* entering the loop (line `1`) and the value *after* the loop (line `4`): variable `x` surely contains the character 'a', and it also may contain the characters '0' and '1'.

4.2 Prefix and Suffix

The next abstract domain we consider approximates strings by their *prefix*. A string will be a sequence of characters which *begins* with a certain sequence of characters and ends with any string (we use $*$ to represent any string, ϵ included). For example, $abc*$ represents all the strings which begin with "*abc*", including "*abc*" itself. Since the asterisk $*$ at the end of the representation is always present, we do not include it in the domain and consider abstract elements made only of sequence of characters: $\overline{\mathcal{PR}} = \mathsf{K}^* \cup \bot_{\overline{\mathcal{PR}}}$ The partial order on this domain is: $\overline{\mathsf{S}} \leq_{\overline{\mathcal{PR}}} \overline{\mathsf{T}} \Leftrightarrow \overline{\mathsf{S}} = \bot_{\overline{\mathcal{PR}}} \vee (\forall \mathsf{i} \in [0, len(\overline{\mathsf{T}}) - 1] : len(\overline{\mathsf{T}}) \leq len(\overline{\mathsf{S}}) \wedge \overline{\mathsf{T}}[\mathsf{i}] = \overline{\mathsf{S}}[\mathsf{i}])$

An abstract string $\overline{\mathsf{S}}$ is smaller than $\overline{\mathsf{T}}$ if $\overline{\mathsf{T}}$ is a prefix of $\overline{\mathsf{S}}$ or if $\overline{\mathsf{S}}$ is the bottom $\bot_{\overline{\mathcal{PR}}}$ of the domain. The least upper bound operator is defined as the longest common prefix of two strings. The greater lower bound is defined by:

$$\sqcap_{\overline{\mathcal{PR}}}(\overline{\mathsf{S}}_1, \overline{\mathsf{S}}_2) = \begin{cases} \overline{\mathsf{S}}_1 & \text{if } \overline{\mathsf{S}}_1 \leq_{\overline{\mathcal{PR}}} \overline{\mathsf{S}}_2 \\ \overline{\mathsf{S}}_2 & \text{if } \overline{\mathsf{S}}_2 \leq_{\overline{\mathcal{PR}}} \overline{\mathsf{S}}_1 \\ \bot_{\overline{\mathcal{PR}}} & \text{otherwise} \end{cases}$$

The widening operator is simply the upper bound operator above, as the latter converges in finite time. Top and bottom elements are, respectively, ϵ (the empty prefix) and $\bot_{\overline{\mathcal{PR}}}$. The function which abstracts a single string is $\alpha'_{\overline{\mathcal{PR}}}(\mathsf{s}) = \mathsf{s}$. The abstraction function is $\alpha_{\overline{\mathcal{PR}}}(\mathsf{S}_1) = \bigsqcup_{\overline{\mathcal{PR}}, \mathsf{s} \in \mathsf{S}_1} \alpha'_{\overline{\mathcal{PR}}}(\mathsf{s})$. This means that we consider the longest common prefix amongst all strings in S_1.

We can track information about the *suffix* of a string as well. We define another abstract domain, $\overline{\mathcal{SU}}$, where a string will be something which *ends* with a certain sequence of characters. The notation and all the operators of this domain are dual to those of the previous domain. The definition of the domain is: $\overline{\mathcal{SU}} = \mathsf{K}^* \cup \bot_{\overline{\mathcal{SU}}}$. The partial order is:

$$\overline{\mathsf{S}} \leq_{\overline{\mathcal{SU}}} \overline{\mathsf{T}} \Leftrightarrow \overline{\mathsf{S}} = \bot_{\overline{\mathcal{SU}}} \vee (\forall \mathsf{i} \in [0, len(\overline{\mathsf{T}}) - 1] : len(\overline{\mathsf{T}}) \leq len(\overline{\mathsf{S}}) \wedge \overline{\mathsf{T}}[\mathsf{i}] = \overline{\mathsf{S}}[\mathsf{i} + len(\overline{\mathsf{S}}) - len(\overline{\mathsf{T}})])$$

The least upper bound $\sqcup_{\overline{\mathcal{SU}}}$ is the longest common suffix, while the greatest lower bound $\sqcap_{\overline{\mathcal{SU}}}$ is the smallest suffix (if they are comparable) or $\bot_{\overline{\mathcal{SU}}}$ (if they are not comparable). The widening operator is the least upper bound operator above. The top element is ϵ. The function which abstracts a single string is: $\alpha'_{\overline{\mathcal{SU}}}(\mathsf{s}) = \mathsf{s}$, and the abstraction function is $\alpha_{\overline{\mathcal{SU}}}(\mathsf{S}_1) = \bigsqcup_{\overline{\mathcal{SU}}, \mathsf{s} \in \mathsf{S}_1} \alpha'_{\overline{\mathcal{SU}}}(\mathsf{s})$.

These abstract domains could be particularly useful to check if some simple syntactic properties (e.g., a string that is used as an SQL command always begins with "`SELECT`" and ends with ";") are respected by all possible executions.

Table 4. The abstract semantics of $\overline{\mathcal{PR}}$

$$\overline{\mathbb{S}_{\mathcal{PR}}}[\![\texttt{new String(str)}]\!]() = \mathsf{str}$$
$$\overline{\mathbb{S}_{\mathcal{PR}}}[\![\texttt{concat}]\!](\overline{\mathsf{p}}_1, \overline{\mathsf{p}}_2) = \overline{\mathsf{p}}_1$$
$$\overline{\mathbb{S}_{\mathcal{PR}}}[\![\texttt{readLine}]\!]() = \epsilon$$
$$\overline{\mathbb{S}_{\mathcal{PR}}}[\![\texttt{substring}^{\mathsf{e}}_{\mathsf{b}}]\!](\overline{\mathsf{p}}) = \begin{cases} \overline{\mathsf{p}}[\mathsf{b} \cdots \mathsf{e}-1] & \text{if } \mathsf{e} \leq len(\overline{\mathsf{p}}) \\ \overline{\mathsf{p}}[\mathsf{b} \cdots len(\overline{\mathsf{p}})-1] & \text{if } \mathsf{e} > len(\overline{\mathsf{p}}) \wedge \mathsf{b} < len(\overline{\mathsf{p}}) \\ \epsilon & \text{otherwise} \end{cases}$$
$$\overline{\mathbb{B}_{\mathcal{PR}}}[\![\texttt{contains}_{\mathsf{c}}]\!](\overline{\mathsf{p}}) = \begin{cases} \mathsf{true} \text{ if } \mathsf{c} \in char(\overline{\mathsf{p}}) \\ \top_{\mathsf{B}} \text{ otherwise} \end{cases}$$

$$\overline{\mathbb{S}_{\mathcal{SU}}}[\![\texttt{new String(str)}]\!]() = \mathsf{str}$$
$$\overline{\mathbb{S}_{\mathcal{SU}}}[\![\texttt{concat}]\!](\overline{\mathsf{s}}_1, \overline{\mathsf{s}}_2) = \overline{\mathsf{s}}_2$$
$$\overline{\mathbb{S}_{\mathcal{SU}}}[\![\texttt{readLine}]\!]() = \epsilon$$
$$\overline{\mathbb{S}_{\mathcal{SU}}}[\![\texttt{substring}^{\mathsf{e}}_{\mathsf{b}}]\!](\overline{\mathsf{s}}) = \epsilon$$
$$\overline{\mathbb{B}_{\mathcal{SU}}}[\![\texttt{contains}_{\mathsf{c}}]\!](\overline{\mathsf{s}}) = \\ = \begin{cases} \mathsf{true} \text{ if } \mathsf{c} \in char(\overline{\mathsf{s}}) \\ \top_{\mathsf{B}} \text{ otherwise} \end{cases}$$

(a) The abstract semantics of $\overline{\mathcal{SU}}$

#I	Var	$\overline{\mathcal{PR}}$	$\overline{\mathcal{SU}}$
1	query	$\overline{\mathsf{s}_1}$	$\overline{\mathsf{s}_1}$
3	l	ϵ	ϵ
3	query	$\overline{\mathsf{s}_1}$	$\overline{\mathsf{s}_3}$
4	query	$\overline{\mathsf{s}_1}$	" "
5	per	$\overline{\mathsf{s}_4}$	$\overline{\mathsf{s}_4}$
7	query	$\overline{\mathsf{s}_1}$	$\overline{\mathsf{s}_6}$

(b) First running example

#I	Var	$\overline{\mathcal{PR}}$	$\overline{\mathcal{SU}}$
1	x	a	a
3	x	0	1
4	x	$\top$	$\top$

(c) Second running example

Fig. 3. The abstract semantics of $\overline{\mathcal{SU}}$ and the running examples

Semantics. Table 4 and 3(a) define the abstract semantics on $\overline{\mathcal{PR}}$ and $\overline{\mathcal{SU}}$ respectively. The most precise suffix and prefix of a constant string are the string itself. When we concatenate two strings, we consider as prefix and suffix of the resulting string the abstract value of the left and right operand respectively. As usual, the semantics of `readLine` returns the top value. The same happens for $\texttt{substring}^{\mathsf{e}}_{\mathsf{b}}$ in $\overline{\mathcal{SU}}$, since we do not know how many characters there are before the suffix. Instead, $\overline{\mathcal{PR}}$ can be more precise if b (and eventually e) are smaller than the length of the prefix we have. Finally, the semantics of $\texttt{contains}_{\mathsf{c}}$ returns true iff c is in the prefix or suffix, and $\top_{\mathsf{B}}$ otherwise, since we have no information at all about which characters are after the prefix or before the suffix.

Running Example. The results of the analyses using the prefix and suffix domains on our running examples are reported in Figures 3(b) and 3(c).

For the first program, at line 1, `query` contains the whole string s_1 as both prefix and suffix. As already pointed out, `l` is an input of the user, so we do not know what its prefix and suffix are. On the other hand, when we concatenate it at line 3, we still have some information on the prefix and suffix of the resulting string. Thus, at the end of the analyses, we get that the prefix of `query` is string s_1, its suffix is s_6, although we lose information about what there is in the middle.

For the second program, before entering the loop we know the prefix and suffix of `x`. Inside the loop after line 3, the convergence for `x` is '0' as prefix and '1' as suffix. This state, combined through the lub operator with the state before the loop, unfortunately goes to $\top$ (the longest common prefixes and suffixes are empty), making us lose all the information.

4.3 Bricks

The next abstract domain, $\overline{\mathcal{BR}}$, captures both *inclusion and order* amongst characters, using a simplification of regular expressions. Therefore, the information tracked by this domain could be adopted to prove more sophisticated properties than the previous domains (e.g., the well-formedness of SQL queries). A string is approximated by a combination of *bricks*. A brick is defined as an element of: $\overline{\mathcal{B}} = [\wp(\mathsf{S})]^{\mathsf{min},\mathsf{max}}$, where min and max are two integer positive values. A brick represents all the strings which can be built through the given strings, taken between min and max times altogether. For example, $[\{\text{"}mo\text{"}, \text{"}de\text{"}\}]^{1,2} = \{mo, de, momo, dede, mode, demo\}$. We represent strings as ordered lists of bricks. For example we have that $[\{\text{"}straw\text{"}\}]^{0,1}[\{\text{"}berry\text{"}\}]^{1,1} = \{berry, strawberry\}$ since $[\{\text{"}straw\text{"}\}]^{0,1}$ concretizes to $\{\epsilon, \text{"}straw\text{"}\}$ and $[\{\text{"}berry\text{"}\}]^{1,1}$ to $\{\text{"}berry\text{"}\}$. Since a particular set of strings could be represented by more than one combination of bricks, we adopted a normalised form in which the lists are made of bricks like $[\mathsf{T}]^{1,1}$ or $[\mathsf{T}]^{0,\mathsf{max}>0}$, where T is a set of strings. We defined a function $\overline{normBricks}(\overline{\mathsf{L}})$ which, given a list of bricks $\overline{\mathsf{L}}$, returns its normalized version.

The abstract domain of bricks is defined as: $\overline{\mathcal{BR}} = \overline{\mathcal{B}}^*$, that is, the set of all finite sequences composed of bricks. The top element $\top_{\overline{\mathcal{BR}}}$ is a list containing only $\top_{\overline{\mathcal{B}}}$. The bottom element is $\bot_{\overline{\mathcal{BR}}}$, an empty list or any list which contains at least one invalid element ($\bot_{\overline{\mathcal{B}}}$). The partial order between single bricks is: $[\overline{\mathsf{C}}_1]^{\mathsf{min}_1,\mathsf{max}_1} \leq_{\overline{\mathcal{B}}} [\overline{\mathsf{C}}_2]^{\mathsf{min}_2,\mathsf{max}_2} \Leftrightarrow (\overline{\mathsf{C}}_1 \subseteq \overline{\mathsf{C}}_2 \wedge \mathsf{min}_1 \geq \mathsf{min}_2 \wedge \mathsf{max}_1 \leq \mathsf{max}_2) \vee [\overline{\mathsf{C}}_2]^{\mathsf{min}_2,\mathsf{max}_2} = \top_{\overline{\mathcal{B}}} \vee [\overline{\mathsf{C}}_1]^{\mathsf{min}_1,\mathsf{max}_1} = \bot_{\overline{\mathcal{B}}}$ where $\top_{\overline{\mathcal{B}}}$ and $\bot_{\overline{\mathcal{B}}}$ are special bricks, respectively greater and smaller than any other brick. The partial order between lists of bricks $\overline{\mathsf{L}}_1$ and $\overline{\mathsf{L}}_2$ is as follows:

$$\overline{\mathsf{L}}_1 \leq_{\overline{\mathcal{BR}}} \overline{\mathsf{L}}_2 \Leftrightarrow (\overline{\mathsf{L}}_2 = \top_{\overline{\mathcal{BR}}}) \vee (\overline{\mathsf{L}}_1 = \bot_{\overline{\mathcal{BR}}}) \vee (\forall \mathsf{i} \in [1,\mathsf{n}] : \overline{\mathsf{L}}_1[\mathsf{i}] \leq_{\overline{\mathcal{B}}} \overline{\mathsf{L}}_2[\mathsf{i}])$$

where we make $\overline{\mathsf{L}}_1$ and $\overline{\mathsf{L}}_2$ have the same size n by adding empty bricks ($[\emptyset]^{0,0}$) at the end of the shorter list. The upper bound operator on a single brick is: $\bigsqcup_{\overline{\mathcal{B}}}([\overline{\mathsf{S}}_1]^{\mathsf{m}_1,\mathsf{M}_1}, [\overline{\mathsf{S}}_2]^{\mathsf{m}_2,\mathsf{M}_2}) = [\overline{\mathsf{S}}_1 \cup \overline{\mathsf{S}}_2]^{\min(\mathsf{m}_1,\mathsf{m}_2),\max(\mathsf{M}_1,\mathsf{M}_2)}$

The upper bound operator on lists of bricks (elements of our domain) is as follows: given two lists $\overline{\mathsf{L}}_1$ and $\overline{\mathsf{L}}_2$, we make them to have the same size n adding empty bricks to the shorter one. Then: $\bigsqcup_{\overline{\mathcal{BR}}}(\overline{\mathsf{L}}_1, \overline{\mathsf{L}}_2) = \overline{\mathsf{L}}_R[1]\overline{\mathsf{L}}_R[2]\ldots\overline{\mathsf{L}}_R[\mathsf{n}]$ where $\forall \mathsf{i} \in [1,\mathsf{n}] : \overline{\mathsf{L}}_R[\mathsf{i}] = \sqcup_{\overline{\mathcal{B}}}(\overline{\mathsf{L}}_1[\mathsf{i}], \overline{\mathsf{L}}_2[\mathsf{i}])$.

Let k_L, k_I and k_S be three constant integer values. The widening operator $\nabla_{\overline{\mathcal{BR}}} : (\overline{\mathcal{BR}} \times \overline{\mathcal{BR}}) \rightarrow \overline{\mathcal{BR}}$ is defined as follows:

$$\nabla_{\overline{\mathcal{BR}}}(\overline{\mathsf{L}}_1, \overline{\mathsf{L}}_2) = \begin{cases} \top_{\overline{\mathcal{BR}}} & \text{if } (\overline{\mathsf{L}}_1 \not\leq_{\overline{\mathcal{BR}}} \overline{\mathsf{L}}_2 \wedge \overline{\mathsf{L}}_2 \not\leq_{\overline{\mathcal{BR}}} \overline{\mathsf{L}}_1) \vee \\ & \quad (\exists \mathsf{i} \in [1,2] : len(\overline{\mathsf{L}}_i) > \mathsf{k}_L) \\ w(\overline{\mathsf{L}}_1, \overline{\mathsf{L}}_2) & \text{otherwise} \end{cases}$$

where $w(\overline{\mathsf{L}}_1, \overline{\mathsf{L}}_2) = [\overline{\mathcal{B}}_1^{\mathsf{new}}(\overline{\mathsf{L}}_1[1], \overline{\mathsf{L}}_2[1]); \overline{\mathcal{B}}_2^{\mathsf{new}}(\overline{\mathsf{L}}_1[2], \overline{\mathsf{L}}_2[2]); \ldots; \overline{\mathcal{B}}_n^{\mathsf{new}}(\overline{\mathsf{L}}_1[\mathsf{n}], \overline{\mathsf{L}}_2[\mathsf{n}])]$, with n being the size of the bigger list (we make them to have the same size n adding empty bricks to the shorter one), and $\overline{\mathcal{B}}_i^{\mathsf{new}}(\overline{\mathsf{L}}_1[\mathsf{i}], \overline{\mathsf{L}}_2[\mathsf{i}])$ is defined by:

Table 5. The abstract semantics of $\overline{\mathcal{BR}}$

$$\overline{\mathbb{S}_{\mathcal{BR}}}[\![\texttt{new String(str)}]\!]() = \overline{[\{\texttt{str}\}]^{1,1}}$$
$$\overline{\mathbb{S}_{\mathcal{BR}}}[\![\texttt{concat}]\!](\bar{\mathsf{b}}_1, \bar{\mathsf{b}}_2) = \overline{normBricks}(\overline{concatList}(\bar{\mathsf{b}}_1, \bar{\mathsf{b}}_2))$$
$$\overline{\mathbb{S}_{\mathcal{BR}}}[\![\texttt{readLine}]\!]() = \top_{\overline{\mathcal{BR}}}$$
$$\overline{\mathbb{S}_{\mathcal{BR}}}[\![\texttt{substring}^{\mathsf{e}}_{\mathsf{b}}]\!](\bar{\mathsf{b}}) = \begin{cases} [\bar{\mathsf{T}}']^{1,1} \text{ if } \bar{\mathsf{b}}[0] = [\bar{\mathsf{T}}]^{1,1} \wedge \forall \bar{\mathsf{t}} \in \bar{\mathsf{T}} : len(\bar{\mathsf{t}}) \geq \mathsf{e} \\ \top_{\overline{\mathcal{BR}}} \quad \text{otherwise} \end{cases}$$
$$\overline{\mathbb{B}_{\mathcal{BR}}}[\![\texttt{contains}_{\mathsf{c}}]\!](\bar{\mathsf{b}}) = \begin{cases} \mathsf{true} \text{ if } \exists \bar{\mathsf{B}} \in \bar{\mathsf{b}} : \bar{\mathsf{B}} = [\bar{\mathsf{T}}]^{m,M} \wedge 1 \leq m \leq M \wedge (\forall \bar{\mathsf{t}} \in \bar{\mathsf{T}} : \mathsf{c} \in char(\bar{\mathsf{t}})) \\ \mathsf{false} \text{ if } \forall [\bar{\mathsf{T}}]^{\mathsf{m},\mathsf{M}} \in \bar{\mathsf{b}}, \forall \bar{\mathsf{t}} \in \bar{\mathsf{T}} : \mathsf{c} \notin char(\bar{\mathsf{t}}) \\ \top_{\mathsf{B}} \quad \text{otherwise} \end{cases}$$

$$\overline{\mathcal{B}}_i^{\mathsf{new}}([\bar{\mathsf{S}}_{1i}]^{\mathsf{m}_{1i},\mathsf{M}_{1i}}, [\bar{\mathsf{S}}_{2i}]^{\mathsf{m}_{2i},\mathsf{M}_{2i}}) = \begin{cases} \top_{\overline{\mathcal{B}}} & \text{if } |\bar{\mathsf{S}}_{1i} \cup \bar{\mathsf{S}}_{2i}| > \mathsf{k}_S \\ & \quad \vee \bar{\mathsf{L}}_1[\mathsf{i}] = \top_{\overline{\mathcal{B}}} \vee \bar{\mathsf{L}}_2[\mathsf{i}] = \top_{\overline{\mathcal{B}}} \\ [\bar{\mathsf{S}}_{1i} \cup \bar{\mathsf{S}}_{2i}]^{(0,\infty)} & \text{if } (\mathsf{M} - \mathsf{m}) > \mathsf{k}_I \\ [\bar{\mathsf{S}}_{1i} \cup \bar{\mathsf{S}}_{2i}]^{(\mathsf{m},\mathsf{M})} & \text{otherwise} \end{cases}$$

where $\mathsf{m} = \min(\mathsf{m}_{1i}, \mathsf{m}_{2i})$ and $\mathsf{M} = \max(\mathsf{M}_{1i}, \mathsf{M}_{2i})$. $\nabla_{\overline{\mathcal{BR}}}$ is an upper bound operator because it returns either $\top_{\overline{\mathcal{BR}}}$ or $w(\bar{\mathsf{L}}_1, \bar{\mathsf{L}}_2)$, which builds a new list of bricks which is bigger (with respect to $\leq_{\overline{\mathcal{BR}}}$) than both $\bar{\mathsf{L}}_1$ and $\bar{\mathsf{L}}_2$. The resulting list is greater or equal because each brick is greater than or equal to the two corresponding bricks in $\bar{\mathsf{L}}_1$ and $\bar{\mathsf{L}}_2$, since we always take the union of the two strings sets and an index range bigger than the initial two. Moreover, this operator converges because a value of an ascending chain can increase along three axes: (i) the length of the brick list, (ii) the indices range of a certain brick, and (iii) the strings contained in a certain brick. The growth of an abstract value is bounded along each axis with the help of the three constants. After the list has reached k_L elements, the entire abstract value is approximated to $\top_{\overline{\mathcal{BR}}}$. If the range of a certain brick becomes larger than k_I, the range is approximated to $(0, +\infty)$. Finally, if the strings set of a certain brick reaches k_S elements, the brick is approximated to $\top_{\overline{\mathcal{B}}}$. The lower bound operator is dual with respect to the upper bound operator above. Formally, $\sqcap_{\overline{\mathcal{B}}}([\bar{\mathsf{S}}_1]^{\mathsf{m}_1,\mathsf{M}_1}, [\bar{\mathsf{S}}_2]^{\mathsf{m}_2,\mathsf{M}_2}) = [\bar{\mathsf{S}}_1 \cap \bar{\mathsf{S}}_2]^{\max(\mathsf{m}_1,\mathsf{m}_2),\min(\mathsf{M}_1,\mathsf{M}_2)}$. The abstraction function is defined by: $\alpha'_{\overline{\mathcal{BR}}}(\mathsf{s}) = [\{\mathsf{s}\}]^{(1,1)}$ and
$$\alpha_{\overline{\mathcal{BR}}}(\mathsf{S}_1) = \bigsqcup_{\overline{\mathcal{BR}},\mathsf{s} \in \mathsf{S}_1} \alpha'_{\overline{\mathcal{BR}}}(\mathsf{s}) = [\mathsf{S}_1]^{(1,1)}$$

Semantics. Table 5 defines the abstract semantics on $\overline{\mathcal{BR}}$. When a constant string is evaluated, the semantics returns a single brick containing exactly that string with $[1, 1]$ as index. For the concatenation of two strings, we rely on the $\overline{concatList}$ function that concatenates two lists of bricks, and then we normalise its result. `readLine` returns the top value, while $\texttt{substring}^{\mathsf{e}}_{\mathsf{b}}$ returns the substring iff the first brick of the list has index $[1, 1]$ and the length of all the strings contained in it is greater than e. Notice that $\bar{\mathsf{T}}' = \{\bar{\mathsf{t}}.\texttt{substring}(\mathsf{b}, \mathsf{e}) \forall \bar{\mathsf{t}} \in \bar{\mathsf{T}}\}$. Finally, the semantics of $\texttt{contains}_{\mathsf{c}}$ returns true iff there is surely at least one brick that contains c and whose minimal index is at least 1. It returns false iff all the bricks do not contain c, and $\top_{\mathsf{B}}$ otherwise.

#I	Var	$\overline{\mathcal{BR}}$
1	query	$[\{\mathsf{s}_1\}]^{1,1}$
3	l	$\top_{\overline{\mathcal{B}}}$
3	query	$[\{\mathsf{s}_1+\mathsf{s}_2\}]^{1,1}\top_{\overline{\mathcal{B}}}[\{\mathsf{s}_3\}]^{1,1}$
4	query	$[\{\mathsf{s}_1,\mathsf{s}_1+\mathsf{s}_2\}]^{1,1}\top_{\overline{\mathcal{B}}}[\{\mathsf{s}_3\}]^{0,1}$
5	per	$[\{\mathsf{s}_4\}]^{1,1}$
7	query	$[\{\mathsf{s}_1,\mathsf{s}_1+\mathsf{s}_2\}]^{1,1}\top_{\overline{\mathcal{B}}}[\{\mathsf{s}_3\}]^{0,1}$ $[\{\mathsf{s}_5+\mathsf{s}_4+\mathsf{s}_6\}]^{1,1}$

(a) First running example

#I	Var	$\overline{\mathcal{BR}}$
1	x	$[\{\text{"}a\text{"}\}]^{1,1}$
3	x	$\top$
4	x	$\top$

(b) Second running example

Fig. 4. The results of $\overline{\mathcal{BR}}$

Running Example. The results of the analysis of the running examples using $\overline{\mathcal{BR}}$ are depicted in Figures 4(a) and 4(b). For the first program, the bricks of the final result on query are four: (i) the first brick represents a string between s_1 and $\mathsf{s}_1 + \mathsf{s}_2$, (ii) the second brick corresponds to the input l, (iii) the third brick could be the empty string ϵ or s_3, and (iv) the fourth brick represents the concatenation of s_5, s_4, and s_6. We can see that the precision is higher than in the previous domains, but still not the best we aim to get: amongst the concrete results we have, for example, $\mathsf{s}_1 + \mathsf{s}_3 + \mathsf{s}_5 + \mathsf{s}_4 + \mathsf{s}_6$, which cannot be computed in any execution of the analysed code. For the second program, the result is unsatisfactory: the use of the widening operator makes us lose all information. At the end of the program, variable x has value $\top$.

4.4 String Graphs

The last abstract domain we introduce exploits type graphs, a data structure which represents tree automata [15], adapting them to represent sets of strings. A type graph $\overline{\mathsf{T}}$ is a triplet $(\overline{\mathsf{N}}, \overline{\mathsf{A}}_F, \overline{\mathsf{A}}_B)$ where $(\overline{\mathsf{N}}, \overline{\mathsf{A}}_F)$ is a rooted tree whose arcs in $\overline{\mathsf{A}}_F$ are called forward arcs, and $\overline{\mathsf{A}}_B$ is a restricted class of arcs, backward arcs, superimposed on $(\overline{\mathsf{N}}, \overline{\mathsf{A}}_F)$. Each node $\overline{\mathsf{n}} \in \overline{\mathsf{N}}$ of a type graph has a label, denoted by $\overline{lb}(\overline{\mathsf{n}})$, indicating the kind of term it describes, and the nodes are divided into three classes: simple, functor and OR nodes. We use the convention that $\overline{\mathsf{n}}/\mathsf{i}$ denotes the i-th son of node $\overline{\mathsf{n}}$, and the set of sons of a node $\overline{\mathsf{n}}$ is then denoted as $\{\overline{\mathsf{n}}/1, \ldots, \overline{\mathsf{n}}/k\}$ with $\mathsf{k} = \overline{outdegree}(\overline{\mathsf{n}})$ where $\overline{outdegree}$ is a function that given a node returns the number of its sons. We define a modified version of type graphs, called string graphs, which represent strings instead of types. String graphs have the same basic structure of type graphs. The following differences distinguish them: (i) simple nodes have labels from the set $\{\mathsf{max}, \bot, \epsilon\} \cup \mathsf{K}$; (ii) the only functor we consider is concat (with its obvious meaning of string concatenation). Thus, functor nodes are labelled with concat/k. An example is depicted in Figure 5. The root of the string graph is an OR node with two sons: a simple node (b) and a concat node with two sons of its own. The second son of the concat node is the root (with the use of a backward arc). Such string graph represents the following set of strings: $\{b, ab, aab, aaab, \ldots\} = a^*b$.

The abstract domain is: $\overline{\mathcal{SG}} = \overline{\mathsf{NSG}}$, where $\overline{\mathsf{NSG}}$ is the set of all Normal String Graphs. In fact, the type graphs are very suitable for representing a set of terms. However, several distinct type graphs can have the same denotation. The existence of superfluous nodes and arcs makes operations needed during abstract interpretation, such as the $\leq$-operation, quite complex and inefficient. In order to reduce this variety of type graphs, additional restrictions are imposed (for details see [15]), defining normal type graphs. We added a few other restrictions (specific for string graphs), thus obtaining the definition of normal string graphs. For example, we impose that concat nodes are not allowed to have only one son (they should be replaced by the son itself) or that a concat node cannot have two successive sons with both label concat (they should be merged together). An algorithm of normalisation ($\overline{normStringGraph}$), encapsulating all those rules, is defined as well.

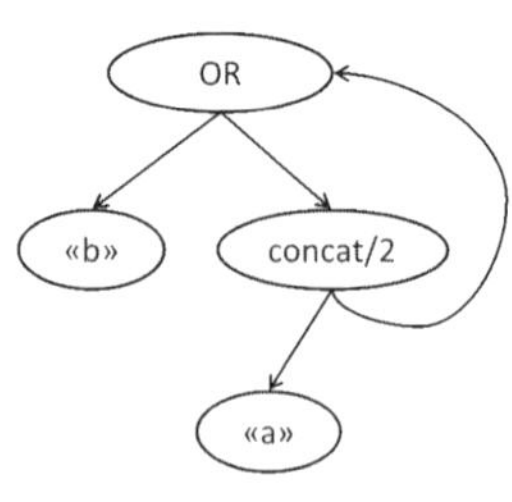

Fig. 5. An example of string graph

The bottom element $\bot_{\overline{\mathcal{SG}}}$ is a string graph made by one bottom node. The top element is a string graph made by only one node, a max-node. To define the partial order of the domain we can exploit an algorithm defined in [15]: $\leq (\overline{\mathsf{n}}, \overline{\mathsf{m}}, \emptyset)$. The algorithm compares the two nodes in input $(\overline{\mathsf{n}}, \overline{\mathsf{m}})$. In some cases the procedure is recursively called, for example if $\overline{\mathsf{n}}$ and $\overline{\mathsf{m}}$ are both concat or OR nodes. Note that the recursive call adds a new edge $(\{\overline{\mathsf{n}}, \overline{\mathsf{m}}\})$ to the third input parameter (a set of edges). If, at the next execution of the procedure $(\leq (\overline{\mathsf{n}'}, \overline{\mathsf{m}'}, \overline{\mathsf{E}}))$, the edge $\{\overline{\mathsf{n}'}, \overline{\mathsf{m}'}\}$ is contained in $\overline{\mathsf{E}}$ then the procedure immediately returns true. The order is then:

$$\overline{\mathsf{T}}_1 \leq_{\overline{\mathcal{SG}}} \overline{\mathsf{T}}_2 \Leftrightarrow \overline{\mathsf{T}}_1 = \bot_{\overline{\mathcal{SG}}} \vee (\leq (\overline{\mathsf{n}}_0, \overline{\mathsf{m}}_0, \emptyset) : \overline{\mathsf{n}}_0 = \overline{root}(\overline{\mathsf{T}}_1) \wedge \overline{\mathsf{m}}_0 = \overline{root}(\overline{\mathsf{T}}_2))$$

where $\overline{root}(\overline{\mathsf{T}})$ is the root element of the tree defined in $\overline{\mathsf{T}}$. The least upper bound between two string graphs $\overline{\mathsf{T}}_1$ and $\overline{\mathsf{T}}_2$ can be computed creating a new string graph $\overline{\mathsf{T}}$ whose root is an OR-node and whose sons are $\overline{\mathsf{T}}_1$ and $\overline{\mathsf{T}}_2$. Then we apply the compaction algorithm that will transform $\overline{\mathsf{T}}$ in a normal string graph:

$$\bigsqcup_{\overline{\mathcal{SG}}}(\overline{\mathsf{T}}_1, \overline{\mathsf{T}}_2) = \overline{normStringGraph}(\mathsf{OR}(\overline{\mathsf{T}}_1, \overline{\mathsf{T}}_2))$$

The greatest lower bound operator is described in the appendix of [15], while the widening operator is described in [23]. The abstraction of a string is: $\alpha'_{\overline{\mathcal{SG}}}(\mathsf{s}) = \mathsf{concat}/\mathsf{k}\{\mathsf{s}[\mathsf{i}] : \mathsf{i} \in [0, \mathsf{k}-1]\}$ where $\mathsf{k} = len(\mathsf{s})$, and the abstraction function is:

$$\alpha_{\overline{\mathcal{SG}}}(\mathsf{S}_1) = \bigsqcup_{\overline{\mathcal{SG}}, \mathsf{s} \in \mathsf{S}_1} \alpha'_{\overline{\mathcal{SG}}}(\mathsf{s}) = \overline{normStringGraph}(\mathsf{OR}\{\alpha'_{\overline{\mathcal{SG}}}(\mathsf{s}) : \mathsf{s} \in \mathsf{S}_1\})$$

Semantics. Table 6 defines the abstract semantics on $\overline{\mathcal{SG}}$. The evaluation of a string returns a concat containing the sequence of all the characters of the string. When we concatenate two strings, the semantics returns the normalisation of a concat node containing the two strings in sequence. As usual, the semantics of `readLine` returns the top value. The semantics of $\texttt{substring}_{\mathsf{b}}^{\mathsf{e}}$ (where $\overline{\mathsf{res}} = \mathsf{concat}/(\mathsf{e}-\mathsf{b})\{(\overline{root}(\overline{\mathsf{t}})/\mathsf{i}) : \mathsf{i} \in [\mathsf{b}, \mathsf{e}-1]\}$) returns a precise value only if the root is a `concat` node with at least `e` characters. Finally, $\texttt{contains}_{\mathsf{c}}$ returns `true` iff there is a concat node containing c in the tree, and without any OR node in the path from the root to this node.

Table 6. The abstract semantics of $\overline{\mathcal{SG}}$

$$\overline{\mathbb{S}_{\mathcal{SG}}}[\![\texttt{new String(str)}]\!]() = \mathsf{concat/k}\{\mathtt{str}[\mathsf{i}] : \mathsf{i} \in [0, \mathsf{k}-1]\}$$
$$\overline{\mathbb{S}_{\mathcal{SG}}}[\![\texttt{concat}]\!](\bar{\mathsf{t}}_1, \bar{\mathsf{t}}_2) = \overline{normStringGraph}(\mathsf{concat/2}\{\bar{\mathsf{t}}_1, \bar{\mathsf{t}}_2\})$$
$$\overline{\mathbb{S}_{\mathcal{SG}}}[\![\texttt{readLine}]\!]() = \top_{\overline{\mathcal{SG}}}$$
$$\overline{\mathbb{S}_{\mathcal{SG}}}[\![\texttt{substring}_{\mathsf{b}}^{\mathsf{e}}]\!](\bar{\mathsf{t}}) = \begin{cases} \overline{\mathsf{res}} & \text{if } \overline{root}(\bar{\mathsf{t}}) = \mathsf{concat/k} \wedge \forall \mathsf{i} \in [0, \mathsf{e}-1] : \overline{lb}(\overline{root}(\bar{\mathsf{t}})/\mathsf{i}) \in \mathsf{K} \\ \top_{\overline{\mathcal{SG}}} & \text{otherwise} \end{cases}$$
$$\overline{\mathbb{B}_{\mathcal{SG}}}[\![\texttt{contains}_{\mathsf{c}}]\!](\bar{\mathsf{t}}) = \begin{cases} \mathsf{true} \text{ if } \exists \overline{\mathsf{m}} \in \bar{\mathsf{t}} : \overline{\mathsf{m}} = \mathsf{concat/k} \wedge \mathsf{OR} \notin \overline{path}(\overline{\mathsf{root}}, \overline{\mathsf{m}}) \wedge \\ \qquad \exists \mathsf{i} : \overline{lb}(\overline{\mathsf{m}}/\mathsf{i}) = \mathsf{c} \\ \mathsf{false} \text{ if } \nexists \overline{\mathsf{n}} \in \bar{\mathsf{t}} : \overline{lb}(\overline{\mathsf{n}}) = \mathsf{max} \vee \overline{lb}(\overline{\mathsf{n}}) = \mathsf{c} \\ \top_{\mathsf{B}} \quad \text{otherwise} \end{cases}$$

#I	Var	$\overline{\mathcal{SG}}$
1	query	$\mathsf{concat}[\mathsf{s}_1]$
3	l	max
3	query	$\mathsf{concat}[\mathsf{s}_1 + \mathsf{s}_2; \mathsf{max}; \mathsf{s}_3]$
4	query	$\mathsf{SG}_1 = \mathsf{OR}[\mathsf{concat}[\mathsf{s}_1]; \mathsf{concat}[\mathsf{s}_1 + \mathsf{s}_2; \mathsf{max}; \mathsf{s}_3]]$
5	per	$\mathsf{concat}[\mathsf{s}_4]$
7	query	$\mathsf{concat}[\mathsf{SG}_1; \mathsf{concat}[\mathsf{s}_5 + \mathsf{s}_4 + \mathsf{s}_6]]$

(a) First running example

#I	Var	$\overline{\mathcal{SG}}$
1	x	$\mathsf{concat}[\text{“}a\text{”}]$
3	x	$\mathsf{OR}_1[\text{“}a\text{”}; \mathsf{concat}[\text{“0”}; OR_1; \text{“1”}]]$
4	x	$\mathsf{OR}_1[\text{“}a\text{”}; \mathsf{concat}[\text{“0”}; OR_1; \text{“1”}]]$

(b) Second running example

Fig. 6. The results of $\overline{\mathcal{SG}}$

Running Example. The results of the analysis of the running examples through string graphs are depicted in Figures 6(a) and 6(b). For sake of simplicity, we adopt the notation $\mathsf{concat}[\mathsf{s}]$ to indicate a string graph with a concat node whose sons are all the characters of string s. The symbol + represents, as usual, string concatenation, while ; is used to separate different sons of a node.

For the first program, the resulting string graph for `query` represents exactly the two possible outcomes of the procedure. For the second program, the resulting string graph for `x` represents exactly all the concrete possible values of `x`. Note that the resulting string graph contains a backward arc to allow the repetition of the pattern $0^n \ldots 1^n$. This abstract domain is the most precise domain for the analysis of both running examples: it tracks information similarly to $\overline{\mathcal{BR}}$ domain, but its lub and widening operators are definitely more accurate.

4.5 Discussion: Relations between the Four Domains

The abstract domains we introduced in the previous sections track different types of information. Let us discuss the relations between different domains. Intuitively, there are two axes on which the analyses of string values can work: the characters contained in a string, and their position inside the string. It is easy to see that the $\overline{\mathcal{CI}}$, $\overline{\mathcal{PR}}$ and $\overline{\mathcal{SU}}$ are less precise than $\overline{\mathcal{BR}}$ and $\overline{\mathcal{SG}}$. In fact, $\overline{\mathcal{CI}}$ domain considers only character inclusion and completely disregards the order. $\overline{\mathcal{PR}}$ and

$\overline{\mathcal{SU}}$ domains consider also the order, but limiting themselves to the initial/final segment of the string, and in the same way they collect only partial information about character inclusion. $\overline{\mathcal{BR}}$ and $\overline{\mathcal{SG}}$, instead, track both inclusion and order along the string. In [3] we studied these relationships in details: we defined pairs of functions (abstraction and concretization) from domain to domain, and showed that $\overline{\mathcal{CI}}$, $\overline{\mathcal{PR}}$ and $\overline{\mathcal{SU}}$ are more abstract (i.e., less precise) than both $\overline{\mathcal{BR}}$ and $\overline{\mathcal{SG}}$. In the case of $\overline{\mathcal{BR}}$ versus $\overline{\mathcal{SG}}$, the comparison is more complex, since they exploit very different data structures. For example, $\overline{\mathcal{SG}}$ has OR-nodes, while $\overline{\mathcal{BR}}$ can only trace alternatives inside bricks but not outside (like: "these three bricks *or* these other two"). From this perspective, $\overline{\mathcal{SG}}$ is more precise than $\overline{\mathcal{BR}}$. Another important difference is that $\overline{\mathcal{SG}}$ has backward arcs which allow repetitions of patterns, but they can be traversed how many times we want (even infinite times). With $\overline{\mathcal{BR}}$, instead, we can indicate exactly how many times a certain pattern should be repeated (through the range of bricks). This makes $\overline{\mathcal{BR}}$ more expressive than $\overline{\mathcal{SG}}$ in that respect. So, these domains are not directly comparable. We obtain the lattice depicted in Figure 7, where the upper domains are more approximated. We denote by $\top$ the abstract domain that does not track any information about string values, and by $\wp(\mathsf{K}^*)$ the (naïve and uncomputable) domain that tracks all the possible strings values we can have.

In conclusion, the first three domains ($\overline{\mathcal{CI}}$, $\overline{\mathcal{PR}}$, $\overline{\mathcal{SU}}$) are not so precise but the complexity is kept linear, whereas the other domains ($\overline{\mathcal{BR}}$ and $\overline{\mathcal{SG}}$) are more demanding (though in the practice complexity is still kept polynomial) but also more precise.

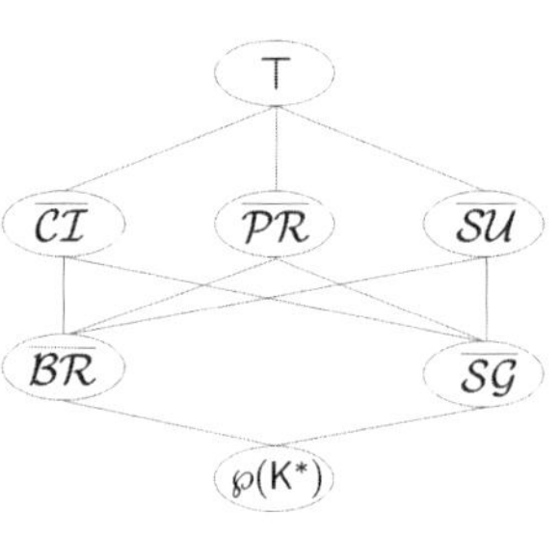

Fig. 7. The hierarchy of abstract domains

5 Related Work

The static analysis of strings was addressed in various directions.

Kim and Choe [16] introduced recently an approach based on abstract interpretation. They abstract strings with pushdown automata (PDA). The result of the analysis is compared with a grammar to determine if all the strings generated by the PDA belong to the grammar. This approach has a fixed precision, and in the worst case (not often encountered in practice) it has exponential complexity.

Hosoya and Pierce [14] used tree automata to verify dynamically generated XML documents. The regular expression types of this approach recall our $\overline{\mathcal{BR}}$ domain, while the tree automata recall our $\overline{\mathcal{SG}}$ domain. However, they are focused on building XML documents, while our focus is on collecting possible values of generic string variables. In addition, they require to manually annotate the code through types while our approach is completely automatic.

A more recent work was developed by Yu *et al.* [24]. It presented an automata-based approach for the verification of string operations in PHP programs. The information tracked by this analysis is fixed, and it is specific for PHP programs.

Tabuchi *et al.* [21] presented a type system based on regular expressions. It is focused on a λ-calculus supporting concatenation, and pattern matching. Some type annotation is required when dealing with recursive function.

Thiemann [22] introduced a type system for string analysis based on context-free grammars. Their analysis is more precise than those based on regular expressions, but the only supported string operator is concatenation, and the analysis is tuned at a fixed level of precision.

Context-free grammars are also the basis of the analysis of Christensen *et al.* [1]. This analysis is tuned at a fixed level of abstraction. In the second running example of this paper, $\overline{\mathcal{SG}}$ domain reaches a better precision than theirs.

Minamide [18] presented an analysis to statically check some properties of Web pages generated dynamically by a server-side program. This work is specific for HTML pages, while we do not need to know the reference grammar *a priori*. Also in this case, $\overline{\mathcal{SG}}$ obtain a better precision on the loop example.

Doh *et al.* [8] proposed a technique called "abstract parsing": it combines LR(k)-parsing technology and data-flow analysis to analyse dynamically generated documents. Their technique is quite precise, but the level of abstraction is fixed, and it cannot be tuned at different levels of precision and efficiency.

Given this context, our work is the first one that (i) is a generic, flexible, and extensible approach to the analysis of string values, and (ii) can be tuned at different levels of precision and efficiency.

6 Conclusion and Future Work

In this paper we introduced a new framework for the static analysis of string values, and four different abstract domains. We chose some string operators on which we focused our approach defining the concrete and the abstract semantics.

Future Work. We are working on the implementation of our approach in Sample (Static Analyzer of Multiple Programming LanguagEs) [9]. We plan to apply our analysis to some case studies to study the precision of our analysis. In order to check the scalability and performances of our approach, we plan to apply our analysis to some Scala standard libraries. Some preliminary experimental results point out that $\overline{\mathcal{CI}}$ and $\overline{\mathcal{PR}} \times \overline{\mathcal{SU}}$ are quite efficient, $\overline{\mathcal{BR}}$ is slower but still fast, while $\overline{\mathcal{SG}}$'s performances seem to be still critical.

Acknowledgments. Work partially supported by RAS project "TESLA - Tecniche di enforcement per la sicurezza dei linguaggi e delle applicazioni", and by SNF project "Verification-Driven Inference of Contracts".

References

1. Christensen, A., Moller, A., Schwartzbach, M.: Precise analysis of string expressions. In: Cousot, R. (ed.) SAS 2003. LNCS, vol. 2694, pp. 1–18. Springer, Heidelberg (2003)
2. Cortesi, A., Zanioli, M.: Widening and narrowing operators for abstract interpretation. Computer Languages, Systems and Structures 37(1), 24–42 (2011)

3. Costantini, G.: Abstract domains for static analysis of strings. Master's thesis, Ca' Foscari University of Venice (2010)
4. Cousot, P., Cousot, R.: Abstract interpretation: a unified lattice model for static analysis of programs by construction or approximation of fixpoints. In: POPL 1977. ACM, New York (1977)
5. Cousot, P., Cousot, R.: Systematic design of program analysis frameworks. In: POPL 1979. ACM, New York (1979)
6. Cousot, P., Cousot, R., Feret, J., Mauborgne, L., Miné, A., Monniaux, D., Rival, X.: The ASTREÉ analyzer. In: Sagiv, M. (ed.) ESOP 2005. LNCS, vol. 3444, pp. 21–30. Springer, Heidelberg (2005)
7. Cousot, P., Halbwachs, N.: Automatic discovery of linear restraints among variables of a program. In: Proceedings of POPL 1978. ACM Press, New York (1978)
8. Doh, K., Kim, H., Schmidt, D.: Abstract parsing: Static analysis of dynamically generated string output using LR-parsing technology. In: Palsberg, J., Su, Z. (eds.) SAS 2009. LNCS, vol. 5673, pp. 256–272. Springer, Heidelberg (2009)
9. Ferrara, P.: Static type analysis of pattern matching by abstract interpretation. In: Hatcliff, J., Zucca, E. (eds.) FMOODS 2010. LNCS, vol. 6117, pp. 186–200. Springer, Heidelberg (2010)
10. Gould, C., Su, Z., Devanbu, P.: Static checking of dynamically generated queries in database applications. In: Proceedings of ICSE 2004, pp. 645–654. IEEE Computer Society, Los Alamitos (2004)
11. Granger, P.: Static analysis of linear congruence equalities among variables of a program. In: Abramsky, S. (ed.) CAAP 1991 and TAPSOFT 1991. LNCS, vol. 493, pp. 169–192. Springer, Heidelberg (1991)
12. Gulwani, S.: Automating string processing in spreadsheets using input-output examples. In: Proceedings of POPL 2011. ACM, New York (2011)
13. Hooimeijer, P., Veanes, M.: An evaluation of automata algorithms for string analysis. In: Jhala, R., Schmidt, D. (eds.) VMCAI 2011. LNCS, vol. 6538, pp. 248–262. Springer, Heidelberg (2011)
14. Hosoya, H., Pierce, B.: Xduce: A statically typed xml processing language. ACM Trans. Internet Technol. 3(2), 117–148 (2003)
15. Janssens, G., Bruynooghe, M.: Deriving description of possible values of program variables by means of abstract interpretation. Journal of Logic Programming 13(2-3), 205–258 (1992)
16. Kim, S.-W., Choe, K.-M.: String analysis as an abstract interpretation. In: Jhala, R., Schmidt, D. (eds.) VMCAI 2011. LNCS, vol. 6538, pp. 294–308. Springer, Heidelberg (2011)
17. Logozzo, F., Fähndrich, M.: Pentagons: A weakly relational domain for the efficient validation of array accesses. In: Proceedings of SAC 2008. ACM Press, New York (2008)
18. Minamide, Y.: Static approximation of dynamically generated web pages. In: Proceedings of WWW 2005, pp. 432–441. ACM, New York (2005)
19. Miné, A.: The octagon abstract domain. Higher-Order and Symbolic Computation (2006)
20. Halder, R., Cortesi, A.: Obfuscation-based analysis of sql injection attacks. In: IEEE (ed.) Proceedings of ISCC 2010 (2010)
21. Tabuchi, N., Sumii, E., Yonezawa, A.: Regular expression types for strings in a text processing language. Electr. Notes Theor. Comput. Sci. 75 (2002)

22. Thiemann, P.: Grammar-based analysis of string expressions. In: Proceedings of TLDI 2005, pp. 59–70. ACM, New York (2005)
23. van Hentenryck, P., Cortesi, A., Le Charlier, B.: Type analysis of prolog using type graphs. Journal of Logic Programming 22(3), 179–208 (1995)
24. Yu, F., Bultan, T., Cova, M., Ibarra, O.: Symbolic string verification: An automata-based approach. In: Havelund, K., Majumdar, R. (eds.) SPIN 2008. LNCS, vol. 5156, pp. 306–324. Springer, Heidelberg (2008)

A Theory of Classes from the Theoretical Foundations of LePUS3

Jonathan Nicholson

University of Essex, UK
johnic@essex.ac.uk

Abstract LePUS3 is a formal design description language for specifying decidable (i.e. automatically verifiable) properties of object-oriented design. LePUS3 has been successfully applied to both design verification and reverse engineering applications. However, LePUS3 is becoming over zealously pragmatic. Its current definition is inflexible, limiting is expressivity, extensibility and reasoning capabilities. We present a new theory of classes derived from the theoretical foundations of LePUS3, and defined in the Typed Predicate Logic. The expressive power of our theory is demonstrated by specifying and reasoning over design patterns.

Keywords: Formal Specification and Modelling, LePUS3, Typed Predicate Logic, Design Patterns.

1 Introduction

LePUS3 is a formal design description language for the specification of design patterns, frameworks, and programs at an appropriate level of abstraction [5]. A LePUS3 specification is called a Codechart, which is constructed from a minimal vocabulary representing the core building-blocks of class-based object-oriented design (Table 1). Codecharts are formal specifications [20] that may be unpacked into the First Order Predicate Logic (**FOPL** [9]).

Table 1. The core building-blocks of object-oriented design representable in LePUS3

Classes, **methods**, and **method signatures**: the primitive entities of LePUS3
Finite sets of entities: particular attention is given to sets of classes that constitute inheritance class hierarchies and sets of dynamically-bound methods
Properties and **relationships** of entities: for example inheritance and aggregation

"Formal verification methods are very hard to put in practice because both the semantics and the specification of a complex system are extremely difficult to define. Even when this is possible, the proof cannot be automated ... without great computational costs" [8]. The building-blocks of LePUS3 do not include generally undecidable concepts such as objects, behaviour, events, or program

S. Qin and Z. Qiu (Eds.): ICFEM 2011, LNCS 6991, pp. 522–536, 2011.

state. Indeed, the scope of LePUS3 is restricted to only those decidable (i.e. *automatically verifiable*) statements of object-oriented design. This sacrifice in expressivity ensures that it is possible (in principle) to create conclusive automated tool support in applications such as design verification [12] and reverse engineering [7] with minimal computational cost[1]. However, these applications have become LePUS3's primary measure of success, and the language is prone to becoming over zealously pragmatic: its definition has become increasingly complex yet reflects a degree of logical innocence. Types are inflexibly defined, lacking notions such as subtyping. Relations are not explicitly typed, and few relations have axioms governing their use. The result of this is a definition that is difficult to reason with, maintain, and extend.

In this paper we present a new theory of classes derived from the theoretical foundations—the relevant definitions, intentions, and intuitions—of LePUS3. That is, we are concerned with capturing the underpinning logic of LePUS3 in a more elegant and rigorous fashion that is open to further investigation and extension, without losing the sight of practical concerns. We build our theory on the Typed Predicate Logic summarised in section 2. In section 3 we present our theory and discuss how it improves on the type system in LePUS3. Finally, in section 4 we apply our theory to representing (specifying) the Factory Method and Abstract Factory design patterns, and prove a relationship between the two.

2 Typed Predicate Logic

Typed Predicate Logic (**TPL** [18]) is "a broad framework in which a rich variety of theories [of types] can be easily and elegantly formulated" that is "sufficiently flexible to elegantly support a wide range of such constructors, including dependent types, subtypes, and polymorphism" [18]. The role that **TPL** type theories play is parallel to first order theories in First Order Predicate Logic (**FOPL**). That is, the bare notions of **FOPL** are operations, properties, relations and objects, which are given substance by first order theories [19]. Although types can be admitted to **FOPL**, this is usually achieved using extensional set-theoretic notions [9]. In comparison, the bare notions of **TPL** are operations, properties, relations, objects *and types*, which are given substance by type theories [19]. Types in **TPL** are *intensional* primitive notions whose contents are determined by axiomatic theories. **TPL** is therefore the ideal framework on which to develop our new theory of classes. As the reader may not be familiar with **TPL**,we devote this section to its very short introduction.

TPL is a many-sorted natural deduction system, where syntax and semantics are both defined with rules: "a type-inference system that is constituted by the *membership* and *formation* rules for types and propositions" [18]. To accomplish this, **TPL** requires the following four judgements (Θ):

$T\ type$	T is a type	$\phi\ prop$	ϕ is a proposition
$t : T$	t is a term of type T	ϕ	ϕ holds

[1] Similar approaches include SPINE [2] and DPML [10], compared to LePUS3 in [11].

where a term t is either a variable (denoted t), or the result of a function (such as $f(t_1, \ldots, t_n)$). A theory's membership rules are those that conclude with a judgement of the form $T\,type$, whereas formation rules conclude in the form of $\phi\,prop$. We show what conclusions follow from a set of premises using the normal sequent notation, $\Gamma \vdash \Theta$, where Θ is a judgement, and Γ is is a finite sequence of judgements of the form $t : T$ or ϕ, called a context. The order that judgements occur within contexts is significant, for example the declaration $t : T$ must occur in the context before the variable t occurs in some proposition ϕ, written $\phi\,[t]$.

The basic structural rules of **TPL** are assumption ($\mathbf{A_{1-2}}$), thinning ($\mathbf{W_{1-2}}$), and substitution (**Sub**). The assumption rules ensure that every term is attached to a type, and permits only grammatically acceptable assumptions. The thinning rules allow weakening under the same grammatical conditions. The substitution rule allows a variable, x, to be replaced (substituted) by another term, t.

$$\mathbf{A_1}\frac{\Gamma \vdash T\,type}{\Gamma, x : T \vdash x : T} \qquad \mathbf{W_1}\frac{\Gamma, \Delta \vdash \Theta \quad \Gamma \vdash T\,type}{\Gamma, x : T, \Delta \vdash \Theta}$$

$$\mathbf{A_2}\frac{\Gamma \vdash \phi\,prop}{\Gamma, \phi \vdash \phi} \qquad \mathbf{W_2}\frac{\Gamma, \Delta \vdash \Theta\ \Gamma \vdash \phi\,prop}{\Gamma, \phi, \Delta \vdash \Theta}$$

$$\mathbf{Sub}\frac{\Gamma, x : T, \Delta \vdash \Theta\,[x] \quad \Gamma \vdash t : T}{\Gamma, \Delta\,[t/x] \vdash \Theta\,[t/x]}$$

where in the rules $\mathbf{A_1}$ and $\mathbf{W_1}$, x is does not already exist in Γ or Δ, and $\Theta\,[t/x]$ is the consistent replacement of variable x with term t in Θ.

The above summarises the very foundation of **TPL** on which axiomatic type theories are built. We discuss how this is accomplished in the following subsections. In §2.1 we discuss how propositions are defined by introducing conjunction. In §2.2 we discuss how types are defined by introducing a simple non-negative integer type and the universe of types. In §2.3 we discuss how we concisely and elegantly define relations via specification. See [18] for a much more detailed and explicit account of **TPL**.

2.1 Propositions

Traditionally, **FOPL** and similar systems are defined using an over-generating context-free grammar where syntactically valid sentences are given an appropriate meaning, or pruned, by semantic rules. For example, the BNF grammar excerpt $\phi ::= \ldots \mid \phi \wedge \phi$ defines the syntax of conjunctions. **TPL** defines its syntax in the same way it defines its semantics: by rules. Consider the rules $\mathbf{Con_{1-4}}$, which introduce the standard notion of conjunction [9] in **TPL** [18].

$$\mathbf{Con_1}\frac{\Gamma \vdash \phi\,prop \quad \Gamma \vdash \varphi\,prop}{\Gamma \vdash \phi \wedge \varphi\,prop} \qquad \mathbf{Con_2}\frac{\Gamma \vdash \phi \quad \Gamma \vdash \varphi}{\Gamma \vdash \phi \wedge \varphi}$$

$$\mathbf{Con_3}\frac{\Gamma \vdash \phi \wedge \varphi}{\Gamma \vdash \phi} \qquad \mathbf{Con_4}\frac{\Gamma \vdash \phi \wedge \varphi}{\Gamma \vdash \varphi}$$

$\mathbf{Con_1}$ is a *formation* rule that defines under what conditions it is grammatically acceptable to use the $\wedge$ symbol. That is, if we know that both ϕ and φ are propositions then we may conclude that $\phi \wedge \varphi$ is also a proposition. This method of defining syntax "permits the expression of systems that involve a rich notion of type including dependency and self application" [19].

The remaining rules should be familiar to the reader. $\mathbf{Con_2}$ is an *introduction* rule that defines under what conditions we may introduce a conjunction. That is, if both ϕ and φ hold then we may conclude that their conjunction holds. Finally, $\mathbf{Con_3}$ and $\mathbf{Con_4}$ are *elimination* rules that define under what conditions we may eliminate a conjunction. That is, if the conjunction $\phi \wedge \varphi$ holds then we may conclude that ϕ ($\mathbf{Con_3}$) and φ ($\mathbf{Con_4}$) hold.

2.2 Types

TPL's treatment of types is non-standard as they are primitive intensional notions, i.e. their equality is not based on shared membership. Types are given meaning through *type theories*. Consider the simple case of natural numbers[2]:

$$\mathbf{N_1}\ \ \mathbb{N}\, type$$

$\mathbf{N_1}$ *introduces* the type of natural numbers, $\mathbb{N}$, which means very little without an associated type theory that describes its members:

$$\mathbf{N_2}\ \ 0 : \mathbb{N} \qquad \mathbf{N_3}\frac{\Gamma \vdash n : \mathbb{N}}{\Gamma \vdash n^+ : \mathbb{N}} \qquad \mathbf{N_4}\frac{\Gamma \vdash a^+ =_{\mathbb{N}} b^+}{\Gamma \vdash a =_{\mathbb{N}} b} \qquad \mathbf{N_5}\frac{\Gamma \vdash n : \mathbb{N}}{\Gamma \vdash n^+ \neq_{\mathbb{N}} 0}$$

$$\mathbf{N_6}\frac{\Gamma, n : \mathbb{N} \vdash \phi\,[n]\ prop \quad \Gamma \vdash \phi\,[0] \quad \Gamma, n : \mathbb{N}, \phi\,[n] \vdash \phi\,[n^+]}{\Gamma, n : \mathbb{N} \vdash \phi\,[n]}$$

These rules admit zero as our only constant natural number ($\mathbf{N_2}$), where every other natural number is obtained by a finite series of applications of the *successor function* ($\mathbf{N_{3-6}}$). $\mathbf{N_3}$ is the successor function's formation rule, $\mathbf{N_4}$ tells us that successor is injective, and $\mathbf{N_5}$ that zero is never a successor. Finally, rule $\mathbf{N_6}$ is the induction principle of $\mathbb{N}$ with the usual interpretation, allowing us to reason over terms of this type. We could further flesh out this theory with addition, multiplication, etc., but doing so is out of the scope of this paper.

We move on to briefly discuss the *universe of types*: a type whose members are themselves types. $\mathbf{U_1}$ introduces the universe of types as a type, which we call $\mathcal{U}$. $\mathbf{U_2}$ ensures all types are members of $\mathcal{U}$, and $\mathbf{U_3}$ ensures all members of $\mathcal{U}$ are types. That is, the universe of types is closed over the type system and includes $\mathcal{U}$ itself.

$$\mathbf{U_1}\ \ \mathcal{U}\, type \qquad \mathbf{U_2}\frac{\Gamma \vdash T\, type}{\Gamma \vdash T : \mathcal{U}} \qquad \mathbf{U_3}\frac{\Gamma \vdash T : \mathcal{U}}{\Gamma \vdash T\, type}$$

[2] $\mathbb{N}$ is not representative of any primitive type in a given programming language, such as **int** in Java, rather it is a simple demonstrative example of types in **TPL**.

The universe of types move type variables from meta-notation to first class citizens of the theory. That is, it facilitates quantification and reasoning over types. This substantially increases the expressive power and polymorphic capabilities of type theories in **TPL**. For example, it allows for notions such as dependent types and subtyping [18].

2.3 Specifications

Specifications elegantly introduce new relations into a theory. They consist of a series of declarations that associate variables with types, and a proposition that articulates relationships between the variables. We write specifications in a box-style format inspired by the *Z* Specification Language [14]:

R

$x_1 : T_1, \ldots, x_n : T_n$
$\phi\,[x_1, \ldots, x_n]$

The following definition gives the logical foundation of specifications:

Definition 1. *Suppose that*[3]*:*

$$\mathbf{R_0} \quad x_1 : T_1, \ldots, x_n : T_n \vdash \phi\,[x_1, \ldots, x_n]\ prop$$

then we may introduce a new relation symbol R governed by the following:

$$\mathbf{R_1} \quad x_1 : T_1, \ldots, x_n : T_n \vdash R\,(x_1, \ldots, x_n)\ prop$$
$$\mathbf{R_2} \quad \forall x_1 : T_1 \cdot \ldots \forall x_n : T_n \cdot \phi\,[x_1, \ldots, x_n] \rightarrow R\,(x_1, \ldots, x_n)$$
$$\mathbf{R_3} \quad \forall x_1 : T_1 \cdot \ldots \forall x_n : T_n \cdot R\,(x_1, \ldots, x_n) \rightarrow \phi\,[x_1, \ldots, x_n]$$

where $\mathbf{R_{1-3}}$ are the formation, introduction and elimination rules respectively.

This forms the basis for more advanced kinds of specification, e.g. dependent and recursive specification. Importantly, relations can also be reasoned over as first class citizens of a theory. For example, the relation R has the type[4]:

$$R : schema\,(T_1, \ldots, T_n)$$

We present several examples of specifications in the next section, where we put these powerful abstraction mechanisms to use in defining our theory of classes.

[3] Where ϕ is restricted to a semi-decidable proposition formed of the basic relations, functions, types, Ω (contradiction) and logical connectives $\wedge$, $\vee$, and $\exists$.

[4] This is the S type constructor in [18], which we rename to *schema* for clarity.

3 Toward a Theory of Classes

We could define our theory of classes by translating each definition from LePUS3 into **TPL**, but doing so does not encourage conceptual clarity. Instead, we build our theory from the ground up, using LePUS3 as a guide, but not as gospel. This affords more flexibility and freedom in our interpretation of LePUS3. When it was appropriate to do so we also took inspiration from [3], which discusses many of the distinctions and common features of object-oriented programming languages, and the Java™ programming language [15]. In the following subsections we present the basic types and relations of our theory of classes.

3.1 Classes and Hierarchies

The most fundamental building-block of object-oriented design is a notion of class. As in LePUS3, we take classes to be atomic elements of our theory, which we introduce[5] in the same way we did for natural numbers (§2.2):

$$\mathbf{CLS_1} \quad \mathbb{CLASS}\, type$$

Note that, as LePUS3, we abstract from distinctions between classes, inner classes, anonymous inner classes, interfaces, primitive types, and so on. This is an appropriate abstraction when designing or visualising systems at this level, as such detail is often unnecessary. If such detail were required, we could easily extend our theory to accommodate them as subtypes of $\mathbb{CLASS}$ without losing clarity of our theory. This simplistic approach to classes serves our purposes.

Next, we give this type some rules to give it meaning in our theory. Perhaps the primary relationship between classes is that of inheritance, which groups classes into hierarchies, facilitating a form of polymorphism in the implementation language. There are many interpretations as to what inheritance means (see [17]), and we do not attempt to capture them all. Instead we follow LePUS3 and restrict ourselves to the two most common interpretations of inheritance, *subclassing* and *subtyping*, as implemented in Java by the **extends** and **implements** keywords respectively. We group these two notions as a single binary relation over classes, $Inherit\,(a, b)$ ($\mathbf{CLS_2}$) meaning a inherits from b, for the same reason we abstracted from the distinctions between kinds of classes. We may always extend our theory if this distinction were required. $Inherit$ is given meaning by rules $\mathbf{CLS_3}$ and $\mathbf{CLS_4}$, which state that a class may not inherit from itself and that there is no direct cyclic inheritance between two distinct[6] classes respectively.

$$\mathbf{CLS_2} \quad Inherit : schema\,(\mathbb{CLASS} \times \mathbb{CLASS})$$

$$\mathbf{CLS_3}\,\frac{\Gamma \vdash c : \mathbb{CLASS}}{\Gamma \vdash \neg Inherit\,(c, c)} \qquad \mathbf{CLS_4}\,\frac{\Gamma \vdash Inherit\,(a, b)}{\Gamma \vdash \neg Inherit\,(b, a)}$$

[5] This partially formalises [5, Definition VI].

[6] If $a = b$ then the premise of $\mathbf{CLS_4}$ cannot hold as it would contradict the conclusion of $\mathbf{CLS_3}$, therefore $a \neq b$.

[11] discusses this relation in more detail, and describes its impact to other relations. For example, we argued that *Inherit* is equivalent to its transitive closure ($Inherit^+$):

$$\mathbf{CLS_I} \quad \Gamma, a, b : \mathbb{CLASS} \vdash Inherit\,(a, b) \leftrightarrow Inherit^+\,(a, b)$$

and that *Inherit* is a strict order relationship over $\mathbb{CLASS}$. Both these results can be observed in [5] and [4] respectively, and are supported by [3]. The interesting consequence of this is that we may deduce the second axiom of class-based programs, that "there are no cycles in the inheritance graph" [5, Definition VIII]. That is, we are able to prove the following proposition:

Proposition 1. $\Gamma, a, b : \mathbb{CLASS} \vdash Inherit^+\,(a, b) \rightarrow \neg Inherit^+\,(b, a)$

Proof. Firstly we assume that $Inherit^+\,(a, b)$ holds. By application of $\mathbf{CLS_I}$ we get $Inherit\,(a, b)$. By application of $\mathbf{CLS_4}$ we get $\neg Inherit\,(b, a)$. Finally, by application of $\mathbf{CLS_I}$ again we get $\neg Inherit^+\,(b, a)$. □

Finally, notice that we declared the *Inherit* relation and constrained its use with axioms rather than defining it in a specification. We treat relations, such as *Inherit*, in the same way that LePUS3 does, i.e. descriptive rather than prescriptive. If we define inheritance by specification (prescriptively) we limit our theory to representing only those implementation languages with exactly the same definition. Our approach allows our theory to represent a greater proportion of implementation languages—any that agree with our descriptive rules.

Let us examine another of the types from LePUS3, inheritance class hierarchies (or simply: *hierarch*ies). A hierarchy is a set of classes that contains a root class, which all other members of the hierarchy (possibly indirectly) inherit from [5, Definition IV]. Unlike the *Inherit* relation, we know exactly what a hierarchy is in this context, so we first capture this knowledge by introducing a new relation, *Hierarchy*, via specification[7]:

Hierarchy

$h : set\,(\mathbb{CLASS})$

$\exists root \in h \cdot \forall x \in h \cdot x \neq root \rightarrow Inherit\,(x, root)$

Notice that our specification is dramatically simpler than its LePUS3 counterpart and permits singleton hierarchies. The *Hierarchy* relation is easily turned into a new type, $\mathbb{HIERARCHY}$, as a subtype of $set\,(\mathbb{CLASS})$ [11]. Explicitly defining $\mathbb{HIERARCHY}$ as a subtype captures implicit implications made in its use and definition in LePUS3 [5, Definition IV], which lacks the notion of subtype.

[7] Where *set* is the type constructor for finite sets with the usual operations of membership, quantification, and so on.

3.2 Methods and Clans

Another of the core building-blocks of object-oriented design representable in LePUS3 (Table 1) are methods and their signatures. Our treatment of methods mirrors their treatment in LePUS3. That is, methods are atomic primitive entities that cannot be decomposed into instructions. We do not distinguish between special kinds of methods, such as static or class (instance) methods. We may extend our theory with further relations/subtypes to capture these details if required. Based on these these assumptions we introduce our type of methods:

$$\mathbf{MTH_1}\quad \mathbb{METHOD}\, type$$

A method is identified by its signature, often taken to be its name (*identifier*), the type and order of its arguments, and its return type. However, method signatures in LePUS3 do not include the return type. The reasoning for this is that the return type does not necessarily distinguish methods in many statically typed object-oriented implementation languages. In Java, for example, it would be a compile-time error if two methods in the same class differ only in their respective return types. LePUS3 therefore abstracts from the return type, modelling only the identifier and argument types. Although we maintain the same abstraction, our theory is flexible enough to accommodate the specification of return types if required at a later date.

Additionally, like classes and methods before them, LePUS3 treats method signatures as atomic entities. This abstraction is extremely useful as we have often found little need to specify identifiers and argument types explicitly [5]. However, specifying and reasoning over method signatures at such a general level prevents reasoning over identifiers or arguments independently. We improve matters, without sacrificing abstraction, by defining method signatures as the Cartesian product ($\times$) of an identifier and a list[8] of classes[9]:

$$\mathbf{MTH_4}\quad \mathbb{IDENTIFIER}\, type$$

$$\mathbf{MTH_5}\quad \mathbb{SIGNATURE} \triangleq \mathbb{IDENTIFIER} \times list\,(\mathbb{CLASS})$$

With our new $\mathbb{SIGNATURE}$ type we introduce a small shorthand notation. Consider a method signature with the identifier i and arguments a and b. In the usual pair notation this would be written $(i, [a, b])$, which gives few visual clues as to its purpose. In our shorthand we may represent this pair as $i\,\langle a, b\rangle$, which is more intuitive as it is closer to how method signatures are written in a programming language such as Java[10]. Importantly, observe that we have not

---

[8] Where *list* is the type constructor for finite lists with the usual operations of membership, quantification, and so on.

[9] As in LePUS3, primitive types from the implementation language are treated as classes. See §3.1. This is sufficient for the current investigation, where our scope is necessarily limited. Future work includes investigating a more generic definition of signature to accommodate arguments of any type.

[10] Although $i\,\langle a, b\rangle$ is not as intuitive as $i\,(a, b)$, the latter would cause confusion with relations and functions.

lost the ability to treat method signatures as atomic entities; we are free to specify and reason over method signatures with in as much detail as we wish.

Let us now give these types some substance. We begin with the *SignatureOf* relation ($\mathbf{MTH_6}$), which maps methods to their signatures. $\mathbf{MTH_7}$ is derived from the third axiom of class-based programs: "every method has exactly one signature" [5, Definition VIII]. $\mathbf{MTH_8}$ ensures that a signature must be associated with at least one method. These rules tell us that *SignatureOf* is a surjective functional relation from $\mathbb{METHOD}$ to $\mathbb{SIGNATURE}$.

$$\mathbf{MTH_6}\ \ SignatureOf : schema\,(\mathbb{SIGNATURE} \times \mathbb{METHOD})$$

$$\mathbf{MTH_7}\frac{\Gamma \vdash m : \mathbb{METHOD}}{\Gamma \vdash \exists! x : \mathbb{SIGNATURE} \cdot SignatureOf\,(x, m)}$$

$$\mathbf{MTH_8}\frac{\Gamma \vdash s : \mathbb{SIGNATURE}}{\Gamma \vdash \exists x : \mathbb{METHOD} \cdot SignatureOf\,(s, x)}$$

Our next relation *MethodMember* ($\mathbf{MTH_9}$) governs how classes and methods are associated, i.e. method membership, primarily characterised by $\mathbf{MTH_{10}}$. This formalises the third axiom of class-based programs: "no two methods with the same signature are members of the same class" [5, Definition VIII].

$$\mathbf{MTH_9}\ \ MethodMember : schema\,(\mathbb{CLASS} \times \mathbb{METHOD})$$

$$\mathbf{MTH_{10}}\frac{\begin{array}{cc}\Gamma \vdash MethodMember\,(c, m_1) & \Gamma \vdash MethodMember\,(c, m_2)\\ \Gamma \vdash SignatureOf\,(s, m_1) & \Gamma \vdash SignatureOf\,(s, m_2)\end{array}}{\Gamma \vdash m_1 = m_2}$$

We could further constrain *MethodMember* as we did *Inherit*. For example, to require that a method must be a member of at least one class, e.g. Java and Smalltalk. But many such rules would not be applicable to languages like C++, where methods can be defined globally. We must be careful in what we choose to include in our theory so as to not specialise our theory to any one set of implementation languages.

The *SignatureOf* and *MethodMember* relations (specifically $\mathbf{MTH_{10}}$) are a linchpin in the core of LePUS3: the *superimposition function* ($\otimes$) [5, Definition V]. This function identifies a unique method by its signature (its name) and a class (its scope), and is designed to extend naturally for nested sets. We introduced the superimposition function into our theory by first defining an appropriate relation[11], and then by proving that it is indeed functional [11]. The superimposition function always favours sets of dynamically-bound methods.

LePUS3 gives special attention to sets of dynamically-bound methods[12] (Table 1). However, neither LePUS3 or our theory represent objects, or attempt to identify exactly which method is executed at runtime. We represent the structure of

[11] We omit the specification for which as it is outside the scope of this paper.

[12] "Dynamic binding means that the operation that is executed when objects are requested to perform an operation is the operation associated with the object itself and not with one of its ancestors" [3].

sets of dynamically-bound methods, i.e. a set of methods that all share the same signature such that one of them may be dynamically selected and executed at runtime. These sets of methods are called *clans*. Although LePUS3 stresses the importance of clans [5], it fails to treat them satisfactorily.

A clan in LePUS3 is defined as a set of methods that all share the same signature. This loose definition allows *any* method with an adequate signature to be in a clan with otherwise unrelated methods. For example, consider the methods java.util.jar.Manifest.fill() and java.util.zip.ZipFile.fill(), which are not dynamically-bound. Despite sharing the same signature, their respective classes are not appropriately related by inheritance. A stronger notion of clan is therefore one parallel to hierarchies, where the key relation is method overriding. To articulate this we begin by specifying what method overriding means in this context:

Overrides

$m_1, m_2 : \mathbb{METHOD}$

$$m_1 \neq m_2 \wedge$$
$$(\exists x : \mathbb{SIGNATURE} \cdot SignatureOf\,(x, m_1) \wedge SignatureOf\,(x, m_2)) \wedge$$
$$\left(\begin{array}{c} \exists x, y : \mathbb{CLASS} \cdot Inherit\,(x, y) \wedge \\ MethodMember\,(x, m_1) \wedge MethodMember\,(y, m_2) \end{array}\right)$$

Where method m_1 *Overrides* m_2 if they are not equal, share the same signature, and their respective classes are related by inheritance[13]. Continuing to mirror hierarchies, a clan is therefore defined as a non-empty (possibly singleton) set of methods that are all related by the *Overrides* relation to a single root:

Clan

$c : set\,(\mathbb{METHOD})$

$$\exists root \in c \cdot \forall x \in c \cdot x \neq root \rightarrow Overrides\,(x, root)$$

Observe that *Clan* requires each method to be a member of a class involved in the same class hierarchy, thus ensuring that a clan may only include dynamically-bound methods. We conclude this extension by treating clans as we did hierarchies by introducing the type $\mathbb{CLAN}$, a subtype of $set\,(\mathbb{METHOD})$ based on the *Clan* relation. This is another example of how our theory opens up and improves on LePUS3.

[13] Note that *Overrides* and its transitive closure $Overrides^+$ are equivalent by virtue of the *Inherit* relation.

3.3 Predicates

This section laid the groundwork for our theory of classes: its types and primary relationships, discussed with respect to its origins in LePUS3. With it we were able to articulate more detailed relationships in object-oriented design, such as *Overrides* and *Clan* (§3.2). Reasoning over sets in our theory, such as clans and hierarchies, can be accomplished using universal and existential quantification. This immediately makes our theory more flexible than LePUS3, in which all quantification is hidden in the meta-language and exposed only within more complex relations called *predicates*: ALL, TOTAL and ISOMORPHIC [5]. These predicates are useful abstractions that are tailored to the domain of object-oriented design. Consequently their definition naturally differs from that traditionally given, therefore we use the names ALL, TOT and ISO respectively to avoid confusion over terminology. Each of the three predicates capture a different sort of abstraction over relations when applied to (possibly) nested sets. The following is a very brief summary of each predicate[14] for the case of unnested sets x, y, and relation R:

- ALL (R, x)–all elements of x are in R. Inspired by universal quantification.
- TOT (R, x, y)–each element of x, excluding abstract methods, relate to some element of y by R. Inspired by total functions.
- ISO (R, x, y)–each element of x, excluding abstract methods, relates to unique element of y by R. Inspired by bijective functions (isomorphisms).

4 Reasoning about Design Patterns

Design patterns [1] (or simply *patterns*) document a "recurring solution to a standard problem" [13] in software design. We focus our attention on object-oriented patterns, specifically those documented in [6]. The principle components of a pattern according to [6] are:

Name. Identifies the pattern.
Problem. Describes when to apply the pattern, often split into *intent*, *motivation*, and *applicability*.
Solution. Describes what design (or variations of) should be employed, often split into *structure*, *participants*, *responsibilities*, and *collaborations*.
Consequences. Arguments for and against applying the pattern.

We do not, nor can we, formalise every aspect of a pattern. The scope of our theory is best suited to formalising a pattern's solution, an area that has received much attention in many pattern formalisation languages [16]. In this section we specify and reason over the Factory Method and Abstract Factory patterns. In Table 2 we present a very brief summary of the Factory Method pattern [6].

By examining this description we observe that the abstract/concrete factory and product classes both constitute inheritance hierarchies, which we call

[14] Each predicate is fully specified for all cases in [11]

Table 2. Summary of the Factory Method pattern [6]

AbstractFactory: Declares the factory method, which produces an AbstractProduct instance. AbstractFactory may also define a default implementation of the factory method that returns a default ConcreteProduct object, but generally relies on its subclasses to define a factory method that returns an instance of the appropriate ConcreteProduct.

ConcreteFactory: Inherits from AbstractFactory, and overrides the factory method to return an instance of a specific ConcreteProduct.

AbstractProduct: Defines the interface of all products.

ConcreteProduct: Inherits from AbstractProduct and implements its interface. There is exactly one ConcreteProduct class for each ConcreteFactory class.

Factories and *Products* respectively. There are no constraints on what the signature of the factory method should be, so we abstract this as a signature variable, *FactoryMth*. As AbstractFactory declares the factory method interface, which is implemented in each ConcreteFactory class, there is a clan of factory methods in the *Factories* hierarchy. For each specific ConcreteFactory class, the respective factory method creates and returns an instance of the appropriate ConcreteProduct class. The Iso predicate appropriately represents this one-to-one relationship between factory methods and their respective products. Indeed, this is the very situation that this predicate is designed to capture. The relation we use with the Iso predicate is *Produce* [11], where $Produce\,(a, b)$ means method a creates and returns (produces) an instance of class b. We consolidate this information in the following specification:

FactoryMethod

$Factories : \mathbb{HIERARCHY}$
$Products : \mathbb{HIERARCHY}$
$FactoryMth : \mathbb{SIGNATURE}$

$\textsc{Iso}\,(Produce, FactoryMth \otimes Factories, Products)$

"One person's pattern can be another person's primitive building block" [6]. Indeed, pattern specifications extend our theory with new relations, thereby allowing patterns to be reused as building-blocks for more complex specifications; a degree of flexibility and freedom that does not currently exist in LePUS3.

Next, consider Table 3, which briefly summarises the Abstract Factory pattern [6]. Notice that this pattern is very similar to the Factory Method we previously examined (Table 2), with two important differences. In this case there are multiple product hierarchies, which we group together as a set of hierarchies called *PRODUCTS*. Additionally, there are multiple factory method signatures, which

Table 3. Summary of the Abstract Factory pattern [6]

AbstractFactory: Declares a set of factory methods, each of which return an AbstractProduct instance. Generally, AbstractFactory defers (via dynamic binding) creation of AbstractProduct instances to the relevant ConcreteFactory subclass.
ConcreteFactory: Inherits from AbstractFactory, and overrides all factory methods to return an instance of a specific ConcreteProduct.
AbstractProduct: Defines the interface of all products. There is exactly one AbstractProduct class for each ConcreteFactory class.
ConcreteProduct: Inherits from AbstractProduct and implements its interface. There is exactly one ConcreteProduct class for each factory method in the respective ConcreteFactory class.

we group together into a set of signatures called $FactoryMths$. Each factory method produces product instances, where there are as many factory methods in each ConcreteFactory class as there are ConcreteProduct classes. This is specified in exactly the same way as the Factory Method pattern with the *Produce* relation and the Iso predicate, which extends naturally to nested sets. Therefore, we arrive at the following specification:

$AbstractFactory$

$$Factories : \mathbb{HIERARCHY}$$
$$PRODUCTS : set\,(\mathbb{HIERARCHY})$$
$$FactoryMths : set\,(\mathbb{SIGNATURE})$$

$$\textsc{Iso}\,(Produce, FactoryMths \otimes Factories, PRODUCTS)$$

With formalisms of each of these patterns we begin to see possible relationships between them. Indeed, the similarities between our $FactoryMethod$ and $AbstractFactory$ relations are visually evident. That is, $AbstractFactory$ looks like it is an abstraction of $FactoryMethod$. We formalise and prove this hypothesis[15] as follows:

Proposition 2. $$\frac{f : \mathbb{HIERARCHY}\ p : \mathbb{HIERARCHY}\ fm : \mathbb{SIGNATURE}}{FactoryMethod\,(f, p, fm) \rightarrow AbstractFactory\,(f, \{p\}, \{fm\})}$$

[15] [5] provides a similar, if inverted, proof in LePUS3. By showing that every program implementing $FactoryMethod$ also implements $AbstractFactory$, it is concluded that the latter is more abstract than the former. Thus, this relationship between patterns is indirectly deduced via their relationship to (theoretical) programs.

Proof. By deduction on the relations $FactoryMethod$ and $AbstractFactory$:

1. We begin by assuming that $FactoryMethod\,(f, p, fm)$ holds.
2. We eliminate the $FactoryMethod$ relation by applying rule $\mathbf{R_3}$, concluding that $\textsc{Iso}\,(\mathit{Produce}, fm \otimes f, p)$ holds.
3. By the definition of the Iso predicate [11] we may abstract this proposition by introducing singleton sets. That is, if $\textsc{Iso}\,(\mathit{Produce}, fm \otimes f, p)$ holds then we know that $\textsc{Iso}\,(\mathit{Produce}, \{fm \otimes f\}, \{p\})$ also holds.
4. By the definition of the superimposition function [11] we know that the same set of methods results from $\{fm \otimes f\}$ and $\{fm\} \otimes f$. By rephrasing the proposition in this way we obtain $\textsc{Iso}\,(\mathit{Produce}, \{fm\} \otimes f, \{p\})$.
5. We introduce the $AbstractFactory$ relation by applying rule $\mathbf{R_2}$, concluding that $AbstractFactory\,(f, \{p\}, \{fm\})$ holds
6. By implication introduction we obtain that which we were required to prove.

□

This proves that $AbstractFactory$ is an abstraction of $FactoryMethod$, i.e. within the scope of our theory, our specification of the Abstract Factory pattern is an abstraction of our specification of the Factory Method pattern. A logical consequence of this is that any program that is shown to satisfy $FactoryMethod$ must also satisfy the $AbstractFactory$. In [11] we also proved that our specification of the State pattern is an abstraction of the Strategy pattern, and similarly that the Object Adaptor pattern is an abstraction of the Proxy pattern.

5 Conclusion

LePUS3 is a formal design description language for specifying decidable (i.e. automatically verifiable) properties of object-oriented design. LePUS3 has had success in applications to design verification [12] and reverse engineering [7], but application has become the language's primary measure of success. LePUS3 is prone to becoming over zealously pragmatic: its definition has become increasingly complex yet reflects a degree of logical innocence [11].

In this paper we presented a theory of classes derived from the theoretical foundations of LePUS3 (§3) that addresses several issues, implicit assumptions, and murky corners in the current definition of LePUS3 [5]. The resultant theory is more open to both theoretical and practical investigation [11]. The scope of our theory mirrors that of LePUS3, i.e. to those properties of design that can (in principle) be automatically verified. However, our theory is more flexible than LePUS3 and may be extended so as to capture more detailed object-oriented design, such as objects and events. Such extensions would greatly increase the expressivity of our theory, but would have consequences to automated verification. Future work includes further research into such extensions, and applications such as reverse engineering and program metrics. Finally, we applied our theory to specifying and reasoning over the Abstract Factory and Factory Method design patterns, and proved that the former is an abstraction of the latter (§4).

Acknowledgements. This work was partially funded by the UK's Engineering and Physical Research Council. The authors wish to thank R. Turner, A.H. Eden, E. Gasparis, and R. Kazman for their contributions to this project.

References

1. Beck, K., Cunningham, W.: Using pattern languages for Object-Oriented programs. In: OOPSLA 1987 workshop on the Specification and Design for Object-Oriented Programming, Florida, USA (September1987)
2. Blewitt, A., Bundy, A., Stark, I.: Automatic verification of design patterns in Java. In: Proceedings of the 20th IEEE/ACM International Conference on Automated Software Engineering, pp. 224–232. ACM, CA (2005)
3. Craig, I.: The Interpretation of Object-Oriented Programming Languages, 2nd edn. Springer, Heidelberg (2000)
4. Eden, A.H., Gasparis, E., Nicholson, J.: LePUS3 and Class-Z reference manual. Technical Report CSM-474, School of Computer Science and Electronic Engineering, University of Essex (December 2007); ISSN 1744-8050
5. Eden, A.H., Nicholson, J.: Codecharts: Roadmaps and Blueprints for Object-Oriented Programs. Wiley-Blackwell (2011)
6. Gamma, E., Helm, R., Johnson, R., Vlissides, J.M.: Design Patterns: Elements of Reusable Object-Oriented Software. Addison-Wesley Professional, Reading (1994)
7. Gasparis, E.: Design Navigation: Recovering Design Charts From Object-Oriented Programs. PhD, University of Essex (February 2010)
8. Hinchey, M., Jackson, M., Cousot, P., Cook, B., Bowen, J.P., Margaria, T.: Software engineering and formal methods. Communications of the ACM 51(9), 54–59 (2008)
9. Huth, M.R.A., Ryan, M.D.: Logic in Computer Science: Modelling and Reasoning about Systems, 2nd edn. Cambridge University Press, Cambridge (2000)
10. Maplesden, D., Hosking, J., Grundy, J.: A visual language for design pattern modeling and instantiation. In: Design Patterns Formalization Techniques. IGI Global, USA (2007)
11. Nicholson, J.: On the Theoretical Foundations of LePUS3 and its Application to Object-Oriented Design Verification. PhD, University of Essex, UK (2011)
12. Nicholson, J., Gasparis, E., Eden, A.H., Kazman, R.: Automated verification of design patterns in LePUS3. In: Proceedings of the 1st NASA Formal Methods Symposium, pp. 76–85. NASA, Moffett Field (2009)
13. Schmidt, D.C., Fayad, M., Johnson, R.E.: Software patterns. Communications of the ACM 39(10), 37–39 (1996)
14. Spivey, J.M.: The Z Notation: a Reference Manual, 2nd edn. Prentice-Hall, Englewood Cliffs (1992)
15. Sun Microsystems Inc.: Java 6 SDK: standard edn. documentation (2006)
16. Taibi, T.: Design Patterns Formalization Techniques. IGI Global, Hershey (2007)
17. Taivalsaari, A.: On the notion of inheritance. ACM Computing Surveys 28(3), 438–479 (1996)
18. Turner, R.: Computable Models. Springer, Heidelberg (2009)
19. Turner, R.: Logic and computation (May 2010), `http://cswww.essex.ac.uk/staff/turnr/Mypapers/TPLessex.pdf`
20. Wing, J.M.: A specifier's introduction to formal methods. Computer 23(9), 8–23 (1990)

Differencing Labeled Transition Systems

Zhenchang Xing[1], Jun Sun[2], Yang Liu[1], and Jin Song Dong[1]

[1] National University of Singapore
{xingzc,liuyang,dongjs}@comp.nus.edu.sg
[2] Singapore University of Technology and Design
sunjun@sutd.edu.sg

Abstract. Concurrent programs often use Labeled Transition Systems (LTSs) as their operational semantic models, which provide the basis for automatic system analysis and verification. System behaviors (generated from the operational semantics) evolve as programs evolve for fixing bugs or implementing new user requirements. Even when a program remains unchanged, its LTS models explored by a model checker or analyzer may be different due to the application of different exploration methods. In this paper, we introduce a novel approach (named SpecDiff) to computing the differences between two LTSs, representing the evolving behaviors of a concurrent program. SpecDiff considers LTSs as Typed Attributed Graphs (TAGs), in which states and transitions are encoded in finite dimensional vector spaces. It then computes a maximum common subgraph of two TAGs, which represents an optimal matching of states and transitions between two evolving LTSs of the concurrent program. SpecDiff has been implemented in our home grown model checker framework PAT. Our evaluation demonstrates that SpecDiff can assist in debugging system faults, understanding the impacts of state reduction techniques, and revealing system change patterns.

1 Introduction

Concurrent programs involve a collection of processes whose behaviors heavily depend on their interactions with other processes and on their reactions to the environment stimuli. The Labeled Transition System (LTS) provides a generic semantic model for capturing the operational semantics of concurrent programs, and is widely used as a basis for automatic software analysis like model based testing [10] or model checking [4]. This semantic model evolves as the program evolves due to bug fixing or implementing new user requirements. A minor syntactic change may lead to significantly different semantic models. For example, a minor change to an atomic step in a concurrent stack program (see Section 3) can lead to very different system behaviors and the violation of critical properties (e.g., linearizability [6]). Even when the program remains syntactically unchanged, its LTS model explored by a model checker or analyzer may be different due to the application of different exploration methods. For example, a model checker may apply partial order reduction [27] or process counter abstraction [21], which can result in a partial LTS compared with the original one.

Identifying the differences in system behaviors of evolving programs is important in debugging and system understanding. Researchers have presented techniques to compute and analyze the changing behavior of programs based on code statements [11],

S. Qin and Z. Qiu (Eds.): ICFEM 2011, LNCS 6991, pp. 537–552, 2011.

control flow [2], data flow [14], and symbolic execution [20,22]. These program representations are not effective in analyzing and verifying the interactions between concurrent processes. Pinpointing differences in the evolving LTSs of a concurrent program can lead to effective analysis of the evolving behaviors of concurrent programs. The underlying assumption is that the evolving LTSs of a program are structurally similar and the structural differences in LTSs can reveal the behavioral changes of a program.

However, computing differences between LTSs is highly nontrivial. The main challenge is how to systematically quantify the similarity of states and transitions and the overall quality of the matching. A state in an LTS can be rather complicated. For concurrent systems, the system configuration has a graph-based structure, in which there are different active processes at different states. The structure of system configuration varies significantly during system transitions. Furthermore, the graph structure of LTSs, such as the incoming and outgoing transitions of states and the transition labels must also be taken into account when comparing two LTSs.

In this paper, we present SpecDiff, an approach to compute and analyze the differences between two evolving LTSs of a concurrent program. The main idea is to represent an LTS as a TAG that encodes the states and transitions in finite dimensional vector spaces, and then exploit the robust graph matching technique to compute an optimal matching of states and transitions between two LTSs. We adopt a modeling language, CSP# [24], for concise behavioral description of concurrent programs. The semantic model of CSP# programs are LTSs. SpecDiff takes as inputs two LTSs of two versions of a CSP# program or of the same program explored with different behavior exploration techniques. It applies GenericDiff framework [28] to compute the differences between two input LTSs. Based on the differences between two LTSs, SpecDiff merges them into a unified model and supports the visualization and query-based analysis of the two LTSs and their differences. Note that our approach is not limited to CSP#, but rather a general method which is capable of identifying the behavioral changes of concurrent programs with LTS-based operational semantic model.

We implement and integrate SpecDiff in our home grown model checker, PAT (Process Analysis Toolkit) [13,25]. We evaluate the applicability of SpecDiff and its potential benefits in debugging and understanding the evolving behaviors of real-life concurrent programs using three scenarios, in which the LTS changes due to three distinct reasons: 1) the system evolution; 2) the application of partial order reduction; and 3) the application of process counter abstraction. These scenarios demonstrate that SpecDiff can assist in debugging system faults, understanding the impacts of state reduction techniques, and revealing system change patterns.

2 Related Work

One notion commonly used for comparison of system behaviors is refinement. Refinement captures the behavioral relationship between an abstract model of a system (e.g., a specification) and a more detailed model (e.g., an implementation). The correctness of the latter with respect to the former can be established by studying their refinement relationship. Transition-system refinement is commonly defined as trace inclusion or simulation [17]. This definition ensures that if the specification satisfies certain property, so does the implementation. This notion of refinement constitutes the foundation of model-based testing [10] and model-based debugging [15].

A symmetric version of the simulation relation is known as bisimulation [16]. Our SpecDiff approach is reminiscent of determining bisimilarity between transition systems. However, bisimilarity requires the behavior of two states to be identical. In contrast, SpecDiff computes a quantitative correspondence value between states, representing how alike they behave. A pair of corresponding states may differ in their system configurations and transitions. Similarly, Girard and Pappas [5] proposed the notion of approximate bisimulation for metric transition systems, whose states and transitions represent quantitative data and computation, such as temperature measurement. The quantitative data constitutes a metric space for measuring the approximate bisimilarity between two metric LTSs. Such approximate bisimilarity allows the possibility of data errors in the analysis of control systems [5]. In our work, the LTSs to be compared do not contain quantitative states and transitions. But SpecDiff encodes the states and transitions of LTSs in finite dimensional vector spaces to quantify their similarities.

If a property is not satisfied, most model checkers will produce a counterexample, which is important in debugging complex systems. For example, Konighofer *et al.* [12] debugs incorrect specifications based on explaining unrealizability using counterexamples. In contrast, SpecDiff analyzes the differences of the evolving LTSs of a concurrent program. It offers more contextual information, since the whole LTSs are compared and differences are highlighted. It can be complementary to counterexample analysis. Furthermore, SpecDiff is also useful in other scenarios, such as assessing the impact of various state space optimization techniques. In such scenarios, model checkers would not provide any counterexamples. However, there is still a need to detect and understand the differences of LTSs.

Program differencing methods [7,9,29] have long been used for identifying syntactic and semantic differences between program versions. Person et al. [20] exploit the over-approximating symbolic execution technique to characterize behavioral program differences. Siegel et al. [23] apply model checking and symbolic execution to verify the equivalence of sequential and parallel versions of a program. A recent work by Qi et al. [22] presents a technique to debug evolving programs using symbolic execution and SAT solver. In our work, SpecDiff exploits a robust model differencing framework (i.e., GenericDiff [28]) to compare the evolving LTSs of a concurrent program.

One of the key steps of GenericDiff is to perform a random walk on graph to propagate the correspondence values of node pairs based on graph structure. This process has close connections to the Markov decision process used in [19,18]. Sokolsky *et al.* [19] compare the LTSs of viruses to classify them into families. Nejati *et al.* [18] compute a similarity measure between Statecharts specifications for finding their correspondences. The goal of our SpecDiff is to detect and analyze the evolving behaviors of a concurrent program, resulted from various reasons.

3 A Motivating Example

We motivate this work with a scenario for an evolving concurrent stack implementation. A concurrent stack is a data structure that provides $push$ and pop operations with

```
1  #define N 2; #define SIZE 2; var H = 0; var HL[N]; Push(i) =
2  τ{HL[i]=H} →
3        ifa(HL[i]==H){ push.i.(H+1){if(H<SIZE){H++}} → Skip }
4        else{ τ → Push(i) };
5  Pop(i) = τ{HL[i]=H;} →
6        ifa(H==0){ pop.i.0 → Skip }
7        else{
8            τ → ifa(HL[i]≠H){τ → Pop(i)}
9                else{ pop.i.H{if(H>0){H--}} → Skip } };
10 Process(i) = (Push(i) □ Pop(i)); Process(i);
11 Stack()=(|||x:{0..N-1}@Process(x))
```

Listing 1.1. A concurrent stack in CSP# - atomic-**ifa**

the usual LIFO (Last In First Out) semantics for concurrent processes. Herlihy and Wing proposed linearizability [6] as an important correctness criterion for implementations of concurrent data structures. For example, the concurrent stack is linearizable if the projection of the operations in time can be matched to a sequence of operations of a sequential stack. The goal of designing concurrent data structures is to achieve the maximum concurrency yet still preserve the linearizability. The critical design decision is to use suitable locks or synchronization primitives, such as *compare-and-swap* (CAS), *load-linked* (LL) or *store-conditional* (SC) to guarantee the exclusive access of concurrent data structures at the critical points (a.k.a. linearization points). If too many steps are executed atomically, then the throughput of the concurrent data structure is low. If too few steps are executed atomically, then linearizability may be violated.

Trieber [26] proposed a concurrent stack implementation using CAS operators. Listing 1.1 shows the algorithm in CSP#. H is the head pointer (being 0 initially) to the top element of stack, $HL[i]$ is a (local) variable of process i to store the value read from the head pointer. The head pointer H is shared by all processes. Each operation tries to update the H until CAS operation succeeds. We will further explain the process definitions in Section 4.2. Here it is important to understand that the CAS operator is implemented using the variable $HL[i]$, which updates H if the value of H is the same as initially read value in $HL[i]$. The operational semantics of **ifa** (line 4 and 7 of Listing 1.1) is that the condition checking and first event execution of true/false branch are done in one atomic step, which gives the power to simulating the CAS operator.

When designing the algorithm, CAS operator should be used with care because it requires additional hardware support and reduces the concurrency. In order to maximize concurrency, a modified implementation of the concurrent stack may decrease the atomicity level by changing atomic conditional choice (**ifa**) at line 4 and 7 in Listing 1.1 into a regular conditional choice (**if**). Unfortunately, this change results in the violation of the linearizability of concurrent stack. It is clear that the change of atomicity level of conditional choice affects the correctness of linearizability. However, this minor change results in significantly different system behavior. The LTS of the correct version contains 438 states and 1120 transitions, while the LTS of the faulty version contains 1102 states and 2642 transitions. It is not obvious that why the change of atomicity of conditional choice introduces the fault.

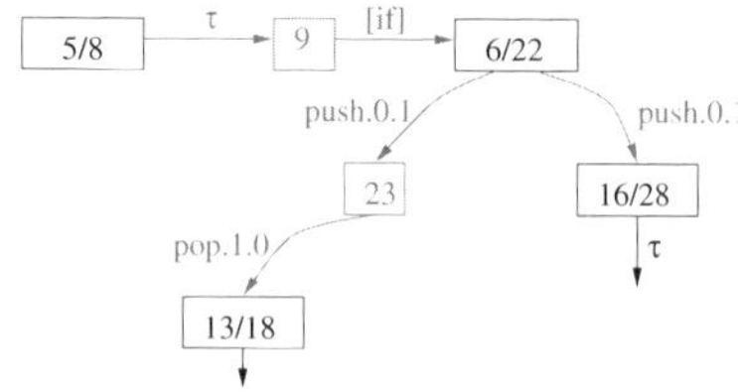

Fig. 1. One incorrect interaction between two processes

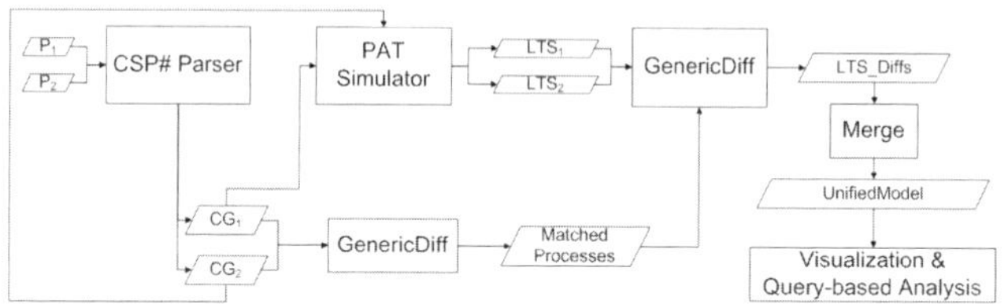

Fig. 2. The architecture of SpecDiff

Our SpecDiff is able to compare the evolving LTSs of the two versions of the concurrent stack. Figure 1 shows one violation of the linearizability of the concurrent stack due to the change of the program. The green states and transitions are reported to be present only in the LTS of the correct version, whereas the red states and transitions are only present in the LTS of the faulty version. SpecDiff reports that the state 6[1] of the correct LTS corresponds to the state 22 of the faulty LTS but the two states behave differently. The state 6 transits to the state 16 by firing a *push.0.1* event in the correct LTS. However, the corresponding state of the state 6, i.e., the state 22 of the faulty LTS does not transit to the corresponding state of the state 16, i.e., the state 28 of the fault LTS by firing a *push.0.1* event. Instead, the state 22 of the faulty LTS transits to the state 23 (a state that is only present in the faulty LTS), by firing a *push.0.1*, from which the system can fire a *pop.1.0* event, which violates the linearizability of the concurrent stack. Essentially, the second process pops nothing after the first process has pushed one item into the stack.

4 The SpecDiff Approach

We begin with an overview of SpecDiff. We then discuss the syntax and semantics of CSP# language. Next, we present how SpecDiff compares the LTSs for detecting the behavioral changes of a concurrent program. Finally, we discuss the visualization and query-based analysis of SpecDiff for inspecting the LTSs and their differences.

4.1 Overview of SpecDiff

Figure 2 presents the architecture of SpecDiff. As a proof of concept, we have implemented SpecDiff in PAT [13] model checker. We adopt CSP# [24] for describing the

[1] The state index is only for illustration purpose.

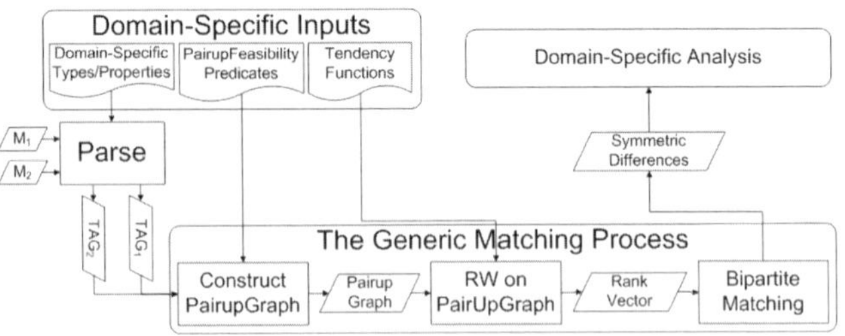

Fig. 3. The architecture of GenericDiff

behavior of concurrent programs, which offers great flexibility in modeling concurrent processes and their interactions.

Given two CSP# programs p_1 and p_2, CSP# parser parses them into two configuration graphs CG_1 and CG_2. The configuration graph is a rooted directed graph, representing the internal syntactic model of a CSP# program. The PAT's simulator that implements the operational semantics of CSP# performs a (bounded) depth-first exploration of configuration graph to generate the LTS model. Given a CSP# program and a particular simulator, the generated LTS is stable across simulations. In our work, the program p_1 and p_2 represent the same program or the two versions of a program. When p_1 and p_2 are the same, different LTSs can be obtained by adopting different simulators that support different behavior exploration methods, such as partial order reduction [27].

The main challenge in comparing the LTSs is quantifying the similarity of states and transitions and the overall quality of the matching. The key idea of SpecDiff is to represent the LTSs as TAGs and exploit the graph matching techniques to determine an optimal correspondence relation over the states and transitions of the input LTSs. More specifically, SpecDiff exploits the GenericDiff framework [28] to compare the evolving LTSs of a CSP# program. First, if the program p_1 and p_2 are different, it applies GenericDiff to compare the configuration graphs (CG_1 and CG_2) of p_1 and p_2 to determine the correspondences between the processes defined in p_1 and p_2, which in turn helps to determine the correspondences between states of two LTSs. Second, it applies GenericDiff to compare the LTSs (LTS_1 and LTS_2) of p_1 and p_2 to determine the correspondences between states and transitions. Based on the matching results of two LTSs, SpecDiff merges the two LTSs into a unified model. It supports visualization and query-based analysis of the two LTSs and their differences.

4.2 Syntax of CSP#

A CSP# [24] program contains the constant and variable definitions, channel definitions and process definitions. Like any program, CSP# programs also evolve. Since the processes are a key factor to determine the state similarity in the corresponding LTSs, given two versions of a program p_1 and p_2, we must first find the syntactic differences between p_1 and p_2. In our work, we compare the configuration graphs CG_1 and CG_2 of p_1 and p_2 to determine the correspondences between processes of p_1 and p_2.

A process is defined as an equation in the following syntax $P(x_1, x_2, \ldots, x_n) = \mathit{ProcessExp}$, where P is the process name, $x_1, x_2, \ldots, x_n$ is an optional list of process parameters and $\mathit{ProcessExp}$ is a process expression. A named process may be referenced by its name (with the valuation of the parameters). The process expression defines the computational logic of the process. The following is a BNF description of process expressions [24]. CSP# supports various types of process constructs, including primitives, event prefixing, channel communication, hiding, and various process compositions. CSP# parser parses a CSP# program into a configuration graph $CG(V, E)$, where the vertex set V contains the processes defined in the program and the edge set E contains the composition relations between processes.

$$
\begin{aligned}
P = \; & \mathit{Stop} \mid \mathit{Skip} \mid e.x\{\mathit{prog}\} \rightarrow P \mid ch!x \rightarrow P \mid ch?x \rightarrow P \mid P \setminus X \\
\mid \; & P \,;\, Q \mid P \,\Box\, Q \mid P \sqcap Q \mid [b]P \mid P \parallel Q \mid P \mid\mid\mid Q \mid P \bigtriangleup Q \\
\mid \; & \mathit{if}\ b\ \{P\}\ \mathit{else}\ \{Q\} \mid \mathit{ifa}\ b\ \{P\}\ \mathit{else}\ \{Q\} \mid \mathit{ref}(Q)
\end{aligned}
$$

The concurrent stack program in Figure 1.1 implements Treiber's lock-free concurrent stack [26] in CSP#. It represents the concurrent stack as a singly-linked list with a head pointer to the top element of the stack and uses `CAS` to modify the value of the head pointer atomically. This program defines two constants (Line 1). N is the number of processes and SIZE is the size bound of the stack. To make the state finite, we bound the size of the stack and the number of processes. Line 2 defines a variable H that records the stack head pointer and a variable HL that records the temporary head value of each process. The process definitions $\mathit{Push}(i)$, $\mathit{Pop}(i)$, $\mathit{Process}(i)$, and $\mathit{Stack}()$ specify the exact behaviors of the concurrent stack.

Figure 4 presents the partial configuration graph of this stack program. The $\mathit{Stack}()$ process is defined as the interleaving (|||) of N $\mathit{Process}(i)$. The $\mathit{Process}(i)$ is defined as the sequential composition (;) of a choice process ([]) and itself (self-loop). The choice process ([]) is composed of two choices ($\mathit{Push}(i)[]\mathit{Pop}(i)$). The process $\mathit{Push}(i)$ is defined as a event prefixing process $\tau\{\mathit{HL}[i] = H\} \rightarrow \ldots$. τ is the event name and the statement block attached to this event is a sequential program that is executed atomically together with the occurrence of the event. In this example, it update $\mathit{HL}[i]$ to be H. The process $\mathit{Push}(i)$ behaves like the atomic conditional choice process $\mathit{ifa}(\mathit{HL}[i] == H)\{\ldots\}\mathit{else}\{\ldots\}$ after performing $\tau\{\mathit{HL}[i] = H\}$. If the boolean expression $\mathit{HL}[i] == H$ evaluates to true, then $\mathit{Push}(i)$ behaves like the event prefixing process $push.i.(H + 1)\{...\} \rightarrow \mathit{Skip}$ that performs $push.i.(H + 1)$, updates H, and then terminate. If $\mathit{HL}[i] == H$ evaluates to false, $\mathit{Push}(i)$ behaves like the event prefixing process $\tau \rightarrow \mathit{Push}(i)$. Similarly, process $\mathit{Pop}(i)$ defines the behavior of pop operation (details are omitted in Figure 4 for the sake of clarity).

4.3 Operational Semantic of CSP#

The operational semantics of CSP# programs is defined in the form of Structural Operational Semantics (SOS) rules [24]. It extends the operational semantics for CSP [3]. These rules translate a CSP# program into an LTS.

An LTS is a 3-tuple $(S, \mathit{init}, \rightarrow)$, which consists of a set of system configurations, i.e., global states, the initial system configuration $\mathit{init} \in S$, and a set of labeled transition relations $\rightarrow$. In CSP#, a state is composed of two components (V, P) where V

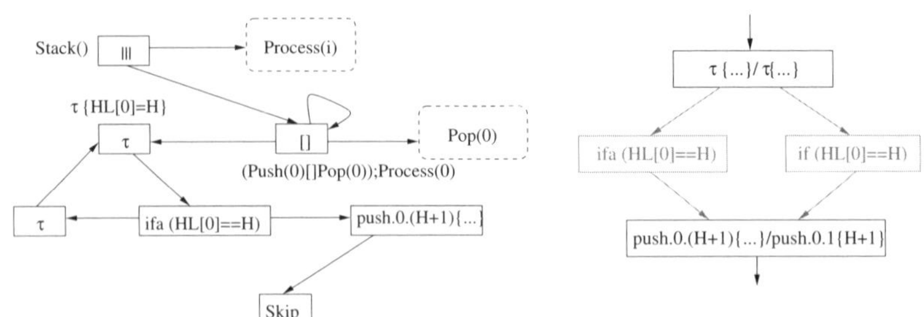

Fig. 4. Stack program configuration graph

Fig. 5. Partial matching result

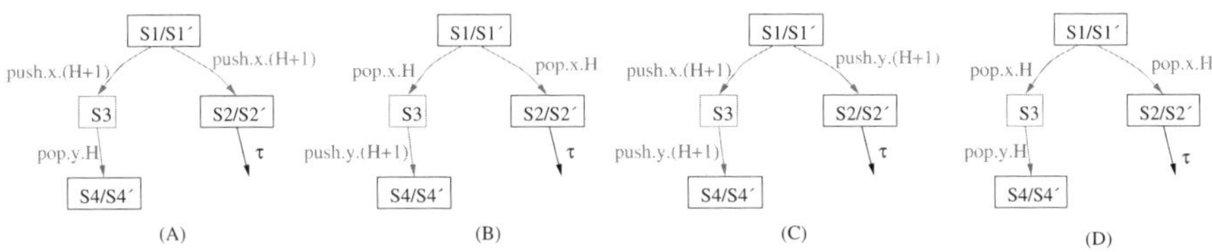

Fig. 6. Four types of incorrect interactions

is a valuation function mapping a variable name (or a channel name) to its value (or a sequence of items in the buffer) and P is the current process expression. A transition is a labeled directed relation from a source state to a target state. The labeled transition relation $\rightarrow$ conforms to the structural operational semantics of CSP# process constructs. The transition label represents the engaged event. This event has a name and an ordered list (possible empty) of parameter expressions, which captures the information such as process id and the valuation of global variables or channel buffers.

For example, in the LTS of the correct version of the stack program in Figure 1.1, the valuation of global variables H and HL at the state 6 is 0 and $[0, 0]$ respectively. The process expression at the state 6 is $ifa(HL[0] == H)\{push.0.(H+1)\{\ldots\} \rightarrow Skip\}\ldots;\ Process(0)\ |||\ ifa(H == 0)\{pop.1.0 \rightarrow Skip\}\ldots$. Since $HL[0] == H$ evaluates to true at the state 6, the first process can perform the event prefixing process $push.0.(H+1)\{\ldots\} \rightarrow Skip$. Consequently, the state 6 transits to the state 16 by a $push.0.1$ transition. The first parameter 0 of the $push.0.1$ event is the id of the first process and the second parameter is the updated head pointer of the shared stack. The valuation of H and HL at the target state 16 is 1 and $[0, 0]$. The process expression at the state 16 is $Skip;\ Process(0)\ |||\ ifa(H == 0)\{pop.1.0 \rightarrow Skip\}\ldots$.

4.4 Comparing Configuration Graphs and Labeled Transition Systems

SpecDiff applies GenericDiff [28] to compare the evolving configuration graphs and LTSs. GenericDiff is a general framework for model comparison. Given two input models, GenericDiff casts the problem of comparing two models as the problem of recognizing the *Maximum Common Subgraph* of two TAGs. The only step required to apply

GenericDiff is to develop the necessary domain-specific inputs (see the architecture of GenericDiff in Figure 3). The *domain-specific types and properties* specify the TAG that GenericDiff builds when parsing the input model and the characteristic properties of model elements and relations that discriminate their instances. The *pairup feasibility predicates* specify rules that a pair of elements (relations) must satisfy so that they can be paired-up as matching candidates. The *random walk tendency functions* specify the parameters for the random walk process that propagates the correspondence values on graph. GenericDiff reports a *symmetric difference* between two input models, i.e., a set of corresponding model elements and relations in two models and two sets of model elements and relations that are only present in one of the two input models respectively. Due to the space limitation, interested readers are referred to [28] for the technical details about how SpecDiff configures GenericDiff framework.

Figure 5 presents the partially matching results of the configuration graphs of the two versions of the stack program. In this example, the program suffers a minor syntactic change. The atomic conditional choice (green) is only present in the configuration graph of the correct stack program, while the regular conditional choice (red) is only present in the faulty version. All other process constructs are matched.

However, this minor syntactic change to the stack program results in significant semantics changes. Figure 1 presents a violation of linearizability of the concurrent stack among these semantics changes as reported by SpecDiff. Due to the decrease of the atomicity level of conditional choice in the faulty version, the condition checking $if(H == 0)$ will not be executed atomically together with either $pop.i.0 \rightarrow Skip$ (then branch) or $tau \rightarrow ifa(HL[i]! = h)\ldots$ (else branch). Consequently, the second process evaluates $H == 0$ at the state 9 (only present in the faulty LTS), the faulty LTS transits to the state 22. However, at the state 22, before the second process executes $pop.1.0 \rightarrow Skip$, the first process executes $push.0.(H + 1)\{\ldots\} \rightarrow Skip$, which update the head pointer of the concurrent stack, i.e., H becomes 1 at the state 23. But the second process is not aware of this update and erroneously execute $pop.1.0 \rightarrow Skip$.

4.5 Analyzing the LTS Differences

Given the matching results of two LTSs, SpecDiff merges the two LTSs into a unified model. The unified model is constructed by first creating the matched parts of two LTSs (i.e., corresponding states and transitions) and then applies a sequence of insert operations to create the unmatched states and transitions on the basis of the matched parts of two LTSs. A pair of matched states and transitions appears only once in the unified model. It is important to note that, in our formulation of the LTS similarity, two states (one from each LTS) being matched only indicates that the two states are similar in terms of their characteristic properties and graph structures. As shown in our running example, two matched states (e.g. $6/22$) may still differ in their system configurations (i.e., the valuation of global variables and channels and/or the process expression) and their incoming and outgoing transitions.

To enable an intuitive means of inspecting the differences between the two LTSs, we have developed two types of visualizations for the unified model: normal and fragmented. The normal view shows the unified model in a whole graph. The fragmented view breaks the unified model into a set of disconnected matched and unmatched fragments. A matched (unmatched) fragment is a maximally connected subgraph of matched (unmatched) states. That is, there are no matched (unmatched) states and transitions in the unified model that could be added to the subgraph and still leave it connected. A unmatched fragment also contains the duplicates of the matched states neighboring with unmatched states. The matched fragments can be hidden in the fragmented view. The detailed state information, i.e., the valuation of global variables and channels as well as the process expression at a state can be inspected in the State Info view or a pop-up window. The visualization supports zooming-in/out and panning the view.

Figure 1 shows partially a normal view of the unified model of the two evolving LTSs of the stack program. The matched states and transitions of two LTSs are shown in black, while the unmatched states and transitions of two LTSs are shown in green and red respectively. In the visualization, the states are indexed with unique ids for illustration purpose. A pair of matched states sid_1 and sid_2 (one from each LTS) is shown in one node labeled sid_1 / sid_2. For example, $6/22$ represents that the state 6 of the correct LTS correspondes to the state 22 of the faulty LTS. Note that the state indices have nothing to do with the similarity between states. A pair of matched transitions (one from each LTS) is shown as one edge labeled tl_1 / tl_2, tl_1 and tl_2 being the labels of two transitions. When tl_1 and tl_2 are the same, tl_2 is omitted for the sake of clarity. For example, the transition $6/22 \stackrel{pop.1.0}{\rightarrow} 9/17$ represents a pair of matched transitions $6 \stackrel{pop.1.0}{\rightarrow} 9$ and $22 \stackrel{pop.1.0}{\rightarrow} 17$.

In addition to the interactive visual inspection of two LTSs and their differences, SpecDiff stores all the data of two LTSs and their differences in a database. We have defined several queries for detecting behavioral change patterns based on the matching results of two LTSs. For example, one query has been defined to search for pairs of matched states with unmatched same-label transitions. The transitions $6/22 \stackrel{push.0.1}{\rightarrow} 16/28$ and $6/22 \stackrel{push.0.1}{\rightarrow} 23$ shown in Figure 1 is an instance returned by this query.

The visual inspection and query-based analysis complement each other. The visualization provides an intuitive means of inspecting the differences between two LTSs. Query-based analysis scales up to large LTSs. It helps to identify the potentially interesting states and transitions that are worth further investigation. The analysts can then visually explore these states and transitions. In fact, we use the visualization and query-based analysis interleavingly to incrementally build up the knowledge about the two compared LTSs and their differences.

5 Evaluation

In this section, we present our preliminary evaluation of SpecDiff. We focus on the general applicability and the potential benefits of SpecDiff in three scenarios, where the LTS models of concurrent programs change due to three distinct reasons.

5.1 The Effectiveness of SpecDiff

We first report our experience in using SpecDiff for debugging and understanding the evolving LTSs of concurrent programs. Three scenarios were illustrated: 1) the evolution of a concurrent stack that results in faulty behaviors; 2) the application of partial order reduction; 3) the application of process counter abstraction. Note that the programs remain unchanged in the second and third scenarios, but the LTS models actually explored are different due to the application of state space reduction or abstraction techniques.

The Evolution of a Concurrent Stack. Concurrent programs are significantly more difficult to design and verify than the sequential ones because process executing concurrently may interleave their steps in many ways, each with a different and potentially unexpected outcome. Our running example demonstrates such a case. A change to the atomicity of conditional choices results in the violation of the linearizability of the concurrent stack. Detecting and analyzing the differences between the correct and faulty LTSs help to debug and understand the evolving behavior of concurrent programs.

In Section 3, we discussed an incorrect interaction between two processes in the faulty concurrent stack (see Figure 1). This incorrect behavior motivated us to define a query searching for pairs of matched states with unmatched same-label transitions. Figure 6 presents four types of incorrect interactions between two processes of the concurrent stack that we have learned from inspecting the SpecDiff results.

Our running example illustrates the first type of incorrect interactions (Figure 6 (A)). The process y pops nothing or an item from the invalid stack top after the process x has pushed one item into the stack. In the second type of incorrect interactions (Figure 6 (B)), one process x executes a pop operation, which updates the head pointer and results in $HL[y] \neq H$, i.e., the temporary head value of the other process y is different from the head pointer. Under this condition, the correct behavior of the process y should perform $\tau \rightarrow Push(y)$ and then update its temporary head value before any $push$ operations. However, due to the non-atomic execution of condition checking $HL[y] == H$ and $push$ operation, the process y pushes one item into the invalid stack top.

In the third type shown in Figure 6 (C), the process x performs a $push$ operation between the condition check $HL[y] == H$ and the $push$ operation of the process y; the process y overrides the item pushed by the process x. In the forth type, the process x performs a pop operation between the condition check $HL[y] == H$ and the pop operation of the process y; the process y pops an item from the invalid stack top.

We also used the PAT model checker to verify the linearizibility of the faulty CSP# concurrent stack program. PAT reports one counterexample $\ldots \rightarrow pop.1.1 \rightarrow pop.0.1$, which represents an instance of the forth type of incorrect interactions between the two processes of concurrent stack. In this particular case, the process 1 pops an item from the stack top (the head pointer H being 1 before the pop operation) such that the stack becomes empty (H being 0). And then the process 0 attempts to pop from the invalid stack top. This counterexample is important in debugging the incorrect program behavior. But it reveals only one case of incorrect interactions. Furthermore, it is not always straightforward to imagine what the corresponding correct behaviors are and what the differences between the correct and incorrect behaviors are. As demonstrated in this case study, our SpecDiff is able to reveal four types of incorrect interactions (see Figure 6) and it is able to offer more contextual information for understanding the evolving behaviors of concurrent programs.

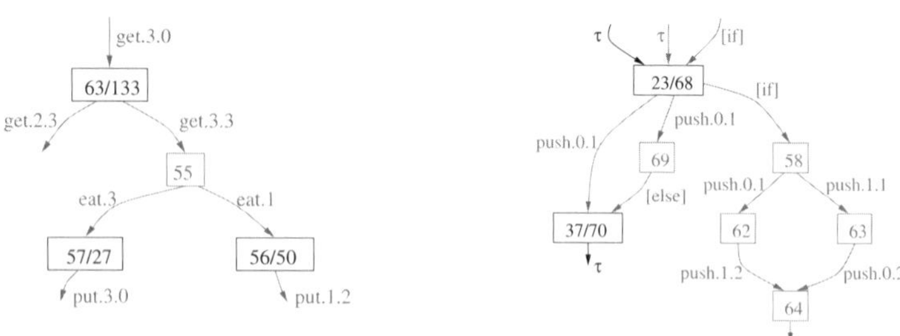

Fig. 7. The impact of partial order reduction **Fig. 8.** An example of false positive match

The Application of Partial Order Reduction. To enable a rigorous correctness proof of a concurrent program, we need to accurately model a concurrent program, for example using formal languages like CSP# [24]. Once the specification of a concurrent program stabilizes, it is often optimized manually or mechanically in order to make verification feasible or efficient [4]. For example, partial order reduction [27] is a technique for reducing the state space to be explored by a model checking algorithm. It exploits the commutativity of concurrently executed independent transitions, which result in the same state when executed in different order. The application of such state reduction techniques can result in the intricate differences in the partial LTS being explored. Identifying these differences helps developers better understand the impact of state space reduction techniques.

In this scenario, we have implemented the classic dining philosophers problem in CSP#, which demonstrates the multi-process synchronization problem in concurrent computing. We simulated two LTSs of this dining philosophers CSP# program with and without partial order reduction respectively. With four philosophers, the LTS obtained without partial order reduction contains 1297 states and 4968 transitions, while the LTS obtained with partial order reduction contains 1214 states and 3396 transitions.

We applied SpecDiff to compare these two LTSs. SpecDiff isolated the 83 states and 1572 transitions that have not been explored when the partial order reduction is in place. Figure 7 presents partially an unmatched LTS fragment. At the state 63 and the state 133, the first philosopher P_1 have grabbed two forks and the third P_3 philosopher have grabbed one fork. Without partial order reduction, there are three ways to proceed, i.e., P_1 eats ($eat.1$ transition, not shown in Figure 7), P_3 grabs another fork ($get.3.3$ transition), or the second philosopher P_2 grabs one fork ($get.2.3$ transition). With partial order reduction, only one way (i.e., P_1 eats) is possible. Consequently, the partial LTS explored with partial order reduction will not consist of the transitions $get.3.3$ and $get.2.3$; the system will not enter the state 55 in which both P_1 and P_3 have grabbed two forks and can eat.

The Application of Process Counter Abstraction. A parameterized system has finite types of processes, but the number of processes of each type can be very large or even unbounded. Such systems frequently arise in concurrent algorithms and protocols, such as the classic readers-writers problem and the Java meta-lock algorithm [1]. Process counter abstraction [21] is a common state abstraction technique for analyzing parameterized systems, which groups the processes based on which state of the local finite state machine they reside in. To achieve a finite state abstract system, one can then adopt a *cutoff* number, so that any counter greater than the *cutoff* number is abstracted to w (unbounded number). This yields a sound but incomplete verification procedure - any linear temporal logical property verified in the abstract system holds for all concrete finite-state instances of the system, but not vice versa. In such cases, it is desirable to find plausible change patterns of system behavior as the *cutoff* number changes, since inspecting such change patterns may lead to effective abstraction acceleration and system verification.

Let us start with the classic readers-writer problem. We implemented the readers-writer lock pattern in a parameterized specification in CSP#. The readers-writer lock allows concurrent read access to an object but requires exclusive access for write. It is a synchronization primitive supported by Java version 5 or above and C#. We simulated 20 LTSs of this CSP# readers-writer lock program by setting the *cutoff* number to $i(i = 1..20)$. We applied SpecDiff to compare the consecutive LTSs lts_i and lts_{i+1} and then inspected the differences between lts_i and lts_{i+1} as the *cutoff* number increases.

Let N be the maximum number of readers that can read concurrently. SpecDiff revealed that, as the *cutoff* number i increases by 1, there will be $N - i - 1$ additional fragments in the lts_{i+1}. An additional fragment links two pairs of matched states SP_1 and SP_2 with $i + 3$ unmatched states in between. At SP_1, an unbounded number of readers do not hold the lock and one reader holds the lock, while at the other pair of matched states SP_2, one reader does not hold the lock and an unbounded number of readers hold the lock. From SP_1, the only reader that holds the lock releases the lock (i.e., stopread); the lts_{i+1} transits to an unmatched state where no readers hold the lock. Then, the readers keep acquiring the lock (i.e., startread) until all the readers hold the lock. Finally, one reader releases the lock and the lts_{i+1} reaches to SP_2 where only one reader does not hold the lock. The transitions from SP_2 to SP_1 is in reverse.

We also implemented a parameterized abstract specification in CSP# for Java metalock algorithm [1]. Java metalock plays an essential role in allowing Java to offer concurrent access to objects. Metalocking can be viewed as a two-tiered scheme. At the metalock level, a thread waits until it can enqueue itself on an object's monitor queue in a mutually exclusive manner. We simulated 9 LTSs of this CSP# program by setting the number of threads that can wait at waiting state to $m(m = 2..10)$. We applied SpecDiff to compare the consecutive LTSs lts_m and lts_{m+1}. SpecDiff revealed that, as m increases by 1, lts_{m+1} will have 40 more states and 90 more transitions. There are 10 pairs of matched states, from which lts_{m+1} transits to unmatched states by $getslow$ transitions (i.e., obtaining an object lock by a slow path). From those unmatched states, lts_{m+1} then transits to other unmatched states until it finally transits back to the 10 pairs of matched states by $request$ transitions (i.e., signaling the request for an object).

5.2 The Robustness of SpecDiff

The quantitative similarities of states and transitions are heuristic estimates, based on the characteristic properties of states and transitions as well as the graph structure of

LTSs (see Section 4.4). In this section, we evaluate how good the heuristics of SpecDiff are in matching the corresponding states and transitions in two evolving LTSs.

In principle, the precision and recall metrics are used to evaluate the quality of such matching tasks. Given the total number of matched states (M_{actual}) and the number of matched states reported by SpecDiff ($M_{reported}$), precision is the percentage of the correctly reported matches ($M_{actual} \cap M_{reported}$)/$M_{reported}$ and recall is the percentage of matches reported ($M_{actual} \cap M_{reported}$)/$M_{actual}$. In this work, we have manually examined two compared LTSs to establish the oracle (i.e., M_{actual}) for the analysis. Overall, the precision and recall of SpecDiff is fairly good. In the first scenario, the precision and recall of SpecDiff is 95% and 95% respectively. SpecDiff achieves 100% precision and 100% recall in the second and third scenarios. We attribute this to the rich domain-specific properties and graph structure of the input LTSs.

Figure 8 presents an example of false positive (i.e., erroneous) match of states in the first scenario. SpecDiff reports the state 23 of the correct LTS and the state 68 of the faulty LTS as a pair of corresponding states. However, the state 23 should be matched to the state 58 of the faulty LTS, as the state pair (23/58) can better reflect the violation of the linearizibility of the concurrent stack. It will be an instance of the third type of violations (see Figure 6).

However, as the set of active processes at the state 23 and the state 58 is “too” different, the state 23 and the state 58 are not paired-up as matching candidates. Consequently, SpecDiff matches the state 23 to the state 68 which is one transition (if) away from the state 58. Since the matching of the state 23 and the state 68 is less intuitive for understanding the violation of the linearizibility of concurrent stack, we consider it as a false positive match. In the first scenario, such erroneous matches prevent the states from being matched to their “real” counterparts, which consequently results in the false negatives (i.e., missed matches).

6 Threats to Validity

In this work, we ground our discussion on CSP# for modeling the behavior of concurrent programs. We exploit the syntax and structural operational semantics of CSP# to quantify the similarity between the LTSs of a concurrent program. However, the foundational concept of SpecDiff is general, i.e., representing a labeled transition system as a typed attributed graph, quantifying the states and transitions in finite dimensional vector spaces, and exploiting the graph differencing framework to compare the LTSs. Given a modeling language with different syntax and operational semantics, SpecDiff should be applicable as long as the language has LTS-based operational semantics.

The SpecDiff is used to compare the evolving LTSs of two versions of a program or the LTSs of a program explored by different behavior exploration techniques. The underlying assumption is that the structural differences of syntactic models and LTSs of a program can reveal the syntactic and behavioral changes of the program under investigation. However, this assumption does not hold for two arbitrary programs. Two different programs may have the same LTSs. On the other hand, the LTSs being different does not indicate that the two programs must behave differently.

While our preliminary evaluations demonstrate the applicability and potential benefits of SpecDiff, its practical utility still needs further assessments. Scalability is an important challenge to our SpecDiff approach. We are currently exploring a few ways to mitigate the scalability issue. First, we may explore syntactic differences (which could be easy to compute) to guide the comparison of large LTSs. While specification remains unchanged, limiting the depth of search could be one solution. Alternatively, we are considering integrating intuitive visualization technique that allows the user to interactively explore the state space and select which part(s) of the LTSs to differentiate. This would incorporate the human intelligence to guide an interactive differencing process, because the user would have clues about which parts most likely go wrong. Second, we are reviewing the current implementation that compares the LTSs rendered in the GUI. Direct comparison of the internal data structures of LTSs could significantly reduce the execution time and memory consumption. Last but not least, our experiment suggests that often the important differences (e.g. faults) would be reflected in the differences of small sized models. Similar experience has been reported by other verification tools like Alloy [8].

7 Conclusions and Future Work

In this paper, we present SpecDiff for identifying the behavioral changes of concurrent programs with LTS-based semantic model. The main challenge in comparing LTSs lies in how to systematically quantify the similarity of states and transitions of the LTSs and the overall quality of the matching. Our solution is to represent the labeled transitions systems as typed attributed graphs, encodes the states and transitions in finite dimensional vector spaces, and exploits the robust graph matching techniques to determine an optimal correspondence relation over the states and transitions of the input LTSs.

We have developed a proof-of-concept implementation of SpecDiff on the PAT model checker. We evaluated the applicability and the potential benefits of SpecDiff in the evolution and optimization of concurrent programs, written in CSP#, a modeling language for concurrent systems. Our evaluation shows that SpecDiff is able to produce an accurate matching results between the evolving LTSs of a concurrent program. The reported differences are useful in debugging program faults and understanding the behavioral change patterns of concurrent programs.

This work is the first step in exploiting the model differencing techniques to support the development and verification of concurrent programs. Our future work will further develop more types of analysis based on the SpecDiff results. We also plan to extend SpecDiff to compare and analyze real-time systems and web services.

References

1. Agesen, O., Detlefs, D., Garthwaite, A., Knippel, R., Ramakrishna, Y., White, D.: An Efficient Meta-Lock for Implementing Ubiquitous Synchronization. In: OOPSLA 1999, pp. 207–222 (1999)
2. Agrawal, H., Horgan, J., London, S., Wong, W.: Fault localization using execution slices and dataflow tests. In: ISSRE 1995, pp. 143–151 (1995)
3. Brookes, S.D., Roscoe, A.W., Walker, D.J.: An Operational Semantics for CSP. Technical report (1986)
4. Clarke, E., Grumberg, O., Peled, D.: Model Checking. The MIT Press, Cambridge (1999)

5. Girard, A., Pappas, G.: Approximation metrics for discrete and continuous systems. IEEE Transactions on Automatic Control 52(5), 782–798 (2005)
6. Herlihy, M., Wing, J.M.: Linearizability: A Correctness Condition for Concurrent Objects. ACM Trans. on Prog. Lang. and Syst (TOPLAS) 12(3), 463–492 (1990)
7. Horwitz, S.: Identifying the semantic and textual differences between two versions of a program. SIGPLAN Not. 25(6), 234–245 (1990)
8. Jackson, D.: Software Abstractions. MIT Press, Cambridge (2006)
9. Jackson, D., Ladd, D.: Semantic diff: A tool for summarizing the effects of modifications. In: ICSM 1994, pp. 243–252 (1994)
10. Jacky, J., Veanes, M., Campbell, C., Schulte, W.: Model-Based Software Testing and Analysis with C#. Cambridge University Press, Cambridge (2007)
11. Jones, J., Harrold, M.: Empirical evaluation of the tarantula automatic fault-localization technique. In: ASE 2005, pp. 273–282 (2005)
12. Könighofer, R., Hofferek, G., Bloem, R.: Debugging formal specifications using simple counterstrategies. In: FMCAD 2009, pp. 152–159 (2009)
13. Liu, Y., Sun, J., Dong, J.S.: An Analyzer for Extended Compositional Process Algebras. In: ICSE 2008 Companion, pp. 919–920 (2008)
14. Masri, W.: Fault localization based on information flow coverage. Technical report, AUB-CMPS-07-10 (2007)
15. Mayer, W., Stumptner, M.: Model-based debugging – state of the art and future challenges. Electron. Notes Theor. Comput. Sci. 174(4), 61–82 (2007)
16. Milner, R.: Communication and Concurrency. Prentice-Hall, Englewood Cliffs (1989)
17. Milner, R.: Operational and algebraic semantics of concurrent processes, pp. 1201–1242 (1990)
18. Nejati, S., Sabetzadeh, M., Chechik, M., Easterbrook, S., Zave, P.: Matching and merging of statecharts specifications. In: ICSE 2007, pp. 54–64 (2007)
19. Sokolsky, S.K.O., Lee, I.: Simulation-based graph similarity. In: Hermanns, H. (ed.) TACAS 2006. LNCS, vol. 3920, pp. 426–440. Springer, Heidelberg (2006)
20. Person, S., Dwyer, M.B., Elbaum, S., Păsăreanu, C.S.: Differential symbolic execution. In: Nyberg, K. (ed.) FSE 2008. LNCS, vol. 5086, pp. 226–237. Springer, Heidelberg (2008)
21. Pnueli, A., Xu, J., Zuck, L.: Liveness with $(0, 1, \infty)$-counter abstraction. In: Brinksma, E., Larsen, K.G. (eds.) CAV 2002. LNCS, vol. 2404, pp. 107–122. Springer, Heidelberg (2002)
22. Qi, D., Roychouhury, A., Liang, Z., Vaswani, K.: Darwin: an approach for debugging evolving programs. In: Dunkelman, O. (ed.) FSE 2009. LNCS, vol. 5665, pp. 33–42. Springer, Heidelberg (2009)
23. Siegel, S.F., Mironova, A., Avrunin, G.S., Clarke, L.A.: Using model checking with symbolic execution to verify parallel numerical programs. In: ISSTA 2006, pp. 157–168 (2006)
24. Sun, J., Liu, Y., Dong, J.S., Chen, C.Q.: Integrating Specification and Programs for System Modeling and Verification. In: TASE 2009, pp. 127–135 (2009)
25. Sun, J., Liu, Y., Dong, J.S., Pang, J.: PAT: Towards Flexible Verification under Fairness. In: Bouajjani, A., Maler, O. (eds.) CAV 2009. LNCS, vol. 5643, pp. 709–714. Springer, Heidelberg (2009)
26. Treiber, R.K.: Systems Programming: Coping with Parallelism. Technical Report RJ 5118, IBM Almaden Research Center (1986)
27. Valmari, A.: Stubborn Set Methods for Process Algebras. In: PMIV 1996, pp. 213–231 (1996)
28. Xing, Z.: Genericdiff: A general framework for model comparison. Technical report, National University of Singpore (2011), `http://www.comp.nus.edu.sg/~pat/publications/gendiff.pdf`
29. Yang, W.: Identifying syntactic differences between two programs. Softw. Pract. Exper. 21(7), 739–755 (1991)

Developing a Consensus Algorithm Using Stepwise Refinement

Jeremy W. Bryans

School of Computing Science, Newcastle University, United Kingdom
Jeremy.Bryans@ncl.ac.uk

Abstract. Consensus problems arise in any area of computing where distributed processes must come to a joint decision. Although solutions to consensus problems have similar aims, they vary according to the processor faults and network properties that must be taken into account, and modifying these assumptions will lead to different algorithms. Reasoning about consensus protocols is subtle, and correctness proofs are often informal. This paper gives a fully formal development and proof of a known consensus algorithm using the stepwise refinement method Event-B. This allows us to manage the complexity of the proof process by factoring the proof of correctness into a number of refinement steps, and to carry out the proof task concurrently with the development. During the development the processor faults and network properties on which the development steps rely are identified. The research outlined here is motivated by the observation that making different choices at these points may lead to alternative algorithms and proofs, leading to a refinement tree of algorithms with partially shared proofs.

Keywords: Consensus Algorithms, Stepwise Refinement, Verification, Event-B.

1 Introduction

A consensus problem is one in which a number of distributed processes must come to a common decision despite different initial proposals from the processors. They arise in many areas of computing, such as the decision to commit to a transaction on a distributed database or agreeing a common value from a number of independent sensors. A consensus algorithm is an algorithm which solves the consensus problem for particular processor and network fault assumptions, timing models and reliability/performance trade-offs. The wide variety of these assumptions has led to the design of a wide variety of bespoke consensus algorithms.

Developing consensus algorithms and proving them to be correct is a challenging task and in many cases informal proofs of correctness are provided. The research in this paper is motivated by the eventual goal of defining a taxonomy of consensus algorithms, in which algorithms are more or less closely related according to the similarity or disparity of their underlying assumptions. Such a taxonomy could then form a basis for a set of stepwise-refined formal developments of consensus algorithms which would share more or less steps according to the similarity of their fault assumptions.

S. Qin and Z. Qiu (Eds.): ICFEM 2011, LNCS 6991, pp. 553–568, 2011.

The purpose of this work is to give a refinement-based approach to the formal development and proof of a well-known consensus algorithm as a means of evaluating the plausibility of a formal taxonomy of consensus protocols. During the development the processor faults and network properties on which the development steps rely are identified. Development using stepwise refinement has a number of benefits. Proof complexity is managed by splitting the proof over a number of refinement steps, so proof invariants may be given and proved at the earliest possible stage, before the introduction of distracting detail. A stepwise development naturally postpones some decisions (such as particular fault and network models) and related algorithms may therefore be developed by making different choices at these points, therefore reusing early parts of a development.

In this paper a formal development of the Floodset consensus algorithm [12] is given, using the modelling language Event-B [1]. Floodset is chosen because it is a relatively straightforward consensus algorithm with strong fault assumptions, and the Event-B formalism is chosen because it supports stepwise refinement by structuring developments into a chain of machines linked by refinement relations, thereby managing the complexity of proof. It is also well supported by proof tools.

Sect. 2 gives the consensus correctness criteria, as well as a description of the Floodset algorithm and assumptions. The modelling technology used is outlined in Sect. 3. The body of the work is in Sect. 4, which describes the development of the Floodset algorithm by stepwise refinement. Sect. 5 draws some conclusions and considers the plausibility of this work as a basis for a taxonomy of consensus algorithms.

Related Work. Event-B is used in [4] to model the distributed reference counting algorithm, which shares and removes resources in a distributed way while ensuring that shared resources currently being used elsewhere are not removed. The given algorithm does not allow for potential faults. In [3] the authors use Event-B to give a stepwise refinement model of the IEEE 1394 Tree Identify Protocol. This is a specialised consensus problem in which participants must elect a leader. A single abstract event is refined into an existing protocol and message-passing between participants is introduced in a later refinement. Potential faults within the system are not considered. In [7] an algorithm for topology discovery is presented in which individual nodes in a network must remain up-to-date about the changing topology of the network.

In [13] security protocols are developed using Isabelle/HOL. Stepwise refinement is exploited to break the development into logical stages, and to allow the possibility of making different choices at various stages in a development. In [8] Event-B is used to model a consensus protocol under similar assumptions to those made here – messages may be dropped but not forged. The initial machine is roughly equivalent to our machine $X4$. The authors do not address the algorithmic description of protocols. Event-B is used to consider consensus analysis in [14]. The focus there is on multi-agent systems and the specification of separate machines which are later composed.

The Heard-Of model [6] is a common representation of a number of standard systems and failure assumptions, and has been used to verify complex protocols [5].

2 The Floodset Algorithm

A consensus algorithm is one which meets a number of correctness properties and there are a number of ways in the literature of formulating these. In this work, the following definitions, taken from [12], are chosen.

Agreement: No two correct processes decide on different values,
Validity: Any decision value for a process is an initial value for some process, and
Termination: All correct processes eventually reach a decision.

The *Floodset* algorithm [12] is a solution to the consensus problem. It assumes a synchronous network model (processor computation takes place in synchronous rounds) and *failstop* processors (processors may only fail by stopping, and once stopped cannot restart during that execution of the algorithm.) Processors may not behave maliciously. Floodset also assumes a reliable network, although messages may not be received if the receiver has failed. The number of rounds executed is a parameter of Floodset, and up to t processor failures may be tolerated, provided $t+1$ rounds are executed, and the original number of processors is greater than t.

The Floodset algorithm proceeds as follows. Each process[1] begins with an initial value. In the first round, every process sends its identity and value to all other processes. Processes retain all received (process, value) pairs. In each subsequent round, all processes send all the pairs they currently know[2]. Faulty processors may fail at any time.

Fig. 1 depicts the first two rounds of an example execution of Floodset on processors p_1, p_2 and p_3. Fig. 1(a) gives the initial state of the three processes. During the first round, processor p_2 fails after process p_2 has sent its name and value to process p_3, but before sending them to process p_1. It receives nothing from either of the other processes. Processes p_1 and p_3 communicate fully with each other. The state after the first round is given in Fig. 1(b). During the second round, processes p_1 and p_3 again communicate fully, leading to the state shown in Fig. 1(c).

After $t+1$ rounds have been carried out, each process arrives at its final value by running a deterministic decision function on its final (local) state, which selects one of the values known to that process. To demonstrate that each correct process arrives at the same value, it is sufficient to ensure that the initial inputs each correct process provides to the deterministic decision function are identical.

To see that Floodset is correct, recall that $t+1$ rounds are executed, up to t failures are tolerated, and that failures are failstop (failed processes do not resume execution.) There must therefore be a round in which no failures occur. After this round (which we refer to later as the *saturation* round) all working processes (a superset of correct processes) must have the information, and this information cannot be added to at later rounds in the protocol. Each correct process therefore has the same input at decision

[1] A process is assumed to run on a single processor, and we therefore conflate process and processor, referring to both in the subsequent text as p_i.

[2] A version of Floodset can be implemented which sends only values, and omits process names. Process names are included to make this model more reusable in the future development of more complex consensus algorithms.

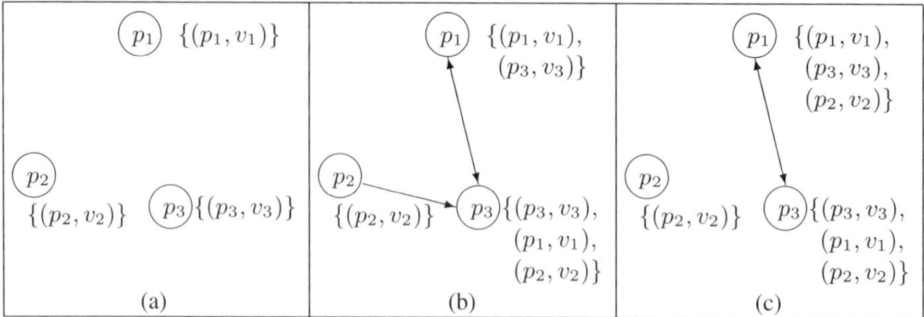

Fig. 1. Example initial rounds of Floodset with three processors

time, and the same value will be reached. Formalising this argument to derive a precise specification of the state information after each round forms the second part of the formal development in Sect. 4.2 – 4.5.

3 Event-B

A Event-B [1] model is composed of a sequence of *machines*, each of which (apart from the first) is linked to its predecessor by a *refinement* relation. A machine contains *variables* modelling state data, *invariants* which restrict the possible values of variables, and *events* which change the values of variables. An event consists of *guards*, which must be true in order for the event to occur, and *actions*, in which the values of variables are changed. Events may be parameterised, and in general an event takes the form

eventname
  any p **where**
    $G(p, v)$
  then
    $S(p, v)$
  end

where p are the event parameters, v are the state variables of the machine, G is a list of guards and S is the list of actions, made up of one or more assignments to variables. Each machine may have associated *carrier sets* and *constants*, which are held in a *context* visible to the machine. A context may be *extended* by another context, visible to subsequent machines in the sequence of refinements.

Proof obligations allow us to establish the internal consistency of individual machines, and the validity of the refinement relation between machines. *Invariant preservation* is the proof obligation that requires each invariant to continue to hold whenever any event occurs.

For any step in the refinement chain, the relationship between the variables in the abstract model and the variables in the concrete model is given by a *gluing invariant*. To show that an event in the concrete model refines an event in the abstract model, it must be shown that the guards of the concrete event imply the guards of the abstract event, and that the variable states reached after the occurrence of the concrete and the abstract event are linked by the gluing invariant.

Proof obligations are generated and in some cases proved automatically by the Rodin Tools [2]. Those that are not proved automatically may be discharged with the help of the interactive theorem prover.

4 Development

The approach taken to the development has three stages[3]. The first stage is the specification of the result of a successful run of any consensus algorithm by giving an abstract description of the chosen consensus properties above. This stage is independent of the algorithm chosen and corresponds to the initial machine in the development ($X0$).

The proof of the agreement property relies on the fact that the local views of correct processes are identical at the end of any execution. To show this, we show that the views of all working processes become equal before the end of an execution, and do not change for the remainder of that execution.

The second stage derives a precise specification of the behaviour of each round of Floodset by formalising the informal proof of correctness given in Sect. 2. The first machine in this stage ($X1$) introduces the round structure of the algorithm, and identifies three *phases* in the execution. The *saturation* round is a separate phase, and is the first round in which no processes fail. All preceding rounds are part of the *pre-saturation* phase, and all subsequent rounds are part of the *post-saturation* phase. The specification of the three phases therefore varies according to phase.

Within an execution, a process cannot know which phase it is in, as phase is a global notion and not a local one. The final specification of the round behaviour must not therefore vary according to phase. However, identifying the phase facilitates our development and proof, so phase distinctions are introduced in $X1$ and used in $X2$ and $X3$. The stronger guards in the saturation round specification in $X1$ play an important role in proving the key invariant at the end of Sect. 4.2. In refinement $X2$ the set $live$ is identified, which is the faulty processes still working during the saturation round. Refinement $X3$ makes further use of the fault assumptions to define a function between round numbers and the processes which fail in that round. This brings the phase descriptions to the point where they are equal but for the phase information. Refinement $X4$ then merges the three events together, producing a common specification for the behaviour of each round of Floodset. The final stage is the final refinement ($X5$) in which the sending and receiving behaviour of individual processes is introduced and an abstract network description is given. It is shown by refinement that this description meets the specification deduced in $X4$.

The first two consensus properties (agreement and validity) are established in $X0$ and demonstrated to hold throughout the development using refinement. The third property (termination) is shown by model-checking the completed development. Termination was therefore shown using ProB, a model-checker for Event-B [11].

[3] The model is available at http://deploy-eprints.ecs.soton.ac.uk/

4.1 The Initial Machine

The purpose of the initial machine is to define the success conditions for Floodset. We begin with some terminology. The distributed system considered contains a finite set of processes, P. Each process p in P has an initial value given by $INIT(p)$ and drawn from a set V, which is proposed to its peers as a possible final value. The set $CORR \subseteq P$ is the set of processes which behave correctly throughout the execution of the algorithm.

After the execution of Floodset each correct process p_c has a *view* – a set containing all the learned (process, value) pairs. The function M gives the final view of each correct process. At termination, each correct process p_c runs the decision function on $M(p_c)$.

The initial machine contains a single success event floodset (see Fig. 2) which will fire when the correctness properties hold. On firing, floodset assigns a value to M which is a correct final outcome of the Floodset algorithm – the properties defining consensus hold over M.

The guards on the floodset event define the correctness conditions by imposing restrictions on the event parameter m, which is then assigned to the final views M. The first guard gives the type of m, which is the same as the variable M: it assigns views to correct processes. The second guard establishes the first two consensus properties. f and g are two arbitrary views from m. The first conjunct of the consequent of guard 2 ensures that these are equal, which is a sufficient condition for the consensus property of agreement. To ensure validity, the second conjunct ($CORR \lhd INIT \subseteq f$) requires that a process is aware of the initial values of all correct processes and the third ($f \subseteq INIT$) conjunct requires that no incorrect values (i.e. ones not in $INIT$) are present in any final view. We assume that the decision function picks one of values given in the final view.

floodset
any m **where**
(1) $m \in CORR \rightarrow (P \leftrightarrow V)$
(2) $\forall f, g \cdot (g \in ran(m) \wedge f \in ran(m)) \Rightarrow$
$f = g \wedge CORR \lhd INIT \subseteq f \wedge f \subseteq INIT$
then
$M := m$
end

Fig. 2. The floodset event in the initial machine

The third consensus property, that of termination, is a consequence of the firing of floodset, rather than being a precondition to its firing. We establish this for the final development using the model checker ProB [11].

4.2 The First Refinement: Introducing Phase Specifications

The first refinement begins the second development stage, in which a specification for the behaviour of a round of Floodset is derived. A different specification is introduced for each of the three phases. Recall that in an execution of Floodset, the *saturation* round is the first round in which no failures occur. In it all currently working processes will learn all known information. Any rounds before the saturation round are modelled by the event presat. The saturation round is modelled by the event saturation, and rounds after the saturation round are modelled by the event postsat. The saturation round may be any round in an execution. We cannot tell in advance which round will be the saturation round, only that there will be one.

In this refinement a progress counter r is introduced. When $r \in 1..t+1$ it records the current round number. $r = t+2$ when the final round is completed, and $r = t+3$ when the floodset event has taken place.

The saturation round is labelled j, where j, where $j \in 1..t+1$. In the presat rounds $r < j$ and in the postsat rounds $r > j$. Since presat, postsat and saturation are new events they are considered to refine the skip event. The final event is floodset, a refinement of floodset in the previous machine. Machines $X0$ and $X1$ and the refinement relationship between them are summarised in Fig. 3.

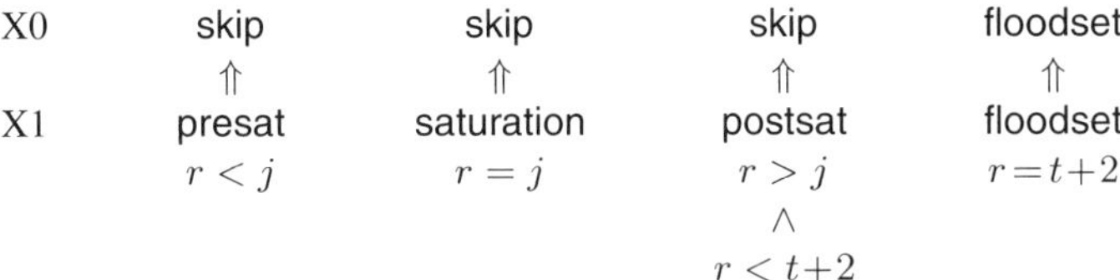

Fig. 3. The refinement relationship between the first two machines

During execution, each process maintains a working view of the information it has received. These working views are given by the global variable $W \in P \rightarrow (P \nrightarrow V)$. Initially $W(p) = \{(p, INIT(p))\}$, since each process begins knowing its own value.

In each round, each process p sends $W(p)$ to all other processes, and at the end of each round W is updated.

The presat event (Fig. 4) defines the intermediate view W for pre-saturation rounds (guard 1). The parameter new gives all the information received by each process during the round. This could include information already known to the process. The only restriction on new is given in guard 4 – no process is sent false information. The parameter w is the updated state of the views of each process when this new information is received (guard 5). It is assigned to the working view W.

After the saturation event (Fig. 4), every correct process will have the same view. At this level of abstraction, it is not possible to give a precise specification of this view, but some restrictions may be identified. The parameter f is a view of an arbitrary process. Guard 4 requires that it may include only correct information (information from the initial state) and guard 5 requires that it must include the proposed values of all correct processes. The parameter w has the same purpose as in the presat event – to identify the updated value of W – but in the saturation round more precise restrictions can be placed on w. Since no processor fails in this round, all currently working processes send and receive all their information successfully. After this round all currently working processors will therefore have the same view. It is not possible at this level of abstraction to identify the set of currently working processes precisely, but it must contain the set

presat
any new, w **where**
(1) $r < j$
(2) $new \in P \rightarrow (P \leftrightarrow V)$
(3) $w \in P \rightarrow (P \leftrightarrow V)$
(4) $\forall p \cdot p \in P \Rightarrow new(p) \subseteq INIT$
(5) $\forall p \cdot w(p) = W(p) \cup new(p)$
then
$W := w$
$r := r + 1$
end

saturation
any f, w **where**
(1) $r = j$
(2) $w \in P \rightarrow (P \leftrightarrow V)$
(3) $f \in (P \leftrightarrow V)$
(4) $f \subseteq INIT$
(5) $CORR \lhd INIT \subseteq f$
(6) $\forall g \cdot g \in ran(CORR \lhd w) \Rightarrow f = g$
then
$W := w$
$r := r + 1$
end

Fig. 4. The presat and saturation events in the first refinement

of correct processes. Thus the only values of W allowed after saturation are those in which all correct processes share the same view (given by the parameter f). This view must be shared by at least all the correct processes (guard 6.)

Since no process can now learn new information, (and therefore W cannot change further) the postsat event simply increments the round counter until the remaining rounds have been completed.

The refined floodset event (not given) simply increments the round counter after the final round.

The invariant below moves the correctness criteria from the floodset event in the previous machine and shows that the first two consensus properties hold for all rounds following the saturation round (rounds in which $r > j$).

$$\begin{aligned} r > j \Rightarrow (\exists f \cdot (& f \in (P \leftrightarrow V) \wedge \\ & CORR \lhd INIT \subseteq f \wedge \\ & f \subseteq INIT \wedge \\ & (\forall g \cdot g \in ran(CORR \lhd W) \Rightarrow f = g))) \end{aligned}$$

4.3 Identifying Live Processes: $X2$

This refinement introduces no new state, but looks more closely at the existing state variable W and strengthens the set of invariants relating to it (Fig. 5). The first invariant gives an upper bound on the information known by a process. It states that all (process,value) pairs known by any process must be valid, in the sense that they are given by the original function $INIT$. This excludes the possibility of a process learning false information at any stage. The second invariant states that every process is aware of its own initial value.

The set of processes which fail in an execution is defined as the $FLT = P \setminus CORR$. The number of failing processes must not be more than the number of faults (failing processes) that can be tolerated: $t \geq card(FLT)$.

(1) $\forall p \cdot p \in dom(W) \Rightarrow W(p) \subseteq INIT$
(2) $\forall p \cdot p \in dom(W) \Rightarrow p \mapsto INIT(p) \in W(p)$

Fig. 5. Invariants in X2

presat
 refines $presat$
 any new, w **where**
  (1) $r < j$
  (2) $new \in P \rightarrow (P \leftrightarrow V)$
  (3) $w \in P \rightarrow (P \leftrightarrow V)$
  (4) $\forall p \cdot p \in CORR \Rightarrow$
    $CORR \lhd INIT \subseteq new(p)$
  (5) $\forall p \cdot p \in CORR \Rightarrow new(p) \subseteq INIT$
  (6) $\forall p \cdot p \in FLT \Rightarrow new(p) \subseteq INIT$
  (7) $\forall p \cdot w(p) = W(p) \cup new(p)$
 then
  $W := w$
  $r := r + 1$
 end

postsat
 refines $postsat$
 any new, w **where**
  (1) $r > j$
  (2) $r \leq t+1$
  (3) $w \in P \rightarrow (P \leftrightarrow V)$
  (4) $new \in P \rightarrow (P \leftrightarrow V)$
  (5) $\forall p \cdot p \in P \Rightarrow new(p) \subseteq W(p)$
  (6) $\forall p \cdot p \in P \Rightarrow$
    $w(p) = W(p) \cup new(p)$
 then
  $W := w$
  $r := r + 1$
 end

Fig. 6. The presat and postsat events in $X2$

The event presat is now refined to the description given in Fig. 6. Since processes may fail during these rounds and therefore fail to send or receive information the value of new is non-deterministic. Guard 4 gives a lower bound: each correct process receives information from all correct processes. Guards 5 and 6 give an upper bound for new for correct and faulty processes respectively – in each case the process receives only valid information. The final guard creates the new value for W using the parameter w.

The refined postsat event (Fig. 6) adds the restriction that no process learns anything new after saturation (guard 6).

The saturation event (Fig. 7) gives the value of W after this round more precisely. The faulty processes which are currently working at the time of the saturation round are identified using the parameter $live \subseteq FLT$ (guard 3). After this round, all currently working processes ($CORR \cup live$) know all that each currently working process knows (guard 4.) Processes that have already failed (those in $FLT \setminus live$) learn nothing new (guard 5). We remove the parameter f from saturation to make it more consistent with the definitions of presat and postsat. The refinement is performed using the witness $f = union(W[CORR \cup live])$. The property that all correct processes have the same view after saturation is therefore recorded in a different way in guard 6.

4.4 Homogenising the Events: $X3$

The events presat, saturation and postsat are still unimplementable, as they rely on processes knowing in advance which round will be the saturation round. Over this

saturation
refines $saturation$
any $w, live$ **where**
(1) $r = j$
(2) $w \in P \to (P \leftrightarrow V)$
(3) $live \subseteq FLT$
(4) $\forall p \cdot p \in CORR \cup live \Rightarrow w(p) = union(W[(CORR \cup live)])$
(5) $\forall p \cdot p \in FLT \setminus live \Rightarrow w(p) = W(p)$
(6) $\forall p, q \cdot \{p, q\} \subseteq CORR \Rightarrow w(p) = w(q)$
then
$W := w$
$r := r + 1$
end

Fig. 7. The saturation event in $X2$

refinement ($X3$) and the next ($X4$) this reliance on the global saturation variable is removed by merging these three events into a single event which does not depend on j. The purpose of this refinement is to finally "set up" this merging by providing versions of the three events in which each event has the same guards and actions (excluding those guards which refer to j). The subsequent refinement then merges these three events into a single event which does not rely on j.

To do this, the set of processes are considered more carefully and those which will fail in each round are identified. The function d (in context $X3\_ctx$) maps each round to the set of processes which fail in that round, and is defined by axioms 1–4 in Fig. 8. Axiom 1 gives the type of d, and axiom 2 ensures that no process can fail in two separate rounds. All processes in FLT will fail (axiom 3), and no process fails in the saturation round (axiom 4). The function d may be any function that satisfies these axioms.

(1) $d : 1..t{+}1 \to \mathbb{P}(FLT)$
(2) $\forall i, k \cdot i \in dom(d) \wedge k \in dom(d) \wedge i \neq k \Rightarrow d(i) \cap d(k) = \varnothing$
(3) $\forall p \cdot p \in FLT \Rightarrow (\exists i \cdot i \in dom(d) \wedge p \in d(i))$
(4) $d(j) = \varnothing$
(5) $dead : 1..t{+}2 \to \mathbb{P}(FLT)$
(6) $dead(1) = \varnothing$
(7) $\forall i \cdot i \in dom(dead) \wedge i \geq 2 \Rightarrow dead(i) = union(d[(1 \,..\, (i{-}1))])$

Fig. 8. The axiomatic definition of d and $dead$ in context $X3\_ctx$

The helper function $dead$ is defined using d in axioms 5–7 in Fig. 8. For each round $dead$ returns all the processes that have failed prior to the start of that round (axiom 7). We assume that no processes fail before the start of the execution (axiom 6).

The descriptions of the events presat, saturation, postsat differ only by their second guard ($r < j, r = j, r > j$ respectively). The definition of presat is given in Fig. 9. The guards distinguish three disjoint sets of processes, depending on whether they will work correctly throughout that round, will fail at some point during the round, or have failed already.

For the first two sets the guards give an upper and lower bound on the new information that can be received in a round. All working processes send and receive to themselves. Since the processes which fail before round r are given by $dead(r)$, processes working at the start of a round r are given by $CORR \cup (FLT \setminus dead(r))$. The processes working correctly at the end of round r are given by $CORR \cup (FLT \setminus dead(r+1))$.

Guard 5 of presat states that the most information a process which works for the whole round may learn is $union(W[CORR \cup (FLT \setminus dead(r))])$. In this case all processes in $d(r)$ transmit all messages before failing. Guard 6 states that the least information a process working for the whole round will receive is everything known by any process which survives the round. In this case all processes in $d(r)$ fail before sending any messages. Processes which have failed before this round and are no longer communicating will learn nothing in this round (guard 7). Guard 8 states that processes in $d(r)$ may learn as much as the processes which continue to function correctly for the whole round. In the worst case, they will fail before receiving any information (guard 9). As previously, the new value for W is identified as w (guard 10). Apart from guard 1, these guards are now identical for each of the three round events.

The invariant on W can now be strengthened, and is given below. It states that every process still operating after the saturation round learns nothing new after the saturation round. The common information known at the saturation round is given by $union(W[CORR \cup (FLT \setminus dead(j))])$.

$$\begin{aligned}\forall p \cdot r \in dom(dead) \wedge p \in CORR \cup (FLT \setminus dead(r)) \wedge r > j \Rightarrow \\ W(p) = union(W[CORR \cup (FLT \setminus dead(j))])\end{aligned}$$

presat
refines $presat$
any w, new **where**
(1) $r < j$
(2) $r < t+2$
(3) $w \in P \rightarrow (P \leftrightarrow V)$
(4) $new \in P \rightarrow (P \leftrightarrow V)$
(5) $\forall p \cdot p \in CORR \cup (FLT \setminus dead(r+1)) \Rightarrow$
$new(p) \subseteq union(W[CORR \cup (FLT \setminus dead(r))])$
(6) $\forall p \cdot p \in CORR \cup (FLT \setminus dead(r+1)) \Rightarrow$
$union(W[(CORR \cup (FLT \setminus dead(r+1)))]) \subseteq new(p)$
(7) $\forall p \cdot p \in dead(r) \Rightarrow new(p) = \varnothing$
(8) $\forall p \cdot p \in d(r) \Rightarrow new(p) \subseteq union(W[CORR \cup (FLT \setminus dead(r))])$
(9) $\forall p \cdot w(p) = W(p) \cup new(p)$
then
$W := w$
$r := r + 1$
end

Fig. 9. The event presat in $X3$

4.5 Refining Out the Saturation Assumption: $X4$

In this refinement, the floodset event remains unchanged and the three events presat, saturation and postsat are *merged* into the single event round (Fig. 10). To perform the merging, it must be shown that the concrete guards of round imply the disjunction of the guards of the merged events. The guards of round are identical to the guards of the three events in the previous refinement, except that the second guard has been removed, so the proof reduces to proving the trivial theorem $r < j \vee r = j \vee r > j$.

This round event is now a sufficiently detailed description of a single round of the algorithm to allow an implementation to be developed and a possible implementation is shown in the next section.

4.6 Implementing the Round Event: $X5$

The round event provides a global specification of the desired behaviour of Floodset at each round. The purpose of this refinement is to define the local behaviour of individual processes. A message passing network model is also introduced.

A round is now split into three phases: $sending$, $receiving$, and $restarting$. In the $sending$ phase messages are sent to the network middleware. In the $receiving$ phase all the messages for each process are sent to that process. The $restarting$ phase is used to reset the state of processes after a round. The variable $phase$ records the phase of the round.

round
refines $presat, saturation, postsat$
any new, w **where**
(1) $r < t + 2$
(2) $w \in P \rightarrow (P \leftrightarrow V)$
(3) $new \in P \rightarrow (P \leftrightarrow V)$
(4) $\forall p \cdot p \in CORR \cup (FLT \setminus dead(r+1)) \Rightarrow new(p) \subseteq union(W[CORR \cup (FLT \setminus dead(r))])$
(5) $\forall p \cdot p \in CORR \cup (FLT \setminus dead(r+1)) \Rightarrow union(W[(CORR \cup (FLT \setminus dead(r+1)))]) \subseteq new(p)$
(6) $\forall p \cdot p \in dead(r) \Rightarrow new(p) = \varnothing$
(7) $\forall p \cdot p \in d(r) \Rightarrow new(p) \subseteq union(W[CORR \cup (FLT \setminus dead(r))])$
(8) $\forall p \cdot w(p) = W(p) \cup new(p)$
then
$W := w$
$r := r + 1$
end

Fig. 10. The event round in $X4$

The point at which a process fails is now identified more accurately using the variables die_in_send and die_in_rec. No process sends or receives messages in the $restarting$ phase, so a process which fails during $restarting$ may be considered to have failed during $receiving$, after all messages have been sent. The important axioms are

$$\forall i \cdot i \in 1\,..\,t{+}1 \Rightarrow die\_in\_send(i) \cap die\_in\_rec(i) = \varnothing$$
$$\forall i \cdot i \in 1\,..\,t{+}1 \Rightarrow die\_in\_send(i) \cup die\_in\_rec(i) = d(i)$$

The network middleware is given the variable mw, where $mw(p)$ is the set of all $(process, value)$ pairs that have been sent to process p. A process p records the processes to which it has sent messages as $sent(p)$.

The $sending$ phase consists of multiple occurrences of the send event (Fig. 11), each parameterised by the sender (fr) and receiver (to). The only processes unable to send information in round r are the ones which have already failed (given by $dead(r)$), so fr may be drawn from any other process (guard 3). Processes do not maintain a record of their failed peers, so each process sends to all other processes. It would also be possible to design a "failure aware" algorithm in which a process learns about and records failed peers, and does not send to processes it knows have failed. The end of the $sending$ phase is marked by a phase transition event (not given.)

In the rec event (Fig. 11) one of the working processes receives all its amalgamated information from the middleware in a single message. The processes which are working at the start of the $receiving$ phase are given by the invariant

$$receiving \subseteq CORR \cup (FLT \setminus dead(r+1)) \cup \; die\_in\_rec(r)$$

and any of these processes may receive from the middleware (guard 2). Those that will fail during this round ($die\_in\_rec(r)$) may or may not receive from the middleware before they fail. Receiving processes are added to the set $received$, which is local to the middleware. W_part is a temporary variable, which contains the partially updated view of W during the $receiving$ phase.

The end of the $receiving$ phase is marked by the event end_rec_phase in Fig. 12 which assigns the partial view W_part to W, and refines the event round from the previous refinement. It may fire once all working processes have received messages from the middleware (guard 3).

send
any fr, to **where**
(1) $r < t + 2$
(2) $phase = sending$
(3) $fr \in CORR \cup (FLT \setminus dead(r))$
(4) $to \in P$
(5) $to \notin sent(fr)$
then
$mw(to) := mw(to) \cup W(fr)$
$sent(fr) := sent(fr) \cup \{to\}$
end

rec
any p **where**
(1) $r < t{+}2$
(2) $p \in CORR \cup (FLT \setminus dead(r{+}1))$
$\cup \; die\_in\_rec(r)$
(3) $p \notin received$
(4) $phase = receiving$
then
$received := received \cup \{p\}$
$W\_part(p) := W\_part(p) \cup mw(p)$
end

Fig. 11. The events send and rec in $X5$

end_rec_phase
refines *round*
when
(1) $r < t{+}2$
(2) $phase = receiving$
(3) $(CORR \cup (FLT \setminus dead(r+1))) \subseteq received$
then
$W := W\_part$
$r := r + 1$
$phase := restarting$
end

Fig. 12. The end_rec_phase event in $X5$

A number of implementation issues remain open. In particular, events which mark the end of the sending or receiving phase are global specifications, using global variables in the guards. The event end_rec_phase refers to *received*, which suggests that processes have knowledge of the internal state of the middleware. In reality this reliance would be removed by implementing these events locally as time-triggered events on each processor. The functions d and $dead$ could be removed from the specification using a description of an explicit fault injector in the network model.

5 Discussion and Conclusions

We have demonstrated the stepwise refinement in the development of a well-known consensus algorithm, Floodset. The initial, most abstract model captured the three generic consensus properties in Sect. 2. The first two (agreement and validity) are demonstrated by construction. They are captured in the initial abstract model, and shown by refinement to continue to hold at each step.

The third property, that all correct processes eventually reach a decision, may be shown by demonstrating deadlock freeness — that each model in a development (apart form the first) does not deadlock more often than its predecessor. That is, the only execution paths permitted are those which eventually satisfy the most abstract specification in the refinement chain. In this development, the description of rounds in $X1$ is deliberately more non-deterministic than necessary. The second refinement introduces no new state, so all properties introduced in $X2$ could have been introduced in $X1$. The more restrictive invariants in $X2$ mean fewer execution paths, and therefore deadlock freedom cannot be proved at this step. However, this refinement is carried out over two steps to simplify the proofs involved at each stage. Termination was therefore shown using the ProB [11] model-checker. It was shown that the development has not introduced a possible deadlock where the floodset event cannot eventually occur. This was shown for three processes with arbitrary initial state, by checking the truth of the temporal logic proposition **F**[floodset] (eventually the floodset event occurs).

A good level of automatic proof ($> 75\%$) is achieved, given the complexity of the development. However the manual proof overhead is still relatively high, and this may lead away from the goal of reusable models and proofs.

A number of decision points were identified during the development. Each of these is a potential point of branching, and so using this development as a basis for a branching taxonomy seems to be a promising approach. On the other hand, the manual proof effort required by this work may be too high to be reused in more complex developments. This work sought to provide a reuseable platform for the development of consensus algorithms with weaker failure and network models and so the algorithm transmits sets of $(process, value)$ pairs, rather than just values. Refactoring the development to use more simple datatypes may lead to improved levels of automatic proof, and therefore improve the potential for reuse. A further possibility is to split the final refinement step to introduce the network model and the individual processes separately.

Floodset relies on the assumption that processes can only fail by stopping entirely. Allowing Byzantine failures naturally leads to more complex algorithms. An interesting intermediate case is to allow only authenticated messages between processes. Furthermore, Floodset relies on a synchronous timing model and is a round-based algorithm, and the development here makes use of that structure. Algorithms developed for asynshronous timing models are less structured, and developing such models using stepwise refinement is a more challenging task. We will investigate these alternative network and timing models using the Byzantine Generals algorithm [10] and the Paxos algorithm [9].

Acknowledgements. This work was supported by the EU Integrated Project DEPLOY (www.deploy-project.eu/) and by the EPSRC Platform Grant TrAmS. John Fitzgerald suggested this line of research. Thanks also to Sascha Romanovsky and Alexei Iliasov, and to the anonymous reviewers who made a number of suggestions which led to improvements in the work.

References

1. Abrial, J.-R.: Modeling in Event-B: System and Software Engineering. Cambridge University Press, Cambridge (2010)
2. Abrial, J.-R., Butler, M., Hallerstede, S., Voisin, L.: An Open Extensible Tool Environment for Event-B. In: Liu, Z., Kleinberg, R.D. (eds.) ICFEM 2006. LNCS, vol. 4260, pp. 588–605. Springer, Heidelberg (2006)
3. Abrial, J.-R., Cansell, D., Méry, D.: A Mechanically Proved and Incremental Development of IEEE 1394 Tree Identify Protocol. Formal Asp. Comput. 14(3), 215–227 (2003)
4. Cansell, D., Méry, D.: Formal and incremental construction of distributed algorithms: On the distributed reference counting algorithm. Theoretical Computer Science 364(3), 318–337 (2006); Applied Semantics
5. Charron-Bost, B., Merz, S.: Formal Verification of a Consensus Algorithm in the Heard-Of Model. Int. J. Software and Informatics 3(2-3), 273–303 (2009)
6. Charron-Bost, B., Schiper, A.: The Heard-Of model: computing in distributed systems with benign faults. Distributed Computing 22, 49–71 (2009)
7. Hoang, T.S., Kuruma, H., Basin, D.A., Abrial, J.-R.: Developing Topology Discovery in Event-B. In: Leuschel, M., Wehrheim, H. (eds.) IFM 2009. LNCS, vol. 5423, pp. 1–19. Springer, Heidelberg (2009)
8. Krenický, R., Ulbrich, M.: Deductive verification of a byzantine agreement protocol. Technical report, Karlsruhe Institute of Technology (April 2010)
9. Lamport, L.: The part-time parliament. ACM Trans. Comput. Syst. 16(2), 133–169 (1998)

10. Lamport, L., Shostak, R., Pease, M.: The byzantine generals problem. ACM Trans. Program. Lang. Syst. 4(3), 382–401 (1982)
11. Leuschel, M., Butler, M.: ProB: A Model Checker for B. In: Araki, K., Gnesi, S., Mandrioli, D. (eds.) FME 2003. LNCS, vol. 2805, pp. 855–874. Springer, Heidelberg (2003)
12. Lynch, N.A.: Distributed Algorithms, 1st edn. Morgan Kaufmann, San Francisco (1997)
13. Sprenger, C., Basin, D.: Developing security protocols by refinement. In: 17th ACM Conference on Computer and Communications Security, CCS 2010 (2010)
14. Truong, N.-T., Trinh, T.-B., Nguyen, V.-H.: Coordinated consensus analysis of multi-agent systems using Event-B. In: Seventh IEEE International Conference on Software Engineering and Formal Methods, pp. 201–209 (2009)

Refining Nodes and Edges of State Machines

Stefan Hallerstede[1] and Colin Snook[2]

[1] University of Düsseldorf
[2] University of Southampton

Abstract. State machines are hierarchical automata that are widely used to structure complex behavioural specifications. We develop two notions of refinement of state machines, node refinement and edge refinement. We compare the two notions by means of examples and argue that, by adopting simple conventions, they can be combined into one method of refinement. In the combined method, node refinement can be used to develop architectural aspects of a model and edge refinement to develop algorithmic aspects. The two notions of refinement are grounded in previous work. Event-B is used as the foundation for our refinement theory and UML-B state machine refinement influences the style of node refinement. Hence we propose a method with direct proof of state machine refinement avoiding the detour via Event-B that is needed by UML-B.

1 Introduction

Theories and calculi of verification and refinement are established: for instance, Hoare logic [4], refinement calculus [13] and Event-B [2]. Hoare logic is difficult to use on a larger scale. Refinement addresses some shortcomings of Hoare logic allowing properties of less detailed abstractions to be proved before turning to the detailed implementation. However, the refinement calculi are rather restrictive when it comes to system modelling. The refinement method of Event-B relaxes some of the restrictions by abandoning most control structure and using a weaker semantic foundation. In [2] a large number of complex models are presented to demonstrate verification on a larger scale. Still, two problems remain: it can be difficult to build larger models that are inherently structured and to master more complex sequences of refinements. Our main concern in this article is making verification and refinement easier to use. To this end, we are interested in methods and techniques for stating, managing and visualising complex verification and refinement proofs.

UML-B, a UML-based notation defined on top of Event-B, has been developed over the last ten years to support the writing of more complex models with consequent structuring needs, in particular, state machines [17]. UML-B was first invented in [18] as a UML profile with translation to B and has been developed into a diagrammatic front-end to Event-B.

UML-B supports refinement of state machines but is not equipped with its own theory of refinement. It relies on a translation to Event-B using explicit

S. Qin and Z. Qiu (Eds.): ICFEM 2011, LNCS 6991, pp. 569–584, 2011.

variables to represent the state machines [14]. Recently we have also evaluated the use of Event-B for the development of sequential programs [8]. The lack of control structures can make modelling of such algorithms difficult. However, the advances made by Event-B with respect to incremental proving [3] are mainly due to the lack of control structures. Avoiding the reintroduction of control structures we use state machine notation to provide the needed features [7]. The refinement method of [14] could be named "node refinement": nodes are replaced by state machines. The choice of [7], "edge refinement" is different: edges are replaced by state machines. In this article we compare the two refinement methods. We are specifically interested in their similarities.[1] For this purpose we have formalised the refinement notion underlying the conventions of UML-B via node refinement. This formalisation of edge and node refinement is independent from Event-B. It is an alternative refinement based on the diagrammatic notations and, unlike UML-B, does not involve translation into the Event-B notation. We suggest a combined method that allows us to switch between the two at any refinement step. In the future, we think they could be merged entirely, so that we would get one refinement method with perspectives of node and edge refinement. However, this is likely to change both refinement methods. We believe it is of interest to present the two methods before unifying them so that it will be easier to judge what is gained and what is lost in the unification.

In our use of state machine diagrams, they serve to describe refinement proofs. The possible execution semantics is secondary. We content ourselves with the potential of an operational interpretation. *Invariant based programming* described in [5] follows a similar approach for the construction of correct programs. It uses refinement in the sense of [19] to construct a correctness proof along with the corresponding correct program. In comparison, our approach is intended to be used for program development but also for systems modelling. Our definitions of refinement obey the "statechart refinement rules for behavioural compatibility" stated in [15]. However, we focus on the development of a proof method whereas [15] uses the rules to formulate an approach for test case generation. The related [12] focuses on common patterns of structural refinement that could be used with state machines. In [11] formal semantics of state machines is discussed and proof rules for superposition refinement are proposed. By contrast, we use the more general Event-B refinement as a foundation of our approach. Comparatively simple structural refinement for state machines based on Event-B has been discussed in [16]. In [6] JSD-like diagrams are used to illustrate concurrent Event-B models and their refinement but the diagrams are not formally linked to Event-B models.

Overview. In Section 2 we briefly introduce the state machine notation that we use and in Section 3 we outline the two refinement methods. In Section 4 we present the construction of an iterative Quicksort algorithm using the two methods side by side. This could give the impression that the two notions are interchangeable. In Section 5 we present a development by node refinement of a simple controller which is not an edge refinement and we suggest a combined

[1] When looking at [14] and [7] the similarities are far from obvious.

refinement method that permits mixing node and edge refinement. Section 6 draws a conclusion and sketches some future work.

2 State Machines

State machines are a diagrammatic modelling notation where the condition of a system is represented by states (denoted by the nodes of a graph) and the behaviour of the system is represented by transitions connecting the nodes (denoted by edges of a graph). The UML contains a hierarchical state machine notation which is widely used in industry and that has been adopted by UML-B. Fig. 1(a) shows a typical UML state machine. For our purposes it is easier

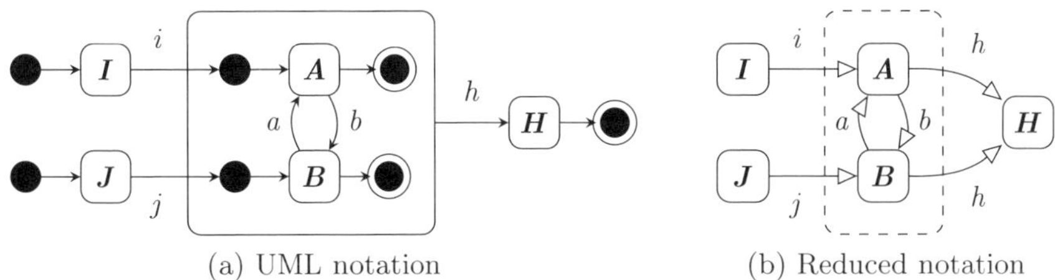

(a) UML notation (b) Reduced notation

Fig. 1. State machine notation

to work with a simpler reduced notation without explicit initial "●" and final states "⦿" as shown in Fig. 1(b). This makes it easier to define (refinement) proof obligations.

In this paper, we represent a node as ▢ and an edge, connecting two nodes, as —▷. Convergent loop edges may be used to indicate that the loop edge may only be followed finitely often before an "ordinary edge" is followed. The restriction to convergent *loops* is inherited from Event-B where event may be marked 'convergent' or 'anticipated'.[2] Loop edges are often used to prepare for introducing and proving the convergence of a more complex loop involving several edges and nodes. Edges are labelled with *events* that describe the effect of following that edge. An event has the shape any p when g then $x := a$. The *parameters* p are non-deterministically chosen when an event occurs. The *guard* g of an event states the condition, a first-order predicate, under which the event may occur.[3] If its guard is true an event is said to be *enabled*. The *action* of an event is an (simultaneous) update statement of the form $x := a$ where x is a variable (list) of the state machine containing the event and a is an expression (list). Clauses of an event are simply left out when they would have no effect. The parameters may be left out if there are none, a guard if it is *true*, an action if it is $x := x$.

[2] We do not distinguish those two concepts but simply allow convergence to be proved at later refinement steps.

[3] Predicates p, q written on consecutive lines are implicitly conjoined.

Nodes are labelled by *assertions*. If $\boldsymbol{A}$ is the label of a node, we write "@$\boldsymbol{A}$ p" to say that "$\boldsymbol{A}$ contains p" or, in other words, "p holds at $\boldsymbol{A}$". We also call assertions of nodes with loop edges *invariants*.[4] In formulas we use $\boldsymbol{A}$ to stand for p. State machines are a notation for proofs similarly to proof outlines [4]. An edge labelled e where $e = \mathsf{any}\ p\ \mathsf{when}\ g\ \mathsf{then}\ x := a$ connecting a node labelled $\boldsymbol{A}$ to a node labelled $\boldsymbol{B}$ corresponds to a proof obligation: $\boldsymbol{A} \wedge g \Rightarrow \boldsymbol{B}[x := a]$. Formal proof is the central aspect of our notation replacing the operational view of UML-B.

State machine notation supports hierarchical construction where state machines may be nested within a node of the parent state-machine. We refer to the node containing the nested state machine as a super-node and represent it as ⬚. Super nodes structure assertions: if a super node $\boldsymbol{A}$ contains a node (or super node) $\boldsymbol{B}$ then $\boldsymbol{B}$ contains all assertions that $\boldsymbol{A}$ contains. This is their only function in our approach. We do not attach any operational meaning to super nodes. Super nodes are essential in our definition of node and edge refinement. Super nodes (themselves) are not connected by edges. Sometimes we draw an edge exiting a super-node as an abbreviation for an edge that exits all contained nodes. This is often used in node refinement diagrams. For edge refinement diagrams we need a third kind of edge: anonymous edges $\rightarrow$ that are not labelled. They can be imagined to be labelled with *skip*, the event that is always enabled and does not change the state. In a state machine we identify *initial nodes* to be those nodes that do not have entering edges, and *final nodes* to be those nodes that do not have exiting edges. An anonymous edge entering a super node is to be connected to the initial nodes of the contained state machine; an anonymous edge exiting a super node is to be connected to the final nodes. An anonymous edge connecting $\boldsymbol{A}$ to $\boldsymbol{B}$ corresponds to the proof obligation $\boldsymbol{A} \Rightarrow \boldsymbol{B}$. Anonymous edges are needed in edge refinement diagrams to model conditional statements.

We have adapted the notation to emphasise similarities between the two notions of refinement. In particular, we do not use the notation of [7] for edge refinement and of [14] for node refinement. This makes it easy to see the differences and similarities and suggests how combined use of the two methods is possible. (The striking similarity that results from the common notation strongly suggests combined use or unification.) We believe that it should be possible to unify the two methods completely into a single refinement method, but as a consequence they could both lose their defining characteristics: specialisation on either architectural or algorithmic refinement. The new method will have to recover the two aspects in order to provide strong methodological guidelines for the use of the unified method.

3 Refinement

We discuss the two refinement notions by means of the refinement diagrams stated in Fig. 2. The concepts are easy to generalise. See, e.g., [11] for node

[4] By contrast, an Event-B model has only one "global" invariant. Nodes of our notation would have to be represented in Event-B by abstract program counters.

refinement and [7] for edge refinement. Fig. 2(a) shows a state machine that we use as an abstraction (also called *abstract model*) for the refinements shown in Fig. 2(b) to Fig. 2(d) (also called *concrete models*). The proof obligations are adapted from corresponding Event-B proof obligations. We use the same

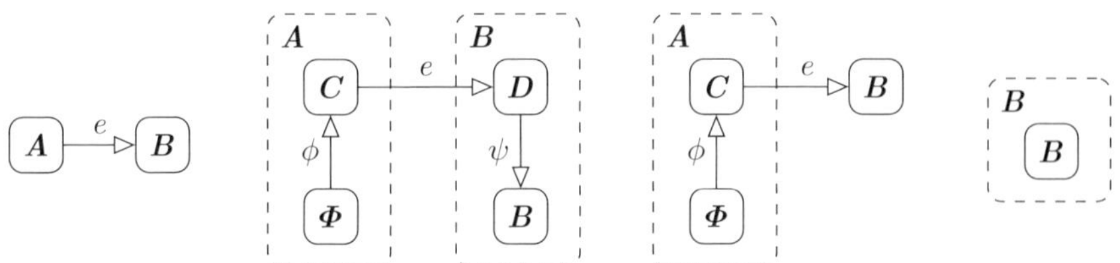

(a) State machine (b) Refinement of $\boldsymbol{A}$ and $\boldsymbol{B}$ (c) Refinement of $\boldsymbol{A}$ (d) Reuse of $\boldsymbol{B}$

Fig. 2. Refinement diagrams

diagrams to describe both refinement methods. Edges of concrete models may be labelled with events e occurring already in the abstract model: the concrete event $e = \mathsf{any}\ q\ \mathsf{when}\ h\ \mathsf{then}\ y := b$ refines the abstract event $e = \mathsf{any}\ p\ \mathsf{when}\ g\ \mathsf{then}\ x := a$. For instance, the proof obligation for the edge labelled e in Fig. 2(b) is: $\boldsymbol{C} \wedge h \wedge W \Rightarrow g \wedge \boldsymbol{D}[x, y := a, b]$, where W is a predicate, called *witness*, that relates the concrete parameters q to the abstract parameters p. The existence of suitable parameters q must be proved: $\boldsymbol{C} \wedge h \Rightarrow (\exists q \cdot W)$. A refinement may also introduce a new name f for a refined event e by stating the abstract name in brackets behind the new concrete name: $f\ (e)$. Concrete edges otherwise labelled with events that do not occur in the abstract model are said to be *new*. New events, e.g., ϕ in Fig. 2(b), must refine *skip*, the event that is always enabled and does not change the state. For $\phi = \mathsf{any}\ q\ \mathsf{when}\ h\ \mathsf{then}\ y := b$ we have to prove: $\boldsymbol{\Phi} \wedge h \Rightarrow \boldsymbol{C}[y := b]$. For a convergent loop edge $\boxed{A}$ e where $e = \mathsf{any}\ p\ \mathsf{when}\ g\ \mathsf{then}\ x := a$ we have to provide a *variant* u and prove $\boldsymbol{A} \wedge g \Rightarrow u \geq 0$ and $\boldsymbol{A} \wedge g \Rightarrow u[x := a] < u$, or the corresponding proof obligation for a refinement of e.[5] While e has not been proved convergent, we have to show for refinements $\mathsf{any}\ q\ \mathsf{when}\ h\ \mathsf{then}\ y := b$ of e that they do not "disturb" new convergent edges introduced in a refinement of $\boldsymbol{A}$ or e. We have to prove: $\boldsymbol{F} \wedge h \Rightarrow u \geq 0$ and $\boldsymbol{F} \wedge h \Rightarrow u[x := a] \leq u$ where $\boldsymbol{F}$ is a node introduced in a refinement of $\boldsymbol{A}$ or e, and u the variant of some other convergent event.

In Fig. 2(c) only (super) node $\boldsymbol{A}$ looks affected by the refinement. However, in a refinement all nodes are replaced. The outgoing edge labelled e is simply connected to node $\boldsymbol{B}$. The node $\boldsymbol{B}$ shown in the figure is considered a node of the concrete model. We can think of it as a node $\boldsymbol{B}$ inside a super node $\boldsymbol{B}$ (see Fig. 2(d)) that is not shown. Assertions in refinements are always added to concrete nodes. This approach avoids adding assertions accidentally to many nodes when data-refining. The super nodes in refinement diagrams are also used

[5] We also allow finite set as variants but do not provide proof obligations here. See [2].

to indicate containment of assertions among concrete nodes. For instance, an assertion added to $\boldsymbol{B}$ in Fig. 2(b) is also added to $\boldsymbol{D}$ as indicated by the super node labelled $\boldsymbol{B}$. Edges in refinement diagrams can only connect concrete nodes. Everything not shown in a refinement diagram stays structurally unchanged.

Node refinement. Node refinement replaces a node with a super-node, hence an assertion with a collection of more precise assertions. The new nodes enable new edges to be added and old edges to be replicated (for instance, elaborating non-deterministic choices present in events, in the diagram). New edges may be added between nodes inside a (refined) super-node and must not exit or enter that super-node. Edges of the abstract state-machine must be preserved: their refinements must connect the corresponding (refined) super-nodes. A loop edge, having the same node for both its source and its target, is refined by a transition between two nodes inside the corresponding refined super-node.

Edge refinement. Edge refinement replaces an edge with a state machine that is to be inserted between the source and the target of the edge. State machines occurring in edge refinements must have at most one initial node where the execution of the modelled algorithm would start. Nodes occurring in state machines introduced by edge refinements may have at most one edge entering from other nodes. But they may have several loops. More complex diagrams can be constructed using super nodes and anonymous edges. The constructed diagrams correspond closely to proof outlines as discussed in [4].

4 Development of a Sequential Algorithm

In [2] it is shown how Event-B can be used for the development of sequential algorithms. The proof method is well-suited for this purpose, providing strong support for finding invariants and carrying complex termination proofs. Recently, we argued [8] that some structuring facilities would benefit the method in terms of proof methodology and potential scaling. State machines could solve some of the issues involved. Developing a sequential algorithm we present the two approaches to state machine refinement side by side. Node and edge refinement provide two different views on the same development with the same proofs, documenting and explaining different aspects of the involved refinement steps. We do not present the proof obligations and proofs in full. It is rather intricate. Instead, we want to convey that using the two refinement techniques, finding the proof and presenting it are made much easier. The associated proof obligations have been produced by imitating the notation in Event-B. That is, we have used Rodin tool [3] to carry out the proofs but the translation into Event-B has been manual.

Fig. 3 gives a brief overview of the development. Along the sequence of (refined) models M1 to M7 a number of variables modelling the state of the algorithm are introduced and removed. The table provides, for each model, a short description of its purpose and mentions the variant used for termination proofs (if any).

model	introduced	removed	description	variant
M0	a		specification of sorting	
M1	b, t, m, n		introduction of outer loop and stack	
M2	C		lexicographic convergence of outer loop	C
M3		C	lexicographic convergence of outer loop	t
M4	L, R, π		introduction of inner loop	$R - L$
M5	u, v		implementation of inner loop	$(v - u) + 1$
M6	s, l, o, p, q	t, m, n	new representation of stack	
M7	h		replacement of pivot index by pivot value	

Fig. 3. Overview of the development

M0. Fig. 4 shows the specification of the sorting algorithm consisting of a state machine, an assertion $a \in D \to \mathbb{Z}$ specified to hold at $\boldsymbol{A}$, and an event *sort* that specifies sorting of array a using a permutation p. Initially, we assert that a is

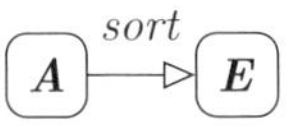

$\boldsymbol{A} \xrightarrow{sort} \boldsymbol{E}$

$$
\begin{aligned}
sort = \ & \textsf{any } p \textsf{ when} \\
& \quad p \in P \\
& \quad \forall x, y \cdot x \in D \wedge y \in D \wedge x \le y \Rightarrow (a \circ p)(x) \le (a \circ p)(y) \\
& \textsf{then} \\
& \quad a := a \circ p
\end{aligned}
$$

$@\boldsymbol{A} \quad a \in D \to \mathbb{Z}$

Fig. 4. Specification of a sorting algorithm

an array with domain D and range $\mathbb{Z}$. There is nothing to prove because no assertion has been specified at $\boldsymbol{E}$. Our aim is to construct a state machine that implements iterative Quicksort based on [4] and [10].

M1. Fig. 5 shows the first node and edge refinement steps. Although the two diagrams look identical they describe different viewpoints of the same proof. Diagram 5(a) describes how the abstract node $\boldsymbol{A}$ can be replaced by a super node, indicating the internal structure of the super node and how the concrete edge *sort* is to be connected to neighbours of the super node. Diagram 5(b) describes how the abstract edge can be replaced by the four edges *init*, *part*, *drop* and *sort*. The super-state node in this diagram only indicates that at $\boldsymbol{I}$ all assertions of $\boldsymbol{A}$ hold. Event *init* sets up the variables for the loop. Event *part* specifies partitioning of the section $m(t) \mathinner{..} n(t)$ of the array b containing at least two elements described by the top of the stack. The sub-sections $m(t) \mathinner{..} r$ and $l \mathinner{..} n(t)$ are stored on the stack and the corresponding partitioning is stored in b,

$$
\begin{aligned}
part = \ & \textsf{any } p\ l\ r\ f \textsf{ when} \\
& \quad t > 0 \wedge m(t) < n(t) \wedge f \in m(t) \mathinner{..} n(t) \wedge p \in P \wedge l > r \wedge \ldots \\
& \quad \forall x \cdot x \in (b \circ p)[m(t) \mathinner{..} l{-}1] \Rightarrow x \le b(f) \\
& \quad \forall x \cdot x \in (b \circ p)[r{+}1 \mathinner{..} n(t)] \Rightarrow b(f) \le x \\
& \textsf{then} \\
& \quad b, m, n, t := b \circ p, m \mathbin{\lhd\!\!-} \{t{+}1 \mapsto l\}, n \mathbin{\lhd\!\!-} \{t \mapsto r, t{+}1 \mapsto n(t)\}, t{+}1\ .
\end{aligned}
$$

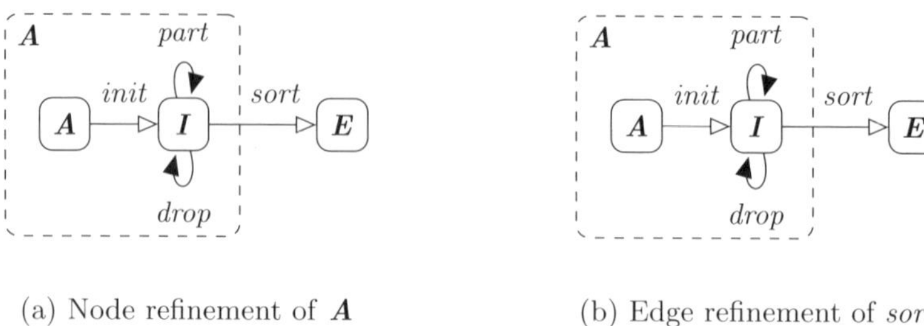

(a) Node refinement of $\boldsymbol{A}$ (b) Edge refinement of *sort*

Fig. 5. First refinement

Event *drop* removes intervals from the stack that contain at most one element. The abstract event *sort* of Fig. 4 is refined by the concrete event *sort* of Fig. 5 (as indicated by the reuse of the name), $sort = \mathsf{when}\ t \leq 0\ \mathsf{then}\ a := b$. We have to prove this: using $p \in P \wedge b = a \circ p$ as a witness for the abstract parameter p —its existence is guaranteed by $\boldsymbol{I}$ below—, the invariant and concrete guard $\boldsymbol{I} \wedge t \leq 0$ imply the guard of the corresponding abstract event *sort* and the equality $a = b$ which establishes the simulation by the abstract event's action $a := a \circ p$. Among other assertions $\boldsymbol{I}$ contains the following:

$$
\begin{array}{ll}
@\boldsymbol{I} & t \geq 0 \wedge n(0) = 0 \wedge (\exists q \cdot q \in P \wedge b = a \circ q) \wedge \ldots \\
& \forall x, y \cdot x \in D \wedge y \in n(t){+}1 \,..\, N \wedge x \leq y \Rightarrow b(x) \leq b(y) \ .
\end{array}
$$

We omit the proofs that the new events *init*, *part* and *drop* refine *skip*. During those proofs more assertions would be added to node $\boldsymbol{I}$ incrementally [3].

M2 and M3. In refinement step M2 convergence of event *part* is proved and convergence of event *drop* in refinement step M3, establishing a lexicographic variant (see [2]). We introduce a variable C to express the variant, adding $C := 0 \,..\, N{+}1 \times 0 \,..\, N{+}1$ to the action of event *init* and $C := C \setminus ((0 \,..\, m(t) \times r{+}1 \,..\, N{+}1) \cup (0 \,..\, l{-}1 \times n(t) \,..\, N{+}1))$ to the action of event *part*. We add some assertions to the node $\boldsymbol{I}$:

$$
\begin{array}{ll}
@\boldsymbol{I} & C \in 0 \,..\, N{+}1 \leftrightarrow 0 \,..\, N{+}1 \\
& \forall i \cdot i \in 1 \,..\, t \Rightarrow m(i) \mapsto n(i) \in C \\
& \forall x, y \cdot x \mapsto y \in C \wedge y \leq N \Rightarrow (\forall v \cdot v \in x{+}1 \,..\, y{+}1 \Rightarrow v \mapsto y \in C) \\
& \forall x, y \cdot x \mapsto y \in C \wedge x \geq 1 \Rightarrow (\forall w \cdot w \in x{-}1 \,..\, y{-}1 \Rightarrow x \mapsto w \in C) \ .
\end{array}
$$

Using C as a variant we can prove that *part* is convergent. Event *drop* obviously does not change C. Compared to direct verification (e.g. [4]) Event-B refinement offers the advantage of introducing and removing auxiliary variables whenever it appears convenient. Compared to program refinement [13] it offers more flexibility with complex refinement steps. Convergence of *drop* can be verified with the variant t, the height of the stack. The first component of the lexicographical variant is a set, the second a number. The chosen proof method frees us from having to construct the lexicographical variant explicitly; or rather, the construction is automated.

M4. We introduce a nested loop to compute the partitioning. In this refinement step the outer loop is introduced, the inner loops in the next step. As this refinement concerns inner nodes, the node refinement diagram becomes more complicated than the edge refinement diagram. The reason for this is that node refinement diagrams can potentially express more complex refinements. An edge refinement replaces always one edge. Node refinements can replace several edges in one go. However, the node refinement diagram contains all elements that are involved in the proof. In this sense the edge refinement diagram is less complete. We have to show that *init* establishes the concrete invariant ***I***. The edge *sort* in Fig. 6(a) is redundant: neither event *sort* nor node ***E*** are changed, and ***I*** may only be stronger than its abstract counterpart. Still, both diagrams represent the same proof.

Note the difference of how loops are refined in node and edge refinement diagrams. Nodes are uniquely identifiable in node refinement diagrams whereas in edge refinement diagrams only edges need to be uniquely identifiable. An edge refinement has start and final nodes that are connected to the start and final node of the refined edge. If a loop is edge-refined, the concerned node is replicated in the refined diagram. E.g., Fig. 6(b) has two copies of node ***I***. The two copies do not denote the same node. If a loop is node-refined, the concerned node is not replicated. Instead, the loop remains in the diagram either as a loop or as a cycle involving several nodes.

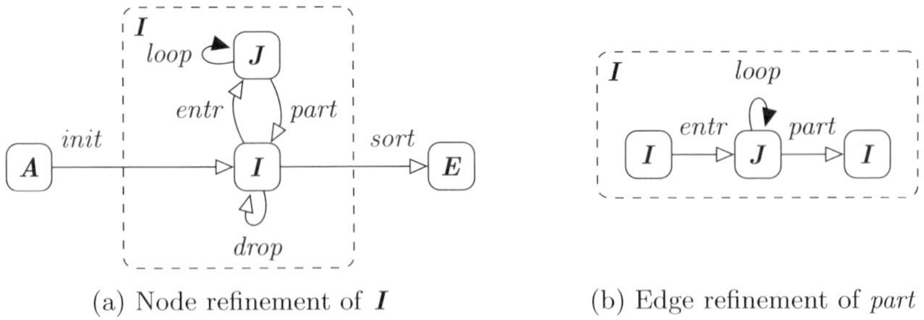

(a) Node refinement of ***I*** (b) Edge refinement of *part*

Fig. 6. Fourth refinement

The node ***J*** specifies the loop invariant. It is established initially by event *entr*, where $entr = \textsf{when}\ t > 0\ \textsf{then}\ c, L, R, \pi := b, m(t), n(t), (m(t)+n(t)) \div 2$. At ***J*** all assertions of ***I*** hold plus the following:

$$@\boldsymbol{J}\quad t > 0 \wedge m(t) < n(t) \wedge \pi \in m(t) \mathinner{..} n(t) \wedge \ldots$$
$$L > R+1 \Rightarrow m(t) < L \wedge R < n(t)$$

Similarly to the first refinement step these assertions are mostly determined by the shape of the guard and action of the abstract event *part* of M1. This is driven by the proof obligations for the refinement of *part*, where $part = \textsf{when}\ L > R\ \textsf{then}\ b, m, n, t := c, m \Leftarrow \{t+1 \mapsto L\}, n \Leftarrow \{t \mapsto R, t+1 \mapsto n(t)\}, t+1$.[6] However,

[6] With appropriate witnesses for the abstract parameters: $f = \pi$ and so on.

during the development, assertions were also propagated bottom up. In refinement M5 the assertions that already hold at $\boldsymbol{J}$ in m4 are essential for refinement proofs of the loop body. Note that the last three assertions at $\boldsymbol{J}$ would be difficult to guess in a top down manner. They were propagated upwards from the refinement proofs of events *swap* and *done* of M5. The guard of event *loop* has subsequently been chosen such that it preserves these assertions:

$$
\begin{array}{ll}
loop = \textsf{any}\ p\ l\ r\ \textsf{when} & \\
\quad L \leq R \wedge p \in P \wedge \ldots & \\
\quad l > r{+}1 \Rightarrow (m(t) < l \wedge r < n(t)) & \\
\textsf{then} & \\
\quad c, L, R := c \circ p, l, r &
\end{array}
$$

The redundancy between *loop* and $\boldsymbol{J}$ is intentional; the assertions that hold at $\boldsymbol{J}$ are established dynamically by choosing appropriate parameters p, l and r nondeterministically. Often the construction is guided by invariant preservation proofs. The same principle is already present in the B-Method [1]: it emphasises assertions and requires statement of suitable events respecting the assertions.

M5. In this refinement the body of the inner loop is implemented. It demonstrates how nested assertions are used in more complex steps of a refinement proof. In refinements M6 and M7 we will show two more refinements of the model that has now become quite complex. The degree of difficulty does not increase as the model grows in complexity. This was the main motivation that started this work on top of Event-B. We preserve the strengths of Event-B: the emphasis on reasoning, formal proof, and incremental modelling [8]. The key to incremental modelling in Event-B is the generation of fine grained proof obligations exploiting proof-oriented facts specified in formal models. Fig. 7(a) shows

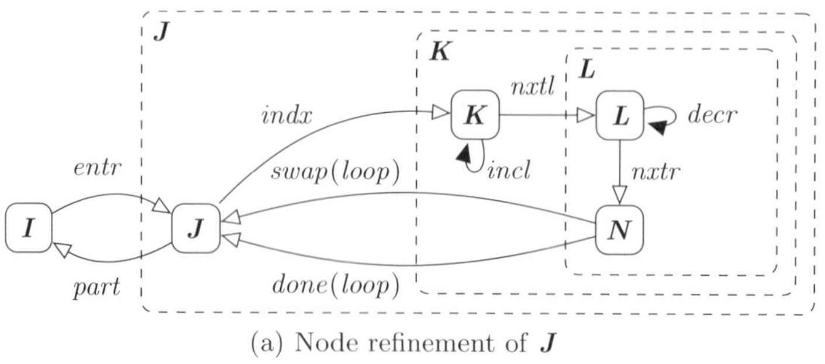

(a) Node refinement of $\boldsymbol{J}$

Fig. 7. Fifth refinement

the node refinement where $\boldsymbol{J}$ is refined and two nested super nodes $\boldsymbol{K}$,

$$@\boldsymbol{K} \quad L \leq R \wedge u \leq v{+}1 \wedge \ldots$$

and $\boldsymbol{L}$, with $@\boldsymbol{L}\ c(u) \geq b(\pi)$, are introduced. So node $\boldsymbol{N}$, with $@\boldsymbol{N}\ b(\pi) \geq c(v)$, contains all assertions of $\boldsymbol{I}$, $\boldsymbol{J}$, $\boldsymbol{K}$ and $\boldsymbol{L}$. Following the nesting the structure could be introduced step-wise but we find that the larger step that we chose is not difficult to prove. Nothing would be gained by using additional refinement steps. In our experience the liberty in choosing the granularity of refinement steps makes it easier to produce the proof for a whole development. The mixture of program verification and step-wise refinement techniques supports the user in choosing appropriate abstractions. Supporting this mixture is not common in verification or refinement methods. The events *done*, with $done = \mathsf{when}\ u > v\ \mathsf{then}\ L, R := u, v$, and *swap*, with $swap = \mathsf{when}\ u \leq v\ \mathsf{then}\ c, L, R := c \Leftarrow \{u \mapsto c(v), v \mapsto c(u)\}, u{+}1, v{-}1$, refine the abstract event *loop* as indicated by writing the name of the abstract event name in brackets behind the concrete event names.

Fig. 7(b) shows the refinement as an edge refinement. It emphasises more how we would read the body of a loop as a sequence of commands. The structure of the inside of the loop is more obvious than in node refinement. In the corresponding node refinement one has to look more closely to identify the relevant part. The

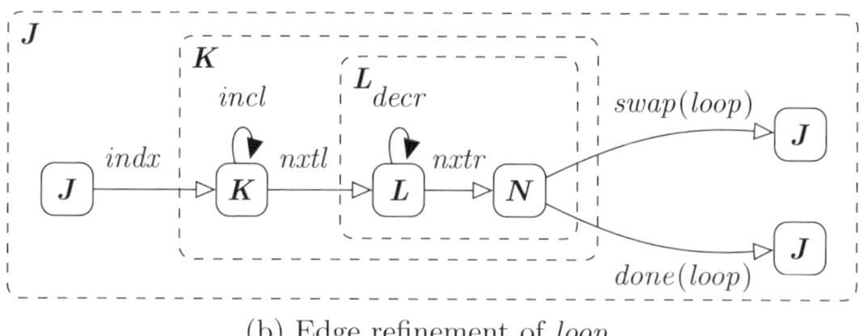

(b) Edge refinement of *loop*

Fig. 7. Fifth refinement

two events *done* and *swap* specify different values for the witnesses of the abstract parameters (of event *loop*). For example, *done* specifies $p = D \lhd id$ and *swap* specifies $p = (D \lhd id) \Leftarrow \{u \mapsto v, v \mapsto u\}$ giving a clue about how *loop* is implemented. Witnesses are a versatile feature of Event-B being applicable to verification techniques besides proof [9].

M6. In the sixth refinement the two nodes $\boldsymbol{I}$ and $\boldsymbol{J}$ are refined simultaneously demonstrating how sub-nodes of the refined nodes are to be connected. This is a data-refinement replacing the pointer to the top of the stack t by a new pointer s such that $t = s{+}1$, storing the top of the stack $m(t)$ and $n(t)$ in dedicated variables p and q, and finally, replacing the stack m and n by the "smaller" stack l and o. In the edge refinement diagram (Fig. 8(b)) we have collected two simultaneous edge refinements. The corresponding two simultaneous node refinements are shown in Fig. 8(a). In the edge refinement diagram we have to draw an additional super node —the inner super node $\boldsymbol{I}$— and connect it using anonymous edges. This is necessary because of restrictions on the shape of edge refinement diagrams that are imposed in order to be able to map such diagrams to customary control structures.

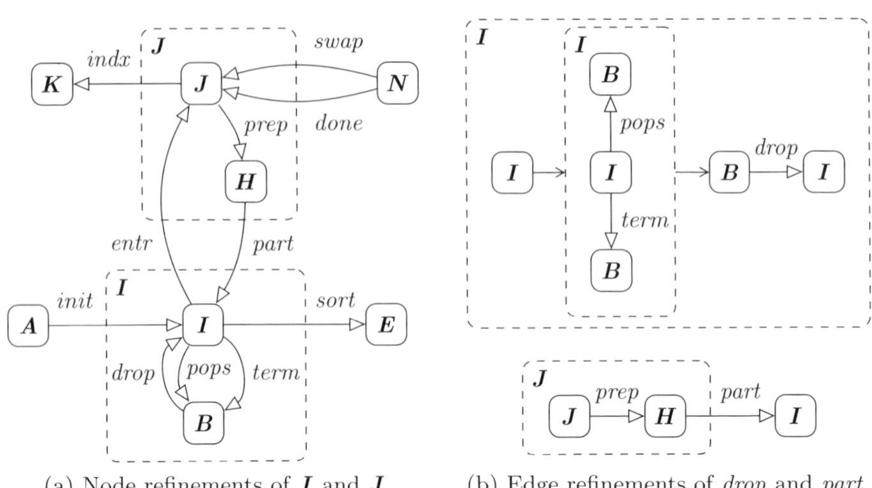

(a) Node refinements of ***I*** and ***J*** (b) Edge refinements of *drop* and *part*

Fig. 8. Sixth refinement

M7. The last refinement step introduces a new variable h to replace $b(\pi)$ in all event guards. In other words we add $h = b(\pi)$ to the nodes $\boldsymbol{J}$, $\boldsymbol{K}$, $\boldsymbol{L}$ and $\boldsymbol{N}$. The new event *setp* contains the assignment $h := b(\pi)$. Note how new events in the

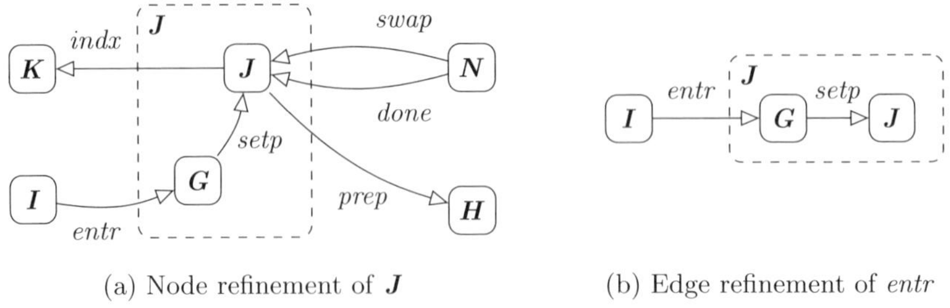

(a) Node refinement of ***J*** (b) Edge refinement of *entr*

Fig. 9. Seventh refinement

refinement diagrams are indicated by the nesting of the (super) nodes; compare Fig. 8 and Fig. 9 in this respect.

Closing remarks. We can carry out a series of data refinements to remove "synonyms" of variables. For instance, a, b and c by a variable h. This does not affect the structure of the diagrams. No further diagrams need to be drawn for these refinements.

We think the diagrams are easy to understand and manipulate. With their help, complex refinement steps using the Event-B refinement method are possible that would not be feasible in Event-B itself. Using multiple refinement steps in Event-B does not always solve the problem. This is particularly important because in Event-B the ordering of the refinement steps influences the shape of the developed program. Using state machines its shape is specified and refinement is only concerned with structuring a complex correctness proof.

5 Design of a Controller

The edge refinement diagrams in Section 4 are simpler than the corresponding node diagrams. The developed algorithmic structure is more discernible. Edge refinement was developed for this purpose and is therefore more specialised towards algorithm development than node refinement. This specialisation is achieved by imposing greater restrictions on the refinements that can be made. Lacking these restrictions, node refinement allows more flexibility in refinements. Node refinement is suited for the modelling and refinement of systems level models. It was developed for this purpose. In this section, we demonstrate the greater generality of node refinement by means of a model of a simple controller system which has mechanisms for responding and recovering from faults. The controller could not be developed using edge refinement. Although this example is simple and somewhat manufactured, it is intuitive and sufficient to illustrate the greater generality of node refinement. One can easily imagine that the model can be expanded in later refinements with similar patterns that would be impossible with edge refinement. Usually, there is a collection of informal requirements describing possible behaviours on which formal system modelling is based. Feedback from the formal model can then be used to improve the requirements: pointing to specification gaps and contradictions. However, for the present purpose we are not concerned with discussing requirements and do not refer to them explicitly. We also do not go into detail concerning the assertions and events that occur in the model.

The controller model. The initial abstract model of the controller (see Fig. 10) has three states: the power is off "***U***"; the power is on "***P***"; the power is on but the controlled is in a fault state "***F***". An edge labelled *pwr* models the power

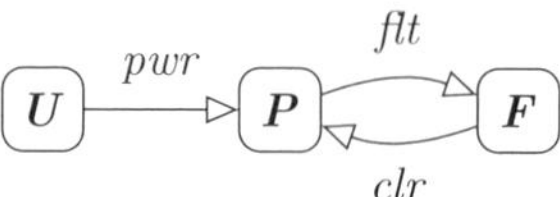

Fig. 10. Abstract controller model

being switched on and while the power is switched on, faults may occur *flt* and are subsequently cleared *clr*.

Firstly, the fault state "***F***" is refined to distinguish two sub-categories of fault (see Fig. 11(a)), ones that can be recovered from "***R***", and ones that require a reset "***E***". This enables the edge *flt* to be refined by spitting it into two edges *uerr* and *rerr* representing the two categories of fault. Similarly, *clr* is refined into *reset* and *recover* originating from their respective fault categories. Recovery may be unsuccessful resulting in a recoverable fault becoming transmuted into a resettable one by edge *rfail*.

The powered state "***P***" is then refined to distinguish two sub-modes of operation (see Fig. 11(b)). The control is switched off "***X***", and the control is switched on "***O***". Edges *on* and *off* form a loop allowing power to be cycled. This enables us to refine edges *uerr*, *reset*, *rerr* and *recover* so that recoverable errors originate and recover to the powered sub-state, "***O***", while unrecoverable ones originate and reset to the unpowered sub-state, "***X***".

The behaviour of the controller while being in one of the states ***P*** or ***F*** is more general than the patterns arrived at by edge refinement. If we were to implement a control program, we would introduce a dedicated variable to model the current operational state of the controller. This would obfuscate the model hiding the control structure in the program text. If we do not insist on program structure, state machines can concisely and clearly capture the behaviour.

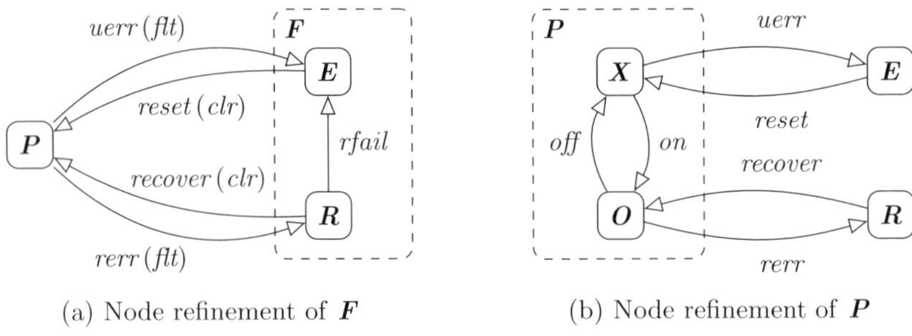

(a) Node refinement of ***F***

(b) Node refinement of ***P***

Fig. 11. Refinements of the controller model

The refinement of node ***F*** splits the incoming and outgoing edges into cases that are revealed by the node refinement. This would not be possible using edge refinement.

The refinement of node ***P*** introduces a cycle between the states ***X*** and ***O***. If this was introduced via edge refinement it would require a loop at ***P*** in the abstraction. This would require prediction of later refinements in the abstract model which would be detrimental to its objective. The aim of abstract system modelling is to simplify the model in order to concentrate on important properties. Abstract models could become unnecessarily complex if stricter rules were imposed.

Allowing more general diagrams to be constructed supports forms of reasoning that would be difficult to achieve using the simpler algorithmic diagrams enforced by edge refinement. For instance, we may want to argue whether edge *rfail* is reasonable: is it reasonable for a supposedly recoverable error to result in a reset of the controller. The explicit modelling of the control states makes it possible to discuss such questions. This would not be possible if the control state was encoded by a program variable.

A combined refinement method. Using node refinement we can deal with more general architectural requirements. Edge refinement on the other hand provides only algorithmic structures that can be safely mapped on to (sequential) programs. A combined method would have the strengths of both. One could, for instance, develop the architecture of the controller using node refinement and implement the code at the edges using edge refinement. We have seen in Section 3 that the proof obligations of the methods could be easily mixed. We could simply consider every edge refinement to be a stylised node refinement allowing them to be mixed freely. Edge refinement can also be used to prove properties of deadlock-freedom [7]. Node refinement does not support this. The main difficulties are to achieve a clear refinement method and to avoid large complex proof obligations. Our next aim is to investigate deadlock-freedom properties of node refinement.

6 Conclusion

We have demonstrated the use of state machines for the formalisation of complex models based on Event-B. We have discussed two approaches to refinement that suggest themselves when modelling with state machines: node refinement and edge refinement. We have defined the two notions of refinement (based on Event-B refinement). Node and edge refinement have similar proof obligations. We have argued that, for the development of programs, they can be seen as providing two views of the same proof of correctness and refinement. However, node refinement is more general. It has been conceived for system-level modelling and it is not so obvious how to develop programs by this means alone. Edge refinement on the other hand has been conceived for program development, but is too restrictive to be used for system modelling. Combined use of both can address a large class of systems using node refinement for architectural modelling aspects and edge refinement for algorithmic aspects. We believe the two notions of refinement could be unified. However, care has to be taken to preserve the strong support of the two modelling aspects: architecture and algorithms. In this article we have not discussed deadlock-freedom. For edge refinement it is obvious how properties of deadlock-freedom can be proved. For node refinement it is less clear how this can be done. We will still be looking for a method that is easy to apply. A unified method could transfer the concept of deadlock-freedom as dealt with by edge refinement to node refinement.

References

1. Abrial, J.-R.: The B-Book: Assigning Programs to Meanings. In: CUP (1996)
2. Abrial, J.-R.: Modeling in Event-B: System and Software Engineering. In: CUP (2010)
3. Abrial, J.-R., Butler, M.J., Hallerstede, S., Hoang, T.S., Mehta, F., Voisin, L.: Rodin: an open toolset for modelling and reasoning in Event-B. STTT 12(6), 447–466 (2010)

4. Apt, K.R., de Boer, F.S., Olderog, E.-R.: Verification of Sequential and Concurrent Programs. Springer, Heidelberg (2009)
5. Back, R.-J.: Invariant based programming: basic approach and teaching experiences. Formal Asp. Comput. 21(3), 227–244 (2009)
6. Fathabadi, A.S., Butler, M.: Applying Event-B Atomicity Decomposition to a Multi Media Protocol. In: de Boer, F.S., Bonsangue, M.M., Hallerstede, S., Leuschel, M. (eds.) FMCO 2009. LNCS, vol. 6286, pp. 89–104. Springer, Heidelberg (2010)
7. Hallerstede, S.: Structured Event-B Models and Proofs. In: Frappier, M., Glässer, U., Khurshid, S., Laleau, R., Reeves, S. (eds.) ABZ 2010. LNCS, vol. 5977, pp. 273–286. Springer, Heidelberg (2010)
8. Hallerstede, S., Leuschel, M.: Experiments in Program Verification using Event-B. In: Formal Asp. Comput. (to appear, 2011)
9. Hallerstede, S., Leuschel, M., Plagge, D.: Refinement-Animation for Event-B — Towards a Method of Validation. In: Frappier, M., Glässer, U., Khurshid, S., Laleau, R., Reeves, S. (eds.) ABZ 2010. LNCS, vol. 5977, pp. 287–301. Springer, Heidelberg (2010)
10. Kaldewaij, A.: Programming: The Derivation of Algorithms. Prentice-Hall, Englewood Cliffs (1990)
11. Knapp, A., Merz, S., Wirsing, M.: Refining Mobile UML State Machines. In: Rattray, C., Maharaj, S., Shankland, C. (eds.) AMAST 2004. LNCS, vol. 3116, pp. 274–288. Springer, Heidelberg (2004)
12. Lano, K., Clark, D.: Semantics and Refinement of Behavior State Machines. In: Filipe, J., Cordeiro, J. (eds.) Enterprise Information Systems. LNBIP, vol. 19, pp. 42–49. Springer, Heidelberg (2009)
13. Morgan, C.C.: Programming from Specifications, 2nd edn. Prentice-Hall, Englewood Cliffs (1994)
14. Said, M.Y., Butler, M.J., Snook, C.F.: Language and tool support for class and state machine refinement in UML-B. In: Cavalcanti, A., Dams, D.R. (eds.) FM 2009. LNCS, vol. 5850, pp. 579–595. Springer, Heidelberg (2009)
15. Simons, A.J.H.: A theory of regression testing for behaviourally compatible object types. Softw. Test, Verif. Reliab. 16(3), 133–156 (2006)
16. Snook, C., Waldén, M.: Refinement of statemachines using event B semantics. In: Julliand, J., Kouchnarenko, O. (eds.) B 2007. LNCS, vol. 4355, pp. 171–185. Springer, Heidelberg (2006)
17. Snook, C.F., Butler, M.J.: UML-B: Formal modeling and design aided by UML. ACM Trans. Softw. Eng. Methodol. 15(1), 92–122 (2006)
18. Snook, C.: Exploring the Barriers to Formal Specification. PhD thesis, Electronics and Computer Science, University of Southampton (2002)
19. Wirth, N.: Program development by stepwise refinement. CACM 14(4), 221–227 (1971)

Some Event-B Specific Symbols

$a \circ p$ denotes composition of a and b: $x \mapsto y \in a \circ p \Leftrightarrow (\exists z \cdot x \mapsto z \in p \land z \mapsto y \in a)$.
$t \lhd r$ denotes domain restriction of r by t: $x \mapsto y \in t \lhd r \Leftrightarrow x \in t \land x \mapsto y \in r$.
$t \mathbin{⩤} r$ denotes domain subtraction of r by t: $x \mapsto y \in t \mathbin{⩤} r \Leftrightarrow x \notin t \land x \mapsto y \in r$.
$s \mathbin{\lhd\!\!\!+} r$ denotes relational override of s by r: $s \mathbin{\lhd\!\!\!+} r \Leftrightarrow (\mathrm{dom}(r) \lhd s) \cup r$.

Managing Complexity through Abstraction: A Refinement-Based Approach to Formalize Instruction Set Architectures

Fangfang Yuan[1,⋆], Stephen Wright[1,⋆⋆], and Kerstin Eder[1] and David May[2]

[1] Computer Science Department, University of Bristol, Bristol BS8 1UB
{fangfang.yuan,stephen.wright,kerstin.eder}@bristol.ac.uk
[2] XMOS Ltd, Venturers House, King St, Bristol BS1 4PB
dave@xmos.com

Abstract. Verifying the functional correctness of a processor requires a sound and complete specification of its Instruction Set Architecture (ISA). Current industrial practice is to describe a processor's ISA informally using natural language often with added semi-formal notation to capture the functional intent of the instructions. This leaves scope for errors and inconsistencies. In this paper we present a method to specify, design and construct sound and complete ISAs by stepwise refinement and formal proof using the formal method Event-B. We discuss how the automatically generated Proof Obligations help to ensure self-consistency of the formal ISA model, and how desirable properties of ISAs can be enforced within this modeling framework. We have developed a generic ISA modeling template in Event-B to facilitate reuse. The key value of reusing such a template is increased model integrity. Our method is now being used to formalize the ISA of the XMOS XCore processor with the aim to guarantee that the documentation of the XCore matches the silicon and the silicon matches the architectural intent.

1 Introduction

The Instruction Set Architecture (ISA) is the part of a computer's architecture visible to programmers. It specifies the basic data types, all instructions, internal storage, addressing modes, memory architecture and interrupt/exception handling. Programmers use the ISA as a reference manual for coding. Design engineers use it as a reference for implementation. Processor verification heavily relies on the ISA [16] because the ISA provides the functional reference specification against which the processor's implementation is verified.

Current industrial practice is to describe a processor's ISA informally using natural language often with added semi-formal notation to capture the functional intent of the instructions. This leaves scope for errors and inconsistencies.

⋆ Funded in part by EPSRC grant EP/E001556/1 "Reassessing Processor Design Assumptions in Cryptography".

⋆⋆ Funded by a one year EPSRC Knowledge Transfer Secondment running since October 2010 under grant EP/H500316/1 and kindly hosted by XMOS Ltd.

S. Qin and Z. Qiu (Eds.): ICFEM 2011, LNCS 6991, pp. 585–600, 2011.

Moreover, in most cases these "specification" documents, often referred to as *Architecture Reference Manuals*, do not have any formal relationship to the actual design nor to the product. One of the recognized challenges in the 2009 issue of the International Technology Roadmap for Semiconductors [1] is *Specification for verifiability*: *"How to specify the desired behavior of a design is a continuing challenge in design verification. ... For instance, there is a need for automatic ways to check the self-consistency of a specification document, so that different specifications don't state conflicting requirements. In addition, specific training is needed for designers to use these notations and to be able to develop formal specifications consistently."*

We present a novel formal modeling method that addresses this challenge in the context of specifying, designing and constructing instruction sets using Event-B [3]. The fundamental principles underlying this method are rigorous application of stepwise formal refinement combined with mathematical proof. The refinement process supports incremental construction of the entire ISA from a simple state machine by repeatedly splitting the instruction set into instruction classes that have common behavior until individual instructions are reached at the bottom level of the model. This refinement strategy promotes reasoning about the model as it is being developed and helps engineers understand the intent of the ISA as a whole as opposed to specifying each instruction in isolation.

Mathematical proof serves three purposes during model construction. One is establishing self-consistency of the formal model. The second is ensuring that each refinement step is valid. Both are enforced in Event-B by default through the generation of Proof Obligations (POs). The third is to demonstrate desirable properties of the model. These can be defined explicitly during modeling through the introduction of invariants and theorems. In the context of ISAs it is, for example, important to ensure that the ISA is complete in terms of covering all possible changes to the processor state. Another desirable property for an ISA may be determinism, *i.e.* the ISA defines exactly one change to the processor state for each input condition. POs are automatically generated to ensure the model satisfies these domain specific properties.

To facilitate uptake of our modeling method we have developed a generic template in Event-B ready to use with the Rodin tool set [4]. The template has been designed to support the ISA development process and is based on the generalization of three ISA models of increasing complexity; from an academic "toy" ISA called MIDAS [24], via the more elaborate ISA of the performance-optimized cryptographic processor CRISP [19] to the ISA of the XMOS XCore processor [17], a fully fledged industrial processor design. Currently, the XCore ISA model is being completed. The template is structured into several abstraction layers, each addressing a set of fundamental design options available for the respective instruction class. The template is generic in that it is parametrized and thus offers design alternatives for later instantiation. We call these alternatives *choice points* because they allow the model to be tailored to a specific ISA or an ISA family. Each refinement step is intentionally kept small enough to remain comprehensible.

While it is difficult to provide precise data on development time with and without using the generic template, an increase in modeling productivity is indicated by the fact that ISAs of increasing numbers of instructions, from ~30 for MIDAS via ~50 for CRISP to ~170 for the XCore, have been (or are being) modeled each within roughly one year of development effort. The key value of such a generic template is more than just the productivity gain during modeling. Re-using this template ensures increased model integrity and results in more reliable and trustworthy models. This gives design and verification engineers a higher degree of confidence in the correctness of the formal model that is used as top-level specification during verification.

2 Event-B and the Rodin Development Platform

Event-B [3] is a formal method that combines mathematical techniques, set theory and first-order logic for the purpose of building and analyzing models of complex systems. Event-B is model-based. The stored state within a system is represented by globally scoped state variables. All modifications to this state are defined by atomic *events*, consisting of *actions* (the description of the state modifications) and *guards* (the conditions under which the actions may occur). Set membership statements, fundamentally derived from integers, Booleans, or completely abstract sets, provide variable type information. In our Event-B ISA models, all the actions of a single instruction's execution are encapsulated within a single event, deliberately abstracting any ordering performed by an actual implementation. Thus the model's independence from any particular implementation is preserved.

An important feature of Event-B is refinement. Abstract model variables may be refined to one or more concrete variables. The relationship between abstract and concrete versions of a variable is stated by a gluing invariant. Thus any events containing refined variables must also be refined in the concrete version of the model in order to maintain the relationship stated in the gluing invariant. Other event refinements are possible: guards may be restated or strengthened, that is replaced by a logical sub-set of the abstract guard. Events may be split during refinement into two or more concrete events, in which the guards and actions of each must be valid refinements of the abstract version. Refinement allows systems to be described at different levels of abstraction which is key to our approach to ISA formalization.

Central to reasoning about Event-B models is the use of proof obligations (POs). By default, Event-B POs ensure a model is sound with respect to the basic rules of set theory, first-order logic and the basic principles of formal refinement. As discussed in [13], provision of a domain specific behavioral semantics is not necessary to establish soundness of a model (in terms of the model being self consistent and all refinements being valid), because the POs are generic and therefore applicable to different modeling domains. Beyond basic soundness, domain specific properties of a model can be introduced through the definition of invariants and theorems for which extra POs will be generated.

POs in Event-B are classified according to type [3]. In our Event-B models the following PO types are of particular relevance:

- WD: A well-definedness PO ensures expressions are properly defined and comply with applicable constraints.
- FIS: A feasibility PO ensures that each non-deterministic action is feasible. In particular, this ensures an action provides a satisfiable post condition when the guards are satisfied.
- THM: A theorem PO ensures an explicitly introduced theorem is provable.
- INV: An invariant preservation PO ensures that each invariant is preserved by each event. This means that invariants must be initiated properly and hold whenever the values of the involved state variables change.
- GRD: A guard strengthening PO ensures for corresponding concrete and abstract events that the concrete guards are stronger (or equally strong) than the abstract ones. As a consequence, whenever a concrete event is enabled so too is the respective abstract event.
- SIM: A simulation PO ensures that the outcome of the concrete event's actions is not contradicting what the related abstract event does.

Rodin is an open-source development platform for Event-B [4]. It provides an environment for system modeling and analysis, including support for refinement, *i.e.* POs are generated automatically, and support for mathematical proof, *i.e.* most POs can be discharged automatically. It also allows model checking and animation via ProB [20].

3 Literature Review

Verification is the process used to demonstrate the correctness of a design with respect to its specification [7]. By its very nature, verification requires descriptions of a design at two levels of abstraction: one higher level, this one is typically referred to as the specification, and one lower level. In addition, a method is needed to establish correctness of the lower-level description with respect to the higher-level one. Methods for simulation-based (dynamic) and formal (static) verification are increasingly successfully used in practice. An introduction to the state of the art in verification can be found in [21].

Verification relies on the fundamental assumption that the higher-level description is functionally correct, self-consistent and also complete in that it must cover all the behaviors of the design. This is very difficult to achieve.[1] In practice, a lot of time is often spent resolving inconsistencies and filling omissions in the ISA during micro-architectural design and verification. Recent work has extended coverage metrics so that the degree of completeness of a specification can be established retrospectively [9]. Ideally, however, a specification should be

[1] It is of increasing importance especially for a business model that aims to license the ISA as separate IP. Ensuring compatibility with third party developments heavily relies on the ISA specification.

developed in such a way that these important properties are an integral part of the description from the outset.

Various Architecture Description Languages have been developed to describe ISAs in order to dynamically explore design features. A typical example is ArchC [6]. While these approaches allow validation of the functional behavior of an ISA via test runs, they do not provide methods to formally reason about an ISA in terms of checking self-consistency and completeness. A formal model provides the most appropriate description for this purpose. The literature contains examples of different kinds of formal models used for microprocessor specification and verification. We now review relevant key contributions.

One of the first attempts to provide a correct and complete description of a microprocessor instruction set was the specification of the 8-bit Motorola 6800 ISA in Z. This formal specification [8] primarily served as documentation. It could also be used to manually prove properties of instruction sequences. One problem identified in [8] was the "possible complexity of the description".

In [14] an algebraic method to model microprocessors at different abstraction levels for the purpose of verification is presented. It uses iterated maps over state sets to describe the functional behavior of a higher-level specification, called the Programmer's Model (*i.e.* the ISA), and of a lower-level implementation, called the Abstract Circuit Design. It then defines under which conditions the lower-level algebraic model correctly implements the higher-level specification. Proof support in HOL was provided for this method [11] and a first formalization of the ARM ISA in HOL was undertaken [10]. Within this HOL specification the ARM ISA is grouped into eight instruction classes. For each instruction class state transforming HOL functions are defined to cover each individual instruction. Tackling complete industrial designs in this way can lead to quite sizable specifications, confirming the observation made in [8] as described above. A more recent formalization of the ARMv7 ISA came to 6500 lines of HOL4 script. In [12] details of the extra effort invested into ensuring this complex model is "valid and trustworthy" are outlined. These primarily include tool support in the form of an instruction evaluator to enable extensive validation of the formal model against ARM hardware. Testing found several bugs in the formal model.

Another early approach to formalize ISAs with a focus on establishing the semantics of an instruction set for later verification is presented in [22]. HOL is used for formalization and to prove internal model consistency, *e.g.* type checking of definitions and ensuring totality of each definition. Exponentially increasing prover time in the size of the ISA model was identified as a problem. Based on the fact that ISAs contain collections of instructions that have similar behavior, instructions with common behavior are represented by special *semantic frameworks*. These provide parametrized abstractions of the behavior of an entire class of instructions (up to the specific operation of individual instructions). While semantic frameworks are acknowledged to facilitate creating and maintaining specifications, the approach in [22] does not take advantage of these abstractions to reduce the size of the formal model which in turn would probably have increased proof efficiency.

Industrial sized ISAs tend to be large and complex. The need to introduce more structure into ISA formalization has already been recognized when first attempts to ISA formalization were made. In [8] it was noted that the stepwise construction of the formal model from "easily assimilated concepts" would help to overcome the difficulty in constructing a complete and correct formal specification for increasingly complex architectures. It was proposed to keep each such concept "readily understandable" and to layer such a formal specification with the aim to facilitate its construction and also to ease readability and comprehension. We aim to achieve exactly this.

We have now reviewed several examples of ISA formalizations. Our work attempts to overcome a limitation common to all these: the lack of a systematic abstraction/refinement hierarchy. Such a hierarchy has several obvious benefits in terms of combating complexity: It provides an overarching description that relates individual instructions and gives a top-down "narrative" allowing engineers to understand the meaning of instructions and their interaction. Layers in the hierarchy also provide natural boundaries to control the size of the formal model so that proofs can be done more efficiently either at higher abstraction levels or by decomposition into a series of locally scoped smaller proofs.

The use of refinement in Event-B supports the creation of a hierarchical model via top-down refinement. The hierarchy provides an intuitive structure that facilitates model construction, maintenance, re-use and comprehension. In comparison, the approaches reviewed above are "flat". Tackling designs of industrial complexity with such "flat" approaches results in increasingly complex formal models and at best ad-hoc solutions to combat the associated problems.

A recent example of modeling the Z80 ISA with the B-Method [2], a predecessor of Event-B, is presented in [18]. Common functionality of individual instructions has been factored into auxiliary functions (re-usable within this model). Proof ensures consistency of the model as well as satisfaction of system and safety properties. Our method goes beyond this work in that it demonstrates how the generalization of common functionality can be extended beyond classes of instructions to modeling entire classes of ISAs.

4 The MIDAS and CRISP ISA Models

The feasibility of formalizing ISAs in Event-B was first demonstrated on the MIDAS ISA model [24]. Re-using this model to formalize the CRISP processor's ISA was a natural next step. This section briefly introduces our refinement strategy, followed by short reviews of key features of both ISA models.

4.1 Refinement Strategy

The entire instruction space of the ISA is initially represented by an abstract set *Inst*. This allows all aspects of the representation to be abstracted, including any numerical values that may be assigned by a particular implementation. *Inst* represents all possible instructions that may be presented to the processor at run-time, including both valid and invalid. Instruction classes are constructed by the successive partitioning of sub-sets of *Inst* based on common features, *e.g.* control flow[2] instructions, instructions which access the internal storage, load/store instructions, etc. This gives rise to a hierarchy of abstraction layers. These sub-sets are then employed in the guards of events describing the possible outcomes of execution of a particular instruction class. An event describing the successful execution of the instruction is initially created by appropriate refinement of its abstract event. To ensure completeness, complementary events describing all possible failure conditions for the instruction are then derived by the negation of each guard in the successful-execution event within the constraints of the corresponding abstract failure event. One failure event is constructed for each negated guard and inherits the actions of the abstract failure event. This refinement strategy is currently performed manually although the provision of tool support within the Rodin environment would be feasible.

4.2 Modeling the MIDAS ISA in Event-B

The MIDAS[3] ISA consists of 35 simple instructions. The salient features of MIDAS are as follows:

a) Both a register file and a stack version were required.
b) Each instruction takes up to 2 source and up to 1 destination operands.
c) Condition flags are used for storing the result of the branch condition that is evaluated by a compare instruction.

The 39/40 refinement steps within the MIDAS derivation can be grouped into distinct layers. At the top is a basic State Machine (SM). It provides the fundamental operations of a processor in terms of a basic next state function. Two abstract events represent successful instruction completion or failure due to any error condition. Following the SM layer, the Control Flow (CF) layer introduces an instruction space and Program Counter (PC). Note that the PC is defined by a variable local to each event, rather than fixing it to a specific location. This allows the PC to be further refined to reside in a special-purpose register, such as in CRISP; or in one of the general-purpose registers, such as in the ARM architecture [5]. Branching is based on a calculated condition flag; Table 1 enumerates all the cases to be considered, based on the result of the condition evaluation wrt status and value, and PC validity, *i.e.* in or outside of range, after PC recalculation.

Next, the Register Array (RA) layer refines the instruction subset that writes to the internal storage. The internal storage is specified in the RA layer context as a *total function*, (represented by $\rightarrow$ in Event-B), called *RA*, from an integer subset, called *RADom*, to a set of bit patterns, called *Data*. The definition in

[2] In this paper, we use *control flow instructions* to refer to instructions that change the flow of control; *compare instructions* for instructions that evaluate (branch) conditions; *branch* means *conditional* change.

[3] **M**icroprocessor **I**nstruction and **D**ata **A**bstraction **S**ystem.

Table 1. Control Flow Layer: Successful and Error Handling Event Refinements

Condition Evaluation		PC Recalculation	Event Refinement
Status	Value		
successful	*true*	*in range*	Event for true-condition error-free case
successful	*true*	$\neg$ *in range*	Event for invalid PC recalculation case
successful	*false*	*in range*	Event for false-condition error-free case
successful	*false*	$\neg$ *in range*	Event for invalid PC increment case
failed	*n/a*	*n/a*	Event for condition evaluation error

Equation 1 ensures that each element in $RADom$ can be mapped to one and only one bit pattern in $Data$.

$$RA \in RADom \rightarrow Data \tag{1}$$

For the register file MIDAS version, the internal storage is accessed using an intermediate variable idx to specify the register position. The action of updating the internal storage is defined in Equation 2, where op is the operation of the instruction, which takes 2 source operands, s_0 and s_1, and produces a bit pattern that fits one element of the internal storage.

$$RA(idx) := op(s_0, s_1) \tag{2}$$

For the stack-based MIDAS version, a set of events is refined to catch illegal accesses such as stack overflow or empty stack. These error cases also give rise to the invalid condition evaluation described in the last row of Table 1. Note that both MIDAS versions have been refined from the same abstract model.

The next layer, the MEmory layer (ME), refines the load/store instruction subset. The instruction and data memories are defined as separate total functions from the memory index domain to a set of bit patterns.

Further MIDAS ISA-specific layers refine the ME layer to a level from which an executable reference model is generated [23] to be used for dynamic model validation. Thus, [24] presents a "correct-by-construction" stepwise refinement of an entire, yet simple ISA down to executable code. The layers of the MIDAS ISA model are depicted on the left in Figure 1.

4.3 Modeling the CRISP ISA in Event-B

The MIDAS ISA model was extended to formalize the more complex CRISP[4] ISA. CRISP is a modified MIPS architecture [15], with 50 instructions, optimized towards fast cryptographic computation. The features of the CRISP ISA are:

a) CRISP uses a register file for internal storage. The number of registers in CRISP is 2 raised to the power of the bit width of the index specifier.
b) Each instruction can take up to 4 source and up to 2 destination operands, enabling special instructions for fast execution of cryptographic algorithms.
c) *Compare-and-branch* instructions comprise both compare and branch operations, so no conditional state is stored. Some of them are bit-addressed.

[4] **C**ryptographic **RISC** **P**rocessor [19].

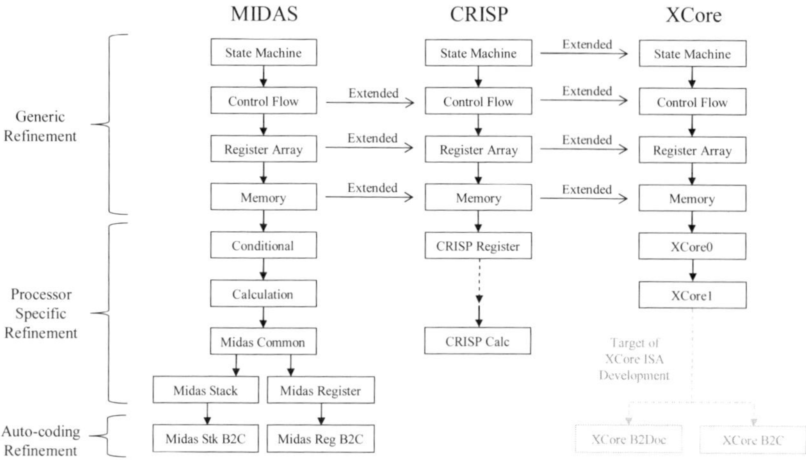

Fig. 1. The derivation and structure of the Generic ISA Model

The CRISP ISA model has 47 refinement steps. The SM layer is identical to the MIDAS model. In the CF layer, where MIDAS uses separate instructions for compare and branch, CRISP merges these two steps into one-step dedicated instructions. CRISP has bit-addressed conditional instructions, which may fail due to invalid indexing causing an "out of register width" error (an instance of the error case in the last row of Table 1). In the model the bit compare function is defined as:

$$BbitComp \in Data \times RADom \rightarrow BOOL \tag{3}$$

When this function is applied in Equation 4, the first parameter is the data in the first register, while the second is the data in the second register.

$$cond = BbitComp(op1Data \mapsto Data2Int(op2Data)) \tag{4}$$

The definition in Equation 3 requires, via a WD PO, that the integer in the second register must be within the register array domain.

In the RA layer, CRISP re-uses the internal storage definition of MIDAS. The instruction format in CRISP permits dual destination instructions. Updating 2 destination registers in one single action is desirable as this maintains consistency with the abstract action, given in Equation 5.

$$RA :\in RADom \rightarrow Data \tag{5}$$

A formal statement describing such a dual-write is given in Equation 6, where the registers indexed by d_0 and d_1 are updated with the two-part result produced by the operation *op* applied to the operands s_0, s_1, s_2, and s_3.

$$RA := RA \Leftarrow \{\ d_0 \ \mapsto \ op(s_0, s_1, s_2, s_3)[0]^5, d_1 \ \mapsto \ op(s_0, s_1, s_2, s_3)[1]\ \} \tag{6}$$

[5] Please note that the use of indexing to access the first segment of the result in "$op(s_0, s_1, s_2, s_3)[0]$" is for the purpose of illustration only; this is not Event-B syntax. The Event-B models use two designated variables to capture the results of "op".

The internal storage RA is specified as a *total function*, which requires that any action must assign a unique value to each updated element. Our refinement gives rise to a SIM PO that ensures the update in Equation 6 simulates the abstract one. Discharging this PO is only possible by adding a new guard that requires the indices d_0 and d_1 are not identical. This is a typical example of requirement discovery as a by-product of the seamless interaction of modeling and proof as promoted in Event-B. The missing requirement was added to the original (informal) CRISP ISA manual to avoid potential race conditions in practice.

The CRISP model was constructed to explore the consistency of the CRISP ISA during ISA design; code generation was not required. The structure of the CRISP ISA model is given in the middle column in Figure 1. The CRISP ISA model demonstrated that the formal model is easily extendable. In the process of modeling new error cases were identified which were missing from the CRISP specification. Note that, this was possible even without a fully refined model.

5 The Generic Modeling Template

The numerous similarities between the MIDAS and CRISP ISA models motivated a generalization of the model to a re-usable template, *i.e.* the *generic model*. This relatively short paper cannot contain all the information needed to use the generic model. Instead, an overview is given of its structure followed by a section that focuses on a generic formalization of the internal storage options.

5.1 Structure of the Generic Modeling Template

The top four layers of the MIDAS and CRISP ISA models, as illustrated in Figure 1, share features commonly found in any ISA. These include a basic state machine to specify how instructions are executed (SM layer), the means to control program execution including the definition of the PC and all control flow instructions (CF layer), the organization of and access to the register array (RA layer) and also the organization of and access to the memory with load/store instructions (ME layer). For each of these aspects there are alternative design options. To accommodate these, *choice points* are built into the generic model. A *choice point* can later be instantiated, *i.e.* further refined, to one particular option. Thus, the resulting hierarchy provides a generic template within which the effects of different design options can be explored at the appropriate level of abstraction. The generic model covers the fundamental design options open at the different layers in accordance with the classification of processors in [15].

The entire generic model consists of 27 refinement steps, yielding 63 events at the final layer, *i.e.* the ME layer of the CRISP column in Table 2. The model is available from `http://www.cs.bris.ac.uk/~yuan/GM.zip`. The next section provides an insight into a generic formalization of the internal storage options.

5.2 Generalization of Internal Storage Options

A basic differentiator between processors is the *internal storage* method; the RA layer addresses this aspect. Conventional options for internal storage are an accumulator, a stack or a register file. All of these may be refined from an addressable contiguous region. The following context fragments show the definitions used in the generic model to capture this internal storage region without committing to any one of the above options.

```
CONSTANTS
    MinRAIdx
    MaxRAIdx
    RADom
AXIOMS
axm1: MinRAIdx ∈ ℕ
axm2: MaxRAIdx ∈ ℕ
axm3: MinRAIdx ≤ MaxRAIdx
axm4: RADom = MinRAIdx .. MaxRAIdx
```

```
CONSTANTS
    instToSrc0Idx
    instToSrc1Idx
    instToDst0Idx
    ...
AXIOMS
axm1: instToSrc0Idx ∈ Inst → ℕ
axm2: instToSrc1Idx ∈ Inst → ℕ
axm3: instToDst0Idx ∈ Inst → ℕ
...: ...
```

To fetch a bit pattern from the internal storage an access function is applied to an instruction, *e.g.* $s_0 = RA(instToSrc0Idx(inst))$ fetches the first source operand of instruction *inst*. The action is guarded to check whether the index belongs to *RADom* which ensures legitimate accesses, especially for stack and accumulator machines. The actual type of internal storage is left as an open choice point. For CRISP, the $instTo\langle operand\rangle Idx$ mappings are refined to implement point a) from Section 4.3 into $Inst \rightarrow RADom$, *i.e.* a one-to-one mapping; this makes the guards that check legitimate accesses to the register file always *true* and the corresponding failure events become obsolete. This is an excellent example of how clever design can reduce verification effort.

Equations 2 and 6 describe internal storage updates for two specific ISAs. The generic model accommodates this functionality by providing a generic update over the entire internal storage region for instructions with m sources and n destinations given in Equation 7, where *op* is the operation of the instruction, which produces a bit pattern to fit n destinations. The update in Equation 7 overrides the existing internal storage region with a new mapping, which assigns the respective result to the n destinations indexed with $idx_0 \dots idx_{n-1}$.

$$\begin{aligned} RA := RA \lhd\!\!\!+ \{\ & idx_0 \mapsto op(s_0, \cdots, s_{m-1})[0], \\ & idx_1 \mapsto op(s_0, \cdots, s_{m-1})[1], \cdots, \\ & idx_{n-1} \mapsto op(s_0, \cdots, s_{m-1})[n-1]\ \} \end{aligned} \tag{7}$$

Equations 2 and 6 are now instantiations of this generic formula, fixing the number of updates to either one or two. The syntax used in Equation 7 contains ellipsis and is for illustration only. The values for m and n have to be instantiated to fit the target instruction format, *e.g.* for CRISP $m = 4$ and $n = 2$. For $n > 1$ the update gives rise to the SIM PO mentioned in Section 4.3. This PO revealed an important practical constraint which is incorporated into the generic model both as a guard and as an error condition in case the guard is not satisfied: *In architectures with multi-destination instructions, the destination registers need to be distinct: writing multiple values into the same register causes a race condition.*

Our formalization greatly benefits from the fact that Event-B by default enforces model consistency and valid refinements. A clear advantage is that important properties can be introduced early, *i.e.* at higher levels of abstraction within the hierarchy. For example, the ARMv7 Reference Manual [5] states that for dual destination instructions, such as the Signed Multiply Accumulate Long Dual `SMLALD` instruction on page A8-338, the two destinations must refer to distinct registers. The CRISP processor has dual destination instructions with a similar requirement, so does the XCore ISA. Instead of repeating this requirement for each individual instruction in the formal ISA model, the requirement is introduced together with the dual destination instruction format in the RA layer because this requirement applies irrespective of the instruction's functionality. By default, any subsequent refinements must preserve this requirement.

6 Modeling the XCore ISA in Event-B

XMOS Ltd is a fab-less semiconductor company that develops multi-core, multi-threaded processors. XMOS has developed several core pieces of technology, including a multi-threaded general purpose processor (XCore), an interconnect switch that routes messages between cores, and a link to interconnect these switches. Support for these features is integrated into the ISA. This greatly improves run-time performance at the cost of introducing specialist instructions. The XCore ISA [17] comprises of $\sim$170 instructions. It has been embodied in the XS1-G4 XCore processor (a four-core device that can run up to 32 real time tasks), and the XS1-L1 (a single core device that can run up to 8 real time tasks). Although the XCore is used as the basis of multi-core devices, the individual cores are entirely symmetric and linked only via asynchronous communication links. Thus the single ISA model is appropriate to each individual core. XMOS also provides a complete software development tool-chain that supports C, C++, and XC (a language developed to best exploit the XCore architecture). The XCore has been exploited in a range of different markets, including audio, display, communications, robotics and motor control.

A one year Knowledge Transfer Secondment started in October 2010 to transfer the modeling method to XMOS in order to formalize the XCore ISA. Our objective is to derive an executable reference model from the formal model of the XCore ISA using the techniques described in [23]. In addition, we intend to use the formal model to generate a document that specifies the XCore ISA behavior under all conditions derived from the formal specification. The formalization is expected to produce two important results: it will guarantee that the documentation of the XCore matches the silicon, and it will guarantee that the silicon matches the architectural intent. The former is important to exclude errors from documentation; the latter will be particularly important for the next generation products. Typically, the next generation of a processor is heavily based on the current one and is obtained by extending the current instruction set architecture. Such extensions, unless rigorously verified, can easily introduce inconsistencies within the newly extended ISA itself, which then propagate into the design and finally, if undetected during design verification, into the end product. The formal ISA model in Event-B lends itself naturally to modification and extension based on the principle of stepwise refinement. The need to formally establish model consistency between refinement levels, which is inherent to the Event-B method, guarantees the absence of inconsistencies being introduced during the ISA extension process.

The first phase of the project, the extension of the generic model to accommodate commercial ISA features, has already been completed (see the right column in Figure 1). Extensions include: Memory alignment requirements for both instruction and data fetches from memory are modeled with uncommitted constants. Vectored jumps on exception detection extend the simple machine-halt defined in the original generic model. Vectored interrupt behavior triggered by modeled external events was added. Other extensions capture less common features. Specifically, an ability to pause in anticipation of external events and the special instructions used to support this behavior. Although unusual, similar features could be provided by other ISAs. The behavior is therefore included at an abstract level within the generic model to permit future re-use.

In the next phase of the project, the processor specific refinement, this enhanced generic model is being used as the basis for refinement to an XCore-specific model. While this phase is labor intensive, it involves formalizing the functional behavior of each instruction, there are no further formalization challenges now that the generic model has been extended to accommodate the XCore ISA features. Instead, this phase will challenge tool capacity.

The value of the modeling approach has already been demonstrated by the discovery of subtle errors in the published specification as compared to the existing product, even prior to the refinement of the current abstract model to full detail. For example, the requirement not to permit the use of equal register indexes as destinations for dual-destination instructions, which is embedded in the generic model, enabled discovery of an undocumented exception implemented by the XCore for these instructions: the actual machine robustly detects this error condition and yields an exception. One instruction was specified with different behaviors, depending on the value of one of its included immediate fields. Separate refinement of the two forms of the instruction from separate abstract events, effectively defining two separate instructions, was found to match the approach taken by the XCore implementation. Thus it was found that in one form there is never a memory access; this form is the faster of the two and can never give rise to an exception. In the other form there is always a memory access. The formal model helps to identify and document such issues, enforcing explicit specification of all exceptions. The cases detected so far had previously not been explicitly documented due to the fact that there is no single model from which documentation and executables are generated. The current state of development of the XCore ISA model is given in the right column of Figure 1.

7 Summary

We have presented a method to formalize ISAs in Event-B using a refinement-based strategy to build a hierarchically structured formal specification. We have intentionally kept each refinement small enough to remain comprehensible and functionally self-contained. To enable re-use of our method we developed a generic ISA modeling template. This template captures all common and differentiating ISA features discussed in [15] by providing choice points at different levels of abstraction. This allows tailoring the model to capture a specific target ISA or ISA family. We noticed that deriving the CRISP ISA model by refining the generic model considerably decreased the effort spent on modeling. Most time was used discharging POs, many of a very similar nature. Defining a set of domain-specific proof tactics, *i.e.* a meta-level ordered sequence of rules akin to the proof commands mentioned in [18], would increase the efficiency of discharging many of these. The generic modeling template is currently being used to formalize the ISA of the XMOS XCore processor. This necessitated the extension of the existing template to accommodate commercial ISA features. In this process, the generic model has already helped to identify some subtle errors. Future re-use of the generic model may require further such extensions. The generic model thus "grows" into an electronic repository of ISA design expertise. The key benefit of deriving an ISA from this template, compared to developing a model from scratch, is the increased model integrity which ensures a more reliable and trustworthy model giving design and verification engineers a higher degree of confidence in the model's correctness.

With reference to Figure 1, Table 2 shows the number of refinement steps within each abstraction layer, the event counts sampled at the bottom of each layer, and the total number of discharged POs in each model.

Table 2. Data from the ISA models of MIDAS (R)egister / (S)tack version, CRISP and XCore

<table>
<tr><th></th><th></th><th colspan="4">MIDAS</th><th colspan="2">CRISP</th><th colspan="2">XCore</th></tr>
<tr><th></th><th>Layers</th><th colspan="2">Steps</th><th colspan="2">#Events</th><th>Steps</th><th>#Events</th><th>Steps</th><th>#Events</th></tr>
<tr><td rowspan="4">Generic Refinement</td><td>SM</td><td colspan="2">5</td><td colspan="2">8</td><td>5</td><td>8</td><td>3</td><td>8</td></tr>
<tr><td>CF</td><td colspan="2">5</td><td colspan="2">17</td><td>5</td><td>17</td><td>13</td><td>18</td></tr>
<tr><td>RA</td><td colspan="2">5</td><td colspan="2">42</td><td>7</td><td>51</td><td>2</td><td>23</td></tr>
<tr><td>ME</td><td colspan="2">9</td><td colspan="2">56</td><td>10</td><td>63</td><td>9</td><td>39</td></tr>
<tr><td rowspan="3">Processor Specific Refinement</td><td>EXT1</td><td colspan="2">4</td><td colspan="2">63</td><td>5</td><td>47</td><td>5</td><td>45</td></tr>
<tr><td>EXT2</td><td colspan="2">2</td><td colspan="2">83</td><td>2</td><td>64</td><td>6</td><td>64</td></tr>
<tr><td>EXT3</td><td colspan="2">7</td><td colspan="2">107</td><td>13</td><td>110</td><td>-</td><td>-</td></tr>
<tr><td>Auto-coding Refinement</td><td>EXT4</td><td>2 (R)</td><td>3 (S)</td><td>109 (R)</td><td>113 (S)</td><td>-</td><td>-</td><td>-</td><td>-</td></tr>
<tr><td></td><td>Total POs</td><td colspan="4">4804</td><td colspan="2">2101</td><td colspan="2">1343</td></tr>
</table>

The differing values for each layer of the generic model reflect its upgrading across successive versions, as illustrated in Figure 1. Modifications include expansion to capture new features (*e.g.* multi-destination instructions for CRISP and interrupt handling for the XCore). In addition, the XCore ISA model is being constructed using Rodin 2.0 taking advantage of the enhancements recently made to the Event-B notation. For MIDAS and CRISP Rodin 0.8.2 was used.

8 Conclusion

Verifying the functional correctness of a processor requires an unambiguous, self-consistent, complete and functionally correct specification of its ISA. Such rigorous specification can most effectively be achieved with formal methods and in practice requires robust tool support. Using Event-B and the Rodin tool set as a formal modeling method and development environment has several advantages.

Firstly, the model can be incrementally developed by following a stepwise refinement strategy. This allows design development and exploration within a hierarchy of increasingly detailed abstraction levels. The hierarchical structure of the generic model provides a means to manage complexity through abstraction. This facilitate model construction, maintenance, re-use and comprehension. The abstraction layers also provide boundaries to control the size of the model so that proof can be done more efficiently.

Secondly, the generation and discharge of POs ensures model consistency and valid refinement by default right from the outset and without the need to explicitly provide a domain-specific semantics. Desirable domain specific properties can additionally be introduced into the model. One such property for ISAs may be *enabledness*, *i.e.* ensuring transitions are defined from all states. Enabledness corresponds to the absence of deadlock at ISA level, which would result in the processor hanging unexpectedly during program execution. Enabledness properties, similar to the ones discussed in [13], could be introduced into the model resulting in extra POs being generated to preserve these. The interaction between modeling and proof can help discover important missing constraints of practical relevance even at an early stage of formalization. The resulting models provide unambiguous, self-consistent and complete specifications. In addition, validation of functional correctness can be achieved by biased random testing of the executable reference model which can be generated from the bottom level of a fully developed ISA model.

Finally, for formal models and methods such as the one presented in this paper, the ultimate test of acceptance in practice is whether or not these can be seamlessly integrated into the tool flow currently used by design and verification engineers. Code and document generation from the bottom level of refinement provides this important link to integrate our method into existing flows. An ISA description and an executable reference model are thus derived from the same formal source. The design verification process, where the reference model serves as executable specification, ensures that the implementation functionally matches the reference model. Our approach thus closes an important gap at the front end of existing design flows by providing a formal link between the documentation, the design and, indirectly, the actual product.

References

1. International Technology Roadmap for Semiconductors, chap. Design, p. 19 (2009), `http://www.itrs.net`
2. Abrial, J.R.: The B-book: Assigning Programs to Meanings. Cambridge University Press, New York (1996)
3. Abrial, J.R.: Modeling in Event-B: System and Software Engineering. Cambridge University Press, Cambridge (2010)

4. Abrial, J.R., Butler, M., Hallerstede, S., Hoang, T.S., Mehta, F., Voisin, L.: Rodin: An open toolset for modelling and reasoning in Event-B. STTT 12(6), 447–466 (2010)
5. ARM Ltd: ARM Architecture Refernce Manual, AMVv7-A and ARMv7-R edn.
6. Azevedo, R., Rigo, S., Bartholomeu, M., Araujo, G., Araujo, C., Barros, E.: The ArchC architecture description language and tools. Int. J. Parallel Program. 33, 453–484 (2005)
7. Bergeron, J.: Writing Testbenches: Functional Verification of HDL Models, 2nd edn. Springer, Heidelberg (2003)
8. Bowen, J.P.: Formal specification and documentation of microprocessor instruction sets. Microprocess. Microprogram 21(1-5), 223–230 (1987)
9. Chockler, H., Halpern, J.Y., Kupferman, O.: What causes a system to satisfy a specification? ACM Transactions on Computational Logic 9, 1–26 (2008)
10. Fox, A.: A HOL specification of the ARM instruction set architecture. Tech. Rep. UCAM-CL-TR-545, University of Cambridge, Computer Laboratory (June 2001)
11. Fox, A.: An algebraic framework for modelling and verifying microprocessors using HOL. Tech. Rep. UCAM-CL-TR-512, University of Cambridge, Computer Laboratory (March 2001)
12. Fox, A., Myreen, M.: A trustworthy monadic formalization of the ARMv7 instruction set architecture. Interactive Theorem Proving, ITP (2010)
13. Hallerstede, S.: On the purpose of Event-B proof obligations. Formal Aspects of Computing 23(1), 133–150 (2011)
14. Harman, N.A., Tucker, J.V.: Algebraic models and the correctness of microprocessors. In: Proceedings of the IFIP WG 10.5 Advanced Research Working Conference on Correct Hardware Design and Verification Methods, pp. 92–108. Springer, Heidelberg (1993)
15. Hennessy, J.L., Patterson, D.A.: Computer Architecture: A Quantitative Approach, 3rd edn. Morgan Kaufmann, San Francisco (2002)
16. Jones, R.B., O'Leary, J.W., Seger, C.J.H., Aagaard, M.D., Melham, T.F.: Practical formal verification in microprocessor design. IEEE Design & Test of Computers 18(4), 16–25 (2001)
17. May, D.: The XMOS XS1 Architecture. XMOS Limited (2009)
18. Medeiros Jr., V., Déharbe, D.: Formal Modelling of a Microcontroller Instruction Set in B. In: Formal Methods: Foundations and Applications: 12th Brazilian Symposium on Formal Methods, pp. 282–289 (2009)
19. Page, D.: CRISP: A Cryptographic RISC Processor, `pagecs.bris.ac.uk`
20. ProB, `http://www.stups.uni-duesseldorf.de/ProB/`
21. Wile, B., Goss, J.C., Roesner, W.: Comprehensive Functional Verification. Morgan Kaufmann, San Francisco (2005)
22. Windley, P.J.: Specifying Instruction-Set Architectures in HOL: A Primer. In: Melham, T.F., Camilleri, J. (eds.) HUG 1994. LNCS, vol. 859, pp. 440–455. Springer, Heidelberg (1994)
23. Wright, S.: Automatic Generation of C from Event-B. In: IM_FMT 2009 Workshop on Integration of Model-based Formal Methods and Tools (February 2009)
24. Wright, S., Eder, K.: Using Event-B to construct instruction set architectures. Formal Aspects of Computing 23(1), 73–89 (2010)

A Language for Test Case Refinement in the Test Template Framework

Maximiliano Cristia[2,3], Diego Hollmann[2], Pablo Albertengo[1], Claudia Frydman[3], and Pablo Rodriguez Monetti[4]

[1] Flowgate Consulting, Rosario, Argentina
[2] CIFASIS-UNR, Rosario Argentina
[3] LSIS-UPCAM, Marseille, France
[4] FCEIA-UNR, Rosario, Argentina
mcristia@flowgate.net

Abstract. Model-based testing (MBT) generates test cases by analysing a formal model of the system under test (SUT). In many MBT methods, these test cases are too abstract to be executed. Therefore, an executable representation of them is necessary to test the SUT. So far, the MBT community has focused on methods that automate the generation of test cases, but less has been done in making them executable. In this paper we propose a language to specify rules that can be automatically applied to produce an executable representation of test cases generated by the Test Template Framework (TTF), a MBT method for the Z notation.

1 The Process of Model-Based Testing

Model-based testing (MBT) is a well-known technique aimed at testing software by analysing a formal model or specification of the system under test (SUT) [1,2]. These techniques have been developed and applied to models written in different formal notations such as Z [3], finite state machines and their extensions [4], B [5], algebraic specifications [6], and so on. The fundamental hypothesis behind MBT is that, as a program is correct if it satisfies its specification, then the specification is an excellent source of test cases.

Figure 1 depicts a possible testing process when a MBT method is applied. So far, the MBT community has focused on the "Generation" step in which testers analyse a model of the SUT and generate test cases by applying different techniques. Test cases produced by the "Generation" step are abstract in the sense that they are written in the same language of the model, making them, in most of the MBT methods, not executable. In effect, during the "Refinement" step these abstract test cases are made executable by a process that can be called *refinement*, *concretization* or *reification*. Note that this not necessarily means that the SUT has been refined from the model; it only says that test cases must be refined. In fact, Hierons and others conclude that the relation between refinement and MBT is still a challenge that would have a very tangible benefit if solved [2]. Besides, test case refinement can require an effort equal to the 25% up to 100% of the time spent on modelling [1], so it is worth to automate this step

S. Qin and Z. Qiu (Eds.): ICFEM 2011, LNCS 6991, pp. 601–616, 2011.

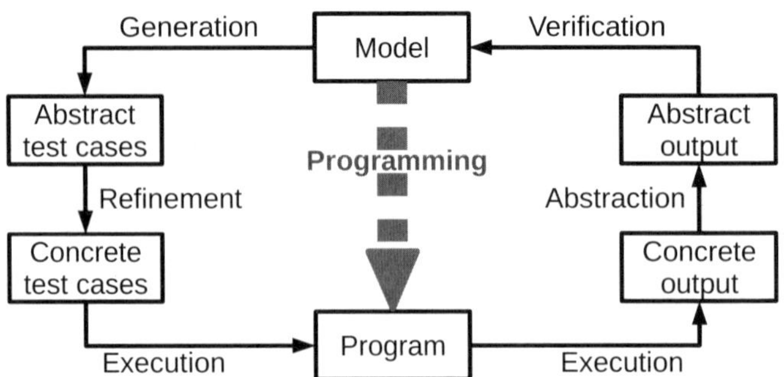

Fig. 1. A general description of a possible MBT process

as much as possible. Furthermore, automating this step enables the automation of the rest of the MBT process. Once test cases have been refined they can be automatically executed by one of the many test execution environments or techniques already developed [7,8]. Hence, the problem we try to solve is the automation of the "Refinement" step and not the automation of the "Execution" step, which has been extensively studied.

As we have said, there is a variety of MBT methods for many formal notations. Our work concentrates in the Z notation [9]. Z is a widely known formal notation based on first order logic and set theory. There are some MBT methods available for the Z notation. In [10] the authors apply category–partition; Hall [11] generates tests by analysing the test domains of Z operations; in [12] the Z information provided in a μSZ specification is used to provide sequences of transitions that covers a EFSM derived from the specification; Hierons [13] also partitions a Z operation and then derives a FSA to control how testing is performed; Horcher and Peleska [14] apply DNF to a Z operation and describe a MBT process similar to the one in Figure 1. However, we think that the Test Template Framework (TTF) [3,15,16] is the MBT method that takes the most of the Z notation, as we will show in Section 2. We have developed the first automatic implementation of the TTF in a tool called Fastest [17,18,19].

Hence, in this paper we propose a test case refinement language (TCRL) as an extension to the TTF. This TCRL does not assume that the SUT has been refined from the Z specification. In fact, if this is the case there might be better options [20]. However, our method does assumes that the SUT's source code is available. We have implemented an interpreter for this TCRL in Fastest following an architecture that allows users to automatically refine test cases to different programming languages after specifying simple refinement rules. Furthermore, the architecture makes it easy to plug in modules that implement the TCRL for programming languages not yet supported by the tool. The implementation is still a research prototype.

This article is a summary of a 65 page long reference manual describing the TCRL [21]. Therefore, due to space restrictions, here we will introduce only its most relevant features by means of some running examples. This document along with examples to be executed on Fastest can be found at `http://www.flowgate.net/pdf/ftcrl.tar.gz`.

In Section 2 we introduce the TTF and in 3 we precisely state the contribution of this article. Section 4 describe the most salient features of our method. A case study is briefly introduced in Section 5. We discuss some similar approaches in Section 6 and our conclusions in Section 7.

2 The Test Template Framework

In this section we briefly introduce those steps of the TTF strongly related to test case refinement—for a thorough introduction see [17,18,3]. The presentation is made by means of an example that we will use throughout this article. It is assumed that the reader is fluent in the Z notation. In the TTF each operation within the specification is analysed to generate abstract test cases, as follows:

1. Consider the valid input space (VIS) of a Z operation.
2. Apply one or more testing tactics in order to partition the VIS.
3. Find one abstract test case from each satisfiable test condition.

We will introduce these steps for the operation named *NewClient* of the Z specification shown in Figure 2. The specification is about the savings accounts of a simple banking system. Table 1 summarizes the meaning of each basic element of the model. We think that this table plus the common knowledge about savings accounts will suffice to understand the model.

$[AN, UID, NAME]$
$BALANCE == \mathbb{N}$

State schema for the savings accounts.

$$
\begin{array}{l}
\textit{Bank} \\
\hline
\textit{clients} : \textit{UID} \pfun \textit{NAME} \\
\textit{balances} : \textit{AN} \pfun \textit{BALANCE} \\
\textit{owners} : \textit{UID} \leftrightarrow \textit{AN} \\
\hline
\end{array}
$$

$$
\begin{array}{l}
\textit{NewClientOk} \\
\hline
\Delta \textit{Bank} \\
u? : \textit{UID} \\
\textit{name}? : \textit{NAME};\ n? : \textit{AN} \\
\hline
u? \notin \operatorname{dom} \textit{clients} \\
n? \notin \operatorname{dom} \textit{balances} \\
\textit{clients}' = \textit{clients} \cup \{u? \mapsto \textit{name}?\} \\
\textit{balances}' = \textit{balances} \cup \{n? \mapsto 0\} \\
\textit{owners}' = \textit{owners} \cup \{u? \mapsto n?\} \\
\hline
\end{array}
$$

$\textit{ClientAlreadyExists} == [\Xi \textit{Bank};\ u? : \textit{UID} \mid u? \in \operatorname{dom} \textit{clients}]$
$\textit{AccountAlreadyExists} == [\Xi \textit{Bank};\ n? : \textit{AN} \mid n? \in \operatorname{dom} \textit{balances}]$
$\textit{NewClient} == \textit{NewClientOk} \lor \textit{ClientAlreadyExists} \lor \textit{AccountAlreadyExists}$

Fig. 2. Part of a Z specification of the savings accounts of a banking system

Table 1. Meaning of the basic elements of the Z model of Figure 2

Term	Meaning
AN	The set of possible savings accounts numbers
UID	The set of identifiers of individuals
$NAME$	The set of names of individuals
$clients\ u$	The name of person u as is recorded in the bank
$balances\ n$	The balance of savings account n
$owners(u, n)$	u is an owner of account n
$NewClient(u, name, n)$	Account n is opened by client u whose name is $name$

Step 1. Since *NewClient* is a total operation, its VIS is the Z schema declaring all the input and before state variables used by it:

$$\begin{array}{l} NewClient_{VIS} == [clients : UID \rightarrow\!\!\!\!\!\!\;\; + NAME;\ balances : AN \rightarrow\!\!\!\!\!\!\;\; + BALANCE; \\ \quad owners : UID \leftrightarrow AN;\ name? : NAME;\ u? : UID;\ n? : AN] \end{array}$$

Step 2. The TTF partitions the VIS by applying one or more *testing tactics*. The result is a set of so-called *test specifications*. Test specifications obtained in this way can be further subdivided into more test specifications by applying other testing tactics. The net effect of this technique is a progressive partition of the VIS into more restrictive test specifications. This procedure can continue until the engineer think that the test specifications will uncover enough errors in the implementation. Each tactic indicates how the current test specification must be partitioned by giving a set of predicates characterizing each resulting test specification. Two of the testing tactics proposed within the TTF are Disjunctive Normal Form (DNF) and Standard Partitions (SP) [3,17].

In this example, we first apply DNF to the VIS of *NewClient*, getting the following test specifications:

$$\begin{array}{l} NewClient_1^{DNF} == [NewClient_{VIS} \mid u? \notin \operatorname{dom} clients \land n? \notin \operatorname{dom} balances] \\ NewClient_2^{DNF} == [NewClient_{VIS} \mid u? \in \operatorname{dom} clients] \\ NewClient_3^{DNF} == [NewClient_{VIS} \mid n? \in \operatorname{dom} balances] \end{array}$$

SP is applied to the set union operator ($\cup$) in $clients \cup \{u? \mapsto name?\}$ in order to partition $NewClient_1^{DNF}$, yielding the following satisfiable test specifications (the unsatisfiable ones have been omitted for brevity):

$$\begin{array}{l} NewClient_2^{SP} == [NewClient_1^{DNF} \mid clients = \varnothing \land \{u? \mapsto name?\} \neq \varnothing] \\ NewClient_4^{SP} == [NewClient_1^{DNF} \mid \\ \quad clients \neq \varnothing \land clients \cap \{u? \mapsto name?\} = \varnothing] \end{array}$$

Step 3. The TTF prescribes to derive abstract test cases only from those test specifications that were not partitioned—we have four in the example. This means to find at least one element satisfying each of them. For example, the following horizontal schemas represent abstract test cases of the corresponding test specifications[1]:

$$
\begin{aligned}
&NewClient_1^{ATC} == [NewClient_2^{SP} \mid balances = \varnothing \land name? = name0 \land \\
&\quad n? = an0 \land u? = uid0 \land clients = \varnothing \land owners = \varnothing] \\
&NewClient_2^{ATC} == [NewClient_4^{SP} \mid u? = uid0 \land name? = name0 \land \\
&\quad n? = an0 \land balances = \{(an1, 20)\} \land \\
&\quad clients = \{(uid1, name0)\} \land owners = \{(uid1, an1)\}] \\
&NewClient_3^{ATC} == [NewClient_2^{DNF} \mid balances = \varnothing \land name? = name0 \land \\
&\quad n? = an0 \land u? = uid0 \land clients = \{(uid0, name0)\} \land owners = \varnothing] \\
&NewClient_4^{ATC} == [NewClient_3^{DNF} \mid n? = an0 \land name? = name0 \land \\
&\quad balances = \{(an0, 0)\} \land u? = uid0 \land clients = \varnothing \land owners = \varnothing]
\end{aligned}
$$

As can be seen, within the TTF an abstract test case is a conjunction of equalities between VIS variables and constant values, rather than a sequence of operations leading to the desired state, as it is suggested by other approaches [1,2]. Some of these equalities specify the initial state for the test, while others specify the values for the input parameters of the SUT. This is a key issue when test case refinement is considered.

Note that test specifications and abstract test cases are all expressed in Z.

In the TTF test cases do not include test oracles because they are provided at the end of the MBT process [3]. Since oracles appear at the end of the process we do not need to deal with them during test case refinement. In the TTF, test case refinement concerns only with state and input data refinement.

3 A Method for Test Case Refinement

The core of this paper is, then, a general method for refining test cases, like $NewClient_4^{ATC}$, written in LaTeX markup, into executable programs or scripts written in some programming language. The result of this refinement is a collection of *concrete test cases*, or just test cases when it is clear from context. This refinement requires: (a) identifying the SUT's state variables and input parameters that correspond to the specification variables; (b) initializing the implementation variables as specified in each abstract test case; (c) initializing implementation variables used by the SUT but not considered in the specification; and (d) performing a sound refinement of the values of the abstract test cases into values for the implementation variables. For instance, if account numbers are implemented as integer numbers, then $an0$ in $NewClient_4^{ATC}$ must be refined as, say, 9711048.

The method yields programs written in the SUT's implementation language because we found it natural to correlate specification and implementation variables and it is easier to initialize them, assuming the SUT's source code is available. The correlation between specification and implementation variables is given

[1] Identifiers like $name0$ are assumed to be declared in axiomatic definitions and are regarded as constants of their types.

by engineers by means of so-called *refinement rules*, written in a declarative TCRL which is, in principle, independent of any programming language.

In summary, the method receives a user-defined refinement rule for a given Z operation, a list of test cases for that operation and the name of a programming language, and automatically applies the refinement rule to the list of test cases outputting a list of concrete test cases written in that programming language, each of which:

1. Sets the initial state of the SUT as specified by the test case.
2. Sets the input parameters expected by the SUT as specified by the test case.
3. Calls the SUT.

As it can be seen, the method we propose can be thought as a lightweight form of what is traditionally called *data refinement* [22, chapter 10]. Furthermore, as we have anticipated in the introduction, this method does not assume that the SUT was formally developed because no information from a possible formal refinement is needed.

All the remaining test activities—i.e. compiling test cases, executing them, capturing their output, etc. (Figure 1)—are beyond the scope of this paper.

4 Fastest Test Case Refinement Language

The method we propose is called Fastest TCRL (FTCRL). FTCRL is an interpreted language whose programs are refinement rules. Refinement rules transform a list of abstract test cases generated by Fastest into a list of concrete test cases in the SUT's programming language. The interpreter receives the target programming language as a parameter. In this paper we show part of the FTCRL semantics when the target programming language is C [23]; in [21] the full operational semantics for C and Java can be found.

The TTF is intended to be used as an MBT method for unit testing. Therefore, given a unit of implementation, P, engineers must find the Z schema, S, that specifies P—this schema may reference other schemas and it can be the specification of other units as well. Then, a refinement rule for the pair (P, S) must be given.

4.1 An Example of a Refinement Rule

Since refinement rules are essentially specifications of how VIS variables must be refined into implementation variables, we need some information about the unit under test (UUT). Below we introduce a typical refinement rule that is explained and analysed in the following sections.

Assume the banking system specified in Section 2 is implemented in the C programming language[2]. Let's say that elements of AN and $NAME$ are implemented as character strings, elements of UID are integer numbers and those

[2] We assume the reader is familiar with the C programming language [23].

of *BALANCE* are floats. Say *clients* is implemented as a simply-linked list, c, declared as:

```
struct cdata {int uid; char *name; struct cdata *n;} *c;
```

balances is implemented as an array, b, declared as:

```
struct bdata {char* num; float bal;} b[100];
```

and there is an integer variable, l, pointing to the last used component of b. *owners* is implemented as a doubly-linked list, o, declared as:

```
struct odata {int *puid; char *pn; struct odata *n,*p;} *o;
```

where puid should point to the uid member of the corresponding node in c; pn should point to the num member of the corresponding b component; and n and p are pointers to the next and previous nodes in the list, respectively. Say that c, b, l and o are global variables. Finally, let's assume that *NewClient* is implemented by a C function with the following signature:

```
int newClient(int u, char *name, char *n)
```

Figure 3 shows the refinement rule for *NewClient*, when it is implemented by newClient() and the data structures described above. Figure 4 shows the concrete test case generated by applying that refinement rule to $NewClient_2^{ATC}$. Note: (a) the kind of information of the UUT that is needed to write a refinement rule; (b) FTCRL assumes that the SUT's source code is available; and (c) Figure 4 is an executable C program. Please, look at these figures while we introduce FTCRL below.

4.2 The Basic Structure of a Refinement Rule

The first line in a refinement rule declares its name. Refinement rules have four mandatory sections that must be written in strict order: @PREAMBLE, @LAWS, @UUT and @EPILOGUE. The interpreter uses the preamble to collect typing information of the UUT and adds it at the beginning of a test case. The preamble should contain all the code necessary to compile the UUT—for instance, UUT's definition, type declarations, sentences to import external resources, header files, etc. The epilogue should contain code to perform clean-up once the test has been run—for instance, deleting a file—and it is blindly copied at the end of each test case. The @UUT section contains only one line of FTCRL code to call the UUT. The value returned by the UUT is not considered since it does not affect refinement, but other steps of the MBT process.

The name of a refinement rule can be used in other refinement rules as shown in Figure 5, with the obvious meaning. Note that this mechanism allows users to use the same @LAWS section with different preambles and epilogues, thus making it possible to refine the same abstract test cases to different programming languages, since all the code of the refinement rule that depends on the target programming language is confined to these two sections. The language includes others forms of reuse [21].

```
@RRULE bank
@PREAMBLE
#include <bank.h>
@LAWS
l1:u?        ==> u
l2:name?     ==> name
l3:n?        ==> n
l4:clients   ==> c AS LIST[SLL,n] WITH[clients.@dom ==> c.uid,
                                       clients.@ran ==> c.name]
l5:balances ==> b AS ARRAY WITH[balances.@dom ==> b.num,
                                balances.@ran ==> b.bal];
                balances.@# ==> l
l6:owners    ==> o AS LIST[DLL,n,p]
                     WITH[owners.@dom ==> o.puid AS REF[c.uid],
                          owners.@ran ==> o.pn AS REF[b.num]]
@UUT newClient(u,name,n)
```

Fig. 3. Refinement rule for *NewClient*. `bank.h` declares all the elements of the UUT

```
#include <bank.h>
int main() {
 int u = 345;
 char *name = "name0", *n = "an0";
 struct cdata cdata0 = {87,"name0",NULL};
 struct bdata bdata0 = {"an1",20};
 struct odata odata0 = {0,0,NULL,NULL};
 c = &cdata0;
 b[0] = bdata0;
 l = 1;
 odata0.puid = &cdata0.uid;
 odata0.pn = bdata0.num;
 o = &odata0;
 newClient(u,name,n);
 return 1;
}
```

Fig. 4. Concrete test case for $NewClient_2^{ATC}$ generated by `bank` of Figure 3

```
@RRULE otherBankingRefRule
@PREAMBLE bank.@PREAMBLE
@LAWS
bank.l04
.....
commercialAccounts.@LAWS
.....
@UUT deposit(....)
```

Fig. 5. Refinement rules can be reused as Z schemas are reused by schema inclusion

4.3 Refinement Laws

The `@LAWS` section is a list of *refinement laws* (or laws), of the following form:

```
ident:list_of_spec_vars ==> refinement
```

where `ident` is an identifier to reuse the law in other rules (Figure 5), `list_of_spec_vars` is a list of one or more specification variables, and `refinement` specifies how the specification variables must be refined. The token `==>` can be read as 'refines to'.

The most simple law is, for instance, `l1` in Figure 3. For each abstract test case, this law makes the interpreter to declare a local variable named `u` of type `int` and to assign it the value of $u?$ in the abstract test case (Figure 4). The type of `u` is deduced as follows: `u` is the first parameter in the call placed in the `@UUT` section, and the first parameter found in the signature of `newClient()` is of type `int`. In general, all the typing information can be deduced by parsing both the LaTeX markup of the Z specification and the source code of the SUT. Constant values of given types at the specification level, such as $uid0$, are translated to the implementation type by applying an arbitrary bijection whenever necessary.

Note that, in this context, the overflow C semantics of the `int` type is not a problem when refining Z's $\mathbb{Z}$, because, if at the Z level a natural number is greater than the C `int` limit, then, precisely, this test case will test how the program deals with the overflow C semantics. It is not the difficulty appearing in classical refinement calculus: the intention is to test the program, not to refine the specification.

Law `l4` specifies that *clients* is implemented as the `c` list. The first parameter of the `LIST` clause indicates that `c` is a simply-linked list and the second one is the name of the variable pointing to the next node in the list—some of these parameters are ignored when refining to some programming languages, Java is an instance. It is necessary to include this information in the law because, in some programming languages, it is impossible to automatically deduce that `c` is a list, solely from its declaration. The `WITH` clause helps to specify how each ordered pair in *clients* must be accommodated in the list. In this case, elements in the domain go to `uid` and elements in the range to `name`. Therefore, the interpreter creates a new variable of type `cdata` for each pair in *clients* and initializes them with the constant values of each pair. The value of the `n` member of each of these new variables is set to point to the address of any other of them—since *clients* is a function, there is no order between its pairs, and so any order in `c` should be correct. In general, FTCRL applies a sort of extensionality to refine Z sets [21].

Note how a specification variable is refined to more than one implementation variable in `l5`; `balances.@#` is the cardinality of *balances*. Had it been necessary to make `l` to point to the first free component in `b`, then we would have written: `balances.@# + 1`—in general, any constant expression is valid.

Regarding `l6`, `DLL` stands for doubly-linked list and the other two parameters are the members pointing to the next and previous nodes, respectively. If an implementation variable is intended to hold a reference (or a pointer) to some data in some other data structure, the `REF` directive must be used. It is possible to generate source code according to this specification because every element of a dynamic data structure is first saved in a new static variable whose name, memory address and value can be freely used by the interpreter.

4.4 More Examples and Features

In this section we will show a few small examples to introduce a variety of FTCRL's features; sometimes we will use the savings account example.

Two specification variables refined into one implementation variable. Consider the following excerpt from some specification:

$$[NAME]$$
$$AddPerson == [first?, last? : NAME \ldots \mid \ldots]$$

Assume the implementation stores the first and last name of persons in a single character string variable, `name`. Then, the law could be as follows:

```
person:first?, last? ==> last? ++ ", " ++ first? ==> name
```

If an abstract test case binds *name*0 to *first*? and *name*1 to *last*?, then the interpreter would generate the following code:

```
char* name = "name1, name0";
```

Implementation details abstracted away in the specification. Now assume the implementation of the banking system introduced in Section 2 stores also the address and age of each client. Specifiers abstracted away these details retaining only the name of the client. Therefore, `cdata` would indeed be:

```
struct cdata {int uid, age; char *name, *addr; struct cdata *n;} c;
```

In this case the refinement law would be:

```
104:clients ==> c AS LIST [SLL,n]
                    WITH [clients.@dom ==> c.uid,
                          clients.@ran ==> c.name,
                          "Road" ==> c.addr,
                          40 ==> c.age]
```

or `@AUTOFILL ==> c.*` can replace `"Road" ==> c.addr, 40 ==> c.age` [21]. In other words, if an implementation detail was abstracted away in the specification, then, in some way, its value is irrelevant with respect to the correctness of the implementation. Hence, the same value can be used in all of the tests.

Refining into external resources. Assume there is an UUT of the banking system that reads client data from a text file. Test cases for this UUT would need to initialize this file according to the value *clients* has in different abstract test cases. Say the file stores one record per line with the format `UID:NAME`. Then, the refinement law would be:

```
file:clients ==> clients.@DOM ++ ":" ++ clients.@RAN
                   ==> clientData.txt AS FILE[/bank]
```

If in some test case we have $clients = \{(uid1, name0), (uid2, name1)\}$ the interpreter would produce roughly the following C code:

```
fd = open(/bank/clientData.txt, O_RDWR | O_TRUNC | O_CREAT);
.......
write(fd, "87:name0", strlen("87:name0"));
write(fd, "91:name1", strlen("91:name1"));
.......
close(fd);
```

where 87 and 91 result from applying an arbitrary bijection between *UID* and `int` as we have said before.

Refining complex Z types. Suppose it is necessary to refine $f : X \rightarrow\!\!\!\!\!\!+ Y \rightarrow\!\!\!\!\!\!+ H \times W$ where X, Y and W are given types and H is the schema $[a : A;\ b : B]$. The recursive nature of FTCRL, Z and all programming languages make it possible to refine such complex types in equally complex implementation data structures. For instance, the dot notation in FTCRL can be recursively applied to cross products, schema types and other constructions [21].

Data structures currently supported. The implementation data structures that are supported by FTCRL depends on the programming language. For C and Java we have [21]:

- C: `int` (plus all the modifiers `short`, `long`, `unsigned` and `signed`), `char`, `float`, `double`, `enum`, arrays, `struct` and pointers to any of them. This implies that all kinds of lists are supported.
- Java: `int`, `short`, `long`, `byte`, `Integer`, `Short`, `Long`, `Byte`, `char`, `Character`, `float`, `double`, `Float`, `Double`, `enum`, arrays, `class`, `List<type>`, `ArrayList<type>`, `LinkedList<type>`, `Attributes`, `HasMap`, `Hashtable`, `IdentityHashMap`, `TreeMap`, `WeakHashMap` and `String`.

Completeness—Refining to possibly unsupported data structures. Say some C program defines a list where each node points to the next node but also to the node five positions ahead. Data structures like this can be arbitrary complex, but, as far as we know, they are seldom used. FTCRL was designed to directly support the most common data structures, but it provides a (low level) language feature that allows to refine to any data structure. This feature involves using the `@PLCODE` optional section. This section can contain only source code (of the

SUT's programming language) and is blindly copied between the code generated after parsing `@LAWS` and the call to the UUT. We expect that users will use this section only when they find no other way of writing their refinement rules, because it increases the dependency of refinement rules on the SUT's programming language. Readers can find more about `@PLCODE` in [21, Section 2.4].

Even considering only the most common data structures, it is very difficult to prove that FTCRL can be used to refine any Z variable into any implementation data structure because it would require to prove that for every programming language. However, since FTCRL supports all the C data structures, we have strong reasons to believe that data structures defined by higher-level programming languages can be supported too. The `@PLCODE` mechanism provides completeness where the proper FTCRL code fails to do so.

Implementation independence. We want to emphasize that refinement rules and all the test cases generated by them are resilient to a number of changes in the implementation. For instance, considering the savings accounts example, if there is some error in updating or walking `c`, or some error in keeping the references of `o`'s nodes, or `l` is not correctly synchronized with the last used component of `b`, and these errors are fixed, the `bank` refinement rule remains the same since `c`, `o`, `b` and `l` all maintain their attributes and roles in the implementation.

Fastest's architecture for test case refinement. Fastest is a Java application, so it is FTCRL's interpreter. Currently, the interpreter is a proof of concept implemented with the ANTLR parser generator [24]—and using a simpler version of FTCRL than the one shown here. The architecture of the interpreter was envisioned to allow for easily plug-in modules implementing FTCRL for new programming languages, as shown in Figure 6. Some of the pluggable modules hide a few technological issues such as connections to databases, operating system interactions, etc.

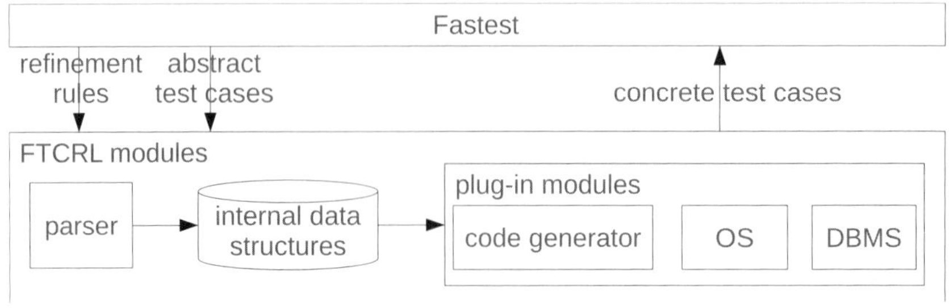

Fig. 6. Simple module diagram of the Fastest's architecture for test case refinement

5 A Case Study

This approach has been used in a contract with Nemo Group (Argentina) to test its core product. Confidentiality issues and space restrictions impede us to include all the information; key data is available at `http://www.flowgate.net/pdf/cacheflight.tar.gz`. Nemo's core business is software development for the travel industry. The SUT is a large Java application whose purpose is to provide booking functionality for flights provided by several major international companies. This program heavily uses a database.

We have written Z specifications for the most critical methods of the key classes of the SUT. The choice of methods and classes as well as the specification for each of them had to be reverse-engineered along with some key Nemo's engineers. This process was carried out in such a way that we did not read the code. First, we asked Nemo's engineers what a particular method should do, then we wrote the specification according to their comments—how they learned the function of a method was transparent for us. Once the specifications were ready we applied Fastest to generate abstract test cases and, at the same time, we wrote the refinement rules—during this activity we seldom needed the assistance of Nemo's personnel since we have already learned the application. Currently, we have refined more than one thousand test cases with a few refinement rules. Refinement rules include database connections, nested classes, lists, etc. However, we cannot give figures about how many errors were found because the experiment concluded when we were able to execute the test cases.

6 Related Work

Refinement calculus or specification refinement has a long and well-established tradition in the formal methods community [25,26]. The Z formal notation is not an exception [22]. However, these theories are aimed at a much harder and general problem than ours: to formally transform an abstract specification into executable code. Usually, these methods list a set of sound refinement rules guaranteeing that every time they are applied, the description so obtained verifies the original specification. Classical refinement has four important differences with our method: (a) we do not try to refine the whole specification but just some constant values of some variables; (b) the implementation is already available, it must not be derived from the specification; (c) we do not attempt to prove that refinement rules are right, precisely, we try to surface problems in the implementation; and (d) we propose that users write refinement rules instead of choosing them from a fixed menu, because implementations can be arbitrarily complex. However, our approach was inspired by the idea of tiered specifications proposed for Larch [27] which can be seen as a form of refinement.

The creators of the TTF applied it to Object-Z to test classes of object-oriented programs [28]. They use the ClassBench testing framework which requires testers to write testgraphs to test the class under test. Once testgraphs are written ClassBench automatically tests the class. The authors propose to generate a finite state machine (FSM) from a test specification and then to transform the FSM to a testgraph. However, it is not clear how easy it might be to semi-automatically derive testgraphs from abstract test cases. Actually, the authors discuss several issues that arise when transforming a FSM to a testgraph because they are models at different levels of abstraction.

Derrick and Boiten [20] analyse the relationship between testing and refinement in the context of Z specifications. However, they apply a different approach because they assume that the implementation has been refined from the specification. Therefore, they first derive abstract test cases from the Z specification—in doing so they apply a different method, not the TTF—and then they use information available in the refinement in order to refine the abstract test cases. Although their method is more formal than FTCRL, it is less applicable than ours since formal refinement is seldom available.

BTT is a MBT method based on the B notation that generates sequences of operation invocations at an abstract level that constitute the abstract test cases [5]. This sequences are made executable by translating them into scripts [29]. These scripts are built by providing a test script pattern and a mapping table. The test script pattern is a source code file in the target language with some tags indicating where to insert sequences of operation invocations. The information present in a mapping table is similar to that of a refinement rule. However, the mapping tables do not seem to be as expressive as FTCRL. Furthermore, in this method testers must provide the test script pattern instead of getting it automatically from the reification information.

AspecT is an aspect-oriented language for the instantiation of abstract test cases from UML statecharts [30]. This approach uses a combination of languages, Ecore, OCL, Phyton, Groovy and AspectT, to refine test cases. It does not seem to clearly define the mapping between specification and implementation variables but to decompose the refinement phase into several steps in which aspects, pointcuts and advices are written.

If some naming conventions are applied and the implementation is conveniently annotated, it might be possible to automatically define many refinement rules. Meyer and et al. manage to automatically test programs by annotating them with contracts written in the implementation language, Eiffel in this case [31]. They, for instance, use the same names for variables in the implementation and in the contracts. We need to further investigate whether this can be applied to Z specifications since they are more abstract than contracts.

7 Conclusions

We have proposed FTCRL, a declarative refinement language that automates test case concretization within the Test Template Framework (TTF), a Z-based MBT method. By defining simple refinement rules, that are independent of test cases and, to a great extent, of the implementation itself, testers can use an interpreter to refine all the abstract test cases generated by Fastest—TTF's implementation. A prototype of this interpreter has been implemented in Fastest by following an architecture that allows developers to plug-in modules supporting different implementation languages.

Refinement rules become, also, a key formal document linking the specification and the implementation. It must be noted, however, that the mere possibility of writing a refinement rule does not necessarily imply that the implementation verifies the specification. Once the implementation has passed all the tests, it can be assumed correct (modulo testing) and, then, refinement rules might be used to perform some lightweight formal analyses.

We plan to improve the interpreter and to add more features to FTCRL. So far, the method is non-intrusive, i.e. it does not modify the SUT to test it—even if it is implemented in Java where reflection is used to access private members from the outside. This property is important since modifying the SUT to get it tested can be a source of artificial errors. However, we have a problem with local static variables declared inside a subroutine since they cannot be initialized from the outside of the unit under test. We need to further investigate this issue.

References

1. Utting, M., Legeard, B.: Practical Model-Based Testing: A Tools Approach. Morgan Kaufmann Publishers Inc., San Francisco (2006)
2. Hierons, R.M., et al.: Using formal specifications to support testing. ACM Comput. Surv. 41(2), 1–76 (2009)
3. Stocks, P., Carrington, D.: A Framework for Specification-Based Testing. IEEE Transactions on Software Engineering 22(11), 777–793 (1996)
4. Grieskamp, W., Gurevich, Y., Schulte, W., Veanes, M.: Generating finite state machines from abstract state machines. In: ISSTA 2002: Proceedings of the 2002 ACM SIGSOFT International Symposium on Software Testing and Analysis, pp. 112–122. ACM, New York (2002)
5. Legeard, B., Peureux, F., Utting, M.: A comparison of the BTT and TTF test-generation methods. In: Bert, D., Bowen, J. (eds.) B 2002 and ZB 2002. LNCS, vol. 2272, pp. 309–329. Springer, Heidelberg (2002)
6. Bernot, G., Gaudel, M.C., Marre, B.: Software testing based on formal specifications: a theory and a tool. Softw. Eng. J. 6(6), 387–405 (1991)
7. Posey, B.: Just Enough Software Test Automation. Prentice Hall PTR, Upper Saddle River (2002)
8. Fewster, M., Graham, D.: Software test automation: effective use of test execution tools. ACM Press/Addison-Wesley Publishing Co. (1999)
9. Information Technology, I.S.O.: – Z Formal Specification Notation – Syntax, Type System and Semantics. Technical Report ISO/IEC 13568, International Organization for Standardization (2002)
10. Ammann, P., Offutt, J.: Using formal methods to derive test frames in category-partition testing. In: Compass 1994: 9th Annual Conference on Computer Assurance, pp. 69–80. National Institute of Standards and Technology, Gaithersburg (1994)
11. Hall, P.A.V.: Towards testing with respect to formal specification. In: Proc. Second IEE/BCS Conference on Software Engineering, IEE/BCS Conference Publication, vol. 290, pp. 159–163 (July 1988)
12. Hierons, R.M., Sadeghipour, S., Singh, H.: Testing a system specified using Statecharts and Z. Information and Software Technology 43(2), 137–149 (2001)
13. Hierons, R.M.: Testing from a Z specification. Software Testing, Verification & Reliability 7, 19–33 (1997)
14. Hörcher, H.M., Peleska, J.: Using Formal Specifications to Support Software Testing. Software Quality Journal 4, 309–327 (1995)

15. Stocks, P.: Applying Formal Methods to Software Testing. PhD thesis, Department of Computer Science, University of Queensland (1993)
16. Maccoll, I., Carrington, D.: Extending the Test Template Framework. In: Proceedings of the Third Northern Formal Methods Workshop (1998)
17. Cristiá, M., Rodríguez Monetti, P.: Implementing and applying the stocks-carrington framework for model-based testing. In: Breitman, K., Cavalcanti, A. (eds.) ICFEM 2009. LNCS, vol. 5885, pp. 167–185. Springer, Heidelberg (2009)
18. Cristiá, M., Albertengo, P., Rodríguez Monetti, P.: Pruning testing trees in the Test Template Framework by detecting mathematical contradictions. In: Fiadeiro, J.L., Gnesi, S. (eds.) SEFM, pp. 268–277. IEEE Computer Society, Los Alamitos (2010)
19. Cristiá, M., Albertengo, P., Rodríguez Monetti, P.: Fastest: a model-based testing tool for the Z notation. In: Mazzanti, F., Trentani, G. (eds.) PTD-SEFM, Consiglio Nazionale della Ricerche, Pisa, Italy, pp. 3–8 (2010)
20. Derrick, J., Boiten, E.: Testing refinements of state-based formal specifications. Software Testing, Verification and Reliability (9), 27–50 (1999)
21. Cristiá, M., Rodríguez Monetti, P., Albertengo, P.: The FTCRL reference guide. Technical report, Flowgate Consulting (2010)
22. Potter, B., Till, D., Sinclair, J.: An introduction to formal specification and Z. Prentice Hall PTR, Upper Saddle River (1996)
23. Kernighan, B.W., Ritchie, D.M.: The C Programming Language, 2nd edn. Prentice-Hall, Inc., Englewood Cliffs (1988)
24. Parr, T.: Language Implementation Patterns: Create Your Own Domain-Specific and General Programming Languages, 1st edn. Pragmatic Bookshelf (2009)
25. Morgan, C.: Programming from specifications, 2nd edn. Prentice Hall International (UK) Ltd., Hertfordshire (1994)
26. Back, R.J., Wright, J.V.: Refinement Calculus: A Systematic Introduction, 1st edn. Springer-Verlag New York, Inc., Secaucus (1998)
27. Guttag, J.V., Horning, J.J.: Larch: languages and tools for formal specification. Springer-Verlag New York, Inc., New York (1993)
28. Carrington, D.A., MacColl, I., McDonald, J., Murray, L., Strooper, P.A.: From object-z specifications to classbench test suites. Softw. Test., Verif. Reliab. 10(2), 111–137 (2000)
29. Bouquet, F., Legeard, B.: Reification of executable test scripts in formal specicifation-based test generation: The Java card transaction mechanism case study. In: Araki, K., Gnesi, S., Mandrioli, D. (eds.) FME 2003. LNCS, vol. 2805, pp. 778–795. Springer, Heidelberg (2003)
30. Benz, S.: Aspectt: aspect-oriented test case instantiation. In: Proceedings of the 7th International Conference on Aspect-oriented Software Development, AOSD 2008, pp. 1–12. ACM, New York (2008)
31. Meyer, B., Fiva, A., Ciupa, I., Leitner, A., Wei, Y., Stapf, E.: Programs that test themselves. Computer 42, 46–55 (2009)

Automating Algebraic Methods in Isabelle

Walter Guttmann[1], Georg Struth[2], and Tjark Weber[3]

[1] Institut für Programmiermethodik und Compilerbau, Universität Ulm
walter.guttmann@uni-ulm.de
[2] Department of Computer Science, The University of Sheffield
g.struth@dcs.shef.ac.uk
[3] Computer Laboratory, University of Cambridge
tw333@cam.ac.uk

Abstract. We implement a large Isabelle/HOL repository of algebras for application in modelling computing systems. They subsume computational logics such as dynamic and Hoare logics and form a basis for various software development methods. Isabelle has recently been extended by automated theorem provers and SMT solvers. We use these integrated tools for automatically proving several rather intricate refinement and termination theorems. We also automate a modal correspondence result and soundness and relative completeness proofs of propositional Hoare logic. These results show, for the first time, that Isabelle's tool integration makes automated algebraic reasoning particularly simple. This is a step towards increasing the automation of formal methods.

1 Introduction

Many popular formalisms for developing and verifying programs and software systems, and many system semantics are based on algebra. Many computational logics, for instance temporal, dynamic or Hoare logics, have algebraic siblings. Algebraic approaches offer simple abstract modelling languages, system analysis via equational reasoning, and a well developed meta-theory, namely universal algebra. In the area of formal methods, algebraic semantics form an important part of, for example, Alloy, B and Z.

Among the above algebraic methods, variants of idempotent semirings and Kleene algebras play a fundamental role. They provide the operations for nondeterministic choice, sequential composition and (in)finite iteration of a system; important semantics—binary relations, computation traces, computation trees—are among their models. They have already been applied widely from compiler optimisation and feature-oriented software development to program transformation and refinement. They are particularly suitable for automation [18,20]; automated theorem proving (ATP) systems were, in fact, instrumental for developing some recent variants [10].

Stand-alone ATP systems, however, do not suffice for coherently implementing and applying algebraic methods. Mechanisms for designing modular theory hierarchies, inheriting and instantiating theorems across hierarchies and models, exploiting dualities, filtering relevant hypotheses, supporting (co)inductive

S. Qin and Z. Qiu (Eds.): ICFEM 2011, LNCS 6991, pp. 617–632, 2011.

reasoning or decision procedures for data types, and integrating domain specific solvers are indispensable for these tasks. Yet all these mechanisms are available through the recent integration of ATP systems and Satisfiability Modulo Theories (SMT) solvers into Isabelle/HOL [28,4]. Our paper shows that this offers new perspectives for algebraic methods in formal software development: we have implemented a large Isabelle/HOL repository for algebraic methods, which contains more than 1000 facts.[1] They have all been obtained by ATP and SMT, using Isabelle's Sledgehammer tool which calls the external provers E, SPASS and Vampire and internally reconstructs their output with the theorem prover Metis or the SMT solver Z3. While some basic features of the repository have been presented in a tutorial paper [13], this paper describes the more advanced implementation of modal algebras and computational logics and discusses several intricate modelling examples. Our main results are as follows:

* In the context of Kleene algebras [6,22] we show how inductive proofs involving finite iteration can be automated and give a new simple automated calculational proof of a well-known termination theorem [2].
* In the context of modal Kleene algebras [8,26] we automatically derive the axioms of propositional dynamic logic, notably Segerberg's formula, show how dualities give theorems for free, discuss how to obtain an algebraic wlp-calculus, and automate a rather complex computational modelling task.
* Based on modal Kleene algebras, we automatically relate three algebraic notions of termination, which implies a modal correspondence result for Löb's formula. We apply these notions in a simple automated proof of a generalisation of the above termination theorem [12].
* From a minimalist set of algebraic axioms we develop the calculus and semantics of propositional Hoare logic and provide simple abstract automated soundness and relative completeness proofs. We instantiate this theory to modal Kleene algebras and further to the relational wlp-semantics.
* We instantiate all abstract concepts and results to binary relations, thus making them available for relational program semantics and development.

In combination, these results yield the main contribution of this paper: Isabelle's Sledgehammer tool enabled us to design and implement a large modular repository for algebraic methods with relative ease by ATP and SMT, to extend it to implementations of various computational logics and program semantics, and to automate some rather complex modelling tasks. Such methods can complement existing Isabelle verification technology [29] by additional support for developing programs that are correct by construction.

This paper can only present some main theorems and proof sketches. A complete documentation of all formal proofs is available in our repository. This paper has been generated by Isabelle's document preparation system. The theory sources and its technical content are formally verified by Isabelle2011.

[1] The repository is available at http://www.dcs.shef.ac.uk/~georg/isa/

2 Preliminaries

This work builds on our large repository for Kleene and relation algebras that contains most of the standard calculational theorems in these areas. We use a relational semantics, but do not need full relation algebras.

An Isabelle theory for dioids is the basis of our formalisation. It covers variants of semirings needed for process algebras, the analysis of probabilistic algorithms, program refinement, formal language theory or relational program semantics. Isabelle's class mechanism [14] is used for implementing this theory hierarchy. For the sake of simplicity we only discuss semirings and dioids. Many theorems hold already in weaker variants.

Formally, a *semiring* is a structure $(S, +, \cdot, 0, 1)$ such that $(S, +, 0)$ is a commutative monoid, $(S, \cdot, 1)$ is a monoid, the distributivity laws $x \cdot (y + z) = x \cdot y + x \cdot z$ and $(x + y) \cdot z = x \cdot z + y \cdot z$ hold and 0 is an annihilator, that is, $0 \cdot x = 0 = x \cdot 0$. A *dioid* is a semiring in which addition is idempotent, that is, $x + x = x$. By idempotency, the additive monoid forms a semilattice and the dioid is ordered by the semilattice order $x \leq y \leftrightarrow x + y = y$. The semiring operations are isotone with respect to $\leq$ and 0 is its least element. The order is instrumental for proving theorems in dioids and Kleene algebras, splitting identities into inequalities: 'Use inequalities wherever possible' [6, page 120].

Each semiring comes with a dual semiring—its *opposite*—in which the order of multiplication is swapped. This is captured in Isabelle by defining $x \odot y = y \cdot x$ and proving the following fact.

Lemma (**in** *semiring-one-zero*) *dual-semiring-one-zero*:
class.semiring-one-zero (*op* +) (*op* $\odot$) *1 0*

We have shown in Isabelle that the binary relations on a set S under union, relational composition, the empty set and the identity relation form a dioid. In this model, $(a, c) \in x \cdot y$ if and only if $(a, b) \in x$ and $(b, c) \in y$ for some $b \in S$, and $1 = \{(a, a) : a \in S\}$. More abstractly, an element x represents an action of a system, $+$ a non-deterministic choice between actions and $\cdot$ the sequential composition of actions; 0 and 1 are the aborting and the ineffective actions.

For modelling iterative behaviour, dioids can be expanded to Kleene algebras. Formally, a *Kleene algebra* is a dioid augmented with a star operation that satisfies the unfold and induction axioms

Assumes *star-unfoldl*: $1{+}x{\cdot}x^* \leq x^*$
Assumes *star-inductl*: $z{+}x{\cdot}y \leq y \rightarrow x^*{\cdot}z \leq y$

and their opposites (with arguments to $\cdot$ swapped). In relation Kleene algebras, x^* is the reflexive transitive closure of the relation x. More abstractly, x^* is the least (pre)fixpoint of the mapping $f(y) = 1 + x \cdot y$ and its opposite. It models finite iteration of x in the sense that, by the unfold law, either 1 is executed (which has no effect) or an x-action is performed before the iteration continues. The next section shows how infinite iteration can be axiomatised similarly.

Kleene algebras were initially conceived as algebras of regular expressions. A classical result states that Kleene algebras are complete for the equational theory of regular expressions [22]. Hence all *regular identities* from formal languages, for instance, $1 + x \cdot x^* = x^* = x^* \cdot x^* = x^{**}$ and $(x + y)^* = x^* \cdot (y \cdot x^*)^*$ and $x \cdot (y \cdot x)^* = (x \cdot y)^* \cdot x$, hold in this setting. The theory of Kleene algebras in our repository contains more than 100 facts for different variants and, by instantiation, for models based on binary relations, languages and traces. Almost all proofs could be fully automated by invoking Sledgehammer. All identities hold in weak variants where the Isabelle decision procedure for regular expression equivalence [24] is not applicable.

3 Warm-Up: Three Proofs in Kleene Algebra

We now set the scene for later results. First, beyond purely equational reasoning and the capabilities of ATP systems, we automate two inductive proofs in Kleene algebras. Second, reasoning about infinite behaviours, we automate a coinductive proof of a well-known termination theorem.

The Kleene star is often defined as a sum of powers: $x^* = \sum_{i \geq 0} x^i$. A benefit of Kleene algebra, which is slightly weaker, is that it replaces higher-order inductive reasoning about powers and unbounded suprema by equational reasoning in first-order logic. Yet many theorems combine the star and finite sums and require both kinds of reasoning. To implement this combination we use a primitive recursive function *power* for x^i with Isabelle's built-in theory of sums and a small set of simple lemmas (see below). Our first induction example is an unfold law that frequently occurs in automata theory.

Lemma *powerstar-unfoldl*: $(\sum i{=}0..n\ .\ x^i) + x^{n+1} \cdot x^* = x^*$
Proof (*induct n*)
  case *0* **show** *?case* **by** *simp* (*smt mult-oner star-unfoldl-eq*)
  case *Suc* **thus** *?case* **by** (*simp add*: *setsum-cl-ivl-Suc*) (*smt add-assoc*
    power.simps(2) *distl mult-oner mult-assoc star-unfoldl-eq power-commutes*)
qed

Isabelle's Isar proof language allows users to obtain human-readable proofs. In our examples, however, the main emphasis is on proof automation beyond the granularity of textbook proofs. Hence the above proof only displays the splitting into inductive cases, which is beyond first-order reasoning. The proofs of the base case and the induction step are fully automatic, using previously verified lemmas that have been selected by Sledgehammer's relevance filter.

In the base case, Isabelle's simplifier strips off the sums before Z3 uses some basic regular identities. In the induction step, we simplify again before Z3 uses the inductive definition of powers $x^{Suc\ n} = x \cdot x^n$, the lemma $x^m \cdot x^n = x^n \cdot x^m$ and further regular identities.

One advantage of the approach is that users can, to a large extent, control the granularity of Isar proofs. In the rest of this paper, we will usually only display Isar proof skeletons, in which the list of lemmas used is omitted. In these cases, we merely indicate whether Metis or the SMT solver has been used.

Our second example is (the dual of) Conway's *powerstar axiom* for Kleene algebras [6]. Its proof requires some inductive facts about sums, but does not need induction itself.

Lemma *conway-powerstar-var*: $x^* = (\sum i{=}0..n\ .\ x^i){\cdot}(x^{n+1})^*$
Proof –
  have $x^* \leq (\sum i{=}0..n\ .\ x^i){\cdot}(x^{n+1})^*$ **by** (*smt star-inductl-eq sum-power-3 distr add-assoc add-comm star-unfoldl-eq mult-onel sum-power-2 mult-assoc mult-oner*)
  thus *?thesis*
  by (*smt power-le-star prod-star-closure star-invol star-iso sum-power-le-star eq-iff*)
qed

The identities $x \cdot \sum_{i=0}^{n} x^i = (\sum_{i=1}^{n} x^i) + x^{n+1}$ and $\sum_{i=0}^{n} x^i = 1 + \sum_{i=1}^{n} x^i$ are used in the first step together with star induction. The second step uses the approximation law $\sum_{i=0}^{n} x^i \leq x^*$. All other properties are again regular identities. We will further need the following instance of the powerstar axiom.

Lemma *conway-powerstar-2*: $x^* = (x^2)^*{+}x{\cdot}(x^2)^*$ — by smt

The above examples show, for the first time, how combined fixpoint-based and inductive reasoning can be fully automated in Isabelle.

To reason about infinite iteration we augment Kleene algebras by an omega operation which is axiomatised as a greatest (post)fixpoint.

Assumes *omega-unfold*: $x^\omega \leq x{\cdot}x^\omega$
Assumes *omega-coinduct*: $y \leq z{+}x{\cdot}y \rightarrow y \leq x^\omega{+}x^*{\cdot}z$

Kleene algebras expanded by this operation are called *omega algebras* [5]. We have shown within Isabelle/HOL that binary relations form omega algebras and developed the basic calculus of omega algebra. The following, for instance, is a new separation theorem for infinite loops.

Theorem *omega-sum-refine*: $y{\cdot}x \leq x{\cdot}(x{+}y)^* \rightarrow (x{+}y)^\omega = x^\omega{+}x^*{\cdot}y^\omega$
Proof
  assume $y{\cdot}x \leq x{\cdot}(x{+}y)^*$
  hence $(x{+}y)^\omega \leq x{\cdot}(x{+}y)^*{\cdot}(x{+}y)^\omega{+}y^\omega$ — by smt
  thus $(x{+}y)^\omega = x^\omega{+}x^*{\cdot}y^\omega$ — by metis
qed

It states that if x *quasicommutes* over y, that is, $y \cdot x \leq x \cdot (x + y)^*$, the infinite loop $(x+y)^\omega$ in which x and y are executed non-deterministically can be refined to the more deterministic loops in $x^\omega{+}x^*{\cdot}y^\omega$. The initial step uses the unfold law $(x{+}y)^\omega = y^\omega{+}y^*{\cdot}x{\cdot}(x{+}y)^\omega$ and then applies the consequence $y^*{\cdot}x \leq x{\cdot}(x{+}y)^*$ of quasicommutation.

In omega algebra, termination can be expressed as the absence of infinite iteration: (iteration of) x *terminates* if and only if $x^\omega = 0$. Our previous refinement theorem then implies the following well-known separation of termination:

Corollary *bd*: $y{\cdot}x \leq x{\cdot}(x{+}y)^* \rightarrow ((x{+}y)^\omega = 0 \leftrightarrow x^\omega{+}y^\omega = 0)$
  by (*smt add-comm annil no-trivial-inverse omega-sum-refine omega-sum-unfold*)

It states that termination of $x + y$ can be separated into individual termination of x and y whenever x quasicommutes over y. An informal proof chasing infinite relational diagrams is due to Bachmair and Dershowitz [2]. In omega algebra, it arises as a simple consequence of the loop refinement law. The proof in this section is significantly simpler and more automatic than earlier proofs [18]. A generalisation of this result in modal Kleene algebra is proved in Section 6.

4 Modal Semirings and Kleene Algebras

Reasoning about computing systems often requires modelling state spaces in addition to actions. One way to achieve this is to define modal operators over dioids or Kleene algebras. For an action x of a system and a set of states p, the forward diamond operator $|x\rangle p$ models the set of all states from which executing x *may* lead into p, whereas the forward box operator $|x]p$ models the set of all states from which executing x *must* lead into that set. Backward boxes and diamonds can be defined as well: $\langle x|p$ describes the set of states one may reach from p by executing x, and $[x|p$ describes the set of all states that can only be reached from p. In relational models (Kripke frames), $|x\rangle p$ is the preimage of the set p under the relation x, that is, the *domain* of x restricted in its range to p: $|x\rangle p = d(x \cdot p)$. Similarly, $\langle x|p = r(p \cdot x)$, where r denotes the range operation.

Modal operators can therefore be obtained in dioids or Kleene algebras by axiomatising domain and range. In fact, an *antidomain* operation a can be introduced in dioids by three simple axioms [10]:

Assumes *a1*: $a(x) \cdot x = 0$
Assumes *a2*: $a(x \cdot y) + a(x \cdot a(a(y))) = a(x \cdot a(a(y)))$
Assumes *a3*: $a(a(x)) + a(x) = 1$

It is the Boolean complement of the domain operation: $a(x)$ describes the set of states *not* in the domain of an action x, that is, the part of the state space where x is not enabled. In the relational model, $a(x) = \{(s,s) : \neg\exists t\,.\,(s,t) \in x\}$. Domain can then be defined as $d(x) = a(a(x))$. It models that part of the state space where the action x is enabled. Thus $d(x) = \{(s,s) : \exists t\,.\,(s,t) \in x\}$ in the relational model. The domain operation induces an appropriate state space: if S is a dioid, then the set of domain elements $d(S) = \{d(x) : x \in S\}$ forms a Boolean algebra with join $+$, meet $\cdot$ and complement a. Moreover, $p \in d(S)$ if and only if $p = d(p)$, whence domain elements can be typed by applying d or a. We use the letters p, q, $\ldots$ to highlight domain elements.

A range operation is axiomatised as domain in the opposite semiring. We have formalised this duality in Isabelle. All theorems about domain semirings have been automatically dualised to range semirings.

Forward diamonds and boxes are then defined in an Isabelle class for forward modal semirings.

Assumes *fdiamond-def*: $|x\rangle y = d(x \cdot y)$
Assumes *fbox-def*: $|x]y = a(x \cdot a(y))$

We have axiomatised backward modal operators dually by using range. Kleene algebras extended by all these operations are called *modal Kleene algebras* [26].

Again, duality has been formally established by Isabelle's locale mechanism and all statements about backward modalities have been obtained directly by duality.

Boxes and diamonds are duals, too: $|x]p = a(|x\rangle a(p))$ and $[x|p = a(\langle x|a(p))$. This De Morgan duality acts on the Boolean subalgebra $d(S)$ of S. Capturing it formally within Isabelle requires axiomatisations based on carrier sets, which have a detrimental effect on proof automation. To dualise diamond statements into box statements, we use a simple trick instead: we provide the dual theorem together with a set of about 10 lemmas, including the De Morgan laws for a and d and similar 'conversion theorems'. We show an example in Section 5.

The interaction between the star, the modalities and (anti)domain elements is particularly interesting. The relational semantics of while-programs can be encoded in this setting, for example, if p then x else y as $d(p) \cdot x + a(p) \cdot y$, and while p do x as $(d(p) \cdot x)^* \cdot a(p)$. This is used in Section 7. Furthermore, modal star induction laws can be derived:

Lemma *dia-star-induct*: $d(p)+(|x\rangle d(q)) \leq d(q) \rightarrow |x^*\rangle d(p) \leq d(q)$
Lemma *box-star-induct*: $d(q) \leq d(p) \cdot |x]d(q) \rightarrow d(q) \leq |x^*]d(p)$

These link modal Kleene algebras with computational logics such as propositional dynamic logic or Hoare logic. In particular, the forward box operator abstractly represents the wlp-operator and the calculus of modal Kleene algebra encompasses the laws of partial correctness for while-programs. Finally, we have instantiated the relational model of modal Kleene algebras in Isabelle.

5 Dynamic Algebras and Segerberg's Formula

We now relate modal Kleene algebras with dynamic algebras, which are algebraic siblings of propositional dynamic logic (PDL). Our repository contains automated proofs of all PDL axioms—in algebraic form—as theorems of modal Kleene algebra. As an example we present the derivation of Segerberg's formula, the only non-trivial proof task, from the modal star induction law. To simplify presentation and proof we introduce an auxiliary function.

Definition $A\ x\ p \equiv d(x \cdot p) \cdot a(p)$

It models those states outside of p from which executing x may lead into that set. Since the domain and antidomain operations are used for complementation and for typing domain elements, type conversions that humans would leave implicit tend to pollute proofs and inhibit automation. We therefore provide helper lemmas, for instance, $|x\rangle p = d(|x\rangle p)$, $|x\rangle p = |x\rangle d(p)$, $A\ x\ p = d(A\ x\ p)$, $A\ x\ p = (|x\rangle p) \cdot a(p)$ and $a(A\ x\ a(p)) = a(p) + |x]d(p)$, to derive Segerberg's formula after splitting into inequalities.

Lemma *fsegerberg*: $|x^*\rangle d(p) = d(p) + |x^*\rangle(A\ x\ p)$
Proof –
  have $|x^*\rangle d(p) \leq d(p) + |x^*\rangle(A\ x\ p)$ — by smt, using diamond star induction
  thus *?thesis* — by smt
qed

Segerberg's formula is perhaps better known and explained in box form. We prove it by duality using the trick described above.

Lemma *fbox-segerberg*: $|x^*]d(p) = d(p)\cdot|x^*](a(p)+|x]d(p))$
by (*smt a-A a-closure a-de-morgan-var-2 antidomain-semiring-domain-def fbox-simp-2 fdia-fbox fsegerberg*)

The list of lemmas contains the diamond variant of Segerberg's formula plus some helpers, including a De Morgan law for domain and antidomain elements. This list has been obtained from a larger one by minimising with Sledgehammer.

In box form, Segerberg's formula expresses induction: its right-hand side states that the system is originally in p and it is always the case (after executing x any number of times) that p will be preserved when executing x once more. The left-hand side states that the system is always in p (after repeatedly executing x). The term $a(p) + |x]d(p)$ corresponds to the Boolean implication $d(p) \rightarrow |x]d(p)$. We introduce special notation in Isabelle,

Definition $p \xrightarrow{x} q \equiv a(p)+|x]d(q)$

expressing that if p holds in the current state, q must hold after executing the action x. We can then rewrite Segerberg's formula as $|x^*]d(p) = d(p) \cdot |x^*](p \xrightarrow{x} p)$.

Modal Kleene algebra supports automated computational modelling by equational reasoning. As an example we prove a rather intricate formula expressing a separation property for alternating transitions between sets of states p and q. Again, we first introduce some helper lemmas: (i) $d(p) \cdot p \xrightarrow{x} q = d(p) \cdot |x]q$, (ii) $p \xrightarrow{x} q \cdot |x]q \xrightarrow{y} s \leq p \xrightarrow{x \cdot y} s$, and (iii) $|x^*](d(p) \cdot |x]d(p)) = |x^*]d(p)$. Equation (i) expresses a (dynamic) form of modus ponens, (ii) a property of sequential composition, as in the wlp-calculus, and (iii) an unfold property for boxes.

Theorem *alternation*:
$d(p)\cdot|x^*]((p \xrightarrow{x} q)\cdot(q \xrightarrow{x} p)) = |(x\cdot x)^*](d(p)\cdot(q \xrightarrow{x} p))\cdot|x\cdot(x\cdot x)^*](d(q)\cdot(p \xrightarrow{x} q))$
Proof –
have $d(p)\cdot|x^*]((p \xrightarrow{x} q)\cdot(q \xrightarrow{x} p)) = d(p)\cdot|(x\cdot x)^*]((p \xrightarrow{x} q)\cdot|x](q \xrightarrow{x} p)\cdot(q \xrightarrow{x} p)\cdot|x](p \xrightarrow{x} q))$
— essentially by powerstar, distributing boxes and regular identities
also have ... $= d(p)\cdot|(x\cdot x)^*](p \xrightarrow{x\cdot x} p)\cdot|(x\cdot x)^*]((p \xrightarrow{x} q)\cdot|x](q \xrightarrow{x} p)\cdot(q \xrightarrow{x} p)\cdot|x](p \xrightarrow{x} q))$
— essentially by the above property (ii)
also have ... $= |(x\cdot x)^*]d(p)\cdot|(x\cdot x)^*]((p \xrightarrow{x} q)\cdot|x](q \xrightarrow{x} p)\cdot(q \xrightarrow{x} p)\cdot|x](p \xrightarrow{x} q))$
— by Segerberg's formula
also have ... $= |(x\cdot x)^*](d(p)\cdot|x\cdot x]d(p))\cdot|(x\cdot x)^*]((q \xrightarrow{x} p)\cdot|x](d(q)\cdot(p \xrightarrow{x} q)))$
— by distributing boxes, property (i) and rearranging terms
finally show *?thesis* — by property (iii) and distributing boxes
qed

By instantiating q with $a(p)$ or p, our separation theorem specialises to an exercise from Harel, Kozen and Tiuryn's book on dynamic logic [15, Exercise 5.6], namely the identity $p \cdot |x^*](p \xrightarrow{x} a(p) \cdot a(p) \xrightarrow{x} p) = |(x \cdot x)^*]p \cdot |x \cdot (x \cdot x)^*]a(p)$, and to Segerberg's formula. Both instances have again been proved automatically.

6 Termination and Löb's Formula

To generalise our termination example from Section 3 we now implement notions of termination in modal Kleene algebra. In particular, we prove a modal correspondence result, namely that Löb's formula expresses wellfoundedness on transitive Kripke frames. We express both the frame property and Löb's formula in modal Kleene algebra and then establish their equivalence.

Definition $\Omega\ x\ p \equiv d(p){\cdot}a(x{\cdot}p)$

If p is a set, then $\Omega\ x\ p$ describes those elements in p from which no further x-transitions inside of p are possible, hence x-maximal elements. We have first proved helper lemmas such as $\Omega\ x\ p = d(p) \cdot a(|x\rangle p) = d(p) \cdot |x]a(p)$. We have also proved that the non-maximal states in p are those from which there is an x-transition into p: $a(\Omega\ x\ p) = a(p) + |x\rangle p$ and $d(p) \cdot a(\Omega\ x\ p) = d(p) \cdot |x\rangle p$. Finally, we have shown that $\Omega\ x\ p = 0$ if and only if $d(p) \leq |x\rangle p$.

Following [9] we have formalised three algebraic notions of termination in Isabelle. In set theory, a relation x on a set q is *Noetherian* if every non-empty subset of q has an x-maximal element, which means that if a subset p of q has no x-maximal elements, then it must be empty:

Definition $\mathit{Noetherian}(x) \equiv (\forall\, p\ .\ \Omega\ x\ p = 0 \rightarrow d(p) = 0)$

This is equivalent to $\forall p\,.\,d(p) \leq |x\rangle p \rightarrow d(p) = 0$. Our abstract notion of Noetherity has been formally linked with the standard relational definition within Isabelle, that is, in the relational model the two definitions are equivalent. The second way of expressing termination is as follows:

Definition $\mathit{PreLoebian}(x) \equiv (\forall\, p\ .\ d(p) \leq |x^*\rangle(\Omega\ x\ p))$

Third, if x is transitive, which implies $x = x \cdot x^*$, we can apply $|x\rangle$ to both sides of this formula and obtain Löb's formula.

Definition $\mathit{Loebian}(x) \equiv (\forall\, p\ .\ |x\rangle p \leq |x\rangle(\Omega\ x\ p))$

We now relate the three properties, formalising the approach in [9]. Noetherity can be interpreted as a frame property via the relational model, and Löb's formula as a formula of modal logic; hence we establish a modal correspondence result. The main step is to show that an element is pre-Löbian if and only if it is Noetherian.

Theorem $\mathit{Noetherian}(x) \leftrightarrow \mathit{PreLoebian}(x)$
Proof –
  have $\forall\, p\ .\ d(p){\cdot}a(|x^*\rangle(\Omega\ x\ p)) \leq |x\rangle(d(p){\cdot}a(|x^*\rangle(\Omega\ x\ p)))$ — mainly star unfold
  hence $\mathit{Noetherian}(x) \rightarrow \mathit{PreLoebian}(x)$ — by Noetherity
  thus *?thesis* — straightforward
qed

The remaining proofs are then straightforward.

Lemma $\mathit{Loebian}(x) \rightarrow \mathit{Noetherian}(x)$
Lemma $(\forall\, p\ .\ |x\rangle(|x\rangle p) \leq |x\rangle p) \rightarrow \mathit{PreLoebian}(x) \rightarrow \mathit{Loebian}(x)$
Theorem $(\forall\, p\ .\ |x\rangle(|x\rangle p) \leq |x\rangle p) \rightarrow (\mathit{Noetherian}(x) \leftrightarrow \mathit{Loebian}(x))$

Finally, we translate Löb's formula into its more conventional box version:

Lemma $(\forall p\ .\ |x\rangle p \leq |x\rangle(\Omega\ x\ p)) \leftrightarrow (\forall p\ .\ |x](a(|x]d(p))+d(p)) \leq |x]d(p))$

As an example for termination analysis with modal Kleene algebra, we now prove a generalisation of Bachmair and Dershowitz's theorem which, in a higher-order relational setting, is due to Doornbos, Backhouse and van der Woude [12]. We expand modal Kleene algebras by an operation ∇ of *divergence* [9], mapping each action x to the set of those states from which infinite x-transition sequences may start. Divergence is modelled as a greatest (post)fixpoint; it is the greatest set of states that is invariant with respect to 'stepping back' with x.

Assumes *nabla-closure*: $d(\nabla x) = \nabla x$
Assumes *nabla-unfold*: $\nabla x \leq |x\rangle \nabla x$
Assumes *nabla-coinduction*: $d(y) \leq |x\rangle d(y)+d(z) \rightarrow d(y) \leq \nabla x+|x^*\rangle d(z)$

We have developed a simple ∇-calculus in Isabelle which is very similar to that of the omega operation. We use the instance $d(y) \leq |x\rangle d(y) \rightarrow d(y) \leq \nabla x$ of nabla coinduction, the fact that nabla is a fixpoint $\nabla x = |x\rangle \nabla x$, subdistributivity $\nabla x \leq \nabla(x+y)$, isotonicity $x \leq y \rightarrow \nabla x \leq \nabla y$, star absorption $|x^*\rangle \nabla x = \nabla x$, and $\Omega\ x\ d(y) = 0 \rightarrow d(y) \leq \nabla x$. We have also formally linked divergence Kleene algebras with the relational model.

In divergence Kleene algebras an action x terminates if and only if $\nabla x = 0$. We have shown that this property implies that x is Noetherian (hence pre-Löbian).

Doornbos, Backhouse and van der Woude's theorem generalises quasicommutation to *lazy commutation*: $y \cdot x \leq x \cdot (x+y)^* + y$. We use that lazy commutation implies $y \cdot x^* \leq x \cdot (x+y)^* + y$.

Theorem *dbw*: $y{\cdot}x \leq x{\cdot}(x+y)^*+y \rightarrow (\nabla x+\nabla y = 0 \leftrightarrow \nabla(x+y) = 0)$
Proof (*rule+*)
assume *lazycomm*: $y{\cdot}x \leq x{\cdot}(x+y)^*+y$ **and** *xy-wf*: $\nabla x+\nabla y = 0$
hence $\nabla(x+y) \leq |x\rangle\nabla(x+y)+|y\rangle|x^*\rangle(\Omega\ x\ (\nabla(x+y)))$
— by nabla unfold and because x is pre-Löbian
hence $\nabla(x+y) \leq |x\rangle\nabla(x+y)+|x\rangle|(x+y)^*\rangle(\Omega\ x\ (\nabla(x+y)))+|y\rangle(\Omega\ x\ (\nabla(x+y)))$
using *lazycomm* — and distributing diamonds
hence $\nabla(x+y) \leq |x\rangle\nabla(x+y)+|y\rangle(\Omega\ x\ (\nabla(x+y)))$ — by star absorption
with *xy-wf* **show** $\nabla(x+y) = 0$ — by Noetherity
next assume $\nabla(x+y) = 0$ **thus** $\nabla x+\nabla y = 0$ — by subdistributivity of nabla
qed

In particular, this theorem holds in the relational model, where $\nabla x = d(x^\omega)$.

7 Hoare Logic

In this section we consider propositional Hoare logic (PHL), a fragment of Hoare logic that abstracts from assignments and focuses on the control structure of while-programs. PHL is also a fragment of PDL [15] and it is subsumed by Kleene algebra with tests [23]. We give an abstract algebraic formalisation and automatically derive soundness and relative completeness of PHL. To link Hoare-style reasoning about programs with modal Kleene algebras, we show that the latter satisfy the abstract axioms.

Soundness and relative completeness of different variants of Hoare logic are well known and have already been proved in Isabelle/HOL [27,29]. Our development abstracts from underlying structures such as state spaces and program executions. By assuming a small axiom set, it generalises previous approaches in modal Kleene algebra [26], benefits automated proving and supports models beyond relational ones. Our proofs are highly automatic using Metis and Z3. Basic algebraic properties, meaningful lemmas and whole cases in inductive proofs can be shown by single calls to these tools.

Our presentation focuses on partial correctness, but this is not an inherent limitation. We take the following steps.

1. Axiomatise tests as a subset of elements that form a Boolean algebra. Tests are needed as conditions in while-programs and as preconditions in correctness statements.
2. Axiomatise preconditions. We use a subset of axioms known from the weakest liberal precondition operator.
3. Axiomatise while-programs. We use equational axioms for the conditional, the unfold rule for the while-loop and an axiom capturing soundness of the loop rule in the Hoare calculus.
4. Derive soundness and relative completeness. We can thus axiomatise validity of Hoare triples and obtain the rules of PHL as consequences.
5. Show that modal Kleene algebras form an instance of the above theory.

We now elaborate these steps.

1. Boolean subset: As described in Section 4, the range of the antidomain operation a forms a Boolean algebra. In program semantics, its elements typically represent conditions on the state space. This motivates the following axiomatisation.

We assume a structure $(S, \cdot, a)$ such that $a(S)$, the range of a, is a Boolean algebra with meet operation $\cdot$ and complement a. Technically, this is achieved by taking an axiomatisation for Boolean algebra and replacing each variable x with $a(x)$, denoting an arbitrary element of the range of a. We use Huntington's axioms [25], which are particularly concise, and therefore yield a small set of axioms for a. Additionally, closure of $a(S)$ under $\cdot$ is asserted by the axiom $a(x) \cdot a(y) = a(a(a(x) \cdot a(y)))$; by definition it is closed under a. The constants 0 and 1, the join operation $+$ and the order $\leq$ can then be expressed in terms of $\cdot$ and a. Laws of Boolean algebra, including [25, Theorems 3, 5, 7], are restricted to the range of a and derived automatically.

It is essential to impose the Boolean algebra only on a subset of elements, because some models of programs are not closed under general complements [17].

2. Preconditions: The elements of the Boolean subset serve as tests, firstly in preconditions. Our axioms for preconditions are motivated by the properties of weakest liberal preconditions [11]. The weakest liberal precondition $\mathsf{wlp}(x, q)$ is the set of initial states from which all terminating executions of the program x

end up in a state satisfying q. While the program x may be an arbitrary element, q and $\mathsf{wlp}(x,q)$ must be tests, that is, in the range of a.

This motivates the introduction of the binary operation $x«q$, our abstract version of $\mathsf{wlp}(x,q)$, with the following axioms in an Isabelle class.

Assumes *pre-closed*: $x « a(q) = a(a(x « a(q)))$
Assumes *pre-seq*: $x \cdot y « a(q) = x « y « a(q)$
Assumes *pre-test*: $a(p) \cdot (a(p) « a(q)) = a(p) \cdot a(q)$
Assumes *pre-distrib*: $x « a(p) \cdot a(q) = (x « a(p)) \cdot (x « a(q))$

Similarly to the axiomatisation of the Boolean subset, we use $a(q)$ to denote an arbitrary element in the range of a. The axiom *pre-closed* states that the result of « is a test, effectively making « an operation which takes an element and a test and yields a test. The axioms *pre-seq* and *pre-test* capture the interaction of preconditions with sequential composition and tests, respectively. The axiom *pre-distrib* separates the conjunction of two postconditions.

3. While-Programs: A second use of tests is as conditions: the statement $\mathsf{if}\ p\ \mathsf{then}\ x\ \mathsf{else}\ y$ is obtained by the ternary operation $x \lhd p \rhd y$, where p is a test. For our derivation of PHL it suffices to characterise the two branches by the following axioms; see [16,21] for more comprehensive axiomatisations.

Assumes $a(p) \cdot (x \lhd a(p) \rhd y) = a(p) \cdot x$
Assumes $a(a(p)) \cdot (x \lhd a(p) \rhd y) = a(a(p)) \cdot y$

The following consequence exemplifies the interaction of the conditional with preconditions. It essentially states soundness of the PHL conditional rule.

Lemma $a(p) \cdot a(q) \le x « a(s) \wedge a(a(p)) \cdot a(q) \le y « a(s) \rightarrow a(q) \le x \lhd a(p) \rhd y « a(s)$
— by smt

Conditions also occur in while-loops: the statement $\mathsf{while}\ p\ \mathsf{do}\ x$ is obtained by the binary operation $p{*}x$, where p is a test. The unfold property of the while-loop is captured by the following axiom.

Assumes $a(p) {*} x = x \cdot (a(p) {*} x) \lhd a(p) \rhd 1$

While-programs can be constructed from atomic programs by the operations of sequential composition, conditional and while-loop. In PHL, atomic programs are an unspecified set; in concrete models they contain, for example, assignments.

Inductive-Set *While-program*
where $x \in$ *Atomic-program* $\Rightarrow x \in$ *While-program*
| $x \in$ *While-program* $\wedge$ $y \in$ *While-program* $\Rightarrow x \cdot y \in$ *While-program*
| $x \in$ *While-program* $\wedge$ $y \in$ *While-program* $\Rightarrow x \lhd a(p) \rhd y \in$ *While-program*
| $x \in$ *While-program* $\Rightarrow a(p) {*} x \in$ *While-program*

Isabelle expects the meta-logic implication $\Rightarrow$ in such inductive definitions; we also use it instead of $\rightarrow$ for subsequent results proved by induction.

For simplicity, we assume that all tests in the range of a can be used as conditions in while-programs. A more detailed theory prescribes how to construct tests from an unspecified set of atomic tests by Boolean operations. It is then necessary to assume that preconditions are such tests; see [7,15,1] for related questions of expressibility.

4. Hoare Calculus: The unfold rule for while-loops is sufficient for proving relative completeness of PHL. Soundness of the partial correctness while-loop rule is essentially captured by the following, additional axiom.

Assumes $a(p) \cdot a(q) \leq x \ll a(q) \rightarrow a(q) \leq a(p) * x \ll a(a(p)) \cdot a(q)$

It can be derived in models where an explicit definition of while-loops is available. The reason for this indirect characterisation is that different models may have different semantics of while-loops.

The calculus makes correctness claims in the form of Hoare triples $p\,\{x\}\,q$. Intuitively, this triple states that all terminating executions of the program x started from a state satisfying p end up in a state satisfying q.

We capture the rules of the Hoare calculus by the following inductive predicate. Hence $p\,(\!|x|\!)\,q$ holds if the triple $p\,\{x\}\,q$ is derivable.

Inductive *derived-hoare-triple* (- (| - |) -)
  where $x \in$ *Atomic-program* $\Rightarrow x \ll a(p) (\!|x|\!) a(p)$
    $|\ a(p)(\!|x|\!)a(q) \wedge a(q)(\!|y|\!)a(s) \Rightarrow a(p)(\!|x \cdot y|\!)a(s)$
    $|\ a(p) \cdot a(q)(\!|x|\!)a(s) \wedge a(a(p)) \cdot a(q)(\!|y|\!)a(s) \Rightarrow a(q)(\!|x \lhd a(p) \rhd y|\!)a(s)$
    $|\ a(p) \cdot a(q)(\!|x|\!)a(q) \Rightarrow a(q)(\!|a(p) * x|\!)a(a(p)) \cdot a(q)$
    $|\ a(p) \leq a(q) \wedge a(q)(\!|x|\!)a(s) \wedge a(s) \leq a(t) \Rightarrow a(p)(\!|x|\!)a(t)$

The calculus has one axiom for atomic programs, one rule for each program construct and the rule of consequence. It follows by induction that only while-programs appear in derivable Hoare triples.

Lemma $p(\!|x|\!)q \Rightarrow p = a(a(p)) \wedge q = a(a(q)) \wedge x \in$ *While-program*
  by (*induct rule*: *derived-hoare-triple.induct*) — and 5 applications of smt

Validity of the Hoare triple $p\,\{x\}\,q$ is defined by the predicate $p\,\langle x\rangle\,q$, which holds if p and q are tests, x is a while-program and the condition p is sufficient to establish the postcondition q:

Definition $p\langle x\rangle q \equiv (p = a(a(p)) \wedge q = a(a(q)) \wedge x \in$ *While-program* $\wedge\ p \leq x \ll q)$

Soundness and relative completeness are proved separately by induction. Reasoning for each case is automated by Metis or Z3.

Theorem *soundness*: $p(\!|x|\!)q \Rightarrow p\langle x\rangle q$
  by (*induct rule*: *derived-hoare-triple.induct*) — and 5 applications of smt

Lemma *pre-completeness*: $x \in$ *While-program* $\Rightarrow x \ll a(q)(\!|x|\!)a(q)$
  by (*induct arbitrary*: *q rule*: *While-program.induct*) — and 4 applications of smt

Theorem *completeness*: $p\langle x\rangle q \rightarrow p(\!|x|\!)q$ — by smt

For convenient application of the calculus, we axiomatise validity of Hoare triples without referring to while-programs, using the predicate $p\,\{\!|x|\!\}\,q$.

Assumes $a(p)\{\!|x|\!\}a(q) \leftrightarrow a(p) \leq x \ll a(q)$

Based on this, we derive the above Hoare rules and further, auxiliary rules [1].

5. Instance for Modal Kleene Algebra: In the richer structure of modal Kleene algebra, we can explicitly define preconditions, the conditional, the while-loop and the validity of Hoare triples. To inherit the results derived above, we establish the subclass relationship by verifying the axioms, again using Z3.

— in the context of modal Kleene algebra
Assumes $x \ll p = |x]p$
Assumes $x \lhd p \rhd y = d(p) \cdot x + a(p) \cdot y$
Assumes $p * x = (d(p) \cdot x)^* \cdot a(p)$
Assumes $p \{\!| x |\!\} q \leftrightarrow d(p) \leq |x]q$

This makes the Hoare calculus available for reasoning about programs in modal Kleene algebra. The following simple example treats a while-loop, whose body contains two sub-programs w and y switching between states p and q. They are surrounded by sub-programs v, x and z for which p and q are invariants. The result shows that p is preserved by the while-loop.

Lemma $d(p) \{\!| v |\!\} d(p) \wedge d(p) \{\!| w |\!\} d(q) \wedge d(q) \{\!| x |\!\} d(q) \wedge d(q) \{\!| y |\!\} d(p) \wedge d(p) \{\!| z |\!\} d(p)$
$\rightarrow d(p) \{\!| d(s) * v \cdot w \cdot x \cdot y \cdot z |\!\} a(s) \cdot d(p)$ — by smt

8 Discussion and Conclusion

Our results show that algebraic formal methods can easily be developed by automated reasoning within Isabelle/HOL. A surprising observation is that the SMT solver Z3 often outperformed Metis and sometimes even the external ATP systems invoked by Sledgehammer. Although not especially designed for proofs in algebra, it could frequently automate proof steps at textbook level. Related empirical evidence supporting this observation has been obtained by using a benchmark suite of seven representative Isabelle formalisations that range from fast Fourier transforms to security protocol analysis [3].

Variants of Kleene algebras and their modal extensions are particularly suitable as algebraic methods because, in general, their theories admit a high degree of automation and important logics of programs and program semantics can be developed from that basis. This also includes temporal logics [18], which we did not discuss in this text. In contrast to previous work that was based solely on ATP [19,20], Isabelle's mechanisms for higher-order reasoning, proof management and theory modularisation are an essential aspect of the formalisation. To highlight the concision and simplicity of the algebraic approach, we only presented some proofs at the algebraic level. The complete formalisation of the relational model can be found in our repository.

While most of the basic proofs in Kleene algebras, omega algebras and modal Kleene algebras could be found automatically based on proof search by Sledgehammer (sometimes after splitting identities into inequalities), most of the more complex proofs in this paper have been engineered: Sledgehammer was often only able to automate individual proof steps at the granularity of handwritten proofs. Sometimes, when the scope of hypotheses was large, it was even unable to filter out the relevant lemmas. We have then merged steps for Metis or Z3 until those failed within reasonable time limits.

Our repository contains a large coherent set of algebraic theorems that require both equational and order-based reasoning. Therefore, it lends itself ideally for empirical investigations, tool optimisation, the design of tactics and the development of proof presentation methods. The repository can be extended for algebraic proof support for existing formal methods. This is promising for applications in formal program development and analysis. It would yield a high degree of automation and the possibility to switch seamlessly between pointwise domain-specific and abstract algebraic reasoning.

Another aspect of tool integration into Isabelle has not been discussed in this paper. Counterexample generators such as Nitpick complement the ATP systems and allow a proof and refutation game which is useful for developing and debugging formal specifications. Examples can be found across the repository.

Our main interest in a repository for algebraic methods and our main motivation for the research in this paper is to devise program development methods that complement and augment existing verification environments and tools. The combination of algebraic methods with proof technology ranging from domain-specific solvers and ATP systems to higher-order reasoning within the Isabelle theorem proving environment could make formal program development significantly simpler and more automatic. Integrating additional statements such as assignments, and data types such as numbers, arrays or lists into our abstract approach, and linking it with state-of-the-art program development methods is therefore the obvious direction for future work.

Acknowledgement. Walter Guttmann was supported by a fellowship within the Postdoc-Programme of the German Academic Exchange Service (DAAD). Georg Struth acknowledges funding from EPSRC grant EP/G031711/1. Tjark Weber acknowledges funding from EPSRC grant EP/F067909/1.

References

1. Apt, K.R., de Boer, F.S., Olderog, E.R.: Verification of Sequential and Concurrent Programs, 3rd edn. Springer, Heidelberg (2009)
2. Bachmair, L., Dershowitz, N.: Commutation, transformation, and termination. In: Siekmann, J.H. (ed.) CADE 1986. LNCS, vol. 230, pp. 5–20. Springer, Heidelberg (1986)
3. Blanchette, J.C., Böhme, S., Paulson, L.C.: Extending sledgehammer with SMT solvers. In: Bjørner, N., Sofronie-Stokkermans, V. (eds.) CADE 2011. LNCS, vol. 6803, pp. 116–130. Springer, Heidelberg (2011)
4. Böhme, S., Weber, T.: Fast LCF-style proof reconstruction for Z3. In: Kaufmann, M., Paulson, L.C. (eds.) ITP 2010. LNCS, vol. 6172, pp. 179–194. Springer, Heidelberg (2010)
5. Cohen, E.: Separation and reduction. In: Backhouse, R., Oliveira, J.N. (eds.) MPC 2000. LNCS, vol. 1837, pp. 45–59. Springer, Heidelberg (2000)
6. Conway, J.H.: Regular Algebra and Finite Machines. Chapman and Hall, Boca Raton (1971)
7. Cook, S.A.: Soundness and completeness of an axiom system for program verification. SIAM J. Comput. 7(1), 70–90 (1978)

8. Desharnais, J., Möller, B., Struth, G.: Kleene algebra with domain. ACM Transactions on Computational Logic 7(4), 798–833 (2006)
9. Desharnais, J., Möller, B., Struth, G.: Algebraic notions of termination. Logical Methods in Computer Science 7(1:1), 1–29 (2011)
10. Desharnais, J., Struth, G.: Internal axioms for domain semirings. Sci. Comput. Program. 76(3), 181–203 (2011)
11. Dijkstra, E.W.: A Discipline of Programming. Prentice-Hall, Englewood Cliffs (1976)
12. Doornbos, H., Backhouse, R., van der Woude, J.: A calculational approach to mathematical induction. Theor. Comput. Sci. 179(1-2), 103–135 (1997)
13. Foster, S., Struth, G., Weber, T.: Automated engineering of relational and algebraic methods in isabelle/HOL. In: de Swart, H. (ed.) RAMICS 2011. LNCS, vol. 6663, pp. 52–67. Springer, Heidelberg (2011)
14. Haftmann, F., Wenzel, M.: Local theory specifications in isabelle/Isar. In: Berardi, S., Damiani, F., de'Liguoro, U. (eds.) TYPES 2008. LNCS, vol. 5497, pp. 153–168. Springer, Heidelberg (2009)
15. Harel, D., Kozen, D., Tiuryn, J.: Dynamic Logic. MIT Press, Cambridge (2000)
16. Hoare, C.A.R., Hayes, I.J., He, J., Morgan, C.C., Roscoe, A.W., Sanders, J.W., Sorensen, I.H., Spivey, J.M., Sufrin, B.A.: Laws of programming. Commun. ACM 30(8), 672–686 (1987)
17. Hoare, C.A.R., He, J.: Unifying theories of programming. Prentice Hall Europe (1998)
18. Höfner, P., Struth, G.: Automated reasoning in kleene algebra. In: Pfenning, F. (ed.) CADE 2007. LNCS (LNAI), vol. 4603, pp. 279–294. Springer, Heidelberg (2007)
19. Höfner, P., Struth, G.: On automating the calculus of relations. In: Armando, A., Baumgartner, P., Dowek, G. (eds.) IJCAR 2008. LNCS (LNAI), vol. 5195, pp. 50–66. Springer, Heidelberg (2008)
20. Höfner, P., Struth, G., Sutcliffe, G.: Automated verification of refinement laws. Annals of Mathematics and Artificial Intelligence 55(1-2), 35–62 (2009)
21. Jackson, M., Stokes, T.: Semigroups with if-then-else and halting programs. International Journal of Algebra and Computation 19(7), 937–961 (2009)
22. Kozen, D.: A completeness theorem for Kleene algebras and the algebra of regular events. Information and Computation 110(2), 366–390 (1994)
23. Kozen, D.: On Hoare logic and Kleene algebra with tests. ACM Transactions on Computational Logic 1(1), 60–76 (2000)
24. Krauss, A., Nipkow, T.: Proof pearl: Regular expression equivalence and relation algebra. Journal of Automated Reasoning (2011), http://dx.doi.org/10.1007/s10817-011-9223-4
25. Maddux, R.D.: Relation-algebraic semantics. Theor. Comput. Sci. 160(1-2), 1–85 (1996)
26. Möller, B., Struth, G.: Algebras of modal operators and partial correctness. Theor. Comput. Sci. 351(2), 221–239 (2006)
27. Nipkow, T.: Hoare logics in Isabelle/HOL. In: Schwichtenberg, H., Steinbrüggen, R. (eds.) Proofs and System-Reliability, pp. 341–367. Kluwer Academic Publishers, Dordrecht (2002)
28. Paulson, L.C., Blanchette, J.C.: Three years of experience with Sledgehammer, a practical link between automatic and interactive theorem provers. In: Sutcliffe, G., Ternovska, E., Schulz, S. (eds.) Proceedings of the 8th International Workshop on the Implementation of Logics, pp. 3–13 (2010)
29. Schirmer, N.: Verification of Sequential Imperative Programs in Isabelle/HOL. Ph.D. thesis, TU München (2006)

Term Rewriting in Logics of Partial Functions

Matthias Schmalz

ETH Zurich, Switzerland*

Abstract. We devise a theoretical foundation of *directed rewriting*, a term rewriting strategy for logics of partial functions, inspired by term rewriting in the Rodin platform. We prove that directed rewriting is sound and show how to supply new rewrite rules in a soundness preserving fashion. In the context of Rodin, we show that directed rewriting makes a significant number of conditional rewrite rules unconditional. Our work not only allows us to point out a number of concrete ways of improving directed rewriting in Rodin, but also has applications in other logics of partial functions. Additionally, we give a semantics for the logic of Event-B.

1 Introduction

Partiality is a common phenomenon in computer science: programs may not terminate, throw exceptions, or have undesired side-effects such as memory corruption. Reasoning about partial functions often involves proving a term to be *well-defined*; informally, a term is *well-defined* if and only if the involved functions are always applied to arguments within their domains. Well-definedness proofs are often perceived as an annoying distraction. Moreover, a theorem prover for a logic of partial functions can be overwhelmed by the number of well-definedness subgoals arising during proofs.

This paper tackles the problem of term rewriting in logics of partial functions. Many unconditional rewrite rules that are sound in logics of total functions become conditional when transferred to logics of partial functions; e.g., rewriting $\$x - \$x$ to 0 is typically sound only under the condition that $\$x$ is well-defined. Note that the '\$' in $\$x$ emphasizes that $\$x$ matches arbitrary, possibly ill-defined, terms. Proving such well-definedness conditions even when applying the simplest rewrite rules constitutes a significant overhead.

In order to make concrete statements about the practical impact of our results, we focus on a particular logic of partial functions, although our results are of a more general nature. *Event-B* [1] is a formal method for modeling discrete state transition systems. Event-B is based on a logic of partial functions. *Rodin* [2] is the corresponding development environment. Interestingly, Rodin often avoids proving well-definedness: Rodin rewrites $\$x - \$x$ to 0 without checking well-definedness of $\$x$, and $\$x \div \$x$ to 1 without proving that $\$x$ differs from 0. This raises several questions, in particular, why term rewriting in Rodin is sound and to what extent Rodin avoids solving well-definedness conditions. The question of soundness has been addressed in [11], but only for a fragment of the logic (see Sect. 6).

In this paper, we provide a theoretical foundation for Rodin's rewriting strategy: *directed rewriting*. Usually, the term t may be rewritten to u if and only if $t \equiv u$, i.e., t

* This research is supported by the EU funded FP7 project Deploy (Grant N° 214158).

S. Qin and Z. Qiu (Eds.): ICFEM 2011, LNCS 6991, pp. 633–650, 2011.

and u are semantically equal. In directed rewriting, t may be rewritten to u if and only if $t \sqsubseteq u$, where $\sqsubseteq$ designates the *flat domain order* $\sqsubseteq$ (see e.g. [18, p. 61]). We explain how conditional directed rewrite rules can be applied within proofs and why their application is sound. Directed rewriting is *unsafe* in general, i.e., it may transform a provable statement into an unprovable one and thus lead a proof attempt into a dead end. However, we show that it is straightforward to avoid this unsafety. Moreover, we provide evidence that directed rewriting significantly reduces the number of well-definedness checks required during proofs.

It is desirable that the set of rewrite rules used in proofs can be extended in a soundness preserving fashion. Event-B requires operators and binders to be monotonic w.r.t. the flat domain order; this is one of the reasons why directed rewriting is successful. However, if all operators are required to be monotonic, it is difficult to express soundness proof obligations for user-supplied rewrite rules. We point out a solution to this problem for a class of rewrite rules that often occur in practice.

Soundness proofs obviously presuppose a well-understood notion of validity. Other work introducing Event-B's logic disregards the details about partial functions [1] or is confined to an untyped fragment of Event-B's logic [12], in particular excluding sets. We therefore start our exposition with a novel presentation of syntax and semantics of Event-B's logic.

The main contribution of this paper is the insight how a simple change in the rewriting strategy makes a significant number of conditional rewrite rules unconditional. Although we present our results in the context of Event-B, they have applications in other logics of partial functions such as LPF [10] and PVS [17], as we will explain in Sect. 6. We believe that our novel presentation of Event-B's logic not only helps to understand directed rewriting, but is also useful for further developments such as mathematical (viz. conservative) extensions [5,20] and generic instantiation [23]. As a direct application, our results suggest several ways of improving Rodin's current implementation of directed rewriting.

2 Abstract Syntax

Sequences. By $t_1, \ldots, t_n$ and $t_1 \; \ldots \; t_n$ we denote the sequence of length n with t_i at position i, for $1 \leq i \leq n$. Variables denoting sequences are written in bold and underlined. We write t_i for the ith element of $\underline{\boldsymbol{t}}$ when it exists, $|\underline{\boldsymbol{t}}|$ for $\underline{\boldsymbol{t}}$'s length, and $\underline{\boldsymbol{t}}, \underline{\boldsymbol{t}}'$ or $(\underline{\boldsymbol{t}}, \underline{\boldsymbol{t}}')$ for the concatenation of $\underline{\boldsymbol{t}}$ and $\underline{\boldsymbol{t}}'$.

2.1 Types and Terms

Types. Roughly speaking, Event-B has a Hindley-Milner style type system, just like HOL [8] and ML. A *signature* Σ consists of three pairwise disjoint sets of *type operators*, *(ordinary) operators*, and *binders*. We assume we are given infinitely many *type variables* that are distinct from the type operators given by signatures. A signature Σ assigns a non-negative integer, called *arity*, to each type operator. The signatures we consider in this paper all include the *boolean* type operator $\mathcal{B}$ of arity zero. The set of *types (over Σ)* is the smallest set such that every type variable is a type, and $\tau(\underline{\boldsymbol{\nu}})$ is a type if $\underline{\boldsymbol{\nu}}$ is a sequence of types and τ a type operator of arity $|\underline{\boldsymbol{\nu}}|$.

Examples of type operators in Rodin include the *integer type* $\mathcal{Z}$ of arity 0 and the *powerset* type operator $\mathcal{P}$ of arity 1. Informally, $\mathcal{Z}$ denotes the set of all integers, $\mathcal{P}(\mathcal{Z})$ the set of all subsets of $\mathcal{Z}$, and $\mathcal{P}(\alpha)$ the set of all subsets of α.

A *(type) substitution σ (over Σ)* consists of a sequence $\underline{\boldsymbol{\alpha}}$ of pairwise distinct type variables and a sequence $\underline{\boldsymbol{\mu}}$ of types, where $|\underline{\boldsymbol{\alpha}}| = |\underline{\boldsymbol{\mu}}|$, and is written $[\underline{\boldsymbol{\alpha}} := \underline{\boldsymbol{\mu}}]$. The substitution σ maps the type ν to the type $\nu\sigma$ obtained by simultaneously replacing every occurrence of α_i by μ_i, $1 \leq i \leq |\underline{\boldsymbol{\alpha}}|$, in ν. The type sequence $\underline{\boldsymbol{\nu}'}$ is an *instance* of $\underline{\boldsymbol{\nu}}$ iff $|\underline{\boldsymbol{\nu}'}| = |\underline{\boldsymbol{\nu}}|$ and there is a substitution σ such that $\nu'_i = \nu_i\sigma$, for $1 \leq i \leq |\underline{\boldsymbol{\nu}}|$.

Terms. The signature Σ associates with each ordinary operator f a sequence of types $\underline{\boldsymbol{\nu}}$ (the *argument type*) and a type μ (the *result type*), written as $f \mathbin{⨾} \underline{\boldsymbol{\nu}} \rightsquigarrow \mu$ or, if $\underline{\boldsymbol{\nu}}$ is empty, also as $f \mathbin{⨾} \mu$. With each binder Q the signature Σ associates a non-empty sequence $\underline{\boldsymbol{\nu}}$ (the *bound variable type*), a non-empty sequence $\underline{\boldsymbol{\mu}}$ (the *argument type*), and a type ξ (the *result type*), written as $Q \mathbin{⨾} (\underline{\boldsymbol{\nu}} \rightsquigarrow \underline{\boldsymbol{\mu}}) \rightsquigarrow \xi$.

Examples of operators in Rodin include $0 \mathbin{⨾} \mathcal{Z}$, *conjunction* $\wedge \mathbin{⨾} (\mathcal{B}, \mathcal{B}) \rightsquigarrow \mathcal{B}$, and *membership* $\in \mathbin{⨾} (\alpha, \mathcal{P}(\alpha)) \rightsquigarrow \mathcal{B}$. An example of a binder is *universal quantification* $\forall \mathbin{⨾} (\alpha \rightsquigarrow \mathcal{B}) \rightsquigarrow \mathcal{B}$, which informally takes a function mapping elements of α to booleans and yields a boolean.

We assume we are given infinitely many *variable names* that always differ from the operators and binders given by signatures. An *(ordinary) variable* $x \mathbin{⨾} \nu$ consists of a variable name x and a type ν. An *operator variable* $\$f \mathbin{⨾} \underline{\boldsymbol{\nu}} \rightsquigarrow \mu$ consists of a variable name f, *argument types* $\underline{\boldsymbol{\nu}}$ and a *result type* μ; if $\underline{\boldsymbol{\nu}}$ is empty, we usually write $\$f \mathbin{⨾} \mu$ instead of $\$f \mathbin{⨾}\!\rightsquigarrow \mu$.

Conditions T1-T4 below inductively define *terms (over Σ)*. By *$\underline{\boldsymbol{t}}$ has type $\underline{\boldsymbol{\nu}}$* (abbreviated as $\underline{\boldsymbol{t}} \mathbin{⨾} \underline{\boldsymbol{\nu}}$) we mean $|\underline{\boldsymbol{t}}| = |\underline{\boldsymbol{\nu}}|$ and t_i is of type ν_i, $1 \leq i \leq |\underline{\boldsymbol{t}}|$.

T1: Every ordinary variable of type ν is a term of type ν.
T2: If $f \mathbin{⨾} \underline{\boldsymbol{\nu}} \rightsquigarrow \mu$ is an operator and $\underline{\boldsymbol{t}} \mathbin{⨾} \underline{\boldsymbol{\nu}'}$ a sequence of terms, then $f(\underline{\boldsymbol{t}} \mathbin{⨾} \underline{\boldsymbol{\nu}'}) \mathbin{⨾} \mu'$ is a term of type μ', provided $(\underline{\boldsymbol{\nu}'}, \mu')$ is an instance of $(\underline{\boldsymbol{\nu}}, \mu)$.
T3: If $\$f \mathbin{⨾} \underline{\boldsymbol{\nu}} \rightsquigarrow \mu$ is an operator variable and $\underline{\boldsymbol{t}} \mathbin{⨾} \underline{\boldsymbol{\nu}}$ a sequence of terms, then $\$f(\underline{\boldsymbol{t}} \mathbin{⨾} \underline{\boldsymbol{\nu}}) \mathbin{⨾} \mu$ is a term of type μ.
T4: If $Q \mathbin{⨾} (\underline{\boldsymbol{\nu}} \rightsquigarrow \underline{\boldsymbol{\mu}}) \rightsquigarrow \xi$ is a binder, $\underline{\boldsymbol{x}} \mathbin{⨾} \underline{\boldsymbol{\nu}'}$ a sequence of pairwise distinct variables, and $\underline{\boldsymbol{t}} \mathbin{⨾} \underline{\boldsymbol{\mu}'}$ a sequence of terms, then $(Q\,\underline{\boldsymbol{x}} \mathbin{⨾} \underline{\boldsymbol{\nu}'} \cdot \underline{\boldsymbol{t}} \mathbin{⨾} \underline{\boldsymbol{\mu}'}) \mathbin{⨾} \xi'$ is a term of type ξ', provided $(\underline{\boldsymbol{\nu}'}, \underline{\boldsymbol{\mu}'}, \xi')$ is an instance of $(\underline{\boldsymbol{\nu}}, \underline{\boldsymbol{\mu}}, \xi)$.

A term of type $\mathcal{B}$ is called *formula*. Rodin imposes further restrictions on terms; in particular, terms containing variables with the same name but different types are in some cases rejected. We ignore these restrictions, because they have no logical significance and would merely complicate our presentation without adding clarity.

Operators and operator variables have much in common, but are used for different purposes. Intuitively, an operator has a fixed meaning, while the meaning of an operator variable is unspecified. A term of the form $\$f(\underline{\boldsymbol{t}})$ serves as place-holder, e.g., when specifying rewrite rules (Sect. 4.1). Rodin does not explicitly support operator variables, which is convenient for term rewriting (Sect. 4.3), but introduces challenges when reasoning about the soundness of rewrite rules (Sect. 5).

We adopt the usual definitions of *bound* and *free* (ordinary) variables. Unless mentioned otherwise, we consider *alpha-congruent* terms, i.e., terms that informally speaking differ only in the names of bound variables (see e.g. [9]), as identical.

2.2 An Example Signature

For the sake of illustration, we define the signature Σ_1 introducing

- the type operators $\mathcal{B}$ and $\mathcal{Z}$ of arity 0 and $\mathcal{P}$ of arity 1,
- the operators $\mathsf{D} \mathbin{⦂} \alpha \rightsquigarrow \mathcal{B}$, $\bullet \mathbin{⦂} \alpha$, and $= \mathbin{⦂} (\alpha, \alpha) \rightsquigarrow \mathcal{B}$,
- the operators $\top \mathbin{⦂} \mathcal{B}$, $\bot \mathbin{⦂} \mathcal{B}$, and $\neg \mathbin{⦂} \mathcal{B} \rightsquigarrow \mathcal{B}$,
- the operators $\wedge \mathbin{⦂} (\mathcal{B}, \mathcal{B}) \rightsquigarrow \mathcal{B}$, $\vee \mathbin{⦂} (\mathcal{B}, \mathcal{B}) \rightsquigarrow \mathcal{B}$, and $\Rightarrow \mathbin{⦂} (\mathcal{B}, \mathcal{B}) \rightsquigarrow \mathcal{B}$,
- the operators $\in \mathbin{⦂} (\alpha, \mathcal{P}(\alpha)) \rightsquigarrow \mathcal{B}$, $\varnothing \mathbin{⦂} \mathcal{P}(\alpha)$, and $\cap \mathbin{⦂} (\mathcal{P}(\alpha), \mathcal{P}(\alpha)) \rightsquigarrow \mathcal{P}(\alpha)$,
- the operators $0 \mathbin{⦂} \mathcal{Z}$ and $1 \mathbin{⦂} \mathcal{Z}$, and $\mathsf{mod} \mathbin{⦂} (\mathcal{Z}, \mathcal{Z}) \rightsquigarrow \mathcal{Z}$, and
- the binders $\forall \mathbin{⦂} (\alpha \rightsquigarrow \mathcal{B}) \rightsquigarrow \mathcal{B}$ and $\mathsf{collect} \mathbin{⦂} (\alpha \rightsquigarrow \mathcal{B}) \rightsquigarrow \mathcal{P}(\alpha)$.

Rodin provides more symbols than those in Σ_1 (see [20]). The operators D and $\bullet$ are not available in Rodin, but simplify our presentation. Intuitively, the term $\mathsf{D}(t)$ is true if t is well-defined and otherwise false. The term $\bullet$ is always ill-defined. Our results do not depend on the availability of $\bullet$. Whenever required, we will discuss the relevance of our results for signatures without D.

To improve readability, we use infix notation and leave out parentheses when the precedence is clear. We leave out type constraints "$⦂ \nu$" when the types are clear or irrelevant. Terms of the form $\mathsf{collect}\, x \cdot \varphi$ are written $\{x \mid \varphi\}$. The formula $\forall x_1 \cdot \ldots \forall x_{|\underline{\boldsymbol{x}}|} \cdot \varphi$ is abbreviated as $\forall \underline{\boldsymbol{x}} \cdot \varphi$. By default, a term is of the most general type, and we assign the same types to different occurrences of a variable name. See [13] for Rodin's concrete syntax conventions.

3 Semantics

An important decision is in which logic to formalize the denotations of Event-B's types and terms. The best option can certainly not be uniquely determined. We have decided to define the semantics of Event-B's logic by an embedding in higher-order logic (HOL) for the following reasons. First, HOL has a well-understood set theoretic semantics [3,8]. Second, Event-B's logic closely resembles HOL; the main difference lies in the treatment of partial functions. This similarity allows us to keep our presentation of semantics concise. Third, there are powerful theorem provers for HOL such as Isabelle/HOL [15]. Hence, an embedding of Event-B's logic into HOL enables us to use Isabelle/HOL as a theorem prover for Rodin. We regard it as promising to integrate Isabelle/HOL into Rodin, because Isabelle/HOL provides powerful proof tactics and Isabelle/HOL's proofs are more trustworthy than Rodin's thanks to Isabelle's LCF architecture. Isabelle/HOL can also be used to prove meta-theorems about Event-B that are hard to formalize in Event-B itself; for example, in [20] we use Isabelle/HOL to prove soundness of Event-B proof rules.

Our main sources of information are [1,12,13]; these sources give an intuition about the intended semantics, but also leave questions open. We have resolved these questions through discussions with other Rodin developers.

3.1 Isabelle/HOL

To make the paper more accessible to readers not familiar with Isabelle/HOL, we summarize the most relevant features. Isabelle [19] is a generic theorem prover supporting various logics. The term HOL from now on refers to the instantiation of Isabelle to HOL.

HOL's type system (see [8,24]) essentially coincides with ML's. The notation $t :: \nu$ indicates that the term t has type ν. A term of type $\nu \Rightarrow \mu$ denotes a function taking one argument of type ν and yielding a result of type μ. Functions taking n arguments, $n > 0$, are represented by terms of type $\nu_1 \Rightarrow \cdots \Rightarrow \nu_{n+1}$. The type operator $\Rightarrow$ associates to the right. The application of the function f to the n arguments $x_1, \ldots, x_n$ is written $f\ x_1\ \ldots\ x_n$ and should be read as $(\ldots(f\ x_1)\ \ldots)\ x_n$. Function application has higher precedence than infix operators: $f\ x + 1$ is to be read as $(f\ x) + 1$.

Terms of type $\nu \Rightarrow \mu$ represent total functions. Partial functions are therefore sometimes approximated by total functions: HOL's integer division div is a total function of type $\mathsf{int} \Rightarrow \mathsf{int} \Rightarrow \mathsf{int}$. The developers of Isabelle/HOL have decided that $x\ \mathsf{div}\ (0 :: \mathsf{int})$ equals 0. The way how a partial function is approximated by a total function varies from case to case: in particular, the "least integer" $\mathsf{Least}\ \{x :: \mathsf{int}.\ \mathsf{True}\}$ is left unspecified.

3.2 Option Types

We develop a theory EB_0 providing auxiliary definitions. The standard theory of HOL introduces *option types*, defined by

$$\textbf{datatype}\ \alpha\ \mathsf{option} = \mathsf{Some}\ \alpha \mid \mathsf{None}.$$

Intuitively, the type α option contains copies of all elements of α and a constant None. If x is of type α, then $\mathsf{Some}\ x$ is the copy of x in α option. The theory EB_0 introduces the notations $\alpha\!\uparrow$ for α option, $x\!\uparrow$ for $\mathsf{Some}\ x$, and $\bullet$ for None.

Moreover, EB_0 defines the functions WD, T, F, WT by

$$\mathsf{WD}\ x = (x \neq \bullet),$$
$$\mathsf{T}\ \varphi = (\varphi = \mathsf{True}\!\uparrow), \qquad \mathsf{F}\ \varphi = (\varphi = \mathsf{False}\!\uparrow), \qquad \mathsf{WT}\ \varphi = (\varphi \neq \mathsf{False}\!\uparrow).$$

The function WD takes a term t of type $\nu\!\uparrow$ and indicates whether t differs from $\bullet$. The term t is *well-defined* iff $\mathsf{WD}\ t$ is valid and *ill-defined* iff $\neg(\mathsf{WD}\ t)$ is valid. The functions T and F take a term φ of type $\mathsf{bool}\!\uparrow$ and indicate whether φ equals $\mathsf{True}\!\uparrow$ or $\mathsf{False}\!\uparrow$, respectively. Moreover, $\mathsf{WT}\ \varphi$ indicates whether φ is *weakly true*, i.e., equal to $\mathsf{True}\!\uparrow$ or equal to $\bullet$. Finally, we say that a function f whose arguments and result have option types is *strict* iff $\mathsf{WD}(f\ \underline{\boldsymbol{x}}) \longrightarrow \mathsf{WD}\ x_1 \wedge \cdots \wedge \mathsf{WD}\ x_{|\underline{\boldsymbol{x}}|}$ is valid.

3.3 Denotations of Types and Terms

Given a signature Σ, a *structure (over Σ)* specifies the *denotations* of Event-B types and terms over Σ. Technically, a structure $(\mathrm{M}, [\![\cdot]\!])$ consists of a HOL theory M extending EB_0 and a *denotation function* $[\![\cdot]\!]$ mapping Event-B symbols, types, and terms to HOL symbols, types, and terms, respectively. For a sequence $\underline{\boldsymbol{t}}$ of types or terms, $[\![\underline{\boldsymbol{t}}]\!]$ abbreviates $([\![t_1]\!], \ldots, [\![t_{|\underline{\boldsymbol{t}}|}]\!])$.

For every Event-B type variable α, we define $[\![\alpha]\!] = \alpha$; here we assume, without loss of generality, that α is a HOL type variable. For every Event-B type operator τ of arity n, $[\![\tau]\!]$ is a HOL type operator taking n arguments[1]. The boolean type $\mathcal{B}$ denotes bool, and a type $\tau(\underline{\nu})$ denotes the type $([\![\underline{\nu}]\!])\ [\![\tau]\!]$, i.e., the result of applying the type operator $[\![\tau]\!]$ to the types $[\![\underline{\nu}]\!]$.

While the denotation of a type is obtained by renaming type operators, the situation is more involved for terms. The denotation function $[\![\cdot]\!]$ maps operators $f \mathbin{⨾} \underline{\nu} \rightsquigarrow \mu$ to HOL constants of type $[\![\nu_1]\!]\!\uparrow \Rightarrow \ldots \Rightarrow [\![\nu_{|\underline{\nu}|}]\!]\!\uparrow \Rightarrow [\![\mu]\!]\!\uparrow$ and binders $Q \mathbin{⨾} (\underline{\nu} \rightsquigarrow \underline{\mu}) \rightsquigarrow \xi$ to HOL constants of type

$$([\![\nu_1]\!] \Rightarrow \ldots \Rightarrow [\![\nu_{|\underline{\nu}|}]\!] \Rightarrow [\![\mu_1]\!]\!\uparrow) \Rightarrow \ldots \Rightarrow ([\![\nu_1]\!] \Rightarrow \ldots \Rightarrow [\![\nu_{|\underline{\nu}|}]\!] \Rightarrow [\![\mu_{|\underline{\mu}|}]\!]\!\uparrow) \Rightarrow [\![\xi]\!]\!\uparrow.$$

An operator is *strict* iff its denotation is strict.

An Event-B term of type ν denotes a HOL term of type $[\![\nu]\!]\!\uparrow$ as follows:

1. $[\![x \mathbin{⨾} \nu]\!] = (x :: [\![\nu]\!])\!\uparrow$.
2. $[\![f(\underline{t}) \mathbin{⨾} \mu']\!] = (([\![f]\!]\ [\![\underline{t}]\!]) :: [\![\mu']\!]\!\uparrow)$.
3. $[\![\$f(\underline{t}) \mathbin{⨾} \mu]\!] = ((\$f\ [\![\underline{t}]\!]) :: [\![\mu]\!]\!\uparrow)$.
4. $[\![(Q\underline{\boldsymbol{x}} \mathbin{⨾} \underline{\boldsymbol{\nu}} \cdot \underline{t}) \mathbin{⨾} \xi']\!] = (([\![Q]\!]\ (\lambda\underline{\boldsymbol{x}} :: [\![\underline{\boldsymbol{\nu}}]\!].\ [\![t_1]\!])\ \ldots\ (\lambda\underline{\boldsymbol{x}} :: [\![\underline{\boldsymbol{\nu}}]\!].\ [\![t_{|\underline{t}|}]\!])) :: [\![\xi']\!]\!\uparrow)$.

For convenience, we assume that, for each Event-B variable name x, both x and $\$x$ are available as variable names in M. In 4, the notation $\underline{\boldsymbol{x}}::\underline{\boldsymbol{\nu}}$ abbreviates $(x_1::\nu_1)\ \ldots\ (x_{|\underline{\boldsymbol{x}}|}:: \nu_{|\underline{\boldsymbol{\nu}}|})$.

An Event-B term is *well-defined* (*ill-defined*) iff its denotation is well-defined (ill-defined). The Event-B terms t and u are *equivalent* iff $[\![t]\!] = [\![u]\!]$ is valid. An Event-B formula φ is *valid* iff $\mathsf{T}[\![\varphi]\!]$ is valid.

Readers familiar with HOL may wonder why Event-B has the syntactic categories of operators and binders. HOL provides only one operator, namely function application, and one binder, namely lambda-abstraction, and views the remaining operators and binders as constants of suitable function types. It would however be difficult to organize the logic of Event-B in a similar way, because Event-B's *constants* (i.e., operators with empty argument types) denote terms of type $\nu\!\uparrow$; hence constants cannot be used to represent operators or binders, simply because they have inappropriate types.

3.4 An Example Structure

We define a structure $(\mathrm{EB}_1, [\![\cdot]\!])$ over Σ_1, the signature introduced in Sect. 2.2. It reflects the intended semantics of the symbols introduced by Σ_1, i.e., the semantics that is used to validate the inference rules implemented in Rodin. The denotations of Rodin's remaining symbols are defined in [20].

We start with the denotations of type operators, D, and $\bullet$:

$$[\![\mathcal{B}]\!] = \mathsf{bool}, \qquad [\![\mathcal{Z}]\!] = \mathsf{int}, \qquad [\![\mathcal{P}]\!] = \mathsf{set},$$
$$[\![\mathsf{D}]\!]\ x = (\mathsf{WD}\ x)\!\uparrow, \qquad [\![\bullet]\!] = \bullet.$$

[1] In this regard, we also view HOL's *type synonyms* as type operators.

The *strict extension* F of a function f taking n arguments, $n \geq 0$, is given by

$$F\ x_1\ \ldots\ x_n = \begin{cases} \bullet & (\neg(\mathsf{WD}\ x_1) \vee \cdots \vee \neg(\mathsf{WD}\ x_n)) \\ (f\ y_1\ \ldots\ y_n)\uparrow & (x_1 = y_1\uparrow \wedge \cdots \wedge x_n = y_n\uparrow). \end{cases}$$

Intuitively, F behaves as f for well-defined arguments and is ill-defined if an argument is ill-defined. The denotations of most operators are strict extensions:

the denotation of	$\top$	$\bot$	$\neg$	$=$	$\varnothing$	$\in$	$\cap$	0	1
is the strict extension of	True	False	$\neg$	$=$	$\{\}$	$\in$	$\cap$	$0 :: \mathsf{int}$	$1 :: \mathsf{int}$

Thus, if x is an ordinary variable, then $x = x$ is valid, because x is well-defined. If however $\$x$ is an operator variable, then $\$x = \$x$ is not valid.

The operator mod is strict; its result is ill-defined if an argument is negative:

$$[\![\mathsf{mod}]\!]\ x\uparrow\ y\uparrow = \begin{cases} (x \bmod y)\uparrow & (x \geq 0 \wedge y > 0) \\ \bullet & (\text{otherwise}). \end{cases}$$

The denotation of conjunction is given by

$$[\![\wedge]\!]\ \varphi\ \psi = \begin{cases} \mathsf{True}\uparrow & (\mathsf{T}\ \varphi \wedge \mathsf{T}\ \psi) \\ \mathsf{False}\uparrow & (\mathsf{F}\ \varphi \vee \mathsf{F}\ \psi) \\ \bullet & (\text{otherwise}). \end{cases}$$

The denotations of disjunction and implication are defined such that $\$\varphi \vee \$\psi$ is equivalent to $\neg(\neg\$\varphi \wedge \neg\$\psi)$ and $\$\varphi \Rightarrow \$\psi$ is equivalent to $\neg\$\varphi \vee \$\psi$.

Note that conjunction, disjunction, and implication are not strict. In particular, both $\bot \wedge \$\varphi$ and $\$\varphi \wedge \bot$ are equivalent to $\bot$. Contrast this to intersection: neither $\varnothing \cap \$R$ nor $\$R \cap \varnothing$ is equivalent to $\varnothing$, because $\$R$ is not necessarily well-defined and intersection is strict.

Finally, $[\![\forall]\!]$ and $[\![\mathsf{collect}]\!]$ are defined such that

$$[\![\forall x \cdot \varphi]\!] = \begin{cases} \mathsf{True}\uparrow & (\forall x.\ \mathsf{T}\ [\![\varphi]\!]) \\ \mathsf{False}\uparrow & (\exists x.\ \mathsf{F}\ [\![\varphi]\!]) \\ \bullet & (\text{otherwise}), \end{cases}$$

$$[\![\{x \mid \varphi\}]\!] = \begin{cases} \{x.\ \mathsf{T}\ [\![\varphi]\!]\}\uparrow & (\forall x.\ \mathsf{WD}\ [\![\varphi]\!]) \\ \bullet & (\text{otherwise}). \end{cases}$$

The universal quantifier may be viewed as generalized conjunction: for instance, $\forall x ⦂ \mathcal{B} \cdot \$\varphi(x)$ is equivalent to $\$\varphi(\top) \wedge \$\varphi(\bot)$. The variables bound by a binder range over well-defined values: $\forall x \cdot x = x$ is valid, and $\{x \mid x \neq x\}$ is equivalent to the empty set $\varnothing$.

3.5 Substitutions

Intuitively, a type substitution $[\underline{\boldsymbol{\alpha}} := \underline{\boldsymbol{\nu}}]$ is applied to a term by simultaneously replacing α_i by ν_i, $1 \leq i \leq |\underline{\boldsymbol{\alpha}}|$. The details are similar as in HOL (cf. [8, CH. 15]) and can be found in [21]. We define the *denotation* $[\![[\underline{\boldsymbol{\alpha}} := \underline{\boldsymbol{\nu}}]]\!]$ of a type substitution by $[\underline{\boldsymbol{\alpha}} := [\![\underline{\boldsymbol{\nu}}]\!]]$. From this, we prove the following duality property:

Lemma 1. *If t is an Event-B term and σ a type substitution, then* $[\![t\sigma]\!] = [\![t]\!][\![\sigma]\!]$.

Type variables intuitively serve as place holders for types. By defining the effect of type substitutions on terms, we make precise how exactly type variables can be instantiated. Lemma 1 provides a semantic characterization of type substitutions σ; in particular, if $\mathsf{T}\ [\![\varphi]\!]$ is valid, then so is $\mathsf{T}\ [\![\varphi\sigma]\!]$.

An *operator substitution* σ is written

$$[\$f_1(\underline{\boldsymbol{\$x^1}}) := u_1, \dots, \$f_n(\underline{\boldsymbol{\$x^n}}) := u_n],$$

where $\$f_1, \dots, \$f_n$ are pairwise distinct, the elements of $\underline{\boldsymbol{\$x^i}}$ are pairwise distinct, the type of $\underline{\boldsymbol{\$x^i}}$ is the argument type of $\$f_i$, and the type of u_i the result type of $\$f_i$, for $1 \leq i \leq n$. Let us consider three examples. First, we will see that $(\$\varphi \wedge \neg\$\varphi)[\$\varphi := \top]$ equals $\top \wedge \neg\top$. Second, consider $\forall x \cdot \$\varphi(x)$; by writing $\$\varphi(x)$ instead of $\$\varphi$, we indicate that the term substituted for $\$\varphi(x)$ may have free occurrences of x. We will see that $(\forall x \cdot \$\varphi(x))[\$\varphi(\$y) := (\$y = 0)]$ equals $\forall x \cdot x = 0$. Finally, $(\forall x \cdot \$\varphi)[\$\varphi := (x = 0)]$ equals $\forall y \cdot x = 0$.

The *denotation* $[\![\sigma]\!]$ of σ is

$$[\$f_1 := \lambda\underline{\boldsymbol{\$x^1}}.\ [\![u_1]\!], \dots, \$f_n := \lambda\underline{\boldsymbol{\$x^n}}.\ [\![u_n]\!]].$$

To obtain a duality property analog to Lemma 1, we define the *result of applying σ to a term* as follows:

1. $x\sigma = x$,
2. $f(\underline{t})\sigma = f(\underline{t\sigma})$,
3. $\$g(\underline{t})\sigma = \$g(\underline{t\sigma})$, provided $\$g$ differs from $\$f_i$, for $1 \leq i \leq n$,
4. $\$f_i(\underline{t})\sigma = u_i[\$x^i_1 := t_1\sigma, \dots, \$x^i_{|\underline{\boldsymbol{\$x^i}}|} := t_{|\underline{t}|}\sigma]$, for $1 \leq i \leq n$,
5. $(Q\underline{\boldsymbol{y}} \cdot \underline{t})\sigma = Q\underline{\boldsymbol{y}} \cdot \underline{t\sigma}$, provided no element of $\underline{\boldsymbol{y}}$ occurs free in $u_1, \dots, u_n$.

In 2, 3, and 5, we adopt the convention that $\underline{t\sigma}$ abbreviates $t_1\sigma, \dots, t_{|\underline{t}|}\sigma$. The proviso of 5 is achieved by suitable renaming of bound variables. Operator substitutions fulfill a duality property analog to Lemma 1:

Lemma 2. *If t is a term and σ an operator substitution, then* $[\![t\sigma]\!] = [\![t]\!][\![\sigma]\!]$.

If we defined substitutions for ordinary variables, they would fail to satisfy a property analog to Lemma 1 and 2. Suppose we define an ordinary substitution σ such that $x\sigma$ is $\bullet$. Then $[\![x\sigma]\!]$ is $\bullet$, but there is no way of defining $[\![\sigma]\!]$ such that $[\![x]\!][\![\sigma]\!]$ equals $\bullet$, because $[\![x]\!]$ is defined as $x\!\uparrow$.

4 Term Rewriting

In the following, the available types and terms, and their denotations are specified by a signature Σ and a structure $(\mathrm{M}, [\![\cdot]\!])$ over Σ. If Σ provides symbols of Σ_1 (cf. Sect. 2.2), we assume that their denotations are given according to $(\mathrm{EB}_1, [\![\cdot]\!])$ (cf. Sect. 3.4).

In Event-B, proofs are organized in terms of hypothetical statements, called *sequents*. A *sequent* $\underline{\psi} \vdash \varphi$ consists of a finite set $\{\underline{\psi}\}$ of formulae, called *hypotheses*, and a single formula φ, called *goal*. When a sequent is used to express a desired property of an Event-B model, we refer to it as *proof obligation*.

We consider several ways of defining denotations of sequents, all of the form

$$[\![\psi_1, \ldots, \psi_n \vdash \varphi]\!] = (\mathcal{H}[\![\psi_1]\!] \wedge \cdots \wedge \mathcal{H}[\![\psi_n]\!] \longrightarrow \mathcal{G}[\![\varphi]\!]).$$

The functions $\mathcal{H}$ and $\mathcal{G}$ range over T and WT. We distinguish *WW-, WS-, SW-, and SS-semantics*, where the first letter indicates the choice of $\mathcal{H}$ and the second the choice of $\mathcal{G}$; the letter S ("strong") represents the choice T, and the letter W ("weak") represents the choice WT. A sequent is *WW-, WS-, SW-, or SS-valid* iff its denotation is valid according to WW-, WS-, SW-, or SS-semantics, respectively. As Event-B is based on SW-validity, we refer to SW-validity also as *validity*.

An *inference rule* is written $\dfrac{\underline{\Gamma}}{\Gamma_0}$ and consists of a possibly empty sequence $\underline{\Gamma}$ of sequents, called *antecedents*, and a single sequent Γ_0, called *consequent*. It is *sound* iff validity of all antecedents implies validity of the consequent. We are interested in *backwards proofs*: in a backwards proof a sequent Δ is proved by first choosing a rule with Δ as consequent and then proving the antecedents of the rule. This is repeated up to the point where no sequents remain to be proved.

Note that rules are schematic in the sense that they may contain operator variables, which can be instantiated by substitution. Because of Lemmas 1 and 2, soundness is closed under substitution, i.e., if an inference rule is sound, then so is the result of applying a substitution to its antecedents and consequent. However, side-conditions that require variables not to occur free in formulae must be stated informally. Defining a formal representation covering all inference rules of Event-B is not in the scope of this paper.

The choice between WW-, WS-, SW-, and SS-semantics influences which inference rules are sound. Unfortunately it is not an easy choice; for each of the four semantics there exist an unsound rules whose unsoundness may be hard to accept for some reader:

semantics	unsound rule	semantics	unsound rule
WW	$\dfrac{\underline{\chi} \vdash \psi}{\underline{\chi}, \neg\psi \vdash \bot}\,\mathsf{not_E}$	WS	$\dfrac{}{\underline{\chi}, \varphi \vdash \varphi}\,\mathsf{hyp}$
SS	$\dfrac{\underline{\chi}, \varphi \vdash \bot}{\underline{\chi} \vdash \neg\varphi}\,\mathsf{not_I}$	SW	$\dfrac{\underline{\chi} \vdash \psi \quad \underline{\chi}, \psi \vdash \varphi}{\underline{\chi} \vdash \varphi}\,\mathsf{cut}$

It is therefore not surprising that different logics are based on different semantics: Event-B [12] and PVS [17] choose SW-semantics; LPF [4], the logic underlying VDM, is based on SS-semantics; Owe [16] favors WS-semantics. To our best knowledge, only Owe explains his choice by a comparison between the four semantics. In Section 4.2, we will show why SW-semantics, and SW-semantics only, is well-suited for term rewriting. We thus provide a novel argument in favor of SW-semantics.

4.1 Rewriting Terms to Equivalent Terms

When rewriting terms to equivalent terms in Event-B's logic, it is often necessary to check well-definedness of the term to be rewritten. Consider for example

$$(\$x = \$x) \equiv \top. \tag{1}$$

A rule $t \equiv u$ is *sound* iff t and u are equivalent; hence, (1) is unsound. The unsoundness becomes evident when rewriting the goal $\mathsf{D}(\bullet = \bullet)$ to $\mathsf{D}(\top)$. However, the rule is sound under the precondition $\mathsf{D}(\$x)$, i.e., whenever a well-defined term is substituted for $\$x$. Similarly, the following rules are sound only under appropriate well-definedness preconditions:

$$\$x \in \$R \cap \$S \equiv \$x \in \$R \wedge \$x \in \$S, \tag{2}$$

$$\$x \in \varnothing \equiv \bot, \tag{3}$$

$$0 \in \{x \mid \$\varphi(x)\} \equiv \$\varphi(0). \tag{4}$$

The need for well-definedness preconditions stems from the special status of $\bullet$, i.e., (1) is unsound because equality is strict and therefore not reflexive, (2) is unsound because intersection is strict and conjunction is not, (3) is unsound because membership is strict, and (4) is unsound because there are substitutions σ such that $\$\varphi(0)\sigma$ is well-defined whereas $\$\varphi(1)\sigma$ is not. Well-definedness preconditions can be avoided to some extent by choosing appropriate semantics. However, this would result in difficulties when applying Event-B to the problems it has initially been designed for.

During conditional rewriting as in, e.g., Isabelle [14], it is often hard to predict and control which conditions can be solved and whether a conditional rewrite rule is applied. The choice of tactic that solves conditions is tricky: if it is too weak, many conditional rewrite rules become useless; if it is too powerful, term rewriting becomes slow. Because solving conditions is undecidable, these problems are inevitable in general; but we will see that we can sometimes do better.

In the following sections, we present *directed rewriting*. *Directed rewrite rules* have well-definedness preconditions, but these preconditions can always be solved, and therefore do not need to be checked. We thus show how the before mentioned problems can be avoided for a non-trivial class of rewrite rules. We will also demonstrate the practical relevance of directed rewriting.

4.2 Directed Rewriting

A *directed rewrite rule* consists of a *(pre)condition* $\varphi \mathbin{⨾} \mathcal{B}$, a *left-hand side* $t \mathbin{⨾} \nu$, and a *right-hand side* $u \mathbin{⨾} \nu$, and is written

$$\frac{\varphi}{t \mathbin{⨾} \nu \sqsubseteq u \mathbin{⨾} \nu}. \tag{5}$$

An *unconditional* rule has the condition $\top$ and is written $t \mathbin{⨾} \nu \sqsubseteq u \mathbin{⨾} \nu$. For the semantics of directed rewrite rules, we recall the *flat domain order* $\sqsubseteq$ defined by

$$\forall x\ y.\ x \sqsubseteq y \longleftrightarrow (\mathsf{WD}\ x \longrightarrow x = y).$$

The rewrite rule (5) denotes $\mathsf{WT}[\![\varphi]\!] \longrightarrow [\![t]\!] \sqsubseteq [\![u]\!]$ and is sound iff its denotation is valid. Directed rewrite rules are not symmetric: soundness of $t \sqsubseteq u$ does not imply soundness of $u \sqsubseteq t$. The reader may want to check that the rules (1 – 4) can be recast as unconditional sound directed rewrite rules.

Alternatively, we could have defined the denotation of (5) by $\mathsf{T}[\![\varphi]\!] \longrightarrow [\![t]\!] \sqsubseteq [\![u]\!]$. Our choice of semantics is motivated by the observation (cf. [21]) that the majority of the conditional rewrite rules available in Rodin are already sound w.r.t. our semantics, which interprets the condition φ as $\mathsf{WT}[\![\varphi]\!]$. The advantage of our semantics over the alternative semantics, which interprets φ as $\mathsf{T}\ [\![\varphi]\!]$, is that $\mathsf{D}(\varphi)$ does not need to be proved when applying the rule; this makes conditional rules more generally applicable. If a rule is sound only w.r.t. the alternative semantics we may replace the condition φ by $\mathsf{D}(\varphi) \wedge \varphi$.

The following lemma shows how to use directed rewrite rules to rewrite formulae:

Lemma 3. *If the rule*

$$\frac{\psi}{\varphi_1 \sqsubseteq \varphi_2} \tag{6}$$

is sound, then so are

$$\frac{\underline{\chi} \vdash \psi \qquad \underline{\chi} \vdash \varphi_2}{\underline{\chi} \vdash \varphi_1} \quad \textit{and} \quad \frac{\underline{\chi} \vdash \psi \qquad \underline{\chi}, \varphi_2 \vdash \varphi}{\underline{\chi}, \varphi_1 \vdash \varphi}. \tag{7}$$

Intuitively, if the rule in (6) is sound, it may be used to rewrite a hypothesis or goal φ_1 to φ_2 in a backwards proof. Moreover, when applying a conditional rule, one has to prove the condition ψ from the other hypotheses $\underline{\chi}$ of the sequent at hand. Note that, although, in general, φ_1 and φ_2 are equivalent only if φ_1 is well-defined, there is no need to prove well-definedness of φ_1 when applying the rewrite rule. This is how directed rewriting avoids solving well-definedness conditions.

Lemma 3 is an immediate consequence of the definitions of soundness and the fact that sequents have SW-semantics. The assertion does not hold if sequents have WW-, WS-, or SS-semantics: take the empty sequence for $\underline{\chi}$, $\top$ for ψ, $\bullet$ for φ_1, and $\top$ or $\bot$ for φ_2. Thus, SW-semantics is the only of the four semantics, under which directed rewriting is sound.

So far we are assuming that we want to apply directed rewrite rules from left to right, i.e., to rewrite φ_1 to φ_2. If we wanted to apply them in reverse direction, i.e., to rewrite φ_2 to φ_1, this would be sound only under WS-semantics. We believe that rewriting in reverse direction is not useful in practice, because it would make rules like $\$x = \$x \sqsubseteq \top$, $\$\varphi \wedge \neg\$\varphi \sqsubseteq \bot$, $\$R \cap \varnothing \sqsubseteq \varnothing$, and many others inapplicable.

4.3 Rewriting Subterms

Term rewriting would not be very useful without the possibility of rewriting subterms. We now explain under which assumptions directed rewriting of subterms is sound.

A HOL function f is *monotonic* iff

$$\forall \underline{\boldsymbol{x}}\, \underline{\boldsymbol{y}}.\, x_1 \sqsubseteq y_1 \wedge \cdots \wedge x_{|\underline{\boldsymbol{x}}|} \sqsubseteq y_{|\underline{\boldsymbol{y}}|} \longrightarrow f\, \underline{\boldsymbol{x}} \sqsubseteq f\, \underline{\boldsymbol{y}}.$$

For uniformity, we also consider terms of type $\nu\!\uparrow$ as *monotonic*. The order $\sqsubseteq$ is lifted to functions in the usual point-wise fashion: $f \sqsubseteq g \longleftrightarrow (\forall x.\ f\ x\ \sqsubseteq g\ x)$. The denotation Q of a binder is *monotonic* iff

$$\forall \underline{\boldsymbol{f}}\ \underline{\boldsymbol{g}}.\ f_1 \sqsubseteq g_1 \wedge \cdots \wedge f_{|\underline{\boldsymbol{f}}|} \sqsubseteq g_{|\underline{\boldsymbol{g}}|} \longrightarrow Q\ \underline{\boldsymbol{f}} \sqsubseteq Q\ \underline{\boldsymbol{g}}.$$

Similarly, an operator or binder is monotonic iff its denotation is.

The following lemma shows that directed rewrite rules may be applied to subterms of the hypothesis or the goal at hand. The restriction is that only arguments of *monotonic* operators and binders may be rewritten.

Lemma 4. *If the directed rewrite rule* $\dfrac{\varphi}{t \sqsubseteq t'}$ *is sound, then so are*

$$\frac{\varphi}{f(\underline{\boldsymbol{u}}, t, \underline{\boldsymbol{u}}') \sqsubseteq f(\underline{\boldsymbol{u}}, t', \underline{\boldsymbol{u}}')} \quad \text{and} \quad \frac{\forall \underline{\boldsymbol{x}} \cdot \varphi}{Q\underline{\boldsymbol{x}} \cdot \underline{\boldsymbol{v}}, t, \underline{\boldsymbol{v}}' \sqsubseteq Q\underline{\boldsymbol{x}} \cdot \underline{\boldsymbol{v}}, t', \underline{\boldsymbol{v}}'},$$

where f is a monotonic operator and Q a monotonic binder.

Note that every strict operator is monotonic. Moreover, every operator and binder of Σ_1 is monotonic; for most operators this is obvious, because they are strict. In fact, all operators and binders available in Rodin are monotonic [20]. However, neither the well-definedness operator D is monotonic, nor the denotations of operator variables that take at least one argument. Hence, rewriting subterms is sound for the logic implemented by Rodin, but rewriting arguments of D or of operator variables is in general unsound.

4.4 Safety

In this section we address the question under which conditions directed rewriting is *safe*. Informally, an *unsafe* backwards step transforms a valid sequent into an invalid one and thus drives the proof into a dead end. We restrict the discussion to unconditional rules, assuming that conditional rules are applied only if their conditions can be solved.

Formally, an inference rule is *safe* iff validity of its consequent implies validity of all antecedents. The inference rules resulting from sound directed rewrite rules are in general unsafe: take the rule rewriting $\vdash \bullet$ to $\vdash \bot$ as an example.

An inference rule is *WS-safe* iff WS-validity of the consequent implies WS-validity of all antecedents. Note that the inference rules resulting from sound directed rewrite rules are WS-safe. Hence, if (i) the sequent at hand is WS-valid, and (ii) only WS-safe rules are applied, then only WS-valid (and therefore valid) sequents will arise during the proof attempt. We will examine under which circumstances Conditions (i) and (ii) are true.

Note that $\underline{\boldsymbol{\psi}} \vdash \varphi$ is valid iff $\mathsf{D}(\underline{\boldsymbol{\psi}}), \mathsf{D}(\varphi), \underline{\boldsymbol{\psi}} \vdash \varphi$ is WS-valid (and therefore also valid). So it is straightforward to establish Condition (i) by a mild (and validity preserving) modification of the proof obligation at hand.

Of course, inference rules may be only safe but not WS-safe: consider $\dfrac{\vdash \bullet}{\vdash \top}$. Such rules need to be avoided to fulfill Condition (ii). We can always transform a safe inference rule into a WS-safe one (in a soundness preserving manner) by adding well-definedness conditions to the antecedents. That is actually unnecessary for the inference rules available in Rodin: by inspecting the list of available rules, we observe that every inference rule of Rodin is safe iff it is WS-safe. So Condition (ii) is fulfilled in Rodin if the user avoids applying unsafe rules.

In summary, directed rewriting is unsafe in general; but after slight modifications of the proof obligation and the proof calculus, directed rewriting is safe whenever only safe inference rules are applied within proofs. For Rodin, such modifications of the proof calculus are unnecessary[2].

4.5 Practical Relevance

We have seen that directed rewriting is sound if (i) sequents are interpreted in SW-semantics and (ii) the operators and binders "surrounding" the term to be rewritten are monotonic. There is no agreement in the literature on which of the four sequent semantics is best; we view directed rewriting as a novel argument in favor of SW-semantics. Clearly, non-monotonic operators are sometimes useful; e.g., we will see how to apply them for reasoning about the soundness of rewrite rules (see Sect. 5). We have however experienced that monotonicity is an acceptable restriction for many applications. Other researchers seem to make similar experiences: Jones et al. [10] point out that non-monotonic operators are "not needed for specifying software systems" or "seldom employed in proofs". PVS [17] supports only monotonic operators and binders.

To understand how often directed rewrite rules arise in practice, we have analyzed the rewrite rules available in the Rodin platform. New rules for Rodin's term rewriter are chosen and implemented based on the requests of Rodin users. The set of available rules therefore reflects which rules are important in practice. The details of our analysis can be found in [21].

We say that a sound directed rewrite rule is *truly* directed iff its condition does *not* imply equivalence of its left- and right-hand side. In total, Rodin implements 453 unconditional directed rewrite rules; 165 of them (about 36%) are truly directed. Without directed rewriting, Rodin would have to prove well-definedness of the left-hand side whenever applying one of these rules. Moreover, Rodin implements 53 conditional directed rewrite rules of which 42 (about 79%) are truly directed. Thus, in a significant number of cases directed rewriting makes conditional rewrite rules unconditional or weakens the condition of a rewrite rule. We therefore conclude that directed rewriting constitutes an important optimization of Rodin's term rewriter.

The reader may have the impression that directed rewriting mainly compensates for problems introduced by the fact that Event-B's logic explicitly supports partial functions. But this is not entirely true. In logics of total functions it is quite common to approximate partial functions by underspecified total functions. In such a logic, $x \mathsf{~mod~} 0$ denotes an unspecified integer. Therefore $x \mathsf{mod} x$ is equivalent to 0 only if $\neg(x = 0)$. In Event-B and with directed rewriting, we can avoid the condition $\neg(x = 0)$ by restating the rule as $\$x \mathsf{~mod~} \$x \sqsubseteq 0$. Thus, directed rewriting not only compensates for problems introduced by explicit partiality, but also makes rules unconditional that are commonly conditional in logics of total functions. In the case of Rodin, there are 35 such rules.

[2] We do not make a statement about required modifications of Rodin's proof obligations, because we are not aware of a document specifying them.

5 Proving User Supplied Rules Sound

Rodin provides a generic term rewriter to which the user can supply new rewrite rules [11]. The term rewriter accepts a new rule only if the user formally proves its soundness. Rules with conjunctions, disjunctions, implications, universal or existential quantifiers on the left-hand side are however rejected, because it has been unclear how to generate the required soundness proof obligations. Operator variables with non-empty argument types are not supported either. Below, we show how to overcome these limitations for a practically relevant class of rewrite rules.

In a logic with the well-definedness operator D and operator variables, it is straightforward to express soundness proof obligations:

Lemma 5. *The directed rewrite rule* $\dfrac{\varphi}{t \sqsubseteq u}$ *is sound iff* $\mathsf{D}(\varphi) \Rightarrow \varphi, \mathsf{D}(t) \vdash \mathsf{D}(u) \wedge t = u$ *is valid.*

However, Rodin supports neither the operator D nor operator variables, which makes Lemma 5 inapplicable. A way out would be to make the operator D and operator variables available. Unfortunately, such a change would not come cheaply, because monotonicity assumptions are hard-wired in several places, in particular in Rodin's term rewriter. Therefore, we develop a method for expressing soundness proof obligations with only monotonic operators and binders and without operator variables.

Before going into the gory details, let us consider an example. For convenience, we introduce the operator restrict with argument type $(\mathcal{B}, \alpha)$ and result type α whose denotation is given by $[\![\mathsf{restrict}]\!]\ \varphi\ x = (\mathsf{if}\ \mathsf{T}\,\varphi\ \mathsf{then}\ x\ \mathsf{else}\ \bullet)$. Consider the rule $(\exists x \cdot x = \$y) \sqsubseteq \top$; Lemma 5 suggests, after slight simplifications, the following soundness proof obligation:

$$\mathsf{D}(\exists x \cdot x = \$y) \vdash \exists x \cdot x = \$y. \tag{8}$$

To eliminate the operator variable $\$y$, we extend the underlying signature by the operators dy and sy; dy is of type $\mathcal{B}$ and sy has the same type as $\$y$. The denotations of dy and sy are left unspecified, except that we require $\mathsf{WD}\ [\![\mathsf{dy}]\!]$ and $\mathsf{WD}\ [\![\mathsf{sy}]\!]$ to be valid. Intuitively, $\mathsf{restrict}(\mathsf{dy}, \mathsf{sy})$ is equivalent to $\$y$. Then, (8) is equivalent to

$$\mathsf{D}(\exists x \cdot x = \mathsf{restrict}(\mathsf{dy}, \mathsf{sy})) \vdash \exists x \cdot x = \mathsf{restrict}(\mathsf{dy}, \mathsf{sy}). \tag{9}$$

The goal of (9) is already built from monotonic operators and binders. The hypothesis of (9) is equivalent to

$$(\exists x \cdot \mathsf{dy} \wedge x = \mathsf{restrict}(\mathsf{dy}, \mathsf{sy})) \vee (\forall x \cdot \mathsf{dy} \wedge \neg(x = \mathsf{restrict}(\mathsf{dy}, \mathsf{sy}))).$$

Note that we are unable to directly eliminate D from (8), because that would require us to eliminate D from terms of the form $\mathsf{D}(\$y)$.

The following theorem shows how to establish the transition from (8) to (9) in general, provided operator variables are applied only to ordinary variables.

Theorem 6. *Suppose all occurrences of the operator variable* $\$f \mathbin{⨾} \underline{\nu} \rightsquigarrow \mu$ *in the sequent* Γ *take only ordinary variables as arguments. Extend the underlying signature* *by the operators* $\mathsf{df} \mathbin{⨾} \underline{\nu} \rightsquigarrow \mathcal{B}$ *and* $\mathsf{sf} \mathbin{⨾} \underline{\nu} \rightsquigarrow \mu$*, and the underlying structure such that* $[\![\mathsf{df}]\!]$ *is specified by* $\mathsf{WD}([\![\mathsf{df}]\!]\ \underline{\boldsymbol{x}}) \longleftrightarrow \mathsf{WD}\ \underline{\boldsymbol{x}}$[3] *and* $[\![\mathsf{sf}]\!]$ *by* $\mathsf{WD}([\![\mathsf{sf}]\!]\ \underline{\boldsymbol{x}}) \longleftrightarrow \mathsf{WD}\ \underline{\boldsymbol{x}}$. *Then* Γ *is valid w.r.t. the original structure iff* $\Gamma[\$f(\underline{\$\boldsymbol{x}}) := \mathsf{restrict}(\mathsf{df}(\underline{\$\boldsymbol{x}}), \mathsf{sf}(\underline{\$\boldsymbol{x}}))]$ *is valid w.r.t. the extended structure.*

Here, $\mathsf{WD}\ \underline{\boldsymbol{x}}$ abbreviates $\mathsf{WD}\ x_1 \wedge \cdots \wedge \mathsf{WD}\ x_{|\underline{\boldsymbol{x}}|}$. A substitution is applied to a sequent by simultaneous application to the hypotheses and the goal.

After applying Theorem 6 to eliminate operator variables, it remains to eliminate well-definedness conditions $\mathsf{D}(t)$. If t is a term over Rodin's signature, it is well-known how to do that (see [6]). The procedure in [6] can be easily extended to terms containing restrict and the ad-hoc operators arising from Theorem 6. The result is a soundness proof obligation containing only monotonic operators and binders and not containing operator variables.

To understand the relevance of the machinery described above, we consider the rewrite rules implemented by Rodin as a benchmark. There are still rules for which the soundness proof obligations cannot be expressed, even with the above procedure. These rules fall in at least one of the following two categories:

1. rules containing associative operators with an arbitrary number of arguments; an example is the rule $\$\varphi_1 \wedge \cdots \wedge \$\psi \wedge \cdots \wedge \$\varphi_n \Rightarrow \$\psi \sqsubseteq \top$.
2. rules that violate the proviso of Theorem 6. An example is the rule $\dfrac{\mathsf{D}(\$y)}{\forall x \cdot x = \$y \Rightarrow \$\varphi(x) \sqsubseteq \$\varphi(\$y)}$, because the $\$y$ in $\$\varphi(\$y)$ is not an ordinary variable.

Only five rewrite rules fall into the second category (cf. [21]).

We admit that our procedure for expressing soundness proof obligations is not straightforward. Rodin's commitment to monotonicity has a price!

6 Related Work

PVS uses predicate subtypes and dependent types to represent partial functions: a partial function is viewed as total function over a restricted domain. Although the semantics of PVS [17] is presented quite differently from the semantics of Event-B's logic, we observe the following similarities: if we view type-correctness in PVS as well-definedness in Event-B, then the operators and binders available in PVS are monotonic, operator variables are unavailable, and PVS inference rules are (SW-)sound. Hence, directed rewriting is sound in PVS and the problem and solution concerning reasoning about soundness (cf. Sect. 5) apply.

We are not aware of a paper devising the foundations of term rewriting in PVS. From the prover guide [22, p. 86], we have the impression that PVS implements directed rewrite rules such as $0 * \$x \sqsubseteq 0$. However, the techniques discussed in Sect. 5 seem to be unavailable: we tried to introduce the rule $\$x \in \varnothing \sqsubseteq \bot$ (and some others), but PVS insisted on checking well-definedness of $\$x$ when applying this rule. Therefore we believe that our results can be used to improve term rewriting in PVS.

[3] This is achieved by **consts** $[\![\mathsf{df}]\!]$ **ax_specification** $([\![\mathsf{df}]\!])$ $\mathsf{WD}(\mathsf{df}\ \underline{x}) \longleftrightarrow \mathsf{WD}\ \underline{x}$.

LPF [10], the logic underlying VDM, is based on SS-semantics. It is therefore sound to apply directed rewrite rules to hypotheses belonging to LPF's monotonic fragment, but unsound to apply directed rewrite rules to goals. Dawson [7] already defines a version of unconditional directed rewriting for quantifier free LPF; we in particular complement his work by providing evidence that directed rewriting is powerful in practice and by our results on safety. The complications when reasoning about soundness of rewrite rules addressed in Sect. 5 do not arise in LPF, because LPF supports non-monotonic operators.

Monotonicity is an important concept in LCF (see e.g. [18]); hence there is a chance of applying directed rewriting. Conjectures in LCF seem however often to be built from $\equiv$ and $\sqsubseteq$ (in Event-B terminology). The challenge is to reorganize proofs in terms of sequents that have SW-semantics. More research is needed to understand whether directed rewriting has applications in LCF.

Maamria and Butler [11] devise directed rewriting for the untyped fragment of Event-B, i.e., the fragment with exactly one non-boolean type. In their setting, the left- and right-hand sides of rewrite rules are built from operator variables with empty argument types and strict operators. In particular, they do not support rewrite rules whose left- or right-hand sides involve boolean connectives or binders. We overcome these restrictions and correct a flaw concerning the application of conditional rewrite rules. (The proviso above (4.2) on p. 11 allows one to apply conditional rewrite rules in an unsound way.)

Our research has been greatly inspired by term rewriting in Isabelle [14].

7 Conclusions and Future Work

We have devised the foundations of directed rewriting, a technique that rewrites not only terms to equivalent terms but also ill-defined to well-defined terms. To make concrete statements about the practical impact of directed rewriting, we have focused on a particular logic of partial functions, namely the logic of Event-B. Applications to other logics of partial functions are described in Sect. 6.

As a prerequisite of our investigations, we have defined a semantics for Event-B's logic (see Sect. 3). Soundness of directed rewriting in Event-B, as manifested by Lemmas 3 and 4, is an immediate consequence of our presentation of semantics, and the observations that sequents have SW-semantics (see Sect. 4), and operators and binders are monotonic (see Sect. 4.3). In particular, we have shown how to apply conditional rewrite rules to the arguments of binders, which is currently not supported in Rodin. Our work on semantics has also helped us to spot inconsistency bugs in earlier versions of Rodin's theorem prover and identify dispensable preconditions of rewrite rules (see [21]).

To understand the practical impact of directed rewriting, we have analyzed the directed rewrite rules implemented by Rodin (see Sect. 4.5). Our conclusion is that directed rewriting makes a significant number of conditional rewrite rules unconditional and thus constitutes an important optimization. Directed rewriting is unsafe it general: it may transform a valid sequent into an invalid one during a backwards proof. This unsafety can however be easily avoided, for reasons explained in Sect. 4.4.

Monotonicity is an important prerequisite for soundness of directed rewriting, but a disturbing restriction when reasoning about soundness of rewrite rules. In Sect. 5

we have shown how to express soundness proof obligations for a practically important class of rewrite rules using only monotonic operators and binders. In particular, we have pointed out how to overcome limitations of Rodin concerning rules that contain boolean connectives or binders.

We are currently integrating Isabelle as an automated theorem prover into Rodin[4]. Our logical embedding of Event-B's logic into HOL serves as a basis. This Isabelle based theorem prover already provides a restricted version of directed rewriting.

Acknowledgements. The author would like to thank several people for their helpful feedback on preliminary versions of this paper: David Basin, Andreas Fürst, Matus Harvan, Thai Son Hoang, Felix Klaedtke, Ognjen Maric, Simon Meier, Patrick Schaller, Benedikt Schmidt, and Laurent Voisin. The author is also grateful for the numerous useful suggestions of the anonymous reviewers.

References

1. Abrial, J.R.: Modeling in Event-B, Cambridge (2010)
2. Abrial, J.R., Butler, M.J., Hallerstede, S., Hoang, T.S., Mehta, F., Voisin, L.: Rodin: an open toolset for modelling and reasoning in Event-B. STTT 12(6), 447–466 (2010)
3. Andrews, P.B.: An Introduction to Mathematical Logic and Type Theory. Kluwer, Dordrecht (2002)
4. Barringer, H., Cheng, J.H., Jones, C.B.: A logic covering undefinedness in program proofs. Acta Inf. 21, 251–269 (1984)
5. Butler, M., Maamria, I.: Mathematical extension in Event-B through the Rodin theory component (2010), `http://deploy-eprints.ecs.soton.ac.uk/251`
6. Darvas, Á., Mehta, F., Rudich, A.: Efficient well-definedness checking. In: Armando, A., Baumgartner, P., Dowek, G. (eds.) IJCAR 2008. LNCS (LNAI), vol. 5195, pp. 100–115. Springer, Heidelberg (2008)
7. Dawson, J.E.: Simulating term-rewriting in LPF and in display logic. In: Supplementary Proc. of TPHOLs, pp. 47–62. Australian National University (1998)
8. Gordon, M.J.C., Melham, T.F.: Introduction to HOL, Cambridge (1993)
9. Hindley, J.R., Seldin, J.P.: Lambda-Calculus and Combinators, Cambridge (2008)
10. Jones, C.B., Middelburg, C.A.: A typed logic of partial functions reconstructed classically. Acta Inf. 31(5), 399–430 (1994)
11. Maamria, I., Butler, M.: Rewriting and well-definedness within a proof system. In: PAR. EPTCS, vol. 43, pp. 49–64 (2010)
12. Mehta, F.: A practical approach to partiality – A proof based approach. In: Liu, S., Araki, K. (eds.) ICFEM 2008. LNCS, vol. 5256, pp. 238–257. Springer, Heidelberg (2008)
13. Metayer, C., Voisin, L.: The Event-B mathematical language (2009), `http://deploy-eprints.ecs.soton.ac.uk/11`
14. Nipkow, T.: Term rewriting and beyond - theorem proving in isabelle. Formal Asp. Comput. 1(4), 320–338 (1989)
15. Nipkow, T., Paulson, L.C., Wenzel, M.T.: Isabelle/HOL - A Proof Assistant for Higher-Order Logic. LNCS, vol. 2283. Springer, Heidelberg (2002)
16. Owe, O.: Partial logics reconsidered: A conservative approach. Formal Asp. Comput. 5(3), 208–223 (1993)

[4] `http://wiki.event-b.org/index.php/Export_to_Isabelle`

17. Owre, S., Shankar, N.: The formal semantics of PVS (1999), http://pvs.csl.sri.com/papers/csl-97-2/csl-97-2.ps
18. Paulson, L.C.: Logic and Computation: Interactive Proof with Cambridge LCF, Cambridge (1987)
19. Paulson, L.C.: The foundation of a generic theorem prover. J. Autom. Reasoning 5(3), 363–397 (1989)
20. Schmalz, M.: The logic of Event-B (2011), ftp://ftp.inf.ethz.ch/pub/publications/tech-reports/6xx/698.pdf
21. Schmalz, M.: Term rewriting in logics of partial functions (2011), ftp://ftp.inf.ethz.ch/pub/publications/tech-reports/7xx/732.pdf
22. Shankar, N., Owre, S., Rushby, J.M., Stringer-Calvert, D.W.J.: PVS prover guide (2001), http://pvs.csl.sri.com/doc/pvs-prover-guide.pdf
23. Silva, R., Butler, M.: Supporting reuse of Event-B developments through generic instantiation. In: Breitman, K., Cavalcanti, A. (eds.) ICFEM 2009. LNCS, vol. 5885, pp. 466–484. Springer, Heidelberg (2009)
24. Wenzel, M.: Type classes and overloading in higher-order logic. In: Gunter, E.L., Felty, A.P. (eds.) TPHOLs 1997. LNCS, vol. 1275, pp. 307–322. Springer, Heidelberg (1997)

Synchronous AADL and Its Formal Analysis in Real-Time Maude

Kyungmin Bae[1] and Peter Csaba Ölveczky[2], Abdullah Al-Nayeem[1], and José Meseguer[1]

[1] University of Illinois at Urbana-Champaign
[2] University of Oslo

Abstract. Distributed Real-Time Systems (DRTS), such as avionics systems and distributed control systems in motor vehicles, are very hard to design because of asynchronous communication, network delays, and clock skews. Furthermore, their model checking problem typically becomes unfeasible due to the large state spaces caused by the interleavings. For many DRTSs, we can use the PALS methodology to reduce the problem of designing and verifying asynchronous DRTSs to the much simpler task of designing and verifying their synchronous versions. AADL is an industrial modeling standard for avionics and automotive systems. We define in this paper the *Synchronous AADL* language for modeling synchronous real-time systems in AADL, and provide a formal semantics for Synchronous AADL in Real-Time Maude. We have integrated into the OSATE modeling environment for AADL a plug-in which allows us to model check Synchronous AADL models in Real-Time Maude within OSATE. We exemplify such verification on an avionics system, whose Synchronous AADL design can be model checked in less than 10 seconds, but whose asynchronous design cannot be feasibly model checked.

1 Introduction

Many real-time systems are distributed due to physical and fault-tolerance requirements. Designing, implementing, and verifying such systems is very difficult and costly. Due to their asynchrony, clock skews, and message delays, such systems may experience race conditions and violations of their safety properties that can be very difficult to uncover by testing. Automated formal verification by model checking is also unfeasible in practice, since, due to asynchrony, there are *too many interleavings*, leading to a veritable combinatorial explosion.

The above remarks apply to the verification of both designs and code. Since design errors are much more expensive than coding errors, there is general agreement that system verification should first be carried out at the level of designs by verifying the *model* representing a system design. For real-time systems such as avionics and automative systems the AADL modeling language [16] is a widely used industrial standard. To make *formal* verification of AADL models possible *two key problems* have to be solved. The first problem is to have a *formal semantics* of AADL models, since without such a semantics there is no *mathematical*

S. Qin and Z. Qiu (Eds.): ICFEM 2011, LNCS 6991, pp. 651–667, 2011.

model satisfying any properties. We have addressed this problem by providing a formal semantics in rewriting logic for a behavioral fragment of AADL [14], and other researchers have carried our related efforts [3,4,5,9,14]. The second problem is the one mentioned above: since AADL models have components that interact asynchronously with each other, their automatic model checking verification becomes *unfeasible* even for simple models. The key point is that the inherent difficulties of verifying a distributed real-time system (DRTS) *do not disappear* at the level of models: they are common to both models and code.

To reduce the difficulties of designing and verifying DRTSs, we and other colleagues at Rockwell-Collins and UIUC have proposed the PALS transformation [1,11,17]. The key idea behind PALS is that the intended behavior of many DRTSs is that they should be *virtually synchronous*. That is, conceptually there is a logical period during which all components perform a transition and send data to each other. The PALS transformation (summarized in Section 2) achieves this virtual synchrony by reducing the design and verification of a DRTS of this nature to that of a much simpler semantically equivalent *synchronous* one [11].

Our Approach and Contributions. Our approach to verifying in practice AADL models that are distributed but virtually synchronous is based on the following ideas and contributions: (i) to specify a fragment of AADL called *Synchronous AADL* in which synchronous models can be defined (Section 3); (ii) to define a formal *synchronous semantics* for this subset (Section 5); (iii) to embody this semantics in a tool called *SynchAADL2Maude* (Section 8), which is an OSATE plugin and maps models in Synchronous AADL to rewrite theories in Real-Time Maude, where such models can be simulated and verified by model checking (Section 6); (iv) to illustrate the effectiveness of the approach by modeling in Synchronous AADL and verifying in *SynchAADL2Maude* an avionics example that we could not verify in its asynchronous version: the requirements for this example can now be verified in 10 seconds or less (Section 7).

Using the PALS transformation it is then possible to transform a Synchronous AADL model into a correct-by-construction asynchronous one [1]. The usefulness of our work is not restricted to PALS: it can be exploited by similar transformations relating synchronous and asynchronous systems for other distributed real-time architectures, such as the time-triggered architecture [10].

The huge state space reduction from the verification of an asynchronous system to that of its synchronous counterpart is not specific to AADL models: for the avionics example in Section 4 a similar reduction was reported by Darren Cofer and Steven Miller in [13] using SMV models. We conducted an experiment modeling the same example directly in Real-Time Maude: the number of states of the synchronous system was 185, and all properties were verified in 0.8 seconds or less, but the simplest possible asynchronous model (no network delays, no execution time, no clock skews) had 3,047,832 states [11]. Although it was possible to verify a property of the asynchronous system in 2000 seconds, as soon as a one-unit delay was possible for messages, model checking became impossible. What this work achieves is to make such a huge reduction possible for AADL models to support their automatic model checking verification.

2 Preliminaries on AADL, Real-Time Maude, and PALS

AADL. The *Architecture Analysis & Design Language* (AADL) [16] is an industrial modeling standard used in avionics, aerospace, automotive, medical devices, and robotics communities to describe an embedded real-time system as an assembly of software components mapped onto an execution platform.

An AADL model describes a system of hardware and software components. Software components include *threads* that model the application software to be executed. Thread behavior is described using the *behavior annex* [8], which models thread behaviors as transition systems with local state variables. The OSATE modeling environment provides a set of Eclipse plug-ins for AADL. The current stable version 1.5.8 of OSATE, that also supports the behavior annex, supports version 1 of the AADL standard; therefore, the language Synchronous AADL defined in this paper is also based on version 1 of AADL.

In the software component subset of AADL that is the focus of this paper, a component *type* specifies the component's *interface* and *properties*, and a component *implementation* specifies the internal structure of the component as a set of *subcomponents* and a set of *connections* linking their ports. *System* components are the top level components, and a set of *thread* components define their dynamic behaviors. Components may have *properties* describing its parameters and other information. The *dispatch protocol* of a thread determines when the thread is executed. For example, a *periodic* thread is activated at fixed time intervals, and an *aperiodic* thread is activated when it receives an event.

Thread behavior is defined by guarded state transitions. The actions performed when a transition is applied may update local variables, generate new outputs, and/or suspend the thread. Actions are built from basic actions using sequencing, conditionals, and finite loops. When a thread is activated, an enabled transition is applied; if the resulting state is not a *complete* state, another transition is applied, until a complete state is reached (or the thread suspends).

Real-Time Maude. A Real-Time Maude [15] *timed module* specifies a *real-time rewrite theory* of the form (Σ, E, IR, TR), where:

- (Σ, E) is a *membership equational logic* [6] theory with Σ a signature[1] and E a set of *confluent and terminating conditional equations*. (Σ, E) specifies the system's states as an algebraic data type.
- IR is a set of (possibly conditional) *labeled instantaneous rewrite rules* specifying the system's *instantaneous* (i.e., zero-time) local transitions.[2]
- TR is a set of *tick rewrite rules* of the form `crl [`l`] : {`u`} => {`v`} in time` τ `if` *cond*. Such a rule specifies a transition with duration τ and label l from an instance of the term u to the corresponding instance of the term v.

[1] i.e., Σ is a set of declarations of *sorts*, *subsorts*, and *function symbols*.

[2] E is a union $E' \cup A$, where A is a set of equational axioms such as associativity, commutativity, and identity, so that deduction is performed *modulo* A. Operationally, a term is reduced to its E'-normal form modulo A before any rewrite rule is applied.

The Real-Time Maude syntax is fairly intuitive (see [6]). A function symbol f is declared with the syntax `op` f `:` $s_1 \ldots s_n$ `->` s, where $s_1 \ldots s_n$ are the sorts of its arguments, and s is its (value) *sort*. Equations are written with syntax `eq` u `=` v, and `ceq` u `=` v `if` *cond* for conditional equations.

A *class* declaration `class` C `|` att_1 `:` s_1 `, ... ,` att_n `:` s_n declares a class C with attributes att_1 to att_n of sorts s_1 to s_n. An *object* of class C is represented as a term `<` $O : C \mid att_1 : val_1, ..., att_n : val_n$ `>` where O is the object's *identifier*, and where val_1 to val_n are the current values of the attributes att_1 to att_n. The global state has the form `{`t`}`, where t is a term of sort `Configuration` that has the structure of a *multiset* of objects and messages, with multiset union denoted by a juxtaposition operator that is declared associative and commutative, so that rewriting is *multiset rewriting* supported in Real-Time Maude. A *subclass* inherits all the attributes and rules of its superclasses.

A Real-Time Maude specification is *executable*, and the tool offers a variety of formal analysis methods. The *rewrite* command simulates *one* behavior of the system, starting with a given initial state. The *search* command uses a breadth-first strategy to analyze all possible behaviors of the system from an initial state, by checking whether a state matching a *pattern* and satisfying a *condition* can be reached from the initial state. Real-Time Maude's *linear temporal logic model checker* checks whether each behavior from an initial state, possibly up to a time bound, satisfies a linear temporal logic formula. *State propositions*, possibly parametrized, are operators of sort `Prop`. A temporal logic *formula* is constructed by state propositions and temporal logic operators such as `True`, `~` (negation), `/\`, `\/`, `->` (implication), `[]` ("always"), `<>` ("eventually"), `U` ("until"), and `O` ("next"). The command (`mc` t `|=u` φ `.`) then checks whether the temporal logic formula φ holds in all behaviors starting from the initial state t.

PALS. In many systems targeted by AADL, such as avionics systems and distributed control systems in motor vehicles, the system design is essentially a *synchronous design* that must be realized in a distributed setting. The design and verification of such distributed real-time systems is a challenging and error-prone task because of asynchronous communication, network delays, clock skews, and because the state space explosion caused by the system's concurrency can make it unfeasible to apply model checking to verify required properties.

The key idea of the *PALS architectural pattern* [1,11,13] is to reduce the design and verification of a distributed real-time system to that of its much simpler synchronous version when the network infrastructure guarantees bounds on the messaging delays and the skews of the local clocks. For a synchronous design SD and network bounds Γ, PALS defines the corresponding asynchronous distributed design $PALS(SD, \Gamma)$. In [12] we formalize PALS and prove that the typically unfeasible task of model checking the asynchronous design $PALS(SD, \Gamma)$ reduces to the feasible task of model checking the synchronous design SD.

The systems we target consist of components that communicate asynchronously and must change state and respond to environment inputs within hard real-time bounds. A synchronous PALS model is therefore formalized as the synchronous composition of a collection of deterministic *typed machines*, a nondeterministic *environment*, and a *wiring diagram* that connects the machines:

Definition 1. *A* typed machine $M = (D_i, S, D_o, \delta_M)$ *consists of:*

- D_i*, called the* input set*, a nonempty set of the form* $D_i = D_{i_1} \times \cdots \times D_{i_n}$*,*
- S*, a nonempty set, called the* set of states.
- D_o*, called the* output set*, a nonempty set of the form* $D_o = D_{o_1} \times \cdots \times D_{o_m}$*,*
- δ_M*, called the* transition function*, a function* $\delta_M : (D_i \times S) \to (S \times D_o)$*.*

That is, a machine has n input ports and m output ports; an input to port k is an element of D_{i_k}, and an output from port j is an element of D_{o_j}.

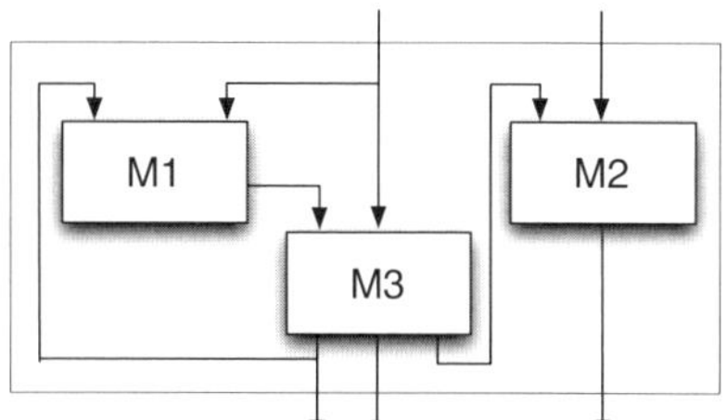

Fig. 1. A machine ensemble

Typed machines can be "wired together" into a *machine ensemble* by means of a "wiring diagram," as shown in Fig. 1. An ensemble has a *synchronous semantics*: all machines perform a transition simultaneously, and whenever a machine has a feedback wire to itself and/or to any other machine, then the corresponding output becomes an input for any such machine at the *next* step. We assume an environment where the *constraints on the values generated by the environment* can be defined as a *satisfiable* predicate $c_e : D_o^e \to Bool$ so that $c_e(d_1, \ldots, d_{m_e})$ is *true* if and only if the environment can generate output $(d_1, \ldots, d_{m_e})$. We refer to [11] for the formal definition of the synchronous system.

3 Synchronous AADL

This section defines the *Synchronous AADL* language that can be used to model synchronous designs in AADL, including both synchronous PALS designs and other synchronous designs that can be mapped onto different distributed real-time architectures, such as the time-triggered architecture [10].

We have defined Synchronous AADL as an annotated sublanguage of AADL, in which the execution of each thread in each "round" is independent of the other threads, and where output generated by a thread in a round is available as input at the receiving thread exactly at the beginning at the next "round." In AADL, such threads would be executed asynchronously. However, since the threads are independent of each other in each round, the "final" states in each round are the same in both any asynchronous execution and in a synchronous execution. Therefore, all AADL constructs in the subset have the same meaning in AADL and Synchronous AADL. Synchronous AADL also adds a *property set* `SynchAADL` to declare Synchronous AADL-specific properties as explained below.

Since Synchronous AADL is intended to model synchronous *designs*, as opposed to asynchronous implementations, it ignores the hardware and scheduling features of AADL. Synchronous AADL therefore focuses on the behavioral and structural subset of AADL, namely, hierarchical system, process, and thread components, ports and connections, and thread behaviors defined in the *behavior annex* standard. We next discuss the definition of Synchronous AADL.

Dispatch. The dispatch protocol is used to trigger an execution of an AADL thread. A *periodic* thread is dispatched at the beginning of each new time period of the thread. In aperiodic, sporadic, timed, and hybrid dispatch, a thread is dispatched when it receives an *event*. Such *event-triggered* dispatch is not suitable to define a system in which all threads (with a possible exception for the environment thread) should execute in lock-step, since the sending thread triggers the execution of the receiving thread, which would read in its ith round the output generated by the sender in the same round. Therefore, each thread must have *periodic* dispatch; furthermore, since each thread must execute in each round, the *period* of all the threads must be the same.

Communication. There are three kinds of ports in AADL: *data*, *event*, and *event data* ports. Event and event data ports can be used to dispatch event-triggered threads. To have only AADL constructs that define "synchronous behaviors," the communication primitives must ensure that all output generated in an iteration is available to the receiver at the beginning of the next iteration, *and not earlier*.

Version 1 of AADL has two kinds of *data* connections: *immediate* and *delayed* connections. For threads with the same dispatch time, the source of an immediate connection must execute before the destination thread, which violates the intended "lock-step" semantics. For a *delayed* connection, the value from the sender is transmitted at its deadline and is available to the receiver at its next dispatch. In our setting, where all threads have periodic dispatch with the same period, the output generated in an iteration is therefore available at the start of the next iteration. Since only data ports have delayed connections, and since event-triggered dispatches are excluded, only *data* ports are used in Synchronous AADL, and connections between non-environment threads must be delayed.

Execution Times. Since the components execute in lock-step, it is natural to assume that they use the same time to perform their execution. For simplicity, and since the PALS synchronous model is untimed, we assume that thread executions are instantaneous.

Deterministic Threads. In the systems targeted by PALS and Synchronous AADL, the nodes that communicate with the environment are invariably deterministic. We therefore assume that the transition system defining the behavior of a non-environment thread is deterministic, and that each such thread has the property `SynchAADL::Deterministic => true`.

Environment Thread. In PALS, the *environment thread* generates output nondeterministically in each iteration. The possible outputs can often be defined by an *environment constraint* c_e so that $c_e(\boldsymbol{o})$ is *true* if and only if the environment can nondeterministically generate output $\boldsymbol{o}$ in any iteration. The property `SynchAADL::IsEnvironment => true` denotes that the thread is an environment thread, and `SynchAADL::InputConstraints => ("Boolean formula")` defines an input constraint on a set of Boolean-valued outputs. We assume that a Synchronous AADL system has *at most one environment thread.*

It seems natural to regard the system as responding to the *current* environment output. We therefore support only *immediate* connections *from* the environment. According to the AADL semantics, this forces the environment to execute before the other nodes in each round.

Declaring Synchronous Systems. The top-level `system` component declares the entire system to execute synchronously by declaring `SynchAADL::Synchronous => true`. The period of the system can be declared by `SynchAADL::SynchPeriod => p`. A Synchronous AADL model defines a synchronous machine ensemble in the obvious way, as explained in [2].

4 An Avionics Example

We exemplify Synchronous AADL with fragments of a model of an avionics system based on a specification by Steve Miller and Darren Cofer at Rockwell-Collins [13]. A full description of this model is given in [2].

In *integrated modular avionics* (IMA), a cabinet is a chassis with a power supply, internal bus, and general purpose computing, I/O, and memory cards. Aircraft applications are implemented using the resources in the cabinets. There are always two or more physically separated cabinets on the aircraft so that physical damage does not take out the computer system. The *active standby* system considers the case of two cabinets and focuses on the logic for deciding which side is *active.* Each side can fail, and a failed side can recover after failure. In case one side fails, the non-failed side should be the active side. In addition, the pilot can toggle the active status of the sides. The full functionality of each side depends on the two sides' perception of the availability of other system components. The architecture of the system is shown in Figure 2. Each time Environment dispatches, it nondeterministically sends 5 Boolean values, one through each ports, so that two sides cannot fail at the same time. Therefore, in each round, the environment can send any one of 24 different 5-tuples.

The Synchronous AADL Model. The following top-level system implementation declares the architecture of the system, with the three subcomponents `sideOne`, `sideTwo`, and `env`, and with immediate data connections (denoted by the arrow '`->`') from the environment to the two sides, and with delayed data connections ('`->>`') between the two sides (parts of the model are replaced by '`...`'):

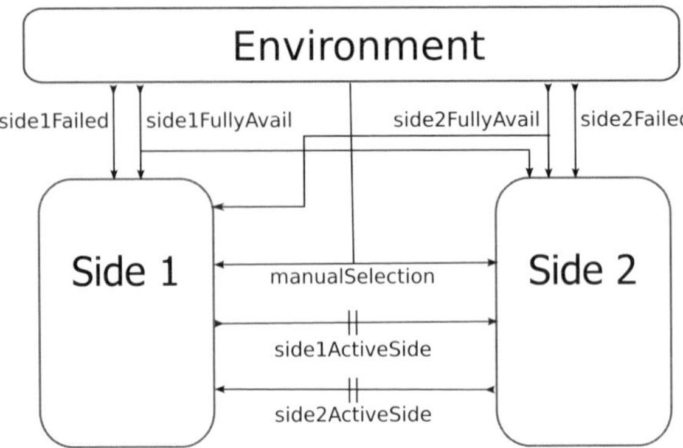

Fig. 2. The architecture of the active standby system

```
system implementation ActiveStandbySystem.impl
  properties
    SynchAADL::Synchronous => true;     SynchAADL::SynchPeriod  => 2 ms;
  subcomponents
    sideOne: system Side1.impl;   sideTwo: system Side2.impl;   env: system Environment.impl;
  connections
    data port sideOne.side1ActiveSide ->> sideTwo.side1ActiveSide;
    data port sideTwo.side2ActiveSide ->> sideOne.side2ActiveSide;
    data port env.side1FullyAvail -> sideOne.side1FullyAvail;
    data port env.side1FullyAvail -> sideTwo.side1FullyAvail;
    ...
end ActiveStandbySystem.impl;
```

We do not show the definition of the system `env`, which contains an instance of the following thread component defining the environment:

```
thread EnvironmentThread
  features
    side1FullyAvail: out data port Behavior::boolean;
    side2FullyAvail: out data port Behavior::boolean;
    manualSelection: out data port Behavior::boolean;
    side1Failed: out data port Behavior::boolean;
    side2Failed: out data port Behavior::boolean;
end EnvironmentThread;

thread implementation EnvironmentThread.impl
  properties
    SynchAADL::InputConstraints => ("not (s1F and s2F)");   SynchAADL::IsEnvironment => true;
    Dispatch_Protocol => Periodic;                            Period => 2 ms;
  annex behavior_specification {**
    states  s0 : initial complete state;
    state variables
      s1FA: Behavior::boolean;    s2FA: Behavior::boolean;    mS: Behavior::boolean;
      s1F: Behavior::boolean;     s2F: Behavior::boolean;
    transitions
      s0 -[]-> s0 {side1FullyAvail := s1FA;  side2FullyAvail := s2FA;
                          manualSelection := mS;    side1Failed := s1F; side2Failed := s2F;};
    **};
end EnvironmentThread.impl;
```

The environment has a single transition, that sends the values of the state variables `s1FA`, `s2FA`, `mS`, `s1F`, and `s2F` to the corresponding output ports. These variables can be assigned any values that satisfy the constraint `not (s1F and s2F)` that states that side 1 and side 2 cannot both fail at the same time.

The following component defines the behavior of side 1:

```
thread Side1Thread
  features
    side2ActiveSide: in data port Behavior::integer;
    manualSelection: in data port Behavior::boolean;
    side1Failed: in data port Behavior::boolean;
    side1FullyAvail: in data port Behavior::boolean;
    side2FullyAvail: in data port Behavior::boolean;
    side1ActiveSide: out data port Behavior::integer;
end Side1Thread;

thread implementation Side1Thread.impl
  properties
    SynchAADL::Deterministic => true;    Dispatch_Protocol => Periodic;    Period => 2 ms;
  annex behavior_specification {**
    states  preInit:  initial complete state;
            initState, side1FailedState, side2FailedState, side1WaitState, side1ActiveState,
            side2ActiveState:  complete state;
    state variables
      prevSide2ActiveStatus: Behavior::integer;  prevManSwitch: Behavior::boolean;
    initially  prevSide2ActiveStatus := 0;   prevManSwitch := false;
    transitions
      ...
      side2ActiveState  -[side1Failed = false and side2ActiveSide != 0 and
                          side1FullyAvail = true and ((prevManSwitch = false and
                          manualSelection = true) or
                          side2FullyAvail = false)]->  side1ActiveState
          {side1ActiveSide := 1;   prevSide2ActiveStatus := side2ActiveSide;
           prevManSwitch := manualSelection;};
      ...
  **};
end Side1Thread.impl;
```

We show only one of the 20 transitions in this thread. The transition takes the thread from state `side2ActiveState` to state `side1ActiveState` if the input received in the `side1Failed` port is `false`, the value received in the port `side2ActiveSide` is different from 0, etc. As a result of applying the transition, the value 1 is sent through the output port `side1ActiveSide`, and the local variables `prevSide2ActiveStatus` and `prevManSwitch` are assigned the values received in the ports `side2ActiveSide` and `manualSelection`, respectively.

5 Real-Time Maude Semantics of Synchronous AADL

This section summarizes the Real-Time Maude semantics of Synchronous AADL. The entire formal semantics of Synchronous AADL is given in [2].

Representing Synchronous AADL Models in Real-Time Maude. The semantics of a component-based language can naturally be defined in an object-oriented style, where each component instance is modeled as an object. The hierarchical structure of Synchronous AADL components is reflected in the nested structure of objects, in which an attribute of an object contains its subcomponents as a multiset of objects. Any Synchronous AADL component instance is represented as an object instance of a subclass of the following class `Component`, which contains the attributes common to all kinds of components:

```
class Component | features : Configuration,  subcomponents : Configuration,
                  properties : Properties,   connections : ConnectionSet .
```

The attribute `features` denotes the ports of a component, represented as a multiset of `Port` objects; `subcomponents` denotes the subcomponents of the object; `properties` denotes its *properties*; and `connections` denotes its connections.

The `Thread` class is declared as follows:

```
class Thread | behaviorRef : ComponentRef,  variables : Valuation,
               currState : Location,        completeStates : LocationSet .
subclass Thread < Component .
```

Since the term representing the transitions of a thread can be fairly large, we do not carry them around in the objects. Instead, a `memo`-ized (see [6]) function `transitions : ComponentRef ~> TransitionSet` contains the transitions of each thread component, represented as a semi-colon-separated multiset of transitions of the form s `-[`*guard*`]->` s' `{`*actions*`}`. The attribute `behaviorRef` denotes the component of the thread; `variables` denotes its local variables *and* their values; `currState` denotes the current "state" of the transition system; and `completeStates` denotes its *complete* states.

Data ports are represented as objects of subclasses of the class `Port`, whose `content` attribute denotes the content of the port, which is either `noMsg` (the port buffer is empty) or contains a data element e, in which case the `content` is `data(`e`)`. Thread input ports also have a flag `fresh`, denoting whether the port received data in the latest dispatch.

```
class Port | content : MsgContent .   class InDataPort .   class OutDataPort .
   subclass InDataPort OutDataPort < Port .
class InDataThreadPort | fresh : Bool .
   subclass InDataThreadPort < InDataPort .

sort MsgContent .
op noMsg : -> MsgContent [ctor] .
op data : Bool -> MsgContent [ctor] .
op data : Int -> MsgContent [ctor] .
```

A level-up *connection*, linking an outgoing port P in a subcomponent C to the outgoing port P' in the "current" component, is modeled as a term C `.` P `-->` P'. Immediate same-level and level-down connections are terms of the forms, respectively, C_1 `.` P_1 `-->` C_2 `.` P_2 and P `-->` C `.` P'. Delayed connections are denoted with the arrow `-->>`. A *connection set* is a semi-colon-separated set of connections.

For example, in our avionics example, an instance of the top-level system component in Section 4 would be represented in Real-Time Maude by the term

```
< MAIN : System | features : none,     properties : Synchronous(true) ; SynchPeriod(2),
                  subcomponents : < sideOne : System | ... >   < sideTwo : System | ... >
                                  < env : System | ... >,
                  connections : sideOne . side1ActiveSide -->> sideTwo . side1ActiveSide ;
                                sideTwo . side2ActiveSide -->> sideOne . side2ActiveSide ;
                                env . side1FullyAvail --> sideOne . side1FullyAvail ;
                                ...
                                env . side2Failed --> sideTwo . side2Failed >
```

The instance `side1Thread` of the component `Side1Thread.impl` in a particular state is represented by the term

```
< side1Thread : Thread |
    features : < side2ActiveSide : InDataThreadPort | content : data(2), fresh : true >
               < manualSelection : InDataThreadPort | content : data(false), fresh : true >
               ...
               < side1ActiveSide : OutDataPort | content : data(0) >,
    subcomponents : none,    properties : periodic-dispatch(2) ; Deterministic(true),
    connections : none,      behaviorRef : thread Side1Thread . impl,
    variables : (prevSide2ActiveStatus |-> 2) (prevManualSwitch |-> false),
    currState : side1FailedState,
    completeStates : preinit initState side1FailedState ... side2ActiveState >
```

Formalizing the Synchronous Steps. Assuming that the system contains one environment thread and that the other threads are deterministic, a synchronous step of the system is formalized by the following tick rewrite rule:

```
var SYSTEM : Object .    var VAL : Valuation .    var VALS : ValuationSet .

crl [syncStepWithTime] :
    {SYSTEM}
 => {applyTransitions(transferData(applyEnvTransitions(VAL, SYSTEM)))}
    in time period(SYSTEM)
 if containsEnvironment(SYSTEM) /\ VAL ;; VALS := allEnvAssignments(SYSTEM) .
```

The function `allEnvAssignments` uses Maude's SAT solver to find all valuations of the Boolean variables in the environment thread that satisfy the environment constraint. The union operator `_;;_` is declared to be associative and commutative; therefore, *any* of these valuations is nondeterministically assigned to the variable `VAL` in the matching condition `VAL ;; VALS := allEnvAssignments(SYSTEM)`. The function `applyEnvTransitions` then performs the environment transition that outputs the values of the variables given by the selected valuation `VAL`. The function `transferData` then transfers the data from the output ports to the receiving input ports and then clears the output ports. Finally, the function `applyTransitions` applies transitions in each non-environment thread until a *complete* state is reached in the thread. The function `period` extracts the period of the system.

The function `applyTrans`, which distributes to the thread objects in the state, is defined as follows for deterministic threads:

```
ceq applyTransitions(
      < O : Thread | properties : Deterministic(true) ; PROPS,
```

```
                     features : PORTS,   currState : L1,   completeStates : LS,
                     variables : VAL,   behaviorRef  :  CR >)
  = if L2 in LS then < O : Thread | features : NEW-PORTS,   currState : L2,
                                    variables : NEW-VALUATION >
    else applyTransitions(< O : Thread | features: NEW-PORTS, currState : L2,
                                       variables  :  NEW-VALUATION >) fi
  if ((L1 -[GUARD]-> L2 {SL}) ; TRANSITIONS) := transitions(CR)
       /\ evalGuard(GUARD, PORTS, VAL)
       /\ transResult(NEW-PORTS, NEW-VALUATION) :=
           executeTransition(L1 -[GUARD]-> L2 {SL}, PORTS, VAL) .
```

The thread is in local state `L1`, and a transition `L1 -[GUARD]-> L2 {SL}`, whose `GUARD` evaluates to `true` in the current state and input port values, is applied from the transitions in `transitions(CR)`. The function `executeTransition` executes a given transition in a state with a given set `PORTS` of ports and assignment `VAL` of the state variables. The function returns a term `transResult`(p, σ), where p is the state of the ports after the execution, and σ denotes the resulting values of the state variables. If the resulting state `L2` is *not* a *complete* state, the function `applyTransitions` is applied again to the new state.

6 Formal Analysis of Synchronous AADL Models

The Real-Time Maude model that can be synthesized from a Synchronous AADL model can be formally analyzed in different ways. This section presents some functions allowing the user to define system properties for a Synchronous AADL model without having to understand its formal representation. For example,

`value of` v `in component` *fullComponentName* `in` *globalComponent*

gives the value of the state variable v in the thread identified by the full component name *fullComponentName* in the system in state *globalComponent*. The full component name is a `->`-separated path of component names. Likewise,

`location of component` *fullComponentName* `in` *globalComponent*

gives the current location/state in the transition system in the given thread.

In our example, if `MAIN` is the name of the top-level component, then the following search command checks whether we can reach a state where the side one thread is in state `side1ActiveState` and the side two thread is in state `side2ActiveState`:

```
Maude> (utsearch [1] {initial} =>* {C:Configuration}
         such that
          ((location of component (MAIN -> sideOne -> sideProcess -> sideThread)
              in C:Configuration) == side1ActiveState
           and (location of component (MAIN -> sideTwo -> sideProcess -> sideThread)
                  in C:Configuration) == side2ActiveState) .)
```

For LTL model checking purposes, our tool has useful pre-defined parametric atomic propositions, such as *full thread name* @ *location*, which holds when the thread is in state *location*, and

`value of` *port*/*variable* `in component` *fullThreadName* `is` v

that holds in a state if the value of the local variable or port of the thread is v.

7 Verifying the Active Standby System

This section shows how we have verified the Synchronous AADL model of the active standby system in Section 4. That model, the synthesized Real-Time Maude specification, and the properties we have verified for this example and another avionics example are given in [2].

The paper [13] lists five properties that the avionics system must satisfy. We explain how we have verified one of these properties ($R1$): *Both sides should agree on which side is active (provided neither side has failed, the availability of a side has not changed, and the pilot has not made a manual selection).*

Side i thinks that side j is active if it sends the number j to its output port `side`*i*`ActiveSide`. Using the predefined proposition `value of` *port* `in` *thread* `is` v, we can easily define the formula `agreeOnActiveSide` to hold when both sides think that side 1 is active or when both sides think that side 2 is active:

```
op agreeOnActiveSide : -> Formula .
eq agreeOnActiveSide =
    ((value of side1ActiveSide in component (MAIN -> sideOne -> sideProcess -> sideThread) is 1)
     /\ (value of side2ActiveSide in component (MAIN -> sideTwo -> sideProcess -> sideThread) is 1))
 \/ ((value of side1ActiveSide in component (MAIN -> sideOne -> sideProcess -> sideThread) is 2)
     /\ (value of side2ActiveSide in component (MAIN -> sideTwo -> sideProcess -> sideThread) is 2)) .
```

Side i has failed if it has received the value `true` in its `side`*i*`Failed` port:

```
ops side1Failed side2Failed neitherSideFailed : -> Formula .
eq side1Failed
 = value of side1Failed in component (MAIN -> sideOne -> sideProcess -> sideThread) is true .
eq side2Failed
 = value of side2Failed in component (MAIN -> sideTwo -> sideProcess -> sideThread) is true .
eq neitherSideFailed = (~ side1Failed) /\ (~ side2Failed) .
```

Likewise, the proposition `side`*i*`FullyAvailable` holds if side i is fully available. There is no change in availability if both sides are equally available in the current state and in the next state:

```
op noChangeAvailability : -> Formula .
eq noChangeAvailability = (side1FullyAvailable <-> O side1FullyAvailable)
                          /\ (side2FullyAvailable <-> O side2FullyAvailable) .
```

We define a property that the pilot has made a manual selection, and then define a formula that says that in the *next* state, the pilot has not made a manual selection, the availability of a side has not changed, and neither side has failed:

```
ops manSelectPressed noChangeAssumptionNextState : -> Formula .
eq manSelectPressed
 = value of manualSelection in component (MAIN -> sideOne -> sideProcess -> sideThread) is true .
eq noChangeAssumptionNextState
 = noChangeAvailability /\ (O ~ manSelectPressed) /\ (O neitherSideFailed) .
```

As explained in [12], the requirement $R1$ is not satisfied in the active standby system; instead, we verify the following weaker property `R1`:

```
op R1 : -> Formula .
eq R1 = [] (noChangeAssumptionNextState
            -> O (agreeOnActiveSide \/ O (neitherSideFailed -> agreeOnActiveSide))) .
```

We then use Real-Time Maude model checking to verify the property `O R1`:

```
Maude> (mc {initial} |=u O R1 .)

rewrites: 1211549 in 9698ms cpu (9918ms real) (124918 rewrites/second)
Result Bool : true
```

We have also verified that the Synchronous AADL model satisfies corrected versions of all the five requirements; in each case, it takes less than 10 seconds.

8 The SynchAADL2Maude Tool

We have integrated the Real-Time Maude verification of Synchronous AADL models into the Open Source AADL Tool Environment (OSATE). The *SynchAADL2Maude* tool is an OSATE plug-in that uses OSATE's model traversal facility to support both checking whether a model is a legal Synchronous AADL model and verifying Synchronous AADL models *within OSATE*.

When OSATE has generated an *AADL instance model* from an AADL specification, we can use the SynchAADL2Maude tool to: (i) check whether the instance model is a Synchronous AADL model, (ii) generate the corresponding Real-Time Maude model, and (iii) model check LTL properties of the instance model. Figure 3 shows the SynchAADL2Maude window for the active standby example. The `Constraints Check` button, the `Code Generation` button, and `Do Verification` button are used to perform, respectively, the static analysis, the Real-Time Maude code generation, and the model checking. The corrected versions of the active standby system requirements have been entered into the tool, and are shown in the "AADL Property Requirement" table. The `Do Verification` button has been clicked and the results of the model checking are shown in the "Maude Console."

The properties to be verified are managed by the associated XML property file. For example, to add an LTL model checking command to verify the property `R1` in Section 7, we just add the following `command` tag to the property file:

```
<command>
 <name>R1</name>
  <value type = "ltl">
    O [] (noChangeAssumptionNextState
           -> O (agreeOnActiveSide \/ O (neitherSideFailed -> agreeOnActiveSide))) .
  </value>
</command>
```

SyncAADL2Maude Verification

AADL Instance Model

Model Location: /ActiveStandBy/aaxl/packages/Main_ActiveStandbySystem_impl_Instance.aaxl

Constraints Check | Code Generation

Simulation Bound: Do Simulation

AADL Property Requirement

Name	Property	Category
R1	O ([] (noChangeAssumptionNextState -> O (agreeOnActiveSide \/ O (neitherSideFailed -> agreeOnActiv	LTL
R2a	O ([] ((noChangeAssumptionNextState /\ O side1FullyAvailable /\ O ~ side2FullyAvailable) -> O (~ side:	LTL
R3g	[] ((~ manSelectPressed /\ agreeOnActiveSide /\ side1FullyAvailable /\ side2FullyAvailable /\ noChang	LTL
R4	[] (((side1Failed /\ ~ side2Failed) -> O (~ side2Failed -> side2Active)) /\ ((side2Failed /\ ~ side1Faile	LTL
R5side1	[] (((side1Active /\ side1FullyAvailable /\ ~ manSelectPressed) -> (side1Active W (~ side1FullyAvailable	LTL

Do Verification

Verification | Main_ActiveStandbySystem_impl_Instance.prop

Problems | Properties | AADL Property Values | Maude Console

Ready.

```
side2FullyAvailable \/ manSelectPressed \/ side1Failed)) in
Main_ActiveStandbySystem_impl_Instance-VERIFICATION-DEF with mode
deterministic time increase

Result Bool :
  true
```

Fig. 3. SynchAADL2Maude window in OSATE

New formulas can be defined in the property file using the `definition` tag. For example, the new constant `side1Failed` is defined as follows:

```
<definition>
 <name>side1Failed</name>
  <value>
    value of side1Failed in component (MAIN -> sideOne -> sideProcess -> sideThread) is true
  </value>
</definition>
```

9 Related Work

The paper [7] formalizes the AADL data port protocol in Event-B. Despite the title of the paper, it does not define a synchronous subset of AADL and therefore does not provide an executable formal semantics of any such subset. There exist a number of formalizations and verification tools for different subsets of AADL (see, e.g., [3,4,5,14]). These approaches target ordinary (asynchronous) AADL models and do not define synchronous subsets of AADL. In [9], the behaviors of single AADL threads are given by synchronous Lustre programs. Since [9] also targets "standard" asynchronous AADL models, the authors show how asynchronous computation can be *encoded* in a synchronous language. This encoding does of course not reduce the state space of the asynchronous system.

Our work is motivated by the PALS pattern [1,11,13] that reduces the design and verification of an asynchronous system to that of its synchronous version.

There is a fair amount of work that relates synchronous and asynchronous models in various ways; we refer to [12] for an extensive discussion on this topic.

10 Concluding Remarks

To the best of our knowledge the work we have presented is the first defining a synchronous subset of AADL. Such a subset is essential to reduce the design and verification complexity of distributed real-time systems that should operate in a virtually synchronous way. The formal semantics of synchronous AADL models we have provided is also essential for formal verification and is supported in practice by the *SynchAADL2Maude* tool in a way that preserves the AADL "look and feel" for users and minimizes the need for a detailed knowledge of the underlying Real-Time Maude tool. In summary, our work makes possible in practice the formal verification of asynchronous AADL models that are virtually synchronous by supporting the definition and verification of their semantically equivalent synchronous counterparts.

As usual much work remains ahead. One natural extension of the proposed AADL subset and the *SynchAADL2Maude* tool is the simultaneous support of synchronous subsystems with different periods and of additional AADL features. Further experimentation and development of additional case studies will also be important to improve the tool and its performance and to facilitate its use.

Acknowledgments. Our design of Synchronous AADL was inspired by our previous work on PALS with Steve Miller and Darren Cofer at Rockwell-Collins corporation, and Lui Sha at UIUC. We have also benefited from many discussions on the design of Synchronous AADL with Lui Sha and Peter Feiler; and from the feedback of the participants at several AADL meetings. We also thank the anonymous reviewers for helpful comments on a previous version of this paper. This work has been partially supported by the Boeing corporation under grant C8088, by the National Science Foundation, including grants CNS 08-34709 and CCF 09-05584, and by the Research Council of Norway, Rockwell Collins Inc., the Office of Naval Research, Lockheed Martin Corporation, and the Software Engineering Institute.

References

1. Al-Nayeem, A., Sun, M., Qiu, X., Sha, L., Miller, S.P., Cofer, D.D.: A formal architecture pattern for real-time distributed systems. In: Proc. RTSS 2009. IEEE, Los Alamitos (2009)
2. Bae, K., Ölveczky, P.C., Al-Nayeem, A., Meseguer, J.: Synchronous AADL and its formal analysis in Real-Time Maude. Department of Computer Science, University of Illinois at Urbana-Champaign (2011), `http://hdl.handle.net/2142/25091`
3. Berthomieu, B., Bodeveix, J.P., Chaudet, C., Dal Zilio, S., Filali, M., Vernadat, F.: Formal verification of AADL specifications in the topcased environment. In: Kordon, F., Kermarrec, Y. (eds.) Ada-Europe 2009. LNCS, vol. 5570, pp. 207–221. Springer, Heidelberg (2009)

4. Bozzano, M., Cimatti, A., Katoen, J.P., Nguyen, V., Noll, T., Roveri, M., Wimmer, R.: A model checker for AADL. In: Touili, T., Cook, B., Jackson, P. (eds.) CAV 2010. LNCS, vol. 6174, pp. 562–565. Springer, Heidelberg (2010)
5. Chkouri, M.Y., Robert, A., Bozga, M., Sifakis, J.: Translating AADL into BIP - application to the verification of real-time systems. In: Chaudron, M.R.V. (ed.) MODELS 2008. LNCS, vol. 5421, pp. 5–19. Springer, Heidelberg (2009)
6. Clavel, M., Durán, F., Eker, S., Lincoln, P., Martí-Oliet, N., Bevilacqua, V., Talcott, C.: All About Maude - A High-Performance Logical Framework. LNCS, vol. 4350. Springer, Heidelberg (2007)
7. Filali, M., Lawall, J.: Development of a synchronous subset of AADL. In: Frappier, M., Glässer, U., Khurshid, S., Laleau, R., Reeves, S. (eds.) ABZ 2010. LNCS, vol. 5977, pp. 245–258. Springer, Heidelberg (2010)
8. França, R., Bodeveix, J.P., Filali, M., Rolland, J.F., Chemouil, D., Thomas, D.: The AADL behaviour annex - experiments and roadmap. In: Proc. ICECCS 2007. IEEE, Los Alamitos (2007)
9. Jahier, E., Halbwachs, N., Raymond, P., Nicollin, X., Lesens, D.: Virtual execution of AADL models via a translation into synchronous programs. In: Proc. EMSOFT 2007. ACM, New York (2007)
10. Kopetz, H., Bauer, G.: The time-triggered architecture. Proc. of the IEEE 93(1) (2003)
11. Meseguer, J., Ölveczky, P.C.: Formalization and correctness of the PALS architectural pattern for distributed real-time systems. In: Dong, J.S., Zhu, H. (eds.) ICFEM 2010. LNCS, vol. 6447, pp. 303–320. Springer, Heidelberg (2010)
12. Meseguer, J., Ölveczky, P.: Formalization and correctness of the PALS architectural pattern for distributed real-time systems. Tech. rep., Department of Computer Science, University of Illinois at Urbana-Champaign (2010), `http://hdl.handle.net/2142/17089`
13. Miller, S.P., Cofer, D.D., Sha, L., Meseguer, J., Al-Nayeem, A.: Implementing logical synchrony in integrated modular avionics. In: Proc. DASC 2009. IEEE, Los Alamitos (2009)
14. Ölveczky, P.C., Boronat, A., Meseguer, J.: Formal semantics and analysis of behavioral AADL models in real-time maude. In: Hatcliff, J., Zucca, E. (eds.) FMOODS 2010. LNCS, vol. 6117, pp. 47–62. Springer, Heidelberg (2010)
15. Ölveczky, P.C., Meseguer, J.: Semantics and pragmatics of Real-Time Maude. Higher-Order and Symbolic Computation 20(1-2), 161–196 (2007)
16. SAE AADL Team: AADL homepage (2009), `http://www.aadl.info/`
17. Sha, L., Al-Nayeem, A., Sun, M., Meseguer, J., Ölveczky, P.: PALS: Physically asynchronous logically synchronous systems. Tech. rep., Department of Computer Science, University of Illinois at Urbana-Champaign (2009), `http://hdl.handle.net/2142/11897`

Author Index